The Editor

LELAND S. PERSON is Professor and Head of the English Department at the University of Cincinnati. He previously taught at the University of Alabama at Birmingham, Southern Illinois University at Carbondale, and Indiana University, Fort Wayne. He is the author of *Henry James and the Suspense of Masculinity; Aesthetic Headaches: Women and a Masculine Poetics in Poe, Melville, and Hawthorne*; and many articles on nineteenth-century American writers, especially Hawthorne, Poe, Melville, Henry James, and James Fenimore Cooper. He recently coedited (with Robert K. Martin) a collection of essays, *Roman Holidays: American Writers and Artists in Nineteenth-Century Italy*.

A NORTON CRITICAL EDITION

Nathaniel Hawthorne

THE SCARLET LETTER

AND OTHER WRITINGS

AUTHORITATIVE TEXTS

CONTEXTS

CRITICISM

Edited by

LELAND S. PERSON

UNIVERSITY OF CINCINNATI

W. W. NORTON & COMPANY

New York • London

W. W. Norton & Company has been independent since its founding in 1923, when William Warder Norton and Mary D. Herter Norton first published lectures delivered at the People's Institute, the adult education division of New York City's Cooper Union. The Nortons soon expanded their program beyond the Institute, publishing books by celebrated academics from America and abroad. By mid-century, the two major pillars of Norton's publishing program—trade books and college texts—were firmly established. In the 1950s, the Norton family transferred control of the company to its employees, and today—with a staff of four hundred and a comparable number of trade, college, and professional titles published each year—W. W. Norton & Company stands as the largest and oldest publishing house owned wholly by its employees.

Composition by PennSet, Inc.
Manufacturing by the Courier Companies—Westford Division.
Production manager: Ben Reynolds.

Library of Congress Cataloging-in-Publication Data
Hawthorne, Nathaniel, 1804–1864.
    The scarlet letter and other writings: authoritative texts, contexts, criticism / Nathaniel Hawthorne; edited by Leland S. Person.
        p. cm.— (A Norton critical edition)
    Includes bibliographical references (p.).

ISBN 0–393–97953–9 (pbk.)

    1. Boston (Mass.)—History—Colonial period, ca. 1600–1775—Fiction. 2. Hawthorne, Nathaniel, 1804–1864. Scarlet letter. 3. Illegitimate children—Fiction. 4. Women immigrants—Fiction. 5. Married women—Fiction. 6. Puritans—Fiction. 7. Adultery—Fiction. 8. Revenge—Fiction. 9. Clergy—Fiction. I. Person, Leland S. II. Title. III. Series.

PS1868.A2P47 2004
813'.3—dc22

2004054775

W. W. Norton & Company, Inc., 500 Fifth Avenue, New York, N.Y. 10110-0017
www.wwnorton.com

W. W. Norton & Company Ltd., Castle House,
75/76 Wells Street, London W1T 3QT

8   9   0

For Nina Baym
in token of my admiration for her career

Contents

Preface

This new edition of Nathaniel Hawthorne's *The Scarlet Letter* appears during the bicentennial anniversary year of Hawthorne's birth (on July 4, 1804). Although there have been three previous Norton Critical Editions of Hawthorne's first major novel, this edition has been designed from the ground up. For copy text, I have chosen to use the third edition of the novel, published in September 1850 by Ticknor, Reed, and Fields, because that edition, the first set in stereotype plates, was the basis of subsequent printings in Hawthorne's lifetime and so represents the text that most nineteenth-century readers actually read.

At the request of W. W. Norton's editors, I have included five of Hawthorne's short prose works that seem most pertinent as supplements to *The Scarlet Letter*. One of Hawthorne's earliest sketches, "Mrs. Hutchinson," deserves a wider readership, especially in view of Hawthorne's famous observation in chapter 1 of *The Scarlet Letter* that the wild rose bush outside the prison door had "sprung up under the feet of the sainted Ann Hutchinson." "Endicott and the Red Cross" includes Hawthorne's earliest mention of a woman wearing a scarlet letter and helps augment the Puritan context of the later novel. "The Minister's Black Veil" can be considered an early trying out of a character and situation Hawthorne would develop in his portrait of Arthur Dimmesdale. "Young Goodman Brown," arguably Hawthorne's most thoughtful treatment of the Salem witchcraft hysteria of 1692, also helps to highlight his use of setting and symbolic spaces in *The Scarlet Letter*, especially the lure of the forest. In its treatment of Georgiana's relationship to Aylmer and its fixation on marked women's bodies, "The Birth-mark" anticipates Hester Prynne's situation and can provide important additional material for gender-oriented analyses of *The Scarlet Letter*.

In addition to those short works, I have also provided a rich sampling from Hawthorne's letters and notebooks—letters he wrote at the time he was writing and publishing the novel and notebook entries that found their way into the narrative. I have included a lengthy passage from Hawthorne's campaign biography of Franklin Pierce because it has so often been cited by scholars interested in Hawthorne's politics and especially his attitude toward slavery and abolition. I have included selected early reviews of *The Scarlet Letter*, including a little-known, arguably feminist review by Jane Swisshelm that Robert S. Levine, who uses that review as the linchpin for a fascinating examination of nineteenth-century women's responses to the novel, has been kind enough to edit for this volume.

Deciding which critical essays to include in this edition has been a wonderfully enjoyable task, as well as an impossible one. I have decided to take a risk and emphasize recent essays and book chapters, recognizing that some readers will regret the omission of "classic" essays, such as Frederick Crews's psychoanalytic treatment of the novel in *The Sins of the Fathers* (1966). I have tried as much as possible to provide examples of most recent approaches to the novel, especially those emphasizing the relationship between the novel and its nineteenth-century context.

Preparing the footnotes for this edition has been a fascinating experience, an opportunity to read Hawthorne in a new way—a hypertextual way. I discovered many live links, or at least found many opportunities to create live links, and many chances to enter portals that took me to new places. I have relied on many different sources, online and print. For definitions I have consulted the *Oxford English Dictionary* and Merriam-Webster's online dictionary. For the many Biblical passages to which Hawthorne refers, the King James Bible available at the University of Virginia's Electronic Text Center <http://etext.lib.virginia.edu/kjv.browse.html>. For biographical information on Hawthorne and his family, I have consulted James R. Mellow, *Nathaniel Hawthorne in His Times*; Arlin Turner, *Nathaniel Hawthorne: A Biography*; and Brenda Wineapple, *Hawthorne: A Life*; as well as Stephen Nissenbaum, "The Firing of Nathaniel Hawthorne"; Margaret Moore, *The Salem World of Nathaniel Hawthorne*; and Joseph B. Felt's *Annals of Salem from Its First Settlement* (1827). For information on the settlement and early governance of the Massachusetts Bay Colony, Caleb Snow, *History of Boston* (Boston, 1825); John Winthrop, *The Journal of John Winthrop, 1630–1649*, ed. Richard S. Dunn, James Savage, and Laetitia Yeandle (Cambridge: Harvard UP, 1996); William Bradford, *Bradford's History of Plymouth Plantation, 1606–1646*, ed. William T. Davis (New York: Scribner's, 1923); Robert Emmet Wall, Jr., *Massachusetts Bay: The Crucial Decade, 1640–1650* (New Haven: Yale UP, 1972); Alfred A. Cave, *The Pequot War* (Amherst: U of Massachusetts P, 1996). On Anne Hutchinson, David D. Hall, *The Antinomian Controversy, 1636–1638* (Middletown: Wesleyan UP, 1968); Amy Schrager Lang, *Prophetic Woman: Anne Hutchinson and the Problem of Dissent in the Literature of New England*. For information on English history, especially the first half of the seventeenth century, Samuel R. Gardiner, *History of England from the Accession of James I to the Outbreak of the Civil War, 1603–1642*, 10 vols. (New York: Longmans, Green, 1909). For additional information about William Prynne, I have read William Lamont, *Puritanism and Historical Controversy* (London: University College of London Press, 1996), 15–25, and Mukhtar Ali Isani, "Hawthorne and the Branding of William Prynne," *New England Quarterly* 45 (1972): 182–95. For additional information on the Thomas Overbury murder case, Alfred S. Reid, *The Yellow Ruff and*

The Scarlet Letter: A Source for Hawthorne's Novel (Gainesville: U of Florida P, 1955); Anne Somerset, *Unnatural Murder: Poison at the Court of James I* (London: Weidenfield & Nicolson, 1997); and David Lindley, *The Trials of Frances Howard: Fact and Fiction at the Court of King James* (New York: Routledge, 1993).

My career-long interest in Hawthorne has been aided by many scholars too numerous to list here. I want to give special thanks, however, to Nina Baym, not only for her own career-long devotion to Hawthorne studies, but also for her friendship and support of my own scholarship. Thanks also to Larry J. Reynolds, who urged me to take on this project. I want to thank my colleagues at the University of Cincinnati, Jon Kamholtz, Jay Twomey, and Marty Wechselblatt, for important pieces of information about Hawthorne's references. Thanks to Geri Hinkle-Wesseling, Nancy Bauman, and Sarah Brown for their help with our balky copy machine. Special thanks to Julia Reidhead and Carol Bemis at W. W. Norton & Company, who gave me this opportunity.

A Note on the Texts

For copy text, I have chosen to use the third edition of the novel, published in September 1850 by Ticknor, Reed, and Fields, because that edition, the first set in stereotype plates (by Hobart & Robins and the New England Type and Stereotype Foundry), was the basis of subsequent printings in Hawthorne's lifetime and so represents the text that most nineteenth-century readers actually read. I have collated that edition with the first edition and the Centenary Edition text published by Ohio State University Press. There is no evidence that Hawthorne examined proofs for any edition of the novel, and since no manuscript pages in Hawthorne's hand survive, Hawthorne's final intentions for the text are impossible to determine.

Differences among these three editions are minor but worth noting. The Centenary text has "roundabout" in several places, where the first and third editions have "round about" (e.g., pages 20, 93, and 161 of this volume); I have kept the two-word form, "round about." The first edition has "heaped up," while the third and Centenary editions have "heaped-up" (p. 24); I have used "heaped-up." The third edition is missing a word in line 21 on p. 32; like the editors of the Centenary Edition, I have inserted the word "form" where it seems called for. The first and third editions have "midday" in line 31 on p. 46; the Centenary Edition has "mid-day." I have kept the word as "midday." The Centenary Edition has "stedfastly" in line 7 on p. 49, in line 11 on p. 152, and in line 6 on p. 156; I have preserved "steadfastly," as in the first and third editions. Hawthorne wrote both "elfish" and "elvish" in *The Scarlet Letter*. The Centenary Edition editors regularized the spelling to "elfish" in every case, but I see no reason to do so and so have preserved Hawthorne's different renderings ("elvish" in line 13 on p. 66; "elfish" in line 19 on p. 67; "elvish" in line 2 on p. 102; "elvish" in line 20 on p. 103). In line 41 on p. 69, the first edition has no comma between "occurrences" and "remembrances." The third and Centenary editions insert the comma, and I have preserved it. In line 1 on p. 74, the Centenary Edition has "hall-window," while the first and third editions have "hall window," which I have preserved. In line 13 on p. 118, the first edition has "die," while the third and Centenary editions have "dye," which I have preserved. In line 28 on p. 121, the Centenary Edition has an exclamation point after "time," but the first and third editions use a comma; I have kept the comma. The first edition has no comma between "painfully" in line 39 on p. 156; I have preserved the comma, as in the third and Centenary editions. In line 34 on p. 158, the first edition has a question mark at the end of the sentence, while the third and Centenary editions have an exclamation point; I have used a question mark. In line 22 on p. 165, the first edition has "sobre-hued," the Centenary Edition has "sombre-hued," while the third edition has "sober-hued," which I have preserved.

For "Mrs. Hutchinson," "Endicott and the Red Cross," "The Minister's Black Veil," "Young Goodman Brown," and "The Birth-mark," I have used the Centenary Edition texts published by Ohio State University Press.

The Texts of
THE SCARLET LETTER
AND OTHER WRITINGS

THE

SCARLET LETTER,

A ROMANCE.

BY

NATHANIEL HAWTHORNE.

BOSTON:
TICKNOR, REED, AND FIELDS.
M DCCC LII.

Preface to the Second Edition.[1]

Much to the author's surprise, and (if he may say so without additional offence) considerably to his amusement, he finds that his sketch of official life, introductory to THE SCARLET LETTER, has created an unprecedented excitement in the respectable community immediately around him. It could hardly have been more violent, indeed, had he burned down the Custom-House, and quenched its last smoking ember in the blood of a certain venerable personage, against whom he is supposed to cherish a peculiar malevolence. As the public disapprobation would weigh very heavily on him, were he conscious of deserving it, the author begs leave to say, that he has carefully read over the introductory pages, with a purpose to alter or expunge whatever might be found amiss, and to make the best reparation in his power for the atrocities of which he has been adjudged guilty. But it appears to him, that the only remarkable features of the sketch are its frank and genuine good-humor, and the general accuracy with which he has conveyed his sincere impressions of the characters therein described. As to enmity, or ill-feeling of any kind, personal or political, he utterly disclaims such motives. The sketch might, perhaps, have been wholly omitted, without loss to the public or detriment to the book; but, having undertaken to write it, he conceives that it could not have been done in a better or a kindlier spirit, nor, so far as his abilities availed, with a livelier effect of truth.

The author is constrained, therefore, to republish his introductory sketch without the change of a word.

SALEM, *March* 30, 1850.

---

1. For the second edition of *The Scarlet Letter*, Hawthorne added this brief preface—an unrepentant response to the anger that his original "Custom-House" preface had provoked from many Salem residents.

Contents.

The Custom-House

Introductory to "The Scarlet Letter"

It is a little remarkable, that—though disinclined to talk overmuch of myself and my affairs at the fireside, and to my personal friends—an autobiographical impulse should twice in my life have taken possession of me, in addressing the public. The first time was three or four years since, when I favored the reader—inexcusably, and for no earthly reason, that either the indulgent reader or the intrusive author could imagine—with a description of my way of life in the deep quietude of an Old Manse.[1] And now—because, beyond my deserts, I was happy enough to find a listener or two on the former occasion—I again seize the public by the button, and talk of my three years' experience in a Custom-House. The example of the famous "P. P., Clerk of this Parish," was never more faithfully followed.[2] The truth seems to be, however, that, when he casts his leaves forth upon the wind, the author addresses, not the many who will fling aside his volume, or never take it up, but the few who will understand him, better than most of his schoolmates or lifemates. Some authors, indeed, do far more than this, and indulge themselves in such confidential depths of revelation as could fittingly be addressed, only and exclusively, to the one heart and mind, of perfect sympathy; as if the printed book, thrown at large on the wide world, were certain to find out the divided segment of the writer's own nature, and complete his circle of existence by bringing him into communion with it. It is scarcely decorous, however, to speak all, even where we speak impersonally. But, as thoughts are frozen and utterance benumbed, unless the speaker stand in some true relation with his audience, it may be pardonable to imagine that a friend, a kind and apprehensive, though not the closest friend, is listening to our talk; and then, a native reserve being thawed by this genial consciousness, we may prate of the circumstances that lie around us, and even of ourself, but still keep the inmost Me behind its veil. To this extent, and within these limits, an author, methinks, may be auto-

---

1. On their wedding day (July 9, 1842), Nathaniel and Sophia Hawthorne moved into the Old Manse in Concord, Massachusetts. The house had been built by Ralph Waldo Emerson's grandfather, William Emerson. The Hawthornes lived there until the fall of 1845, when they moved in with Hawthorne's mother and sisters in Salem. Hawthorne's second short story collection, *Mosses from an Old Manse* (1846), included a prefatory essay entitled "The Old Manse."
2. In 1728 Alexander Pope published "Memoirs of P. P., Clerk of This Parish," a satire on contemporary memoirs, especially *The History of His Own Times* (1724), a posthumous publication by Gilbert Burnett, Lord Bishop of Salisbury. Literary London assumed that it was this work Pope meant to burlesque.

7

biographical, without violating either the reader's rights or his own.

It will be seen, likewise, that this Custom-House sketch has a certain propriety, of a kind always recognized in literature, as explaining how a large portion of the following pages came into my possession, and as offering proofs of the authenticity of a narrative therein contained. This, in fact,—a desire to put myself in my true position as editor, or very little more, of the most prolix among the tales that make up my volume,—this, and no other, is my true reason for assuming a personal relation with the public.[3] In accomplishing the main purpose, it has appeared allowable, by a few extra touches, to give a faint representation of a mode of life not heretofore described, together with some of the characters that move in it, among whom the author happened to make one.

In my native town of Salem, at the head of what, half a century ago, in the days of old King Derby,[4] was a bustling wharf,—but which is now burdened with decayed wooden warehouses, and exhibits few or no symptoms of commercial life; except, perhaps, a bark or brig, half-way down its melancholy length, discharging hides; or, nearer at hand, a Nova Scotia schooner, pitching out her cargo of fire-wood,—at the head, I say, of this dilapidated wharf, which the tide often overflows, and along which, at the base and in the rear of the row of buildings, the track of many languid years is seen in a border of unthrifty grass,—here, with a view from its front windows adown this not very enlivening prospect, and thence across the harbor, stands a spacious edifice of brick. From the loftiest point of its roof, during precisely three and a half hours of each forenoon, floats or droops, in breeze or calm, the banner of the republic; but with the thirteen stripes turned vertically, instead of horizontally, and thus indicating that a civil, and not a military post of Uncle Sam's government, is here established. Its front is ornamented with a portico of half a dozen wooden pillars, supporting a balcony, beneath which a flight of wide granite steps descends towards the street. Over the entrance hovers an enormous specimen of the American eagle, with outspread wings, a shield before her breast, and, if I recollect aright, a bunch of intermingled thunderbolts and barbed arrows in each claw. With the customary infirmity of temper that characterizes this unhappy fowl, she appears, by the fierceness of her beak and eye, and the general truculency of her attitude, to threaten mischief to the inoffensive community; and especially to warn all citizens, careful of their safety, against intruding on the premises which she overshadows with her wings. Nevertheless, vixenly as she looks, many people are seeking, at this very moment, to shelter themselves under the wing of the federal eagle; imagining, I presume, that her bosom has all the softness and snugness of an eider-down pillow. But she has no great tenderness, even in her best of

---

3. Hawthorne initially intended *The Scarlet Letter* to be a short story and part of another collection, tentatively entitled *Old Time Legends*. The story grew long enough that his editor, James T. Fields, encouraged him to publish it separately as a novel, but he did not remove several references in "The Custom-House" to the original project.
4. Elias Haskett Derby (1739–1799), Salem merchant and ship owner.

moods, and, sooner or later,—oftener soon than late,—is apt to fling off her nestlings, with a scratch of her claw, a dab of her beak, or a rankling wound from her barbed arrows.

The pavement round about the above-described edifice—which we may as well name at once as the Custom-House of the port—has grass enough growing in its chinks to show that it has not, of late days, been worn by any multitudinous resort of business. In some months of the year, however, there often chances a forenoon when affairs move onward with a livelier tread. Such occasions might remind the elderly citizen of that period, before the last war with England,[5] when Salem was a port by itself; not scorned, as she is now, by her own merchants and ship-owners, who permit her wharves to crumble to ruin, while their ventures go to swell, needlessly and imperceptibly, the mighty flood of commerce at New York or Boston. On some such morning, when three or four vessels happen to have arrived at once,—usually from Africa or South America,—or to be on the verge of their departure thitherward, there is a sound of frequent feet, passing briskly up and down the granite steps. Here, before his own wife has greeted him, you may greet the sea-flushed ship-master, just in port, with his vessel's papers under his arm, in a tarnished tin box. Here, too, comes his owner, cheerful or sombre, gracious or in the sulks, accordingly as his scheme of the now accomplished voyage has been realized in merchandise that will readily be turned to gold, or has buried him under a bulk of incommodities, such as nobody will care to rid him of. Here, likewise,—the germ of the wrinkle-browed, grizzly-bearded, care-worn merchant,—we have the smart young clerk, who gets the taste of traffic as a wolf-cub does of blood, and already sends adventures in his master's ships, when he had better be sailing mimic-boats upon a mill-pond. Another figure in the scene is the outward-bound sailor in quest of a protection; or the recently arrived one, pale and feeble, seeking a passport to the hospital. Nor must we forget the captains of the rusty little schooners that bring fire-wood from the British provinces; a rough-looking set of tarpaulins, without the alertness of the Yankee aspect, but contributing an item of no slight importance to our decaying trade.

Cluster all these individuals together, as they sometimes were, with other miscellaneous ones to diversify the group, and, for the time being, it made the Custom-House a stirring scene. More frequently, however, on ascending the steps, you would discern—in the entry, if it were summer time, or in their appropriate rooms, if wintry or inclement weather—a row of venerable figures, sitting in old-fashioned chairs, which were tipped on their hind legs back against the wall. Oftentimes they were asleep, but occasionally might be heard talking together, in voices between speech and a snore, and with that lack of energy that distinguishes the occupants of alms-houses, and all other human beings who depend for subsistence on charity, on monopolized labor, or anything else but their own independent exertions. These old

5. The War of 1812 (1812–14).

gentlemen—seated, like Matthew, at the receipt of customs, but not very liable to be summoned thence, like him, for apostolic errands— were Custom-House officers.[6]

Furthermore, on the left hand as you enter the front door, is a certain room or office, about fifteen feet square, and of a lofty height; with two of its arched windows commanding a view of the aforesaid dilapidated wharf, and the third looking across a narrow lane, and along a portion of Derby-street. All three give glimpses of the shops of grocers, block-makers, slop-sellers, and ship-chandlers; around the doors of which are generally to be seen, laughing and gossiping, clusters of old salts, and such other wharf-rats as haunt the Wapping[7] of a seaport. The room itself is cobwebbed, and dingy with old paint; its floor is strewn with gray sand, in a fashion that has elsewhere fallen into long disuse; and it is easy to conclude, from the general slovenliness of the place, that this is a sanctuary into which womankind, with her tools of magic, the broom and mop, has very infrequent access. In the way of furniture, there is a stove with a voluminous funnel; an old pine desk, with a three-legged stool beside it; two or three wooden-bottom chairs, exceedingly decrepit and infirm; and—not to forget the library—on some shelves, a score or two of volumes of the Acts of Congress, and a bulky Digest of the Revenue Laws. A tin pipe ascends through the ceiling, and forms a medium of vocal communication with other parts of the edifice. And here, some six months ago,—pacing from corner to corner, or lounging on the long-legged stool, with his elbow on the desk, and his eyes wandering up and down the columns of the morning newspaper,—you might have recognized, honored reader, the same individual who welcomed you into his cheery little study, where the sunshine glimmered so pleasantly through the willow branches, on the western side of the Old Manse. But now, should you go thither to seek him, you would inquire in vain for the Locofoco Surveyor.[8] The besom of reform has swept him out of office; and a worthier successor wears his dignity, and pockets his emoluments.

This old town of Salem—my native place, though I have dwelt much away from it, both in boyhood and maturer years—possesses, or did possess, a hold on my affections, the force of which I have never realized during my seasons of actual residence here. Indeed, so far as its physical aspect is concerned, with its flat, unvaried surface, covered chiefly with wooden houses, few or none of which pretend to architectural beauty,—its irregularity, which is neither picturesque nor quaint, but only tame,—its long and lazy street, lounging wearisomely through the whole extent of the peninsula, with Gallows Hill and New

6. See Matthew 9:9: "And as Jesus passed forth from thence, he saw a man, named Matthew, sitting at the receipt of custom: and he saith unto him, Follow me. And he arose, and followed him."
7. A suburb of East London on the river Thames, Wapping provided the main entrance to the London docks. *Slop-sellers*: "Slop" could refer to several things, including inexpensive clothes.
8. A reform-minded faction of the Democratic party in New York, called the Equal Rights party. *Locofoco*: a type of friction match that party members used for illumination when conservative Democrats turned out the lights in Tammany Hall before one of their meetings.

Guinea at one end, and a view of the alms-house at the other,[9]—such being the features of my native town, it would be quite as reasonable to form a sentimental attachment to a disarranged checker-board. And yet, though invariably happiest elsewhere, there is within me a feeling for old Salem, which, in lack of a better phrase, I must be content to call affection. The sentiment is probably assignable to the deep and aged roots which my family has struck into the soil. It is now nearly two centuries and a quarter since the original Briton, the earliest emigrant of my name, made his appearance in the wild and forest-bordered settlement, which has since become a city.[1] And here his descendants have been born and died, and have mingled their earthy substance with the soil; until no small portion of it must necessarily be akin to the mortal frame wherewith, for a little while, I walk the streets. In part, therefore, the attachment which I speak of is the mere sensuous sympathy of dust for dust. Few of my countrymen can know what it is; nor, as frequent transplantation is perhaps better for the stock, need they consider it desirable to know.

But the sentiment has likewise its moral quality. The figure of that first ancestor, invested by family tradition with a dim and dusky grandeur, was present to my boyish imagination, as far back as I can remember. It still haunts me, and induces a sort of home-feeling with the past, which I scarcely claim in reference to the present phase of the town. I seem to have a stronger claim to a residence here on account of this grave, bearded, sable-cloaked and steeple-crowned progenitor,—who came so early, with his Bible and his sword, and trode the unworn street with such a stately port, and made so large a figure, as a man of war and peace,—a stronger claim than for myself, whose name is seldom heard and my face hardly known. He was a soldier, legislator, judge; he was a ruler in the Church; he had all the Puritanic traits, both good and evil. He was likewise a bitter persecutor; as witness the Quakers, who have remembered him in their histories, and relate an incident of his hard severity towards a woman of their sect, which will last longer, it is to be feared, than any record of his better deeds, although these were many.[2] His son, too, inherited the persecuting spirit, and made himself so conspicuous in the martyrdom of the witches, that their blood may fairly be said to have left a stain upon him.[3] So deep a stain, indeed, that his old dry bones, in the Charter-street burial-ground, must still retain it, if they have not crumbled utterly to dust! I know not whether these ancestors of mine bethought themselves to repent, and ask pardon of heaven for their cruelties; or whether they are now groaning under the heavy consequences of them,

9. Gallows Hill, at the southern edge of Salem, is the area where nineteen witches were hanged in the summer of 1692.
1. Hawthorne's great-great-great grandfather, William Hathorne (c. 1606–1681), became a notable public figure in Salem after he settled there in 1636. He served on the Board of Selectmen for many years and fought in King Philip's War. Hawthorne added the "w" to the family name when he was in his twenties.
2. William Hathorne ordered a Quaker woman, Ann Coleman, to be whipped through the streets of Salem.
3. John Hathorne (1641–1717), William's son and Hawthorne's great-great grandfather, presided at the Salem witch trials.

in another state of being. At all events, I, the present writer, as their representative, hereby take shame upon myself for their sakes, and pray that any curse incurred by them—as I have heard, and as the dreary and unprosperous condition of the race, for many a long year back, would argue to exist—may be now and henceforth removed.

Doubtless, however, either of these stern and black-browed Puritans would have thought it quite a sufficient retribution for his sins, that, after so long a lapse of years, the old trunk of the family tree, with so much venerable moss upon it, should have borne, as its top-most bough, an idler like myself. No aim, that I have ever cherished, would they recognize as laudable; no success of mine—if my life, beyond its domestic scope, had ever been brightened by success—would they deem otherwise than worthless, if not positively disgraceful. "What is he?" murmurs one gray shadow of my forefathers to the other. "A writer of story-books! What kind of a business in life,—what mode of glorifying God, or being serviceable to mankind in his day and genera- tion,—may that be? Why, the degenerate fellow might as well have been a fiddler!" Such are the compliments bandied between my great- grandsires and myself, across the gulf of time! And yet, let them scorn me as they will, strong traits of their nature have intertwined them- selves with mine.

Planted deep, in the town's earliest infancy and childhood, by these two earnest and energetic men, the race has ever since subsisted here; always, too, in respectability; never, so far as I have known, disgraced by a single unworthy member; but seldom or never, on the other hand, after the first two generations, performing any memorable deed, or so much as putting forward a claim to public notice. Gradually, they have sunk almost out of sight; as old houses, here and there about the streets, get covered half-way to the eaves by the accumulation of new soil. From father to son, for above a hundred years, they followed the sea; a gray-headed shipmaster, in each generation, retiring from the quarter-deck to the homestead, while a boy of fourteen took the hereditary place before the mast, confronting the salt spray and the gale, which had blustered against his sire and grandsire.[4] The boy, also, in due time, passed from the forecastle to the cabin, spent a tem- pestuous manhood, and returned from his world-wanderings, to grow old, and die, and mingle his dust with the natal earth. This long con- nection of a family with one spot, as its place of birth and burial, cre- ates a kindred between the human being and the locality, quite independent of any charm in the scenery or moral circumstances that surround him. It is not love, but instinct. The new inhabitant—who came himself from a foreign land, or whose father or grandfather came—has little claim to be called a Salemite; he has no conception of the oyster-like tenacity with which an old settler, over whom his third century is creeping, clings to the spot where his successive gen- erations have been imbedded. It is no matter that the place is joyless

---

4. Hawthorne's father, Nathaniel Hathorne, was a sea captain who died of yellow fever in Suri- nam in 1808, when Hawthorne was not quite four.

for him; that he is weary of the old wooden houses, the mud and dust, the dead level of site and sentiment, the chill east wind, and the chillest of social atmospheres;—all these, and whatever faults besides he may see or imagine, are nothing to the purpose. The spell survives, and just as powerfully as if the natal spot were an earthly paradise. So has it been in my case. I felt it almost as a destiny to make Salem my home; so that the mould of features and cast of character which had all along been familiar here—ever, as one representative of the race lay down in his grave, another assuming, as it were, his sentry-march along the main street—might still in my little day be seen and recognized in the old town. Nevertheless, this very sentiment is an evidence that the connection, which has become an unhealthy one, should at last be severed. Human nature will not flourish, any more than a potato, if it be planted and replanted, for too long a series of generations, in the same worn-out soil. My children have had other birthplaces, and, so far as their fortunes may be within my control, shall strike their roots into unaccustomed earth.

On emerging from the Old Manse, it was chiefly this strange, indolent, unjoyous attachment for my native town, that brought me to fill a place in Uncle Sam's brick edifice, when I might as well, or better, have gone somewhere else.[5] My doom was on me. It was not the first time, nor the second, that I had gone away,—as it seemed, permanently,—but yet returned, like the bad half-penny; or as if Salem were for me the inevitable centre of the universe. So, one fine morning, I ascended the flight of granite steps, with the President's commission in my pocket, and was introduced to the corps of gentlemen who were to aid me in my weighty responsibility, as chief executive officer of the Custom-House.

I doubt greatly—or, rather, I do not doubt at all—whether any public functionary of the United States, either in the civil or military line, has ever had such a patriarchal body of veterans under his orders as myself. The whereabouts of the Oldest Inhabitant was at once settled, when I looked at them. For upwards of twenty years before this epoch, the independent position of the Collector had kept the Salem Custom-House out of the whirlpool of political vicissitude, which makes the tenure of office generally so fragile. A soldier,—New England's most distinguished soldier,—he stood firmly on the pedestal of his gallant services; and, himself secure in the wise liberality of the successive administrations through which he had held office, he had been the safety of his subordinates in many an hour of danger and heart-quake. General Miller was radically conservative; a man over whose kindly nature habit had no slight influence; attaching himself strongly to familiar faces, and with difficulty moved to change, even when change might have brought unquestionable improvement.[6]

5. Hawthorne was appointed surveyor of the Salem Custom House by President James K. Polk and took office in the spring of 1846. His annual salary was $1,200 (about $25,000 in 2004 dollars).
6. General James F. Miller (1776–1851) fought in the War of 1812, served as the first territorial governor of Arkansas (1819–25), and held the position of collector of the Port of Salem from 1825 until 1849.

Thus, on taking charge of my department, I found few but aged men. They were ancient sea-captains, for the most part, who, after being tost on every sea, and standing up sturdily against life's tempestuous blast, had finally drifted into this quiet nook; where, with little to disturb them, except the periodical terrors of a Presidential election, they one and all acquired a new lease of existence. Though by no means less liable than their fellow-men to age and infirmity, they had evidently some talisman or other that kept death at bay. Two or three of their number, as I was assured, being gouty and rheumatic, or perhaps bed-ridden, never dreamed of making their appearance at the Custom-House, during a large part of the year; but, after a torpid winter, would creep out into the warm sunshine of May or June, go lazily about what they termed duty, and, at their own leisure and convenience, betake themselves to bed again. I must plead guilty to the charge of abbreviating the official breath of more than one of these venerable servants of the republic. They were allowed, on my representation, to rest from their arduous labors, and soon afterwards—as if their sole principle of life had been zeal for their country's service; as I verily believe it was— withdrew to a better world. It is a pious consolation to me, that, through my interference, a sufficient space was allowed them for repentance of the evil and corrupt practices, into which, as a matter of course, every Custom-House officer must be supposed to fall. Neither the front nor the back entrance of the Custom-House opens on the road to Paradise.

The greater part of my officers were Whigs.[7] It was well for their venerable brotherhood that the new Surveyor was not a politician, and though a faithful Democrat in principle, neither received nor held his office with any reference to political services.[8] Had it been otherwise,—had an active politician been put into this influential post, to assume the easy task of making head against a Whig Collector, whose infirmities withheld him from the personal administration of his office,—hardly a man of the old corps would have drawn the breath of official life, within a month after the exterminating angel had come up the Custom-House steps. According to the received code in such matters, it would have been nothing short of duty, in a politician, to bring every one of those white heads under the axe of the guillotine. It was plain enough to discern, that the old fellows dreaded some such discourtesy at my hands. It pained, and at the same time amused me, to behold the terrors that attended my advent; to see a furrowed cheek, weather-beaten by half a century of storm, turn ashy pale at the glance of so harmless an individual as myself; to detect, as one or another addressed me, the tremor of a voice, which, in long-past days, had been

7. The Democrats and Whigs were the two major political parties in the middle of the nineteenth century until a coalition of Whig, Free-Soil, and abolitionist northern Democrats formed the Republican party in the 1850s. Abraham Lincoln was elected the first Republican president in 1860.
8. Hawthorne had a vested interest in claiming little interest in politics. He was fired from his position as surveyor after Zachary Taylor became president in 1848. He lobbied to retain his position on the grounds that he was apolitical, but local Whigs, led by the Reverend Charles W. Upham, claimed with some truth that he had been more politically active than he acknowledged.

wont to bellow through a speaking-trumpet, hoarsely enough to frighten Boreas[9] himself to silence. They knew, these excellent old persons, that, by all established rule,—and, as regarded some of them, weighed by their own lack of efficiency for business,—they ought to have given place to younger men, more orthodox in politics, and altogether fitter than themselves to serve our common Uncle. I knew it too, but could never quite find in my heart to act upon the knowledge. Much and deservedly to my own discredit, therefore, and considerably to the detriment of my official conscience, they continued, during my incumbency, to creep about the wharves, and loiter up and down the Custom-House steps. They spent a good deal of time, also, asleep in their accustomed corners, with their chairs tilted back against the wall; awaking, however, once or twice in a forenoon, to bore one another with the several thousandth repetition of old sea-stories, and mouldy jokes, that had grown to be pass-words and countersigns among them.

The discovery was soon made, I imagine, that the new Surveyor had no great harm in him. So, with lightsome hearts, and the happy consciousness of being usefully employed,—in their own behalf, at least, if not for our beloved country,—these good old gentlemen went through the various formalities of office. Sagaciously, under their spectacles, did they peep into the holds of vessels! Mighty was their fuss about little matters, and marvellous, sometimes, the obtuseness that allowed greater ones to slip between their fingers! Whenever such a mischance occurred,—when a wagon-load of valuable merchandise had been smuggled ashore, at noonday, perhaps, and directly beneath their unsuspicious noses,—nothing could exceed the vigilance and alacrity with which they proceeded to lock, and double-lock, and secure with tape and sealing-wax, all the avenues of the delinquent vessel. Instead of a reprimand for their previous negligence, the case seemed rather to require an eulogium on their praiseworthy caution, after the mischief had happened; a grateful recognition of the promptitude of their zeal, the moment that there was no longer any remedy.

Unless people are more than commonly disagreeable, it is my foolish habit to contract a kindness for them. The better part of my companion's character, if it have a better part, is that which usually comes uppermost in my regard, and forms the type whereby I recognize the man. As most of these old Custom-House officers had good traits, and as my position in reference to them, being paternal and protective, was favorable to the growth of friendly sentiments, I soon grew to like them all. It was pleasant, in the summer forenoons,—when the fervent heat, that almost liquefied the rest of the human family, merely communicated a genial warmth to their half-torpid systems,—it was pleasant to hear them chatting in the back entry, a row of them all tipped against the wall, as usual; while the frozen witticisms of past generations were thawed out, and came bubbling with laughter from their lips. Externally, the jollity of aged men has much in common

9. God of the north wind in Greek mythology.

with the mirth of children; the intellect, any more than a deep sense of humor, has little to do with the matter; it is, with both, a gleam that plays upon the surface, and imparts a sunny and cheery aspect alike to the green branch, and gray, mouldering trunk. In one case, however, it is real sunshine; in the other, it more resembles the phosphorescent glow of decaying wood.

It would be sad injustice, the reader must understand, to represent all my excellent old friends as in their dotage. In the first place, my coadjutors were not invariably old; there were men among them in their strength and prime, of marked ability and energy, and altogether superior to the sluggish and dependent mode of life on which their evil stars had cast them. Then, moreover, the white locks of age were sometimes found to be the thatch of an intellectual tenement in good repair. But, as respects the majority of my corps of veterans, there will be no wrong done, if I characterize them generally as a set of wearisome old souls, who had gathered nothing worth preservation from their varied experience of life. They seemed to have flung away all the golden grain of practical wisdom, which they had enjoyed so many opportunities of harvesting, and most carefully to have stored their memories with the husks. They spoke with far more interest and unction of their morning's breakfast, or yesterday's, to-day's, or to-morrow's dinner, than of the shipwreck of forty or fifty years ago, and all the world's wonders which they had witnessed with their youthful eyes.

The father of the Custom-House—the patriarch, not only of this little squad of officials, but, I am bold to say, of the respectable body of tide-waiters all over the United States—was a certain permanent Inspector.[1] He might truly be termed a legitimate son of the revenue system, dyed in the wool, or, rather, born in the purple; since his sire, a Revolutionary colonel, and formerly collector of the port, had created an office for him, and appointed him to fill it, at a period of the early ages which few living men can now remember. This Inspector, when I first knew him, was a man of four-score years, or thereabouts, and certainly one of the most wonderful specimens of winter-green that you would be likely to discover in a lifetime's search. With his florid cheek, his compact figure, smartly arrayed in a bright-buttoned blue coat, his brisk and vigorous step, and his hale and hearty aspect, altogether he seemed—not young, indeed—but a kind of new contrivance of Mother Nature in the shape of man, whom age and infirmity had no business to touch. His voice and laugh, which perpetually reëchoed through the Custom-House, had nothing of the tremulous quaver and cackle of an old man's utterance; they came strutting out of his lungs, like the crow of a cock, or the blast of a clarion. Looking at him merely as an animal,—and there was very little else to look at,—he was a most satisfactory object, from the thorough healthfulness and wholesomeness of his system, and his capacity, at that extreme age, to enjoy all, or nearly all, the delights which he had ever aimed at, or conceived of. The careless

---

1. William Lee served as inspector. According to Margaret Moore, Lee's daughters never forgave Hawthorne for his "trivializing" sketch, and Hawthorne later regretted having written disparagingly about him. See Moore, 182.

security of his life in the Custom-House, on a regular income, and with but slight and infrequent apprehensions of removal, had no doubt contributed to make time pass lightly over him. The original and more potent causes, however, lay in the rare perfection of his animal nature, the moderate proportion of intellect, and the very trifling admixture of moral and spiritual ingredients; these latter qualities, indeed, being in barely enough measure to keep the old gentleman from walking on all-fours. He possessed no power of thought, no depth of feeling, no troublesome sensibilities; nothing, in short, but a few commonplace instincts, which, aided by the cheerful temper that grew inevitably out of his physical well-being, did duty very respectably, and to general acceptance, in lieu of a heart. He had been the husband of three wives, all long since dead; the father of twenty children, most of whom, at every age of childhood or maturity, had likewise returned to dust. Here, one would suppose, might have been sorrow enough to imbue the sunniest disposition, through and through, with a sable tinge. Not so with our old Inspector! One brief sigh sufficed to carry off the entire burden of these dismal reminiscences. The next moment, he was as ready for sport as any unbreeched infant; far readier than the Collector's junior clerk, who, at nineteen years, was much the elder and graver man of the two.

I used to watch and study this patriarchal personage with, I think, livelier curiosity, than any other form of humanity there presented to my notice. He was, in truth, a rare phenomenon; so perfect, in one point of view; so shallow, so delusive, so impalpable, such an absolute nonentity, in every other. My conclusion was that he had no soul, no heart, no mind; nothing, as I have already said, but instincts; and yet, withal, so cunningly had the few materials of his character been put together, that there was no painful perception of deficiency, but, on my part, an entire contentment with what I found in him. It might be difficult—and it was so—to conceive how he should exist hereafter, so earthly and sensuous did he seem; but surely his existence here, admitting that it was to terminate with his last breath, had been not unkindly given; with no higher moral responsibilities than the beasts of the field, but with a larger scope of enjoyment than theirs, and with all their blessed immunity from the dreariness and duskiness of age.

One point, in which he had vastly the advantage over his four-footed brethren, was his ability to recollect the good dinners which it had made no small portion of the happiness of his life to eat. His gourmandism was a highly agreeable trait; and to hear him talk of roast-meat was as appetizing as a pickle or an oyster. As he possessed no higher attribute, and neither sacrificed nor vitiated any spiritual endowment by devoting all his energies and ingenuities to subserve the delight and profit of his maw, it always pleased and satisfied me to hear him expatiate on fish, poultry, and butcher's meat, and the most eligible methods of preparing them for the table. His reminiscences of good cheer, however ancient the date of the actual banquet, seemed to bring the savor of pig or turkey under one's very nostrils. There were flavors on his palate, that had lingered there not less than sixty or seventy years, and were still apparently as fresh as that of the mutton-chop which he had just devoured for his breakfast. I have heard him smack his lips over dinners, every guest at which, except himself, had long been food for worms. It was marvellous to observe how the ghosts of bygone meals were continually rising up before him; not in anger or retribution, but as if grateful for his former appreciation, and seeking to repudiate an endless series of enjoyment, at once shadowy and sensual. A tender-loin of beef, a hind-quarter of veal, a spare-rib of pork, a particular chicken, or a remarkably praiseworthy turkey, which had perhaps adorned his board in the days of the elder Adams, would be remembered;[2] while all the subsequent experience of our race, and all the events that brightened or darkened his individual career, had gone over him with as little permanent effect as the passing breeze. The chief tragic event of the old man's life, so far as I could judge, was his mishap with a certain goose, which lived and died some twenty or forty years ago; a goose of most promising figure, but which, at table, proved so inveterately tough that the carving-knife would make no impression on its carcass, and it could only be divided with an axe and and handsaw.

But it is time to quit this sketch; on which, however, I should be glad to dwell at considerably more length, because, of all men whom I have ever known, this individual was fittest to be a Custom-House officer. Most persons, owing to causes which I may not have space to hint at, suffer moral detriment from this peculiar mode of life. The old Inspector was incapable of it; and, were he to continue in office to the end of time, would be just as good as he was then, and sit down to dinner with just as good an appetite.

There is one likeness, without which my gallery of Custom-House portraits would be strangely incomplete; but which my comparatively few opportunities for observation enable me to sketch only in the merest outline. It is that of the Collector, our gallant old General, who, after his brilliant military service, subsequently to which he had ruled over a wild Western territory, had come hither, twenty years before, to spend the decline of his varied and honorable life. The brave soldier had already numbered, nearly or quite, his threescore years and ten, and was pursuing the remainder of his earthly march, burdened with infirmities which even the martial music of his own spirit-stirring recollections could do little towards lightening. The step was palsied now, that had been foremost in the charge. It was only with the assistance of a servant, and by leaning his hand heavily on the iron balustrade, that he could slowly and painfully ascend the Custom-House steps, and, with a toilsome progress across the floor, attain his customary chair beside the fireplace. There he used to sit, gazing with a somewhat dim serenity of aspect at the figures that came and went; amid the rustle of papers, the administering of oaths, the discussion of business, and the casual talk of the office; all which sounds and circumstances seemed but indistinctly to impress his senses, and hardly to

---

2. John Adams (1735–1826), second president (1797–1801) of the United States.

make their way into his inner sphere of contemplation. His countenance, in this repose, was mild and kindly. If his notice was sought, an
expression of courtesy and interest gleamed out upon his features;
proving that there was light within him, and that it was only the outward medium of the intellectual lamp that obstructed the rays in their
passage. The closer you penetrated to the substance of his mind, the
sounder it appeared. When no longer called upon to speak, or listen,
either of which operations cost him an evident effort, his face would
briefly subside into its former not uncheerful quietude. It was not
painful to behold this look; for, though dim, it had not the imbecility
of decaying age. The framework of his nature, originally strong and
massive, was not yet crumbled into ruin.

To observe and define his character, however, under such disadvan-
tages, was as difficult a task as to trace out and build up anew, in
imagination, an old fortress, like Ticonderoga, from a view of its gray
and broken ruins.[3] Here and there, perchance, the walls may remain
almost complete; but elsewhere may be only a shapeless mound, cumbrous with its very strength, and overgrown, through long years of
peace and neglect, with grass and alien weeds.

Nevertheless, looking at the old warrior with affection,—for, slight
as was the communication between us, my feeling towards him, like
that of all bipeds and quadrupeds who knew him, might not improp-
erly be termed so,—I could discern the main points of his portrait. It
was marked with the noble and heroic qualities which showed it to be
not by a mere accident, but of good right, that he had won a distinguished name. His spirit could never, I conceive, have been characterized by an uneasy activity; it must, at any period of his life, have
required an impulse to set him in motion; but, once stirred up, with
obstacles to overcome, and an adequate object to be attained, it was
not in the man to give out or fail. The heat that had formerly pervaded
his nature, and which was not yet extinct, was never of the kind that
flashes and flickers in a blaze; but, rather, a deep, red glow, as of iron
in a furnace. Weight, solidity, firmness; this was the expression of his
repose, even in such decay as had crept untimely over him, at the period of which I speak. But I could imagine, even then, that, under
some excitement which should go deeply into his consciousness,—
roused by a trumpet-peal, loud enough to awaken all of his energies
that were not dead, but only slumbering,—he was yet capable of flinging off his infirmities like a sick man's gown, dropping the staff of age
to seize a battle-sword, and starting up once more a warrior. And, in so
intense a moment, his demeanor would have still been calm. Such
an exhibition, however, was but to be pictured in fancy; not to be anticipated, nor desired. What I saw in him—as evidently as the indestructible ramparts of Old Ticonderoga, already cited as the most
appropriate simile—were the features of stubborn and ponderous endurance, which might well have amounted to obstinacy in his earlier

3. One of the first major battles of the Revolutionary War occurred on May 10, 1775, when
Ethan Allen led his Green Mountain Boys in a successful attack on British troops at Fort
Ticonderoga in what is now upstate New York.

days; of integrity, that, like most of his other endowments, lay in a somewhat heavy mass, and was just as unmalleable and unmanageable as a ton of iron ore; and of benevolence, which, fiercely as he led the bayonets on at Chippewa or Fort Erie, I take to be of quite as genuine a stamp as what actuates any or all the polemical philanthropists of the age.[4] He had slain men with his own hand, for aught I know;— certainly, they had fallen, like blades of grass at the sweep of the scythe, before the charge to which his spirit imparted its triumphant energy;—but, be that as it might, there was never in his heart so much cruelty as would have brushed the down off a butterfly's wing. I have not known the man, to whose innate kindliness I would more confidently make an appeal.

Many characteristics—and those, too, which contribute not the least forcibly to impart resemblance in a sketch—must have vanished, or been obscured, before I met the General. All merely graceful attributes are usually the most evanescent; nor does Nature adorn the human ruin with blossoms of new beauty, that have their roots and proper nutriment only in the chinks and crevices of decay, as she sows wall-flowers over the ruined fortress of Ticonderoga. Still, even in respect of grace and beauty, there were points well worth noting. A ray of humor, now and then, would make its way through the veil of dim obstruction, and glimmer pleasantly upon our faces. A trait of native elegance, seldom seen in the masculine character after childhood or early youth, was shown in the General's fondness for the sight and fragrance of flowers. An old soldier might be supposed to prize only the bloody laurel on his brow; but here was one, who seemed to have a young girl's appreciation of the floral tribe.

There, beside the fireplace, the brave old General used to sit; while the Surveyor—though seldom, when it could be avoided, taking upon himself the difficult task of engaging him in conversation—was fond of standing at a distance, and watching his quiet and almost slumberous countenance. He seemed away from us, although we saw him but a few yards off; remote, though we passed close beside his chair; unattainable, though we might have stretched forth our hands and touched his own. It might be that he lived a more real life within his thoughts, than amid the unappropriate environment of the Collector's office. The evolutions of the parade; the tumult of the battle; the flourish of old, heroic music, heard thirty years before;—such scenes and sounds, perhaps, were all alive before his intellectual sense. Meanwhile, the merchants and ship-masters, the spruce clerks and uncouth sailors, entered and departed; the bustle of this commercial and Custom-House life kept up its little murmur round about him; and neither with the men nor their affairs did the General appear to sustain the most distant relation. He was as much out of place as an old sword—now rusty, but which had flashed once in the battle's front, and showed still a bright gleam along its blade—would have been,

---

4. In the War of 1812, American troops won important battles at Fort Erie and at Chippewa (near Niagara Falls) in the summer of 1814. General Miller fought at the Battle of Chippewa (July 5, 1814), the day after Hawthorne's tenth birthday.

among the inkstands, paper-folders, and mahogany rulers, on the Deputy Collector's desk.

There was one thing that much aided me in renewing and re-creating the stalwart soldier of the Niagara frontier,—the man of true and simple energy. It was the recollection of those memorable words of his,—"I'll try, Sir!"—spoken on the very verge of a desperate and heroic enterprise, and breathing the soul and spirit of New England hardihood, comprehending all perils, and encountering all.[5] If, in our country, valor were rewarded by heraldic honor, this phrase—which it seems so easy to speak, but which only he, with such a task of danger and glory before him, has ever spoken—would be the best and fit test of all mottoes for the General's shield of arms.

It contributes greatly towards a man's moral and intellectual health, to be brought into habits of companionship with individuals unlike himself, who care little for his pursuits, and whose sphere and abilities he must go out of himself to appreciate. The accidents of my life have often afforded me this advantage, but never with more fulness and variety than during my continuance in office. There was one man, especially, the observation of whose character gave me a new idea of talent.[6] His gifts were emphatically those of a man of business; prompt, acute, clear-minded; with an eye that saw through all perplexi-ties, and a faculty of arrangement that made them vanish, as by the waving of an enchanter's wand. Bred up from boyhood in the Custom-House, it was his proper field of activity; and the many intrica-cies of business, so harassing to the interloper, presented themselves be-fore him with the regularity of a perfectly comprehended system. In my contemplation, he stood as the ideal of his class. He was, indeed, the Custom-House in himself; or, at all events, the main spring that kept its variously revolving wheels in motion; for, in an institution like this, where its officers are appointed to subserve their own profit and conven-ience, and seldom with a leading reference to their fitness for the duty to be performed, they must perforce seek elsewhere the dexterity which is not in them. Thus, by an inevitable necessity, as a magnet attracts steel-filings, so did our man of business draw to himself the difficulties which everybody met with. With an easy condescension, and kind forbearance towards our stupidity,—which, to his order of mind, must have seemed little short of crime,—would he forthwith, by the merest touch of his fin-ger, make the incomprehensible as clear as daylight. The merchants val-ued him not less than we, his esoteric friends. His integrity was perfect; it was a law of nature with him, rather than a choice or a principle; nor can it be otherwise than the main condition of an intellect so remarkably clear and accurate as his, to be honest and regular in the administration of affairs. A stain on his conscience, as to anything that came within the range of his vocation, would trouble such a man very much in the same

5. When General Winfield Scott commanded General Miller to take a British battery at Lundy's Lane on July 25, 1814, he reportedly replied, "I'll try, Sir!"
6. Zachariah Burchmore (1809–1884), secretary of the Democratic Party in Salem, served as Custom House clerk and was one of Hawthorne's allies in his effort to retain his job. Burch-more was fired from his position shortly after Hawthorne's own dismissal. See Nissenbaum, 73–75.

way, though to a far greater degree, than an error in the balance of an account, or an ink-blot on the fair page of a book of record. Here, in a
word,—and it is a rare instance in my life,—I had met with a person
thoroughly adapted to the situation which he held.

Such were some of the people with whom I now found myself connected. I took it in good part, at the hands of Providence, that I was
thrown into a position so little akin to my past habits; and set myself
seriously to gather from it whatever profit was to be had. After my fellowship of toil and impracticable schemes with the dreamy brethren of
Brook Farm;[7] after living for three years within the subtile influence of
an intellect like Emerson's; after those wild, free days on the Assabeth,
indulging fantastic speculations, beside our fire of fallen boughs, with
Ellery Channing; after talking with Thoreau about pine-trees and Indian relics, in his hermitage at Walden; after growing fastidious by
sympathy with the classic refinement of Hillard's culture; after becoming imbued with poetic sentiment at Longfellow's hearth-stone;—it
was time, at length, that I should exercise other faculties of my nature,
and nourish myself with food for which I had hitherto had little appetite. Even the old Inspector was desirable, as a change of diet, to a
man who had known Alcott.[8] I looked upon it as an evidence, in some
measure, of a system naturally well balanced, and lacking no essential
part of a thorough organization, that, with such associates to remember, I could mingle at once with men of altogether different qualities,
and never murmur at the change.

Literature, its exertions and objects, were now of little moment in
my regard. I cared not, at this period, for books; they were apart from
me. Nature,—except it were human nature,—the nature that is developed in earth and sky, was, in one sense, hidden from me; and all the
imaginative delight, wherewith it had been spiritualized, passed away
out of my mind. A gift, a faculty, if it had not departed, was suspended
and inanimate within me. There would have been something sad, unutterably dreary, in all this, had I not been conscious that it lay at my
own option to recall whatever was valuable in the past. It might be
true, indeed, that this was a life which could not, with impunity, be
lived too long; else, it might make me permanently other than I had
been, without transforming me into any shape which it would be
worth my while to take. But I never considered it as other than a transitory life. There was always a prophetic instinct, a low whisper in my
ear, that, within no long period, and whenever a new change of custom should be essential to my good, a change would come.

7. George Ripley (1802–1880) founded the utopian community Brook Farm in 1841 at a site
   near West Roxbury, Massachusetts, just west of Boston. Hawthorne invested $1,000
   (the price of two shares) in the experiment and lived at the farm for several months (April–
   October) in 1841, but he quickly grew disenchanted. His experiences at Brook Farm form
   the pretext for *The Blithedale Romance* (1852).
8. Hawthorne recalls his three years at the Old Manse in Concord. He lived about a mile from
   Ralph Waldo Emerson (1803–1882), enjoyed the company of William Ellery Channing
   (1818–1901) and Henry David Thoreau (1817–1862), whose Walden cabin he visited
   shortly before leaving Concord in 1845. Boston attorney George Hillard (1808–1879) became a good friend. Hawthorne knew poet Henry Wadsworth Longfellow (1807–1882) from
   their days as students at Bowdoin College. Bronson Alcott (1799–1888), father of Louisa
   May Alcott, was a prominent, if eccentric, Concord intellectual.

Meanwhile, there I was, a Surveyor of the Revenue, and, so far as I have been able to understand, as good a Surveyor as need be. A man of thought, fancy, and sensibility, (had he ten times the Surveyor's proportion of those qualities,) may, at any time, be a man of affairs, if he will only choose to give himself the trouble. My fellow-officers, and the merchants and sea-captains with whom my official duties brought me into any manner of connection, viewed me in no other light, and probably knew me in no other character. None of them, I presume, had ever read a page of my inditing, or would have cared a fig the more for me, if they had read them all; nor would it have mended the matter, in the least, had those same unprofitable pages been written with a pen like that of Burns or of Chaucer, each of whom was a Custom-House officer in his day, as well as I.[9] It is a good lesson— though it may often be a hard one—for a man who has dreamed of literary fame, and of making for himself a rank among the world's dignitaries by such means, to step aside out of the narrow circle in which his claims are recognized, and to find how utterly devoid of significance, beyond that circle, is all that he achieves, and all he aims at. I know not that I especially needed the lesson, either in the way of warning or rebuke; but, at any rate, I learned it thoroughly; nor, it gives me pleasure to reflect, did the truth, as it came home to my perception, ever cost me a pang, or require to be thrown off in a sigh. In the way of literary talk, it is true, the Naval Officer—an excellent fellow, who came into office with me and went out only a little later—would often engage me in a discussion about one or the other of his favorite topics, Napoleon or Shakspeare. The Collector's junior clerk, too,—a young gentleman who, it was whispered, occasionally covered a sheet of Uncle Sam's letter-paper with what (at the distance of a few yards) looked very much like poetry,—used now and then to speak to me of books, as matters with which I might possibly be conversant. This was my all of lettered intercourse; and it was quite sufficient for my necessities.

No longer seeking nor caring that my name should be blazoned abroad on title-pages, I smiled to think that it had now another kind of vogue. The Custom-House marker imprinted it, with a stencil and black paint, on pepper-bags, and baskets of anatto, and cigar-boxes, and bales of all kinds of dutiable merchandise, in testimony that these commodities had paid the impost, and gone regularly through the office.[1] Borne on such queer vehicle of fame, a knowledge of my existence, so far as a name conveys it, was carried where it had never been before, and, I hope, will never go again.

But the past was not dead. Once in a great while, the thoughts, that had seemed so vital and so active, yet had been put to rest so quietly, revived again. One of the most remarkable occasions, when the habit of bygone days awoke in me, was that which brings it within the law of literary propriety to offer the public the sketch which I am now writing.

9. Poets Robert Burns and Geoffrey Chaucer had held jobs similar to Hawthorne's at the Custom House.
1. Hawthorne refers to the seal that labeled each box, "Salem / N Hawthorne / Sur / 1847."
   Anatto: a small evergreen tree whose seeds are used to produce an orange-red dye.

In the second story of the Custom-House, there is a large room, in which the brick-work and naked rafters have never been covered with panelling and plaster. The edifice—originally projected on a scale adapted to the old commercial enterprise of the port, and with an idea of subsequent prosperity destined never to be realized—contains far more space than its occupants know what to do with. This airy hall, therefore, over the Collector's apartments, remains unfinished to this day, and, in spite of the aged cobwebs that festoon its dusky beams, appears still to await the labor of the carpenter and mason. At one end of the room, in a recess, were a number of barrels, piled one upon another, containing bundles of official documents. Large quantities of similar rubbish lay lumbering the floor. It was sorrowful to think how many days, and weeks, and months, and years of toil, had been wasted on these musty papers, which were now only an encumbrance on earth, and were hidden away in this forgotten corner, never more to be glanced at by human eyes. But, then, what reams of other manuscripts—filled not with the dulness of official formalities, but with the thought of inventive brains and the rich effusion of deep hearts—had gone equally to oblivion; and that, moreover, without serving a purpose in their day, as these heaped-up papers had, and—saddest of all—without purchasing for their writers the comfortable livelihood which the clerks of the Custom-House had gained by these worthless scratchings of the pen! Yet not altogether worthless, perhaps, as materials of local history. Here, no doubt, statistics of the former commerce of Salem might be discovered, and memorials of her princely merchants,—old King Derby,—old Billy Gray,—old Simon Forrester,—and many another magnate in his day; whose powdered head, however, was scarcely in the tomb, before his mountain-pile of wealth began to dwindle.[2] The founders of the greater part of the families which now compose the aristocracy of Salem might here be traced, from the petty and obscure beginnings of their traffic, at periods generally much posterior to the Revolution, upward to what their children look upon as long-established rank.

Prior to the Revolution, there is a dearth of records; the earlier documents and archives of the Custom-House having, probably, been carried off to Halifax, when all the King's officials accompanied the British army in its flight from Boston. It has often been a matter of regret with me; for, going back, perhaps, to the days of the Protectorate, those papers must have contained many references to forgotten or remembered men, and to antique customs, which would have affected me with the same pleasure as when I used to pick up Indian arrowheads in the field near the Old Manse.[3]

2. William Gray (1750–1825), a very wealthy Massachusetts merchant who began his career in Salem before settling in Boston and being elected lieutenant governor of Massachusetts. Simon Forrester (1748–1817), a wealthy Salem merchant and ship owner, and brother-in-law to Hawthorne's father.
3. The Protectorate is the name given to the English government under Oliver Cromwell that formed in the aftermath of the English Civil War (1642–49) and the execution of King Charles I. The Protectorate ended in 1660 with the restoration of the monarchy and the ascension of Charles II to the throne.

But, one idle and rainy day, it was my fortune to make a discovery of some little interest. Poking and burrowing into the heaped-up rubbish in the corner; unfolding one and another document, and reading the names of vessels that had long ago foundered at sea or rotted at the wharves, and those of merchants, never heard of now on 'Change,[4] nor very readily decipherable on their mossy tomb-stones; glancing at such matters with the saddened, weary, half-reluctant interest which we bestow on the corpse of dead activity,—and exerting my fancy, sluggish with little use, to raise up from these dry bones an image of the old town's brighter aspect, when India was a new region, and only Salem knew the way thither,—I chanced to lay my hand on a small package, carefully done up in a piece of ancient yellow parchment. This envelope had the air of an official record of some period long past, when clerks engrossed their stiff and formal chirography on more substantial materials than at present. There was something about it that quickened an instinctive curiosity, and made me undo the faded red tape, that tied up the package, with the sense that a treasure would here be brought to light. Unbending the rigid folds of the parchment cover, I found it to be a commission, under the hand and seal of Governor Shirley, in favor of one Jonathan Pue, as Surveyor of his Majesty's Customs for the port of Salem, in the Province of Massachusetts Bay.[5] I remembered to have read (probably in Felt's Annals) a notice of the decease of Mr. Surveyor Pue, about fourscore years ago; and likewise, in a newspaper of recent times, an account of the digging up of his remains in the little grave-yard of St. Peter's Church, during the renewal of that edifice. Nothing, if I rightly call to mind, was left of my respected predecessor, save an imperfect skeleton, and some fragments of apparel, and a wig of majestic frizzle; which, unlike the head that it once adorned, was in very satisfactory preservation. But, on examining the papers which the parchment commission served to envelop, I found more traces of Mr. Pue's mental part, and the internal operations of his head, than the frizzled wig had contained of the venerable skull itself.

They were documents, in short, not official, but of a private nature, or, at least, written in his private capacity, and apparently with his own hand. I could account for their being included in the heap of Custom-House lumber only by the fact, that Mr. Pue's death had happened suddenly; and that these papers, which he probably kept in his official desk, had never come to the knowledge of his heirs, or were supposed to relate to the business of the revenue. On the transfer of the archives to Halifax, this package, proving to be of no public concern, was left behind, and had remained ever since unopened.

The ancient Surveyor—being little molested, I suppose, at that early day, with business pertaining to his office—seems to have devoted some of his many leisure hours to researches as a local antiquarian,

---

4. Merchant's Exchange in Boston.
5. William Shirley (1694–1771) was royal governor of Massachusetts from 1741 to 1756. According to Joseph B. Felt's *Annals of Salem*, Jonathan Pue was appointed surveyor of Salem in 1752.

and other inquisitions of a similar nature. These supplied material for
petty activity to a mind that would otherwise have been eaten up with
rust. A portion of his facts, by the by, did me good service in the preparation of the article entitled "MAIN STREET," included in the
present volume.[6] The remainder may perhaps be applied to purposes equally
valuable, hereafter; or not impossibly may be worked up, so far as they
go, into a regular history of Salem, should my veneration for the natal
soil ever impel me to so pious a task. Meanwhile, they shall be at the
command of any gentleman, inclined, and competent, to take the unprofitable labor off my hands. As a final disposition, I contemplate de-
positing them with the Essex Historical Society.

But the object that most drew my attention, in the mysterious package, was a certain affair of fine red cloth, much worn and faded. There
were traces about it of gold embroidery, which, however, was greatly
frayed and defaced; so that none, or very little, of the glitter was left.[7]
It had been wrought, as was easy to perceive, with wonderful skill of
needlework; and the stitch (as I am assured by ladies conversant with
such mysteries) gives evidence of a now forgotten art, not to be recovered even by the process of picking out the threads. This rag of scarlet
cloth,—for time, and wear, and a sacrilegious moth, had reduced it to
little other than a rag,—on careful examination, assumed the shape of
a letter. It was the capital letter A. By an accurate measurement, each
limb proved to be precisely three inches and a quarter in length. It had
been intended, there could be no doubt, as an ornamental article of
dress; but how it was to be worn, or what rank, honor, and dignity, in
by-past times, were signified by it, was a riddle which (so evanescent
are the fashions of the world in these particulars) I saw little hope of
solving. And yet it strangely interested me. My eyes fastened themselves upon the old scarlet letter, and would not be turned aside.
Certainly, there was some deep meaning in it, most worthy of interpretation, and which, as it were, streamed forth from the mystic symbol, subtly communicating itself to my sensibilities, but evading the
analysis of my mind.

While thus perplexed,—and cogitating, among other hypotheses,
whether the letter might not have been one of those decorations
which the white men used to contrive, in order to take the eyes of Indians,—I happened to place it on my breast. It seemed to me,—the
reader may smile, but must not doubt my word,—it seemed to me,
then, that I experienced a sensation not altogether physical, yet almost
so, as of burning heat; and as if the letter were not of red cloth, but
red-hot iron. I shuddered, and involuntarily let it fall upon the floor.

In the absorbing contemplation of the scarlet letter, I had hitherto
neglected to examine a small roll of dingy paper, around which it had
been twisted. This I now opened, and had the satisfaction to find,

---

6. Hawthorne originally intended "Main Street," a lengthy sketch about Salem, to form part of
Old Time Legends. He ended up publishing the sketch in *Aesthetic Papers* (1849), a collection edited by Sophia's sister, Elizabeth Palmer Peabody.
7. Hawthorne may be thinking of his own early story, "Endicott and the Red Cross" (1837),
which includes a woman wearing a scarlet letter that she has embroidered with gold thread.
See p. 174 of this Norton Critical Edition.

recorded by the old Surveyor's pen, a reasonably complete explanation of the whole affair. There were several foolscap sheets, containing many particulars respecting the life and conversation of one Hester Prynne, who appeared to have been rather a noteworthy personage in the view of our ancestors. She had flourished during the period between the early days of Massachusetts and the close of the seventeenth century.[8] Aged persons, alive in the time of Mr. Surveyor Pue, and from whose oral testimony he had made up his narrative, remembered her, in their youth, as a very old, but not decrepit woman, of a stately and solemn aspect. It had been her habit, from an almost immemorial date, to go about the country as a kind of voluntary nurse, and doing whatever miscellaneous good she might; taking upon herself, likewise, to give advice in all matters, especially those of the heart; by which means, as a person of such propensities inevitably must, she gained from many people the reverence due to an angel, but, I should imagine, was looked upon by others as an intruder and a nuisance. Prying further into the manuscript, I found the record of other doings and sufferings of this singular woman, for most of which the reader is referred to the story entitled "THE SCARLET LETTER"; and it should be borne carefully in mind, that the main facts of that story are authorized and authenticated by the document of Mr. Surveyor Pue. The original papers, together with the scarlet letter itself,—a most curious relic,—are still in my possession, and shall be freely exhibited to whomsoever, induced by the great interest of the narrative, may desire a sight of them.[9] I must not be understood as affirming, that, in the dressing up of the tale, and imagining the motives and modes of passion that influenced the characters who figure in it, I have invariably confined myself within the limits of the old Surveyor's half a dozen sheets of foolscap. On the contrary, I have allowed myself, as to such points, nearly or altogether as much license as if the facts had been entirely of my own invention. What I contend for is the authenticity of the outline.

This incident recalled my mind, in some degree, to its old track. There seemed to be here the ground-work of a tale. It impressed me as if the ancient Surveyor, in his garb of a hundred years gone by, and wearing his immortal wig,—which was buried with him, but did not perish in the grave,—had met me in the deserted chamber of the Custom-House. In his port was the dignity of one who had borne his Majesty's commission, and who was therefore illuminated by a ray of the splendor that shone so dazzlingly about the throne. How unlike, alas! the hang-dog look of a republican official, who, as the servant of the people, feels himself less than the least, and below the lowest, of his masters. With his own ghostly hand, the obscurely seen but majestic figure had imparted to me the scarlet symbol, and the little roll of

8. Roughly 1640 and 1690. Hester Prynne must have arrived in Boston in 1640 since she has been in residence for two years when the novel opens in 1642. Roughly speaking, her life encompassed the period between 1620, the year the Pilgrims emigrated to Plymouth, and the Salem witch trials in 1692.
9. There is no evidence that the scarlet letter or these papers ever existed outside Hawthorne's imagination.

explanatory manuscript. With his own ghostly voice, he had exhorted me, on the sacred consideration of my filial duty and reverence towards him,—who might reasonably regard himself as my official ancestor,—to bring his mouldy and moth-eaten lucubrations before the public. "Do this," said the ghost of Mr. Surveyor Pue, emphatically nodding the head that looked so imposing within its memorable wig, "do this, and the profit shall be all your own! You will shortly need it; for it is not in your days as it was in mine, when a man's office was a life-lease, and oftentimes an heirloom. But, I charge you, in this matter of old Mistress Prynne, give to your predecessor's memory the credit which will be rightfully due!" And I said to the ghost of Mr. Surveyor Pue,—"I will!"

On Hester Prynne's story, therefore, I bestowed much thought. It was the subject of my meditations for many an hour, while pacing to and fro across my room, or traversing, with a hundred-fold repetition, the long extent from the front-door of the Custom-House to the side-entrance, and back again. Great were the weariness and annoyance of the old Inspector and the Weighers and Gaugers, whose slumbers were disturbed by the unmercifully lengthened tramp of my passing and returning footsteps. Remembering their own former habits, they used to say that the Surveyor was walking the quarter-deck. They probably fancied that my sole object—and, indeed, the sole object for which a sane man could ever put himself into voluntary motion—was, to get an appetite for dinner. And to say the truth, an appetite, sharpened by the east wind that generally blew along the passage, was the only valuable result of so much indefatigable exercise. So little adapted is the atmosphere of a Custom-House to the delicate harvest of fancy and sensibility, that, had I remained there through ten Presidencies yet to come, I doubt whether the tale of "The Scarlet Letter" would ever have been brought before the public eye. My imagination was a tarnished mirror. It would not reflect, or only with miserable dimness, the figures with which I did my best to people it. The characters of the narrative would not be warmed and rendered malleable by any heat that I could kindle at my intellectual forge. They would take neither the glow of passion nor the tenderness of sentiment, but retained all the rigidity of dead corpses, and stared me in the face with a fixed and ghastly grin of contemptuous defiance. "What have you to do with us?" that expression seemed to say. "The little power you might once have possessed over the tribe of unrealities is gone! You have bartered it for a pittance of the public gold. Go, then, and earn your wages!" In short, the almost torpid creatures of my own fancy twitted me with imbecility, and not without fair occasion.

It was not merely during the three hours and a half which Uncle Sam claimed as his share of my daily life, that this wretched numbness held possession of me. It went with me on my sea-shore walks, and rambles into the country, whenever—which was seldom and reluctantly—I bestirred myself to seek that invigorating charm of Nature, which used to give me such freshness and activity of thought, the moment that I stepped across the threshold of the Old Manse. The same torpor, as regarded the capacity for intellectual effort, accompanied me home, and weighed upon me in the chamber which I most absurdly termed my study. Nor did it quit me, when, late at night, I sat in the deserted parlor, lighted only by the glimmering coal-fire and the moon, striving to picture forth imaginary scenes, which, the next day, might flow out on the brightening page in many-hued description.

If the imaginative faculty refused to act at such an hour, it might well be deemed a hopeless case. Moonlight, in a familiar room, falling so white upon the carpet, and showing all its figures so distinctly,—making every object so minutely visible, yet so unlike a morning or noontide visibility,—is a medium the most suitable for a romance-writer to get acquainted with his illusive guests.[1] There is the little domestic scenery of the well-known apartment; the chairs, with each its separate individuality; the centre-table, sustaining a work-basket, a volume or two, and an extinguished lamp; the sofa; the book-case; the picture on the wall;—all these details, so completely seen, are so spiritualized by the unusual light, that they seem to lose their actual substance, and become things of intellect. Nothing is too small or too trifling to undergo this change, and acquire dignity thereby. A child's shoe; the doll, seated in her little wicker carriage; the hobby-horse;—whatever, in a word, has been used or played with, during the day, is now invested with a quality of strangeness and remoteness, though still almost as vividly present as by daylight. Thus, therefore, the floor of our familiar room has become a neutral territory, somewhere between the real world and fairy-land, where the Actual and the Imaginary may meet, and each imbue itself with the nature of the other. Ghosts might enter here, without affrighting us. It would be too much in keeping with the scene to excite surprise, were we to look about us and discover a form, beloved, but gone hence, now sitting quietly in a streak of this magic moonshine, with an aspect that would make us doubt whether it had returned from afar, or had never once stirred from our fireside.

The somewhat dim coal-fire has an essential influence in producing the effect which I would describe. It throws its unobtrusive tinge throughout the room, with a faint ruddiness upon the walls and ceiling, and a reflected gleam from the polish of the furniture. This warmer light mingles itself with the cold spirituality of the moonbeams, and communicates, as it were, a heart and sensibilities of human tenderness to the forms which fancy summons up. It converts them from snow-images into men and women. Glancing at the looking-glass, we behold—deep within its haunted verge—the smouldering glow of the half-extinguished anthracite, the white moonbeams on the floor, and a repetition of all the gleam and shadow of the picture, with one remove further from the actual, and nearer to the imaginative. Then, at such an hour, and with this scene before him, if a man, sitting all alone, cannot dream strange things, and make them look like truth, he need never try to write romances.

---

1. Compare the passage from Hawthorne's notebook on pp. 215–16 of this Norton Critical Edition.

But, for myself, during the whole of my Custom-House experience, moonlight and sunshine, and the glow of fire-light, were just alike in my regard; and neither of them was of one whit more avail than the twinkle of a tallow-candle. An entire class of susceptibilities, and a gift connected with them,—of no great richness or value, but the best I had,—was gone from me.

It is my belief, however, that, had I attempted a different order of composition, my faculties would not have been found so pointless and inefficacious. I might, for instance, have contented myself with writing out the narratives of a veteran shipmaster, one of the Inspectors, whom I should be most ungrateful not to mention, since scarcely a day passed that he did not stir me to laughter and admiration by his marvellous gifts as a story-teller. Could I have preserved the picturesque force of his style, and the humorous coloring which nature taught him how to throw over his descriptions, the result, I honestly believe, would have been something new in literature. Or I might readily have found a more serious task. It was a folly, with the materiality of this daily life pressing so intrusively upon me, to attempt to fling myself back into another age; or to insist on creating the semblance of a world out of airy matter, when, at every moment, the impalpable beauty of my soap-bubble was broken by the rude contact of some actual circumstance. The wiser effort would have been, to diffuse thought and imagination through the opaque substance of to-day, and thus to make it a bright transparency; to spiritualize the burden that began to weigh so heavily; to seek, resolutely, the true and indestructible value that lay hidden in the petty and wearisome incidents, and ordinary characters, with which I was now conversant. The fault was mine. The page of life that was spread out before me seemed dull and commonplace, only because I had not fathomed its deeper import. A better book than I shall ever write was there; leaf after leaf presenting itself to me, just as it was written out by the reality of the flitting hour, and vanishing as fast as written, only because my brain wanted the insight and my hand the cunning to transcribe it. At some future day, it may be, I shall remember a few scattered fragments and broken paragraphs, and write them down, and find the letters turn to gold upon the page.

These perceptions have come too late. At the instant, I was only conscious that what would have been a pleasure once was now a hopeless toil. There was no occasion to make much moan about this state of affairs. I had ceased to be a writer of tolerably poor tales and essays, and had become a tolerably good Surveyor of the Customs. That was all. But, nevertheless; it is anything but agreeable to be haunted by a suspicion that one's intellect is dwindling away; or exhaling, without your consciousness, like ether out of a phial; so that, at every glance, you find a smaller and less volatile residuum. Of the fact, there could be no doubt; and, examining myself and others, I was led to conclusions, in reference to the effect of public office on the character, not very favorable to the mode of life in question. In some other form, perhaps, I may hereafter develop these effects. Suffice it here to say, that a Custom-House officer, of long continuance, can hardly be a very praiseworthy or respectable personage, for many reasons; one of them, the tenure by which he holds his situation, and another, the very nature of his business, which—though, I trust, an honest one—is of such a sort that he does not share in the united effort of mankind.

An effect—which I believe to be observable, more or less, in every individual who has occupied the position—is, that, while he leans on the mighty arm of the Republic, his own proper strength departs from him. He loses, in an extent proportioned to the weakness or force of his original nature, the capability of self-support. If he possess an unusual share of native energy, or the enervating magic of place do not operate too long upon him, his forfeited powers may be redeemable. The ejected officer—fortunate in the unkindly shove that sends him forth betimes, to struggle amid a struggling world—may return to himself, and become all that he has ever been. But this seldom happens. He usually keeps his ground just long enough for his own ruin, and is then thrust out, with sinews all unstrung, to totter along the difficult footpath of life as he best may. Conscious of his own infirmity,—that his tempered steel and elasticity are lost,—he forever afterwards looks wistfully about him in quest of support external to himself. His pervading and continual hope—a hallucination, which, in the face of all discouragement, and making light of impossibilities, haunts him while he lives, and, I fancy, like the convulsive throes of the cholera, torments him for a brief space after death—is, that finally, and in no long time, by some happy coincidence of circumstances, he shall be restored to office. This faith, more than anything else, steals the pith and availability out of whatever enterprise he may dream of undertaking. Why should he toil and moil, and be at so much trouble to pick himself up out of the mud, when, in a little while hence, the strong arm of his Uncle will raise and support him? Why should he work for his living here, or go to dig gold in California, when he is so soon to be made happy, at monthly intervals, with a little pile of glittering coin out of his Uncle's pocket?[2] It is sadly curious to observe how slight a taste of office suffices to infect a poor fellow with this singular disease. Uncle Sam's gold—meaning no disrespect to the worthy old gentleman—has, in this respect, a quality of enchantment like that of the Devil's wages. Whoever touches it should look well to himself, or he may find the bargain to go hard against him, involving, if not his soul, yet many of its better attributes; its sturdy force, its courage and constancy, its truth, its self-reliance, and all that gives the emphasis to manly character.

Here was a fine prospect in the distance! Not that the Surveyor brought the lesson home to himself, or admitted that he could be so utterly undone, either by continuance in office, or ejectment. Yet my reflections were not the most comfortable. I began to grow melancholy and restless; continually prying into my mind, to discover which

2. Gold was discovered at Sutter's Mill in California in January 1848, and the first wave of gold seekers arrived in 1849.

of its poor properties were gone, and what degree of detriment had already accrued to the remainder. I endeavored to calculate how much longer I could stay in the Custom-House, and yet go forth a man. To confess the truth, it was my greatest apprehension,—as it would never be a measure of policy to turn out so quiet an individual as myself, and it being hardly in the nature of a public officer to resign,—it was my chief trouble, therefore, that I was likely to grow gray and decrepit in the Surveyorship, and become much such another animal as the old Inspector. Might it not, in the tedious lapse of official life that lay before me, finally be with me as it was with this venerable friend,—to make the dinner-hour the nucleus of the day, and to spend the rest of it, as an old dog spends it, asleep in the sunshine or in the shade? A dreary look-forward this, for a man who felt it to be the best definition of happiness to live throughout the whole range of his faculties and sensibilities! But, all this while, I was giving myself very unnecessary alarm. Providence had meditated better things for me than I could possibly imagine for myself.

A remarkable event of the third year of my Surveyorship—to adopt the tone of "P. P."—was the election of General Taylor to the Presidency.[3] It is essential, in order to form a complete estimate of the advantages of official life, to view the incumbent at the in-coming of a hostile administration. His position is then one of the most singularly irksome, and, in every contingency, disagreeable, that a wretched mortal can possibly occupy; with seldom an alternative of good, on either hand, although what presents itself to him as the worst event may very probably be the best. But it is a strange experience, to a man of pride and sensibility, to know that his interests are within the control of individuals who neither love nor understand him, and by whom, since one or the other must needs happen, he would rather be injured than obliged. Strange, too, for one who has kept his calmness throughout the contest, to observe the bloodthirstiness that is developed in the hour of triumph, and to be conscious that he is himself among its objects! There are few uglier traits of human nature than this tendency—which I now witnessed in men no worse than their neighbors—to grow cruel, merely because they possessed the power of inflicting harm. If the guillotine, as applied to office-holders, were a literal fact, instead of one of the most apt of metaphors, it is my sincere belief, that the active members of the victorious party were sufficiently excited to have chopped off all our heads, and have thanked Heaven for the opportunity![4] It appears to me—who have been a calm and curious observer, as well in victory as defeat—that this fierce and bitter spirit of malice and revenge has never distinguished the many triumphs of my own party as it now did that of the Whigs. The Democrats take the offices, as a general rule, because they need them, and

3. General Zachary Taylor, a Whig, was elected president in 1848 and fired Hawthorne from his surveyor job in the early summer of 1849.
4. As Larry J. Reynolds notes in an essay reprinted in this Norton Critical Edition, Zachary Taylor's political appointments in 1849 were reported in Democratic papers as beheadings of Democratic Party members. The guillotine, infamous for its use during the French Revolution, decapitated its victims.

because the practice of many years has made it the law of political warfare, which, unless a different system be proclaimed, it were weakness and cowardice to murmur at. But the long habit of victory has made them generous. They know how to spare, when they see occasion; and when they strike, the axe may be sharp, indeed, but its edge is seldom poisoned with ill-will; nor is it their custom ignominiously to kick the head which they have just struck off.

In short, unpleasant as was my predicament, at best, I saw much reason to congratulate myself that I was on the losing side, rather than the triumphant one. If, heretofore, I had been none of the warmest of partisans, I began now, at this season of peril and adversity, to be pretty acutely sensible with which party my predilections lay; nor was it without something like regret and shame, that, according to a reasonable calculation of chances, I saw my own prospect of retaining office to be better than those of my Democratic brethren. But who can see an inch into futurity, beyond his nose? My own head was the first that fell!

The moment when a man's head drops off is seldom or never, I am inclined to think, precisely the most agreeable of his life. Nevertheless, like the greater part of our misfortunes, even so serious a contingency brings its remedy and consolation with it, if the sufferer will but make the best, rather than the worst, of the accident which has befallen him. In my particular case, the consolatory topics were close at hand, and, indeed, had suggested themselves to my meditations a considerable time before it was requisite to use them. In view of my previous weariness of office, and vague thoughts of resignation, my fortune somewhat resembled that of a person who should entertain an idea of committing suicide, and, although beyond his hopes, meet with the good hap to be murdered. In the Custom-House, as before in the Old Manse, I had spent three years; a term long enough to rest a weary brain; long enough to break off old intellectual habits, and make room for new ones; long enough, and too long, to have lived in an unnatural state, doing what was really of no advantage nor delight to any human being, and withholding myself from toil that would, at least, have stilled an unquiet impulse in me. Then, moreover, as regarded his unceremonious ejectment, the late Surveyor was not altogether ill-pleased to be recognized by the Whigs as an enemy; since his inactivity in political affairs,—his tendency to roam, at will, in that broad and quiet field where all mankind may meet, rather than confine himself to those narrow paths where brethren of the same household must diverge from one another,—had sometimes made it questionable with his brother Democrats whether he was a friend. Now, after he had won the crown of martyrdom, (though with no longer a head to wear it on,) the point might be looked upon as settled. Finally, little heroic as he was, it seemed more decorous to be overthrown in the downfall of the party with which he had been content to stand, than to remain a forlorn survivor, when so many worthier men were falling; and, at last, after subsisting for four years on the mercy of a hostile administration, to be compelled then to define his position anew, and claim the yet more humiliating mercy of a friendly one.

Meanwhile the press had taken up my affair, and kept me, for a week or two, careering through the public prints, in my decapitated state, like Irving's Headless Horseman; ghastly and grim, and longing to be buried, as a politically dead man ought.[5] So much for my figurative self. The real human being, all this time, with his head safely on his shoulders, had brought himself to the comfortable conclusion that everything was for the best; and, making an investment in ink, paper, and steel-pens, had opened his long-disused writing-desk, and was again a literary man.

Now it was, that the lucubrations of my ancient predecessor, Mr. Surveyor Pue, came into play. Rusty through long idleness, some little space was requisite before my intellectual machinery could be brought to work upon the tale, with an effect in any degree satisfactory. Even yet, though my thoughts were ultimately much absorbed in the task, it wears, to my eye, a stern and sombre aspect; too much ungladdened by genial sunshine; too little relieved by the tender and familiar influences which soften almost every scene of nature and real life, and, undoubtedly, should soften every picture of them. This uncaptivating effect is perhaps due to the period of hardly accomplished revolution, and still seething turmoil, in which the story shaped itself. It is no indication, however, of a lack of cheerfulness in the writer's mind; for he was happier, while straying through the gloom of these sunless fantasies, than at any time since he had quitted the Old Manse. Some of the briefer articles, which contribute to make up the volume, have likewise been written since my involuntary withdrawal from the toils and honors of public life, and the remainder are gleaned from annuals and magazines, of such antique date that they have gone round the circle, and come back to novelty again.* Keeping up the metaphor of the political guillotine, the whole may be considered as the POSTHUMOUS PAPERS OF A DECAPITATED SURVEYOR; and the sketch which I am now bringing to a close, if too autobiographical for a modest person to publish in his lifetime, will readily be excused in a gentleman who writes from beyond the grave. Peace be with all the world! My blessing on my friends! My forgiveness to my enemies! For I am in the realm of quiet!

The life of the Custom-House lies like a dream behind me. The old Inspector,—who, by the by, I regret to say, was overthrown and killed by a horse, some time ago; else he would certainly have lived forever,—he, and all those other venerable personages who sat with him at the receipt of custom, are but shadows in my view; white-headed and wrinkled images, which my fancy used to sport with, and has now flung aside forever. The merchants,—Pingree, Phillips, Shepard, Up-

5. A reference to Washington Irving's "The Legend of Sleepy Hollow" (1820), which includes the Headless Horseman (in keeping with Hawthorne's decapitation theme).
* At the time of writing this article, the author intended to publish, along with "The Scarlet Letter," several shorter tales and sketches. These it has been thought advisable to defer [Author's Note].

ton, Kimball, Bertram, Hunt,—these, and many other names, which had such a classic familiarity for my ear six months ago,—these men of traffic, who seemed to occupy so important a position in the world,—how little time has it required to disconnect me from them all, not merely in act, but recollection! It is with an effort that I recall the figures and appellations of these few. Soon, likewise, my old native town will loom upon me through the haze of memory, a mist brooding over and around it; as if it were no portion of the real earth, but an overgrown village in cloud-land, with only imaginary inhabitants to people its wooden houses, and walk its homely lanes, and the un-picturesque prolixity of its main street. Henceforth, it ceases to be a reality of my life. I am a citizen of somewhere else. My good towns-people will not much regret me; for—though it has been as dear an object as any, in my literary efforts, to be of some importance in their eyes, and to win myself a pleasant memory in this abode and burial-place of so many of my forefathers—there has never been, for me, the genial atmosphere which a literary man requires, in order to ripen the best harvest of his mind. I shall do better amongst other faces; and these familiar ones, it need hardly be said, will do just as well without me.

It may be, however,—O, transporting and triumphant thought!—that the great-grandchildren of the present race may sometimes think kindly of the scribbler of bygone days, when the antiquary of days to come, among the sites memorable in the town's history, shall point out the locality of THE TOWN PUMP![6]

---

6. Hawthorne had published another Salem sketch, "A Rill from the Town Pump," in 1835.

The Scarlet Letter

I. The Prison-Door

A throng of bearded men, in sad-colored garments, and gray, steeple-crowned hats, intermixed with women, some wearing hoods, and others bareheaded, was assembled in front of a wooden edifice, the door of which was heavily timbered with oak, and studded with iron spikes.

The founders of a new colony, whatever Utopia of human virtue and happiness they might originally project, have invariably recognized it among their earliest practical necessities to allot a portion of the virgin soil as a cemetery, and another portion as the site of a prison. In accordance with this rule, it may safely be assumed that the forefathers of Boston had built the first prison-house somewhere in the vicinity of Cornhill, almost as seasonably as they marked out the first burial-ground, on Isaac Johnson's lot, and round about his grave, which subsequently became the nucleus of all the congregated sepulchres in the old church-yard of King's Chapel.[1] Certain it is, that, some fifteen or twenty years after the settlement of the town, the wooden jail was already marked with weather-stains and other indications of age, which gave a yet darker aspect to its beetle-browed and gloomy front.[2] The rust on the ponderous iron-work of its oaken door looked more antique than anything else in the New World. Like all that pertains to crime, it seemed never to have known a youthful era. Before this ugly edifice, and between it and the wheel-track of the street, was a grass-plot, much overgrown with burdock, pig-weed, apple-peru, and such unsightly vegetation, which evidently found something congenial in the soil that had so early borne the black flower of civilized society, a prison. But, on one side of the portal, and rooted almost at the threshold, was a wild rose-bush, covered, in this month of June, with its delicate gems, which might be imagined to offer their fragrance and fragile beauty to the prisoner as he went in, and to the condemned criminal as he came forth to his doom, in token that the deep heart of Nature could pity and be kind to him.

---

1. Caleb Snow calls Isaac Johnson the "father of Boston" because he was instrumental in encouraging John Winthrop's party to settle on the south side of the Charles River. According to Snow, Johnson died in 1630 and asked to be buried at the southwest corner of his property, the site of the old courthouse. This is the origin of the first burying ground to which Hawthorne refers.
2. See Charles Ryskamp's essay in this Norton Critical Edition. Hawthorne sets the novel between 1642 and 1649. Governor John Winthrop, whose death occurs in chapter 12, died on March 26, 1649. Richard Bellingham was governor of the Massachusetts Bay Colony in 1642, but he had in fact just been replaced by Winthrop at the time Hester stands on the scaffold.

This rose-bush, by a strange chance, has been kept alive in history; but whether it had merely survived out of the stern old wilderness, so long after the fall of the gigantic pines and oaks that originally over-shadowed it,—or whether, as there is fair authority for believing, it had sprung up under the footsteps of the sainted Ann Hutchinson, as she entered the prison-door,—we shall not take upon us to deter-mine.[3] Finding it so directly on the threshold of our narrative, which is now about to issue from that inauspicious portal, we could hardly do otherwise than pluck one of its flowers, and present it to the reader. It may serve, let us hope, to symbolize some sweet moral blossom, that may be found along the track, or relieve the darkening close of a tale of human frailty and sorrow.

II. The Market-Place

The grass-plot before the jail, in Prison-lane, on a certain summer morning, not less than two centuries ago, was occupied by a pretty large number of the inhabitants of Boston; all with their eyes intently fastened on the iron-clamped oaken door. Amongst any other popula-tion, or at a later period in the history of New England, the grim rigid-ity that petrified the bearded physiognomies of these good people would have augured some awful business in hand. It could have be-tokened nothing short of the anticipated execution of some noted cul-prit, on whom the sentence of a legal tribunal had but confirmed the verdict of public sentiment. But, in that early severity of the Puritan character, an inference of this kind could not so indubitably be drawn. It might be that a sluggish bond-servant, or an undutiful child, whom his parents had given over to the civil authority, was to be corrected at the whipping-post. It might be, that an Antinomian,[1] a Quaker, or other heterodox religionist, was to be scourged out of the town, or an idle and vagrant Indian, whom the white man's fire-water had made ri-otous about the streets, was to be driven with stripes into the shadow of the forest. It might be, too, that a witch, like old Mistress Hibbins, the bitter-tempered widow of the magistrate, was to die upon the gal-lows.[2] In either case, there was very much the same solemnity of de-meanor on the part of the spectators; as befitted a people amongst whom religion and law were almost identical, and in whose character both were so thoroughly interfused, that the mildest and the severest acts of public discipline were alike made venerable and awful. Meagre, indeed, and cold, was the sympathy that a transgressor might look

3. Anne Hutchinson (1591–1643) was banished from Massachusetts (to Rhode Island) in 1638 for unlawful preaching and, in Governor John Winthrop's words, for "being a woman not fit for our society." She had been hosting prayer meetings for women and had re-proached most of the ministers, including Reverend John Wilson, for preaching a covenant of works rather than a covenant of grace—behavior, in Winthrop's terms, not "fitting for your sex."
1. One who believes that faith alone can merit salvation and, conversely, that neither good nor evil works affect salvation.
2. Ann Hibbins, sister of Governor Richard Bellingham, was executed as a witch in 1656. See Ellen Weinauer's essay reprinted in this Norton Critical Edition, especially pp. 377–80.

for, from such bystanders, at the scaffold. On the other hand, a penalty which, in our days, would infer a degree of mocking infamy and ridicule, might then be invested with almost as stern a dignity as the punishment of death itself.

It was a circumstance to be noted, on the summer morning when our story begins its course, that the women, of whom there were several in the crowd, appeared to take a peculiar interest in whatever penal infliction might be expected to ensue. The age had not so much refinement, that any sense of impropriety restrained the wearers of petticoat and farthingale from stepping forth into the public ways, and wedging their not unsubstantial persons, if occasion were, into the throng nearest to the scaffold at an execution. Morally, as well as materially, there was a coarser fibre in those wives and maidens of old English birth and breeding, than in their fair descendants, separated from them by a series of six or seven generations; for, throughout that chain of ancestry, every successive mother has transmitted to her child a fainter bloom, a more delicate and briefer beauty, and a slighter physical frame, if not a character of less force and solidity, than her own. The women who were now standing about the prison-door stood within less than half a century of the period when the man-like Elizabeth had been the not altogether unsuitable representative of the sex.[3] They were her countrywomen; and the beef and ale of their native land, with a moral diet not a whit more refined, entered largely into their composition. The bright morning sun, therefore, shone on broad shoulders and well-developed busts, and on round and ruddy cheeks, that had ripened in the far-off island, and had hardly yet grown paler or thinner in the atmosphere of New England. There was, moreover, a boldness and rotundity of speech among these matrons, as most of them seemed to be, that would startle us at the present day, whether in respect to its purport or its volume of tone.

"Goodwives," said a hard-featured dame of fifty, "I'll tell ye a piece of my mind. It would be greatly for the public behoof, if we women, being of mature age and church-members in good repute, should have the handling of such malefactresses as this Hester Prynne.[4] What think ye, gossips? If the hussy stood up for judgment before us five, that are now

---

3. Queen Elizabeth I ruled England from 1558 to 1603. She was succeeded by James I, who ruled from 1603 to 1625. Charles I was king of England during most of the period in which Hawthorne sets the novel, although he was beheaded on January 30, 1649, six months before the main action of the novel comes to a close.
4. Hawthorne probably took the name "Prynne" from William Prynne (1600–1669), a vehement anti-Catholic Puritan, who devoted a lengthy book, *Histriomastix; A Scourge of Stage Players* (1632), to castigating Englishmen (and implicitly King Charles) for attending plays. When he published diatribes against Archbishop of Canterbury William Laud, whom he considered a Catholic in disguise, he was punished by having his ears cut off and the letters "SL" (for "Seditious Libeller") burnt into his cheeks. Hawthorne undoubtedly appreciated the coincidence of writing a story about a similar punishment that bore the same initials (see Isani and Alfred Reid). Uncannily anticipating Hester's alteration of the scarlet letter and its meaning, William Prynne responded to his branding by composing a Latin distich, "in which he interpreted the S L which he now bore indelibly on his cheeks as *Stigmata Laudis*, the Scars of Laud" (Samuel R. Gardiner, *History of England from the Accession of James I to the Outbreak of the Civil War, 1603–1642*, 10 vols. [New York: Longmans, Green, 1909], 8:232). Isani notes the feud between Prynne and Archbishop Laud, one of whose protégés was William Chillingworth.

here in a knot together, would she come off with such a sentence as the worshipful magistrates have awarded? Marry, I trow not!"[5]

"People say," said another, "that the Reverend Master Dimmesdale, her godly pastor, takes it very grievously to heart that such a scandal should have come upon his congregation."

"The magistrates are God-fearing gentlemen, but merciful over-much,—that is a truth," added a third autumnal matron. "At the very least, they should have put the brand of a hot iron on Hester Prynne's forehead. Madam Hester would have winced at that, I warrant me. But she,—the naughty baggage,—little will she care what they put upon the bodice of her gown! Why, look you, she may cover it with a brooch, or such like heathenish adornment, and so walk the streets as brave as ever!"

"Ah, but," interposed, more softly, a young wife, holding a child by the hand, "let her cover the mark as she will, the pang of it will be always in her heart."

"What do we talk of marks and brands, whether on the bodice of her gown, or the flesh of her forehead?" cried another female, the ugliest as well as the most pitiless of these self-constituted judges. "This woman has brought shame upon us all, and ought to die.[6] Is there not law for it? Truly there is, both in the Scripture and the statute-book. Then let the magistrates, who have made it of no effect, thank themselves if their own wives and daughters go astray!"[7]

"Mercy on us, goodwife," exclaimed a man in the crowd, "is there no virtue in woman, save what springs from a wholesome fear of the gallows? That is the hardest word yet! Hush, now, gossips! for the lock is turning in the prison door, and here comes Mistress Prynne herself."

The door of the jail being flung open from within, there appeared, in the first place, like a black shadow emerging into sunshine, the grim and grisly presence of the town-beadle, with a sword by his side, and his staff of office in his hand. This personage prefigured and represented in his aspect the whole dismal severity of the Puritanic code

---

5. Think or believe not.
6. John Winthrop notes that Mary Latham of Plymouth Colony and James Britton were condemned to die for adultery in March 1644. Winthrop explains that Mary Latham had been rejected by a young man she loved, vowed to marry the "next that came to her," and ended up "matched with an ancient man" for whom she had no affection (*Journal*, 500–01). Charles Boewe and Murray G. Murphy (see Bibliography) also note the case of Salem's Hester Craford, who in 1688 was ordered to be "severely whipped" for fornicating with John Wedg. The judgment, which was carried out by William Hathorne, was suspended for a month or so because of the birth of the child.
7. Magistrates were elected officials of the Massachusetts Bay Colony, whose government was organized, by the Royal Charter, under a governor, a deputy governor, and a group of assistants (elected from among the freemen, who were church members and stockholders of the company). Although they were elected, the magistrates formed an exclusive group of the wealthiest and highest-born settlers. Shortly before the novel opens, as Robert Emmet Wall explains, the colonists had approved a "Body of Liberties" that gave slightly more power to the whole body of freemen and even nonfreemen. During the years of the novel's action (1642–1649) the magistrates faced more democratic challenges to their authority. Hawthorne's repeated references to the magistrates help to generalize the colonists' challenges to government authority beyond Hester's individual case (*Massachusetts Bay: The Crucial Decade, 1640–1650* [New Haven: Yale UP, 1972], 18).

of law, which it was his business to administer in its final and closest
application to the offender. Stretching forth the official staff in his left
hand, he laid his right upon the shoulder of a young woman, whom he
thus drew forward; until, on the threshold of the prison-door, she repelled him, by an action marked with natural dignity and force of character, and stepped into the open air, as if by her own free will. She bore
in her arms a child, a baby of some three months old, who winked and
turned aside its little face from the too vivid light of day; because its existence, heretofore, had brought it acquainted only with the gray twilight of a dungeon, or other darksome apartment of the prison.

When the young woman—the mother of this child—stood fully revealed before the crowd, it seemed to be her first impulse to clasp the
infant closely to her bosom; not so much by an impulse of motherly
affection, as that she might thereby conceal a certain token, which
was wrought or fastened into her dress. In a moment, however, wisely
judging that one token of her shame would but poorly serve to hide
another, she took the baby on her arm, and, with a burning blush, and
yet a haughty smile, and a glance that would not be abashed, looked
around at her townspeople and neighbors. On the breast of her gown,
in fine red cloth, surrounded with an elaborate embroidery and fantastic flourishes of gold thread, appeared the letter A. It was so artistically
done, and with so much fertility and gorgeous luxuriance of fancy, that
it had all the effect of a last and fitting decoration to the apparel
which she wore; and which was of a splendor in accordance with the
taste of the age, but greatly beyond what was allowed by the sumptuary regulations of the colony.[8]

The young woman was tall, with a figure of perfect elegance on a
large scale. She had dark and abundant hair, so glossy that it threw off
the sunshine with a gleam, and a face which, besides being beautiful
from regularity of feature and richness of complexion, had the impres-
siveness belonging to a marked brow and deep black eyes. She was
lady-like, too, after the manner of the feminine gentility of those days;
characterized by a certain state and dignity, rather than by the delicate, evanescent, and indescribable grace, which is now recognized as
its indication. And never had Hester Prynne appeared more lady-like,
in the antique interpretation of the term, than as she issued from the
prison. Those who had before known her, and had expected to behold
her dimmed and obscured by a disastrous cloud, were astonished, and
even startled, to perceive how her beauty shone out, and made a halo
of the misfortune and ignominy in which she was enveloped. It may be
true, that, to a sensitive observer, there was something exquisitely
painful in it. Her attire, which, indeed, she had wrought for the occasion, in prison, and had modelled much after her own fancy, seemed
to express the attitude of her spirit, the desperate recklessness of her

8. In his *History of Boston*, Caleb Snow mentions the Puritans' regulation of fashion in the observation that the Reverend John Cotton "found it necessary to exert his influence to suppress superfluous and unnecessarily expensive fashions. . . . Gold or silver laces, girdles, or
hat-bands, embroidered caps, immoderate great veils and immoderate great sleeves incurred
special disapprobation" (55).

mood, by its wild and picturesque peculiarity. But the point which drew all eyes, and, as it were, transfigured the wearer,—so that both men and women, who had been familiarly acquainted with Hester Prynne, were now impressed as if they beheld her for the first time,—was that SCARLET LETTER, so fantastically embroidered and illuminated upon her bosom. It had the effect of a spell, taking her out of the ordinary relations with humanity, and enclosing her in a sphere by herself.

"She hath good skill at her needle, that's certain," remarked one of her female spectators; "but did ever a woman, before this brazen hussy, contrive such a way of showing it! Why, gossips, what is it but to laugh in the faces of our godly magistrates, and make a pride out of what they, worthy gentlemen, meant for a punishment?"

"It were well," muttered the most iron-visaged of the old dames, "if we stripped Madam Hester's rich gown off her dainty shoulders; and as for the red letter, which she hath stitched so curiously, I'll bestow a rag of mine own rheumatic flannel, to make a fitter one!"

"O, peace, neighbors, peace!" whispered their youngest companion; "do not let her hear you! Not a stitch in that embroidered letter, but she has felt it in her heart."

The grim beadle now made a gesture with his staff.

"Make way, good people, make way, in the King's name!" cried he. "Open a passage; and, I promise ye, Mistress Prynne shall be set where man, woman and child, may have a fair sight of her brave apparel, from this time till an hour past meridian. A blessing on the righteous Colony of the Massachusetts, where iniquity is dragged out into the sunshine! Come along, Madam Hester, and show your scarlet letter in the market-place!"

A lane was forthwith opened through the crowd of spectators. Preceded by the beadle, and attended by an irregular procession of stern-browed men and unkindly visaged women, Hester Prynne set forth towards the place appointed for her punishment. A crowd of eager and curious school-boys, understanding little of the matter in hand, except that it gave them a half-holiday, ran before her progress, turning their heads continually to stare into her face, and at the winking baby in her arms, and at the ignominious letter on her breast. It was no great distance, in those days, from the prison-door to the market-place. Measured by the prisoner's experience, however, it might be reckoned a journey of some length; for, haughty as her demeanor was, she perchance underwent an agony from every footstep of those that thronged to see her, as if her heart had been flung into the street for them all to spurn and trample upon. In our nature, however, there is a provision, alike marvellous and merciful, that the sufferer should never know the intensity of what he endures by its present torture, but chiefly by the pang that rankles after it. With almost a serene deportment, therefore, Hester Prynne passed through this portion of her ordeal, and came to a sort of scaffold, at the western extremity of the market-place. It stood nearly beneath the eaves of Boston's earliest church, and appeared to be a fixture there.

In fact, this scaffold constituted a portion of a penal machine, which now, for two or three generations past, has been merely historical and traditionary among us, but was held, in the old time, to be as effectual an agent, in the promotion of good citizenship, as ever was the guillotine among the terrorists of France. It was, in short, the platform of the pillory; and above it rose the framework of that instrument of discipline, so fashioned as to confine the human head in its tight grasp, and thus hold it up to the public gaze. The very ideal of ignominy was embodied and made manifest in this contrivance of wood and iron. There can be no outrage, methinks, against our common nature,—whatever be the delinquencies of the individual,—no outrage more flagrant than to forbid the culprit to hide his face for shame; as it was the essence of this punishment to do. In Hester Prynne's instance, however, as not unfrequently in other cases, her sentence bore, that she should stand a certain time upon the platform, but without undergoing that gripe about the neck and confinement of the head, the proneness to which was the most devilish characteristic of this ugly engine. Knowing well her part, she ascended a flight of wooden steps, and was thus displayed to the surrounding multitude, at about the height of a man's shoulders above the street.

Had there been a Papist among the crowd of Puritans, he might have seen in this beautiful woman, so picturesque in her attire and mien, and with the infant at her bosom, an object to remind him of the image of Divine Maternity, which so many illustrious painters have vied with one another to represent; something which should remind him, indeed, but only by contrast, of that sacred image of sinless motherhood, whose infant was to redeem the world. Here, there was the taint of deepest sin in the most sacred quality of human life, working such effect, that the world was only the darker for this woman's beauty, and the more lost for the infant that she had borne.

The scene was not without a mixture of awe, such as must always invest the spectacle of guilt and shame in a fellow-creature, before society shall have grown corrupt enough to smile, instead of shuddering, at it. The witnesses of Hester Prynne's disgrace had not yet passed beyond their simplicity. They were stern enough to look upon her death, had that been the sentence, without a murmur at its severity, but had none of the heartlessness of another social state, which would find only a theme for jest in an exhibition like the present. Even had there been a disposition to turn the matter into ridicule, it must have been repressed and overpowered by the solemn presence of men no less dignified than the Governor, and several of his counsellors, a judge, a general, and the ministers of the town; all of whom sat or stood in a balcony of the meeting-house, looking down upon the platform. When such personages could constitute a part of the spectacle, without risking the majesty or reverence of rank and office, it was safely to be inferred that the infliction of a legal sentence would have an earnest and effectual meaning. Accordingly, the crowd was sombre and grave. The unhappy culprit sustained herself as best a woman might, under the heavy weight of a thousand unrelenting eyes, all fastened upon her, and concentred at her bosom. It was almost intolerable to be borne. Of an impulsive and passionate nature, she had fortified herself to encounter the stings and venomous stabs of public contumely, wreaking itself in every variety of insult; but there was a quality so much more terrible in the solemn mood of the popular mind, that she longed rather to behold all those rigid countenances contorted with scornful merriment, and herself the object. Had a roar of laughter burst from the multitude,—each man, each woman, each little shrill-voiced child, contributing their individual parts,—Hester Prynne might have repaid them all with a bitter and disdainful smile. But, under the leaden infliction which it was her doom to endure, she felt, at moments, as if she must needs shriek out with the full power of her lungs, and cast herself from the scaffold down upon the ground, or else go mad at once.

Yet there were intervals when the whole scene, in which she was the most conspicuous object, seemed to vanish from her eyes, or, at least, glimmered indistinctly before them, like a mass of imperfectly shaped and spectral images. Her mind, and especially her memory, was preternaturally active, and kept bringing up other scenes than this roughly hewn street of a little town, on the edge of the Western wilderness; other faces than were lowering upon her from beneath the brims of those steeple-crowned hats. Reminiscences, the most trifling and immaterial, passages of infancy and school-days, sports, childish quarrels, and the little domestic traits of her maiden years, came swarming back upon her, intermingled with recollections of whatever was gravest in her subsequent life; one picture precisely as vivid as another; as if all were of similar importance, or all alike a play. Possibly, it was an instinctive device of her spirit, to relieve itself, by the exhibition of these phantasmagoric forms, from the cruel weight and hardness of the reality.

Be that as it might, the scaffold of the pillory was a point of view that revealed to Hester Prynne the entire track along which she had been treading, since her happy infancy. Standing on that miserable eminence, she saw again her native village, in Old England, and her paternal home; a decayed house of gray stone, with a poverty-stricken aspect, but retaining a half-obliterated shield of arms over the portal, in token of antique gentility. She saw her father's face, with its bald brow, and reverend white beard, that flowed over the old-fashioned Elizabethan ruff; her mother's, too, with the look of heedful and anxious love which it always wore in her remembrance, and which, even since her death, had so often laid the impediment of a gentle remonstrance in her daughter's pathway. She saw her own face, glowing with girlish beauty, and illuminating all the interior of the dusky mirror in which she had been wont to gaze at it. There she beheld another countenance, of a man well stricken in years, a pale, thin, scholar-like visage, with eyes dim and bleared by the lamp-light that had served them to pore over many ponderous books. Yet those same bleared optics had a strange, penetrating power, when it was their owner's purpose to read the human soul. This figure of the study and the cloister, as Hester Prynne's womanly fancy failed not to recall, was slightly deformed, with the left shoulder a trifle higher than the right. Next rose before her, in memory's picture-gallery, the intricate and narrow thoroughfares, the tall, gray houses, the huge cathedrals, and the public edifices, ancient in date and quaint in architecture, of a Continental city;[9] where a new life had awaited her, still in connection with the misshapen scholar; a new life, but feeding itself on time-worn materials, like a tuft of green moss on a crumbling wall. Lastly, in lieu of these shifting scenes, came back the rude market-place of the Puritan settlement, with all the townspeople assembled and levelling their stern regards at Hester Prynne,—yes, at herself,—who stood on the scaffold of the pillory, an infant on her arm, and the letter A, in scarlet, fantastically embroidered with gold thread, upon her bosom!

Could it be true? She clutched the child so fiercely to her breast, that it sent forth a cry; she turned her eyes downward at the scarlet letter, and even touched it with her finger, to assure herself that the infant and the shame were real. Yes!—these were her realities,—all else had vanished!

III. The Recognition

From this intense consciousness of being the object of severe and universal observation, the wearer of the scarlet letter was at length relieved, by discerning, on the outskirts of the crowd, a figure which irresistibly took possession of her thoughts. An Indian, in his native garb, was standing there; but the red men were not so infrequent visitors of the English settlements, that one of them would have attracted any notice from Hester Prynne, at such a time; much less would he have excluded all other objects and ideas from her mind. By the Indian's side, and evidently sustaining a companionship with him, stood a white man, clad in a strange disarray of civilized and savage costume.

He was small in stature, with a furrowed visage, which, as yet, could hardly be termed aged. There was a remarkable intelligence in his features, as of a person who had so cultivated his mental part that it could not fail to mould the physical to itself, and become manifest by unmistakable tokens. Although, by a seemingly careless arrangement of his heterogeneous garb, he had endeavored to conceal or abate the peculiarity, it was sufficiently evident to Hester Prynne, that one of this man's shoulders rose higher than the other. Again, at the first instant of perceiving that thin visage, and the slight deformity of the figure, she pressed her infant to her bosom, with so convulsive a force that the poor babe uttered another cry of pain. But the mother did not seem to hear it.

At his arrival in the market-place, and some time before she saw him, the stranger had bent his eyes on Hester Prynne. It was care-

---

9. Amsterdam, where the Puritans had lived after leaving England.

lessly, at first, like a man chiefly accustomed to look inward, and to whom external matters are of little value and import, unless they bear relation to something within his mind. Very soon, however, his look became keen and penetrative. A writhing horror twisted itself across his features, like a snake gliding swiftly over them, and making one little pause, with all its wreathed intervolutions in open sight. His face darkened with some powerful emotion, which, nevertheless, he so instantaneously controlled by an effort of his will, that, save at a single moment, its expression might have passed for calmness. After a brief space, the convulsion grew almost imperceptible, and finally subsided into the depths of his nature. When he found the eyes of Hester Prynne fastened on his own, and saw that she appeared to recognize him, he slowly and calmly raised his finger, made a gesture with it in the air, and laid it on his lips.

Then, touching the shoulder of a townsman who stood next to him, he addressed him, in a formal and courteous manner.

"I pray you, good Sir," said he, "who is this woman?—and wherefore is she here set up to public shame?"

"You must needs be a stranger in this region, friend," answered the townsman, looking curiously at the questioner and his savage companion, "else you would surely have heard of Mistress Hester Prynne, and her evil doings. She hath raised a great scandal, I promise you, in godly Master Dimmesdale's church."

"You say truly," replied the other. "I am a stranger, and have been a wanderer, sorely against my will. I have met with grievous mishaps by sea and land, and have been long held in bonds among the heathen-folk, to the southward; and am now brought hither by this Indian, to be redeemed out of my captivity. Will it please you, therefore, to tell me of Hester Prynne's,—have I her name rightly?—of this woman's offences, and what has brought her to yonder scaffold?"

"Truly, friend; and methinks it must gladden your heart, after your troubles and sojourn in the wilderness," said the townsman, "to find yourself, at length, in a land where iniquity is searched out, and punished in the sight of rulers and people; as here in our godly New England. Yonder woman, Sir, you must know, was the wife of a certain learned man, English by birth, but who had long dwelt in Amsterdam, whence, some good time agone, he was minded to cross over and cast in his lot with us of the Massachusetts. To this purpose, he sent his wife before him, remaining himself to look after some necessary affairs. Marry, good Sir, in some two years, or less, that the woman has been a dweller here in Boston, no tidings have come of this learned gentleman, Master Prynne; and his young wife, look you, being left to her own misguidance——"

"Ah!—aha!—I conceive you," said the stranger, with a bitter smile. "So learned a man as you speak of should have learned this too in his books. And who, by your favor, Sir, may be the father of yonder babe—it is some three or four months old, I should judge—which Mistress Prynne is holding in her arms?"

"Of a truth, friend, that matter remaineth a riddle; and the Daniel who shall expound it is yet a-wanting,"[1] answered the townsman. "Madam Hester absolutely refuseth to speak, and the magistrates have laid their heads together in vain. Peradventure the guilty one stands looking on at this sad spectacle, unknown of man, and forgetting that God sees him."

"The learned man," observed the stranger, with another smile, "should come himself, to look into the mystery."

"It behooves him well, if he be still in life," responded the townsman. "Now, good Sir, our Massachusetts magistracy, bethinking themselves that this woman is youthful and fair, and doubtless was strongly tempted to her fall;—and that, moreover, as is most likely, her husband may be at the bottom of the sea;—they have not been bold to put in force the extremity of our righteous law against her. The penalty thereof is death. But in their great mercy and tenderness of heart, they have doomed Mistress Prynne to stand only a space of three hours on the platform of the pillory, and then and thereafter, for the remainder of her natural life, to wear a mark of shame upon her bosom."

"A wise sentence!" remarked the stranger, gravely bowing his head. "Thus she will be a living sermon against sin, until the ignominious letter be engraved upon her tomb-stone. It irks me, nevertheless, that the partner of her iniquity should not, at least, stand on the scaffold by her side. But he will be known!—he will be known!—he will be known!"

He bowed courteously to the communicative townsman, and, whispering a few words to his Indian attendant, they both made their way through the crowd.

While this passed, Hester Prynne had been standing on her pedestal, still with a fixed gaze towards the stranger; so fixed a gaze, that, at moments of intense absorption, all other objects in the visible world seemed to vanish, leaving only him and her. Such an interview, perhaps, would have been more terrible than even to meet him as she now did, with the hot, midday sun burning down upon her face, and lighting up its shame; with the scarlet token of infamy on her breast; with the sin-born infant in her arms; with a whole people, drawn forth as to a festival, staring at the features that should have been seen only in the quiet gleam of the fireside, in the happy shadow of a home, or beneath a matronly veil, at church. Dreadful as it was, she was conscious of a shelter in the presence of these thousand witnesses. It was better to stand thus, with so many betwixt him and her, than to greet him, face to face, they two alone. She fled for refuge, as it were, to the public exposure, and dreaded the moment when its protection should be withdrawn from her. Involved in these thoughts, she scarcely heard a voice behind her, until it had repeated her name more than once, in a loud and solemn tone, audible to the whole multitude.

---

1. See Daniel 5:12: "Forasmuch as an excellent spirit, and knowledge, and understanding, interpreting of dreams, and shewing of hard sentences, and dissolving of doubts, were found in the same Daniel, whom the king named Belteshazzar: now let Daniel be called, and he will shew the interpretation."

"Hearken unto me, Hester Prynne!" said the voice.

It has already been noticed, that directly over the platform on which Hester Prynne stood was a kind of balcony, or open gallery, appended to the meeting-house. It was the place whence proclamations were wont to be made, amidst an assemblage of the magistracy, with all the ceremonial that attended such public observances in those days. Here, to witness the scene which we are describing, sat Governor Bellingham himself, with four sergeants about his chair, bearing halberds, as a guard of honor.[2] He wore a dark feather in his hat, a border of embroidery on his cloak, and a black velvet tunic beneath; a gentleman advanced in years, with a hard experience written in his wrinkles. He was not ill fitted to be the head and representative of a community, which owed its origin and progress, and its present state of development, not to the impulses of youth, but to the stern and tempered energies of manhood, and the sombre sagacity of age; accomplishing so much, precisely because it imagined and hoped so little. The other eminent characters, by whom the chief ruler was surrounded, were distinguished by a dignity of mien, belonging to a period when the forms of authority were felt to possess the sacredness of Divine institutions. They were, doubtless, good men, just, and sage. But, out of the whole human family, it would not have been easy to select the same number of wise and virtuous persons, who should be less capable of sitting in judgment on an erring woman's heart, and disentangling its mesh of good and evil, than the sages of rigid aspect towards whom Hester Prynne now turned her face. She seemed conscious, indeed, that whatever sympathy she might expect lay in the larger and warmer heart of the multitude; for, as she lifted her eyes towards the balcony, the unhappy woman grew pale and trembled.

The voice which had called her attention was that of the reverend and famous John Wilson, the eldest clergyman of Boston, a great scholar, like most of his contemporaries in the profession, and withal a man of kind and genial spirit.[3] This last attribute, however, had been less carefully developed than his intellectual gifts, and was, in truth, rather a matter of shame than self-congratulation with him. There he stood, with a border of grizzled locks beneath his skull-cap; while his gray eyes, accustomed to the shaded light of his study, were winking, like those of Hester's infant, in the unadulterated sunshine. He looked like the darkly engraved portraits which we see prefixed to old volumes

2. As Charles Ryskamp points out in his essay in this Norton Critical Edition, Hawthorne takes a small liberty with dates. Bellingham's term ended in May 1642, a month or so before this scene occurs. John Winthrop would have been governor in June 1642. Hawthorne's decision to identify Bellingham as governor is ironic, because Bellingham was prosecuted in June 1642 by the General Court for improper behavior. According to Winthrop's journal, Bellingham had "obtained" for himself a wife (Penelope Pelham) who was already "contracted to a friend of his, who lodged in his house," and he had "married himself"—that is, conducted their marriage ceremony. Given Hester's later justification of her behavior, Bellingham's rationale for his behavior—"the strength of his affection, and that she was not absolutely promised to the other gentleman"—seems especially ironic (Winthrop, *Journal*, 367). Bellingham would seem to have little moral authority to judge Hester Prynne. See Michael Colacurcio's essay in this Norton Critical Edition for more on Bellingham's role.

3. John Wilson (1588–1667), one of the first settlers of the Massachusetts Bay Colony, pronounced the sentence of excommunication upon Anne Hutchinson just before her banishment in 1638, labeling her a heathen and a leper (Hall, 388).

of sermons; and had no more right than one of those portraits would have, to step forth, as he now did, and meddle with a question of human guilt, passion and anguish.

"Hester Prynne," said the clergyman, "I have striven with my young brother here, under whose preaching of the word you have been privileged to sit,"—here Mr. Wilson laid his hand on the shoulder of a pale young man beside him,—"I have sought, I say, to persuade this godly youth, that he should deal with you, here in the face of Heaven, and before these wise and upright rulers, and in hearing of all the people, as touching the vileness and blackness of your sin. Knowing your natural temper better than I, he could the better judge what arguments to use, whether of tenderness or terror, such as might prevail over your hardness and obstinacy; insomuch that you should no longer hide the name of him who tempted you to this grievous fall. But he opposes to me, (with a young man's over-softness, albeit wise beyond his years,) that it were wronging the very nature of woman to force her to lay open her heart's secrets in such broad daylight, and in presence of so great a multitude. Truly, as I sought to convince him, the shame lay in the commission of the sin, and not in the showing of it forth. What say you to it, once again, brother Dimmesdale? Must it be thou, or I, that shall deal with this poor sinner's soul?"

There was a murmur among the dignified and reverend occupants of the balcony; and Governor Bellingham gave expression to its purport, speaking in an authoritative voice, although tempered with respect towards the youthful clergyman whom he addressed.

"Good Master Dimmesdale," said he, "the responsibility of this woman's soul lies greatly with you. It behooves you, therefore, to exhort her to repentance, and to confession, as a proof and consequence thereof."

The directness of this appeal drew the eyes of the whole crowd upon the Reverend Mr. Dimmesdale; a young clergyman, who had come from one of the great English universities,[4] bringing all the learning of the age into our wild forest-land. His eloquence and religious fervor had already given the earnest of high eminence in his profession. He was a person of very striking aspect, with a white, lofty, and impending brow, large, brown, melancholy eyes, and a mouth which, unless when he forcibly compressed it, was apt to be tremulous, expressing both nervous sensibility and a vast power of self-restraint. Notwithstanding his high native gifts and scholar-like attainments, there was an air about this young minister,—an apprehensive, a startled, a half-frightened look,—as of a being who felt himself quite astray and at a loss in the pathway of human existence, and could only be at ease in some seclusion of his own. Therefore, so far as his duties would permit, he trod in the shadowy by-paths, and thus kept himself simple and childlike; coming forth, when occasion was, with a freshness, and fragrance, and dewy purity of thought, which, as many people said, affected them like the speech of an angel.

4. Oxford. See p. 80.

Such was the young man whom the Reverend Mr. Wilson and the Governor had introduced so openly to the public notice, bidding him speak, in the hearing of all men, to that mystery of a woman's soul, so sacred even in its pollution. The trying nature of his position drove the blood from his cheek, and made his lips tremulous.

"Speak to the woman, my brother," said Mr. Wilson. "It is of moment to her soul, and therefore, as the worshipful Governor says, momentous to thine own, in whose charge hers is. Exhort her to confess the truth!"

The Reverend Mr. Dimmesdale bent his head, in silent prayer, as it seemed, and then came forward.

"Hester Prynne," said he, leaning over the balcony, and looking down steadfastly into her eyes, "thou hearest what this good man says, and seest the accountability under which I labor. If thou feelest it to be for thy soul's peace, and that thy earthly punishment will thereby be made more effectual to salvation, I charge thee to speak out the name of thy fellow-sinner and fellow-sufferer! Be not silent from any mistaken pity and tenderness for him; for, believe me, Hester, though he were to step down from a high place, and stand there beside thee, on thy pedestal of shame, yet better were it so, than to hide a guilty heart through life. What can thy silence do for him, except it tempt him—yea, compel him, as it were—to add hypocrisy to sin? Heaven hath granted thee an open ignominy, that thereby thou mayest work out an open triumph over the evil within thee, and the sorrow without. Take heed how thou deniest to him—who, perchance, hath not the courage to grasp it for himself—the bitter, but wholesome, cup that is now presented to thy lips!"

The young pastor's voice was tremulously sweet, rich, deep, and broken. The feeling that it so evidently manifested, rather than the direct purport of the words, caused it to vibrate within all hearts, and brought the listeners into one accord of sympathy. Even the poor baby, at Hester's bosom, was affected by the same influence; for it directed its hitherto vacant gaze towards Mr. Dimmesdale, and held up its little arms, with a half pleased, half plaintive murmur. So powerful seemed the minister's appeal, that the people could not believe but that Hester Prynne would speak out the guilty name; or else that the guilty one himself, in whatever high or lowly place he stood, would be drawn forth by an inward and inevitable necessity, and compelled to ascend the scaffold.

Hester shook her head.

"Woman, transgress not beyond the limits of Heaven's mercy!" cried the Reverend Mr. Wilson, more harshly than before. "That little babe hath been gifted with a voice, to second and confirm the counsel which thou hast heard. Speak out the name! That, and thy repentance, may avail to take the scarlet letter off thy breast."

"Never!" replied Hester Prynne, looking, not at Mr. Wilson, but into the deep and troubled eyes of the younger clergyman. "It is too deeply branded. Ye cannot take it off. And would that I might endure his agony, as well as mine!"

"Speak, woman!" said another voice, coldly and sternly, proceeding from the crowd about the scaffold. "Speak; and give your child a father!"

"I will not speak!" answered Hester, turning pale as death, but responding to this voice, which she too surely recognized. "And my child must seek a heavenly Father; she shall never know an earthly one!"

"She will not speak!" murmured Mr. Dimmesdale, who, leaning over the balcony, with his hand upon his heart, had awaited the result of his appeal. He now drew back, with a long respiration. "Wondrous strength and generosity of a woman's heart! She will not speak!"

Discerning the impracticable state of the poor culprit's mind, the elder clergyman, who had carefully prepared himself for the occasion, addressed to the multitude a discourse on sin, in all its branches, but with continual reference to the ignominious letter. So forcibly did he dwell upon this symbol, for the hour or more during which his periods were rolling over the people's heads, that it assumed new terrors in their imagination, and seemed to derive its scarlet hue from the flames of the infernal pit. Hester Prynne, meanwhile, kept her place upon the pedestal of shame, with glazed eyes, and an air of weary indifference. She had borne, that morning, all that nature could endure; and as her temperament was not of the order that escapes from too intense suffering by a swoon, her spirit could only shelter itself beneath a stony crust of insensibility, while the faculties of animal life remained entire. In this state, the voice of the preacher thundered remorselessly, but unavailingly, upon her ears. The infant, during the latter portion of her ordeal, pierced the air with its wailings and screams; she strove to hush it, mechanically, but seemed scarcely to sympathize with its trouble. With the same hard demeanor, she was led back to prison, and vanished from the public gaze within its iron-clamped portal. It was whispered, by those who peered after her, that the scarlet letter threw a lurid gleam along the dark passage-way of the interior.

IV. The Interview

After her return to the prison, Hester Prynne was found to be in a state of nervous excitement that demanded constant watchfulness, lest she should perpetrate violence on herself, or do some half-frenzied mischief to the poor babe. As night approached, it proving impossible to quell her insubordination by rebuke or threats of punishment, Master Brackett, the jailer,[1] thought fit to introduce a physician. He described him as a man of skill in all Christian modes of physical science, and likewise familiar with whatever the savage people could teach, in respect to medicinal herbs and roots that grew in the forest. To say the truth, there was much need of professional assistance, not merely for Hester herself, but still more urgently for the child; who, drawing its sustenance from the maternal bosom, seemed

---

1. Caleb Snow mentions Brackett as "prison keeper," beginning in 1633 (116).

to have drank in with it all the turmoil, the anguish and despair, which pervaded the mother's system. It now writhed in convulsions of pain, and was a forcible type, in its little frame, of the moral agony which Hester Prynne had borne throughout the day.

Closely following the jailer into the dismal apartment, appeared that individual, of singular aspect, whose presence in the crowd had been of such deep interest to the wearer of the scarlet letter. He was lodged in the prison, not as suspected of any offence, but as the most convenient and suitable mode of disposing of him, until the magistrates should have conferred with the Indian sagamores respecting his ransom. His name was announced as Roger Chillingworth. The jailer, after ushering him into the room, remained a moment, marvelling at the comparative quiet that followed his entrance; for Hester Prynne had immediately become as still as death, although the child continued to moan.

"Prithee, friend, leave me alone with my patient," said the practitioner. "Trust me, good jailer, you shall briefly have peace in your house; and, I promise you, Mistress Prynne shall hereafter be more amenable to just authority than you may have found her heretofore."

"Nay, if your worship can accomplish that," answered Master Brackett, "I shall own you for a man of skill indeed! Verily, the woman hath been like a possessed one; and there lacks little, that I should take in hand to drive Satan out of her with stripes."

The stranger had entered the room with the characteristic quietude of the profession to which he announced himself as belonging. Nor did his demeanor change, when the withdrawal of the prison-keeper left him face to face with the woman, whose absorbed notice of him, in the crowd, had intimated so close a relation between himself and her. His first care was given to the child; whose cries, indeed, as she lay writhing on the trundle-bed, made it of peremptory necessity to postpone all other business to the task of soothing her. He examined the infant carefully, and then proceeded to unclasp a leathern case, which he took from beneath his dress. It appeared to contain medical preparations, one of which he mingled with a cup of water.

"My old studies in alchemy,"[2] observed he, "and my sojourn, for above a year past, among a people well versed in the kindly properties of simples, have made a better physician of me than many that claim the medical degree. Here, woman! The child is yours,—she is none of mine,—neither will she recognize my voice or aspect as a father's. Administer this draught, therefore, with thine own hand."

Hester repelled the offered medicine, at the same time gazing with strongly marked apprehension into his face.

"Wouldst thou avenge thyself on the innocent babe?" whispered she.

"Foolish woman!" responded the physician, half coldly, half soothingly. "What should ail me, to harm this misbegotten and miserable

---

2. Experiments for turning common metals, such as lead, into gold. Aylmer in Hawthorne's "The Birth-mark" is also associated with alchemy.

babe? The medicine is potent for good; and were it my child,—yea, mine own, as well as thine!—I could do no better for it."

As she still hesitated, being, in fact, in no reasonable state of mind, he took the infant in his arms, and himself administered the draught. It soon proved its efficacy, and redeemed the leech's[3] pledge. The moans of the little patient subsided; its convulsive tossings gradually ceased; and, in a few moments, as is the custom of young children after relief from pain, it sank into a profound and dewy slumber. The physician, as he had a fair right to be termed, next bestowed his attention on the mother. With calm and intent scrutiny, he felt her pulse, looked into her eyes,—a gaze that made her heart shrink and shudder, because so familiar, and yet so strange and cold,—and, finally, satisfied with his investigation, proceeded to mingle another draught.

"I know not Lethe nor Nepenthe," remarked he; "but I have learned many new secrets in the wilderness, and here is one of them,—a recipe that an Indian taught me, in requital of some lessons of my own, that were as old as Paracelsus.[4] Drink it! It may be less soothing than a sinless conscience. That I cannot give thee. But it will calm the swell and heaving of thy passion, like oil thrown on the waves of a tempestuous sea."

He presented the cup to Hester, who received it with a slow, earnest look into his face; not precisely a look of fear, yet full of doubt and questioning, as to what his purposes might be. She looked also at her slumbering child.

"I have thought of death," said she,—"have wished for it,—would even have prayed for it, were it fit that such as I should pray for anything. Yet, if death be in this cup, I bid thee think again, ere thou beholdest me quaff it. See! It is even now at my lips."

"Drink, then," replied he, still with the same cold composure. "Dost thou know me so little, Hester Prynne? Are my purposes wont to be so shallow? Even if I imagine a scheme of vengeance, what could I do better for my object than to let thee live,—than to give thee medicines against all harm and peril of life,—so that this burning shame may still blaze upon thy bosom?" As he spoke, he laid his long forefinger on the scarlet letter, which forthwith seemed to scorch into Hester's breast, as if it had been red-hot. He noticed her involuntary gesture, and smiled. "Live, therefore, and bear about thy doom with thee, in the eyes of men and women,—in the eyes of him whom thou didst call thy husband,—in the eyes of yonder child! And, that thou mayest live, take off this draught."

Without further expostulation or delay, Hester Prynne drained the cup, and, at the motion of the man of skill, seated herself on the bed where the child was sleeping; while he drew the only chair which the room afforded, and took his own seat beside her. She could not but

---

3. An archaic term for physician; in the seventeenth century, it was applied in ordinary prose only to veterinary practitioners (*OED*).
4. A sixteenth-century Swiss alchemist (1493–1541). *Lethe*: in Greek mythology, one of the rivers of Hades, associated with forgetfulness. *Nepenthe*: a drug that purportedly assuaged grief.

tremble at these preparations; for she felt that—having now done all that humanity, or principle, or, if so it were, a refined cruelty, impelled him to do, for the relief of physical suffering—he was next to treat with her as the man whom she had most deeply and irreparably injured.

"Hester," said he, "I ask not wherefore, nor how, thou hast fallen into the pit, or say, rather, thou hast ascended to the pedestal of infamy, on which I found thee. The reason is not far to seek. It was my folly, and thy weakness. I,—a man of thought,—the book-worm of great libraries,—a man already in decay, having given my best years to feed the hungry dream of knowledge,—what had I to do with youth and beauty like thine own! Misshapen from my birth-hour, how could I delude myself with the idea that intellectual gifts might veil physical deformity in a young girl's fantasy! Men call me wise. If sages were ever wise in their own behoof, I might have foreseen all this. I might have known that, as I came out of the vast and dismal forest, and entered this settlement of Christian men, the very first object to meet my eyes would be thyself, Hester Prynne, standing up, a statue of ignominy, before the people. Nay, from the moment when we came down the old church-steps together, a married pair, I might have beheld the bale-fire of that scarlet letter blazing at the end of our path!"

"Thou knowest," said Hester,—for, depressed as she was, she could not endure this last quiet stab at the token of her shame,—"thou knowest that I was frank with thee. I felt no love, nor feigned any."

"True," replied he. "It was my folly! I have said it. But, up to that epoch of my life, I had lived in vain. The world had been so cheerless! My heart was a habitation large enough for many guests, but lonely and chill, and without a household fire. I longed to kindle one! It seemed not so wild a dream,—old as I was, and sombre as I was, and misshapen as I was,—that the simple bliss, which is scattered far and wide, for all mankind to gather up, might yet be mine. And so, Hester, I drew thee into my heart, into its innermost chamber, and sought to warm thee by the warmth which thy presence made there!"

"I have greatly wronged thee," murmured Hester.

"We have wronged each other," answered he. "Mine was the first wrong, when I betrayed thy budding youth into a false and unnatural relation with my decay. Therefore, as a man who has not thought and philosophized in vain, I seek no vengeance, plot no evil against thee. Between thee and me, the scale hangs fairly balanced. But, Hester, the man lives who has wronged us both! Who is he?"

"Ask me not!" replied Hester Prynne, looking firmly into his face. "That thou shalt never know!"

"Never, sayest thou?" rejoined he, with a smile of dark and self-relying intelligence. "Never know him! Believe me, Hester, there are few things,—whether in the outward world, or to a certain depth, in the invisible sphere of thought,—few things hidden from the man who devotes himself earnestly and unreservedly to the solution of a mystery. Thou mayest cover up thy secret from the prying multitude. Thou mayest conceal it, too, from the ministers and magistrates, even as thou didst this day, when they sought to wrench the name out of thy heart, and give thee a partner on thy pedestal. But, as for me, I come to the inquest with other senses than they possess. I shall seek this man, as I have sought truth in books; as I have sought gold in alchemy. There is a sympathy that will make me conscious of him. I shall see him tremble. I shall feel myself shudder, suddenly and unawares. Sooner or later, he must needs be mine!"

The eyes of the wrinkled scholar glowed so intensely upon her, that Hester Prynne clasped her hands over her heart, dreading lest he should read the secret there at once.

"Thou wilt not reveal his name? Not the less he is mine," resumed he, with a look of confidence, as if destiny were at one with him. "He bears no letter of infamy wrought into his garment, as thou dost; but I shall read it on his heart. Yet fear not for him! Think not that I shall interfere with Heaven's own method of retribution, or, to my own loss, betray him to the gripe of human law. Neither do thou imagine that I shall contrive aught against his life; no, nor against his fame, if, as I judge, he be a man of fair repute. Let him live! Let him hide himself in outward honor, if he may! Not the less he shall be mine!"

"Thy acts are like mercy," said Hester, bewildered and appalled. "But thy words interpret thee as a terror!"

"One thing, thou that wast my wife, I would enjoin upon thee," continued the scholar. "Thou hast kept the secret of thy paramour. Keep, likewise, mine! There are none in this land that know me. Breathe not, to any human soul, that thou didst ever call me husband! Here, on this wild outskirt of the earth, I shall pitch my tent; for, elsewhere a wanderer, and isolated from human interests, I find here a woman, a man, a child, amongst whom and myself there exist the closest ligaments. No matter whether of love or hate; no matter whether of right or wrong! Thou and thine, Hester Prynne, belong to me. My home is where thou art, and where he is. But betray me not!"

"Wherefore dost thou desire it?" inquired Hester, shrinking, she hardly knew why, from this secret bond. "Why not announce thyself openly, and cast me off at once?"

"It may be," he replied, "because I will not encounter the dishonor that besmirches the husband of a faithless woman. It may be for other reasons. Enough, it is my purpose to live and die unknown. Let, therefore, thy husband be to the world as one already dead, and of whom no tidings shall ever come. Recognize me not, by word, by sign, by look! Breathe not the secret, above all, to the man thou wottest of. Shouldst thou fail me in this, beware! His fame, his position, his life, will be in my hands. Beware!"

"I will keep thy secret, as I have his," said Hester.

"Swear it!" rejoined he.

And she took the oath.

"And now, Mistress Prynne," said old Roger Chillingworth, as he was hereafter to be named, "I leave thee alone; alone with thy infant, and the scarlet letter! How is it, Hester? Doth thy sentence bind thee to wear the token in thy sleep? Art thou not afraid of nightmares and hideous dreams?"

"Why dost thou smile so at me?" inquired Hester, troubled at the expression of his eyes. "Art thou like the Black Man that haunts the forest round about us? Hast thou enticed me into a bond that will prove the ruin of my soul?"

"Not thy soul," he answered, with another smile. "No, not thine!"

V. Hester at Her Needle

Hester Prynne's term of confinement was now at an end. Her prison-door was thrown open, and she came forth into the sunshine, which, falling on all alike, seemed, to her sick and morbid heart, as if meant for no other purpose than to reveal the scarlet letter on her breast. Perhaps there was a more real torture in her first unattended footsteps from the threshold of the prison, than even in the procession and spectacle that have been described, where she was made the common infamy, at which all mankind was summoned to point its finger. Then, she was supported by an unnatural tension of the nerves, and by all the combative energy of her character, which enabled her to convert the scene into a kind of lurid triumph. It was, moreover, a separate and insulated event, to occur but once in her lifetime, and to meet which, therefore, reckless of economy, she might call up the vital strength that would have sufficed for many quiet years. The very law that condemned her—a giant of stern features, but with vigor to support, as well as to annihilate, in his iron arm—had held her up, through the terrible ordeal of her ignominy. But now, with this un-attended walk from her prison-door, began the daily custom; and she must either sustain and carry it forward by the ordinary resources of her nature, or sink beneath it. She could no longer borrow from the future to help her through the present grief. To-morrow would bring its own trial with it; so would the next day, and so would the next; each its own trial, and yet the very same that was now so unutterably griev-ous to be borne. The days of the far-off future would toil onward, still with the same burden for her to take up, and bear along with her, but never to fling down; for the accumulating days, and added years, would pile up their misery upon the heap of shame. Throughout them all, giving up her individuality, she would become the general symbol at which the preacher and moralist might point, and in which they might vivify and embody their images of woman's frailty and sinful passion. Thus the young and pure would be taught to look at her, with the scarlet letter flaming on her breast,—at her, the child of honorable parents,—at her, the mother of a babe, that would hereafter be a woman,—at her, who had once been innocent,—as the figure, the body, the reality of sin. And over her grave, the infamy that she must carry thither would be her only monument.

It may seem marvellous, that, with the world before her,—kept by no restrictive clause of her condemnation within the limits of the Puritan settlement, so remote and so obscure,—free to return to her birth-place, or to any other European land, and there hide her character and identity under a new exterior, as completely as if emerging into another state of being,—and having also the passes of the dark, inscrutable forest open to her, where the wildness of her nature might assimilate itself with a people whose customs and life were alien from the law that had condemned her,—it may seem marvellous, that this woman should still call that place her home, where, and where only, she must needs be the type of shame. But there is a fatality, a feeling so irresistible and inevitable that it has the force of doom, which almost invariably compels human beings to linger around and haunt, ghost-like, the spot where some great and marked event has given the color to their lifetime; and still the more irresistibly, the darker the tinge that saddens it. Her sin, her ignominy, were the roots which she had struck into the soil. It was as if a new birth, with stronger assimilations than the first, had converted the forest-land, still so uncongenial to every other pilgrim and wanderer, into Hester Prynne's wild and dreary, but life-long home. All other scenes of earth—even that village of rural England, where happy infancy and stainless maidenhood seemed yet to be in her mother's keeping, like garments put off long ago—were foreign to her, in comparison. The chain that bound her here was of iron links, and galling to her inmost soul, but could never be broken.

It might be, too,—doubtless it was so, although she hid the secret from herself, and grew pale whenever it struggled out of her heart, like a serpent from its hole,—it might be that another feeling kept her within the scene and pathway that had been so fatal. There dwelt, there trode the feet of one with whom she deemed herself connected in a union, that, unrecognized on earth, would bring them together before the bar of final judgment, and make that their marriage-altar, for a joint futurity of endless retribution. Over and over again, the tempter of souls had thrust this idea upon Hester's contemplation, and laughed at the passionate and desperate joy with which she seized, and then strove to cast it from her. She barely looked the idea in the face, and hastened to bar it in its dungeon. What she compelled herself to believe,—what, finally, she reasoned upon, as her motive for continuing a resident of New England,—was half a truth, and half a self-delusion. Here, she said to herself, had been the scene of her guilt, and here should be the scene of her earthly punishment; and so, perchance, the torture of her daily shame would at length purge her soul, and work out another purity than that which she had lost; more saint-like, because the result of martyrdom.

Hester Prynne, therefore, did not flee. On the outskirts of the town, within the verge of the peninsula, but not in close vicinity to any other habitation, there was a small thatched cottage. It had been built by an earlier settler, and abandoned, because the soil about it was too sterile for cultivation, while its comparative remoteness put it out of the sphere of that social activity which already marked the habits of the emigrants. It stood on the shore, looking across a basin of the sea at the forest-covered hills, towards the west. A clump of scrubby trees, such as alone grew on the peninsula, did not so much conceal the cottage from view, as seem to denote that here was some object which would fain have been, or at least ought to be, concealed. In this little, lonesome dwelling, with some slender means that she possessed, and by the license of the magistrates, who still kept an inquisitorial watch over her, Hester established herself, with her infant child. A mystic shadow of suspicion immediately attached itself to the spot. Children, too young to comprehend wherefore this woman should be shut out from the sphere of human charities, would creep nigh enough to behold her plying her needle at the cottage-window, or standing in the doorway, or laboring in her little garden, or coming forth along the pathway that led townward; and, discerning the scarlet letter on her breast, would scamper off with a strange, contagious fear.

Lonely as was Hester's situation, and without a friend on earth who dared to show himself, she, however, incurred no risk of want. She possessed an art that sufficed, even in a land that afforded comparatively little scope for its exercise, to supply food for her thriving infant and herself. It was the art—then, as now, almost the only one within a woman's grasp—of needle-work. She bore on her breast, in the curiously embroidered letter, a specimen of her delicate and imaginative skill, of which the dames of a court might gladly have availed themselves, to add the richer and more spiritual adornment of human ingenuity to their fabrics of silk and gold. Here, indeed, in the sable simplicity that generally characterized the Puritanic modes of dress, there might be an infrequent call for the finer productions of her handiwork. Yet the taste of the age, demanding whatever was elaborate in compositions of this kind, did not fail to extend its influence over our stern progenitors, who had cast behind them so many fashions which it might seem harder to dispense with. Public ceremonies, such as ordinations, the installation of magistrates, and all that could give majesty to the forms in which a new government manifested itself to the people, were, as a matter of policy, marked by a stately and well-conducted ceremonial, and a sombre, but yet a studied magnificence. Deep ruffs, painfully wrought bands, and gorgeously embroidered gloves, were all deemed necessary to the official state of men assuming the reins of power; and were readily allowed to individuals dignified by rank or wealth, even while sumptuary laws forbade these and similar extravagances to the plebeian order. In the array of funerals, too,—whether for the apparel of the dead body, or to typify, by manifold emblematic devices of sable cloth and snowy lawn, the sorrow of the survivors,—there was a frequent and characteristic demand for such labor as Hester Prynne could supply. Baby-linen—for babies then wore robes of state—afforded still another possibility of toil and emolument.

By degrees, nor very slowly, her handiwork became what would now be termed the fashion. Whether from commiseration for a woman of so miserable a destiny; or from the morbid curiosity that gives a fictitious value even to common or worthless things; or by whatever other intangible circumstance was then, as now, sufficient to bestow, on some persons, what others might seek in vain; or because Hester really filled a gap which must otherwise have remained vacant; it is certain that she had ready and fairly requited employment for as many hours as she saw fit to occupy with her needle. Vanity, it may be, chose to mortify itself, by putting on, for ceremonials of pomp and state, the garments that had been wrought by her sinful hands. Her needle-work was seen on the ruff of the Governor; military men wore it on their scarfs, and the minister on his band; it decked the baby's little cap; it was shut up, to be mildewed and moulder away, in the coffins of the dead. But it is not recorded that, in a single instance, her skill was called in aid to embroider the white veil which was to cover the pure blushes of a bride. The exception indicated the ever relentless vigor with which society frowned upon her sin.

Hester sought not to acquire anything beyond a subsistence, of the plainest and most ascetic description, for herself, and a simple abundance for her child. Her own dress was of the coarsest materials and the most sombre hue; with only that one ornament,—the scarlet letter,—which it was her doom to wear. The child's attire, on the other hand, was distinguished by a fanciful, or, we might rather say, a fantastic ingenuity, which served, indeed, to heighten the airy charm that early began to develop itself in the little girl, but which appeared to have also a deeper meaning. We may speak further of it hereafter. Except for that small expenditure in the decoration of her infant, Hester bestowed all her superfluous means in charity, on wretches less miserable than herself, and who not unfrequently insulted the hand that fed them. Much of the time, which she might readily have applied to the better efforts of her art, she employed in making coarse garments for the poor. It is probable that there was an idea of penance in this mode of occupation, and that she offered up a real sacrifice of enjoyment, in devoting so many hours to such rude handiwork. She had in her nature a rich, voluptuous, Oriental characteristic,—a taste for the gorgeously beautiful, which, save in the exquisite productions of her needle, found nothing else, in all the possibilities of her life, to exercise itself upon. Women derive a pleasure, incomprehensible to the other sex, from the delicate toil of the needle. To Hester Prynne it might have been a mode of expressing, and therefore soothing, the passion of her life. Like all other joys, she rejected it as sin. This morbid meddling of conscience with an immaterial matter betokened, it is to be feared, no genuine and steadfast penitence, but something doubtful, something that might be deeply wrong, beneath.

In this manner, Hester Prynne came to have a part to perform in the world. With her native energy of character, and rare capacity, it could not entirely cast her off, although it had set a mark upon her, more intolerable to a woman's heart than that which branded the brow of Cain.[1] In all her intercourse with society, however, there was nothing that made her feel as if she belonged to it. Every gesture, every word, and even the silence of those with whom she came in contact, implied, and often expressed, that she was banished, and as much alone

1. See Genesis 4:1–16. For killing his brother, Abel, Cain was sentenced to be "a fugitive and a vagabond." When Cain protested that he would be killed, "the LORD set a mark upon Cain, lest any finding him should kill him" (4:15).

as if she inhabited another sphere, or communicated with the common nature by other organs and senses than the rest of human kind. She stood apart from moral interests, yet close beside them, like a ghost that revisits the familiar fireside, and can no longer make itself seen or felt; no more smile with the household joy, nor mourn with the kindred sorrow; or, should it succeed in manifesting its forbidden sympathy, awakening only terror and horrible repugnance. These emotions, in fact, and its bitterest scorn besides, seemed to be the sole portion that she retained in the universal heart. It was not an age of delicacy; and her position, although she understood it well, and was in little danger of forgetting it, was often brought before her vivid self-perception, like a new anguish, by the rudest touch upon the tenderest spot. The poor, as we have already said, whom she sought out to be the objects of her bounty, often reviled the hand that was stretched forth to succor them. Dames of elevated rank, likewise, whose doors she entered in the way of her occupation, were accustomed to distil drops of bitterness into her heart; sometimes through that alchemy of quiet malice, by which women can concoct a subtile poison from ordinary trifles; and sometimes, also, by a coarser expression, that fell upon the sufferer's defenceless breast like a rough blow upon an ulcerated wound. Hester had schooled herself long and well; she never responded to these attacks, save by a flush of crimson that rose irrepressibly over her pale cheek, and again subsided into the depths of her bosom. She was patient,—a martyr, indeed,—but she forebore to pray for her enemies; lest, in spite of her forgiving aspirations, the words of the blessing should stubbornly twist themselves into a curse.

Continually, and in a thousand other ways, did she feel the innumerable throbs of anguish that had been so cunningly contrived for her by the undying, the ever-active sentence of the Puritan tribunal. Clergymen paused in the street to address words of exhortation, that brought a crowd, with its mingled grin and frown, around the poor, sinful woman. If she entered a church, trusting to share the Sabbath smile of the Universal Father, it was often her mishap to find herself the text of the discourse. She grew to have a dread of children; for they had imbibed from their parents a vague idea of something horrible in this dreary woman, gliding silently through the town, with never any companion but one only child. Therefore, first allowing her to pass, they pursued her at a distance with shrill cries, and the utterance of a word that had no distinct purport to their own minds, but was none the less terrible to her, as proceeding from lips that babbled it unconsciously. It seemed to argue so wide a diffusion of her shame, that all nature knew of it; it could have caused her no deeper pang, had the leaves of the trees whispered the dark story among themselves,—had the summer breeze murmured about it—had the wintry blast shrieked it aloud! Another peculiar torture was felt in the gaze of a new eye. When strangers looked curiously at the scarlet letter,—and none ever failed to do so,—they branded it afresh into Hester's soul; so that, oftentimes, she could scarcely refrain, yet always did refrain, from covering the symbol with her hand. But then, again, an accus-

tomed eye had likewise its own anguish to inflict. Its cool stare of familiarity was intolerable. From first to last, in short, Hester Prynne
had always this dreadful agony in feeling a human eye upon the token;
the spot never grew callous; it seemed, on the contrary, to grow more
sensitive with daily torture.

But sometimes, once in many days, or perchance in many months,
she felt an eye—a human eye—upon the ignominious brand, that
seemed to give a momentary relief, as if half of her agony were shared.
The next instant, back it all rushed again, with still a deeper throb of
pain; for, in that brief interval, she had sinned anew. Had Hester
sinned alone?

Her imagination was somewhat affected, and, had she been of a
softer moral and intellectual fibre, would have been still more so, by
the strange and solitary anguish of her life. Walking to and fro, with
those lonely footsteps, in the little world with which she was outwardly connected, it now and then appeared to Hester,—if altogether
fancy, it was nevertheless too potent to be resisted,—she felt or fancied, then, that the scarlet letter had endowed her with a new sense.
She shuddered to believe, yet could not help believing, that it gave her
a sympathetic knowledge of the hidden sin in other hearts. She was
terror-stricken by the revelations that were thus made. What were
they? Could they be other than the insidious whispers of the bad angel, who would fain have persuaded the struggling woman, as yet only
half his victim, that the outward guise of purity was but a lie, and that,
if truth were everywhere to be shown, a scarlet letter would blaze forth
on many a bosom besides Hester Prynne's? Or, must she receive those
intimations—so obscure, yet so distinct—as truth? In all her miserable
experience, there was nothing else so awful and so loathsome as this
sense. It perplexed, as well as shocked her, by the irreverent inoppor-
tuneness of the occasions that brought it into vivid action. Sometimes
the red infamy upon her breast would give a sympathetic throb, as she
passed near a venerable minister or magistrate, the model of piety and
justice, to whom that age of antique reverence looked up, as to a mortal man in fellowship with angels. "What evil thing is at hand?" would
Hester say to herself. Lifting her reluctant eyes, there would be nothing human within the scope of view, save the form of this earthly saint!
Again, a mystic sisterhood would contumaciously assert itself, as she
met the sanctified frown of some matron, who, according to the rumor
of all tongues, had kept cold snow within her bosom throughout life.
That unsunned snow in the matron's bosom, and the burning shame
on Hester Prynne's,—what had the two in common? Or, once more,
the electric thrill would give her warning,—"Behold, Hester, here is a
companion!"—and, looking up, she would detect the eyes of a young
maiden glancing at the scarlet letter, shyly and aside, and quickly
averted, with a faint, chill crimson in her cheeks; as if her purity were
somewhat sullied by that momentary glance. O Fiend, whose talisman
was that fatal symbol, wouldst thou leave nothing, whether in youth or
age, for this poor sinner to revere?—such loss of faith is ever one of
the saddest results of sin. Be it accepted as a proof that all was not

corrupt in this poor victim of her own frailty, and man's hard law, that Hester Prynne yet struggled to believe that no fellow-mortal was guilty like herself.

The vulgar, who, in those dreary old times, were always contributing a grotesque horror to what interested their imaginations, had a story about the scarlet letter which we might readily work up into a terrific legend. They averred, that the symbol was not mere scarlet cloth, tinged in an earthly dye-pot, but was red-hot with infernal fire, and could be seen glowing all alight, whenever Hester Prynne walked abroad in the night-time. And we must needs say, it seared Hester's bosom so deeply, that perhaps there was more truth in the rumor than our modern incredulity may be inclined to admit.

VI. Pearl

We have as yet hardly spoken of the infant; that little creature, whose innocent life had sprung, by the inscrutable decree of Providence, a lovely and immortal flower, out of the rank luxuriance of a guilty passion. How strange it seemed to the sad woman, as she watched the growth, and the beauty that became every day more brilliant, and the intelligence that threw its quivering sunshine over the tiny features of this child! Her Pearl!—For so had Hester called her; not as a name expressive of her aspect, which had nothing of the calm, white, unimpassioned lustre that would be indicated by the comparison. But she named the infant "Pearl," as being of great price,—purchased with all she had,—her mother's only treasure![1] How strange, indeed! Man had marked this woman's sin by a scarlet letter, which had such potent and disastrous efficacy that no human sympathy could reach her, save it were sinful like herself. God, as a direct consequence of the sin which man thus punished, had given her a lovely child, whose place was on that same dishonored bosom, to connect her parent forever with the race and descent of mortals, and to be finally a blessed soul in heaven! Yet these thoughts affected Hester Prynne less with hope than apprehension. She knew that her deed had been evil; she could have no faith, therefore, that its result would be good. Day after day, she looked fearfully into the child's expanding nature; ever dreading to detect some dark and wild peculiarity, that should correspond with the guiltiness to which she owed her being.

Certainly, there was no physical defect. By its perfect shape, its vigor, and its natural dexterity in the use of all its untried limbs, the infant was worthy to have been brought forth in Eden; worthy to have been left there, to be the plaything of the angels, after the world's first parents were driven out. The child had a native grace which does not invariably coëxist with faultless beauty; its attire, however simple, always impressed the beholder as if it were the very garb that precisely

---

1. See Matthew 13:45–46: "The kingdom of heaven is like unto a merchant man, seeking goodly pearls: Who, when he had found one pearl of great price, went and sold all that he had, and bought it."

became it best. But little Pearl was not clad in rustic weeds. Her
mother, with a morbid purpose that may be better understood hereafter, had bought the richest tissues that could be procured, and allowed her imaginative faculty its full play in the arrangement and
decoration of the dresses which the child wore, before the public eye.
So magnificent was the small figure, when thus arrayed, and such was
the splendor of Pearl's own proper beauty, shining through the gorgeous robes which might have extinguished a paler loveliness, that
there was an absolute circle of radiance around her, on the darksome
cottage floor. And yet a russet gown, torn and soiled with the child's
rude play, made a picture of her just as perfect. Pearl's aspect was imbued with a spell of infinite variety; in this one child there were many
children, comprehending the full scope between the wild-flower prettiness of a peasant-baby, and the pomp, in little, of an infant princess.
Throughout all, however, there was a trait of passion, a certain depth
of hue, which she never lost; and if, in any of her changes, she had
grown fainter or paler, she would have ceased to be herself;—it would
have been no longer Pearl!

This outward mutability indicated, and did not more than fairly express, the various properties of her inner life. Her nature appeared to
possess depth, too, as well as variety; but—or else Hester's fears deceived her—it lacked reference and adaptation to the world into which
she was born. The child could not be made amenable to rules. In giving her existence, a great law had been broken; and the result was a
being whose elements were perhaps beautiful and brilliant, but all in
disorder; or with an order peculiar to themselves, amidst which the
point of variety and arrangement was difficult or impossible to be discovered. Hester could only account for the child's character—and
even then most vaguely and imperfectly—by recalling what she herself
had been, during that momentous period while Pearl was imbibing her
soul from the spiritual world, and her bodily frame from its material of
earth. The mother's impassioned state had been the medium through
which were transmitted to the unborn infant the rays of its moral life;
and, however white and clear originally, they had taken the deep stains
of crimson and gold, the fiery lustre, the black shadow, and the untempered light, of the intervening substance. Above all, the warfare of
Hester's spirit, at that epoch, was perpetuated in Pearl. She could recognize her wild, desperate, defiant mood, the flightiness of her temper,
and even some of the very cloud-shapes of gloom and despondency
that had brooded in her heart. They were now illuminated by the
morning radiance of a young child's disposition, but, later in the day of
earthly existence, might be prolific of the storm and whirlwind.

The discipline of the family, in those days, was of a far more rigid
kind than now. The frown, the harsh rebuke, the frequent application
of the rod, enjoined by Scriptural authority, were used, not merely in
the way of punishment for actual offences, but as a wholesome regi-
men for the growth and promotion of all childish virtues.[2] Hester

2. See Proverbs 13:24: "He that spareth his rod hateth his son: but he that loveth him chas-
teneth him betimes."

Prynne, nevertheless, the lonely mother of this one child, ran little risk
of erring on the side of undue severity. Mindful, however, of her own
errors and misfortunes, she early sought to impose a tender, but strict
control over the infant immortality that was committed to her charge.
But the task was beyond her skill. After testing both smiles and
frowns, and proving that neither mode of treatment possessed any cal-
culable influence, Hester was ultimately compelled to stand aside, and
permit the child to be swayed by her own impulses. Physical compulsion or restraint was effectual, of course, while it lasted. As to any
other kind of discipline, whether addressed to her mind or heart, little
Pearl might or might not be within its reach, in accordance with the
caprice that ruled the moment. Her mother, while Pearl was yet an infant, grew acquainted with a certain peculiar look, that warned her
when it would be labor thrown away to insist, persuade, or plead. It
was a look so intelligent, yet inexplicable, so perverse, sometimes so
malicious, but generally accompanied by a wild flow of spirits, that
Hester could not help questioning, at such moments, whether Pearl
was a human child.[3] She seemed rather an airy sprite, which, after
playing its fantastic sports for a little while upon the cottage-floor,
would flit away with a mocking smile. Whenever that look appeared in
her wild, bright, deeply black eyes, it invested her with a strange remoteness and intangibility; it was as if she were hovering in the air
and might vanish, like a glimmering light, that comes we know not
whence, and goes we know not whither. Beholding it, Hester was constrained to rush towards the child,—to pursue the little elf in the
flight which she invariably began,—to snatch her to her bosom, with a
close pressure and earnest kisses,—not so much from overflowing
love, as to assure herself that Pearl was flesh and blood, and not utterly delusive. But Pearl's laugh, when she was caught, though full of
merriment and music, made her mother more doubtful than before.
    Heart-smitten at this bewildering and baffling spell, that so often
came between herself and her sole treasure, whom she had bought so
dear, and who was all her world, Hester sometimes burst into passionate tears. Then, perhaps,—for there was no foreseeing how it might
affect her,—Pearl would frown, and clench her little fist, and harden
her small features into a stern, unsympathizing look of discontent. Not
seldom, she would laugh anew, and louder than before, like a thing incapable and unintelligent of human sorrow. Or—but this more rarely
happened—she would be convulsed with a rage of grief, and sob out
her love for her mother, in broken words, and seem intent on proving
that she had a heart, by breaking it. Yet Hester was hardly safe in con-
fiding herself to that gusty tenderness; it passed, as suddenly as it
came. Brooding over all these matters, the mother felt like one who
has evoked a spirit, but, by some irregularity in the process of conjura-
tion, has failed to win the master-word that should control this new
and incomprehensible intelligence. Her only real comfort was when
the child lay in the placidity of sleep. Then she was sure of her, and

3. Compare the passage from Hawthorne's notebook on pp. 218–19 of this Norton Critical
    Edition.

tasted hours of quiet, sad, delicious happiness; until—perhaps with that perverse expression glimmering from beneath her opening lids— little Pearl awoke!

How soon—with what strange rapidity, indeed!—did Pearl arrive at an age that was capable of social intercourse, beyond the mother's ever-ready smile and nonsense-words![4] And then what a happiness would it have been, could Hester Prynne have heard her clear, bird-like voice mingling with the uproar of other childish voices, and have distinguished and unravelled her own darling's tones, amid all the en-tangled outcry of a group of sportive children! But this could never be. Pearl was a born outcast of the infantile world. An imp of evil, emblem and product of sin, she had no right among christened infants. Noth-ing was more remarkable than the instinct, as it seemed, with which the child comprehended her loneliness; the destiny that had drawn an inviolable circle round about her; the whole peculiarity, in short, of her position in respect to other children. Never, since her release from prison, had Hester met the public gaze without her. In all her walks about the town, Pearl, too, was there; first as the babe in arms, and afterwards as the little girl, small companion of her mother, holding a forefinger with her whole grasp, and tripping along at the rate of three or four footsteps to one of Hester's. She saw the children of the settle-ment, on the grassy margin of the street, or at the domestic thresh-olds, disporting themselves in such grim fashion as the Puritanic nurture would permit; playing at going to church, perchance; or at scourging Quakers; or taking scalps in a sham-fight with the Indians; or scaring one another with freaks of imitative witchcraft. Pearl saw, and gazed intently, but never sought to make acquaintance. If spoken to, she would not speak again. If the children gathered about her, as they sometimes did, Pearl would grow positively terrible in her puny wrath, snatching up stones to fling at them, with shrill, incoherent ex-clamations, that made her mother tremble, because they had so much the sound of a witch's anathemas in some unknown tongue.[5]

The truth was, that the little Puritans, being of the most intolerant brood that ever lived, had got a vague idea of something outlandish, unearthly, or at variance with ordinary fashions, in the mother and child; and therefore scorned them in their hearts, and not unfre-quently reviled them with their tongues. Pearl felt the sentiment, and requited it with the bitterest hatred that can be supposed to rankle in a childish bosom. These outbreaks of a fierce temper had a kind of value, and even comfort, for her mother; because there was at least an intelligible earnestness in the mood, instead of the fitful caprice that so often thwarted her in the child's manifestations. It appalled her, nevertheless, to discern here, again, a shadowy reflection of the evil that had existed in herself. All this enmity and passion had Pearl in-herited, by inalienable right, out of Hester's heart. Mother and daugh-

---

4. Hawthorne uses Pearl's aging in this chapter to move the novel forward approximately three years.
5. In Hawthorne's "The Gentle Boy" (1832), the Quaker child Ilbrahim is persecuted and ulti-mately killed by Puritan children.

ter stood together in the same circle of seclusion from human society; and in the nature of the child seemed to be perpetuated those unquiet elements that had distracted Hester Prynne before Pearl's birth, but had since begun to be soothed away by the softening influences of maternity.

At home, within and around her mother's cottage, Pearl wanted not a wide and various circle of acquaintance. The spell of life went forth from her ever creative spirit, and communicated itself to a thousand objects, as a torch kindles a flame wherever it may be applied. The unlikeliest materials,—a stick, a bunch of rags, a flower,—were the puppets of Pearl's witchcraft, and, without undergoing any outward change, became spiritually adapted to whatever drama occupied the stage of her inner world. Her one baby-voice served a multitude of imaginary personages, old and young, to talk withal. The pine-trees, aged, black and solemn, and flinging groans and other melancholy utterances on the breeze, needed little transformation to figure as Puritan elders; the ugliest weeds of the garden were their children, whom Pearl smote down and uprooted, most unmercifully. It was wonderful, the vast variety of forms into which she threw her intellect, with no continuity, indeed, but darting up and dancing, always in a state of preternatural activity,—soon sinking down, as if exhausted by so rapid and feverish a tide of life,—and succeeded by other shapes of a similar wild energy. It was like nothing so much as the phantasmagoric play of the northern lights. In the mere exercise of the fancy, however, and the sportiveness of a growing mind, there might be little more than was observable in other children of bright faculties; except as Pearl, in the dearth of human playmates, was thrown more upon the visionary throng which she created. The singularity lay in the hostile feelings with which the child regarded all these offspring of her own heart and mind. She never created a friend, but seemed always to be sowing broadcast the dragon's teeth, whence sprung a harvest of armed enemies, against whom she rushed to battle.[6] It was inexpressibly sad—then what depth of sorrow to a mother, who felt in her own heart the cause!—to observe, in one so young, this constant recognition of an adverse world, and so fierce a training of the energies that were to make good her cause, in the contest that must ensue.

Gazing at Pearl, Hester Prynne often dropped her work upon her knees, and cried out with an agony which she would fain have hidden, but which made utterance for itself, betwixt speech and a groan,—"O Father in Heaven,—if Thou art still my Father,—what is this being which I have brought into the world!" And Pearl, overhearing the ejaculation, or aware, through some more subtle channel, of those throbs of anguish, would turn her vivid and beautiful little face upon her mother, smile with sprite-like intelligence, and resume her play.

One peculiarity of the child's deportment remains yet to be told. The very first thing which she had noticed, in her life, was—what?—

---

6. In Greek mythology, Cadmus planted dragon's, or serpent's, teeth in the ground, and soldiers sprang up from the seeds.

not the mother's smile, responding to it, as other babies do, by that faint, embryo smile of the little mouth, remembered so doubtfully afterwards, and with such fond discussion whether it were indeed a smile. By no means! But that first object of which Pearl seemed to become aware was—shall we say it?—the scarlet letter on Hester's bosom! One day, as her mother stooped over the cradle, the infant's eyes had been caught by the glimmering of the gold embroidery about the letter; and, putting up her little hand, she grasped at it, smiling, not doubtfully, but with a decided gleam, that gave her face the look of a much older child. Then, gasping for breath, did Hester Prynne clutch the fatal token, instinctively endeavoring to tear it away; so infinite was the torture inflicted by the intelligent touch of Pearl's baby-hand. Again, as if her mother's agonized gesture were meant only to make sport for her, did little Pearl look into her eyes, and smile! From that epoch, except when the child was asleep, Hester had never felt a moment's safety; not a moment's calm enjoyment of her. Weeks, it is true, would sometimes elapse, during which Pearl's gaze might never once be fixed upon the scarlet letter; but then, again, it would come at unawares, like the stroke of sudden death, and always with that peculiar smile, and odd expression of the eyes.

Once, this freakish, elvish cast came into the child's eyes, while Hester was looking at her own image in them, as mothers are fond of doing; and, suddenly,—for women in solitude, and with troubled hearts, are pestered with unaccountable delusions,—she fancied that she beheld, not her own miniature portrait, but another face, in the small black mirror of Pearl's eye. It was a face, fiend-like, full of smiling malice, yet bearing the semblance of features that she had known full well, though seldom with a smile, and never with malice in them. It was as if an evil spirit possessed the child, and had just then peeped forth in mockery. Many a time afterwards had Hester been tortured, though less vividly, by the same illusion.[7]

In the afternoon of a certain summer's day, after Pearl grew big enough to run about, she amused herself with gathering handfuls of wild-flowers, and flinging them, one by one, at her mother's bosom; dancing up and down, like a little elf, whenever she hit the scarlet letter. Hester's first motion had been to cover her bosom with her clasped hands. But, whether from pride or resignation, or a feeling that her penance might best be wrought out by this unutterable pain, she resisted the impulse, and sat erect, pale as death, looking sadly into little Pearl's wild eyes. Still came the battery of flowers, almost invariably hitting the mark, and covering the mother's breast with hurts for which she could find no balm in this world, nor knew how to seek it in another. At last, her shot being all expended, the child stood still and gazed at Hester, with that little, laughing image of a fiend peeping out—or, whether it peeped or no, her mother so imagined it—from the unsearchable abyss of her black eyes.

"Child, what art thou?" cried the mother.

---

7. Compare the passage in Hawthorne's notebook on p. 218 of this Norton Critical Edition.

"O, I am your little Pearl!" answered the child.

But, while she said it, Pearl laughed, and began to dance up and down, with the humorsome gesticulation of a little imp, whose next freak might be to fly up the chimney.

"Art thou my child, in very truth?" asked Hester.

Nor did she put the question altogether idly, but, for the moment, with a portion of genuine earnestness; for, such was Pearl's wonderful intelligence, that her mother half doubted whether she were not acquainted with the secret spell of her existence, and might not now reveal herself.

"Yes; I am little Pearl!" repeated the child, continuing her antics.

"Thou art not my child! Thou art no Pearl of mine!" said the mother, half playfully; for it was often the case that a sportive impulse came over her, in the midst of her deepest suffering. "Tell me, then, what thou art, and who sent thee hither?"

"Tell me, mother!" said the child, seriously, coming up to Hester, and pressing herself close to her knees. "Do thou tell me!"

"Thy Heavenly Father sent thee!" answered Hester Prynne.

But she said it with a hesitation that did not escape the acuteness of the child. Whether moved only by her ordinary freakishness, or because an evil spirit prompted her, she put up her small forefinger, and touched the scarlet letter.

"He did not send me!" cried she, positively. "I have no Heavenly Father!"

"Hush, Pearl, hush! Thou must not talk so!" answered the mother, suppressing a groan. "He sent us all into this world. He sent even me, thy mother. Then, much more, thee! Or, if not, thou strange and elfish child, whence didst thou come?"

"Tell me! Tell me!" repeated Pearl, no longer seriously, but laughing, and capering about the floor. "It is thou that must tell me!"

But Hester could not resolve the query, being herself in a dismal labyrinth of doubt. She remembered—betwixt a smile and a shudder—the talk of the neighboring townspeople; who, seeking vainly elsewhere for the child's paternity, and observing some of her odd attributes, had given out that poor little Pearl was a demon offspring; such as, ever since old Catholic times, had occasionally been seen on earth, through the agency of their mother's sin, and to promote some foul and wicked purpose. Luther, according to the scandal of his monkish enemies, was a brat of that hellish breed; nor was Pearl the only child to whom this inauspicious origin was assigned, among the New England Puritans.[8]

---

8. Martin Luther (1483–1546), leader of the Protestant Reformation. Hawthorne refers to a legend that Luther's mother had intercourse with the devil. Heiko A. Oberman says that the rumor persisted into the nineteenth century; see *Luther: Man Between God and the Devil* (New Haven: Yale UP, 1989), 88.

VII. The Governor's Hall

Hester Prynne went, one day, to the mansion of Governor Bellingham, with a pair of gloves, which she had fringed and embroidered to his order, and which were to be worn on some great occasion of state; for, though the chances of a popular election had caused this former ruler to descend a step or two from the highest rank, he still held an honorable and influential place among the colonial magistracy.[1]

Another and far more important reason than the delivery of a pair of embroidered gloves impelled Hester, at this time, to seek an interview with a personage of so much power and activity in the affairs of the settlement. It had reached her ears, that there was a design on the part of some of the leading inhabitants, cherishing the more rigid order of principles in religion and government, to deprive her of her child. On the supposition that Pearl, as already hinted, was of demon origin, these good people not unreasonably argued that a Christian interest in the mother's soul required them to remove such a stumbling-block from her path. If the child, on the other hand, were really capable of moral and religious growth, and possessed the elements of ultimate salvation, then, surely, it would enjoy all the fairer prospect of these advantages, by being transferred to wiser and better guardianship than Hester Prynne's. Among those who promoted the design, Governor Bellingham was said to be one of the most busy. It may appear singular, and, indeed, not a little ludicrous, that an affair of this kind, which, in later days, would have been referred to no higher jurisdiction than that of the selectmen of the town, should then have been a question publicly discussed, and on which statesmen of eminence took sides. At that epoch of pristine simplicity, however, matters of even slighter public interest, and of far less intrinsic weight, than the welfare of Hester and her child, were strangely mixed up with the deliberations of legislators and acts of state. The period was hardly, if at all, earlier than that of our story, when a dispute concerning the right of property in a pig, not only caused a fierce and bitter contest in the legislative body of the colony, but resulted in an important modification of the framework itself of the legislature.[2]

Full of concern, therefore,—but so conscious of her own right that it seemed scarcely an unequal match between the public, on the one side, and a lonely woman, backed by the sympathies of nature, on the other,—Hester Prynne set forth from her solitary cottage. Little Pearl, of course, was her companion. She was now of an age to run lightly

---

1. Richard Bellingham's term as governor ended in May 1642. He would be re-elected in 1654 and again in 1665.
2. Caleb Snow discusses this incident at length. A "thoughtless pig strayed from its owner, one good Mrs. Sherman," and "wandered through the town, breaking into every body's corn as its hunger dictated." The pig was apparently kept by a Captain Keayne for nearly a year before he decided to kill it. At that point, the owner of the stray pig demanded restitution, which Keayne refused. The matter went to church court, which found in Keayne's favor. The case was appealed several times, and eventually caused a rift between the magistrates and their deputies such that two houses of government were created. As Snow concludes, "this was the origin of our present Senate" (*History of Boston*, 95–97).

along by her mother's side, and, constantly in motion, from morn till sunset, could have accomplished a much longer journey than that before her. Often, nevertheless, more from caprice than necessity, she demanded to be taken up in arms; but was soon as imperious to be set down again, and frisked onward before Hester on the grassy pathway, with many a harmless trip and tumble. We have spoken of Pearl's rich and luxuriant beauty; a beauty that shone with deep and vivid tints; a bright complexion, eyes possessing intensity both of depth and glow, and hair already of a deep, glossy brown, and which, in after years, would be nearly akin to black. There was fire in her and throughout her; she seemed the unpremeditated offshoot of a passionate moment. Her mother, in contriving the child's garb, had allowed the gorgeous tendencies of her imagination their full play; arraying her in a crimson velvet tunic, of a peculiar cut, abundantly embroidered with fantasies and flourishes of gold thread. So much strength of coloring, which must have given a wan and pallid aspect to cheeks of a fainter bloom, was admirably adapted to Pearl's beauty, and made her the very brightest little jet of flame that ever danced upon the earth.

But it was a remarkable attribute of this garb, and, indeed, of the child's whole appearance, that it irresistibly and inevitably reminded the beholder of the token which Hester Prynne was doomed to wear upon her bosom. It was the scarlet letter in another form; the scarlet letter endowed with life! The mother herself—as if the red ignominy were so deeply scorched into her brain that all her conceptions assumed its form—had carefully wrought out the similitude; lavishing many hours of morbid ingenuity, to create an analogy between the object of her affection and the emblem of her guilt and torture. But, in truth, Pearl was the one, as well as the other; and only in consequence of that identity had Hester contrived so perfectly to represent the scarlet letter in her appearance.

As the two wayfarers came within the precincts of the town, the children of the Puritans looked up from their play,—or what passed for play with those sombre little urchins,—and spake gravely one to another:—

"Behold, verily, there is the woman of the scarlet letter; and, of a truth, moreover, there is the likeness of the scarlet letter running along by her side! Come, therefore, and let us fling mud at them!"

But Pearl, who was a dauntless child, after frowning, stamping her foot, and shaking her little hand with a variety of threatening gestures, suddenly made a rush at the knot of her enemies, and put them all to flight. She resembled, in her fierce pursuit of them, an infant pestilence,—the scarlet fever, or some such half-fledged angel of judgment,—whose mission was to punish the sins of the rising generation. She screamed and shouted, too, with a terrific volume of sound, which, doubtless, caused the hearts of the fugitives to quake within them. The victory accomplished, Pearl returned quietly to her mother, and looked up, smiling, into her face.

Without further adventure, they reached the dwelling of Governor Bellingham. This was a large wooden house, built in a fashion of which there are specimens still extant in the streets of our elder towns; now moss-grown, crumbling to decay, and melancholy at heart with the many sorrowful or joyful occurrences, remembered or forgotten, that have happened, and passed away, within their dusky chambers. Then, however, there was the freshness of the passing year on its exterior, and the cheerfulness, gleaming forth from the sunny windows, of a human habitation, into which death had never entered. It had, indeed, a very cheery aspect; the walls being overspread with a kind of stucco, in which fragments of broken glass were plentifully intermixed; so that, when the sunshine fell aslant-wise over the front of the edifice, it glittered and sparkled as if diamonds had been flung against it by the double handful. The brilliancy might have befitted Aladdin's palace, rather than the mansion of a grave old Puritan ruler. It was further decorated with strange and seemingly cabalistic figures and diagrams, suitable to the quaint taste of the age, which had been drawn in the stucco when newly laid on, and had now grown hard and durable, for the admiration of after times.

Pearl, looking at this bright wonder of a house, began to caper and dance, and imperatively required that the whole breadth of sunshine should be stripped off its front, and given her to play with.

"No, my little Pearl!" said her mother. "Thou must gather thine own sunshine. I have none to give thee!"

They approached the door; which was of an arched form, and flanked on each side by a narrow tower or projection of the edifice, in both of which were lattice-windows, with wooden shutters to close over them at need. Lifting the iron hammer that hung at the portal, Hester Prynne gave a summons, which was answered by one of the Governor's bond-servants; a free-born Englishman, but now a seven years' slave. During that term he was to be the property of his master, and as much a commodity of bargain and sale as an ox, or a joint-stool. The serf wore the blue coat, which was the customary garb of serving-men at that period, and long before, in the old hereditary halls of England.

"Is the worshipful Governor Bellingham within?" inquired Hester.

"Yea, forsooth," replied the bond-servant, staring with wide-open eyes at the scarlet letter, which, being a new-comer in the country, he had never before seen. "Yea, his honorable worship is within. But he hath a godly minister or two with him, and likewise a leech. Ye may not see his worship now."

"Nevertheless, I will enter," answered Hester Prynne; and the bond-servant, perhaps judging from the decision of her air, and the glittering symbol in her bosom, that she was a great lady in the land, offered no opposition.

So the mother and little Pearl were admitted into the hall of entrance. With many variations, suggested by the nature of his building-materials, diversity of climate, and a different mode of social life, Governor Bellingham had planned his new habitation after the residences of gentlemen of fair estate in his native land. Here, then, was a wide and reasonably lofty hall, extending through the whole depth of the house, and forming a medium of general communication, more or less directly, with all the other apartments. At one extremity, this spacious room was lighted by the windows of the two towers, which formed a small recess on either side of the portal. At the other end, though partly muffled by a curtain, it was more powerfully illuminated by one of those embowed hall-windows which we read of in old books, and which was provided with a keep and cushioned seat. Here, on the cushion, lay a folio tome, probably of the Chronicles of England, or other such substantial literature; even as, in our own days, we scatter gilded volumes on the centre-table, to be turned over by the casual guest. The furniture of the hall consisted of some ponderous chairs, the backs of which were elaborately carved with wreaths of oaken flowers; and likewise a table in the same taste; the whole being of the Elizabethan age, or perhaps earlier, and heirlooms, transferred hither from the Governor's paternal home. On the table—in token that the sentiment of old English hospitality had not been left behind—stood a large pewter tankard, at the bottom of which, had Hester or Pearl peeped into it, they might have seen the frothy remnant of a recent draught of ale.

On the wall hung a row of portraits, representing the forefathers of the Bellingham lineage, some with armor on their breasts, and others with stately ruffs and robes of peace. All were characterized by the sternness and severity which old portraits so invariably put on; as if they were the ghosts, rather than the pictures, of departed worthies, and were gazing with harsh and intolerant criticism at the pursuits and enjoyments of living men.

At about the centre of the oaken panels, that lined the hall, was suspended a suit of mail, not, like the pictures, an ancestral relic, but of the most modern date; for it had been manufactured by a skilful armorer in London, the same year in which Governor Bellingham came over to New England. There was a steel head-piece, a cuirass, a gorget, and greaves, with a pair of gauntlets and a sword hanging beneath; all, and especially the helmet and breastplate, so highly burnished as to glow with white radiance, and scatter an illumination everywhere about upon the floor.[3] This bright panoply was not meant for mere idle show, but had been worn by the Governor on many a solemn muster and training field, and had glittered, moreover, at the head of a regiment in the Pequod war.[4] For, though bred a lawyer, and accustomed to speak of Bacon, Coke, Noye, and Finch, as his profes-

---

3. Hawthorne lists several pieces of armor: *cuirass* (breastplate), *gorget* (throat protector), *greaves* (shin guards), *gauntlets* (gloves).
4. Histories of the Pequot War do not mention Bellingham's participation in the war, which occurred during the late spring and summer of 1637. Hawthorne undoubtedly knew of the internal political wrangling among the Massachusetts Bay contingent, the result, as Alfred Cave explains, of the Puritans' giving high military rank to magistrates such as Winthrop and Dudley while the actual field commanders received lesser ranks. The man who actually led the Massachusetts Bay forces, Captain John Underhill, complained about this practice. Underhill also strongly supported Anne Hutchinson, an allegiance that cost him his rank and position after the war. Hawthorne may, then, be making a visual joke at Bellingham's expense by placing an empty suit of armor on the wall of his house. The Pequots were nearly wiped out by a coalition of Puritan forces from Massachusetts and Connecticut. These forces set fire to the Pequot fort at Mystic (May 26, 1637) and killed more than 500 members of the tribe, including women and children.

sional associates,[5] the exigencies of this new country had transformed Governor Bellingham into a soldier, as well as a statesman and ruler.

Little Pearl—who was as greatly pleased with the gleaming armor as she had been with the glittering frontispiece of the house—spent some time looking into the polished mirror of the breastplate.

"Mother," cried she, "I see you here. Look! Look!"

Hester looked, by way of humoring the child; and she saw that, owing to the peculiar effect of this convex mirror, the scarlet letter was represented in exaggerated and gigantic proportions, so as to be greatly the most prominent feature of her appearance. In truth, she seemed absolutely hidden behind it. Pearl pointed upward, also, at a similar picture in the head-piece; smiling at her mother, with the elfish intelligence that was so familiar an expression on her small physiognomy. That look of naughty merriment was likewise reflected in the mirror, with so much breadth and intensity of effect, that it made Hester Prynne feel as if it could not be the image of her own child, but of an imp who was seeking to mould itself into Pearl's shape.

"Come along, Pearl," said she, drawing her away. "Come and look into this fair garden. It may be, we shall see flowers there; more beautiful ones than we find in the woods."

Pearl, accordingly, ran to the bow-window, at the further end of the hall, and looked along the vista of a garden-walk, carpeted with closely shaven grass, and bordered with some rude and immature attempt at shrubbery. But the proprietor appeared already to have relinquished, as hopeless, the effort to perpetuate on this side of the Atlantic, in a hard soil and amid the close struggle for subsistence, the native English taste for ornamental gardening. Cabbages grew in plain sight; and a pumpkin-vine, rooted at some distance, had run across the intervening space, and deposited one of its gigantic products directly beneath the hall-window; as if to warn the Governor that this great lump of vegetable gold was as rich an ornament as New England earth would offer him. There were a few rose-bushes, however, and a number of apple-trees, probably the descendants of those planted by the Reverend Mr. Blackstone, the first settler of the peninsula; that half mythological personage, who rides through our early annals, seated on the back of a bull.[6]

5. Francis Bacon, Sir Edward Coke, William Noy, and Sir John Finch played prominent political roles during the reigns of King James I and King Charles I, and each played a part in one of the sensational legal cases (the Thomas Overbury murder case and William Prynne's prosecution) that lurk in the background of The Scarlet Letter. Finch (1584–1634), for example, served as chief justice of the Common Pleas (1634–1640) and in that role prosecuted Prynne for libel. As Samuel R. Gardiner notes, it was Finch who "savagely added a wish that Prynne should be branded on the cheeks with the letters S.L., as a Seditious Libeller" (8:229). Noy (1577–1634), King Charles I's attorney general from 1632 until 1634, was also involved in Prynne's prosecution (Gardiner 7:334). Bacon (1561–1626), member of the House of Commons, is considered one of the founders of modern science. He and Coke (1552–1634), also a prominent member of the House of Commons and political rival of Bacon, prosecuted the murderers of Thomas Overbury, including Lord (Robert Carr) and Lady (Frances Howard) Somerset. For more on that case see n. 5, p. 85, of this Norton Critical Edition.

6. Blackstone was an early settler who built his house on a peninsula at the mouth of the Charles River. According to Caleb Snow, in April 1633 Blackstone was granted fifty acres in return for the peninsula, called Blackstone's Neck (50). Snow calls Blackstone a "very eccentrick character" (51) and reports that when he grew old and unable to travel on foot, "he used to ride on a bull, which he had tamed and tutored to that use" (53).

Pearl, seeing the rose-bushes, began to cry for a red rose, and would not be pacified.

"Hush, child, hush!" said her mother, earnestly. "Do not cry, dear little Pearl! I hear voices in the garden. The Governor is coming, and gentlemen along with him!"

In fact, adown the vista of the garden avenue, a number of persons were seen approaching towards the house. Pearl, in utter scorn of her mother's attempt to quiet her, gave an eldritch scream, and then became silent; not from any notion of obedience, but because the quick and mobile curiosity of her disposition was excited by the appearance of these new personages.

VIII. The Elf-Child and the Minister

Governor Bellingham, in a loose gown and easy cap,—such as elderly gentlemen loved to endue themselves with, in their domestic privacy,—walked foremost, and appeared to be showing off his estate, and expatiating on his projected improvements. The wide circumference of an elaborate ruff, beneath his gray beard, in the antiquated fashion of King James' reign, caused his head to look not a little like that of John the Baptist in a charger.[1] The impression made by his aspect, so rigid and severe, and frost-bitten with more than autumnal age, was hardly in keeping with the appliances of worldly enjoyment wherewith he had evidently done his utmost to surround himself. But it is an error to suppose that our grave forefathers—though accustomed to speak and think of human existence as a state merely of trial and warfare, and though unfeignedly prepared to sacrifice goods and life at the behest of duty—made it a matter of conscience to reject such means of comfort, or even luxury, as lay fairly within their grasp. This creed was never taught, for instance, by the venerable pastor, John Wilson, whose beard, white as a snow-drift, was seen over Governor Bellingham's shoulder; while its wearer suggested that pears and peaches might yet be naturalized in the New England climate, and that purple grapes might possibly be compelled to flourish, against the sunny garden-wall. The old clergyman, nurtured at the rich bosom of the English Church, had a long-established and legitimate taste for all good and comfortable things; and however stern he might show himself in the pulpit, or in his public reproof of such transgressions as that of Hester Prynne, still, the genial benevolence of his private life had won him warmer affection than was accorded to any of his professional contemporaries.

Behind the Governor and Mr. Wilson came two other guests; one, the Reverend Arthur Dimmesdale, whom the reader may remember, as

---

1. See Mark 6:21–29. The daughter of Herodias asked King Herod for the head of John the Baptist on a charger (platter): "And immediately the king sent an executioner, and commanded his head to be brought: and he went and beheaded him in the prison / And brought his head in a charger, and gave it to the damsel: and the damsel gave it to her mother / And when his disciples heard of it, they came and took up his corpse, and laid it in a tomb."

having taken a brief and reluctant part in the scene of Hester Prynne's disgrace; and, in close companionship with him, old Roger Chillingworth, a person of great skill in physic, who, for two or three years past, had been settled in the town. It was understood that this learned man was the physician as well as friend of the young minister, whose health had severely suffered, of late, by his too unreserved self-sacrifice to the labors and duties of the pastoral relation.

The Governor, in advance of his visitors, ascended one or two steps, and, throwing open the leaves of the great hall window, found himself close to little Pearl. The shadow of the curtain fell on Hester Prynne, and partially concealed her.

"What have we here?" said Governor Bellingham, looking with surprise at the scarlet little figure before him. "I profess, I have never seen the like, since my days of vanity, in old King James' time, when I was wont to esteem it a high favor to be admitted to a court mask! There used to be a swarm of these small apparitions, in holiday time; and we called them children of the Lord of Misrule.[2] But how gat such a guest into my hall?"

"Ay, indeed!" cried good old Mr. Wilson. "What little bird of scarlet plumage may this be? Methinks I have seen just such figures, when the sun has been shining through a richly painted window, and tracing out the golden and crimson images across the floor. But that was in the old land. Prithee, young one, who art thou, and what has ailed thy mother to bedizen thee in this strange fashion? Art thou a Christian child,—ha? Dost know thy catechism? Or art thou one of those naughty elfs or fairies, whom we thought to have left behind us, with other relics of Papistry, in merry old England?"

"I am mother's child," answered the scarlet vision, "and my name is Pearl!"

"Pearl?—Ruby, rather!—or Coral!—or Red Rose, at the very least, judging from thy hue!" responded the old minister, putting forth his hand in a vain attempt to pat little Pearl on the cheek. "But where is this mother of thine? Ah! I see," he added; and, turning to Governor Bellingham, whispered, "This is the selfsame child of whom we have held speech together; and behold here the unhappy woman, Hester Prynne, her mother!"

"Sayest thou so?" cried the Governor. "Nay, we might have judged that such a child's mother must needs be a scarlet woman, and a worthy type of her of Babylon![3] But she comes at a good time; and we will look into this matter forthwith."

Governor Bellingham stepped through the window into the hall, followed by his three guests.

"Hester Prynne," said he, fixing his naturally stern regard on the wearer

---

2. The master of Christmas revels in medieval England, associated with pleasure and rule-breaking.
3. Bellingham compares Hester to the Whore of Babylon. See Revelation 17:4–5: "And the woman was arrayed in purple and scarlet colour, and decked with gold and precious stones and pearls, having a golden cup in her hand full of abominations and filthiness of her fornication: / And upon her forehead was a name written, MYSTERY, BABYLON THE GREAT, THE MOTHER OF HARLOTS AND ABOMINATIONS OF THE EARTH."

of the scarlet letter, "there hath been much question concerning thee, of late. The point hath been weightily discussed, whether we, that are of authority and influence, do well discharge our consciences by trusting an immortal soul, such as there is in yonder child, to the guidance of one who hath stumbled and fallen, amid the pitfalls of this world. Speak thou, the child's own mother! Were it not, thinkest thou, for thy little one's temporal and eternal welfare, that she be taken out of thy charge, and clad soberly, and disciplined strictly, and instructed in the truths of heaven and earth? What canst thou do for the child, in this kind?"

"I can teach my little Pearl what I have learned from this!" answered Hester Prynne, laying her finger on the red token.

"Woman, it is thy badge of shame!" replied the stern magistrate. "It is because of the stain which that letter indicates, that we would transfer thy child to other hands."

"Nevertheless," said the mother, calmly, though growing more pale, "this badge hath taught me,—it daily teaches me,—it is teaching me at this moment,—lessons whereof my child may be the wiser and better, albeit they can profit nothing to myself."

"We will judge warily," said Bellingham, "and look well what we are about to do. Good Master Wilson, I pray you, examine this Pearl,—since that is her name,—and see whether she hath had such Christian nurture as befits a child of her age."

The old minister seated himself in an arm-chair, and made an effort to draw Pearl betwixt his knees. But the child, unaccustomed to the touch or familiarity of any but her mother, escaped through the open window, and stood on the upper step, looking like a wild tropical bird, of rich plumage, ready to take flight into the upper air. Mr. Wilson, not a little astonished at this outbreak,—for he was a grandfatherly sort of personage, and usually a vast favorite with children,—essayed, however, to proceed with the examination.

"Pearl," said he, with great solemnity, "thou must take heed to instruction, that so, in due season, thou mayest wear in thy bosom the pearl of great price. Canst thou tell me, my child, who made thee?"

Now Pearl knew well enough who made her; for Hester Prynne, the daughter of a pious home, very soon after her talk with the child about her Heavenly Father, had begun to inform her of those truths which the human spirit, at whatever stage of immaturity, imbibes with such eager interest. Pearl, therefore, so large were the attainments of her three years' lifetime, could have borne a fair examination in the New England Primer, or the first column of the Westminster Catechisms, although unacquainted with the outward form of either of those celebrated works.[4] But that perversity, which all children have more or less

4. *The New England Primer*, first published probably in 1690, was designed to teach children the alphabet. The best-known verse is undoubtedly the one for the letter A: "In ADAM'S Fall / We sinned all." The verse for the letter Q might also be pertinent: "Queen Esther sues / And saves the Jews." *The Westminster Catechism*, which was published in 1647, included a series of more than 100 questions and answers based on Biblical passages. The closest question to the one Reverend Wilson asks Pearl is "How did God create man?" The answer, from Genesis, is that God created man in His own image. Given the time of the novel's action, Pearl could not have "borne a fair examination" in either of these works.

of, and of which little Pearl had a ten-fold portion, now, at the most inopportune moment, took thorough possession of her, and closed her lips, or impelled her to speak words amiss. After putting her finger in her mouth, with many ungracious refusals to answer good Mr. Wilson's question, the child finally announced that she had not been made at all, but had been plucked by her mother off the bush of wild roses that grew by the prison-door.

This fantasy was probably suggested by the near proximity of the Governor's red roses, as Pearl stood outside of the window; together with her recollection of the prison rose-bush, which she had passed in coming hither.

Old Roger Chillingworth, with a smile on his face, whispered something in the young clergyman's ear. Hester Prynne looked at the man of skill, and even then, with her fate hanging in the balance, was startled to perceive what a change had come over his features,—how much uglier they were,—how his dark complexion seemed to have grown duskier, and his figure more misshapen,—since the days when she had familiarly known him. She met his eyes for an instant, but was immediately constrained to give all her attention to the scene now going forward.

"This is awful!" cried the Governor, slowly recovering from the astonishment into which Pearl's response had thrown him. "Here is a child of three years old, and she cannot tell who made her! Without question, she is equally in the dark as to her soul, its present depravity, and future destiny! Methinks, gentlemen, we need inquire no further."

Hester caught hold of Pearl, and drew her forcibly into her arms, confronting the old Puritan magistrate with almost a fierce expression. Alone in the world, cast off by it, and with this sole treasure to keep her heart alive, she felt that she possessed indefeasible rights against the world, and was ready to defend them to the death.

"God gave me the child!" cried she. "He gave her in requital of all things else, which ye had taken from me. She is my happiness!—she is my torture, none the less! Pearl keeps me here in life! Pearl punishes me too! See ye not, she is the scarlet letter, only capable of being loved, and so endowed with a million-fold the power of retribution for my sin? Ye shall not take her! I will die first!"

"My poor woman," said the not unkind old minister, "the child shall be well cared for!—far better than thou canst do it."

"God gave her into my keeping," repeated Hester Prynne, raising her voice almost to a shriek. "I will not give her up!"—And here, by a sudden impulse, she turned to the young clergyman, Mr. Dimmesdale, at whom, up to this moment, she had seemed hardly so much as once to direct her eyes.—"Speak thou for me!" cried she. "Thou wast my pastor, and hadst charge of my soul, and knowest me better than these men can. I will not lose the child! Speak for me! Thou knowest,—for thou hast sympathies which these men lack!—thou knowest what is in my heart, and what are a mother's rights, and how much the stronger they are, when that mother has but her child and the scarlet letter! Look thou to it! I will not lose the child! Look to it!"

At this wild and singular appeal, which indicated that Hester Prynne's situation had provoked her to little less than madness, the young minister at once came forward, pale, and holding his hand over his heart, as was his custom whenever his peculiarly nervous temperament was thrown into agitation. He looked now more careworn and emaciated than as we described him at the scene of Hester's public ignominy; and whether it were his failing health, or whatever the cause might be, his large dark eyes had a world of pain in their troubled and melancholy depth.

"There is truth in what she says," began the minister, with a voice sweet, tremulous, but powerful, insomuch that the hall reëchoed, and the hollow armor rang with it,—"truth in what Hester says, and in the feeling which inspires her! God gave her the child, and gave her, too, an instinctive knowledge of its nature and requirements,—both seemingly so peculiar,—which no other mortal being can possess. And, moreover, is there not a quality of awful sacredness in the relation between this mother and this child?"

"Ay!—how is that, good Master Dimmesdale?" interrupted the Governor. "Make that plain, I pray you!"

"It must be even so," resumed the minister. "For, if we deem it otherwise, do we not thereby say that the Heavenly Father, the Creator of all flesh, hath lightly recognized a deed of sin, and made of no account the distinction between unhallowed lust and holy love? This child of its father's guilt and its mother's shame hath come from the hand of God, to work in many ways upon her heart, who pleads so earnestly, and with such bitterness of spirit, the right to keep her. It was meant for a blessing; for the one blessing of her life! It was meant, doubtless, as the mother herself hath told us, for a retribution too; a torture to be felt at many an unthought of moment; a pang, a sting, an ever-recurring agony, in the midst of a troubled joy! Hath she not expressed this thought in the garb of the poor child, so forcibly reminding us of that red symbol which sears her bosom?"

"Well said, again!" cried good Mr. Wilson. "I feared the woman had no better thought than to make a mountebank[5] of her child!"

"O, not so!—not so!" continued Mr. Dimmesdale. "She recognizes, believe me, the solemn miracle which God hath wrought, in the existence of that child. And may she feel, too,—what, methinks, is the very truth—that this boon was meant, above all things else, to keep the mother's soul alive, and to preserve her from blacker depths of sin into which Satan might else have sought to plunge her! Therefore it is good for this poor, sinful woman that she hath an infant immortality, a being capable of eternal joy or sorrow, confided to her care,—to be trained up by her to righteousness,—to remind her, at every moment, of her fall,—but yet to teach her, as it were by the Creator's sacred pledge, that, if she bring the child to heaven, the child also will bring its parent thither! Herein is the sinful mother happier than the sinful father. For Hester Prynne's sake, then, and no less for the poor child's sake, let us leave them as Providence hath seen fit to place them!"

5. Charlatan or pretender.

"You speak, my friend, with a strange earnestness," said old Roger Chillingworth, smiling at him.

"And there is a weighty import in what my young brother hath spoken," added the Reverend Mr. Wilson. "What say you, worshipful Master Bellingham? Hath he not pleaded well for the poor woman?"

"Indeed hath he," answered the magistrate, "and hath adduced such arguments, that we will even leave the matter as it now stands; so long, at least, as there shall be no further scandal in the woman. Care must be had, nevertheless, to put the child to due and stated examination in the catechism, at thy hands or Master Dimmesdale's. Moreover, at a proper season, the tithing-men must take heed that she go both to school and to meeting."[6]

The young minister, on ceasing to speak, had withdrawn a few steps from the group, and stood with his face partially concealed in the heavy folds of the window-curtain; while the shadow of his figure, which the sunlight cast upon the floor, was tremulous with the vehemence of his appeal. Pearl, that wild and flighty little elf, stole softly towards him, and taking his hand in the grasp of both her own, laid her cheek against it; a caress so tender, and withal so unobtrusive, that her mother, who was looking on, asked herself,—"Is that my Pearl?" Yet she knew that there was love in the child's heart, although it mostly revealed itself in passion, and hardly twice in her lifetime had been softened by such gentleness as now. The minister,—for, save the long-sought regards of woman, nothing is sweeter than these marks of childish preference, accorded spontaneously by a spiritual instinct, and therefore seeming to imply in us something truly worthy to be loved,—the minister looked round, laid his hand on the child's head, hesitated an instant, and then kissed her brow. Little Pearl's unwonted mood of sentiment lasted no longer; she laughed, and went capering down the hall, so airily, that old Mr. Wilson raised a question whether even her tiptoes touched the floor.

"The little baggage hath witchcraft in her, I profess," said he to Mr. Dimmesdale. "She needs no old woman's broomstick to fly withal!"

"A strange child!" remarked old Roger Chillingworth. "It is easy to see the mother's part in her. Would it be beyond a philosopher's research, think ye, gentlemen, to analyze that child's nature, and, from its make and mould, to give a shrewd guess at the father?"

"Nay; it would be sinful, in such a question, to follow the clew of profane philosophy," said Mr. Wilson. "Better to fast and pray upon it; and still better, it may be, to leave the mystery as we find it, unless Providence reveal it of its own accord. Thereby, every good Christian man hath a title to show a father's kindness towards the poor, deserted babe."

The affair being so satisfactorily concluded, Hester Prynne, with Pearl, departed from the house. As they descended the steps, it is averred that the lattice of a chamber-window was thrown open, and forth into the sunny day was thrust the face of Mistress Hibbins, Gov-

---

6. Tithing men collect church taxes, typically, one tenth of one's income.

ernor Bellingham's bitter-tempered sister, and the same who, a few years later, was executed as a witch.[7]

"Hist, hist!" said she, while her ill-omened physiognomy seemed to cast a shadow over the cheerful newness of the house. "Wilt thou go with us to-night? There will be a merry company in the forest; and I well-nigh promised the Black Man that comely Hester Prynne should make one."[8]

"Make my excuse to him, so please you!" answered Hester, with a triumphant smile. "I must tarry at home, and keep watch over my little Pearl. Had they taken her from me, I would willingly have gone with thee into the forest, and signed my name in the Black Man's book too, and that with mine own blood!"

"We shall have thee there anon!" said the witch-lady, frowning, as she drew back her head.

But here—if we suppose this interview betwixt Mistress Hibbins and Hester Prynne to be authentic, and not a parable—was already an illustration of the young minister's argument against sundering the relation of a fallen mother to the offspring of her frailty. Even thus early had the child saved her from Satan's snare.

IX. The Leech

Under the appellation of Roger Chillingworth, the reader will remember, was hidden another name, which its former wearer had resolved should never more be spoken. It has been related, how, in the crowd that witnessed Hester Prynne's ignominious exposure, stood a man, elderly, travel-worn, who, just emerging from the perilous wilderness, beheld the woman, in whom he hoped to find embodied the warmth and cheerfulness of home, set up as a type of sin before the people. Her matronly fame was trodden under all men's feet. Infamy was babbling around her in the public market-place. For her kindred, should the tidings ever reach them, and for the companions of her unspotted life, there remained nothing but the contagion of her dishonor; which would not fail to be distributed in strict accordance and proportion with the intimacy and sacredness of their previous relationship. Then why—since the choice was with himself—should the individual, whose connection with the fallen woman had been the most intimate and sacred of them all, come forward to vindicate his claim to an inheritance so little desirable? He resolved not to be pilloried beside her on her pedestal of shame. Unknown to all but Hester Prynne, and possessing the lock and key of her silence, he chose to withdraw his name from the roll of mankind, and, as regarded his former ties and interests, to vanish out of life as completely as if he indeed lay at the bottom of the ocean, whither rumor had long ago consigned him. This purpose once effected, new interests would immediately spring up,

---

7. As noted, Ann Hibbins was executed as a witch in 1656.
8. Compare the forest scene in "Young Goodman Brown," in which both Brown and his wife Faith apparently meet the devil, or the Black Man, in the forest.

and likewise a new purpose; dark, it is true, if not guilty, but of force enough to engage the full strength of his faculties.

In pursuance of this resolve, he took up his residence in the Puritan town, as Roger Chillingworth, without other introduction than the learning and intelligence of which he possessed more than a common measure. As his studies, at a previous period of his life, had made him extensively acquainted with the medical science of the day, it was as a physician that he presented himself, and as such was cordially received. Skilful men, of the medical and chirurgical[1] profession, were of rare occurrence in the colony. They seldom, it would appear, partook of the religious zeal that brought other emigrants across the Atlantic. In their researches into the human frame, it may be that the higher and more subtile faculties of such men were materialized, and that they lost the spiritual view of existence amid the intricacies of that wondrous mechanism, which seemed to involve art enough to comprise all of life within itself. At all events, the health of the good town of Boston, so far as medicine had aught to do with it, had hitherto lain in the guardianship of an aged deacon and apothecary, whose piety and godly deportment were stronger testimonials in his favor than any that he could have produced in the shape of a diploma. The only surgeon was one who combined the occasional exercise of that noble art with the daily and habitual flourish of a razor. To such a professional body Roger Chillingworth was a brilliant acquisition. He soon manifested his familiarity with the ponderous and imposing machinery of antique physic; in which every remedy contained a multitude of far-fetched and heterogeneous ingredients, as elaborately compounded as if the proposed result had been the Elixir of Life.[2] In his Indian captivity, moreover, he had gained much knowledge of the properties of native herbs and roots; nor did he conceal from his patients, that these simple medicines, Nature's boon to the untutored savage, had quite as large a share of his own confidence as the European pharmacopœia, which so many learned doctors had spent centuries in elaborating.

This learned stranger was exemplary, as regarded, at least, the outward forms of a religious life, and, early after his arrival, had chosen for his spiritual guide the Reverend Mr. Dimmesdale. The young divine, whose scholar-like renown still lived in Oxford, was considered by his more fervent admirers as little less than a heavenly-ordained apostle, destined, should he live and labor for the ordinary term of life, to do as great deeds for the now feeble New England Church, as the early Fathers had achieved for the infancy of the Christian faith. About this period, however, the health of Mr. Dimmesdale had evidently begun to fail. By those best acquainted with his habits, the paleness of the young minister's cheek was accounted for by his too earnest devotion to study, his scrupulous fulfilment of parochial duty, and, more than all, by the fasts and vigils of which he made a frequent practice, in order to keep the grossness of this earthly state from clog-

---

1. Surgical (archaic form).
2. From alchemy, a potion for making one immortal.

ging and obscuring his spiritual lamp. Some declared, that, if Mr. Dimmesdale were really going to die, it was cause enough, that the world was not worthy to be any longer trodden by his feet. He himself, on the other hand, with characteristic humility, avowed his belief, that, if Providence should see fit to remove him, it would be because of his own unworthiness to perform its humblest mission here on earth. With all this difference of opinion as to the cause of his decline, there could be no question of the fact. His form grew emaciated; his voice, though still rich and sweet, had a certain melancholy prophecy of decay in it; he was often observed, on any slight alarm or other sudden accident, to put his hand over his heart, with first a flush and then a paleness, indicative of pain.

Such was the young clergyman's condition, and so imminent the prospect that his dawning light would be extinguished, all untimely, when Roger Chillingworth made his advent to the town. His first entry on the scene, few people could tell whence, dropping down, as it were, out of the sky, or starting from the nether earth, had an aspect of mystery, which was easily heightened to the miraculous. He was now known to be a man of skill; it was observed that he gathered herbs, and the blossoms of wild-flowers, and dug up roots, and plucked off twigs from the forest-trees, like one acquainted with hidden virtues in what was valueless to common eyes. He was heard to speak of Sir Kenelm Digby,[3] and other famous men,—whose scientific attainments were esteemed hardly less than supernatural,—as having been his correspondents or associates. Why, with such rank in the learned world, had he come hither? What could he, whose sphere was in great cities, be seeking in the wilderness? In answer to this query, a rumor gained ground,—and, however absurd, was entertained by some very sensible people,—that Heaven had wrought an absolute miracle, by transporting an eminent Doctor of Physic, from a German university, bodily through the air, and setting him down at the door of Mr. Dimmesdale's study! Individuals of wiser faith, indeed, who knew that Heaven promotes its purposes without aiming at the stage-effect of what is called miraculous interposition, were inclined to see a providential hand in Roger Chillingworth's so opportune arrival.

This idea was countenanced by the strong interest which the physician ever manifested in the young clergyman; he attached himself to him as a parishioner, and sought to win a friendly regard and confidence from his naturally reserved sensibility. He expressed great alarm at his pastor's state of health, but was anxious to attempt the cure, and, if early undertaken, seemed not despondent of a favorable result. The elders, the deacons, the motherly dames, and the young and fair maidens, of Mr. Dimmesdale's flock, were alike importunate that he should make trial of the physician's frankly offered skill. Mr. Dimmesdale gently repelled their entreaties.

"I need no medicine," said he.

3. Sir Kenelm Digby (1603–1665), physical scientist and naval commander, authored *Nature of Bodies* and *The Immortality of Reasonable Souls* in 1644. An alchemist and astrologer, he would have shared interests with Chillingworth.

But how could the young minister say so, when, with every successive Sabbath, his cheek was paler and thinner, and his voice more
tremulous than before,—when it had now become a constant habit,
rather than a casual gesture, to press his hand over his heart? Was
he weary of his labors? Did he wish to die? These questions were
solemnly propounded to Mr. Dimmesdale by the elder ministers of
Boston and the deacons of his church, who, to use their own phrase,
"dealt with him" on the sin of rejecting the aid which Providence so
manifestly held out. He listened in silence, and finally promised to
confer with the physician.

"Were it God's will," said the Reverend Mr. Dimmesdale, when, in
fulfilment of this pledge, he requested old Roger Chillingworth's professional advice, "I could be well content, that my labors, and my sorrows, and my sins, and my pains, should shortly end with me, and
what is earthly of them be buried in my grave, and the spiritual go
with me to my eternal state, rather than that you should put your skill
to the proof in my behalf."

"Ah," replied Roger Chillingworth, with that quietness which,
whether imposed or natural, marked all his deportment, "it is thus
that a young clergyman is apt to speak. Youthful men, not having
taken a deep root, give up their hold of life so easily! And saintly men,
who walk with God on earth, would fain be away, to walk with him on
the golden pavements of the New Jerusalem."

"Nay," rejoined the young minister, putting his hand to his heart,
with a flush of pain fitting over his brow, "were I worthier to walk
there, I could be better content to toil here."

"Good men ever interpret themselves too meanly," said the physician.

In this manner, the mysterious old Roger Chillingworth became the
medical adviser of the Reverend Mr. Dimmesdale. As not only the disease interested the physician, but he was strongly moved to look into
the character and qualities of the patient, these two men, so different
in age, came gradually to spend much time together. For the sake of
the minister's health, and to enable the leech to gather plants with
healing balm in them, they took long walks on the sea-shore, or in the
forest; mingling various talk with the plash and murmur of the waves,
and the solemn wind-anthem among the tree-tops. Often, likewise,
one was the guest of the other, in his place of study and retirement.
There was a fascination for the minister in the company of the man of
science, in whom he recognized an intellectual cultivation of no moderate depth or scope; together with a range and freedom of ideas, that
he would have vainly looked for among the members of his own profession. In truth, he was startled, if not shocked, to find this attribute
in the physician. Mr. Dimmesdale was a true priest, a true religionist,
with the reverential sentiment largely developed, and an order of mind
that impelled itself powerfully along the track of a creed, and wore its
passage continually deeper with the lapse of time. In no state of society would he have been what is called a man of liberal views; it would
always be essential to his peace to feel the pressure of a faith about

him, supporting, while it confined him within its iron framework. Not the less, however, though with a tremulous enjoyment, did he feel the occasional relief of looking at the universe through the medium of another kind of intellect than those with which he habitually held converse. It was as if a window were thrown open, admitting a freer atmosphere into the close and stifled study, where his life was wasting itself away, amid lamp-light, or obstructed day-beams, and the musty fragrance, be it sensual or moral, that exhales from books. But the air was too fresh and chill to be long breathed with comfort. So the minister, and the physician with him, withdrew again within the limits of what their church defined as orthodox.

Thus Roger Chillingworth scrutinized his patient carefully, both as he saw him in his ordinary life, keeping an accustomed pathway in the range of thoughts familiar to him, and as he appeared when thrown amidst other moral scenery, the novelty of which might call out something new to the surface of his character. He deemed it essential, it would seem, to know the man, before attempting to do him good. Wherever there is a heart and an intellect, the diseases of the physical frame are tinged with the peculiarities of these. In Arthur Dimmesdale, thought and imagination were so active, and sensibility so intense, that the bodily infirmity would be likely to have its ground-work there. So Roger Chillingworth—the man of skill, the kind and friendly physician—strove to go deep into his patient's bosom, delving among his principles, prying into his recollections, and probing everything with a cautious touch, like a treasure-seeker in a dark cavern. Few secrets can escape an investigator, who has opportunity and license to undertake such a quest, and skill to follow it up. A man burdened with a secret should especially avoid the intimacy of his physician. If the latter possess native sagacity, and a nameless something more,—let us call it intuition; if he show no intrusive egotism, nor disagreeably prominent characteristics of his own; if he have the power, which must be born with him, to bring his mind into such affinity with his patient's, that this last shall unawares have spoken what he imagines himself only to have thought; if such revelations be received without tumult, and acknowledged not so often by an uttered sympathy as by silence, an inarticulate breath, and here and there a word, to indicate that all is understood; if to these qualifications of a confidant be joined the advantages afforded by his recognized character as a physician;—then, at some inevitable moment, will the soul of the sufferer be dissolved, and flow forth in a dark, but transparent stream, bringing all its mysteries into the daylight.

Roger Chillingworth possessed all, or most, of the attributes above enumerated. Nevertheless, time went on; a kind of intimacy, as we have said, grew up between these two cultivated minds, which had as wide a field as the whole sphere of human thought and study, to meet upon; they discussed every topic of ethics and religion, of public affairs, and private character; they talked much, on both sides, of matters that seemed personal to themselves; and yet no secret, such as the physician fancied must exist there, ever stole out of the minister's consciousness into his companion's ear. The latter had his suspicions, indeed, that even the nature of Mr. Dimmesdale's bodily disease had never fairly been revealed to him. It was a strange reserve!

After a time, at a hint from Roger Chillingworth, the friends of Mr. Dimmesdale effected an arrangement by which the two were lodged in the same house; so that every ebb and flow of the minister's life-tide might pass under the eye of his anxious and attached physician. There was much joy throughout the town, when this greatly desirable object was attained. It was held to be the best possible measure for the young clergyman's welfare; unless, indeed, as often urged by such as felt authorized to do so, he had selected some one of the many blooming damsels, spiritually devoted to him, to become his devoted wife. This latter step, however, there was no present prospect that Arthur Dimmesdale would be prevailed upon to take; he rejected all suggestions of the kind, as if priestly celibacy were one of his articles of church-discipline. Doomed by his own choice, therefore, as Mr. Dimmesdale so evidently was, to eat his unsavory morsel always at another's board, and endure the life-long chill which must be his lot who seeks to warm himself only at another's fireside, it truly seemed that this sagacious, experienced, benevolent old physician, with his concord of paternal and reverential love for the young pastor, was the very man, of all mankind, to be constantly within reach of his voice.

The new abode of the two friends was with a pious widow, of good social rank, who dwelt in a house covering pretty nearly the site on which the venerable structure of King's Chapel has since been built. It had the grave-yard, originally Isaac Johnson's home-field, on one side, and so was well adapted to call up serious reflections, suited to their respective employments, in both minister and man of physic. The motherly care of the good widow assigned to Mr. Dimmesdale a front apartment, with a sunny exposure, and heavy window-curtains, to create a noontide shadow, when desirable. The walls were hung round with tapestry, said to be from the Gobelin looms, and, at all events, representing the Scriptural story of David and Bathsheba, and Nathan the Prophet, in colors still unfaded, but which made the fair woman of the scene almost as grimly picturesque as the woe-denouncing seer.[4] Here, the pale clergyman piled up his library, rich with parchment-bound folios of the Fathers, and the lore of Rabbis, and monkish erudition, of which the Protestant divines, even while they vilified and decried that class of writers, were yet constrained often to avail themselves. On the other side of the house, old Roger Chillingworth arranged his study and laboratory; not such as a modern man of science would reckon even tolerably complete, but provided with a

---

4. The widow's choice of tapestries could hardly be more appropriate or better designed to keep Dimmesdale's guilt before his eyes. See 2 Samuel 11–12. David committed adultery with Bathsheba, wife of Uriah the Hittite. He then sent Uriah to die in battle and married Bathsheba, but the Lord sent Nathan the Prophet to chastise and punish David. In his comment upon a case involving William Hathorne (who in 1641 argued for punishment according to the letter of the law), John Winthrop used the example of David and Bathsheba to argue that punishments for crimes should be discretionary because God himself had not chosen to put David and Bathsheba to death for their adultery (*Journal*, 381–82).

distilling apparatus, and the means of compounding drugs and chemicals, which the practised alchemist knew well how to turn to purpose. With such commodiousness of situation, these two learned persons sat themselves down, each in his own domain, yet familiarly passing from one apartment to the other, and bestowing a mutual and not incurious inspection into one another's business.

And the Reverend Arthur Dimmesdale's best discerning friends, as we have intimated, very reasonably imagined that the hand of Providence had done all this, for the purpose—besought in so many public, and domestic, and secret prayers—of restoring the young minister to health. But—it must now be said—another portion of the community had latterly begun to take its own view of the relation betwixt Mr. Dimmesdale and the mysterious old physician. When an uninstructed multitude attempts to see with its eyes, it is exceedingly apt to be deceived. When, however, it forms its judgment, as it usually does, on the intuitions of its great and warm heart, the conclusions thus attained are often so profound and so unerring, as to possess the character of truths supernaturally revealed. The people, in the case of which we speak, could justify its prejudice against Roger Chillingworth by no fact or argument worthy of serious refutation. There was an aged handicraftsman, it is true, who had been a citizen of London at the period of Sir Thomas Overbury's murder, now some thirty years agone; he testified to having seen the physician, under some other name, which the narrator of the story had now forgotten, in company with Doctor Forman, the famous old conjurer, who was implicated in the affair of Overbury.[5] Two or three individuals hinted, that the man of skill, during his Indian captivity, had enlarged his medical attainments by joining in the incantations of the savage priests; who were universally acknowledged to be powerful enchanters, often performing seemingly miraculous cures by their skill in the black art. A large number—and many of these were persons of such sober sense and practical observation that their opinions would have been valuable, in other matters—affirmed that Roger Chillingworth's aspect had undergone a remarkable change while he had dwelt in town, and especially since his abode with Mr. Dimmesdale. At first, his expression had been calm, meditative, scholar-like. Now, there was something ugly and evil

---

5. The murder of Sir Thomas Overbury (1581–1613) was a sensational sex scandal involving adultery and murder during the reign of James I. Overbury protested the plan of his friend, Robert Carr, to marry Frances Howard, wife of the Earl of Essex, who sought an annulment of her marriage. Lady Essex claimed that her husband was impotent, and she and Carr (Viscount of Rochester) entered into an adulterous affair, even though a gynecological exam (probably of a substitute her family supplied) vouched for her virginity. Overbury was imprisoned by King James in 1613 and apparently poisoned to death. Frances Howard received an annulment, and married Carr. Two years later, six of the plotters were tried and convicted of Overbury's murder, and four were executed. Robert Carr and Frances Howard, now Lord and Lady Somerset, were convicted and imprisoned but then pardoned by King James. The prosecution emphasized adultery at Howard's trial in order to establish motive for the murder. Sir Edward Coke (see n. 5, p. 72) drew a connection to David and Bathsheba. Frances Howard consulted Dr. Simon Forman, a wizard, astrologer, and fortune-teller, to whom she confided her fear of having to "lie" with her husband and her sexual desire for Carr. Forman was also a prolific adulterer who kept meticulous records of his conquests. Alfred S. Reid, *The Yellow Ruff and The Scarlet Letter: A Source of Hawthorne's Novel* (1955), offers an extended treatment of connections between these events and Hawthorne's novel.

in his face, which they had not previously noticed, and which grew still the more obvious to sight, the oftener they looked upon him. According to the vulgar idea, the fire in his laboratory had been brought from the lower regions, and was fed with infernal fuel; and so, as might be expected, his visage was getting sooty with the smoke.

To sum up the matter, it grew to be a widely diffused opinion, that the Reverend Arthur Dimmesdale, like many other personages of especial sanctity, in all ages of the Christian world, was haunted either by Satan himself, or Satan's emissary, in the guise of old Roger Chillingworth. This diabolical agent had the Divine permission, for a season, to burrow into the clergyman's intimacy, and plot against his soul. No sensible man, it was confessed, could doubt on which side the victory would turn. The people looked, with an unshaken hope, to see the minister come forth out of the conflict, transfigured with the glory which he would unquestionably win. Meanwhile, nevertheless, it was sad to think of the perchance mortal agony through which he must struggle towards his triumph.

Alas! to judge from the gloom and terror in the depths of the poor minister's eyes, the battle was a sore one, and the victory anything but secure.

X. The Leech and His Patient

Old Roger Chillingworth, throughout life, had been calm in temperament, kindly, though not of warm affections, but ever, and in all his relations with the world, a pure and upright man. He had begun an investigation, as he imagined, with the severe and equal integrity of a judge, desirous only of truth, even as if the question involved no more than the air-drawn lines and figures of a geometrical problem, instead of human passions, and wrongs inflicted on himself. But, as he proceeded, a terrible fascination, a kind of fierce, though still calm, necessity seized the old man within its gripe, and never set him free again, until he had done all its bidding. He now dug into the poor clergyman's heart, like a miner searching for gold; or, rather, like a sexton delving into a grave, possibly in quest of a jewel that had been buried on the dead man's bosom, but likely to find nothing save mortality and corruption. Alas for his own soul, if these were what he sought!

Sometimes, a light glimmered out of the physician's eyes, burning blue and ominous, like the reflection of a furnace, or, let us say, like one of those gleams of ghastly fire that darted from Bunyan's awful door-way in the hill-side, and quivered on the pilgrim's face.[1] The soil where this dark miner was working had perchance shown indications that encouraged him.

"This man," said he, at one such moment, to himself, "pure as they deem him,—all spiritual as he seems,—hath inherited a strong animal

---

1. In John Bunyan's allegorical *Pilgrim's Progress* (1678), Christian encounters fire flashing out of a hill on his journey from the City of Destruction to the Celestial City.

nature from his father or his mother. Let us dig a little further in the direction of this vein!"

Then, after long search into the minister's dim interior, and turning over many precious materials, in the shape of high aspirations for the welfare of his race, warm love of souls, pure sentiments, natural piety, strengthened by thought and study, and illuminated by revelation,—all of which invaluable gold was perhaps no better than rubbish to the seeker,—he would turn back, discouraged, and begin his quest towards another point. He groped along as stealthily, with as cautious a tread, and as wary an outlook, as a thief entering a chamber where a man lies only half asleep,—or, it may be, broad awake,—with purpose to steal the very treasure which this man guards as the apple of his eye. In spite of his premeditated carefulness, the floor would now and then creak; his garments would rustle; the shadow of his presence, in a forbidden proximity, would be thrown across his victim. In other words, Mr. Dimmesdale, whose sensibility of nerve often produced the effect of spiritual intuition, would become vaguely aware that something inimical to his peace had thrust itself into relation with him. But old Roger Chillingworth, too, had perceptions that were almost intuitive; and when the minister threw his startled eyes towards him, there the physician sat; his kind, watchful, sympathizing, but never intrusive friend.

Yet Mr. Dimmesdale would perhaps have seen this individual's character more perfectly, if a certain morbidness, to which sick hearts are liable, had not rendered him suspicious of all mankind. Trusting no man as his friend, he could not recognize his enemy when the latter actually appeared. He therefore still kept up a familiar intercourse with him, daily receiving the old physician in his study; or visiting the laboratory, and, for recreation's sake, watching the processes by which weeds were converted into drugs of potency.

One day, leaning his forehead on his hand, and his elbow on the sill of the open window, that looked towards the grave-yard, he talked with Roger Chillingworth, while the old man was examining a bundle of unsightly plants.

"Where," asked he, with a look askance at them,—for it was the clergyman's peculiarity that he seldom, now-a-days, looked straight-forth at any object, whether human or inanimate—"where, my kind doctor, did you gather those herbs, with such a dark, flabby leaf?"

"Even in the grave-yard here at hand," answered the physician, continuing his employment. "They are new to me. I found them growing on a grave, which bore no tomb-stone, nor other memorial of the dead man, save these ugly weeds, that have taken upon themselves to keep him in remembrance. They grew out of his heart, and typify, it may be, some hideous secret that was buried with him, and which he had done better to confess during his lifetime."

"Perchance," said Mr. Dimmesdale, "he earnestly desired it, but could not."

"And wherefore?" rejoined the physician. "Wherefore not; since all the powers of nature call so earnestly for the confession of sin, that

these black weeds have sprung up out of a buried heart, to make manifest an unspoken crime?"

"That, good Sir, is but a fantasy of yours," replied the minister.
"There can be, if I forebode aright, no power, short of the Divine
mercy, to disclose, whether by uttered words, or by type or emblem,
the secrets that may be buried with a human heart. The heart, making
itself guilty of such secrets, must perforce hold them, until the day
when all hidden things shall be revealed. Nor have I so read or interpreted Holy Writ, as to understand that the disclosure of human
thoughts and deeds, then to be made, is intended as a part of the retribution. That, surely, were a shallow view of it. No; these revelations,
unless I greatly err, are meant merely to promote the intellectual satisfaction of all intelligent beings, who will stand waiting, on that day, to
see the dark problem of this life made plain. A knowledge of men's
hearts will be needful to the completest solution of that problem. And
I conceive, moreover, that the hearts holding such miserable secrets as
you speak of will yield them up, at that last day, not with reluctance,
but with a joy unutterable."

"Then why not reveal them here?" asked Roger Chillingworth,
glancing quietly aside at the minister. "Why should not the guilty ones
sooner avail themselves of this unutterable solace?"

"They mostly do," said the clergyman, griping hard at his breast, as
if afflicted with an importunate throb of pain. "Many, many a poor
soul hath given its confidence to me, not only on the death-bed, but
while strong in life, and fair in reputation. And ever, after such an out-
pouring, O, what a relief have I witnessed in those sinful brethren!
even as in one who at last draws free air, after long stifling with
his own polluted breath. How can it be otherwise? Why should a
wretched man, guilty, we will say, of murder, prefer to keep the dead
corpse buried in his own heart, rather than fling it forth at once, and
let the universe take care of it!"

"Yet some men bury their secrets thus," observed the calm physician.

"True; there are such men," answered Mr. Dimmesdale. "But, not to
suggest more obvious reasons, it may be that they are kept silent by
the very constitution of their nature. Or,—can we not suppose it?—
guilty as they may be, retaining, nevertheless, a zeal for God's glory
and man's welfare, they shrink from displaying themselves black and
filthy in the view of men; because, thenceforward, no good can be
achieved by them; no evil of the past be redeemed by better service.
So, to their own unutterable torment, they go about among their
fellow-creatures, looking pure as new-fallen snow; while their hearts
are all speckled and spotted with iniquity of which they cannot rid
themselves."

"These men deceive themselves," said Roger Chillingworth, with
somewhat more emphasis than usual, and making a slight gesture with
his forefinger. "They fear to take up the shame that rightfully belongs
to them. Their love for man, their zeal for God's service,—these holy
impulses may or may not coëxist in their hearts with the evil inmates

to which their guilt has unbarred the door, and which must needs propagate a hellish breed within them. But, if they seek to glorify God, let them not lift heavenward their unclean hands! If they would serve their fellow-men, let them do it by making manifest the power and reality of conscience, in constraining them to penitential self-abasement! Wouldst thou have me to believe, O wise and pious friend, that a false show can be better—can be more for God's glory, or man's welfare—than God's own truth? Trust me, such men deceive themselves!"

"It may be so," said the young clergyman, indifferently, as waiving a discussion that he considered irrelevant or unseasonable. He had a ready faculty, indeed, of escaping from any topic that agitated his too sensitive and nervous temperament.—"But, now, I would ask of my well-skilled physician, whether, in good sooth, he deems me to have profited by his kindly care of this weak frame of mine?"

Before Roger Chillingworth could answer, they heard the clear, wild laughter of a young child's voice, proceeding from the adjacent burial-ground. Looking instinctively from the open window,—for it was summer-time,—the minister beheld Hester Prynne and little Pearl passing along the foot-path that traversed the enclosure. Pearl looked as beautiful as the day, but was in one of those moods of perverse merriment which, whenever they occurred, seemed to remove her entirely out of the sphere of sympathy or human contact. She now skipped irreverently from one grave to another; until, coming to the broad, flat, armorial tomb-stone of a departed worthy,—perhaps of Isaac Johnson himself,—she began to dance upon it. In reply to her mother's command and entreaty that she would behave more decorously, little Pearl paused to gather the prickly burrs from a tall burdock which grew beside the tomb. Taking a handful of these, she arranged them along the lines of the scarlet letter that decorated the maternal bosom, to which the burrs, as their nature was, tenaciously adhered. Hester did not pluck them off.

Roger Chillingworth had by this time approached the window, and smiled grimly down.

"There is no law, nor reverence for authority, no regard for human ordinances or opinions, right or wrong, mixed up with that child's composition," remarked he, as much to himself as to his companion. "I saw her, the other day, bespatter the Governor himself with water, at the cattle-trough in Spring-lane. What, in Heaven's name, is she? Is the imp altogether evil? Hath she affections? Hath she any discoverable principle of being?"

"None,—save the freedom of a broken law," answered Mr. Dimmesdale, in a quiet way, as if he had been discussing the point within himself. "Whether capable of good, I know not."

The child probably overheard their voices; for, looking up to the window, with a bright, but naughty smile of mirth and intelligence, she threw one of the prickly burrs at the Reverend Mr. Dimmesdale. The sensitive clergyman shrunk, with nervous dread, from the light missile. Detecting his emotion, Pearl clapped her little hands, in the most extravagant ecstasy. Hester Prynne, likewise, had involuntarily looked up; and all these four persons, old and young, regarded one another in silence, till the child laughed aloud, and shouted,—"Come away, mother! Come away, or yonder old Black Man will catch you! He hath got hold of the minister already. Come away, mother, or he will catch you! But he cannot catch little Pearl!"

So she drew her mother away, skipping, dancing, and frisking fantastically, among the hillocks of the dead people, like a creature that had nothing in common with a bygone and buried generation, nor owned herself akin to it. It was as if she had been made afresh, out of new elements, and must perforce be permitted to live her own life, and be a law unto herself, without her eccentricities being reckoned to her for a crime.

"There goes a woman," resumed Roger Chillingworth, after a pause, "who, be her demerits what they may, hath none of that mystery of hidden sinfulness which you deem so grievous to be borne. Is Hester Prynne the less miserable, think you, for that scarlet letter on her breast?"

"I do verily believe it," answered the clergyman. "Nevertheless, I cannot answer for her. There was a look of pain in her face, which I would gladly have been spared the sight of. But still, methinks, it must needs be better for the sufferer to be free to show his pain, as this poor woman Hester is, than to cover it all up in his heart."

There was another pause; and the physician began anew to examine and arrange the plants which he had gathered.

"You inquired of me, a little time agone," said he, at length, "my judgment as touching your health."

"I did," answered the clergyman, "and would gladly learn it. Speak frankly, I pray you, be it for life or death."

"Freely, then, and plainly," said the physician, still busy with his plants, but keeping a wary eye on Mr. Dimmesdale, "the disorder is a strange one; not so much in itself, nor as outwardly manifested,—in so far, at least, as the symptoms have been laid open to my observation. Looking daily at you, my good Sir, and watching the tokens of your aspect, now for months gone by, I should deem you a man sore sick, it may be, yet not so sick but that an instructed and watchful physician might well hope to cure you. But—I know not what to say—the disease is what I seem to know, yet know it not."

"You speak in riddles, learned Sir," said the pale minister, glancing aside out of the window.

"Then, to speak more plainly," continued the physician, "and I crave pardon, Sir,—should it seem to require pardon,—for this needful plainness of my speech. Let me ask,—as your friend,—as one having charge, under Providence, of your life and physical well-being,—hath all the operation of this disorder been fairly laid open and recounted to me?"

"How can you question it?" asked the minister. "Surely, it were child's play, to call in a physician, and then hide the sore!"

"You would tell me, then, that I know all?" said Roger Chillingworth, deliberately, and fixing an eye, bright with intense and concentrated intelligence, on the minister's face. "Be it so! But, again! He to whom only the outward and physical evil is laid open, knoweth, oftentimes, but half the evil which he is called upon to cure. A bodily disease, which we look upon as whole and entire within itself, may, after all, be but a symptom of some ailment in the spiritual part. Your pardon, once again, good Sir, if my speech give the shadow of offence. You, Sir, of all men whom I have known, are he whose body is the closest conjoined, and imbued, and identified, so to speak, with the spirit whereof it is the instrument."

"Then I need ask no further," said the clergyman, somewhat hastily rising from his chair. "You deal not, I take it, in medicine for the soul!"

"Thus, a sickness," continued Roger Chillingworth, going on, in an unaltered tone, without heeding the interruption,—but standing up, and confronting the emaciated and white-cheeked minister, with his low, dark, and misshapen figure,—"a sickness, a sore place, if we may so call it, in your spirit, hath immediately its appropriate manifestation in your bodily frame. Would you, therefore, that your physician heal the bodily evil? How may this be, unless you first lay open to him the wound or trouble in your soul?"

"No!—not to thee!—not to an earthly physician!" cried Mr. Dimmesdale, passionately, and turning his eyes, full and bright, and with a kind of fierceness, on old Roger Chillingworth. "Not to thee! But, if it be the soul's disease, then do I commit myself to the one Physician of the soul! He, if it stand with his good pleasure, can cure; or he can kill! Let him do with me as, in his justice and wisdom, he shall see good. But who art thou, that meddlest in this matter?—that dares thrust himself between the sufferer and his God?"

With a frantic gesture, he rushed out of the room.

"It is as well to have made this step," said Roger Chillingworth to himself, looking after the minister, with a grave smile. "There is nothing lost. We shall be friends again anon. But see, now, how passion takes hold upon this man, and hurrieth him out of himself! As with one passion, so with another! He hath done a wild thing ere now, this pious Master Dimmesdale, in the hot passion of his heart!"

It proved not difficult to reëstablish the intimacy of the two companions, on the same footing and in the same degree as heretofore. The young clergyman, after a few hours of privacy, was sensible that the disorder of his nerves had hurried him into an unseemly outbreak of temper, which there had been nothing in the physician's words to excuse or palliate. He marvelled, indeed, at the violence with which he had thrust back the kind old man, when merely proffering the advice which it was his duty to bestow, and which the minister himself had expressly sought. With these remorseful feelings, he lost no time in making the amplest apologies, and besought his friend still to continue the care, which, if not successful in restoring him to health, had, in all probability, been the means of prolonging his feeble existence to that hour. Roger Chillingworth readily assented, and went on with his medical supervision of the minister; doing his best for him, in all good

faith, but always quitting the patient's apartment, at the close of a professional interview, with a mysterious and puzzled smile upon his lips.
This expression was invisible in Mr. Dimmesdale's presence, but grew
strongly evident as the physician crossed the threshold.

"A rare case!" he muttered. "I must needs look deeper into it. A
strange sympathy betwixt soul and body! Were it only for the art's sake,
I must search this matter to the bottom!"

It came to pass, not long after the scene above recorded, that the
Reverend Mr. Dimmesdale, at noon-day, and entirely unawares, fell
into a deep, deep slumber, sitting in his chair, with a large black-letter
volume open before him on the table. It must have been a work of vast
ability in the somniferous school of literature. The profound depth of
the minister's repose was the more remarkable, inasmuch as he was
one of those persons whose sleep, ordinarily, is as light, as fitful, and
as easily scared away, as a small bird hopping on a twig. To such an
unwonted remoteness, however, had his spirit now withdrawn into itself, that he stirred not in his chair, when old Roger Chillingworth,
without any extraordinary precaution, came into the room. The physician advanced directly in front of his patient, laid his hand upon his
bosom, and thrust aside the vestment, that, hitherto, had always covered it even from the professional eye.

Then, indeed, Mr. Dimmesdale shuddered, and slightly stirred.

After a brief pause, the physician turned away.

But, with what a wild look of wonder, joy, and horror! With what a
ghastly rapture, as it were, too mighty to be expressed only by the eye
and features, and therefore bursting forth through the whole ugliness
of his figure, and making itself even riotously manifest by the extravagant gestures with which he threw up his arms towards the ceiling,
and stamped his foot upon the floor! Had a man seen old Roger Chillingworth, at that moment of his ecstacy, he would have had no need to
ask how Satan comports himself, when a precious human soul is lost
to heaven, and won into his kingdom.

But what distinguished the physician's ecstacy from Satan's was the
trait of wonder in it!

XI. The Interior of a Heart

After the incident last described, the intercourse between the clergyman and the physician, though externally the same, was really of another character than it had previously been. The intellect of Roger
Chillingworth had now a sufficiently plain path before it. It was not,
indeed, precisely that which he had laid out for himself to tread.
Calm, gentle, passionless, as he appeared, there was yet, we fear, a
quiet depth of malice, hitherto latent, but active now, in this unfortunate old man, which led him to imagine a more intimate revenge than
any mortal had ever wreaked upon an enemy. To make himself the one
trusted friend, to whom should be confided all the fear, the remorse,
the agony, the ineffectual repentance, the backward rush of sinful

thoughts, expelled in vain! All that guilty sorrow, hidden from the world, whose great heart would have pitied and forgiven, to be revealed to him, the Pitiless, to him, the Unforgiving! All that dark treasure to be lavished on the very man, to whom nothing else could so adequately pay the debt of vengeance!

The clergyman's shy and sensitive reserve had balked this scheme. Roger Chillingworth, however, was inclined to be hardly, if at all, less satisfied with the aspect of affairs, which Providence—using the avenger and his victim for its own purposes, and, perchance, pardoning, where it seemed most to punish—had substituted for his black devices. A revelation, he could almost say, had been granted to him. It mattered little, for his object, whether celestial, or from what other region. By its aid, in all the subsequent relations betwixt him and Mr. Dimmesdale, not merely the external presence, but the very inmost soul, of the latter, seemed to be brought out before his eyes, so that he could see and comprehend its every movement. He became, thenceforth, not a spectator only, but a chief actor, in the poor minister's interior world. He could play upon him as he chose. Would he arouse him with a throb of agony? The victim was forever on the rack; it needed only to know the spring that controlled the engine;—and the physician knew it well! Would he startle him with sudden fear? As at the waving of a magician's wand, uprose a grisly phantom,—uprose a thousand phantoms,—in many shapes, of death, or more awful shame, all flocking round about the clergyman, and pointing with their fingers at his breast!

All this was accomplished with a subtlety so perfect, that the minister, though he had constantly a dim perception of some evil influence watching over him, could never gain a knowledge of its actual nature. True, he looked doubtfully, fearfully,—even, at times, with horror and the bitterness of hatred,—at the deformed figure of the old physician. His gestures, his gait, his grizzled beard, his slightest and most indifferent acts, the very fashion of his garments, were odious in the clergyman's sight; a token implicitly to be relied on, of a deeper antipathy in the breast of the latter than he was willing to acknowledge to himself. For, as it was impossible to assign a reason for such distrust and abhorrence, so Mr. Dimmesdale, conscious that the poison of one morbid spot was infecting his heart's entire substance, attributed all his presentiments to no other cause. He took himself to task for his bad sympathies in reference to Roger Chillingworth, disregarded the lesson that he should have drawn from them, and did his best to root them out. Unable to accomplish this, he nevertheless, as a matter of principle, continued his habits of social familiarity with the old man, and thus gave him constant opportunities for perfecting the purpose to which—poor, forlorn creature that he was, and more wretched than his victim—the avenger had devoted himself.

While thus suffering under bodily disease, and gnawed and tortured by some black trouble of the soul, and given over to the machinations of his deadliest enemy, the Reverend Mr. Dimmesdale had achieved a brilliant popularity in his sacred office. He won it, indeed, in great

part, by his sorrows. His intellectual gifts, his moral perceptions, his
power of experiencing and communicating emotion, were kept in a
state of preternatural activity by the prick and anguish of his daily life.
His fame, though still on its upward slope, already overshadowed
the soberer reputations of his fellow-clergymen, eminent as several of
them were. There were scholars among them, who had spent more
years in acquiring abstruse lore, connected with the divine profession,
than Mr. Dimmesdale had lived; and who might well, therefore, be
more profoundly versed in such solid and valuable attainments than
their youthful brother. There were men, too, of a sturdier texture of
mind then his, and endowed with a far greater share of shrewd, hard,
iron, or granite understanding; which, duly mingled with a fair proportion of doctrinal ingredient, constitutes a highly respectable, efficacious, and unamiable variety of the clerical species. There were
others, again, true saintly fathers, whose faculties had been elaborated
by weary toil among their books, and by patient thought, and etherealized, moreover, by spiritual communications with the better world,
into which their purity of life had almost introduced these holy personages, with their garments of mortality still clinging to them. All
that they lacked was the gift that descended upon the chosen disciples
at Pentecost, in tongues of flame; symbolizing, it would seem, not the
power of speech in foreign and unknown languages, but that of addressing the whole human brotherhood in the heart's native language.
These fathers, otherwise so apostolic, lacked Heaven's last and rarest
attestation of their office, the Tongue of Flame.[1] They would have
vainly sought—had they ever dreamed of seeking—to express the
highest truths through the humblest medium of familiar words and
images. Their voices came down, afar and indistinctly, from the upper
heights where they habitually dwelt.

Not improbably, it was to this latter class of men that Mr. Dimmesdale, by many of his traits of character, naturally belonged. To the high
mountain-peaks of faith and sanctity he would have climbed, had not
the tendency been thwarted by the burden, whatever it might be, of
crime or anguish, beneath which it was his doom to totter. It kept him
down, on a level with the lowest; him, the man of ethereal attributes,
whose voice the angels might else have listened to and answered! But
this very burden it was, that gave him sympathies so intimate with the
sinful brotherhood of mankind; so that his heart vibrated in unison
with theirs, and received their pain into itself, and sent its own throb
of pain through a thousand other hearts, in gushes of sad, persuasive
eloquence. Oftenest persuasive, but sometimes terrible! The people
knew not the power that moved them thus. They deemed the young
clergyman a miracle of holiness. They fancied him the mouth-piece of
Heaven's messages of wisdom, and rebuke, and love. In their eyes, the

---

1. See Acts 2:1–11: "And when the day of Pentecost was fully come . . . suddenly there came a
   sound from heaven as of a rushing mighty wind, and it filled all the house where they were
   sitting. / And there appeared unto them cloven tongues like as of fire, and it sat upon each
   of them. / And they were all filled with the Holy Ghost, and began to speak with other
   tongues, as the Spirit gave them utterance" (1–4).

very ground on which he trod was sanctified. The virgins of his church grew pale around him, victims of a passion so imbued with religious sentiment that they imagined it to be all religion, and brought it openly, in their white bosoms, as their most acceptable sacrifice before the altar. The aged members of his flock, beholding Mr. Dimmesdale's frame so feeble, while they were themselves so rugged in their infirmity, believed that he would go heavenward before them, and enjoined it upon their children, that their old bones should be buried close to their young pastor's holy grave. And, all this time, perchance, when poor Mr. Dimmesdale was thinking of his grave, he questioned with himself whether the grass would ever grow on it, because an accursed thing must there be buried!

It is inconceivable, the agony with which this public veneration tortured him! It was his genuine impulse to adore the truth, and to reckon all things shadow-like, and utterly devoid of weight or value, that had not its divine essence as the life within their life. Then, what was he?—a substance?—or the dimmest of all shadows? He longed to speak out, from his own pulpit, at the full height of his voice, and tell the people what he was. "I, whom you behold in these black garments of the priesthood,—I, who ascend the sacred desk, and turn my pale face heavenward, taking upon myself to hold communion, in your behalf, with the Most High Omniscience,—I, in whose daily life you discern the sanctity of Enoch,[2]—I, whose footsteps, as you suppose, leave a gleam along my earthly track, whereby the pilgrims that shall come after me may be guided to the regions of the blest,—I, who have laid the hand of baptism upon your children,—I, who have breathed the parting prayer over your dying friends, to whom the Amen sounded faintly from a world which they had quitted,—I, your pastor, whom you so reverence and trust, am utterly a pollution and a lie!"

More than once, Mr. Dimmesdale had gone into the pulpit, with a purpose never to come down its steps, until he should have spoken words like the above. More than once, he had cleared his throat, and drawn in the long, deep, and tremulous breath, which, when sent forth again, would come burdened with the black secret of his soul. More than once—nay, more than a hundred times—he had actually spoken! Spoken! But how? He had told his hearers that he was altogether vile, a viler companion of the vilest, the worst of sinners, an abomination, a thing of unimaginable iniquity; and that the only wonder was, that they did not see his wretched body shrivelled up before their eyes, by the burning wrath of the Almighty! Could there be plainer speech than this? Would not the people start up in their seats, by a simultaneous impulse, and tear him down out of the pulpit which he defiled? Not so, indeed! They heard it all, and did but reverence him the more. They little guessed what deadly purport lurked in those self-condemning words. "The godly youth!" said they among themselves. "The saint on earth! Alas, if he discern such sinfulness in his

---

2. Enoch offers one of several examples of the power of faith. See Hebrews 11:5: "By faith Enoch was translated that he should not see death." Others mentioned in Hebrews 11 are Abel, Noah, Abraham, and Sarah.

own white soul, what horrid spectacle would he behold in thine or mine!" The minister well knew—subtle, but remorseful hypocrite that he was!—the light in which his vague confession would be viewed. He had striven to put a cheat upon himself by making the avowal of a guilty conscience, but had gained only one other sin, and a self-acknowledged shame, without the momentary relief of being self-deceived. He had spoken the very truth, and transformed it into the veriest falsehood. And yet, by the constitution of his nature, he loved the truth, and loathed the lie, as few men ever did. Therefore, above all things else, he loathed his miserable self!

His inward trouble drove him to practices more in accordance with the old, corrupted faith of Rome, than with the better light of the church in which he had been born and bred. In Mr. Dimmesdale's secret closet, under lock and key, there was a bloody scourge.[3] Oftentimes, this Protestant and Puritan divine had plied it on his own shoulders; laughing bitterly at himself the while, and smiting so much the more pitilessly because of that bitter laugh. It was his custom, too, as it has been that of many other pious Puritans, to fast,—not, however, like them, in order to purify the body and render it the fitter medium of celestial illumination, but rigorously, and until his knees trembled beneath him, as an act of penance. He kept vigils, likewise, night after night, sometimes in utter darkness; sometimes with a glimmering lamp; and sometimes, viewing his own face in a looking-glass, by the most powerful light which he could throw upon it. He thus typified the constant introspection wherewith he tortured, but could not purify, himself. In these lengthened vigils, his brain often reeled, and visions seemed to flit before him; perhaps seen doubtfully, and by a faint light of their own, in the remote dimness of the chamber, or more vividly, and close beside him, within the looking-glass. Now it was a herd of diabolic shapes, that grinned and mocked at the pale minister, and beckoned him away with them; now a group of shining angels, who flew upward heavily, as sorrow-laden, but grew more ethereal as they rose. Now came the dead friends of his youth, and his white-bearded father, with a saint-like frown, and his mother, turning her face away as she passed by. Ghost of a mother,—thinnest fantasy of a mother,—methinks she might yet have thrown a pitying glance towards her son! And now, through the chamber which these spectral thoughts had made so ghastly, glided Hester Prynne, leading along little Pearl, in her scarlet garb, and pointing her forefinger, first at the scarlet letter on her bosom, and then at the clergyman's own breast.

None of these visions ever quite deluded him. At any moment, by an effort of his will, he could discern substances through their misty lack of substance, and convince himself that they were not solid in their nature, like yonder table of carved oak, or that big, square, leathern-bound and brazen-clasped volume of divinity. But, for all that, they were, in one sense, the truest and most substantial things which the

---

3. A bloody whip. See 2 Maccabees 9:11: "Here therefore, being plagued, he began to leave off his great pride, and to come to the knowledge of himself by the scourge of God, his pain increasing every moment."

poor minister now dealt with. It is the unspeakable misery of a life so false as his, that it steals the pith and substance out of whatever realities there are around us, and which were meant by Heaven to be the spirit's joy and nutriment. To the untrue man, the whole universe is false,—it is impalpable,—it shrinks to nothing within his grasp. And he himself, in so far as he shows himself in a false light, becomes a shadow, or, indeed, ceases to exist. The only truth that continued to give Mr. Dimmesdale a real existence on this earth, was the anguish in his inmost soul, and the undissembled expression of it in his aspect. Had he once found power to smile, and wear a face of gayety, there would have been no such man!

On one of those ugly nights, which we have faintly hinted at, but forborne to picture forth, the minister started from his chair. A new thought had struck him. There might be a moment's peace in it. Attiring himself with as much care as if it had been for public worship, and precisely in the same manner, he stole softly down the staircase, undid the door, and issued forth.

XII. The Minister's Vigil

Walking in the shadow of a dream, as it were, and perhaps actually under the influence of a species of somnambulism, Mr. Dimmesdale reached the spot, where, now so long since, Hester Prynne had lived through her first hours of public ignominy. The same platform or scaffold, black and weather-stained with the storm or sunshine of seven long years, and foot-worn, too, with the tread of many culprits who had since ascended it, remained standing beneath the balcony of the meeting-house. The minister went up the steps.

It was an obscure night of early May.[1] An unvaried pall of cloud muffled the whole expanse of sky from zenith to horizon. If the same multitude which had stood as eye-witnesses while Hester Prynne sustained her punishment could now have been summoned forth, they would have discerned no face above the platform, nor hardly the outline of a human shape, in the dark gray of the midnight. But the town was all asleep. There was no peril of discovery. The minister might stand there, if it so pleased him, until morning should redden in the east, without other risk than that the dank and chill night-air would creep into his frame, and stiffen his joints with rheumatism, and clog his throat with catarrh and cough; thereby defrauding the expectant audience of to-morrow's prayer and sermon. No eye could see him, save that ever-wakeful one which had seen him in his closet, wielding the bloody scourge. Why, then, had he come hither? Was it but the mockery of penitence? A mockery, indeed, but in which his soul trifled with itself! A mockery at which angels blushed and wept, while fiends rejoiced, with jeering laughter! He had been driven hither by the im-

---

1. John Winthrop died March 26, 1649, so Hawthorne is taking a small liberty with history by moving this scene to May. Much as he had done in chapter 6, Hawthorne uses chapter 11 to advance the action of the novel—in this case, four more years.

pulse of that Remorse which dogged him everywhere, and whose own sister and closely linked companion was that Cowardice which invariably drew him back, with her tremulous gripe, just when the other impulse had hurried him to the verge of a disclosure. Poor, miserable man! what right had infirmity like his to burden itself with crime? Crime is for the iron-nerved, who have their choice either to endure it, or, if it press too hard, to exert their fierce and savage strength for a good purpose, and fling it off at once! This feeble and most sensitive of spirits could do neither, yet continually did one thing or another, which intertwined, in the same inextricable knot, the agony of heaven-defying guilt and vain repentance.

And thus, while standing on the scaffold, in this vain show of expiation, Mr. Dimmesdale was overcome with a great horror of mind, as if the universe were gazing at a scarlet token on his naked breast, right over his heart. On that spot, in very truth, there was, and there had long been, the gnawing and poisonous tooth of bodily pain. Without any effort of his will, or power to restrain himself, he shrieked aloud; an outcry that went pealing through the night, and was beaten back from one house to another, and reverberated from the hills in the background; as if a company of devils, detecting so much misery and terror in it, had made a plaything of the sound, and were bandying it to and fro.

"It is done!" muttered the minister, covering his face with his hands. "The whole town will awake, and hurry forth, and find me here!"

But it was not so. The shriek had perhaps sounded with a far greater power, to his own startled ears, than it actually possessed. The town did not awake; or, if it did, the drowsy slumberers mistook the cry either for something frightful in a dream, or for the noise of witches; whose voices, at that period, were often heard to pass over the settlements or lonely cottages, as they rode with Satan through the air. The clergyman, therefore, hearing no symptoms of disturbance, uncovered his eyes and looked about him. At one of the chamber-windows of Governor Bellingham's mansion, which stood at some distance, on the line of another street, he beheld the appearance of the old magistrate himself, with a lamp in his hand, a white night-cap on his head, and a long white gown enveloping his figure. He looked like a ghost, evoked unseasonably from the grave. The cry had evidently startled him. At another window of the same house, moreover, appeared old Mistress Hibbins, the Governor's sister, also with a lamp, which, even thus far off, revealed the expression of her sour and discontented face. She thrust forth her head from the lattice, and looked anxiously upward. Beyond the shadow of a doubt, this venerable witch-lady had heard Mr. Dimmesdale's outcry, and interpreted it, with its multitudinous echoes and reverberations, as the clamor of the fiends and night-hags, with whom she was well known to make excursions into the forest.

Detecting the gleam of Governor Bellingham's lamp, the old lady quickly extinguished her own, and vanished. Possibly, she went up among the clouds. The minister saw nothing further of her motions. The magistrate, after a wary observation of the darkness—into which, nevertheless, he could see but little further than he might into a mill-stone—retired from the window.

The minister grew comparatively calm. His eyes, however, were soon greeted by a little, glimmering light, which, at first a long way off, was approaching up the street. It threw a gleam of recognition on here a post, and there a garden-fence, and here a latticed window-pane, and there a pump, with its full trough of water, and here, again, an arched door of oak, with an iron knocker, and a rough log for the door-step. The Reverend Mr. Dimmesdale noted all these minute particulars, even while firmly convinced that the doom of his existence was stealing onward, in the footsteps which he now heard; and that the gleam of the lantern would fall upon him, in a few moments more, and reveal his long-hidden secret. As the light drew nearer, he beheld, within its illuminated circle, his brother clergyman,—or, to speak more accurately, his professional father, as well as highly valued friend,—the Reverend Mr. Wilson; who, as Mr. Dimmesdale now conjectured, had been praying at the bedside of some dying man. And so he had. The good old minister came freshly from the death-chamber of Governor Winthrop, who had passed from earth to heaven within that very hour. And now, surrounded, like the saint-like personages of olden times, with a radiant halo, that glorified him amid this gloomy night of sin,—as if the departed Governor had left him an inheritance of his glory, or as if he had caught upon himself the distant shine of the celestial city, while looking thitherward to see the triumphant pilgrim pass within its gates,—now, in short, good Father Wilson was moving homeward, aiding his footsteps with a lighted lantern! The glimmer of this luminary suggested the above conceits to Mr. Dimmesdale, who smiled,—nay, almost laughed at them,—and then wondered if he were going mad.

As the Reverend Mr. Wilson passed beside the scaffold, closely muffling his Geneva cloak about him with one arm, and holding the lantern before his breast with the other, the minister could hardly restrain himself from speaking.

"A good evening to you, venerable Father Wilson! Come up hither, I pray you, and pass a pleasant hour with me!"

Good heavens! Had Mr. Dimmesdale actually spoken? For one instant, he believed that these words had passed his lips. But they were uttered only within his imagination. The venerable Father Wilson continued to step slowly onward, looking carefully at the muddy pathway before his feet, and never once turning his head towards the guilty platform. When the light of the glimmering lantern had faded quite away, the minister discovered, by the faintness which came over him, that the last few moments had been a crisis of terrible anxiety; although his mind had made an involuntary effort to relieve itself by a kind of lurid playfulness.

Shortly afterwards, the like grisly sense of the humorous again stole in among the solemn phantoms of his thought. He felt his limbs growing stiff with the unaccustomed chilliness of the night, and doubted whether he should be able to descend the steps of the scaffold. Morn-

ing would break, and find him there. The neighborhood would begin
to rouse itself. The earliest riser, coming forth in the dim twilight,
would perceive a vaguely defined figure aloft on the place of shame;
and, half crazed betwixt alarm and curiosity, would go, knocking from
door to door, summoning all the people to behold the ghost—as he
needs must think it—of some defunct transgressor. A dusky tumult
would flap its wings from one house to another. Then—the morning
light still waxing stronger—old patriarchs would rise up in great haste,
each in his flannel gown, and matronly dames, without pausing to put
off their night-gear. The whole tribe of decorous personages, who had
never heretofore been seen with a single hair of their heads awry,
would start into public view, with the disorder of a nightmare in their
aspects. Old Governor Bellingham would come grimly forth, with his
King James' ruff fastened askew; and Mistress Hibbins, with some
twigs of the forest clinging to her skirts, and looking sourer than ever,
as having hardly got a wink of sleep after her night ride; and good Father Wilson, too, after spending half the night at a death-bed, and lik-
ing ill to be disturbed, thus early, out of his dreams about the glorified
saints. Hither, likewise, would come the elders and deacons of Mr.
Dimmesdale's church, and the young virgins who so idolized their
minister, and had made a shrine for him in their white bosoms; which
now, by the by, in their hurry and confusion, they would scantly have
given themselves time to cover with their kerchiefs. All people, in a
word, would come stumbling over their thresholds, and turning up
their amazed and horror-stricken visages around the scaffold. Whom
would they discern there, with the red eastern light upon his brow?
Whom, but the Reverend Arthur Dimmesdale, half frozen to death,
overwhelmed with shame, and standing where Hester Prynne had
stood!

Carried away by the grotesque horror of this picture, the minister,
unawares, and to his own infinite alarm, burst into a great peal of
laughter. It was immediately responded to by a light, airy, childish
laugh, in which with a thrill of the heart,—but he knew not whether
of exquisite pain, or pleasure as acute,—he recognized the tones of little Pearl.

"Pearl! Little Pearl!" cried he, after a moment's pause; then, suppressing his voice,—"Hester! Hester Prynne! Are you there?"

"Yes; it is Hester Prynne!" she replied, in a tone of surprise; and the
minister heard her footsteps approaching from the sidewalk, along
which she had been passing. "It is I, and my little Pearl."

"Whence come you, Hester?" asked the minister. "What sent you
hither?"

"I have been watching at a death-bed," answered Hester Prynne;—
"at Governor Winthrop's death-bed, and have taken his measure for a
robe, and am now going homeward to my dwelling."

"Come up hither, Hester, thou and little Pearl," said the Reverend
Mr. Dimmesdale. "Ye have both been here before, but I was not with
you. Come up hither once again, and we will stand all three together!"

She silently ascended the steps, and stood on the platform, holding little Pearl by the hand. The minister felt for the child's other hand, and took it. The moment that he did so, there came what seemed a tumultuous rush of new life, other life than his own, pouring like a torrent into his heart, and hurrying through all his veins, as if the mother and the child were communicating their vital warmth to his half-torpid system. The three formed an electric chain.

"Minister!" whispered little Pearl.

"What wouldst thou say, child?" asked Mr. Dimmesdale.

"Wilt thou stand here with mother and me, to-morrow noontide?" inquired Pearl.

"Nay; not so, my little Pearl," answered the minister; for, with the new energy of the moment, all the dread of public exposure, that had so long been the anguish of his life, had returned upon him; and he was already trembling at the conjunction in which—with a strange joy, nevertheless—he now found himself. "Not so, my child. I shall, indeed, stand with thy mother and thee one other day, but not to-morrow."

Pearl laughed, and attempted to pull away her hand. But the minister held it fast.

"A moment longer, my child!" said he.

"But wilt thou promise," asked Pearl, "to take my hand, and mother's hand, to-morrow noontide?"

"Not then, Pearl," said the minister, "but another time."

"And what other time?" persisted the child.

"At the great judgment day," whispered the minister,—and, strangely enough, the sense that he was a professional teacher of the truth impelled him to answer the child so. "Then, and there, before the judgment-seat, thy mother, and thou, and I, must stand together. But the daylight of this world shall not see our meeting!"

Pearl laughed again.

But, before Mr. Dimmesdale had done speaking, a light gleamed far and wide over all the muffled sky. It was doubtless caused by one of those meteors, which the night-watcher may so often observe burning out to waste, in the vacant regions of the atmosphere. So powerful was its radiance, that it thoroughly illuminated the dense medium of cloud betwixt the sky and earth. The great vault brightened, like the dome of an immense lamp. It showed the familiar scene of the street, with the distinctness of mid-day, but also with the awfulness that is always imparted to familiar objects by an unaccustomed light. The wooden houses, with their jutting stories and quaint gable-peaks; the door-steps and thresholds, with the early grass springing up about them; the garden-plots, black with freshly turned earth; the wheel-track, little worn, and, even in the market-place, margined with green on either side;—all were visible, but with a singularity of aspect that seemed to give another moral interpretation to the things of this world than they had ever borne before. And there stood the minister, with his hand over his heart; and Hester Prynne, with the embroidered letter glimmering on her bosom; and little Pearl, herself a symbol, and the connecting link between those two. They stood in the noon of that strange and solemn splendor, as if it were the light that is to reveal all secrets, and the daybreak that shall unite all who belong to one another.

There was witchcraft in little Pearl's eyes; and her face, as she glanced upward at the minister, wore that naughty smile which made its expression frequently so elvish. She withdrew her hand from Mr. Dimmesdale's and pointed across the street. But he clasped both his hands over his breast, and cast his eyes towards the zenith.

Nothing was more common, in those days, than to interpret all meteoric appearances, and other natural phenomena, that occurred with less regularity than the rise and set of sun and moon, as so many revelations from a supernatural source. Thus, a blazing spear, a sword of flame, a bow, or a sheaf of arrows, seen in the midnight sky, prefigured Indian warfare. Pestilence was known to have been foreboded by a shower of crimson light. We doubt whether any marked event, for good or evil, ever befell New England, from its settlement down to Revolutionary times, of which the inhabitants had not been previously warned by some spectacle of this nature. Not seldom, it had been seen by multitudes. Oftener, however, its credibility rested on the faith of some lonely eye-witness, who beheld the wonder through the colored, magnifying, and distorting medium of his imagination, and shaped it more distinctly in his after-thought. It was, indeed, a majestic idea, that the destiny of nations should be revealed, in these awful hieroglyphics, on the cope of heaven. A scroll so wide might not be deemed too expansive for Providence to write a people's doom upon. The belief was a favorite one with our forefathers, as betokening that their infant commonwealth was under a celestial guardianship of peculiar intimacy and strictness. But what shall we say, when an individual discovers a revelation, addressed to himself alone, on the same vast sheet of record! In such a case, it could only be the symptom of a highly disordered mental state, when a man, rendered morbidly self-contemplative by long, intense, and secret pain, had extended his egotism over the whole expanse of nature, until the firmament itself should appear no more than a fitting page for his soul's history and fate!

We impute it, therefore, solely to the disease in his own eye and heart, that the minister, looking upward to the zenith, beheld there the appearance of an immense letter,—the letter A,—marked out in lines of dull red light. Not but the meteor may have shown itself at that point, burning duskily through a veil of cloud; but with no such shape as his guilty imagination gave it; or, at least, with so little definiteness, that another's guilt might have seen another symbol in it.

There was a singular circumstance that characterized Mr. Dimmesdale's psychological state, at this moment. All the time that he gazed upward to the zenith, he was, nevertheless, perfectly aware that little Pearl was pointing her finger towards old Roger Chillingworth, who stood at no great distance from the scaffold. The minister appeared to see him, with the same glance that discerned the miraculous letter. To his features, as to all other objects, the meteoric light imparted a new expression; or it might well be that the physician was not careful then, as at all other times, to hide the malevolence with which he looked upon his victim. Certainly, if the meteor kindled up the sky, and disclosed the earth, with an awfulness that admonished Hester Prynne and the clergyman of the day of judgment, then might Roger Chillingworth have passed with them for the arch-fiend, standing there with a smile and scowl, to claim his own. So vivid was the expression, or so intense the minister's perception of it, that it seemed still to remain painted on the darkness, after the meteor had vanished, with an effect as if the street and all things else were at once annihilated.

"Who is that man, Hester?" gasped Mr. Dimmesdale, overcome with terror. "I shiver at him! Dost thou know the man? I hate him, Hester!"

She remembered her oath, and was silent.

"I tell thee, my soul shivers at him!" muttered the minister again. "Who is he? Who is he? Canst thou do nothing for me? I have a nameless horror of the man!"

"Minister," said little Pearl, "I can tell thee who he is!"

"Quickly, then, child!" said the minister, bending his ear close to her lips. "Quickly!—and as low as thou canst whisper."

Pearl mumbled something into his ear, that sounded, indeed, like human language, but was only such gibberish as children may be heard amusing themselves with, by the hour together. At all events, if it involved any secret information in regard to old Roger Chillingworth, it was in a tongue unknown to the erudite clergyman, and did but increase the bewilderment of his mind. The elvish child then laughed aloud.

"Dost thou mock me now?" said the minister.

"Thou was not bold!—thou wast not true!"—answered the child. "Thou wouldst not promise to take my hand, and mother's hand, tomorrow noontide!"

"Worthy Sir," answered the physician, who had now advanced to the foot of the platform. "Pious Master Dimmesdale! can this be you? Well, well, indeed! We men of study, whose heads are in our books, have need to be straitly looked after! We dream in our waking moments, and walk in our sleep. Come, good Sir, and my dear friend, I pray you, let me lead you home!"

"How knewest thou that I was here?" asked the minister, fearfully.

"Verily, and in good faith," answered Roger Chillingworth, "I knew nothing of the matter. I had spent the better part of the night at the bedside of the worshipful Governor Winthrop, doing what my poor skill might to give him ease. He going home to a better world, I, likewise, was on my way homeward, when this strange light shone out. Come with me, I beseech you, Reverend Sir; else you will be poorly able to do Sabbath duty to-morrow. Aha! see now, how they trouble the brain,—these books!—these books! You should study less, good Sir, and take a little pastime; or these night-whimseys will grow upon you."

"I will go home with you," said Mr. Dimmesdale.

With a chill despondency, like one awaking, all nerveless, from an ugly dream, he yielded himself to the physician, and was led away.

The next day, however, being the Sabbath, he preached a discourse

which was held to be the richest and most powerful, and the most replete with heavenly influences, that had ever proceeded from his lips.
Souls, it is said, more souls than one, were brought to the truth by the
efficacy of that sermon, and vowed within themselves to cherish a holy
gratitude towards Mr. Dimmesdale throughout the long hereafter. But,
as he came down the pulpit steps, the gray-bearded sexton met him,
holding up a black glove, which the minister recognized as his own.

"It was found," said the sexton, "this morning, on the scaffold where
evil-doers are set up to public shame. Satan dropped it there, I take it,
intending a scurrilous jest against your reverence. But, indeed, he was
blind and foolish, as he ever and always is. A pure hand needs no glove
to cover it!"

"Thank you, my good friend," said the minister, gravely, but startled
at heart; for, so confused was his remembrance, that he had almost
brought himself to look at the events of the past night as visionary.
"Yes, it seems to be my glove, indeed!"

"And, since Satan saw fit to steal it, your reverence must needs handle him without gloves, henceforward," remarked the old sexton,
grimly smiling. "But did your reverence hear of the portent that was
seen last night?—a great red letter in the sky,—the letter A, which we
interpret to stand for Angel. For, as our good Governor Winthrop was
made an angel this past night, it was doubtless held fit that there
should be some notice thereof!"

"No," answered the minister, "I had not heard of it."

XIII. Another View of Hester

In her late singular interview with Mr. Dimmesdale, Hester Prynne
was shocked at the condition to which she found the clergyman reduced. His nerve seemed absolutely destroyed. His moral force was
abased into more than childish weakness. It grovelled helpless on the
ground, even while his intellectual faculties retained their pristine
strength, or had perhaps acquired a morbid energy, which disease only
could have given them. With her knowledge of a train of circumstances hidden from all others, she could readily infer that, besides
the legitimate action of his own conscience, a terrible machinery had
been brought to bear, and was still operating, on Mr. Dimmesdale's
well-being and repose. Knowing what this poor, fallen man had once
been, her whole soul was moved by the shuddering terror with which
he had appealed to her,—the outcast woman,—for support against his
instinctively discovered enemy. She decided, moreover, that he had a
right to her utmost aid. Little accustomed, in her long seclusion from
society, to measure her ideas of right and wrong by any standard external to herself, Hester saw—or seemed to see—that there lay a responsibility upon her, in reference to the clergyman, which she owed to no
other, nor to the whole world besides. The links that united her to the
rest of human kind—links of flowers, or silk, or gold, or whatever the
material—had all been broken. Here was the iron link of mutual

crime, which neither he nor she could break. Like all other ties, it brought along with it its obligations.

Hester Prynne did not now occupy precisely the same position in which we beheld her during the earlier periods of her ignominy. Years had come and gone. Pearl was now seven years old. Her mother, with the scarlet letter on her breast, glittering in its fantastic embroidery, had long been a familiar object to the townspeople. As is apt to be the case when a person stands out in any prominence before the community, and, at the same time, interferes neither with public nor individual interests and convenience, a species of general regard had ultimately grown up in reference to Hester Prynne. It is to the credit of human nature, that, except where its selfishness is brought into play, it loves more readily than it hates. Hatred, by a gradual and quiet process, will even be transformed to love, unless the change be impeded by a continually new irritation of the original feeling of hostility. In this matter of Hester Prynne, there was neither irritation nor irksomeness. She never battled with the public, but submitted, uncomplainingly, to its worst usage; she made no claim upon it, in requital for what she suffered; she did not weigh upon its sympathies. Then, also, the blameless purity of her life during all these years in which she had been set apart to infamy, was reckoned largely in her favor. With nothing now to lose, in the sight of mankind, and with no hope, and seemingly no wish, of gaining anything, it could only be a genuine regard for virtue that had brought back the poor wanderer to its paths.

It was perceived, too, that while Hester never put forward even the humblest title to share in the world's privileges,—further than to breathe the common air, and earn daily bread for little Pearl and herself by the faithful labor of her hands,—she was quick to acknowledge her sisterhood with the race of man, whenever benefits were to be conferred. None so ready as she to give of her little substance to every demand of poverty; even though the bitter-hearted pauper threw back a gibe in requital of the food brought regularly to his door, or the garments wrought for him by the fingers that could have embroidered a monarch's robe. None so self-devoted as Hester, when pestilence stalked through the town. In all seasons of calamity, indeed, whether general or of individuals, the outcast of society at once found her place. She came, not as a guest, but as a rightful inmate, into the household that was darkened by trouble; as if its gloomy twilight were a medium in which she was entitled to hold intercourse with her fellow-creatures. There glimmered the embroidered letter, with comfort in its unearthly ray. Elsewhere the token of sin, it was the taper of the sick-chamber. It had even thrown its gleam, in the sufferer's hard extremity, across the verge of time. It had shown him where to set his foot, while the light of earth was fast becoming dim, and ere the light of futurity could reach him. In such emergencies, Hester's nature showed itself warm and rich; a well-spring of human tenderness, unfailing to every real demand, and inexhaustible by the largest. Her breast, with its badge of shame, was but the softer pillow for the head that needed one. She was self-ordained a Sister of Mercy; or, we may rather say, the world's heavy hand had so ordained her, when neither the world nor she looked forward to this result. The letter was the symbol of her calling. Such helpfulness was found in her,—so much power to do, and power to sympathize,—that many people refused to interpret the scarlet A by its original signification. They said that it meant Able; so strong was Hester Prynne, with a woman's strength.

It was only the darkened house that could contain her. When sunshine came again, she was not there. Her shadow had faded across the threshold. The helpful inmate had departed, without one backward glance to gather up the meed of gratitude, if any were in the hearts of those whom she had served so zealously. Meeting them in the street, she never raised her head to receive their greeting. If they were resolute to accost her, she laid her finger on the scarlet letter, and passed on. This might be pride, but was so like humility, that it produced all the softening influence of the latter quality on the public mind. The public is despotic in its temper; it is capable of denying common justice, when too strenuously demanded as a right; but quite as frequently it awards more than justice, when the appeal is made, as despots love to have it made, entirely to its generosity. Interpreting Hester Prynne's deportment as an appeal of this nature, society was inclined to show its former victim a more benign countenance than she cared to be favored with, or, perchance, than she deserved.

The rulers, and the wise and learned men of the community, were longer in acknowledging the influence of Hester's good qualities than the people. The prejudices which they shared in common with the latter were fortified in themselves by an iron framework of reasoning, that made it a far tougher labor to expel them. Day by day, nevertheless, their sour and rigid wrinkles were relaxing into something which, in the due course of years, might grow to be an expression of almost benevolence. Thus it was with the men of rank, on whom their eminent position imposed the guardianship of the public morals. Individuals in private life, meanwhile, had quite forgiven Hester Prynne for her frailty; nay, more, they had begun to look upon the scarlet letter as the token, not of that one sin, for which she had borne so long and dreary a penance, but of her many good deeds since. "Do you see that woman with the embroidered badge?" they would say to strangers. "It is our Hester,—the town's own Hester,—who is so kind to the poor, so helpful to the sick, so comfortable to the afflicted!" Then, it is true, the propensity of human nature to tell the very worst of itself, when embodied in the person of another, would constrain them to whisper the black scandal of bygone years. It was none the less a fact, however, that, in the eyes of the very men who spoke thus, the scarlet letter had the effect of the cross on a nun's bosom. It imparted to the wearer a kind of sacredness, which enabled her to walk securely amid all peril. Had she fallen among thieves, it would have kept her safe. It was reported, and believed by many, that an Indian had drawn his arrow against the badge, and that the missile struck it, but fell harmless to the ground.

The effect of the symbol—or, rather, of the position in respect to society that was indicated by it—on the mind of Hester Prynne herself, was powerful and peculiar. All the light and graceful foliage of her character had been withered up by this red-hot brand, and had long ago fallen away, leaving a bare and harsh outline, which might have been repulsive, had she possessed friends or companions to be repelled by it. Even the attractiveness of her person had undergone a similar change. It might be partly owing to the studied austerity of her dress, and partly to the lack of demonstration in her manners. It was a sad transformation, too, that her rich and luxuriant hair had either been cut off, or was so completely hidden by a cap, that not a shining lock of it ever once gushed into the sunshine. It was due in part to all these causes, but still more to something else, that there seemed to be no longer anything in Hester's face for Love to dwell upon; nothing in Hester's form, though majestic and statue-like, that Passion would ever dream of clasping in its embrace; nothing in Hester's bosom, to make it ever again the pillow of Affection. Some attribute had departed from her, the permanence of which had been essential to keep her a woman. Such is frequently the fate, and such the stern development, of the feminine character and person, when the woman has encountered, and lived through, an experience of peculiar severity. If she be all tenderness, she will die. If she survive, the tenderness will either be crushed out of her, or—and the outward semblance is the same—crushed so deeply into her heart that it can never show itself more. The latter is perhaps the truest theory. She who has once been woman, and ceased to be so, might at any moment become a woman again, if there were only the magic touch to effect the transfiguration. We shall see whether Hester Prynne were ever afterwards so touched, and so transfigured.

Much of the marble coldness of Hester's impression was to be attributed to the circumstance, that her life had turned, in a great measure, from passion and feeling, to thought. Standing alone in the world,—alone, as to any dependence on society, and with little Pearl to be guided and protected,—alone, and hopeless of retrieving her position, even had she not scorned to consider it desirable,—she cast away the fragments of a broken chain. The world's law was no law for her mind. It was an age in which the human intellect, newly emancipated, had taken a more active and a wider range than for many centuries before. Men of the sword had overthrown nobles and kings. Men bolder than these had overthrown and rearranged—not actually, but within the sphere of theory, which was their most real abode—the whole system of ancient prejudice, wherewith was linked much of ancient principle. Hester Prynne imbibed this spirit. She assumed a freedom of speculation, then common enough on the other side of the Atlantic, but which our forefathers, had they known it, would have held to be a deadlier crime than that stigmatized by the scarlet letter.[1] In her lone-

---

1. Hawthorne is probably referring to the English Civil War, whose dates parallel those of the novel. By May 1649, King Charles I had been overthrown and beheaded (in January 1649). Hawthorne invites us to see Hester as an American version of such British revolutionaries as Oliver Cromwell.

some cottage, by the sea-shore, thoughts visited her, such as dared to enter no other dwelling in New England; shadowy guests, that would have been as perilous as demons to their entertainer, could they have been seen so much as knocking at her door.

It is remarkable, that persons who speculate the most boldly often conform with the most perfect quietude to the external regulations of society. The thought suffices them, without investing itself in the flesh and blood of action. So it seemed to be with Hester. Yet, had little Pearl never come to her from the spiritual world, it might have been far otherwise. Then, she might have come down to us in history, hand in hand with Ann Hutchinson, as the foundress of a religious sect. She might, in one of her phases, have been a prophetess. She might, and not improbably would, have suffered death from the stern tribunals of the period, for attempting to undermine the foundations of the Puritan establishment. But, in the education of her child, the mother's enthusiasm of thought had something to wreak itself upon. Providence, in the person of this little girl, had assigned to Hester's charge the germ and blossom of womanhood, to be cherished and developed amid a host of difficulties. Everything was against her. The world was hostile. The child's own nature had something wrong in it, which continually betokened that she had been born amiss,—the effluence of her mother's lawless passion,—and often impelled Hester to ask, in bitterness of heart, whether it were for ill or good that the poor little creature had been born at all.

Indeed, the same dark question often rose into her mind, with reference to the whole race of womanhood. Was existence worth accepting, even to the happiest among them? As concerned her own individual existence, she had long ago decided in the negative, and dismissed the point as settled. A tendency to speculation, though it may keep woman quiet, as it does man, yet makes her sad. She discerns, it may be, such a hopeless task before her. As a first step, the whole system of society is to be torn down, and built up anew. Then, the very nature of the opposite sex, or its long hereditary habit, which has become like nature, is to be essentially modified, before woman can be allowed to assume what seems a fair and suitable position. Finally, all other difficulties being obviated, woman cannot take advantage of these preliminary reforms, until she herself shall have undergone a still mightier change; in which, perhaps, the ethereal essence, wherein she has her truest life, will be found to have evaporated. A woman never overcomes these problems by any exercise of thought. They are not to be solved, or only in one way. If her heart chance to come uppermost, they vanish. Thus, Hester Prynne, whose heart had lost its regular and healthy throb, wandered without a clew in the dark labyrinth of mind; now turned aside by an insurmountable precipice; now starting back from a deep chasm. There was wild and ghastly scenery all around her, and a home and comfort nowhere. At times, a fearful doubt strove to possess her soul, whether it were not better to send Pearl at once to heaven, and go herself to such futurity as Eternal Justice should provide.

The scarlet letter had not done its office.

Now, however, her interview with the Reverend Mr. Dimmesdale, on the night of his vigil, had given her a new theme of reflection, and held up to her an object that appeared worthy of any exertion and sacrifice for its attainment. She had witnessed the intense misery beneath which the minister struggled, or, to speak more accurately, had ceased to struggle. She saw that he stood on the verge of lunacy, if he had not already stepped across it. It was impossible to doubt, that, whatever painful efficacy there might be in the secret sting of remorse, a deadlier venom had been infused into it by the hand that proffered relief. A secret enemy had been continually by his side, under the semblance of a friend and helper, and had availed himself of the opportunities thus afforded for tampering with the delicate springs of Mr. Dimmesdale's nature. Hester could not but ask herself, whether there had not originally been a defect of truth, courage and loyalty, on her own part, in allowing the minister to be thrown into a position where so much evil was to be foreboded, and nothing auspicious to be hoped. Her only justification lay in the fact, that she had been able to discern no method of rescuing him from a blacker ruin than had overwhelmed herself, except by acquiescing in Roger Chillingworth's scheme of disguise. Under that impulse, she had made her choice, and had chosen, as it now appeared, the more wretched alternative of the two. She determined to redeem her error, so far as it might yet be possible. Strengthened by years of hard and solemn trial, she felt herself no longer so inadequate to cope with Roger Chillingworth as on that night, abased by sin, and half maddened by the ignominy that was still new, when they had talked together in the prison-chamber. She had climbed her way, since then, to a higher point. The old man, on the other hand, had brought himself nearer to her level, or perhaps below it, by the revenge which he had stooped for.

In fine, Hester Prynne resolved to meet her former husband, and do what might be in her power for the rescue of the victim on whom he had so evidently set his gripe. The occasion was not long to seek. One afternoon, walking with Pearl in a retired part of the peninsula, she beheld the old physician, with a basket on one arm, and a staff in the other hand, stooping along the ground, in quest of roots and herbs to concoct his medicines withal.

XIV. Hester and the Physician

Hester bade little Pearl run down to the margin of the water, and play with the shells and tangled seaweed, until she should have talked awhile with yonder gatherer of herbs. So the child flew away like a bird, and, making bare her small white feet, went pattering along the moist margin of the sea. Here and there she came to a full stop, and peeped curiously into a pool, left by the retiring tide as a mirror for Pearl to see her face in. Forth peeped at her, out of the pool, with dark, glistening curls around her head, and an elf-smile in her eyes, the image of a little maid, whom Pearl, having no other playmate, invited to take her hand, and run a race with her. But the visionary little maid, on her part, beckoned likewise, as if to say,—"This is a better place! Come thou into the pool!" And Pearl, stepping in, mid-leg deep, beheld her own white feet at the bottom; while, out of a still lower depth, came the gleam of a kind of fragmentary smile, floating to and fro in the agitated water.

Meanwhile, her mother had accosted the physician.

"I would speak a word with you," said she,—"a word that concerns us much."

"Aha! and is it Mistress Hester that has a word for old Roger Chillingworth?" answered he, raising himself from his stooping posture. "With all my heart! Why, Mistress, I hear good tidings of you, on all hands! No longer ago than yester-eve, a magistrate, a wise and godly man, was discoursing of your affairs, Mistress Hester, and whispered me that there had been question concerning you in the council. It was debated whether or no, with safety to the common weal, yonder scarlet letter might be taken off your bosom. On my life, Hester, I made my entreaty to the worshipful magistrate that it might be done forthwith!"

"It lies not in the pleasure of the magistrates to take off this badge," calmly replied Hester. "Were I worthy to be quit of it, it would fall away of its own nature, or be transformed into something that should speak a different purport."

"Nay, then, wear it, if it suit you better," rejoined he. "A woman must needs follow her own fancy, touching the adornment of her person. The letter is gayly embroidered, and shows right bravely on your bosom!"

All this while, Hester had been looking steadily at the old man, and was shocked, as well as wonder-smitten, to discern what a change had been wrought upon him within the past seven years. It was not so much that he had grown older; for though the traces of advancing life were visible, he bore his age well, and seemed to retain a wiry vigor and alertness. But the former aspect of an intellectual and studious man, calm and quiet, which was what she best remembered in him, had altogether vanished, and been succeeded by an eager, searching, almost fierce, yet carefully guarded look. It seemed to be his wish and purpose to mask this expression with a smile; but the latter played him false, and flickered over his visage so derisively, that the spectator could see his blackness all the better for it. Ever and anon, too, there came a glare of red light out of his eyes; as if the old man's soul were on fire, and kept on smouldering duskily within his breast, until, by some casual puff of passion, it was blown into a momentary flame. This he repressed, as speedily as possible, and strove to look as if nothing of the kind had happened.

In a word, old Roger Chillingworth was a striking evidence of man's faculty of transforming himself into a devil, if he will only, for a reasonable space of time, undertake a devil's office. This unhappy person had effected such a transformation, by devoting himself, for seven years, to the constant analysis of a heart full of torture, and deriving his enjoyment thence, and adding fuel to those fiery tortures which he analyzed and gloated over.

The scarlet letter burned on Hester Prynne's bosom. Here was another ruin, the responsibility of which came partly home to her.

"What see you in my face," asked the physician, "that you look at it so earnestly?"

"Something that would make me weep, if there were any tears bitter enough for it," answered she. "But let it pass! It is of yonder miserable man that I would speak."

"And what of him?" cried Roger Chillingworth, eagerly, as if he loved the topic, and were glad of an opportunity to discuss it with the only person of whom he could make a confidant. "Not to hide the truth, Mistress Hester, my thoughts happen just now to be busy with the gentleman. So speak freely; and I will make answer."

"When we last spake together," said Hester, "now seven years ago, it was your pleasure to extort a promise of secrecy, as touching the former relation betwixt yourself and me. As the life and good fame of yonder man were in your hands, there seemed no choice to me, save to be silent, in accordance with your behest. Yet it was not without heavy misgivings that I thus bound myself; for, having cast off all duty towards other human beings, there remained a duty towards him; and something whispered me that I was betraying it, in pledging myself to keep your counsel. Since that day, no man is so near to him as you. You tread behind his every footstep. You are beside him, sleeping and waking. You search his thoughts. You burrow and rankle in his heart! Your clutch is on his life, and you cause him to die daily a living death; and still he knows you not. In permitting this, I have surely acted a false part by the only man to whom the power was left me to be true!"

"What choice had you?" asked Roger Chillingworth. "My finger, pointed at this man, would have hurled him from his pulpit into a dungeon,—thence, peradventure, to the gallows!"

"It had been better so!" said Hester Prynne.

"What evil have I done the man?" asked Roger Chillingworth again. "I tell thee, Hester Prynne, the richest fee that ever physician earned from monarch could not have bought such care as I have wasted on this miserable priest! But for my aid, his life would have burned away in torments, within the first two years after the perpetration of his crime and thine. For, Hester, his spirit lacked the strength that could have borne up, as thine has, beneath a burden like thy scarlet letter. O, I could reveal a goodly secret! But enough! What art can do, I have exhausted on him. That he now breathes, and creeps about on earth, is owing all to me!"

"Better he had died at once!" said Hester Prynne.

"Yea, woman, thou sayest truly!" cried old Roger Chillingworth, letting the lurid fire of his heart blaze out before her eyes. "Better had he died at once! Never did mortal suffer what this man has suffered. And all, all, in the sight of his worst enemy! He has been conscious of me. He has felt an influence dwelling always upon him like a curse. He knew, by some spiritual sense,—for the Creator never made another being so sensitive as this,—he knew that no friendly hand was pulling at his heart-strings, and that an eye was looking curiously into him, which sought only evil, and found it. But he knew not that the eye and hand were mine! With the superstition common to his brotherhood, he fancied himself given over to a fiend, to be tortured with frightful dreams, and desperate thoughts, the sting of remorse, and despair of pardon; as a foretaste of what awaits him beyond the grave. But it was the constant shadow of my presence!—the closest propinquity of the man whom he had most vilely wronged!—and who had grown to exist only by this perpetual poison of the direst revenge! Yea, indeed!—he did not err!—there was a fiend at his elbow! A mortal man, with once a human heart, has become a fiend for his especial torment!"

The unfortunate physician, while uttering these words, lifted his hands with a look of horror, as if he had beheld some frightful shape, which he could not recognize, usurping the place of his own image in a glass. It was one of those moments—which sometimes occur only at the interval of years—when a man's moral aspect is faithfully revealed to his mind's eye. Not improbably, he had never before viewed himself as he did now.

"Hast thou not tortured him enough?" said Hester, noticing the old man's look. "Has he not paid thee all?"

"No!—no!—He has but increased the debt!" answered the physician; and as he proceeded, his manner lost its fiercer characteristics, and subsided into gloom. "Dost thou remember me, Hester, as I was nine years agone? Even then, I was in the autumn of my days, nor was it the early autumn. But all my life had been made up of earnest, studious, thoughtful, quiet years, bestowed faithfully for the increase of mine own knowledge, and faithfully, too, though this latter object was but casual to the other,—faithfully for the advancement of human welfare. No life had been more peaceful and innocent than mine; few lives so rich with benefits conferred. Dost thou remember me? Was I not, though you might deem me cold, nevertheless a man thoughtful for others, craving little for himself,—kind, true, just, and of constant, if not warm affections? Was I not all this?"

"All this, and more," said Hester.

"And what am I now?" demanded he, looking into her face, and permitting the whole evil within him to be written on his features. "I have already told thee what I am! A fiend! Who made me so?"

"It was myself!" cried Hester, shuddering. "It was I, not less than he. Why hast thou not avenged thyself on me?"

"I have left thee to the scarlet letter," replied Roger Chillingworth. "If that have not avenged me, I can do no more!"

He laid his finger on it, with a smile.

"It has avenged thee!" answered Hester Prynne.

"I judged no less," said the physician. "And now, what wouldst thou with me touching this man?"

"I must reveal the secret," answered Hester, firmly. "He must discern thee in thy true character. What may be the result, I know not.

But this long debt of confidence, due from me to him, whose bane and ruin I have been, shall at length be paid. So far as concerns the over-throw or preservation of his fair fame and his earthly state, and per-chance his life, he is in thy hands. Nor do I,—whom the scarlet letter has disciplined to truth, though it be the truth of red-hot iron, enter-ing into the soul,—nor do I perceive such advantage in his living any longer a life of ghastly emptiness, that I shall stoop to implore thy mercy. Do with him as thou wilt! There is no good for him,—no good for me,—no good for thee! There is no good for little Pearl! There is no path to guide us out of this dismal maze!"

"Woman, I could well-nigh pity thee!" said Roger Chillingworth, un-able to restrain a thrill of admiration too; for there was a quality al-most majestic in the despair which she expressed. "Thou hadst great elements. Peradventure, hadst thou met earlier with a better love than mine, this evil had not been. I pity thee, for the good that has been wasted in thy nature!"

"And I thee," answered Hester Prynne, "for the hatred that has transformed a wise and just man to a fiend! Wilt thou yet purge it out of thee, and be once more human? If not for his sake, then doubly for thine own! Forgive, and leave his further retribution to the Power that claims it! I said, but now, that there could be no good event for him, or thee, or me, who are here wandering together in this gloomy maze of evil, and stumbling, at every step, over the guilt wherewith we have strewn our path. It is not so! There might be good for thee, and thee alone, since thou hast been deeply wronged, and hast it at thy will to pardon. Wilt thou give up that only privilege? Wilt thou reject that priceless benefit?"

"Peace, Hester, peace!" replied the old man, with gloomy sternness. "It is not granted me to pardon. I have no such power as thou tellest me of. My old faith, long forgotten, comes back to me, and explains all that we do, and all we suffer. By thy first step awry, thou didst plant the germ of evil; but since that moment, it has all been a dark neces-sity. Ye that have wronged me are not sinful, save in a kind of typical il-lusion; neither am I fiend-like, who have snatched a fiend's office from his hands. It is our fate. Let the black flower blossom as it may! Now go thy ways, and deal as thou wilt with yonder man."

He waived his hand, and betook himself again to his employment of gathering herbs.

XV. Hester and Pearl

So Roger Chillingworth—a deformed old figure, with a face that haunted men's memories longer than they liked—took leave of Hester Prynne, and went stooping away along the earth. He gathered here and there an herb, or grubbed up a root, and put it into the basket on his arm. His gray beard almost touched the ground, as he crept on-ward. Hester gazed after him a little while, looking with a half fantas-tic curiosity to see whether the tender grass of early spring would not be blighted beneath him, and show the wavering track of his footsteps, sere and brown, across its cheerful verdure. She wondered what sort of herbs they were, which the old man was so sedulous to gather. Would not the earth, quickened to an evil purpose by the sympathy of his eye, greet him with poisonous shrubs, of species hitherto unknown, that would start up under his fingers? Or might it suffice him, that every wholesome growth should be converted into something deleterious and malignant at his touch? Did the sun, which shone so brightly everywhere else, really fall upon him? Or was there, as it rather seemed, a circle of ominous shadow moving along with his deformity, whichever way he turned himself? And whither was he now going? Would he not suddenly sink into the earth, leaving a barren and blasted spot, where, in due course of time, would be seen deadly nightshade, dogwood, henbane,[1] and whatever else of vegetable wickedness the climate could produce, all flourishing with hideous luxuriance? Or would he spread bat's wings and flee away, looking so much the uglier, the higher he rose towards heaven?

"Be it sin or no," said Hester Prynne, bitterly, as she still gazed after him, "I hate the man!"

She upbraided herself for the sentiment, but could not overcome or lessen it. Attempting to do so, she thought of those long-past days, in a distant land, when he used to emerge at eventide from the seclusion of his study, and sit down in the fire-light of their home, and in the light of her nuptial smile. He needed to bask himself in that smile, he said, in order that the chill of so many lonely hours among his books might be taken off the scholar's heart. Such scenes had once appeared not otherwise than happy, but now, as viewed through the dismal medium of her subsequent life, they classed themselves among her ugliest remembrances. She marvelled how such scenes could have been! She marvelled how she could ever have been wrought upon to marry him! She deemed it her crime most to be repented of, that she had ever endured, and reciprocated, the lukewarm grasp of his hand, and had suffered the smile of her lips and eyes to mingle and melt into his own. And it seemed a fouler offence committed by Roger Chillingworth, than any which had since been done him, that, in the time when her heart knew no better, he had persuaded her to fancy herself happy by his side.

"Yes, I hate him!" repeated Hester, more bitterly than before. "He betrayed me! He has done me worse wrong than I did him!"

Let men tremble to win the hand of woman, unless they win along with it the utmost passion of her heart! Else it may be their miserable fortune, as it was Roger Chillingworth's, when some mightier touch than their own may have awakened all her sensibilities, to be reproached even for the calm content, the marble image of happiness, which they will have imposed upon her as the warm reality. But Hester ought long ago to have done with this injustice. What did it be-

---

1. The poison (Hyoscyamus niger) Claudius poured into King Hamlet's ear in Shakespeare's play. *Nightshade* (Atropa belladonna): contains atropine.

token? Had seven long years, under the torture of the scarlet letter, inflicted so much of misery, and wrought out no repentance?

The emotions of that brief space, while she stood gazing after the crooked figure of old Roger Chillingworth, threw a dark light on Hester's state of mind, revealing much that she might not otherwise have acknowledged to herself.

He being gone, she summoned back her child.

"Pearl! Little Pearl! Where are you?"

Pearl, whose activity of spirit never flagged, had been at no loss for amusement while her mother talked with the old gatherer of herbs. At first, as already told, she had flirted fancifully with her own image in a pool of water, beckoning the phantom forth, and—as it declined to venture—seeking a passage for herself into its sphere of impalpable earth and unattainable sky. Soon finding, however, that either she or the image was unreal, she turned elsewhere for better pastime. She made little boats out of birch-bark, and freighted them with snail-shells, and sent out more ventures on the mighty deep than any merchant in New England; but the larger part of them foundered near the shore. She seized a live horse-shoe by the tail, and made prize of several five-fingers,[2] and laid out a jelly-fish to melt in the warm sun. Then she took up the white foam, that streaked the line of the advancing tide, and threw it upon the breeze, scampering after it, with winged footsteps, to catch the great snow-flakes ere they fell. Perceiving a flock of beach-birds, that fed and fluttered along the shore, the naughty child picked up her apron full of pebbles, and, creeping from rock to rock after these small sea-fowl, displayed remarkable dexterity in pelting them. One little gray bird, with a white breast, Pearl was almost sure, had been hit by a pebble, and fluttered away with a broken wing. But then the elf-child sighed, and gave up her sport; because it grieved her to have done harm to a little being that was as wild as the sea-breeze, or as wild as Pearl herself.

Her final employment was to gather sea-weed, of various kinds, and make herself a scarf, or mantle, and a head-dress, and thus assume the aspect of a little mermaid. She inherited her mother's gift for devising drapery and costume. As the last touch to her mermaid's garb, Pearl took some eel-grass, and imitated, as best she could, on her own bosom, the decoration with which she was so familiar on her mother's. A letter,—the letter A,—but freshly green, instead of scarlet! The child bent her chin upon her breast, and contemplated this device with strange interest; even as if the one only thing for which she had been sent into the world was to make out its hidden import.

"I wonder if mother will ask me what it means?" thought Pearl.

Just then, she heard her mother's voice, and flitting along as lightly as one of the little sea-birds, appeared before Hester Prynne, dancing, laughing, and pointing her finger to the ornament upon her bosom.

"My little Pearl," said Hester, after a moment's silence, "the green letter, and on thy childish bosom, has no purport. But dost thou know,

2. Starfish. *Horse-shoe*: horseshoe crab.

my child, what this letter means which thy mother is doomed to wear?"

"Yes, mother," said the child. "It is the great letter A. Thou hast taught me in the horn-book."[3]

Hester looked steadily into her little face; but, though there was that singular expression which she had so often remarked in her black eyes, she could not satisfy herself whether Pearl really attached any meaning to the symbol. She felt a morbid desire to ascertain the point.

"Dost thou know, child, wherefore thy mother wears this letter?"

"Truly do I!" answered Pearl, looking brightly into her mother's face. "It is for the same reason that the minister keeps his hand over his heart!"

"And what reason is that?" asked Hester, half smiling at the absurd incongruity of the child's observation; but, on second thoughts, turning pale. "What has the letter to do with any heart, save mine?"

"Nay, mother, I have told all I know," said Pearl, more seriously than she was wont to speak. "Ask yonder old man whom thou hast been talking with! It may be he can tell. But in good earnest now, mother dear, what does this scarlet letter mean?—and why dost thou wear it on thy bosom?—and why does the minister keep his hand over his heart?"

She took her mother's hand in both her own, and gazed into her eyes with an earnestness that was seldom seen in her wild and capricious character. The thought occurred to Hester, that the child might really be seeking to approach her with child-like confidence, and doing what she could, and as intelligently as she knew how, to establish a meeting-point of sympathy. It showed Pearl in an unwonted aspect. Heretofore, the mother, while loving her child with the intensity of a sole affection, had schooled herself to hope for little other return than the waywardness of an April breeze; which spends its time in airy sport, and has its gusts of inexplicable passion, and is petulant in its best of moods, and chills oftener than caresses you, when you take it to your bosom; in requital of which misdemeanors, it will sometimes, of its own vague purpose, kiss your cheek with a kind of doubtful tenderness, and play gently with your hair, and then begone about its other idle business, leaving a dreamy pleasure at your heart. And this, moreover, was a mother's estimate of the child's disposition. Any other observer might have seen few but unamiable traits, and have given them a far darker coloring. But now the idea came strongly into Hester's mind, that Pearl, with her remarkable precocity and acuteness, might already have approached the age when she could be made a friend, and intrusted with as much of her mother's sorrows as could be imparted, without irreverence either to the parent or the child. In the little chaos of Pearl's character, there might be seen emerging—and could have been, from the very first—the steadfast principles of an unflinching courage,—an uncontrollable will,—a sturdy pride, which might be disciplined into self-respect,—and a bitter scorn of many things, which, when examined, might be found to have the taint of

---

3. An early reader made by gluing a piece of parchment to a board and covering it with a piece of transparent horn.

falsehood in them. She possessed affections, too, though hitherto acrid and disagreeable, as are the richest flavors of unripe fruit. With all these sterling attributes, thought Hester, the evil which she inherited from her mother must be great indeed, if a noble woman do not grow out of this elfish child.

Pearl's inevitable tendency to hover about the enigma of the scarlet letter seemed an innate quality of her being. From the earliest epoch of her conscious life, she had entered upon this as her appointed mission. Hester had often fancied that Providence had a design of justice and retribution, in endowing the child with this marked propensity; but never, until now, had she bethought herself to ask, whether, linked with that design, there might not likewise be a purpose of mercy and beneficence. If little Pearl were entertained with faith and trust, as a spirit messenger no less than an earthly child, might it not be her errand to soothe away the sorrow that lay cold in her mother's heart, and converted it into a tomb?—and to help her to overcome the passion, once so wild, and even yet neither dead nor asleep, but only imprisoned within the same tomb-like heart?

Such were some of the thoughts that now stirred in Hester's mind, with as much vivacity of impression as if they had actually been whispered into her ear. And there was little Pearl, all this while, holding her mother's hand in both her own, and turning her face upward, while she put these searching questions, once, and again, and still a third time.

"What does the letter mean, mother?—and why dost thou wear it?—and why does the minister keep his hand over his heart?"

"What shall I say?" thought Hester to herself. "No! If this be the price of the child's sympathy, I cannot pay it."

Then she spoke aloud.

"Silly Pearl," said she, "what questions are these? There are many things in this world that a child must not ask about. What know I of the minister's heart? And as for the scarlet letter, I wear it for the sake of its gold thread."

In all the seven bygone years, Hester Prynne had never before been false to the symbol on her bosom. It may be that it was the talisman of a stern and severe, but yet a guardian spirit, who now forsook her; as recognizing that, in spite of his strict watch over her heart, some new evil had crept into it, or some old one had never been expelled. As for little Pearl, the earnestness soon passed out of her face.

But the child did not see fit to let the matter drop. Two or three times, as her mother and she went homeward, and as often at suppertime, and while Hester was putting her to bed, and once after she seemed to be fairly asleep, Pearl looked up, with mischief gleaming in her black eyes.

"Mother," said she, "what does the scarlet letter mean?"

And the next morning, the first indication the child gave of being awake was by popping up her head from the pillow, and making that other inquiry, which she had so unaccountably connected with her investigations about the scarlet letter:—

"Mother!—Mother!—Why does the minister keep his hand over his heart?"

"Hold thy tongue, naughty child!" answered her mother, with an asperity that she had never permitted to herself before. "Do not tease me; else I shall shut thee into the dark closet!"

XVI. A Forest Walk

Hester Prynne remained constant in her resolve to make known to Mr. Dimmesdale, at whatever risk of present pain or ulterior consequences, the true character of the man who had crept into his intimacy. For several days, however, she vainly sought an opportunity of addressing him in some of the meditative walks which she knew him to be in the habit of taking, along the shores of the peninsula, or on the wooded hills of the neighboring country. There would have been no scandal, indeed, nor peril to the holy whiteness of the clergyman's good fame, had she visited him in his own study; where many a penitent, ere now, had confessed sins of perhaps as deep a dye as the one betokened by the scarlet letter. But, partly that she dreaded the secret or undisguised interference of old Roger Chillingworth, and partly that her conscious heart imputed suspicion where none could have been felt, and partly that both the minister and she would need the whole wide world to breathe in, while they talked together,—for all these reasons, Hester never thought of meeting him in any narrower privacy than beneath the open sky.

At last, while attending in a sick-chamber, whither the Reverend Mr. Dimmesdale had been summoned to make a prayer, she learnt that he had gone, the day before, to visit the Apostle Eliot, among his Indian converts.[1] He would probably return, by a certain hour, in the afternoon of the morrow. Betimes, therefore, the next day, Hester took little Pearl,—who was necessarily the companion of all her mother's expeditions, however inconvenient her presence,—and set forth.

The road, after the two wayfarers had crossed from the peninsula to the mainland, was no other than a foot-path. It straggled onward into the mystery of the primeval forest. This hemmed it in so narrowly, and stood so black and dense on either side, and disclosed such imperfect glimpses of the sky above, that, to Hester's mind, it imaged not amiss the moral wilderness in which she had so long been wandering. The day was chill and sombre. Overhead was a gay expanse of cloud, slightly stirred, however, by a breeze; so that a gleam of flickering sunshine might now and then be seen at its solitary play along the path. This flitting cheerfulness was always at the further extremity of some long vista through the forest. The sportive sunlight—feebly sportive, at best, in the predominant pensiveness of the day and scene—withdrew

---

1. John Eliot (1604–1690), commonly called "Apostle Eliot," sought to convert Massachusetts Indians to Christianity. He translated the Bible into Algonquin beginning in the 1640s. He also testified against Anne Hutchinson at her trial. Hawthorne's *Grandfather's Chair* (1840) includes a chapter on Eliot.

itself as they came nigh, and left the spots where it had danced the drearier, because they had hoped to find them bright.

"Mother," said little Pearl, "the sunshine does not love you. It runs away and hides itself, because it is afraid of something on your bosom. Now, see! There it is, playing, a good way off. Stand you here, and let me run and catch it. I am but a child. It will not flee from me; for I wear nothing on my bosom yet!"

"Nor ever will, my child, I hope," said Hester.

"And why not, mother?" asked Pearl, stopping short, just at the beginning of her race. "Will not it come of its own accord, when I am a woman grown?"

"Run away, child," answered her mother, "and catch the sunshine! It will soon be gone."

Pearl set forth, at a great pace, and, as Hester smiled to perceive, did actually catch the sunshine, and stood laughing in the midst of it, all brightened by its splendor, and scintillating with the vivacity excited by rapid motion. The light lingered about the lonely child, as if glad of such a playmate, until her mother had drawn almost nigh enough to step into the magic circle too.

"It will go now," said Pearl, shaking her head.

"See!" answered Hester, smiling. "Now I can stretch out my hand, and grasp some of it."

As she attempted to do so, the sunshine vanished; or, to judge from the bright expression that was dancing on Pearl's features, her mother could have fancied that the child had absorbed it into herself, and would give it forth again, with a gleam about her path, as they should plunge into some gloomier shade. There was no other attribute that so much impressed her with a sense of new and untransmitted vigor in Pearl's nature, as this never-failing vivacity of spirits; she had not the disease of sadness, which almost all children, in these latter days, inherit, with the scrofula,[2] from the troubles of their ancestors. Perhaps this too was a disease, and but the reflex of the wild energy with which Hester had fought against her sorrows, before Pearl's birth. It was certainly a doubtful charm, imparting a hard, metallic lustre to the child's character. She wanted—what some people want throughout life—a grief that should deeply touch her, and thus humanize and make her capable of sympathy. But there was time enough yet for little Pearl.

"Come, my child!" said Hester, looking about her from the spot where Pearl had stood still in the sunshine. "We will sit down a little way within the wood, and rest ourselves."

"I am not aweary, mother," replied the little girl. "But you may sit down, if you will tell me a story meanwhile."

"A story, child!" said Hester. "And about what?"

"O, a story about the Black Man," answered Pearl, taking hold of her mother's gown, and looking up, half earnestly, half mischievously, into her face. "How he haunts this forest, and carries a book with him,—a big, heavy book, with iron clasps; and how this ugly Black

2. A tubercular neck infection.

Man offers his book and an iron pen to everybody that meets him here among the trees; and they are to write their names with their own blood. And then he sets his mark on their bosoms! Didst thou ever meet the Black Man, mother?"

"And who told you this story, Pearl?" asked her mother, recognizing a common superstition of the period.

"It was the old dame in the chimney-corner, at the house where you watched last night," said the child. "But she fancied me asleep while she was talking of it. She said that a thousand and a thousand people had met him here, and had written in his book, and have his mark on them. And that ugly-tempered lady, old Mistress Hibbins, was one. And, mother, the old dame said that this scarlet letter was the Black Man's mark on thee, and that it glows like a red flame when thou meetest him at midnight, here in the dark wood. Is it true, mother? And dost thou go to meet him in the night-time?"

"Didst thou ever awake, and find thy mother gone?" asked Hester.

"Not that I remember," said the child. "If thou fearest to leave me in our cottage, thou mightest take me along with thee. I would very gladly go! But, mother, tell me now! Is there such a Black Man? And didst thou ever meet him? And is this his mark?"

"Wilt thou let me be at peace, if I once tell thee?" asked her mother.

"Yes, if thou tellest me all," answered Pearl.

"Once in my life I met the Black Man!" said her mother. "This scarlet letter is his mark!"

Thus conversing, they entered sufficiently deep into the wood to secure themselves from the observation of any casual passenger along the forest track. Here they sat down on a luxuriant heap of moss; which, at some epoch of the preceding century, had been a gigantic pine, with its roots and trunk in the darksome shade, and its head aloft in the upper atmosphere. It was a little dell where they had seated themselves, with a leaf-strewn bank rising gently on either side, and a brook flowing through the midst, over a bed of fallen and drowned leaves. The trees impending over it had flung down great branches, from time to time, which choked up the current, and compelled it to form eddies and black depths at some points; while, in its swifter and livelier passages, there appeared a channel-way of pebbles, and brown, sparkling sand. Letting the eyes follow along the course of the stream, they could catch the reflected light from its water, at some short distance within the forest, but soon lost all traces of it amid the bewilderment of tree-trunks and underbrush, and here and there a huge rock covered over with gray lichens. All these giant trees and boulders of granite seemed intent on making a mystery of the course of this small brook; fearing, perhaps, that, with its never-ceasing loquacity, it should whisper tales out of the heart of the old forest whence it flowed, or mirror its revelations on the smooth surface of a pool. Continually, indeed, as it stole onward, the streamlet kept up a babble, kind, quiet, soothing, but melancholy, like the voice of a young child that was spending its infancy without playfulness, and knew not how to be merry among sad acquaintance and events of sombre hue.

"O brook! O foolish and tiresome little brook!" cried Pearl, after listening awhile to its talk. "Why art thou so sad? Pluck up a spirit, and
do not be all the time sighing and murmuring!"

But the brook, in the course of its little lifetime among the forest-
trees, had gone through so solemn an experience that it could not help
talking about it, and seemed to have nothing else to say. Pearl resembled the brook, inasmuch as the current of her life gushed from a
well-spring as mysterious, and had flowed through scenes shadowed
as heavily with gloom. But, unlike the little stream, she danced and
sparkled, and prattled airily along her course.

"What does this sad little brook say, mother?" inquired she.

"If thou hadst a sorrow of thine own, the brook might tell thee of
it," answered her mother, "even as it is telling me of mine! But now,
Pearl, I hear a foot-step along the path, and the noise of one putting
aside the branches. I would have thee betake thyself to play, and leave
me to speak with him that comes yonder."

"Is it the Black Man?" asked Pearl.

"Wilt thou go and play, child?" repeated her mother. "But do not
stray far into the wood. And take heed that thou come at my first call."

"Yes, mother," answered Pearl. "But if it be the Black Man, wilt thou
not let me stay a moment, and look at him, with his big book under his
arm?"

"Go, silly child!" said her mother, impatiently. "It is no Black Man!
Thou canst see him now, through the trees. It is the minister!"

"And so it is!" said the child. "And, mother, he has his hand over his
heart! Is it because, when the minister wrote his name in the book,
the Black Man set his mark in that place? But why does he not wear it
outside his bosom, as thou dost, mother?"

"Go now, child, and thou shalt tease me as thou wilt another time,"
cried Hester Prynne. "But do not stray far. Keep where thou canst
hear the babble of the brook."

The child went singing away, following up the current of the brook,
and striving to mingle a more lightsome cadence with its melancholy
voice. But the little stream would not be comforted, and still kept
telling its unintelligible secret of some very mournful mystery that had
happened—or making a prophetic lamentation about something that
was yet to happen—within the verge of the dismal forest. So Pearl,
who had enough of shadow in her own little life, chose to break off all
acquaintance with this repining brook. She set herself, therefore, to
gathering violets and wood-anemones, and some scarlet columbines
that she found growing in the crevices of a high rock.

When her elf-child had departed, Hester Prynne made a step or two
towards the track that led through the forest, but still remained under
the deep shadow of the trees. She beheld the minister advancing along
the path, entirely alone, and leaning on a staff which he had cut
by the way-side. He looked haggard and feeble, and betrayed a nerveless despondency in his air, which had never so remarkably characterized him in his walks about the settlement, nor in any other situation
where he deemed himself liable to notice. Here it was wofully visible,

in this intense seclusion of the forest, which of itself would have been a heavy trial to the spirits. There was a listlessness in his gait; as if he saw no reason for taking one step further, nor felt any desire to do so, but would have been glad, could he be glad of anything, to fling himself down at the root of the nearest tree, and lie there passive, forevermore. The leaves might bestrew him, and the soil gradually accumulate and form a little hillock over his frame, no matter whether there were life in it or no. Death was too definite an object to be wished for, or avoided.

To Hester's eye, the Reverend Mr. Dimmesdale exhibited no symptom of positive and vivacious suffering, except that, as little Pearl had remarked, he kept his hand over his heart.

XVII. The Pastor and His Parishioner

Slowly as the minister walked, he had almost gone by, before Hester Prynne could gather voice enough to attract his observation. At length, she succeeded.

"Arthur Dimmesdale!" she said, faintly at first; then louder, but hoarsely. "Arthur Dimmesdale!"

"Who speaks?" answered the minister.

Gathering himself quickly up, he stood more erect, like a man taken by surprise in a mood to which he was reluctant to have witnesses. Throwing his eyes anxiously in the direction of the voice, he indistinctly beheld a form under the trees, clad in garments so sombre, and so little relieved from the gray twilight into which the clouded sky and the heavy foliage had darkened the noontide, that he knew not whether it were a woman or a shadow. It may be, that his pathway through life was haunted thus, by a spectre that had stolen out from among his thoughts.

He made a step nigher, and discovered the scarlet letter.

"Hester! Hester Prynne!" said he. "Is it thou? Art thou in life?"

"Even so!" she answered. "In such life as has been mine these seven years past! And thou, Arthur Dimmesdale, dost thou yet live?"

It was no wonder that they thus questioned one another's actual and bodily existence, and even doubted of their own. So strangely did they meet, in the dim wood, that it was like the first encounter, in the world beyond the grave, of two spirits who had been intimately connected in their former life, but now stood coldly shuddering, in mutual dread; as not yet familiar with their state, nor wonted to the companionship of disembodied beings. Each a ghost, and awe-stricken at the other ghost! They were awe-stricken likewise at themselves; because the crisis flung back to them their consciousness, and revealed to each heart its history and experience, as life never does, except at such breathless epochs. The soul beheld its features in the mirror of the passing moment. It was with fear, and tremulously, and, as it were, by a slow, reluctant necessity, that Arthur Dimmesdale put forth his hand, chill as death, and touched the chill hand of Hester Prynne. The grasp, cold as it was, took away what was dreariest in the interview. They now felt themselves, at least, inhabitants of the same sphere.

Without a word more spoken,—neither he nor she assuming the guidance, but with an unexpressed consent,—they glided back into the shadow of the woods, whence Hester had emerged, and sat down on the heap of moss where she and Pearl had before been sitting. When they found voice to speak, it was, at first, only to utter remarks and inquiries such as any two acquaintance might have made, about the gloomy sky, the threatening storm, and, next, the health of each. Thus they went onward, not boldly, but step by step, into the themes that were brooding deepest in their hearts. So long estranged by fate and circumstances, they needed something slight and casual to run before, and throw open the doors of intercourse, so that their real thoughts might be led across the threshold.

After a while, the minister fixed his eyes on Hester Prynne's.

"Hester," said he, "hast thou found peace?"

She smiled drearily, looking down upon her bosom.

"Hast thou?" she asked.

"None!—nothing but despair!" he answered. "What else could I look for, being what I am, and leading such a life as mine? Were I an atheist,—a man devoid of conscience,—a wretch with coarse and brutal instincts,—I might have found peace, long ere now. Nay, I never should have lost it! But, as matters stand with my soul, whatever of good capacity there originally was in me, all of God's gifts that were the choicest have become the ministers of spiritual torment. Hester, I am most miserable!"

"The people reverence thee," said Hester. "And surely thou workest good among them! Doth this bring thee no comfort?"

"More misery, Hester!—only the more misery!" answered the clergyman, with a bitter smile. "As concerns the good which I may appear to do, I have no faith in it. It must needs be a delusion. What can a ruined soul, like mine, effect towards the redemption of other souls?—or a polluted soul, towards their purification? And as for the people's reverence, would that it were turned to scorn and hatred! Canst thou deem it, Hester, a consolation, that I must stand up in my pulpit, and meet so many eyes turned upward to my face, as if the light of heaven were beaming from it!—must see my flock hungry for the truth, and listening to my words as if a tongue of Pentecost were speaking!—and then look inward, and discern the black reality of what they idolize? I have laughed, in bitterness and agony of heart, at the contrast between what I seem and what I am! And Satan laughs at it!"

"You wrong yourself in this," said Hester, gently. "You have deeply and sorely repented. Your sin is left behind you, in the days long past. Your present life is not less holy, in very truth, than it seems in people's eyes. Is there no reality in the penitence thus sealed and witnessed by good works?[1] And wherefore should it not bring you peace?"

---

1. Anne Hutchinson had been charged with claiming that several Puritan ministers, including John Wilson, had preached a covenant of works, rather than a covenant of grace, as a way to salvation.

"No, Hester, no!" replied the clergyman. "There is no substance in it! It is cold and dead, and can do nothing for me! Of penance, I have had enough! Of penitence, there has been none! Else, I should long ago have thrown off these garments of mock holiness, and have shown myself to mankind as they will see me at the judgment-seat. Happy are you, Hester, that wear the scarlet letter openly upon your bosom! Mine burns in secret! Thou little knowest what a relief it is, after the torment of a seven years' cheat, to look into an eye that recognizes me for what I am! Had I one friend,—or were it my worst enemy!—to whom, when sickened with the praises of all other men, I could daily betake myself, and be known as the vilest of all sinners, methinks my soul might keep itself alive thereby. Even thus much of truth would save me! But, now, it is all falsehood!—all emptiness!—all death!"

Hester Prynne looked into his face, but hesitated to speak. Yet, uttering his long-restrained emotions so vehemently as he did, his words here offered her the very point of circumstances in which to interpose what she came to say. She conquered her fears, and spoke.

"Such a friend as thou hast even now wished for," said she, "with whom to weep over thy sin, thou hast in me, the partner of it!"—Again she hesitated, but brought out the words with an effort.—"Thou hast long had such an enemy, and dwellest with him, under the same roof!"

The minister started to his feet, gasping for breath, and clutching at his heart, as if he would have torn it out of his bosom.

"Ha! What sayest thou!" cried he. "An enemy! And under mine own roof! What mean you?"

Hester Prynne was now fully sensible of the deep injury for which she was responsible to this unhappy man, in permitting him to lie for so many years, or, indeed, for a single moment, at the mercy of one whose purposes could not be other than malevolent. The very contiguity of his enemy, beneath whatever mask the latter might conceal himself, was enough to disturb the magnetic sphere of a being so sensitive as Arthur Dimmesdale. There had been a period when Hester was less alive to this consideration; or, perhaps, in the misanthropy of her own trouble, she left the minister to bear what she might picture to herself as a more tolerable doom. But of late, since the night of his vigil, all her sympathies towards him had been both softened and invigorated. She now read his heart more accurately. She doubted not, that the continual presence of Roger Chillingworth,—the secret poison of his malignity, infecting all the air about him,—and his authorized interference, as a physician, with the minister's physical and spiritual infirmities,—that these bad opportunities had been turned to a cruel purpose. By means of them, the sufferer's conscience had been kept in an irritated state, the tendency of which was, not to cure by wholesome pain, but to disorganize and corrupt his spiritual being. Its result, on earth, could hardly fail to be insanity, and hereafter, that eternal alienation from the Good and True, of which madness is perhaps the earthly type.

Such was the ruin to which she had brought the man, once,—nay, why should we not speak it?—still so passionately loved! Hester felt that the sacrifice of the clergyman's good name, and death itself, as she had already told Roger Chillingworth, would have been infinitely preferable to the alternative which she had taken upon herself to choose. And now, rather than have had this grievous wrong to confess, she would gladly have lain down on the forest-leaves, and died there, at Arthur Dimmesdale's feet.

"O Arthur," cried she, "forgive me! In all things else, I have striven to be true! Truth was the one virtue which I might have held fast, and did hold fast, through all extremity; save when thy good,—thy life,— thy fame,—were put in question! Then I consented to a deception. But a lie is never good, even though death threaten on the other side! Dost thou not see what I would say? That old man!—the physician!— he whom they call Roger Chillingworth!—he was my husband!"

The minister looked at her, for an instant, with all that violence of passion, which—intermixed, in more shapes than one, with his higher, purer, softer qualities,—was, in fact, the portion of him which the Devil claimed, and through which he sought to win the rest. Never was there a blacker or a fiercer frown than Hester now encountered. For the brief space that it lasted, it was a dark transfiguration. But his character had been so much enfeebled by suffering, that even its lower energies were incapable of more than a temporary struggle. He sank down on the ground, and buried his face in his hands.

"I might have known it," murmured he. "I did know it! Was not the secret told me, in the natural recoil of my heart, at the first sight of him, and as often as I have seen him since? Why did I not under-stand? O Hester Prynne, thou little, little knowest all the horror of this thing! And the shame!—the indelicacy!—the horrible ugliness of this exposure of a sick and guilty heart to the very eye that would gloat over it! Woman, woman, thou art accountable for this! I cannot forgive thee!"

"Thou shalt forgive me!" cried Hester, flinging herself on the fallen leaves beside him. "Let God punish! Thou shalt forgive!"

With sudden and desperate tenderness, she threw her arms around him, and pressed his head against her bosom; little caring though his cheek rested on the scarlet letter. He would have released himself, but strove in vain to do so. Hester would not set him free, lest he should look her sternly in the face. All the world had frowned on her,—for seven long years had it frowned upon this lonely woman,—and still she bore it all, nor ever once turned away her firm, sad eyes. Heaven, likewise, had frowned upon her, and she had not died. But the frown of this pale, weak, sinful, and sorrow-stricken man was what Hester could not bear, and live!

"Wilt thou yet forgive me!" she repeated, over and over again. "Wilt thou not frown? Wilt thou forgive?"

"I do forgive you, Hester," replied the minister, at length, with a deep utterance, out of an abyss of sadness, but no anger. "I freely for-give you now. May God forgive us both! We are not, Hester, the worst sinners in the world. There is one worse than even the polluted priest! That old man's revenge has been blacker than my sin. He has violated, in cold blood, the sanctity of a human heart. Thou and I, Hester, never did so!"

"Never, never!" whispered she. "What we did had a consecration of its own. We felt it so! We said so to each other! Hast thou forgotten it?"

"Hush, Hester!" said Arthur Dimmesdale, rising from the ground. "No; I have not forgotten!"

They sat down again, side by side, and hand clasped in hand, on the mossy trunk of the fallen tree. Life had never brought them a gloomier hour; it was the point whither their pathway had so long been tending, and darkening ever, as it stole along;—and yet it enclosed a charm that made them linger upon it, and claim another, and another, and, after all, another moment. The forest was obscure around them, and creaked with a blast that was passing through it. The boughs were tossing heavily above their heads; while one solemn old tree groaned dolefully to another, as if telling the sad story of the pair that sat beneath, or constrained to forebode evil to come.

And yet they lingered. How dreary looked the forest-track that led backward to the settlement, where Hester Prynne must take up again the burden of her ignominy, and the minister the hollow mockery of his good name! So they lingered an instant longer. No golden light had ever been so precious as the gloom of this dark forest. Here, seen only by her eyes, the scarlet letter need not burn into the bosom of the fallen woman! Here, seen only by her eyes, Arthur Dimmesdale, false to God and man, might be, for one moment, true!

He started at a thought that suddenly occurred to him.

"Hester," cried he, "here is a new horror! Roger Chillingworth knows your purpose to reveal his true character. Will he continue, then, to keep our secret? What will now be the course of his revenge?"

"There is a strange secrecy in his nature," replied Hester, thoughtfully; "and it has grown upon him by the hidden practices of his revenge. I deem it not likely that he will betray the secret. He will doubtless seek other means of satiating his dark passion."

"And I!—how am I to live longer, breathing the same air with this deadly enemy?" exclaimed Arthur Dimmesdale, shrinking within himself, and pressing his hand nervously against his heart,—a gesture that had grown involuntary with him. "Think for me, Hester! Thou art strong. Resolve for me!"

"Thou must dwell no longer with this man," said Hester, slowly and firmly. "Thy heart must be no longer under his evil eye!"

"It were far worse than death!" replied the minister. "But how to avoid it? What choice remains to me? Shall I lie down again on these withered leaves, where I cast myself when thou didst tell me what he was? Must I sink down there, and die at once?"

"Alas, what a ruin has befallen thee!" said Hester, with the tears gushing into her eyes. "Wilt thou die for very weakness? There is no other cause!"

"The judgment of God is on me," answered the conscience-stricken priest. "It is too mighty for me to struggle with!"

"Heaven would show mercy," rejoined Hester, "hadst thou but the strength to take advantage of it."

"Be thou strong for me!" answered he. "Advise me what to do."

"Is the world, then, so narrow?" exclaimed Hester Prynne, fixing her deep eyes on the minister's, and instinctively exercising a magnetic power over a spirit so shattered and subdued that it could hardly hold itself erect. "Doth the universe lie within the compass of yonder town, which only a little time ago was but a leaf-strewn desert, as lonely as this around us? Whither leads yonder forest track? Backward to the settlement, thou sayest! Yes; but onward, too! Deeper it goes, and deeper, into the wilderness, less plainly to be seen at every step; until, some few miles hence, the yellow leaves will show no vestige of the white man's tread. There thou art free! So brief a journey would bring thee from a world where thou hast been most wretched, to one where thou mayest still be happy! Is there not shade enough in all this boundless forest to hide thy heart from the gaze of Roger Chillingworth?"

"Yes, Hester; but only under the fallen leaves!" replied the minister, with a sad smile.

"Then there is the broad pathway of the sea!" continued Hester. "It brought thee hither. If thou so choose, it will bear thee back again. In our native land, whether in some remote rural village or in vast London,—or, surely, in Germany, in France, in pleasant Italy,—thou wouldst be beyond his power and knowledge! And what hast thou to do with all these iron men, and their opinions? They have kept thy better part in bondage too long already!"

"It cannot be!" answered the minister, listening as if he were called upon to realize a dream. "I am powerless to go! Wretched and sinful as I am, I have had no other thought than to drag on my earthly existence in the sphere where Providence hath placed me. Lost as my own soul is, I would still do what I may for other human souls! I dare not quit my post, though an unfaithful sentinel, whose sure reward is death and dishonor, when his dreary watch shall come to an end!"

"Thou art crushed under this seven years' weight of misery," replied Hester, fervently resolved to buoy him up with her own energy. "But thou shalt leave it all behind thee! It shall not cumber thy steps, as thou treadest along the forest-path; neither shalt thou freight the ship with it, if thou prefer to cross the sea. Leave this wreck and ruin here where it hath happened. Meddle no more with it! Begin all anew! Hast thou exhausted possibility in the failure of this one trial? Not so! The future is yet full of trial and success. There is happiness to be enjoyed! There is good to be done! Exchange this false life of thine for a true one. Be, if thy spirit summon thee to such a mission, the teacher and apostle of the red men. Or,—as is more thy nature,—be a scholar and a sage among the wisest and the most renowned of the cultivated world. Preach! Write! Act! Do anything, save to lie down and die! Give up this name of Arthur Dimmesdale, and make thyself another, and a high one, such as thou canst wear without fear or shame. Why shouldst thou tarry so much as one other day in the torments that have so gnawed into thy life!—that have made thee feeble to will and to do!—that will leave thee powerless even to repent! Up, and away!"

"O Hester!" cried Arthur Dimmesdale, in whose eyes a fitful light, kindled by her enthusiasm, flashed up and died away, "thou tellest of running a race to a man whose knees are tottering beneath him! I must die here! There is not the strength or courage left me to venture into the wide, strange, difficult world, alone!"

It was the last expression of the despondency of a broken spirit. He lacked energy to grasp the better fortune that seemed within his reach.

He repeated the word.

"Alone, Hester!"

"Thou shalt not go alone!" answered she, in a deep whisper.

Then, all was spoken!

XVIII. A Flood of Sunshine

Arthur Dimmesdale gazed into Hester's face with a look in which hope and joy shone out, indeed, but with fear betwixt them, and a kind of horror at her boldness, who had spoken what he vaguely hinted at, but dared not speak.

But Hester Prynne, with a mind of native courage and activity, and for so long a period not merely estranged, but outlawed, from society, had habituated herself to such latitude of speculation as was altogether foreign to the clergyman. She had wandered, without rule or guidance, in a moral wilderness; as vast, as intricate and shadowy, as the untamed forest, amid the gloom of which they were now holding a colloquy that was to decide their fate. Her intellect and heart had their home, as it were, in desert places, where she roamed as freely as the wild Indian in his woods. For years past she had looked from this estranged point of view at human institutions, and whatever priests or legislators had established; criticising all with hardly more reverence than the Indian would feel for the clerical band, the judicial robe, the pillory, the gallows, the fireside, or the church. The tendency of her fate and fortunes had been to set her free. The scarlet letter was her passport into regions where other women dared not tread. Shame, Despair, Solitude! These had been her teachers,—stern and wild ones,—and they had made her strong, but taught her much amiss.

The minister, on the other hand, had never gone through an experience calculated to lead him beyond the scope of generally received laws; although, in a single instance, he had so fearfully transgressed one of the most sacred of them. But this had been a sin of passion, not of principle, nor even purpose. Since that wretched epoch, he had watched, with morbid zeal and minuteness, not his acts,—for those it was easy to arrange,—but each breath of emotion, and his every thought. At the head of the social system, as the clergymen of that day stood, he was only the more trammelled by its regulations, its principles, and even its prejudices. As a priest, the framework of his order inevitably hemmed him in. As a man who had once sinned, but who kept his conscience all alive and painfully sensitive by the fretting of an unhealed wound, he might have been supposed safer within the line of virtue than if he had never sinned at all.

Thus, we seem to see that, as regarded Hester Prynne, the whole seven years of outlaw and ignominy had been little other than a preparation for this very hour. But Arthur Dimmesdale! Were such a man once more to fall, what plea could be urged in extenuation of his crime? None; unless it avail him somewhat, that he was broken down by long and exquisite suffering; that his mind was darkened and confused by the very remorse which harrowed it; that, between fleeing as an avowed criminal, and remaining as a hypocrite, conscience might find it hard to strike the balance; that it was human to avoid the peril of death and infamy, and the inscrutable machinations of an enemy; that, finally, to this poor pilgrim, on his dreary and desert path, faint, sick, miserable, there appeared a glimpse of human affection and sympathy, a new life, and a true one, in exchange for the heavy doom which he was now expiating. And be the stern and sad truth spoken, that the breach which guilt has once made into the human soul is never, in this mortal state, repaired. It may be watched and guarded; so that the enemy shall not force his way again into the citadel, and might even, in his subsequent assaults, select some other avenue, in preference to that where he had formerly succeeded. But there is still the ruined wall, and, near it, the stealthy tread of the foe that would win over again his unforgotten triumph.

The struggle, if there were one, need not be described. Let it suffice, that the clergyman resolved to flee, and not alone.

"If, in all these past seven years," thought he, "I could recall one instant of peace or hope, I would yet endure, for the sake of that earnest of Heaven's mercy. But now,—since I am irrevocably doomed,—wherefore should I not snatch the solace allowed to the condemned culprit before his execution? Or, if this be the path to a better life, as Hester would persuade me, I surely give up no fairer prospect by pursuing it! Neither can I any longer live without her companionship; so powerful is she to sustain,—so tender to soothe! O Thou to whom I dare not lift mine eyes, wilt Thou yet pardon me!"

"Thou wilt go!" said Hester, calmly, as he met her glance.

The decision once made, a glow of strange enjoyment threw its flickering brightness over the trouble of his breast. It was the exhilarating effect—upon a prisoner just escaped from the dungeon of his own heart—of breathing the wild, free atmosphere of an unredeemed, unchristianized, lawless region. His spirit rose, as it were, with a bound, and attained a nearer prospect of the sky, than throughout all the misery which had kept him grovelling on the earth. Of a deeply religious temperament, there was inevitably a tinge of the devotional in his mood.

"Do I feel joy again?" cried he, wondering at himself. "Methought the germ of it was dead in me! O Hester, thou art my better angel! I seem to have flung myself—sick, sin-stained, and sorrow-blackened—

down upon these forest-leaves, and to have risen up all made anew, and with new powers to glorify Him that hath been merciful! This is already the better life! Why did we not find it sooner?"

"Let us not look back," answered Hester Prynne. "The past is gone! Wherefore should we linger upon it now? See! With this symbol, I undo it all, and make it as it had never been!"

So speaking, she undid the clasp that fastened the scarlet letter, and, taking it from her bosom, threw it to a distance among the withered leaves. The mystic token alighted on the hither verge of the stream. With a hand's breadth further flight it would have fallen into the water, and have given the little brook another woe to carry onward, besides the unintelligible tale which it still kept murmuring about. But there lay the embroidered letter, glittering like a lost jewel, which some ill-fated wanderer might pick up, and thenceforth be haunted by strange phantoms of guilt, sinkings of the heart, and unaccountable misfortune.

The stigma gone, Hester heaved a long, deep sigh, in which the burden of shame and anguish departed from her spirit. O exquisite relief! She had not known the weight, until she felt the freedom! By another impulse, she took off the formal cap that confined her hair; and down it fell upon her shoulders, dark and rich, with at once a shadow and a light in its abundance, and imparting the charm of softness to her features. There played around her mouth, and beamed out of her eyes, a radiant and tender smile, that seemed gushing from the very heart of womanhood. A crimson flush was glowing on her cheek, that had been long so pale. Her sex, her youth, and the whole richness of her beauty, came back from what men call the irrevocable past, and clustered themselves, with her maiden hope, and a happiness before unknown, within the magic circle of this hour. And, as if the gloom of the earth and sky had been but the effluence of these two mortal hearts, it vanished with their sorrow. All at once, as with a sudden smile of heaven, forth burst the sunshine, pouring a very flood into the obscure forest, gladdening each green leaf, transmuting the yellow fallen ones to gold, and gleaming adown the gray trunks of the solemn trees. The objects that had made a shadow hitherto, embodied the brightness now. The course of the little brook might be traced by its merry gleam afar into the wood's heart of mystery, which had become a mystery of joy.

Such was the sympathy of Nature—that wild, heathen Nature of the forest, never subjugated by human law, nor illumined by higher truth—with the bliss of these two spirits! Love, whether newly born, or aroused from a death-like slumber, must always create a sunshine, filling the heart so full of radiance, that it overflows upon the outward world. Had the forest still kept its gloom, it would have been bright in Hester's eyes, and bright in Arthur Dimmesdale's!

Hester looked at him with the thrill of another joy.

"Thou must know Pearl!" said she. "Our little Pearl! Thou hast seen her,—yes, I know it!—but thou wilt see her now with other eyes. She is a strange child! I hardly comprehend her! But thou wilt love her dearly, as I do, and wilt advise me how to deal with her."

"Dost thou think the child will be glad to know me?" asked the minister, somewhat uneasily. "I have long shrunk from children, because they often show a distrust,—a backwardness to be familiar with me. I have even been afraid of little Pearl!"

"Ah, that was sad!" answered the mother. "But she will love thee dearly, and thou her. She is not far off. I will call her! Pearl! Pearl!"

"I see the child," observed the minister. "Yonder she is, standing in a streak of sunshine, a good way off, on the other side of the brook. So thou thinkest the child will love me?"

Hester smiled, and again called to Pearl, who was visible, at some distance, as the minister had described her, like a bright-apparelled vision, in a sunbeam, which fell down upon her through an arch of boughs. The ray quivered to and fro, making her figure dim or distinct,—now like a real child, now like a child's spirit,—as the splendor went and came again. She heard her mother's voice, and approached slowly through the forest.

Pearl had not found the hour pass wearisomely, while her mother sat talking with the clergyman. The great black forest—stern as it showed itself to those who brought the guilt and troubles of the world into its bosom—became the playmate of the lonely infant, as well as it knew how. Sombre as it was, it put on the kindest of its moods to welcome her. It offered her the partridge-berries, the growth of the preceding autumn, but ripening only in the spring, and now red as drops of blood upon the withered leaves. These Pearl gathered, and was pleased with their wild flavor. The small denizens of the wilderness hardly took pains to move out of her path. A partridge, indeed, with a brood of ten behind her, ran forward threateningly, but soon repented of her fierceness, and clucked to her young ones not to be afraid. A pigeon, alone on a low branch, allowed Pearl to come beneath, and uttered a sound as much of greeting as alarm. A squirrel, from the lofty depths of his domestic tree, chattered either in anger or merriment,— for a squirrel is such a choleric and humorous little personage, that it is hard to distinguish between his moods,—so he chattered at the child, and flung down a nut upon her head. It was a last year's nut, and already gnawed by his sharp tooth. A fox, startled from his sleep by her light footstep on the leaves, looked inquisitively at Pearl, as doubting whether it were better to steal off, or renew his nap on the same spot. A wolf, it is said,—but here the tale has surely lapsed into the improbable,—came up, and smelt of Pearl's robe, and offered his savage head to be patted by her hand. The truth seems to be, however, that the mother-forest, and these wild things which it nourished, all recognized a kindred wildness in the human child.

And she was gentler here than in the grassy-margined streets of the settlement, or in her mother's cottage. The flowers appeared to know it; and one and another whispered as she passed, "Adorn thyself with me, thou beautiful child, adorn thyself with me!"—and, to please them, Pearl gathered the violets, and anemones, and columbines, and some twigs of the freshest green, which the old trees held down before her eyes. With these she decorated her hair, and her young waist, and became a nymph-child, or an infant dryad,[1] or whatever else was in closest sympathy with the antique wood. In such guise had Pearl adorned herself, when she heard her mother's voice, and came slowly back.

Slowly; for she saw the clergyman!

XIX. The Child at the Brook-Side

"Thou wilt love her dearly," repeated Hester Prynne, as she and the minister sat watching little Pearl. "Dost thou not think her beautiful? And see with what natural skill she has made those simple flowers adorn her! Had she gathered pearls, and diamonds, and rubies, in the wood, they could not have become her better. She is a splendid child! But I know whose brow she has!"

"Dost thou know, Hester," said Arthur Dimmesdale, with an unquiet smile, "that this dear child, tripping about always at thy side, hath caused me many an alarm? Methought—O Hester, what a thought is that, and how terrible to dread it!—that my own features were partly repeated in her face, and so strikingly that the world might see them! But she is mostly thine!"

"No, no! Not mostly!" answered the mother, with a tender smile. "A little longer, and thou needest not to be afraid to trace whose child she is. But how strangely beautiful she looks, with those wild flowers in her hair! It is as if one of the fairies, whom we left in our dear old England, had decked her out to meet us."

It was with a feeling which neither of them had ever before experienced, that they sat and watched Pearl's slow advance. In her was visible the tie that united them. She had been offered to the world, these seven years past, as the living hieroglyphic, in which was revealed the secret they so darkly sought to hide,—all written in this symbol,—all plainly manifest,—had there been a prophet or magician skilled to read the character of flame! And Pearl was the oneness of their being. Be the foregone evil what it might, how could they doubt that their earthly lives and future destinies were conjoined, when they beheld at once the material union, and the spiritual idea, in whom they met, and were to dwell immortally together? Thoughts like these—and perhaps other thoughts, which they did not acknowledge or define— threw an awe about the child, as she came onward.

"Let her see nothing strange—no passion nor eagerness—in thy way of accosting her," whispered Hester. "Our Pearl is a fitful and fantastic little elf, sometimes. Especially, she is seldom tolerant of emotion, when she does not fully comprehend the why and wherefore. But the child hath strong affections! She loves me, and will love thee!"

"Thou canst not think," said the minister, glancing aside at Hester Prynne, "how my heart dreads this interview, and yearns for it! But, in truth, as I already told thee, children are not readily won to be famil-

1. Wood nymph.

iar with me. They will not climb my knee, nor prattle in my ear, nor answer to my smile; but stand apart, and eye me strangely. Even little babes, when I take them in my arms, weep bitterly. Yet Pearl, twice in her little lifetime, hath been kind to me! The first time,—thou knowest it well! The last was when thou ledst her with thee to the house of yonder stern old Governor."

"And thou didst plead so bravely in her behalf and mine!" answered the mother. "I remember it; and so shall little Pearl. Fear nothing! She may be strange and shy at first, but will soon learn to love thee!"

By this time Pearl had reached the margin of the brook, and stood on the further side, gazing silently at Hester and the clergyman, who still sat together on the mossy tree-trunk, waiting to receive her. Just where she had paused, the brook chanced to form a pool, so smooth and quiet that it reflected a perfect image of her little figure, with all the brilliant picturesqueness of her beauty, in its adornment of flowers and wreathed foliage, but more refined and spiritualized than the reality. This image, so nearly identical with the living Pearl, seemed to communicate somewhat of its own shadowy and intangible quality to the child herself. It was strange, the way in which Pearl stood, looking so steadfastly at them through the dim medium of the forest-gloom; herself, meanwhile, all glorified with a ray of sunshine, that was attracted thitherward as by a certain sympathy. In the brook beneath stood another child,—another and the same,—with likewise its ray of golden light. Hester felt herself, in some indistinct and tantalizing manner, estranged from Pearl; as if the child, in her lonely ramble through the forest, had strayed out of the sphere in which she and her mother dwelt together, and was now vainly seeking to return to it.

There was both truth and error in the impression; the child and mother were estranged, but through Hester's fault, not Pearl's. Since the latter rambled from her side, another inmate had been admitted within the circle of the mother's feelings, and so modified the aspect of them all, that Pearl, the returning wanderer, could not find her wonted place, and hardly knew where she was.

"I have a strange fancy," observed the sensitive minister, "that this brook is the boundary between two worlds, and that thou canst never meet thy Pearl again. Or is she an elfish spirit, who, as the legends of our childhood taught us, is forbidden to cross a running stream? Pray hasten her; for this delay has already imparted a tremor to my nerves."

"Come, dearest child!" said Hester, encouragingly, and stretching out both her arms. "How slow thou art! When hast thou been so sluggish before now? Here is a friend of mine, who must be thy friend also. Thou wilt have twice as much love, henceforward, as thy mother alone could give thee! Leap across the brook, and come to us. Thou canst leap like a young deer!"

Pearl, without responding in any manner to these honey-sweet expressions, remained on the other side of the brook. Now she fixed her bright, wild eyes on her mother, now on the minister, and now included them both in the same glance; as if to detect and explain to herself the relation which they bore to one another. For some unaccountable reason, as Arthur Dimmesdale felt the child's eyes upon himself, his hand—with that gesture so habitual as to have become involuntary—stole over his heart. At length, assuming a singular air of authority, Pearl stretched out her hand, with the small forefinger extended, and pointing evidently towards her mother's breast. And beneath, in the mirror of the brook, there was the flower-girdled and sunny image of little Pearl, pointing her small forefinger too.

"Thou strange child, why dost thou not come to me?" exclaimed Hester.

Pearl still pointed with her forefinger; and a frown gathered on her brow; the more impressive from the childish, the almost baby-like aspect of the features that conveyed it. As her mother still kept beckoning to her, and arraying her face in a holiday suit of unaccustomed smiles, the child stamped her foot with a yet more imperious look and gesture. In the brook, again, was the fantastic beauty of the image, with its reflected frown, its pointed finger, and imperious gesture, giving emphasis to the aspect of little Pearl.

"Hasten, Pearl; or I shall be angry with thee!" cried Hester Prynne, who, however inured to such behavior on the elf-child's part at other seasons, was naturally anxious for a more seemly deportment now. "Leap across the brook, naughty child, and run hither! Else I must come to thee!"

But Pearl, not a whit startled at her mother's threats, any more than mollified by her entreaties, now suddenly burst into a fit of passion, gesticulating violently, and throwing her small figure into the most extravagant contortions. She accompanied this wild outbreak with piercing shrieks, which the woods reverberated on all sides; so that, alone as she was in her childish and unreasonable wrath, it seemed as if a hidden multitude were lending her their sympathy and encouragement. Seen in the brook, once more, was the shadowy wrath of Pearl's image, crowned and girdled with flowers, but stamping its foot, wildly gesticulating, and, in the midst of all, still pointing its small forefinger at Hester's bosom!

"I see what ails the child," whispered Hester to the clergyman, and turning pale in spite of a strong effort to conceal her trouble and annoyance. "Children will not abide any, the slightest, change in the accustomed aspect of things that are daily before their eyes. Pearl misses something which she has always seen me wear!"

"I pray you," answered the minister, "if thou hast any means of pacifying the child, do it forthwith! Save it were the cankered wrath of an old witch, like Mistress Hibbins," added he, attempting to smile, "I know nothing that I would not sooner encounter than this passion in a child. In Pearl's young beauty, as in the wrinkled witch, it has a preternatural effect. Pacify her, if thou lovest me!"

Hester turned again towards Pearl, with a crimson blush upon her cheek, a conscious glance aside at the clergyman, and then a heavy sigh; while, even before she had time to speak, the blush yielded to a deadly pallor.

"Pearl," said she, sadly, "look down at thy feet! There!—before thee!—on the hither side of the brook!"

The child turned her eyes to the point indicated; and there lay the scarlet letter, so close upon the margin of the stream, that the gold embroidery was reflected in it.

"Bring it hither!" said Hester.

"Come thou and take it up!" answered Pearl.

"Was ever such a child!" observed Hester, aside to the minister. "O, I have much to tell thee about her! But, in very truth, she is right as regards this hateful token. I must bear its torture yet a little longer,— only a few days longer,—until we shall have left this region, and look back hither as to a land which we have dreamed of. The forest cannot hide it! The mid-ocean shall take it from my hand, and swallow it up forever!"

With these words, she advanced to the margin of the brook, took up the scarlet letter, and fastened it again into her bosom. Hopefully, but a moment ago, as Hester had spoken of drowning it in the deep sea, there was a sense of inevitable doom upon her, as she thus received back this deadly symbol from the hand of fate. She had flung it into infinite space!—she had drawn an hour's free breath!—and here again was the scarlet misery, glittering on the old spot! So it ever is, whether thus typified or no, that an evil deed invests itself with the character of doom. Hester next gathered up the heavy tresses of her hair, and confined them beneath her cap. As if there were a withering spell in the sad letter, her beauty, the warmth and richness of her womanhood, departed, like fading sunshine; and a gray shadow seemed to fall across her.

When the dreary change was wrought, she extended her hand to Pearl.

"Dost thou know thy mother now, child?" asked she, reproachfully, but with a subdued tone. "Wilt thou come across the brook, and own thy mother, now that she has her shame upon her,—now that she is sad?"

"Yes; now I will!" answered the child, bounding across the brook, and clasping Hester in her arms. "Now thou art my mother indeed! And I am thy little Pearl!"

In a mood of tenderness that was not usual with her, she drew down her mother's head, and kissed her brow and both her cheeks. But then—by a kind of necessity that always impelled this child to alloy whatever comfort she might chance to give with a throb of anguish— Pearl put up her mouth, and kissed the scarlet letter too!

"That was not kind!" said Hester. "When thou hast shown me a little love, thou mockest me!"

"Why doth the minister sit yonder?" asked Pearl.

"He waits to welcome thee," replied her mother. "Come thou, and entreat his blessing! He loves thee, my little Pearl, and loves thy mother too. Wilt thou not love him? Come! he longs to greet thee!"

"Doth he love us?" said Pearl, looking up, with acute intelligence, into her mother's face. "Will he go back with us, hand in hand, we three together, into the town?"

"Not now, dear child," answered Hester. "But in days to come he will walk hand in hand with us. We will have a home and fireside of our own; and thou shalt sit upon his knee; and he will teach thee many things, and love thee dearly. Thou wilt love him; wilt thou not?"

"And will he always keep his hand over his heart?" inquired Pearl.

"Foolish child, what a question is that!" exclaimed her mother. "Come and ask his blessing!"

But, whether influenced by the jealousy that seems instinctive with every petted child towards a dangerous rival, or from whatever caprice of her freakish nature, Pearl would show no favor to the clergyman. It was only by an exertion of force that her mother brought her up to him, hanging back, and manifesting her reluctance by odd grimaces; of which, ever since her babyhood, she had possessed a singular variety, and could transform her mobile physiognomy into a series of different aspects, with a new mischief in them, each and all. The minister—painfully embarrassed, but hoping that a kiss might prove a talisman to admit him into the child's kindlier regards—bent forward, and impressed one on her brow. Hereupon, Pearl broke away from her mother, and, running to the brook, stooped over it, and bathed her forehead, until the unwelcome kiss was quite washed off, and diffused through a long lapse of the gliding water. She then remained apart, silently watching Hester and the clergyman; while they talked together, and made such arrangements as were suggested by their new position, and the purposes soon to be fulfilled.

And now this fateful interview had come to a close. The dell was to be left a solitude among its dark, old trees, which, with their multitudinous tongues, would whisper long of what had passed there, and no mortal be the wiser. And the melancholy brook would add this other tale to the mystery with which its little heart was already overburdened, and whereof it still kept up a murmuring babble, with not a whit more cheerfulness of tone than for ages heretofore.

XX. The Minister in a Maze

As the minister departed, in advance of Hester Prynne and little Pearl, he threw a backward glance; half expecting that he should discover only some faintly traced features or outline of the mother and the child, slowly fading into the twilight of the woods. So great a vicissitude in his life could not at once be received as real. But there was Hester, clad in her gray robe, still standing beside the tree-trunk, which some blast had overthrown a long antiquity ago, and which time had ever since been covering with moss, so that these two fated ones, with earth's heaviest burden on them, might there sit down together, and find a single hour's rest and solace. And there was Pearl, too, lightly dancing from the margin of the brook,—now that the intrusive third person was gone,—and taking her old place by her mother's side. So the minister had not fallen asleep, and dreamed!

In order to free his mind from this indistinctness and duplicity of impression, which vexed it with a strange disquietude, he recalled and more thoroughly defined the plans which Hester and himself had sketched for their departure. It had been determined between them, that the Old World, with its crowds and cities, offered them a more eligible shelter and concealment than the wilds of New England, or all America, with its alternatives of an Indian wigwam, or the few settlements of Europeans, scattered thinly along the seaboard. Not to speak of the clergyman's health, so inadequate to sustain the hardships of a forest life, his native gifts, his culture, and his entire development, would secure him a home only in the midst of civilization and refinement; the higher the state, the more delicately adapted to it the man. In furtherance of this choice, it so happened that a ship lay in the harbor; one of those questionable cruisers, frequent at that day, which, without being absolutely outlaws of the deep, yet roamed over its surface with a remarkable irresponsibility of character. This vessel had recently arrived from the Spanish Main, and, within three days' time, would sail for Bristol. Hester Prynne—whose vocation, as a self-enlisted Sister of Charity, had brought her acquainted with the captain and crew—could take upon herself to secure the passage of two individuals and a child, with all the secrecy which circumstances rendered more than desirable.

The minister had inquired of Hester, with no little interest, the precise time at which the vessel might be expected to depart. It would probably be on the fourth day from the present. "That is most fortunate!" he had then said to himself. Now, why the Reverend Mr. Dimmesdale considered it so very fortunate, we hesitate to reveal. Nevertheless,—to hold nothing back from the reader,—it was because, on the third day from the present, he was to preach the Election Sermon; and, as such an occasion formed an honorable epoch in the life of a New England clergyman, he could not have chanced upon a more suitable mode and time of terminating his professional career.[1] "At least, they shall say of me," thought this exemplary man, "that I leave no public duty unperformed, nor ill performed!" Sad, indeed, that an introspection so profound and acute as this poor minister's should be so miserably deceived! We have had, and may still have, worse things to tell of him; but none, we apprehend, so pitiably weak; no evidence, at once so slight and irrefragable, of a subtle disease, that had long since begun to eat into the real substance of his character. No man, for any considerable period, can wear one face to himself, and another to the multitude, without finally getting bewildered as to which may be the true.

The excitement of Mr. Dimmesdale's feelings, as he returned from his interview with Hester, lent him unaccustomed physical energy, and hurried him townward at a rapid pace. The pathway among the woods

---

1. The Puritans elected a new governor every year. In this church state, Dimmesdale has been accorded the honor of preaching a sermon as part of the inaugural celebration. Although Hawthorne does not identify the new governor, John Endicott was elected in 1649.

seemed wilder, more uncouth with its rude natural obstacles, and less trodden by the foot of man, than he remembered it on his outward journey. But he leaped across the plashy places, thrust himself through the clinging underbrush, climbed the ascent, plunged into the hollow, and overcame, in short, all the difficulties of the track, with an unweariable activity that astonished him. He could not but recall how feebly, and with what frequent pauses for breath, he had toiled over the same ground, only two days before. As he drew near the town, he took an impression of change from the series of familiar objects that presented themselves. It seemed not yesterday, not one, nor two, but many days, or even years ago, since he had quitted them. There, indeed, was each former trace of the street, as he remembered it, and all the peculiarities of the houses, with the due multitude of gable-peaks, and a weather-cock at every point where his memory suggested one. Not the less, however, came this importunately obtrusive sense of change. The same was true as regarded the acquaintances whom he met, and all the well-known shapes of human life, about the little town. They looked neither older nor younger now; the beards of the aged were no whiter, nor could the creeping babe of yesterday walk on his feet to-day; it was impossible to describe in what respect they differed from the individuals on whom he had so recently bestowed a parting glance; and yet the minister's deepest sense seemed to inform him of their mutability. A similar impression struck him most remarkably, as he passed under the walls of his own church. The edifice had so very strange, and yet so familiar, an aspect, that Mr. Dimmesdale's mind vibrated between two ideas; either that he had seen it only in a dream hitherto, or that he was merely dreaming about it now.[2]

This phenomenon, in the various shapes which it assumed, indicated no external change, but so sudden and important a change in the spectator of the familiar scene, that the intervening space of a single day had operated on his consciousness like the lapse of years. The minister's own will, and Hester's will, and the fate that grew between them, had wrought this transformation. It was the same town as heretofore; but the same minister returned not from the forest. He might have said to the friends who greeted him,—"I am not the man for whom you take me! I left him yonder in the forest, withdrawn into a secret dell, by a mossy tree-trunk, and near a melancholy brook! Go, seek your minister, and see if his emaciated figure, his thin cheek, his white, heavy, pain-wrinkled brow, be not flung down there, like a cast-off garment!" His friends, no doubt, would still have insisted with him,—"Thou art thyself the man!"—but the error would have been their own, not his.

Before Mr. Dimmesdale reached home, his inner man gave him other evidences of a revolution in the sphere of thought and feeling. In truth, nothing short of a total change of dynasty and moral code, in that interior kingdom, was adequate to account for the impulses now communicated to the unfortunate and startled minister. At every step

2. Compare the experiences of young Goodman Brown after he returns from the forest.

he was incited to do some strange, wild, wicked thing or other, with a sense that it would be at once involuntary and intentional; in spite of himself, yet growing out of a profounder self than that which opposed the impulse. For instance, he met one of his own deacons. The good old man addressed him with the paternal affection and patriarchal privilege, which his venerable age, his upright and holy character, and his station in the Church, entitled him to use; and, conjoined with this, the deep, almost worshipping respect, which the minister's professional and private claims alike demanded. Never was there a more beautiful example of how the majesty of age and wisdom may comport with the obeisance and respect enjoined upon it, as from a lower social rank, and inferior order of endowment, towards a higher. Now, during a conversation of some two or three moments between the Reverend Mr. Dimmesdale and this excellent and hoary-bearded deacon, it was only by the most careful self-control that the former could refrain from uttering certain blasphemous suggestions that rose into his mind, respecting the communion-supper. He absolutely trembled and turned pale as ashes, lest his tongue should wag itself, in utterance of these horrible matters, and plead his own consent for so doing, without his having fairly given it. And, even with this terror in his heart, he could hardly avoid laughing, to imagine how the sanctified old patriarchal deacon would have been petrified by his minister's impiety!

Again, another incident of the same nature. Hurrying along the street, the Reverend Mr. Dimmesdale encountered the eldest female member of his church; a most pious and exemplary old dame; poor, widowed, lonely, and with a heart as full of reminiscences about her dead husband and children, and her dead friends of long ago, as a burial-ground is full of storied grave-stones. Yet all this, which would else have been such heavy sorrow, was made almost a solemn joy to her devout old soul, by religious consolations and the truths of Scripture, wherewith she had fed herself continually for more than thirty years. And, since Mr. Dimmesdale had taken her in charge, the good grandam's chief earthly comfort—which, unless it had been likewise a heavenly comfort, could have been none at all—was to meet her pastor, whether casually, or of set purpose, and be refreshed with a word of warm, fragrant, heaven-breathing Gospel truth, from his beloved lips, into her dulled, but rapturously attentive ear. But, on this occasion, up to the moment of putting his lips to the old woman's ear, Mr. Dimmesdale, as the great enemy of souls would have it, could recall no text of Scripture, nor aught else, except a brief, pithy, and, as it then appeared to him, unanswerable argument against the immortality of the human soul. The instilment thereof into her mind would probably have caused this aged sister to drop down dead, at once, as by the effect of an intensely poisonous infusion. What he really did whisper, the minister could never afterwards recollect. There was, perhaps, a fortunate disorder in his utterance, which failed to impart any distinct idea to the good widow's comprehension, or which Providence interpreted after a method of its own. Assuredly, as the minister looked back, he beheld an expression of divine gratitude and ecstasy that seemed like the shine of the celestial city on her face, so wrinkled and ashy pale.

Again, a third instance. After parting from the old church-member, he met the youngest sister of them all. It was a maiden newly won— and won by the Reverend Mr. Dimmesdale's own sermon, on the Sabbath after his vigil—to barter the transitory pleasures of the world for the heavenly hope, that was to assume brighter substance as life grew dark around her, and which would gild the utter gloom with final glory. She was fair and pure as a lily that had bloomed in Paradise. The minister knew well that he was himself enshrined within the stainless sanctity of her heart, which hung its snowy curtains about his image, imparting to religion the warmth of love, and to love a religious purity. Satan, that afternoon, had surely led the poor young girl away from her mother's side, and thrown her into the pathway of this sorely tempted, or—shall we not rather say?—this lost and desperate man. As she drew nigh, the arch-fiend whispered him to condense into small compass and drop into her tender bosom a germ of evil that would be sure to blossom darkly soon, and bear black fruit betimes. Such was his sense of power over this virgin soul, trusting him as she did, that the minister felt potent to blight all the field of innocence with but one wicked look, and develop all its opposite with but a word. So—with a mightier struggle than he had yet sustained—he held his Geneva cloak before his face, and hurried onward, making no sign of recognition, and leaving the young sister to digest his rudeness as she might. She ransacked her conscience,—which was full of harmless little matters, like her pocket or her work-bag,—and took herself to task, poor thing! for a thousand imaginary faults; and went about her household duties with swollen eyelids the next morning.

Before the minister had time to celebrate his victory over this last temptation, he was conscious of another impulse, more ludicrous, and almost as horrible. It was,—we blush to tell it,—it was to stop short in the road, and teach some very wicked words to a knot of little Puritan children who were playing there, and had but just begun to talk. Denying himself this freak, as unworthy of his cloth, he met a drunken seaman, one of the ship's crew from the Spanish Main. And, here, since he had so valiantly forborne all other wickedness, poor Mr. Dimmesdale longed, at least, to shake hands with the tarry blackguard, and recreate himself with a few improper jests, such as dissolute sailors so abound with, and a volley of good, round, solid, satisfactory, and heaven-defying oaths! It was not so much a better principle, as partly his natural good taste, and still more his buckramed[3] habit of clerical decorum, that carried him safely through the latter crisis.

"What is it that haunts and tempts me thus?" cried the minister to himself, at length, pausing in the street, and striking his hand against his forehead. "Am I mad? or am I given over utterly to the fiend? Did I make a contract with him in the forest, and sign it with my blood? And

3. Stiffened.

does he now summon me to its fulfilment, by suggesting the performance of every wickedness which his most foul imagination can conceive?"

At the moment when the Reverend Mr. Dimmesdale thus communed with himself, and struck his forehead with his hand, old Mistress Hibbins, the reputed witch-lady, is said to have been passing by. She made a very grand appearance; having on a high head-dress, a rich gown of velvet, and a ruff done up with the famous yellow starch, of which Ann Turner, her especial friend, had taught her the secret, before this last good lady had been hanged for Sir Thomas Overbury's murder.[4] Whether the witch had read the minister's thoughts, or no, she came to a full stop, looked shrewdly into his face, smiled craftily, and—though little given to converse with clergymen—began a conversation.

"So, reverend Sir, you have made a visit into the forest," observed the witch-lady, nodding her high head-dress at him. "The next time, I pray you to allow me only a fair warning, and I shall be proud to bear you company. Without taking overmuch upon myself, my good word will go far towards gaining any strange gentleman a fair reception from yonder potentate you wot of!"

"I profess, madam," answered the clergyman, with a grave obeisance, such as the lady's rank demanded, and his own good-breeding made imperative,—"I profess, on my conscience and character, that I am utterly bewildered as touching the purport of your words! I went not into the forest to seek a potentate; neither do I, at any future time, design a visit thither, with a view to gaining the favor of such personage. My one sufficient object was to greet that pious friend of mine, the Apostle Eliot, and rejoice with him over the many precious souls he hath won from heathendom!"

"Ha, ha, ha!" cackled the old witch-lady, still nodding her high head-dress at the minister. "Well, well, we must needs talk thus in the day-time! You carry it off like an old hand! But at midnight, and in the forest, we shall have other talk together!"

She passed on with her aged stateliness, but often turning back her head and smiling at him, like one willing to recognize a secret intimacy of connection.

"Have I then sold myself," thought the minister, "to the fiend whom, if men say true, this yellow-starched and velveted old hag has chosen for her prince and master!"

The wretched minister! He had made a bargain very like it! Tempted by a dream of happiness, he had yielded himself, with deliberate choice, as he had never done before, to what he knew was deadly sin. And the infectious poison of that sin had been thus rapidly diffused throughout his moral system. It had stupefied all blessed impulses, and awakened into vivid life the whole brotherhood of bad ones.

---

4. Anne Turner was one of the conspirators convicted of the murder of Thomas Overbury. See n. 5, p. 85, for more information. Mrs. Turner helped Frances Howard arrange assignations with Carr and confessed to providing the poison to Overbury's jailer, who gave it to Overbury.

Scorn, bitterness, unprovoked malignity, gratuitous desire of ill, ridicule of whatever was good and holy, all awoke, to tempt, even while they frightened him. And his encounter with old Mistress Hibbins, if it were a real incident, did but show his sympathy and fellowship with wicked mortals, and the world of perverted spirits.

He had, by this time, reached his dwelling, on the edge of the burial-ground, and, hastening up the stairs, took refuge in his study. The minister was glad to have reached this shelter, without first betraying himself to the world by any of those strange and wicked eccentricities to which he had been continually impelled while passing through the streets. He entered the accustomed room, and looked around him on its books, its windows, its fireplace, and the tapestried comfort of the walls,[5] with the same perception of strangeness that had haunted him throughout his walk from the forest-dell into the town, and thitherward. Here he had studied and written; here, gone through fast and vigil, and come forth half alive; here, striven to pray; here, borne a hundred thousand agonies! There was the Bible, in its rich old Hebrew, with Moses and the Prophets speaking to him, and God's voice through all! There, on the table, with the inky pen beside it, was an unfinished sermon, with a sentence broken in the midst, where his thoughts had ceased to gush out upon the page, two days before. He knew that it was himself, the thin and white-cheeked minister, who had done and suffered these things, and written thus far into the Election Sermon! But he seemed to stand apart, and eye this former self with scornful, pitying, but half-envious curiosity. That self was gone. Another man had returned out of the forest; a wiser one; with a knowledge of hidden mysteries which the simplicity of the former never could have reached. A bitter kind of knowledge that!

While occupied with these reflections, a knock came at the door of the study, and the minister said, "Come in!"—not wholly devoid of an idea that he might behold an evil spirit. And so he did! It was old Roger Chillingworth that entered. The minister stood, white and speechless, with one hand on the Hebrew Scriptures, and the other spread upon his breast.

"Welcome home, reverend Sir," said the physician. "And how found you that godly man, the Apostle Eliot? But methinks, dear Sir, you look pale; as if the travel through the wilderness had been too sore for you. Will not my aid be requisite to put you in heart and strength to preach your Election Sermon?"

"Nay, I think not so," rejoined the Reverend Mr. Dimmesdale. "My journey, and the sight of the holy Apostle yonder, and the free air which I have breathed, have done me good, after so long confinement in my study. I think to need no more of your drugs, my kind physician, good though they be, and administered by a friendly hand."

All this time, Roger Chillingworth was looking at the minister with the grave and intent regard of a physician towards his patient. But, in spite of this outward show, the latter was almost convinced of the old

5. A joke, assuming the David and Bathsheba tapestry still adorns Dimmesdale's wall. See n. 4, p. 84.

man's knowledge, or, at least, his confident suspicion, with respect to his own interview with Hester Prynne. The physician knew then, that, in the minister's regard, he was no longer a trusted friend, but his bitterest enemy. So much being known, it would appear natural that a part of it should be expressed. It is singular, however, how long a time often passes before words embody things; and with what security two persons, who choose to avoid a certain subject, may approach its very verge, and retire without disturbing it. Thus, the minister felt no apprehension that Roger Chillingworth would touch, in express words, upon the real position which they sustained towards one another. Yet did the physician, in his dark way, creep frightfully near the secret.

"Were it not better," said he, "that you use my poor skill to-night? Verily, dear Sir, we must take pains to make you strong and vigorous for this occasion of the Election discourse. The people look for great things from you; apprehending that another year may come about, and find their pastor gone."

"Yea, to another world," replied the minister, with pious resignation. "Heaven grant it be a better one; for, in good sooth, I hardly think to tarry with my flock through the flitting seasons of another year! But, touching your medicine, kind Sir, in my present frame of body, I need it not."

"I joy to hear it," answered the physician. "It may be that my remedies, so long administered in vain, begin now to take due effect. Happy man were I, and well deserving of New England's gratitude, could I achieve this cure!"

"I thank you from my heart, most watchful friend," said the Reverend Mr. Dimmesdale, with a solemn smile. "I thank you, and can but requite your good deeds with my prayers."

"A good man's prayers are golden recompense!" rejoined old Roger Chillingworth, as he took his leave. "Yea, they are the current gold coin of the New Jerusalem, with the King's own mint-mark on them!"

Left alone, the minister summoned a servant of the house, and requested food, which, being set before him, he ate with ravenous appetite. Then, flinging the already written pages of the Election Sermon into the fire, he forthwith began another, which he wrote with such an impulsive flow of thought and emotion, that he fancied himself inspired; and only wondered that Heaven should see fit to transmit the grand and solemn music of its oracles through so foul an organ-pipe as he. However, leaving that mystery to solve itself, or go unsolved forever, he drove his task onward, with earnest haste and ecstasy. Thus the night fled away, as if it were a winged steed, and he careering on it; morning came, and peeped, blushing, through the curtains; and at last sunrise threw a golden beam into the study, and laid it right across the minister's bedazzled eyes. There he was, with the pen still between his fingers, and a vast, immeasurable tract of written space behind him!

XXI. The New England Holiday

Betimes in the morning of the day on which the new Governor was to receive his office at the hands of the people, Hester Prynne and little Pearl came into the market-place. It was already thronged with the craftsmen and other plebeian inhabitants of the town, in considerable numbers; among whom, likewise, were many rough figures, whose attire of deer-skins marked them as belonging to some of the forest settlements, which surrounded the little metropolis of the colony.

On this public holiday, as on all other occasions, for seven years past, Hester was clad in a garment of coarse gray cloth. Not more by its hue than by some indescribable peculiarity in its fashion, it had the effect of making her fade personally out of sight and outline; while, again, the scarlet letter brought her back from this twilight indistinctness, and revealed her under the moral aspect of its own illumination. Her face, so long familiar to the townspeople, showed the marble quietude which they were accustomed to behold there. It was like a mask; or, rather, like the frozen calmness of a dead woman's features; owing this dreary resemblance to the fact that Hester was actually dead, in respect to any claim of sympathy, and had departed out of the world with which she still seemed to mingle.

It might be, on this one day, that there was an expression unseen before, nor, indeed, vivid enough to be detected now; unless some preternaturally gifted observer should have first read the heart, and have afterwards sought a corresponding development in the countenance and mien. Such a spiritual seer might have conceived, that, after sustaining the gaze of the multitude through seven miserable years as a necessity, a penance, and something which it was a stern religion to endure, she now, for one last time more, encountered it freely and voluntarily, in order to convert what had so long been agony into a kind of triumph. "Look your last on the scarlet letter and its wearer!"—the people's victim and life-long bond-slave, as they fancied her, might say to them. "Yet a little while, and she will be beyond your reach! A few hours longer, and the deep, mysterious ocean will quench and hide forever the symbol which ye have caused to burn upon her bosom!" Nor were it an inconsistency too improbable to be assigned to human nature, should we suppose a feeling of regret in Hester's mind, at the moment when she was about to win her freedom from the pain which had been thus deeply incorporated with her being. Might there not be an irresistible desire to quaff a last, long, breathless draught of the cup of wormwood and aloes, with which nearly all her years of womanhood had been perpetually flavored? The wine of life, henceforth to be presented to her lips, must be indeed rich, delicious, and exhilarating, in its chased[1] and golden beaker; or else leave an inevitable and weary languor, after the lees of bitterness wherewith she had been drugged, as with a cordial of intensest potency.

1. Engraved or embossed.

Pearl was decked out with airy gayety. It would have been impossible to guess that this bright and sunny apparition owed its existence to
the shape of gloomy gray; or that a fancy, at once so gorgeous and so
delicate as must have been requisite to contrive the child's apparel,
was the same that had achieved a task perhaps more difficult, in imparting so distinct a peculiarity to Hester's simple robe. The dress, so
proper was it to little Pearl, seemed an effluence, or inevitable development and outward manifestation of her character, no more to be
separated from her than the many-hued brilliancy from a butterfly's
wing, or the painted glory from the leaf of a bright flower. As with
these, so with the child; her garb was all of one idea with her nature.
On this eventful day, moreover, there was a certain singular inqui-
etude and excitement in her mood, resembling nothing so much as the
shimmer of a diamond, that sparkles and flashes with the varied throb-
bings of the breast on which it is displayed. Children have always a
sympathy in the agitations of those connected with them; always, especially, a sense of any trouble or impending revolution, of whatever
kind, in domestic circumstances; and therefore Pearl, who was the
gem on her mother's unquiet bosom, betrayed, by the very dance of
her spirits, the emotions which none could detect in the marble pas-
siveness of Hester's brow.

This effervescence made her flit with a birdlike movement, rather
than walk by her mother's side. She broke continually into shouts of a
wild, inarticulate, and sometimes piercing music. When they reached
the market-place, she became still more restless, on perceiving the stir
and bustle that enlivened the spot; for it was usually more like the
broad and lonesome green before a village meeting-house, than the
centre of a town's business.

"Why, what is this, mother?" cried she. "Wherefore have all the people left their work to-day? Is it a play-day for the whole world? See,
there is the black-smith! He has washed his sooty face, and put on his
Sabbath-day clothes, and looks as if he would gladly be merry, if any
kind body would only teach him how! And there is Master Brackett,
the old jailer, nodding and smiling at me. Why does he do so, mother?"

"He remembers thee a little babe, my child," answered Hester.

"He should not nod and smile at me, for all that,—the black, grim,
ugly-eyed old man!" said Pearl. "He may nod at thee, if he will; for
thou art clad in gray, and wearest the scarlet letter. But see, mother,
how many faces of strange people, and Indians among them, and
sailors! What have they all come to do, here in the market-place?"

"They wait to see the procession pass," said Hester. "For the Governor and the magistrates are to go by, and the ministers, and all the
great people and good people, with the music and the soldiers marching before them."

"And will the minister be there?" asked Pearl. "And will he hold out
both his hands to me, as when thou ledst me to him from the brook-
side?"

"He will be there, child," answered her mother. "But he will not
greet thee to-day; nor must thou greet him."

"What a strange, sad man is he!" said the child, as if speaking partly to herself. "In the dark night-time he calls us to him, and holds thy hand and mine, as when we stood with him on the scaffold yonder! And in the deep forest, where only the old trees can hear, and the strip of sky see it, he talks with thee, sitting on a heap of moss! And he kisses my forehead, too, so that the little brook would hardly wash it off! But here, in the sunny day, and among all the people, he knows us not; nor must we know him! A strange, sad man is he, with his hand always over his heart!"

"Be quiet, Pearl! Thou understandest not these things," said her mother. "Think not now of the minister, but look about thee, and see how cheery is every-body's face to-day. The children have come from their schools, and the grown people from their workshops and their fields, on purpose to be happy. For, to-day, a new man is beginning to rule over them; and so—as has been the custom of mankind ever since a nation was first gathered—they make merry and rejoice; as if a good and golden year were at length to pass over the poor old world!"

It was as Hester said, in regard to the unwonted jollity that brightened the faces of the people. Into this festal season of the year—as it already was, and continued to be during the greater part of two centuries—the Puritans compressed whatever mirth and public joy they deemed allowable to human infirmity; thereby so far dispelling the customary cloud, that, for the space of a single holiday, they appeared scarcely more grave than most other communities at a period of general affliction.

But we perhaps exaggerate the gray or sable tinge, which undoubtedly characterized the mood and manners of the age. The persons now in the market-place of Boston had not been born to an inheritance of Puritanic gloom. They were native Englishmen, whose fathers had lived in the sunny richness of the Elizabethan epoch; a time when the life of England, viewed as one great mass, would appear to have been as stately magnificent, and joyous, as the world has ever witnessed. Had they followed their hereditary taste, the New England settlers would have illustrated all events of public importance by bonfires, banquets, pageantries, and processions. Nor would it have been impracticable, in the observance of majestic ceremonies, to combine mirthful recreation with solemnity, and give, as it were, a grotesque and brilliant embroidery to the great robe of state, which a nation, at such festivals, puts on. There was some shadow of an attempt of this kind in the mode of celebrating the day on which the political year of the colony commenced. The dim reflection of a remembered splendor, a colorless and manifold diluted repetition of what they had beheld in proud old London,—we will not say at a royal coronation, but at a Lord Mayor's show,[2]—might be traced in the customs which our forefathers instituted, with reference to the annual installation of magistrates. The fathers and founders of the commonwealth—the

---

2. In London, Lord Mayor's day (November 9) featured a similar procession and celebration, as the lord mayor processed to and from Westminster, where he received from the lord chancellor the assent of the Crown to his election (*OED*).

statesman, the priest, and the soldier—deemed it a duty then to assume the outward state and majesty, which, in accordance with antique style, was looked upon as the proper garb of public or social eminence. All came forth, to move in procession before the people's eye, and thus impart a needed dignity to the simple framework of a government so newly constructed.

Then, too, the people were countenanced, if not encouraged, in relaxing the severe and close application to their various modes of rugged industry, which, at all other times, seemed of the same piece and material with their religion. Here, it is true, were none of the appliances which popular merriment would so readily have found in the England of Elizabeth's time, or that of James;—no rude shows of a theatrical kind; no minstrel, with his harp and legendary ballad, nor gleeman, with an ape dancing to his music; no juggler, with his tricks of mimic witchcraft; no Merry Andrew,[3] to stir up the multitude with jests, perhaps hundreds of years old, but still effective, by their appeals to the very broadest sources of mirthful sympathy. All such professors of the several branches of jocularity would have been sternly repressed, not only by the rigid discipline of law, but by the general sentiment which gives law its vitality. Not the less, however, the great, honest face of the people smiled, grimly, perhaps, but widely too. Nor were sports wanting, such as the colonists had witnessed, and shared in, long ago, at the country fairs and on the village-greens of England; and which it was thought well to keep alive on this new soil, for the sake of the courage and manliness that were essential in them. Wrestling-matches, in the different fashions of Cornwall and Devonshire, were seen here and there about the market-place; in one corner, there was a friendly bout at quarterstaff; and—what attracted most interest of all—on the platform of the pillory, already so noted in our pages, two masters of defence were commencing an exhibition with the buckler and broadsword.[4] But, much to the disappointment of the crowd, this latter business was broken off by the interposition of the town beadle, who had no idea of permitting the majesty of the law to be violated by such an abuse of one of its consecrated places.

It may not be too much to affirm, on the whole, (the people being then in the first stages of joyless deportment, and the offspring of sires who had known how to be merry, in their day,) that they would compare favorably, in point of holiday keeping, with their descendants, even at so long an interval as ourselves. Their immediate posterity, the generation next to the early emigrants, wore the blackest shade of Puritanism, and so darkened the national visage with it, that all the subsequent years have not sufficed to clear it up. We have yet to learn again the forgotten art of gayety.

The picture of human life in the market-place, though its general tint was the sad gray, brown, or black of the English emigrants, was yet

---

3. Clown or entertainer. *Gleeman:* minstrel.
4. A large, wide sword designed for cutting. *Quarterstaff:* a long pole used as a weapon. *Buckler:* small shield.

enlivened by some diversity of hue. A party of Indians—in their savage finery of curiously embroidered deer-skin robes, wampum-belts, red and yellow ochre, and feathers, and armed with the bow and arrow and stone-headed spear—stood apart, with countenances of inflexible gravity, beyond what even the Puritan aspect could attain. Nor, wild as were these painted barbarians, were they the wildest feature of the scene. This distinction could more justly be claimed by some mariners,—a part of the crew of the vessel from the Spanish Main,— who had come ashore to see the humors of Election Day. They were rough-looking desperadoes, with sun-blackened faces, and an immensity of beard; their wide, short trousers were confined about the waist by belts, often clasped with a rough plate of gold, and sustaining always a long knife, and, in some instances, a sword. From beneath their broad-brimmed hats of palm-leaf, gleamed eyes which, even in good nature and merriment, had a kind of animal ferocity. They transgressed, without fear or scruple, the rules of behavior that were binding on all others; smoking tobacco under the beadle's very nose, although each whiff would have cost a townsman a shilling; and quaffing, at their pleasure, draughts of wine or aqua-vitæ from pocketflasks, which they freely tendered to the gaping crowd around them. It remarkably characterized the incomplete morality of the age, rigid as we call it, that a license was allowed the seafaring class, not merely for their freaks on shore, but for far more desperate deeds on their proper element. The sailor of that day would go near to be arraigned as a pirate in our own. There could be little doubt, for instance, that this very ship's crew, though no unfavorable specimens of the nautical brotherhood, had been guilty, as we should phrase it, of depredations on the Spanish commerce, such as would have perilled all their necks in a modern court of justice.

But the sea, in those old times, heaved, swelled and foamed, very much at its own will, or subject only to the tempestuous wind, with hardly any attempts at regulation by human law. The buccaneer on the wave might relinquish his calling, and become at once, if he chose, a man of probity and piety on land; nor, even in the full career of his reckless life, was he regarded as a personage with whom it was disreputable to traffic, or casually associate. Thus, the Puritan elders, in their black cloaks, starched bands, and steeple-crowned hats, smiled not unbenignantly at the clamor and rude deportment of these jolly seafaring men; and it excited neither surprise nor animadversion, when so reputable a citizen as old Roger Chillingworth, the physician, was seen to enter the market-place, in close and familiar talk with the commander of the questionable vessel.

The latter was by far the most showy and gallant figure, so far as apparel went, anywhere to be seen among the multitude. He wore a profusion of ribbons on his garment, and gold lace on his hat, which was also encircled by a gold chain, and surmounted with a feather. There was a sword at his side, and a sword-cut on his forehead, which, by the arrangement of his hair, he seemed anxious rather to display than hide. A landsman could hardly have worn this garb and shown this face, and worn and shown them both with such a galliard[5] air, without undergoing stern question before a magistrate, and probably incurring fine or imprisonment, or perhaps an exhibition in the stocks. As regarded the shipmaster, however, all was looked upon as pertaining to the character, as to a fish his glistening scales.

After parting from the physician, the commander of the Bristol ship strolled idly through the market-place; until, happening to approach the spot where Hester Prynne was standing, he appeared to recognize, and did not hesitate to address her. As was usually the case wherever Hester stood, a small vacant area—a sort of magic circle—had formed itself about her, into which, though the people were elbowing one another at a little distance, none ventured, or felt disposed to intrude. It was a forcible type of the moral solitude in which the scarlet letter enveloped its fated wearer; partly by her own reserve, and partly by the instinctive, though no longer so unkindly, withdrawal of her fellow-creatures. Now, if never before, it answered a good purpose, by enabling Hester and the seaman to speak together without risk of being overheard; and so changed was Hester Prynne's repute before the public, that the matron in town most eminent for rigid morality could not have held such intercourse with less result of scandal than herself.

"So, mistress," said the mariner, "I must bid the steward make ready one more berth than you bargained for! No fear of scurvy or ship-fever, this voyage! What with the ship's surgeon and this other doctor, our only danger will be from drug or pill; more by token, as there is a lot of apothecary's stuff aboard, which I traded for with a Spanish vessel."

"What mean you?" inquired Hester, startled more than she permitted to appear. "Have you another passenger?"

"Why, know you not," cried the shipmaster, "that this physician here—Chillingworth, he calls himself—is minded to try my cabin-fare with you? Ay, ay, you must have known it; for he tells me he is of your party, and a close friend to the gentleman you spoke of,—he that is in peril from these sour old Puritan rulers!"

"They know each other well, indeed," replied Hester, with a mien of calmness, though in the utmost consternation. "They have long dwelt together."

Nothing further passed between the mariner and Hester Prynne. But, at that instant, she beheld old Roger Chillingworth himself, standing in the remotest corner of the market-place, and smiling on her; a smile which—across the wide and bustling square, and through all the talk and laughter, and various thoughts, moods, and interests of the crowd—conveyed secret and fearful meaning.

XXII. The Procession

Before Hester Prynne could call together her thoughts, and consider what was practicable to be done in this new and startling aspect of af-

---

5. Spirited, gay.

fairs, the sound of military music was heard approaching along a contiguous street. It denoted the advance of the procession of magistrates and citizens, on its way towards the meeting-house; where, in compliance with a custom thus early established, and ever since observed, the Reverend Mr. Dimmesdale was to deliver an Election Sermon.

Soon the head of the procession showed itself, with a slow and stately march, turning a corner, and making its way across the market-place. First came the music. It comprised a variety of instruments, perhaps imperfectly adapted to one another, and played with no great skill; but yet attaining the great object for which the harmony of drum and clarion addresses itself to the multitude,—that of imparting a higher and more heroic air to the scene of life that passes before the eye. Little Pearl at first clapped her hands, but then lost, for an instant, the restless agitation that had kept her in a continual effervescence throughout the morning; she gazed silently, and seemed to be borne upward, like a floating sea-bird, on the long heaves and swells of sound. But she was brought back to her former mood by the shimmer of the sunshine on the weapons and bright armor of the military company, which followed after the music, and formed the honorary escort of the procession. This body of soldiery—which still sustains a corporate existence, and marches down from past ages with an ancient and honorable fame—was composed of no mercenary materials. Its ranks were filled with gentlemen, who felt the stirrings of martial impulse, and sought to establish a kind of College of Arms, where, as in an association of Knights Templars,[1] they might learn the science, and, so far as peaceful exercise would teach them, the practices of war. The high estimation then placed upon the military character might be seen in the lofty port of each individual member of the company. Some of them, indeed, by their services in the Low Countries[2] and on other fields of European warfare, had fairly won their title to assume the name and pomp of soldiership. The entire array, moreover, clad in burnished steel, and with plumage nodding over their bright morions,[3] had a brilliancy of effect which no modern display can aspire to equal.

And yet the men of civil eminence, who came immediately behind the military escort, were better worth a thoughtful observer's eye. Even in outward demeanor, they showed a stamp of majesty that made the warrior's haughty stride look vulgar, if not absurd. It was an age when what we call talent had far less consideration than now, but the massive materials which produce stability and dignity of character a great deal more. The people possessed, by hereditary right, the quality of reverence; which, in their descendants, if it survive at all, exists in smaller proportion, and with a vastly diminished force, in the selection

1. A military order founded in the Catholic church early in the twelfth century. Members wore white habits with a distinctive red cross. They grew in power and wealth, becoming a transnational order answerable only to papal authority. In 1307, King Philip IV of France had all Templars arrested and tried for heresy upon accusations of denying Christ, spitting on the Cross, and sodomy. The order was formally dissolved in 1312. By the nineteenth century, the Knights Templar were popularly associated with occult magic (astrology and alchemy) and freemasonry.
2. The area now comprising the Netherlands, Luxembourg, and Belgium.
3. Brimmed helmets.

and estimate of public men. The change may be for good or ill, and is partly, perhaps, for both. In that old day, the English settler on these rude shores—having left king, nobles, and all degrees of awful rank behind, while still the faculty and necessity of reverence were strong in him—bestowed it on the white hair and venerable brow of age; on long-tried integrity; on solid wisdom and sad-colored experience; on endowments of that grave and weighty order which gives the idea of permanence, and comes under the general definition of respectability. These primitive statesmen, therefore,—Bradstreet, Endicott, Dudley, Bellingham, and their compeers,—who were elevated to power by the early choice of the people, seem to have been not often brilliant, but distinguished by a ponderous sobriety, rather than activity of intellect.[4] They had fortitude and self-reliance, and, in time of difficulty or peril, stood up for the welfare of the state like a line of cliffs against a tempestuous tide. The traits of character here indicated were well represented in the square cast of countenance and large physical development of the new colonial magistrates. So far as a demeanor of natural authority was concerned, the mother country need not have been ashamed to see these foremost men of an actual democracy adopted into the House of Peers, or made the Privy Council[5] of the sovereign.

Next in order to the magistrates came the young and eminently distinguished divine, from whose lips the religious discourse of the anniversary was expected. His was the profession, at that era, in which intellectual ability displayed itself far more than in political life; for—leaving a higher motive out of the question—it offered inducements powerful enough, in the almost worshipping respect of the community, to win the most aspiring ambition into its service. Even political power—as in the case of Increase Mather[6]—was within the grasp of a successful priest.

It was the observation of those who beheld him now, that never, since Mr. Dimmesdale first set his foot on the New England shore, had he exhibited such energy as was seen in the gait and air with which he kept his pace in the procession. There was no feebleness of step, as at other times; his frame was not bent; nor did his hand rest ominously upon his heart. Yet, if the clergyman were rightly viewed, his strength seemed not of the body. It might be spiritual, and imparted to him by angelic ministrations. It might be the exhilaration of that potent cordial, which is distilled only in the furnace-glow of

---

4. Simon Bradstreet (1604–1697), John Endicott (1588–1665), Thomas Dudley (1576–1653), and Richard Bellingham (1592–1672) each served as governor of Massachusetts Bay Colony. During the seven years encompassed by the novel, Bellingham, Endicott, Dudley, and John Winthrop served as governor. Bradstreet was not elected governor until 1679. His wife, poet Anne Bradstreet, was Thomas Dudley's daughter. Bradstreet, Dudley, Endicott, and Winthrop interrogated Anne Hutchinson at her General Court appearance in November 1637.

5. A group of advisors selected by the king. *House of Peers*: House of Lords, the second chamber of British Parliament; the other is the House of Commons.

6. A prominent minister, Increase Mather (1639–1723) was the first president of Harvard College. In referring to Mather's political power, Hawthorne probably refers to Mather's responsibility for negotiating a new charter for the colony. Mather and his son, Cotton, were both involved in the Salem witch trials of 1692.

earnest and long-continued thought. Or, perchance, his sensitive temperament was invigorated by the loud and piercing music, that swelled
heavenward, and uplifted him on its ascending wave. Nevertheless, so
abstracted was his look, it might be questioned whether Mr. Dimmesdale even heard the music. There was his body, moving onward, and
with an unaccustomed force. But where was his mind? Far and deep
in its own region, busying itself, with preternatural activity, to marshal
a procession of stately thoughts that were soon to issue thence; and so
he saw nothing, heard nothing, knew nothing, of what was around
him; but the spiritual element took up the feeble frame, and carried it
along, unconscious of the burden, and converting it to spirit like itself.
Men of uncommon intellect, who have grown morbid, possess this occasional power of mighty effort, into which they throw the life of many
days, and then are lifeless for as many more.

Hester Prynne, gazing steadfastly at the clergyman, felt a dreary influence come over her, but wherefore or whence she knew not; unless
that he seemed so remote from her own sphere, and utterly beyond
her reach. One glance of recognition, she had imagined, must needs
pass between them. She thought of the dim forest, with its little dell of
solitude, and love, and anguish, and the mossy tree-trunk, where, sitting hand in hand, they had mingled their sad and passionate talk with
the melancholy murmur of the brook. How deeply had they known
each other then! And was this the man? She hardly knew him now!
He, moving proudly past, enveloped, as it were, in the rich music, with
the procession of majestic and venerable fathers; he, so unattainable
in his worldly position, and still more so in that far vista of his unsympathizing thoughts, through which she now beheld him! Her spirit
sank with the idea that all must have been a delusion, and that, vividly
as she had dreamed it, there could be no real bond betwixt the clergyman and herself. And thus much of woman was there in Hester,
that she could scarcely forgive him,—least of all now, when the heavy
footstep of their approaching Fate might be heard, nearer, nearer,
nearer!—for being able so completely to withdraw himself from their
mutual world; while she groped darkly, and stretched forth her cold
hands, and found him not.

Pearl either saw and responded to her mother's feelings, or herself
felt the remoteness and intangibility that had fallen around the minister. While the procession passed, the child was uneasy, fluttering up
and down, like a bird on the point of taking flight. When the whole
had gone by, she looked up into Hester's face.

"Mother," said she, "was that the same minister that kissed me by
the brook?"

"Hold thy peace, dear little Pearl!" whispered her mother. "We must
not always talk in the market-place of what happens to us in the forest."

"I could not be sure that it was he; so strange he looked," continued
the child. "Else I would have run to him, and bid him kiss me now, before all the people; even as he did yonder among the dark old trees.
What would the minister have said, mother? Would he have clapped
his hand over his heart, and scowled on me, and bid me begone?"

"What should he say, Pearl," answered Hester, "save that it was no time to kiss, and that kisses are not to be given in the market-place? Well for thee, foolish child, that thou didst not speak to him!"

Another shade of the same sentiment, in reference to Mr. Dimmesdale, was expressed by a person whose eccentricities—or insanity, as we should term it—led her to do what few of the townspeople would have ventured on; to begin a conversation with the wearer of the scarlet letter, in public. It was Mistress Hibbins, who, arrayed in great magnificence, with a triple ruff, a broidered stomacher,[7] a gown of rich velvet, and a gold-headed cane, had come forth to see the procession. As this ancient lady had the renown (which subsequently cost her no less a price than her life) of being a principal actor in all the works of necromancy that were continually going forward, the crowd gave way before her, and seemed to fear the touch of her garment, as if it carried the plague among its gorgeous folds. Seen in conjunction with Hester Prynne,—kindly as so many now felt towards the latter,—the dread inspired by Mistress Hibbins was doubled, and caused a general movement from that part of the market-place in which the two women stood.

"Now, what mortal imagination could conceive it!" whispered the old lady, confidentially, to Hester. "Yonder divine man! That saint on earth, as the people uphold him to be, and as—I must needs say—he really looks! Who, now, that saw him pass in the procession, would think how little while it is since he went forth out of his study,—chewing a Hebrew text of Scripture in his mouth, I warrant,—to take an airing in the forest! Aha! we know what that means, Hester Prynne! But, truly, forsooth, I find it hard to believe him the same man. Many a church-member saw I, walking behind the music, that has danced in the same measure with me, when Somebody was fiddler, and, it might be, an Indian powwow or a Lapland[8] wizard changing hands with us! That is but a trifle, when a woman knows the world. But this minister! Couldst thou surely tell, Hester, whether he was the same man that encountered thee on the forest-path?"

"Madam, I know not of what you speak," answered Hester Prynne, feeling Mistress Hibbins to be of infirm mind; yet strangely startled and awe-stricken by the confidence with which she affirmed a personal connection between so many persons (herself among them) and the Evil One. "It is not for me to talk lightly of a learned and pious minister of the Word, like the Reverend Mr. Dimmesdale!"

"Fie, woman, fie!" cried the old lady, shaking her finger at Hester. "Dost thou think I have been to the forest so many times, and have yet no skill to judge who else has been there? Yea; though no leaf of the wild garlands, which they wore while they danced, be left in their hair! I know thee, Hester; for I behold the token. We may all see it in the sunshine; and it glows like a red flame in the dark. Thou wearest it openly; so there need be no question about that. But this minister! Let

7. Waistcoat.
8. Northernmost Sweden, Norway, and Finland.

me tell thee, in thine ear! When the Black Man sees one of his own servants, signed and sealed, so shy of owning to the bond as is the Reverend Mr. Dimmesdale, he hath a way of ordering matters so that the mark shall be disclosed in open daylight to the eyes of all the world! What is it that the minister seeks to hide, with his hand always over his heart? Ha, Hester Prynne!"

"What is it, good Mistress Hibbins?" eagerly asked little Pearl. "Hast thou seen it?"

"No matter, darling!" responded Mistress Hibbins, making Pearl a profound reverence. "Thou thyself wilt see it, one time or another. They say, child, thou art of the lineage of the Prince of the Air! Wilt thou ride with me, some fine night, to see thy father? Then thou shalt know wherefore the minister keeps his hand over his heart!"

Laughing so shrilly that all the market-place could hear her, the weird old gentlewoman took her departure.

By this time the preliminary prayer had been offered in the meeting-house, and the accents of the Reverend Mr. Dimmesdale were heard commencing his discourse. An irresistible feeling kept Hester near the spot. As the sacred edifice was too much thronged to admit another auditor, she took up her position close beside the scaffold of the pillory. It was in sufficient proximity to bring the whole sermon to her ears, in the shape of an indistinct, but varied, murmur and flow of the minister's very peculiar voice.

This vocal organ was in itself a rich endowment; insomuch that a listener, comprehending nothing of the language in which the preacher spoke, might still have been swayed to and fro by the mere tone and cadence. Like all other music, it breathed passion and pathos, and emotions high or tender, in a tongue native to the human heart, wherever educated. Muffled as the sound was by its passage through the church-walls, Hester Prynne listened with such intentness, and sympathized so intimately, that the sermon had throughout a meaning for her, entirely apart from its indistinguishable words. These, perhaps, if more distinctly heard, might have been only a grosser medium, and have clogged the spiritual sense. Now she caught the low undertone, as of the wind sinking down to repose itself; then ascended with it, as it rose through progressive gradations of sweetness and power, until its volume seemed to envelop her with an atmosphere of awe and solemn grandeur. And yet, majestic as the voice sometimes became, there was forever in it an essential character of plaintiveness. A loud or low expression of anguish,—the whisper, or the shriek, as it might be conceived, of suffering humanity, that touched a sensibility in every bosom! At times this deep strain of pathos was all that could be heard, and scarcely heard, sighing amid a desolate silence. But even when the minister's voice grew high and commanding,—when it gushed irrepressibly upward,—when it assumed its utmost breadth and power, so overfilling the church as to burst its way through the solid walls, and diffuse itself in the open air,—still, if the auditor listened intently, and for the purpose, he could detect the same cry of pain. What was it? The complaint of a human heart, sorrow-laden, perchance guilty, telling its secret, whether of guilt or sorrow, to the great heart of mankind; beseeching its sympathy or forgiveness,—at every moment,—in each accent,—and never in vain! It was this profound and continual undertone that gave the clergyman his most appropriate power.

During all this time, Hester stood, statue-like, at the foot of the scaffold. If the minister's voice had not kept her there, there would nevertheless have been an inevitable magnetism in that spot, whence she dated the first hour of her life of ignominy. There was a sense within her,—too ill-defined to be made a thought, but weighing heavily on her mind,—that her whole orb of life, both before and after, was connected with this spot, as with the one point that gave it unity.

Little Pearl, meanwhile, had quitted her mother's side, and was playing at her own will about the market-place. She made the sombre crowd cheerful by her erratic and glistening ray; even as a bird of bright plumage illuminates a whole tree of dusky foliage, by darting to and fro, half seen and half concealed amid the twilight of the clustering leaves. She had an undulating, but, oftentimes, a sharp and irregular movement. It indicated the restless vivacity of her spirit, which to-day was doubly indefatigable in its tiptoe dance, because it was played upon and vibrated with her mother's disquietude. Whenever Pearl saw anything to excite her ever active and wandering curiosity, she flew thitherward, and, as we might say, seized upon that man or thing as her own property, so far as she desired it; but without yielding the minutest degree of control over her motions in requital. The Puritans looked on, and, if they smiled, were none the less inclined to pronounce the child a demon offspring, from the indescribable charm of beauty and eccentricity that shone through her little figure, and sparkled with its activity. She ran and looked the wild Indian in the face; and he grew conscious of a nature wilder than his own. Thence, with native audacity, but still with a reserve as characteristic, she flew into the midst of a group of mariners, the swarthy-cheeked wild men of the ocean, as the Indians were of the land; and they gazed wonderingly and admiringly at Pearl, as if a flake of the sea-foam had taken the shape of a little maid, and were gifted with a soul of the sea-fire, that flashes beneath the prow in the night-time.

One of these seafaring men—the shipmaster, indeed, who had spoken to Hester Prynne—was so smitten with Pearl's aspect, that he attempted to lay hands upon her, with purpose to snatch a kiss. Finding it as impossible to touch her as to catch a humming-bird in the air, he took from his hat the gold chain that was twisted about it, and threw it to the child. Pearl immediately twined it around her neck and waist, with such happy skill, that, once seen there, it became a part of her, and it was difficult to imagine her without it.

"Thy mother is yonder woman with the scarlet letter," said the seaman. "Wilt thou carry her a message from me?"

"If the message pleases me, I will," answered Pearl.

"Then tell her," rejoined he, "that I spake again with the black-a-visaged, hump-shouldered old doctor, and he engages to bring his friend, the gentleman she wots of, aboard with him. So let thy mother take no thought, save for herself and thee. Wilt thou tell her this, thou witch-baby?"

"Mistress Hibbins says my father is the Prince of the Air!" cried Pearl, with a naughty smile. "If thou callest me that ill name, I shall tell him of thee; and he will chase thy ship with a tempest!"

Pursuing a zigzag course across the market-place, the child returned to her mother, and communicated what the mariner had said. Hester's strong, calm, steadfastly enduring spirit almost sank, at last, on beholding this dark and grim countenance of an inevitable doom, which—at the moment when a passage seemed to open for the minister and herself out of their labyrinth of misery—showed itself, with an unrelenting smile, right in the midst of their path.

With her mind harassed by the terrible perplexity in which the shipmaster's intelligence involved her, she was also subjected to another trial. There were many people present, from the country round about, who had often heard of the scarlet letter, and to whom it had been made terrific by a hundred false or exaggerated rumors, but who had never beheld it with their own bodily eyes. These, after exhausting other modes of amusement, now thronged about Hester Prynne with rude and boorish intrusiveness. Unscrupulous as it was, however, it could not bring them nearer than a circuit of several yards. At that distance they accordingly stood, fixed there by the centrifugal force of the repugnance which the mystic symbol inspired. The whole gang of sailors, likewise, observing the press of spectators, and learning the purport of the scarlet letter, came and thrust their sunburnt and desperado-looking faces into the ring. Even the Indians were affected by a sort of cold shadow of the white man's curiosity, and, gliding through the crowd, fastened their snake-like black eyes on Hester's bosom; conceiving, perhaps, that the wearer of this brilliantly embroidered badge must needs be a personage of high dignity among her people. Lastly the inhabitants of the town (their own interest in this worn-out subject languidly reviving itself, by sympathy with what they saw others feel) lounged idly to the same quarter, and tormented Hester Prynne, perhaps more than all the rest, with their cool, well-acquainted gaze at her familiar shame. Hester saw and recognized the self-same faces of that group of matrons, who had awaited her forthcoming from the prison-door, seven years ago; all save one, the youngest and only compassionate among them, whose burial-robe she had since made. At the final hour, when she was so soon to fling aside the burning letter, it had strangely become the centre of more remark and excitement, and was thus made to sear her breast more painfully, than at any time since the first day she put it on.

While Hester stood in that magic circle of ignominy, where the cunning cruelty of her sentence seemed to have fixed her forever, the admirable preacher was looking down from the sacred pulpit upon an audience, whose very inmost spirits had yielded to his control. The sainted minister in the church! The woman of the scarlet letter in the market-place! What imagination would have been irreverent enough to surmise that the same scorching stigma was on them both!

XXIII. The Revelation of the Scarlet Letter

The eloquent voice, on which the souls of the listening audience had been borne aloft as on the swelling waves of the sea, at length came to a pause. There was a momentary silence, profound as what should follow the utterance of oracles. Then ensued a murmur and half-hushed tumult; as if the auditors, released from the high spell that had transported them into the region of another's mind, were returning into themselves, with all their awe and wonder still heavy on them. In a moment more, the crowd began to gush forth from the doors of the church. Now that there was an end, they needed other breath, more fit to support the gross and earthly life into which they relapsed, than that atmosphere which the preacher had converted into words of flame, and had burdened with the rich fragrance of his thought.

In the open air their rapture broke into speech. The street and the market-place absolutely babbled, from side to side, with applauses of the minister. His hearers could not rest until they had told one another of what each knew better than he could tell or hear. According to their united testimony, never had man spoken in so wise, so high, and so holy a spirit, as he that spake this day; nor had inspiration ever breathed through mortal lips more evidently than it did through his. Its influence could be seen, as it were, descending upon him, and possessing him, and continually lifting him out of the written discourse that lay before him, and filling him with ideas that must have been as marvellous to himself as to his audience. His subject, it appeared, had been the relation between the Deity and the communities of mankind, with a special reference to the New England which they were here planting in the wilderness. And, as he drew towards the close, a spirit as of prophecy had come upon him, constraining him to its purpose as mightily as the old prophets of Israel were constrained; only with this difference, that, whereas the Jewish seers had denounced judgments and ruin on their country, it was his mission to foretell a high and glorious destiny for the newly gathered people of the Lord. But, throughout it all, and through the whole discourse, there had been a certain deep, sad undertone of pathos, which could not be interpreted otherwise than as the natural regret of one soon to pass away. Yes; their minister whom they so loved—and who so loved them all, that he could not depart heavenward without a sigh—had the foreboding of untimely death upon him, and would soon leave them in their tears! This idea of his transitory stay on earth gave the last emphasis to the effect which the preacher had produced; it was as if an angel, in his passage to the skies, had shaken his bright wings over the people for an instant,—at once a shadow and a splendor,—and had shed down a shower of golden truths upon them.

Thus, there had come to the Reverend Mr. Dimmesdale—as to most men, in their various spheres, though seldom recognized until they see it far behind them—an epoch of life more brilliant and full of triumph than any previous one, or than any which could hereafter be. He stood, at this moment, on the very proudest eminence of superiority, to which the gifts of intellect, rich lore, prevailing eloquence, and a reputation of whitest sanctity, could exalt a clergyman in New England's earliest days, when the professional character was of itself a lofty pedestal. Such was the position which the minister occupied, as he bowed his head forward on the cushions of the pulpit, at the close of his Election Sermon. Meanwhile Hester Prynne was standing beside the scaffold of the pillory, with the scarlet letter still burning on her breast!

Now was heard again the clangor of the music, and the measured tramp of the military escort, issuing from the church-door. The procession was to be marshalled thence to the town-hall, where a solemn banquet would complete the ceremonies of the day.

Once more, therefore, the train of venerable and majestic fathers was seen moving through a broad pathway of the people, who drew back reverently, on either side, as the Governor and magistrates, the old and wise men, the holy ministers, and all that were eminent and renowned, advanced into the midst of them. When they were fairly in the market-place, their presence was greeted by a shout. This—though doubtless it might acquire additional force and volume from the child-like loyalty which the age awarded to its rulers—was felt to be an irrepressible outburst of enthusiasm kindled in the auditors by that high strain of eloquence which was yet reverberating in their ears. Each felt the impulse in himself, and, in the same breath, caught it from his neighbor. Within the church, it had hardly been kept down; beneath the sky, it pealed upward to the zenith. There were human beings enough, and enough of highly wrought and symphonious feeling, to produce that more impressive sound than the organ tones of the blast, or the thunder, or the roar of the sea; even that mighty swell of many voices, blended into one great voice by the universal impulse which makes likewise one vast heart out of the many. Never, from the soil of New England, had gone up such a shout! Never, on New England soil, had stood the man so honored by his mortal brethren as the preacher!

How fared it with him then? Were there not the brilliant particles of a halo in the air about his head? So etherealized by spirit as he was, and so apotheosized by worshipping admirers, did his footsteps, in the procession, really tread upon the dust of earth?

As the ranks of military men and civil fathers moved onward, all eyes were turned towards the point where the minister was seen to approach among them. The shout died into a murmur, as one portion of the crowd after another obtained a glimpse of him. How feeble and pale he looked, amid all his triumph! The energy—or say, rather, the inspiration which had held him up, until he should have delivered the sacred message that brought its own strength along with it from heaven—was withdrawn, now that it had so faithfully performed its office. The glow, which they had just before beheld burning on his cheek, was extinguished, like a flame that sinks down hopelessly among the late-decaying embers. It seemed hardly the face of a man alive, with such a deathlike hue; it was hardly a man with life in him, that tottered on his path so nervelessly, yet tottered, and did not fall!

One of his clerical brethren,—it was the venerable John Wilson,— observing the state in which Mr. Dimmesdale was left by the retiring wave of intellect and sensibility, stepped forward hastily to offer his support. The minister tremulously, but decidedly, repelled the old man's arm. He still walked onward, if that movement could be so described, which rather resembled the wavering effort of an infant, with its mother's arms in view, outstretched to tempt him forward. And now, almost imperceptible as were the latter steps of his progress, he had come opposite the well-remembered and weather-darkened scaffold, where, long since, with all that dreary lapse of time between, Hester Prynne had encountered the world's ignominious stare. There stood Hester, holding little Pearl by the hand! And there was the scarlet letter on her breast! The minister here made a pause; although the music still played the stately and rejoicing march to which the procession moved. It summoned him onward,—onward to the festival!—but here he made a pause.

Bellingham, for the last few moments, had kept an anxious eye upon him. He now left his own place in the procession, and advanced to give assistance; judging, from Mr. Dimmesdale's aspect, that he must otherwise inevitably fall. But there was something in the latter's expression that warned back the magistrate, although a man not readily obeying the vague intimations that pass from one spirit to another. The crowd, meanwhile, looked on with awe and wonder. This earthly faintness was, in their view, only another phase of the minister's celestial strength; nor would it have seemed a miracle too high to be wrought for one so holy, had he ascended before their eyes, waxing dimmer and brighter, and fading at last into the light of heaven!

He turned towards the scaffold, and stretched forth his arms.

"Hester," said he, "come hither! Come, my little Pearl!"

It was a ghastly look with which he regarded them; but there was something at once tender and strangely triumphant in it. The child, with the bird-like motion which was one of her characteristics, flew to him, and clasped her arms about his knees. Hester Prynne—slowly, as if impelled by inevitable fate, and against her strongest will—likewise drew near, but paused before she reached him. At this instant, old Roger Chillingworth thrust himself through the crowd,—or, perhaps, so dark, disturbed and evil, was his look, he rose up out of some nether region,—to snatch back his victim from what he sought to do! Be that as it might, the old man rushed forward, and caught the minister by the arm.

"Madman, hold! what is your purpose?" whispered he. "Wave back that woman! Cast off this child! All shall be well! Do not blacken your fame, and perish in dishonor! I can yet save you! Would you bring infamy on your sacred profession?"

"Ha, tempter! Methinks thou art too late!" answered the minister, encountering his eye, fearfully, but firmly. "Thy power is not what it was! With God's help, I shall escape thee now!"

He again extended his hand to the woman of the scarlet letter.

"Hester Prynne," cried he, with a piercing earnestness, "in the name of Him, so terrible and so merciful, who gives me grace, at this last moment, to do what—for my own heavy sin and miserable agony—I withheld myself from doing seven years ago, come hither now, and twine thy strength about me! Thy strength, Hester; but let it be guided by the will which God hath granted me! This wretched and wronged old man is opposing it with all his might!—with all his own might, and the fiend's! Come, Hester, come! Support me up yonder scaffold!"

The crowd was in a tumult. The men of rank and dignity, who stood more immediately around the clergyman, were so taken by surprise, and so perplexed as to the purport of what they saw,—unable to receive the explanation which most readily presented itself, or to imagine any other,—that they remained silent and inactive spectators of the judgment which Providence seemed about to work. They beheld the minister, leaning on Hester's shoulder, and supported by her arm around him, approach the scaffold, and ascend its steps; while still the little hand of the sin-born child was clasped in his. Old Roger Chillingworth followed, as one intimately connected with the drama of guilt and sorrow in which they had all been actors, and well entitled, therefore, to be present, at its closing scene.

"Hadst thou sought the whole earth over," said he, looking darkly at the clergyman, "there was no one place so secret,—no high place nor lowly place, where thou couldst have escaped me,—save on this very scaffold!"

"Thanks be to Him who hath led me hither!" answered the minister.

Yet he trembled, and turned to Hester with an expression of doubt and anxiety in his eyes, not the less evidently betrayed, that there was a feeble smile upon his lips.

"Is not this better," murmured he, "than what we dreamed of in the forest?"

"I know not! I know not!" she hurriedly replied. "Better? Yea; so we may both die, and little Pearl die with us!"

"For thee and Pearl, be it as God shall order," said the minister; "and God is merciful! Let me now do the will which he hath made plain before my sight. For, Hester, I am a dying man. So let me make haste to take my shame upon me!"

Partly supported by Hester Prynne, and holding one hand of little Pearl's, the Reverend Mr. Dimmesdale turned to the dignified and venerable rulers; to the holy ministers, who were his brethren; to the people, whose great heart was thoroughly appalled, yet overflowing with tearful sympathy, as knowing that some deep life-matter—which, if full of sin, was full of anguish and repentance likewise—was now to be laid open to them. The sun, but little past its meridian, shone down upon the clergyman, and gave a distinctness to his figure, as he stood out from all the earth, to put in his plea of guilty at the bar of Eternal Justice.

"People of New England!" cried he, with a voice that rose over them, high, solemn, and majestic,—yet had always a tremor through it, and sometimes a shriek, struggling up out of a fathomless depth of remorse and woe,—"ye, that have loved me!—ye, that have deemed me holy!—behold me here, the one sinner of the world! At last!—at last!—I stand upon the spot where, seven years since, I should have stood; here, with this woman, whose arm, more than the little strength wherewith I have crept hitherward, sustains me, at this dreadful moment, from grovelling down upon my face! Lo, the scarlet letter which Hester wears! Ye have all shuddered at it! Wherever her walk hath been,—wherever, so miserably burdened, she may have hoped to find repose,—it hath cast a lurid gleam of awe and horrible repugnance round about her. But there stood one in the midst of you, at whose brand of sin and infamy ye have not shuddered!"

It seemed, at this point, as if the minister must leave the remainder of his secret undisclosed. But he fought back the bodily weakness,—and, still more, the faintness of heart,—that was striving for the mastery with him. He threw off all assistance, and stepped passionately forward a pace before the woman and the child.

"It was on him!" he continued, with a kind of fierceness; so determined was he to speak out the whole. "God's eye beheld it! The angels were forever pointing at it! The Devil knew it well, and fretted it continually with the touch of his burning finger! But he hid it cunningly from men, and walked among you with the mien of a spirit, mournful, because so pure in a sinful world!—and sad, because he missed his heavenly kindred! Now, at the death-hour, he stands up before you! He bids you look again at Hester's scarlet letter! He tells you, that, with all its mysterious horror, it is but the shadow of what he bears on his own breast, and that even this, his own red stigma, is no more than the type of what has seared his inmost heart! Stand any here that question God's judgment on a sinner? Behold! Behold a dreadful witness of it!"

With a convulsive motion, he tore away the ministerial band from before his breast. It was revealed! But it were irreverent to describe that revelation. For an instant, the gaze of the horror-stricken multitude was concentred on the ghastly miracle; while the minister stood, with a flush of triumph in his face, as one who, in the crisis of acutest pain, had won a victory. Then, down he sank upon the scaffold! Hester partly raised him, and supported his head against her bosom. Old Roger Chillingworth knelt down beside him, with a blank, dull countenance, out of which the life seemed to have departed.

"Thou hast escaped me!" he repeated more than once. "Thou hast escaped me!"

"May God forgive thee!" said the minister. "Thou, too, hast deeply sinned!"

He withdrew his dying eyes from the old man, and fixed them on the woman and the child.

"My little Pearl," said he, feebly,—and there was a sweet and gentle smile over his face, as of a spirit sinking into deep repose; nay, now that the burden was removed, it seemed almost as if he would be sportive with the child,—"dear little Pearl, wilt thou kiss me now? Thou wouldst not, yonder, in the forest! But now thou wilt?"

Pearl kissed his lips. A spell was broken. The great scene of grief, in which the wild infant bore a part, had developed all her sympathies; and as her tears fell upon her father's cheek, they were the pledge that she would grow up amid human joy and sorrow, nor forever do battle with the world, but be a woman in it. Towards her mother, too, Pearl's errand as a messenger of anguish was all fulfilled.

"Hester," said the clergyman, "farewell!"

"Shall we not meet again?" whispered she, bending her face down close to his. "Shall we not spend our immortal life together? Surely, surely, we have ransomed one another, with all this woe! Thou lookest far into eternity, with those bright dying eyes! Then tell me what thou seest?"

"Hush, Hester, hush!" said he, with tremulous solemnity. "The law we broke!—the sin here so awfully revealed!—let these alone be in thy thoughts! I fear! I fear! It may be, that, when we forgot our God,— when we violated our reverence each for the other's soul,—it was thenceforth vain to hope that we could meet hereafter, in an ever-lasting and pure reunion. God knows; and He is merciful! He hath proved his mercy, most of all, in my afflictions. By giving me this burn-ing torture to bear upon my breast! By sending yonder dark and terri-ble old man, to keep the torture always at red-heat! By bringing me hither, to die this death of triumphant ignominy before the people! Had either of these agonies been wanting, I had been lost forever! Praised be his name! His will be done! Farewell!"

That final word came forth with the minister's expiring breath. The multitude, silent till then, broke out in a strange, deep voice of awe and wonder, which could not as yet find utterance, save in this mur-mur that rolled so heavily after the departed spirit.

XXIV. Conclusion

After many days, when time sufficed for the people to arrange their thoughts in reference to the foregoing scene, there was more than one account of what had been witnessed on the scaffold.

Most of the spectators testified to having seen, on the breast of the unhappy minister, a SCARLET LETTER—the very semblance of that worn by Hester Prynne—imprinted in the flesh. As regarded its origin, there were various explanations, all of which must necessarily have been conjectural. Some affirmed that the Reverend Mr. Dimmesdale, on the very day when Hester Prynne first wore her ignominious badge, had begun a course of penance,—which he afterwards, in so many fu-tile methods, followed out,—by inflicting a hideous torture on himself. Others contended that the stigma had not been produced until a long time subsequent, when old Roger Chillingworth, being a potent necro-mancer, had caused it to appear, through the agency of magic and poisonous drugs. Others, again,—and those best able to appreciate the minister's peculiar sensibility, and the wonderful operation of his spirit upon the body,—whispered their belief, that the awful symbol was the effect of the ever active tooth of remorse, gnawing from the inmost heart outwardly, and at last manifesting Heaven's dreadful judgment by the visible presence of the letter. The reader may choose among these theories. We have thrown all the light we could acquire upon the portent, and would gladly, now that it has done its office, erase its deep print out of our own brain; where long meditation has fixed it in very undesirable distinctness.

It is singular, nevertheless, that certain persons, who were spectators of the whole scene, and professed never once to have removed their eyes from the Reverend Mr. Dimmesdale, denied that there was any mark whatever on his breast, more than on a new-born infant's. Neither, by their report, had his dying words acknowledged, nor even remotely implied, any, the slightest connection, on his part, with the guilt for which Hester Prynne had so long worn the scarlet letter. According to these highly respectable witnesses, the minister, conscious that he was dying,—conscious, also, that the reverence of the multitude placed him already among saints and angels,—had desired, by yielding up his breath in the arms of that fallen woman, to express to the world how utterly nugatory[1] is the choicest of man's own righteousness. After exhausting life in his efforts for mankind's spiritual good, he had made the manner of his death a parable, in order to impress on his admirers the mighty and mournful lesson, that, in the view of Infinite Purity, we are sinners all alike. It was to teach them, that the holiest among us has but attained so far above his fellows as to discern more clearly the Mercy which looks down, and repudiate more utterly the phantom of human merit, which would look aspiringly upward. Without disputing a truth so momentous, we must be allowed to consider this version of Mr. Dimmesdale's story as only an instance of that stubborn fidelity with which a man's friends—and especially a clergyman's—will sometimes uphold his character, when proofs, clear as the mid-day sunshine on the scarlet letter, establish him a false and sin-stained creature of the dust.

The authority which we have chiefly followed,—a manuscript of old date, drawn up from the verbal testimony of individuals, some of whom had known Hester Prynne, while others had heard the tale from contemporary witnesses,—fully confirms the view taken in the foregoing pages. Among many morals which press upon us from the poor minister's miserable experience, we put only this into a sentence:— "Be true! Be true! Be true! Show freely to the world, if not your worst, yet some trait whereby the worst may be inferred!"

Nothing was more remarkable than the change which took place, almost immediately after Mr. Dimmesdale's death, in the appearance and demeanor of the old man known as Roger Chillingworth. All his strength and energy—all his vital and intellectual force—seemed at

1. Worthless.

once to desert him; insomuch that he positively withered up, shrivelled away, and almost vanished from mortal sight, like an uprooted weed that lies wilting in the sun. This unhappy man had made the very principle of his life to consist in the pursuit and systematic exercise of revenge; and when, by its completest triumph and consummation, that evil principle was left with no further material to support it, when, in short, there was no more Devil's work on earth for him to do, it only remained for the unhumanized mortal to betake himself whither his Master would find him tasks enough, and pay him his wages duly. But, to all these shadowy beings, so long our near acquaintances,—as well Roger Chillingworth as his companions,—we would fain be merciful. It is a curious subject of observation and inquiry, whether hatred and love be not the same thing at bottom. Each, in its utmost development, supposes a high degree of intimacy and heart-knowledge; each renders one individual dependent for the food of his affections and spiritual life upon another; each leaves the passionate lover, or the no less passionate hater, forlorn and desolate by the withdrawal of his subject. Philosophically considered, therefore, the two passions seem essentially the same, except that one happens to be seen in a celestial radiance, and the other in a dusky and lurid glow. In the spiritual world, the old physician and the minister—mutual victims as they have been—may, unawares, have found their earthly stock of hatred and antipathy transmuted into golden love.

Leaving this discussion apart, we have a matter of business to communicate to the reader. At old Roger Chillingworth's decease, (which took place within the year,) and by his last will and testament, of which Governor Bellingham and the Reverend Mr. Wilson were executors, he bequeathed a very considerable amount of property, both here and in England, to little Pearl, the daughter of Hester Prynne.

So Pearl—the elf-child,—the demon offspring, as some people, up to that epoch, persisted in considering her,—became the richest heiress of her day, in the New World. Not improbably, this circumstance wrought a very material change in the public estimation; and, had the mother and child remained here, little Pearl, at a marriageable period of life, might have mingled her wild blood with the lineage of the devoutest Puritan among them all. But, in no long time after the physician's death, the wearer of the scarlet letter disappeared, and Pearl along with her. For many years, though a vague report would now and then find its way across the sea,—like a shapeless piece of driftwood tost ashore, with the initials of a name upon it,—yet no tidings of them unquestionably authentic were received. The story of the scarlet letter grew into a legend. Its spell, however, was still potent, and kept the scaffold awful where the poor minister had died, and likewise the cottage by the sea-shore, where Hester Prynne had dwelt. Near this latter spot, one afternoon, some children were at play, when they beheld a tall woman, in a gray robe, approach the cottage-door. In all those years it had never once been opened; but either she unlocked it, or the decaying wood and iron yielded to her hand, or she glided shadow-like through these impediments,—and, at all events, went in.

On the threshold she paused,—turned partly round,—for, per-chance, the idea of entering all alone, and all so changed, the home of so intense a former life, was more dreary and desolate than even she could bear. But her hesitation was only for an instant, though long enough to display a scarlet letter on her breast.

And Hester Prynne had returned, and taken up her long-forsaken shame! But where was little Pearl? If still alive, she must now have been in the flush and bloom of early womanhood. None knew—nor ever learned, with the fulness of perfect certainty—whether the elf-child had gone thus untimely to a maiden grave; or whether her wild, rich nature had been softened and subdued, and made capable of a woman's gentle happiness. But, through the remainder of Hester's life, there were indications that the recluse of the scarlet letter was the ob-ject of love and interest with some inhabitant of another land. Letters came, with armorial seals upon them, though of bearings unknown to English heraldry. In the cottage there were articles of comfort and lux-ury, such as Hester never cared to use, but which only wealth could have purchased, and affection have imagined for her. There were tri-fles, too, little ornaments, beautiful tokens of a continual remem-brance, that must have been wrought by delicate fingers, at the impulse of a fond heart. And, once, Hester was seen embroidering a baby-garment, with such a lavish richness of golden fancy as would have raised a public tumult, had any infant, thus apparelled, been shown to our sober-hued community.

In fine, the gossips of that day believed,—and Mr. Surveyor Pue, who made investigations a century later, believed,—and one of his re-cent successors in office, moreover, faithfully believes,—that Pearl was not only alive, but married, and happy, and mindful of her mother; and that she would most joyfully have entertained that sad and lonely mother at her fireside.

But there was a more real life for Hester Prynne, here, in New En-gland, than in that unknown region where Pearl had found a home. Here had been her sin; here, her sorrow; and here was yet to be her penitence. She had returned, therefore, and resumed,—of her own free will, for not the sternest magistrate of that iron period would have imposed it,—resumed the symbol of which we have related so dark a tale. Never afterwards did it quit her bosom. But, in the lapse of the toilsome, thoughtful, and self-devoted years that made up Hester's life, the scarlet letter ceased to be a stigma which attracted the world's scorn and bitterness, and became a type of something to be sorrowed over, and looked upon with awe, yet with reverence too. And, as Hes-ter Prynne had no selfish ends, nor lived in any measure for her own profit and enjoyment, people brought all their sorrows and perplexi-ties, and besought her counsel, as one who had herself gone through a mighty trouble. Women, more especially,—in the continually recurring trials of wounded, wasted, wronged, misplaced, or erring and sinful passion,—or with the dreary burden of a heart unyielded, because un-valued and unsought,—came to Hester's cottage, demanding why they were so wretched, and what the remedy! Hester comforted and coun-

selled them, as best she might.[2] She assured them, too, of her firm belief, that, at some brighter period, when the world should have grown
ripe for it, in Heaven's own time, a new truth would be revealed, in order to establish the whole relation between man and woman on a
surer ground of mutual happiness.[3] Earlier in life, Hester had vainly
imagined that she herself might be the destined prophetess, but had
long since recognized the impossibility that any mission of divine and
mysterious truth should be confided to a woman stained with sin,
bowed down with shame, or even burdened with a life-long sorrow.
The angel and apostle of the coming revelation must be a woman, indeed, but lofty, pure, and beautiful; and wise, moreover, not through
dusky grief, but the ethereal medium of joy; and showing how sacred
love should make us happy, by the truest test of a life successful to
such an end!

So said Hester Prynne, and glanced her sad eyes downward at the
scarlet letter. And, after many, many years, a new grave was delved,
near an old and sunken one, in that burial-ground beside which King's
Chapel has since been built. It was near that old and sunken grave, yet
with a space between, as if the dust of the two sleepers had no right to
mingle. Yet one tombstone served for both. All around, there were
monuments carved with armorial bearings; and on this simple slab of
slate—as the curious investigator may still discern, and perplex himself with the purport—there appeared the semblance of an engraved
escutcheon. It bore a device, a herald's wording of which might serve
for a motto and brief description of our now concluded legend; so
sombre is it, and relieved only by one ever-glowing point of light
gloomier than the shadow:—

"ON A FIELD, SABLE, THE LETTER A, GULES."[4]

---

2. It is worth recalling that Anne Hutchinson had been charged with unlawfully hosting weekly
   meetings for women. Under interrogation by John Winthrop, Hutchinson cited the New Testament passage in Titus that the "older women should instruct the younger." See Titus
   2:3–5: "The aged women likewise, that they be in behaviour as becometh holiness, not false
   accusers, not given to much wine, teachers of good things; / That they may teach the young
   women to be sober, to love their husbands, to love their children, / To be discreet, chaste,
   keepers at home, good, obedient to their own husbands, that the word of God be not blas-
   phemed."
3. Compare the passage in Hawthorne's campaign biography of Franklin Pierce on pp. 232–34.
   As Thomas Mitchell argues in *Hawthorne's Fuller Mystery*, Hawthorne may also be echoing
   passages in Margaret Fuller's *Woman in the Nineteenth Century* (1845). Early in the book
   Fuller comments, "Yet, then and only then, will mankind be ripe for this, when inward and
   outward freedom for woman as much as for man shall be acknowledged as a right, not
   yielded as a concession" (20). Near the conclusion she observes, "And will not she soon appear? The woman who shall vindicate their birthright for all women; who shall teach them
   what to claim, and how to use what they obtain? Shall not her name be for her era Victoria,
   for her country and life Virginia. Yet predictions are rash; she herself must teach us to give
   her the fitting name" (104). See Margaret Fuller, *Woman in the Nineteenth Century*, ed.
   Larry J. Reynolds (New York: Norton, 1998).
4. "On a black background, the letter A in red." *Sable*: one of the colors of English heraldry, indicated by horizontal and vertical lines crossing each other. *Gules*: the color red, represented
   by vertical lines (*OED*).

Other Writings

Mrs. Hutchinson†

The character of this female suggests a train of thought which will form as natural an introduction to her story as most of the prefaces to Gay's Fables or the tales of Prior,[1] besides that the general soundness of the moral may excuse any want of present applicability. We will not look for a living resemblance of Mrs. Hutchinson, though the search might not be altogether fruitless.—But there are portentous indications, changes gradually taking place in the habits and feelings of the gentle sex, which seem to threaten our posterity with many of those public women, whereof one was a burthen too grievous for our fathers. The press, however, is now the medium through which feminine ambition chiefly manifests itself, and we will not anticipate the period, (trusting to be gone hence ere it arrive,) when fair orators shall be as numerous as the fair authors of our own day. The hastiest glance may show, how much of the texture and body of cis-atlantic literature is the work of those slender fingers, from which only a light and fanciful embroidery has heretofore been required, that might sparkle upon the garment without enfeebling the web. Woman's intellect should never give the tone to that of man, and even her morality is not exactly the material for masculine virtue. A false liberality which mistakes the strong division lines of Nature for arbitrary distinctions, and a courtesy, which might polish criticism but should never soften it, have done their best to add a girlish feebleness to the tottering infancy of our literature. The evil is likely to be a growing one. As yet, the great body of American women are a domestic race; but when a continuance of ill-judged incitements shall have turned their hearts away from the fire-side, there are obvious circumstances which will render female pens more numerous and more prolific than those of men, though but equally encouraged; and (limited of course by the scanty support of the public, but increasing indefinitely within those limits) the ink-stained Amazons will expel their rivals by actual pressure, and petticoats wave triumphant over all the field.[2] But, allowing that

---

† First published in the Salem *Gazette* (December 7, 1830) and not collected until *Miscellaneous Prose and Verse*, vol. 23 of the *Centenary Edition of the Works of Nathaniel Hawthorne*, ed. Thomas Woodson, Claude M. Simpson, and L. Neal Smith (Columbus: Ohio State UP, 1994), 66–74.
1. John Gay (1685–1732) published his *Fables* in 1727. An expanded version appeared in 1738 after his death. Matthew Prior (1664–1721) is perhaps best-known for *The Hind and the Panther Transvers'd to the Story of the Country and the City Mouse* (1687).
2. This characterization of women writers anticipates by twenty-five years Hawthorne's notorious remark in a January 19, 1855, letter to George Ticknor that "America is now wholly given over to a d—d mob of scribbling women" with whose "trash" the "public taste is occupied."

such forebodings are slightly exaggerated, is it good for woman's self that the path of feverish hope, of tremulous success, of bitter and ignominious disappointment, should be left wide open to her? Is the prize worth her having if she win it? Fame does not increase the peculiar respect which men pay to female excellence, and there is a delicacy, (even in rude bosoms, where few would think to find it) that perceives, or fancies, a sort of impropriety in the display of woman's naked mind to the gaze of the world, with indications by which its inmost secrets may be searched out. In fine, criticism should examine with a stricter, instead of a more indulgent eye, the merits of females at its bar, because they are to justify themselves for an irregularity which men do not commit in appearing there; and woman, when she feels the impulse of genius like a command of Heaven within her, should be aware that she is relinquishing a part of the loveliness of her sex, and obey the inward voice with sorrowing reluctance, like the Arabian maid who bewailed the gift of Prophecy. Hinting thus imperfectly at sentiments which may be developed on a future occasion, we proceed to consider the celebrated subject of this sketch.

Mrs. Hutchinson was a woman of extraordinary talent and strong imagination, whom the latter quality, following the general direction taken by the enthusiasm of the times, prompted to stand forth as a reformer in religion. In her native country, she had shown symptoms of irregular and daring thought, but, chiefly by the influence of a favorite pastor, was restrained from open indiscretion. On the removal of this clergyman, becoming dissatisfied with the ministry under which she lived, she was drawn in by the great tide of Puritan emigration, and visited Massachusetts within a few years after its first settlement. But she bore trouble in her own bosom, and could find no peace in this chosen land.—She soon began to promulgate strange and dangerous opinions, tending, in the peculiar situation of the colony, and from the principles which were its basis and indispensable for its temporary support, to eat into its very existence. We shall endeavor to give a more practical idea of this part of her course.

It is a summer evening. The dusk has settled heavily upon the woods, the waves, and the Trimontane peninsula,[3] increasing that dismal aspect of the embryo town which was said to have drawn tears of despondency from Mrs. Hutchinson, though she believed that her mission thither was divine. The houses, straw-thatched and lowly roofed, stand irregularly along streets that are yet roughened by the roots of the trees, as if the forest, departing at the approach of man, had left its reluctant foot prints behind. Most of the dwellings are lonely and silent; from a few we may hear the reading of some sacred text, or the quiet voice of prayer; but nearly all the sombre life of the scene is collected near the extremity of the village. A crowd of hooded women, and of men in steeple-hats and close cropt hair, are assembled at the door and open windows of a house newly built. An earnest expression glows in every face, and some press inward as if the bread of

---

3. The site of Boston on the south side of the Charles River.

life were to be dealt forth, and they feared to lose their share, while others would fain hold them back, but enter with them since they may not be restrained. We also will go in, edging through the thronged doorway to an apartment which occupies the whole breadth of the house. At the upper end, behind a table on which are placed the Scriptures and two glimmering lamps, we see a woman, plainly attired as befits her ripened years; her hair, complexion, and eyes are dark, the latter somewhat dull and heavy, but kindling up with a gradual brightness. Let us look round upon the hearers. At her right hand, his countenance suiting well with the gloomy light which discovers it, stands Vane the youthful governor, preferred by a hasty judgment of the people over all the wise and hoary heads that had preceded him to New-England.[4] In his mysterious eyes we may read a dark enthusiasm, akin to that of the woman whose cause he has espoused, combined with a shrewd worldly foresight, which tells him that her doctrines will be productive of change and tumult, the elements of his power and delight. On her left, yet slightly drawn back so as to evince a less decided support, is Cotton, no young and hot enthusiast, but a mild, grave man in the decline of life, deep in all the learning of the age, and sanctified in heart and made venerable in feature by the long exercise of his holy profession.[5] He also is deceived by the strange fire now laid upon the altar, and he alone among his brethren is excepted in the denunciation of the new Apostle, as sealed and set apart by Heaven to the work of the ministry. Others of the priesthood stand full in front of the woman, striving to beat her down with brows of wrinkled iron, and whispering sternly and significantly among themselves, as she unfolds her seditious doctrines and grows warm in their support. Foremost is Hugh Peters, full of holy wrath, and scarce containing himself from rushing forward to convict her of damnable heresies; there also is Ward, meditating a reply of empty puns, and quaint antitheses, and tinkling jests that puzzle us with nothing but a sound.[6] The audience are variously affected, but none indifferent. On the foreheads of the aged, the mature, and strong-minded, you may generally read steadfast disapprobation, though here and there is one, whose faith seems shaken in those whom he had trusted for years; the females, on the other hand, are shuddering and weeping, and at times they cast a desolate look of fear around them; while the young men lean forward, fiery and impatient, fit instruments for whatever rash deed may be suggested. And what is the eloquence that gives rise to all these passions? The woman tells them, (and cites texts from the Holy Book to prove her words,) that they have put their trust in unregener-

---

4. Henry Vane (1613–1662), who supported Hutchinson, served as governor in 1636–37 and thus preceded John Winthrop, who presided at Hutchinson's "trial." Vane was only twenty-four years old in 1637.
5. John Cotton (1584–1652) was centrally involved in the Antinomian controversy of 1636–38 that resulted in Hutchinson's banishment from the colony. Cotton was called as a witness at Hutchinson's trial and testified that he had not heard her claim that his "brother" ministers were preaching a covenant of works.
6. Hugh Peter (1598–1660) replaced Roger Williams as pastor in Salem. Nathaniel Ward (1578–1652), author of *The Simple Cobler of Aggawam* (1647), wrote the *Body of Liberties* (1641) that constrained the power of Massachusetts Bay Colony magistrates.

ated and uncommissioned men, and have followed them into the wilderness for naught. Therefore their hearts are turning from those whom they had chosen to lead them to Heaven, and they feel like children who have been enticed far from home, and see the features of their guides change all at once, assuming a fiendish shape in some frightful solitude.

These proceedings of Mrs. Hutchinson could not long be endured by the provincial government. The present was a most remarkable case, in which religious freedom was wholly inconsistent with public safety, and where the principles of an illiberal age indicated the very course which must have been pursued by worldly policy and enlightened wisdom. Unity of faith was the star that had guided these people over the deep, and a diversity of sects would either have scattered them from the land to which they had as yet so few attachments, or perhaps have excited a diminutive civil war among those who had come so far to worship together. The opposition to what may be termed the established church had now lost its chief support, by the removal of Vane from office and his departure for England, and Mr. Cotton began to have that light in regard to his errors, which will sometimes break in upon the wisest and most pious men, when their opinions are unhappily discordant with those of the Powers that be. A Synod, the first in New England, was speedily assembled, and pronounced its condemnation of the obnoxious doctrines.[7] Mrs. Hutchinson was next summoned before the supreme civil tribunal, at which, however, the most eminent of the clergy were present, and appear to have taken a very active part as witnesses and advisers. We shall here resume the more picturesque style of narration.

It is a place of humble aspect where the Elders of the people are met, sitting in judgment upon the disturber of Israel. The floor of the low and narrow hall is laid with planks hewn by the axe,—the beams of the roof still wear the rugged bark with which they grew up in the forest, and the hearth is formed of one broad unhammered stone, heaped with logs that roll their blaze and smoke up a chimney of wood and clay. A sleety shower beats fitfully against the windows, driven by the November blast, which comes howling onward from the northern desert, the boisterous and unwelcome herald of a New England winter.[8] Rude benches are arranged across the apartment and along its sides, occupied by men whose piety and learning might have entitled them to seats in those high Councils of the ancient Church, whence opinions were sent forth to confirm or supersede the Gospel in the belief of the whole world and of posterity.—Here are collected all those blessed Fathers of the land, who rank in our veneration next to the Evangelists of Holy Writ, and here also are many, unpurified from the fiercest errors of the age and ready to propagate the religion of peace by violence. In the highest place sits Winthrop, a man by whom the innocent and the guilty might alike desire to be judged, the first con-

---

7. The synod convened on August 30, 1637. John Winthrop was re-elected governor in 1637 and again in 1638 and 1639.
8. November 2, 1637.

fiding in his integrity and wisdom, the latter hoping in his mildness. Next is Endicott, who would stand with his drawn sword at the gate of Heaven, and resist to the death all pilgrims thither, except they travelled his own path.[9] The infant eyes of one in this assembly beheld the faggots blazing round the martyrs, in bloody Mary's time;[1] in later life he dwelt long at Leyden, with the first who went from England for conscience sake; and now, in his weary age, it matters little where he lies down to die. There are others whose hearts were smitten in the high meridian of ambitious hope, and whose dreams still tempt them with the pomp of the old world and the din of its crowded cities, gleaming and echoing over the deep. In the midst, and in the centre of all eyes, we see the Woman. She stands loftily before her judges, with a determined brow, and, unknown to herself, there is a flash of carnal pride half hidden in her eye, as she surveys the many learned and famous men whom her doctrines have put in fear. They question her, and her answers are ready and acute; she reasons with them shrewdly, and brings scripture in support of every argument; the deepest controversialists of that scholastic day find here a woman, whom all their trained and sharpened intellects are inadequate to foil. But by the excitement of the contest, her heart is made to rise and swell within her, and she bursts forth into eloquence. She tells them of the long unquietness which she had endured in England, perceiving the corruption of the church, and yearning for a purer and more perfect light, and how, in a day of solitary prayer, that light was given; she claims for herself the peculiar power of distinguishing between the chosen of man and the Sealed of Heaven, and affirms that her gifted eye can see the glory round the foreheads of the Saints, sojourning in their mortal state.—She declares herself commissioned to separate the true shepherds from the false, and denounces present and future judgments on the land, if she be disturbed in her celestial errand. Thus the accusations are proved from her own mouth. Her judges hesitate, and some speak faintly in her defence; but, with a few dissenting voices, sentence is pronounced, bidding her go out from among them, and trouble the land no more.

Mrs. Hutchinson's adherents throughout the colony were now disarmed, and she proceeded to Rhode Island, an accustomed refuge for the exiles of Massachusetts, in all seasons of persecution.[2] Her enemies believed that the anger of Heaven was following her, of which Governor Winthrop does not disdain to record a notable instance, very interesting in a scientific point of view, but fitter for his old and homely narrative than for modern repetition. In a little time, also, she lost her husband, who is mentioned in history only as attending her footsteps, and whom we may conclude to have been (like most husbands of celebrated women) a mere insignificant appendage of his

9. John Endicott was deputy governor of Massachusetts Bay Colony in 1637.
1. The Catholic Queen Mary, or "Bloody Mary," ruled England briefly (1553–58) as a fierce anti-Protestant. She was succeeded by the Protestant Queen Elizabeth I.
2. After Roger Williams was banished in 1635, he settled in Rhode Island. Because it was winter when Hutchinson was sentenced, she was allowed to postpone her departure until the spring.

mightier wife.[3] She now grew uneasy among the Rhode-Island colonists, whose liberality towards her, at an era when liberality was not esteemed a christian virtue, probably arose from a comparative insolicitude on religious matters, more distasteful to Mrs. Hutchinson than even the uncompromising narrowness of the Puritans. Her final movement was to lead her family within the limits of the Dutch Jurisdiction, where, having felled the trees of a virgin soil, she became herself the virtual head, civil and ecclesiastical, of a little colony.

Perhaps here she found the repose, hitherto so vainly sought. Secluded from all whose faith she could not govern, surrounded by the dependents over whom she held an unlimited influence, agitated by none of the tumultuous billows which were left swelling behind her, we may suppose, that, in the stillness of Nature, her heart was stilled. But her impressive story was to have an awful close. Her last scene is as difficult to be portrayed as a shipwreck, where the shrieks of the victims die unheard along a desolate sea, and a shapeless mass of agony is all that can be brought home to the imagination. The savage foe was on the watch for blood. Sixteen persons assembled at the evening prayer; in the deep midnight, their cry rang through the forest; and daylight dawned upon the lifeless clay of all but one. It was a circumstance not to be unnoticed by our stern ancestors, in considering the fate of her who had so troubled their religion, that an infant daughter, the sole survivor amid the terrible destruction of her mother's household, was bred in a barbarous faith, and never learned the way to the Christian's Heaven. Yet we will hope, that there the mother and the child have met.[4]

Endicott and the Red Cross[†]

At noon of an autumnal day, more than two centuries ago, the English colors were displayed by the standard-bearer of the Salem trainband, which had mustered for martial exercise under the orders of John Endicott.[1] It was a period, when the religious exiles were accustomed often to buckle on their armour, and practise the handling of their weapons of war. Since the first settlement of New England, its prospects had never been so dismal. The dissensions between Charles the First and his subjects were then, and for several years afterwards, confined to the floor of Parliament.[2] The measures of the King and min-

---

3. William Hutchinson died in 1642, whereupon Anne Hutchinson moved her family to New Amsterdam (New York).
4. Hutchinson and all but one of the six children who had accompanied her died in an Indian attack in 1643.
† First published in *The Token* (1837) and collected in the second edition of *Twice-Told Tales* (1642). Reprinted from *Twice-Told Tales*, vol. 9 of *The Centenary Edition of the Works of Nathaniel Hawthorne*, ed. William Charvat, Roy Harvey Pearce, and Claude Simpson (Columbus: Ohio State UP, 1974), 433–41.
1. The incident on which Hawthorne based this tale occurred in November 1634.
2. King Charles I of England had ascended to the throne in 1625 upon the death of his father, James I. As a result of the English Civil War (1642–49), he would be overthrown and beheaded. Puritanism arose in opposition to the Church of England, which Puritans accused of leaning toward Catholicism. Charles I tried to suppress Puritan and Presbyterian dissent within the Church.

istry were rendered more tyrannically violent by an opposition, which had not yet acquired sufficient confidence in its own strength, to resist royal injustice with the sword. The bigoted and haughty primate, Laud, Archbishop of Canterbury, controlled the religious affairs of the realm, and was consequently invested with powers which might have wrought the utter ruin of the two Puritan colonies, Plymouth and Massachusetts.[3] There is evidence on record, that our forefathers perceived their danger, but were resolved that their infant country should not fall without a struggle, even beneath the giant strength of the King's right arm.

Such was the aspect of the times, when the folds of the English banner, with the Red Cross in its field, were flung out over a company of Puritans.[4] Their leader, the famous Endicott, was a man of stern and resolute countenance, the effect of which was heightened by a grizzled beard that swept the upper portion of his breastplate. This piece of armour was so highly polished, that the whole surrounding scene had its image in the glittering steel. The central object, in the mirrored picture, was an edifice of humble architecture, with neither steeple nor bell to proclaim it,—what nevertheless it was,—the house of prayer. A token of the perils of the wilderness was seen in the grim head of a wolf, which had just been slain within the precincts of the town, and, according to the regular mode of claiming the bounty, was nailed on the porch of the meetinghouse. The blood was still plashing on the door-step. There happened to be visible, at the same noontide hour, so many other characteristics of the times and manners of the Puritans, that we must endeavour to represent them in a sketch, though far less vividly than they were reflected in the polished breastplate of John Endicott.

In close vicinity to the sacred edifice appeared that important engine of Puritanic authority, the whipping-post,—with the soil around it well trodden by the feet of evil-doers, who had there been disciplined. At one corner of the meetinghouse was the pillory, and at the other the stocks; and, by a singular good fortune for our sketch, the head of an Episcopalian and suspected Catholic was grotesquely encased in the former machine; while a fellow-criminal, who had boisterously quaffed a health to the King, was confined by the legs in the latter. Side by side, on the meetinghouse steps, stood a male and a female figure. The man was a tall, lean, haggard personification of fanaticism, bearing on his breast this label,—A WANTON GOSPELLER,—which betokened that he had dared to give interpretations of Holy Writ, unsanctioned by the infallible judgment of the civil and religious rulers. His aspect showed no lack of zeal to maintain his heterodoxies, even at the stake. The woman wore a cleft stick on her tongue, in appropriate retribution for having wagged that unruly member against the elders of the church; and her countenance and gestures gave much cause to apprehend, that, the moment the stick should be removed, a

---

3. Archbishop of Canterbury William Laud (1573–1645) headed the Church of England and, along with King Charles I, became the target of Puritan protest.
4. The English flag, with its red cross, symbolized the power of the Church of England.

repetition of the offence would demand new ingenuity in chastising it.[5]

The abovementioned individuals had been sentenced to undergo their various modes of ignominy, for the space of one hour at noonday. But among the crowd were several, whose punishment would be life-long; some, whose ears had been cropt, like those of puppy-dogs; others, whose cheeks had been branded with the initials of their misdemeanors; one, with his nostrils slit and seared; and another, with a halter about his neck, which he was forbidden ever to take off, or to conceal beneath his garments. Methinks he must have been grievously tempted to affix the other end of the rope to some convenient beam or bough. There was likewise a young woman, with no mean share of beauty, whose doom it was to wear the letter A on the breast of her gown, in the eyes of all the world and her own children. And even her own children knew what that initial signified. Sporting with her infamy, the lost and desperate creature had embroidered the fatal token in scarlet cloth, with golden thread, and the nicest art of needle-work; so that the capital A might have been thought to mean Admirable, or any thing rather than Adulteress.[6]

Let not the reader argue, from any of these evidences of iniquity, that the times of the Puritans were more vicious than our own, when, as we pass along the very street of this sketch, we discern no badge of infamy on man or woman. It was the policy of our ancestors to search out even the most secret sins, and expose them to shame, without fear or favor, in the broadest light of the noonday sun. Were such the custom now, perchance we might find materials for a no less piquant sketch than the above.

Except the malefactors whom we have described, and the diseased or infirm persons, the whole male population of the town, between sixteen years and sixty, were seen in the ranks of the trainband. A few stately savages, in all the pomp and dignity of the primeval Indian, stood gazing at the spectacle. Their flint-headed arrows were but childish weapons, compared with the matchlocks[7] of the Puritans, and would have rattled harmlessly against the steel caps and hammered iron breastplates, which enclosed each soldier in an individual fortress. The valiant John Endicott glanced with an eye of pride at his sturdy followers, and prepared to renew the martial toils of the day.

"Come, my stout hearts!" quoth he, drawing his sword. "Let us show these poor heathen that we can handle our weapons like men of might. Well for them, if they put us not to prove it in earnest!"

The iron-breasted company straightened their line, and each man

5. The gruesome punishments that Hawthorne details in these two paragraphs have been gathered from various times and places in the seventeenth-century history of the Massachusetts Bay Colony. In his *Annals of Salem*, for example, Joseph Felt mentions branding with letters, cropping ears, putting a cleft stick on the tongue, as well as placing individuals in the stocks and the pillory.
6. Hawthorne's "camera" lingers on this anonymous woman, whose situation provides many seeds that germinate and sprout in *The Scarlet Letter*—the woman's beauty, the letter itself, with its embroidery in gold thread and its subtle change in meaning at the woman's hand, as well as the negotiation of meaning between the woman and the people observing her.
7. Muskets fired by holding a match over a hole in the breech.

drew the heavy butt of his matchlock close to his left foot, thus awaiting the orders of the captain. But, as Endicott glanced right and left
along the front, he discovered a personage at some little distance,
with whom it behoved him to hold a parley. It was an elderly gentleman, wearing a black cloak and band, and a high-crowned hat, beneath which was a velvet skull-cap, the whole being the garb of a
Puritan minister.[8] This reverend person bore a staff, which seemed to
have been recently cut in the forest, and his shoes were bemired,
as if he had been travelling on foot through the swamps of the wilderness. His aspect was perfectly that of a pilgrim, heightened also by
an apostolic dignity. Just as Endicott perceived him, he laid aside
his staff, and stooped to drink at a bubbling fountain, which gushed
into the sunshine about a score of yards from the corner of the meetinghouse. But, ere the good man drank, he turned his face heavenward in thankfulness, and then, holding back his gray beard with
one hand, he scooped up his simple draught in the hollow of the
other.

"What, ho! good Mr. Williams," shouted Endicott. "You are welcome
back again to our town of peace. How does our worthy Governor
Winthrop?[9] And what news from Boston?"

"The Governor hath his health, worshipful Sir," answered Roger
Williams, now resuming his staff, and drawing near. "And, for the
news, here is a letter, which, knowing I was to travel hitherward to-
day, his Excellency committed to my charge. Belike it contains tidings
of much import; for a ship arrived yesterday from England."

Mr. Williams, the minister of Salem, and of course known to all the
spectators, had now reached the spot where Endicott was standing under the banner of his company, and put the Governor's epistle into his
hand. The broad seal was impressed with Winthrop's coat of arms. Endicott hastily unclosed the letter, and began to read; while, as his eye
passed down the page, a wrathful change came over his manly countenance. The blood glowed through it, till it seemed to be kindling with
an internal heat; nor was it unnatural to suppose that his breastplate
would likewise become red-hot, with the angry fire of the bosom
which it covered. Arriving at the conclusion, he shook the letter
fiercely in his hand, so that it rustled as loud as the flag above his
head.

"Black tidings these, Mr. Williams," said he; "blacker never came to
New England. Doubtless you know their purport?"

"Yea, truly," replied Roger Williams; "for the Governor consulted, respecting this matter, with my brethren in the ministry at Boston; and
my opinion was likewise asked. And his Excellency entreats you by me,
that the news be not suddenly noised abroad, lest the people be stirred

8. Roger Williams (1603–1683) became pastor at Salem in 1634, but he was hardly an "elderly
   gentleman," being only thirty at the time. Less than a year later, Williams was banished from
   the colony and, rather than be deported to England, he fled to what is now Rhode Island,
   where he lived in close proximity to the Narragansett Indians.
9. Thomas Dudley, not John Winthrop, was governor of the Massachusetts Bay Colony in November 1634. Winthrop's term had ended in May, and he would not be re-elected until
   1637.

up unto some outbreak, and thereby give the King and the Archbishop a handle against us."[1]

"The Governor is a wise man,—a wise man, and a meek and moderate," said Endicott, setting his teeth grimly. "Nevertheless, I must do according to my own best judgment. There is neither man, woman, nor child in New England, but has a concern as dear as life in these tidings; and, if John Endicott's voice be loud enough, man, woman, and child shall hear them. Soldiers, wheel into a hollow square! Ho, good people! Here are news for one and all of you."

The soldiers closed in around their captain; and he and Roger Williams stood together under the banner of the Red Cross; while the women and the aged men pressed forward, and the mothers held up their children to look Endicott in the face. A few taps of the drum gave signal for silence and attention.

"Fellow-soldiers,—fellow-exiles," began Endicott, speaking under strong excitement, yet powerfully restraining it, "wherefore did ye leave your native country? Wherefore, I say, have we left the green and fertile fields, the cottages, or, perchance, the old gray halls, where we were born and bred, the church-yards where our forefathers lie buried? Wherefore have we come hither to set up our own tombstones in a wilderness? A howling wilderness it is! The wolf and the bear meet us within halloo of our dwellings. The savage lieth in wait for us in the dismal shadow of the woods. The stubborn roots of the trees break our ploughshares, when we would till the earth. Our children cry for bread, and we must dig in the sands of the sea-shore to satisfy them. Wherefore, I say again, have we sought this country of a rugged soil and wintry sky? Was it not for the enjoyment of our civil rights? Was it not for liberty to worship God according to our conscience?"

"Call you this liberty of conscience?" interrupted a voice on the steps of the meetinghouse.

It was the Wanton Gospeller. A sad and quiet smile flitted across the mild visage of Roger Williams. But Endicott, in the excitement of the moment, shook his sword wrathfully at the culprit,—an ominous gesture from a man like him.

"What hast thou to do with conscience, thou knave?" cried he. "I said, liberty to worship God, not license to profane and ridicule him. Break not in upon my speech; or I will lay thee neck and heels till this time to-morrow![2] Hearken to me, friends, nor heed that accursed rhapsodist. As I was saying, we have sacrificed all things, and have come to a land whereof the old world hath scarcely heard, that we might make a new world unto ourselves, and painfully seek a path from hence to Heaven. But what think ye now? This son of a Scotch tyrant,—this grandson of a papistical and adulterous Scotch woman, whose death proved that a golden crown doth not always save an anointed head from the block—"[3]

---

1. Actually, Williams was more radical than Endicott. He denied, for example, that King Charles had any right to grant title to Indian lands.
2. Place the man in the pillory, where his neck and feet would be secured.
3. King James I (of Scotland) was the father of King Charles I, who succeeded him in 1625. The Catholic Mary (Stuart), Queen of Scots (b. 1542), became Queen of Scotland when only six days old. She was executed by order of Queen Elizabeth in 1587.

"Nay, brother, nay," interposed Mr. Williams; "thy words are not meet for a secret chamber, far less for a public street."

"Hold thy peace, Roger Williams!" answered Endicott, imperiously. "My spirit is wiser than thine, for the business now in hand. I tell ye, fellow-exiles, that Charles of England, and Laud, our bitterest persecutor, arch-priest of Canterbury, are resolute to pursue us even hither. They are taking counsel, saith this letter, to send over a governor-general, in whose breast shall be deposited all the law and equity of the land. They are minded, also, to establish the idolatrous forms of English Episcopacy; so that, when Laud shall kiss the Pope's toe, as cardinal of Rome, he may deliver New England, bound hand and foot, into the power of his master!"

A deep groan from the auditors,—a sound of wrath, as well as fear and sorrow,—responded to this intelligence.

"Look ye to it, brethren," resumed Endicott, with increasing energy. "If this king and this arch-prelate have their will, we shall briefly behold a cross on the spire of this tabernacle which we have builded, and a high altar within its walls, with wax tapers burning round it at noonday. We shall hear the sacring-bell, and the voices of the Romish priests saying the mass. But think ye, Christian men, that these abominations may be suffered without a sword drawn? without a shot fired? without blood spilt, yea, on the very stairs of the pulpit? No,—be ye strong of hand, and stout of heart! Here we stand on our own soil, which we have bought with our goods, which we have won with our swords, which we have cleared with our axes, which we have tilled with the sweat of our brows, which we have sanctified with our prayers to the God that brought us hither! Who shall enslave us here? What have we to do with this mitred prelate,—with this crowned king? What have we to do with England?"

Endicott gazed round at the excited countenances of the people, now full of his own spirit, and then turned suddenly to the standard-bearer, who stood close behind him.

"Officer, lower your banner!" said he.

The officer obeyed; and, brandishing his sword, Endicott thrust it through the cloth, and, with his left hand, rent the Red Cross completely out of the banner. He then waved the tattered ensign above his head.[4]

"Sacrilegious wretch!" cried the high-churchman in the pillory, unable longer to restrain himself; "thou hast rejected the symbol of our holy religion!"

"Treason, treason!" roared the royalist in the stocks. "He hath defaced the King's banner!"

"Before God and man, I will avouch the deed," answered Endicott. "Beat a flourish, drummer!—shout, soldiers and people!—in honor of

4. Endicott defaced the English flag in November 1634. As John Winthrop notes, he was "admonished" for giving the English an excuse for thinking "ill" of the colonists and "disabled" for one year from holding any public office. The court declined any heavier sentence on the grounds that Endicott acted from "tenderness of conscience" rather than any "evil intent," and he was restored to his position as magistrate at the next election in 1636.

the ensign of New England. Neither Pope nor Tyrant hath part in it now!"

With a cry of triumph, the people gave their sanction to one of the boldest exploits which our history records. And, for ever honored be the name of Endicott! We look back through the mist of ages, and recognize, in the rending of the Red Cross from New England's banner, the first omen of that deliverance which our fathers consummated, after the bones of the stern Puritan had lain more than a century in the dust.[5]

Young Goodman Brown[†]

Young Goodman Brown came forth, at sunset, into the street of Salem village, but put his head back, after crossing the threshold, to exchange a parting kiss with his young wife. And Faith, as the wife was aptly named, thrust her own pretty head into the street, letting the wind play with the pink ribbons of her cap, while she called to Goodman Brown.[1]

'Dearest heart,' whispered she, softly and rather sadly, when her lips were close to his ear, 'pr'y[2] thee, put off your journey until sunrise, and sleep in your own bed to-night. A lone woman is troubled with such dreams and such thoughts, that she's afeard of herself, sometimes. Pray, tarry with me this night, dear husband, of all nights in the year!'

'My love and my Faith,' replied young Goodman Brown, 'of all nights in the year, this one night must I tarry away from thee. My journey, as thou callest it, forth and back again, must needs be done 'twixt now and sunrise. What, my sweet, pretty wife, dost thou doubt me already, and we but three months married!'

'Then, God bless you!' said Faith, with the pink ribbons, 'and may you find all well, when you come back.'

'Amen!' cried Goodman Brown. 'Say thy prayers, dear Faith, and go to bed at dusk, and no harm will come to thee.'

So they parted; and the young man pursued his way, until, being about to turn the corner by the meeting-house, he looked back, and saw the head of Faith still peeping after him, with a melancholy air, in spite of her pink ribbons.

'Poor little Faith!' thought he, for his heart smote him. 'What a wretch am I, to leave her on such an errand! She talks of dreams, too. Methought, as she spoke, there was trouble in her face, as if a dream had warned her what work is to be done to-night. But, no, no! 'twould kill her to think it. Well; she's a blessed angel on earth; and after this one night, I'll cling to her skirts and follow her to Heaven.'

5. Hawthorne suggests that Endicott's actions look forward to the Revolutionary War.
† First published in the *New England Magazine* (1835) and collected in *Mosses from an Old Manse* (1846). Reprinted from *Mosses from an Old Manse*, vol. 10 of the *Centenary Edition of the Works of Nathaniel Hawthorne*, ed. William Charvat, Roy Harvey Pearce, and Claude Simpson (Columbus: Ohio State UP, 1974), 74–90.
1. Goodman, like Goody, is a common term for an individual, along the lines of "Mister."
2. An abbreviation of "pray." With "thee," the phrase "pray thee" often becomes "prithee."

With this excellent resolve for the future, Goodman Brown felt himself justified in making more haste on his present evil purpose. He had taken a dreary road, darkened by all the gloomiest trees of the forest, which barely stood aside to let the narrow path creep through, and closed immediately behind. It was all as lonely as could be; and there is this peculiarity in such a solitude, that the traveller knows not who may be concealed by the innumerable trunks and the thick boughs overhead; so that, with lonely footsteps, he may yet be passing through an unseen multitude.

'There may be a devilish Indian behind every tree,' said Goodman Brown, to himself; and he glanced fearfully behind him, as he added, 'What if the devil himself should be at my very elbow!'

His head being turned back, he passed a crook of the road, and looking forward again, beheld the figure of a man, in grave and decent attire, seated at the foot of an old tree. He arose, at Goodman Brown's approach, and walked onward, side by side with him.

'You are late, Goodman Brown,' said he. 'The clock of the Old South was striking as I came through Boston; and that is full fifteen minutes agone.'[3]

'Faith kept me back awhile,' replied the young man, with a tremor in his voice, caused by the sudden appearance of his companion, though not wholly unexpected.

It was now deep dusk in the forest, and deepest in that part of it where these two were journeying. As nearly as could be discerned, the second traveller was about fifty years old, apparently in the same rank of life as Goodman Brown, and bearing a considerable resemblance to him, though perhaps more in expression than features. Still, they might have been taken for father and son. And yet, though the elder person was as simply clad as the younger, and as simple in manner too, he had an indescribable air of one who knew the world, and would not have felt abashed at the governor's dinner-table, or in King William's court, were it possible that his affairs should call him thither.[4] But the only thing about him, that could be fixed upon as remarkable, was his staff, which bore the likeness of a great black snake, so curiously wrought, that it might almost be seen to twist and wriggle itself, like a living serpent. This, of course, must have been an ocular deception, assisted by the uncertain light.

'Come, Goodman Brown!' cried his fellow-traveller, 'this is a dull pace for the beginning of a journey. Take my staff, if you are so soon weary.'

'Friend,' said the other, exchanging his slow pace for a full stop, 'having kept covenant by meeting thee here, it is my purpose now to return whence I came. I have scruples, touching the matter thou wot'st[5] of.'

---

3. Old South Meeting House, built in 1729, was a gathering place for American revolutionists—the place, for example, where the idea for the Boston Tea Party was publicly discussed.
4. King William III ruled England from 1689 to 1702, and so was king during the Salem witch trials in 1692.
5. An abbreviation of "wotest," "to know."

'Sayest thou so?' replied he of the serpent, smiling apart. 'Let us walk on, nevertheless, reasoning as we go, and if I convince thee not, thou shalt turn back. We are but a little way in the forest, yet.'

'Too far, too far!' exclaimed the goodman, unconsciously resuming his walk. 'My father never went into the woods on such an errand, nor his father before him. We have been a race of honest men and good Christians, since the days of the martyrs. And shall I be the first of the name of Brown, that ever took this path, and kept—'

'Such company, thou wouldst say,' observed the elder person, interpreting his pause. 'Well said, Goodman Brown! I have been as well acquainted with your family as with ever a one among the Puritans; and that's no trifle to say. I helped your grandfather, the constable, when he lashed the Quaker woman so smartly through the streets of Salem.[6] And it was I that brought your father a pitch-pine knot, kindled at my own hearth, to set fire to an Indian village, in King Philip's war.[7] They were my good friends, both; and many a pleasant walk have we had along this path, and returned merrily after midnight. I would fain be friends with you, for their sake.'

'If it be as thou sayest,' replied Goodman Brown, 'I marvel they never spoke of these matters. Or, verily, I marvel not, seeing that the least rumor of the sort would have driven them from New-England. We are a people of prayer, and good works, to boot, and abide no such wickedness.'

'Wickedness or not,' said the traveller with the twisted staff, 'I have a very general acquaintance here in New-England. The deacons of many a church have drunk the communion wine with me; the selectmen, of divers towns, make me their chairman; and a majority of the Great and General Court are firm supporters of my interest. The governor and I, too—but these are state-secrets.'[8]

'Can this be so!' cried Goodman Brown, with a stare of amazement at his undisturbed companion. 'Howbeit, I have nothing to do with the governor and council; they have their own ways, and are no rule for a simple husbandman, like me. But, were I to go on with thee, how should I meet the eye of that good old man, our minister, at Salem village? Oh, his voice would make me tremble, both Sabbath-day and lecture-day!'

Thus far, the elder traveller had listened with due gravity, but now burst into a fit of irrepressible mirth, shaking himself so violently, that his snake-like staff actually seemed to wriggle in sympathy.

'Ha! ha! ha!' shouted he, again and again; then composing himself,

---

6. As Hawthorne also notes in "The Custom-House" preface to *The Scarlet Letter*, his paternal great-great grandfather, William Hathorne (1606–1681), had ordered a Quaker woman, Ann Coleman, to be whipped through the streets of Salem.
7. In his *Annals of Salem*, Joseph Felt notes that Hawthorne's great-great uncle, Captain William Hathorne (son of the William Hathorne mentioned in n. 6 above), and his company surprised four hundred Indians at Cocheco during King Philip's War. He captured two hundred Indians and sent them to Boston; seven or eight were sentenced to "immediate death, and the rest were transported and sold as slaves" (2:507).
8. The General Court was the ruling body of the Massachusetts Bay Colony. William Phips was appointed governor during the Salem witch trials in 1692 and eventually put an end to the proceedings.

'Well, go on, Goodman Brown, go on; but pr'y thee, don't kill me with laughing!'

'Well, then, to end the matter at once,' said Goodman Brown, considerably nettled, 'there is my wife, Faith. It would break her dear little heart; and I'd rather break my own!'

'Nay, if that be the case,' answered the other, 'e'en go thy ways, Goodman Brown. I would not, for twenty old women like the one hobbling before us, that Faith should come to any harm.'

As he spoke, he pointed his staff at a female figure on the path, in whom Goodman Brown recognized a very pious and exemplary dame, who had taught him his catechism, in youth, and was still his moral and spiritual adviser, jointly with the minister and Deacon Gookin.[9]

'A marvel, truly, that Goody Cloyse[1] should be so far in the wilderness, at night-fall!' said he. 'But, with your leave, friend, I shall take a cut through the woods, until we have left this Christian woman behind. Being a stranger to you, she might ask whom I was consorting with, and whither I was going.'

'Be it so,' said his fellow-traveller. 'Betake you to the woods, and let me keep the path.'

Accordingly, the young man turned aside, but took care to watch his companion, who advanced softly along the road, until he had come within a staff's length of the old dame. She, meanwhile, was making the best of her way, with singular speed for so aged a woman, and mumbling some indistinct words, a prayer, doubtless, as she went. The traveller put forth his staff, and touched her withered neck with what seemed the serpent's tail.

'The devil!' screamed the pious old lady.

'Then Goody Cloyse knows her old friend?' observed the traveller, confronting her, and leaning on his writhing stick.

'Ah, forsooth, and is it your worship, indeed?' cried the good dame. 'Yea, truly is it, and in the very image of my old gossip, Goodman Brown, the grandfather of the silly fellow that now is. But—would your worship believe it?—my broomstick hath strangely disappeared, stolen, as I suspect, by that unhanged witch, Goody Cory,[2] and that, too, when I was all anointed with the juice of smallage and cinque-foil and wolf's-bane—'

'Mingled with fine wheat and the fat of a new-born babe,' said the shape of old Goodman Brown.

'Ah, your worship knows the receipt,'[3] cried the old lady, cackling

---

9. Daniel Gookin (1612–1687) served as superintendent of all Massachusetts Indians from 1656 until his death. He supported Apostle Eliot in his missionary work.

1. Sarah Cloyce was accused of witchcraft and imprisoned during the Salem witch trials of 1692. She was not executed.

2. Deliberately or not, Hawthorne deviates from the historical record and switches the identities of two women. Sarah Cloyce is undoubtedly the "unhanged witch" to whom he refers. As noted above, she was arrested and imprisoned for witchcraft, but Governor Phips dissolved the special court in October 1692 before she could be executed. Martha Cory, on the other hand, was hanged on September 22, 1692, part of the last group of accused witches to be executed. Her husband, Giles, was pressed to death on September 19 for refusing to stand trial.

3. Recipe. Hawthorne lists ingredients for a witch's flying potion. *Smallage:* a form of wild celery. *Cinque-foil,* or potentilla: in the rose family. *Wolf's-bane,* or monkshood: a poisonous herb.

aloud. 'So, as I was saying, being all ready for the meeting, and no horse to ride on, I made up my mind to foot it; for they tell me, there is a nice young man to be taken into communion to-night. But now your good worship will lend me your arm, and we shall be there in a twinkling.'

'That can hardly be,' answered her friend. 'I may not spare you my arm, Goody Cloyse, but here is my staff, if you will.'

So saying, he threw it down at her feet, where, perhaps, it assumed life, being one of the rods which its owner had formerly lent to the Egyptian Magi.[4] Of this fact, however, Goodman Brown could not take cognizance. He had cast up his eyes in astonishment, and looking down again, beheld neither Goody Cloyse nor the serpentine staff, but his fellow-traveller alone, who waited for him as calmly as if nothing had happened.

'That old woman taught me my catechism!' said the young man; and there was a world of meaning in this simple comment.

They continued to walk onward, while the elder traveller exhorted his companion to make good speed and persevere in the path, discoursing so aptly, that his arguments seemed rather to spring up in the bosom of his auditor, than to be suggested by himself. As they went, he plucked a branch of maple, to serve for a walking-stick, and began to strip it of the twigs and little boughs, which were wet with evening dew. The moment his fingers touched them, they became strangely withered and dried up, as with a week's sunshine. Thus the pair proceeded, at a good free pace, until suddenly, in a gloomy hollow of the road, Goodman Brown sat himself down on the stump of a tree, and refused to go any farther.

'Friend,' said he, stubbornly, 'my mind is made up. Not another step will I budge on this errand. What if a wretched old woman do choose to go to the devil, when I thought she was going to Heaven! Is that any reason why I should quit my dear Faith, and go after her?'

'You will think better of this, by-and-by,' said his acquaintance, composedly. 'Sit here and rest yourself awhile; and when you feel like moving again, there is my staff to help you along.'

Without more words, he threw his companion the maple stick, and was as speedily out of sight, as if he had vanished into the deepening gloom. The young man sat a few moments, by the road-side, applauding himself greatly, and thinking with how clear a conscience he should meet the minister, in his morning-walk, nor shrink from the eye of good old Deacon Gookin. And what calm sleep would be his, that very night, which was to have been spent so wickedly, but purely and sweetly now, in the arms of Faith! Amidst these pleasant and praiseworthy meditations, Goodman Brown heard the tramp of horses along the road, and deemed it advisable to conceal himself within the

---

4. See Exodus 7:9–10: "When Pharaoh shall speak unto you, saying, Shew a miracle for you: then thou shalt say unto Aaron, Take thy rod, and cast it before Pharaoh, and it shall become a serpent. / And Moses and Aaron went in unto Pharaoh, and they did so as the LORD had commanded: and Aaron cast down his rod before Pharaoh, and before his servants, and it became a serpent."

verge of the forest, conscious of the guilty purpose that had brought him thither, though now so happily turned from it.

On came the hoof-tramps and the voices of the riders, two grave old voices, conversing soberly as they drew near. These mingled sounds appeared to pass along the road, within a few yards of the young man's hiding-place; but owing, doubtless, to the depth of the gloom, at that particular spot, neither the travellers nor their steeds were visible. Though their figures brushed the small boughs by the way-side, it could not be seen that they intercepted, even for a moment, the faint gleam from the strip of bright sky, athwart which they must have passed. Goodman Brown alternately crouched and stood on tip-toe, pulling aside the branches, and thrusting forth his head as far as he durst, without discerning so much as a shadow. It vexed him the more, because he could have sworn, were such a thing possible, that he recognized the voices of the minister and Deacon Gookin, jogging along quietly, as they were wont to do, when bound to some ordination or ecclesiastical council. While yet within hearing, one of the riders stopped to pluck a switch.

'Of the two, reverend Sir,' said the voice like the deacon's, 'I had rather miss an ordination-dinner than to-night's meeting. They tell me that some of our community are to be here from Falmouth and beyond, and others from Connecticut and Rhode-Island; besides several of the Indian powows,[5] who, after their fashion, know almost as much deviltry as the best of us. Moreover, there is a goodly young woman to be taken into communion.'

'Mighty well, Deacon Gookin!' replied the solemn old tones of the minister. 'Spur up, or we shall be late. Nothing can be done, you know, until I get on the ground.'

The hoofs clattered again, and the voices, talking so strangely in the empty air, passed on through the forest, where no church had ever been gathered, nor solitary Christian prayed. Whither, then, could these holy men be journeying, so deep into the heathen wilderness? Young Goodman Brown caught hold of a tree, for support, being ready to sink down on the ground, faint and overburthened with the heavy sickness of his heart. He looked up to the sky, doubting whether there really was a Heaven above him. Yet, there was the blue arch, and the stars brightening in it.

'With Heaven above, and Faith below, I will yet stand firm against the devil!' cried Goodman Brown.

While he still gazed upward, into the deep arch of the firmament, and had lifted his hands to pray, a cloud, though no wind was stirring, hurried across the zenith, and hid the brightening stars. The blue sky was still visible, except directly overhead, where this black mass of cloud was sweeping swiftly northward. Aloft in the air, as if from the depths of the cloud, came a confused and doubtful sound of voices. Once, the listener fancied that he could distinguish the accents of town's-people of his own, men and women, both pious and ungodly,

---

5. Medicine men; also called powwows.

many of whom he had met at the communion-table, and had seen others rioting at the tavern. The next moment, so indistinct were the sounds, he doubted whether he had heard aught but the murmur of the old forest, whispering without a wind. Then came a stronger swell of those familiar tones, heard daily in the sunshine, at Salem village, but never, until now, from a cloud of night. There was one voice, of a young woman, uttering lamentations, yet with an uncertain sorrow, and entreating for some favor, which, perhaps, it would grieve her to obtain. And all the unseen multitude, both saints and sinners, seemed to encourage her onward.

'Faith!' shouted Goodman Brown, in a voice of agony and desperation; and the echoes of the forest mocked him, crying—'Faith! Faith!' as if bewildered wretches were seeking her, all through the wilderness.

The cry of grief, rage, and terror, was yet piercing the night, when the unhappy husband held his breath for a response. There was a scream, drowned immediately in a louder murmur of voices, fading into far-off laughter, as the dark cloud swept away, leaving the clear and silent sky above Goodman Brown. But something fluttered lightly down through the air, and caught on the branch of a tree. The young man seized it, and beheld a pink ribbon.

'My Faith is gone!' cried he, after one stupefied moment. 'There is no good on earth; and sin is but a name. Come, devil! for to thee is this world given.'

And maddened with despair, so that he laughed loud and long, did Goodman Brown grasp his staff and set forth again, at such a rate, that he seemed to fly along the forest-path, rather than to walk or run. The road grew wilder and drearier, and more faintly traced, and vanished at length, leaving him in the heart of the dark wilderness, still rushing onward, with the instinct that guides mortal man to evil. The whole forest was peopled with frightful sounds; the creaking of the trees, the howling of wild beasts, and the yell of Indians; while, sometimes, the wind tolled like a distant church-bell, and sometimes gave a broad roar around the traveller, as if all Nature were laughing him to scorn. But he was himself the chief horror of the scene, and shrank not from its other horrors.

'Ha! ha! ha!' roared Goodman Brown, when the wind laughed at him. 'Let us hear which will laugh loudest! Think not to frighten me with your deviltry! Come witch, come wizard, come Indian powow, come devil himself! and here comes Goodman Brown. You may as well fear him as he fear you!'

In truth, all through the haunted forest, there could be nothing more frightful than the figure of Goodman Brown. On he flew, among the black pines, brandishing his staff with frenzied gestures, now giving vent to an inspiration of horrid blasphemy, and now shouting forth such laughter, as set all the echoes of the forest laughing like demons around him. The fiend in his own shape is less hideous, than when he rages in the breast of man. Thus sped the demoniac on his course, until, quivering among the trees, he saw a red light before him, as when the felled trunks and branches of a clearing have been set on fire, and throw up their lurid blaze against the sky, at the hour of midnight. He paused, in a lull of the tempest that had driven him onward, and heard the swell of what seemed a hymn, rolling solemnly from a distance, with the weight of many voices. He knew the tune; it was a familiar one in the choir of the village meeting-house. The verse died heavily away, and was lengthened by a chorus, not of human voices, but of all the sounds of the benighted wilderness, pealing in awful harmony together. Goodman Brown cried out; and his cry was lost to his own ear, by its unison with the cry of the desert.

In the interval of silence, he stole forward, until the light glared full upon his eyes. At one extremity of an open space, hemmed in by the dark wall of the forest, arose a rock, bearing some rude, natural resemblance either to an altar or a pulpit, and surrounded by four blazing pines, their tops aflame, their stems untouched, like candles at an evening meeting. The mass of foliage, that had overgrown the summit of the rock, was all on fire, blazing high into the night, and fitfully illuminating the whole field. Each pendent twig and leafy festoon was in a blaze. As the red light arose and fell, a numerous congregation alternately shone forth, then disappeared in shadow, and again grew, as it were, out of the darkness, peopling the heart of the solitary woods at once.

'A grave and dark-clad company!' quoth Goodman Brown.

In truth, they were such. Among them, quivering to-and-fro, between gloom and splendor, appeared faces that would be seen, next day, at the council-board of the province, and others which, Sabbath after Sabbath, looked devoutly heavenward, and benignantly over the crowded pews, from the holiest pulpits in the land. Some affirm, that the lady of the governor was there. At least, there were high dames well known to her, and wives of honored husbands, and widows, a great multitude, and ancient maidens, all of excellent repute, and fair young girls, who trembled, lest their mothers should espy them. Either the sudden gleams of light, flashing over the obscure field, bedazzled Goodman Brown, or he recognized a score of the church-members of Salem village, famous for their especial sanctity. Good old Deacon Gookin had arrived, and waited at the skirts of that venerable saint, his revered pastor. But, irreverently consorting with these grave, reputable, and pious people, these elders of the church, these chaste dames and dewy virgins, there were men of dissolute lives and women of spotted fame, wretches given over to all mean and filthy vice, and suspected even of horrid crimes. It was strange to see, that the good shrank not from the wicked, nor were the sinners abashed by the saints. Scattered, also, among their pale-faced enemies, were the Indian priests, or powows, who had often scared their native forest with more hideous incantations than any known to English witchcraft.

'But, where is Faith?' thought Goodman Brown; and, as hope came into his heart, he trembled.

Another verse of the hymn arose, a slow and mournful strain, such as the pious love, but joined to words which expressed all that our nature can conceive of sin, and darkly hinted at far more. Unfathomable to mere mortals is the lore of fiends. Verse after verse was sung, and still the chorus of the desert swelled between, like the deepest tone of a mighty organ. And, with the final peal of that dreadful anthem, there came a sound, as if the roaring wind, the rushing streams, the howling beasts, and every other voice of the unconverted wilderness, were mingling and according with the voice of guilty man, in homage to the prince of all. The four blazing pines threw up a loftier flame, and obscurely discovered shapes and visages of horror on the smoke-wreaths, above the impious assembly. At the same moment, the fire on the rock shot redly forth, and formed a glowing arch above its base, where now appeared a figure. With reverence be it spoken, the figure bore no slight similitude, both in garb and manner, to some grave divine of the New-England churches.

'Bring forth the converts!' cried a voice, that echoed through the field and rolled into the forest.

At the word, Goodman Brown stept forth from the shadow of the trees, and approached the congregation, with whom he felt a loathful brotherhood, by the sympathy of all that was wicked in his heart. He could have well nigh sworn, that the shape of his own dead father beckoned him to advance, looking downward from a smoke-wreath, while a woman, with dim features of despair, threw out her hand to warn him back.[6] Was it his mother? But he had no power to retreat one step, nor to resist, even in thought, when the minister and good old Deacon Gookin seized his arms, and led him to the blazing rock. Thither came also the slender form of a veiled female, led between Goody Cloyse, that pious teacher of the catechism, and Martha Carrier, who had received the devil's promise to be queen of hell. A rampant hag was she![7] And there stood the proselytes, beneath the canopy of fire.

'Welcome, my children,' said the dark figure, 'to the communion of your race! Ye have found, thus young, your nature and your destiny. My children, look behind you!'

They turned; and flashing forth, as it were, in a sheet of flame, the fiend-worshippers were seen; the smile of welcome gleamed darkly on every visage.

'There,' resumed the sable form, 'are all whom ye have reverenced from youth. Ye deemed them holier than yourselves, and shrank from your own sin, contrasting it with their lives of righteousness, and prayerful aspirations heavenward. Yet, here are they all, in my wor-

---

6. The cases against the witches depended on "specter evidence"—claims that the shapes or specters of the witches had tormented the accusers by pinching, biting, and tempting them. A key question was whether the devil could take over the "shape" of and impersonate an innocent person without that person's consent. Eventually, as doubts about the trials spread, a consensus developed that the devil could in fact impersonate an innocent person, casting into doubt nearly all of the convictions. As Governor Phips explained in a February 21, 1693, letter to the Earl of Nottingham, "Mr. Increase Mather and several other Divines did give it as their Judgment that the Devil might afflict in the shape of an innocent person and that the look and touch of the suspected persons was not sufficient proof against them" (Boyer and Nissenbaum, 121).

7. Martha Carrier was hanged for witchcraft on August 19, 1692. In his *Wonders of the Invisible World* (1693), Cotton Mather refers to her as a "Rampant Hag" who the devil had promised would be "Queen of Hell."

shipping assembly! This night it shall be granted you to know their secret deeds; how hoary-bearded elders of the church have whispered
wanton words to the young maids of their households; how many a
woman, eager for widow's weeds, has given her husband a drink at
bed-time, and let him sleep his last sleep in her bosom; how beardless
youths have made haste to inherit their fathers' wealth; and how fair
damsels—blush not, sweet ones!—have dug little graves in the garden,
and bidden me, the sole guest, to an infant's funeral. By the sympathy
of your human hearts for sin, ye shall scent out all the places—
whether in church, bed-chamber, street, field, or forest—where crime
has been committed, and shall exult to behold the whole earth one
stain of guilt, one mighty blood-spot. Far more than this! It shall be
yours to penetrate, in every bosom, the deep mystery of sin, the fountain of all wicked arts, and which inexhaustibly supplies more evil impulses than human power—than my power, at its utmost!—can make
manifest in deeds. And now, my children, look upon each other.'

They did so; and, by the blaze of the hell-kindled torches, the
wretched man beheld his Faith, and the wife her husband, trembling
before that unhallowed altar.

'Lo! there ye stand, my children,' said the figure, in a deep and
solemn tone, almost sad, with its despairing awfulness, as if his once
angelic nature could yet mourn for our miserable race. 'Depending
upon one another's hearts, ye had still hoped, that virtue were not all
a dream.[8] Now are ye undeceived! Evil is the nature of mankind. Evil
must be your only happiness. Welcome, again, my children, to the
communion of your race!'

'Welcome!' repeated the fiend-worshippers, in one cry of despair and
triumph.

And there they stood, the only pair, as it seemed, who were yet hes-
itating on the verge of wickedness, in this dark world. A basin was hol-
lowed, naturally, in the rock. Did it contain water, reddened by the
lurid light? or was it blood? or, perchance, a liquid flame? Herein did
the Shape of Evil dip his hand, and prepare to lay the mark of baptism
upon their foreheads, that they might be partakers of the mystery of
sin, more conscious of the secret guilt of others, both in deed and
thought, than they could now be of their own. The husband cast one
look at his pale wife, and Faith at him. What polluted wretches would
the next glance shew them to each other, shuddering alike at what
they disclosed and what they saw!

'Faith! Faith!' cried the husband. 'Look up to Heaven, and resist the
Wicked One!'

Whether Faith obeyed, he knew not. Hardly had he spoken, when
he found himself amid calm night and solitude, listening to a roar of
the wind, which died heavily away through the forest. He staggered

---

8. When John Hathorne questioned Rebecca Nurse, who was being tried for witchcraft, he re-
proached her for her lack of emotion: "It is very awful for all to see these agonies, and you,
an old professor [of witchcraft], thus charged with contracting with the devil by the effects
of it, and yet to see you stand with dry eyes when there are so many wet." Her reply: "You do
not know my heart" (see Boyer and Nissenbaum, 24).

against the rock and felt it chill and damp, while a hanging twig, that had been all on fire, besprinkled his cheek with the coldest dew.

The next morning, young Goodman Brown came slowly into the street of Salem village, staring around him like a bewildered man. The good old minister was taking a walk along the grave-yard, to get an appetite for breakfast and meditate his sermon, and bestowed a blessing, as he passed, on Goodman Brown. He shrank from the venerable saint, as if to avoid an anathema. Old Deacon Gookin was at domestic worship, and the holy words of his prayer were heard through the open window. 'What God doth the wizard pray to?' quoth Goodman Brown. Goody Cloyse, that excellent old Christian, stood in the early sunshine, at her own lattice, catechising a little girl, who had brought her a pint of morning's milk. Goodman Brown snatched away the child, as from the grasp of the fiend himself. Turning the corner by the meeting-house, he spied the head of Faith, with the pink ribbons, gazing anxiously forth, and bursting into such joy at sight of him, that she skipt along the street, and almost kissed her husband before the whole village. But, Goodman Brown looked sternly and sadly into her face, and passed on without a greeting.

Had Goodman Brown fallen asleep in the forest, and only dreamed a wild dream of a witch-meeting?

Be it so, if you will. But, alas! it was a dream of evil omen for young Goodman Brown. A stern, a sad, a darkly meditative, a distrustful, if not a desperate man, did he become, from the night of that fearful dream. On the Sabbath-day, when the congregation were singing a holy psalm, he could not listen, because an anthem of sin rushed loudly upon his ear, and drowned all the blessed strain. When the minister spoke from the pulpit, with power and fervid eloquence, and, with his hand on the open Bible, of the sacred truths of our religion, and of saint-like lives and triumphant deaths, and of future bliss or misery unutterable, then did Goodman Brown turn pale, dreading, lest the roof should thunder down upon the gray blasphemer and his hearers. Often, awakening suddenly at midnight, he shrank from the bosom of Faith, and at morning or eventide, when the family knelt down at prayer, he scowled, and muttered to himself, and gazed sternly at his wife, and turned away. And when he had lived long, and was borne to his grave, a hoary corpse, followed by Faith, an aged woman, and children and grandchildren, a goodly procession, besides neighbors, not a few, they carved no hopeful verse upon his tombstone; for his dying hour was gloom.

The Minister's Black Veil†

A Parable*

The sexton stood in the porch of Milford[1] meeting-house, pulling lustily at the bell-rope. The old people of the village came stooping along the street. Children, with bright faces, tript merrily beside their parents, or mimicked a graver gait, in the conscious dignity of their Sunday clothes. Spruce bachelors looked sidelong at the pretty maidens, and fancied that the Sabbath sunshine made them prettier than on week-days. When the throng had mostly streamed into the porch, the sexton began to toll the bell, keeping his eye on the Reverend Mr. Hooper's door. The first glimpse of the clergyman's figure was the signal for the bell to cease its summons.

'But what has good Parson Hooper got upon his face?' cried the sexton in astonishment.

All within hearing immediately turned about, and beheld the semblance of Mr. Hooper, pacing slowly his meditative way towards the meeting-house. With one accord they started, expressing more wonder than if some strange minister were coming to dust the cushions of Mr. Hooper's pulpit.

'Are you sure it is our parson?' inquired Goodman Gray of the sexton.

'Of a certainty it is good Mr. Hooper,' replied the sexton. 'He was to have exchanged pulpits with Parson Shute of Westbury; but Parson Shute sent to excuse himself yesterday, being to preach a funeral sermon.'

The cause of so much amazement may appear sufficiently slight. Mr. Hooper, a gentlemanly person of about thirty, though still a bachelor, was dressed with due clerical neatness, as if a careful wife had starched his band, and brushed the weekly dust from his Sunday's garb. There was but one thing remarkable in his appearance. Swathed about his forehead, and hanging down over his face, so low as to be shaken by his breath, Mr. Hooper had on a black veil. On a nearer view, it seemed to consist of two folds of crape, which entirely concealed his features, except the mouth and chin, but probably did not intercept his sight, farther than to give a darkened aspect to all living and inanimate things. With this gloomy shade before him, good Mr. Hooper walked onward, at a slow and quiet pace, stooping somewhat and looking on the ground, as is customary with abstracted men, yet nodding kindly to those of his parishioners who still waited on the meeting-house steps. But so wonder-struck were they, that his greeting hardly met with a return.

---

† First published in *The Token* (1835) and collected in *Twice-Told Tales* (1837). Reprinted from *Twice-Told Tales*, vol. 9 of the *Centenary Edition of the Works of Nathaniel Hawthorne*, ed. William Charvat, Roy Harvey Pearce, and Claude Simpson (Columbus: Ohio State UP, 1974), 37–53.

* Another clergyman in New England, Mr. Joseph Moody, of York, Maine, who died about eighty years since, made himself remarkable by the same eccentricity that is here related of the Reverend Mr. Hooper. In his case, however, the symbol had a different import. In early life he had accidentally killed a beloved friend; and from that day till the hour of his own death, he hid his face from men [*Hawthorne's note*].

1. Milford, Massachusetts, about thirty miles west of Boston.

'I can't really feel as if good Mr. Hooper's face was behind that piece of crape,' said the sexton.

'I don't like it,' muttered an old woman, as she hobbled into the meeting-house. 'He has changed himself into something awful, only by hiding his face.'

'Our parson has gone mad!' cried Goodman Gray, following him across the threshold.

A rumor of some unaccountable phenomenon had preceded Mr. Hooper into the meeting-house, and set all the congregation astir. Few could refrain from twisting their heads towards the door; many stood upright, and turned directly about; while several little boys clambered upon the seats, and came down again with a terrible racket. There was a general bustle, a rustling of the women's gowns and shuffling of the men's feet, greatly at variance with that hushed repose which should attend the entrance of the minister. But Mr. Hooper appeared not to notice the perturbation of his people. He entered with an almost noiseless step, bent his head mildly to the pews on each side, and bowed as he passed his oldest parishioner, a white-haired great-grandsire, who occupied an arm-chair in the centre of the aisle. It was strange to observe, how slowly this venerable man became conscious of something singular in the appearance of his pastor. He seemed not fully to partake of the prevailing wonder, till Mr. Hooper had ascended the stairs, and showed himself in the pulpit, face to face with his con-gregation, except for the black veil. That mysterious emblem was never once withdrawn. It shook with his measured breath as he gave out the psalm; it threw its obscurity between him and the holy page, as he read the Scriptures; and while he prayed, the veil lay heavily on his uplifted countenance. Did he seek to hide it from the dread Being whom he was addressing?

Such was the effect of this simple piece of crape, that more than one woman of delicate nerves was forced to leave the meeting-house. Yet perhaps the pale-faced congregation was almost as fearful a sight to the minister, as his black veil to them.

Mr. Hooper had the reputation of a good preacher, but not an ener-getic one: he strove to win his people heavenward, by mild persuasive influences, rather than to drive them thither, by the thunders of the Word. The sermon which he now delivered, was marked by the same characteristics of style and manner, as the general series of his pulpit oratory. But there was something, either in the sentiment of the dis-course itself, or in the imagination of the auditors, which made it greatly the most powerful effort that they had ever heard from their pastor's lips. It was tinged, rather more darkly than usual, with the gen-tle gloom of Mr. Hooper's temperament. The subject had reference to secret sin, and those sad mysteries which we hide from our nearest and dearest, and would fain conceal from our own consciousness, even forgetting that the Omniscient can detect them. A subtle power was breathed into his words. Each member of the congregation, the most innocent girl, and the man of hardened breast, felt as if the preacher had crept upon them, behind his awful veil, and discovered their hoarded iniquity of deed or thought. Many spread their clasped hands on their bosoms. There was nothing terrible in what Mr. Hooper said; at least, no violence; and yet, with every tremor of his melancholy voice, the hearers quaked. An unsought pathos came hand in hand with awe. So sensible were the audience of some unwonted attribute in their minister, that they longed for a breath of wind to blow aside the veil, almost believing that a stranger's visage would be discovered, though the form, gesture, and voice were those of Mr. Hooper.

At the close of the services, the people hurried out with indecorous confusion, eager to communicate their pent-up amazement, and conscious of lighter spirits, the moment they lost sight of the black veil. Some gathered in little circles, huddled closely together, with their mouths all whispering in the centre; some went homeward alone, wrapt in silent meditation; some talked loudly, and profaned the Sabbath-day with ostentatious laughter. A few shook their sagacious heads, intimating that they could penetrate the mystery; while one or two affirmed that there was no mystery at all, but only that Mr. Hooper's eyes were so weakened by the midnight lamp, as to require a shade. After a brief interval, forth came good Mr. Hooper also, in the rear of his flock. Turning his veiled face from one group to another, he paid due reverence to the hoary heads, saluted the middle-aged with kind dignity, as their friend and spiritual guide, greeted the young with mingled authority and love, and laid his hands on the little children's heads to bless them. Such was always his custom on the Sabbath-day. Strange and bewildered looks repaid him for his courtesy. None, as on former occasions, aspired to the honor of walking by their pastor's side. Old Squire Saunders,[2] doubtless by an accidental lapse of memory, neglected to invite Mr. Hooper to his table, where the good clergyman had been wont to bless the food, almost every Sunday since his settlement. He returned, therefore, to the parsonage, and, at the moment of closing the door, was observed to look back upon the people, all of whom had their eyes fixed upon the minister. A sad smile gleamed faintly from beneath the black veil, and flickered about his mouth, glimmering as he disappeared.

'How strange,' said a lady, 'that a simple black veil, such as any woman might wear on her bonnet, should become such a terrible thing on Mr. Hooper's face!'

'Something must surely be amiss with Mr. Hooper's intellects,' observed her husband, the physician of the village. 'But the strangest part of the affair is the effect of this vagary, even on a sober-minded man like myself. The black veil, though it covers only our pastor's face, throws its influence over his whole person, and makes him ghost-like from head to foot. Do you not feel it so?'

'Truly do I,' replied the lady; 'and I would not be alone with him for the world. I wonder he is not afraid to be alone with himself!'

'Men sometimes are so,' said her husband.

2. Michael J. Colacurcio links Old Squire Saunders to "Poor Richard" Saunders in Benjamin Franklin's *Almanac* and *Way to Wealth* (*The Province of Piety*, 351–53).

The afternoon service was attended with similar circumstances. At its conclusion, the bell tolled for the funeral of a young lady. The relatives and friends were assembled in the house, and the more distant acquaintances stood about the door, speaking of the good qualities of the deceased, when their talk was interrupted by the appearance of Mr. Hooper, still covered with his black veil. It was now an appropriate emblem. The clergyman stepped into the room where the corpse was laid, and bent over the coffin, to take a last farewell of his deceased parishioner. As he stooped, the veil hung straight down from his forehead, so that, if her eye-lids had not been closed for ever, the dead maiden might have seen his face. Could Mr. Hooper be fearful of her glance, that he so hastily caught back the black veil? A person, who watched the interview between the dead and living, scrupled not to affirm, that, at the instant when the clergyman's features were disclosed, the corpse had slightly shuddered, rustling the shroud and muslin cap, though the countenance retained the composure of death.[3] A superstitious old woman was the only witness of this prodigy. From the coffin, Mr. Hooper passed into the chamber of the mourners, and thence to the head of the staircase, to make the funeral prayer. It was a tender and heart-dissolving prayer, full of sorrow, yet so imbued with celestial hopes, that the music of a heavenly harp, swept by the fingers of the dead, seemed faintly to be heard among the saddest accents of the minister. The people trembled, though they but darkly understood him, when he prayed that they, and himself, and all of mortal race, might be ready, as he trusted this young maiden had been, for the dreadful hour that should snatch the veil from their faces. The bearers went heavily forth, and the mourners followed, saddening all the street, with the dead before them, and Mr. Hooper in his black veil behind.

'Why do you look back?' said one in the procession to his partner.

'I had a fancy,' replied she, 'that the minister and the maiden's spirit were walking hand in hand.'

'And so had I, at the same moment,' said the other.

That night, the handsomest couple in Milford village were to be joined in wedlock. Though reckoned a melancholy man, Mr. Hooper had a placid cheerfulness for such occasions, which often excited a sympathetic smile, where livelier merriment would have been thrown away. There was no quality of his disposition which made him more beloved than this. The company at the wedding awaited his arrival with impatience, trusting that the strange awe, which had gathered over him throughout the day, would now be dispelled. But such was not the result. When Mr. Hooper came, the first thing that their eyes rested on was the same horrible black veil, which had added deeper gloom to the funeral, and could portend nothing but evil to the wed-

---

3. Hawthorne refers to the folk superstition that a corpse will move or sometimes bleed from the nose in the presence of the murderer. Edgar Allan Poe apparently caught the hint because he claimed that the "*true* import of the narrative" involves a "crime of dark dye, (having reference to the 'young lady')." See review of *Twice-Told Tales*, *Graham's Magazine* 20 (May 1842): 298–300.

ding. Such was its immediate effect on the guests, that a cloud seemed to have rolled duskily from beneath the black crape, and dimmed the light of the candles. The bridal pair stood up before the minister. But the bride's cold fingers quivered in the tremulous hand of the bridegroom, and her death-like paleness caused a whisper, that the maiden who had been buried a few hours before, was come from her grave to be married. If ever another wedding were so dismal, it was that famous one, where they tolled the wedding-knell.[4] After performing the ceremony, Mr. Hooper raised a glass of wine to his lips, wishing happiness to the new-married couple, in a strain of mild pleasantry that ought to have brightened the features of the guests, like a cheerful gleam from the hearth. At that instant, catching a glimpse of his figure in the looking-glass, the black veil involved his own spirit in the horror with which it overwhelmed all others. His frame shuddered— his lips grew white—he spilt the untasted wine upon the carpet—and rushed forth into the darkness. For the Earth, too, had on her Black Veil.

The next day, the whole village of Milford talked of little else than Parson Hooper's black veil. That, and the mystery concealed behind it, supplied a topic for discussion between acquaintances meeting in the street, and good women gossiping at their open windows. It was the first item of news that the tavern-keeper told to his guests. The children babbled of it on their way to school. One imitative little imp covered his face with an old black handkerchief, thereby so affrighting his playmates, that the panic seized himself, and he well nigh lost his wits by his own waggery.

It was remarkable, that, of all the busy-bodies and impertinent people in the parish, not one ventured to put the plain question to Mr. Hooper, wherefore he did this thing. Hitherto, whenever there appeared the slightest call for such interference, he had never lacked advisers, nor shown himself averse to be guided by their judgment. If he erred at all, it was by so painful a degree of self-distrust, that even the mildest censure would lead him to consider an indifferent action as a crime. Yet, though so well acquainted with this amiable weakness, no individual among his parishioners chose to make the black veil a subject of friendly remonstrance. There was a feeling of dread, neither plainly confessed nor carefully concealed, which caused each to shift the responsibility upon another, till at length it was found expedient to send a deputation of the church, in order to deal with Mr. Hooper about the mystery, before it should grow into a scandal. Never did an embassy so ill discharge its duties. The minister received them with friendly courtesy, but became silent, after they were seated, leaving to his visiters the whole burthen of introducing their important business. The topic, it might be supposed, was obvious enough. There was the black veil, swathed round Mr. Hooper's forehead, and concealing every feature above his placid mouth, on which, at times, they could

---

4. Hawthorne refers to his own tale, "The Wedding Knell" (1836), in which a funeral bell begins to toll as the bride enters the church.

perceive the glimmering of a melancholy smile. But that piece of crape, to their imagination, seemed to hang down before his heart, the symbol of a fearful secret between him and them. Were the veil but cast aside, they might speak freely of it, but not till then. Thus they sat a considerable time, speechless, confused, and shrinking uneasily from Mr. Hooper's eye, which they felt to be fixed upon them with an invisible glance. Finally, the deputies returned abashed to their constituents, pronouncing the matter too weighty to be handled, except by a council of the churches, if, indeed, it might not require a general synod.[5]

But there was one person in the village, unappalled by the awe with which the black veil had impressed all beside herself. When the deputies returned without an explanation, or even venturing to demand one, she, with the calm energy of her character, determined to chase away the strange cloud that appeared to be settling round Mr. Hooper, every moment more darkly than before. As his plighted wife, it should be her privilege to know what the black veil concealed. At the minister's first visit, therefore, she entered upon the subject, with a direct simplicity, which made the task easier both for him and her. After he had seated himself, she fixed her eyes steadfastly upon the veil, but could discern nothing of the dreadful gloom that had so overawed the multitude: it was but a double fold of crape, hanging down from his forehead to his mouth, and slightly stirring with his breath.

'No,' said she aloud, and smiling, 'there is nothing terrible in this piece of crape, except that it hides a face which I am always glad to look upon. Come, good sir, let the sun shine from behind the cloud. First lay aside your black veil: then tell me why you put it on.'

Mr. Hooper's smile glimmered faintly.

'There is an hour to come,' said he, 'when all of us shall cast aside our veils. Take it not amiss, beloved friend, if I wear this piece of crape till then.'[6]

'Your words are a mystery too,' returned the young lady. 'Take away the veil from them, at least.'

'Elizabeth, I will,' said he, 'so far as my vow may suffer me. Know, then, this veil is a type and a symbol, and I am bound to wear it ever, both in light and darkness, in solitude and before the gaze of multitudes, and as with strangers, so with my familiar friends. No mortal eye will see it withdrawn. This dismal shade must separate me from the world: even you, Elizabeth, can never come behind it!'

'What grievous affliction hath befallen you,' she earnestly inquired, 'that you should thus darken your eyes for ever?'

'If it be a sign of mourning,' replied Mr. Hooper, 'I, perhaps, like most other mortals, have sorrows dark enough to be typified by a black veil.'

'But what if the world will not believe that it is the type of an innocent sorrow?' urged Elizabeth. 'Beloved and respected as you are, there

---

5. A church court, as in the case of Anne Hutchinson, when a synod was convened to examine and judge her.
6. Judgment Day.

may be whispers, that you hide your face under the consciousness of secret sin. For the sake of your holy office, do away this scandal!'

The color rose into her cheeks, as she intimated the nature of the rumors that were already abroad in the village. But Mr. Hooper's mildness did not forsake him. He even smiled again—that same sad smile, which always appeared like a faint glimmering of light, proceeding from the obscurity beneath the veil.

'If I hide my face for sorrow, there is cause enough,' he merely replied; 'and if I cover it for secret sin, what mortal might not do the same?'

And with this gentle, but unconquerable obstinacy, did he resist all her entreaties. At length Elizabeth sat silent. For a few moments she appeared lost in thought, considering, probably, what new methods might be tried, to withdraw her lover from so dark a fantasy, which, if it had no other meaning, was perhaps a symptom of mental disease. Though of a firmer character than his own, the tears rolled down her cheeks. But, in an instant, as it were, a new feeling took the place of sorrow: her eyes were fixed insensibly on the black veil, when, like a sudden twilight in the air, its terrors fell around her. She arose, and stood trembling before him.

'And do you feel it then at last?' said he mournfully.

She made no reply, but covered her eyes with her hand, and turned to leave the room. He rushed forward and caught her arm.

'Have patience with me, Elizabeth!' cried he passionately. 'Do not desert me, though this veil must be between us here on earth. Be mine, and hereafter there shall be no veil over my face, no darkness between our souls! It is but a mortal veil—it is not for eternity! Oh! you know not how lonely I am, and how frightened to be alone behind my black veil. Do not leave me in this miserable obscurity for ever!'

'Lift the veil but once, and look me in the face,' said she.

'Never! It cannot be!' replied Mr. Hooper.

'Then, farewell!' said Elizabeth.

She withdrew her arm from his grasp, and slowly departed, pausing at the door, to give one long, shuddering gaze, that seemed almost to penetrate the mystery of the black veil. But, even amid his grief, Mr. Hooper smiled to think that only a material emblem had separated him from happiness, though the horrors which it shadowed forth, must be drawn darkly between the fondest of lovers.

From that time no attempts were made to remove Mr. Hooper's black veil, or, by a direct appeal, to discover the secret which it was supposed to hide. By persons who claimed a superiority to popular prejudice, it was reckoned merely an eccentric whim, such as often mingles with the sober actions of men otherwise rational, and tinges them all with its own semblance of insanity. But with the multitude, good Mr. Hooper was irreparably a bugbear.[7] He could not walk the streets with any peace of mind, so conscious was he that the gentle and timid would turn aside to avoid him, and that others would make

7. A goblin or specter.

it a point of hardihood to throw themselves in his way. The imperti-
nence of the latter class compelled him to give up his customary walk,
at sunset, to the burial ground; for when he leaned pensively over the
gate, there would always be faces behind the grave-stones, peeping at
his black veil. A fable went the rounds, that the stare of the dead people drove him thence. It grieved him, to the very depth of his kind
heart, to observe how the children fled from his approach, breaking up
their merriest sports, while his melancholy figure was yet afar off.
Their instinctive dread caused him to feel, more strongly than aught
else, that a preternatural horror was interwoven with the threads of
the black crape. In truth, his own antipathy to the veil was known to
be so great, that he never willingly passed before a mirror, nor stooped
to drink at a still fountain, lest, in its peaceful bosom, he should be affrighted by himself. This was what gave plausibility to the whispers,
that Mr. Hooper's conscience tortured him for some great crime, too
horrible to be entirely concealed, or otherwise than so obscurely intimated. Thus, from beneath the black veil, there rolled a cloud into the
sunshine, an ambiguity of sin or sorrow, which enveloped the poor
minister, so that love or sympathy could never reach him. It was said,
that ghost and fiend consorted with him there. With self-shudderings
and outward terrors, he walked continually in its shadow, groping
darkly within his own soul, or gazing through a medium that saddened
the whole world. Even the lawless wind, it was believed, respected his
dreadful secret, and never blew aside the veil. But still good Mr.
Hooper sadly smiled, at the pale visages of the worldly throng as he
passed by.

Among all its bad influences, the black veil had the one desirable effect, of making its wearer a very efficient clergyman. By the aid of his
mysterious emblem—for there was no other apparent cause—he became a man of awful power, over souls that were in agony for sin. His
converts always regarded him with a dread peculiar to themselves, affirming, though but figuratively, that, before he brought them to celestial light, they had been with him behind the black veil. Its gloom,
indeed, enabled him to sympathize with all dark affections. Dying sinners cried aloud for Mr. Hooper, and would not yield their breath till
he appeared; though ever, as he stooped to whisper consolation, they
shuddered at the veiled face so near their own. Such were the terrors
of the black veil, even when Death had bared his visage! Strangers
came long distances to attend service at his church, with the mere idle
purpose of gazing at his figure, because it was forbidden them to behold his face. But many were made to quake ere they departed! Once,
during Governor Belcher's administration, Mr. Hooper was appointed
to preach the election sermon.[8] Covered with his black veil, he stood
before the chief magistrate, the council, and the representatives, and

---

8. Jonathan Belcher (1681–1757), royal governor of Massachusetts and New Hampshire
(1730–41) and later royal governor of New Jersey (1747–57) and founder of Princeton University. As in *The Scarlet Letter*, Hawthorne refers to the tradition of having a religious service to celebrate the election of a new governor. Being asked to preach the election sermon
was a great honor.

THE MINISTER'S BLACK VEIL   197

wrought so deep an impression, that the legislative measures of that year, were characterized by all the gloom and piety of our earliest ancestral sway.

In this manner Mr. Hooper spent a long life, irreproachable in outward act, yet shrouded in dismal suspicions; kind and loving, though unloved, and dimly feared; a man apart from men, shunned in their health and joy, but ever summoned to their aid in mortal anguish. As years wore on, shedding their snows above his sable veil, he acquired a name throughout the New-England churches, and they called him Father Hooper. Nearly all his parishioners, who were of mature age when he was settled, had been borne away by many a funeral: he had one congregation in the church, and a more crowded one in the church-yard; and having wrought so late into the evening, and done his work so well, it was now good Father Hooper's turn to rest.

Several persons were visible by the shaded candlelight, in the death-chamber of the old clergyman. Natural connections he had none. But there was the decorously grave, though unmoved physician, seeking only to mitigate the last pangs of the patient whom he could not save. There were the deacons, and other eminently pious members of his church. There, also, was the Reverend Mr. Clark, of Westbury, a young and zealous divine, who had ridden in haste to pray by the bed-side of the expiring minister.[9] There was the nurse, no hired hand-maiden of death, but one whose calm affection had endured thus long, in secresy, in solitude, amid the chill of age, and would not perish, even at the dying hour. Who, but Elizabeth! And there lay the hoary head of good Father Hooper upon the death-pillow, with the black veil still swathed about his brow and reaching down over his face, so that each more difficult gasp of his faint breath caused it to stir. All through life that piece of crape had hung between him and the world: it had separated him from cheerful brotherhood and woman's love, and kept him in that saddest of all prisons, his own heart; and still it lay upon his face, as if to deepen the gloom of his darksome chamber, and shade him from the sunshine of eternity.

For some time previous, his mind had been confused, wavering doubtfully between the past and the present, and hovering forward, as it were, at intervals, into the indistinctness of the world to come. There had been feverish turns, which tossed him from side to side, and wore away what little strength he had. But in his most convulsive struggles, and in the wildest vagaries of his intellect, when no other thought retained its sober influence, he still showed an awful solicitude lest the black veil should slip aside. Even if his bewildered soul could have forgotten, there was a faithful woman at his pillow, who, with averted eyes, would have covered that aged face, which she had last beheld in the comeliness of manhood. At length the death-stricken old man lay quietly in the torpor of mental and bodily exhaustion, with an imperceptible pulse, and breath that grew fainter and

9. Michael J. Colacurcio considers Peter Clark the most likely model for Hawthorne's Reverend Mr. Clark (*Province of Piety*, 355–57). In 1739, Peter Clark preached the official election sermon before Governor Belcher.

fainter, except when a long, deep, and irregular inspiration seemed to prelude the flight of his spirit.

The minister of Westbury approached the bedside.

'Venerable Father Hooper,' said he, 'the moment of your release is at hand. Are you ready for the lifting of the veil, that shuts in time from eternity?'

Father Hooper at first replied merely by a feeble motion of his head; then, apprehensive, perhaps, that his meaning might be doubtful, he exerted himself to speak.

'Yea,' said he, in faint accents, 'my soul hath a patient weariness until that veil be lifted.'

'And is it fitting,' resumed the Reverend Mr. Clark, 'that a man so given to prayer, of such a blameless example, holy in deed and thought, so far as mortal judgment may pronounce; is it fitting that a father in the church should leave a shadow on his memory, that may seem to blacken a life so pure? I pray you, my venerable brother, let not this thing be! Suffer us to be gladdened by your triumphant aspect, as you go to your reward. Before the veil of eternity be lifted, let me cast aside this black veil from your face!'

And thus speaking, the Reverend Mr. Clark bent forward to reveal the mystery of so many years. But, exerting a sudden energy, that made all the beholders stand aghast, Father Hooper snatched both his hands from beneath the bed-clothes, and pressed them strongly on the black veil, resolute to struggle, if the minister of Westbury would contend with a dying man.

'Never!' cried the veiled clergyman. 'On earth, never!'

'Dark old man!' exclaimed the affrighted minister, 'with what horrible crime upon your soul are you now passing to the judgment?'

Father Hooper's breath heaved; it rattled in his throat; but, with a mighty effort, grasping forward with his hands, he caught hold of life, and held it back till he should speak. He even raised himself in bed; and there he sat, shivering with the arms of death around him, while the black veil hung down, awful, at that last moment, in the gathered terrors of a life-time. And yet the faint, sad smile, so often there, now seemed to glimmer from its obscurity, and linger on Father Hooper's lips.

'Why do you tremble at me alone?' cried he, turning his veiled face round the circle of pale spectators. 'Tremble also at each other! Have men avoided me, and women shown no pity, and children screamed and fled, only for my black veil? What, but the mystery which it obscurely typifies, has made this piece of crape so awful? When the friend shows his inmost heart to his friend; the lover to his best-beloved; when man does not vainly shrink from the eye of his Creator, loathsomely treasuring up the secret of his sin; then deem me a monster, for the symbol beneath which I have lived, and die! I look around me, and, lo! on every visage a Black Veil!'

While his auditors shrank from one another, in mutual affright, Father Hooper fell back upon his pillow, a veiled corpse, with a faint smile lingering on the lips. Still veiled, they laid him in his coffin, and a veiled corpse they bore him to the grave. The grass of many years has sprung up and withered on that grave, the burial-stone is moss-grown, and good Mr. Hooper's face is dust; but awful is still the thought, that it mouldered beneath the Black Veil!

The Birth-mark†

In the latter part of the last century, there lived a man of science—an eminent proficient in every branch of natural philosophy—who, not long before our story opens, had made experience of a spiritual affinity, more attractive than any chemical one. He had left his laboratory to the care of an assistant, cleared his fine countenance from the furnace-smoke, washed the stain of acids from his fingers, and persuaded a beautiful woman to become his wife. In those days, when the comparatively recent discovery of electricity, and other kindred mysteries of nature, seemed to open paths into the region of miracle, it was not unusual for the love of science to rival the love of woman, in its depth and absorbing energy. The higher intellect, the imagination, the spirit, and even the heart, might all find their congenial aliment[1] in pursuits which, as some of their ardent votaries believed, would ascend from one step of powerful intelligence to another, until the philosopher should lay his hand on the secret of creative force, and perhaps make new worlds for himself. We know not whether Aylmer possessed this degree of faith in man's ultimate control over nature. He had devoted himself, however, too unreservedly to scientific studies, ever to be weaned from them by any second passion. His love for his young wife might prove the stronger of the two; but it could only be by intertwining itself with his love of science, and uniting the strength of the latter to its own.

Such a union accordingly took place, and was attended with truly remarkable consequences, and a deeply impressive moral. One day, very soon after their marriage, Aylmer sat gazing at his wife, with a trouble in his countenance that grew stronger, until he spoke.

"Georgiana," said he, "has it never occurred to you that the mark upon your cheek might be removed?"

"No, indeed," said she, smiling; but perceiving the seriousness of his manner, she blushed deeply. "To tell you the truth, it has been so often called a charm, that I was simple enough to imagine it might be so."

"Ah, upon another face, perhaps it might," replied her husband. "But never on yours! No, dearest Georgiana, you came so nearly perfect from the hand of Nature, that this slightest possible defect—which we hesitate whether to term a defect or a beauty—shocks me, as being the visible mark of earthly imperfection."

---

† First published in *The Pioneer* and collected in *Mosses from an Old Manse* (1846). Reprinted from *Mosses from an Old Mause*, vol. 10 of the *Centenary Edition of the Works of Nathaniel Hawthorne*, ed. William Charvat, Roy Harvey Pearce, and Claude Simpson (Columbus: Ohio State UP, 1974), 36–56.
1. Food, sustenance.

"Shocks you, my husband!" cried Georgiana, deeply hurt; at first reddening with momentary anger, but then bursting into tears. "Then why did you take me from my mother's side? You cannot love what shocks you!"

To explain this conversation, it must be mentioned, that, in the centre of Georgiana's left cheek, there was a singular mark, deeply interwoven, as it were, with the texture and substance of her face. In the usual state of her complexion,—a healthy, though delicate bloom,—the mark wore a tint of deeper crimson, which imperfectly defined its shape amid the surrounding rosiness. When she blushed, it gradually became more indistinct, and finally vanished amid the triumphant rush of blood, that bathed the whole cheek with its brilliant glow. But, if any shifting emotion caused her to turn pale, there was the mark again, a crimson stain upon the snow, in what Aylmer sometimes deemed an almost fearful distinctness. Its shape bore not a little similarity to the human hand, though of the smallest pigmy size. Georgiana's lovers were wont to say, that some fairy, at her birth-hour, had laid her tiny hand upon the infant's cheek, and left this impress there, in token of the magic endowments that were to give her such sway over all hearts. Many a desperate swain would have risked life for the privilege of pressing his lips to the mysterious hand. It must not be concealed, however, that the impression wrought by this fairy sign-manual varied exceedingly, according to the difference of temperament in the beholders. Some fastidious persons—but they were exclusively of her own sex—affirmed that the Bloody Hand, as they chose to call it, quite destroyed the effect of Georgiana's beauty, and rendered her countenance even hideous. But it would be as reasonable to say, that one of those small blue stains, which sometimes occur in the purest statuary marble, would convert the Eve of Powers to a monster.[2] Masculine observers, if the birth-mark did not heighten their admiration, contented themselves with wishing it away, that the world might possess one living specimen of ideal loveliness, without the semblance of a flaw. After his marriage—for he thought little or nothing of the matter before—Aylmer discovered that this was the case with himself.

Had she been less beautiful—if Envy's self could have found aught else to sneer at—he might have felt his affection heightened by the prettiness of this mimic hand, now vaguely portrayed, now lost, now stealing forth again, and glimmering to-and-fro with every pulse of emotion that throbbed within her heart. But, seeing her otherwise so perfect, he found this one defect grow more and more intolerable, with every moment of their united lives. It was the fatal flaw of humanity, which Nature, in one shape or another, stamps ineffaceably on all her productions, either to imply that they are temporary and finite,

---

2. Vermont-born sculptor Hiram Powers (1805–1873), whom Hawthorne would get to know when he lived in Rome, was best known for his *Greek Slave*, a controversial sculpture that toured the United States in 1847–48. Hawthorne probably refers to the sculpture *Eve Tempted* (1842), Powers's first full-length nude (National Museum of American Art in Washington, D.C.).

or that their perfection must be wrought by toil and pain. The Crimson Hand expressed the ineludible gripe, in which mortality clutches the highest and purest of earthly mould, degrading them into kindred with the lowest, and even with the very brutes, like whom their visible frames return to dust. In this manner, selecting it as the symbol of his wife's liability to sin, sorrow, decay, and death, Aylmer's sombre imagination was not long in rendering the birth-mark a frightful object, causing him more trouble and horror than ever Georgiana's beauty, whether of soul or sense, had given him delight.

At all the seasons which should have been their happiest, he invariably, and without intending it—nay, in spite of a purpose to the contrary—reverted to this one disastrous topic. Trifling as it at first appeared, it so connected itself with innumerable trains of thought, and modes of feeling, that it became the central point of all. With the morning twilight, Aylmer opened his eyes upon his wife's face, and recognized the symbol of imperfection; and when they sat together at the evening hearth, his eyes wandered stealthily to her cheek, and beheld, flickering with the blaze of the wood fire, the spectral Hand that wrote mortality, where he would fain have worshipped. Georgiana soon learned to shudder at his gaze. It needed but a glance, with the peculiar expression that his face often wore, to change the roses of her cheek into a deathlike paleness, amid which the Crimson Hand was brought strongly out, like a bas-relief of ruby on the whitest marble.

Late, one night, when the lights were growing dim, so as hardly to betray the stain on the poor wife's cheek, she herself, for the first time, voluntarily took up the subject.

"Do you remember, my dear Aylmer," said she, with a feeble attempt at a smile—"have you any recollection of a dream, last night, about this odious Hand?"

"None!—none whatever!" replied Aylmer, starting; but then he added in a dry, cold tone, affected for the sake of concealing the real depth of his emotion:—"I might well dream of it; for before I fell asleep, it had taken a pretty firm hold of my fancy."

"And you did dream of it," continued Georgiana, hastily; for she dreaded lest a gush of tears should interrupt what she had to say—"A terrible dream! I wonder that you can forget it. Is it possible to forget this one expression?—'It is in her heart now—we must have it out!'— Reflect, my husband; for by all means I would have you recall that dream."

The mind is in a sad note, when Sleep, the all-involving, cannot confine her spectres within the dim region of her sway, but suffers them to break forth, affrighting this actual life with secrets that perchance belong to a deeper one. Aylmer now remembered his dream. He had fancied himself, with his servant Aminadab,[3] attempting an operation for the removal of the birth-mark. But the deeper went the knife, the deeper sank the Hand, until at length its tiny grasp appeared

---

3. See Matthew 1:4. As critics have pointed out, spelled backwards, "Aminadab" becomes "bad anima" (evil female spirit).

to have caught hold of Georgiana's heart; whence, however, her husband was inexorably resolved to cut or wrench it away.

When the dream had shaped itself perfectly in his memory, Aylmer sat in his wife's presence with a guilty feeling. Truth often finds its way to the mind close-muffled in robes of sleep, and then speaks with uncompromising directness of matters in regard to which we practise an unconscious self-deception, during our waking moments. Until now, he had not been aware of the tyrannizing influence acquired by one idea over his mind, and of the lengths which he might find in his heart to go, for the sake of giving himself peace.

"Aylmer," resumed Georgiana, solemnly, "I know not what may be the cost to both of us, to rid me of this fatal birth-mark. Perhaps its removal may cause cureless deformity. Or, it may be, the stain goes as deep as life itself. Again, do we know that there is a possibility, on any terms, of unclasping the firm gripe of this little Hand, which was laid upon me before I came into the world?"

"Dearest Georgiana, I have spent much thought upon the subject," hastily interrupted Aylmer—"I am convinced of the perfect practicability of its removal."

"If there be the remotest possibility of it," continued Georgiana, "let the attempt be made, at whatever risk. Danger is nothing to me; for life—while this hateful mark makes me the object of your horror and disgust—life is a burthen which I would fling down with joy. Either remove this dreadful Hand, or take my wretched life! You have deep science! All the world bears witness of it. You have achieved great wonders! Cannot you remove this little, little mark, which I cover with the tips of two small fingers? Is this beyond your power, for the sake of your own peace, and to save your poor wife from madness?"

"Noblest—dearest—tenderest wife!" cried Aylmer, rapturously. "Doubt not my power. I have already given this matter the deepest thought—thought which might almost have enlightened me to create a being less perfect than yourself. Georgiana, you have led me deeper than ever into the heart of science. I feel myself fully competent to render this dear cheek as faultless as its fellow; and then, most beloved, what will be my triumph, when I shall have corrected what Nature left imperfect, in her fairest work! Even Pygmalion, when his sculptured woman assumed life, felt not greater ecstasy than mine will be."[4]

"It is resolved, then," said Georgiana, faintly smiling,—"And, Aylmer, spare me not, though you should find the birth-mark take refuge in my heart at last."

Her husband tenderly kissed her cheek—her right cheek—not that which bore the impress of the Crimson Hand.

The next day, Aylmer apprized his wife of a plan that he had formed, whereby he might have opportunity for the intense thought and constant watchfulness, which the proposed operation would require;

4. In Greek mythology, Pygmalion sculpted a female figure, Galatea, with whom he fell in love. The goddess Aphrodite brought Galatea to life, Pygmalion married her, and they conceived a son, Paphos. See Book 10 of Ovid's *Metamorphoses*. Also see the well-known painting, *Pygmalion and Galatea*, by Jean-Léon Gérôme (1824–1904), available for viewing online.

while Georgiana, likewise, would enjoy the perfect repose essential to its success. They were to seclude themselves in the extensive apartments occupied by Aylmer as a laboratory, and where, during his toilsome youth, he had made discoveries in the elemental powers of nature, that had roused the admiration of all the learned societies in Europe. Seated calmly in this laboratory, the pale philosopher had investigated the secrets of the highest cloud-region, and of the profoundest mines; he had satisfied himself of the causes that kindled and kept alive the fires of the volcano; and had explained the mystery of fountains, and how it is that they gush forth, some so bright and pure, and others with such rich medicinal virtues, from the dark bosom of the earth. Here, too, at an earlier period, he had studied the wonders of the human frame, and attempted to fathom the very process by which Nature assimilates all her precious influences from earth and air, and from the spiritual world, to create and foster Man, her masterpiece. The latter pursuit, however, Aylmer had long laid aside, in unwilling recognition of the truth, against which all seekers sooner or later stumble, that our great creative Mother, while she amuses us with apparently working in the broadest sunshine, is yet severely careful to keep her own secrets, and, in spite of her pretended openness, shows us nothing but results. She permits us indeed, to mar, but seldom to mend, and, like a jealous patentee, on no account to make. Now, however, Aylmer resumed these half-forgotten investigations; not, of course, with such hopes or wishes as first suggested them; but because they involved much physiological truth, and lay in the path of his proposed scheme for the treatment of Georgiana.

As he led her over the threshold of the laboratory, Georgiana was cold and tremulous. Aylmer looked cheerfully into her face, with intent to reassure her, but was so startled with the intense glow of the birth-mark upon the whiteness of her cheek, that he could not restrain a strong convulsive shudder. His wife fainted.

"Aminadab! Aminadab!" shouted Aylmer, stamping violently on the floor.

Forthwith, there issued from an inner apartment a man of low stature, but bulky frame, with shaggy hair hanging about his visage, which was grimed with the vapors of the furnace. This personage had been Aylmer's under-worker during his whole scientific career, and was admirably fitted for that office by his great mechanical readiness, and the skill with which, while incapable of comprehending a single principle, he executed all the practical details of his master's experiments. With his vast strength, his shaggy hair, his smoky aspect, and the indescribable earthiness that incrusted him, he seemed to represent man's physical nature; while Aylmer's slender figure, and pale, intellectual face, were no less apt a type of the spiritual element.

"Throw open the door of the boudoir, Aminadab," said Aylmer, "and burn a pastille."[5]

"Yes, master," answered Aminadab, looking intently at the lifeless

5. An aromatic paste.

form of Georgiana; and then he muttered to himself:—"If she were my wife, I'd never part with that birth-mark."

When Georgiana recovered consciousness, she found herself breathing an atmosphere of penetrating fragrance, the gentle potency of which had recalled her from her deathlike faintness. The scene around her looked like enchantment. Aylmer had converted those smoky, dingy, sombre rooms, where he had spent his brightest years in recondite pursuits, into a series of beautiful apartments, not unfit to be the secluded abode of a lovely woman. The walls were hung with gorgeous curtains, which imparted the combination of grandeur and grace, that no other species of adornment can achieve; and as they fell from the ceiling to the floor, their rich and ponderous folds, conceal-ing all angles and straight lines, appeared to shut in the scene from in-finite space. For aught Georgiana knew, it might be a pavilion among the clouds. And Aylmer, excluding the sunshine, which would have in-terfered with his chemical processes, had supplied its place with per-fumed lamps, emitting flames of various hue, but all uniting in a soft, empurpled radiance. He now knelt by his wife's side, watching her earnestly, but without alarm; for he was confident in his science, and felt that he could draw a magic circle round her, within which no evil might intrude.

"Where am I?—Ah, I remember!" said Georgiana, faintly; and she placed her hand over her cheek, to hide the terrible mark from her husband's eyes.

"Fear not, dearest!" exclaimed he. "Do not shrink from me! Believe me, Georgiana, I even rejoice in this single imperfection, since it will be such rapture to remove it."

"Oh, spare me!" sadly replied his wife—"Pray do not look at it again. I never can forget that convulsive shudder."

In order to soothe Georgiana, and, as it were, to release her mind from the burthen of actual things, Aylmer now put in practice some of the light and playful secrets, which science had taught him among its profounder lore. Airy figures, absolutely bodiless ideas, and forms of unsubstantial beauty, came and danced before her, imprinting their momentary footsteps on beams of light. Though she had some indis-tinct idea of the method of these optical phenomena, still the illusion was almost perfect enough to warrant the belief, that her husband possessed sway over the spiritual world. Then again, when she felt a wish to look forth from her seclusion, immediately, as if her thoughts were answered, the procession of external existence flitted across a screen. The scenery and the figures of actual life were perfectly repre-sented, but with that bewitching, yet indescribable difference, which always makes a picture, an image, or a shadow, so much more attrac-tive than the original. When wearied of this, Aylmer bade her cast her eyes upon a vessel, containing a quantity of earth. She did so, with lit-tle interest at first, but was soon startled, to perceive the germ of a plant, shooting upward from the soil. Then came the slender stalk— the leaves gradually unfolded themselves—and amid them was a per-fect and lovely flower.

"It is magical!" cried Georgianna, "I dare not touch it."

"Nay, pluck it," answered Aylmer, "pluck it, and inhale its brief perfume while you may. The flower will wither in a few moments, and leave nothing save its brown seed-vessels—but thence may be perpetuated a race as ephemeral as itself."

But Georgianna had no sooner touched the flower than the whole plant suffered a blight, its leaves turning coal-black, as if by the agency of fire.

"There was too powerful a stimulus," said Aylmer thoughtfully.

To make up for this abortive experiment, he proposed to take her portrait by a scientific process of his own invention. It was to be effected by rays of light striking upon a polished plate of metal. Georgiana assented—but, on looking at the result, was affrighted to find the features of the portrait blurred and indefinable; while the minute figure of a hand appeared where the cheek should have been. Aylmer snatched the metallic plate, and threw it into a jar of corrosive acid.[6]

Soon, however, he forgot these mortifying failures. In the intervals of study and chemical experiment, he came to her, flushed and exhausted, but seemed invigorated by her presence, and spoke in glowing language of the resources of his art. He gave a history of the long dynasty of the Alchemists, who spent so many ages in quest of the universal solvent, by which the Golden Principle might be elicted from all things vile and base. Aylmer appeared to believe, that, by the plainest scientific logic, it was altogether within the limits of possibility to discover this long-sought medium; but, he added, a philosopher who should go deep enough to acquire the power, would attain too lofty a wisdom to stoop to the exercise of it. Not less singular were his opinions in regard to the Elixir Vitæ. He more than intimated, that it was his option to concoct a liquid that should prolong life for years—perhaps interminably—but that it would produce a discord in nature, which all the world, and chiefly the quaffer of the immortal nostrum, would find cause to curse.

"Aylmer, are you in earnest?" asked Georgiana, looking at him with amazement and fear; "it is terrible to possess such power, or even to dream of possessing it!"

"Oh, do not tremble, my love!" said her husband, "I would not wrong either you or myself by working such inharmonious effects upon our lives. But I would have you consider how trifling, in comparison, is the skill requisite to remove this little Hand."

At the mention of the birth-mark, Georgiana, as usual, shrank, as if a red-hot iron had touched her cheek.

Again Aylmer applied himself to his labors. She could hear his voice in the distant furnace-room, giving directions to Aminadab, whose harsh, uncouth, misshapen tones were audible in response, more like the grunt or growl of a brute than human speech. After hours of ab-

6. Hawthorne is describing daguerreotypy, an early form of photography developed in France and very popular in America in the 1840s. Daguerreotypes were made by focusing an image on a silver-plated copper sheet and then treating the plate with mercury vapors. Hawthorne used daguerreotypy more extensively in *The House of the Seven Gables* (1851).

sence, Aylmer reappeared, and proposed that she should now examine his cabinet of chemical products, and natural treasures of the earth. Among the former he showed her a small vial, in which, he remarked, was contained a gentle yet most powerful fragrance, capable of impregnating all the breezes that blow across a kingdom. They were of inestimable value, the contents of that little vial; and, as he said so, he threw some of the perfume into the air, and filled the room with piercing and invigorating delight.

"And what is this?" asked Georgiana, pointing to a small crystal globe, containing a gold-colored liquid. "It is so beautiful to the eye, that I could imagine it the Elixir of Life."

"In one sense it is," replied Aylmer, "or rather the Elixir of Immortality. It is the most precious poison that ever was concocted in this world. By its aid, I could apportion the lifetime of any mortal at whom you might point your finger. The strength of the dose would determine whether he were to linger out years, or drop dead in the midst of a breath. No king, on his guarded throne, could keep his life, if I, in my private station, should deem that the welfare of millions justified me in depriving him of it."

"Why do you keep such a terrific drug?" inquired Georgiana in horror.

"Do not mistrust me, dearest!" said her husband, smiling; "its virtuous potency is yet greater than its harmful one. But, see! here is a powerful cosmetic. With a few drops of this, in a vase of water, freckles may be washed away as easily as the hands are cleansed. A stronger infusion would take the blood out of the cheek, and leave the rosiest beauty a pale ghost."

"Is it with this lotion that you intend to bathe my cheek?" asked Georgiana anxiously.

"Oh, no!" hastily replied her husband—"this is merely superficial. Your case demands a remedy that shall go deeper."

In his interviews with Georgiana, Aylmer generally made minute inquiries as to her sensations, and whether the confinement of the rooms, and the temperature of the atmosphere, agreed with her. These questions had such a particular drift, that Georgiana began to conjecture that she was already subjected to certain physical influences, either breathed in with the fragrant air, or taken with her food. She fancied, likewise—but it might be altogether fancy—that there was a stirring up of her system,—a strange indefinite sensation creeping through her veins, and tingling, half painfully, half pleasurably, at her heart. Still, whenever she dared to look into the mirror, there she beheld herself, pale as a white rose, and with the crimson birth-mark stamped upon her cheek. Not even Aylmer now hated it so much as she.

To dispel the tedium of the hours which her husband found it necessary to devote to the processes of combination and analysis, Georgiana turned over the volumes of his scientific library. In many dark old tomes, she met with chapters full of romance and poetry. They were the works of the philosophers of the middle ages, such as Albertus Magnus, Cornelius Agrippa, Paracelsus, and the famous friar who created the prophetic Brazen Head.[7] All these antique naturalists stood in advance of their centuries, yet were imbued with some of their credulity, and therefore were believed, and perhaps imagined themselves, to have acquired from the investigation of nature a power above nature, and from physics a sway over the spiritual world. Hardly less curious and imaginative were the early volumes of the Transactions of the Royal Society,[8] in which the members, knowing little of the limits of natural possibility, were continually recording wonders, or proposing methods whereby wonders might be wrought.

But, to Georgiana, the most engrossing volume was a large folio from her husband's own hand, in which he had recorded every experiment of his scientific career, with its original aim, the methods adopted for its development, and its final success or failure, with the circumstances to which either event was attributable. The book, in truth, was both the history and emblem of his ardent, ambitious, imaginative, yet practical and laborious, life. He handled physical details, as if there were nothing beyond them; yet spiritualized them all, and redeemed himself from materialism, by his strong and eager aspiration towards the infinite. In his grasp, the veriest clod of earth assumed a soul. Georgiana, as she read, reverenced Aylmer, and loved him more profoundly than ever, but with a less entire dependence on his judgment than heretofore. Much as he had accomplished, she could not but observe that his most splendid successes were almost invariably failures, if compared with the ideal at which he aimed. His brightest diamonds were the merest pebbles, and felt to be so by himself, in comparison with the inestimable gems which lay hidden beyond his reach. The volume, rich with achievements that had won renown for its author, was yet as melancholy a record as ever mortal hand had penned. It was the sad confession, and continual exemplification, of the short-comings of the composite man—the spirit burthened with clay and working in matter—and of the despair that assails the higher nature, at finding itself so miserably thwarted by the earthly part. Perhaps every man of genius, in whatever sphere, might recognize the image of his own experience in Aylmer's journal.

So deeply did these reflections affect Georgiana, that she laid her face upon the open volume, and burst into tears. In this situation she was found by her husband.

"It is dangerous to read in a sorcerer's books," said he, with a smile, though his countenance was uneasy and displeased. "Georgiana, there

---

7. Albertus Magnus (c. 1220–1280), a Dominican bishop and philosopher best known as a teacher of St. Thomas Aquinas and as a proponent of Aristotelianism at the University of Paris. Cornelius Agrippa (1486–1535), a German alchemist notable for his works on occult philosophy. Paracelsus (1493–1541), a sixteenth-century Swiss alchemist. Roger Bacon (c. 1214–1294), a thirteenth-century friar, was reputed to have created a talking head out of brass.

8. The oldest scientific journal in continuous publication, *Philosophical Transactions* of the Royal Society of London was first published in 1665.

are pages in that volume, which I can scarcely glance over and keep my senses. Take heed lest it prove as detrimental to you!"

"It has made me worship you more than ever," said she.

"Ah! wait for this one success," rejoined he, "then worship me if you will. I shall deem myself hardly unworthy of it. But, come! I have sought you for the luxury of your voice. Sing to me, dearest!"

So she poured out the liquid music of her voice to quench the thirst of his spirit. He then took his leave, with a boyish exuberance of gaiety, assuring her that her seclusion would endure but a little longer, and that the result was already certain. Scarcely had he departed, when Georgiana felt irresistibly impelled to follow him. She had forgotten to inform Aylmer of a symptom, which, for two or three hours past, had begun to excite her attention. It was a sensation in the fatal birth-mark, not painful, but which induced a restlessness throughout her system. Hastening after her husband, she intruded, for the first time, into the laboratory.

The first thing that struck her eye was the furnace, that hot and feverish worker, with the intense glow of its fire, which, by the quantities of soot clustered above it, seemed to have been burning for ages. There was a distilling apparatus in full operation. Around the room were retorts, tubes, cylinders, crucibles, and other apparatus of chemical research. An electrical machine stood ready for immediate use. The atmosphere felt oppressively close, and was tainted with gaseous odors, which had been tormented forth by the processes of science. The severe and homely simplicity of the apartment, with its naked walls and brick pavement, looked strange, accustomed as Georgiana had become to the fantastic elegance of her boudoir. But what chiefly, indeed almost solely, drew her attention, was the aspect of Aylmer himself.

He was pale as death, anxious, and absorbed, and hung over the furnace as if it depended upon his utmost watchfulness whether the liquid, which it was distilling, should be the draught of immortal happiness or misery. How different from the sanguine and joyous mien that he had assumed for Georgiana's encouragement!

"Carefully now, Aminadab! Carefully, thou human machine! Carefully, thou man of clay!" muttered Aylmer, more to himself than his assistant. "Now, if there be a thought too much or too little, it is all over!"

"Hoh! hoh!" mumbled Aminadab—"look, master, look!"

Aylmer raised his eyes hastily, and at first reddened, then grew paler than ever, on beholding Georgiana. He rushed towards her, and seized her arm with a gripe that left the print of his fingers upon it.

"Why do you come hither? Have you no trust in your husband?" cried he impetuously. "Would you throw the blight of that fatal birth-mark over my labors? It is not well done. Go, prying woman, go!"

"Nay, Aylmer," said Georgiana, with the firmness of which she possessed no stinted endowment, "it is not you that have a right to complain. You mistrust your wife! You have concealed the anxiety with which you watch the development of this experiment. Think not so unworthily of me, my husband! Tell me all the risk we run; and fear not that I shall shrink, for my share in it is far less than your own!"

"No, no, Georgiana!" said Aylmer impatiently, "it must not be."

"I submit," replied she calmly. "And, Aylmer, I shall quaff whatever draught you bring me; but it will be on the same principle that would induce me to take a dose of poison, if offered by your hand."

"My noble wife," said Aylmer, deeply moved, "I knew not the height and depth of your nature, until now. Nothing shall be concealed. Know, then, that this Crimson Hand, superficial as it seems, has clutched its grasp into your being, with a strength of which I had no previous conception. I have already administered agents powerful enough to do aught except to change your entire physical system. Only one thing remains to be tried. If that fail us, we are ruined!"

"Why did you hesitate to tell me this?" asked she.

"Because, Georgiana," said Aylmer, in a low voice, "there is danger!"

"Danger? There is but one danger—that this horrible stigma shall be left upon my cheek!" cried Georgiana. "Remove it! remove it!—whatever be the cost—or we shall both go mad!"

"Heaven knows, your words are too true," said Aylmer, sadly. "And now, dearest, return to your boudoir. In a little while, all will be tested."

He conducted her back, and took leave of her with a solemn tenderness, which spoke far more than his words how much was now at stake. After his departure, Georgiana became wrapt in musings. She considered the character of Aylmer, and did it completer justice than at any previous moment. Her heart exulted, while it trembled, at his honorable love, so pure and lofty that it would accept nothing less than perfection, nor miserably make itself contented with an earthlier nature than he had dreamed of. She felt how much more precious was such a sentiment, than that meaner kind which would have borne with the imperfection for her sake, and have been guilty of treason to holy love, by degrading its perfect idea to the level of the actual. And, with her whole spirit, she prayed, that, for a single moment, she might satisfy his highest and deepest conception. Longer than one moment, she well knew, it could not be; for his spirit was ever on the march—ever ascending—and each instant required something that was beyond the scope of the instant before.

The sound of her husband's footsteps aroused her. He bore a crystal goblet, containing a liquor colorless as water, but bright enough to be the draught of immortality. Aylmer was pale; but it seemed rather the consequence of a highly wrought state of mind, and tension of spirit, than of fear or doubt.

"The concoction of the draught has been perfect," said he, in answer to Georgiana's look. "Unless all my science have deceived me, it cannot fail."

"Save on your account, my dearest Aylmer," observed his wife, "I might wish to put off this birth-mark of mortality by relinquishing mortality itself, in preference to any other mode. Life is but a sad possession to those who have attained precisely the degree of moral advancement at which I stand. Were I weaker and blinder, it might be happiness. Were I stronger, it might be endured hopefully. But, being what I find myself, methinks I am of all mortals the most fit to die."

"You are fit for heaven without tasting death!" replied her husband. "But why do we speak of dying? The draught cannot fail. Behold its effect upon this plant!"

On the window-seat there stood a geranium, diseased with yellow blotches, which had overspread all its leaves. Aylmer poured a small quantity of the liquid upon the soil in which it grew. In a little time, when the roots of the plant had taken up the moisture, the unsightly blotches began to be extinguished in a living verdure.

"There needed no proof," said Georgiana, quietly. "Give me the goblet. I joyfully stake all upon your word."

"Drink, then, thou lofty creature!" exclaimed Aylmer, with fervid admiration. "There is no taint of imperfection on thy spirit. Thy sensible frame, too, shall soon be all perfect!"

She quaffed the liquid, and returned the goblet to his hand.

"It is grateful," said she, with a placid smile. "Methinks it is like water from a heavenly fountain; for it contains I know not what of unobtrusive fragrance and deliciousness. It allays a feverish thirst, that had parched me for many days. Now, dearest, let me sleep. My earthly senses are closing over my spirit, like the leaves round the heart of a rose, at sunset."

She spoke the last words with a gentle reluctance, as if it required almost more energy than she could command to pronounce the faint and lingering syllables. Scarcely had they loitered through her lips, ere she was lost in slumber. Aylmer sat by her side, watching her aspect with the emotions proper to a man, the whole value of whose existence was involved in the process now to be tested. Mingled with this mood, however, was the philosophic investigation, characteristic of the man of science. Not the minutest symptom escaped him. A heightened flush of the cheek—a slight irregularity of breath—a quiver of the eyelid—a hardly perceptible tremor through the frame—such were the details which, as the moments passed, he wrote down in his folio volume. Intense thought had set its stamp upon every previous page of that volume; but the thoughts of years were all concentrated upon the last.

While thus employed, he failed not to gaze often at the fatal Hand, and not without a shudder. Yet once, by a strange and unaccountable impulse, he pressed it with his lips. His spirit recoiled, however, in the very act, and Georgiana, out of the midst of her deep sleep, moved uneasily and murmured, as if in remonstrance. Again, Aylmer resumed his watch. Nor was it without avail. The Crimson Hand, which at first had been strongly visible upon the marble paleness of Georgiana's cheek now grew more faintly outlined. She remained not less pale than ever; but the birth-mark, with every breath that came and went, lost somewhat of its former distinctness. Its presence had been awful; its departure was more awful still. Watch the stain of the rainbow fading out of the sky; and you will know how that mysterious symbol passed away.

"By Heaven, it is well nigh gone!" said Aylmer to himself, in almost irrepressible ecstasy. "I can scarcely trace it now. Success! Success! And now it is like the faintest rose-color. The slightest flush of blood across her cheek would overcome it. But she is so pale!"

He drew aside the window-curtain, and suffered the light of natural day to fall into the room, and rest upon her cheek. At the same time, he heard a gross, hoarse chuckle, which he had long known as his servant Aminadab's expression of delight.

"Ah, clod! Ah, earthly mass!" cried Aylmer, laughing in a sort of frenzy. "You have served me well! Matter and Spirit—Earth and Heaven—have both done their part in this! Laugh, thing of senses! You have earned the right to laugh."

These exclamations broke Georgiana's sleep. She slowly unclosed her eyes, and gazed into the mirror, which her husband had arranged for that purpose. A faint smile flitted over her lips, when she recognized how barely perceptible was now that Crimson Hand, which had once blazed forth with such disastrous brilliancy as to scare away all their happiness. But then her eyes sought Aylmer's face, with a trouble and anxiety that he could by no means account for.

"My poor Aylmer!" murmured she.

"Poor? Nay, richest! Happiest! Most favored!" exclaimed he. "My peerless bride, it is successful! You are perfect!"

"My poor Aylmer!" she repeated, with a more than human tenderness. "You have aimed loftily!—you have done nobly! Do not repent, that, with so high and pure a feeling, you have rejected the best that earth could offer. Aylmer—dearest Aylmer—I am dying!"

Alas, it was too true! The fatal Hand had grappled with the mystery of life, and was the bond by which an angelic spirit kept itself in union with a mortal frame. As the last crimson tint of the birth-mark—that sole token of human imperfection—faded from her cheek, the parting breath of the now perfect woman passed into the atmosphere, and her soul, lingering a moment near her husband, took its heavenward flight. Then a hoarse, chuckling laugh was heard again! Thus ever does the gross Fatality of Earth exult in its invariable triumph over the immortal essence, which, in this dim sphere of half-development, demands the completeness of a higher state. Yet, had Aylmer reached a profounder wisdom, he need not thus have flung away the happiness, which would have woven his mortal life of the self-same texture with the celestial. The momentary circumstance was too strong for him; he failed to look beyond the shadowy scope of Time, and living once for all in Eternity, to find the perfect Future in the present.

CONTEXTS

NATHANIEL HAWTHORNE

From American Notebooks†

January 4, 1839.

Letters in the shape of figures of men, &c. At a distance, the words composed by the letters are alone distinguishable. Close at hand, the figures alone are seen, and not distinguished as letters. Thus things may have a positive, a relative, and a composite meaning, according to the point of view.

October 27, 1841.

To symbolize moral or spiritual disease by disease of the body;—thus, when a person committed any sin, it might cause a sore to appear on the body;—this to be wrought out.

1844.

The Unpardonable Sin might consist in a want of love and reverence for the Human Soul; in consequence of which, the investigator pried into its dark depths, not with a hope or purpose of making it better, but from a cold philosophical curosity,—content that it should be wicked in whatever kind or degree, and only desiring to study it out. Would not this, in other words, be the separation of the intellect from the heart?

Late 1844 or early 1845.

The life of a woman, who, by the old colony law, was condemned always to wear the letter A, sewed on her garment, in token of her having committed adultery.

August 9, 1845.

In the eyes of a young child, or other innocent person, the image of a cherub or an angel to be seen peeping out;—in those of a vicious person, a devil.

[*Monday, August 22d, 1842.*]

I took a walk through the woods, yesterday afternoon, to Mr. Emerson's, with a book which Margaret Fuller had left behind her, after a call on Saturday eve. I missed the nearest way, and wandered into a very secluded portion of the forest—for forest it might justly be called,

† From *The American Notebooks*, vol. 8 of *The Centenary Edition of the Works of Nathaniel Hawthorne*, ed. Claude M. Simpson (Columbus: Ohio State UP, 1972). Reprinted by permission.

so dense and sombre was the shade of oaks and pines. Once I wandered into a tract so overgrown with bushes and underbrush that I could scarcely force a passage through. * * *

* * *

After leaving the book at Mr. Emerson's, I returned through the woods, and entering Sleepy Hollow, I perceived a lady reclining near the path which bends along its verge. It was Margaret herself. She had been there the whole afternoon, meditating or reading; for she had a book in her hand, with some strange title, which I did not understand and have forgotten. She said that nobody had broken her solitude, and was just giving utterance to a theory that no inhabitant of Concord ever visited Sleepy Hollow, when we saw a whole group of people entering the sacred precincts. Most of them followed a path that led them remote from us; but an old man passed near us, and smiled to see Margaret lying on the ground, and me sitting by her side. He made some remark about the beauty of the afternoon, and withdrew himself into the shadow of the wood. Then we talked about Autumn—and about the pleasures of getting lost in the woods—and about the crows, whose voices Margaret had heard—and about the experiences of early childhood, whose influence remains upon the character after the collection of them has passed away—and about the sight of mountains from a distance, and the view from their summits—and about other matters of high and low philosophy. In the midst of our talk, we heard footsteps above us, on the high bank; and while the intruder was still hidden among the trees, he called to Margaret, of whom he had gotten a glimpse. Then he emerged from the green shade; and, behold, it was Mr. Emerson, who, in spite of his clerical consecration, had found no better way of spending the Sabbath than to ramble among the woods. He appeared to have had a pleasant time; for he said that there were Muses in the woods to-day, and whispers to be heard in the breezes. It being now nearly six o'clock, we separated, Mr. Emerson and Margaret towards his house, and I towards mine, where my little wife was very busy getting tea. By the bye, Mr. Emerson gave me an invitation to dinner to-day, to be complied with or not, as might suit my convenience at the time; and it happens not to suit.

[*Friday*] *October 13th, 1848.*

During this moon, I have two or three evenings, sat sometime in our sitting-room, without light, except from the coal-fire and the moon. Moonlight produces a very beautiful effect in the room; falling so white upon the carpet, and showing its figures so distinctly; and making all the room so visible, and yet so different from a morning or noontide visibility. There are all the familiar things;—every chair, the tables, the couch, the bookcase, all the things that we are accustomed to in the daytime; but now it seems as if we were remembering them through a lapse of years rather than seeing them with the immediate eye. A child's shoe—the doll, sitting in her little wicker-carriage—all objects, that have been used or played with during the day, though still as familiar as ever, are invested with something like strangeness and remoteness. I cannot in any measure express it. Then the somewhat dim coal-fire throws its unobtrusive tinge through the room—a faint ruddiness upon the wall—which has a not unpleasant effect in taking from the colder spirituality of the moonbeams. Between both these lights, such a medium is created that the room seems just fit for the ghosts of persons very dear, who have lived in the room with us, to glide noiselessly in, and sit quietly down, without affrighting us. It would be like a matter of course, to look round, and find some familiar form in one of the chairs. If one of the white curtains happen to be down before the windows, the moonlight makes a delicate tracery with the branches of the trees, the leaves somewhat thinned by the progress of autumn, but still pretty abundant. It is strange how utterly I have failed to give anything of the effect of moonlight in a room.

The fire-light diffuses a mild, heart-warm influence through the room; but is scarcely visible, unless you particularly look for it—and then you become conscious of a faint tinge upon the cieling [sic], of a reflected gleam from the mahogany furniture; and if your eyes fall on the glass, deep within it you perceive the glow of the burning anthracite.

I hate to leave such a scene; and when retiring to bed, after closing the sitting-room door, I re-open it, again and again, to peep back at the warm, cheerful, solemn repose, the white light, the faint ruddiness, the dimness,—all like a dream, and which makes me feel as if I were in a conscious dream.

PASSAGES ABOUT UNA

January 28, 1849

* * * Una is now teazing her mother to go out to walk with her, and will not accept of the compromise of going out to play in the yard by herself, but continually recurs to the subject—"Mother, I wish you would take me one little walk:—Mother, if I could but take one little walk—Mother, if you would but let me go with Dora." She is certainly a most pertinacious teaser. Mamma has now proposed that Una shall walk up and down the street by herself—to which she consents with alacrity, never, I believe, having been so far trusted before. "How I do want to go out in the street alone!" says she. It is one step forward, in her existence. So she is dressed up in her purple pelisse, white satin bonnet, with a green veil, and white muff, with woolen gaiters on her well-calved pedestals; in which garb she looks anything but beautiful. Her beauty is the most flitting, transitory, most uncertain and unaccountable affair, that ever had a real existence; it beams out when nobody expects it; it has mysteriously passed away, when you think yourself sure of it;—if you glance sideways at her, you perhaps think it is illuminating her face, but, turning full round to enjoy it, it is gone again. Her mother sees it much oftener than I do; yet, neither is the revelation always withheld from me. When really visible, it is rare and

precious as the vision of an angel; it is a transfiguration—a grace, delicacy, an ethereal fineness, which, at once, in my secret soul, makes me give up all severe opinions that I may have begun to form respecting her. It is but fair to conclude, that, on these occasions, we see her real soul; when she seems less lovely, we merely see something external. But, in truth, one manifestation belongs to her as much as another; for, before the establishment of principles, what is character but the series and succession of moods?

February 1, 1849

* * * It is a very good discipline for Una to carry a book on her head; not merely physical discipline, but moral as well; for it implies a restraint upon her usual giddy, impetuous demeanor. She soon, however, begins to move with great strides, and sudden jerks, and to tumble about in extravagant postures;—a very unfortunate tendency that she has; for she is never graceful or beautiful, except when perfectly quiet. Violence—exhibitions of passion—strong expression of any kind—destroy her beauty. Her voice, face, gestures—every manifestation, in short—becomes disagreeable.

The children have been playing ball together; and Una, heated by the violence with which she plays, sits down on the floor, and complains grievously of warmth—opens her breast. This is the physical manifestation of the evil spirit that struggles for the mastery of her; he is not a spirit at all, but an earthy monster, who lays his grasp on her spinal marrow, her brain, and other parts of her body that lie in closest contiguity to her soul; so that the soul has the discredit of these evil deeds. She is recovered now, and is bounding across the room with a light and graceful motion; but soon sinks down on the floor, complaining of being tired. Her mood, to-day, is less tempestuous than usual—yet it has no settled level.

[Monday] July 30th [1849], 1/2 past 10 o'clock.

Another bright forenoon, warmer than yesterday, with flies buzzing through the sunny air. Mother still lives, but is gradually growing weaker, and appears to be scarcely sensible. Julian is playing quietly about, and is now out of doors, probably hanging on the gate. Una takes a strong and strange interest in poor mother's condition, and can hardly be kept out of the chamber—endeavoring to thrust herself into the door, whenever it is opened, and continually teazing me to be permitted to go up. This is partly the intense curiosity of her active mind—partly, I suppose, natural affection. I know not what she supposes is to be the final result to which grandmamma is approaching. She talks of her being soon to go to God, and probably thinks that she will be taken away bodily. Would to God it were to be so! Faith and trust would be far easier than they are now. But, to return to Una, there is something that almost frightens me about the child—I know not whether elfish or angelic, but, at all events, supernatural. She steps so boldly into the midst of everything, shrinks from nothing, has such a comprehension of everything, seems at times to have but little delicacy, and anon shows that she possesses the finest essence of it; now so hard, now so tender; now so perfectly unreasonable, soon again so wise. In short, I now and then catch an aspect of her, in which I cannot believe her to be my own human child, but a spirit strangely mingled with good and evil, haunting the house where I dwell. The little boy is always the same child, and never varies in his relation to me.

NATHANIEL HAWTHORNE

From Letters†

To H. W. Longfellow, Cambridge

Custom-House,
Salem. Novr 11, '47.

Dear Longfellow,

I have read Evangeline with more pleasure than it would be decorous to express. It cannot fail, I think, to prove the most triumphant of all your successes. Everybody likes it. I wrote a notice of it for our democratic paper, which Conolly edits; but he has not inserted it[1]— why I know not, unless he considers it unworthy of the subject; as it undoubtedly was. But let him write a better if he can. I have heard the poem—and other of your poems, the Wreck of the Hesperus[2] among them—discussed here in the Custom-House. It was very queer, and would have amused you much.

How seldom we meet! It would do me good to see you occasionally; but my duties, official, marital, and paternal, keep me pretty constantly at home; and when I do happen to have a day of leisure, it might chance to be a day of occupation with you—so I do not come.[3] I live at No. 14 Mall-street now. May I not hope to see you there?

I am trying to resume my pen;[4] but the influences of my situation and customary associates are so anti-literary, that I know not whether I shall succeed. Whenever I sit alone, or walk alone, I find myself dreaming about stories, as of old; but these forenoons in the Custom House undo all that the afternoons and evenings have done. I should be happier if I could write—also, I should like to add something to my

† From *The Letters, 1843–1853*, vol. 16 of *The Centenary Edition of the Works of Nathaniel Hawthorne*, ed. Thomas Woodson, L. Neal Smith, and Norman Holmes Pearson (Columbus: Ohio State UP, 1985). Reprinted by permission.

1. NH's notice appeared in the Salem *Advertiser*, November 13: it is rpt. in Randall Stewart, "Hawthorne's Contributions . . . ," *AL*, V (1934), 333–35. Longfellow's reply of November 29 to NH is in his *Letters*, III, 145–46.

2. In Longfellow's *Ballads and Other Poems* (1841).

3. Longfellow had invited NH to dine at Nahant in August, but had received no answer from him; see *Letters*, III, 146.

4. The next day, SH [Sophia Hawthorne] wrote to her mother that NH had begun to write, and on November 23 informed her: "My husband began retiring to his study on the first November and writes every afternoon" (MSS, Berg [Collection. New York Public Library]).

income, which, though tolerable, is a tight fit. If you can suggest any work of pure literary drudgery, I am the very man for it.

I have heard nothing of Hillard, since his departure.[5] Cannot you tell me something about him?

Your friend,
Nathl Hawthorne.

To G. S. Hillard, Boston

Salem, March 5th. 1849.

Dear Hillard,

It is a very long time since I have held converse with you by tongue or pen; but I have thought of you none the less, and have enjoyed Europe with you,[1] and rejoiced at your safe return. My present object in writing is one with which you would hardly imagine yourself to have anything to do.

I am informed that there is to be a strong effort among the politicians here to remove me from office, and that my successor is already marked out. I do not think that this ought to be done; for I was not appointed to office as a reward for political services, nor have I acted as a politician since. A large portion of the local Democratic party look coldly on me, for not having used the influence of my position to obtain the removal of whigs—which I might have done, but which I in no case did. Neither was my own appointment made at the expense of a Whig; for my predecessor[2] was appointed by Tyler, in his latter days, and called himself a Democrat. Nor can any charge of inattention to duty, or other official misconduct, be brought against me; or, if so, I could easily refute it. There is therefore no ground for disturbing me, except on the most truculent party system. All this, however, will be of little avail with the slang-whangers[3]—the vote-distributors—the Jack Cades[4]—who assume to decide upon these matters, after a political triumph; and as to any literary claims of mine, they would not weigh a feather, nor be thought worth weighing at all.

But it seems to me that an inoffensive man of letters—having

---

5. [George] Hillard [classmate at Bowdoin] had sailed for England on July 1, and reached Italy on September 2. During his trip, he sent long descriptive letters to his wife that were shared by his friends George Ticknor, Sumner, and Longfellow, and were eventually transformed into his popular *Six Months in Italy* (1853). See Longfellow, *The Letters of Henry Wadsworth Longfellow*, ed. Andrew Hilen (Cambridge: Harvard UP, 1966–82), III, 131–32, 139, 155–56, 167–69.

1. Presumably NH had read Hillard's letters from Europe. Hillard had returned to Boston on October 19, 1848.

2. Nehemiah Brown was surveyor, 1843–46. In a letter to President Polk, November 1, 1845, Zachariah Burchmore, secretary of the Essex County Democratic Committee, and A. D. Wait, chairman, stressed that "N. Brown, the person who now holds the office of surveyor, is at present moment Whig Sheriff in Essex County," and that Brown had "always been" a Whig (MS, National Archives). See Paul Cortissoz, "The Political Life of Nathaniel Hawthorne," Diss. New York U, 1955, 58. NH elaborates his contrary claim in his letter of June 18, 1849, pp. 223–25 of this Norton Critical Edition.

3. Noisy or abusive talkers or writers.

4. Cade was the leader of a rebellion in southern England in 1450. As dramatized in Shakespeare's *II Henry VI*, Act IV, he is a ranting, anti-intellectual demagogue who orders the beheading of a learned and loyal nobleman.

obtained a pitiful little office on no other plea than his pitiful little literature—ought not to be left to the mercy of these thick-skulled and no-hearted ruffians. It is for this that I now write to you. There are men in Boston—Mr Rufus Choate,[5] for instance—whose favorable influence with the administration would make it impossible to remove me, and whose support and sympathy might fairly be claimed in my behalf—not on the ground that I am a very good writer, but because I gained my position, such as it is, by my literary character, and have done nothing to forfeit that tenure. I do not think that you can have any objection to bringing this matter under the consideration of such men; but if you do so object, I am sure it will be for some good reason, and therefore beg you not to stir in it. I do not want any great fuss to be made; the whole thing is not worth it; but I should like to have the Administration enlightened by a few such testimonials as would take my name out of the list of ordinary office-holders, and at least prevent any hasty action. I think, too, that the letters (if you obtain any) had better contain no allusion to the proposed attack on me, as it may possibly fall through of itself. Certainly, the general feeling here in Salem would be in my favor; but I have seen too much of the modes of political action to lay any great stress on that.

Be pleased on no account to mention this matter to any Salem man, however friendly to me he may profess himself. If any movement on my part were heard of, it would precipitate their assault.

So much for business. I do not let myself be disturbed by these things, but employ my leisure hours in writing, and go on as quietly as ever. I see that Longfellow has written a prose-tale.[6] How indefatigable he is!—and how adventurous! Well he may be, for he never fails.

Remember me to Mrs. Hillard. Sophia is well, and our children continue to flourish famously. Why do you not come to see us?

Your friend,
Nathl Hawthorne.

To H. W. Longfellow, Cambridge

[Salem] Custom House, June 5th. 1849

Dear Longfellow,

I meant to have written you before now about Kavanaugh,[1] but have had no quiet time, during my letter-writing hours; and now the fresh-

---

5. A famous lawyer (1799–1859) who had been an organizer of the Whig party in Massachusetts, and had served as a congressman, 1830–34, and U.S. senator, 1841–45. See *Dictionary of American Biography*, ed. Allen Johnson and Dumas Malone (New York: Scribner, 1943); Jean V. Matthews, *Rufus Choate: The Law and Civic Virtue* (Philadelphia: Temple UP, 1980). In a letter to Louisa, October 5, 1848, SH described a recent evening rally for Choate in Salem that she and NH had observed, and said that she was "very glad . . . to hear the heavy hurrah" (MS, Berg). Hillard, a Whig, persuaded Choate to write on NH's behalf to Secretary Meredith immediately after his dismissal, on June 9. Choate characterized NH as "a writer of rare beauty, & merit & fame, a person of the purest character, & in politics perfectly quiet & silent" (MS, National Archives; see Nevins, p. 128).

6. *Kavanagh: A Tale*, to be published May 12.

1. Longfellow had sent NH an inscribed copy, dated May 19 (now in Berg).

ness of my thoughts has exhaled away. It is a most precious and rare book—as fragrant as a bunch of flowers, and as simple as one flower. A true picture of life, moreover—as true as those reflections of the trees and banks that I used to see in the Concord, but refined to a higher degree than they; as if the reflection were itself reflected. Nobody but yourself would dare to write so quiet a book; nor could any other succeed in it. It is entirely original; a book by itself; a true work of genius, if ever there were one; and yet I should not wonder if many people (God confound them!) were to see no such matter in it. In fact, I doubt whether hardly anybody else has enjoyed it so much as I; although I have heard or seen none but favorable opinions.

I should like to have written a long notice of it, and would have done so for the Salem Advertiser; but, on the strength of my notice of Evangeline and some half-dozen other books, I have been accused of a connection with the editorship of that paper, and of writing political articles—which I never did one single time in my whole life![2] I must confess, it stirs up a little of the devil within me, to find myself hunted by these political bloodhounds. If they succeed in getting me out of office, I will surely immolate one or two of them. Not that poor monster of a Conolly,[3] whom I desire only to bury in oblivion, far out of my own remembrance. Nor any of the common political brawlers, who work on their own level, and can conceive of no higher ground than what they occupy. But if there be among them (as there must be, if they succeed) some men who claim a higher position, and ought to know better, I may perhaps select a victim,[4] and let fall one little drop of venom on his heart, that shall make him writhe before the grin of the multitude for a considerable time to come. This I will do, not as an act of individual vengeance, but in your behalf as well as mine, because he will have violated the sanctity of the priesthood to which we both, in our different degrees, belong. I do not claim to be a poet; and yet I cannot but feel that some of the sacredness of that character adheres to me, and ought to be respected in me, unless I step out of its immunities, or make it a plea for violating any of the rules of ordinary life. When other people concede me this privilege, I never think that I possess it; but when they disregard it, the consciousness makes itself felt. If they will pay no reverence to the imaginative power when it causes herbs of grace and sweet-scented flowers to spring up along their pathway, then they should be taught what it can do in the way of producing nettles, skunk-

2. Eben N. Walton (1825–1907), editor of the *Advertiser* since 1847, was to write to NH on June 30 to deny this charge, in a letter intended to be forwarded to Washington as evidence. Walton stated that "only two articles from your pen have appeared in its columns, one a notice of a dramatic company, the other a notice of Longfellow's 'Evangeline' " (Nevins, pp. 129–30).
3. Horace Conolly had been chairman of the Second Congressional District Democratic Committee, and had written to President Polk in 1845 supporting NH's candidacy for surveyor. Now he had joined the Whigs, and was to participate in the unanimous resolution on July 3 by the Whig Ward Committees and the Government of the Taylor Club to approve NH's removal. See Nevins, pp. 99–100, 105–6.
4. SH's letters to her father, June 10, and to her mother, June 21, suggest that the most likely victims were Charles W. Upham; Richard Saltonstall Rogers (1792–1873), a merchant; Nathaniel Silsbee, Jr. (1804–1881), a merchant, brother of NH's former friend Mary Silsbee Sparks, and current mayor of Salem; and George Humphrey Devereux (1809–1878), a lawyer (Lathrop, *Memories*, p. 96; MS, Berg).

cabbage, deadly night-shade, wolf's bane, dog-wood.[5] If they will not be grateful for its works of beauty and beneficence, then let them dread it as a pervasive and penetrating mischief, that can reach them at their firesides and in their bedchambers, follow them to far countries, and make their very graves refuse to hide them. I have often thought that there must be a good deal of enjoyment in writing personal satire; but, never having felt the slightest ill-will towards any human being, I have hitherto been debarred from this peculiar source of pleasure. I almost hope I shall be turned out, so as to have an opportunity of trying it. I cannot help smiling in anticipation of the astonishment of some of these local magnates here, who suppose themselves quite out of the reach of any retribution on my part.

I have spent a good deal of time in Boston, within a few weeks; my two children having been ill of the scarlet-fever there; and the little boy was in quite an alarming way. I could not have submitted in the least, had it gone ill with him; but God spared me that trial—and there are no real misfortunes, save such as that. Other troubles may irritate me superficially; nothing else can go near the heart.

I mean to come and dine with you, the next time you invite me; and Hillard said he would come too.[6] Do not let it be within a week, however; for Bridge and his wife expect to be here in the course of that time.

Please to present my regards to Mrs. Longfellow, and believe me

ever your friend,
Nath Hawthorne.

To G. S. Hillard, Boston

Salem, June 18th, 1849.

My dear Hillard,

There is an article respecting me in the Boston Atlas of Saturday, which seems to require some notice from my pen;[1] and I choose to give my answer in the form of a letter to yourself, because I would be understood as speaking with a more than common carefulness in regard to the accuracy of what I say.[2] For, what a man should I be, my dear Hillard, if I could dream of connecting your stainless integrity,

5. Compare the narrator's (or Hester's) speculation about Chillingworth's grave, "where, in due course of time, would be seen deadly nightshade, dogwood, henbane, and whatever else of vegetable wickedness the climate could produce, all flourishing with hideous luxuriance" (SL, pp. 175–76) [p. 114 of this Norton Critical Edition].

6. Longfellow suggested June 21. He noted in his journal, June 10: "Sumner dined with us; and we discussed Hawthorne's dismissal from the Custom House in terms not very complimentary to General Taylor and his cabinet" (MS, Harvard; Life. II, 142).

1. The militantly Whig Atlas published in an editorial on June 16 an anonymous letter, perhaps by Charles Upham, attacking NH's alleged political innocence. See Cortissoz, pp. 81–82; Stephen Nissenbaum, "The Firing of Nathaniel Hawthorne," EIHC, CXIV (1978): 67.

2. This letter was published in the Boston Advertiser "at the request of a friend," as the prefatory note stated. The Whig Advertiser "would not be understood as expressing any opinion on the question of Mr. Hawthorne's removal from office" and published the letter "because we consider it due to the writer, that he should have the opportunity to lay before the public his own statement of his position." Elizabeth Peabody wrote to her mother from Boston, June 15: "Hawthorne was here today & wrote a letter. . . . He seems to be all in a rouse" (MS, Antioch).

and honorable name, with any statement which I did not believe to be strictly true!

The article first charges me with never having received the approbation of the Democrats of Salem for the Surveyorship; an accusation which I do not think it necessary, just at this time, to repel. As respects the imputation of having been an office-seeker, I would say, that while residing at Concord, I was earnestly and repeatedly urged to become a candidate for the post office in Salem, by a person who claimed to be the representative of the great majority of the local Democratic party. My consent being reluctantly given, the attempt was made and failed; not from any defect in me, as a candidate, but because the incumbent—my present esteemed friend, Dr. Brown—contrary to what had been told me, was an excellent officer, and had the great bulk of the party with him. Subsequently, without solicitition on my part, two offices were successively tendered to me by Mr Bancroft, each of larger emolument than the one which it afterwards suited me to take.

The article further says, that my predecessor in the Surveyorship was a Whig. Mr. Nehemiah Brown, the gentleman in question, obtained the office through the following succession of changes:—Mr. Daniels,[3] a Whig, appointed in 1840, had been succeeded, after the Tyler revolution, by the late Mr. Edward Palfrey,[4] a Democrat, who held the office for a considerable time during the recess of the Senate. The nomination of Mr. Palfrey not being confirmed, Mr. George W. Mullet,[5] another Democrat, was nominated by President Tyler, and likewise rejected by the Senate. The President, in this emergency, having no opportunity to take the wishes of the local party, and the session drawing to a close, nominated Mr. Brown, who, then and subsequently, was one of that peculiar class of politicians styled Tyler Democrats.[6] I refer, in proof of his democracy, to the records and members of the Hickory Club. I refer to a crowd of witnesses, as well Whigs as Democrats. I refer, among others—and am most happy so to do—to a gentleman now very prominent and active in our local politics, the Rev. Charles Wentworth Upham, who told me, in presence of David Roberts, Esq., that I need never fear removal under a Whig administration, inasmuch as my appointment had not displaced a Whig. Lastly, I refer, frankly and fearlessly, and with entire confidence in his response, to Mr. Nehemiah Brown himself.

In the second year of President Polk's administration, Mr. Brown was removed, and succeeded by myself—not on any charge derogatory to his character—but simply because, as was the predicament of many other Tyler Democrats, his appointment had not been based on any mode of selection by the local party.

I am further accused of having been an active politician, while in of-

3. Stephen Daniels (1798–1872), officially surveyor, 1841–43, now operated a grocery store.
4. Edward Palfrey, surveyor, 1838–41.
5. Mullett (1809–1893) had been chairman of the Democratic Committee of Salem.
6. John Tyler, a Virginia aristocrat elected vice-president by the Whigs in 1840, had become president upon W. H. Harrison's death in April 1841. He soon quarreled with Whig leaders, and they expelled him from their party. Tyler thereupon led a return of disaffected Whigs to the Democratic party, forming an alliance with conservative, pro-slavery Democrats.

fice; in proof of which, it is averred that I have been a member, during two years, of the Democratic Town Committee, and a delegate, last year, to the Democratic State Convention. As respects the latter, I do not remember ever being chosen a delegate to that, or any convention, and certainly never was present at one, in my whole life. I do remember having seen my name, in the Salem Advertiser, as a member of the Democratic Town Committee; but I never was otherwise notified of the fact, never attended a meeting, never acted officially, and have no other knowledge of my membership than having seen my name, as aforesaid.[7] I never in my life walked in a torch light procession, and— I am almost tempted to say—would hardly have done any thing so little in accordance with my tastes and character, had the result of the Presidential election depended on it. My contributions to the Salem Advertiser have been a few notices of books, and other miscellaneous paragraphs, perhaps a dozen in all; never a single line of politics. I have ceased, for upwards of three years, to write for the Democratic Review, and never did write a political article for that, or any other journal or newspaper; nor an article that had the remotest reference to politics, with the single exception of a biographical sketch of Cilley, written at the request of the editor, as a tribute to the memory of an early and very dear friend.

The article further insinuates, as I apprehend it, the charge of fraud or dishonesty against me, and refers for proof to the Blue Book,[8] where, as it affirms, the Democratic officers of the Custom House, appear to have received larger amounts than the Whigs.[9] In reply, I have merely to state that the emoluments of the officers are strictly and necessarily commensurate with the amount of service rendered; and that, in all matters relating to this point, I have been under the constant supervision, as well as general direction, of Colonel Miller, a Whig, the Deputy Collector, and now the Collector of the port.

I have thus, I believe, responded to all the charges, point by point. I am happy that my accuser has given me the opportunity, and should have been still more so, had he come forward under his own name, and met me, face to face, before the public. But, now, if he be a gentleman,—as not improbably he may be—he will be willing, I trust, to acknowledge, that the slanders of private animosity and the distorting medium of party prejudice may have deceived him, as to my position, my conduct, and my character. This frank acknowledgement is all I ask.

Affectionately yours,
Nathl Hawthorne.

George S. Hillard, Esq, Boston.

7. NH was listed as a member of the Democratic Town Committee in the Salem *Advertiser*, November 9, 1846, and November 6, 1847. He was listed as a delegate to the Democratic State Convention in Worcester in the *Advertiser* on August 30, 1848 (Cortissoz, p. 85).
8. Of the U.S. Treasury Department.
9. The charge is detailed in Upham's "Memorial" to Secretary Meredith of July 6 (Nevins, p. 116; Cortissoz, p. 270).

To J. T. Fields, Boston

Salem, Jan. 15th 1850.

My dear Fields,

I send you, at last, the manuscript portion of my volume; not quite all of it, however, for there are three chapters still to be written of "The Scarlet Letter." I have been much delayed by illness in my family and other interruptions. Perhaps you will not like the book nor think well of its prospects with the public. If so (I need not say) I shall not consider you under any obligation to publish it. 'The Scarlet Letter' is rather a delicate subject to write upon, but in the way in which I have treated it, it appears to me there can be no objections on that score. The article entitled "Custom House" is introductory to the volume, so please read it first. In the process of writing, all political and official turmoil has subsided within me, so that I have not felt inclined to execute justice on any of my enemies. I have not yet struck out a title, but may possibly hit on one before I close the package. If not, there need be no running title of the book over each page, but only of the individual articles. Calculating the page of the new volume at the size of that of the 'Mosses,' I can supply 400 and probably more. "The Scarlet Letter," I suppose, will make half of that number; otherwise, the calculation may fall a little short, though I think not.

Very truly yours,
Nathl Hawthorne.

P.S. The proof-sheets will need to be revised by the author. I write such an infernal hand that this is absolutely indispensable.

If my wife approves—whom I have made the umpire in the matter—I shall call the book Old-Time Legends; together with *sketches, experimental and ideal.* I believe we must consider the book christened as above. Of course, it will be called simply "Old-Time Legends," and the rest of the title will be printed in small capitals. I wish I could have brought a definition of the whole book within the compass of a single phrase, but it is impossible. If you think it essentially a bad title, I will make further trials.

To J. T. Fields, Boston

Salem, January 20th. 1850.

My dear Fields,

I am truly glad that you like the introduction; for I was rather afraid that it might appear absurd and impertinent to be talking about myself, when nobody, that I know of, has requested any information on that subject.

As regards the size of the book, I have been thinking a good deal about it. Considered merely as a matter of taste and beauty, the form of publication which you recommend seems to me much preferable to that of the 'Mosses.'[1] In the present case, however, I have some doubts

---

1. In *Yesterdays with Authors*, p. 51, James T. Fields claimed that "after reading the first chapters of the story," he persuaded NH "to elaborate it, and publish it as a separate work."

of the expediency; because, if the book is made up entirely of 'The Scarlet Letter,' it will be too sombre. I found it impossible to relieve the shadows of the story with so much light as I would gladly have thrown in. Keeping so close to its point as the tale does, and diversified no otherwise than by turning different sides of the same dark idea to the reader's eye, it will weary very many people, and disgust some. Is it safe, then, to stake the fate of the book entirely on this one chance? A hunter loads his gun with a bullet and several buck-shot; and, following his sagacious example, it was my purpose to conjoin the one long story with half a dozen shorter ones; so that, failing to kill the public outright with my biggest and heaviest lump of lead, I might have other chances with the smaller bits, individually and in the aggregate.

However, I am willing to leave these considerations to your judgment, and should not be sorry to have you decide for the separate publication.

In this latter event, it appears to me that the only proper title for the book would be 'The Scarlet Letter'; for 'The Custom House' is merely introductory—an entrance-hall to the magnificent edifice which I throw open to my guests. It would be funny, if, seeing the further passages so dark and dismal, they should all choose to stop there!

If 'The Scarlet Letter' is to be the title, would it not be well to print it on the title-page in red ink? I am not quite sure about the good taste of so doing; but it would certainly be piquant and appropriate—and, I think, attractive to the great gull whom we are endeavoring to circumvent.

Very truly Yours,
Nathl Hawthorne

J. T. Fields, Esq.

[*An undated draft of the letter*:]

As regards the book, I have been thinking and considering—I was rather afraid that it appears sagacious absurd and impertinent to have some doubts, of the introduction to the book, which you recommend. I have found it impossible to relieve the shadows of the story with so much light as I would gladly stake the fate of the book entirely on the public. However, I am willing to leave these considerations to your judgment, and should not be sorry to have you decide for the separate publication.

If the Judgment Letter is to be the title—print it on the title page in red ink. I think that the only proper title for the book would be the Scarlet Letter. I am quite sure about the taste of so doing. I think it is attractive and appropriate—

To Horatio Bridge, Portsmouth

Salem, Feby 4th. 1850.

Dear Bridge,

I finished my book only yesterday; one end being in the press in Boston, while the other was in my head here in Salem—so that, as you see, the story is at least fourteen miles long.

I should make you a thousand apologies for being so negligent a correspondent; if you did not know me of old, and as you have tolerated me so many years, I do not fear that you will give me up now. The fact is, I have a natural abhorrence of pen and ink, and nothing short of absolute necessity ever drives me to them.[1]

My book, the publisher tells me, will not be out before April.[2] He speaks of it in tremendous terms of approbation; so does Mrs Hawthorne, to whom I read the conclusion, last night. It broke her heart and sent her to bed with a grievous headache—which I look upon as triumphant success![3] Judging from its effect on her and the publisher, I may calculate on what bowlers call a 'ten-strike.'[4] Yet I do not make any such calculation. Some portions of the book are powerfully written; but my writings do not, nor ever will, appeal to the broadest class of sympathies, and therefore will not attain a very wide popularity. Some like them very much; others care nothing for them, and see nothing in them. There is an introduction to this book—giving a sketch of my Custom-House life, with an imaginative touch here and there—which perhaps may be more widely attractive than the main narrative. The latter lacks sunshine. To tell you the truth it is— (I hope Mrs. Bridge is not present)—it is positively a h–ll-fired story, into which I found it almost impossible to throw any cheering light.

This house on Goose Creek,[5] which you tell me of, looks really attractive; but I am afraid there must be a flaw somewhere. I like the rent amazingly. I wish you would look at it, and form your own judgement, and report accordingly; and should you decide favorably I will come myself and see it. But if it appears ineligible to you, I shall let

---

1. In a letter to John Jay of June 12, 1849, Bridge had mentioned NH's "peculiarly retiring disposition" that "prevents him from applying to anyone for literary employment, or authorizing his friends to do so." See Lease, "Hawthorne and *Blackwood's* in 1849," *Jahrbuch für Amerikastudien*, XIV (1969): 153.

2. *SL* was published March 16.

3. SH wrote to Mary Mann on February 12: "I do not know what you will think of the Romance. It is most powerful, & contains a moral as terrific & stunning as a thunder bolt. It shows that the Law cannot be broken" (MS, Berg). See also *English Notebooks*, vols. 21 and 22 of the *Centenary Edition of the Works of Nathaniel Hawthorne*, ed. Thomas Woodson and Bill Ellis (Columbus: Ohio State UP, 1997), p. 225.

4. Five years later Hawthorne would enter another account of this moment in his *English Notebooks*. He recalls his "emotions when I read the last scene of the Scarlet Letter to my wife, just after writing it—tried to read it, rather, for my voice swelled and heaved, as if I were tossed up and down on an ocean, as it subsided after a storm. But I was in a very nervous state, then, having gone through a great diversity and severity of emotion, for many months past. I think I have never overcome my own adamant in any other instance" [*Editor*].

5. NH had first written to Bridge around August 3, 1849, asking him to look for a house in or near Portsmouth. Bridge replied August 6, describing a house "two stories in height; has twelve acres of good land attached; is a mile from the corner in Kittery" (MS, Berg; see John D. Gordan, "Nathaniel Hawthorne, The Years of Fulfillment, 1804–1853," *Bulletin of the New York Public Library*, 59 [1955], p. 216).

the matter rest there; it being inconvenient for me to leave home—
partly because funds are to be husbanded at this juncture of my affairs; and partly because I can ill spare the time, as the winter is the
season when my brain-work is chiefly accomplished.

As regards the African Journals, the next time I see my publisher, I
will make inquiries and ask advice as to how it is best to use them up.
It appeared to me that the additional matter would not be copious
enough to make a volume by itself; so that the basis would have to be
the African Cruiser. If I settle down by you, you could easily talk a volume, which I would write down.

I should like to give up the house which I now occupy, at the beginning of April; and must soon make a decision as to where I shall go.[6] I
long to get into the country; for my health, latterly, is not quite what it
has been, for many years past. I should not long stand such a life of
bodily inactivity and mental exertion as I have led for the last few
months. An hour or two of daily labor in a garden, and a daily ramble
in country air or on the seashore, would keep all right. Here, I hardly
go out once a week. Do not allude to this matter in your letters to me;
as my wife already sermonizes me quite sufficiently on my habits—and
I never own up to not feeling perfectly well. Neither do I feel anywise
ill, but only a lack of physical vigor and energy, which re-acts upon the
mind. I detest this town so much that I hate to go into the streets, or
to have the people see me. Anywhere else, I shall at once be entirely
another man.

With our best regards to Mrs. Bridge, I remain,

truly Your friend,
Nath Hawthorne

To Horatio Bridge, Portsmouth

Salem, April 13th. 1850.

Dear Bridge,

I am glad you like the Scarlet Letter; it would have been a sad matter indeed, if I had missed the favorable award of my oldest and
friendliest critic. The other day, I met with your notice of 'Twice-told
Tales,' for the Augusta Age;[1] and I really think that nothing better has
been said about them since. This book has been highly successful; the
first edition having been exhausted in ten days, and the second (5000
copies in all) promising to go off rapidly.

As to the Salem people, I really thought that I had been exceedingly

6. SH wrote to Mary Mann on February 12 that since NH wanted seclusion they were considering a house at "the Upper Falls" (Essex Falls), and one at Hamilton, villages in Essex
County; on the fourteenth she wrote to her mother that they were considering a house in
West Cambridge, near the Longfellows. She also inquired of Longfellow about Caroline Tap-
pan's "Red House" in *Lenox*, presently occupied by S. G. Ward's farmer, Luther Butler
(MSS, Berg).
1. Bridge's review had appeared in his hometown newspaper in 1837, but has not yet been
found. Franklin Pierce, to whom Bridge had sent the review at the time of its appearance,
may have given it to NH in Boston in mid-February. See SH to her mother, February 16,
1850 (MS, Berg).

good-natured in my treatment of them. They certainly do not deserve good usage at my hands, after permitting me—(their most distinguished citizen; for they have no other that was ever heard of beyond the limits of the Congressional district)—after permitting me to be deliberately lied down, not merely once, but at two separate attacks, on two false indictments, without hardly a voice being raised in my behalf; and then sending one of the false witnesses to Congress, others to the State legislature, and choosing another as their Mayor.[2] I feel an infinite contempt for them, and probably have expressed more of it than I intended; for my preliminary chapter has caused the greatest uproar that ever happened here since witch-times. If I escape from town without being tarred-and-feathered, I shall consider it good luck. I wish they *would* tar-and-feather me—it would be such an entirely novel kind of distinction for a literary man! And from such judges as my fellow-citizens, I should look upon it as a higher honor than a laurel-crown.

I have taken a cottage in Lenox, and mean to take up my residence there, about the first of May. In the interim, my wife and children are going to stay in Boston, and nothing could be more agreeable to myself than to spend a week or so with you; so that your invitation comes extremely apropos. In fact, I was on the point of writing to propose a visit. We shall remove our household gods from this infernal locality, tomorrow or next day. I will leave my family at Dr. Peabody's, and come to Portsmouth on Friday of this week—or on Saturday at furthest, unless prevented from coming at all. I shall take the train that leaves Boston at 11 o' clock; so, if you happen to be in Portsmouth, that afternoon, please to look after me. I am very glad of this opportunity of seeing you; for I am afraid you will never find your way to Lenox.

I thank Mrs. Bridge for her good wishes as respects my future removals from office; but I should be sorry to anticipate such bad fortune as being ever again appointed to one.[3]

Truly Your friend,
Nathl Hawthorne

---

2. Daniel P. King was reelected to a fourth term in the U.S. House of Representatives in 1848, and Charles W. Upham had served in the Massachusetts House of Representatives from 1840 to 1849. Nathaniel Silsbee, Jr., was mayor of Salem.

3. Bridge had written to Franklin Pierce, November 4, 1849: "Perhaps [NH] may remain [at Lenox] unless at the end of this Administration, he should have a good office tendered him. He deserves it richly, for his removal has made a great flutter in the Whig flock. I trust that this change will be beneficial to H. in two ways—first by making him work with his pen; and then by giving him an office which will enable him to lay up something beyond a bare support. The Democrats will be sure to remember him for his removal showed how popular and how deserving he is" (MS, Library of Congress).

To J. T. Fields, Boston

Lenox, Jany 27. 1851

Dear Fields,

I intend to put the House of the Seven Gables into the express man's hands to-day; so that, if you do not soon receive it, you may conclude that it has miscarried—in which case, I shall not consent to the Universe existing a moment longer. I have no copy of it, except the wildest scribble of a first draught; so that it could never be restored.[1]

It has met with extraordinary success from that portion of the public to whose judgement it has been submitted;—viz, from my wife.[2] I likewise prefer it to the Scarlet Letter; but an author's opinion of his book, just after completing it, is worth little or nothing; he being then in the hot or cold fit of a fever, and certain to rate it too high or too low.

It has undoubtedly one disadvantage, in being brought so close to the present time; whereby its romantic improbabilities become more glaring.

I deem it indispensable that the proof-sheets should be sent me for correction. It will cause some delay, no doubt, but probably not much more than if I lived at Salem. At all events, I don't see how it can be helped. My autography is sometimes villainously blind; and it is odd enough that wherever the printers do mistake a word, it is just the very jewel of a word, worth all the rest of the Dictionary. When the Twice-told Tales are ready, I wish you would give a copy to Longfellow and another to Hillard on my part. I should be glad to have two or three sent hither.

I observe, in one of your catalogues, that you advertise a handsome edition of the New Testament.[3] Will you be kind enough to send it to me, when next you are making up a packet? Did not I suggest to you, last summer, the publication of the Bible, in ten or twelve 12mo. volumes? I think it would have great success; and, at least (but, as a bookseller, I suppose this is the very smallest of your cares) it would result in the salvation of a great many souls, who will never find their way to Heaven, if left to learn it from the inconvenient editions of the Scriptures, now in use. It is very singular that this form of publishing the Bible, in a single bulky or closely-printed volume, should be so long continued. It was first adopted I suppose as being the universal mode of publication at the time when the Bible was translated. Shakespeare, and the other old dramatists and poets, were first published in the same form; but all of them have long since been broken into

---

1. Fields had written on January 22, "it will be a great thing to get out the Vol. before March as at that time I shall go to the South & intend to sell a great many copies among the Book-sellers. Take this with yr plans if you please & decide with me it will be well on receipt of this, if you are all ready, to send me at once the Mss." (MS, Berg).
2. SH wrote to her mother on this date of *HSG:* "its depth of wisdom, its high tone, the flowers of Paradise scattered over all the dark places . . ." (MS, Berg).
3. Probably *The New Testament of Our Lord and Saviour Jesus Christ,* published by Ticknor in 1842 and 1844. See *The Cost Books of Ticknor and Fields and Their Predecessors, 1832–1858,* ed. Warren S. Tryon and William Charvat (New York: Bibliographical Society of America, 1949), p. 73.

dozens and scores of portable and readable volumes—and why not the Bible?[4]

I congratulate you on the laurels (additional to those already encircling your brow) which you will gain as poet of the P. B. K.[5] I am very proud of my publisher.

Those Osgood monumental scamps have paid me nothing.

Somebody has written to condole with me on an attack in the Church Review, in reference to the Introduction to the Scarlet Letter, and the work itself.[6] If really good, I should be glad to see it; but unless particularly so, I do not care about it. I think it essential to my success as an author, to have some bitter enemies.

The certificate of deposit of one hundred dollars was duly received. I had something else to say, but have forgotten what.

Truly Yours,
Nathl Hawthorne.

NATHANIEL HAWTHORNE

From The Life of Franklin Pierce (1852)†

When the series of measures, known under the collective term of the Compromise, were passed by Congress, in 1850, and put to so searching a test, here at the North, the reverence of the people for the Constitution, and their attachment to the Union, General Pierce was true to the principles which he had long ago avowed. At an early period of his Congressional service, he had made known, with the perfect frankness of his character, those opinions upon the slavery question, which he has never since seen occasion to change, in the slightest degree. There is an unbroken consistency in his action with regard to this matter. It is entirely of a piece, from his first entrance upon public life until the moment when he came forward, while many were faultering, to throw the great weight of his character and influence into the scale in favor of those measures, through which it was intended to redeem

---

4. Fields replied on January 30 that such a plan "would be very well for a rich concern able and willing to lose a vast sum of money in the Cause of human salvation. We have the will but not the lucre" (MS, Berg).
5. Fields's poem, delivered before the Harvard chapter of Phi Beta Kappa July 26, 1853, has never been published.
6. L. W. Mansfield had written on January 22. See *Memories*, pp. 140–41. Arthur Cleveland Coxe, "The Writings of Hawthorne," *Church Review*, III (January, 1851), 489–511. See Faust, pp. 79–85; *The Critical Heritage*, pp. 179–84; and pp. 254–63 of this Norton Critical Edition.
† From *Miscellaneous Prose and Poetry*, vol. 23 of *The Centenary Edition of the Works of Nathaniel Hawthorne*, ed. Thomas Woodson, Claude M. Simpson, and L. Neal Smith (Columbus: Ohio State UP, 1994), pp. 350–52. Reprinted by permission.
  Franklin Pierce, Hawthorne's classmate at Bowdoin College, had been nominated for president by the Democratic Party in the summer of 1852. Hawthorne volunteered to write Pierce's campaign biography, from which this selection has been taken. Pierce won the election, but Hawthorne's support for him and seeming lack of support for the abolition of slavery caused much consternation among Hawthorne's family and friends. See Sacvan Bercovitch's essay in this Norton Critical Edition for more on this issue.

the pledges of the Constitution, and to preserve and renew the old love and harmony among the sisterhood of states. His approval embraced the whole series of these acts,—as well those which bore hard upon Northern views and sentiments, as those in which the South deemed itself to have made more than reciprocal concessions.

No friend nor enemy, that knew Franklin Pierce, would have expected him to act otherwise. With his view of the whole subject, whether looking at it through the medium of his conscience, his feelings, or his intellect, it was impossible for him not to take his stand as the unshaken advocate of Union, and of the mutual steps of compromise which that great object unquestionably demanded. The fiercest, the least scrupulous, and the most consistent of those, who battle against slavery, recognize the same fact that he does. They see that merely human wisdom and human efforts cannot subvert it, except by tearing to pieces the Constitution, breaking the pledges which it sanctions, and severing into distracted fragments that common country, which Providence brought into one nation through a continued miracle of almost two hundred years, from the first settlement of the American wilderness until the Revolution. In the days when, a young member of Congress, he first raised his voice against agitation, Pierce saw these perils and their consequences. He considered, too, that the evil would be certain, while the good was, at best, a contingency, and (to the clear, practical foresight with which he looked into the future) scarcely so much as that;—attended as the movement was, and must be, during its progress, with the aggravated injury of those whose condition it aimed to ameliorate, and terminating, in its possible triumph—if such possibility there were—with the ruin of two races which now dwelt together in greater peace and affection, it is not too much to say, than had ever elsewhere existed between the taskmaster and the serf.

Of course, there is another view of all these matters. The theorist may take that view in his closet; the philanthropist by profession may strive to act upon it, uncompromisingly, amid the tumult and warfare of his life. But the statesman of practical sagacity—who loves his country as it is, and evolves good from things as they exist, and who demands to feel his firm grasp upon a better reality before he quits the one already gained—will be likely, here, with all the greatest statesmen of America, to stand in the attitude of a conservative. Such, at all events, will be the attitude of Franklin Pierce. We have sketched some of the influences amid which he grew up, inheriting his father's love of country, mindful of the old patriot's valor in so many conflicts of the Revolution, and having close before his eyes the example of brothers and relatives, more than one of whom have bled for America, both at the extremest North and farthest South;—himself, too, in early manhood, serving the Union in its legislative halls, and, at a maturer age, leading his fellow-citizens, his brethren, from the widest sundered states, to redden the same battlefields with their kindred blood, to unite their breath into one shout of victory, and perhaps to sleep, side by side, with the same sod over them. Such a man, with such hereditary recollections, and such a personal experience, must not narrow himself to adopt the cause of one section of his native country against another. He will stand up, as he has always stood, among the patriots of the whole land. And if the work of anti-slavery agitation—which, it is undeniable, leaves most men, who earnestly engage in it, with only half a country in their affections—if this work must be done, let others do it.

Those Northern men, therefore, who deem the great cause of human welfare all represented and involved in this present hostility against Southern institutions—and who conceive that the world stands still, except so far as that goes forward—these, it may be allowed, can scarcely give their sympathy or their confidence to the subject of this memoir. But there is still another view, and probably as wise a one. It looks upon Slavery as one of those evils, which Divine Providence does not leave to be remedied by human contrivances, but which, in its own good time, by some means impossible to be anticipated, but of the simplest and easiest operation, when all its uses shall have been fulfilled, it causes to vanish like a dream. There is no instance, in all history, of the human will and intellect having perfected any great moral reform by methods which it adapted to that end; but the progress of the world, at every step, leaves some evil or wrong on the path behind it, which the wisest of mankind, of their own set purpose, could never have found the way to rectify. Whatever contributes to the great cause of good, contributes to all its subdivisions and varieties; and, on this score, the lover of his race, the enthusiast, the philanthropist of whatever theory, might lend his aid to put a man, like the one before us, into the leadership of the world's affairs.

CRITICISM

CRITICISM

Nineteenth-Century Reviews of *The Scarlet Letter*

EVERT A. DUYCKINCK

From Literary World†

MR. HAWTHORNE introduces his new story to the public, the longest of all that he has yet published, and most worthy in this way to be called a romance, with one of those pleasant personal descriptions which are the most charming of his compositions, and of which we had so happy an example in the preface to his last collection, the Mosses from an Old Manse. In these narratives everything seems to fall happily into its place. The style is simple and flowing, the observation accurate and acute; persons and things are represented in their minutest shades, and difficult traits of character presented with an instinct which art might be proud to imitate. They are, in fine, little cabinet pictures exquisitely painted. The readers of the Twice Told Tales will know the pictures to which we allude. They have not, we are sure, forgotten Little Annie's Ramble, or the Sights from a Steeple. This is the Hawthorne of the present day in the sunshine. There is another Hawthorne less companionable, of sterner Puritan aspect, with the shadow of the past over him, a reviver of witchcrafts and of those dark agencies of evil which lurk in the human soul, and which even now represent the old gloomy historic era in the microcosm and eternity of the individual; and this Hawthorne is called to mind by such tales as the Minister's Black Veil or the Old Maid in the Winding Sheet, and reappears in the Scarlet Letter, a romance. Romantic in sooth! Such romance as you may read in the intensest sermons of old Puritan divines, or in the mouldy pages of that Marrow of Divinity, the ascetic Jeremy Taylor.[1]

The Scarlet Letter is a psychological romance. The hardiest Mrs. Malaprop[2] would never venture to call it a novel. It is a tale of remorse, a study of character in which the human heart is anatomized, carefully, elaborately, and with striking poetic and dramatic power. Its incidents are simply these. A woman in the early days of Boston becomes the subject of the discipline of the court of those times, and is condemned to stand

† From *Literary World* (March 30, 1850). A few months later, Duyckinck would publish Herman Melville's well-known review essay, "Hawthorne and His Mosses," in the *Literary World*. Melville would suggest the existence of "two Hawthornes" (one light, one dark) in very similar terms to those Duyckinck uses early in this review.
1. Jeremy Taylor (1613–1667), English bishop and theologian.
2. Character in Richard Sheridan's comedy *The Rivals* (1775), whose humor resulted from substituting an incorrect but similar-sounding word.

in the pillory and wear henceforth, in token of her shame, the scarlet letter A attached to her bosom. She carries her child with her to the pillory.
Its other parent is unknown. At this opening scene her husband from
whom she had been separated in Europe, preceding him by ship across
the Atlantic, reappears from the forest, whither he had been thrown by
shipwreck on his arrival. He was a man of a cold intellectual temperament, and devotes his life thereafter to search for his wife's guilty partner
and a fiendish revenge. The young clergyman of the town, a man of a devout sensibility and warmth of heart, is the victim, as this Mephistoph-
ilean old physician fixes himself by his side to watch over him and protect
his health, an object of great solicitude to his parishioners, and, in reality,
to detect his suspected secret and gloat over his tortures. This slow, cool,
devilish purpose, like the concoction of some sublimated hell broth, is
perfected gradually and inevitably. The wayward, elfish child, a concentration of guilt and passion, binds the interests of the parties together,
but throws little sunshine over the scene. These are all the characters,
with some casual introductions of the grim personages and manners of
the period, unless we add the scarlet letter, which, in Hawthorne's hands,
skilled to these allegorical, typical semblances, becomes vitalized as the
rest. It is the hero of the volume. The denouement is the death of
the clergyman on a day of public festivity, after a public confession in the
arms of the pilloried, branded woman. But few as are these main incidents thus briefly told, the action of the story, or its passion, is "long, obscure, and infinite." It is a drama in which thoughts are acts. The
material has been thoroughly fused in the writer's mind, and springs
forth an entire, perfect creation. We know of no American tales except
some of the early ones of Mr. Dana,[3] which approach it in conscientious
completeness. Nothing is slurred over, superfluous, or defective. The
story is grouped in scenes simply arranged, but with artistic power, yet
without any of those painful impressions which the use of the words, as
it is the fashion to use them, "grouping" and "artistic" excite, suggesting
artifice and effort at the expense of nature and ease.

   Mr. Hawthorne has, in fine, shown extraordinary power in this volume, great feeling and discrimination, a subtle knowledge of character
in its secret springs and outer manifestations. He blends, too, a delicate fancy with this metaphysical insight. We would instance the
chapter towards the close, entitled "The Minister in a Maze," where
the effects of a diabolic temptation are curiously depicted, or "The
Minister's Vigil," the night scene in the pillory. The atmosphere of the
piece also is perfect. It has the mystic element, the weird forest influences of the old Puritan discipline and era. Yet there is no affright-
ment which belongs purely to history, which has not its echo even in
the unlike and perversely commonplace custom-house of Salem. Then
for the moral. Though severe, it is wholesome; and is a sounder bit of
Puritan divinity than we have been of late accustomed to hear from
the degenerate successors of Cotton Mather. We hardly know another

---

3. Richard Henry Dana (1815–1882), American writer best known for *Two Years Before the
   Mast* (1840).

writer who has lived so much among the new school who would have handled this delicate subject without an infusion of George Sand.[4] The spirit of his old Puritan ancestors, to whom he refers in the preface, lives in Nathaniel Hawthorne.

We will not mar the integrity of the Scarlet Letter by quoting detached passages. Its simple and perfect unity forbids this. Hardly will the introductory sketch bear this treatment without exposing the writer to some false impressions; but as evidence of the possession of a style faithfully and humorously reflective of the scenes of the passing hour, which we earnestly wish he may pursue in future volumes, we may give one or two separable sketches.

There is a fine, natural portrait of General Miller, the collector; equal in its way to the Old Inspector, the self-sufficing gourmand lately presented in our journal; and there are other officials as well done. A page, however, of as general application, and of as sound profit as any in this office-seeking age, is that which details, in its mental bearing, "The Paralysis of Office."

* * *

The personal situation of Nathaniel Hawthorne—in whom the city by his removal lost an indifferent official, and the world regained a good author—is amusingly presented in this memoir of "A Decapitated Surveyor."

* * *

And a literary man long may he remain, an honor and a support to the craft, of genuine worth and fidelity, to whom no word is idle, given to the world no truer product of the American soil, though of a peculiar culture, than Nathaniel Hawthorne.

[EDWIN PERCY WHIPPLE]

From Graham's Magazine†

In this beautiful and touching romance Hawthorne has produced something really worthy of the fine and deep genius which lies within him. The "Twice Told Tales," and "Mosses from an Old Manse," are composed simply of sketches and stories, and although such sketches and stories as few living men could write, they are rather indications of the possibilities of his mind than realizations of its native power, penetration, and creativeness. In "The Scarlet Letter" we have a complete work, evincing a true artist's certainty of touch and expression in the exhibition of characters and events, and a keen-sighted and far-sighted vision into the essence and purpose of spiritual laws. There is a profound philosophy underlying the story which will escape many of the readers whose attention is engrossed by the narrative.

4. George Sand (1804–1876), pseudonym of Amandine-Aurore-Lucile Dupin, French Romantic novelist, noted for her numerous love affairs, and considered risqué by nineteenth-century standards.

† From *Graham's Magazine* 36, no. 5 (May 1850): 345–46.

The book is prefaced by some fifty pages of autobiographical matter, relating to the author, his native city of Salem, and the Custom House, from which he was ousted by the Whigs. These pages, instinct with the vital spirit of humor, show how rich and exhaustless a fountain of mirth Hawthorne has at his command. The whole representation has the dreamy yet distinct remoteness of the purely comic ideal. The view of Salem streets; the picture of the old Custom House at the head of Derby's wharf, with its torpid officers on a summer's afternoon, their chairs all tipped against the wall, chatting about old stories, "while the frozen witticisms of past generations were thawed out, and came bubbling with laughter from their lips"—the delineation of the old Inspector, whose "reminiscences of good cheer, however ancient the date of the actual banquet, seemed to bring the savor of pig or turkey under one's very nostrils," and on whose palate there were flavors "which had lingered there not less than sixty or seventy years, and were still apparently as fresh as that of the mutton-chop which he had just devoured for his breakfast," and the grand view of the stout Collector, in his aged heroism, with the honors of Chippewa and Fort Erie on his brow, are all encircled with that visionary atmosphere which proves the humorist to be a poet, and indicates that his pictures are drawn from the images which observation has left on his imagination. The whole introduction, indeed, is worthy of a place among the essays of Addison and Charles Lamb.[1]

With regard to "The Scarlet Letter," the readers of Hawthorne might have expected an exquisitely written story; expansive in sentiment, and suggestive in characterization, but they will hardly be prepared for a novel of so much tragic interest and tragic power, so deep in thought and so condensed in style, as is here presented to them. It evinces equal genius in the region of great passions and elusive emotions, and bears on every page the evidence of a mind thoroughly alive, watching patiently the movements of morbid hearts when stirred by strange experiences, and piercing, by its imaginative power, directly through all the externals to the core of things. The fault of the book, if fault it have, is the almost morbid intensity with which the characters are realized, and the consequent lack of sufficient geniality in the delineation. A portion of the pain of the author's own heart is communicated to the reader, and although there is great pleasure received while reading the volume, the general impression left by it is not satisfying to the artistic sense. Beauty bends to power throughout the work, and therefore the power displayed is not always beautiful. There is a strange fascination to a man of contemplative genius in the psychological details of a strange crime like that which forms the plot of the Scarlet Letter, and he is therefore apt to become, like Hawthorne, too painfully anatomical in his exhibition of them.

If there be, however, a comparative lack of relief to the painful emotions which the novel excites, owing to the intensity with which the au-

1. Charles Lamb (1775–1834), English essayist and poet, most famous for his collection *Essays of Elia* (1823, 1833). Joseph Addison (1672–1719), English writer and poet, co-author and co-editor, with Richard Steele, of *The Tatler* and *The Spectator*.

thor concentrates attention on the working of dark passions, it must be confessed that the moral purpose of the book is made more definite by this very deficiency. The most abandoned libertine could not read the volume without being thrilled into something like virtuous resolution, and the roué would find that the deep-seeing eye of the novelist had mastered the whole philosophy of that guilt of which practical roués are but childish disciples. To another class of readers, those who have theories of seduction and adultery modeled after the French school of novelists, and whom libertinism is of the brain, the volume may afford matter for very instructive and edifying contemplation; for, in truth, Hawthorne, in The Scarlet Letter, has utterly undermined the whole philosophy on which the French novels rest, by seeing farther and deeper into the essence both of conventional and moral laws; and he has given the results of his insight, not in disquisitions and criticisms, but in representations more powerful even than those of Sue, Dumas, or George Sand.[2] He has made his guilty parties end, not as his own fancy or his own benevolent sympathies might dictate, but as the spiritual laws, lying back of all persons, dictated to him. In this respect there is hardly a novel in English literature more purely objective.

As everybody will read "The Scarlet Letter," it would be impertinent to give a synopsis of the plot. The principal characters, Dimmesdale, Chillingworth, Hester, and little Pearl, all indicate a firm grasp of individualities, although from the peculiar method of the story, they are developed more in the way of logical analysis than by events. The descriptive portions of the novel are in a high degree picturesque and vivid, bringing the scenes directly home to the heart and imagination, and indicating a clear vision of the life as well as forms of nature. Little Pearl is perhaps Hawthorne's finest poetical creation, and is the very perfection of ideal impishness.

In common, we trust, with the rest of mankind, we regretted Hawthorne's dismissal from the Custom House, but if that event compels him to exert his genius in the production of such books as the present, we shall be inclined to class the Honorable Secretary of the Treasury among the great philanthropists. In his next work we hope to have a romance equal to The Scarlet Letter in pathos and power, but more relieved by touches of that beautiful and peculiar humor, so serene and so searching, in which he excels almost all living writers.

[ANNE W. ABBOTT]

From North American Review†

That there is something not unpleasing to us in the misfortunes of our best friends, is a maxim we have always spurned, as a libel on human

---

2. Alexandre Dumas (1802–1870), French historical novelist best known for *The Three Musketeers* (1844) and *The Count of Monte Cristo* (1845). Eugène Sue (1804–1857), French novelist of the Parisian underworld and slum life.
† From *North American Review* 71, no. 148 (July 1850): 135–48.

nature. But we must be allowed, in behalf of Mr. Hawthorne's friend and gossip, the literary public, to rejoice in the event—a "removal" from the office of Surveyor of the Customs for the port of Salem,—which has brought him back to our admiring, and, we modestly hope, congenial society, from associations and environments which have confessedly been detrimental to his genius, and to those qualities of heart, which, by an unconscious revelation through his style, like the involuntary betrayal of character in a man's face and manners, have won the affection of other than personal friends. We are truly grieved at the savage "scratches" our phœnix has received from the claws of the national eagle, scratches gratuitous and unprovoked, whereby his plumage remains not a little ruffled, if his breast be not very deeply lacerated. We hope we do not see tendencies to *self immolation* in the introductory chapter to this volume. It seems suicidal to a most envi-able fame, to show the fine countenance of the sometime denizen of Concord Parsonage, once so serene and full of thought, and at the same time so attractively arch, now cloudy and peevish, or dressed in sardonic smiles, which would scare away the enthusiasm of less hearty admirers than those he "holds by the button." The pinnacle on which the "conscience of the beautiful" has placed our author's graceful im-age is high enough, however, to make slight changes from the wear and tear of out-door elements, highway dust, and political vandalism, little noticed by those accustomed to look lovingly up to it. Yet they cannot be expected to regret a "removal," which has saved those finer and more delicate traits, in which genius peculiarly manifests itself, from being worn away by rough contact, or obliterated by impercepti-ble degrees through the influence of the atmosphere.

Mr. Hawthorne's serious apprehensions on this subject are thus candidly expressed:—

> "I began to grow melancholy and restless; continually prying into my mind, to discover which of its poor properties were gone, and what degree of detriment had already accrued to the remain-der. I endeavored to calculate how much longer I could stay in the Custom House, and yet go forth a man. To confess the truth, it was my greatest apprehension,—as it would never be a measure of policy to turn out so quiet an individual as myself, and it being hardly in the nature of a public officer to resign,—it was my chief trouble, therefore, that I was likely to grow gray and decrepit in the Surveyorship, and become much such another animal as the old Inspector. Might it not, in the tedious lapse of official life that lay before me, finally be with me as it was with this venerable friend,—to make the dinner hour the nucleus of the day, and to spend the rest of it, as an old dog spends it, asleep in the sun-shine or the shade? A dreary look-forward this, for a man who felt it to be the best definition of happiness to live throughout the whole range of his faculties and sensibilities! But, all this while, I was giving myself very unnecessary alarm. Providence had medi-tated better things for me than I could possibly imagine for my-self."

A man who has so rare an individuality to lose may well shudder at the idea of becoming a soulless machine, a sort of official scarecrow, having only so much of manly semblance left as will suffice to warn plunderers from the property of "Uncle Sam." Haunted by the horror of mental annihilation, it is not wonderful that he should look askance at the drowsy row of officials, as they reclined uneasily in tilted chairs, and should measure their mental torpidity by the length of time they had been subjected to the soul-exhaling process in which he had not yet got beyond the conscious stage. It was in pure apprehension, let us charitably hope, and not in a satirical, and far less a malicious, mood, that he describes one of them as retaining barely enough of the moral and spiritual nature to keep him from going upon all fours, and possessing neither soul, heart, nor mind more worthy of immortality than the spirit of the beast, which "goeth downward." Judging his aged colleagues thus, well might the young publican, as yet spiritually alive, stand aghast! A man may be excusable for starving his *intellect*, if Providence has thrown him into a situation where its dainty palate cannot be gratified. But for the well being of his *moral nature*, he is more strictly responsible, and has no right, under any circumstances, to remain in a position where, from causes beyond his control, his conscience is deprived of its supremacy over the will, and policy or expediency, whether public or selfish, placed upon its throne. "Most men," says our honest author, "suffer moral detriment from this mode of life," from causes which, (having just devoted four pages to a full-length caricature,) he had not space to hint at, except in the following pithy admonition to the aspirants after a place in the Blue Book.

> "Uncle Sam's gold—meaning no disrespect to the worthy old gentleman—has, in this respect, a quality of enchantment, like that of the Devil's wages. Whoever touches it should look well to himself, or he may find the bargain to go hard against him, involving, if not his soul, yet many of his better attributes; its sturdy force, its courage and constancy, its truth, its self-reliance, and all that gives the emphasis to manly character."

It was great gain for a man like Mr. Hawthorne to depart this truly unprofitable life; but we wish that his demise had been quiet and Christian, and not by violence. We regret that any of the bitterness of heart engendered by the political battle, and by his subsequent decapitulation without being judged by his peers, should have come with him to a purer and higher state of existence. That a head should fall, and even receive "an ignominious kick," is but a common accident in a party struggle, and would be of no more consequence to the world in Mr. Hawthorne's case than any other, (the metaphorical head not including brains,) provided the spirit had suffered no material injury in the encounter. Of that, however, we have no means of judging, except by comparing this book of recent production with his former writings. Of the "stern and sombre" pictures of the world and human life, external and internal, found in the Scarlet Letter, we shall speak anon. The preface claims some farther notice.

One would conclude, that the mother on whose bosom the writer was cherished in his urchinhood had behaved herself like a very stepmother towards him, showing a vulgar preference of those sons who have gathered, and thrown into her lap, gifts more substantial than garlands and laurel wreaths. This appears from his reluctant and half ashamed confession of attachment to her, and his disrespectful remarks upon her homely and commonplace features, her chilly and unsocial disposition, and those marks of decay and premature age which needed not to be pointed out. The portrait is like, no doubt; but we cannot help imagining the ire of the ancient dame at the unfilial satire. Indeed, a faint echo of the voice of her indignation has arrived at our ears. She complains, that, in anatomizing the characters of his former associates for the entertainment of the public, he has used the scalpel on some subjects, who, though they could not defend themselves, might possibly wince; and that all who came under his hand, living or dead, had probably relatives among his readers, whose affections might be wounded.

Setting this consideration apart, we confess that, to our individual taste, this naughty chapter is more piquant than any thing in the book; the style is racy and pungent, not elaborately witty, but stimulating the reader's attention agreeably by original turns of expression, and unhackneyed combinations of words, falling naturally into their places, as if of their own accord, and not obtained by far seeking and impressment into the service. The sketch of General Miller is airily and lightly done; no other artist could have given so much character to each fine drawn line as to render the impression almost as distinct to the reader's fancy as a portrait drawn by rays of light is to the bodily vision. Another specimen of his word painting, the lonely parlor seen by the moonlight melting into the warmer glow of the fire, while it reminds us of Cowper's much quoted and admired verse, has truly a great deal more of genuine poetry in it. The delineations of wharf scenery, and of the Custom House, with their appropriate figures and personages, are worthy of the pen of Dickens; and really, so far as mere style is concerned, Mr. Hawthorne has no reason to thank us for the compliment; he has the finer touch, if not more genial feeling, of the two. Indeed, if we except a few expressions which savor somewhat strongly of his late unpoetical associations, and the favorite metaphor of the guillotine, which, however apt, is not particularly agreeable to the imagination in such detail, we like the preface better than the tale.

No one who has taken up the Scarlet Letter will willingly lay it down till he has finished it; and he will do well not to pause, for he cannot resume the story where he left it. He should give himself up to the magic power of the style, without stopping to open wide the eyes of his good sense and judgment, and shake off the spell; or half the weird beauty will disappear like a "dissolving view." To be sure, when he closes the book, he will feel very much like the giddy and bewildered patient who is just awaking from his first experiment of the effects of sulphuric ether. The soul has been floating or flying between earth and heaven, with dim ideas of pain and pleasure strangely mingled, and all things earthly swimming dizzily and dreamily, yet most beautiful, before the half shut eye. That the author himself felt this sort of intoxication as well as the willing subjects of his enchantment, we think, is evident in many pages of the last half of the volume. His imagination has sometimes taken him fairly off his feet, insomuch that he seems almost to doubt if there be any firm ground at all,—if we may so judge from such mist-born ideas as the following.

> "But, to all these shadowy beings, so long our near acquaintances,—as well Roger Chillingworth as his companions,—we would fain be merciful. It is a curious subject of observation and inquiry, whether hatred and love be not the same thing at bottom. Each, in its utmost development, supposes a high degree of intimacy and heart-knowledge; each renders one individual dependent for the food of his affections and spiritual life upon another; each leaves the passionate lover, or the no less passionate hater, forlorn and desolate by the withdrawal of his object. Philosophically considered, therefore, the two passions seem essentially the same, except the one happens to be seen in a celestial radiance, and the other in a dusky and lurid glow. In the spiritual world, the old physician and the minister—mutual victims as they have been—may, unawares, have found their earthly stock of hatred and antipathy transmuted into golden love."

Thus devils and angels are alike beautiful, when seen through the magic glass; and they stand side by side in heaven, however the former may be supposed to have come there. As for Roger Chillingworth, he seems to have so little in common with man, he is such a gnome-like phantasm, such an unnatural personification of an abstract idea, that we should be puzzled to assign him a place among angels, men, or devils. He is no more a man than Mr. Dombey,[1] who sinks down a mere *caput mortuum*, as soon as pride, the only animating principle, is withdrawn. These same "shadowy beings" are much like "the changeling the fairies made o' a benweed." Hester at first strongly excites our pity, for she suffers like an immortal being; and our interest in her continues only while we have hope for her soul, that its baptism of tears will reclaim it from the foul stain which has been cast upon it. We see her humble, meek, self-denying, charitable, and heart-wrung with anxiety for the moral welfare of her wayward child. But anon her humility catches a new tint, and we find it pride; and so a vague unreality steals by degrees over all her most humanizing traits—we lose our confidence in all—and finally, like Undine,[2] she disappoints us, and shows the dream-land origin and nature, when we were looking to behold a Christian.

There is rather more power, and better keeping, in the character of Dimmesdale. But here again we are cheated into a false regard and interest, partly perhaps by the associations thrown around him without

---

1. The rich, arrogant father in Charles Dickens's *Dombey and Son* (1848) who is finally humbled by the loss of his business, wife, and son.
2. A mythical female water nymph who acquires a soul through marriage to a mortal.

the intention of the author, and possibly contrary to it, by our habitual respect for the sacred order, and by our faith in religion, where it has once been rooted in the heart. We are told repeatedly, that the Christian element yet pervades his character and guides his efforts; but it seems strangely wanting. "High aspirations for the welfare of his race, warm love of souls, pure sentiments, natural piety, strengthened by thought and study, and illuminated by revelation—all of which invaluable gold was little better than rubbish" to Roger Chillingworth, are little better than rubbish at all, for any use to be made of them in the story. Mere suffering, aimless and without effect for purification or blessing to the soul, we do not find in God's moral world. The sting that follows crime is most severe in the purest conscience and the tenderest heart, in mercy, not in vengeance, surely; and we can conceive of any cause constantly exerting itself without its appropriate effects, as soon as of a seven years' agony without penitence. But here every pang is wasted. A most obstinate and unhuman passion, or a most unwearying conscience it must be, neither being worn out, or made worse or better, by such a prolonged application of the scourge. Penitence may indeed be life-long; but as for this, we are to understand that there is no penitence about it. We finally get to be quite of the author's mind, that "the only truth that continued to give Mr. Dimmesdale a real existence on this earth, was the anguish in his inmost soul, and the undissembled expression of it in his aspect. Had he once found power to smile, and wear an aspect of gayety, there had been no such man." He duly exhales at the first gleam of hope, an uncertain and delusive beam, but fatal to his misty existence. From that time he is a fantasy, an opium dream, his faith a vapor, his reverence blasphemy, his charity mockery, his sanctity impurity, his love of souls a ludicrous impulse to teach little boys bad words; and nothing is left to bar the utterance of "a volley of good, round, solid, satisfactory, heaven-defying oaths," (a phrase which seems to smack its lips with a strange *goût!*) but good taste and the mere outward shell, "the buckramed habit of clerical decorum." The only conclusion is, that the shell never possessed any thing real,—never was the Rev. Arthur Dimmesdale, as we have foolishly endeavored to suppose; that he was but a changeling, or an imp in grave apparel, not an erring, and consequently suffering human being, with a heart still upright enough to find the burden of conscious unworthiness and undeserved praise more intolerable than open ignominy and shame, and refraining from relieving his withering conscience from its load of unwilling hypocrisy, if partly from fear, more from the wish to be yet an instrument of good to others, not an example of evil which should weaken their faith in religion. The closing scene, where the satanic phase of the character is again exchanged for the saintly, and the pillory platform is made the stage for a triumphant *coup de théatre*, seems to us more than a failure.

But Little Pearl—gem of the purest water—what shall we say of her? That if perfect truth to childish and human nature can make her a mortal, she is so; and immortal, if the highest creations of genius have any claim to immortality. Let the author throw what light he will upon her, from his magical prism, she retains her perfect and vivid human individuality. When he would have us call her elvish and implike, we persist in seeing only a capricious, roguish, untamed child, such as many a mother has looked upon with awe, and a feeling of helpless incapacity to rule. Every motion, every feature, every word and tiny shout, every naughty scream and wild laugh, come to us as if our very senses were conscious of them. The child is a true child, the only genuine and consistent mortal in the book; and wherever she crosses the dark and gloomy track of the story, she refreshes our spirit with pure truth and radiant beauty, and brings to grateful remembrance the like ministry of gladsome childhood, in some of the saddest scenes of actual life. We feel at once that the author must have a "Little Pearl" of his own, whose portrait, consciously or unconsciously, his pen sketches out. Not that we would deny to Mr. Hawthorne the power to call up any shape, angel or goblin, and present it before his readers in a striking and vivid light. But there is something more than imagination in the picture of "Little Pearl." The heart takes a part in it, and puts in certain inimitable touches of nature here and there, such as fancy never dreamed of, and only a long and loving observation of the ways of childhood could suggest. The most characteristic traits are so interwoven with the story, (on which we do not care to dwell,) that it is not easy to extract a paragraph which will convey much of the charming image to our readers. The most convenient passage for our purpose is the description of Little Pearl playing upon the sea-shore. We take in the figure of the old man as a dark back-ground, or contrast, to heighten the effect.

* * *

[Quotes passage in which Pearl plays on the shore.]

Here follows a dialogue in the spirit of the idea that runs through the book,—that revenge may exist without any overt act of vengeance that could be called such, and that a man who refrains from avenging himself, may be more diabolical in his very forbearance than he who in his passionate rage inflicts what evil he may upon his enemy; the former having that spirit of cold hate which could gloat for years, or forever, over the agonies of remorse and despair, over the anguish bodily and mental, and consequent death or madness, of a fellow man, and never relent—never for a moment be moved to pity. This master passion of hatred, swallowing up all that is undevilish and human in Roger Chillingworth, makes him a pure abstraction at last, a sort of mythical fury, a match for Alecto the Unceasing.

* * *

[Quotes a long passage describing Hester's meeting with Chillingworth in the forest, followed by a long passage describing Pearl at play.]

We know of no writer who better understands and combines the elements of the picturesque in writing than Mr. Hawthorne. His style may be compared to a sheet of transparent water, reflecting from its surface blue skies, nodding woods, and the smallest spray or flower that peeps over grassy margin; while in its clear yet mysterious depths we espy rarer and stranger things, which we must dive for, if we would examine. Whether they might prove gems or pebbles, when taken out of the fluctuating medium through which the sun-gleams reach them, is of no consequence to the effect. Every thing charms the eye and ear, and nothing looks like art and pains-taking. There is a naturalness and a continuous flow of expression in Mr. Hawthorne's books, that makes them delightful to read, especially in this our day, when the fear of triteness drives some writers, (even those who might otherwise avoid that reproach,) to adopt an abrupt and dislocated style, administering to our jaded attention frequent thumps and twitches, by means of outlandish idioms and forced inversions, and now and then flinging at our heads an incomprehensible, break-jaw word, which uncivilized missile stuns us to a full stop, and an appeal to authority. No authority can be found, however, which affords any remedy or redress against determined outlaws. After bumping over "rocks and ridges, and grid-iron bridges," in one of these prosaic latter-day omnibuses, how pleasant it is to move over flowery turf upon a spirited, but properly trained Pegasus, who occasionally uses his wings, and skims along a little above *terra firma*, but not with an alarming preference for cloudland or rarefied air. One cannot but wonder, by the way, that the master of such a wizard power over language as Mr. Hawthorne manifests should not choose a less revolting subject than this of the Scarlet Letter, to which fine writing seems as inappropriate as fine embroidery. The ugliness of pollution and vice is no more relieved by it than the gloom of the prison is by the rose tree at its door. There are some palliative expressions used, which cannot, even as a matter of taste, be approved.

Regarding the book simply as a picture of the olden time, we have no fault to find with costume or circumstance. All the particulars given us, (and he is not wearisomely anxious to multiply them to show his research,) are in good keeping and perspective, all in softened outlines and neutral tint, except the ever fresh and unworn image of childhood, which stands out from the canvas in the gorgeously attired "Little Pearl." He forbears to mention the ghastly gallows-tree, which stood hard by the pillory and whipping-post, at the city gates, and which one would think might have been banished with them from the precincts of Boston, and from the predilections of the community of whose opinions it is the focus. When a people have opened their eyes to the fact, that it is not the best way of discountenancing vice to harden it to exposure and shame, and make it brazen-faced, reckless, and impudent, they might also be convinced, it would seem, that respect for human life would not be promoted by publicly violating it, and making a spectacle, or a newspaper theme, of the mental agony and dying struggles of a human being, and of him least fit, in the common belief, to be thus hurried to his account. "Blood for blood!" We are shocked at the revengeful custom among uncivilized tribes, when it bears the aspect of private revenge, because the executioners must be of the kindred of the slain. How much does the legal retribution in kind, which civilized man exacts, differ in reality from the custom of the savage? The law undertakes to avenge its own dignity, to use a popular phrase; that is, it regards the community as one great family, and constitutes itself the avenger of blood in its behalf. It is not punishment, but retaliation, which does not contemplate the reform of the offender as well as the prevention of crime; and where it wholly loses the remedial element, and cuts off the opportunity for repentance which God's mercy allows, it is worthy of a barbarous, not a Christian, social alliance. What sort of combination for mutual safety is it, too, when no man feels safe, because fortuitous circumstances, ingeniously bound into a chain, may so entangle Truth that she cannot bestir herself to rescue us from the doom which the judgment of twelve fallible men pronounces, and our protector, the law, executes upon us?

But we are losing sight of Mr. Hawthorne's book, and of the old Puritan settlers, as he portrays them with few, but clearly cut and expressive, lines. In these sketchy groupings, Governor Bellingham is the only prominent figure, with the Rev. John Wilson behind him, "his beard, white as a snowdrift, seen over the Governor's shoulder."

> "Here, to witness the scene which we are describing, sat Governor Bellingham himself, with four sergeants about his chair, bearing halberds as a guard of honor. He wore a dark feather in his hat, a border of embroidery on his cloak, and a black velvet tunic beneath; a gentleman advanced in years, and with a hard experience written in his wrinkles. He was not ill-fitted to be the head and representative of a community, which owed its origin and progress, and its present state of development, not to the impulses of youth, but to the stern and tempered energies of manhood, and the sombre sagacity of age; accomplishing so much, precisely because it imagined and hoped so little."

With this portrait, we close our remarks on the book, which we should not have criticized at so great length, had we admired it less. We hope to be forgiven, if in any instance our strictures have approached the limits of what may be considered personal. We would not willingly trench upon the right which an individual may claim, in common courtesy, not to have his private qualities or personal features discussed to his face, with everybody looking on. But Mr. Hawthorne's example in the preface, and the condescending familiarity of the attitude he assumes therein, are at once our occasion and our apology.

ORESTES BROWNSON

From Brownson's Quarterly†

Mr. Hawthorne is a writer endowed with a large share of genius, and in the species of literature he cultivates has no rival in this country, unless it be Washington Irving. His *Twice-told Tales*, his *Mosses from an Old Manse*, and other contributions to the periodical press, have made him familiarly known, and endeared him to a large circle of readers. The work before us is the largest and most elaborate of the romances he has as yet published, and no one can read half a dozen pages of it without feeling that none but a man of true genius and a highly cultivated mind could have written it. It is a work of rare, we may say of fearful power, and to the great body of our countrymen who have no well defined religious belief, and no fixed principles of virtue, it will be deeply interesting and highly pleasing.

We have neither the space nor the inclination to attempt an analysis of Mr. Hawthorne's genius, after the manner of the fashionable criticism of the day. Mere literature for its own sake we do not prize, and we are more disposed to analyze an author's work than the author himself. Men are not for us mere psychological phenomena, to be studied, classed, and labelled. They are moral and accountable beings, and we look only to the moral and religious effect of their works. Genius perverted, or employed in perverting others, has no charms for us, and we turn away from it with sorrow and disgust. We are not among those who join in the worship of passion, or even of intellect. God gave us our faculties to be employed in his service, and in that of our fellow-creatures for his sake, and our only legitimate office as critics is to inquire, when a book is sent us for review, if its author in producing it has so employed them.

Mr. Hawthorne, according to the popular standard of morals in this age and this community, can hardly be said to pervert God's gifts, or to exert an immoral influence. Yet his work is far from being unobjectionable. The story is told with great naturalness, ease, grace, and delicacy, but it is a story that should not have been told. It is a story of crime, of an adulteress and her accomplice, a meek and gifted and highly popular Puritan minister in our early colonial days,—a purely imaginary story, though not altogether improbable. Crimes like the one imagined were not unknown even in the golden days of Puritanism, and are perhaps more common among the descendants of the Puritans than it is at all pleasant to believe; but they are not fit subjects for popular literature, and moral health is not promoted by leading the imagination to dwell on them. There is an unsound state of public morals when the novelist is permitted, without a scorching rebuke, to select such crimes, and invest them with all the fascinations of genius, and all the charms of a highly polished style. In a moral community such crimes are spoken

† From "Literary Notices and Criticisms," *Brownson's Quarterly* 4 (October 1850): 528–32.

of as rarely as possible, and when spoken of at all, it is always in terms which render them loathsome, and repel the imagination.

Nor is the conduct of the story better than the story itself. The author makes the guilty parties suffer, and suffer intensely, but he nowhere manages so as to make their sufferings excite the horror of his readers for their crime. The adulteress suffers not from remorse, but from regret, and from the disgrace to which her crime has exposed her, in her being condemned to wear emblazoned on her dress the Scarlet Letter which proclaims to all the deed she has committed. The minister, her accomplice, suffers also, horribly, and feels all his life after the same terrible letter branded on his heart, but not from the fact of the crime itself, but from the consciousness of not being what he seems to the world, from his having permitted the partner in his guilt to be disgraced, to be punished, without his having the manliness to avow his share in the guilt, and to bear his share of the punishment. Neither ever really repents of the criminal deed; nay, neither ever regards it as really criminal, and both seem to hold it to have been laudable, because they *loved* one another,—as if the love itself were not illicit, and highly criminal. No man has the right to love another man's wife, and no married woman has the right to love any man but her husband. Mr. Hawthorne in the present case seeks to excuse Hester Prynne, a married woman, for loving the Puritan minister, on the ground that she had no love for her husband, and it is hard that a woman should not have some one to love; but this only aggravated her guilt, because she was not only forbidden to love the minister, but commanded to love her husband, whom she had vowed to love, honor, cherish, and obey. The modern doctrine that represents the affections as fatal, and wholly withdrawn from voluntary control, and then allows us to plead them in justification of neglect of duty and breach of the most positive precepts of both the natural and the revealed law, cannot be too severely reprobated.

Human nature is frail, and it is necessary for every one who standeth to take heed lest he fall. Compassion for the fallen is a duty which we all owe, in consideration of our own failings, and especially in consideration of the infinite mercy our God has manifested to his erring and sinful children. But however binding may be this duty, we are never to forget that sin is sin, and that it is pardonable only through the great mercy of God, on condition of the sincere repentance of the sinner. But in the present case neither of the guilty parties repents of the sin, neither exclaims with the royal prophet, who had himself fallen into the sin of adultery and murder, *Misere mei Deus, secundum magnam misericordiam; et secundum multitudinem miserationum tuarum, dele iniquitatem meam. Amplius lava me ab iniquitate mea; et a peccato munda me. Quoniam iniquitatem meam cognosco, et peccatum meum contra me est semper.*[1] They hug their il-

---

1. Psalm 51: 1–3: "Have mercy upon me, O God, according to thy loving kindness: according unto the multitude of thy tender mercies blot out my transgressions. / Wash me thoroughly from mine iniquity, and cleanse me from my sin. / For I acknowledge my transgressions: and my sin is ever before me."

licit love; they cherish their sin; and after the lapse of seven years are ready, and actually agree, to depart into a foreign country, where they may indulge it without disguise and without restraint. Even to the last, even when the minister, driven by his agony, goes so far as to throw off the mask of hypocrisy, and openly confess his crime, he shows no sign of repentance, or that he regarded his deed as criminal.

The Christian who reads *The Scarlet Letter* cannot fail to perceive that the author is wholly ignorant of Christian asceticism, and that the highest principle of action he recognizes is pride. In both the criminals, the long and intense agony they are represented as suffering springs not from remorse, from the consciousness of having offended God, but mainly from the feeling, especially on the part of the minister, that they have failed to maintain the integrity of their character. They have lowered themselves in their own estimation, and cannot longer hold up their heads in society as honest people. It is not their conscience that is wounded, but their pride. *He* cannot bear to think that he wears a disguise, that he cannot be the open, frank, stainless character he had from his youth aspired to be, and *she*, that she is driven from society, lives a solitary outcast, and has nothing to console her but her fidelity to her paramour. There is nothing Christian, nothing really moral, here. The very pride itself is a sin; and pride often a greater sin than that which it restrains us from committing. There are thousands of men and women too proud to commit carnal sins, and to the indomitable pride of our Puritan ancestors we may attribute no small share of their external morality and decorum. It may almost be said, that, if they had less of that external morality and decorum, their case would be less desperate; and often the violation of them, or failure to maintain them, by which their pride receives a shock, and their self-complacency is shaken, becomes the occasion, under the grace of God, of their conversion to truth and holiness. As long as they maintain their self-complacency, are satisfied with themselves, and feel that they have outraged none of the decencies of life, no argument can reach them, no admonition can startle them, no exhortation can move them. Proud of their supposed virtue, free from all self-reproach, they are as placid as a summer morning, pass through life without a cloud to mar their serenity, and die as gently and as sweetly as the infant falling asleep in its mother's arms. We have met with these people, and after laboring in vain to waken them to a sense of their actual condition, till completely discouraged, we have been tempted to say, Would that you might commit some overt act, that should startle you from your sleep, and make you feel how far pride is from being either a virtue, or the safeguard of virtue,—or convince you of your own insufficiency for yourselves, and your absolute need of Divine grace. Mr. Hawthorne seems never to have learned that pride is not only sin, but the root of all sin, and that humility is not only a virtue, but the root of all virtue. No genuine contrition or repentance ever springs from pride, and the sorrow for sin because it mortifies our pride, or lessens us in our own eyes, is nothing but the effect of pride. All true remorse, all genuine repentance, springs from humility, and is sorrow for having offended God, not sorrow for having offended ourselves.

Mr. Hawthorne also mistakes entirely the effect of Christian pardon upon the interior state of the sinner. He seems entirely ignorant of the religion that can restore peace to the sinner,—true, inward peace, we mean. He would persuade us, that Hester had found pardon, and yet he shows us that she had found no inward peace. Something like this is common among popular Protestant writers, who, in speaking of great sinners among Catholics that have made themselves monks or hermits to expiate their sins by devoting themselves to prayer, and mortification, and the duties of religion, represent them as always devoured by remorse, and suffering in their interior agony almost the pains of the damned. An instance of this is the Hermit of Engeddi in Sir Walter Scott's *Talisman*. These men know nothing either of true remorse, or of the effect of Divine pardon. They draw from their imagination, enlightened, or rather darkened, by their own experience. Their speculations are based on the supposition that the sinner's remorse is the effect of wounded pride, and that during life the wound can never be healed. All this is false. The remorse does not spring from wounded pride, and the greatest sinner who really repents, who really does penance, never fails to find interior peace. The mortifications he practises are not prompted by his interior agony, nor designed to bring peace to his soul; they are a discipline to guard against his relapse, and an expiation that his interior peace already found, and his overflowing love to God for his superabounding mercy, lead him to offer to God, in union with that made by his blessed Lord and Master on the cross.

Again, Mr. Hawthorne mistakes the character of confession. He does well to recognize and insist on its necessity; but he is wrong in supposing that its office is simply to disburden the mind by communicating its secrets to another, to restore the sinner to his self-complacency, and to relieve him from the charge of cowardice and hypocrisy. Confession is a duty we owe to God, and a means, not of restoring us to our self-complacency, but of restoring us to the favor of God, and reëstablishing us in his friendship. The work before us is full of mistakes of this sort, in those portions where the author really means to speak like a Christian, and therefore we are obliged to condemn it, where we acquit him of all unchristian intention.

As a picture of the old Puritans, taken from the position of a moderate transcendentalist and liberal of the modern school, the work has its merits; but as little as we sympathize with those stern old Popery-haters, we do not regard the picture as at all just. We should commend where the author condemns, and condemn where he commends. Their treatment of the adulteress was far more Christian than his ridicule of it. But enough of fault-finding, and as we have no praise, except what we have given, to offer, we here close this brief notice.

[ARTHUR CLEVELAND COXE]

From The Church Review†

Current Literature, in America, has generally been forced to depend, for criticism, upon personal partiality or personal spleen. We have had very little reviewing on principle; almost none with the pure motive of building up a sound and healthful literature for our country, by cultivating merit, correcting erratic genius, abasing assumption and imposture, and insisting on the fundamental importance of certain great elements, without which no literature can be either beneficial or enduring. Our reviews have, accordingly, exercised very little influence over public taste. They have been rather tolerated than approved; and, for the most part, have led a very precarious existence, rather as attempts than as achievements; creditable make-believes; tolerable domestic imitations of the imported article; well enough in their way, but untrustworthy for opinion, and worthless for taste. Their reviewals of contemporary authors have too commonly been a mere daubing of untempered mortar, or else a deliberate assault, with intent to kill. In either case the reviewer has betrayed himself, as writing, not for the public, but for the satisfaction or the irritation of the author; and the game of mock reviewing has become as notorious as that of mock auctions. The intelligent public hears the hammering and the outcry, but has got used to it, and passes by. Nobody's opinion of a book is the more or less favorable for anything that can be said in this or that periodical. * * *

So it must be, however, till our periodicals become something more than repositories of sophomorical eulogy, or ribaldry, upon literary toys and trifles. Reviews are superfluous, except as they represent a want, which they undertake to supply, from competent resources, and in an earnest spirit of accomplishing an honorable purpose. We make no apology, therefore, for becoming reviewers, when we acknowledge our earnest hope, not only that we may do something to assist the literary and theological studies of Anglo-American Churchmen, but that we may make the voice of the Church more audible to the American public in general, and thus may exercise, for the benefit of popular authors, some salutary influence upon public taste. Our mission—to borrow a little cant from the times—is, indeed, rather religious than literary; yet, in an age when literature makes very free with religion, we must be pardoned for supposing that religion owes some attention to literature. * * * We know not the literary world, except from a distant view, and have nothing in common with its aims or its occupations; but we think it high time that the literary world should learn that Churchmen are, in a very large proportion, their readers and book-buyers, and that the tastes and principles of Churchmen have as

---

† From "The Writings of Hawthorne," *The Church Review* 3, no. 4 (January 1851): 489–511. Coxe's well-known condemnation of *The Scarlet Letter* also includes a lengthy review of *Mosses from an Old Manse*.

good a right to be respected as those of Puritans and Socialists. It is in this relation to our subject that we have taken up the clever and popular writings of Hawthorne; and we propose to consider them, without any attempt to give them a formal review, just in the free and conversational manner which is permitted to table-talk or social intercourse; and if we can thus afford our author a candid exhibition of the impressions he is producing on a large, but quiet portion of the community, and prompt him to a future career more worthy of their entire regard, we shall feel that we have done the State, as well as the Church, some service; and no anxiety for our reputation as critics shall spoil our appetite for a smoking plum-pudding at Christmas.

In taking up Mr. Hawthorne's volumes, we are happy to particularize our general professions of impartiality, and to describe ourselves as heartily his well-wishers, knowing nothing either of him or his works, beyond what is patent to all men, in his own published confessions, or in other publications of the popular character. True we must own to a little prejudice against him, as a conspicuous member of the Bay School, but, in counterpoise, we must put in a profession of a specific feeling in his favor, as at all events one of the best of them, the very Irving of Down-East. He is one of the few Bays whose freest egotism seldom moves our disgust, and whom we are, in truth, disposed to thank for gossiping at random about himself and friends, as if every one knew both him and them, and were anxiously watching them with telescopes and lorgnettes. In fact, we were particularly interested in his graphic description of that ancient seat of witchcraft in which he tells us he was born, for having had forefathers of our own among the broad-banded and steeple-crowned worthies of old Salem, we were glad to learn, more than geographies and gazetteers are wont to tell us, of its appearance and present condition. Nay, we began to feel a degree of cousinry with our author, in spite of ourselves, when, in an old family record of a marriage not very remotely connected with our own existence, we found the name of his ancestor, *Colonel Hathorn*, familiarly mentioned, with those of other Salemites who hasted to the wedding, in the year of Grace 1713, and were there gravely lectured, over their sack-posset, by godly Master Noyes, the Puritan parson. With such, and many other feelings in our author's favor, we take up his works. In fact, who can resist a pleasant influence in his behalf, exhaling from his very name, redolent as it is of guilelessness and springtide, and rich with associations derived from old ballads and madrigals that celebrate the garden-like agriculture of England? In faint suggestiveness too of "Hawthornden," it has a flavor of Scots poesy and the English drama; of Drummond and of Jonson; and if some patriot Pope or Gifford wants a name whose easy lubricity of pronunciation just suits a flowing line, who would not wish that Hawthorne's might be paired with Irving's, as indissolubly as Beaumont's with Fletcher's, and that the twain might be freely allowed to rank as the *lucida sidera* of our literary horizon? It is not for want of a predisposition to admire and praise our author and his performances, that we shall be obliged to say many things in a different humor.

* * *

* * * It is chiefly, in hopes, to save our author from embarking largely into this business of Fescennine romance, that we enter upon a brief examination of his latest and most ambitious production, "The Scarlet Letter."

The success which seems to have attended this bold advance of Hawthorne, and the encouragement which has been dealt out by some professed critics, to its worst symptoms of malice prepense, may very naturally lead, if unbalanced by a moderate dissent, to his further compromise of his literary character. We are glad, therefore, that "The Scarlet Letter" is, after all, little more than an experiment, and need not be regarded as a step necessarily fatal. It is an attempt to rise from the composition of petty tales, to the historical novel; and we use the expression *an attempt*, with no disparaging significance, for it is confessedly a trial of strength only just beyond some former efforts, and was designed as part of a series. It may properly be called a novel, because it has all the ground-work, and might have been very easily elaborated into the details, usually included in the term; and we call it *historical*, because its scene-painting is in a great degree true to a period of our Colonial history, which ought to be more fully delineated. We wish Mr. Hawthorne would devote the powers which he only partly discloses in this book, to a large and truthful portraiture of that period, with the patriotic purpose of making us better acquainted with the stern old worthies, and all the *dramatis personæ* of those times, with their yet surviving habits, recollections, and yearnings, derived from maternal England. Here is, in fact, a rich and even yet an unexplored field for historic imagination; and touches are given in "The Scarlet Letter," to secret springs of romantic thought, which opened unexpected and delightful episodes to our fancy, as we were borne along by the tale. Here a maiden reminiscence, and here a grave ecclesiastical retrospection, clouding the brow of the Puritan colonists, as they still remembered home, in their wilderness of lasting exile! Now a lingering relic of Elizabethan fashion in dress, and now a turn of expression, betraying the deep traces of education under influences renounced and foresworn, but still instinctively prevalent!

Time has just enough mellowed the facts, and genealogical research has made them just enough familiar, for their employment as material for descriptive fiction; and the New England colonies might now be made as picturesquely real to our perception, as the Knickerbocker tales have made the Dutch settlements of the Hudson. This, however, can never be done by the polemical pen of a blind partisan of the Puritans; it demands Irving's humorously insinuating gravity, and all his benevolent satire, with a large share of honest sympathy for at least the earnestness of wrong-headed enthusiasm. We are stimulated to this suggestion by the very life-like and striking manner in which the days of Governor Winthrop are sketched in the book before us, by the beautiful picture the author has given us of the venerable old pastor Wilson, and by the outline portraits he has thrown in, of several of their contemporaries. We like him all the better for his tenderness of the less exceptionable features of the Puritan character; but we are hardly sure that we like his flings at their failings. If it should provoke a smile to find us sensitive in this matter, our consistency may be very briefly demonstrated. True, we have our own fun with the follies of the Puritans; it is our inseparable privilege as Churchmen, thus to compensate ourselves for many a scar which their frolics have left on our comeliness. But when a degenerate Puritan, whose Socinian conscience is but the skimmed-milk of their creamy fanaticism, allows such a conscience to curdle within him, in dyspeptic acidulation, and then belches forth derision at the sour piety of his forefathers—we snuff at him, with an honest scorn, knowing very well that he likes the Puritans for their worst enormities, and hates them only for their redeeming merits.

The Puritan rebelling against the wholesome discipline of that Ecclesiastical Law, which Hooker has demonstrated, with Newtonian evidence, to be but a moral system of central light with its dependent order and illumination; the Puritan with his rough heel and tough heart, mounted upon altars, and hacking down crosses, and sepulchres, and memorials of the dead; the Puritan with his axe on an Archbishop's neck, or holding up in his hand the bleeding head of a martyred king; the Puritan in all this guilt, has his warmest praise, and his prompt witness that he allows the deeds of his fathers, and is ready to fill up the measure of their iniquity; but the Puritans, with a blessed inconsistency, repeating liturgic doxologies to the triune GOD, or, by the domestic hearth, bowing down with momentary conformity, to invoke the name of Jesus, whom the Church had taught him to adore as an atoning Saviour—these are the Puritans at whom the driveler wags his head, and shoots out his tongue! We would not laugh in that man's company. No—no! we heartily dislike the Puritans, so far as they were Puritan; but even in them we recognize many good old English virtues, which Puritanism could not kill. They were in part our ancestors, and though we would not accept the bequest of their enthusiasm, we are not ashamed of many things to which they clung, with principle quite as characteristic. We see no harm in a reverent joke now and then, at an abstract Puritan, in spite of our duty to our progenitors, and Hudibras shall still be our companion, when, at times, the mental bow requires fresh elasticity, and bids us relax its string. There is, after all, something of human kindness, in taking out an old grudge in the comfort of a hearty, side-shaking laugh, and we think we are never freer from bitterness of spirit, than when we contemplate the Banbury zealot hanging his cat on Monday, and reflect that Strafford and Montrose fell victims to the same mania that destroyed poor puss. But there is another view of the same Puritan, which even a Churchman may charitably allow himself to respect, and when precisely that view is chosen by his degenerate offspring for unfilial derision, we own to a sympathy for the grim old Genevan features, at which their seventh reproduction turns up a repugnant nose; for sure we are that the young Ham is gloating over his father's nakedness, with far less of sorrow for the ebriety of a parent, than of satisfaction in the degradation of an orthodox patriarch. Now without asserting that it is so, we are not quite so sure, as we would like to be, that our author is not venting something of this spirit against the Puritans, in his rich delineation of "godly Master Dimmesdale," and the sorely abused confidence of his flock. There is a provoking concealment of the author's motive, from the beginning to the end of the story; we wonder what he would be at; whether he is making fun of all religion, or only giving a fair hint of the essential sensualism of enthusiasm. But, in short, we are astonished at the kind of incident which he has selected for romance. It may be such incidents were too common, to be wholly out of the question, in a history of the times, but it seems to us that good taste might be pardoned for not giving them prominence in fiction. In deference to the assertions of a very acute analyst, who has written ably on the subject of colonization, we are inclined to think, as we have said before, that barbarism was indeed "the first danger" of the pilgrim settlers. Of a period nearly contemporary with that of Mr. Hawthorne's narrative, an habitual eulogist has recorded that "on going to its Church and court records, we discover mournful evidences of incontinence, even in the respectable families; as if, being cut off from the more refined pleasures of society, their baser passions had burnt away the restraints of delicacy, and their growing coarseness of manners had allowed them finally to seek, in these baser passions, the spring of their enjoyments." We are sorry to be told so, by so unexceptionable a witness.* We had supposed, with the Roman satirist, that purity might at least be credited to those primitive days, when a Saturnian simplicity was necessarily revived in primeval forests, by the New England colonists:

> Quippe aliter tunc orbe novo, cœloque recenti
> Vivebant homines.[1]

but a Puritan doctor in divinity publishes the contrary, and a Salemite novelist selects the intrigue of an adulterous minister, as the groundwork of his ideal of those times! We may acknowledge, with reluctance, the historical fidelity of the picture, which retailers of fact and fiction thus concur in framing, but we cannot but wonder that a novelist should select, of all features of the period, that which reflects most discredit upon the cradle of his country, and which is in itself so revolting, and so incapable of receiving decoration from narrative genius.

And this brings inquiry to its point. Why has our author selected such a theme? Why, amid all the suggestive incidents of life in a wilderness; of a retreat from civilization to which, in every individual case, a thousand circumstances must have concurred to reconcile human nature with estrangement from home and country; or amid the historical connections of our history with Jesuit adventure, savage invasion, regicide outlawry, and French aggression, should the taste of Mr. Hawthorne have preferred as the proper material for romance, the

---

* Barbarism the first Danger, by H. Bushnell, D. D.
1. "Indeed, then, when earth was new and heaven young, men lived differently" (Juvenal, Satire 6).

nauseous amour of a Puritan pastor, with a frail creature of his charge, whose mind is represented as far more debauched than her body? Is it, in short, because a running undertide of filth has become as requisite to a romance, as death in the fifth act to a tragedy? Is the French era actually begun in our literature? And is the flesh, as well as the world and the devil, to be henceforth dished up in fashionable novels, and discussed at parties, by spinsters and their beaux, with as unconcealed a relish as they give to the vanilla in their ice cream? We would be slow to believe it, and we hope our author would not willingly have it so, yet we honestly believe that "the Scarlet Letter" has already done not a little to degrade our literature, and to encourage social licentiousness: it has started other pens on like enterprises, and has loosed the restraint of many tongues, that have made it an apology for "the evil communications which corrupt good manners." We are painfully tempted to believe that it is a book made for the market, and that the market has made it merchantable, as they do game, by letting everybody understand that the commodity is in high condition, and smells strongly of incipient putrefaction.

We shall entirely mislead our reader if we give him to suppose that "the Scarlet Letter" is coarse in its details, or indecent in its phraseology. This very article of our own, is far less suited to ears polite, than any page of the romance before us; and the reason is, we call things by their right names, while the romance never hints the shocking words that belong to its things, but, like Mephistophiles, insinuates that the arch-fiend himself is a very tolerable sort of person, if nobody would call him Mr. Devil. We have heard of persons who could not bear the reading of some Old Testament Lessons in the service of the Church: such persons would be delighted with our author's story; and damsels who shrink at the reading of the Decalogue, would probably luxuriate in bathing their imagination in the crystal of its delicate sensuality. The language of our author, like patent blacking, "would not soil the whitest linen," and yet the composition itself, would suffice, if well laid on, to Ethiopize the snowiest conscience that ever sat like a swan upon that mirror of heaven, a Christian maiden's imagination. We are not sure we speak quite strong enough, when we say, that we would much rather listen to the coarsest scene of Goldsmith's "Vicar," read aloud by a sister or daughter, than to hear from such lips, the perfectly chaste language of a scene in "the Scarlet Letter," in which a married wife and her reverend paramour, with their unfortunate offspring, are introduced as the actors, and in which the whole tendency of the conversation is to suggest a sympathy for their sin, and an anxiety that they may be able to accomplish a successful escape beyond the seas, to some country where their shameful commerce may be perpetuated. Now, in Goldsmith's story there are very coarse words, but we do not remember anything that saps the foundations of the moral sense, or that goes to create unavoidable sympathy with unrepenting sorrow, and deliberate, premeditated sin. The "Vicar of Wakefield" is sometimes coarsely virtuous, but "the Scarlet Letter" is delicately immoral.

There is no better proof of the bad tendency of a work, than some unintentional betrayal on the part of a young female reader, of an instinctive consciousness against it, to which she has done violence, by reading it through. In a beautiful region of New England, where stage-coaches are not yet among things that were, we found ourselves, last summer, one of a traveling party, to which we were entirely a stranger, consisting of young ladies fresh from boarding-school, with the proverbial bread-and-butter look of innocence in their faces, and a nursery thickness about their tongues. Their benevolent uncle sat outside upon the driver's box, and ours was a seat next to a worshipful old dowager, who seemed to bear some matronly relation to the whole coach-load, with the single exception of ourselves. In such a situation it was ours to keep silence, and we soon relapsed into nothingness and a semi-slumberous doze. Meanwhile our young friends were animated and talkative, and as we were approaching the seat of a College, their literature soon began to expose itself. They were evidently familiar with the Milliners' Magazines in general, and even with Graham's and Harper's. They had read James, and they had read Dickens; and at last their criticisms rose to Irving and Walter Scott, whose various merits they discussed with an artless anxiety to settle forever the question whether the one was not "a charming composer," and the other "a truly beautiful writer." Poor girls! had they imagined how much harmless amusement they were furnishing to their drowsy, dusty, and very unentertaining fellow traveler, they might, quite possibly, have escaped both his praise and his censure! They came at last to Longfellow and Bryant, and rhythmically regaled us with the "muffled drum" of the one, and the somewhat familiar opinion of the other, that

"Truth crushed to earth will rise again."

And so they came to Hawthorne, of whose "Scarlet Letter" we then knew very little, and that little was favorable, as we had seen several high encomiums of its style. We expected a quotation from the "Celestial Railroad," for we were traveling at a rate which naturally raised the era of railroads in one's estimation, by rule of contrary; but no—the girls went straight to "the Scarlet Letter." We soon discovered that one Hester Prynne was the heroine, and that she had been made to stand in the pillory, as, indeed, her surname might have led one to anticipate. We discovered that there was a mysterious little child in the question, that she was a sweet little darling, and that her "sweet, pretty little name," was "Pearl." We discovered that mother and child had a meeting, in a wood, with a very fascinating young preacher, and that there was a hateful creature named Chillingworth, who persecuted the said preacher, very perseveringly. Finally, it appeared that Hester Prynne was, in fact, Mrs. Hester Chillingworth, and that the hateful old creature aforesaid had a very natural dislike to the degradation of his spouse, and quite as natural a hatred of the wolf in sheep's clothing who had wrought her ruin. All this leaked out in conversation, little by little, on the hypothesis of our protracted somnolency. There was a very gradual approximation to the point, till one inquired—"didn't you think, from the first, that he was the one?" A

modest looking creature, who evidently had not read the story, art-
lessly inquired—"what one?"—and then there was a titter at the
child's simplicity, in the midst of which we ventured to be quite awake,
and to discover by the scarlet blush that began to circulate, that the
young ladies were not unconscious to themselves that reading "the
Scarlet Letter" was a thing to be ashamed of. These school-girls had,
in fact, done injury to their young sense of delicacy, by devouring such
a dirty story; and after talking about it before folk, inadvertently, they
had enough of mother Eve in them, to know that they were ridiculous,
and that shame was their best retreat.

Now it would not have been so if they had merely exhibited a familiarity with "the Heart of Mid-Lothian,"[2] and yet there is more mention
of the foul sin in its pages, than there is in "the Scarlet Letter." Where
then is the difference? It consists in this—that the holy innocence of
Jeanie Deans, and not the shame of Effie, is the burthen of that story,
and that neither Effie's fall is made to look like virtue, nor the truly
honorable agony of her stern old father, in bewailing his daughter's
ruin, made a joke, by the insinuation that it was quite gratuitous. But
in Hawthorne's tale, the lady's frailty is philosophized into a natural
and necessary result of the Scriptural law of marriage, which, by holding her irrevocably to her vows, as plighted to a dried up old book-
worm, in her silly girlhood, is viewed as making her heart an easy
victim to the adulterer. The sin of her seducer too, seems to be considered as lying not so much in the deed itself, as in his long concealment of it, and, in fact, the whole moral of the tale is given in the
words—"Be true—be true," as if sincerity in sin were virtue, and as if
"Be clean—be clean," were not the more fitting conclusion. "The untrue man" is, in short, the hang-dog of the narrative, and the unclean
one is made a very interesting sort of a person, and as the two qualities
are united in the hero, their composition creates the interest of his
character. Shelley himself never imagined a more dissolute conversation than that in which the polluted minister comforts himself with
the thought, that the revenge of the injured husband is worse than his
own sin in instigating it. "Thou and I never did so, Hester"—he suggests: and she responds—"never, never! What we did had *a consecration of its own*, we felt it so—we said so to each other!" This is a little
too much—it carries the Bay-theory a little too far for our stomach!
"Hush, Hester!" is the sickish rejoinder; and fie, Mr. Hawthorne! is the
weakest token of our disgust that we can utter. The poor bemired hero
and heroine of the story should not have been seen wallowing in their
filth, at such a rate as this.

We suppose this sort of sentiment must be charged to the doctrines
enforced at "Brook-farm," although "Brook-farm" itself could never
have been Mr. Hawthorne's home, had not other influences prepared
him for such a Bedlam. At all events, this is no mere slip of the pen; it
is the essential morality of the work. If types, and letters, and words

2. *The Heart of Midlothian* (1818), novel by Sir Walter Scott. When Effie Deans is sentenced
to death for murdering her child, her sister Jeanie obtains a pardon from Queen Caroline.

can convey an author's idea, he has given us the key to the whole, in a very plain intimation that the Gospel has not set the relations of man and woman where they should be, and that a new Gospel is needed to supersede the seventh commandment, and the bond of Matrimony. Here it is, in full: our readers shall see what the world may expect from Hawthorne, if he is not stopped short, in such brothelry. Look at this conclusion:—

"*Women*—in the continually recurring trials of wounded, wasted, wronged, misplaced, or erring and sinful passion, or with the dreary burden of a heart unyielded, because unvalued and unsought—came to Hester's cottage, demanding why they were so wretched, and what the remedy! Hester comforted and counseled them as best she might. She assured them too *of her firm belief,* that, at some brighter period, when the world should have grown ripe for it, in Heaven's own time, *a new truth would be revealed, in order to establish the whole relation between man and woman on a surer ground of mutual happiness.*"

This is intelligible English; but are Americans content that such should be the English of their literature? This is the question on which we have endeavored to deliver our own earnest convictions, and on which we hope to unite the suffrages of all virtuous persons, in sympathy with the abhorrence we so unhesitatingly express. To think of making such speculations the amusement of the daughters of America! The late Convention of females at Boston, to assert the "rights of woman," may show us that there are already some, who think the world is even now *ripe for it*; and safe as we may suppose our own fair relatives to be above such a low contagion, we must remember that to a woman, the very suggestion of a mode of life for her, as preferable to that which the Gospel has made the glorious sphere of her duties and her joys, is an insult and a degradation, to which no one that loves her would allow her to be exposed.

We assure Mr. Hawthorne, in conclusion, that nothing less than an earnest wish that his future career may redeem this misstep, and prove a blessing to his country, has tempted us to enter upon a criticism so little suited to our tastes, as that of his late production. We commend to his attention the remarks of Mr. Alison, on cotemporary popularity, to be found in the review of Bossuet. We would see him, too, rising to a place among those immortal authors who have "clothed the lessons of religion in the burning words of genius;" and let him be assured, that, however great his momentary success, there is no lasting reputation for such an one as he is, except as it is founded on real worth, and fidelity to the morals of the Gospel. The time is past, when mere authorship provokes posthumous attention; there are too many who write with ease, and too many who publish books, in our times, for an author to be considered anything extraordinary. Poems perish in newspapers, now-a-days, which, at one time, would have made, at least, a name for biographical dictionaries; and stories lie dead in the pages of magazines, which would once have secured their author a mention with posterity. Hereafter those only will be thought of, who have enbalmed their writings in the hearts and lives of a few, at least, who learned from them to love truth and follow virtue. The age of "mute inglorious Miltons," is as dead as the age of chivalry. Everybody can write, and everybody can publish. But still, the wise are few; and it is only the wise, who can attain, in any worthy sense, to shine as the stars forever.

AMORY DWIGHT MAYO

From Universalist Quarterly†

* * *

* * * In the remarks we propose to make on this author, there are no pretensions to an exhaustive criticism. It is more than a spring-day's journey to walk around the boundaries, and explore all the paths of his remarkable mind; and he who would attempt to do it, may be compelled to reverse his decision by a deeper insight into his books, or a new manifestation of his power. We only say that we have faithfully read the half-dozen volumes by which he is known, and will try to convey the impression they leave upon our mind. The task of describing their contents and quoting fine passages, we leave to the newspapers. We write for those who have read, and, like ourselves, wish to talk an hour of "things seen and heard" in this new world of genius.

The first thing which attracts our notice upon these pages, is the acuteness and extent of the writer's power of observation. His eye adjusts itself to objects beyond and within the ordinary circle of vision. Wherever he looks, he sees distinctly, and the sweep of his gaze comprehends a wide area. His perception of beauty in nature is singularly keen and comprehensive. He paints an object in the light as with sunbeams, while the shadow or the transition to it are transferred with equal fidelity. We think the works of few poets will present so accurate and extensive portraiture of nature as his; of living nature, for he sees the characteristic points in a landscape, and in a high degree possesses the Spenserian power of transforming, by one magic word, a lifeless pictured catalogue of natural objects, to an actual breathing and moving scene. Perhaps he dwells with more fondness upon the minute and evanescent, than the grand and substantial in nature. Yet he is not incompetent to interpret its noble appearances.

The same clearness of vision he carries into life. He has a vivid perception of historical events and periods, no less than of the actual existence of to-day. He pictures a street with such fidelity that we walk upon its pavements, elbow our way through its shadowy throngs, and raise our voices above the clatter of omnibus wheels, to shout into ghostly ears. Whether it be little Ned Higgins offering his cent to Hepzibah[1] for the gingerbread Jim Crow—"the one that has not a broken

---

† From "The Works of Nathaniel Hawthorne," *Universalist Quarterly* 8 (July 1851): 272–93.
1. Ned Higgins and Hepzibah Pyncheon are characters in Hawthorne's *The House of the Seven Gables* (1851).

foot," or Peter Goldthwaite[2] swinging his axe through the cloud of dust in his own attic, or Hester Prynne walking to the scene of public exposure, wearing the scarlet letter upon her bosom, or Judge Pyncheon sitting dead in the low-studded room, with the mouse at his foot, and grimalkin looking in at the window, and the fly walking across his naked eyeball, or the crowd of dancers in the hall of the old Province-House, and the shadowy procession of governors down its steps,—everywhere is the same wonderful daguerreo-typing of the facts, and the same reproduction of the essential principle of life, which is the chief fact of the spectacle.

His eye does not fail, but increases in power, when directed to the world of thought and feeling. Mr. Hawthorne's books are tables of spiritual statistics, embracing the natural history of the human mind in its ordinary, but oftener in its extraordinary conditions. One would think he had ransacked the experience of all the men, women and children in his neighborhood, been the chaplain of the state prison and madhouse, beside having telegraphic intelligence of the mental state of every out-of-the-way, queer creature in the land. He is a man to whom we would not care to talk an hour if we had any secrets, for as sure as we have a tongue, without invitation we should tell them all to him, even on the top of a mail coach, or in the Merchants' Exchange. If he ever seems to overlook common traits of character, or ordinary states of mind, it is only from the absorbing interest attached to half developed germs of individuality, and flitting or profound spiritual appearances. Like all soul-gazers, he loves to walk along the dim labyrinthine passages of the mind, and poke his head into its cobwebbed closets, and clamber up stairways which are peculiarly unsafe. At all the critical moments of life,—when a man is trying to choke down his confession of love, or holds his first child in his arms, or topples over into the gulf of some terrible sin, he is sure to be a spectator. Yet in moments of less intensity he loves to hear a child prattle, or the old gravestone-cutter of Martha's Vineyard gossip over his epitaphs, or the six vagabonds in the moving show-cart retail their miscellaneous experience.

But he looks further than this. Nature, life, and the soul are only the foreground in his perspective, for beyond them he sees those spiritual laws, which sweep down ages of time, athwart the world, cross each other without confusion and almost annihilate human freedom by their fatal execution. All things are guarded by these relentless keepers, and if they ever escape for a moment, a million of eyes track the fugitives, and an unseen power compels them to walk of their own accord back through their open prison doors. We believe the faculty which perceives the invisible highways of God running up and down the universe, is the author's rarest gift,—more than any other, modifies the ordinary operations of his mind, and is the source of the chief characteristics in his method of delineation.

*   *   *

2. The title character in Hawthorne's tale "Peter Goldthwaite's Treasure" (1838).

* * * Now and then a man is born who can look straight down into the spirit without searing his eyeballs, witness this awful conflict of law and will, trace its results, know the impotence as well as the strength of man, and not lose his balance of mind, or health of affections. One poet alone looked through the length and breadth and depth of life, and unscared by the awful spectacle, with the ease and joy of a little child, wove a few of its groupings into dramas, by which all the poets in the world now swear. But this could not be until a greater than man had affirmed the paternity of God, and by the revelation of Christianity at once secured the welfare of the race, and widened to infinity the possibilities of art. Christianity alone made a Shakespeare possible, for no human creature without peril of insanity, could have looked so deeply into the very heart of existence, unless guarded by its love and faith, and arched over by its firmament of immortal hopes.

Among the few American writers who have the peculiarity of genius which consists of insight into this fact of the soul, Mr. Hawthorne occupies a prominent position. We are convinced that the rarest quality of his mind is the power of tracing the relations of spiritual laws to character. He looks at the soul, life, and nature, from the stand-point of Providence. He follows the track of one of God's mental or moral laws. Every thing which appears along its borders is minutely investigated, though sometimes appreciated rather for its nearness to his path than its own value. If we mistake not, this is the clue to all his works. Even his lightest tale gains a peculiarity of treatment and depth of tone from it, though the tendency of his mind is better perceived in his more elaborate works. Wherever he goes, whoever he meets, or whatever may be the scenes amid which he mingles, this thought is uppermost:—How are these things related to each other, and to those great spiritual agencies which underlie and encompass them? Whatever else Mr. Hawthorne may be, and we do not deny to him great versatility of powers, he is, more than any thing else, a seer.

His view of human nature determines his treatment of individuals. He can hardly be called a truthful delineator of character. His men and women have the elements of life, though not arranged in harmonious proportions. Our interest is concentrated upon the point, in the nature of each, where the battle is raging between human will and spiritual laws. How far has the man obeyed or disobeyed these rules of life, by what process is he receiving reward or retribution, does he accept or resist it, and how are other men implicated in his fate,—are the chief objects of inquiry. A few remarkable exceptions to this mode of treatment will not disturb this assertion. His people either enlist our admiration by a single intense devotion to some high purpose, or compel our sympathies by their struggles to escape the ruin which their own sins or errors have invited. They are analyzed, rather than created, and we obtain from them the impression received from a crowd elated beyond measure by some absorbing enthusiasm, or writhing under the infliction of some terrible chastisement. An artist who should fill his gallery with portraits of inmates of lunatic asylums,

disciples of Miller in their ascension robes, and orators at the top of
their happiest climax, would hardly be regarded as a correct delineation of the human face, neither will consummate skill of analysis
and execution redeem the ghostly family of our author's spiritual offspring from the charge of untruth to a healthy nature.

And his pictures of life are generally from the same point of view.
He shows us a street, a domestic circle, a public assembly, or a whole
village, describes them with wonderful fidelity, yet just as we think we
have them securely located upon solid ground, by one magic sentence
the whole is transmuted to a symbolic picture, and a witch element in
the atmosphere makes us doubt whether we are not in dream-land.
Even the beautiful introductions to the "Mosses from an old Manse,"
and the "Scarlet Letter," are tinged with this peculiarity. The Concord
there, is hardly the one that appears from the rail-track; and the Salem
custom-house and its inmates, are judged from that point whence we
all should put on a somewhat sorry aspect, whence the mercantile life
of New England especially will not bear severe criticism. An observing
reader will be struck by this tendency to symbolism on every page of
these books.

So nature is regarded oftener by him in its relations to the human
mind, and mental and moral laws, than as existing for any independent purpose. His exquisite pencilling of her beautiful scenes is generally illustrative of the person who is the central figure of the
landscape. His winds howl a warning through open doors on the advent of some critical moment. "Alice's Posies," and "The Pyncheon
Elm," the garden of "The House of the Seven Gables," the wood
where Hester and Dimmesdale talked, and the midnight sky, seen by
the minister from the pillory, all prefigure in outline and detail the
spiritual states of those who lived among them. No strange cat walks
across a path, no mouse ventures out of the wainscot, no robin sings
upon the house-top, or bee dives into a squash blossom, which does
not know its business and fulfil its destiny, in his drama.

This prominent tendency in Mr. Hawthorne's mind, at times assumes the form of disease. Doubtless the most profound, and from an
angel's point of view, the truest estimate of man, life and nature, is
that in which they are woven into a spectacle illustrative of spiritual
laws. God is indeed "above all, through all, and in all," yet this doctrine must be held in connection with all we have before said of man's
consciousness of freedom, or it becomes a false statement of our relations to Providence. No man can reconcile this apparent contradiction, but any man knows that he must stand by himself, or go adrift to
foolishness and ruin. Therefore this Providential view of life cannot legitimately occupy the foreground in a correct delineation of existence,
but should rather be the mountain range, and the horizon line, and
the forces beneath the surface; and he who ignores the more obvious
relations of the spirit, to live always near its central blaze, must obtain
and impart false impressions, and become an unfit medium for its
complete interpretation. So is it to a degree with Mr. Hawthorne. A
tendency to disease in his nature, appears in the fearful intensity of

his narratives. There is also a sort of unnaturalness in his world. It is seen not in the noon-day sun, so often as by moon-beams, and by auroral or volcanic lights. All that he describes may and does actually happen, but something else happens, by the omission of which we fail sometimes to acknowledge the reality of his delineation. This tendency appears in many of the tales in the "Mosses from an Old Manse," and reached its climax in the "Scarlet Letter." In "The House of the Seven Gables," we see the author struggling out of its grasp, with a vigor which we believe ensures a final recovery.

The constitution of Mr. Hawthorne's mind, in other respects, is admirably calculated to fit him for his primary office of seer. For all danger of that godless or misanthropic spirit, which so often destroys men who know much of human nature, is averted by his great affections. He follows the track of a spiritual law into the darkest or wildest scene, without losing his faith in God, or his love for humanity. With an impressibility that makes him alive even to the buttons of his overcoat, with the quickest insight through motives, and the sophistry of sin, and an overpowering sense of the ludicrous, he never loses his human sympathies. He looks upon the spectacle of existence, with the same pensive smile always upon his face, changing only to a more touching gleam of joy and sadness. He is one whose eye we feel upon our souls, yet to whom we cheerfully confide their treasures. His humor, too, seems only a part of his great love, so innocently does it play over the surface of every thing he touches; it is beyond our power to analyze it, and were it not, we are sure we should hardly risk the loss of a tithe of the pleasure we receive from it, by the attempt. We know of no modern writer who holds us so completely at his will in this respect; not Emerson, or Lamb. Neither he, nor his readers, can ever be thrown into utter desperation, for thought of the very absurdity of the position.

* * *

Perhaps four years were never spent to better purpose, than those in Mr. Hawthorne's life, between the publication of "Mosses from an Old Manse," and "The Scarlet Letter." The only account we have of them, is in the sketch of the "Custom House," which introduces the latter work. Like most men of genius, our author is not disposed to do full justice to those influences which have powerfully contributed to the growth of his mind. Often when such men are receiving and appropriating most rapidly, they are tormented with a nervous suspicion of the decay of their power. But never was such want of faith more signally rebuked, than in the writer we are reviewing, for we suspect that "spacious edifice of brick" has seldom been turned to so good use, as by this man who looked through its machinery and its occupants to the facts which they unconsciously represent. The portrait of this place is wonderfully vivid, and from the author's point of observation, doubtless true.

The story so gracefully introduced, is the most remarkable of Mr. Hawthorne's works, whether we consider felicity of plot, sustained interest of development, analysis of character, or the witchery of a style

which invests the whole with a strange, ethereal beauty. These qualities of the book are so evident, that we now desire to go beneath them
to those which make it, in many respects, the most powerful imaginative work of the present era of English literature. No reader possessing
the slightest portion of spiritual insight, can fail to perceive that the
chief value of this romance is religious. It is an attempt to delineate
the involved action of spiritual laws, and their effects upon individual
character, with an occasional glimpse into the organization of society.
Of course it has been a puzzle to the critics, and a pebble between the
teeth of the divines, transcending the artificial rules of the former, and
making sad work with the creeds and buckram moralities of the latter.

Standing as "The Scarlet Letter" does, at the junction of several
moral highways, it is not easy to grasp the central idea around which it
instinctively arranged itself in the author's mind. The most obvious
fact upon its pages is, that the only safety for a human soul consists in
appearing to be exactly what it is. If holy, it must not wrench itself out
of its sphere to become a part in any satanic spectacle; if corrupt, it
must heroically stand upon the low ground of its own sinfulness, and
rise through penitence and righteousness.

This law of life is exhibited in the contrasted characters of Dimmesdale and Hester. Whatever errors of head or heart, or infelicity of circumstances, prevent Hester from fully realizing the Christian ideal of
repentance, she sternly respects her moral relations to society. She
embroiders the badge of her own infamy, and without complaint submits to isolation, the pity, scorn and indifference of the world, and the
withering of her own nature under the blaze of a noonday exposure to
the hot sun of social displeasure; she turns her face toward humanity,
and begins the life-long task of beating up to virtue against the pitiless
storm which overthrows so many an offender. If the impending fate of
the minister forces her to catch at the sole hope of escaping from her
penance, and the closing scenes of the drama are necessary to make
her an angel of mercy to the very community she had outraged by the
sin of her youth, we may in mercy impute her falterings to that infirmity of our nature, which its greatest interpreter has represented by
the concession of Isabella to the artifice of Mariana, and the untruth
of Desdemona. As far as human fidelity to a spiritual law can go, did
Hester live out the fact of the correspondence of seeming and being.
Not so with the less heroic partner of her guilt. We cannot deny that
all the arguments which may be used to palliate insincerity apply to
Dimmesdale. The voluntary step he must take by confession, was from
a more than mortal elevation to a more than human abasement. His
constitutional weakness, too, is an excusing circumstance, and especially the genuineness of his repentance up to a certain point. Yet the
radical vice of his soul was not submission to his passions, but cowardice; and the reflex action of this cowardice disarranged his whole
life, placing him in false relations to the community and the woman
he had wronged, and laying open his naked heart to the eye of the demon that was the appointed agent of his final ruin. Of the value of
these two persons, considered as accurate delineations of character,

nothing very flattering can be said. We see them in the midst of conflict, and in the strife of soul and law many wonderful revelations of human nature appear. Yet a strict fidelity to the engrossing object of the book, renders the author unfaithful to individual humanity. Dimmesdale and Hester are the incarnate action and reaction of the law of sincerity.

Another fact which appears in this book, is the downward tendency of sin; once let a soul be untrue, even though half in ignorance of its duty, and its world is disorganized, so that every step in its new path involves it in greater difficulties. The cardinal error, in this maze of guilt and wretchedness, is Hester's marriage with Chillingworth. She committed that sin which women are every day repeating, though never without retribution, as certain, if not as visible as hers, of giving her hand to a man she did not entirely love. There are souls great and good enough to stand firmly against the recoil of such an act, but Hester was not one of these. Her true husband at last came, and she could only give him a guilty love. By her fatal error she had cut herself off from the power to bless him by her affection as long as God should keep her in the bonds of a false marriage. The proclivity of her former error drove her on to sin again with more obvious consequences, if not with deeper guilt. And then came, in rapid succession, the ruin of Dimmesdale, the transformation of Chillingworth, the transmission of a diseased nature to her child, and the wide spread scandal of a whole community.

And growing out of this act, and its retribution, is the whole question of the relation of the sexes, and the organization of society. The author does not grapple with these intricate problems, though he knows as much of the falsity of what is called marriage, and the unnatural position of woman, as those who are more ready to undertake the cure of the world. And the hypocrisy of Dimmesdale, and the searing of heart in Hester, point to a social state in which purity will exist in connection with a mercy which shall throw no artificial obstacles in the way of a sinner's repentance.

Another fact more perplexing to a Christian moralist is here illustrated,—that a certain experience in sin enlarges the spiritual energies and the power to move the souls of men to noble results. The effects of Dimmesdale's preaching are perfectly credible, and moral, although he stood in false relations to those he addressed. True, the limitation at last came in his public exposure, yet we had almost said he could not have left his mark so deep upon the conscience of that community, had he lived and died otherwise. And Hester's error was the downward step in the winding stair leading to a higher elevation. This feature of the work, so far from being a blemish, is only a proof of the writer's insight, and healthy moral philosophy. He has portrayed sin with all its terrible consequences, yet given the other side of a problem which must excite our wonder, rebuke our shallow theories, and direct us to an all-embracing, infinite love for its solution.

In the character of Chillingworth appears another law,—the danger of cherishing a merely intellectual interest in the human soul. The

Leech, is a man of diseased mental acuteness, changed to a demon by yielding to an unholy curiosity. Seduced by the opportunity to know the nature of Dimmesdale, he is drawn to the discovery of the fatal secret,—a discovery which he is not strong enough to bear. His character and fate are an awful rebuke to that insatiable desire for soul-gazing, which is the besetting devil of many men. Our human nature is too sacred to be applied to such uses, and he who enters its guarded enclosure from the mere impulse for intellectual analysis, risks his own soul as surely as he outrages that of another.

Passing from these points of the book to its general moral tone, we find the author's delineation of spiritual laws equalled by his healthy and profound religious sentiment. In justice to human nature, he shows all the palliative circumstances to guilt, while he is sternly true to eternal facts of morality. It is not improper for a novelist to do the former, if he leave the latter uppermost in the mind of the reader. Throughout the work we have not once detected the writer in a concession to that sophistical philanthropy, which, from the vantage-ground of mercy, would pry up the foundation of all religious obligation. His book is a fine contrast to the volumes of a class of modern novelists, who with a large developement of the humane sentiment, and an alarming briskness at catching the palliations of transgression, seem to have lost the sense of immutable moral distinctions. One side of Mr. Hawthorne's mind would furnish the heads of several first class French romancers. It may be that some of his statements on the side of destiny are too strong, and that human will appears to have a play too limited in his world, yet we look upon such passages rather as exaggerations of his idea of the omnipotence of God's law, than as indications of an irreligious fatalism.

We have already noticed the tendency to a symbolical view of nature and life, in this author's genius. In "The Scarlet Letter," it supplies the complete frame-work of the story—the age and social state in which the drama is cast being merely subsidiary to it. The gleam of the symbolical letter invests every object with a typical aspect. The lonely shores along which the minister walked, the wood in which he met Hester, the pillory and the street lit up by Mr. Wilson's lantern, are seen in this mysterious relation to the characters and plot of the story. But all the symbolism of the tale concentrates in the witch-child, Pearl. She seems to absorb and render back, by each development of her versatile being, the secret nature of every thing with which she comes in contact. She is the microcosm of the whole history with its surroundings. As a poetical creation, we know not where to look for her equal in modern literature. She is the companion of Mignon and Little Nell,[3] more original in conception than either, if not as strong in her hold upon our affections.

As a work of art, this book has great merits, shaded by a few conspicuous faults. We cannot too much admire the skill with which

---

3. Child character in Charles Dickens's *The Old Curiosity Shop* (1841). Mignon: a fairylike child in Goethe's *Wilhelm Meister's Apprentice* (1796).

the tangled skein of counteracting law and character is unravelled, the compact arrangement and suggestive disposition of the parts. The analysis of character is also inimitable, and the style is a fit dress for the strange and terrible history it rehearses. Yet we shall be disappointed if we look for any remarkable delineation of character, or portraiture of historical manners. There is a certain ghastliness about the people and life of the book, which comes from its exclusively subjective character and absence of humor. The world it describes is untrue to actual existence; for, although such a tragedy may be acting itself in many a spot upon earth, yet it is hidden more deeply beneath the surface of existence than this, modified by a thousand trivialities, and joys, and humorous interludes of humanity. No puritan city ever held such a throng as stalks through the "Scarlet Letter;" even in a well conducted mad-house, life is not so lurid and intense. The author's love for symbolism occasionally amounts to a ridiculous melodramatic perversity, as when it fathers such things as the minister's hand over his heart, and the hideous disfigurement of his bosom, Dame Hibbins from Gov. Bellingham's window screeching after Hester to go into the forest and sign the black man's book, and the meteoric "A" seen upon the sky during the mid-night vigil.

* * *

[JANE SWISSHELM]

From the *Saturday Visiter*†

This appears to be *the* romance of the day, and is decidedly a curiosity. The author opens with a most humorous description of the Custom House at Salem, and its numerous officers, including himself, during his time of service, or rather leisure, in the establishment. While there employed in serving our mutual uncle Samuel, he spent a portion of his time burrowing amongst a pile of old manuscript which had accumulated in one of the unfinished rooms, and one day found a roll in which he discovered a bit of old worm-eaten scarlet embroidery, which had once been in the form of the letter A. The manuscript was found to contain an outline history of this curious shred; and our author tells of his many futile endeavors to weave of this material a romance. When he was about giving up in despair, Gen. Taylor's election sealed his political death; he was released from the task of doing nothing, and then comes the story. We incline to think much of the fame of the book was acquired by the introduction, which contains most amusing portraits of persons still living, or recently dead, and many decided political hits. But the tale itself is unique, and told in a most masterly manner.

It opens with a description of the jail at Boston in the early times, its dingy walls and iron-barred portal, with the wild rose-bush which grew

† From the *Saturday Visiter* (Sept. 28, 1850), 146.

close by. On a bright morning a solemn and expectant crowd had assembled here, from whose looks and demeanor one might have expected an execution. Presently from the dingy doorway the Beadle comes, leading forward a woman of commanding mien and surpassing beauty, clad in sombre gray, and on her bosom the letter A blazing in embroidery of scarlet and gold. In her arms she carried an infant of two months, which, upon seeing the crowd, she clasps so as to cover the badge upon her breast. Then, as if remembering the folly of covering one emblem of her disgrace with another, she set the child on one arm, and with a firm step proceeded to the pillory, which she ascended, and where she was secured in the usual position which prevented the hiding of the face. Here for many hours she sat bearing the reproving looks of the assembled throng, and listening to lectures from the clergy and elders of the church, and exhortations to reveal the name of her partner in sin. This she refused, and the Rev. Arthur Dimmesdale, her pastor, a young man of great beauty and talent, and of commanding reputation for sanctity, is called upon to address her, which he does in a most impressive speech, begging her to name him who had caused her fall, and thus aid him in coming to repentance—reminding her that as he was too weak to acknowledge his sin she would do him a great service by preventing his living in hypocrisy, &c. &c.—to all which she replies by a short and peremptory refusal to implicate any one. He turns away with an apostrophe to the constancy of woman, which leads the reader to suspect he himself is the sinner thus screened; but of this the spectators never dream; none except one old man who has just arrived with an Indian, that comes to receive a ransom for him who has long been his prisoner. This old man, Hester Prynne, the heroine on the scaffold, sees and recognizes as her husband, a preacher, whom she had preceded to the colony two years, and who had been thought dead. When she is released from the pillory and taken back to prison, the old man visits her in the character of physician, and endeavors to wring from her the name of her seducer. She is firm on this point, but finally promises under oath not to reveal their previous connection, but to permit him to live under an assumed name. He already suspected Rev. Dimmesdale, and in the character of physician and friend devoted his life to a most subtle and fiend-like vengeance. When Hester is released from prison she takes up her abode in a lonely cabin on the seaside, where she maintains herself and child by needlework. Her poetic imagination and inventive genius find outlet in her employment, and her embroidery becomes the fashion. Her child is a perfect incarnation of the spirit of beauty—a wild, fitful, impulsive little sprite, who was even in babyhood attracted by the blazing insignia on her mother's sombre dress. This becomes a bitter portion of Hester's punishment, and every fit of passion in little Pearl the author attributes to the circumstances of her birth—paints the child's fitful spirit as a mark of the Divine displeasure, on account of the law broken by her parents. Whenever mother and child appear they are greeted by the Puritans, old and young, with cold and silent contempt, or hootings and epithets of infamy. If they appeared in church, all shrank from them, and the language of every one was, "Come not near me! I am holier than thou!" In no crowd did Hester stand in fear of being jostled. She was the moral leper whom none might dare to touch—the blazing emblem of the virtuous indignation of an entire community. Yet Hester went quietly on her way. Was any sick, or suffering in great distress, Hester was there to minister to every want. Even scorn and insults from those she aided, did not drive her from their side while aid was wanted, but that time past she never recognized them more. Did gratitude prompt them to notice her kindly in public, she laid her finger on the scarlet letter—the emblem of her shame, and passed on in silence. So the years sped, and after a while she acquired the title of "our Hester," and many said the A upon her breast meant Able, she was so strong to assist and comfort. In the mean time poor Dimmesdale underwent most terrible penance from the serpent-cunning of his old tormentor—the lashings of conscience, and the enthusiastic admiration of his parishioners. He becomes a monomaniac, and one night at midnight and during a storm, he goes and mounts the pillory, there alone and unseen to undergo the ordeal Hester had passed. Here Hester and Pearl find him as they return from a death-bed. They go up and sit with him there, and the old doctor comes to witness the scene. This showed Hester the state of abject misery to which her weak lover was reduced, and she resolves to free him from the fangs of the old serpent, the doctor. So she meets him in the forest and reveals the identity of the doctor and her former husband—advises, urges him to fly to Europe, and offers to accompany him. A plan is fixed upon, and he falls into a state of fiendish excitement, which to us appears somewhat preposterous. He is strangely impelled to blaspheme and swear, indulge in brutal jests, and mock at every thing he believes to be sacred! In this frame of mind he composes a sermon to be preached on the occasion of the installation of a new governor. This sermon is a miracle, and electrifies collected thousands. In the crowd without stands Hester, at the foot of the pillory, within sound of his voice, and surrounded by the circle of infamy which kept all from approaching within some yards. Here she learns their plan of flight has been discovered and frustrated by the old doctor, and stood in her despair when her lover came out of the church, tottering and pale, surrounded by admiring, almost worshipping thousands. When he sees Hester he approaches and asks her to aid him in ascending the scaffold. They and Pearl go up, and there to the electrified crowd he proclaims his guilt, and dies. The old doctor had now nothing to live for, and soon died, leaving Pearl heiress to a large fortune. Pearl's nature appears changed from the time of her father's death, and she becomes gentle, affectionate—comprehensible. She and her mother disappear for some years, and then Hester returns to the cabin alone. It is supposed from signs that Pearl is the wife of some nobleman in a foreign land, but Hester voluntarily returns, takes up her badge of shame, lives and dies in the cabin by the sea side, and finally sleeps beside her lover.

When one has read the book the query is, "what did the author mean! What moral lesson did he want to inculcate? What philosophy did he want to teach?"

If he meant to teach the sinfulness of Hester's sin—the great and divine obligation and sanctity of a legal marriage contract, and the monstrous depravity of a union sanctioned only by affection, his book is the most sublime failure of the age. Hester Prynne stands morally, as Saul did physically amongst his contemporaries, the head and shoulders taller than the tallest. She is the most glorious creation of fiction that has ever crossed our path. We never dreamed of any thing so sublime as the moral force and grandeur of her character. Scott's Jeanie Deans sinks into insignificance beside her. Jane Eyer [sic] is a chip floating with the current of popular opinion, while Hester rows her boat up from the brink of Niagara, and lands at Buffalo as calm and self-possessed as ordinary people from a ride on the "raging canal." The Divines and Elders and Governors and Magistrates and honorably married dames of her day, look like pasteboard puppets beside breathing men and women, when they come in contact with "their Hester." What one instinctively blames her for is, that she did not save her poor imbecile lover from the insane persecutions of the old sinner who was putting him to death by slow tortures. She should have protected Dimmesdale as well as kept his secret. It was not like herself to desert him, and leave him in the embrace of such a wily old serpent.

As for the author's lame attempts to make Pearl a punishment sent to her mother, we never saw a mother who would not be happy to be so punished—never knew a child who did not give fifty times the evidence of being sent in wrath. If any argument, pro or con, could be drawn from Pearl, she was surely a special evidence of the Divine approbation of the law which governed her birth. If such a little "jet of flame" as Pearl can be considered a sign of a broken law, we do wonder what Hawthorne thinks of the royal idiots whose existence testifies to the validity and legality of the pompous marriage rites of Queens and Empresses?

If Hawthorne really wants to teach the lesson ostensibly written on the pages of his book, he had better try again. For our part if we knew there was such another woman as Hester Prynne in Boston now, we should travel all the way there to pay our respects, while the honorable characters of the book are such poor affairs it would scarce be worth while throwing a mud-ball at the best of them.

ROBERT S. LEVINE

Antebellum Feminists on Hawthorne: Reconsidering the Reception of *The Scarlet Letter*†

A number of antebellum feminists greatly admired *The Scarlet Letter*, but readers of the standard reception histories of Hawthorne would be unable to find a record of their responses. J. Donald Crowley's

† An essay written for this Norton Critical Edition; printed with the author's permission.

Nathaniel Hawthorne: The Critical Heritage includes only one selection from a nineteenth-century American woman writer, a review of *The Scarlet Letter* by Anne W. Abbott, the pious daughter of a Massachusetts clergyman. Gary Scharnhorst's *The Critical Response to Nathaniel Hawthorne's* The Scarlet Letter fails to include an example from any nineteenth-century American woman writer; and in the section on *The Scarlet Letter* in John L. Idol, Jr., and Buford Jones's *Nathaniel Hawthorne: The Contemporary Reviews*, the only response by an American woman writer (either in the reprinted reviews or the checklist of other reviews) is Anne W. Abbott's. The review by Abbott, which is regularly cited by Hawthorne critics, is worth our brief attention. Appearing in the *North American Review* shortly after the publication of *The Scarlet Letter*, Abbott's review offers an appreciation of Hawthorne's portrayal of "mental torpidity" in the prefatory "The Custom-House," but for the most part focuses on Hawthorne's failure to invest the novel with a proper Christian spirit. The initially appealing Hester Prynne, Abbott says, finally "disappoints us, and shows the dreamland origin and nature, when we were looking to behold a Christian." Abbott had hoped to find a truer Christian in Dimmesdale, but here, too, she is disappointed, proclaiming that "the Christian element . . . seems strangely wanting" in the minister. Though she is more tolerant and admiring of the book than most other writers of the religious press, there are no great differences between Abbott's response and, say, that of the clergyman Arthur Cleveland Coxe, who stated with respect to *The Scarlet Letter* in the *Church Review and Ecclesiastical Register*: "We protest against any toleration to a popular and gifted writer, when he perpetrates bad morals."[1]

In a useful recent volume, *Hawthorne and Women: Engendering and Expanding the Hawthorne Tradition*, the editors John L. Idol, Jr., and Melinda M. Ponder present essays that illuminate Hawthorne's interactions with women writers and intellectuals, such as Margaret Fuller and Elizabeth Palmer Peabody, and his influence on a range of women fiction writers, including Harriet Beecher Stowe, Elizabeth Stoddard, and Rebecca Harding Davis. But with only one important exception, which I will discuss below, this revisionary volume ultimately works to perpetuate the notion that there were virtually no antebellum feminists who responded to *The Scarlet Letter* in the wake of its publication, and that those women of the 1850s who did respond to Hawthorne's novels responded in the manner of Abbott. Thus Idol and Ponder assert in their introduction that the contemporary reviews of Hawthorne written by women "differ little from those written by men. In subjects treated, style, and perceptions of Hawthorne's genius and

---

1. [Anne W. Abbott], "The Scarlet Letter," *North American Review* 71 (July 1850), rpt. in *Nathaniel Hawthorne: The Contemporary Reviews*, ed. John L. Idol, Jr., and Buford Jones (New York: Cambridge UP, 1994), 129–30, and on pp. 241–49 of this Norton Critical Edition; [Arthur Cleveland Coxe], "The Writings of Hawthorne," *Church Review and Ecclesiastical Register* 3 (January 1851), rpt. in Idol and Jones, *Nathaniel Hawthorne*, 146, and on pp. 254–63 of this Norton Critical Edition. See also *Nathaniel Hawthorne: The Critical Heritage*, ed J. Donald Crowley (1970; rpt. London and New York: Routledge, 1997); and *The Critical Response to Nathaniel Hawthorne's* The Scarlet Letter, ed. Gary Scharnhorst (New York: Greenwood P, 1992).

character, women reviewers generally responded to Hawthorne's fiction as if they were integral members of the New England (or national) clerisy."[2]

Ironically, the apparent existence of only conventional responses to Hawthorne's romances from antebellum women writers has contributed to the notion that Hawthorne, seemingly ignored by more radical women, was as conventional and moralistic as the critics like Abbott who attacked him. In a recent polemic, *The Scarlet Mob of Scribblers: Rereading Hester Prynne*, Jamie Barlowe suggests as much, taking Hawthorne's conventionality as a given and thus excoriating male critics who "admire the duplicitous radical subversion of men like Nathaniel Hawthorne and hold up as a model his male fantasy of a radical, subversive woman, Hester Prynne."[3] But how "duplicitous" was Hawthorne in his conception of Hester as a subversive? Michael T. Gilmore has argued that Hester's "dissident side . . . associates her with antebellum feminism,"[4] and it is the contention of this reception study that Gilmore's view of such an association is no male fantasy. The noted antebellum feminists Jane Swisshelm, Amelia Bloomer, Grace Greenwood, and Charlotte Forten all admired *The Scarlet Letter*, and yet their responses to the novel have not made a mark on the historical record. Some of the fault may lie with the nature of the "contemporary responses" book, for such books tend to focus on full-length reviews at the expense of shorter reviews and different forms of contemporary responses, such as letters and journals or essays not principally devoted to reviewing particular works. In her polemic, Barlowe attacks what she regards as a male Hawthorne industry for overlooking the responses of twentieth-century women writers to *The Scarlet Letter*. One could argue similarly that, with respect to the responses of antebellum feminists, the predominately male critics of twentieth-century Hawthorne studies (and women critics as well, including Barlowe) did not care to take note of, or did not know how to look for, such responses. How else to explain the neglect until 1999 (and beyond) of the popular writer Jane Swisshelm's extensive review of *The Scarlet Letter*, which is among the most incisive short essays on the novel ever published?

Jane Grey Swisshelm (1815–1884) was born Jane Grey Cannon in Pittsburgh and emerged as a major voice in women's rights, antislavery, and temperance reform. In 1836 she married the Methodist farmer James Swisshelm, a man she came to regard as a tyrant. She

2. John L. Idol, Jr., and Melinda M. Ponder, eds., *Hawthorne and Women: Engendering and Expanding the Hawthorne Tradition* (Amherst: U of Massachusetts P, 1999), 13.
3. Jamie Barlowe, *The Scarlet Mob of Scribblers: Rereading Hester Prynne* (Carbondale: Southern Illinois UP, 2000), 18. On the important role of male elites in the making of Hawthorne's canonical reputation, see also Jane Tompkins, "Masterpiece Theater: The Politics of Hawthorne's Literary Reputation," in *Sensational Designs: The Cultural Work of American Fiction, 1790–1860* (New York: Oxford UP, 1985) and Richard Brodhead, *The School of Hawthorne* (New York: Oxford UP, 1986).
4. Michael T. Gilmore, "Hawthorne and the Making of the Middle Class," in *Rethinking Class: Literary Studies and Social Formations*, ed. Wai Chee Dimock and Gilmore (New York: Columbia UP, 1994), 227 [p. 607 in this Norton Critical Edition].

left him on several occasions and in the early 1840s began writing feminist essays for local newspapers. In 1847 she founded and edited the Pittsburgh *Saturday Visiter* [*sic*] as an antislavery and women's rights paper, building a circulation of around 6,000 subscribers by 1850. Swisshelm remarked in her autobiography that men were outraged that "a woman had started a political paper," but according to her probably overstated testimony, the "*Visiter* had thousands of readers scattered over every State and Territory in the nation, in England and the Canadas. It was quoted more perhaps than any other paper in the country."[5] In 1852 she sold her interest in the paper while remaining an important contributor. Continuing to find life with her husband intolerable, she left him for good in 1857, moving with her six-year-old daughter to St. Cloud, Minnesota, where she founded the *St. Cloud Visiter*, one of the most vigorously antislavery newspapers in the western territories. Unfazed when a proslavery group destroyed her printing press in 1858, she started up the *St. Cloud Democrat* in its place. In 1863 she volunteered to serve as a nurse in the Union army, and after the war she retired to Swissvale, Pennsylvania, where she eventually wrote her memoir, *Half a Century* (1880).

As a writer and social critic, Swisshelm is best on display in her most popular book, *Letters to Country Girls* (1853), which collects a number of her weekly opinion pieces from the *Saturday Visiter*. Deploying a comic, aggressive, "impudent" voice similar to that of the popular columnist Fanny Fern, Swisshelm sought to remedy what she termed the "masculine-superiority fever," "a deeply-rooted and unsightly cancer, which disfigures the entire face of the body-politic." Complaining of men's efforts to keep women at home in " 'a woman's place,' " Swisshelm asserted about women who attempt to do something more or different: "let her aspire to turn editor, public speaker, doctor, lawyer—take up any profession or avocation which is deemed honorable and requires talent, and O! bring the Cologne, get a cambric kerchief and a feather fan, unloose his corsets and take off his cravat!"[6] The same sort of spirited antipatriarchal energy informed her 1850 review of *The Scarlet Letter* in the September 28 issue of the Pittsburgh *Saturday Visiter*. That review had not been reprinted or even mentioned in Hawthorne criticism until 1999, when it was reprinted as an Appendix to Idol and Ponder's *Hawthorne and Women*. Oddly, Idol and Ponder supply no introduction to the review, no biographical or historical contextualization. Moreover, not one of the essays in the volume mentions the review, which seems to have had no impact on Idol and Ponder's conception of antebellum women's responses to Hawthorne's fiction as elaborated in their introduction. The review is thus both there and not there in *Hawthorne and Women*; I have transcribed the review from its

---

5. Jane Grey Swisshelm, *Half a Century* (Chicago: Jansen, McClurg & Company, 1880), 113, 123. For additional biographical background on Swisshelm, see *Crusader and Feminist: Letters of Jane Grey Swisshelm, 1858–1865*, ed. Arthur J. Larsen (1934; rpt. Westport, Connecticut: Hyperion P, 1976).
6. Jane G. Swisshelm, *Letters to Country Girls* (New York: John R. Riker, 1853), 79, 77, 78.

original source in the *Saturday Visiter* and it is printed in its entirety in this Norton Critical Edition.[7]

Swisshelm's review of *The Scarlet Letter* is notable for what could be termed its Hester-centric reading of the novel. Rather than morally condemn Hester, Swisshelm hails her as "the most glorious creation of fiction that has ever crossed our path,"[8] a woman who, in a world of timorous and judgmental men, bravely acts on her romantic and sexual desires. Thus Swisshelm begins her review by making it clear that the genius of Hawthorne's romance lies not in the gossipy and political "The Custom-House," but in the "unique" tale central to the novel itself, "told in a most masterly manner." Having made great claims for the novel, Swisshelm, following the conventions of the time, then launches into an extended, approximately 1,200-word reading of the plot, which of course is not simply a plot summary but a reorchestration of the story lines and motifs that had most engaged her, particularly Hester's refusal to succumb to a bad marriage. In her columns in the Pittsburgh *Saturday Visiter*, Swisshelm regularly insisted that marriage should be "a spirit union . . . designed to make one out of two" and thus railed against marriages in which women were subordinated to a brutal, unloving master.[9] Swisshelm's rehearsal of plot has little to say about Dimmesdale and Chillingworth. Instead, the emphasis is on Hester's sexuality, her "commanding mien and surpassing beauty," her relation to Pearl, and her efforts to negotiate her place in the hostile Puritan community. There is considerable psychological acuity in Swisshelm's reading of Hester's efforts to find new outlets for her "poetic imagination and inventive genius" and sympathy for the plight of the reviled adulterous mother and for the child herself. As Swisshelm nicely remarks about the transformed Pearl at the end of the novel: "she becomes gentle, affectionate—comprehensible." Swisshelm remains puzzled and even annoyed by Hawthorne's depiction of Hester's voluntary return to Boston to once again take up the scarlet letter. Why would Hester capitulate in such a way? The implicit answer supplied by Swisshelm helps to keep the novel true to her sense of its romantic vision: the return will enable Hester at her death to "sleep[ ] beside her lover."

In her review, then, Swisshelm celebrates a novel that, perhaps despite itself, depicts the bankruptcy of a loveless marriage, raises questions about a woman's legal obligation to remain confined within such a marriage, and supports a woman's desire for sexual fulfillment (even if the result is a child out of wedlock). My "perhaps" is deliberate here, for it gets at Swisshelm's own uncertainty about Hawthorne's didactic aims, as suggested by her repeated use of "if" when considering

---

7. See pp. 271–74. It needs to be noted that there are over twenty transcription errors in the 1999 reprinting of Swisshelm's review in Idol and Ponder's *Hawthorne and Women*, pp. 288–91. Among the errors are "is even" for "was even," "administer" for "minister," "the state of abject misery" for "the abject state," "persecutions" for "insane persecutions," and "no one" for "none."

8. All citations from Jane Swisshelm's "The Scarlet Letter" are from the original publication in the *Saturday Visiter* 28 Sept. 1850, 2 (p. 146 of the 1850 volume).

9. See the Pittsburgh *Saturday Visiter* 24 Nov. 1849, 2; and for Swisshelm's related comments on marriage, see her editorials in the *Saturday Visiter*, especially 1 June 1850, 27 July 1850, and 3 Aug. 1850.

whether his politics might more resemble someone like Anne Abbott's than her own. "If he meant to teach the sinfulness of Hester's sin— the great and divine obligation and sanctity of a legal marriage contract, and the monstrous depravity of a union sanctioned only by affection," she writes, "his book is the most sublime failure of the age." But she goes on to suggest that it would be absurd to condemn Hester as a sinner, drawing on Hawthorne's romance to support her argument. So perhaps Hawthorne did not mean to condemn her; perhaps he meant to argue for the "moral force and grandeur of [Hester's] character." As for the men of the novel, Swisshelm perceives little more than intolerant Puritan leaders, a "poor imbecile lover" (Dimmesdale), and an "insane . . . old sinner" (Chillingworth). "If," she comically writes, "such a little 'jet of flame' as Pearl can be considered a sign of a broken law, we do wonder what Hawthorne thinks of the royal idiots whose existence testifies to the validity and legality of the pompous marriage rites of Queens and Empresses." Instead of regarding Pearl as punishment for her mother's adulterous sexuality, Swisshelm, quite unlike Abbott, sees "Divine approbation of the law which governed her birth." When Swisshelm writes in her concluding paragraph that "[i]f Hawthorne really wants to teach the lesson ostensibly written on the pages of his book, he had better try again," the suggestion is that if Hawthorne did *not* want to teach that lesson, then he got things just right. Ultimately what Swisshelm emphasizes in *The Scarlet Letter* through her "if" 's is Hawthorne's conflict between his attraction to the subversive Hester and his desire to contain her. In her own way, Swisshelm anticipates by 125 years or so the critical insights of Nina Baym and other feminist readers of the novel who, in the words of Robert K. Martin, regard Hawthorne as speaking "his Romantic desire through Hester as he also speaks his sense of guilt and shame."[1] The shape of Hawthorne criticism over the course of the twentieth century could well have had a significantly different arc had more readers known of Swisshelm's pioneering review before 1999.

Swisshelm is not the only antebellum feminist neglected by Hawthorne scholars. Two months before Swisshelm published her review in the *Saturday Visiter*, there appeared an admiring literary notice of *The Scarlet Letter* in the July 1850 issue of Amelia Bloomer's *The Lily: A Ladies Journal, Devoted to Temperance and Literature*. I have been unable to find any mention of this evocative notice in Hawthorne bibliography or scholarship. Best known for her championing of dress reform for women (she promoted Turkish-style pantaloons, which came to be known as "Bloomers"), Amelia Jenks Bloomer (1818–1894) during most of her life as a reformer was primarily committed to temperance. From

1. Robert K. Martin, "Hester Prynne, *C'est Moi*: Nathaniel Hawthorne and the Anxieties of Gender," in *Engendering Men: The Question of Male Feminist Criticism*, ed. Joseph A. Boone and Michael Cadden (New York: Routledge, 1990), 129 [p. 521 in this Norton Critical Edition]. The only discussion of Swisshelm's review of *The Scarlet Letter* that I have been able to locate is in the historian Peter F. Walker's *Moral Choices: Memory, Desire, and Imagination in Nineteenth-Century American Abolition* (Baton Rouge: Louisiana State UP, 1978), 133–35. Walker reads the review, and indeed Swisshelm's entire career, mainly in terms of her troubled marriage; in his rendering, her political engagement is a kind of "symptom" of the marriage.

her feminist perspective, temperance reform promised to put a check on patriarchal power, which she conceived of both literally and metaphorically as a form of intoxication that threatened the stability of the home. Born Amelia Jenks in Homer, New York, she married the Quaker antislavery lawyer Dexter Bloomer in 1840, and shortly thereafter began contributing temperance writings to local newspapers and journals. She attended the Seneca Falls Woman's Rights Convention in 1848 and around the same time helped to form a women's temperance organization in Seneca Falls. One year later she founded *The Lily*, the second newspaper, after Swisshelm's, to be established and edited entirely by a woman. The paper had a subscription base of around 4,000 and remained a vigorous forum for women's reform causes until Bloomer sold the paper in 1855. Subsequently she moved to Iowa with her husband, where she continued her temperance work until her death in 1894.

Though *The Lily* announced itself as a journal devoted to temperance and literature, Bloomer printed virtually no literary reviews or notices. One of the few was of Hawthorne's *The Scarlet Letter*, which appeared on the front page of the issue of July 1850, followed immediately, on the front and second page, by a reprinting of Hawthorne's "A Rill from the Town-Pump." The notice, offered here in its entirety, came in the form of a letter from "T" to Amelia Bloomer:

> MRS. BLOOMER—The perusal of "The Scarlet Letter," a new work by NATHANIEL HAWTHORNE, has naturally recalled to mind the earlier productions by the same author. Some time ago some of his most beautiful sketches were collected and published, with the title of "Twice Told Tales," which have taken a high place among the literary works of our day, and would, alone, mark the author as one possessed of rare mental endowments. Although a writer of prose, Hawthorne always sees Nature with the eye of a poet, and yet, his descriptions are so accurate and finished, he may fairly be ranked among her true interpreters. His pictures have all the truthfulness of the Daguerreotype, and, at the same time, that warm and golden light upon them which the hand of genius alone can impart. Judging of the merits of the productions, from the impressions they have left upon me to this day, I may safely say one of the best is that entitled "A Rill from the Town Pump"; and I ask for it a place in your monthly, because, while it shows the peculiar power Hawthorne possesses of throwing a charm around even the commonest subject, it carries with it a lesson in morals which few can forget, and is, in fact, one of the best temperance lectures extant. "A Vision of the Fountain," another of his productions, which describes water gushing forth, pure and bright, from its home in the woods, untrammelled by the hand of art, yet adorned with the highest order of natural beauty, would not be inappropriate to your columns; but your readers shall first admire the speech supposed to have been delivered by a resident of the old town of Salem, Mass, the birth-place of at least one great orator.   T.[2]

2. *The Lily: A Ladies Journal, Devoted to Temperance and Literature*, 2 (1 July 1850): 49; "A Rill from the Town-Pump" appeared on pp. 49–50 (which were actually pp. 1–2 of the July issue).

Of course the large irony of this notice is that it identifies the worth of *The Scarlet Letter* in the very terms that Hawthorne in "The Custom-House" claims to have rejected: in relation to his popular "A Rill from the Town-Pump" (1835). For Bloomer, "T," and presumably other feminist-temperance women associated with *The Lily*, "Rill," in which a talking town pump makes a millennialist case for the value of pure water, was not simply a quaint, sentimental, evangelical, or "puritanical" piece of temperance writing, but a work that engaged issues of health, body, and gender. In short, "Rill" for these readers remained a charged aesthetic and political document well worth reprinting fifteen years after its initial publication. Hawthorne wrote "Rill" at a time when temperance reform was predominately in the hands of elites who were concerned about controlling male workers' drinking at the newly developing factories. Bloomer republished the sketch shortly after the Seneca Falls Convention had helped to redefine temperance as a major concern of women reformers.

To a certain extent, then, it can be argued that Bloomer, through "T" 's notice and the reprinting of "A Rill from the Town-Pump," appropriated *The Scarlet Letter* for her own feminist-temperance purposes, but such an argument would obscure the fact that Hawthorne's antipatriarchal politics of the body may not have been considerably different from hers. In *The Lily*, Bloomer printed numerous accounts of the connections between male drinking and abusive husbands, beginning with the inaugural issue of January 1, 1849, when she remarked in a squib on the "fearful sight" of a young woman marrying a man "who loves to linger around the wine cup": "wealth, talents, fame can never gild the drunkard's home, nor sooth the sorrows of a drunkard's wife." Jane Swisshelm herself wrote in the October 1850 issue of *The Lily* that the "drunkard," by giving "himself up to a base, sordid selfish appetite . . . [is] a monster!"[3] In *The Scarlet Letter* Hawthorne works metaphorically to present Chillingworth as a kind of monster driven by an intemperate appetite for revenge. In his next novel, *The House of the Seven Gables* (1851), Hawthorne conceptualizes issues of temperance more explicitly in the manner of writers for *The Lily*, portraying Judge Pyncheon as a husband literally intoxicated by such stimulants as wine and coffee, who reveals the full extent of his intemperate patriarchal authority immediately after his marriage: "the lady got her death-blow in the honey-moon, and never smiled again, because her husband compelled her to serve him with coffee, every morning, at his bedside, in token of fealty to her liege-lord and master."[4] When Hawthorne mentions in the same paragraph that the wife

---

3. *The Lily* 1 (1 Jan. 1849): 3; "Mrs. Swisshelm's Opinion of Drunkards," *The Lily*, 2 (1 Oct. 1850): 78. On women and temperance, see Carol Mattingly, ed., *Water Drops from Women Writers: A Temperance Reader* (Carbondale: Southern Illinois UP, 2001). Though Swisshelm would contribute a number of pieces to *The Lily*, she remained distrustful of two key aspects of Bloomer's feminism. She believed that Bloomer's dress reforms mistakenly attempted to cover up what she regarded as the very real differences between the sexes; and she believed that Bloomer put too much emphasis on women's rights at the expense of antislavery; see Swisshelm, *Half a Century*, chap. 29.

4. Nathaniel Hawthorne, *The House of the Seven Gables*, ed. William Charvat et al. (Columbus: Ohio State UP, 1965), 123.

died three or four years later, the suggestion is that her death can be taken as a form of rebellious suicide.

The notice on *The Scarlet Letter* in *The Lily*, along with the reprinting of "Rill," would thus have worked to focus attention on the politics of gender in the novel, creating sympathy for Hester as a "victim" of intemperate patriarchal authority. Though "T" does not develop an explicit argument along those lines, we can extrapolate such a reading from her praise of "natural beauty," which in the novel is regularly associated with Hester. For "T," that which is most valued is "water gushing forth, untrammelled by the hand of art, yet adorned with the highest order of natural beauty." In *The Scarlet Letter*, there is a clear divide between the artifice of the town and the naturalness of the woods, with the town regularly associated with the patriarchal authority of the Puritan masters and the woods with the antipatriarchal revolutionism of Mistress Hibbins and Hester. True, the fact that Hester is also an artist makes the gender dichotomy that I am suggesting somewhat tenuous. But in her celebration of the natural, "T" does suggest an alliance with the Hester whose "beauty shone out" on the scaffold at the opening of the novel and who seven years later manages to restore that natural beauty during her forest walk with Dimmesdale. In this great revolutionary moment, Hester tosses aside the scarlet letter and declares to Dimmesdale, "What we did had a consecration of its own." At which point, Hawthorne wryly points to the dynamic of gender and interpretation by remarking that the "whole richness of her beauty came back from what men call the irrevocable past."[5] In her ability in the woods to state her views and desires and annunciate a millennial vision of freedom, Hester has, to push the metaphor just a bit, achieved a natural gushing forth of feeling that links her to the purity celebrated by "T" in both "Rill" and "A Vision of the Fountain."

As the favorable notice in *The Lily* suggests, Hawthorne was regarded by some activist women as a critic of patriarchal authority. But did this writer who spoke to women who were concerned about the slavery of the bottle speak to women concerned about slavery on the southern plantation? Jane Swisshelm, who advocated both temperance and antislavery, was certainly responsive to *The Scarlet Letter*, even as she suspected that Hawthorne may have fled from some of the radical implications of his novel. Was such a flight the result of his contradictory relation to slavery? In an influential article of 1986, Jonathan Arac linked the compromise of the novel's ending (Hester's willingness to return to Boston and keep herself in a sort of irresolute relation to patriarchal civil authority) to the Compromise of 1850, which was generally supported by Hawthorne's friends in the Democratic party. In the compromise of *The Scarlet Letter* and in the Compromise of 1850, Arac argues, there was an effort to balance conservative and radical tendencies into a somewhat mystified func-

---

5. Nathaniel Hawthorne, *The Scarlet Letter*, pp. 40, 126, and 130 in this Norton Critical Edition.

tional order.[6] Far more critical of Hawthorne's Democratic politics is Jean Fagan Yellin, who criticizes him for his failure to "exhort his readers to act to end human bondage, as William Lloyd Garrison had been doing in his newspaper the *Liberator* every Friday since 1831."[7] In her essay "Hawthorne and the Slavery Question," Yellin adduces evidence of Hawthorne's racism and unwillingness to challenge slavery head-on, but her comparison to Garrison is tendentious, given that virtually no antebellum white American author was engaged in antislavery at the level of Garrison (who, it is worth recalling, was regarded by Frederick Douglass and others as a paternalistic racist).[8] Viewed from our present moment, Hawthorne indeed failed the test of slavery, but viewed from within the context of his times, there is compelling evidence that feminist-abolitionists held him in high regard, perhaps because they didn't see him as such a failure after all. I will be examining two antislavery women writers who praised *The Scarlet Letter*, but first it would be useful to consider a notable attack on Hawthorne's politics of slavery, which appeared in the leading African American newspaper of the time.

Yellin's criticisms of Hawthorne were anticipated in an anonymous squib in an 1855 issue of *Frederick Douglass' Paper*. At the conclusion of the essay, which praised Emerson for his antislavery politics, the writer (perhaps Douglass) states: "The fact is, that with the exception of Mr. Hawthorne, every New England author who is likely to be heard of a hundred years hence, is in favor of freedom."[9] During the 1850s such criticism of Hawthorne's politics was rather unusual, in part, I would argue, because his fictions suggested a propensity in favor of freedom, with the mesmerical motifs of *The House of the Seven Gables* and *The Blithedale Romance*, for instance, conveying a genuine revulsion towards patriarchal enslavers. The propensity for freedom discernible in his romances was not merely rhetorical, for there is evidence that Hawthorne, despite his hostility toward abolitionists, was opposed to slavery. In a letter to Longfellow of 8 May 1851, Hawthorne voiced his objection to the Fugitive Slave Law, and in his 1852 campaign biography of Franklin Pierce, he called slavery one of the "evils" of the world. Despite these beliefs, Hawthorne, as he stated in an infamous passage in the Pierce biography, argued that the actual job of ending slavery should be left to the mysterious workings of "divine Providence."[1] Hawthorne's resistance to political antislavery had much to do with the fact that his closest friends dating back to his Bowdoin College days were active members of the Democratic party—a party that, it is worth remembering, despite its support for the Com-

6. Jonathan Arac, "The Politics of *The Scarlet Letter*," in *Ideology and Classic American Literature*, ed. Sacvan Bercovitch and Myra Jehlen (New York: Cambridge UP, 1986), 247–66.
7. Jean Fagan Yellin, "Hawthorne and the Slavery Question," in *A Historical Guide to Nathaniel Hawthorne*, ed. Larry J. Reynolds (New York: Oxford UP, 2001), 137.
8. See Frederick Douglass, *My Bondage and My Freedom*, ed. William L. Andrews (1855; Urbana: U of Illinois P, 1987), 220.
9. *Frederick Douglass' Paper* 23 Feb. 1855, 2.
1. See Hawthorne, *The Letters, 1843–1853*, ed. Thomas Woodson, L. Neal Smith, and Norman Holmes Pearson (Columbus: Ohio State UP, 1985), 431; Hawthorne, *Life of Franklin Pierce* (1852), in *Miscellanies: Biographical and Other Sketches and Letters by Nathaniel Hawthorne* (Boston and New York: Houghton Mifflin Company, 1900), 166 (p. 234 of this Norton Critical Edition).

promise of 1850, was radical at its inception in its hostility toward class privilege. As Yellin points out, Hawthorne's friendship with Pierce in particular got him into trouble during the Civil War, when he chose to dedicate *Our Old Home* (1863) to his friend, who was rightly regarded in antislavery circles as having been sympathetic to southern slave interests during his presidency. Hawthorne's Unionist acquaintances were appalled by this apparent sign of disloyalty, as they had been appalled a year earlier by his skeptical remarks on Abraham Lincoln in his 1862 *Atlantic* essay, "Chiefly about War-Matters."

The relatively mild contempt expressed toward Hawthorne in *Frederick Douglass' Paper* is actually not representative of the views of the temperance women and feminist-abolitionists who commented on *The Scarlet Letter* during the 1850s, and it is notable that at least two antislavery women writers of the period, Grace Greenwood and Charlotte Forten, regarded Hawthorne favorably within the context of their own antislavery politics. Greenwood's remarks on *The Scarlet Letter* appeared in the *National Era*, the antislavery newspaper based in Washington, D.C., which would become famous when it serialized *Uncle Tom's Cabin* in 1851–52. Hawthorne was treated with great respect in this paper throughout the 1850s, beginning with an enthusiastic review of *The Scarlet Letter* in an April 1850 issue. Because the anonymous review (perhaps written by Greenwood) has hitherto not been noted or reprinted in the various collections of contemporary responses to Hawthorne's fiction, I offer it here in its entirety:

> The introductory chapter to this work, containing a description of the Custom House, its life and inmates, reminds one of the happiest and quaintest portraitures of Charles Lamb. The Romance itself is complete in design and execution. Simple in its action, with few incidents, and few characters, it is yet rich in thought, in feeling, and in philosophy. The story is one of crime and its punishment, dating back a century ago, the scene being laid in the colony of Massachusetts. The characters, in the exhibition of which the author displays extraordinary psychological skill, are Hester Prynne, a woman, young, beautiful, proud, daring, full of passion, of inexhaustible energy of character, branded with a crime that banishes her from the sympathies of society, amidst which she lives and moves, all alone, with the symbol of her shame blazoned upon her:—a minister, of brilliant endowments, fearing God, loving man; but suffering for years the gnawing pangs of deadly remorse for a sin, he would not repeat, but dares not confess—and a student, advanced in years, once amiable, devoted to the pursuit of knowledge, but transformed into a fiend by cherishing and feeding a terrible appetite for revenge, which in the end works the death of the minister through the influence of spiritual torture, utterly ruins himself, and blasts the earthly hopes of the unfortunate woman. In the subtle, thrilling analysis of these characters, and of the workings of the passions and sentiments by which they were controlled, consists the extraordinary power of this singular romance.[2]

2. "THE SCARLET LETTER," *National Era* 4. 171 (11 April 1850): 59.

As would be the case in Swisshelm's review published later in the year, the anonymous writer celebrates Hawthorne's psychological acuity, focusing on the splendor of his creation of Hester Prynne. The clear expression of sympathy for Hester works to condemn a society that fails to offer a similar sympathy, and thus, by extension, raises questions about reviewers like Anne Abbott, who ultimately want to bring the novel into the realm of a conventional Christian moral ethic. The review is extraordinary, then, for its utter lack of moral judgment on the behavior of a woman who has an adulterous affair resulting in a child. Moreover, the antislavery reviewer's description of Hester as "branded" implicitly links her to the slaves, many of whom were branded, thus anticipating by around 150 years Leland S. Person's argument that Hester "resembles the slave mothers like Harriet Jacobs," and that "in representing her maternally, Hawthorne shows more sympathy and ironic understanding of the politics of her motherhood than his nineteenth- and twentieth-century detractors have allowed."[3]

Later in 1850, around the time of Swisshelm's review, the *National Era* printed two travel letters that commented favorably on *The Scarlet Letter*. These were the work of the writer Grace Greenwood, the pen name of Sarah Jane Lippincott (1823–1904). Born Sara Jane Clarke in Pompey, New York, she began writing under the pen name of Grace Greenwood in the early 1840s, publishing essays on domesticity and reform in *Godey's Lady's Book* and numerous other newspapers and journals. She opposed the Mexican War, capital punishment, African colonization, and slavery. Her poem "The Leap from the Long Bridge" (1851) helped to inspire William Wells Brown's *Clotel* (1853), the first published novel by an African American; and during the Civil War she earned President Lincoln's praise for her visits to Union hospitals and camps. Her antislavery politics were on display in many of her letters to the *National Era*, but she also published letters that simply focused on her travels. In a letter of 18 September 1850 from Lynn, Massachusetts, for instance, Greenwood described her pleasant visit to the Gloucester seashore and her subsequent visit to Boston, where she attended the theater and visited the studio of the painter C. G. Thompson. At the studio, she admired his great portrait of Hawthorne, and her reflections on Hawthorne's physiognomy allowed her to comment on his widely discussed recent novel, *The Scarlet Letter*. She writes of Thompson's oil painting:

> In the deep, dark eye of Hawthorne lies the secret of that wonderful mastery—that half-beautiful, half-fearful power—that strange, weird-like fascination, which so enchain one in "THE SCARLET LETTER"; while, in the warm fulness and quiet scorn of the lips, we re-read that memorable "Preface," wherein the play of delicate fancy and a delicious humor alternated with cold, sharp strokes of merciless satire.
> Mr. Hawthorne is, according to this portrait, a singularly hand-

3. Leland S. Person, "The Dark Labyrinth of Mind: Hawthorne, Hester, and the Ironies of Racial Mothering." *Studies in American Fiction* 29 (2001): 44 (p. 669 in this Norton Critical Edition).

some man, but his face wears an expression of unconsciousness, or rather disdain, of his beauty.[4]

Granted, Greenwood doesn't say all that much about Hawthorne in this short description. But it is worth noticing that Greenwood and, as we will see, Charlotte Forten place great emphasis on what can be learned about an author by looking at his portrait. As in Hawthorne's *House*, there is a sense that a portrait, whether a painting or a daguerreotype, can supply access to something more "natural," "real," and essential than the living, breathing personage viewed in the midst of daily activities. Looking into Hawthorne's dark eye, Greenwood discovers the "secret" of the "wonderful mastery" that "so enchain one" in *The Scarlet Letter*. In the context of the aesthetic vocabulary of the time, that enchaining power would have been the power of sympathy. I would posit, then, on the basis of this short reflection, that Greenwood's viewing of the portrait helped her better to understand Hawthorne's ability to sympathize with a figure like Hester Prynne who, like Hawthorne at the Custom-House, was a "beauty" who became a victim of patriarchal authority. Two months later Greenwood presented patriarchal authority in terms more specific to slavery in a highly political letter from Boston of 9 November 1850. In the midst of a long letter on the injustices of the Fugitive Slave Bill, Greenwood took the occasion not to lambaste Hawthorne for his Democratic politics, but to note his forthcoming publications: "I have a bit of literary intelligence for you. The title of the forthcoming romance, by the author of THE SCARLET LETTER, is 'THE HOUSE OF SEVEN GABLES [*sic*].' Is it not quaint and Hawthornish? Another work by this most delightful author is a volume for children, entitled 'TRUE STORIES FROM HISTORY AND BIOGRAPHY.' This Ticknor is bringing out in fine style."[5]

The fact that Hawthorne and Greenwood had the same publisher in George Ticknor may help to explain Greenwood's graciousness toward Hawthorne and, in the early 1850s, Hawthorne's toward Greenwood. (Hawthorne would eventually have unkind things to say about Greenwood in letters of 1854 and 1856.) Hawthorne, for instance, wrote Greenwood on 17 April 1852 to praise her 1852 *Greenwood Leaves: A Collection of Sketches and Letters, Second Series*, commenting that her letters "are the best that any woman writes—of course, better than any man's." In her excellent assessment of the relationship between Greenwood and Hawthorne, Nina Baym speculates that Hawthorne may have not even read *Greenwood Leaves*, and had simply offered his praise as a form of male noblesse oblige. But she goes on to argue that if this man, who regularly instructed his wife that women should remain out of the public eye, had read *Leaves*, "he could not possibly

4. "Letters from Grace Greenwood. From the Shore. Lynn, September 18, 1850," *National Era* 4.195 (26 Sept. 1850): 155. For a reproduction of Cephas Thompson's magnificent 1850 oil painting of Hawthorne, see Rita K. Gollin, *Portraits of Nathaniel Hawthorne: An Iconography* (DeKalb: Northern Illinois UP, 1983), 30.
5. "Letter of Grace Greenwood. Boston, November 9, 1850," *National Era* 4.203 (21 Nov. 1850): 18.

have escaped awareness of their openly political and fundamentally public nature." Baym thus concludes that there is much more in common between Hawthorne and Greenwood than Hawthorne would want to concede. I would add to Baym's analysis another reason for Hawthorne's warm letter of 1852 to Greenwood: that even if he had not read *Greenwood Leaves*, he would have read or heard about Greenwood's flattering mentions of him in the *National Era*. (*Greenwood Leaves* reprints a number of Greenwood's letters in the *National Era*, but *not* the two she wrote about Hawthorne.) And I would underscore the significance of the fact that those flattering mentions appeared in a journal devoted to antislavery.[6]

The African American diarist and antislavery reformer Charlotte L. Forten [Grimké] was also quite taken with *The Scarlet Letter*, commenting on it both in her private journals and in a published newspaper report on Salem. The granddaughter of the prosperous sailmaker and antislavery activist James Forten, Charlotte Forten (1837–1914) was born in Philadelphia and raised by her father, Robert Forten, an abolitionist whose wife died three years after Charlotte's birth. Objecting to Philadelphia's segregated schools, Robert sent Charlotte to Salem in 1853, and there she lived with the antislavery activists Charles Lenox Remond and his wife, Amy Matilda Remond, while attending Higginson Grammar School. She began keeping her diary in 1854 and published several poems and essays in the late 1850s. Moving back and forth between Salem and Philadelphia, she taught for a while at Epes Grammar School in Salem, and eventually got a federal teaching position in 1862 at Port Royal, St. Helena Island, where she taught recently freed South Carolina slaves. Until her diaries were published in the twentieth century, her most famous piece of writing was her two-part essay about that teaching experience, "Life on the Sea Islands," which appeared in the May and June 1864 issues of the *Atlantic Monthly*.[7] She married the Presbyterian minister Francis J. Grimké in 1878 and eventually settled with him in Washington, D.C., where she remained active in African American political and intellectual affairs.

Shortly after moving to Salem in 1853, Forten became a close friend of Hawthorne's sister Elizabeth. Perhaps because of that friendship, Forten's journals register a regular, enthusiastic reading of Hawthorne, taking special note of *The Scarlet Letter*, *The House of the Seven Gables*, and *Tanglewood Tales*, even as she is responding to the political controversies of the day. Outraged by the Massachusetts Supreme Court's ruling against the fugitive slave Anthony Burns,

6. Hawthorne, *The Letters, 1843–1853*, 532; Nina Baym, "Again and Again, the Scribbling Women," in *Hawthorne and Women*, 31–32. See also Hawthorne, *The Letters, 1853–1856*, ed. Thomas Woodson, L. Neal Smith, and Norman Holmes Pearson (Columbus: Ohio State UP, 1987), 166, 456–57. Throughout the 1850s, the *National Era* would continue to write only good things about Hawthorne, even noting in 1857, after he left his Democratic patronage position as consul to Liverpool: "[A]s the 'Scarlet Letter' followed his retirement from one office, we may expect, as an early result of this resignation, a book in no wise inferior to that remarkable romance in power and popularity" (11.558 [10 Sept. 1857]: 147).

7. Charlotte L. Forten's "Life on the Sea Islands" may be found in William L. Andrews, *Classic African American Women's Narratives* (New York: Oxford UP, 2003), 364–91.

Forten wrote on 2 June 1854: "To-day Massachusetts has again been disgraced; again she has showed her submissions to the Slave Power; and Oh! with what deep sorrow do we think of what will doubtless be the fate of that poor man, when he is again consigned to the horrors of slavery." One month later, in an entry of 17 July 1854, she remarked with anger and dismay on the pervasive antiblack racism of "my native land—where I am hated and oppressed because God has given me a *dark skin.* How did this cruel this absurd prejudice ever exist?"[8] Between these 1854 entries on Anthony Burns and antiblack racism, she wrote her most substantial entry on Hawthorne, which has nothing but good things to say about this prominent supporter of the Democratic Party.

Like Grace Greenwood, Forten responds to Hawthorne through a reading of a portrait, in this case a daguerreotype. She is shown the daguerreotype and another Hawthorne portrait (perhaps an 1840 oil painting by Charles Osgood) by his sister Elizabeth, whom she describes as having an "eerie, spectral look which instantly brought to my mind the poem of 'The Ancient Mariner.' " Forten responds quite differently to the supposedly gloomy Nathaniel Hawthorne:

> I have seen to-day a portrait of Hawthorne, one of the finest that has ever been taken of him. He has a splendid head. That noble, expansive brow bears the unmistakeable impress of genius and superior intellect. And in the depths of those dark, expressive eyes there is a strange, mysterious influence which one feels in reading his works, and which I felt most forcible when reading that thrilling story "The Scarlet Letter." Yet there is in his countenance no trace of that gloom which pervades some of his writings; particularly that strange tale "The Unpardonable Sin" and many of the "Twice Told Tales." After reading them, I had pictured the author to myself as very dark and gloomy-looking. But I was agreeably disappointed. Grave, earnest, thoughtful, he appears but not gloomy. His sister, who, with much kindness showed me his portrait, is very singular-looking. . . . She showed me another portrait of Hawthorne taken when he was very young. His countenance, though glowing with genius, has more of the careless, sanguine expression of youth than profound, elevated thought which distinguishes his maturer years, and gives to his fine face and to his deeply interesting writings that mysterious charm which is felt and acknowledged by all.[9]

In many respects, what is most interesting about this reflection is what is not there: criticism of Hawthorne's politics. Instead, as in Greenwood's comments on Thompson's painting, one discerns an admiration for a writer whose fiction, one has to assume, was not viewed as radically at odds with her commitment to antislavery. That said, what mainly comes across in Forten's remarks is a lack of concern about connections between politics and art. Forten's Hawthorne,

---

8. *The Journals of Charlotte Forten Grimké,* ed. Brenda Stevenson (New York: Oxford UP, 1988), 65, 87.
9. *Journals of Charlotte Forten Grimké,* 84–85.

specifically the Hawthorne of *The Scarlet Letter*, is a playful, mysterious, and even elusive presence whose novel cannot be reduced to a single meaning, political or otherwise. Taking an interpretive position quite different from that of Yellin over a century later, she seems simply moved by a text that she cannot quite pin down, but that certainly speaks in inspiring ways to a reader who was also concerned about racism and slavery in her contemporary culture. Compared to Swisshelm, Bloomer, and even Greenwood, then, Forten seems the least willing to appropriate the novel for a specific end, ultimately admiring the novel for its hard-to-describe otherness and aesthetic power. One suspects that if she had thought the novel's main objective was to discipline the heroine and reinforce white patriarchy, she would have been a far less appreciative reader.

The following year, Forten commented again on *The Scarlet Letter* in her diary. In an entry of 26 November 1855, she remarked: "Saw for the first time the Custom House of which I read Hawthorne's descriptions in the introduction to that thrilling story—the 'Scarlet Letter.' I should have known it at once by the description. I wonder that I have not visited it before." What is striking here, in addition to Forten's terming of the novel as "thrilling," is her understanding of Hawthorne's investment in the real, despite his protestations to the contrary in the prefaces of his three romances of the 1850s. She links *The Scarlet Letter* to the real again in her first published essay, "Glimpses of New England," which appeared anonymously in the 1858 *National Anti-Slavery Standard*. In a somewhat veiled reference to *The House of the Seven Gables*, she refers to "the Old Witch House," which, she says, "has recently been defaced and desecrated by the erection of an apothecary shop in front of one of its wings." But she is explicit with her reference to *The Scarlet Letter*, which draws from her diary: "On Derby street, a street of wharves, stands the old Custom-House, which Hawthorne has so minutely described in his introduction to 'The Scarlet Letter.'" Again, her admiration for Hawthorne's fidelity to the real dominates both short mentions of his romances in an essay that, unsurprisingly, given its publication in an antislavery newspaper, has as one of its main concerns the situation of antislavery in Salem. The essay concludes by lamenting that it is only "the faithful few, too, few alas!" who fight the antislavery struggle.[1]
Given her interest in the real, and her politics of antislavery, it is somewhat surprising that Forten, unlike the anonymous critic in *Frederick Douglass' Paper*, can continue to read Hawthorne, the known Democrat, the author of the biography of Franklin Pierce, so enthusiastically. Some might regret Forten's naiveté in ignoring connections between Hawthorne's politics and art; I find inspiring her ability to read across the color line and against the grain of a political reductionism. At the very least, Forten's appreciations of Hawthorne should help to prompt critics toward more capacious and unpredictable ex-

---

1. *Journals of Charlotte Forten Grimké*, 145; [Charlotte Forten], "Glimpses of New England, *National Anti-Slavery Standard* 19 June 1858: 4.

plorations of Hawthorne's relationship to the slave culture of his time.

Writing about neglected African American perspectives in antebellum slave culture, Frederick Douglass stressed the importance of bringing African Americans more to the center of historical narratives by attending to "marks, traces, possibles, and probabilities."[2] In my survey of responses to *The Scarlet Letter* by the antebellum feminists Swisshelm, Bloomer, Greenwood, and Forten, I have similarly considered marks, traces, possibilities, and probabilities, and I would suggest that there are in all likelihood many more marks and traces still to be detected. We do not yet have a full grasp of the reception of *The Scarlet Letter* in the many strata of antebellum culture. Swisshelm in particular represents and anticipates an important school of criticism that is both exhilarated by Hawthorne's bold conception of the rebellious Hester and skeptical about the extent of his investment in the containment strategies of his novel. In a "Postscript" appended to one of the best studies that we have of *The Scarlet Letter*'s containment strategies, Sacvan Bercovitch suggests the possibility of what he terms an "aversive" reading of the novel, one that, going against the grain of his overall argument about the novel as "an agent of socialization," emphasizes dissent over containment and takes as a measure of Hawthorne's own identification with the radicalism of Hester "unerased traces of contradiction in the novel—undesired silences that . . . do not quite succeed in silencing conflict."[3] Such a reading, I have been suggesting, is both hinted at and sanctioned by the enthusiastic response of the antebellum feminists under consideration in this essay. These commentators appreciate an imaginative writer who, despite his possible containment strategies, was responsive to feminist issues of the time, and thus could be read in the context of their own political projects, or, as would appear to be the case with Forten, in an awed dis-relation from any particular political project. Their Hawthorne needs to become a more central constituent of our Hawthorne.

2. Frederick Douglass, "The Heroic Slave" (1853), in *The Oxford Frederick Douglass Reader*, ed. William L. Andrews (New York: Oxford UP, 1996), 132.
3. Sacvan Bercovitch, *The Office of the Scarlet Letter* (Baltimore: Johns Hopkins UP, 1991), xii, 155, 157.

Puritan Background and Sources

CHARLES RYSKAMP

The New England Sources of *The Scarlet Letter*†

After all the careful studies of the origins of Hawthorne's tales and the extensive inquiry into the English sources of *The Scarlet Letter*,[1] it is surprising that the American sources for the factual background of his most famous novel have been largely unnoticed. As would seem only natural, Hawthorne used the most creditable history of Boston available to him at that time, and one which is still an important source for the identification of houses of the early settlers and for landmarks in the city. The book is Dr. Caleb H. Snow's *History of Boston*. Study and comparison of the many histories read by Hawthorne reveal his repeated use of it for authentication of the setting of *The Scarlet Letter*. Consequently, for the most part this article will be concerned with Snow's book.

If we are to see the accurate background Hawthorne created, some works other than Snow's must also be mentioned, and the structure of time as well as place must be established. Then it will become apparent that although Hawthorne usually demanded authentic details of colonial history, some small changes were necessary in his portrayal of New England in the 1640's. These were not made because of lack of knowledge of the facts, nor merely by whim, but according to definite purposes—so that the plot would develop smoothly to produce the grand and simple balance of the book as we know it.

During the "solitary years," 1825–37, Hawthorne was "deeply engaged in reading everything he could lay his hands on. It was said in those days that he had read every book in the Athenaeum. . . ."[2] Yet no

---

† From *American Literature* 31.3 (1959): 257–72. Copyright © Duke University Press. All rights reserved. Used by permission of the publisher. Page numbers in square brackets refer to this Norton Critical Edition.

1. I shall make no reference to the English sources of *The Scarlet Letter* which have been investigated by Alfred S. Reid in *The Yellow Ruff and The Scarlet Letter* (Gainesville, 1955) and in his edition of *Sir Thomas Overbury's Vision . . . and Other English Sources of Nathaniel Hawthorne's "The Scarlet Letter"* (Gainesville, 1957). Most of this article was written before the publication of Reid's books. It may serve, however, as a complement or corrective to the central thesis put forth by Reid: "that accounts of the murder of Sir Thomas Overbury were Hawthorne's principal sources in composing *The Scarlet Letter*" (*The Yellow Ruff*, 112).

2. James T. Fields, *Yesterdays with Authors* (Boston, 1900), 47. For a list of books which Hawthorne borrowed from the Salem Athenaeum, see Marion L. Kesselring, *Hawthorne's Reading 1828–1850* (New York, 1949). All of my sources are included in this list, except the second edition (1845) of Felt's *Annals of Salem*.

scholar has studied his notebooks without expressing surprise at the exceptionally few remarks there on his reading. Infrequently one will find a bit of "curious information, sometimes with, more often without, a notation of the source; and some of these passages find their way into his creative work."[3] But for the most part Hawthorne did not reveal clues concerning the books he read and used in his own stories. About half of his writings deal in some way with colonial American history, and Professor Turner believes that "Hawthorne's indebtedness to the history of New England was a good deal larger than has ordinarily been supposed."[4] Certainly in *The Scarlet Letter* the indebtedness was much more direct than has hitherto been known.

Any work on the exact sources would have been almost impossible if it had not been for Hawthorne's particular use of the New England annals. Most of these are similar in content. The later historian builds on those preceding, who, in turn, must inevitably base all history on the chronicles, diaries, and records of the first settlers. Occasionally an annalist turns up a hitherto unpublished fact, a new relationship, a fresh description. It is these that Hawthorne seizes upon for his stories, for they would, of course, strike the mind of one who had read almost all the histories, and who was intimate with the fundamentals of colonial New England government.

As a young bachelor in Salem Hawthorne, according to his future sister-in-law, Elizabeth Peabody, "made himself thoroughly acquainted with the ancient history of Salem, and especially with the witchcraft era."[5] This meant that he studied Increase Mather's *Illustrious Providences* and Cotton Mather's *Magnalia Christi Americana*. He read the local histories of all the important New England towns. He read—and mentioned in his works—Bancroft's *History of the United States*, Hutchinson's *History of Massachusetts*, Snow's *History of Boston*, Felt's *Annals of Salem*, and Winthrop's *Journal*.[6] His son reported that Hawthorne pored over the daily records of the past: newspapers, magazines, chronicles, English state trials, "all manner of lists of things. . . . The forgotten volumes of the New England Annalists were favorites of his, and he drew not a little material from them."[7] He used these works to establish verisimilitude and greater materiality for his own books. His reading was perhaps most often chosen to help him— as he wrote to Longfellow—"give a life-like semblance to such shadowy stuff"[8] as formed his romances. Basically it was an old method of achieving reality, most successfully accomplished in his own day by

3. *The American Notebooks*, ed. Randall Stewart (New Haven, 1932), xxxii.
4. H. Arlin Turner, "Hawthorne's Literary Borrowings," *PMLA*, LI, 545 (June, 1936).
5. Moncure D. Conway, *Life of Nathaniel Hawthorne* (New York, 1890), 31.
6. Edward Dawson, *Hawthorne's Knowledge and Use of New England History: A Study of Sources* (Nashville, Tenn., 1939), 5–6; Turner, 551.
7. Julian Hawthorne, *Hawthorne Reading* (Cleveland, 1902), 107–108, 111, 132. Hawthorne's sister Elizabeth wrote to James T. Fields: "There was [at the Athenaeum] also much that related to the early History of New England. . . . I think if you looked over a file of old Colonial Newspapers you would not be surprised at the fascination my brother found in them. There were a few volumes in the Salem Athenaeum; he always complained because there were no more" (Randall Stewart, "Recollections of Hawthorne by His Sister Elizabeth," *American Literature*, XVI, 324, 330, Jan., 1945).
8. *The American Notebooks*, xlii.

Scott; but for Hawthorne the ultimate effects were quite different. Here and there Hawthorne reported actual places, incidents, and people—historical facts—and these were united with the creations of his mind. His explicitly stated aim in *The Scarlet Letter* was that "the Actual and the Imaginary may meet, and each imbue itself with the nature of the other" (55) [29]. His audience should recognize "the authenticity of the outline" (52) [27] of the novel, and this would help them to accept the actuality of the passion and guilt which it contained. For the author himself, the strongest reality of outline or scene was in the past, especially the history of New England.

The time scheme of the plot of *The Scarlet Letter* may be dated definitely. In chapter 12, "The Minister's Vigil," the event which brings the various characters together is the death of Governor Winthrop. From the records we know that the old magistrate died on March 26, 1649.[9] However, Hawthorne gives the occasion as Saturday, "an obscure night of early May" (179) [97]. Some suggestions may be made as reasons for changing the date. It would be difficult to have a night-long vigil in the cold, blustery month of March without serious plot complications. The rigidly conceived last chapters of the book require a short period of time to be dramatically and psychologically effective. The mounting tension in the mind and heart of the Reverend Mr. Dimmesdale cries for release, for revelation of his secret sin. Hawthorne realized that for a powerful climax, not more than a week, or two weeks at the most, should elapse between the night of Winthrop's death, when Dimmesdale stood on the scaffold, and the public announcement of his sin to the crowd on Election Day. The Election Day (275) [143–44] and the Election Sermons (257) [137] were well-known and traditionally established in the early colony in the months of May or June.[1] (The election of 1649, at which John Endicott became governor, was held on May 2.) Consequently Hawthorne was forced to choose between two historical events, more than a month apart. He wisely selected May, rather than March, 1649, for the time of the action of the last half of the book (chapters 12–23).

The minister's expiatory watch on the scaffold is just seven years after Hester Prynne first faced the hostile Puritans on the same platform

9. William Allen, *An American Biographical and Historical Dictionary* (Cambridge, Mass., 1809), 616; Caleb H. Snow, *A History of Boston* (Boston, 1825), 104; Thomas Hutchinson, *The History of Massachusetts* (Salem, 1795), I, 142.

1. John Winthrop, *The History of New England from 1630 to 1649* (Boston, 1825–1826), II, 31, 218 (a note on p. 31 states that the charter of 1629 provided for a general election on "the last Wednesday in Easter term yearly"; after 1691, on the last Wednesday of May); also Daniel Neal, *The History of New-England . . . to . . . 1700* (London, 1747), II, 252. Speaking of New England festivals, Neal writes: "their Grand Festivals are the Day of the annual Election of Magistrates at *Boston*, which is the latter End of *May*; and the Commencement at *Cambridge*, which is the last *Wednesday* in *July*, when Business is pretty much laid aside, and the People are as chearful among their Friends and Neighbours, as the *English* are at *Christmas*." Note Hawthorne's description of Election Day (*The Scarlet Letter*, [146]): "Had they followed their hereditary taste, the New England settlers would have illustrated all events of public importance by bonfires, banquets, pageantries and processions. . . . There was some shadow of an attempt of this kind in the mode of celebrating the day on which the political year of the colony commenced. The dim reflection of a remembered splendor, a colorless and manifold diluted repetition of what they had beheld in proud old London . . . might be traced in the customs which our forefathers instituted, with reference to the annual installation of magistrates."

(179, 194, 205) [97, 105, 110]. Therefore, the first four chapters of
The Scarlet Letter may be placed in June, 1642 (see 68) [37].
Hawthorne says that at this time Bellingham was governor (85–86)
[47]. Again one does not find perfect historical accuracy; if it were so,
then Winthrop would have been governor, for Bellingham had finished
his term of office just one month before.[2] A possible reason for
Hawthorne's choice of Bellingham will be discussed later.

The next major scene—that in which Hester Prynne goes to the
mansion of Bellingham—takes place three years later (1645).[3]
Hawthorne correctly observes: "though the chances of a popular election had caused this former ruler to descend a step or two from the
highest rank, he still held an honorable and influential place among
the colonial magistracy" (125) [67].[4] From the description of the garden of Bellingham's house we know that the time of the year was late
summer (132–133) [72].

With these references to time, as Edward Dawson has suggested,[5]
we can divide the major action of the novel as follows:

Act One

i. Chapters 1–3. The Market-Place, Boston. A June morning,
1642.

ii. Chapter 4. The Prison, Boston. Afternoon of the same day.

Act Two

Chapters 7–8. The home of Richard Bellingham, Boston. Late
summer, 1645.

Act Three

i. Chapter 12. The Market-Place. Saturday night, early May,
1649.

ii. Chapters 14–15. The sea coast, "a retired part of the peninsula" (202) [109]. Several days later.

iii. Chapters 16–19. The forest. Several days later.

Act Four

Chapters 21–23. The Market-Place. Three days later (see 257)
[137].

The place of each action is just as carefully described as is the time.
Hawthorne's picture of Boston is done with precise authenticity. A detailed street-by-street and house-by-house description of the city in
1650 is given by Snow in his *History of Boston*. It is certainly the most
complete history of the early days in any work available to Hawthorne.
Whether he had an early map of Boston cannot be known, but it is
doubtful that any existed from the year 1650. However, the City of

2. Winthrop, II, 31: June 2, 1641, Richard Bellingham elected governor. Winthrop, II, 63: May
18, 1642, John Winthrop elected governor.
3. *The Scarlet Letter*, 138 [75]: "Pearl, therefore, so large were the attainments of her three
years' lifetime, could have borne a fair examination in the New England Primer, or the first
column of the Westminster Catechisms, although unacquainted with the outward form of
either of those celebrated works." The Westminster Catechisms were not formulated until
1647; the New England Primer was first brought out ca. 1690.
4. Winthrop, II, 220: on May 14, 1645, Thomas Dudley had been elected governor.
5. I am largely indebted to Dawson, 17, for this time scheme.

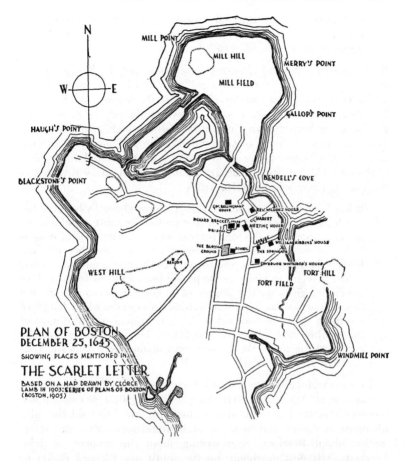

PLAN OF BOSTON
DECEMBER 25, 1645
SHOWING PLACES MENTIONED IN
THE SCARLET LETTER
BASED ON A MAP DRAWN BY GEORGE
LAMB IN 1903: SERIES OF PLANS OF BOSTON
(BOSTON, 1905)

Boston Records, 1634–1660, and the "Book of Possessions" with the reconstructed maps (made in 1903–1905 by George Lamb, based on the original records)[6] prove conclusively the exactness of the descriptions written by Snow and Hawthorne.

Hawthorne locates the first scene of *The Scarlet Letter* in this way:

> . . . it may safely be assumed that the forefathers of Boston had built the first prison-house somewhere in the vicinity of Cornhill, almost as seasonably as they marked out the first burial-ground, on Isaac Johnson's lot, and round about his grave, which subsequently became the nucleus of all the congregated sepulchres in the old churchyard of King's Chapel. (67) [36].[7]

> It was no great distance, in those days, from the prison-door to the market-place. . . . Hester Prynne . . . came to a sort of scaf-

6. For the drawing of the map reproduced with this essay, I am grateful to Professor W. F. Shellman, Jr., of the School of Architecture, Princeton University.

7. Concerning Isaac Johnson, Snow writes: "According to his particular desire expressed on his death bed, he was buried at the Southwest corner of the lot, and the people exhibited their attachment to him, by ordering their bodies to be buried near him. This was the origin of the first burying place, at present the Chapel burial ground" (37).

fold, at the western extremity of the market-place. It stood nearly beneath the eaves of Boston's earliest church, and appeared to be a fixture there. (75–76) [41][8]

Snow says that in 1650 Governor Bellingham and the Rev. John Wilson lived on one side of the Market-Place and Church Square (Snow, 117). Near Spring Lane on the other side of the Square (mentioned by Hawthorne when little Pearl says, "I saw her, the other day, bespatter the Governor himself with water, at the cattle-trough in Spring Lane," 164) [89] was the home of Governor Winthrop (Snow, 108). All the action of *The Scarlet Letter* set in Boston is thus centered in the heart of the city. This, as Snow takes great pains to point out, was where all the leading townsmen lived. He writes:

> It has been so often repeated that it is now generally believed the north part of the town was at that period the most populous. We are convinced that the idea is erroneous. . . . The book of possessions records the estates of about 250, the number of their houses, barns, gardens, and sometimes the measurement of their lands. It seems to embrace the period from 1640 to 1650, and we conclude, gives us the names of almost, if not quite, all the freemen of Boston. They were settled through the whole length of the main street on both sides. . . . It is evident too, that most of the wealthy and influential characters lived in what is now the centre of the town. We discover only about thirty names of residents north of the creek. (128–129)

A clear instance of Hawthorne's borrowing a fact from Snow is in the naming of "Master Brackett, the jailer" (92) [50]. Few colonial historians mention a jailer in Boston at this time, and if they do, they give his name as Parker. But Snow, alone it would seem, gives this information about Brackett, after writing about the property of John Leverett: "His next neighbour on the south was Richard Parker or Brackett, whose name we find on the colony records as prison keeper so early as 1638. He had '*the market stead*' on the east, the prison yard west, and the meeting house on the south" (Snow, 116). This last sentence taken from Snow gives the exact location of the action of the early chapters of *The Scarlet Letter*.

Another example of Hawthorne's use of Snow is shown in the description of Governor Bellingham's house. Here Hawthorne builds a vivid image of the old mansion. He writes of Hester and Pearl:

> Without further adventure, they reached the dwelling of Governor Bellingham. This was a large wooden house, built in a fashion of which there are specimens still extant in the streets of our

8. Justin Winsor, in *The Memorial History of Boston* (Boston, 1881), I, 506, 539, writes: "The whipping-post appears as a land-mark in the Boston records in 1639, and the frequent sentences to be whipped must have made the post entirely familiar to the town. It stood in front of the First Church, and was probably thought to be as necessary to good discipline as a police-station now is. . . . The stocks stood sometimes near the whipping-post. . . . And here, at last, before the very door of the sanctuary, perhaps to show that the Church and State went hand-in-hand in precept and penalty, stood the first whipping-post,—no unimportant adjunct of Puritan life."

older towns. . . . It had, indeed, a very cheery aspect; the walls being overspread with a kind of stucco, in which fragments of broken glass were plentifully intermixed; so that, when the sunshine
fell aslant-wise over the front of the edifice, it glittered and
sparkled as if diamonds had been flung against it by the double
handful. . . . It was further decorated with strange and seemingly
cabalistic figures and diagrams, suitable to the quaint taste of the
age, which had been drawn in the stucco when newly laid on, and
had now grown hard and durable, for the admiration of after
times. (128–129) [69–70][9]

There are almost no representations of the first settlers' houses in the
New England annals. But Snow on one occasion does print an old
plate showing an "Ancient building at the corner of Ann-Street and
Market-Square" (166). And he describes the house in a way which
bears a remarkable resemblance to the sketch written by Hawthorne
twenty-five years later:

This, says a description furnished by a friend, is perhaps the only
wooden building now standing in the city to show what was considered elegance of architecture here, a century and a half ago.
. . . The outside is covered with plastering, or what is commonly
called rough-cast. But instead of pebbles, which are generally
used at the present day to make a hard surface on the mortar,
broken glass was used. This glass appears like that of common
junk bottles, broken into pieces of about half an inch diameter.
. . . This surface was also variegated with ornamental squares, diamonds and flowers-de-luce. (167)[1]

Snow is also the only historian who tells the story of Mrs. Sherman's pig in order to bring out its effect upon the early Massachusetts
government.[2] Hawthorne, with his characteristic interest in the unusual fact from the past, refers to this strange incident:

At that epoch of pristine simplicity, however, matters of even
slighter public interest, and of far less intrinsic weight, than the
welfare of Hester and her child, were strangely mixed up with the
deliberations of legislators and acts of state. The period was
hardly, if at all, earlier than that of our story, when a dispute concerning the right of property in a pig not only caused a fierce and
bitter contest in the legislative body of the colony, but resulted in
an important modification of the framework itself of the legislature. (126) [68]

In his version of the story Snow said that the incident "gave rise to a
change also in regard to the Assistants" (95) and that because of the
confusion and dissatisfaction over the decision of the court, "provision

---

9. Hawthorne also accurately noted that Governor Bellingham was "bred a lawyer." Snow
writes of Bellingham: "He was by education a lawyer" (159).
1. For a possible source for details concerning the interior of Bellingham's house, the front
door, knocker, etc., see Joseph B. Felt, *Annals of Salem* (2nd ed.; Salem, 1845), I, 403–406.
2. Snow, 95–96. Hutchinson, I, 135–136 also refers to the incident, but not in this particular
way.

was made for some cases in which, if the two houses differed, it was
agreed that the major vote of the whole should be decisive. This was
the origin of our present Senate" (96).

The characters named in *The Scarlet Letter*—other than Hester,
Pearl, Chillingworth, and Dimmesdale, for whom we can find no real
historical bases—were actual figures in history. The fictional protagonists of the action move and gain their being in part through their realistic meetings with well-known people of colonial Boston. Even the
fantastic Pearl grows somewhat more substantial in the light of the
legend and story of her primitive world. She is seen, for example,
against the silhouette of the earlier Mr. Blackstone. When describing
Bellingham's garden Hawthorne relates: "There were a few rose-
bushes, however, and a number of apple-trees, probably the descendants of those planted by the Reverend Mr. Blackstone, the first
settler of the peninsula; that half-mythological personage, who rides
through our early annals, seated on the back of a bull" (133) [72].
Snow had said:

> By right of previous possession, Mr. Blackstone had a title to pro-
> prietorship in the whole peninsula. It was in fact for a time called
> Blackstone's neck. . . . Mr. Blackstone was a very eccentrick char-
> acter. He was a man of learning, and had received episcopal ordi-
> nation in England. . . . It was not very long before Mr. Blackstone
> found that there might be more than one kind of nonconformity,
> and was virtually obliged to leave the remainder of his estate here.
> . . . Let the cause of his removal have been what it may, certain it
> is that he went and settled by the Pawtucket river. . . . At this his
> new plantation he lived uninterrupted for many years, and there
> raised an orchard, the first that ever bore apples in Rhode Island.
> He had the first of the sort called yellow sweetings, that were ever
> in the world, and is said to have planted the first orchard in Mas-
> sachusetts also. . . . Though he was far from agreeing in opinion
> with Roger Williams, he used frequently to go to Providence to
> preach the gospel; and to encourage his younger hearers, while
> he gratified his own benevolent disposition, he would give them
> of his apples, which were the first they ever saw. It was said that
> when he grew old and unable to travel on foot, not having any
> horse, he used to ride on a bull, which he had tamed and tutored
> to that use. (50–53)

This account is taken virtually word for word from a series of articles
called "The Historical Account of the Planting and Growth of Providence" published in the Providence *Gazette* (January 12 to March 30,
1765).[3] However, Snow adds to this narrative the application to
Boston, which would be of special interest to Hawthorne (the phrase,
"and is said to have planted the first orchard in Massachusetts also").

The only minor characters that are developed to such an extent that
they become in any way memorable figures are Mrs. Hibbins and the

---

3. These were reprinted in the Massachusetts Historical Society's *Collections*, 2nd Ser., IX,
166–203 (1820).

Rev. John Wilson. Hawthorne's use of Mrs. Hibbins shows again a precise interest in the byways of Boston history. He describes the costume of the "reputed witch-lady" carefully (264, 286) [141, 153]. He refers to her as "Governor Bellingham's bitter-tempered sister, . . . the same who, a few years later, was executed as a witch" (44) [37]. And again, during the minister's vigil, Hawthorne writes that Dimmesdale beheld "at one of the chamber-windows of Governor Bellingham's mansion . . . the appearance of the old magistrate himself. . . . At another window of the same house, moreover, appeared old Mistress Hibbins, the Governor's sister . . ." (181) [98]. In Snow's book there is this account of Mrs. Ann Hibbins:

> The most remarkable occurrence in the colony in the year 1655 was the trial and condemnation of Mrs. Ann Hibbins of Boston for witchcraft. Her husband, who died July 23, 1654, was an agent for the colony in England, several years one of the assistants, and a merchant of note in the town; but losses in the latter part of his life had reduced his estate, and increased the natural crabbedness of his wife's temper, which made her turbulent and quarrelsome, and brought her under church censures, and at length rendered her so odious to her neighbours as to cause some of them to accuse her of witchcraft. The jury brought her in guilty, but the magistrates refused to accept the verdict; so the cause came to the general court, where the popular clamour prevailed against her, and the miserable old lady was condemned and executed in June 1656. (140)[4]

There seems to be only one source for Hawthorne's reference to Mrs. Hibbins as Bellingham's sister. That is in a footnote by James Savage in the 1825 edition of John Winthrop's *History of New England*, and it was this edition that Hawthorne borrowed from the Salem Athenaeum.[5] Savage writes that Mrs. Hibbins "suffered the punishment of death, for the ridiculous crime, the year after her husband's decease; her brother, Bellingham, not exerting, perhaps, his highest influence for her preservation."[6] Hawthorne leads the reader to assume that Mrs. Hibbins, nine years before the death of her husband, is living at the home of her brother. Hawthorne uses this relationship between Bellingham and Mrs. Hibbins in order to have fewer stage directions and explanations. It helps him to establish a more realistic unity in the tale. It partially explains the presence of the various people at the Market-Place the night of the minister's vigil, since Bellingham's house was just north of the scaffold. It also suggests why Bellingham is the governor chosen for the opening scenes of the novel, to prevent the plot from becoming encumbered with too many minor figures.

---

4. This is almost a literal copy from Hutchinson, I, 173. See also William Hubbard, "A General History of New England," Massachusetts Historical Society *Collections*, 2nd Ser., V, 574 (1815); Winthrop, I, 321.
5. Kesselring, 64.
6. Winthrop, I, 321 n. This contradicts Julian Hawthorne's observation: "As for Mistress Hibbins, history describes her as Bellingham's relative, but does not say that she was his sister, as is stated in the 'Romance' " ("Scenes of Hawthorne's Romances," *Century Magazine*, XXVIII, 391, July, 1884).

The Reverend John Wilson's description is sympathetically done, and it is for the most part historically accurate. Hawthorne presents him as "the reverend and famous John Wilson, the eldest clergyman of Boston, a great scholar, like most of his contemporaries in the profession, and withal a man of kind and genial spirit" (86) [47]. Cotton Mather,[7] William Hubbard,[8] and Caleb Snow testify to his remarkable "compassion for the distressed and . . . affection for all" (Snow, 156). William Allen, in his *American Biographical and Historical Dictionary*, writes that "Mr. Wilson was one of the most humble, pious, and benevolent men of the age, in which he lived. Kind affections and zeal were the prominent traits in his character. . . . Every one loved him. . . ."[9] Hawthorne, to gain dramatic opposition to Dimmesdale, makes the preacher seem older than he really was. He pictures the man of fifty-seven as "the venerable pastor, John Wilson . . . [with a] beard, white as a snow-drift"; and later, as the "good old minister" (182) [99].

Hawthorne's description of Puritan costuming has been substantiated by twentieth-century research. Although the elders of the colonial church dressed in "sad-colored garments, and gray, steeple-crowned hats" (67) [36][1] and preached simplicity of dress, Hawthorne recognized that "the church attendants never followed that preaching."[2] "Lists of Apparell" left by the old colonists in their wills, inventories of estates, ships' bills of lading, laws telling what must *not* be worn, ministers' sermons denouncing excessive ornamentation in dress, and portraits of the leaders prove that "little of the extreme Puritan is found in the dress of the first Boston colonists."[3] Alice Morse Earle, after going over the lists of clothing brought by the Puritans, concludes:

> From all this cheerful and ample dress, this might well be a Cavalier emigration; in truth, the apparel supplied as an outfit to the Virginia planters (who are generally supposed to be far more given over to rich dress) is not as full nor as costly as this apparel of Massachusetts Bay. In this as in every comparison I make, I find little to indicate any difference between Puritan and Cavalier in quantity of garments, in quality, or cost—or, indeed, in form. The differences in England were much exaggerated in print; in America they often existed wholly in men's notions of what a Puritan must be. (I, 34)

Hawthorne's descriptions agree with the early annals. The embroideries and bright colors worn by Pearl, the silks and velvets of Mrs.

---

7. *Magnalia Christi Americana* (London, 1702), bk. III, 46.
8. Hubbard, 604.
9. Allen, 613. The Reverend John Wilson was born in 1588; he died in 1667.
1. The phrase, "steeple-crowned hats," is used by Hawthorne each time he describes the dress of the Puritan elders (*The Scarlet Letter*, 24, 67, 79, 278) [11, 36, 43, 148]. The only source that I have been able to find for this particular phrase is in an essay on hats in a series of articles on clothing worn in former times: Joseph Moser, "Vestiges, Collected and Recollected, Number XXIV," *European Magazine*, XLV, 409–415 (1804). The Charge-Books of the Salem Athenaeum show that Hawthorne read the magazine in which this article appeared. Moser wrote about the "elevated and solemn beavers of the Puritans" (414) and the "high and steeple-crowned hats, probably from an idea, that the conjunction of Church and State was necessary to exalt their archetype in the manner that it was exalted" (411).
2. Alice Morse Earle, *Two Centuries of Costume in America* (New York, 1903), I, 8.
3. Earle, I, 13.

Hibbins, Hester's needlework—the laces, "deep ruffs . . . and gorgeously embroidered gloves"—were, as he said, "readily allowed to individuals dignified by rank or wealth, even while sumptuary laws forbade these and similar extravagances to the plebeian order" (105–106) [57]. The Court in 1651 had recorded "its utter detestation and dislike that men or women of mean condition should take upon them the garb of Gentlemen, by wearing gold or silver lace . . . which, though allowable to persons of greater Estates or more liberal Education, yet we cannot but judge it intolerable in persons of such like condition."[4] Hawthorne's attempt to create an authentic picture of the seventeenth century is shown in *The American Notebooks* where he describes the "Dress of an old woman, 1656."[5] But all of Hawthorne's description is significant beyond the demands of verisimilitude. In *The Scarlet Letter* he is repeating the impressions which are characteristic of his tales: the portrayal of color contrasts for symbolic purposes, the play of light and dark, the rich color of red against black, the brilliant embroideries[6] on the sable background of the "sad-colored garments."

So far there has been slight mention of the influence of Cotton Mather's writings on *The Scarlet Letter*. These surely require our attention in any study such as this one. Professor Turner believes that certain elements of Mather's *Magnalia Christi Americana*, "and in particular the accounts of God's judgment on adulterers [in II, 397–398], may also have influenced *The Scarlet Letter*. Mather relates [II, 404–405] that a woman who had killed her illegitimate child was exhorted by John Wilson and John Cotton to repent while she was in prison awaiting execution. In like manner, as will be recalled, John Wilson joins with Governor Bellingham and Arthur Dimmesdale in admonishing Hester Prynne to reveal the father of her child."[7] It is possible that an echo of the witch tradition in the *Magnalia Christi Americana* may also be found in *The Scarlet Letter*. "The proposal by Mistress Hibbins that Hester accompany her to a witch meeting is typical of the Mather witch tradition, which included, in accordance with the well known passage in *The Scarlet Letter*, the signing in the devil's book with an iron pen and with blood for ink. . . ."[8] The Black Man mentioned so often by Hawthorne (100, 144, 222–225) [54, 79, 119–20] was familiar to the Puritan settlers of New England. Pearl tells her mother "a story about the Black Man. . . . How he haunts this forest, and carries a book with him,—a big, heavy book, with iron clasps; and how this ugly Black Man offers his book and an iron pen to everybody that meets him here among the trees; and they are to

4. Winsor, I, 484–85. Hawthorne had read the *Acts and Laws . . . of the Massachusetts-Bay in New-England* (Boston, 1726)—see Kesselring, 56.
5. *The American Notebooks*, 109.
6. One of Hawthorne's favorite words—for example, see *The American Notebooks*, 97.
7. Turner, 550; Turner is using the Hartford (1855) edition of the *Magnalia Christi Americana*. See *The Scarlet Letter*, 86–91 [47–50].
8. Turner, 546—see *The Scarlet Letter*, 143–144 [79], and *Magnalia Christi Americana*, bk. VI, 81: "It was not long before *M. L.* . . . confess'd that *She* rode with her Mother to the said Witch-meeting. . . . At another time *M. L. junior*, the Grand-daughter, aged about 17 Years . . . declares that . . . they . . . rode on a *Stick* or *Pole* in the *Air* . . . and that they set their Hands to the Devil's Book. . . ."

write their names with their own blood" (222) [119–20]. Concerning the Black Man, Cotton Mather had written: "These *Tormentors* tendred unto the afflicted a *Book*, requiring them to *Sign* it, or *Touch* it at least, in token of their consenting to be Listed in the Service of the *Devil*; which they refusing to do, the *Spectres* under the Command of that *Blackman*, as they called him, would apply themselves to Torture them with prodigious Molestations."[9]

Even the portent in the sky, the great red letter A, which was seen on the night of the revered John Winthrop's death (and Dimmesdale's vigil), would not have seemed too strange to Puritan historians. To them it would certainly not have been merely an indication of Hawthorne's gothic interests. Snow had related that when John Cotton had died on Thursday, December 23, 1652, "strange and alarming signs appeared in the heavens, while his body lay, according to the custom of the times, till the Tuesday following" (133).

The idea of the scarlet A had been in Hawthorne's mind for some years before he wrote the novel. In 1844 he had made this comment in his notebooks as a suggestion for a story: "The life of a woman, who, by the old colony law, was condemned always to wear the letter A, sewed on her garment, in token of her having committed adultery."[1] Before that, in "Endicott and the Red Cross," he had told of a "woman with no mean share of beauty" who wore a scarlet A [p. 174 of this Norton Critical Edition]. It has commonly been accepted that the "old colony law" which he had referred to in his notebooks had been found in Felt's *Annals of Salem*, where we read under the date of May 5, 1694: "Among such laws, passed this session, were two against Adultery and Polygamy. Those guilty of the first crime, were to sit an hour on the gallows, with ropes about their necks,—be severely whipt not above 40 stripes; and forever after wear a capital A, two inches long, cut out of cloth coloured differently from their clothes, and sewed on the arms, or back parts of their garments so as always to be seen when they were about."[2]

Exactly when Hawthorne began writing *The Scarlet Letter* is not known, but by September 27, 1849, he was working on it throughout every day. It was finished by February 3, 1850.[3] In the novel there is the same rapid skill at composition which is typical of the notebooks. From the multitude of historical facts he knew he could call forth with severe economy only a few to support the scenes of passion or punishment. Perhaps it does not seem good judgment to claim that Hawthorne wrote *The Scarlet Letter* with a copy of Snow's *History of Boston* on the desk. But it does not appear believable that all these incidental facts from New England histories, the exacting time scheme, the authentic description of Boston in the 1640's, should have remained so extremely clear and perfect in his mind when he was under the ex-

9. *Magnalia Christi Americana*, bk. II, 60; see also Massachusetts Historical Society *Collections*, V, 64 (1708); Neal, II, 131, 133–135, 144, 150, 158, 160, 169.
1. *The American Notebooks*, 107 [p. 215 of this Norton Critical Edition].
2. Joseph B. Felt, *The Annals of Salem, from Its First Settlement* (Salem, 1827), 317.
3. Randall Stewart, *Nathaniel Hawthorne* (New Haven, 1948), 93–95.

traordinary strain of writing the story. Here the studies of Hawthorne's literary borrowings made by Dawson, Turner, and others must be taken into account. They have shown that in certain of his tales, he "seems to have written with his original open before him."[4] To claim a firm dependence upon certain New England histories for the background of *The Scarlet Letter* should therefore not seem unreasonable.

The incidents, places, and persons noticed in this article are the principal New England historical references in *The Scarlet Letter*. A study like this of Hawthorne's sources shows something of his thorough method of reading; it reveals especially his certain knowledge of colonial history and his interest in the unusual, obscure fact. But these are side lights of an author's mind. His steady determination was to make the romances of his imagination as real as the prison-house and the grave.

It would be unfair to leave the study of Hawthorne's historical approach here. His final concern in history was the attempt to find the "spiritual significance"[5] of the facts. As his sister Elizabeth had said of the young man: "He was not very fond of history in general."[6] Hawthorne stated concretely his conception of history and the novel in a review (1846) of W. G. Simms's *Views and Reviews in American History*:

> . . . we cannot help feeling that the real treasures of his subject have escaped the author's notice. The themes suggested by him, viewed as he views them, would produce nothing but historical novels, cast in the same worn out mould that has been in use these thirty years, and which it is time to break up and fling away. To be the prophet of Art requires almost as high a gift as to be a fulfiller of the prophecy. Mr. Simms has not this gift; he possesses nothing of the magic touch that should cause new intellectual and moral shapes to spring up in the reader's mind, peopling with varied life what had hitherto been a barren waste.[7]

With the evocation of the spirit of the colonial past, and with a realistic embodiment of scene, Hawthorne repeopled a landscape wherein new intellectual and moral shapes could dwell. The new fiction of Hester Prynne and the old appearances of Mrs. Hibbins could not be separated. Time past and time present became explicable as they were identified in the same profound moral engagement.

4. Turner, 547.
5. Julian Hawthorne, *Hawthorne Reading*, 100.
6. "Recollections of Hawthorne by His Sister Elizabeth," 324.
7. Stewart, "Hawthorne's Contributions to *The Salem Advertiser*," *American Literature*, V (Jan., 1934): 331–332.

MICHAEL J. COLACURCIO

Footsteps of Ann Hutchinson: The Context of *The Scarlet Letter*†

I

In the first brief chapter of *The Scarlet Letter*, the narrator pays almost as much attention to a rose bush as he does to the appearance and moral significance of Puritan America's first prison. That "wild rose-bush, covered, in this month of June, with its delicate gems," contrasts with the "burdock, pig-weed, apple-peru" and other "unsightly vegetation"; yet all flourish together in the same "congenial" soil which has so early brought forth "the black flower of civilized society, a prison" (48) [36].[1] And thus early are we introduced to the book's extremely complicated view of the natural and the social. Moreover, as the rose bush seems to offer Nature's sympathy to society's criminal, it becomes essentially associated with Hester Prynne, almost as *her* symbol. Accordingly, criticism has been lavish in its own attention to that rose bush: it has, out of perfect soundness of instinct, been made the starting point of more than one excellent reading of *The Scarlet Letter*; indeed the explication of this image and symbol is one of the triumphs of the "new" Hawthorne criticism.[2]

But if the "natural" and internal associations of this rose bush have been successfully elaborated, its external and "historic" implications have been largely ignored. And yet not for any fault of the narrator. This rose bush "has been kept alive in history," he assures us; and it may even be, as "there is fair authority for believing," that "it had sprung up under the footsteps of the sainted Ann Hutchinson, as she entered the prison-door" [36–37].

We are, I suppose, free to ignore this critical invitation if we choose. Obviously we are being offered a saint's legend in which Hawthorne expects no reader literally to believe. Perhaps it is there only for the irony of "sainted"—a trap for D. H. Lawrence or other romantic (later, feminist) readers; for Hawthorne will have nearly as many reservations about Hester's sainthood as John Winthrop had about Mrs. Hutchinson's. Certainly the natural language of flowers is a more available and universal sort of literary knowledge than that overdetermined system of historical fixities and definites which laborers in the field of American studies call "Antinomianism." And is not Hawthorne himself responsible for the idea that he was not all *that* serious about those old books he borrowed from the Salem Athenaeum or went up to Boston to buy?

---

† From *ELH* 39.3 (1972): 459–94. Copyright © by The Johns Hopkins University Press. Reprinted with permission of The Johns Hopkins University Press. Page numbers in square brackets refer to this Norton Critical Edition.
1. All quotations from *The Scarlet Letter*, identified by page numbers in the text, refer to the Centenary Edition, Vol. 1 (Columbus, Ohio, 1962).
2. See, particularly, Hyatt H. Waggoner's *Hawthorne* (Cambridge, Mass., 1955, 1963) and Roy R. Male's "From the Innermost Germ," *ELH*, 20 (1953).

Still, a conscious decision *not* to look for and press a Hester Prynne-Ann Hutchinson analogy might be risky, the result of a critical bias. We should not, it seems to me, want to believe Hawthorne a casual name dropper unless he prove himself one. We should prefer a more rather than a less precise use of literary allusion, not only in this opening reference but also in a later one which suggests that, except for the existence of Pearl, Hester "might have come down to us in history, hand in hand with Ann Hutchinson, as the foundress of a religious sect" (165) [108]. The references are, after all, pretty precise: Hester walks in the footsteps of (but not quite hand-in-hand with) Ann Hutchinson. And before we invest too heavily in Hawthorne's well-known demurrer to Longfellow, we might remind ourselves that Hawthorne did write—near the outset of his career, in clear and close dependence on "a good many books"[3]—a well informed sketch called "Mrs. Hutchinson." He mentions her again, prominently, in those reviews of New England history entitled *Grandfather's Chair* and "Main Street." Now he seems to be apprising us of a relationship between Hester Prynne and that famous lady heretic. The man who created the one and memorialized the other ought to be in a position to know.

Clearly the relationship is not one of "identity": tempting as the view can be made to appear, *The Scarlet Letter* is probably not intended as an allegory of New England's Antinomian Crisis. Hawthorne's historical tales never work quite that simply: "The Gentle Boy," "Young Goodman Brown," and "The Minister's Black Veil" all have something quite precise and fundamental to say about the Puritan mind but, in spite of the precision with which they are set or "dated," they are not primarily "about" (respectively) the Quaker problem, the witchcraft delusion, or the great awakening.[4] Their history is not quite that literalistic. And here, of course, the setting is "literally" Boston, 1642 to 1649—not 1636 and 1637.[5] More importantly, but equally obviously, the career of Hawthorne's fictional Hester Prynne is far from identical with that of the historical Mrs. Hutchinson. However "antinomian" Hester becomes, it would be positively ludicrous to forget that her philosophical career is inseparable from adultery and illegitimate childbirth, events which have no very real counterpart in the life of that enthusiastic prophetess Hawthorne calls her prototype.

But as important as are the simple differences, and as dangerous as

3. The critic must always be alert for tones of mock self-condescension in Hawthorne. In the famous letter to Longfellow (4 June 1837) Hawthorne calls his "studious life" at Salem a "desultory" one; but when he complains that his reading has not brought him "the fruits of study," he may well be remembering that it is *Longfellow* who went on from Bowdoin to become Professor of Modern Languages in Harvard University, rather than "the obscurest man of letters in America."

4. I have explored these relationships, among others, in a book-length manuscript on the "history" in Hawthorne's early stories, which I hope to publish within the next year. [See Colacurcio, *The Province of Piety*.] The clue to the "unobvious" relation here—that between *MBV* and the Awakening—comes from the similarity of some of Hooper's concerns with those expressed in various election sermons preached "during Governor Belcher's administration" (I, 65).

5. For the "dates" of *The Scarlet Letter*, see Charles Ryskamp, "The New England Sources of *The Scarlet Letter*," *AL*, 31 (1959) and pp. 291–303 in this Norton Critical Edition; and for a speculation about the "libertarian" meaning of those dates, see H. Bruce Franklin's "Introduction" to *The Scarlet Letter and Related Writings* (Philadelphia and New York, 1967).

it must always seem to turn away from the richness and particularity of Hester's own love story, Hawthorne himself seems to have invited us temporarily to do so. And if we follow his suggestion, a number of similarities come teasingly to mind.

Like Ann Hutchinson, Hester Prynne is an extraordinary woman who falls afoul of a theocratic and male-dominated society; and the problems which cause them to be singled out for exemplary punishment both begin in a special sort of relationship with a pastor who is one of the acknowledged intellectual and spiritual leaders of that society. No overt sexual irregularity seems to have been associated with Mrs. Hutchinson's denial that converted saints were under the moral law, but (as we shall see later) no one could read what seventeenth-century Puritan observers said about the "seductiveness" of her doctrines without sensing sexual implications everywhere. Evidently such implications were not lost on Hawthorne. Further, though with increasing complications, both of these remarkable and troublesome women have careers as nurses and counsellors to other women: Ann Hutchinson begins her prophetic career this way, whereas Hester Prynne moves in this direction as a result of her punishment. And most significantly—if most problematically—both make positive pronouncements about the inapplicability of what the majority of their contemporaries take to be inviolable moral law.[6]

To be sure, it takes Hester Prynne some time to catch up with Ann Hutchinson; but when Hawthorne says of Hester, in the full tide of her later speculative freedom, that "the world's law was no law to her mind" (164) [107], we may well suspect that he intends some conscious pun on the literal meaning of "antinomianism." If Hester's problems begin with sex more literally than do Ann Hutchinson's, her thinking eventually ranges far outward from that domestic subject. In some way, and for complicated reasons that need to be examined, Hester Prynne and sex are associated in Hawthorne's mind with Ann Hutchinson and spiritual freedom.

So teasing do Hawthorne's connections and analogies come to seem, that we are eventually led to wonder whether *The Scarlet Letter* shows only this one set of historical footprints. If Hester Prynne bears relation to Ann Hutchinson, would it be too outrageous to look for similarities between Arthur Dimmesdale and John Cotton, that high

6. I have assumed a basic familiarity with the career and heresies, spoken and alleged, of Ann Hutchinson. A full study of her "influence," at least indirect, leads virtually everywhere in the seventeenth century. The following items seem most relevant: for primary sources beyond those *demonstrably* read by Hawthorne (Winthrop's *Journal*, Edward Johnson's *Wonder-Working Providence of Sion's Savior*, Cotton Mather's *Magnalia*, and Thomas Hutchinson's *History of Massachusetts Bay*), consult Charles Francis Adams' collection of material on *Antinomianism in the Colony of Massachusetts Bay, 1636–1638*, published as Volume 21 of the *Publications of the Prince Society* (Boston, 1894), and David D. Hall's *The Antinomian Controversy: A Documentary History* (Middletown, Conn., 1968). This last contains some sources which Hawthorne probably could *not* have seen; but both contain the crucial transcripts of her two "trials" as well as Winthrop's *Short Story of the Rise, Reign, and Ruine of the Antinomians, Familists, and Libertines* (1644). For modern commentary on the meaning of Mrs. Hutchinson's ideas and career, two works seem indispensable: Emery Battis, *Saints and Sectaries* (Chapel Hill, N.C., 1962) and Larzer Ziff, *John Cotton* (Princeton, N.J., 1962). Also useful is Part Two of C. F. Adams' *Three Episodes in Massachusetts History*, 2 vols. (Boston, 1893).

Calvinist who was variously asserted and denied to be the partner in heresy? And—granting that what is involved is neither allegory nor *roman à clef*—might there not be some fundamental relation between the deepest philosophical and theological "issues" raised by the Antinomian Controversy and the "themes" of Hawthorne's romance?

To the first of these questions, a certain kind of answer comes readily enough. Although the portrait of Dimmesdale is physically unlike the one Hawthorne gives of Cotton in his early sketch of "Mrs. Hutchinson," their positions are disturbingly similar: both are singled out from among distinguished colleagues as models of learning and piety; and both relate very ambiguously to a wayward woman on trial. It is impossible not to feel that John Cotton's drastic change of relation to Ann Hutchinson—a phenomenon as fascinating to scholars now as it was momentous to Puritans then—lies somewhere behind Dimmesdale's movement from partner in to judge of Hester's adultery. Both men sit in public judgment of an outrage against public order in which there is reason to believe they bear equal responsibility with the criminal.

Although his sketch of "Mrs. Hutchinson" suggests in one place that her enthusiasm had earlier been restrained from public manifestation by the influence of her favorite pastor, Hawthorne actually takes a rather harsh view of Cotton's role in her trial: "Mr. Cotton began to have that light in regard to her errors, which will sometimes break in upon the wisest and most pious men, when their opinions are unhappily discordant with those of the powers that be" (XII, 222) [170].[7] That is to say: Cotton and his female parishioner have been what their society calls "antinomians" together, both "deceived by the fire" (221) [169]: but the respected minister saves himself. Not all modern commentators would agree that Cotton's behavior is to be judged this harshly, but that is not the issue here. At some point Cotton did clearly reverse his relationship to Ann Hutchinson, reproving doctrines she thought were his own offspring; and clearly Hawthorne's view of Cotton has influenced his treatment of Dimmesdale.[8] Except for the rather too delicate question of who first lit the strange fires, both Mrs. Hutchinson's treatment by Cotton and Hester's by Dimmesdale might almost be subtitled "Seduced and Abandoned in Old Boston."

Although the significance is completely ironic in *The Scarlet Letter*, both pastors are reminded by their colleagues that "the responsibility of [the] woman's soul" is largely within their sphere; Wilson's urging Dimmesdale to press repentance and confession upon Hester sounds a good deal like an ironic version of the ministerial pleas which Cotton, because of his doctrinal affinities with Ann Hutchinson, so long

---

7. "Mrs. Hutchinson" first appeared in the *Salem Gazette* for 7 December 1830. Quotations in this essay are from the "Riverside Edition" of *Hawthorne's Works*, Vol. 12 (Boston, 1882–83).

8. The harshest modern judgment is that of Perry Miller: "Cotton tried hard to adhere to the Protestant line until his colleagues forced him to recognize that he, for all his great position, would be sacrificed along with Mistress Hutchinson unless he yielded. As many another man in a similar predicament, Cotton bent" (*The New England Mind: From Colony to Province* [Cambridge, Mass., 1953], 59–60). For a view which emphasizes Cotton's "idealistic" naivete see Ziff, *Cotton*, 106–48.

refused to heed. And to the end, both men are spared from denunciation by their partners. Although Puritan defenders of Cotton's doctrinal reputation (like Cotton Mather) insisted he had been slandered by even being named in the same breath with the seductive Mrs. Hutchinson, there is no evidence to suggest that the "abandoned" one ever pointed a finger of public accusation at Cotton, or reproached him for infidelity to what she continued to believe were their shared experiences and beliefs. Cotton alone, Hawthorne reports, is excepted from her final denunciations. And in spite of Dimmesdale's false and unfaithful position on the balcony overlooking her scaffold, of his own part in her troubles, Hester "will not speak."

The Cotton-Dimmesdale analogy may seem treacherous on these internal grounds alone. After all, Cotton is not named by Hawthorne and Mrs. Hutchinson is. But there are also arguments which "implicate" Cotton in Dimmesdale—external reasons for believing that John Cotton could not be far from Hawthorne's mind when he wrote of the Reverend Mr. Dimmesdale. And in the light of these, the very omission of the name of Cotton seems glaringly to call attention to itself. The historically alert reader of *The Scarlet Letter* comes to sense the presence of Cotton's absence on almost every page.

First of all, in the public judgment of Hester, Dimmesdale stands as the partner of John Wilson, at the head of the Boston church of which Hester is a member: Wilson is the fervent, Dimmesdale the reluctant enforcer of discipline. Now it seems to me inconceivable that the man who wrote about the Hutchinson situation explicitly three separate times, using highly detailed contemporary sources as well as later histories (and who built into *The Scarlet Letter* certain colonial details so minutely accurate as to convince one recent critic that he wrote the romance with a number of books open before him) would *not* know that the famous partnership at Boston throughout the 1630's and 1640's was Wilson and Cotton.[9] It might be too much to suggest that Dimmesdale is conceived and dramatized as a younger version of Cotton, one whose pastoral involvement with Hester Prynne amounted to a less metaphorical seduction than Cotton's relationship with Ann Hutchinson; but it is hard to believe Hawthorne could pair Wilson with *Dimmesdale* without thinking *Cotton*.

Several other, more curious "displacements" also implicate Cotton. Hawthorne had certainly read in Mather's *Magnalia* of a case in which John Wilson and John Cotton joined together publicly to urge public repentance upon a woman who had killed an illegitimate child; Mather's account surely lies somewhere behind Hawthorne's first scaffold scene. Also he could scarcely have *not* known that it was with Cotton's death in 1652 that the fiery signs in the sky were associated—not with Winthrop's in 1649. One could argue, of course, that this points *away* from Cotton; but just as cogently one can say that Hawthorne cannot *make* the transference without having Cotton in

9. For an account of the un-desultory scholarship behind *The Scarlet Letter*, see Ryskamp, "New England Sources."

mind; and that the reader who knows the facts will make the application, especially when, standing on his midnight scaffold, Dimmesdale applies "Cotton's" sign to himself. And finally, it was not exactly a secret (despite Mather's silence) that Cotton's son, John Cotton, *Junior*, was deprived of his pastorship and excommunicated from church membership at Plymouth for adultery. Perhaps Dimmesdale is to be thought of—metaphorically, and with a certain irony—as a sort of offspring of Cotton's principles.[1]

Now all of this may not add up to a completely rational calculus of "influence," but it does suggest that, at some level, *The Scarlet Letter* reflects a complicated response to more in the historic Puritan world than Ann Hutchinson alone. To this point, however, we still know very little about the importance of historical context to the realized intentions of Hawthorne's first long romance—as opposed, that is, to some complex, Road-to-Xanadu association that lies somewhere behind it, perhaps even close to its source. The rest of this essay is conceived as a cautious and tentative answer to the less positivistic, more pragmatic question of what *The Scarlet Letter* may mean if it does indeed call up a fairly extensive set of associations from Puritanism's most crucial theological controversy.[2]

II

The place to begin an exploration of the inner similarities between Hester Prynne and Ann Hutchinson is with a closer look at Hawthorne's early sketch. In many ways a puzzling piece of historical fiction, the sketch does clear up one fundamental point immediately: Hester's sexual problems can be related to those of Mrs. Hutchinson because the latter are, in Hawthorne's view, themselves flagrantly sexual.

The sketch introduces itself, too heavily, as a lesson in that forlorn subject we used to call the nature and place of women. Mrs. Hutchinson is first presented as "the female"; she is offered as a forerunner of certain nameless public ladies of 1830, and the line from Hawthorne's remark here about "how much of the texture and body of cisatlantic literature is the work of those slender fingers" (XII, 217) [167] to the more famous but equally sexist one later about "the damned mob of scribbling women" seems to run direct. The revelation is damaging enough, but fairly simple: Hawthorne enjoyed competing with women

---

1. The facts in this paragraph have been noticed by other Hawthorne critics, but they have not pressed the Cotton-Dimmesdale implication. Besides Ryskamp, see Austin Warren's "Introduction" to the Rinehart Edition of *The Scarlet Letter* (New York, 1947).

2. In "spirit" this essay derives from a suggestion by Roy Harvey Pearce that Hawthorne criticism has "tended to rush on, identifying and collocating his symbols and their forms, and then pursuing them out of time—out of space, too often beyond the consciousness of those whose life in art they make possible" ("Romance and the Study of History," in *Hawthorne Centenary Essays*, Columbus, Ohio, 1964). My general view of Hawthorne is also congruent with that elaborated by Q. D. Leavis in "Hawthorne as Poet," *Sewanee Review*, 59 (1951). I have not tried to reread all *Scarlet Letter* criticism in preparing this essay, nor to cite specific debts at every point. I should, however, acknowledge the special influence of Austin Warren, "*The Scarlet Letter*: A Literary Exercise in Moral Theology," *Southern Review*, 1 (1965); and E. W. Baughman, "Public Confessions and *The Scarlet Letter*," *NEQ*, 40 (1967).

for the readership of magazines and gift books at the outset of his career as little as he did for the "gentle reader" of romances later.[3]

But if Hawthorne's own sexual politics are easy and largely irrelevant to the present question, certain subtler forms of the feminist problem treated in "Mrs. Hutchinson" throw an important light on Hester Prynne (as well as on a significant woman-problem in Hawthorne's larger career). Once we read on and apprehend Hawthorne's dominant image of Ann Hutchinson—formerly a spiritual counsellor to Puritan women, interpreting to them the best of the male theological mind; now a prophet in her own right, giving voice to a new spirit of freedom and embodying within herself a new awareness of female intelligence and social power—we immediately grasp the significant context of Hawthorne's views of the later Hester Prynne.

In the epilogue which Hawthorne calls a "Conclusion," Hester has returned to Boston to wear her scarlet letter "of her own free will," with something like an internalized acceptance of its appropriateness. She now accepts as reasonable what in the forest she tried to deny and many years earlier she could, in very much the same words, only rationalize: "Here had been her sin; here, her sorrow; and here was yet to be her penitence" (263) [165].[4] But this is not the whole story. Whether to affirm a yet undestroyed inner-direction and unreconstructed self-reliance, or else to assert once again the mortal irreparability of ruined walls, the narrator informs us that Hester is still a visionary and has become a counsellor to women. Earlier—even in her most antinomian moments—she had stopped short of that critical move from undisciplined private speculation to unsanctioned public prophecy; providentially she had been prevented from joining hands (metaphorically) with her sister Hutchinson because "in the education of the child, the mother's enthusiasm of thought had something to wreak itself upon" (165) [108]. Now, although Hester has apparently picked up and pieced together again "the fragments of [the] broken chain" formerly cast away; although "the world's law" is now apparently *some* law to her mind; and although she would not now presumably claim for her adultery a totally sufficient "consecration" in feeling, she has now found a way to make public her ideas about sexual justice.

Earlier she had pondered the "dark question" of the "whole race of womanhood": could its lot ever be a happy one without a tearing down of "the whole system of society" and an essential modification of "the very nature of the opposite sex" (165) [108]? Now—with important

3. After lecturing on Hawthorne to a course on "Women in Literature," my Cornell colleague Dan McCall reported to me that, in such a context, Hawthorne is a "sitting duck." He also suggested, quite cogently, that Hawthorne's later statements about women writers being interesting only when they expose their "natal mind" and come before the public as it were "naked" are not to be separated from the sexual overtones of the early sketch of Ann Hutchinson; perhaps not even from his historical memory of certain Quaker women whipped half-naked through the streets of New England by his ancestor.
4. The earlier form is in chapter 5: "Here, she said to herself, had been the scene of her guilt, and here should be the scene of her earthly punishment." The change from "punishment" to "penitence" is obviously significant. Also notice that the earlier paragraph in question begins by suggesting that "doubtless" she has a "secret" reason for remaining (80) [56].

modifications of tone and in separation from all traces of antimonian self-justification—her ideas are expressed to other women, especially those whose lives have been made miserable through excess or absence of passion.

> Hester comforted and counseled them, as best she might. She assured them, too, of her firm belief, that, at some brighter period, when the world should have grown ripe for it, in Heaven's own time, a new truth would be revealed, in order to establish the whole relation between man and woman on a surer ground of mutual happiness. (263) [165–66]

What Hester's experience comes to finally—in an epilogue, and after a painful and complicated development forced upon her by others—is some insight about the double standard, or perhaps about the new morality.

Thus, if we can bear the temporary critical reduction, it is easy to see that Hester passes through a phase of antinomianism comparable to (though not identical with) that of the historical Ann Hutchinson, only to emerge as a version of the sexual reformer already "typed out" in Hawthorne's "figure" of Mrs. Hutchinson as independent and reforming "female." And though the equation might need to be clarified by an examination of the precise quality of Hester's anti-legal phase, we can already calculate that her final position is, in Hawthorne's mental universe, just about half way between Ann Hutchinson and Margaret Fuller; and we can sense that when Hawthorne describes her later career as counsellor to troubled and searching women, he has certain seventeenth-century, Sunday-evening doctrinal meetings and certain nineteenth-century "Conversations" just about equally in mind. (What this clearly suggests, in consequence, is that interpreters of the problem of women in Hawthorne can make a less autonomous use of Margaret Fuller than they have often supposed.)[5]

To this point, as I have indicated, Hawthorne seems open to the charge of a fairly radical sort of reductivism: he seems to have presented an historical woman whose heretical ideas once caused a profound religious and social crisis as a simple case of uneasy or misplaced sexuality; and the opportunity to reduce Hester Prynne to a woman whose sexuality got quite literally out of control and never did entirely recover itself is therefore ready to hand. Such a reduction is, presumably, as distasteful to old male literary critics as it is to new women.

The way to stop being reductive and offensive about Hawthorne's use of the "female" Mrs. Hutchinson as a type of Hester Prynne is not, therefore, to appeal to the masterful modern psycho-historical interpretation of Mrs. Hutchinson's career. It is probably of some value to notice that its author (Emery Battis) devotes almost as many pages to the complicated female problems of her relation to her strong father,

---

5. Even as the abundant and familiar discussion of Margaret Fuller and Zenobia reaches the point of diminishing returns, criticism is proposing "Margaret Fuller as a Model for Hester Prynne"; see the article by Francis E. Kearns in *Jahrbuch Für Amerikastudien* 10 (1965).

her weak husband, and her beloved pastor as he does to her ideas; that
he convincingly urges a relation between menstrual cycle, pregnancy,
menopause and the more public aspects of her career; and that he introduces his treatment of the character of this unusual woman with
the astonishingly Hawthornean speculation that "had she been born
into a later age, Mrs. Hutchinson might have crusaded for women's
rights."[6] It is perhaps more than a nice polemical point to observe that
Hawthorne is not alone in reading sexual implications in Mrs. Hutchinson's theologic and prophetic career, but the observation leaves out
all the subtle considerations. They concern not only the ways in which
Ann Hutchinson and Hester Prynne are related in a very serious approach to the "theological" meaning of sexuality, but also the historical
reasons Hawthorne had for linking enthusiasm, individualism, and femaleness.

If we glance again at the early sketch, we can notice that, embattled
and argumentative as it is, it is yet about sex in some more elemental
way than our discussion about "feminism" has so far indicated. With
structural intention (and not, clearly, by obsession), the sketch tries
hard to focus on several scenes in which Mrs. Hutchinson is the center of all male attention, prophesying doctrines that astound the male
intellect. Most of the "historical" facts are there, but only a fairly well
informed reader can feel assured of this; and except for an initial, one-
paragraph reminder, the facts seem to fall out incidentally, so as not to
distract from the dramatic confrontation. The implications, in turn,
are not in the ordinary sense "theological": there is no mention of the
famous eighty-two errors Mrs. Hutchinson is said to have spawned—
as there is, self-consciously, in *Grandfather's Chair*; we are, historically
and psychologically, beyond that sort of consideration. The issue is not
sanctification as an evidence of justification, but the woman's own
prophetic abilities. Having formerly cast aspersions on legal doctrines
of salvation, the enthusiast now claims the spiritual "power of distinguishing between the chosen of man and the sealed of heaven" (XII,
224) [171]. What further need of witnesses? Clearly the progress of
the strange fire of her enthusiasm is far advanced.

Nor is there any significant ambiguity about the source and significance of that fire: Mrs. Hutchinson's spiritual openings and leadings
are inseparable from her female sexuality. Although her "dark enthusiasm" has deceived the impetuous Vane and the learned but mildly il-
luministic Cotton, it is clearly her own "strange fire now laid upon the
altar" (XII, 221) [169]. The men, variously affected, must make of it
whatever they can. Hawthorne does not quite identify enthusiasm
with "the female," but we do not distort his intentions if—supplying
our own italics—we take as the very heart of the sketch the following
sentence: "In the midst, and in the center of all eyes, we see *the
woman*" (XII, 224) [171].

This may still be sexist, but it is no longer petty or carping. Mrs.
Hutchinson's influence is indeed profound. Even the male chauvinist

6. *Saints and Sectaries*, 6.

is compelled to admit it. The impulse to challenge the Puritan theocracy's dominant (and socially conservative) assumptions about "visible sanctity" evidently comes from a fairly deep and powerful source. It seems to be coming from—"the woman."

Evidently, in Hawthorne's view, fully awakened women accept the inevitability of a given legal order far less easily than their male counterparts. And clearly this is the central issue. What caused a state of near civil war in Boston and what creates the crackling tension in Hawthorne's sketch is Mrs. Hutchinson's proclamation—variously worded at various times, but always as far beyond the reach of the "trained and sharpened intellects" of the most scholastic Puritan controversialists as are Hester Prynne's sexual secrets—that "the chosen of man" are not necessarily "the sealed of heaven." Here, in her last, most devastating, and for Hawthorne most insupportable formulation, Mrs. Hutchinson is claiming that sort of direct inspiration and divine guidance necessary to distinguish between true and false, spiritual and legal teachers. But she has been forced to this last claim by the pressure of investigation and over-response; this, presumably, is what you are made bold to say when facing the legalistic integrity of John Winthrop—not to mention the holy wrath of Hugh Peters, the satiric antifeminism of Nathaniel Ward, and the sheer adamant intolerance of John Endicott. Behind her last claim—as Hawthorne well knows—lies a series of far less drastic attempts to affirm that the Spirit does not always obey the laws of ordinary moral appearance. And even though she has moved from the dangerous to the intolerable, the weight of Hawthorne's subtlest moral judgment falls no more heavily on her head than on those of her judges.

In simple ironic fact, she is their natural opposite—induced into individualistic heresy by their organized, legalistic intolerance in much the same way as Hester's later denials are induced by the violence of the community's over-response. Beginning, apparently, with only a purer sort of Calvinism than was customarily preached in New England, Mrs. Hutchinson's ultimate claim to a totally self-sufficient private illumination seems the inevitable response to an emerging Puritan orthodoxy which, in its undeniable tendency to conflate the visible with the invisible church, was really claiming that for nearly all valid human purposes the "chosen of men" *were* the "sealed of heaven."[7] If the community overextends and mystifies its authority, the individual will trust the deepest passional self to nullify it all. Or at least "the woman" will.

What Hawthorne's figure of Mrs. Hutchinson suggests is that "the woman" is not by essence the safe and conserving social force the seventeenth and the nineteenth century (and much Hawthorne criticism)

7. For an authoritative discussion of the way Puritan theory made the visible church *nearly* identical with the *invisible* (i.e., mystified the prime agent of "discipline") see Edmund Morgan, *Visible Saints* (New York, 1963). Some strong sense of the process seems implied everywhere in Hawthorne's writings about the Puritans; and, indeed, one could scarcely read Mather's *Magnalia* without grasping that it was with the Ann Hutchinson affair that the mystified public achieved precedence, in the Puritan world, over the mystical private.

decreed her to be.[8] On the contrary female sexuality seems, in its concentration and power, both a source for and a type of individualistic nullification of social restraint. Obviously Hawthorne's feelings about this are not without ambivalence. Personally, of course, he would always prefer some less powerful, more submissive "Phoebe"; and in one way or another he would continue to protest that "Woman's intellect should never give the tone to that of man," that her "morality is not exactly the material for masculine virtue" (XII, 217–18) [167]. But his clear recognition of the antisocial meaning of self-conscious female sexuality, first formulated in the theological context of Puritan heresy, goes a long way toward explaining the power and the pathos of Hester Prynne.

Hawthorne reformulates his insight in "The Gentle Boy." Despite the complexities introduced by a "calm" male enthusiast and by the presence of the "rational piety" of that unreconstructed lover of home and children named Dorothy Pearson, we can hardly miss the elemental clash between "the female," Quaker Catherine, and the entire legalistic, repressive Puritan establishment. Against that male system of enforced rationalistic uniformity, she extravagantly testifies to the reality of an inspired and pluralistic freedom. Her response is, of course, extreme; Hawthorne is no more than faithful to history in judging it so (even though he does not have her walk naked through the streets of the Puritan capital). But, in a terrifying and elemental way, her response is effective. Tobias Pearson can only puzzle over and feel guilty about his drift toward the sect whose doctrines he thinks quite irresponsible; but this "muffled female" *must* stand up in the midst of a Puritan congregation (authoritatively and symbolically divided, by a wide aisle, into male and female) and denounce the minister's cruel and sterile formulation of the Puritan way.

The relevance of Quaker Catherine for Hester Prynne is simple and evident: here is the woman who has *not* been prevented from joining hands with Ann Hutchinson; her enthusiasm (and her sufferings) are such that not even little Ilbrahim can hold her back from a career of public testimony to the autonomous authority of conscience itself. Quaker Catherine does "come down to us *in history*, hand in hand with Ann Hutchinson." No doubt several historical women lie behind Hawthorne's figural portrait of Quaker Catherine, but surely none more powerfully than Mary Dyer, Ann Hutchinson's strongest female ally—who literally took her hand and accompanied her out of Cotton's church after her excommunication, went with her into exile, and (years after Mrs. Hutchinson had been providentially slaughtered by the Indians) went on to become notorious in the Quaker invasion of Massachusetts.[9]

Accordingly, another level of history is also involved: virtually all commentators have recognized that in New England, in dialectic with

8. This point is made very effectively in an article by Nina Baym, in spite of an ill-informed and logically inconclusive "negative" argument about the lack of meaningful Puritan categories in *The Scarlet Letter*. See "Passion and Authority in *The Scarlet Letter*," *NEQ* 43 (1970).

9. There is no satisfactory reading of "The Gentle Boy" in print. The basic, old-fashioned "source" study—which includes some relevant material on Mary Dyer—is G. H. Orians, "Sources and Themes of 'The Gentle Boy,' " *NEQ* 14 (1941).

the Puritan Way, Ann Hutchinson and the Quakers go together; that the latter represent, chiefly, a more organized and self-consciously sectarian espousal of the values of individualistic (or "spiritual") freedom which is the essence of Ann Hutchinson's doctrine. If one is committed and hostile, the cry against both is simply devilish and seductive enthusiasm, unregenerate impulse breaking all bonds of restraint and decorum. If one is committed and sympathetic, the cry is just as simple: the martyrdom of human dignity and divine freedom by aggressive repression. If one is a cautious modern commentator, one can only pity the victims and worry that both the Hutchinsonian and the (seventeenth-century) Quaker doctrines do rather tend to elevate the "individual conscience above all authority"; that both promote a "monistic egotism" which tends to dissolve "all those psychological distinctions man had invented to 'check, circumscribe, and surpass himself.' "[1]

None of these formulations would have been unfamiliar to Hawthorne. And neither would his knowledge or speculation be significantly advanced by the modern historian who, after discussing the Ann Hutchinson question as a "Pre-Quaker Movement," begins his chapters on Quakerism proper with the observation that as in London and at the great Universities of England, "so too, the first Quakers to reach the American hemisphere were women."[2] In every way it comes to seem the reverse of surprising that radical freedom and awakened female sexuality are inextricably linked in Hawthorne's most obviously historical romance. History itself had forged the link.

What is perhaps surprising is that Hawthorne is as sympathetic to a sex-related understanding of freedom as he is. His "Mrs. Hutchinson" is a profoundly troubled and dangerous woman; his Quaker Catherine becomes, in her "unbridled fanaticism," guilty of violating her most sacred duties (even if Ilbrahim is *not* a Christ-figure); even his Hester Prynne is far from the "Saint" she has occasionally been made out to be. But Hawthorne sympathizes with the problems as deeply as he fears the dangers; his compulsion to record warnings is no stronger than his desire to discover the laws by which powerful half truths generate their opposites or to feel the pain of those being destroyed by that implacable dialectic. The context of the sex-freedom link in *The Scarlet Letter* is not adequately sensed, therefore, until we are in a position to measure Hawthorne's emotional distance from his seventeenth-century sources who first raised the issue of sex in connection with Ann Hutchinson's law-denying theology.

The measurement is swiftly made. It begins with Cotton Mather

---

1. The larger quotation is from Battis (287); he, in turn, is quoting from Gertrude Huehns' *Antinomianism in English History* (London, 1951). The same sentiments can be found in many modern treatments of any of the more individualistic or "spiritual" forms of religious experience in the seventeenth century.
2. Rufus Jones, *The Quakers in the American Colonies* (London, 1911), 26. See also Geoffrey Nuttall, *The Holy Spirit in Puritan Experience* (London, 1946). Nuttall treats early Quakerism as a "limit" of one sort of Puritan logic and experience; though he does not argue the case, one cannot help being struck by the prominence of women in his accounts of early Quaker prophecy.

and runs backward directly to John Winthrop and Edward Johnson.[3] All three are, through the typology of Ann Hutchinson, important sources for *The Scarlet Letter*. And except that they are all highy scornful in tone, it might almost be said that these Puritan historians began the tranformation of Ann Hutchinson into Hester Prynne. Certainly they reduced Ann Hutchinson to a sexual phenomenon far more egregiously than did Hawthorne.

The emphasis of Cotton Mather's treatment of the Hutchinson controversy is double—but not very complex or subtle. On the one hand he utterly rejects the charge that his grandfather John Cotton was hypocritical in declining to espouse Ann Hutchinson as his partner in heresy: it is not, he pedantically insists, a case of a Montanus refusing to stand by the side of his Maxilla; rather, obviously, of a notorious woman whom an infamous calumny connected with the name of an Athanasius. (One thinks, perhaps, of certain obdurate refusals to believe Dimmesdale's final confession.) On the other hand, more expansively and with more literary flair, he is determined to treat the sectaries themselves in a frankly sexual way.

The following reflection—from a special sub-section titled "Dux Faemina Facta"—may stand for Mather's theological antifeminism:

> It is the *mark of seducers* that *they lead captive silly women;* but what will you say, when you hear *subtil women* becoming the most *remarkable* of the *seducers*? . . . Arius promoted his blasphemies by first proselyting seven hundred *virgins* thereunto. Indeed, a *poyson* does never insinuate so quickly, nor operate so strongly, as when *women's milk* is the *vehicle* wherein 'tis given. Whereas the prime seducer of the whole faction which now began to threaten the country with something like a Munster tragedy, was a woman, a gentlewoman, of "an haughty carriage, busie spirit, competent wit, and a voluble tongue."[4]

The quotation marks around the final descriptive phrase point back, of course, to a contemporary phase of antifeminist response to Ann Hutchinson. As usual Mather is only elaborating what has come down to him.

But equally important in the "Wonderbook" which so pervasively influenced Hawthorne is the primary sexual language which informs Mather's account. Far more memorable than any formulation concerning the self-evidence of justification is a bastardy metaphor which helped to shape *The Scarlet Letter*: the doctrines of the Antinomians are "brats" whose "true parents" are to be discovered by the guardians of orthodoxy. And related to this basic concept is the whole grotesque

---

3. Thomas Hutchinson's masterful, three-volume *History of Massachusetts Bay* probably provided Hawthorne with his most judicious account of the Hutchinson affair; certainly it was useful in providing the transcript of Mrs. Hutchinson before the General Court at Newtown in November, 1637—where she gave a far better account of herself than would appear from Winthrop's *Short Story*. But the account given by *this* Hutchinson contains no hint of sexual language. For Hawthorne's reading of Hutchinson, Mather, Johnson, and Winthrop, see Marion L. Kesselring, *Hawthorne's Reading* (New York, 1949).

4. Of necessity I quote from a nineteenth-century edition: *Magnalia Christi Americana* (Hartford, Conn., 1855), II, 516.

business of the "very surprising *prodigies*" which were looked upon as
testimonies from heaven against the ways of the arch-heretic: "The erroneous gentlewoman herself, convicted of holding about *thirty* monstrous opinions, growing big with child . . . was delivered of about
thirty monstrous births at once." Or—behold the Puritan wit—perhaps "these were no more *monstrous births* than what is frequent for
women, laboring with *false conceptions*, to produce."

Again, none of this is strictly original with Cotton Mather: the hereti-
cal-idea-as-illegitimate-child conceit is in the windy pages of Edward
Johnson, and Winthrop himself labors the ugly details of monstrous
births—which are at least the providential consequence of her criminal
heresies. But the full "literary" elaboration of this sort of talk is
Mather's, and his account seems most to have influenced Hawthorne.[5]

The influence is very curious. On the one hand, Hawthorne specifically declines to repeat the story of monstrous births in his "Mrs.
Hutchinson"; such details are fitter for the "old and homely narrative
than for modern repetition" (XII, 225) [171]. And the sketch makes no
use of any bastardy metaphor. On the other hand, however, in a rather
startling display of creative process, it all comes back in the story of
Ann Hutchinson's typic sister, Hester Prynne. Not only does Hester
conceive a very real, natural child to accompany (and in some measure embody) her quasi-Hutchinsonian conception of spiritual freedom; but she finds it almost impossible to convince herself that Pearl
is not in some sense a monstrous birth. Along with many other characters in *The Scarlet Letter* (and not a few critics) Hester daily stares
at the child, waiting "to detect some dark and wild peculiarity" (90)
[61], unable to believe that a sinful conception can come to any valid
issue. This *might* be no more than the too-simply Puritan inability ever
to separate the moral order from the physical (like looking for "A's" in
the midnight sky), but with Mather's elaboration of Johnson and
Winthrop behind it, it is evidently a bit more. As almost everywhere,
Hawthorne seems to be making Hester Prynne literally what orthodox
Puritan metaphor said Ann Hutchinson was "really" or spiritually.

One more telling detail from Mather—to which we can only imagine Hawthorne's convoluted reaction. Not quite faithful to the wording of Winthrop, Mather has John Cotton express the opinion that
Mrs. Hutchinson ought "to be cast out with them that 'love and make
a lie.' "[6]

Except for this peculiar formulation—which is not really related to
Mather's basic set of sexual equivalences, but which just happens to
read like an epitome of Dimmesdale's career—nearly all of Mather's
basic vocabulary is second-hand. Mather's own debts are tedious to
detail, and clearly Hawthorne could have got all he needed from the

---

5. The heresy-bastard conceit is also in Thomas Weld's "Preface" to Winthrop's *Short Story*
(reprinted in Adams and Hall; see n. 6, p. 306); the *Short Story* is, in turn, the main source
of Mather's account. It is not certain, but it seems likely, that Hawthorne saw Winthrop's
book independently.

6. *Magnalia*, II, 518. Probably this is only Mather's pedantry at work—re-translating from Revelations. In Winthrop's *Short Story* Cotton says "make and maintaine a lye" (see Hall, *Antinomian Controversy*, 307).

Magnalia (though it is certain he read most of Mather's sources independently). The basic antifeminist construction seems to originate with Winthrop—not only with his specific characterization of Mrs. Hutchinson as "a woman of a haughty and fierce carriage, of a nimble wit and active spirit, and a very voluble tongue" but also with the clear implication in his whole account that one very deep issue is Mrs. Hutchinson's female invasion of male "literary" prerogative. Mrs. Hutchinson insists, out of *Titus*, that "elder women should instruct the younger"; Winthrop might admit, under exegetical duress, that "elder women must instruct the younger about their business, and to love their husbands and not to make them to clash," but his deeper feeling is rationalized in *Timothy*: "I permit not a woman to teach."[7]

This last makes the sexual politics of Hawthorne's remark about women's intellect not giving the tone to men's seem liberal. It also enables us to imagine, by simple contraries, what new and surer "relation between man and woman" Hester is teaching at the end of *The Scarlet Letter*. But, again, this is too easy.

If there is one formulation behind those of Cotton Mather worth savoring on its own, it is something from Edward Johnson. His impassioned account of the seductive appeal of Mrs. Hutchinson's doctrines gives us the clearest sense that Puritans themselves feared sexual implications more profound than those involving ordinary decorum. Upon Johnson's return to New England, he was alarmed to discover that a "Masterpiece of Woman's wit" had been set up by her own sex as a "Priest"; and Johnson was invited to join the cult:

> There was a little nimble tongued Woman among them, who said she could bring me acquainted with one of her own Sex that would shew me a way, if I could attaine it, even Revelations, full of such ravishing joy that I should never have cause to be sorry for sinne, so long as I live.

Here, as clearly as we need, is the simply hostile version of Hawthorne's suggestion that "woman's morality it not quite the standard for masculine virtue"—as well as the perception, registered in anger and in fear, that antinomian doctrine is not separable from the tone and from the unsettling consequences of awakened female sexuality.[8]

To write *The Scarlet Letter* out of Hutchinsonian materials Hawthorne would have to feel that tone, but he would have to feel others as well. Fear "the woman" as he might, he would yet feel the justice of setting her—in reality, and as a symbol of radical and self-contained moral freedom—against the omnivorous legalism of the Puritan establishment. If he would reduce Ann Hutchinson to a female

---

7. Quoted from Hall, *Antinomian Controversy*, 315–16, 267. Hawthorne would have found all he needed in the "Appendix" to Thomas Hutchinson's second volume; see his *History* (Cambridge, Mass., 1936), II, 366–91, esp. 368–69.
8. *Wonder-Working Providence of Sion's Saviour*, ed. by Franklin L. Jameson (New York, 1910), 134. Note also that Winthrop, besides his relentless pursuit of "monstrous" evidences against both Ann Hutchinson and Mary Dyer, does not overlook instances of irregular sexual practice resulting from Hutchinsonian principles; see his *Journal*, ed. James Kendall Hosmer, 2 vols. (New York, 1908), esp. II, 28.

"case," his reduction would be less drastic than that of his ancestors. And he would preserve, amplify, and revalue certain deeper hints. *The Scarlet Letter* might not be "about" Ann Hutchinson, but it would be, consciously and emphatically, about antinomianism and "the woman."

III

We are now, finally, in a position to "begin"—to look directly at Hester walking in the footsteps of Ann Hutchinson, and to approach *The Scarlet Letter* itself in the one historical context Hawthorne seems most urgently to suggest. Legitimately, that task would require twice as many pages and distinctions as we have already set down. But perhaps the sympathetic reader will waive his right to charge reductive or text-ignoring historicism against a necessarily schematic suggestion about Hawthorne's romance in the Antinomian context.

The Scarlet Letter is, as I have suggested, not *roman à clef*: we are not to look for secret informations about literal, existent singulars in the seventeenth-century world. Neither is it quite an "allegory" of the real significance of a theological controversy: the Antinomian Crisis has historical ramifications which defy critical ingenuity to discover in *The Scarlet Letter*. And yet, to repeat, it is about antinomianism and "the woman."

It is, as in one recent formulation, about "passion and authority," but it is not about those timeless human realities *as such*. The experiences of Hester and Dimmesdale are subject to an exquisite (and painful) historical conditioning. Their Puritan world may be, as in another formulation, some version of the "modern" world, but this is far too imprecise to account for the historical specificity of Hawthorne's intention and achievement. To be sure, *The Scarlet Letter* details the items of Hester's beliefs even less than the early sketch specifies those of Mrs. Hutchinson; and yet the romance undoubtedly is, as one very excellent reading describes it, a "literary exercise in moral theology."[9]

That theology is, so far as the *characters* are concerned, "Puritan." So profoundly Puritan are the historically conditioned experiences of Hester and Dimmesdale, in fact, that *The Scarlet Letter* must be seen as Hawthorne's way of testing the limits of Puritan theology as a way of making sense out of the deepest and most passionate human experience. The limits of that theology are understood by Hawthorne to be—what I take it in fact they are—antinomian; and those antinomian limits of Puritan theology are associated by Hawthorne—as they were by his orthodox predecessors—with "the woman." When the limits are reached, as historically they were and as philosophically they must be, the theology fails what a twentieth-century critic of Puritanism has called "the pragmatic test." And as the theology fails, *The Scarlet Letter* becomes (in the context of the Ann Hutchinson problem, at least)

9. The three formulations are, respectively, those of Nina Baym, "Passion and Authority," Charles Feidelson, Jr., "*The Scarlet Letter*," *Hawthorne Centenary Essays* (Columbus, Ohio, 1964), and Austin Warren, "*The Scarlet Letter*: A Literary Exercise in Moral Theology."

a powerful contribution to what a nineteenth-century critic called "the moral argument against Calvinism."[1]

The Scarlet Letter is about the reasons why "the woman" Hester Prynne reaches certain antinomian conclusions not unlike those of Ann Hutchinson; and why, though her progress seems somehow necessary, and though personally she enlists our deepest sympathies, both the tale and the teller force her to abandon those conclusions. More elliptically, it is also about Dimmesdale's lesser portion of the "strange fire"; about the failure of his Cottonesque, semi-antinomian theology; and, in the end, about his much-misunderstood "neonomian" emphasis on "the law" and "the sin." If we understand Hawthorne's relation to Mather, Johnson, and Winthrop properly, we can profitably view *The Scarlet Letter* as Hawthorne's own *Short Story of the Rise, Reign and Ruine of the Antinomians, Familists, and Libertines.*

In these terms, Hester's career is fairly easy to plot. At the outset she is not unambiguously antinomian. But she is conceived, like Hawthorne's Ann Hutchinson, as a woman who bears "trouble in her own bosom" (XII, 219) [168]; and her "desperate recklessness" on the scaffold, symbolized by the flagrancy of her embroidered "A," and issuing in "a haughty smile, and a glance that would not be abashed" (52) [40], seems deliberately to recall Mrs. Hutchinson's courtroom defiance:

> She stands loftily before her judges with a determined brow; and, unknown to herself, there is a flash of carnal pride half hidden in her eye, as she surveys the many learned and famous men whom her doctrines have put in fear. (XII, 224) [171]

That might describe Hester easily enough. She begins, let us say, in a not very repentant spirit. Strong hints of her later denials and unorthodox affirmations are already there.

To be sure, Hester feels a deep sense of shame, and we scarcely need the still, small quasi-authorial voice of a young-woman spectator to tell us so; the "reduction" of Ann Hutchinson's doctrinal bastard to a living illegitimate child must, in a Puritan community, at least, count for something. And yet even here Hester feels little enough of what we should call "guilt."[2] Just after the trauma of public exposure, she does confess a real wrong done to Chillingworth; but defiance of hopelessly unqualified and painfully uncomprehending male judges seems clearly the dominant element in her early characterization. It is probably true to say that (ignoring the "epilogue") Hester is nearer to "repentance" at the very opening of *The Scarlet Letter* than she ever is again. But she is not very near it. And by the time she finds herself in the forest

---

1. The "pragmatic" (or moral) argument against Calvinism runs backwards from Henry Bamford Parkes' essay "The Puritan Heresy" (in *The Pragmatic Test* [New York, 1941]) to William Ellery Channing, at least (probably to Jonathan Mayhew). Only critics who do not feel themselves challenged by Puritan beliefs fail to argue from Puritanism's seeming inability to square with natural conscience and adequately to interpret moral experience.
2. My Cornell colleague Michael Kammen first suggested to me that the modern sociological and anthropological distinction between "guilt" and the more primitive, less rational and internalized "shame" was useful in distinguishing Dimmesdale's from Hester's response to their adultery.

with Dimmesdale, she has evidently found that she "should never have cause to be sorry for sinne" again.

For that antinomian moment, the narrator severely instructs us, Hester's "whole seven years of outlaw and ignominy had been little other than a preparation" (200) [129]. The moment includes not only the decision to cast by all outward pretence of living by the Puritan "world's law" and run away with Dimmesdale but also, and even more radically, her attempt to convince that unreconstructed Puritan theologian that what they earlier did "had a consecration of its own"—they having felt it so and said so to each other. The painfulness of Hester's development toward this moment in no way lessens our sense of its inevitability. From the first she has seemed perilously close to defying her judges with the affirmation that her spirit posits and obeys its own law.

The narrator seems convinced that Hester has indeed sinned—deeply, and "in the most sacred quality of human life" (56) [42]; at one level of our response, the seventh commandment remains real enough. But what he urges far more strongly is the outrage to both human privacy and human conscience perpetrated by the "unpardonable" Puritan practice of exposure and enforced confession.[3] And he also feels—with Hester—that her adultery was, in quality, not entirely evil: the sacred is present along with the sinful; or, less paradoxically, that Hester has fulfilled her passionate self for the first time in her life.

But of course there are no Puritan categories for this ambiguity. There is no way for Hester to say to herself that her action had been naturally perfect and yet had introduced an element of profound social disharmony. And no way for the Puritan mind to treat her evident unwillingness *fully* to disown and un-will the affections and natural motions which caused the disorder as anything but evidence of unregenerated natural depravity. She evidently loves her sin, and theocrats in the business of inferring the ultimate moral quality of the self from the prevailing outward signs can reach only one conclusion. And, thus, when the Puritan establishment moves from the *fact* that Hester *has sinned* to the *conclusion* that she in essence *is sinful*, her rich and ambiguous personality has no life-saving resource but to begin a career of antinomian speculation, of internal resistance to all Puritan categories.

If Society must treat the negative implications of one mixed act as the symbol of the natural depravity of the Self, that Self is likely to respond with a simple affirmation of all its own profound impulses. If the Puritans begin by turning Hester into a sermon, a type, and an allegory of "Sin," she will end by nullifying their entire world of external law and interference with her own pure freedom. Ideally we might wish for Hester to cease feeling shame and to discover the real though limited extent of her guilt. But this, in the Puritan mental and social world seems impossible. Extremes of public legalism seem to breed

---

3. For the Puritan doctrine and practice of confession—and for a very useful approach to *The Scarlet Letter*, which I regard as supplementary to my own—see Baughman, "Public Confession and *The Scarlet Letter*."

their antinomian opposite by natural law.[4] At any rate, Hester finds no way to affirm the legitimacy of her powerful sexual nature without also affirming total, anarchic spiritual freedom.

Of course she begins in outward conformity, playing the game of "sanctification"—the single rule of which is that the true Self is the sum of all its outward works; indeed, by the time we see her in the chapter called "Another View of Hester," she has learned the game so well as to have covered her undestroyed inner pride with an external appearance "so like humility, that it produced all the softening influence of that latter quality on the public mind" (162) [106]. But all the while she is "preparing," moving toward the moment when she announces a doctrine of personal freedom which every orthodox Puritan sensed would lead directly to passionate license and judged a more serious threat to public order than adultery itself.

Her own version of the antinomian heresy does not, obviously, express itself in theological jargon; for the most part Hawthorne eschewed it even in treating Mrs. Hutchinson. No dogmatist, Hawthorne is looking for differences that *make* a difference; and the antinomian difference is identically expressed in Mrs. Hutchinson and Hester Prynne, in association with but not quite reduced to a discovery and affirmation of the legitimacy of their female sexuality. Call it Spirit with the seventeenth, or Passional Self with a later century, one's affirmation is not very different: the significance of a life is *not* the sum of its legally regulated outward works; or, more radically, what one does has a consecration of its own provided the quality of deep inner feeling is right—i.e., authentic.

Now plainly this is all too partial a truth for Hawthorne; we are not wrong in hearing his own advice when Dimmesdale twice bids Hester's revolutionary voice to "Hush." And yet he understands how it all comes about. He even presents it as necessary for Hester to reach this stage of self-affirmation and release from shame before she can settle into anything approaching final peace.

While she cannot affirm her adultery, she cannot truly accept Pearl as a valid human person. It is probably too much to ask her to accept a good-out-of-evil doctrine all at once. Certainly it is better to affirm the natural order than to treat Pearl chiefly as a living sermon; clearly nothing good can happen as long as the mother is allegorizing the child even as the community has allegorized the mother; and surely a

---

4. Though John Winthrop is only a background figure in *The Scarlet Letter*, his moral presence is strongly felt. It is surely the famous "little speech" on liberty of this most energetic opponent of Ann Hutchinson that Hawthorne had in mind when he wrote in "Main Street" that what the Puritans "called Liberty" was very much "like an iron cage" (III, 449). In fact, it is Winthrop's doctrine of liberty as holy obedience which sinews the clerical doctrines of visible sanctity, preparation, and sanctification, to make the Puritan world the massive and unitary legal construct Hawthorne represents it to be in the opening pages of *The Scarlet Letter*. Hawthorne gives us that world as of the 1640's: one could argue that rigidification was not complete by that point and that Hawthorne is really describing a later stage of development, when "one generation had bequeathed . . . the counterfeit of its religious ardor to the next" (III, 460); for this view see E. H. Davidson, "The Question of History in *The Scarlet Letter*," *ESQ*, 25 (1951); but one can also argue that, though Hawthorne does indeed "encapsulate" a long historical sequence into the moments of its beginning, he clearly intends to point us to the banishment of Ann Hutchinson (1636–38) as the crucial defeat of spiritual libertarianism in the Puritan world.

parent who is watching for a child to become a moral monster will not be disappointed.

And then there is the simple matter of Hester's integrity. Speculating so boldly and conforming so relentlessly, she has become—no less than Dimmesdale himself—two people. At one primal level, the whole antinomian controversy is about the inner and the outer, the private and the public person: what do our outward works, positive and negative, really reveal about our salvation status, or, in naturalized form, about our selves? Hawthorne's romance is, of course, busy denying total autonomous validity to the private or "spiritual" self; and the explicit "moral" about freely "showing forth" some inferential "token" clearly embodies the authorial realization that inner and outer can never be completely congruent. Hawthorne has not written "Young Goodman Brown" and "The Minister's Black Veil" for nothing. And yet Hester must stop living a life so completely double. Quite like Dimmesdale, she must heal the wide and deep, "hypocritical" split between her outer and inner self. She may never realize as clearly as Dimmesdale finally does the extent to which (or the profound reasons why) the Self must accept the demystified implications of the visible, and dwell—though not as the great body of Puritans do—among moral surfaces.[5] But in the terms of her own developing theory of spiritual self-reliance, she must be, as fully as possible, whatever she truly is.

And we sense her self-acceptance and self-affirmation coming. She may seem to wander in confusion—thinking the sun of universal benevolence shines only to illuminate her scarlet letter, and deceiving herself about why she remains in New England; but from time to time, when a human eye (presumably Dimmesdale's) falls upon her "ignominious brand," she wills her old passion anew. She may worry about the condition and quality of Pearl's right to existence; but when the watchful theocratic government considers removing her natural child to some more socialized context of Christian nurture, Hester is simply defiant: "I will not lose the child!" (113) [76]. She may argue from Pearl's moral use, but she is also affirming the validity of her sexual nature.

We can say—if we wish to maintain a *modern only* reading of *The Scarlet Letter*—that this is *all* Hester is affirming when she argues, finally, that her adultery had "a consecration of its own"; that Hawthorne has engaged Hester *entirely* in an *overt* struggle with the unruly and unsatisfied sexual emotions which the Puritans obscurely felt to lie unsublimated behind Mrs. Hutchinson's public career, and which they clearly felt would be unleashed upon their community by a public acceptance of her doctrine. (Male self-control being difficult enough when all women are passive or frigid.) But if our conclusions concern only Hester's movement from sexual shame to sexual affirmation, then Hawthorne has wasted a good deal of historic under-

---

5. The lesson of the ultimate autonomy of the spiritual self, along with the coordinate subjection of the outward man to civil authority, is (presumably) the lesson Hawthorne learned from the career of Roger Williams—of whom Hawthorne seems a true spiritual disciple.

standing and surmise as mere costume and color. It seems far more adequate to say—as we have already said—that Hawthorne regards awakened and not conventionally invested female sexual power as a source and type of individualistic nullification of social restraint.

Waiving the problem of vehicle and tenor, we may validly conclude that in *The Scarlet Letter* "the woman's" discovery of an authentic, valid, and not shameful sexual nature is not unlike the Self's discovery of its own interior, "spiritual" sanction. The *donnée* of Hawthorne's romance is such that Hester discovers both together, and each reinforces the other.

And further, by way of completing our contextual approach to *The Scarlet Letter*, it seems appropriate to suggest that Hawthorne's treatment of Dimmesdale, the less clearly antinomian partner, provides cogent reasons for not divorcing the theology from, or reducing it too simply to, the sexuality. For Dimmesdale's predicament is not to be understood without some fairly explicit reference to the most theological of the antinomian questions—certainly not without a sense of the peculiar moral shapes one can be molded into only by a fairly high Calvinism. Indeed there is, as I have already suggested, strong evidence that Hawthorne thought of Dimmesdale as some intellectual and literary relative of John Cotton.

IV

In a number of related senses, Dimmesdale's problem is "hypocrisy." Most simply, he is not what he outwardly appears; he may or may not be "vile," but he is not the apotheosis of saintly purity the Puritan community takes him for. More technically, he is an enforcing agent of public discipline who has himself sinned against a clear and serious public law whose absolute validity he (unlike Hester) never questions for a moment; and who refuses to confess and submit to the discipline he has sworn by covenant to uphold and enforce. In so refusing, he may very well be avoiding the question of whether he is really sorry for his sin, or whether in fact he loves his own satisfactions more than he loves God; if so, if Dimmesdale's adultery is really "idolatry," as in the common religious equivalence, then of course he is a "hypocrite" in the very most technical Puritan sense of all: he is an unconverted man who has found his way not only *in to* but to the very *apex* of the purest church the world has ever known. This is clearly what he fears: that the minister, whose election is sure if anyone's is, whose conversion is the norm for the members' admission, and who—at this level, incidentally—is universally revered as a miracle of preternatural holiness and supernatural humility, is really an unregenerate sinner simply.

He fears, but he is not certain. He also hopes. In such tension Dimmesdale is a classic Puritan case of conscience—an advanced and exacerbated form of the too-common problem of lingering sinfulness and naturally attendant doubt which seems to have followed most honest Puritans into full communion with New England's congregations of "visible saints." What, after all, could the unreconstructed Arminianism of natural conscience make of the fact that after one professed to have received saving grace by the direct operation of the spirit (and had that profession accepted by all other spiritual men) one continued to be roughly the same sort of moral person one was before?[6]

The *simple* answer is antinomianism: "works" argue nothing. The sons of God being under no law, it is as fatal a confusion to argue from the presence of sin to the absence of grace as it is to infer justification of the person from sanctification of the life. Grace is a spiritual indwelling, and whatever the Spirit is, is right. Just ask Hester.

Dimmesdale, of course, can accept this limit-interpretation of Pauline and Protestant theology as little as Cotton could. And yet Dimmesdale seems caught in a trap set for him by certain of the spiritual principles Cotton laid down carefully to distinguish himself from both the covenant legalists on the one side and the "antinomians, familists, and libertines" on the other. Everyone wanted to admit that the forensic transaction of justification did not imply or create immediate and perfect operational sanctity, but Cotton's critics wanted him to narrow the gap as much as Protestant loyalty could possibly admit. They put it to him: when you say "A Christian may have assurance of his good estate maintained to him when the frame of his Spirit and course is grown much degenerate, we want much satisfaction." Your doctrine is very dangerous, they instructed him; there ought to be more "symmetry and proportion" in this matter of "faith and holiness" or you "open a wide door of temptation, as into Sin with less fear, so into a bold continuance and slight healing of sin, and breaches thereby."[7]

As always, the legalists have conceived the problem rather too crudely: Dimmesdale's "continuance," for example, is far from "bold," and his physical and moral self-flagellations amount at some level to more than a "slight healing of sin." And yet there is sense in their position. A man who *fears* he may be a hypocrite and yet has good theological reasons to *hope* that even gross sins do not necessarily prove the case either way is likely to clutch at every available theological straw. And indeed Cotton's answer to the legalists offers far more than a straw. It is worth quoting at some length for it marvellously illuminates Dimmesdale's predicament. If a man

> know the riches of Gods grace in Christ, he ordinarily both may, and (by ordinary rule) ought to believe that his justified estate doth still remain unshaken, not withstanding his grievous sin. For

6. Conveniently, one might look at *The Diary of Michael Wigglesworth*, ed. by Edmund Morgan (New York, 1956), for a sense of the painful doubts experienced by the already encovenanted saints. I have studied a coordinate problem—how could the sinning and doubting Christian really see fit to *declare* himself a saint?—in an analysis of Edward Taylor: "*Gods Determinations* Touching Half-Way Membership," *AL*, 39 (1967). If Solomon Stoddard is to be believed (that Puritan theory had turned Communion Sundays into "days of torment") then *some* version of Dimmesdale's problem was widespread indeed.

7. Quoted from Hall, *Antinomian Controversy*, 65–66. The document in question is "The Elders Reply"—to the answers Cotton had given to sixteen questions addressed to him by those same "Elders."

> as Justification and the faith of it doth not stand upon his good
> works, so neither doth it fall or fail upon his evil work.[8]

Cotton's difference from the antinomians is, evidently, a fairly subtle
one—and not of primary interest to us here. Of significance is the fact
that the strictest Calvinist of New England's first generation provides
Dimmesdale with a perfectly plausible way to avoid the obvious, most
"natural" conclusion about his technical hypocrisy.

And Cotton brings the case even closer to our own:

> Because men of great measure of holiness be apt to live besides
> their faith, in the strength of their own gifts and not in the
> strength of Christ, it pleaseth the Lord sometimes to leave them
> to greater falls, than other weaker Christians, who being of
> weaker gifts do find more need to live by faith in Christ than
> upon the strength of their gifts.

It seems to me entirely likely that some conception such as this—a
highly religious man being tested by a great fall—lies very close to
Hawthorne's idea of Dimmesdale.[9] And that Hawthorne is testing this
Cottonesque way of conceptualizing the problem of sin and sainthood
as he watches Dimmesdale fail to work out his salvation in these
terms.

For the terms do fail him, even more plainly than, in the epilogue,
Hester's appear to have failed her. The psychological dynamic of their
failure is delicately wrought, but it is "there," in the romance. To see it
requires only to look at Dimmesdale's few key speeches very closely.

We do not begin to get inside Dimmesdale until Chapter 10, where
"The Leech" is working on "His Patient." With the worst imaginable
motives, Chillingworth is trying to get Dimmesdale to do what the
structure and basic conception of the romance clearly indicates he
must if he is to save his soul, in any imaginable sense—clearly and
openly admit his guilt, whatever the consequences. Dimmesdale offers
several "good" reasons why some men find it impossible to confess before the Last Day, or to any but the Searcher of Hearts. His reasons are
all, we easily sense, speculative or notional, unreal; the two men are
talking "objectively" about "some men." And yet before Dimmesdale
waives the whole subject as if "irrelevant or unreasonable," he is betrayed into a modestly revealing hint. The best of his rationalizations is
that "some men" do not confess because in spite of their sin they yet
retain "a zeal for God's glory and man's welfare"; they realize that once
exposed "no good can be achieved by them; no evil of the past be redeemed by better service" (132) [88]. Hypocrisy, Dimmesdale seems to
argue, is not without an important social, even spiritual use.

8. From "Mr. Cotton's Rejoynder," quoted in Hall, 88.
9. "Rejoynder," in Hall, 88–89. I do not suppose that Hawthorne could have seen this then-
unpublished document. I do assume, however, that Hawthorne did somewhere acquire a
first-hand familiarity with some of Cotton's works, or with at least some Puritan writers who
introduced the problem of justification *in spite of* a rather imperfect sanctification. It would
be very naive to assume that Hawthorne's reading of Puritan writers is exhausted by the list
of his borrowings from the Salem Athenaeum, when so many of them were available on the
bookstands of the 1830's.

Chillingworth, however, that perfect devil's advocate, recognizes the desperate character of this logic at once. Hypocrisy for the sake of the kingdom is the worst hypocrisy of all. Would Dimmesdale have us believe "that a false show can be better—can be more for God's glory, or man's welfare—than God's own truth" (133) [89]?

The irony here is very keen. It seems impossible to escape the sense that Hawthorne is deliberately playing with one of the most famous arguments in a massive Puritan literature of propagandistic self-defense—the idea of "the usefulness of hypocrites." Attacked by En-glish Presbyterians for a wildly utopian collapse of the invisible church into the visible, defenders of the New England Way loudly protested that they fully *expected* to receive hypocrites into their churches, despite the revolutionary tests for saving grace; that they indeed could rest easy in this practical knowledge, despite their purist theoretic aims, because in outward practice the hypocrite was very often more zealous, set a more striking public example than the true saint. The most authoritative spokesman for this Puritan "foreign policy" was—of course—John Cotton.[1]

The irony is only slightly less telling when we remember that neither Dimmesdale nor Hawthorne really sees the case in these terms. Hawthorne could very *easily* accept hypocrites into *his* church, since it is universal and consists *only* of hypocrites who never *can* fully "show forth" what they ultimately are. Limited to his historic world, however, Dimmesdale is obviously far from this insight. Indeed he is even farther away from it than his use-of-hypocrites rationalization would indicate.

Where he is, morally and theologically speaking, becomes perfectly clear only in the forest with Hester—though anyone versed in the literary cure of Puritan souls senses it long before. The meaning of his entire predicament is encapsulated into two sentences, and logically enough he speaks them in direct reply to Hester's antinomian plan for adulterous escape:

> "If, in all these past seven years," thought he, "I could recall one instant of peace or hope, I would yet endure, for the sake of that earnest of Heaven's mercy. But now,—since I am irrevocably doomed,—wherefore should I not snatch the solace allowed to the condemned culprit before his execution?" (201) [129]

Again the irony is fairly complex. First of all we recognize in Dimmesdale's decision to "seize the day" the crassest sort of antinomian response possible for a Calvinist to make: since I am predestined to hell anyway, I might as well. . . . But this is the least of it.

More crucially, Dimmesdale reveals that he has to this point been looking at his life in a way that is very "properly" Calvinist: he has been regarding his acts, good and evil, and his spiritual states, hopeful and discouraging, not as sequential parts of a moral life that he is *building*, bit by bit, but rather as *evidences* of his status relative to di-

1. See Miller, *Colony to Province*, 79–80.

vine decree. The difference may often seem subtle in practice, but it is absolutely profound; and the meaning is to be read in any Puritan diary. One does not repent sin in order to undo it and atone for it and get back into divine favor; only Catholics and other Arminians think this. Rather one examines sins along with every other significant fact about the moral life in order to detect, if one possibly can, whether or not an eternal decree of salvation has made itself temporally manifest as a spiritual experience of justification, usually issuing more or less "proportionally and symmetrically" in sanctification.

For *most* Puritans sins are, therefore, an essential sign; for *all*, repentance is an absolutely necessary one. Even for Cotton. The great man may have great sins and not lose heart and hope; but even the great man must find that he truly *can* repent. Gross outward lapses may be at best a crude indicator of the spiritual estate, but enduring love of sin is not.

"Of penance," Dimmesdale admits—of that melodramatic outward punishment and gothic inward torture—there has been a surfeit; "Of penitence," however—of that true spiritual rejection of the soul's rejection of God—"there has been none!" (192) [124]. And now, he concludes, things look very bad indeed. He may as well admit he has been, all along, the hypocrite he feared he might be and yet hoped (in spite of his rationalization to Chillingworth) he might not be. In the forest then, finally, after seven years of self-torturing hope against hope, Dimmesdale gives over the attempt to see himself as the man whose justification does not, in Cotton's words, "Fall or fail upon his evil works." Semi-antinomian to this point, he now concludes that his hope has all been in vain—that he has not repented his sin, that he has been granted no further spiritual assurances, and that his crime of adultery is precisely what all vulgar Puritanism would take it to be, "visible" (if only to himself) evidence of manifest unregeneracy.

Spiritually, then, Dimmesdale is further from Hester Prynne during their sexual reunion in the forest than he has ever been before—as far away, in fact, as it is possible to be within a Puritan world. Their decision to escape, though they may "say it" to each other, means two dramatically opposed things. To Hester it is that triumphant escape into the higher antinomian freedom of spiritual self-reliance; to Dimmesdale it is a pitiful retreat from the hope-against-hope to that miserable alternative of sinful freedom left to the despairing reprobate. One may wish their original adulterous meeting involved more of real mutuality.

Thus Hawthorne's subtlest view of Dimmesdale is as a man who is so ineffectual an antinomian as not to be able to overcome the conscientious suspicion that his serious sin proves him a hypocrite; not even with the subtle categories of John Cotton. Hawthorne's men, as we know, are weaker than his women. Or perhaps it is simply that "woman's morality is not quite the standard for masculine virtue." Or perhaps he is simply honest. In any event, neither his sexuality nor his doctrine can justify the life he has been leading or, now, sanctify the new freedom he has been seduced into accepting. He will run away, in

a sense, to settle his doubts, once and for all, into a certainty of repro-
bation.

If we are sufficiently aware of the positivistic pitfalls, it becomes
useful to speculate about Dimmesdale's fictional relation to John Cotton. Should we say he is some curious version of Cotton's son, who
did commit adultery and suffer ignominious excommunication? Or
might we see him as a provisional John Cotton who by Providential
mischance happened to seduce (or be seduced by) Ann Hutchinson?
What if, Hawthorne might have brooded, what if Ann Hutchinson had
literally been what Puritan metaphor implied she was? And what if
Cotton were implicated, literally, to the very extent his English detractors said he metaphorically was? What, in short, would a "high" but
not antinomian Calvinist do if he *had* played the part of a sexual Montanus to some sexual Maxilla? What would a real sin, all passionate
and ambiguous, do to the delicate balances of personality required to
maintain that exquisite "Doctrine of the Saints' Infirmities"? What
sense might a younger, less robust, less settled version (or disciple) of
Cotton be able to make out of a passionate adultery?

In this light, it is just possible that Dimmesdale owes something to
the writings (*not* to the *life*) of John Preston, Cotton's most famous orthodox convert and disciple. Mather's *Magnalia* calls Cotton the "spiritual father" of Preston, and his most famous work (*The Doctrine of
the Saints' Infirmities*, 1638) owes a profound debt to Cotton's ideas
about assurance in spite of sin. Like Cotton, Preston is at great pains
to prove that the Puritan saint "may have many infirmities, and the
covenant remain unbroken." But there is one peculiar and illuminating hesitation in Preston that is entirely lacking in Cotton's answers to
the American legalists of the 1630's. Unlike Cotton, Preston is anxious
about an exception—or at least a possible misunderstanding. Not *all*
sins can be written off as mere "infirmities"; "some sins" are so radically idolatrous that they must be taken to mean that a person has not
been in the covenant—that he has been a hypocrite all along. Preston
does not specify; but his one hint is telling indeed: the exceptions are
sins which "untye the marriage knot" as, in human marriage, "Adultery."[2] That revelation would seem to explain Dimmesdale's career
pretty well: the reason he *cannot* repent is that he *is not* a saint; *probably* Preston's emphasis is sounder than Cotton's. And so he gives
over the desperate seven-year effort to believe himself *not* a hypocrite in the worst sense. His peculiar "infirmity" is too real, too true
a sign of unregenerate infidelity. Justification and sanctification are

2. *The Doctrine of the Saints' Infirmities* (London, 1638), 36–38. No less a scholar than John F.
H. New has interpreted the passage in question to mean, simply, that adultery is a cardinal
example of a sin which disproves covenant status—whereas, according to my reading, only
some analogy is intended (see *Anglican and Puritan* [1964], 93). The critic of *The Scarlet
Letter* will be rewarded by a reading of Preston's treatise, especially the first sermon. His encouragement to even a *lifelong* struggle against "infirmities" forms an appropriate background to Dimmesdale's weakening after seven years; and, on the other side, his clear
statement that "a sin committed simply with deliberation cannot be an infirmity" seems to
supply the ironic context for Hawthorne's comment on Dimmesdale's state just *after* he has
lost the *struggle*: "he had yielded himself, with deliberate choice, as he had never done before, to what he knew was deadly sin" (222) [141]. Thus, in a sense, it is only when
Dimmesdale gives up the belief that is sin that is an infirmity that it truly ceases to be one.

not to be conflated, but "some sins" are unsupportable. And thus, until Dimmesdale's very last moment, Puritan doctrines with sexual implications and overtones seem to be damning him as surely as they seem to be saving Hester.

At the last moment, of course, a major reversal occurs. Ceasing to "live in the strength of [his] own gifts"—even though he has just exercised them magnificently in a bad-faith election sermon—Dimmesdale asks for Hester's strength and God's grace to help him up the scaffold. Once there, his words indicate that somehow he has freed himself from his old Calvinist entrapment. If he has not entirely de-theologized himself, at least he has got his doctrine down to certain saving essentials. Hester calls on his far-seeing vision to predict their final destiny. But Dimmesdale, who has been reading evidences of *faits accomplis* for too long, rightly refuses to predict: "Hush, Hester, hush!" What has often been called his final "gloom" is no more than elemental moral and theological honesty. "The law we broke!—the sin here so awfully revealed!" Stern instructions to an Antinomian. Yet these alone must be in their thoughts, their only proper concern. For the rest, "God knows; and He is merciful!" (256) [162].

Law, Sin, Mercy—these are now the only terms in Dimmesdale's new moral scheme. We know there are laws to restrict our Selves in the name of our communities which, well or ill, sustain our common life; we know we break these laws; the rest is up to God. This may or may not conceal Arminian heresy, but "neonomian" Hawthorne has clearly designed it to be. I think we may grant the writer of "Young Goodman Brown" and "The Minister's Black Veil," and the creator of Dimmesdale's problems of ever "outering" what he truly is inside, the right to affirm the operational primacy of "the public."

It takes Hester longer, and it requires a years-later epilogue, but she too relents from her doctrine of the autonomous private—she repents, turns her game of "penance" into authentic "penitence." She still holds out for a feminist reformer, but she can now separate the valid sexual expectations of her sisterhood from the supposed spiritual freedom of the Self from the world's law.

The final ironies of Hawthorne's use of Hutchinsonian motifs and antinomian ideas are striking indeed. If his early sketch seems to reduce a dangerous female heretic to a sexual case, his effort can be regarded as a commentary on a Puritan response as validly as it can be taken for his own; and, he puts *all* the subtlety back into *The Scarlet Letter*. He maintains, even literalizes, all the sexual suggestions in his creation of Hester Prynne, but he leaves them in tension with some very profound (if, for him, dangerous) religious ideas. With Dimmesdale he allows the full theological complexity to operate, though we never forget that Dimmesdale is related to Hester in the sexual problems which form the context of their spiritual struggles. The perfect context, we feel, given Puritan problems with "privacy" of all sorts. And in the end, after he has fully explored the antinomian and Cottonesque ramifications of his imaginative vision of a Puritan heresy, in doctrine and in metaphoric implication, Hawthorne brings both his principal characters back to something like his own "neonomian" norm. The ending is by no means "happy"—any more than Hawthorne's "Antinomians" and "Libertines" are in any sense that would satisfy Winthrop or Mather "Ruined." But their "Short Story" does end in an important doctrinal transformation.

The Self is not to be regularly inferred from its Works; it is quite naive to think so. But human sin, guilt, and sorrow are not to be transcended or "spiritually" suspended in this life. The Self is spiritually more free than any human establishment, theocratic or otherwise, can recognize or "tolerate." But the world's law validly exists to restrain our disruptive social excesses, however powerful and authentic we feel or "say" their private consecration to be. That, or something like it, equally simple, was the usable historical truth to be discovered from a tracing of Ann Hutchinson's footsteps.

FREDERICK NEWBERRY

A Red-Hot *A* and a Lusting Divine: Sources for *The Scarlet Letter*†

While there has been no shortage of studies on Hawthorne's literary borrowings in *The Scarlet Letter*, little has been found concerning historical sources of the letter *A* itself and virtually nothing has been uncovered concerning adulterous figures in Puritan history who might have been the prototypes of Hester Prynne and the Reverend Arthur Dimmesdale. We do know that by 1838, when an early version of Hester appeared in "Endicott and the Red Cross," Hawthorne was aware of the 1694 law enacted in Salem that required a woman convicted of adultery to wear a capital *A* sewn conspicuously on her garments.[1] Although the appearance of this law so late in the century might seem anomalous to the 1634 setting of "Endicott and the Red Cross" or to the 1642–49 setting of *The Scarlet Letter*, we may easily resolve the discrepancy by assuming either that Hawthorne had been influenced instead by the early seventeenth-century case of Goodwife Mendame, sentenced to wear an *AD* on her sleeve, or that, contrary to his usual practice, he felt the need in this instance to take liberties with the historical record.[2] Yet the burning sensation described by the narrator in

---

† From *New England Quarterly* 60.2 (June 1987): 256–64. Copyright © *The New England Quarterly*. Reproduced by permission of the publisher and the author. Page numbers in square brackets refer to this Norton Critical Edition.

1. Edward Dawson, *Hawthorne's Knowledge and Use of New England History: A Study in Sources* (Nashville: Vanderbilt UP, 1939), 19, first proposed that Hawthorne discovered this source in Joseph Felt, *The Annals of Salem, from Its First Settlement* (Salem, 1827), 317. Hawthorne consulted Felt in 1833, 1834, and 1849. See Marion L. Kesselring, *Hawthorne's Reading, 1828–1850: A Transcription and Identification of Titles Recorded in the Charge-Books of the Salem Athenæum* (1949; reprinted, Folcroft, Pa.: Folcroft Library Editions, 1975), 50.

2. The time frame of *The Scarlet Letter* is well established. See Charles Ryskamp, "The New England Sources of *The Scarlet Letter*," pp. 291–303 in this Norton Critical Edition. See also H. Bruce Franklin's introduction to *"The Scarlet Letter" and Other Writings* (Philadelphia: Lippincott, 1967), 13–14.

"The Custom-House" when he places the faded badge on his breast and feels "as if the letter were not of red cloth, but red-hot iron" and Hester's searing torment when observers fix their eyes on the emblem, causing it to be "branded . . . afresh into Hester's soul," may well be based on an actual incident [26, 59].[3] In three separate sources, Hawthorne could have read about a woman who, at a moment very close to the novel's setting, had the letter A branded upon her. Perhaps just as curious, this woman was married to a former Puritan minister who had been previously censured for adulterous behavior. Hawthorne was undoubtedly acquainted with the fall of this Puritan divine, the implication being that the adultery of the Reverend Dimmesdale was not entirely the product of Hawthorne's irreverent imagination after all.[4] As the scholarship on Hawthorne's historical works has consistently revealed, the "Actual and the Imaginary" do indeed meet, and "each imbue[s] itself with the nature of the other" (36) [29].

The case of the woman branded for adultery first appeared in the records of York, in what is now Maine. Dated 15 October 1651, the entry reads:

> We do present George Rogers for, & Mary Batcheller the wife of Mr. Steven Batcheller ministr for adultery. It is ordered by ye Court yt George Rogers for his adultery with mis Batcheller shall forthwith have fourty stripes save one upon the bare skine given him: It is ordered yt mis Batcheller for her adultery shall receave 40 stroakes save one at ye First Towne meeting held at Kittery. 6 weeks after her delivery & be branded with the letter A.

Beside that entry, written in the same hand, is the notation, "Execution Done."[5] It appears that Charles Edward Banks, in his *History of*

Austin Warren first mentioned the case of Goodwife Mendame's adultery with an Indian in his introduction to *The Scarlet Letter* (New York: Holt, 1947), vii. Charles Boewe and Murray G. Murphy, "Hester Prynne in History," *American Literature* 32 (1960): 202–4, unconvincingly argue for Hawthorne's potential knowledge of this undated case, based upon the undocumented account in George Willison's *Saints and Strangers* (New York: Regnal and Hitchcock, 1945), 324. Goodwife Mendame was sentenced under a Plymouth law passed in 1636, first noticed and reproduced by Randall Stewart in his edition of Hawthorne's *The American Notebooks* (New Haven: Yale University Press, 1932), 229.

Neither the Plymouth law nor the case of Goodwife Mendame appears in the histories of Plymouth colony familiar to Hawthorne: Edward Johnson's *The Wonder-Working Providence of Sions Savior in New England*, which appeared in the *Massachusetts Historical Society Collections*, 2d ser., vols. 2–4 (1814–16), and vols. 7–8 (1818–19); William Hubbard's *General History of New England*, which also appeared in *MHSC*, 2d ser., vols. 5–6 (1815); William Prince's *Annals of New England*, which appeared in *MHSC*, 2d ser., vol. 7 (1819) and which concludes its coverage in 1633; and Nathaniel Morton's *New-England's Memorial* (Boston, 1826). For Hawthorne's repeated reading of the *MHSC* and his reading of Morton, see Kesselring, *Hawthorne's Reading*, 56, 57.

3. Cited from *The Centenary Edition of the Works of Nathaniel Hawthorne*, ed. William Charvat, Roy Harvey Pearce, and Claude M. Simpson (Columbus: Ohio State UP, 1962), 32, 86.

4. In his introduction to *The Scarlet Letter*, Charvat says, "No historical equivalents of Dimmesdale and Chillingworth are known, but there are records of scandals in seventeenth-century Massachusetts similar to Dimmesdale's case" (xxvii). As far as I am aware, no one has specified any of these similarities except Michael Colacurcio, who anticipated my independent discovery of the Reverend Stephen Batchellor in Winthrop's *History of New England*. See " 'The Woman's Own Choice': Sex, Metaphor, and the Puritan 'Sources' of *The Scarlet Letter*," in *New Essays on "The Scarlet Letter*," ed. Michael Colacurcio (New York: Cambridge UP, 1985), 110.

5. From a microfilm copy of York County Court Records (1636–1671), roll no. 1, 173–74, located at the County Court House, Alfred, Maine. The original records are deposited in the

York, Maine (1935), recognized the connection between Hawthorne's novel and this case, for he refers to Mary Batchellor's branding in a section titled "The Scarlet Letter."[6]

Hawthorne did not have to read the original records in order to become acquainted with the punishment of Mary Batchellor. In the first volume of *Collections of the Maine Historical Society* he could have read an account of the sentence passed on George Rogers and Mary Batchellor.[7] We know that Hawthorne had a personal interest in Maine's history. Not only had he attended Bowdoin College during the years immediately following the excitement over Maine's admission to statehood, but his father's family had claims to land there, and his mother's family still lived in Maine.[8] It would not be surprising if, in the course of his research, he came across the reference to Mary Batchellor's sentence.

Still another report of the sentence appears in the second edition of Alonzo Lewis's *History of Lynn* (1844), which also includes a lengthy biographical sketch of Mary's husband, the Reverend Stephen Batchellor.[9] Hawthorne, it is true, had read the first edition of Lewis's *History* (1829), which contains most of the sketch on Stephen Batchellor found in the second edition as well as information on his marital troubles with Mary, but the original does not mention Mary's adultery.[1] Nevertheless, Hawthorne may also have consulted the second edition. Having published several volumes of poetry, Alonzo Lewis was both fondly and jokingly known around Boston and Salem as the

Maine State Archives. Although I have not located evidence to prove that Hawthorne ever saw these early county records, the possibility does exist. In 1820, soon after Maine was admitted to the Union, the records were moved from York, the crossroads of southern Maine, to the new county seat of Alfred. Using the road map of H. S. Tanner, *Map of the States of Maine, New Hampshire, Vermont, Massachusetts, Connecticut, and Rhode Island* (n.p., 1820), we can see that Hawthorne probably traveled the coastal route from York to Brunswick when he first set out from Salem to attend Bowdoin College in 1821, and thus did not pass through Alfred. The same route would have been the quickest way to reach Augusta in 1837 when he visited his friend Horatio Bridge. It seems unlikely that Hawthorne ventured south to Alfred during college vacations spent with his Manning relations in Raymond. But in 1826, on a trip from Salem to Raymond and back, he may very well have taken the inland route from York to Alfred, and, because it was the largest town in southernmost Maine, he could well have laid over there. For the details of Hawthorne's trips to Maine, see Arlin Turner, *Nathaniel Hawthorne: A Biography* (New York: Oxford UP, 1980), 92–94, 46.

6. Charles Edward Banks, *History of York, Maine,* 3 vols. (Boston: n.p., 1935), 2:241. The Batchellor name is spelled in various ways in historical records. Except in a quotation, I use the spelling as it appears in Winthrop's *History.*

7. *Collections of the Maine Historical Society,* 1st ser., vol. 1 (1831), 276.

8. For the Hawthorne land claims in Maine, see Vernon Loggins, *The Hawthornes* (New York: Columbia UP, 1951), 109, 155, 169–70. For Hawthorne's maternal connection to Maine, see Turner, *Nathaniel Hawthorne,* 13–30. We know, of course, that Hawthorne was familiar with James Sullivan, *The History of the District of Maine,* 2 vols. (Boston: I. Thomas & E. T. Andrews, 1795), because he refers to the work in a footnote to "The Great Carbuncle"—see the *Centenary Edition,* 9:149. And in Thomas Hutchinson, *The History of the Colony and Province of Massachusetts-Bay,* ed. Lawrence Shaw Mayo, 3 vols. (Cambridge: Harvard UP, 1936), 1:150–52, Hawthorne would have read that his first American ancestor, William Hathorne, had been one of the commissioners sent to York in 1651 to resolve a boundary dispute, which eventually brought Kittery and York under the jurisdiction of Massachusetts Bay. For Hawthorne's reading in Hutchinson, see Kesselring, *Hawthorne's Reading,* 53. Hawthorne may have known the fuller details of his ancestor's role in this boundary dispute from William D. Williamson, *The History of the State of Maine,* 2 vols. (Hallowell, Maine: Glazier, Masters, 1832), 1:334–48.

9. Alonzo Lewis, *The History of Lynn, Including Nahant* (Boston: n.p., 1844), 93–97.

1. See Alonzo Lewis, *The History of Lynn* (Boston: J. H. Eastburn, 1829), 54–57. Hawthorne consulted this edition in 1833. See Kesselring, *Hawthorne's Reading,* 55.

"Bard of Lynn," and he was a town character frequently subjected to controversy.[2] Hawthorne must have been acquainted with Lewis through local gossip, and he may even have known him by sight, since Lewis habitually walked several miles from his home in Lynn throughout the 1820s and 1830s in order to attend Episcopal services at St. Peter's Church in Salem.[3] These circumstances, in addition to specific reports by word or print, might have elicited Hawthorne's interest in the second edition of the *History*, which was available during the Custom-House period when Hawthorne began rereading historical materials in preparation for writing *The Scarlet Letter*.

One would prefer a more compelling claim than plausibility for Hawthorne's knowledge of Mary Batchellor's case. Indeed, the similarities between Hester Prynne and Mary Batchellor are so outstanding that it is tempting to argue for a direct source. For example, Mary Batchellor's adultery is the only known case involving a child that can be linked to Hester's plight. By postponing execution of the sentence until six weeks after Mrs. Batchellor's delivery, the officials of York obviously considered the health of the unborn child. Hawthorne suggests a similar delay in the novel, for when Hester and Pearl appear in the opening scaffold scene, Pearl is "some three months old" (52) [40]. Although Hester is not physically punished, the account of Mary Batchellor might have provided factual warrant for postponing Hester's sentence to stand exposed to public disgrace and ridicule.

The striking feature of Mary Batchellor's case, however, is the form of punishment. Hawthorne certainly knew that adultery was sometimes a capital offense in Massachusetts Bay. In John Winthrop's *History of New England*, for example, he would have read about James Britton and Mary Latham, who were executed for adultery in 1643. Britton appealed to the General Court for his life, "but they would not grant it, though some of the magistrates spake much for it, and questioned the letter, whether adultery was death by God's law now."[4] Accordingly, in the opening scaffold scene, "the ugliest as well as the most pitiless" of the women spectators says that Hester "has brought shame upon us all, and ought to die. Is there not law for it? Truly there is, both in the Scripture and the statute-book" (51–52) [39].

Another disgruntled woman in this scene would like to see Hester suffer the punishment of Mary Batchellor: "The magistrates are God-fearing gentlemen, but merciful overmuch. . . . At the very least, they should have put the brand of a hot iron on Hester Prynne's forehead" (51) [39]. Although Hawthorne knew that branding was used to punish diverse crimes in early New England, the association of branding with the letter A in Mrs. Batchellor's punishment is reflected not only

2. See *Dictionary of American Biography*; see also the biographical sketch of Lewis written by James R. Newhall (son-in-law of Lewis) in his updated version of *The History of Lynn* (Boston: John L. Shorey, 1865), 544–48. An anonymous broadside attacking Lewis on several counts can be found among the unnumbered Alonzo Lewis folders at the Lynn Historical Society.
3. See Alonzo Lewis, *Poetical Works*, ed. Ion Lewis (Boston: n.p., 1883), xxi.
4. John Winthrop, *The History of New England from 1630 to 1649*, ed. James Savage, 2 vols. in 1 (1825; reprinted, New York: Arno P, 1972), 2:157–59. For Hawthorne's reading in Winthrop, see Kesselring, *Hawthorne's Reading*, 64.

in Hester's sense of the scarlet letter as an "ignominious brand" (86) [59] that is "flaming" (79) [55], which of course also suggests the figurative heat of shame or passion, but also in the narrator's description of the letter as a brand in "The Custom-House."

If Hawthorne was aware of Mary Batchellor's marriage to Stephen Batchellor, it could well have inspired the creation not only of Arthur Dimmesdale but also of Roger Chillingworth. Batchellor himself was no stranger to Hawthorne. In the edition of Winthrop's *History* familiar to him, editor James Savage calls special attention to the "unfortunate" Stephen Batchellor, who arrived in Massachusetts Bay on 5 June 1632 at the age of seventy-one.[5] Batchellor was the subject of two controversies in the 1630s concerning his unsanctioned methods of establishing separate churches at Lynn, but these squabbles were insignificant compared to the one at Hampton in 1641, which Winthrop describes at some length:

> Mr. Stephen Batchellor, the pastor of the church at Hampton, who had suffered much at the hands of the bishops in England, being about 80 years of age, and having a lusty comely woman to his wife, did solicit the chastity of his neighbour's wife, who acquainted her husband therewith; whereupon he was dealt with, but denied it, as he had told the woman he would do, and complained to the magistrates against the woman and her husband for slandering him. The church likewise dealing with him, he stiffly denied it, but soon after, when the Lord's supper was to be administered, he did voluntarily confess the attempt, and that he did intend to have defiled her, if she would have consented. The church, being moved with his free confession and tears, silently forgave him, and communicated with him: but after, finding how scandalous it was, they took advice of other elders, and after long debate and much pleading and standing upon the church's forgiving and being reconciled to him in communicating with him after he had confessed it, they proceeded to cast him out. After this he went on in a variable course, sometimes seeming very penitent, soon after again excusing himself, and casting blame upon others. . . . He was off and on for a long time, and when he had seemed most penitent, so as the church were ready to have received him in again, he would fall back again, and as it were repent of his repentance.[6]

Hawthorne could have found all but the last sentence and clause of this case quoted from Winthrop in the second edition of Lewis's *History*.[7] In the first edition, however, Hawthorne would have learned only that Batchellor had been "excommunicated" in 1641 for "irregular conduct," although this edition does mention that Batchellor was ninety at the time of his remarriage in 1650 to Mary (the "lusty comely" wife of 1641 having died).[8] Their union drew the attention of

5. Winthrop, *History of New England*, 1:78n.
6. Winthrop, *History of New England*, 2:44–45.
7. Lewis, *History of Lynn* (1844), 94.
8. Lewis, *History of Lynn* (1829), 55.

Bay authorities when Batchellor was "fined ten pounds, for not publishing his intention of marriage, according to law," and again, later in 1650, when the General Court ordered the couple to "lyve together as man and wife," thereby denying both of their petitions for divorce.[9] Sometime in 1651, Batchellor returned to England, where he remarried and lived another ten years, his polygamy apparently undetected.[1] One cannot determine from either Lewis's first or second edition whether Batchellor left America before or after Mary's trial for adultery. Within the narrow time margins involved, however, he probably knew that Mary was pregnant from an extra-marital union. The would-be adulterer had himself become a cuckold, and his response was to flee.

Few details in Batchellor's life invite comparison with Hawthorne's Dimmesdale. Indeed, Batchellor's advanced age, his young and wayward wife, and his incorrigibility attracting public censure are more reminiscent of Chillingworth. But Batchellor's attempt to seduce another man's wife links his American experience to Dimmesdale's. Moreover, Batchellor's attempted adultery, followed by his repeated confessions and denials, suggests the major dilemma tormenting Dimmesdale throughout *The Scarlet Letter*. Knowing at the outset that he should confess, yet perhaps fearing that he will be excommunicated (as Batchellor had been for a seemingly lesser offense), Dimmesdale cannot bring himself to reveal his role in Hester's sin until seven years later in the climactic scaffold scene.[2] It is also worth considering that Batchellor's return to England might have given Hawthorne the idea of having Hester propose to Dimmesdale that they escape to the Old World. Alternately, knowing that Mary Batchellor was left with the difficulty of providing for family after her husband's flight, Hawthorne might have seen the need to discover the moral necessity and the future independence of America lying behind Hester's ultimate decision to remain in New England.

Finally, the year of Batchellor's attempted seduction probably influenced Hawthorne's manipulation of the historical time frame of *The Scarlet Letter*. When that attempt took place in 1641, Richard Bellingham was governor. Bellingham is clearly the governor, "the chief ruler," in the opening scaffold scene of *The Scarlet Letter* (64) [47]. And yet, because that scene takes place in June 1642, Hawthorne should have designated Winthrop, who had become governor in May.[3] Hawthorne, who had a high opinion of Winthrop, may have created this anachronism among the otherwise accurate details of the novel's

---

9. Lewis, *History of Lynn* (1829), 55–56.
1. Lewis, *History of Lynn* (1829), 56. In 1656, Mary petitioned the Court to be free of her marriage to Batchellor in order to remarry for the sake of her children (56–57). Earlier, however, she had demonstrated that the branding and stripes did not change her behavior, for in March 1652 (1651 old style), she was again sentenced to be whipped for adultery. See York County Court Records, 188. Both her first and second punishments are recorded in *Province and Court Records of Maine* (Portland: Maine Historical Society, 1928), 1:164, 176.
2. For the necessity of public confession in Puritan Massachusetts Bay, see Ernest W. Baughman, "Public Confession and *The Scarlet Letter*," *New England Quarterly* 40 (1967): 532–50.
3. Winthrop replaced Bellingham on 18 May—see Winthrop, *History of New England*, 2:63.

historical setting in order to dissociate Winthrop from the Puritan "sages of rigid aspect" who rule in Hester's case but who are not "capable of sitting in judgment on an erring woman's heart" (64) [64]. Hawthorne surely knew from his reading in Winthrop, however, that the historical Bellingham would have been as unqualified to judge Hester as he was to rule in Batchellor's case. While governor in 1641, not long before he presided over the General Court's arraignment of Batchellor, Bellingham had won the hand of a woman who had previously pledged herself to his friend. The governor not only circumvented the law by failing to publish the banns but also performed his own marriage ceremony.[4] As reported by Winthrop, Bellingham refused to disqualify himself when the General Court convened to take up charges brought against him by the "great inquest." The Court was "unwilling to command him publicly to go off the bench, and yet not thinking it fit he should sit as a judge, when he was by law to answer as an offender."[5] That he subsequently sat on the bench when the Reverend Batchellor's case came before the Court would no doubt have pleased Hawthorne's sense of irony and may further have prompted him to allow the unworthy Bellingham to preside over Hester's public humiliation.

One of the more unique aspects of Hawthorne's fiction is how it sends us back to the record books in search of individuals and events that, through the force of his art, he has made us experience as historically real. We do know that Hawthorne did not entirely invent the circumstances and dilemmas of his characters, but we cannot always be sure that he knew what we have discovered in the historical record available to him. While he almost certainly drew upon the life of the Reverend Batchellor, the case of his ill-fated wife is more problematic. Even if, however, we were to dismiss the possibility that Hawthorne knew about Mary Batchellor—which I do not think we can or should do—the historical analogy remains tantalizing. Had *The Scarlet Letter* never been written, many of us would never have been aware that in mid-seventeenth-century New England even Puritan divines were implicated in cases of adultery and that wayward women faced the threat of being physically as well as socially stigmatized by a burning *A*. One of Hawthorne's particular gifts is that he not only brings such facts to light but also that from them he spins stories of such psychological and moral power that they have fascinated readers for generations and promise to do so for generations to come.

4. Without mentioning his source, Franklin, *"The Scarlet Letter" and Other Writings*, 13, mentions these details.
5. The full case and the quotations come from Winthrop, *History of New England*, 2:43. In connection to Hawthorne's likely appreciation of the irony involved in Bellingham's case, it seems worth recording Winthrop's preface to the account: "Query, whether the following be fit to be published."

KRISTIN BOUDREAU

Hawthorne's Model of Christian Charity†

Jefferson's belief that fiction could be used to bind the nation in ideological unity was shared by those who followed him into the nineteenth century. In 1833 the criminal lawyer Rufus Choate addressed a crowd in Salem on the topic of historical novels and their usefulness in "illustrating New-England History." In doing so, he used terms even more charged with overt political motives, even less distinguished by references to moral sentiments than those used by earlier leaders of the republic. The significant historical American romance, he argued, had not yet been written, even though such a work could surpass conventional histories in "speak[ing] directly to the heart and affections and imagination of the whole people" (3). The notion that the affections have cultural and political work to do should by now be familiar—as it was to Choate's audience—though the faith in such a creature as a "whole people" may have been new to Choate's generation. Like Thomas Jefferson and Benjamin Rush, Choate wanted desperately to consider his nation a single entity bound by common sentiments. Indeed, in his address the stakes seem even higher than they were when the country was still very young. A new generation of authors was coming of age, and while the great literary renaissance was still a few years away, writers like Washington Irving had already begun to establish national pride in the native cultural resources of the United States. If the political experiment known as the United States were to fail, it would be a great loss to local literature and the arts, which had only recently begun to develop independently of their European roots. Choate thought these cultural productions might help to unify the nation.

Toward the close of his address, Choate proposed that a series of historical romances like those of Walter Scott "might do *something* to perpetuate the Union itself" (36). The tone of his recommendation seemed to indicate that the union was already in a state of peril. A successful attempt to illustrate our common history in fictional form

> would turn back our thoughts from these recent and overrated diversities of interest,—these controversies about negro-cloth, coarse-woolled sheep, and cotton bagging,—to the day when our fathers walked hand in hand together through the valley of the Shadow of Death in the War of Independence. Reminded of our fathers, we should remember that we are brethren. The exclusiveness of State pride, the narrow selfishness of a mere local policy, and the small jealousies of vulgar minds, would be merged in an expanded, comprehensive, constitutional sentiment of old, family, fraternal regard. (37)

† From *Sympathy in American Literature: American Sentiments from Jefferson to the Jameses* (Gainesville: UP of Florida, 2002), 49–82, 212–14. Reprinted by permission of the University Press of Florida. Page references in square brackets refer to this Norton Critical Edition.

Choate understood that regional interests, some of the same issues that would explode in civil war twenty-seven years later, were "overrated" in comparison with the longer-standing, more natural family sentiment. Like Jefferson appealing to "consanguinity," Choate worried that "diversities of interest" would break through the affections that an earlier generation of cultural leaders had worked so hard to develop. Though Choate didn't indicate whether these affections were natural or produced, he did believe that a step backward in time, taking the people closer to the source of their common experiences, would help to heal the wounds caused by diversity, would help to recreate one people.

Choate called emphatically upon writers to produce literature that could properly be called national, given that it would become the "common property of all the States" (36). He imagined ideal reading communities dotting the American landscape, uniting distant regions. "Poems and romances which shall be read in every parlor, by every fireside, in every school-house, behind every counter, in every printing-office, in every lawyer's office, at every weekly evening club, in all the States of this Confederacy, must do something, along with more palpable if not more powerful agents, toward moulding and fixing that final, grand, complex result,—the national character" (36).

Although the previously dominant term "sensibility" had been replaced by "character," Choate was still referring to the ties of affection that came from common exposure to a carefully constructed and well-regulated model of morality. Faced with regional disputes and the threat of disunion, Choate echoed the sentiments of his eighteenth-century predecessors and called upon novelists to bind an otherwise dispersed nation. The only difference is that Choate considered that the common topic of these romances would be history rather than the American family. Otherwise, his project resembled that of the early novels we have already considered, which exhort their readers to share in the sensibilities of an ideal American.

Was it only coincidence that Choate, speaking to a Salem audience that may have included Nathaniel Hawthorne, suggested "the *old Puritan character*" as a particularly rich topic (21–22)?[1] Implicitly, Choate was raising the possibility that the "particular duty" of the Puritan character might be called for once again on behalf of a nation that, though secularized almost beyond recognition, still needed a disciplined conscience to hold it together. If the Puritan character was once "dissolved . . . into its elements" (22), perhaps it might be summoned forth in a time of national crisis. The novelist was the ideal soldier for a such a task.

Nathaniel Hawthorne's most successful novel, of course, answers

---

1. Although there is no direct evidence that Hawthorne was present at Choate's lecture (his extant journals begin in 1835), there is strong circumstantial evidence that he was at least acquainted with Choate's argument, perhaps having heard an account of the address. In October and December of 1833, and again in February of 1834, Hawthorne's aunt borrowed the works of Walter Scott from the Salem Athenaeum. It is possible that Hawthorne's interest in the historical novel began with Choate's public lecture. For Hawthorne's sources, see Kesselring.

Choate's call for a historical romance while developing the genre of the seduction novel. *The Scarlet Letter*, published in 1850, in many ways restores a sense of the past to Hawthorne's nineteenth-century audience. A number of excellent studies have demonstrated the complicated historical issues submerged beneath the romantic plot of the fallen woman Hester Prynne.[2] The novel also speaks to its own historical context, as Sacvan Bercovitch has splendidly shown.[3] Students of Hawthorne are now familiar with the historical details, both accurate and inaccurate, that he wrote into our seven-year encounter with Hester, Dimmesdale, Pearl, and Chillingworth, the only purely fictional characters in the novel. The others, Governors Bellingham and Winthrop, the Reverend Mr. Wilson, Mistress Hibbins, and even the jailer, Master Brackett, are historical figures that Hawthorne drew from his intense reading in colonial history: Increase Mather's *Illustrious Providences*, Cotton Mather's *Magnalia Christi Americana*, George Bancroft's *History of the United States*, Thomas Hutchinson's *History of the Colony and Province of Massachusetts Bay*, Caleb H. Snow's *History of Boston*, John Winthrop's *Journal*.[4]

Hawthorne was also familiar with European and American seduction novels. Although the records of his adolescent reading are scant, he does tell us that as a boy he read any "light books within [his] reach" (J. Hawthorne 1:96). Nina Baym notes that "he particularly loved the books that were popular successes in the early decades of the nineteenth century" (*Shape* 16). Baym cites English novels, but there is every reason to suppose that Hawthorne had also read the most popular American novels. These included a large number of seduction novels, which took part in a "national debate over the uses of a woman's body" (Williams, "Victims" 60). Unfortunately, the detailed records of the Hawthorne and Manning activity at the Salem Athenaeum do not begin until 1828, when Hawthorne had put the lightest reading behind him. By that time, he was probably familiar with the conventional plot of the seduction novel. To be sure, the novelist made many changes in shaping this transhistorical genre to a precise historical context. *The Scarlet Letter* begins after the heroine's fall, so we do not see how Hester Prynne was tempted and how she might have resisted the Reverend Mr. Dimmesdale. The conventional moral, to avoid sins of passion, appears most emphatically only in the early chapters, and is voiced not by the narrator but by an array of characters (magistrates, ministers, and vindictive townspeople) who should not be taken to represent the author's position. Still, *The Scarlet Letter* is indebted to the plot of the seduction novel.

Like those stories, Hawthorne's romance is fairly pessimistic about the American family: marriage ties are dissolved, and the one human relation with "a consecration of its own" does not promise to be re-

---

2. Colacurcio has done impressive work here. See also Baughman, Ryskamp, Bell, and Hugh J. Dawson.
3. Others who have explored the antebellum context include Leverenz, Douglas Anderson, Michael T. Gilmore, Larry Reynolds, Railton, and Van Leer.
4. Edward Dawson, 5–6, explains Hawthorne's sources for *The Scarlet Letter*.

newed after death, whatever Hester's wishes (1:195) [126]. As the dying Dimmesdale tells her, "when we violated our reverence each for the other's soul,—it was thenceforth vain to hope that we could meet hereafter" (256) [162]. Their American offspring, Pearl, does not remain in the New World but returns to the Old, the place of her mother's origins. While Hester returns to counsel other unhappy women, to see the office of the scarlet letter fulfilled, Hawthorne gives us no model family to carry on the New England Way.

But Hawthorne introduced important innovations to the conventional seduction novel. The moral of seduction novels, like that of public punishments, was clear: Spectators must avoid the errors that brought this spectacle to her unhappy end. In Hawthorne's romance, though public scrutiny is certainly fastened upon the erring Hester, we are not meant to read her story merely in order to avoid her trespasses. Hawthorne has other uses in mind for his character and his readers. Hester's story, that is, concerns not her fall but her punishment, her place in the community that condemns her, and the roles of mercy and justice in seeing to the reformation of erring colonists. In this regard Hawthorne wrote the historical romance that Choate had demanded.

Of all the historical figures who enter *The Scarlet Letter*, it is appropriate that John Winthrop presides most influentially over Hawthorne's text, for he was the Puritan most concerned with binding his fellow colonists together in ties of mutual affection.[5] Writing as civil war loomed, but before it seemed inevitable, Hawthorne too was wary of deep political differences: an expanding market economy, violent labor and political disputes, and a culture whose emerging ethos was based on individualism. He turned to Winthrop as a model peacemaker. In recalling the colonial figure most concerned with binding his fellow colonists together in bonds of mutual affection, Hawthorne also participated in the project that Choate and earlier writers had called for. We might say, to use Choate's words, that Hawthorne "mould[ed] and fix[ed] that final, grand, complex result,—the national character."

A Sweet Moral Blossom

Ostensibly, of course, Hawthorne's moral involves a condemnation of Dimmesdale and his deceptive life. "Be true! Be true! Be true!" urges the narrator. "Show freely to the world, if not your worst, yet some trait whereby the worst may be inferred!" (260) [263]. In this exhortation, the narrator resembles the magistrates and ministers, most notably the Reverend Mr. Wilson, who call upon Hester to "lay open her

5. For an excellent analysis of the uses of sympathy in "mediat[ing] between, rather than iso-lat[ing], individuals who themselves have successfully internalized regulatory functions," see Alkana, 56–81. Throughout this book Alkana traces the nineteenth-century "social self" to Common Sense philosophers who sought to use moral sentiments to unite diverse populations. His chapter on *The Scarlet Letter* considers the novel mainly in the context of Hawthorne's own time, while I am attempting to look more closely at his historical sources. For Hawthorne's debt to Adam Smith's conception of sympathy, see Hunt.

heart's secrets in such broad daylight, and in presence of so great a multitude" (65) [48]. But the directness of this particular moral conceals the ambiguity with which Hawthorne conveys it, giving us his lesson only obliquely and calling it only one "among many morals" (260) [163]. The author leaves us to guess that other lessons are not laid out so clearly, that we must search for them in the shadows of his text. But one moral is equally clear, though it is put into a metaphor rather than a sentence. The "sweet moral blossom" that the narrator hopes for in the opening chapter is figured by the rosebush outside the prison door: "we could hardly do otherwise than pluck one of its flowers and present it to the reader. It may serve, let us hope, to symbolize some sweet moral blossom, that may be found along the track, or relieve the darkening close of a tale of human frailty and sorrow" (48) [37]. A moral blossom meant to "relieve" the close of the romance: Hawthorne's language is very much like Adam Smith's discussion of sympathy, the only sentiment, Smith claims, that can relieve human suffering (15). Perhaps Hawthorne, anticipating Henry James's criticism, means only aesthetic, rather than moral, relief. As James later wrote, this work is "densely dark, with a single spot of vivid colour in it; and it will probably long remain the most consistently gloomy of English novels of the first order" (*Hawthorne* 87). Although Hawthorne clearly had aesthetic issues on his mind, he was also considering moral, social, and historical ones, and what the metaphorical flower does aesthetically for the reader, the actual flower does sympathetically for the suffering prisoner. The "delicate gems" of the rosebush, the narrator of *The Scarlet Letter* notes, "might be imagined to offer their fragrance and fragile beauty to the prisoner as he went in, and to the condemned criminal as he came forth to his doom, in token that the deep heart of Nature could pity and be kind to him" (48) [36]. Pitted against other flowers—"the black flower of civilized society, a prison" (48) [36] and the black flower of fate that prevents Chillingworth from forgiving his enemy (174) [113]—this blossom evokes a decades-long debate in the colonies about the treatment of transgressions. That Hawthorne draws on this pitying flower as the image of his moral suggests that whatever lesson we find will tell us something about the justice of mercy. Whatever the attitudes of Hester's fellow townspeople, the narrator draws our attention to the heart of Nature, thereby giving us a model, as John Winthrop called it, of "Christian charity."

A Story and a By-Word

Winthrop's most famous document informs Hawthorne's most famous novel. "A Model of Christian Charity" was delivered in 1630 to the passengers aboard the *Arbella*, as they contemplated their roles in the settlement of the Bay Colony. The Reverend Mr. John Wilson, who appears prominently at Hester's public punishment, was one of those passengers. So was Richard Bellingham, whom Hawthorne designates as governor during the period that includes the opening scene of *The*

Scarlet Letter. Hester Prynne, on the other hand, was not present among the charter members of Massachusetts Bay. Hawthorne puts her in New England no earlier than 1640, fully ten years after Winthrop delivered his speech. Whether the Prynnes were Puritans, as is likely from their association with Amsterdam, or whether they had more secular interests in the colony, the principles of these Puritan families applied to all colonists alike. Chillingworth learns that theirs is "a land where iniquity is searched out, and punished in the sight of rulers and people" (62) [45].

As if prophesying the fate of the errant Hester, poised high on a scaffold in a crowded marketplace, Winthrop had told his fellow passengers that "we shall be as a city upon a Hill, the eyes of all people are upon us; so that if we shall deal falsely with our god in this work we have undertaken and so cause him to withdraw his present help from us, we shall be made a story and a by-word through the world" (295). Hawthorne literalizes this image in Hester, who must serve, as Chillingworth observes, as "a living sermon against sin" (63) [46]. The novel opens with a crowd of spectators, "all with their eyes intently fastened on the iron-clamped oaken door" of the prison (49) [37]. Upon the scaffold, Hester feels "the heavy weight of a thousand unrelenting eyes, all fastened upon her, and concentred at her bosom" (57) [42], as she enacts the most memorable lines in Winthrop's address, the lines that insist upon public scrutiny.

As Q. D. Leavis, Larry Reynolds, and others have noted, the novel seems to be structured according to the three scenes located at the scaffold. Before Hester's entrance, moreover, the narrator suggests a range of public punishments and the offenses that might bring a malefactor to the scaffold: heterodoxy, sluggishness, disobedience, idleness, drunkenness, and witchcraft all provoked "the same solemnity" among the spectators, for whom "the mildest and the severest acts of public discipline were alike made venerable and awful" (49–50) [37]. As Winthrop's speech closes with strong words of warning, so Hawthorne's novel opens with the horror of strict justice meted out in a public place. Hyperconscious of the public scrutiny under which they lived, the people of Massachusetts were uneasily aware of the many transgressions that might bring one of them into the marketplace. And while there might seem to be a world of difference between shiftlessness and witchcraft, the shame that followed from the revelation of these sins was equally painful. While Hester considers her position, she fears "she must needs shriek out with the full power of her lungs, and cast herself from the scaffold down upon the ground, or else go mad at once" (57) [43]. The unsympathetic eyes of her spectators drive home to her the almost corporal violence of exhibitionist justice. Using a metaphor drawn from the tradition of punitive mutilations, Hester claims that the letter "is too deeply branded" to be removed (68) [49].

The gathering of Bostonians enacts a central component of Winthrop's famous speech. Even Hester, "knowing well her part," performs according to apparently familiar conventions (55) [42]. And the success of those conventions depends upon the distance between the criminal and her audience. Though a limited identification is necessary for the spectators to fear their own passions and avoid Hester's missteps, they must not feel sympathy for the criminal. The eyes of the crowd must be fastened in judgment alone, lest the spectators feel too deeply for Hester and lay the blame for her suffering upon the prominent men who are responsible for her public exposure. The narrator comes close to such a conclusion: "They were, doubtless, good men, just, and sage," he admits, yet "out of the whole human family, it would not have been easy to select the same number of wise and virtuous persons, who should be less capable of sitting in judgment on an erring woman's heart" (64) [47]. But Hawthorne's narrator is not representative of these practiced Puritans, determined to bestow justice rather than mercy. Typically, he tells us, "the sympathy that a transgressor might look for, from such bystanders at the scaffold," was "meagre, indeed, and cold" (50) [37].

Hawthorne's Puritans understood well the roles that justice called them to perform. But Hawthorne's readers, promised a "sweet moral blossom," might be dismayed to find that mercy is represented by such "meager" and "cold" sympathy. The dominant theme of Winthrop's sermon, Christian charity, seems mostly to have dried up; among most of the citizens, sweet mercy and charity are replaced with adamant justice.

The point of public punishments, of course, was to bind the colonists in a mutual sense of proper behavior. The culprit exhibited upon the scaffold symbolized a breach of law, but in so doing she served to rally her townspeople in an affirmation of the specific law that was broken and the idea of law itself. Public spectacles of discipline helped to remind the people of their consent to the laws that governed them; by publicly greeting the offender with opprobrium, they acted as agents of the law and strengthened the regulations that held the community together (Erikson 6).

What are the implications of linking the affections and the law? A Marxist or feminist reading—or indeed any reading that seeks to understand how literature participates in hegemonic values—might condemn both Hawthorne and Winthrop for masking ideological apparatuses in moral sentiments. A sympathetic reading of Hawthorne and Winthrop, however, can overcome the need to see the forces lurking at the heart of sentimental culture as either subversive or repressive. In reading *The Scarlet Letter* against the backdrop of seventeenth-century political and social crises, we shall see that the association between sentiments and the law is not necessarily oppressive; neither is the deployment of sympathy simply subversive. Hawthorne's novel demonstrates that sympathy, though perhaps a "natural" sentiment, can lie dormant in the face of deep suffering or long-standing self-absorption. Likewise, it can be coaxed back to life in order to revitalize both the individual and the social institutions that serve communities. Though we may understand the relationship between individuals and communities to be antagonistic, even Thoreau never claimed that such antagonism was inevitable.

The Rule of Mercy

As John Winthrop well knew, justice is not the only implement that fortifies a community. For him, the affections that prompted sympathy were at times stronger and more appropriate mechanisms for binding a community that might otherwise be tempted to disperse. His "Model of Christian Charity" distinguishes between the "two rules whereby we are to walk one towards another: JUSTICE and MERCY" (283). Winthrop contended that the second law was inspired by a natural human sentiment, meant "to strengthen defend preserve and comfort" fellow citizens (289). Such affection and sympathy, furthermore, would operate as an invisible bond between the people: "though we were absent from each other many miles, and had our employments as far distant, yet we ought to account our selves knit together by this bond of love, and live in the exercise of it" (292). The rule of justice applied in ordinary times, but a "community of peril" required the rule of mercy, which Winthrop described as "more enlargement towards others and less respect towards ourselves" (287).

Until the end of his life in 1649, Winthrop considered Massachusetts Bay Colony to be one such imperiled community, in need of more mercy than justice. Though his "Model" was well received by his fellow Puritans, his policy on mercy caused him subsequent political problems. A dispute in 1635 between Winthrop and Thomas Dudley, the longtime deputy governor, concerned a difference of opinion regarding the severity of punishments called for by the magistrates. While Dudley advocated severity, Winthrop called for "more lenyte" (*Journal* 165). Although Winthrop, learning that public opinion was against him, eventually modified his position, his words do not indicate a true change of heart. He answered his fellow magistrates "that his speeches & carriage had been in part mistaken, but withall professed, that it was his judgment . . . that in the infancy of plantations justice should be administered with more lenyte than in a settled state, because people were then more apt to transgress partly of ignorance of new laws & Orders, partly through oppression of business & other straits" (167).

The cause of this dispute, according to some historians, was the treatment of Roger Williams, the religious dissident who was forced out of the Bay Colony in 1635. Although the magistrates issued a warrant requiring Williams, a Puritan much more radical than the non-Separatists of Boston, to be returned on the next ship to England, he received advance warning, which allowed him to escape to Rhode Island. James G. Moseley speculates that "the warmth of Williams's lifelong affection and respect for Winthrop suggests that he may have been the one who helped Williams elude the Puritans' grasp" (72).

That lifelong affection, the fruit of Winthrop's mercy, was at no time regrettable, either for Winthrop or the colony itself. Although the wording of a parliamentary letter of safe conduct of 1644 may be slightly exaggerated, Winthrop's and Williams's sentiments for each other remained warm: Williams and the Massachusetts magistrates, the letter indicates, "mutually give good testimony each of other, as we observe you do of him, and he abundantly of you" (*Journal* 541).

For all of their doctrinal disputes—and they were significant— Winthrop's affection for Williams, like his public policy, kept pace with the theory of sentiments he had sketched out in his "Model." That theory included two kinds of arguments, those of a fervently religious man and those of a pragmatic political leader. Winthrop was both.[6] The exercise of charity, he argued, helped every person to "have need of other, and from hence they might be all knit more nearly together in the Bond of brotherly affection" ("Model" 283). The alliance between Williams and Winthrop proved the truth of this claim. A second reason, though strictly religious on the face of it, was also pragmatic: "That [God] might have the more occasion to manifest the work of his Spirit . . . in the regenerate in exercising his graces in them, as in the great ones, their love, mercy, gentleness, temperance etc." (283). Here Winthrop's argument resembles Jefferson's a century later. In exercising our charity, we learn to be more charitable. A society of charitable citizens, whose private interests "stand aside" until the good of the whole is served, cannot help but survive (286).

In Hawthorne's novel we see a model of sympathy in the narrator, who, by acknowledging the ministers' and magistrates' inability to judge Hester, implicitly refuses to judge her as they do. We see a clearer model in the young woman who tries to moderate the self-righteous utterances of her companions. Those companions, women who "appeared to take a peculiar interest" in Hester's punishment (1:50) [38], speak with derision of the malefactor and invent even more shameful punishments for her: branding her forehead and replacing her ornate letter with "a rag of mine own rheumatic flannel" (54) [41].

The compassionate woman, in contrast, wishes to alleviate Hester's shame. As she tries to silence her companions, there is gentle scolding in her words: "O, peace, neighbours, peace! . . . Do not let her hear you! Not a stitch in that embroidered letter, but she has felt it in her heart!" (54) [41]. She alone among these women has entered into the feelings of the suffering Hester.

The argument among the ordinary townspeople in this early scene echoes an ongoing debate between the magistrates and deputies of John Winthrop's time. As a number of scholars have pointed out, the period covered by the novel, 1642 to 1649, coincides almost precisely with struggles for political power waged between the petty bourgeoisie, represented by the deputies, and the governing aristocracy, represented by the magistrates.[7] One of those debates, directly reflected in the story of Hester's adultery and public punishment, concerned the degree to which the magistrates should be free to assign

6. Cotton Mather mentions Winthrop's double sense of vocation: "But though he would rather have Devoted himself unto the Study of Mr. *John Calvin*, than of Sir *Edward Cooke*; nevertheless, the Accomplishments of a *Lawyer*, were those wherewith Heaven made his chief Opportunities to be Serviceable" (2:213–14).

7. See, for instance, Berlant's reading of the novel in the context of these political crises. Wall provides a detailed account of these years. Colacurcio notes that a major theme throughout Winthrop's journal is "democratic excess" (" 'The Woman's Own Choice' " 106).

penalties for crimes. The issue came before the General Court in March 1638, when three people had been convicted of adultery, a capital offense in Massachusetts.[8] Because the magistrates were uncertain whether the law had been clearly publicized, the three criminals had been sitting in jail since June 1637. As the prisoners awaited sentencing, the magistrates concluded that "if the law had been sufficiently published, they ought to be put to death." But after discussion, "it was thought safest, that these three persons should be whipped and banished; and the law was confirmed and published" (Winthrop, *Journal* 249).

When, in March of 1644, Mary Latham and James Britton were convicted of adultery and executed according to this law, they became the only two persons ever executed for adultery in Massachusetts. Even this one case was controversial, as Winthrop notes: "some of the magistrates thought the evidence not sufficient against her, because there were not two direct witnesses; but the jury [convicted] her" (*Journal* 501). As Hugh J. Dawson explains, "the members of that unhappy couple's court searched the Bible and the Colony's stipulated penalty in an anguished effort to find some escape from imposing the prescribed sentence" (228–29).[9] Winthrop wrote that "some of the magistrates spake much for [the sparing of Britton's life], and questioned the letter, whether adultery was death by God's law now" (*Journal* 502).

Representing the will of the people, the jury condemned this couple to death, even while some of the magistrates, again, representing the will of God, objected.[1] The question again concerned the choice between justice and mercy, particularly, in this case, whether a sentence of death could be just in the absence of irrefutable evidence. Being closer to God than the people were, the magistrates felt that they were better qualified to determine penalties in specific cases.[2]

In other words, while the people may have been more rigid than their elected governors, their legalistic ardor may have limited their capacity to be merciful. One of Hawthorne's characters makes this point explicitly, when she observes that the punishment settled upon by the magistrates was much lighter than what Hester would have received from her peers. "It would be greatly for the public behoof," this "hard-featured dame of fifty" says, "if we women, being of mature age and church-members in good repute, should have the handling of

---

8. In 1631 the Court of Assistants had ruled that "if any man shall have carnall copulacon with another mans wife <be she English or Indian> they both shalbe punished by death" (*Records of the Court* 2:19, 66, 70).

9. Dawson's brief essay contains a remarkably thorough and insightful discussion of the treatment of adulterers and the role that William Hathorne played in insisting on the letter of the law.

1. While the deputies represented the freemen, magistrates held a higher power, one that they sought to protect against the deputies' mounting demand for more influence. In a 1636 letter stating the magistratical position, John Cotton asked, "If the people be governors, who shall be governed?" (Hutchinson 1:415). For divine sanction of the magistrates, see Wall, 78–80.

2. For this reason, perhaps, Massachusetts magistrates generally opposed the use of juries for criminal cases. For an evaluation of seventeenth-century attitudes toward the jury system, see Murrin.

such malefactresses as this Hester Prynne. What think ye, gossips? If the hussy stood up for judgment before us five, that are now here in a knot together, would she come off with such a sentence as the worshipful magistrates have awarded? Marry, I trow not!" (1:51) [38].

Popular opinion, which Winthrop often dismissed as "mere democracy" (*Journal* 456) was just as distasteful to Hawthorne, who in "The Custom House" is deeply critical of democratic excess. Aesthetically and ethically, Hawthorne preferred the "sweet moral blossom" to the shrill cries for justice that greet Hester's entrance into the marketplace. While the woman who clamors to bestow her "rheumatic flannel" upon Hester Prynne may be an extreme example of sanctimonious passion, however, Hawthorne has added other, more complicated voices to the assembly, reenacting among his fictional community the contentions that had engaged Massachusetts governors for an entire decade.

Just as the narrator concedes the godliness of the magistrates but hints that they may be too severe, too little capable of mercy when the crime involves the heart, so the townspeople recognize the righteousness of their leaders. But their conclusion is far different: these men have been too lenient. One woman observes, "The magistrates are God-fearing gentlemen, but merciful overmuch" (51) [39]. Another, "the ugliest as well as the most pitiless of these self-constituted judges," calls for the ultimate penalty: "This woman has brought shame upon us all, and ought to die" (51) [39]. Although Hawthorne may seem to have made it easy for his readers to condemn this merciless woman, attaching ugliness to her hard justice, she speaks with political sense. "Is there not law for it? Truly there is, both in the Scripture and the statute-book. Then let the magistrates, who have made it of no effect, thank themselves if their own wives and daughters go astray!" (51–52) [39].

In his careful reading, Hawthorne encountered this argument repeatedly. The pages of Winthrop's journal are full of references to this question of whether specific penalties should be fixed with certainty. If a law is published but never enforced, how effective a deterrent is the fear of punishment? If punishments are always commuted, why specify them at all? Many New Englanders insisted that specific penalties should be the inevitable result of particular crimes. As early as 1641, according to Winthrop, the General Court "was full of uncomfortable agitations and contentions," as people had been calling for the passage and publication of precise punishments for a number of offenses (*Journal* 376). During a three-week session in 1641, one hundred laws, called the Body of Liberties, were drawn up against the will of John Winthrop with his belief that magistrates should have discretionary power to assign penalties.

Winthrop believed that severity was not necessarily the best instrument of government. Though he had little patience for sin, especially when the stability of the colony was threatened, his compassion toward sinners was genuine. In the words of one biographer, "Winthrop portrayed life as a purposeful process of enduring struggle, rather than as a one-time contest between absolute good and evil" (Moseley 93). During the 1640s a series of bestiality cases occurred both in Boston and in Plymouth, cases that indicate Winthrop's sympathy for the human struggle against sin in contrast to the response of his neighbor, Governor William Bradford of Plymouth. Moseley argues that whereas Winthrop's narrative of the Boston sex offender, Hackett, "expresses the characteristic Puritan concern with the struggle between sin and grace in each individual's life, . . . Bradford's account of Granger's fate articulates a typical Separatist desire to weed out wicked people who may have crept into the community of the saints" (132). While Moseley's comparison may be unfair to Bradford, it may also be too generous to the non-Separatists whom Winthrop represented, especially when we note how often the Massachusetts governor found himself pleading for leniency. The death penalty might indeed assure the colony that a sinner had been eradicated, but Winthrop believed that penitence and conversion were the greater victories. Furthermore, he thought that most virtuous behavior was not motivated by fear. He classified people into two types: those "who are godly & virtuous" and observed the law "for Conscience, & Virtue's sake" and those who "must be held in by fear of punishment" ("Arbitrary Government" 453). Although the social and political community consisted of both types, the covenant with God involved only the first kind of person. Winthrop felt a stronger commitment to the spiritual welfare of this first group.

When the citizens in Hawthorne's romance debate the purpose and severity of punitive treatment, they are repeating the terms of a familiar argument. The ugliest and most merciless woman in the crowd calls for the preservation of social order when she advocates capital punishment. If Hester Prynne's sentence is commuted, she warns, even the wives and daughters of the magistrates themselves will "go astray." She is answered in words very much like those Winthrop might have used: " 'Mercy on us, goodwife,' exclaimed a man in the crowd, 'is there no virtue in woman, save what springs from a wholesome fear of the gallows? That is the hardest word yet!' " (52) [39]. The two compassionate characters in the marketplace, this man and the young woman, use rhetorical terms that are loaded with political significance: "mercy" and "peace." Hawthorne has overshadowed the immediate occasion for the novel, the revelation of Hester's adultery, with a broader moral and political debate that engrossed the Massachusetts governors and their subjects. What role does mercy play in the governance of a Christian community? Must peace depend upon justice alone? Not surprisingly, the words "mercy" and "justice" and "sympathy" are far more conspicuous in Hawthorne's novel than the merely nominal problem of adultery.[3]

Although Hawthorne displaces the magistratical debate onto the villagers in the square, we do see signs that a discussion has transpired

---

3. The point that I am arguing—that Hester's adultery is only a specific occasion for the introduction of much broader political and social issues—has an actual historical precedent. As Moseley observes about the many sexual misconduct cases of the 1640s, "However grievous

among the governors and magistrates, who have commuted Hester's sentence from death and are willing to be even more lenient if she speaks the name of her partner. The removal of the letter would indicate visually what Hester's utterance would enact symbolically. As Ernest W. Baughman has explained, public confession was not merely a part of the penalty for sin; it was the entrance into forgiveness, "the means by which an individual can remain a part of society; lacking confession, the sinner ceases to be a part of that society, or he is so much at odds with it that his functioning is seriously impaired" (540). The connection between mercy and confession—urged vehemently upon Hester by the Reverend Mr. Wilson, weakly and ambivalently by Dimmesdale—is made explicit in the New England *Platform of Church Discipline*, published in 1649: "If the Lord sanctify the censure to the offender, so as by the grace of Christ, he doth testify his repentance, with humble confession of his sin, and judging of himself, giving glory unto God; the Church is then to *forgive* him, and to *comfort* him, and to *restore* him to the wonted brotherly communion, which formerly he enjoyed with them" (228).

Although the *Platform* was written by New England church elders and representatives of their congregations, it was done at the request of the General Court, and received unanimous approval from the magistrates, including John Winthrop. While Winthrop was not personally responsible for the language of this passage, he most likely endorsed its sentiments and agreed that one important goal of church censure is "the reclaiming and gaining of offending brethren" (227). Sacvan Bercovitch has argued convincingly that the strength of Hawthorne's Puritan community "lies not in coercion but, on the contrary, in their susceptibility to reassessment and change." The Massachusetts leaders have chosen "not to apply the letter of the law . . . but instead to define it through the ambiguities of mercy and justice" (47). In offering to remove Hester's letter, Wilson indicates his eagerness to accept her once again into the community, to suspend strict justice in favor of mercy.

The Politics of Charity

The question of how to treat a single sinner, whether to exile or rehabilitate her, had particular relevance to the larger political issues confronting antebellum America. David S. Reynolds has pointed out that Hawthorne's contemporary culture was dominated by "intensifying moral wars" (*Beneath the American Renaissance* 113). Political and social enthusiasms, evangelical fervor, and moral absolutes abounded in the political and social contests of the day—discussions in which the word "compromise" usually provoked virulent condemnation. Haw-

---

such personal matters were, though, the Bay Colony's problems in these years went well beyond instances of individual immorality. Indeed, upon the heels of their victory in the Pequod war and their resolution of the Antinomian crisis, the Puritans faced a broader, more far-reaching challenge, involving their relationship with England and raising unavoidable questions about the stability, success, and meaning of their entire errand" (87).

thorne's own ruminations on the Civil War sound distinctly familiar when we consider the pedagogical, reformist uses of punishment. In 1861 he wrote: "though I approve the war . . . I don't quite understand what we are fighting for, or what definite result can be expected. If we pummel the South ever so hard, they will love us none the better for it; and even if we subjugate them, our next step should be to cut them adrift."[4]

Bercovitch explains the influence of nineteenth-century domestic political conflicts on *The Scarlet Letter*. Hawthorne clearly recognized these episodes of confrontation—slavery, westward expansion, industrialization, regional disputes, and conflicts over the treatment of women, blacks, laborers, the poor—as the modern versions of political differences that had challenged the colony some two hundred years earlier. When Bercovitch points to the cultural work of *The Scarlet Letter*, he dwells on a political gesture, a ritual of consensus. The word "consensus," like "compromise," is a term based on political expedience—which, Thoreau argued, has no place in the realm of moral issues. In returning to Winthrop, an astute political thinker who drew on the bonds of love and charity to secure political stability, Hawthorne inflects that expedient term "compromise" with the ethically sublime concept of charity. *The Scarlet Letter* is saturated with Winthrop's influence.

Apart from his death, which provides the occasion for a midnight reunion between Hester and Dimmesdale, John Winthrop is absent from the novel. Lauren Berlant is correct in claiming that the "absent" Winthrop is nevertheless "woven into the novel" (74). Berlant is referring to the "struggles over legal representation that fractured the state apparatus of the Massachusetts Bay Colony in the 1630s and 1640s" (73–74). I would add that Hawthorne's interest in Winthrop had less to do with the precise political arguments of the seventeenth century than with the role of sympathy in binding together an otherwise dispersing population in Hawthorne's own day.

The novel's treatment of the Reverend John Wilson furnishes one such example. Edward Johnson, a contemporary chronicler of the colony, notes that Wilson, pastor of the Second Church of Christ, "made a powerful instrument in [Christ's] hands for the cutting down of Error, and Schism" (67). Johnson's description does not seem to indicate tolerance; rather, it resembles the language used by Hawthorne in "The Maypole of Merry-Mount," where John Endicott ruthlessly hacks away at the sign of error and revelry. Johnson was writing generally about the Antinomian crisis of 1637, but we also have evidence of particular occasions when Wilson was unyielding. In a case of heresy in 1643, John Wilson was the most vehement of the elders in calling for Samuel Gorton's execution, even swaying the more temperate John Cotton. As Robert Emmet Wall Jr. writes, "Cotton may have called for reasonableness initially, but his final preachings before the sentencing had called for the most serious of punishments. In this, he was in full

---

4. Letter to Horatio Bridge, 26 May 1861, cited in Masur, "*The Real War*," 164.

accord with his colleague in the Boston pulpit, John Wilson" (140).[5]
Wilson, who constantly clamored in his sermons for Gorton's death, is
here used as a model of rigidity. In Hawthorne's romance, however, he
appears to be much more lenient. Though the novelist makes Wilson
significantly older than he was in 1642, he describes him as "a man of
kind and genial spirit" (65) [47]. Of course, Hawthorne tells us that
this spirit "was, in truth, rather a matter of shame than self-
congratulation with him" (65) [47], as if to note that Wilson's charity
is not his most prized quality among the stern leaders of Massachusetts. Nevertheless, the nineteenth-century narrator clearly approves
of these sentiments. Like Winthrop, Wilson does not assume that
severity is his only course, but considers "what arguments to use,
whether of tenderness or terror," to draw a confession from Hester
(65) [48]. And it is Wilson himself, finally, who tries to negotiate with
Hester by offering to remove her letter.

I have been arguing that John Winthrop, though not actually present as a character in *The Scarlet Letter*, in fact permeates the novel.
His character is suggested by the pitying rosebush, which "by a
strange chance, has been kept alive in history" (1:48) [36]. If we continue to read this passage metaphorically, we shall see that Hawthorne
has an interest in keeping this tradition alive into the nineteenth century, a tradition that comes to us here in the guise of the shadowy
John Winthrop. His influence is clear in the softening of John Wilson,
the senior church leader at Hester's punishment. The civil representative, Governor Bellingham, also speaks briefly, and though he does not
speak of mercy, he hints at it, urging Dimmesdale to extract a confession "as a proof and consequence" of Hester's repentance (66) [48].

It is appropriate, given Hawthorne's indebtedness to Winthrop, that
these high-ranking officials recommend mercy, while the people call
for justice. During the many years in which he battled the people
(through the deputies, their political representatives), Winthrop maintained that the magistrates had a more direct link with God, and thus
were better qualified to assign the penalties for crime and sin. Arguing
in 1641 for the continuance of discretionary power, he contended that
"all punishments, except such as are made certain in the law of God,
or are not subject to variation by merit of circumstances, ought to be
left arbitrary to the wisdom of the judges" (*Journal* 381). In 1644 he
recommended that magistrates "be guided by the word of God" rather
than the prescribed penalties written by mere men (*Journal* 554).
Winthrop even went so far as to claim that judges "are Gods upon
earth: therefore, in their Administrations, they are to hold forth the
wisdom & mercy of God, . . . as well as his Justice" ("Arbitrary Government" 448). He made his case most emphatically in 1645, after
having survived a petition for his impeachment: "The great Questions
that have troubled the Country, are about the Authority of the magistrates & the Liberty of the people: It is your selves, who have called us
to this office, & being called by you, we have our Authority from God,

5. A compromise was reached, and Gorton was first imprisoned and then exiled. See Wall,
   121–56, for an extended discussion of the case.

in way of an Ordinance, such as hath the image of God eminently stamped upon it" ("Speech on Authority and Liberty" in *Journal* 586).

Winthrop's defense of discretionary power for the magistrates, an argument he was forced to repeat frequently during his many years as governor,[6] was fairly simple. The argument is best articulated in his address "Arbitrary Government," delivered in 1644 after an unpleasant confrontation between the deputies and magistrates. Because there was no clear rule about whether to exercise mercy or justice upon a sinner, Winthrop contended, these decisions should be left open to those who were best able to see as God sees. Juries could be trusted to use discretion in civil cases, but they did not have the requisite wisdom to decide criminal cases, where a person's soul was at stake. Winthrop held that the law of the land, by which "the Officers of this Body politick" must walk, was "the Word of God" ("Arbitrary Government" 445). But the Word of God required interpretation, and the governor believed that interpretation often involved the individual circumstances of a case. A fixed penalty for a specific crime, decided in the abstract, could not take account of mitigating circumstances. "If all penalties were prescribed," he asked, "then what need were there of any special wisdom, learning, Courage, zeal, or faithfulness in a Judge?" (446). Winthrop was particularly troubled by the prospect of setting penalties for crimes whose penalties were unspecified in Scripture: "I would know by what Rule we may take upon us, to prescribe penalties, where God prescribes none" (449).

The deputies were clearly right in understanding that the higher-ranking magistrates wielded considerable power. Winthrop had a definite sense of social and political hierarchy, and he supported the clear differences in power between the several groups. "The determination of Law belongs properly to God," he conceded, but God "hath given power & gifts to men to interpret his Laws: & this belongs principally to the highest Authority in a Commonwealth & subordinately to other magistrates & Judges according to their several places" (453). Winthrop had no interest in seeing these hierarchies leveled. Such distinctions were the self-evident truths of his generation of magistrates, and the deputies could not ask for greater powers without hearing the sneering term "mere democracy."

Still, Winthrop's obstinacy on this issue did not make him a tyrant. Because he believed so firmly that he was one of the "Gods upon earth," he was careful not to abuse his power but to represent God's law as truthfully as he could. For this reason, he was much more apt to call for mercy than some of the other political leaders, who saw their roles largely in secular and social terms, and thus were willing to destroy or exile anyone who threatened the status of the community. Halfway through his discourse on arbitrary government, Winthrop turned to the issue of adultery, which, as we have seen, occupied much of the colony's attention during the 1640s, as sex crimes were becoming more prevalent. The example surely resonated with his au-

6. As early as 3 August 1632, Winthrop's *Journal* records such a defense.

dience, many of whom had been present at the double execution for adultery only seven months earlier.

In a significant passage on adultery, Winthrop cites a number of Scriptural cases where the law calling for the death of adulterers was overlooked:

> Adultery & incest deserved death, by the Law, in Jacob's time . . . yet Ruben was punished only with loss of his Birthright, because he was a Patriarch. David his life was not taken away for his Adultery & murder, (but he was otherwise punished) in respect of public interest & advantage, he was valued at 10000 common men. Bathsheba was not put to death for her Adultery, because the Kings desire had with her the force of a Law. . . . But if Judges be tied to a prescript punishment, & no liberty left for dispensation or mitigation in any case, here is no place left for wisdom or mercy. (449)[7]

The point, says Winthrop, is "to show how God hath sometimes (in his wisdom & mercy) dispensed with the rigor of his own Law: & that Princes have sometimes done the like, upon public or other prevalent considerations" (457).

Winthrop does not explain what these considerations might be. As a political leader with deeply religious sentiments, his reasons were probably twofold. First, although he was a civil leader, his authority over the realm of crime and punishment meant that he had a stake in the spiritual condition of all convicted criminals.[8] In Hester Prynne, Hawthorne gives us a fine example of a criminal whose life was spared and soul rehabilitated. Though it takes many years for the scarlet letter to do its office, by the end of the novel she has become an exemplary citizen and Christian, sharing with her townspeople tokens of the same mercy that was exercised upon her. Winthrop was reluctant to practice strict justice while compelling spiritual reasons might be found for substituting mercy and thus for saving both a life and a soul. He felt, moreover, genuine affection for his fellow colonists who, like himself, had forsaken more comfortable lives in Europe in order to participate in a godly mission in a new world. This affection caused him to look mercifully upon their transgressions, to plead for their lives in capital cases, and to look for extenuating circumstances.

A second, more pragmatic reason for his leaning toward mercy had to do with the many battles over political authority waged during what Wall calls the colony's "crucial decade." As a political leader, Winthrop understood the important role of public consent to the authority of a political system and its heads of state. He begins his discourse on arbitrary government by recognizing what John Locke and other theorists would later describe more fully, that governments derive their just

7. The story of Bathsheba and David is represented on a tapestry that hangs in Dimmesdale's apartment. See p. 84 of this Norton Critical Edition.
8. Early on, the Massachusetts Bay Colony decided upon a separation of religious and civil leadership. Although church elders and court magistrates frequently consulted with each other, Winthrop records in July 1632 that the Boston congregation decided that no civil magistrate could be nominated as a ruling elder (*Journal* 71).

authority from the consent of the governed. "Arbitrary government," he writes, "is, where a people have men set over them, without their choice, or allowance: who have power to govern them, & Judge their Causes without a Rule. God only hath this prerogative" (440). Because governors were elected each year, Winthrop was acutely aware of the role of public choice in the development of a healthy political system. He also understood that the colonists of Massachusetts would not long tolerate harsh and judgmental political leaders. As his "Model of Christian Charity" suggests, the welfare of the whole colony was Winthrop's foremost concern, and the colony would never be unified if the people distrusted their leaders.

Resistance might be futile, but desertion was a distinct possibility, and one that Winthrop feared from the beginning. In his "Model" he urged his listeners to consider themselves a body knit together: "though we were absent from each other many miles, and had our employments as far distant, yet we ought to account ourselves knit together by this bond of love" (292). Winthrop had hoped that the absences he alluded to were only temporary. He lived, however, to see the strands of his community come apart, as economic interests and love of liberty prevailed over the sense of charity that he had hoped would hold the community together. One moving passage from his journal is worth citing at length. Following an economic crisis caused by declining immigration, as the people debated their right to leave Massachusetts for "outward advantages," he wrote in September 1642:

> For such as come together into a wilderness, where are nothing but wild beasts and beastlike men, and there confederate together in civil and church estate, whereby they do, implicitly at least, bind themselves to support each other, . . . how they can break from this without free consent, is hard to find, so as may satisfy a tender or good conscience in time of trial. Ask thy conscience, if thou wouldst have plucked up thy stakes, and brought thy family 3000 miles, if thou hadst expected that all, or most, would have forsaken thee there. Ask again, what liberty thou hast towards others, which thou likest not to allow others towards thyself; for if one may go, another may, and so the greater part, and so church and commonwealth may be left destitute in a wilderness, exposed to misery and reproach, and all for thy ease and pleasure. (416)

In this remarkable passage, Winthrop ceases to be a historian of the colony and assumes the role of preacher, appealing to the conscience of his imagined reader, and reminding future generations that a covenant had been broken and a people betrayed. Charity might have held the community together, but selfishness and love of liberty threatened the ruin of the colony. For Winthrop, even the ultimate economic success of Massachusetts would have signified little, so long as that success resulted from the pursuit of private interests. He could take little joy in overall prosperity when it was merely the sum total of private gains.

Winthrop wrote this lament in 1642, the year that Hawthorne chose for the opening scene of his romance. He lived another seven years, long enough to preside over some of the most unsettling political events in the colony's history: the struggle between the deputies and magistrates, prompted by questions about the ownership of a sow (an episode that Hawthorne alludes to in his romance); news of the English civil war, where victory by their Puritan brethren left the New Englanders abandoned as the tides of emigration dried up; and an impeachment trial, which (though the charges were ludicrous and the victory easy) surely caused Winthrop great pain.[9] Through all these episodes, the governor remained true to his policy on mercy, and sincerely regretted having listened to those who had advised greater strictness. Until his dying hour, Winthrop's advocacy of mercy waned only once, in his uncharacteristically severe management of the Antinomian controversy surrounding Anne Hutchinson. Thomas Hutchinson reports that "upon [Winthrop's] death-bed, when Mr. Dudley pressed him to sign an order of banishment of an heterodox person, he refused, saying, 'he had done too much of that work already' " (1:129).

Winthrop's deathbed intimation resonates in Hawthorne's romance, where Hester Prynne is compared to the "sainted" Anne Hutchinson (48) [37]. While it may be tempting to understand this early characterization of the Antinomian leader as Hawthorne's defense of her conduct, such a reading is unconvincing when we consider that Hester is nearly identified with "the image of Divine Maternity" (1:56) [42]. In neither case does the narrator exonerate the woman for her lawlessness. Rather, the association between Hester and Hutchinson reminds us, if only by allusion, that merciful conduct does not come easily. Even the angelic John Winthrop shared some of Chillingworth's least attractive impulses.

By all accounts, Winthrop's death in 1649 signaled the end of charity as a quasi-official policy. According to George Bancroft (whom Hawthorne had read), Massachusetts became much more harsh after losing Winthrop's tolerant leadership, ruthlessly prosecuting Quakers, witches, and other heterodox people. Hutchinson writes of one petty example of Puritan intolerance. "Soon after Mr. Winthrop's death, Mr. Endicott, the most rigid of any of the magistrates, being governor, he joined with the other assistants in an association against long hair" (130). Wall calls the orthodoxy following Winthrop's death "uncompromising and harsh" (233).

A sign of that rigidity might be found in one response to the *Book of General Laws*, finally published in 1648 after years of battle between the magistrates and the deputies. In the end, the magistrates acquiesced in the project. But Winthrop was clearly reluctant, as we have seen. Edward Johnson's *Wonder-Working Providence*, published four years after Winthrop's death, describes the work of the government in

9. Wall writes: "Apparently several of the magistrates thought there were grounds for refusing to entertain the petition. Winthrop was accused for doing what he had every right to do, and the charges against him were ridiculous. Winthrop disagreed. He was anxious to clear his name and by so doing to uphold the authority of his fellow magistrates" (106).

compiling the code of laws. His unmistakable enthusiasm for law and order clearly indicates the changes in the colony during the four short years since Winthrop's death:

> but let not any ill-affected persons find fault with [the laws], be-
> cause they suit not with their own humour, or because they med-
> dle with matters of Religion, for it is no wrong to any man, that a
> people who have spent their estates, many of them, and ventured
> their lives for to keep faith and a pure conscience, to use all
> means that the Word of God allows for maintenance and contin-
> uance of the same, especially they have taken up a desolate
> Wilderness to be their habitation, and not deluded any by keeping
> their profession in huggermug, but print and proclaim to all the
> way and course they intend, God willing, to walk in. (244–45)

Johnson's ideas, of course, are similar to the ones we find in Win-throp's lament about the breakup of his community: the sacrifices of those who have come to the new world, the dangers posed by individual whims, and the sanctity of conscience. But the tone could not be more different. Johnson defends the use of "all means that the Word of God allows" to protect the community, whereas Winthrop sadly accedes to the dispersal of his people because he cannot bring himself to use any means necessary. Hoping to preserve the community by appealing to charity and affection alone, he found that these instruments were insufficient. And yet, even to the end of his life, he refused to use harsher methods.

The Golden Bonds of Love

In Hawthorne's novel, the death of John Winthrop is notable beyond its use in bringing Hester, Pearl, and Arthur together at the scaffold. While the scaffold remains in its usual place, the emblems of mercy have disappeared. On the day of election, when the people will choose Winthrop's successor, his fictional counterpart, the sympathetic young woman of the opening scene, has also passed on to a more merciful world. These absences are consequential for the long-suffering Hester, whose apparently hopeful words to Pearl are surely ironic. Explaining the election-day events, she tells Pearl that "the children have come from their schools, and the grown people from their workshops and their fields, on purpose to be happy. For to-day, a new man is beginning to rule over them; and so—as has been the custom of mankind ever since a nation was first gathered—they make merry and rejoice; as if a good and golden year were at length to pass over the poor old world!" (229) [146]. We must doubt Hester's faith in the reality of this congregated mirth, since her last encounter with the public holiday, when the children were released from their schoolwork, was the scene of her ignominious display seven years earlier. Then, as now, the children did not understand the political significance of the event, only that they were given a "half-holiday" (54) [41]. The two events, indicating shame and happiness, flow together in Hester's experience. Even now, after years of being accustomed to her scarlet letter, Hester's neighbors rediscover their pleasure in her discomfort. As new-comers stare at the letter for the first time, "the inhabitants of the town (their own interest in this worn-out subject languidly reviving it-self, by sympathy with what they saw others feel) lounged idly to the same quarter, and tormented Hester Prynne, perhaps more than all the rest, with their cool, well-acquainted gaze at her familiar shame" (246) [156]. The original scene of Hester's humiliation is nearly repli-cated, except that she encounters no expressions of mercy, but antici-pates that "a new man is beginning to rule over them." Furthermore, as Michael Davitt Bell has pointed out, the "new man" is none other than the despotic John Endicott, who "went on to dominate the gov-ernment of Massachusetts until his own death in 1665." Though Hawthorne does not mention the name of the new governor, "the sup-pressed 'truth' about Endicott's succession is intended ironically to un-dercut the hopefulness of Hester and Dimmesdale" (141). Hester, we must conclude, fully intends all of the ironies of her political lesson to Pearl.

With the death of Winthrop, charity seems to have evaporated among the political and religious leaders of New England; conse-quently, so have the real bonds of community. We see this point most clearly in Arthur Dimmesdale's election-day sermon, delivered as he is planning his covert departure from the colony. On the face of it, the sermon describes the very preoccupation that had consumed John Winthrop: the future of this godly experiment called New England, and the reward that God meant to bestow upon those who remained faithful to the covenant. "His subject, it appeared, had been the rela-tion between the Deity and the communities of mankind, with a spe-cial reference to the New England which they were here planting in the wilderness. And, as he drew towards the close, a spirit as of prophecy had come upon him, constraining him to its purpose as mightily as the old prophets of Israel were constrained; only with this difference, that, whereas the Jewish seers had denounced judgments and ruin on their country, it was his mission to foretell a high and glo-rious destiny for the newly gathered people of the Lord" (249) [157]. The conclusion of the sermon is one for which Winthrop himself, writing in 1630, could only hope. Dimmesdale's apparent certainty, "constraining" him to this prophecy of congregational victory, is espe-cially incriminating when we consider that the preacher is plotting his escape from the very community that has selected him as its prophet and saint. He is constrained by nothing but his desire to escape the grasp of Chillingworth, accompanied by Hester and Pearl. He com-poses his inspired sermon in the afterglow of his forest meeting with Hester, in anticipation of his escape. Returning to his study after the encounter, he flings "the already written pages of the Election Sermon into the fire," and "forthwith beg[ins] another." Writing "with earnest haste and ecstasy," he consumes the entire night at his desk and dis-covers himself, at dawn, with "a vast, immeasurable tract of written space behind him!" (225) [143]. The metaphor clearly indicates that Dimmesdale's mind is fastened not on spiritual matters but on the open space that he plans to put between himself and his tormentor, and also, unavoidably, between himself and the people who share in his covenant with God. We might almost hear Winthrop's lament in the background of Dimmesdale's sermon; here, indeed, is a man ready to take the "liberty of removing for outward advantages." Perhaps Dimmesdale has heard these echoes from the dead Winthrop. After all, his newfound attraction to "ease and pleasure" is just as alienating as his habitual penance and solitude have been. In his case, neither punishment nor its escape brings him any closer to his community. In this gifted minister, Hawthorne has given us a clear sign that Winthrop's New England has forgotten its covenant of charity.

Another sign that true charity is a thing of the past is that those who pretend to it inspire nothing but horror in the observant reader. For all of his malice, Roger Chillingworth is a keen student of Winthrop and understands better than Dimmesdale that community ties cannot be so easily dissolved. Echoing Winthrop and poisoning his meaning, Chillingworth explains to Hester why he cannot leave New England: "elsewhere a wanderer, and isolated from human interests, I find here a woman, a man, a child, amongst whom and myself there exist the closest ligaments. No matter whether of love or hate; no matter whether of right or wrong!" (76) [54]. The ligaments that for Winthrop were made of love become for Chillingworth ties of "interests" that have nothing to do with affection. What matters to him is the compulsion to recognize and pursue those claims to human community. As he tells the dying Dimmesdale, "Hadst thou sought the whole earth over, . . . there was no one place so secret,—no high place nor lowly place, where thou couldst have escaped me,—save on this very scaffold!" (253) [160]. However vast the geographic distance the minister might put between himself and his tormentor, only the moral space afforded by Dimmesdale's confession could have severed the ligaments of guilt and retribution connecting the two men.

Chillingworth understands these things because he has sought to master what Winthrop described as the "sensibleness and sympathy of [an]other's conditions" ("Model" 289). To gain this sympathy, Winthrop advised, we must practice "more enlargement towards others and less respect towards ourselves" (287). Chillingworth satisfies this condition in the extreme, exchanging his own subjectivity for whatever elements of another consciousness might flow into his own. He is able to "go deep into his patient's bosom" precisely because he can put his own personality aside (124) [83]. Seeing the success of Chillingworth's practice, the narrator issues this warning:

> A man burdened with a secret should especially avoid the intimacy of his physician. If the latter possess native sagacity, and a nameless something more,—let us call it intuition; if he show no intrusive egotism, nor disagreeably prominent characteristics of his own; if he have the power, which must be born with him, to bring his mind into such affinity with his patient's, that this last shall unawares have spoken what he imagines himself only to have thought; . . . then, at some inevitable moment, will the soul

of the sufferer be dissolved, and flow forth in a dark, but transparent stream, bringing all its mysteries into the daylight. (124)
[83]

The language here is very like that used by Hawthorne in his famous
description of mesmerism. To enter into the feelings of another, that
is, one must put one's own feelings aside and imagine what the object
of the gaze is undergoing; the result is a flowing of the soul of the observed, often unawares, into the grasp of the observer. Only the observer's motives can protect the object of sympathy. If the practitioner
of sympathy has pernicious designs on his companion, designs that
Hawthorne feared in a mesmerist and dramatized in Chillingworth,
the transaction is formidable. Amazed to see sympathy used for malicious ends, Hester articulates some of the awe with which her author
regarded complete sympathy. " 'Thy acts are like mercy,' said Hester,
bewildered and appalled. 'But thy words interpret thee as a terror!' "
(76) [54].

Dimmesdale, in contrast, becomes a victim precisely because he is
unable to escape his own ego and thereby enter into the feelings and
motives of others. On the night of Winthrop's death, the minister suffers from "a highly disordered mental state" because he misreads the
token in the sky as a reference to his own private sin. "Rendered morbidly self-contemplative by long, intense, and secret pain," Dimmesdale has "extended his egotism over the whole expanse of nature, until
the firmament itself should appear no more than a fitting page for his
soul's history and fate" (155) [102]. The sign and the cause of this
morbidity are the same: Dimmesdale's secret sin has become the one
significant fact in his life, and it colors his perceptions of the world.
Preoccupied with his own sin, he assumes that all humans are likewise fallen, likewise suspect. "Trusting no man as his friend, he could
not recognize his enemy when the latter actually appeared" (130) [87].

Hester suffers from the same solipsism, but unlike Dimmesdale she
recognizes it as a symptom of her own subjectivism rather than as a
truth of the universe. When "the red infamy upon her breast would
give a sympathetic throb" (87) [60] indicating "the hidden sin in other
hearts" (86) [60], Hester resists the conclusion that the world is as
fallen as she. "Be it accepted as a proof that all was not corrupt in this
poor victim of her own frailty, and man's hard law, that Hester Prynne
yet struggled to believe that no fellow-mortal was guilty like herself"
(87) [60].

Chillingworth, suffering from no such intrusive egotism, knows that
his conclusions are accurate. As he explains to Hester, the science of
sympathy, learned well, is just as reliable as other sciences. "I shall
seek this man, as I have sought truth in books; as I have sought gold
in alchemy. There is a sympathy that will make me conscious of him. I
shall see him tremble. I shall feel myself shudder, suddenly and unawares. Sooner or later, he must needs be mine!" (75) [53]. Chillingworth is concerned with science, not art, but his language curiously
echoes the passage in "The Custom-House" where Hawthorne describes how the letter "on [his] breast" provoked "a sensation not alto-

gether physical, yet almost so, as of burning heat; and as if the letter were not of red cloth, but red-hot iron. I shuddered, and involuntarily let it fall upon the floor" (32) [26]. "Suddenly and unawares," Hawthorne experiences the sensations of a perfect sympathetic encounter, producing an involuntary bodily reaction. Like Chillingworth, the author identifies fully with Hester herself, who experiences the letter as an almost literal wound, "the tenderest spot" of her sore consciousness (84) [59], a spot that seems "to grow more sensitive with daily torture" (86) [59]. Unlike Chillingworth, who rejoices in the shudder that constitutes the proof he has sought, Hawthorne would like to escape the sympathetic encounter embodied in the scarlet letter. As the narrator admits at the close of the novel, he "would gladly, now that it has done its office, erase its deep print out of [his] own brain; where long meditation has fixed it in very undesirable distinctness" (259) [163]. He does not tell us whether such a wish is realistic or whether, like Hester's, his mark is "too deeply branded" to be removed. Like Dimmesdale, the narrator has developed a sympathetic replica of Hester's mark of shame; unlike Dimmesdale, he sees it as a link between himself and the human community, a token of what Winthrop called the "sensibleness and sympathy" of another's condition.

Hester, who comes to be known through the town as a "Sister of Mercy" (161) [105], likewise performs deeds that look like mercy but are really quite different. If, as Winthrop believed, charity arises out of ligaments of affection, then Hester's acts of mercy are not true charity, though they eventually restore her to her community and make true charity possible. While she "came to have a part to perform in the world," Hester does not feel as though she belongs; all of her encounters "implied, and often expressed, that she was banished, and as much alone as if she inhabited another sphere" (84) [58]. Though this banishment is imposed on Hester by the token that she must wear, during her years of exile she comes to internalize the judgment of the people and extricate herself from the grasp of human sympathies. Her face typically shows "the frozen calmness of a dead woman's features; owing this dreary resemblance to the fact that Hester was actually dead, in respect to any claim of sympathy, and had departed out of the world with which she still seemed to mingle" (226) [144]. While she comes to be known by a "blameless purity" that is taken to indicate her "genuine regard for virtue" (160) [105], we learn that she does not share in her community's sense of virtue: "The world's law was no law for her mind" (164) [107].

Whatever motivates her kind deeds, then, they are not acts of charity, since she seems actively to eschew the "sensibleness and sympathy" of another's condition that prompt charitable work. Instead, the narrator dismisses Hester's apparently charitable acts as mere "morbid meddling of conscience with an immaterial matter" (84) [58], like the impulses that drive the minister to fast and scourge himself "as an act of penance" (144) [96]. Hawthorne wishes us to recognize the difference between the appearance of charity and its deeper reality, even if the community does not. Indeed the one person of whose condition she is most apt to be sensible does not gain Hester's immediate sympathy. She feels the solace of Arthur Dimmesdale's "human eye," giving her "momentary relief, as if half of her agony were shared" (86) [60], but the glance does not also offer her entrance into his suffering. Wandering "without a clew in the dark labyrinth of mind" (166) [108], Hester forgets that she is not the only one undergoing torment.

Only when she sees him upon the scaffold, occupying the same place where she had stood in her own ignominy and torment, does Hester begin to understand the depth of her lover's suffering. Hawthorne has nearly literally enacted the scene of sympathy as Adam Smith describes it, where we can understand another person's pain only by imagining how it would feel for ourselves. Only in imaginatively exchanging places with the object of suffering can we enter into that suffering. Dimmesdale attempts to take on his due share of punishment by occupying the same ground where Hester had stood; Hester, having stood there once before, is able to feel the torment that Dimmesdale has endured at the hands of his physician. The moment proves pivotal for the socially estranged woman, who, "in the misanthropy of her own trouble, [had] left the minister to bear what she might picture to herself as a more tolerable doom. But of late, since the night of his vigil, all her sympathies towards him had been both softened and invigorated. She now read his heart more accurately" (193) [124]. Hester's egotism and sense of her own estrangement have made her nearly impervious to the sufferings of the one person whose pain she should have intuited. Hardened by years of loneliness, she overlooks the obligations demanded by the "iron link of mutual crime" (160) [104].

It is notable that one of the most arresting statements in the novel—"The scarlet letter had not done its office"—is immediately followed by an indication that Hester is about to acknowledge her debt to Dimmesdale (166) [108]. The moment is significant because, rather than reintegrating her into the community, as punishments should do, the scarlet letter has instead alienated Hester from the sentiments that must seem natural in order to provide a sense of communal identity. Looking at Dimmesdale now with sympathy rather than solipsism, Hester begins to feel the tug of communal loyalties for the first time in seven years:

> The scarlet letter had not done its office.
> Now, however, her interview with the Reverend Mr. Dimmesdale, on the night of his vigil, had given her a new theme of reflection, and held up to her an object that appeared worthy of any exertion and sacrifice for its attainment. She had witnessed the intense misery beneath which the minister struggled, or, to speak more accurately, had ceased to struggle. (166) [108–09]

Hester's newfound sense of responsibility for another person, unlike her other charitable acts, can be considered real charity in Winthrop's sense: she decides to lay aside her own concerns, including her promise to Chillingworth and the consequences of breaking it, and "redeem her error" (167) [109]. One such consequence might well be the deaths of Hester and Arthur. Since the statute calls for the death of adulterers, the revelation that Hester's husband is still alive could result in a double execution. Of course, given the length of time since the crime, it is possible that the magistrates would not insist on the extreme penalty. But Chillingworth, "the man whom [they have] most vilely wronged," has every right to demand the lives of these sinners, and his voice would be a powerful argument in favor of execution (172) [112]. As he tells Hester, "My finger, pointed at this man, would have hurled him from his pulpit into a dungeon,—thence, peradventure, to the gallows!" (171) [111]. Since the death of Winthrop, furthermore, mercy could not be expected at the hands of the law.

As one of the first signs that she has rejoined her Christian community, Hester begins to speak of mercy and charity. Since, for many years, "there seemed to be no longer any thing in Hester's face for Love to dwell upon" (163) [107], Hester's association with these words, rather than with judgment and revenge, signifies a dramatic change, and hints that the letter is finally doing its office. Calling upon Chillingworth to give up his fiendish revenge, Hester asks him to "purge it out of thee, and be once more human. . . . Forgive, and leave [Arthur's] further retribution to the Power that claims it!" (173–74) [113].

Though Chillingworth refuses Hester's appeal, she has gained something from contemplating the benefits of charity and the effects of unmerciful thoughts on her former husband. No longer seeing the world through the single lens of retribution, she considers that mercy might also be part of her lot. Hester has long understood that it is Pearl's role to "connect her parent for ever with the race and descent of mortals" (89) [61], but until she opens her heart to the redemptive power of mercy, the mother recognizes that relation as primarily punitive. Though she admits that Pearl "is my happiness," she dwells on the child's function as a representative of the law. "Pearl punishes me too! See ye not, she is the scarlet letter . . . endowed with a millionfold the power of retribution for my sin" (113) [76].

But after beginning to understand and sympathize with the sufferings of others, Hester recognizes that perhaps Pearl might offer more than "justice and retribution": "never, until now, had she bethought herself to ask, whether, linked with that design, there might not likewise be a purpose of mercy and beneficence. If little Pearl were entertained with faith and trust, as a spirit-messenger no less than an earthly child, might it not be her errand to soothe away the sorrow that lay cold in her mother's heart, and converted it into a tomb?" (180) [117]. Hester rejects Pearl's silent offer of sympathy, but the child's work has nevertheless begun. It will be finished at the scene of Dimmesdale's death, where "Pearl's errand as a messenger of anguish was all fulfilled" (256) [162]. Hester's tomblike heart becomes a scene of resurrection when she allows her sorrows to stir again and become a conduit to other sorrows than her own.

In accepting her link with the human community, moreover, Hester embodies Winthrop's connection between the affections and the social order. Covenants, that is, can only be upheld when the bonds of affection unite all members. As Hawthorne explains, a "general sentiment . . . gives law its vitality" (231) [147]. Before her seven years of alienation, Hester had understood that law was deeply rooted in the affections, not wicked and repressive but gentle and firm. Standing upon the scaffold, she recalls the deepest influence over her past life, the "look of heedful and anxious love" in her mother's face, "which, even since her death, had so often laid the impediment of a gentle remonstrance in her daughter's pathway" (58) [43]. Likewise, Hester seems to intuit the good motives of the magistrates; even during these early days of her humiliation, she regards the law with mixed feelings, understanding that "the very law that condemned her—a giant of stern features, but with vigor to support, as well as to annihilate, in his iron arm—had held her up, through the terrible ordeal of her ignominy" (78) [55]. This law seems almost parental, offering Hester mercy and support when it might have called for her death.

But after years of enduring "the ever relentless vigor with which society frowned upon her sin" (83) [58], Hester comes to confuse official law with the way it takes root in the popular imagination. On the first day of her punishment, these two sources of discipline are not the same. "Amongst any other population," the narrator explains, "the grim rigidity that petrified the bearded physiognomies of these good people . . . could have betokened nothing short of the anticipated execution of some noted culprit, on whom the sentence of a legal tribunal had but confirmed the verdict of public sentiment" (49) [37]. The point is easy to miss: the spectacle will not be an execution, but, just as significantly, the legal tribunal has refrained from confirming the verdict of the public. Rather, as we have seen, the magistrates have been much more gentle, almost parental in their censure.

By conflating these two sources of penance and dismissing abstract law as mere vindictiveness, Hester has fully alienated herself from her community and rejected law altogether. Hester's treatment of Pearl indicates how unlike her own mother she has become. Though "she early sought to impose a tender, but strict, control over the infant immortality that was committed to her charge," she eventually learns that the lawless Pearl will not be governed (91–92) [62–63]. Pearl's disorderly nature is only one reason why Hester relinquishes her motherly control of the child; for, in her long alienation from human society, Hester has set herself free from the forms of human restraint. "For years past she had looked from this estranged point of view at human institutions, and whatever priests or legislators had established; criticizing all with hardly more reverence than the Indian would feel for the clerical band, the judicial robe, the pillory, the gallows, the fireside, or the church" (199) [128].

The narrator, as we have seen, shares some of Hester's ambivalence about the men who judge her and the peculiar penalty they have assigned. Almost literally calling upon her to bare her soul, requiring her to write her sin upon her bosom, they have, as Dimmesdale says of the physician, "violated, in cold blood, the sanctity of a human heart" (195) [125–26]. Describing the effect of the pillory, the narrator steps forth with vehement condemnation of an unnatural punishment: "There can be no outrage, methinks, against our common nature,—whatever be the delinquencies of the individual,—no outrage more flagrant than to forbid the culprit to hide his face for shame; as it was the essence of this punishment to do" (55) [42]. Though Hester is spared this particular torment, her punishment is very similar: she cannot hide the mark of her sin, but must become "the general symbol at which the preacher and moralist might point" (79) [55].

Both Hester and the narrator shift between condemnation of the Puritan leaders and a grudging respect for their piety. These shifting positions are also more objectively apparent in the relative tolerance of the magistrates and elders in the opening chapters, as opposed to their "iron framework of reasoning" that prevents them from forgiving Hester as fully as her townspeople do (162) [106]. In the actions of his Puritan characters Hawthorne demonstrates his own complicated attitudes toward the Puritan elders. As Joseph Alkana and Lawrence Buell have persuasively demonstrated, these shifting attitudes toward official Puritan culture coincide with the conventional and ongoing tension among historians of Hawthorne's generation between filiopiety and criticism of the Puritan founding fathers. The unstable attitudes of Hester's neighbors also reflect an antebellum ambivalence toward an earlier generation, whose moral firmness must have seemed to Hawthorne at times admirable, at times disappointing.

Hawthorne's narrator does not oppose the magistrates or impugn their character. His criticism has only to do with the sanctity of a soul and his horror at seeing it exposed. Even as the chronicler of this tragic tale, he often discreetly turns aside from private details. While Dimmesdale contemplates his escape from New England, the narrator admits to an act of narrative omission: "The struggle, if there were one, need not be described. Let it suffice, that the clergyman resolved to flee, and not alone" (201) [129]. At the climax of the novel, while he relays the many accounts of Dimmesdale's dying revelation, he refrains from giving us the true one, explaining that "it were irreverent to describe that revelation" (255) [161].

As if to correct Hester's mistakes, the narrator reiterates the forgotten message of charity. Even toward Roger Chillingworth, he claims he "would fain be merciful" (260) [164], and so he consigns the leech to a benevolent afterlife, where he and the minister "may, unawares, have found their earthly stock of hatred and antipathy transmuted into golden love" (261) [164].

In this image we again hear the words of John Winthrop resonating through Hawthorne's romance, long after we have forgotten the man himself. The narrator helps Hester to transmute her own anger into golden love, tempering her irreverent judgment of the New England authorities with his own description. The magistrates "had fortitude and self-reliance, and, in time of difficulty or peril, stood up for the welfare of the state like a line of cliffs against a tempestuous tide" (238) [151]. Like Hester's anxious mother, the statesmen wish mainly to protect their charges. Although they have not arranged the election and invited the people "on purpose to be happy," neither do the stern rulers wish to impose sorrow on the world. As a sign that Hester's antipathy has also been transmuted into golden love, she once more joins her community and abides by its laws. For Winthrop as for this narrator whom he so deeply influenced, love and law are one and the same.

With the death of John Winthrop, as we have seen, charity all but disappeared from the official policy of New England. But Hawthorne restored Winthrop's most prized sentiments to the New England of his romance and of his antebellum reader. Though mercy and sympathy are not fully developed until the end of the novel, when Hester Prynne returns to New England and assumes the scarlet letter "of her own free will" (263) [165], the seeds of these virtues are first sown at the scaffold on the night of Winthrop's death, when Dimmesdale enacts Hester's penance and Hester first recognizes the extent of his.

Just as the citizens in the opening scenes articulate the public debates over mercy and judgment that have consumed the political leaders, in the closing scene Hawthorne grants to Hester, a woman estranged from the court, the church, and the meeting-house, the power to realize Winthrop's ideal of charity. When she returns to New England, it is to a "real life" (262) [165], not to the "labyrinth of mind" that had been her home for seven years. Her charity, like her life, also becomes real; it springs from common experiences and true sympathy for "the continually recurring trials of wounded, wasted, wronged, misplaced, or erring and sinful passion" (263) [165]. No longer ridiculed by those she tries to help, she is instead sought out and finally understood by those who value her sympathetic counsel as coming from "one who had herself gone through a mighty trouble" (263) [165].

In this "Sister of Mercy," Hawthorne offers his nineteenth-century readers a modern model of the politically specific charity that had gone out of circulation with the death of John Winthrop in 1649. By the end of the romance, all of the major characters have learned the lesson of charity. We are given hope that Dimmesdale and Chillingworth, each "dependent for the food of his affections and spiritual life upon [the] other" (260) [164], are bound by the ligaments of "golden love" (261) [164]. As for Pearl, the scene of her father's death has "developed all her sympathies" (256) [162]. The unnamed women of the village, once represented by the most pitiless of all the Puritans, now look to Hester's letter with "awe, yet with reverence too" (263) [165]. And Hester's affections (sorrow and penitence) draw her back into the community she once tried to escape.

When Hawthorne railed against the "mob of scribbling women," he was attacking, I suspect, neither literary women nor what we have come to call "sentimental novels," if by that we mean novels that share a preoccupation with the moral sentiments, particularly sympathy.

Clearly *The Scarlet Letter* is one such sentimental novel. Instead, Hawthorne's impatience was directed not only at the literary market but also at the peculiar nineteenth-century American manifestation of sympathy, a vague, free-floating sentimentalism that encouraged inconsequential expressions of feeling. Hawthorne considered moral sentiments deeply significant. If sympathy helped to bring human beings together, then communities governed by sympathy, he believed, were not oppressive, and laws motivated by love should be gratefully upheld.

Both Rufus Choate and John Winthrop, arguably the only early Americans who inspired Hawthorne with unqualified filiopiety, would have approved of Hester's return to New England. In restoring this most alienated Puritan to the land that had made her a story and a byword, and in giving her the task of counseling other disaffected members and thereby helping them to accept their burdens, Hawthorne expressed his hope that, to recall Choate, "overrated diversities of interest" might be overlooked in favor of a larger social good, the "constitutional sentiment of old, family, fraternal regard." In so doing he countered both versions of sentiment prevalent in his own age: the generalized and effete sentimental response to all scenes of pathos, and the politically contentious sympathies often stridently aligned with moral and political absolutes. Rewriting the history of New England, Hawthorne corrected what he saw as the errors of the past, granting the lowliest of our ancestors the task of internalizing and dispersing, rather than losing, the greatest of Winthrop's political contributions: the understanding that law derives its fortitude from general sentiments.

WORKS CITED

Alkana, Joseph. *The Social Self: Hawthorne, Howells, William James, and Nineteenth-Century Psychology.* Lexington: UP of Kentucky, 1977.

Anderson, Douglas. "Jefferson, Hawthorne, and 'The Custom-House.'" *Nineteenth-Century Literature* 46 (1991): 309–26.

Baughman, Ernest W. "Public Confession and *The Scarlet Letter.*" *New England Quarterly* 40 (1967): 532–50.

Bell, Michael Davitt. *Hawthorne and the Historical Romance of New England.* Princeton: Princeton UP, 1971.

Bercovitch, Sacvan. *The Office of* The Scarlet Letter. Baltimore: Johns Hopkins UP, 1991.

Berlant, Lauren. *The Anatomy of National Fantasy: Hawthorne, Utopia, and Everyday Life.* Chicago: U of Chicago P, 1991.

Buell, Lawrence. *New England Literary Culture: From Revolution Through Renaissance.* New York: Cambridge UP, 1986.

Choate, Rufus. "The Importance of Illustrating New-England History by a Series of Romances like the Waverly Novels." In *Addresses and Orations of Rufus Choate.* Boston: Little, Brown, 1878. 1–39.

Dawson, Edward. *Hawthorne's Knowledge and Use of New England History: A Study of Sources.* Nashville: Vanderbilt UP, 1939.

Dawson, Hugh J. "Hester Prynne, William Hawthorne, and the Bay Colony Adultery Laws of 1641–42." *ESQ* 32 (1986): 225–31.

Erickson, Kai T. *Wayward Puritans: A Study in the Sociology of Deviance.* New York: Wiley, 1966.

Gilmore, Michael T. "Hawthorne and the Making of the Middle Class." *Discovering Difference: Contemporary Essays in American Culture.* Ed. Christoph Lohmann. Bloomington: Indiana UP, 1993. 88–104. Pp. 597–613 in this Norton Critical Edition.

Hunt, Lester. "*The Scarlet Letter*: Hawthorne's Theory of Moral Sentiments." *Philosophy and Literature* 8 (1984): 78–88.

Hutchinson, Thomas. *The History of the Colony and Province of Massachusetts Bay.* 1764. Ed. Lawrence Shaw Mayo. 3 vols. Cambridge: Harvard UP, 1936.

Johnson, Edward. *Johnson's Wonder-Working Providence 1628–1651*. 1653. Ed J. Franklin Jameson. New York: Scribner's, 1910.

Kesselring, Marion L. *Hawthorne's Reading, 1828–1850*. New York: New York Public Library, 1949.

Leavis, Q. D. "Hawthorne as Poet." *Sewanee Review* 59 (1951): 426–58.

Leverenz, David. "Mrs. Hawthorne's Headache: Reading *The Scarlet Letter*." *Nineteenth-Century Fiction* 37 (1983): 552–573. Pp. 463–81 in this Norton Critical Edition.

Masur, Louis P., ed. *"The Real War Will Never Get in the Books": Selections from Writers during the Civil War*. New York: Oxford UP, 1993.

Mather, Cotton. *Magnalia Christi Americana, Books I and II*. Ed. Kenneth B. Murdock. Cambridge: Harvard UP, 1977.

Moseley, James G. *John Winthrop's World: History as a Story, the Story as History*. Madison: U of Wisconsin P, 1992.

Murrin, John M. "Magistrates, Sinners, and a Precarious Liberty: Trial by Jury in Seventeenth-Century New England." In *Saints and Revolutionaries: Essays on Early American History*. Ed. David D. Hall, John M. Murrin, and Thad Tate. New York: W. W. Norton and Company, 1984. 152–206.

Railton, Stephen. "The Address of *The Scarlet Letter*." *Readers in History: Nineteenth-Century American Literature and the Contexts of Response*. Ed. James L. Machor. Baltimore: Johns Hopkins UP, 1993. 138–63. Pp. 481–500 in this Norton Critical Edition.

Reynolds, David S. *Beneath the American Renaissance: The Subversive Imagination in the Age of Emerson and Whitman*. Cambridge: Harvard UP, 1988.

Reynolds, Larry J. "*The Scarlet Letter* and Revolutions Abroad." *American Literature* 57.1 (March 1985): 44–67. Pp. 614–32 in this Norton Critical Edition.

Ryskamp, Charles. "The New England Sources of *The Scarlet Letter*." *American Literature* 31 (1959): 257–72. Pp. 291–304 in this Norton Critical Edition.

Van Leer, David. "Hester's Labyrinth: Transcendental Rhetoric in Puritan Boston." *New Essays on* The Scarlet Letter. Ed. Michael J. Colacurcio. New York: Cambridge UP, 1985. 57–100.

Wall, Robert Emmet, Jr. *Massachusetts Bay: The Crucial Decade, 1640–1650*. New Haven: Yale UP, 1972.

Williams, Daniel E. "Victims of Narrative Seduction: The Literary Translations of Elizabeth (and 'Miss Harriot') Wilson." *Early American Literature* 28 (1993): 148–70.

Winthrop, John. "Arbitrary Government, Described." 1645. In *Life and Letters of John Winthrop*. Boston: Ticknor and Fields, 1867. 440–59.

———. *The Journal of John Winthrop, 1630–1649*. Ed. Richard S. Dunn, James Savage, and Laetitia Yeandle. Cambridge: Harvard UP, 1996.

———. "A Model of Christian Charity." In *Winthrop Papers*. New York: Russell and Russell, 1968–. 2: 282–95.

ELLEN WEINAUER

Considering Possession in *The Scarlet Letter*†

In the much-discussed first line of "The Custom-House," Nathaniel Hawthorne announces not only his text's complicated attitude toward its audience, but also its even more complicated treatment of issues of demonic possession. "It is a little remarkable," Hawthorne writes, "that—though disinclined to talk overmuch of myself and my affairs at the fireside, and to my personal friends—an autobiographical impulse should twice in my life have taken possession of me, in addressing the public."[1] This line is interesting, of course, for what it suggests about Hawthorne's discomfort with the autobiographical mode. It is also interesting, I think, for the particular and peculiar trope with which Hawthorne figures that discomfort. In suggesting that the desire to disclose has "taken possession of me," Hawthorne intriguingly pres-

† From *Studies in American Fiction* 29 (Spring 2001): 93–112. Copyright © Northeastern University. Reprinted by permission of the publisher and the author. Page numbers in square brackets refer to this Norton Critical Edition.

1. Nathaniel Hawthorne, *The Scarlet Letter: A Romance* (New York: Penguin Books, 1983), 7; hereafter cited parenthetically.

ents himself as the resistant victim of a sort of witchcraft, as one whose subjective mastery has been undermined by an apparently irresistible and demonic force.

Nor do these associations end here: indeed, the trope of demonic possession that is launched in this line makes insistent, one might even say obsessive, re-appearances in "The Custom-House." "This old town of Salem," Hawthorne tells us early in the sketch, "possesses, or did possess, a hold on my affections, the force of which I have never realized during my seasons of actual residence here" (11) [10]. Hawthorne attempts to explain this "hold" by describing ancestral connections, noting that the "figure of that first ancestor . . . still haunts me" (12) [11], and that he feels tied to Salem as by a "spell" (14) [13]. Later, when he has "found" the scarlet letter in the second story of the Custom House but cannot, as he articulates it, bring the "dead corpses" of the narrative characters to life, those corpses stare at him with "a fixed and ghastly grin": " 'What have you to do with us?' that expression seemed to say. 'The little power you might once have possessed over the tribe of unrealities is gone!' " (34) [28]. Hawthorne cannot create: a "wretched numbness held possession of me" (35) [28]. He is "haunted by a suspicion that [his] intellect is dwindling away" (37) [30] and that he has lost the "poor properties" of his mind (39) [32]; he suggests that the man in civil service is, if ejected from office, "haunt[ed]" by a "hope" that he will be "restored to office" (38) [31]; having himself been ejected from his position as Custom-House surveyor, he describes his now positionless and "figurative self" as one who has been "decapitated" and is writing "from beyond the grave" (42) [34].

With these descriptions, Hawthorne provides us with a return to and redaction of one of his most prevalent themes: the perils of authorship, which he variously figures in his sketches, short stories, and novels as both dangerously powerful and dangerously disempowering. It is precisely in the context of issues of craft and creativity—in the context of issues of literary power—that critics such as Millicent Bell, Maria Tatar, and Samuel Chase Coale have read Hawthorne's treatment of witchcraft, mesmerism, spiritualism, and other "popular supernaturalisms."[2] Hawthorne himself makes an explicit link between his authorship and witchcraft, in a letter commenting upon the furor that ensued in Salem in the wake of the publication of "The Custom-House." Writing to Horatio Bridge, Hawthorne noted that "my preliminary chapter has caused the greatest uproar that ever happened here since witch-times." Through his authorship of this apparently incendiary sketch, Hawthorne becomes in his own configuration much like

2. See Samuel Chase Coale, *Mesmerism and Hawthorne: Mediums of American Romance* (Tuscaloosa: U of Alabama P, 1998); Maria M. Tatar, *Spellbound: Studies in Mesmerism and Literature* (Princeton: Princeton UP, 1978); Millicent Bell, *Hawthorne's View of the Artist* (New York: State UP, 1962). For an alternative reading, briefly articulated, see Mary E. Rucker, "The Art of Witchcraft in Hawthorne's 'Feathertop: A Moralized Legend,' " *Studies in Short Fiction* 24 (1987): 31–39. The phrase "popular supernaturalism" comes from Howard Kerr, John W. Crowley, and Charles L. Crow, "Introduction," *The Haunted Dusk: American Supernatural Fiction, 1820–1920* (Athens: U of Georgia P, 1983), 4.

the Salem witches—a heretic who will only with great "good luck" be able to "escape from town without being tarred-and-feathered."[3]

It is undeniable, I think, that Hawthorne's use of metaphors of witchcraft and demonic possession signals complex attitudes toward the act of literary creation; but it is also worth noting that, unlike in his letter to Bridge, in "The Custom-House" Hawthorne is, for the most part, not the witch but the victim of witchcraft, not the demonic possessor but the demonically (dis)possessed. Taking note of this, I want to offer another way of reading the issue of witchcraft in *The Scarlet Letter*, one that draws explicitly on some of Hawthorne's critical seventeenth-century sources. In particular, I want to resituate the text's treatment of witchcraft in a Puritan history that insistently associates witchcraft with disruptions by women of male ownership of property. Like the witches and proto-witches with which she is associated throughout the novel—Anne Hibbins, Anne Hutchinson— Hawthorne's heroine claims an authority over property that leaves the text, and its author, deeply troubled, raising as it does the specter of male dispossession.

Indeed, the novel's disturbed iteration of this theme reflects a kind of textual urgency, reminding us that, far from being put to rest along with the witchcraft trials, this specter was hauntingly present in Hawthorne's own day. The antebellum years saw a great deal of public debate about laws of "coverture"—laws designating, among other things, the distribution of property in marriage. By the year of *The Scarlet Letter*'s publication, in fact, seventeen states had passed laws giving married women significantly more control over both personal and real property. Hawthorne's own state of Massachusetts passed acts—albeit limited ones—in both 1845 and 1846.[4] I do not intend to reduce *The Scarlet Letter* to a simple "thumbs-up" or "thumbs-down" on these matters; but in suggesting that we resituate the novel's treatment of witchcraft in a history of the meanings of (women-as-) property in marriage, I am also suggesting that Hawthorne's text exists as an anxious meditation on a pressing issue of its own contemporary moment. By examining the ways in which Hawthorne's seventeenth-century sources serve to frame and mediate that issue, we can make more sense, I think, of the ambivalence with which Hester's insurgency is depicted in *The Scarlet Letter*. We can also return to "The Custom-House" with a perspective that allows us to better understand the anxiety about male (self-)possession—an anxiety captured in its proliferating metaphors of witchcraft—that so haunts *The Scarlet Letter*'s "Introductory."

Hawthorne, of course, knew his Bible as well as he knew his history. In his readings of the latter, then, he might well have noticed the rather curious reappearance of a Jewish sect, the Sadducees, when

---

3. Nathaniel Hawthorne, *The Letters, 1843–1853*, ed. Thomas Woodson, L. Neal Smith, and Norman Holmes Pearson, *The Centenary Edition of the Works of Nathaniel Hawthorne*, vol. 16 (Columbus: Ohio State UP, 1985), 329–30.
4. Marylynn Salmon, *Women and the Law of Property in Early America* (Chapel Hill: U of North Carolina P, 1986), 140.

women heretics in particular are under discussion. In her 1637 ecclesiastical trial, for example, Anne Hutchinson is accused of Sadducism; Cotton Mather uses the term repeatedly in his treatment of witchcraft in the *Magnalia Christi Americana*.[5] On a quite basic level, the Sadducees, who denied the existence of resurrection, come to function in Puritan sources as a collective emblem of theological doubt. Mather makes this usage explicit in a story about a group of Indians who had once widely participated in "witchcrafts" and "confederacies with devils" but who became, finally, "serious Christians." Mather offers this section of the *Magnalia* (entitled "SADDUCISMUS TRIUMPHATUS," or "Sadducism vanquished") as a hortatory against doubt: "Come hither, ye prophane Sadducees, that will not believe the being of a devil, for fear lest you must thence infer the being of a God," he writes; "We will relate some things well known to prudent and honest witnesses: And when you have read this relation, mock on!"[6] In his chapter on the "wonders of the invisible world," Mather carries this notion of Sadducism forward, quoting a preface to a "true" witchcraft narrative which claims that "This great instance [of possession] comes with such convincing evidence, that he must be a very obdurate Sadducee, that will not believe it." Perhaps most importantly, Mather refers to the Salem witchcraft trials as "SADDUCISMUS DEBELLATUS," or "Sadducism stormed," presumably because, after the trials, confessions, convictions, and executions in Salem, one can no longer offer plausible denial of a spiritual world beyond the earthly one.[7] According to Mather and his Puritan contemporaries, in other words, witchcraft "proved" what Ann Kibbey has called the "fact of spiritual intervention in the natural world."[8] Witchcraft, therefore, undermined "Sadducaical" skepticism.

But the connections between Sadducism and witchcraft exceed these theologically instrumental ones, as a look at *how* the Sadducees' denial of resurrection is framed in the New Testament will suggest. Repeated in the books of Luke, Mark, and Matthew, the story of the Sadducees involves a debate with Jesus on the matter of resurrection. Interested in "entangling him in his talk," the Sadducees approach Jesus with an intriguing hypothetical problem. "Now there were seven brothers among us," they begin: "the first married, and died, and hav-

5. I am indebted to my colleague Tamara Harvey for the insight into the role of Sadducism in these contexts and its pertinence to *The Scarlet Letter*.
6. Cotton Mather, *Magnalia Christi Americana; or, The Ecclesiastical History of New England* (Hartford: Silas Andrus & Son, 1853), vol. 2, 445.
7. Mather, 465, 471.
8. Ann Kibbey, "Mutations of the Supernatural: Witchcraft, Remarkable Providences, and the Power of Puritan Men," *American Quarterly* 34 (1982): 137. Kibbey's essay offers a fascinating reading of the complications posed for Puritan authorities by the fact that "the image of the deity as the author of remarkable providences, and the image of the witch as the author of *maleficia* [evil deeds or mischief] were positive and negative forms of a single idea about supernatural power" (137). Kibbey notes in particular that both "forms" of such power were associated with men, thereby working against a traditional reading that associates witchcraft largely with women. Indeed, Kibbey asks, "since Puritan culture so strongly associated the power of *maleficia* with adult males, we need to ask seriously why and how were women accused of witchcraft at Salem at all?" (147). The answer, she suggests, lies at least in part in the effort by men to criminalize women's efforts to "take for themselves a power that Puritan culture had come to associate with adult male sexual identity" (149).

ing no children left his wife to his brother. So too the second and third, down to the seventh. After them all, the woman died. In the resurrection, therefore, to which of the seven will she be wife? For they all had her."[9] Less interesting for my purposes than Jesus' answer to the Sadducees (he tells them, in essence, that worldly laws do not attend the risen soul, that the very "problem" they pose is moot) is the fact that, as Tamara Harvey has pointed out, resurrection is here debated via the "vehicle" of "marriage and the possession of women."[1]

That this connection between the "heretical" views of the Sadducees and the idea of secure ownership of women in marriage is not merely incidental to Puritan histories is made clear in the ecclesiastical trial of Anne Hutchinson, whose own denial of resurrection seems to threaten the very institution of marriage itself. Indeed, Harvey comments, "Part of what is at stake in the theological debates of the Antinomian Controversy is the status of women as possessions in marriage."[2] John Cotton makes Hutchinson's challenge to this status explicit, begging her to "consider" that

> *if the Resurection be past than you cannot Evade the Argument* that was prest upon you by *our Brother Buckle* and others, that filthie Sinne of the Comunitie of Woemen and all promiscuus and filthie cominge togeather of men and Woemen without Distinction or Relation of Marriage, will necessarily follow. And though I have not herd, nayther do I thinke, you have bine unfaythfull to your Husband in his Marriage Covenant, *yet that will follow upon it*, for it is the very argument that the Saduces bringe to our Saviour Christ agaynst the Resurrection . . .[3]

Cotton is clearly interested in the issue of doubt here; but at least as important for him are the implications of that doubt for civil authority: without the idea of an extraworldly judgment to follow, what is to hold people (and, in particular, women) to their worldly covenants (and, in particular, the covenant of marriage)? Cotton's specific reference to the debate between Jesus and the Sadducees reveals the secular nature of his concerns: as Harvey observes, whereas Jesus "deemphasizes the human covenant of marriage" in his answer to the Sadducees, Hutchinson's judges "reemphasize it, shifting attention from the resurrection to worldly morality" and to the threats to that morality that Hutchinson poses.[4] From Hutchinson's "mortalist" rejection of the resurrection of the soul/body, Cotton insists, "will necessarily follow" disruptions in the social—and particularly the marital—body: "that filthie Sinne of the Comunitie of Woemen," the "promiscuus and filthie cominge togeather of men and Woemen with-

9. *The New Oxford Annotated Bible*, ed. Herbert G. May and Bruce M. Metzger (New York: Oxford UP, 1973), 1201.
1. Tamara Harvey, *Modesty's Charge: The Body and Feminist Tactics in Early American Women's Discourse* (Diss. U of California, 1998), 128.
2. Harvey, 128–29.
3. David D. Hall, *The Antinomian Controversy, 1636–1638: A Documentary History*, 2d ed. (Durham: Duke UP, 1990), 372.
4. Harvey, 128.

out Distinction or Relation of Marriage."[5] Although Cotton indicates his awareness that Hutchinson has not yet been involved in such a "filthie cominge togeather," that she has not literally violated the marriage covenant, she is clearly heading in that direction: inevitably, he proclaims, *"that will follow upon it."* And all the examiners seem to believe in any case that the marriage covenant has already been *figuratively* violated: "you have stept out of your place," Hugh Peters tells her; *"you have rather bine a Husband than a Wife."*[6]

Hutchinson's "sadducism" thus comes to be connected to her usurpation of a husband's prerogative in marriage, to her usurpation of male authority over her and her body. Despite Hutchinson's acknowledgment in her civil trial—published in an appendix to Thomas Hutchinson's *History of Massachusetts Bay*, an important source for Hawthorne—that the judges "have power over my body," her position on resurrection implicitly denies the ultimate meaning of that power. Indeed, Hutchinson goes on to deny the magistrates' authority, telling them that only "the Lord Jesus hath power over my body and soul," and noting ominously that "if you go on in this course you begin you will bring a curse upon you and your posterity, and the mouth of the Lord hath spoken it."[7]

Considering how her "heresies" are framed in her trials, and considering the sort of "curse" that apparently issued from her, it seems somewhat surprising that Anne Hutchinson was never formally accused of witchcraft. Historian Carol Karlsen has attempted to account for this, noting that, while witchcraft was much prosecuted in seventeenth-century England and was also included in colonial legal codes as a capital crime, the "demographic and economic conditions of early settlement" delayed witchcraft prosecutions in the colonies.[8] But, as Karlsen also points out, many of the stories that circulated about Hutchinson—particularly in the writings of John Winthrop, with which Hawthorne was thoroughly familiar—draw on long-held associations with and images of witchcraft. Carrying with them beliefs originating in their native England, most colonists, Karlsen suggests, would have associated witches with a variety of "sins," including "discontent, anger, envy, malice, seduction, lying, and pride."[9] Hutchinson was, of course,

5. It is precisely such a "cominge togeather of men and Woemen without Distinction or Relation of Marriage" in which Hester and Dimmesdale participate in *The Scarlet Letter*. I do not intend to read Hawthorne's text as an allegory of the Antinomian Crisis, or even to parse out detail by detail the much-discussed relationship between the historical Anne Hutchinson and the fictional Hester Prynne. Rather, I am interested more generally in the ways in which Hawthorne's Puritan sources lead to an almost inevitable association between strong (read "heretical") women and the violation of patriarchal principles of (male) ownership. The most fully enacted reading of the relationship between Hutchinson and Hester Prynne is still Michael Colacurcio's "Footsteps of Ann Hutchinson: The Context of *The Scarlet Letter*," *ELH* 39 (1972): 459–94 (pp. 304–31 of this Norton Critical Edition). Also see Amy Schrager Lang, *Prophetic Woman: Anne Hutchinson and the Problem of Dissent in the Literature of New England* (Berkeley: U of California P, 1987) (pp. 670–79 of this Norton Critical Edition).
6. Hall, *The Antinomian Controversy*, 382–83.
7. Hall, *The Antinomian Controversy*, 338.
8. Carol Karlsen, *The Devil in the Shape of a Woman: Witchcraft in Colonial New England* (New York: Vintage Books, 1989), 14. The first witchcraft prosecution occurred in Connecticut in 1647.
9. Karlsen, 119.

accused of all of these (seduction is perhaps most interesting in this regard, carrying us back to Cotton's jeremiad regarding the "promiscuus
and filthie cominge togeather of men and Woemen" that Hutchinson's
views allegedly promoted). Winthrop's *A Short Story of the Rise, reign,
and ruine of the Antinomians, Familists, and Libertines* recounts, for example, Hutchinson's response to a visit made to her after her banishment by "foure . . . members" of the Church of Boston. In his retelling,
Winthrop stresses the "disdain" (read "pride") and "bitterness" of
"spirit" (read "discontent, anger, envy, malice") with which Hutchinson
greets her visitors, along with her defiant rejection of their spiritual authority: "What, from the Church at Boston? I know no such Church,
neither will I owne it, call it the Whore and Strumpet of Boston, no
Church of Christ," she allegedly declares.[1]

Drawing on Hutchinson's deviance from accepted (female) norms—
her bitterness, her pride, her unruly speech—Winthrop places Hutchinson in a field of associations that renders her analogous, if not
identical, to the colonial witch. This field is even more spectacularly
elaborated in the famous and oft-repeated description of Hutchinson's
"monstrous birth."[2] Like Mary Dyer, one of Hutchinson's followers
and loyal supporters whose own "monstrous birth" testifies to the
monstrosity of her theological positions, Hutchinson is depicted as delivering a kind of demon offspring.[3] Indeed, according to Winthrop,
Hutchinson "brought forth not one, (as Mistris Dier did) but . . .
30 monstrous births or thereabouts, at once; some of them bigger,
some lesser, some of one shape, some of another; few of any perfect
shape, none at all of them . . . of humane shape."[4] Winthrop insists, of
course, that in these "demon offspring" one can see the hand of God,
who has been "pleased to step in with his casting voice, and bring in
his owne vote and suffrage from heaven, by testifying his displeasure
against their opinions and practises, as clearly as if he had pointed
with his finger."[5]

As if to reassert the corporeal power that Hutchinson had earlier
granted and then promptly denied him, Winthrop clearly works to exercise interpretive authority over Hutchinson's body. In her discussion
of Hutchinson's "mortalist" views, Tamara Harvey explains that

1. Hall, *The Antinomian Controversy*, 215.
2. That Hawthorne was aware of these descriptions and that they come to him from Winthrop's
A Short Story seem clear from his 1830 sketch, "Mrs. Hutchinson," where he notes that
"Governor Winthrop does not disdain to record a notable instance, very interesting in a scientific point of view, but fitter for his old and homely narrative than for modern repetition."
See "Mrs. Hutchinson" in this Norton Critical Edition, 171. The story of the "monstrous
birth" is repeated in Mather's *Magnalia*, which may also have functioned as the source for
Hawthorne's reference.
3. Gabriele Schwab suggests that it was Mary Dyer who just before her execution pronounces
the "curse on the Salem judges and their descendants to which Nathaniel Hawthorne refers"
in "The Custom-House." See "Seduced by Witches: Nathaniel Hawthorne's *The Scarlet Letter* in the Context of New England Witchcraft Fictions," in *Seduction and Theory: Readings
of Gender, Representation, and Rhetoric*, ed. Dianne Hunter (Urbana: U of Illinois P, 1989),
177. For the reference in "The Custom-House," see p. 11.
4. For a contemporary diagnosis of Hutchinson's miscarriage, see Emery Battis, *Saints and Sectaries: Anne Hutchinson in the Antinomian Controversy in the Massachusetts Bay Colony*
(Chapel Hill: U of North Carolina P, 1962), 247–48, 346–48; and Bethany Reid, " 'Unfit
for Light': Anne Bradstreet's Monstrous Birth," *New England Quarterly* 71 (1998): 517–42.
5. Hall, *The Antinomian Controversy*, 214.

"Hutchinson and her followers . . . reject the significance of the body except as a vehicle for immediate union with Christ, and in doing so undermine the system that authorized the judges and sustains patriarchal privilege."[6] In his description of the "monstrous birth," we witness Winthrop reinstating the very "system" that Hutchinson undermines: he insists precisely on the significance of her body—a body the offspring of which marks Hutchinson's seduction by the devil—in order to show that God's judgment is consonant with that of the magistrates, whose theological and social authority is thereby underscored. Hutchinson is, in short, as much marked by Satan as are the colonial witches whose bodies would later be "searched" for devils' "teats" or who "gave birth to and suckled demons instead of children."[7] And ultimately, her "witchcraft" can be traced back to her Sadducaical "heresies"—those heresies that "necessarily" lead to the disruption of the "proper" and accepted relations between men and women, husbands and wives, that was so widely feared by Puritan authorities.

I would suggest that this same set of associations is at work in the *Magnalia Christi Americana*, when Mather makes his even more direct links between Sadducism and witchcraft. Like Winthrop during the Antinomian Crisis, Mather is as interested in the temporal disturbances the witchcraft outbreaks map as he is in their theological implications. Offering himself as witness to one family's victimization at the hands of a witch, for example, Mather explains that he brought the family's oldest daughter into his own home, "partly out of compassion to her parents, but chiefly that I might be a critical eye-witness to things that would enable me to confute the sadducism of this debauch'd age."[8] Here, the "debauchery" seems at least in part to refer to the worldly sins into which Mather believed that later generations of colonists had descended. He can "confute . . . sadducism" not only by bearing witness to the "truth" of spiritual life, but also by showing just how strongly implicated the "devil" had become in the daily ("debauch'd") lives of the colonists.

Whatever specific sins and debaucheries Mather had in mind, it is worth taking note of the historical commonplace that the vast majority of those accused, prosecuted, and executed for witchcraft in the colonies were women. In recent years, historians have turned increasingly to the economic disputes that lie at the root of witchcraft outbreaks. Perhaps most famously, Paul Boyer and Stephen Nissenbaum have argued that the Salem outbreak of 1692 was fuelled by conflict between an emergent mercantile class and a group tied to a traditional, land-based economic order.[9] But, as Carol Karlsen asserts, while this move to identify the central role that economic considerations played in accusations of and prosecutions for witchcraft is cru-

---

6. Harvey, 129.
7. Karlsen, 144. Karlsen also notes that, like witches, Hutchinson was depicted as "dispens[ing]" theological "poisons" (144) throughout the Puritan community.
8. Mather, 460.
9. Paul Boyer and Stephen Nissenbaum, *Salem Possessed: The Social Origins of Witchcraft* (Cambridge: Harvard UP, 1974).

cial, Boyer and Nissenbaum do not "tell[ ] us very much about why witches were primarily women."[1] Karlsen attempts to fill in this gap: carrying forward the correlation that Boyer and Nissenbaum find between witchcraft outbreaks and wide-spread anxieties over changing economic (and therefore social) relations, Karlsen argues persuasively that women came to stand in for and in fact to provoke such anxiety. In particular, she notes, "Whether as actual or potential inheritors of property, as healers or tavern-keepers or merchants, most accused witches were women who symbolized the obstacles to [male ownership] of property and [male] prosperity." "[A]ll witches," Karlsen asserts, "stood symbolically opposed to—and therefore were subversive of—that order, in that they did not accept their assigned place within it."[2] David D. Hall makes a similar claim, noting that "[t]he prosecution of women as witches occurred in a society in which men exercised substantial authority—legal, political, ideological, and economic—over women. It is possible to interpret witch-hunting as a means of reaffirming this authority at a time when some women (like the charismatic spiritual leader Anne Hutchinson) were testing these constraints, and when others were experiencing a degree of independence, as when women without husbands or male siblings inherited property."[3]

Here, then, one might bring another perspective to bear on the analogy between the Sadducees, women, and witchcraft made by both Winthrop and Mather. Like the Sadducees, whose denial of resurrection appeared to the Puritans to open the door to a denial of the covenant of marriage, the witch also threatened that covenant (hence witches were often accused of promiscuity, sexual laxity, and adultery). Further, the witch also threatened the ownership of property by men (whether of the woman or of her land and personality) which that covenant was intended to ensure. In this context, it makes sense that much of the "evidence" lodged against accused witches involved *maleficia*—evil deeds or mischief—allegedly performed against personal and real property: cows and chickens inexplicably become sick, household objects and farming equipment go missing or get damaged, crops are destroyed.

The case of accused witch Katherine Harrison offers insight into the role women's claims to property might have played in witchcraft accusations and prosecution. Harrison was a widow whose husband left her the bulk of his large estate—789 pounds; the remainder of the 929-pound estate went to his three daughters at his death in 1666, making her at once very wealthy and in control of a good deal of real and personal property. Significantly, it was after her husband's death, between 1668 and 1670, that Harrison was accused of and tried for witchcraft multiple times, and convicted at least once.[4] Testimony against Harrison indicates the usual accusations of unruly speech,

1. Karlsen, 214.
2. Karlsen, 217.
3. David D. Hall, ed., *Witch-Hunting in Seventeenth-Century New England: A Documentary History* (Boston: Northeastern UP, 1991), 7. Also see Kibbey, 147–49.
4. Both Carol Karlsen and David Hall take up Harrison's case. See Karlsen, 84–89; and Hall, *Witch-Hunting*, 170–84.

threatening behavior, and *maleficia* against people and property. But records also reveal the extent to which Harrison recognized that the accusations signaled a battle for, and the extent to which she was determined to preserve, her property. In 1668, around the time of her first witchcraft accusation, Harrison presented a formal petition of grievances in court, accusing her neighbors of vandalism and attacks on her estate. Among other complaints, she testifies that many of her horses, sows, cows and oxen have been "spoiled," their backs or ribs broken, "hole[s] bored" in their sides or "legs cut off"; that her corn was "damnified with horses" and that "30 poles of hops [were] cut and spoiled." Perhaps most interestingly, Harrison observes that her very marks of ownership have been effaced and re-written: "I had a heifer in my barnyard," she testifies, "my earmark of which was cut out, and other earmarks set on; nextly I had a sow that had young pigs earmarked (in the sty) after the same manner." Taking note of the specific timing at work in this worldly *maleficia*—"all which things have happened since my husband['s] death," she writes—Harrison seems to have been well aware of the threat she posed as a *feme sole* property owner.[5] Not surprisingly, among her earliest accusers was one John Chester, with whom Harrison was involved in a land dispute.[6]

Katherine Harrison was not the first wealthy widow to be accused of and indicted for witchcraft. A few years earlier, in fact, a more widely known widow—one who makes repeated appearances in *The Scarlet Letter* itself—was not only tried and convicted, but also executed as a witch. In 1656, Anne Hibbins was sentenced by the General Court of Massachusetts to "hang till she was dead."[7] Hibbins serves as another salient example of the link between women, property ownership, and witchcraft. Her case also reminds us of the ways in which the marriage covenant operated to contain the threat to male ownership of property posed by strong women. In 1640, long before she was formally convicted of witchcraft, Hibbins was brought to trial for "false accusations and contentious behavior," after having publicly aired complaints about the quality and cost of work done by a joiner in her house.[8] While much of her church trial concerns the extent to which her "censurings, and judgings" of her "brethren" were "uncharitable," of even greater concern appears to be the extent to which Anne Hibbins' accusations against the joiner involved her usurpation of husbandly authority. In her "examination," one "Sargent Savage" notes that "if all other offenses were passed by, . . . yet she hath shed forth one sin in the face of the congregation worthy of reproof: and that is transgressing the rule of the apostle in usurping authority over him whom God hath made her head and husband, and in taking the power

5. All quotations regarding Harrison's case come from Hall, *Witch-Hunting*, 171–72.
6. According to both Karlsen and Hall, Harrison kept working to find ways to render her estate less vulnerable and to protect it for her daughters. Although she seems to have held on to some of her real property, she had in 1668 signed much of her estate over to her daughters and by 1669 "disposed of a great part of her estate to others in trust" (quoted in Karlsen, 88).
7. Hall, *Witch-Hunting*, 90.
8. Nancy F. Cott, *The Root of Bitterness: Documents of the Social History of American Women* (Boston: Northeastern UP, 1986), 47.

and authority . . . out of his hands; and when he was satisfied and sits down contented she . . . will stir in it, as if she were able to manage it better than her husband, which is a plain breach of the rule of Christ."[9]

By taking up a cause her husband had been willing to lay aside, Hibbins appears to have nullified his authority; in doing so, or so the complaints suggest, she seems to have nullified *him*. Under the (common law) principles of coverture in operation in virtually all of the New England colonies at this time, the married woman lost any agency she might have possessed as a *feme sole* to her husband. As legal commentator William Blackstone would later explain it, "the very being or legal existence of the woman is suspended during the marriage, or at least is incorporated and consolidated into that of the husband."[1] Complaints against Hibbins indicate a perception that she has (sinfully) violated and inverted these principles: "some do think she doth but make a wisp of her husband" one examiner acknowledges; another complains, "she makes a cipher of her husband."[2] By coming out from under her husband's "cover," Hibbins has apparently rendered *him* meaningless.

For such threats to her husband's very meaning and identity, Hibbins is severely punished: she is first formally admonished, then excommunicated. But these attempts to contain the threats Hibbins posed to male meaning were themselves nullified by Hibbins' widowhood in 1654. Threatening enough as a married woman who exerts control of her husband's property, Hibbins would appear to have been even more threatening as a *feme sole*. Much like Katherine Harrison, Hibbins was left a substantial property-owner upon her husband's death. Again like Harrison, just two years after being widowed, Hibbins was tried as a witch. In Hibbins' case, however, the results of the trial were far more dire. She was executed in June of 1656.

Anne Hibbins is, of course, the only explicitly identified witch in *The Scarlet Letter*. Consideration of her case therefore invites us back into Hawthorne's text and its treatment of the threat one individual woman poses to the covenant of marriage and (male) property ownership. In recent years, critics such as Carol Bensick, Gordon Hutner, and Ken Egan have turned to the question of Hawthorne's complex and revisionary representation of adultery in *The Scarlet Letter*.[3] The issues of property and possession at work in Hester's adulterous act, however, have received less attention. Perhaps because the text itself displaces the issue of cuckoldry onto issues of sin, penitence, and re-

9. Cott, 56, 48.
1. William Blackstone, *Commentaries on the Laws of England*, vol. 1, ed. Stanley N. Katz (Chicago: U of Chicago P, 1979), 430.
2. Cott, 48, 54.
3. See Carol Bensick, "His Folly, Her Weakness: Demystified Adultery in *The Scarlet Letter*," *New Essays on The Scarlet Letter*, ed. Michael J. Colacurcio (Cambridge: Cambridge UP, 1985), 137–59. Bensick offers the most thorough reading of Hawthorne's novel within the "novel of adultery" tradition, suggesting persuasively that under Hawthorne's treatment adultery becomes not "a fateful tragedy to be ritually suffered," but rather "a practical human problem that the individuals involved have, along with their society, a common obligation to address" (137). Also see Gordon Hutner, *Secrets and Sympathy: Forms of Disclosure in Hawthorne's Novels* (Athens: U of Georgia P, 1988); and Ken Egan, "The Adulteress in the Marketplace: Hawthorne and *The Scarlet Letter*," *Studies in the Novel* 27 (1995): 26–41.

demption, it is tempting *not* to consider that what Hester has done is, in essence, to give herself to another—to exert a kind of agency and self-proprietorship that the laws of marriage simply do not grant her. Gillian Brown, who sees issues of inheritance and women's property at the center of Hawthorne's novel, suggests that this displacement emerges from the novel itself, which effectively "erases" the issue of adultery in order to "make property safely heritable" for Pearl. Thus, Brown claims, "the original crime, the usurpation of Chillingworth's marital property in Hester's person, has practically disappeared even at the outset of the story."[4] I submit, however, that this "crime" does not "disappear," for both Hawthorne's seventeenth-century sources and his own society, occupied itself with debates about marital property law, continue to insist on it. Like Anne Hibbins and Anne Hutchinson, the "witches" with whom she is associated throughout the novel, Hester's violation of the marriage covenant—in her case a violation that is quite literal—sets in motion troubling questions of male authority over property. The question to which *The Scarlet Letter* finally points, then, is this: who can claim ownership of Hester?

Just as she is with Anne Hutchinson, Hester is associated with Anne Hibbins from the beginning of *The Scarlet Letter*, when the narrator sets the stage for Hester's emergence from the Boston jail. Noting the possible reasons for the gathering of a "pretty large number of the inhabitants of Boston" before the prison-door—perhaps an Antinomian or a Quaker is to be "scourged out of the town," or "an idle and vagrant Indian" whipped "into the shadow of the forest"—the narrator moves to the scenario that will prove most appropriate to Hester's own: "It might be, too, that a witch, like old Mistress Hibbins, the bitter-tempered widow of the magistrate, was to die upon the gallows" (47) [37]. Scott Harshbarger has noticed the lack of critical commentary on "Hawthorne's characterization, and condemnation, of Hibbins as a full-fledged witch." While one might "reasonably expect" Hawthorne to "exonerate Hibbins from charges of witchcraft" in a novel "dedicated to expiating the sins of Hawthorne's persecuting forebears," Harshbarger writes, "the author heads in the opposite direction," so that by the end of the novel "Hibbins emerges as self-confessed disciple" of Satan.[5] In short, Hawthorne seems notably uncritical of his Puritan sources in this case, drawing on such representations of Hibbins as that offered by Thomas Hutchinson, who takes pains in his 1765 *History of Massachusetts Bay* to describe the "natural crabbedness" of Hibbins' character, along with the "turbulent

4. Gillian Brown, "Hawthorne, Inheritance, and Women's Property," *Studies in the Novel* 23 (1991): 110, 113. Brown argues that Hawthorne works to "purify" property by vesting it in women—in this case, Pearl: "Though set in the seventeenth century, the story of Hester and her daughter registers in its redemptive vision of the sin of adultery a liberalization of nineteenth-century American moral and economic conventions of property and family" (111). Although Brown recognizes the problematic place that Hester assumes in such "redemption," I would argue that Hester's displacement from the "inheritance plot" suggests a more thoroughgoing ambivalence on Hawthorne's part about women and property ownership.
5. Scott Harshbarger, " 'A H—LL—Fired Story': Hawthorne's Rhetoric of Rumor," *College English* 56 (1994): 32, 39.

and quarrelsome" nature that "brought her under church censures, and at length rendered her so odious to her neighbours as to cause some of them to accuse her of witchcraft," and who questions the validity of neither her condemnation nor her execution.[6]

Hibbins always appears in *The Scarlet Letter* at the moments of greatest vulnerability for the protagonists: she is rumored to have approached Hester upon her departure from Governor Bellingham's mansion, where Hester has gone to appeal for permission to keep Pearl (103) [78–79]; she "is said to have" confronted Dimmesdale upon his reentrance into the village from the forest, where he has sealed a pact to leave the colony with Hester (192) [141]. In these contexts, Hibbins seems to be used as a marker for what Harshbarger calls the main characters' "proximity" to "radical evil."[7] It is thereby significant, of course, that Hester repeatedly resists Hibbins' invitations into the forest: " 'Make my excuse to [the Black Man],' " Hester says "with a triumphant smile. 'I must tarry at home, and keep watch over my little Pearl. Had they taken her from me, I would willingly have gone with thee into the forest, and signed my name in the Black Man's book too' " (103) [79]. Hester may be proximate to, but she has not apparently crossed over into, the "evil" that Hibbins represents.

Hester's resistance to Hibbins is figured in terms of her commitment to her daughter, to her status as mother. But while Hester remains true to her domesticity, however painful and problematic that domesticity is for her, we know that she has once, and irrevocably, transgressed the legal bounds of domestic relations. Hester has, to use the phrase deployed by John Cotton in Anne Hutchinson's trial, "bine unfaythfull to [her] Husband in his Marriage Covenant"; and it is this violation to which Hester refers when she confesses to Pearl that "Once in my life I met the Black Man" (162) [120]. By figuring her adultery as a mark of having compacted with the Devil, Hester connects herself to both Hutchinson and Hibbins, who violated the marriage covenant by usurping their husbands' proprietorship in their persons. Like both of these precursors, Hester claims an authority over "personal" property—in this case, her property in herself—that transgresses the very principal of marital unity upon which colonial marriage and its attendant property laws were based.

Chillingworth tacitly admits as much in a scene that offers a series of complicated witchcraft/marriage/property associations. In his first face-to-face confrontation with Hester, Chillingworth reveals through his language just how central the issue of ownership is to the complex of relations between the three protagonists. Like an accused witch pressured to name her "confederates," Hester is queried by Chillingworth: "the man lives who has wronged us both! Who is he?" (69) [53]. Hester's refusal to name her confederate proves to Chilling-

6. Thomas Hutchinson, *The History of the Colony and Province of Massachusetts Bay* (London: 1765–68), vol. 2, 173.
7. Harshbarger, 39.

worth, as Carol Bensick asserts, that "she will not be reunited with him on any terms."[8] The "unity" between husband and wife has been irrevocably violated: Hester has come out permanently from under Chillingworth's "cover."

Having been thus forced to relinquish property in Hester, Chilling-worth (in three variations) claims ownership of the yet-undiscovered lover: "he must needs be mine!," "he is mine," and "he shall be mine!," he announces with a "look of confidence" perhaps belied by his rather anxious repetitions of the phrase (69) [53–54]. Chillingworth's inter-est in reestablishing himself as a secure proprietor is borne out again later in the same scene, when he goes from overtly divesting himself of ownership of Hester ("thou that wast my wife," he proclaims her [69] [54]) to reclaiming property in her that, under common law, vests in him as husband. Drawing on principles of marital unity, according to which a wife could not testify against her husband because she would thereby incriminate herself,[9] he enjoins her to silence about his true identity, reminding her as he does so that "Thou and thine, Hester Prynne, belong to me" (70) [54].

The narrative sympathies in this scene are complicated.[1] Having made her promise, Hester queries Chillingworth as to whether she has made another demonic compact: "Art thou like the Black Man, that haunts the forest round about us? Hast thou enticed me into a bond that will prove the ruin of my soul?" (70) [54]. At this moment, of course, it is not Hester but Chillingworth who is associated with witchcraft.[2] Here, the legal "bond" of marriage, under the principles of which Hester "belongs" to Chillingworth and so cannot bear witness against him, draws Hester into a clear moral violation. By returning to her role as *feme covert*, Hester betrays Dimmesdale, who remains ig-norant of Chillingworth's true identity. The narrative thus seems to critique legal marriage as an institution which, by denying Hester pro-prietorship of herself, draws her into a bond with the "Black Man" who seeks to claim her.[3]

But at the same time, as readers and critics have long recognized, *The Scarlet Letter* remains deeply ambivalent about Hester's resistance to the secular laws of men and marriage, as much repelled as com-pelled by the various forms of insurgency that she represents. Like

8. Bensick, 144.
9. See Blackstone, 431.
1. For a thoughtful reading of the ways in which the narrator extends a kind of sympathy and understanding to Chillingworth here, see Bensick, 141–46.
2. Along with Hester and Chillingworth, Pearl is also represented as a witch in *The Scarlet Let-ter*. I am less interested in understanding the larger "witchcraft themes" than I am in think-ing through the particular field of witchcraft associations with which Hester and her marital insurgency can be located. For a basic overview of the theme of witchcraft in *The Scarlet Letter*, see Claudia Durst Johnson, *Understanding* The Scarlet Letter: *A Student Casebook to Issues, Sources, and Historical Documents* (Westport: Greenwood P, 1995).
3. T. Walter Herbert suggests that Hawthorne draws on emergent ideas about companionate marriage in order to make a distinction between "legal" and "moral" marriage. According to this model, Hester's legal marriage to Chillingworth is itself a kind of adultery. In *The Scar-let Letter*, "the anguish of the principal characters results from the inopportune social arrangements in which they are fated to live." See Herbert, *Dearest Beloved: The Hawthornes and the Making of the Middle-Class Family* (Berkeley: U of California P, 1993), 184 and fol-lowing.

Anne Hutchinson, who believed, as she made clear in her civil trial, that the magistrates owned her body but not her "body and soul," Hester has, in exerting her own (sexual and social) agency, laid claim to radical properties in herself. But try as Hawthorne might to ratify those claims, the narrative he creates argues against him, associating Hester's freedom of thought both with a kind of unsexing (she has lost "[s]ome attribute . . . the permanence of which had been essential to keep her a woman" [143] [107]) and with the capital crime of witchcraft. Having announced that "the world's law was no law for [Hester's] mind," the narrator points out that "our forefathers" would have "held [her freedom of speculation] to be a deadlier crime than that stigmatized by the scarlet letter" (143) [107].

It is significant that, just after we get "another view" (139) [104] of Hester's fully anarchic tendencies, we watch her break her promise of (wifely) silence to Chillingworth, confess her sin of silence to Dimmesdale, and then propose a new life elsewhere for her, Dimmesdale, and Pearl. And it is just after Dimmesdale agrees to flee with Hester that Anne Hibbins makes a brief but potent reappearance in the text, meeting Dimmesdale on his return to Boston from his walk with Hester. "So, reverend Sir, you have made a visit into the forest," the "witch-lady" remarks, drawing Dimmesdale into the witchcraft associations with which the text is replete (193) [141].

A curious detail in this scene, however, reminds us that it is not Dimmesdale but Hester who has initiated the new transgression. Hibbins, we are told, "made a very grand appearance; having on a high head-dress, a rich gown of velvet, and a ruff done up with the famous yellow starch, of which Ann Turner, her especial friend, had taught her the secret, before this last good lady had been hanged for Sir Thomas Overbury's murder" (193) [141]. With the reference to Anne Turner, who, in addition to being convicted of murder, was also accused of being "a witch, a trafficker in necromancy," and a "sorceress," the issue of witchcraft reverts back to Hester herself.[4] Turner's "yellow ruff," for example, is linked not just to Hibbins but also to Hester, whose needlework resembles Turner's own: according to Alfred Reid, Turner "made ruffs and cuffs and introduced fashions of dress into courtly circles. The starched yellow ruff is said to have been her invention."[5] It should come as no surprise, then, that in addition to being a witch, Turner was also an adulteress. Hawthorne may have earlier drawn a distinction between Hester and Hibbins, but that distinction breaks down here as, *via* Anne Turner, the relationship between witchcraft and marital "violation" returns with a subtle but insistent force. Indeed, in a final marketplace scene that loops us back to the opening of the text, we see Hibbins, wearing in this case a "triple ruff," in direct "conjunction with Hester Prynne" (209) [153].

4. Alfred S. Reid, *The Yellow Ruff and* The Scarlet Letter: *A Source of Hawthorne's Novel* (Gainesville: U of Florida P, 1955), 3. Noting that Turner "was executed . . . for magic and witchcraft as much as for procuring poisons in the murder of Overbury" (4), Reid takes up at length the connections between Turner and Hester Prynne, and teases out a variety of other connections between the Overbury case and *The Scarlet Letter*.
5. Reid, 49.

Clearly, the narrative cannot let Hester's "witchcraft" go. Finally, Hawthorne seems unable to do other than concur with his forefathers, the judging "iron men" for whom a woman's resistance—Hutchinson's, Hibbens', Hester's—to the laws of patriarchal marriage was viewed as a "deadly" crime indeed.[6]

Why is it, then, that Hawthorne's text cannot finally break free from those patriarchal, persecuting ancestors—the very forefathers against whom he sets himself in "The Custom-House"? Referring to some literary forefathers in his analysis of Hawthorne's use of Anne Hutchinson, Michael Colacurcio provides a possible answer, one that moves away from the situation of marriage and toward matters of the literary market. Noting the ways in which Cotton Mather's depictions of Hutchinson emerge from those of John Winthrop, Colacurcio writes, "The basic antifeminist construction seems to originate with Winthrop—not only with his specific characterization of Mrs. Hutchinson as 'a woman of a haughty and fierce carriage, of a nimble wit and active spirit, and a very voluble tongue' but also with the clear implication in his whole account that one very deep issue is Mrs. Hutchinson's female invasion of male 'literary' prerogative."[7] Hawthorne's familiarity with this perception of Hutchinson (which draws not only on the "teaching" function she exerted in the Puritan community, but also on her resistant readings of scripture) is made plain in his 1830 sketch, "Mrs. Hutchinson," which begins with a prefatory meditation on the "portentous" rise of literary women. "[T]here are obvious circumstances which will render female pens more numerous and more prolific than those of men," Hawthorne writes; soon, he goes on, "the ink-stained Amazons will expel their rivals by actual pressure, and petticoats wave triumphant over all the field."[8]

Hawthorne's use of the battle metaphor lends credence to a remark made many years later by one of those "ink-stained Amazons," Elizabeth Stoddard. Writing to Rufus Griswold in 1856, Stoddard described her authorship in terms of "guerrilla . . . warfare," noting that "The Literary Female is abroad and the souls of the literary men are tried."[9] Coupled with Hawthorne's earlier rendition, Stoddard's depiction of the "warfare" between literary women and literary men facilitates the now-familiar reading of what, precisely, is at issue in the contest: the battlefield is the literary marketplace, and the clear victor, by 1850, is the "Literary Female," whose prominence and salability far exceeds that of the sorely tried "Literary Male." This is, of course, the war for readers that led Hawthorne to make his infamous complaint to William D. Ticknor, quoted *ad infinitum*, about the "mob of scribbling women" and the "trash" they "sell by the 100,000."[1]

---

6. In contrast to this reading, Schwab makes a strong distinction between Hawthorne's moralizing narrator and Hawthorne himself, suggesting that the "attributes condemned by the narrator" are "precisely" those that "make for the strength of Hester as a literary character" and arguing that Hester breaks free from the "witch stereotype" (189).

7. Colacurcio, 477.

8. Hawthorne, "Mrs. Hutchinson," 18 [167].

9. James H. Matlack, "The *Alta-California*'s Lady Correspondent," *New-York Historical Society Quarterly* 58 (1974): 281–303.

1. Hawthorne, *The Letters, 1853–1856*, 303.

Certainly one can see the ways in which Hawthorne's uneasiness with Hester's power—a power notably figured, via references to Hester's needlework, as in part artistic—reflects anxieties about an ongoing literary battle in which men appeared (in Hawthorne's own moment, in any case) to be the losers. But while admitting the significance of these issues, I want also to read the matter much less metaphorically, to revert the discussion back to the literal problem being negotiated in *The Scarlet Letter* and its sources: men's property in women. I have already suggested how witchcraft trials in general, and the trial of Anne Hibbins in particular, manifested concerns about the "witch's" violation of principles of coverture, according to which the married woman's existence is "incorporated" into that of her husband. The issue of coverture, I have also noted, had resurfaced as the focus of one of many "reform" movements in the antebellum period. Emerging in the wake of the Panic of 1837, which prompted concerns about how to protect men's property from creditors, and fuelled by both legal codification movements and woman's rights agitation, the effort to modify the laws governing women's rights to property in marriage intensified in the years just prior to *The Scarlet Letter*'s publication. Debates about laws took place not only in the more rarified forums of the "Woman's Rights Convention," but also in mainstream publications like *Godey's Lady's Book* and "high culture" magazines like *U. S. Magazine and Democratic Review*.

In this context, we should not find it remarkable that Hawthorne engages matters of property and marriage in *The Scarlet Letter*. But to understand the urgency—the anxiety—with which those matters are treated, we have to recognize that coverture designates not just the distribution of property in marriage, but the distribution of subjectivity as well. Legal historian Margaret Radin has noted that, according to one "strand" of liberal property theory (a strand clearly applicable to the U.S. context), to "achieve proper self-development—to be a *person*—an individual needs some control" over property.[2] According to this theory, one is literally constituted by the property to which one lays claim. To the "personality" thus constructed C. B. Macpherson has offered the now-famous designation, "possessive individual." Property, according to the theory of possessive individualism, is not merely something the individual has the right to claim; it is something the individual must claim, in order to *be* an individual: "the man without property in things loses that full proprietorship of his own person," Macpherson explains.[3] Insofar as they ratify men's control both over any real and personal property a woman might have controlled before marriage and, importantly, over the woman herself, laws of coverture operate in a quite obvious way to underwrite the possessive individual (whose gendered contours are thereby made plain). By codifying women's object-status, marital laws attempted to make "one plus one

2. Margaret Jane Radin, *Reinterpreting Property* (Chicago: U of Chicago P, 1993), 35.
3. C. B. Macpherson, *The Political Theory of Possessive Individualism: Hobbes to Locke* (Oxford: Oxford UP, 1962), 231.

equal one."[4] That final "one" is the possessive individual, the liberal subject whose ownership in "things"—in this case, a wife—ratifies his "proprietorship in his own person." It is precisely this proprietorship, this distinctive form of self-possession, which the wife threatens when she refuses to exist under the cover of male control. It is no wonder that we find one of Anne Hibbins' examiners fretfully protesting that she "makes a cipher of her husband."

Given the high stakes of this proprietary contest, it becomes less remarkable that *The Scarlet Letter*, like its colonial sources, figures woman's effort to exert more control over herself and her property in terms of witchcraft. Indeed, Hawthorne would not have been alone in making the association. In the aftermath of the 1848 Seneca Falls Convention, which highlighted laws of coverture in its manifesto, *The Declaration of Sentiments*, one commentator remarked that a "new element" (women's activism) had been "thrown into the cauldron of agitation which is now bubbling around us with such fury."[5] In even more hysterical rhetoric, assemblyman Jonathan Burnet responded to an 1854 speech to the New York legislature by Elizabeth Cady Stanton—a speech in which Stanton argued for changes in New York's property laws—by proclaiming that Stanton and her cohorts "do not appear to be satisfied with having unsexed themselves, but they desire to unsex every female in the land, and to set the whole community ablaze with unhallowed fire." "[I]t is well known," Burnet went on, "that the object of these unsexed women is to overthrow the most sacred of our institutions, to set at defiance the Divine law which declares man and wife to be one, and establish on its ruins what will be in fact and in principle but a species of legalized adultery."[6]

Hawthorne's treatment of Hester's marital insurgency is, of course, a great deal more tempered than this. But the text's inability to fully ratify that insurgency suggests that Hawthorne is perhaps no less anxious than assemblyman Burnet about its consequences. That anxiety is put on display even more obviously in *The Scarlet Letter*'s pre-text, "The Custom-House," which is, as I noted at the outset of this essay, riddled with metaphors of witchcraft and (male dis-)possession. We are now, I think, in a better position to understand these metaphors, and to recognize the ways in which that text, along with the narrative that follows it, might function as an effort to beat back the very forces that threaten to "possess" the writer by challenging his subjective mastery. For having begun "The Custom-House" with an assertion regarding his own passive experience of dispossession (the writer has been "taken possession of" by an "autobiographical impulse"), Hawthorne ends with an assertion of his own proprietorship over the materials of his narrative. This assertion begins early in "The Custom-House," when Hawthorne argues for the "propriety" of his sketch by alleging

4. Norma Basch, *In the Eyes of the Law: Women, Marriage, and Property in Nineteenth-Century New York* (Ithaca: Cornell UP, 1982), 17.
5. Elizabeth Cady Stanton, Susan B. Anthony, and Matilda Joslyn Gage, eds., *The History of Woman Suffrage*, Volume 1: 1848–1861 (New York: Arno and the New York Times, 1969), 805.
6. Stanton, 613.

that it "explain[s] how a large portion of the following pages came into my possession" (8) [8]. Following this lead, he moves in the sketch from viewing himself as one who has lost subjective mastery to constructing himself as a proprietor of certain self-constituting materials. Having claimed those materials he can, by the end of his introductory sketch, declare himself a self-owning "citizen of somewhere else" (43) [35]: Hawthorne has liberated himself from the Custom-House, from imaginative imprisonment, from Salem, and, most importantly, from the condition of subjective alienation and dispossession that he finds so troubling.

But while Hawthorne seeks to assert, by the end of his introductory sketch, such liberation, the narrative that follows, as we have already seen, reverberates against and unsettles this claim. In recent years, we have increasingly explored how Hawthorne might be less the slayer of middle-class ideology than he is a sometimes reluctant, sometimes enthusiastic participant in it. The discomfort about female (self)ownership registered throughout *The Scarlet Letter* in its associations between Hester, Hutchinson, and Hibbins exposes another layer of that participation. Despite his effort to situate himself in an alternative and indeed antipatriarchal history, *The Scarlet Letter* taken as a whole suggests that, like Winthrop and Mather before him, and like his own middle-class culture, Hawthorne needs the possessed female body. For it would appear that only through that body can doubts about male subjective mastery—fears about becoming, like Anne Hibbins' husband, a "wisp" and a "cipher"—be contained and controlled.

The Custom-House

JOHN FRANZOSA

"The Custom-House," *The Scarlet Letter*, and Hawthorne's Separation from Salem†

I desire to set before my fellows the likeness of a man in all the truth of nature, and that man myself. Myself alone! I know the feelings of my heart, and I know men. I am not made like any of those I have seen. I venture to believe that I am not made like any of those who are in existence. If I am not better, at least I am different.

—*Confessions,* Rousseau

On March 21, 1850, the Salem *Register* printed a long review of Nathaniel Hawthorne's *The Scarlet Letter,* published just five days previous. In the opening paragraph, the reviewer praised the "exquisiteness of Hawthorne's genius" and the "affluence of imagination and bold and striking thought" which sustained his narrative.[1] This much took up less than a quarter of the review; for the rest, the reviewer felt that "justice compels us to notice some other things": the "small sneers at Salem," and the "calumnious caricatures of inoffensive men," one of whom was a "venerable gentleman, whose chief crime seems to be that he loves a good dinner, has preserved a youthful flow of cheerfulness, and can tell a graphic story." The reviewer likened such "refinement of cruelty" to the vengeance of Roger Chillingworth but asserted that Hawthorne had no "visible motive for so much malice."

There was, of course, sufficient motive in the matter of Hawthorne's removal from the Custom House amid charges of untoward partisanship and corruption.[2] Hawthorne had threatened his revenge in a letter to Longfellow, and in later correspondence he wrote somewhat

---

† From *ESQ* 24 (1978): 57–71. Reprinted by permission of the author. Page numbers in square brackets refer to this Norton Critical Edition.
1. This review, probably written by John Chapman, the paper's editor and a virulent Whig, is reprinted in Benjamin Lease, "Salem vs. Hawthorne: an Early Review of *The Scarlet Letter,*" *New England Quarterly* 44 (1971): 110–117.
2. For the particulars of this case, including a reprint of the "Memorial" signed by Charles W. Upham for the Salem Whig committee which brought these charges against Hawthorne, see Winfield S. Nevins, "Nathaniel Hawthorne's Removal from the Salem Custom House," *Essex Institute Historical Collections* 53 (1917): 97–132. Ephraim Miller, the old general's son, was the main target of the Whigs and not Hawthorne, who was felt to be "the abused instrument of others" (118). See also B. Bernard Cohen, "Edward Everett and Hawthorne's Removal from the Salem Custom House," *American Literature* 27 (1955): 245–49; and Kenneth W. Cameron, "New Light on Hawthorne's Removal from the Salem Custom House," *Emerson Society Quarterly* 23 (2nd quarter 1961), 2–5.

approvingly of the notoriety this sketch had won for him.[3] His response to the *Register's* criticism in his preface to the second edition
was "surprise" and "amusement" at the "respectable community" for
having been aroused to such a pitch of "unprecedented excitement" by
the "atrocities" committed in his introduction. He defended the "general accuracy" of his characterizations, affirmed the "genuine good humor" of the sketch and—perhaps mocking the *Register's* compelling
need to attack him—felt "constrained" to reprint the entire sketch
"without the change of a word" (I, 1–2) [5].

In this preface, Hawthorne demonstrates a precious obstinacy which
underscores the *Register's* complaints through his diffident rejection of
them. Perhaps the "outrageous personalities" portrayed had served him
as objects on which to "vent his spite"; perhaps ineffectual old men had
been vilified for their dependency and particularly their love of food;
and perhaps a "strange antipathy toward the aged" had manifested itself and had apparently infected the romance as well. As evidence of
that antipathy, a passage had been quoted at length which appeared to
satirize the piety of a widow with a "heart full of reminiscences about
her dead husband and children" who had "fed herself" with "religious
consolations" (I, 218) [139]. More accurately than many modern readings of the romance, I think, this first criticism not only demonstrated
the unity of this sketch and the narrative it introduces, but unwittingly
identified the important psychological themes operating in *The Scarlet
Letter*. Where psychoanalytic and less doctrinaire "Romantic" readers
have discussed the individual's rebellion against authority, the self's
struggle to mediate desire and guilt, the isolated individual's effort to
realize a viable self against an alienating community, this reviewer responded to themes of dependence—nourishment, loss, and rejection—
themes which because of their developmental priority shape more
mature relationships between self and other.[4]

3. See Frank MacShane, "The House of the Dead: Hawthorne's 'The Custom-House' and *The
   Scarlet Letter*," *New England Quarterly* 35 (1962): 98; Horatio Bridge, *Personal Recollections
   of Nathaniel Hawthorne* (New York: Harper & Bros., 1893), 114; and Lease, 112. See also
   William Charvat, "Introduction," *The Scarlet Letter*, Centenary Edition (Columbus: Ohio
   State UP, 1962), xxiii. All references to Hawthorne's writing will note volume and page of
   this edition.
4. In its psychological implications, most Hawthorne criticism—and criticism of "The Custom-
   House" in particular—proceeds from an essentially Freudian view of conflict. MacShane;
   and David Stouck, "The Surveyor of the Custom-House: A Narrator for *The Scarlet Letter*,"
   The Centennial Review 15 (1971): 309–329, are most explicit in this regard. But other crit-
   ics, such as Nina Baym, "The Romantic *Malgré Lui*: Hawthorne in the Custom House,"
   ESQ 19 (1973): 14–25; Dan McCall, "The Design of Hawthorne's Custom-House,"
   Nineteenth-Century Fiction 21 (1967): 349–58; Charles R. O'Donnell, "Hawthorne and
   Dimmesdale: The Search for the Realm of Quiet," *Nineteenth-Century Fiction* 14 (1960):
   317–32; and Marshall Van Deusen, "Narrative Tone in 'The Custom-House' and *The Scarlet
   Letter*," *Nineteenth-Century Fiction* 21 (1967): 61–71, also frame their arguments in terms
   of a struggle between authority and the beleaguered individual. Paul John Eakin,
   "Hawthorne's Imagination and the Structure of 'The Custom-House,'" *American Literature*
   43 (1971): 346–58, on the other hand, views this authority as dead: there is a necessary
   journey to the source of creative power, a necessary "communion with the dead," that pre-
   cedes Hawthorne's "salvation." See also Jean Normand, *Nathaniel Hawthorne: An Approach
   to an Analysis of Artistic Creation*, trans. Derek Coltman (Cleveland: Case Western Reserve
   UP, 1970). James M. Cox, "*The Scarlet Letter*: Through the Old Manse and the Custom
   House," *Virginia Quarterly Review* 51 (1975): 432–47; Thomas H. Pauly, "Hawthorne's
   Houses of Fiction," *American Literature* 48 (1976): 271–91; and Harry C. West,
   "Hawthorne's Editorial Pose," *American Literature*, 44 (1972): 208–221, though explicitly

I

According to contemporary psychoanalytic theory, the key relationship in the first year of life is the "symbiotic dyad." Within weeks after its biological separation from the mother, the infant is "seduced" into a psychological symbiosis with a maternal figure. Words cannot adequately describe this relationship, since it predates the infant's acquisition of language and use of symbols; and the term "relationship" is misleading because in this experience there is no differentiation between self and other.[5] Using a biological metaphor, Heinz Lichtenstein describes this dyadic relationship as a "schema" or a maternal *Umwelt*—not an environment, but a range of experience in which the infant figures as an organ within a larger organism. The mother "imprints" the infant with a specific mode of being for her, a specific way of relating. This experience will have a determining effect on the infant's separation from the maternal *Umwelt*, its sense of itself as different from its mother and its ability to individuate itself as a separate entity, a self. At a later time, the child enters into triadic relationships—typically the oedipal configuration—when sexual differences are realized, gender identity is formed, language is acquired, and the experiences of conflict and ambivalence arise. For a boy, the father is not merely the prohibitive Victorian censor but a mediator between boy and mother—an object which the boy's emergent identity requires to complement his identification with his mother and to complete the process of separating from her and individuating as a male person in his own right. Throughout life, as Lichtenstein argues, identity remains most fundamentally an "experience of a potential instrumentality for another."[6]

As *The Scarlet Letter* opens, a "throng of bearded men . . . intermixed with women" is seen gathered outside the prison door from which Hester Prynne and her infant will emerge. It is the figure of maternity which immediately captures interest: the metaphoric, the literal, and, I suggest, the latent maternal women who, through the figure of Hester, provide the matrix from which characters, motives, and meanings will separate, clarify, conflict, and resolve. The roses near the threshold of the prison seem outward signs of the "deep heart" of "Nature," just as the prison itself is described as the "black

---

non-psychoanalytic—in fact, Cox carefully distinguishes his position from that of Frederick Crews, *The Sins of the Fathers* (New York: Oxford UP, 1966)—have offered the most useful insights for a psychoanalytic reading of "The Custom-House." All three see Hawthorne in a sense as a man "whose art caused his life"; all three comment on the way Hawthorne focused (and still focuses) discussion on the processes of writing and not on self-revelation. I think implicit in their views is a psychological argument that as a person, Hawthorne was first and foremost a performer. A glance at his early letters to his mother, sisters, uncles, and wife should confirm the primacy of literary performance in even his most intimate social and personal relationships.

5. Heinz Lichtenstein, "Identity and Sexuality," *Journal of the American Psychoanalytic Association*, 9 (1961): 200. See also Margaret Mahler, *On Human Symbiosis and the Vicissitudes of Individuation* (New York: International UP, 1966); Michael Balint, *The Basic Fault: Therapeutic Aspects of Regression* (London: Tavistock Publications, 1968); and Phyllis Greenacre, *Emotional Growth* (New York: International UP, 1971).

6. Lichtenstein, 203.

flower of civilization." That these roses might have "sprung up under the footsteps of the sainted Ann Hutchinson" suggests perhaps a "civilized" matrix born of a more natural one, or perhaps the possibility that history mediates between repressive civilizing forces and natural, creative ones. At any rate, the figure of maternity seems to provide the ground on which the drama is played out, be it the "native soil" (or the "infertile soil" on which Hester lives in exile), the legacy of the ancestral martyr, the larger comprehensiveness of Nature, the influence of the spectral Mistress Hibbins, the piety of Dimmesdale's housekeeper, or the community of vindictive Puritan women.

From the beginning, *The Scarlet Letter* offers a particular type of maternal figure which embodies both masculine and feminine characteristics. As the reader awaits Hester's entrance, Hawthorne provides examples of criminals likely to be punished, all of them implying transgressions of dependency relationships. Those guilty of such private crimes would ordinarily be punished in public, according to Hawthorne, because religious and legal authority were "almost identical" and "interfused" (I, 50) [37] in the Puritan theocracy. Symbolically, the law is associated with masculine characters and images such as "iron" and "oak"; religion is associated more with women: Anne Hutchinson, the Quaker woman whipped by Major Hathorne, and the "whore of Babylon," the Catholic Church. The social structure suggests a composite parental figure, and so does history: Anne Hutchinson—whose footsteps germinate roses—and Queen Elizabeth.[7] Fed on the "beef and ale of their native land," the "not unsubstantial" Puritan women of Boston "stood within less than half a century of the period when the man-like Elizabeth had been the not altogether unsuitable representative of the sex" (I, 50) [38].[8]

These conflated parental figures suggest a fantasy of a "man-like" or phallic mother, a fantasy which dominates this romance. Such a fantasy ordinarily serves to deny the fact of sexual difference by fusing both parents in one image. In cases where the father is absent (as Hawthorne's was), it can serve to deny this loss and allow a boy to identify with his lost father by identifying with a fantasy of his mother somehow embodying his father.[9] Such a strategy, however, can obviously lead to role and gender confusions. "Plying her needle," Hester Prynne "possessed an art" which "might have been a mode of expressing and therefore soothing, the passion of her life," except that she "rejected it as sin" (I, 84) [58]. As it is, her "rich, voluptuous and Ori-

7. Footsteps, particularly when combined with thresholds, usually imply a phallic significance for Hawthorne: in one of his earliest stories, "My Kinsman, Major Molineux," a lady with scarlet petticoats takes the young Robin and draws "his half-willing footsteps nearly to the threshold" before the "keeper of midnight order" scares her away; and one of the unfinished romances concerns a blood-stained footprint on a threshold, the sign of a lost ancestor. Characters do not merely walk through doorways—Jaffrey Pyncheon in *The House of the Seven Gables*, for instance, intrudes, penetrates, or thrusts himself into others' private spaces.
8. The "man-like Elizabeth" suggests an implied pun, since, as he wrote, Hawthorne "stood within less than half a century" of the time when his mother had been Elizabeth Manning.
9. See Greenacre, I, 81–82; also Melanie Klein, *The Psychoanalysis of Children* (London: Hogarth Press, 1932), 188–190. Hawthorne's father, a sea captain, died when the boy was four years old.

ental" character found nothing else to "exercise itself upon" but the "exquisite productions of her needle," commissioned by the more affluent women of Boston. Such "delicate toil" is a pleasure "incomprehensible to the other sex" (I, 83) [58]. In contrast to her phallic, active qualities, the dominant features of her partner in sin, Arthur Dimmesdale, are his "tremulous lips" and his hand compulsively clutching his heart. It is Hester's needle which affords her—in her privacy—a "part to perform in the world" even if, in her "intercourse with society," there was "nothing that made her feel as if she belonged to it."

With the absence of Pearl's father, Hester as mother has been forced to become active and self-reliant—in nineteenth-century terms, "manly." And the effect of such a maternal figure on succeeding generations is painfully obvious to Hawthorne. The particular importance of the mother's influence on the child is demonstrated as Hester recalls her mother's face with the "look of heedful and anxious love which it always wore," a look which since her death had proved an "impediment" (I, 58) [43]. And if Hester's own "impassioned state" was the "medium through which were transmitted to the unborn infant the rays of its moral life" (I, 91) [62], we can see the problem of identity when the maternal *Umwelt* includes not only a maternal presence but an absent father. Being in the world, for Hester, means activity, particularly the alienated activity of her needlework, and this affects Dimmesdale as well as her daughter. "Exchange this false life of thine for a true one. . . . Preach! Write! Act!" she charges him as he lies prostrate on a "luxuriant heap of moss" (I, 198) [127]. But of course, Dimmesdale cannot act on his own, condemned as he is to "eat his unsavory morsel at another's board" and "to warm himself by another's fire." "Think for me, Hester," he pleads: "Be thou strong for me" (I, 196) [126]. There is no authentic core to Dimmesdale's character; thus to "be . . . for" Hester is to fuse with her will and to identify with a fantasy of her "masculine" qualities, and to "be . . . for" himself is to be isolated and empty.

Central to *The Scarlet Letter* is the figure of the maternal woman, not only the matrix from which characters separate and act, but also a type of phallic mother. To this extent, the maternal figure is a denial of loss—an important consideration for Hawthorne, who had lost his position at the Salem Custom House and shortly thereafter had lost his mother, another Elizabeth, with whom his relationship had been admittedly ambivalent.[1] The romance is framed by allusions to "the man-like Elizabeth" (I, 50) [38] and to "the sunny richness of the Elizabethan epoch" (I, 230) [146], and, like the figures of maternal women, it contains a paternal absence: the central chapter, "The Minister's Vigil," takes place on the night of John Winthrop's death which occurs beyond the periphery of the setting. One recent critic, noting that this date (1649) fixes the chronology of *The Scarlet Letter*, has argued that the romance, "above all else, is about history," specifically about the Pu-

---

1. In *The American Notebooks*, Hawthorne writes: "I love my mother; but there has been, ever since my boyhood, a sort of coldness of intercourse between us, such as is apt to come between persons of strong feelings, if they are not managed rightly" (VIII, 429).

ritans' definitive turning away from their English (although Hawthorne emphasizes Elizabethan) past and its "gentle" qualities.[2] More importantly, *The Scarlet Letter* is also about the resolution of a personal conflict in 1849.[3] As he looks back on what has been lost—whether mother, Salem, Custom House, or Elizabethan gaiety—Hawthorne finds those "gentle" qualities intermixed with a more disturbing absence, all figured in the "man-like" woman. *The Scarlet Letter* and "The Custom-House" are representations of Hawthorne's attempt to come to terms with a significant loss, to articulate the "basic fault" in a particular maternal relationship, and to frame a profound self-discovery.[4]

II

When Hawthorne apologizes for his "autobiographical impulse" in his introductory sketch, it is more likely that he had failed in *The Scarlet Letter*—and not in "The Custom-House"—to keep the "inmost Me behind a veil," and that this sketch is intended to dispel the "stern and somber aspect" of self-discovery. His claim that he was happy while "straying through the gloom of these sunless fantasies" (I, 43) [34] is sheer fabrication. According to his wife, he apparently "came near a brain fever" when his mother died; a month later he was writing "*immensely*" so that she was "almost frightened about it."[5] The moth-eaten scarlet letter, whose discovery among the dusty bins of the Custom House places the sketch "within the law of literary propriety," is a more obvious fiction, despite Hawthorne's curiously adamant contention: the letter and manuscript "are still in my possession, and shall be freely exhibited" (I, 33) [27]. Such fictions—even such a time-worn convention as the recovered lost manuscript—are significant in the context of a sketch whose most insistent concern is "authenticity." They deflect attention from Hawthorne the man and artist toward Hawthorne the perceiver and editor; thus, psychological and moral issues seem to evaporate in mists of aesthetics and epistemology.[6] In ironic self-deprecation, Hawthorne

2. Frederick Newberry, "Tradition and Disinheritance in *The Scarlet Letter*," *ESQ* 23 (1977): 1–26.

3. Hawthorne's penchant for anniversaries—using historical material from fifty, one hundred or two hundred years previous in order to illuminate contemporary conflicts—may be seen in such tales as "My Kinsman, Major Molineux," "Roger Malvin's Burial," and "Endicott and the Red Cross." See, for example, Robert Daly, "History and Chivalric Myth in 'Roger Malvin's Burial,' " *Essex Institute Historical Collections* 109 (1973): 99–115; and Roy Harvey Pearce, "Hawthorne and the Sense of the Past or, the Immortality of Major Molineux" (1954), rpt. in *Historicism Once More: Problems & Occasions for the American Scholar* (Princeton, N.J.: Princeton UP, 1969).

4. Balint, 21, describes this "fault" in the self—which derives from the experience in the dyadic relationship—as a "sudden irregularity in the overall structure, an irregularity which in normal circumstances might be hidden, but, if strains and stresses occur, may lead to a break, profoundly disrupting the overall structure." Except for the aspect of "shame" which Balint discusses elsewhere, this might be Hawthorne writing of a "secret guilt."

5. Julian Hawthorne, *Nathaniel Hawthorne and His Wife* (Boston: J. R. Osgood & Co., 1884), I, 352–354.

6. The ethical questions raised by "The Custom-House" are treated by Larzer Ziff, "The Ethical Dimension of 'The Custom-House,' " *Modern Language Notes* 73 (1958): 338–44, who finds Hawthorne's idea of the "good life" involves "an enrichment of the material by the inner self, an appreciation of the present through a consciousness of the past" (341). Van Deusen reads "The Custom-House" as an epistemological problem. Despite the fine readings that their approaches yield, there is a danger of being led away from the heart of the matter by following Hawthorne's intellectual speculation. West and Pauly, for instance, see a

equates the inevitability of his returns to Salem with that of a "bad half-penny," and I think "The Custom-House" must be read in that spirit: its truths must be taken seriously but not at face value. Hawthorne's fictions do not conceal truths, but, like the "scrubby trees" that hide Hester Prynne's cottage, they "denote that here was some object which would fain have been, or at least ought to be, concealed" (I, 81) [56].

In contrast to Hawthorne's reticence concerning self-exposure, his initial description of the Custom House confronts the reader with an interpretation of its essential qualities. The dominant symbol of the Custom House and the republic for which it is an emblem is "an enormous specimen of the American eagle" which "hovers" over the entrance (I, 5) [8]. Despite her expansive wings to which many flock for "shelter," Hawthorne finds "the fierceness of her beak and eye" posing a threat of "mischief to the inoffensive community." While others may imagine that "her bosom has all the softness and snugness of an eider-down pillow," Hawthorne notes a "shield before her breast" and a "bunch of intermingled thunderbolts and arrows in each claw." Left alone to rule her roost, this "unhappy fowl" has incorporated the emblems of patriarchal authority, but the "dignity" of "his Majesty" has been transformed into a "bunch" of destructive weapons. So awful are these nether regions, apparently, that Hawthorne equivocates in his description, prefacing his remarks with "if I recollect aright." Even so, Americans are drawn to her in search of shelter, as if they must return to her to actualize their identities as her instruments. The "patriarchal" civil servants are reduced to "dependents"; for their "half-torpid systems," the Custom House has become "the sole principle of life."

By his own admission, Hawthorne's relation to Salem is similar to that dependency he patronizes in his fellow civil servants. Salem is his "native place" and he returns as if under a "spell." His desire to return is "not love, but instinct," as if Salem were "the inevitable centre of the universe" for him (I, 12) [13]. Like his paternal ancestors who "followed the sea," Hawthorne has obtained a post related to maritime commerce; but unlike them, he has remained home, near his "native soil."[7] His post places him in relation to both paternal and

---

complex process of transforming facts into significance, but their arguments rest on unexamined assertions of "spiritual significance" in Hawthorne's material, or Hawthorne's "intentions." In the famous aesthetic passage on the "neutral territory" in "The Custom-House," it is interesting that the "material" is enriched by the "inner self" only after an elaborate abstraction. Hawthorne begins with "my imagination," then "the imaginative faculty"; but finally it is "the Imaginary" that intermixes with "the Actual." Hawthorne is distanced from the fusion that takes place and participates only visually: among the "domestic scenery of the well-known apartment" transfigured by moonlight, we may "look about us and discover a form, beloved, but gone hence, now sitting quietly" (I, 34–36) [29]. Contrast this with his more immediate experience a little earlier on finding the scarlet letter. Imagining the decoration to be—of all things—a contrivance to "take eyes of Indians," "I happened to place it on my breast"; he imagines the reader smiling as he reports a "sensation not altogether physical, yet almost so, as of burning heat" (I, 32) [26]. Both passages imply a recovery of something lost, one by conjuring a "ghost," the other by identification with a lost maternal figure: but though framed in a tentative fiction, the latter experience communicates a fear of fusion that the former defends against through a process of intellectualizing.

7. According to Randall Stewart, *Nathaniel Hawthorne: A Biography* (New Haven: Yale UP, 1948), 76, Hawthorne had turned down several appointments—clerk in the Charlestown Navy Yard and naval storekeeper in Portsmouth were two—because he apparently wanted a post in Salem.

maternal qualities, yet the paternal elements—like those of the Custom House eagle—are merged, engulfed, or incorporated into a larger matrix. For example, the once bustling wharf is now dilapidated: the "tide often overflows" it at one end and grass has grown up around it at the other (I, 5) [8].[8] Hawthorne's "affection" for Salem is "assignable to the deep and aged roots which my family has struck into the soil" (I, 8) [11]. The dust of his immigrant ancestor is mingled in that soil and "the attachment of which I speak is the mere sensuous sympathy of dust for dust." That "deep and aged roots" had been "struck into" the "native soil" suggests that, though the fathers are absent, their phallic qualities remain present—if only as "dust" within an essentially maternal configuration, Hawthorne's "natal spot." The return to Salem thus implies not only a regression, but a search through a maternal configuration for a lost paternal ancestor.[9] It is not quite accurate to speak of a search, however, for Hawthorne is not really distinct from Salem (he must distinguish himself first as "surveyor"), nor are the objects of his search separate or individualized (hence, there is no "love" but "instinct"). Rather, there is a range of experience from which Hawthorne must differentiate himself and other objects.

Symptomatic of the relationships possible with the republican eagle is the "frozen thought and benumbed language" which pervades the Custom House. The "dependent mode of life" (I, 16) [16] Hawthorne finds among the "patriarchs" there has apparently obviated any need for speech or action. They would view his nervous pacing as useful only insofar as it served him "to get an appetite for dinner" (I, 34) [28]; their discourse has been reduced to "pass words and countersigns," to "frozen witticisms," its content more likely to center on "their morning's breakfast, or yesterday's, to-day's or to-morrow's dinner" than "the shipwreck of forty or fifty years ago" (I, 15–16) [15–16].[1] Their debased language implies that their relationships have regressed to a stage of development characterized by the symbiotic fusion of self and object, and for Hawthorne the problem is compounded by the general ineffectiveness of language even in describing such regressed states: "A better book than I shall ever write was there" (I, 37) [30].[2] Yet having returned to his "native place," Hawthorne realizes, I think, that this area, describable only by indirection, is central to his experience. It remains for him to separate himself and to estab-

---

8. The "wheel-track" at the Old Manse was also "overgrown with grass" (X, 3), but there the image was of nourishment, not decay. That grass afforded "dainty mouthfuls to two or three vagrant cows" (X, 3); and the orchard planted by the late minister suggested the "idea of an infinite generosity and exhaustless bounty, on the part of our Mother Nature" (X, 13). The garret of the Old Manse contained "nooks, or rather caverns of deep obscurity, the secrets of which I never learned" (X, 16); and consequently, Hawthorne produced "no profound treatise of ethics—no philosophic history—no novel" (X, 34).
9. Hawthorne's ancestral roots had been "planted deep, in the town's earliest infancy and childhood" (I, 10) [12]. This suggests the process of "imprinting" an identity and ties that identity to a fantasy of a fused parental image.
1. Hawthorne's father had died at sea forty-one years before.
2. It is possible to view this quotation as Hawthorne's choice—despite himself—to write romance rather than realism, to express the "inner light" rather than adapt to authoritarian conventions (see Baym, 16). But if The Scarlet Letter speaks "a reality far more powerful than the quotidian" (16), why should a novel of the Custom House have been a "better

lish a relationship between himself as surveyor and the world as a cluster of distinct objects. As with any separation, however, there is a danger that the psychological separation of self and object may not conform to the "real" separation of two physical bodies: some aspects of the world may appear as elements of himself, while other aspects of himself may be projected onto the world. In his native town of Salem, for instance, his "name is seldom heard" and his "face hardly known." Yet, as surveyor, his name is stenciled on dutiable merchandise to be shipped across the globe. In Salem, he has a sense of identity based on his "attachment" to his ancestors, an identity which is not confirmed by his social experience; outside Salem, he has a social role as surveyor of customs which does not feel real—a "false self." In Salem, he is "in possession" of a secret identity which he defends against the intrusion of the social world; outside Salem his "autobiographical impulse" might itself be considered an "intrusion."

As surveyor, Hawthorne finds himself balanced precariously between the themes of possession and intrusion, engaged now in a dependency relationship with the republican eagle. For Hawthorne, possession and intrusion are really two aspects of the same theme. Since the separation of self and other appears problematic, the self cannot feel complete unless it can intrude on the other and possess those contents which it fantasizes as part of itself. At the same time, the self may harbor contents which it fantasizes as parts of the other, which it fears the other may reclaim by some act of intrusion. Such an experience, then, cannot be analyzed (much less moralized) unless the objects differentiate from each other and one becomes the intruder and the other the object of intrusion. Hawthorne attempts to separate and individuate these themes in the persons of the Inspector and Collector (as well as in the romance at times between the Reverend Mr. Wilson and Hester Prynne, for instance, or Chillingworth and Dimmesdale). The Inspector, as we might expect, is a hyper-intrusive surveyor, whereas the Collector is an object of intrusion: "The closer you penetrated to the substance of his mind, the sounder it appeared"

---

book?" Is that merely the guilty Hawthorne heaping conventional judgments on himself? In part, yes, but there is more involved: Hawthorne cannot write of the Custom House unless he can satisfactorily separate himself from it. His art (and most psychoanalysts would include language generally) requires distance, a separation of self from other objects which language mediates by providing a space where self and objects can merge while retaining their distinctness. Inside the Custom House, this distance is insufficient—Hawthorne is overwhelmed by an otherness and his vestigial literary capacities atrophy (I, 34 [28], 38 [31]); outside the distance is too great to be bridged by language—"it ceases to be a reality of my life" (I, 44) [35]. To write a "better book" Hawthorne would have to find a language (and by implication, a mode of relating) which could present his world and himself in it—in a sense, he would have to be able to stand alternately inside and outside himself and other objects. More than "the individual in conflict with authority" (Baym, 18), the issue of "The Custom-House" concerns the establishing of a "true relation"; and from the moment of Hawthorne's instinctive return to his "natal spot," the ontological basis of the "individual" is called into question. If he cannot accept otherness (not merely "conventional modes," but the existence of objects outside himself), if he cannot establish an authentic relation with "individuals unlike himself" (I, 24) [21], Hawthorne is forced to people his world with parts of himself: his ancestors, Surveyor Pue, even Hester Prynne. What Baym celebrates as Hawthorne's "turning into the self" (19) is really a symptom of his inability to "open an intercourse with the world" (IX, 6).

(I, 20) [19]. The themes of possession and intrusion, within the dependency mode, have a two-fold significance: some characters use their own or others' dependence as a way of intruding (at the risk of being intruded upon), while other characters strive to remain independent as a way of retaining their possessions (at the risk of cutting themselves off from others).

The Inspector is emblematic of the first type and significantly is identified only by his role.[3] He "possessed no power of thought, no depth of feeling, no troublesome sensibilities; nothing, in short, but a few commonplace instincts" (I, 17) [17]. A man of roughly eighty years, he appears "as ready for sport as any unbreeched infant." He seems "earthy and sensuous," the quality of his life little better than a beast's, except in one "advantage over his four-footed brethren"—"his ability to recollect the good dinners" which he had eaten. This "contrivance of Mother Nature," too shallow to mourn the loss of three wives and most of his twenty children, too devoted to "the delight and profit of his maw" to have corrupted any "spiritual endowment," is human only in his ability to recollect and tell stories. "I have heard him smack his lips over dinners, every guest at which, except himself, had long been food for worms." With life reduced to the proposition that one must eat or be eaten, Hawthorne apparently finds it necessary to place certain limits on such unbridled sensuality. "The chief tragic event of the old man's life . . . was his mishap with a certain goose" which was "so inveterately tough that the carving-knife would make no impression on its carcass" (I, 18–19) [18]. Hawthorne seems bound to assert an impenetrable object with contents safe from even an inspector's intrusion.

One such impenetrable object is the Collector, identified by name as General James F. Miller, hero of the Battle of Lundy's Lane in the War of 1812. Hawthorne is able to "sketch only the merest outline" of the general, only "the main points of his portrait": his "step was palsied" and only with aid could he "slowly and painfully ascend the Custom-House steps." Like Fort Ticonderoga, some areas of his aspect were "almost complete" but others could be aptly described as "a shapeless mound, cumbrous with its very strength." Nonetheless, Hawthorne finds a "light within him," a wholeness of character discoverable when his "notice was sought" and a discourse established. This wholeness includes not only a "stubborn and ponderous endurance," but "benevolence," and a foundation of "innate kindliness,"

---

3. Hawthorne must have known the response this characterization would engender. When Evert Duyckinck requested an excerpt of Hawthorne's new novel for his *Literary World*, Hawthorne's publisher advised him to use this one, the "Old Gourmand." Hawthorne preferred the passage on General Miller, but the former was used over his objections (Charvat, xvii). The Collector's portrait is obviously more reverential and its stance differs little from Upham's in "The Memorial": "His powers of locomotion are wholly destroyed, and his articulation rendered quite difficult, but his mental faculties have not shared the decrepitude of his physical frame" (in Nevins, 115). The Whigs approved of Miller, appointed as he was "before the parties that now divide the country had been formed" (110), and advocated his re-appointment as Collector at the expense of his son's (and Hawthorne's) removal from office. Hawthorne's reverence is part of a complex relation to others, and Duyckinck as well as Chapman at the *Register* were astute enough to read through Hawthorne's pieties to find the barbs.

"humor" and "native elegance, seldom seen in the masculine character after childhood and early youth." He seemed, for instance, to have a "young girl's appreciation of the floral tribe." For the surveyor, it is much more satisfying "standing at a distance and watching" the Collector than "engaging him in conversation" which is a "difficult task." Thus distanced, he is safe to surmise that the old warrior "lived a more real life within his own thoughts" and recollections. Indeed, it is the recollection of his famous "I'll try, Sir" (I, 20–23) [18–21] which not only provides Hawthorne with the contour of the general's character, but a spur to his own activity: when he imagines Surveyor Pue's ghost charging him to dispose properly of his tale, he responds, "I will" (I, 34) [28].

The quality of recollection, then, would seem to be that quality which humanizes the beast by distancing him from his objects. Even the Inspector rises above other animals because of this quality; and because of his delight in memories, he stands far above the chorus of torpid "patriarchs." This quality is also the "bright gleam" along the blade of the "rusty . . . old sword" which is General Miller. Similarly, the documents of the part-time antiquarian, Surveyor Pue, provide "petty activity" for Hawthorne's mind and keep it from being "eaten up with rust" (I, 30) [26]. Dredging up and collecting bits of the past afford an escape from being metaphorically consumed in the present. Hawthorne, speaking of the positive aspects of the Custom House, had noted his desire to "nourish myself with food for which I had hitherto had little appetite" (I, 25) [22]. But such a "change of diet" has placed him in the relation of a dependent, and while being nourished he is also being consumed. Recollection, it seems, is his escape: "there would have been something sad, unutterably dreary in all this, had I not been conscious that it lay at my own option to recall whatever was valuable in the past" (I, 26) [22].

III

Dependence on an external object weakens a person's "own proper strength" and condemns him to a search for "support external to himself." Only a "slight . . . taste of office" infects one with a "singular disease" which torments the victim even after life has ceased. Public office robs the soul of its "sturdy force, its courage and constancy, its truth, its self-reliance, and all that gives the emphasis to manly character" (I, 39) [31]. Yet it is difficult to take this prating on self-reliance at face value, considering Hawthorne's own dependence on either "our common Uncle" or his maternal uncle, Robert Manning, for almost every position he ever held. An impenetrable goose may frustrate the Inspector but does not mediate the processes of consumption; recollection may provide temporary escape but cannot finally ameliorate the condition of decay. The surveyor, trapped in these processes which threaten to distintegrate him—he fears his intellect is "dwindling away; or exhaling . . . like ether out of a phial" (I, 38) [30], begins to drift toward paranoia.

Recollection is not only limited in its positive effect, but reveals a darker side as well. Hawthorne discovers the tale of the scarlet letter through "poking and burrowing," "unfolding" and "unbending" and "prying." He finds "traces of Mr. Pue's mental part, and the internal operations of his head" (I, 29–30) [25]. As if to absolve himself of a wrongful "intrusiveness" more characteristic of Chillingworth's "delving," "prying" and "probing" (I, 124) [83], he fantasizes the old surveyor delivering the manuscript to his hand. His intrusion into Surveyor Pue's "private" documents is sanctioned by his "filial duty and reverence" towards the surveyor's ghost. He becomes a collector of documents, not an inspector; and as if to discourage further intrusion, he vouches only for the "authenticity" of the "outline" of the tale, claiming nothing for its contents. Obsession with secrets implies not only the keeping of one's own but the disclosing of others', just as an obsession with eating implies not only consuming but being consumed. The two-person relationship, which allows for fusion and separation between self and other, cannot provide for a mediation between the two.

Hawthorne's attempt to mediate the processes of possession and intrusion forces him to become the "inevitable centre of the universe"; he is the one chosen by Surveyor Pue to bring Hester Prynne's tale to light and the one to assume his family's shame and to absolve the Hathornes of their "curse." Refusing to become "thoroughly adapted" to the Custom House, like the nameless and titleless "man of talent," Hawthorne recalls his Puritan ancestors, the witchcraft judge and the persecutor of the Quakers. When he takes their "shame" upon himself (I, 10) [12], he asserts for himself an objective identity, a self that distances him from his contemporaries even as it makes him visible to them. Through his family name, the spelling of which he altered slightly when he became a writer, he claims continuity with the Hathornes whose "persecuting spirit" had made them "conspicuous." Their shame protects the civil servant from anonymity, from being consumed by the present: even though an identification with his ancestors affords him a rather negative distinction, it makes him, if not noteworthy, then perhaps notorious.[4] It provides him with a kind of social reality, though perhaps incongruous or inappropriate, which suggests the possibility of a "real" Hawthorne. Though he takes upon himself their two-hundred-year-old shame, he only hints at the "strong traits of their natures"—perhaps a "hard severity" or a "persecuting spirit"—which remain hidden in his otherwise "inoffensive" character. The identification with his "great-grandsires" is further complicated, qualified by his professed guilt and inadequacy, his confessing himself an "idler" and his works "worthless, if not positively disgraceful."[5] He

4. Heinz Lichtenstein, "The Dilemma of Human Identity: Notes on Self-Transformation, Self-Objectivation, and Metamorphosis," *Journal of the American Psychoanalytic Association* 11 (1963): 215: "Shame occurs in such situations where the burden of identity and separateness, the loneliness of autonomy has become unbearable: the temptation to abandon it, to give up one's will, to become a slave, a physical thing, triumphs over our defenses."
5. Although the context renders these judgments ironic, Hawthorne did refer to *The Scarlet Letter* in a more serious vein as "positively a hell-fired story." Bridge, 112.

imagines their "compliments": "Why, the degenerate fellow might as well have been a fiddler!" (I, 10) [12]. Inward guilt in the face of his ancestors, like outward shame in the face of his community, seems to provide Hawthorne with a coherent sense of self, if coherent only insofar as the self focuses attacks from the community outside or from the guilt inside. As Frederick Crews has remarked, "Hawthorne's evocations of Puritan times gave him *a guilty identity, which was better than none*."[6] Hawthorne himself explains his need for social animosity: since, as a civil servant, "his interests are within the control of individuals who neither love nor understand him, . . . he would rather be injured than obliged" (I, 40) [32].

Throughout the sketch, he seems to invite notoriety, identifying himself with radical Jacksonians (as a "Loco-Foco Surveyor") and needling the Whigs whenever possible. Alternately, he identifies his interests with the loyal monarchist, Surveyor Pue, or his own shameful ancestors. These are, of course, so many more fictions, masks manipulated by Hawthorne. It is as if each pose, each objective identity, were calculated to entice the reader to infer the essential subjective Hawthorne, but each pose reveals a mass of contradiction on closer inspection. The Salem Whigs, led by the Reverend Charles W. Upham, accused Hawthorne of partisanship, of belonging to certain radical Democratic clubs, and of marching in torchlight parades. Hawthorne's defense was that he not only never belonged to such organizations, but he rarely even voted in elections—an admission which lost much of what little support he had among local Democrats. This is not to say that Hawthorne was a lukewarm Democrat or that he was politically naive; rather, he would prefer to present and manipulate an objective identity of his own. Careful readers may have found in the words of Hawthorne's "great-grandsires" not his ancestors' view of storytellers, but a close paraphrase of the "Loco-Foco" attack on anti-Democratic literature. When Hawthorne's friend, John L. O'Sullivan, assumed full control of *The Democratic Review*, he began by publishing literary manifestoes, one of which denounced aristocratic poets as "fiddlers." Petrarch was a prime example: a "passion suddenly conceived . . . by a priest . . . for the wife of another"—such a topic was "too nonsensical for a Yankee imagination" and could "never, under any circumstances, become popular" in America. The poetry, though "exquisite," was thus as "worthless . . . as a penny-whistle."[7] Hawthorne seems to have effectively criticized his own efforts through the words of his political allies and distanced himself—at least in his own mind, perhaps—from his most ardent political and literary supporters. They had cited Hawthorne as one of the "writers of the first class" who "have . . . expressed themselves plainly in the terms of the democratic creed," the foundation of which was the belief that "there is no hereditary line" of genius, intellect, or manly character.[8] Thus, it is doubly ironic that Hawthorne's ancestors, from whom he

6. Crews, 38.
7. "Petrarch," *The Democratic Review*, 11 (1842): 279–80.
8. "Democracy and Literature," *The Democratic Review*, 11 (1842), 199.

had inherited "strong traits," should condemn him on Democratic principles.

There is a further irony in the "shame" Hawthorne assumes on behalf of his ancestors. Upham had accused Hawthorne specifically of fraud and corruption and had compounded the insult by charging Hawthorne to have been the "abused instrument of others."[9] In his *Lectures on Witchcraft*, however, Upham had virtually ignored Hawthorne's ancestors, only twice even mentioning Judge John Hathorne. Years later, he would praise the Hawthorne family: "No one in our annals fills a larger space" than William Hathorne, and John "succeeded him in all his public honors." "The name is indelibly stamped on the hills and meadows of the region, as it was in the civil history of that age, and has been in the elegant literature of the present."[1] Hawthorne would probably have known Upham's earlier work, although the ironic nature of his family's shame would certainly have been lost on his readers. It is evident, however, that the shame he takes upon himself is largely of his own invention. Since he is dealing with those who "neither love nor understand him" and must be either injured or obliged (I, 40) [32], he at least chooses the shameful identity he will assume, the particular injury he will suffer. Of primary importance is self-preservation. He will not seem to be the "abused instrument" of petty grafters or political hacks, but an estranged Salemite, brooding guiltily over a shameful past. In this way, Hawthorne presents an invented self which seems to denote an almost inaccessible secret self that would rather be, or ought to be, hidden. The shameful, objective identity he adopts, then, allows him to balance between the threats of the intrusion of a hostile community and the isolation of absolute self-possession.

This compromise, which allows him to exist—albeit inauthentically—within the political community, is short-lived, however. The dependence which consumes the "manly" strength of the individual and the process of recollection, which is ultimately the self's intrusion into the contents of the past, are the positive aspects of life with the republican eagle. Negatively, the barbed arrows and thunderbolts in her claws threaten the young from their nest and this "inoffensive" public official with decapitation. Hawthorne seems to prefer this alternative, however, for half a man seems better than none and persecution does

---

9. Nevins, 118. This further insult must have been the cruelest blow for Hawthorne. Not only was he blamed for wrongdoing; he was not even given credit for having willfully done wrong. A similar situation had developed when Hawthorne was caught gambling while a college student, and his response is indicative of his need to control his own self-presentation. The Reverend William Allen, President of Bowdoin College, wrote to Mrs. Hawthorne, informing her of her son's transgressions but blaming them on "the influence of a student whom we have dismissed." Hawthorne wrote a rather perfunctory letter to his mother, admitting the charge, asking her not to show the official letter of reprimand to anyone, and adding a more serious charge of his own—the "Card Players" had gambled for a quart of wine. If to his mother he was unrepentant, to his sister he was defiant: "I was fully as willing to play as the person he suspects of having enticed me, and would have been influenced by no one. I have a great mind to commence playing again, merely to show him that I scorn to be seduced by another into anything wrong." Letters quoted in Manning Hawthorne, "Nathaniel Hawthorne at Bowdoin," *New England Quarterly* 13 (1940): 260–62.

1. Charles W. Upham, *Lectures on Witchcraft* (Boston: Carter, Hendee and Babcock, 1831), 24, 71–80; *Salem Witchcraft* (Boston: Wiggin and Lunt, 1867), I, 99–100.

imply a certain measure of notoriety. Life in the Custom House was "an unnatural state," and, like a person contemplating suicide who meets with "the good hap to be murdered," Hawthorne is freed from a false relation blamelessly when he is turned out of office. His "autobiographical impulse," too immodest for a living person, can "be excused in a gentleman who writes from beyond the grave" (I, 44) [34]. The "true relation" to the audience as a negation of the self, however, seems to defeat its purpose.

But Hawthorne is not content to leave himself dead and outcast, if true and free at last. The "real human being," he says, resides elsewhere. The Custom House and its circumstances are disconnected from his "recollections": "it ceases to be a reality of my life. I am a citizen of somewhere else" (I, 44) [35]. He resurrects himself to reject the Salem that rejected him and dreams of a future time when the locality of "The Town-Pump" will have been immortalized by one of his tales. The reversal is complete: through a fortuitous decapitation, Hawthorne has become central to Salem, eminently famous and totally untouchable.

IV

When Dimmesdale returns from the forest, possessed by an uncharacteristic energy, he views the settlement from a new perspective, as if all before had been a dream, or as if this new view were a dream. He realizes "wicked impulses" toward an old man and a devout widow. The voice of the "arch-fiend" tempts him, on seeing a young maiden, to "drop into her bosom a germ of evil that would be sure to blossom darkly soon, and bear black fruit betimes" (I, 220) [140].[2] He feels a secret camaraderie with "heaven-defying" seamen and with Mistress Hibbins, the "bitter-tempered widow of the magistrate." He returns home to his unfinished sermon, separates from Chillingworth his leech ("no more of your drugs"), and instead eats "with ravenous appetite" and gives vent to an "impulsive flow of thought and emotion," feeling himself all the while a "foul" medium for this energy (I, 224–25) [143]. All Hester can hear of this sermon on Election Day is an "indistinct, but varied, murmur,"[3] yet her sympathy is aroused in fairly sensual terms without benefit of the "grosser medium" of words. The "tone and cadence" of his "vocal organ" (a "rich endowment") communicates immediately "the complaint of a human heart, sorrow laden, perchance guilty, telling its secret" (I, 243) [154]. It is a sermon whose significance cannot adequately be expressed in words—only in a "tongue native to the human heart"—whose undercurrent of emo-

---

2. In his letter to Longfellow, Hawthorne threatened: "I may perhaps select a victim and let fall one little drop of venom on his heart, that shall make him writhe before the grin of the multitude for a considerable time to come" (MacShane, 98).
3. Compare *The American Notebooks*: Hawthorne's dying mother "could only murmur a few indistinct words. . . . I found the tears slowly gathering in my eyes. I tried to keep them down; but it would not be—I kept filling up, till, for a few moments, I shook with sobs. For a long time, I knelt there, holding her hand; and surely it is the darkest hour I have ever lived" (VIII, 429). Here, as in the romance, there is a communication immediately heard and felt, not distanced through sight or words.

tion cannot be mediated by the social and cultural institutions which frame it.

The background to this revelation is the resurgence of Elizabethan custom, not merely the conflated religious and legal rituals of the first chapters, but the melding of law and license in the carnival, the fusion of town and country, of sober Indians and drunken mariners, of law-abiding Puritans and men of the sea "unregulated by human law." At the center of this tumult, Hester is saved from "indistinctness" by the "talisman" of her letter, her public shame.[4] Pearl, too, as the "gem on her mother's unquiet bosom," stands in a "charmed circle," a space created by the simultaneous "attraction and repugnance of the mystic symbol" (I, 246) [156]. Dimmesdale, like an "oracle," speaks and en-rapts his listeners in a "high spell"; yet, as they "gush forth from the doors of the church" all in a "babble" with "applause for the minister," he appears spent, "deathlike." An uncharacteristic energy (which "might be spiritual") had propelled Dimmesdale's body in the proces-sion to the meeting house: "There was no feebleness of step . . . his frame was not bent" (I, 238) [151]. But leaving the church, he walks toward Hester with "the wavering effort of an infant, with its mother's arms in view, outstretched to tempt him forward" (I, 251) [159].

Dimmesdale will not be "tempted forward" in the way that Hester had wished, however, because he has annihilated himself and all ob-jects. He proclaims himself "the one sinner of the world," and through this act not only does he escape from Chillingworth, but from Hester too, to whom his feeble body finally "crept." There is little hope for re-union hereafter, he tells her rather unfeelingly (I, 256) [162], and Hawthorne surmises that even their dust has "no right to mingle" in the cemetery (I, 264) [166]. Dimmesdale's identification with a heav-enly father provides the hope which is the necessary motive for resolv-ing his torment in self-annihilation.[5] Within the religious schema, he

---

4. In his fine historical reading, Newberry argues that *The Scarlet Letter* concerns the conflict between a dominant Puritan militancy and recessive—primarily English—forces of "sympa-thy, charity, gaiety, respect for tradition, and appreciation of art" (1). "Hawthorne unmistak-ably presents English forms and traditions as positive historical origins from which, by and large, the Puritans have dissociated themselves" (19). Unfortunately, this view takes Hawthorne's nostalgia at face value. The recessive (actually, *regressive*) forces do not always yield "fond" memories of an English past (6); they provide Hester with an escape from the here-and-now of the scaffold in Boston, but they present her with—among other images—a "decayed house," her father's "bald brow," her mother's "look of heedful and anxious love" (I, 58) [43]. Origins are really the not-now for Hawthorne, just as England is the not-here. Threatened with an "intolerable burden of identity and separateness," as Lichtenstein would put it, Hester denies her reality: "Standing on that miserable eminence, she saw again her native village" (I, 58) [43]. Election Day presents the reverse situation: the Elizabethan fes-tival threatens to dissolve separate identities, transforming individuals into a motley throng: "rough figures" in "deer-skins" (I, 226) [144], groups of "painted barbarians," sailors with their "animal ferocity" (I, 232) [148], and the brown- and gray-clad Puritans. Here, Hester's gray cloth "had the effect of making her fade" while the scarlet letter "brought her back from this twilight indistinctness" (I, 226) [144]. These festivities—saved from their traditional ex-cesses by the grim keepers of Puritan law—seem more threatening than gay; and it is only Hester's shameful though exquisite production (whether her child or her art) that allows her an identity. For the community at large—as for Hawthorne personally—the choices are ex-treme: engulfment or isolation.

5. David Holbrook, "R. D. Laing & the Death Circuit," *Encounter* 31 (1968): 35–45, describes what he calls "schizoid suicide," a delusion that the suicide harbors (Sylvia Plath and Dylan Thomas are his prime examples): that he (or someone else) will rescue his true self from the torments of inauthenticity through his suicide.

has grasped God's will and thus has become a type of His justice and mercy; at the same time, he has delved within himself and exposed his secret to the world. As Hester supports Dimmesdale's body ("twine thy strength around me," he had asked), she becomes a type of medium through which these complementary revelations are accomplished. But when inner contents (His mercy, Dimmesdale's guilt) are revealed, Dimmesdale dies and with him all the relationships which those contents had "twined" together so hopelessly. Chillingworth's "life seemed to have departed" already on the scaffold and soon Hester and Pearl "disappeared," Hester to return later to her exile near Boston and Pearl to live forever "elsewhere." Dimmesdale's revelation itself becomes garbled in a host of conflicting reports and contradictory interpretations, and Hawthorne urges us to "Be true" by showing the world some "trait by which our worst may be inferred" (I, 260) [163]. At least, of all the morals which Dimmesdale's end brings to mind, this injunction only is "put . . . into a sentence." Relationships wind up split or fragmented with the disclosure of the secret.

Dimmesdale's experience is the tragic complement to Surveyor Hawthorne's and the decapitation and resurrection of the latter should alert us to the truths expressed in *The Scarlet Letter* as well as "The Custom-House." Unlike Dimmesdale, whose loss of self is irrevocable, Hawthorne seems content to give up pieces of himself—not his heart "delicately fried, with brain-sauce" (X, 33) to be sure—but enough of himself to entice his audience to infer his character from the traits he has offered. This is not Romantic self-expression by any means but an attempt to achieve fame without exposing the "inmost Me," to invent a self which appears real but in which he has a minimal investment. Hawthorne's insight into this problem of inauthenticity and his ambivalence concerning fusion and separation are particularly noteworthy because he is able to faithfully render such a dilemma while exerting a remarkable control over his material and his audience. His presentation is clearly manipulative—there is little feeling for a person suffering intolerably because he does not feel real, a person driven to suicide in the delusional hope that the "real human being" can be released from the sway of a false self. But this real human being did read Dimmesdale's rejection of life and Hester Prynne to Sophia Hawthorne shortly after writing it—"tried to read it, rather, for my voice swelled and heaved, as if I were tossed up and down on an ocean, as it subsides after a storm."[6] The next day he wrote his friend Horatio Bridge: the conclusion of the romance "broke her heart, and sent her to bed with a grievous headache, which I look upon as a triumphant success."[7]

I think Hawthorne realized at some level that, given his psychology, the alternative to self-annihilation was a denial of the claims of the

6. *The English Notebooks*, ed. Randall Stewart (New York: MLA, 1941), 225. The passage continues, "But I was in a very nervous state, then, having gone through a great diversity and severity of emotion, for many months past. I think I have never overcome my own adamant in any other instance."
7. Hawthorne to Bridge, February 4, 1850; quoted in Bridge, 111.

real world—a rejection on the order of Dimmesdale's though perhaps on a smaller scale. With his mother gone, there was no tie to Salem or to his paternal ancestors; and in the letter to Bridge quoted above, he expresses his desire to leave Salem, to invigorate himself elsewhere. Significantly, he asks Bridge not to mention his health in his own letters since "my wife already sermonizes me quite sufficiently on my habits; and I never own up to not feeling perfectly well." He never returned to Salem, and although he bought and christened "The Wayside" in Concord after his year in the Berkshires, he never felt as if he had a home again.[8]

With "The Custom-House," Hawthorne claims to give up that part of himself which has identified with Salem, with the ancestral dust in the native soil. But in the next year, he wrote *The House of the Seven Gables* from his rented house in Lenox, taking his revenge on Upham thinly disguised as Jaffrey Pyncheon; he tried to escape the hold of this fantasy of a dead patriarch within a maternal configuration, this time through an almost ritualistic repetition and undoing. His characters all leave Salem, but Hawthorne could never escape from that fantasy; it haunts his fiction, obsessively so in *The Marble Faun* and the unfinished romances. Salem might be rejected, as feared maternal figures could be rejected, but these are types of a deep fault which provided the design for his best fiction as it bound him to its psychological demands. Serving up "traits" to be analyzed, claiming nothing for their truth and denying any single interpretation, Hawthorne was able to maintain his "intercourse with the world"; but like Dimmesdale's more drastic loss of self, such a strategy could not resolve his dilemma. For Hawthorne, the problem seems only aggravated: to live is to exist inauthentically; to give up the falsehood, to expose the secret, to "Be true," is to perish.

DOUGLAS ANDERSON

Jefferson, Hawthorne, and "The Custom-House"†

The fullest accounts of the relationship of *The Scarlet Letter* to the political circumstances in which the book was written suggest that the novel's politics are every bit as complex as its formal, ethical, or psychological properties. Stephen Nissenbaum pointed out over a decade ago the extent to which Hawthorne's involvement in the local machinery of Democratic party patronage may well have shaped the moral and dramatic structure of the book. In the same year that Nissenbaum wrote, Henry Nash Smith suggested that the "ontological as well as

---

8. According to Julian Hawthorne, I, 429, "after freeing himself from Salem, Hawthorne never found any permanent rest anywhere. . . . A novelist would say that he inherited the roving disposition of his seafaring ancestors."
† From *Nineteenth-Century Literature* 46.3 (December 1991): 309–26. Copyright © 1991 by the Regents of the University of California. Reprinted by permission of the publisher. Page numbers in square brackets refer to this Norton Critical Edition.

epistemological uncertainties" of Hawthorne's text constituted a challenge to the public morality upon which American political life had
come to rely. Michael Davitt Bell insisted earlier still, in *Hawthorne
and the Historical Romance of New England*, that *The Scarlet Letter*
reflected its author's sense of the failure of the American utopian experiment. Perhaps most recently, Jonathan Arac has found the book to
be a complex fusion of radical and conservative elements—"propaganda," as Arac describes it, "*not* to change your life."[1]

Twenty years of concentrated attention upon the political implications of Hawthorne's book have produced no consensus on the author's purposes and sympathies. The subversive mingles with the
apologist in our accounts of Hawthorne's character, the artist with the
place-seeker, the critic with the defender of the status quo. Nor is it
reasonable to expect a less confused picture of personal and public
loyalties to emerge from a book published during one of the nation's
most dramatically divided periods by a writer with Hawthorne's complex personal and public history. What it is reasonable to require from
Hawthorne, however, is some recognition of the political entangle-
ments within which he works, a recognition that matches the degree
of sophistication he accords to his treatments of guilt, repentance, and
revenge in the body of the novel itself. Arac views the problem of accommodating the *Life of Franklin Pierce* to *The Scarlet Letter* as if it
were almost exclusively a task for modern criticism, when in fact it is
Hawthorne's personal dilemma to begin with and one that he chooses
to address by making textual adulteration a central concern of both his
book and his community. Acts of adulteration play a much more conspicuous and explicit part in the creation of Hester Prynne's story than
does the single act of adultery that leads to her disgrace.[2] The first of
those acts is one that Hawthorne takes as the basis of his response to
critics of "The Custom-House" in his preface to the second edition of
The Scarlet Letter. In its own way as extraordinary as "The Custom-
House" itself, this brief preface manages to evoke, as a background for
Hawthorne's own consideration of revisions and emendations in his
sketch of Salem life, the publicly amended status of the Declaration of
Independence.

It is not particularly surprising that Hawthorne should employ Jefferson's work as part of his own artistic and political design. Marion L.
Kesselring and Michael J. Colacurcio have reminded us repeatedly

---

1. See Nissenbaum, "The Firing of Nathaniel Hawthorne," *Essex Institute Historical Collec-
tions*, 114 (1978): 57–86; Smith, *Democracy and the Novel: Popular Resistance to Classic
American Writers* (New York: Oxford UP, 1978), 16–34; Bell, *Hawthorne and the Historical
Romance of New England* (Princeton, N.J.: Princeton UP, 1971), 190; Arac, "The Politics of
The Scarlet Letter," in *Ideology and Classic American Literature*, ed. Sacvan Bercovitch and
Myra Jehlen (New York: Cambridge UP, 1986), 247–66. A good biographical account of
Hawthorne's political circumstances between 1845 and 1850 is James R. Mellow's chapter
"A Dark Necessity," in *Nathaniel Hawthorne in His Times* (Boston: Houghton-Mifflin,
1980), 266–308.
2. Arac makes a point of connecting the absence of the words "adulterer" and "adultery" in *The
Scarlet Letter* with the omission of "slavery" from the Declaration of Independence and
the Constitution. But Hawthorne does call the bright sunshine that makes Pearl blink in the
novel's opening scene "unadulterated" and uses synonyms for the phenomenon of adulteration (to temper or to mingle, in most cases) pervasively in the book.

that Hawthorne's researches into the colonial past included a fascination with the central figures of the Revolution as well as with his seventeenth-century Puritan "fathers."[3] The disposition of patronage in
the Salem customhouse in Hawthorne's own day was still affected by
key appointments made as a result of service in the Revolution, among
them the appointment of the Permanent Inspector, the son of a Revolutionary War veteran, whose father had created a sinecure for him
and whose sensual nature becomes the butt of Hawthorne's humor in
"The Custom-House."[4] Surveyor Pue's fictive account of the life of
Hester Prynne remained in the customhouse attic, Hawthorne claims,
because the British did not think it had any official significance and so
left it behind in their withdrawal from Boston in 1775. And "The
Custom-House" itself amounts to a personal declaration of independence on Hawthorne's own part. Like the beleaguered British in some
respects, he too, with his family, is withdrawing from Salem, though
not as an unwelcome invader but as a native son with an intensely ambivalent relation to his ancestors.

All these connections to the historical and ideological background
of the Revolution are clear enough from "The Custom-House" alone,
without any additional assistance from the preface that Hawthorne
added less than a month after the first edition of *The Scarlet Letter*
had appeared. This rapid sale of his first novel was a triumphant exception to Hawthorne's previous literary experience, and the sense of
triumph shows in the tone he ultimately adopts in the preface toward
the "respectable community" that had taken offense at the excesses of
"The Custom-House." Hawthorne confesses to a mixture of surprise
and amusement at the outrage he has provoked, declares his determination to respond to "the public disapprobation" by editing his text,
but discovers upon rereading it nothing but "frank and genuine good-
humor" along with "general accuracy" in the portrayal of character:
"The sketch might, perhaps, have been wholly omitted, without loss to
the public, or detriment to the book; but, having undertaken to write
it, he conceives that it could not have been done in a better or a kindlier spirit, nor, so far as his abilities availed, with a livelier effect of
truth." The preface closes with Hawthorne's announcement that he is
"constrained, therefore, to republish his introductory sketch without
the change of a word."

The reasons why "The Custom-House" should have produced such
a "violent" response among Hawthorne's Salem neighbors are not immediately apparent even to historically informed readers. Before we
turn to some consideration of those reasons, however, it is important
to recognize that Hawthorne's professed intention, as he put it, "to al-

---

3. See Kesselring, *Hawthorne's Reading, 1828–1850: A Transcription and Identification of Titles
   Recorded in the Charge-Books of the Salem Athenaeum* (New York: New York Public Library,
   1949); and Colacurcio, *The Province of Piety: Moral History in Hawthorne's Early Tales*
   (Cambridge, Mass.: Harvard UP, 1984), 75.
4. See "The Custom-House" in *The Scarlet Letter*, ed. William Charvat, et al., vol. 1 of *The
   Centenary Edition of the Works of Nathaniel Hawthorne* (Columbus: Ohio State UP, 1962),
   16 [16]. Since the preface to the second edition is brief, and is quoted in full below, I have
   not included page numbers for it.

ter or expunge" his offending text, to make "reparation . . . for the
atrocities of which he has been adjudged guilty," echoes in an unmistakable way the key infinitives and the informing legal structure of the
Declaration of Independence. Like Jefferson's celebrated preamble,
Hawthorne's preface opens in an atmosphere of "decent respect to the
opinions of mankind" and closes—as the Declaration closes its recita-
tion of English atrocities—by acquiescing in the "necessity" to adhere to the truth of his introductory sketch of contemporary life.
Hawthorne even transplants the conclusive "therefore" of Jefferson's
peroration—"We therefore the representatives of the United States
of America"—to the one-sentence declaration of his own final intentions. Jefferson's more potent act of social revision—rooted in the
seventeenth- and eighteenth-century evolution of the concept of popular sovereignty and the nature of parliamentary representation—entails the power "to alter or abolish" inadequate governmental forms, a
power Jefferson further characterizes as the right "to expunge" former
systems of government.[5] The Continental Congress later rejected "to
expunge" in favor of repeating "to alter" in the Declaration's second
paragraph.[6] The Congress retained Jefferson's depiction of "the necessity which constrains" the colonies to act, and Hawthorne draws on all
these stages and features in the language of the Declaration in his
own assertions of revisionary power, "to alter or expunge," and in his
own surrender to the constraints of higher necessity. The language of
the opening paragraphs of the Declaration of Independence is familiar
to most readers, but it may prove useful to reproduce Hawthorne's
brief preface here in order to emphasize the care with which the allusion is woven into Hawthorne's own purposes:

> Much to the author's surprise, and (if he may say so without ad-
> ditional offence) considerably to his amusement, he finds that his
> sketch of official life, introductory to THE SCARLET LETTER, has
> created an unprecedented excitement in the respectable commu-
> nity immediately around him. It could hardly have been more
> violent, indeed, had he burned down the Custom-House, and
> quenched its last smoking ember in the blood of a certain venera-
> ble personage, against whom he is supposed to cherish a peculiar
> malevolence. As the public disapprobation would weigh very
> heavily on him, were he conscious of deserving it, the author begs
> leave to say, that he has carefully read over the introductory
> pages, with a purpose to alter or expunge whatever might be
> found amiss, and to make the best reparation in his power for the
> atrocities of which he has been adjudged guilty. But it appears to
> him, that the only remarkable features of the sketch are its frank
> and genuine good-humor, and the general accuracy with which
> he has conveyed his sincere impressions of the characters therein

5. For complete accounts of the tradition Jefferson wrote in, see Edmund S. Morgan, *Inventing the People: The Rise of Popular Sovereignty in England and America* (New York: W. W. Nor-ton & Company, 1988); and Garry Wills, *Inventing America: Jefferson's Declaration of Inde-pendence* (Garden City, N.Y.: Doubleday, 1978).
6. For Jefferson's text of the draft and emendations of the Declaration of Independence, see *Writings* (New York: The Library of America, 1984), 19–24.

described. As to enmity, or ill-feeling of any kind, personal or political, he utterly disclaims such motives. The sketch might, perhaps, have been wholly omitted, without loss to the public, or detriment to the book; but, having undertaken to write it, he conceives that it could not have been done in a better or a kindlier spirit, nor, so far as his abilities availed, with a livelier effect of truth.

The author is constrained, therefore, to republish his introductory sketch without the change of a word. [5]

Suggestive as the rhetorical and textual similarities are, it is the differences between Hawthorne's posture in his preface and that of Jefferson in the Declaration that matter. For one thing, Jefferson is writing on behalf of a community in response to offences committed against it. He is the plaintiff executing the right of petition in its final, revolutionary stage. Hawthorne, on the other hand, is the defendant answering communal accusations. His position is analogous to that of King George rather than the Continental Congress, a role that seems to suit the antidemocratic animus of "The Custom-House," in which Hawthorne portrays himself as the victim of the guillotine of the electoral spoils system (41) [32]. But more critical than this contrast in roles is the contrast between Jefferson's heavily edited language in the Declaration and Hawthorne's determination to let his own words stand. Part of the effect of the incorporation of Jefferson's deleted infinitive, "to expunge," into Hawthorne's preface is to call attention both to Hawthorne's own resolution and to the expedient nature of the Declaration itself. The first acts of alteration performed by the independent colonies were verbal rather than geopolitical, producing the first of several adulterated texts with which *The Scarlet Letter* deals.

Hawthorne's acquaintance with Jefferson's draft for the Declaration dates from the early 1830s, when he first read Jefferson's *Memoir* in an edition that included Jefferson's own meticulous system for indicating changes in the language of his most famous work.[7] The Fourth of July is Hawthorne's birthday, as well as the nation's, and year after year the conjunction of those two events must have come to seem peculiarly significant to an artist with a taste for the symbolically fateful coincidence. In his notebooks Hawthorne recorded at some length the holiday festivities in Salem on one such Fourth of July (1838), in which confectionery booths, spruce beer, wax exhibits, and all the details of the local celebration on the common conclude with Hawthorne's visit to the Charter Street burial ground, where he notes the sunken, moss-covered gravestone of John Hathorne, "the witch judge," surrounded by long grass.[8] Family identity and national identity mingled easily and vividly in Hawthorne's experience. His formal

---

7. Hawthorne checked out of the Salem Athenaeum the second edition of Jefferson's papers, *Memoir, Correspondence, and Miscellanies, from the Papers of Thomas Jefferson*, ed. Thomas Jefferson Randolph, 4 vols. (Boston: Gray and Bowen, 1830). The book's first edition appeared in Charlottesville, Virginia, a year earlier (see Kesselring, *Hawthorne's Reading*).
8. See *Hawthorne's Lost Notebook, 1835–1841: Facsimile from the Pierpont Morgan Library*, transcript and preface by Barbara S. Mouffe (University Park: Pennsylvania State UP, 1978), 66–67.

dismissal from his customhouse post came on 8 June 1849, but by his own account (and to some extent through his own efforts) his case was kept alive in the press "for a week or two" before all hope of rein-statement disappeared.[9] Independence Day 1849 marked in some measure, then, the resumption of the writer's vocation for Hawthorne, much as Hester Prynne's release from her confinement falls sometime in June or early July 1642, when she takes up residence and begins raising her child in a small cottage on the outskirts of Boston.

None of these details or biographical curiosities can really account for the verbal echoes of the Declaration of Independence in the pref-ace to *The Scarlet Letter*, but they tend to make a more convincing case for dwelling on Hawthorne's preoccupation with the mixed na-ture of ceremonial texts. Hester clearly is the first of these. Her puni-tive letter incorporates certain ornamental embellishments that some members of her audience find unacceptable or offensive. She has cos-tumed herself for her scaffold ordeal in a way that clashes both with her personal circumstances and with sumptuary law. The moment at which she steps forth into the public eye, she shrugs off the hand of the beadle and asserts her independence, though a few moments later she mounts the scaffold in a somewhat less rebellious manner, "know-ing well her part" in the theatrics of public punishment (55–56) [42].

The other two performers on this occasion convey equally mixed messages. Dimmesdale's appeal to Hester to name her lover seems ir-resistibly powerful to the crowd witnessing Hester's punishment, but Hawthorne makes its duplicity plain in his emphasis on the sensual intensity of Dimmesdale's pastoral exhortation. John Wilson professes to be reluctant to supplant Dimmesdale in the exercise of his respon-sibilities, but he proves to have supplied himself with a carefully crafted discourse "on sin, in all its branches" (68) [50] filled with timely references to Hester and consuming more than an hour of her ordeal. As his "periods were rolling over the people's heads" in a cas-cade of distinctly romantic rather than priestly oratory, it becomes clear that Wilson's sense of his occasion is as much political as it is re-ligious. In every respect Hester's punishment is a pre-vision of the Election festival at the close of the book, where Dimmesdale delivers another, more famous speech marked still more memorably in Hawthorne's account by its adulterated meanings: a triumphant pre-diction of a glorious future for New England, and an abject plea for forgiveness from a painfully burdened heart.

Dimmesdale makes a specialty of sermons that are really two texts rather than one. In this respect, however, he follows Hawthorne him-self, who claims in "The Custom-House" to be guided in the writing of

9. Nissenbaum points out that Hawthorne's successor in the customhouse did not receive his official commission until 24 July 1849 and that Hawthorne does not record his abandon-ment of hope (in a letter to Horace Mann) until 8 August 1849. But Edward Everett, then president of Harvard and one of Hawthorne's most influential allies, had read Charles Up-ham's decisive "Memorial" of accusations against Hawthorne's official conduct by late June 1849 and had formally withdrawn his letter of support for Hawthorne on 27 June 1849. Un-der these circumstances it would have been clear by Independence Day that Hawthorne's campaign for reinstatement would fail (see Nissenbaum, "The Firing of Nathaniel Haw-thorne," 71).

the novel by Surveyor Pue's manuscript report of Hester's life, but not at the expense of his own imagination. Indeed, he confesses to having "allowed myself . . . nearly or altogether as much license as if the facts had been entirely of my own invention" (33) [27], a fair description of Hawthorne's actual method of employing source material from Felt's *Annals of Salem*, *Magnalia Christi Americana*, or the *Collections* of the Massachusetts Historical Society in his tales and sketches. "The Custom-House" in effect describes a method of systematic adulteration that is only nominally a fiction. *The Scarlet Letter* is make-believe, but the process of writing that Hawthorne describes is not.

The pointed allusion to yet another conspicuously adulterated text in the preface to the book's second edition, then, is not so much an accident of birthdays and firings as it is fundamental to Hawthorne's procedures and meaning. Moreover, the particular adulterations of Jefferson's text of the Declaration, as his *Memoirs* record them, play a more decisive role in the writing of "The Custom-House" than may at first appear. The single change to which Hawthorne's preface calls our attention—the substitution of "to alter" for "to expunge" in Jefferson's second assertion of the fundamental right of revolution—is among the least consequential of Congress's modifications. But it does alert the reader to one pattern in those modifications: a consistent effort on the part of Congress as a whole to restrain Jefferson's most fervent rhetoric. The most extensive instance of this restraint occurs in the conclusion of the Declaration, where Congress opts "to publish and declare" their independence, to "absolve" themselves of allegiance to the crown, and to announce that their former political connections are "totally dissolved." Jefferson's draft text had begun its last paragraph with the determination "to reject & renounce all allegiance & subjection to the kings of Great Britain & all others who may hereafter claim by, through or under them," to "utterly dissolve" all connection not only with "the state of Great Britain" but with its people as well, and finally to "assert & declare" American independence (*Writings*, 24). Congress's final language is by no means ambiguous, but Jefferson's original text must have struck many of the representatives as overly impassioned for a public document, however appropriate it might have been to the impassioned sentiments of the time. The final version of the Declaration (not unlike the three central figures of *The Scarlet Letter*) represses the most turbulent emotions behind its composition. As Garry Wills has observed, the Continental "Congress" tended to be intensely interested in "egress"—in maintaining a possibility of withdrawal even from its most irrevocable acts, at least partly in response to the difficulty that the Congress confronted in securing any sort of consensus among its disparate and fragmented membership.[1]

More critical than this dimension of its repressed meaning, however, are the two other significant exclusions from the final text of the

1. See Wills, 49–64. See also Robert A. Ferguson, " 'We Hold These Truths': Strategies of Control in the Literature of the Founders," in *Reconstructing American Literary History*, ed. Sacvan Bercovitch (Cambridge, Mass.: Harvard UP, 1986), 1–28.

Declaration to which Wills and many others have called attention: the deletion of Jefferson's painfully contorted attempt to blame the King of England for imposing slavery upon the unwilling colonies, and the removal of Jefferson's implied defense of independence by virtue of expatriation—an argument that Wills convincingly connects with the earliest stages of awareness that an act of political "secession" conducted against England and based in part on geographic grounds held dangerous implications for the survival of any degree of unity among the geographically distinct American colonies themselves.[2] The Declaration of Independence, then, was a pivotal document in the history of disunion as well as union. The central position of the Fourth of July in American political life, particularly after the publication of Jefferson's *Autobiography* in 1829, only served to emphasize this paradox, as indeed Jefferson himself had done in 1821 when he recorded in papers he clearly envisioned for publication the Declaration's potentially very disturbing draft text.

Jefferson, then, is an early practitioner in the tradition of subversive oratory with which Michael T. Gilmore and John P. McWilliams have associated Hawthorne's first novel, but subversion scarcely seems adequate as a description of Jefferson's and Hawthorne's purposes.[3] Completeness was Jefferson's personal goal in the printing of his adulterated text of the Declaration, since (as he wrote in his *Autobiography*) "the sentiments of men are known not only by what they receive, but what they reject also" (*Writings*, 18). The deletions relating to slavery Jefferson explains in his introduction to the text of the Declaration as gestures of "complaisance" to South Carolina and Georgia, as well as to certain "northern brethren" who "felt a little tender" on the issue of northern involvement in the slave trade. Jefferson was willing to accommodate that tenderness in 1776, but he was not willing to forget it, particularly at the beginning of the series of political compromises with which the nineteenth century sought to address the ongoing dilemma of the existence and the potential extension of slavery. Indeed, Jefferson began composing his *Autobiography* in the months immediately following the resolution of the Missouri controversy, "a fire bell in the night," as Jefferson described it, which prompted him to wonder in a letter to John Adams whether the United States was destined to fragment into its own Athenian and Spartan camps, waging "another Peloponnesian war to settle the ascendancy between them."[4] A few months before that letter to Adams—after the first of the two compromises that permitted Missouri to enter the Union as a slave state while prohibiting the extension of slavery into other western territories north of a fixed line of latitude—Jefferson made clear the ominous implications he saw in permitting the country to divide itself in such a geographically stigmatized fashion: "A geo-

2. See Wills, 89.
3. See Gilmore, *The Middle Way: Puritanism and Ideology in American Romantic Fiction* (New Brunswick, N.J.: Rutgers UP, 1977), 107–14; and McWilliams, *Hawthorne, Melville, and the American Character: A Looking-Glass Business* (New York: Cambridge UP, 1984), 25–70.
4. *The Works of Thomas Jefferson*, ed. Paul Leicester Ford, 12 vols. (New York: Putnam, 1905), XII, 198.

graphical line," he wrote to John Holmes, "coinciding with a marked principle, moral and political, once conceived and held up to the angry passions of men, will never be obliterated; and every new irritation will mark it deeper and deeper" (*Works*, XII, 158).

It is a fairly modest imaginative leap from Jefferson's image of the acute sensitivities awakened by such a deepening mark in the national landscape to the acute sensitivities awakened in Hester Prynne by the analogous act of moral inscription that she experiences. Hawthorne is probably not engaged in excavating metaphors out of Jefferson's correspondence, but he clearly seems to be thinking along lines similar to those that prompted Jefferson's letter to Holmes. Jefferson's larger point in that letter is that the temporary accommodation reached by the Missouri Compromises of 1820 and 1821 was achieved at the price of a potentially catastrophic act of moral and political simplification. The immensely appealing duality of a pure versus an impure geography takes its first official form, as Jefferson sees it, in the language of these compromises. Colonial political experience and the history of the Revolution were inconsistent with that dualism, as was the textual evolution of the Declaration of Independence. Jefferson's decision to prepare his draft for publication at the time and in the manner that he did seems clearly motivated by a determination to resist that simplification and to make dramatically evident that a consensus for American liberty in 1776 was a consensus for American slavery as well. A painful adulteration of principle and of character is Jefferson's start-ing point for coming to grips with the unacceptable predicament of slavery in 1821, and to a surprising extent just such a painful adulteration forms the dramatic basis of "The Custom-House" as well, an adulteration less of principle directly than of community and of regional identity.

The single most insistent motif of Hawthorne's introductory biographical sketch is the phenomenon of adulterated identity invoked as a formal property of "The Custom-House" in its opening paragraphs, where Hawthorne characterizes his intentions as a peculiar mixture of confession and concealment. The process of adulteration extends itself thereafter to every term and character in the sketch. The present and the past, Hawthorne and his Salem ancestors, experience a sensuous sympathy of flesh with dust that unites them in spite of the profound spiritual and political differences that form part of Hawthorne's decision to break with his native town. The life of the artist and the life of the bureaucrat are apparently hostile to one another, yet an artist may at any time (Hawthorne claims) become a "man of affairs" and the customhouse itself contains the materials of great art: "A better book than I shall ever write was there; leaf after leaf presenting itself to me, just as it was written out by the reality of the flitting hour" (37) [30]. Great energy and great repose fuse in the beautiful inertia of General Miller, the Collector of the Customs at Salem and Hawthorne's immediate superior. For all of these instances of mingled or adulterated meaning Hawthorne's image of the artistically indispensable mingling of moonlight and firelight on his parlor floor serves as the emblem, but none of them suggests the same range of political ambition and political risk as does the author's conflation of "family" and "race" in his consideration of the Hawthorne ancestry.

To some degree the use of "race" as a synonym for "family" is conventional in Hawthorne's day, but the convention is an uneasily suggestive one in the context of the congressional debates leading to the Compromise of 1850—a package of legislation with which Hawthorne would later closely identify his friend Franklin Pierce—and in the town with the largest black population in Essex County.[5] When Hawthorne addresses himself to the "curse" incurred by the cruelties of his Puritan ancestors, and blames the bleak condition of the "race" of Hawthornes upon that inheritance, he openly invites his reader to recall the apocalyptic rhetoric of abolitionism, the spurious arguments of slaveholders appealing for justification to the biblical curse of Ham, and the present condition of the several hundred residents of Salem described in the official census as "colored persons." The town of Salem had segregated its public schools in 1807, when Hawthorne was three years old, and as late as 1834 the Salem School Committee reaffirmed its policy by voting to create a new North Salem school for blacks so that the town's regular schools would not have to accept black students.[6] Charles Wentworth Upham, Hawthorne's chief antagonist in the struggle to retain his customhouse post, was a member of that school committee. Much as the moral geography of Hester Prynne's Boston is distinguished by its twin landmarks of a prison and a cemetery, the landscape of Salem as Hawthorne depicts it in "The Custom-House" stretches down its "long and lazy" Main Street from Gallows Hill and New Guinea to the Almshouse (8) [10–11]—emblems of poverty and of the witchcraft persecution linked by Hawthorne in a grimly significant relation to the colloquial term for the local black ghetto. Even Hawthorne's passing reference in "The Custom-House" to the former glories of Salem's commercial life—"the old town's brighter aspect, when India was a new region, and only Salem knew the way thither" (29) [25]—may be a veiled reference to a less romantic, more complicated commerce. It was not India that formed Salem's chief trading partner in the years following the War of 1812, but Africa, the ports of Zanzibar and of the Gold Coast, where Salem's merchants exchanged calico cloth manufactured in New England mills out of Southern cotton for ivory, hides, pepper, and a gum resin used in the production of lacquers and varnishes in New England.[7]

---

5. See Barbara M. Solomon, "The Growth of the Population in Essex County, 1850–1860," *Essex Institute Historical Collections*, 95 (1959): 82–103.
6. For a summary discussion of the Salem schools, see Bernard Farber, *Guardians of Virtue: Salem Families in 1800* (New York: Basic Books, 1972), 167–72. Farber's chief source is "Extracts from the Salem School Committee Records," *Essex Institute Historical Collections*, 91 (1955): 24–74 (the passage in the records showing Upham's involvement in creating the North Salem school is on p. 71).
7. Salem's merchants did trade extensively with India, Sumatra, and the Philippines in the eighteenth century, but after the War of 1812 (in which most of Salem's merchant vessels were seized or destroyed) the Zanzibar trade—managed cleverly as a Salem monopoly—played a critical role in the town's economic survival. During Hawthorne's surveyorship, in fact, the Naumkeag Steam Cotton Company began operating in Salem to produce cloth locally for the Africa trade (see Richard H. Gates-Hunt, "Salem and Zanzibar: A Special Relationship," *Essex Institute Historical Collections*, 117 [1981]: 1–26).

This is not a commercial pyramid built upon the trade in rum and slaves, but moral complicity in Hawthorne does not have to be blatant in order to be telling. Like Jefferson's "northern brethren," Hawthorne's Salem neighbors were likely to be a little tender upon the subject of their relationship to the economics and the politics of race. "The Custom-House" touches upon that relationship with just enough authority to awaken that tenderness and—so Hawthorne must have felt—with just enough delicacy to avoid offense, at least in these preliminary details. The author has a bit of Roger Chillingworth's fine capacity to calculate just the degree of pressure to apply to Arthur Dimmesdale's tortured conscience without arousing his victim's suspicion.[8]

As "The Custom-House" presents the portrait of Hawthorne's fellow employees, however, the suspicion grows progressively more definite that the laziness, the inefficiency, the childlike "jollity," the sleepy conviviality of these old retired sea captains bears an uncomfortably close resemblance to the developing stereotypes of "southern" character in the years immediately preceding the Civil War. Hawthorne himself traces the behavior of his colleagues not to age but to the debilitating effects of a dependence "on charity, on monopolized labor, or any thing else but their own independent exertions" for existence (7) [9]. A little more than a year after the publication of *The Scarlet Letter* Harriet Beecher Stowe had Augustine St. Clare trace his own laziness to just these debilitating effects, but Hawthorne suggests that his own shiftless colleagues combine traits of the languid master and the childish slave: they lead lives of enervating leisure punctuated by the terrors of presidential elections that bring with them the prospect of losing their comfortable jobs. Hawthorne himself, as the new Surveyor, has the nearly anagrammatical double role of "overseer" among these aged public servants, and until he makes his generally sympathetic nature known, they view him with a degree of fear that Hawthorne finds painfully inconsistent with their age and experience, and at the same time amusing.

In the sketch of the Permanent Inspector a degree of amusement and of pain are evident as well, but Hawthorne's ridicule of this figure's robust indifference to every dimension of life outside of his digestion just thinly masks the metaphor of livestock that summarizes the repellent image of the slave auction in the highly charged political rhetoric of abolitionism. The analogies between Hester's exposure on the scaffold and the exposure of a slave for sale are clear enough in the opening scene of the novel, even to Chillingworth's distant admonishment to his wife, from the edge of the marketplace, that begins with a raised finger and the "gesture" of a bid (61) [45]. But no one in

---

8. Hawthorne's own conscience too is implicated in this network of trade. As he observes in "The Custom-House," his name was stenciled on all the bales of incoming merchandise to prove that they had paid the import duty: "Borne on such queer vehicle of fame, a knowledge of my existence, so far as a name conveys it, was carried where it had never been before, and, I hope, will never go again" (27) [23].

Hester's audience underestimates her dignity or the seriousness of her emotional and spiritual plight. In Hawthorne's caricature of the Permanent Inspector, on the other hand, all of the invidious assumptions of slavery are present. A life of "careless security" had left this "patriarch" of all customhouse officials little better than an animal, the "very trifling admixture of moral and spiritual ingredients" in his nature being "in barely enough measure to keep the old gentleman from walking on all-fours" (17) [17]. His age belies his remarkable vigor, his "thorough healthfulness and wholesomeness," and he is not encumbered with inconvenient family sentiments. Wives and children have come and gone in his existence and left not the least residue of sorrow. In effect, in every respect except his physical health, he is a kind of anticipatory inversion of Uncle Tom—an exemplary slave by Haley's standards rather than Stowe's—and Hawthorne does everything in his power except comment on the condition of the Permanent Inspector's teeth to make the nature of the characterization clear. Part of Stephen Nissenbaum's admiration for "The Custom-House" derives from the extent to which Hawthorne appears to have resisted the temptation to retaliate directly upon his political opponents among Salem's Whigs, and it is true that to this local degree at least Hawthorne depoliticizes his text. But in the process of doing so he elicits and sets in motion the deepest political and moral passions of his time, far more consequential and menacing issues than the effects of the party spoils system on the livelihood of Nathaniel Hawthorne.

It is not whether the Salem customhouse is Whig or Democrat that engages Hawthorne's interest for the moment but whether it, or the community it serves, is implicated in and perhaps degraded by a far more extensive and truly inhumane system of "spoils." This is the question that is implicit in many of the features of the sketch, in Hawthorne's evocation of the idea of "race," in the segregated geography of the town, in the portrait of his fellow workers, and to some extent in the architecture of the customhouse itself. Salem by the time of Hawthorne's surveyorship had become an economic backwater and the facilities of its port were in decline, the wharf "dilapidated," grass growing up around little-used warehouses, the customhouse unfinished and likely to remain so (4–5) [8]. In every detail the port of Salem was the opposite of the ideal Yankee standard of bustling enterprise, a perfect setting for the shiftless loafers who inhabited it and an equally perfect New England version of the kind of decayed commercial life that John Pendleton Kennedy described in parts of *Swallow Barn* (1832), his sketchbook of "A Sojourn in the Old Dominion." It is difficult to confirm that Hawthorne had read Kennedy's book. Unlike his well-documented historical researches in the library of the Salem Athenaeum, most of the contemporary novels he read seem to have come from a local circulating library (or from personal collections) from which no records survive. He knew Kennedy well enough by name to seek him out in Rome in 1858, however, and in all likelihood it was an acquaintance Hawthorne sought because of the popular reputation of *Swallow Barn* more than twenty years earlier.[9] One of Kennedy's sketches in the book is of a Fourth of July discussion on states' rights that takes place at "The Landing," a plantation river port that, like Salem, has fallen on hard times:

> The Landing, which we had now reached, had originally been used for a foreign trade, in which vessels of a large class, a long time ago, were accustomed to receive freights of tobacco, and deposit the commodities required by the country, in return. It is now, however, nothing more than the place of resort for a few river craft, used in carrying the country produce to market. There were two or three dilapidated buildings in view, and, among these, one of larger dimensions than the rest, a brick house, with a part of the roof entirely gone. A rank crop of Jamestown weed grew up within, so as to be seen through the windows of the first story. Indian corn was planted on the adjacent ground up to the walls, and extended partly under the shelter of a few straggling old apple-trees, that seemed to stand as living mementoes of an early family that had long since been swept from beneath their shade . . . What was once the warehouse, but now used for a ferry-house, stood with its gable end at the extremity of a mouldering wharf of logs. In this end there was a door studded with nails and another above it opening into the loft. The ridge of the roof projected over these doors and terminated in a beam, where were yet to be seen the remains of a block and tackle. On the land side the building was enlarged by sheds, to which was appended a rude porch. A sun-dried post supported what was once a sign, whereon a few hieroglyphics denoted that this was a place of entertainment, notwithstanding its paper-patched windows and scanty means of accommodation.[1]

The national holiday brings out a larger and livelier crowd around Kennedy's wharf than generally circulates around Hawthorne's, but the settings are sufficiently similar to suggest the sort of implication an alert reader of "The Custom-House" might reasonably have drawn from Hawthorne's characterization of the Salem economy.

The adulterations that shape "The Custom-House," then, range more widely than the personal history of the Hawthorne family and the peculiar needs of a literary artist at first suggest. Hawthorne's subtext is Salem and slavery, New England and the South, drawn together in an intricate network of associations that resembles the complex art of Hester's embroidered letter—needlework that is too subtle to unravel in either its literal or its metaphorical implications. Like Jefferson's more intricate presentation of the Declaration of Independence in his *Autobiography*, Hawthorne's Salem appears as an amalgam both of what it receives and what it rejects. More importantly, Salem itself is a part of the larger political and moral adulteration that is expressed

9. See Hawthorne, *The French and Italian Notebooks*, ed. Thomas Woodson, vol. 14 of *The Centenary Edition* (Columbus: Ohio State UP, 1980), 105.
1. *Swallow Barn; or, A Sojourn in the Old Dominion* (Baton Rouge: Louisiana State UP, 1986), 158–59.

in its national government, in the formative documents of that government, and in the character of the founders. Strong traits of their nature too, Hawthorne seems to suggest, have intertwined themselves with our own, and if the results are indeterminate, as many readers have been inclined to claim, then it is an indeterminacy that springs from the textual condition of Jefferson's indeterminate Declaration. The act of asserting such a lineage is in many respects conservative, just as the *Life of Franklin Pierce* bases its political case in large part upon the candidate's distinguished father, General Benjamin Pierce, a hero of the Revolution, to whom Hawthorne repeatedly refers as the primary moral influence upon the mind and career of his son. The preface to *The Scarlet Letter*, however, reaches behind acts of hagiography, justified or unjustified, to a moment when Thomas Jefferson was (like Hawthorne himself) seized by an autobiographical impulse and, without violating his own impenetrable reserve, showed freely to the world traits by which the worst might be inferred.

The Scarlet Letter

MICHAEL WINSHIP

Hawthorne and the "Scribbling Women": Publishing *The Scarlet Letter* in the Nineteenth-Century United States†

Besides, America is now wholly given over to a d——d mob of scribbling women, and I should have no chance of success while the public taste is occupied with their trash—and should be ashamed of myself if I did succeed. What is the mystery of these innumerable editions of the Lamplighter, and other books neither better nor worse?—worse they could not be, and better they need not be, when they sell by 100,000.

It may well be that no single passage written by Nathaniel Hawthorne is better known than this or, at least over the past few decades, more widely quoted.[1] An extraordinary possibility, especially as the passage comes from the middle of a rather long private letter, written to his publisher and friend William D. Ticknor on January 19, 1855, and first published only in 1910.[2] Nevertheless, this passage has resonated through recent discussions of American literary history, for it raises questions that are key to our understandings of that tradition: What is the relationship between popular success and literary quality? What role do gender politics play in our assessment of a work? In what ways have the economic factors facing authors and publishers fostered or discouraged authorship in the United States? And how is it that during the 1850s, a decade that came to be dubbed the "American Renaissance," sentimental novels could have enjoyed such popular success, while the "classics" by Hawthorne, Melville, Thoreau, and Whitman did not?

Although he could hardly have thought in such terms, clearly these issues bothered Hawthorne as he pondered in what direction to continue his literary career. He returned to the subject in his very next let-

† From *Studies in American Fiction* 29 (Spring 2001): 3–11. Copyright © Northeastern University. Reprinted by permission of the publisher and the author.

1. Letter, Nathaniel Hawthorne to William D. Ticknor, January 19, 1855, in Nathaniel Hawthorne, *The Letters, 1853–1856*, ed. Thomas Woodson et al., *The Centenary Edition of the Works of Nathaniel Hawthorne*, vol. 16 (Columbus: Ohio State UP, 1987), 304. Hereafter cited parenthetically by volume and page number.
2. In Nathaniel Hawthorne, *Letters of Hawthorne to William D. Ticknor, 1851–1864* (Newark: Carteret Book Club, 1910), 73–76, and again in Caroline Ticknor, *Hawthorne and His Publisher* (Boston: Houghton Mifflin, 1913), 141.

ter to Ticknor, written two weeks later, but here at least he selects one of that "scribbling mob," Fanny Fern, for praise.[3] His original outburst had been directed specifically at the work of another, Maria Susannah Cummins, whose best-selling novel *The Lamplighter* was making a tremendous success. Published in early March 1854, this work is reported to have sold 20,000 copies in twenty days, and 40,000 copies in eight weeks. By year's end, nearly 75,000 copies had been produced; by the end of the decade, total sales in the United States were somewhere around 90,000.[4] Nevertheless, Hawthorne clearly exaggerated when in his exasperation he claimed that books written by women were selling by the hundred thousand. Although sales of *The Lamplighter* approached that figure, its success was exceptional, and its sales were not matched by other novels of the decade. The exception, of course, was Harriet Beecher Stowe's *Uncle Tom's Cabin*, which indeed did sell in the hundred thousands—around 310,000 copies during the 1850s.[5]

Hawthorne's frustration is understandable. Consider his most popular work, *The Scarlet Letter*, which was published in March 1850: only 11,800 copies had been produced by 1860. For the short term at least, sales of his works had to be reckoned in the thousands instead of tens of thousands, much less hundreds of thousands. But as we pass the sesquicentennial of the original publication of *The Scarlet Letter*, it pays to look at the longer term. What was the publication history of the work for the remainder of the nineteenth century? And how does this history compare to that of *Uncle Tom's Cabin*? What can the comparison tell us about these works' subsequent histories and reputations?

The story of the composition and original publication of *The Scarlet Letter* is well known.[6] Hawthorne, who was an established writer of short stories and sketches, began work on the manuscript sometime—probably late summer—during 1849, the same year that he was dismissed from his job at the Salem Custom House. Before year's end, the Boston publisher James T. Fields called on Hawthorne in Salem and came away with a draft of "The Scarlet Letter," which Hawthorne imagined as one of several stories in a collection to be called *Old-Time Legends* (or possibly *The Custom-House*). Fields encouraged Hawthorne to consider expanding the work for separate publication,

3. Letter, Nathaniel Hawthorne to William D. Ticknor, February 2, 1855, CE 16: 307–8.
4. See advertisements and notices in *Norton's Literary Gazette* April 1, 1854, May 1, 1854, and Dec. 15, 1854. The total sales are difficult to know precisely: the work's publisher, John P. Jewett, lists the eighty-ninth thousand in his catalog dated April 1, 1858; *American Publishers' Circular* 4 (Aug. 14, 1858): 391, gives the total as 90,000. These figures do not account for the many thousands that must have been produced and sold in Great Britain.
5. *American Publishers' Circular* 4 (Aug. 14, 1858): 391, gives the following totals for American fiction: Stowe's *Uncle Tom's Cabin* (1852), 310,000; Cummins's *The Lamplighter* (1854), 90,000; Fanny Fern's *Fern Leaves* (1853), 70,000, and *Ruth Hall* (1855), 55,000; Martha Stone Hubbell's *The Shady Side* (1853), 42,000; Marion Harland's *Alone* (1854), *The Hidden Path* (1855), and *Moss Side* (1857), 25,000 each.
6. The following account is based on William Charvat, "Introduction," in *The Scarlet Letter*, ed. William Charvat et al., *The Centenary Edition of the Works of Nathaniel Hawthorne*, vol. 1 (Columbus: Ohio State UP, 1962), xv–xxviii, supplemented with information taken from *The Cost Books of Ticknor and Fields and Their Predecessors, 1832–1858*, ed. Warren S. Tryon and William Charvat (New York: Bibliographical Society of America, 1949), and C.E. Frazer Clark, *Nathaniel Hawthorne: A Descriptive Bibliography* (Pittsburgh: U of Pittsburgh P, 1978).

and Hawthorne eventually agreed. On January 15, 1850, Hawthorne sent the revised manuscript to Fields, including the introductory "Custom-House" sketch but missing three chapters, which were sent on to Boston on February 3. In the meanwhile, Fields had gone ahead with production, putting typesetters to work, and by February 18 he was able to include the sheets "as far as printed" in a parcel sent to the London publisher Richard Bentley. On March 16 the first edition of 2,500 copies appeared at a retail price of 75 cents and bound in the characteristic Ticknor and Fields binding of brown ribbed T cloth.

As Fields had hoped but to Hawthorne's apparent surprise, the work was both well received and a moderate success.[7] A second edition of 2,500 copies was issued on April 22, containing a new preface by Hawthorne dated "March 30, 1850," and a third edition of 1,000 copies, for the first time printed from stereotype plates, followed on September 9. By year's end, Hawthorne had earned $663.75 in royalties—his royalty was reckoned at fifteen percent of the retail price—while the publisher's profits came to roughly $900, even after paying for the cost of the stereotype plates. These results were in part due to Fields's talents as a publisher, for he was skilled at managing the publicity of announcements, advertisements, and a network of sympathetic reviewers to push his firm's publications.[8]

In one regard, though, Fields fell short, for in rushing the work into publication, he failed to allow time for arrangements for an authorized English edition. British copyright law required that such an edition appear before or simultaneously with the American edition, but by the time that Bentley, the London publisher that Fields had approached, received the entire text, it had already been published in Boston. Bentley reported that two other firms were preparing unauthorized editions and declined to publish the work. In the event the work was not reprinted in England until May 1851, though imported copies of the American sheets had been available earlier.

The wish to rush the work into publication may also explain in part why the firm printed the first two editions from type instead of from stereotype plates, although this is not as surprising as it may at first appear. Only a few years later, the firm's standard practice would become to print most of its new publications from plates; in 1850, however, only four of its eighteen new works were stereotyped for the first printing. The reason may have been financial, as the firm was in the process of expanding its list and may have wished to avoid the extra investment that plates entailed. The cost of producing stereotype plates nearly doubled the cost of composition: in the case of *The Scarlet Letter* composition for the first two editions came to $130.11 and

7. The reception history of *The Scarlet Letter* can be traced in *The Critical Response to Nathaniel Hawthorne's* The Scarlet Letter, ed. Gary Scharnhorst (New York: Greenwood P, 1992). For a more general discussion of Hawthorne's reputation over time, see Richard H. Brodhead, *The School of Hawthorne* (Oxford: Oxford UP, 1986).

8. *Cost Books of Ticknor and Fields*, entries A173a, A79a, A189a; see also William Charvat, "James T. Fields and the Beginnings of Book Promotion," in *The Profession of Authorship in America, 1800–1870: The Papers of William Charvat*, ed. Matthew J. Bruccoli (Columbus: Ohio State UP, 1968), [168]–189.

$121.57, respectively, whereas the cost of composition and stereotyping for the third was $233.39. Clearly it would have been more economical to produce the plates immediately, though the firm may not have expected the work to have such success.[9]

Despite these oversights, Hawthorne was surely pleased with Fields's handling of the work's publication, for over the next several years Fields's firm, Ticknor and Fields, was to reissue many of Hawthorne's earlier works and to publish his new works as they were finished. Hawthorne himself was to form close personal ties with both partners, and Ticknor and Fields and its successor firms remained Hawthorne's primary publisher for the rest of the century. Thus, Hawthorne's works formed a key part of the core list of canonical American literary works—including those of Emerson and Thoreau—that modern scholars have come to associate with Houghton, Mifflin & Co., the firm into which Ticknor and Fields evolved.

Harriet Beecher Stowe was less fortunate in her original choice of publisher for *Uncle Tom's Cabin*, Boston's John P. Jewett. Despite the work's tremendous initial success, and despite the skillful promotional efforts of its publisher, demand fell off markedly after little over a year. Shortly thereafter Stowe fell out with Jewett over contract terms, and for future works she turned for a second time to another Boston publisher, Phillips, Sampson & Co., a firm that had originally declined to publish her anti-slavery masterpiece. After the break with Stowe, Jewett remained the publisher of *Uncle Tom's Cabin*, but it cannot have brought him much profit: he nearly failed during the Panic of 1857 and finally dissolved his publishing business in 1860. In 1859 Stowe's chief publishers, Phillips, Sampson & Co., also went out of business, and in consequence she approached Fields to act as her publisher. When Stowe's works joined those of Hawthorne on the list of Ticknor and Fields in 1860, *Uncle Tom's Cabin* had been, for all intents and purposes, out of print for many years.[1]

In the meanwhile Hawthorne's *Scarlet Letter* had remained happily in print with steady sales, which declined only slightly as time passed. The investment in stereotype plates for the third edition of September 1850 allowed the firm to produce small impressions over time as demand required. A second printing from these plates—the fourth printing of the work over all—of 800 copies was produced in June 1851, and between then and Hawthorne's death on May 19, 1864, the plates were used for thirteen impressions of 500 copies each, a total of 6,500 copies at an average of one impression per year.[2]

9. *Cost Books of Ticknor and Fields*, entries A173a, A79a, A189a. For a general discussion of the firm's practice in regard to printing from plates, see Michael Winship, *American Literary Publishing in the Mid-Nineteenth Century: The Business of Ticknor and Fields* (Cambridge: Cambridge UP, 1995), 103–10, 142–47. It should be noted that the relatively large press runs for the first two editions reflect the fact that they were printed from type instead of plates.

1. Fields was in no hurry to rush it back into print: his firm's first printing, a mere 270 copies, was not completed until November 1862. For the history of the publication of *Uncle Tom's Cabin*, see Michael Winship, " 'The Greatest Book of Its Kind': A Publishing History of *Uncle Tom's Cabin*," *Proceedings of the American Antiquarian Society* 109 (1999): 309–32.

2. Ticknor and Fields, Cost Books, fair, A–D, in the Houghton Library, Harvard University (MS Am 2030–2, items 14–17).

Hawthorne's death occurred a little over a month after that of William D. Ticknor, the senior partner of Ticknor and Fields, which had occurred on April 10, 1864, while Hawthorne and Ticknor were on a vacation trip to the South that, it was hoped, would revive Hawthorne's failing health. Inevitably, these deaths had an effect on the publication of Hawthorne's works, including *The Scarlet Letter*. Hawthorne's business relations with Ticknor and Fields had been complicated, based on a series of verbal agreements that stipulated that the royalties on his works were set at varying terms, at ten percent of the retail price for some and fifteen percent for others. Once the firm was reorganized and Fields firmly in charge as senior partner, he arranged to regularize matters, and it was agreed that the firm would in future pay a flat sum of 12 cents for each copy sold of any of Hawthorne's works.[3]

The fairness of this new arrangement is difficult to assess. At the time, it certainly seemed generous, for 12 cents a copy represented an increase in royalty on *The Scarlet Letter*, from 11 1/4 cents to 12 cents. Similarly, it meant an increase in royalty for all of Hawthorne's other works save two—*The House of the Seven Gables* and *Our Old Home*—that were earning 15 cents per copy under the old arrangement. The problem, however, arises from the shift in the method of determining royalties from a percentage basis to a flat fee. Retail prices for books had remained remarkably stable throughout the 1840s and 1850s, but the Civil War had brought about a period of inflation and a consequent increase in book production costs, which in turn inevitably led to an increase in retail prices, a result that Fields must have foreseen. By the late 1860s, retail prices on all of Hawthorne's works had risen to $1.50 or $2.00, which meant that the royalty on *The Scarlet Letter*, for example, would have risen under the old agreement to 30 cents a copy. From this perspective, Fields had struck a very hard bargain indeed.

Conflict was inevitable. Hawthorne's widow, Sophia, raising three children alone, found herself strapped financially and sensed that perhaps Hawthorne's royalties were less than they should be. Her suspicions seemed confirmed in 1868, when Gail Hamilton, another Ticknor and Fields author whose royalty terms had been changed in 1864 in a manner similar to Hawthorne's, began to raise questions. Upset, Sophia Hawthorne even went so far as to threaten to transfer future rights in her husband's works to another firm. Fields reacted quickly: he prepared an explanation, backed by figures, and offered to submit the matter to arbitration. Eventually Sophia Hawthorne's sister Elizabeth Peabody intervened. After examining the firm's accounts, she came to the conclusion that, despite several clerical errors and other carelessness, the firm's records were consistent with each other, but she also noted that demand had been such that neither author nor firm had received as much as $1000 per year on average in income from Hawthorne's books. Ticknor and Fields was technically vindi-

---

3. For this and the next paragraph, see Ellen B. Ballou, *The Building of the House: Houghton Mifflin's Formative Years* (Boston: Houghton Mifflin, 1970), 142–56; Tryon, 333–49.

cated, but relations were soured. In an attempt to placate Sophia Hawthorne, Fields offered to pay in future a royalty of ten percent on all of Hawthorne's works. These terms were agreed to and remained in force until 1875, when Hawthorne's heirs accepted the firm's offer of a regular annuity of $2,000 in lieu of royalties.[4]

Hawthorne's death in 1864 was to have another important impact on the publication of *The Scarlet Letter*, for in the fall of that year the firm issued the first collected edition of Hawthorne's works. *The Scarlet Letter*, printed from the 1850 plates, appeared as volume six of fourteen in this so-called "Tinted Edition" (A16.3q; B1). A second collected edition was issued in 1871, and the same plates were used for *The Scarlet Letter*, which appeared bound with *The Blithedale Romance* as volume four in a twelve-volume "Illustrated Library Edition" (A16.3.w; B2). This trend continued, for when new plates for *The Scarlet Letter* were finally cast in 1875, they were for use in the twenty-three-volume "Little Classic Edition" of Hawthorne's collected works (A16.8.a; B5). A third set of plates, cast in 1883, was prepared for the "Riverside Edition" (A16.13.a; B9), where *The Scarlet Letter* appeared, again bound with *The Blithedale Romance*, as volume five of twelve. These sets of Hawthorne's collected works were expanded as posthumous works appeared and, over the years, were repackaged and reissued in a variety of formats and bindings at a range of prices, but for the rest of the century *The Scarlet Letter* was generally speaking marketed as part of his collected works, and not singly as Hawthorne's greatest masterpiece.[5]

Hawthorne and Stowe shared the same publisher from 1860, but the pattern of publication of their works was quite different. *Uncle Tom's Cabin* clearly stood out among Stowe's works, not just in terms of importance but also income: by the end of the 1880s her earnings from *Uncle Tom's Cabin* equaled nearly two and a half times the combined royalty on all her other books. Unlike *The Scarlet Letter*, which had been chiefly available as part of a set of Hawthorne's collected works since his death in 1864, *Uncle Tom's Cabin* was chiefly sold by itself. Stowe, who survived Hawthorne by over thirty years, continued to produce new works through the 1870s, and there was no collected edition of Stowe's works until after her death in 1896.

And what of the sales of the two works? *The Scarlet Letter* started out at considerable disadvantage, but as time passed and sales increased, the difference grew less striking. During the 1860s, roughly 6,500 copies of *The Scarlet Letter* were produced, compared to 8,000 copies of *Uncle Tom's Cabin*; during the 1870s, roughly 20,000 copies, compared to 26,000 copies of *Uncle Tom's Cabin*.[6] In 1878, with the formation of a new business partnership, the stereotype plates of the

4. Ballou, 242, states that the offer was not accepted due to wrangling among Hawthorne's children but the firm's records indicate otherwise; see "Agreement No. 2," May 1, 1875, in the uncataloged Houghton Mifflin contract files in the Houghton Library, Harvard University (MS Storage 288, box 34).

5. See Frazer Clark, *Nathaniel Hawthorne*, for details; references to entries to this bibliography are given in parentheses in text.

6. These figures are based on Ticknor and Fields & Houghton, Osgood & Co., Sheet Stock Books, in the Houghton Library, Harvard University (fMS Am 2030.2, item 22–23, & fMS AM 2030, item 16).

two works were inventoried and valued, a figure that served as a guide to estimating the worth of the rights to their publication: the plates of *The Scarlet Letter* were valued at \$4,792.38; those for *Uncle Tom's Cabin* at \$4,524.60.[7]

Although *The Scarlet Letter* was chiefly marketed as part of Hawthorne's collected works, it was also issued from time to time in separate editions. In late 1877, as the end of the original copyright term of twenty-eight years approached, James R. Osgood & Co., a successor firm to Ticknor and Fields, issued the first new separate edition of *The Scarlet Letter* (A16.10). With rather lavish illustrations by Mary Hallock Foote, this was an expensive volume at \$4 in cloth, \$9 in leather. The illustrations may have been intended to support the firm's claim in the work, though the copyright in the text could be and was renewed and protected for a further fourteen years. In 1879 Houghton, Osgood & Co., another successor firm, issued for \$10 F. O. C. Darley's *Compositions in Outline from Hawthorne's* Scarlet Letter, a series of 12 illustrated prints, each accompanied by a page of text extracted from Hawthorne's work.[8]

During the 1880s, both Hawthorne's works and *Uncle Tom's Cabin* continued as steady sellers, although developments in the book trade were troubling. Throughout the decade the market for books was bedeviled by pirates and undersellers, an emerging group of publishers and booksellers who took advantage of the lack of international copyright on British works and the increasing use of trade sales as a means of dumping surplus or out-of-date stock to flood the market with cheap books. As an established trade publisher, Houghton, Mifflin & Co., the final inheritor of the rights to the works of both authors, was well aware of the losses caused by these practices. The threat was exacerbated by the fact that early in the 1890s the copyrights on both *The Scarlet Letter* and *Uncle Tom's Cabin* were due to expire, and these works were destined to enter the public domain.[9]

During fall 1891, the editors at Houghton, Mifflin discussed strategies for the continued publication of both works while they planned new and cheap editions that they hoped would maintain their control of the market. The main issue under discussion was the timing for issuing these new editions, but things came to a head in spring 1892, when the firm learned that new plates of both works were already being prepared for sale to the publishers of cheap publications. Legal

7. Ticknor and Fields, "Plate Inventory (1873–77)" in the Houghton Library, Harvard University (fMS Am 2030.2, item 25).

8. For a full discussion of the illustrated editions of *The Scarlet Letter*, see Rita K. Gollin, "The Scarlet Letter" in "From Cover to Cover: The Presentation of Hawthorne's Major Romances," *Essex Institute Historical Collections* 127 (1991): 12–30.

9. Curiously, Houghton, Mifflin & Co. seems to have been confused about the actual date that both works were destined to become public property. At this period legal copyright in a work was established when it was registered and a pre-publication title page was filed in the District Court Clerk's office: the original term of twenty-eight years thus established could then be renewed for a further fourteen years. The copyright on *Uncle Tom's Cabin* was thus destined to expire on May 12, 1893, though in late 1891 Henry Oscar Houghton was under the mistaken impression that the date was 1892. Similarly, the firm maintained that the copyright on *The Scarlet Letter* expired on November 15, 1892, though it seems very probable that the title page had been deposited in late 1849, meaning that it would enter the public domain in 1891 rather than 1892.

advice was sought, and although the copyright technicalities were obscure, the firm put up a bold front and succeeded in driving off the competition, but only for the time being.[1]

By early 1892, Houghton, Mifflin had prepared and issued new and cheap separate editions of both *The Scarlet Letter* and *Uncle Tom's Cabin*, for the most part printed from plates that were already in use. In its spring announcement of March, the firm listed two new separate editions of *The Scarlet Letter*: the "Universal Edition" (printed from plates of the "Riverside Edition"),[2] which cost 50 cents in cloth, 25 cents in paper, and an even cheaper "Salem Edition" (A16.8.d; printed from the plates of the "Little Classic Edition"), at 30 cents in cloth, 15 cents in paper. These were followed in May by an expensive edition, illustrated with photogravures based on Darley's outline drawings: the "trade edition" cost $2.50 (A16.13.g; printed from plates of the "Riverside Edition"), and also issued in a special "Large Paper Edition," limited to 200 numbered copies and bound in vellum, $7.50 (A16.13.h). These joined the "Popular Edition" of *The Scarlet Letter* (A16.13.d; printed from the plates of the "Riverside Edition"), the only other separate edition that had been issued, which had been in print since 1885 and was priced at $1 in cloth, 50 cents in paper. When the work entered the public domain, its authorized publisher Houghton, Mifflin & Co. made sure it was available separately in a range of formats and prices that appealed to as broad a market as possible.

The copyright on *Uncle Tom's Cabin* expired in May 1893. As with *The Scarlet Letter*, the firm had already issued a range of new editions, both cheap and expensive, in an attempt to maintain their hold over the market. After both works entered the public domain, however, they were quickly reprinted in unauthorized editions. By century's end, separate editions of *The Scarlet Letter* were available from many of the firms that specialized in cheap publishing—Altemus, Bay View, Burt, Caldwell, Coates, Crowell, Donohue, Hill, Hurst, Lupton, McKay, Mershon, Ogilvie, Page, Rand, Stokes, Truslove, Warne, Ziegler—a list that closely matches that for *Uncle Tom's Cabin*.[3] Houghton, Mifflin & Co. continued as an important publisher of both works, but was no longer able to control the ways in which they were packaged and marketed.

For much of the twentieth century, critical opinion of the two works followed different paths. *Uncle Tom's Cabin* came to be viewed as flawed, overly sentimental, and frankly racist, in fact an embarrassment—an assessment that has only recently been revised. In the meanwhile, *The Scarlet Letter* emerged, along with Melville's *Moby-Dick*, as one of the "two most nearly undisputed classics of American

---

1. See letters, Francis Jackson Garrison to Henry Oscar Houghton, July 14, 1891, to December 4, 1891, in the Houghton Library, Harvard University (Ms Am 1648 [330]), and letters regarding the Liberty Book Company in the Houghton Mifflin contract files.
2. This "edition" is not listed in Frazer Clark, *Nathaniel Hawthorne*, but most likely it is that listed as A16.13.f.
3. See *The United States Catalog: Books in Print, 1899 (Part 1: Author Index)*, ed. George Flavel Danforth and Marion E. Potter (Minneapolis: H. W. Wilson, 1900), 290, 631.

fiction."[4] Clearly, reception history cannot be explained only by a work's publication and marketing, but it is interesting to speculate on the extent to which they have influenced the critical understanding of the importance of *The Scarlet Letter* in Hawthorne's oeuvre, for as the twentieth century dawned it was for the first time readily and widely available to readers not as one volume from his collected works, but as a distinct and separate work.

LAURA HANFT KOROBKIN

The Scarlet Letter of the Law: Hawthorne and Criminal Justice†

I.

In the scene of public witnessing that begins *The Scarlet Letter*, the Governor, magistrates, and elders look down from their balcony to the platform where Hester Prynne stands in proud shame, raised in turn above the grim faces of the milling crowd. The ground-level voices we hear express a resentment quite appropriate to a townspeople both beneath and outside the nexus of unassailable power represented by that balcony, "the place whence proclamations were wont to be made" (64) [46]. Though they hold varying opinions of the letter-wearing sentence, in one thing the townspeople's comments are consistent: not they but the magistrates have had the sole power and authority to deal with Hester Prynne. "This woman has brought shame upon us all and ought to die," rants one woman. "Is there not law for it? Truly there is, both in the Scripture and the statute-book. Then let the magistrates, who have made it of no effect, thank themselves if their own wives and daughters go astray!" (51–52) [39].

In Hawthorne's Puritan world, the only decision-makers standing between Hester and the gallows are the all-powerful magistrates. Their word is law, their discretion untrammeled. If the colony has a fully developed criminal justice system—grand juries returning indictments, juries assessing trial testimony and returning verdicts, pre-determined criminal penalties governing the sentencing of offenders—we don't hear about it. Instead, the entire apparatus of the Puritan Rule of Law in *The Scarlet Letter* is signified by this small group of powerful men, accountable apparently to none but themselves and their God. The first three chapters create the clear impression that the townspeople are wholly excluded from any decision-making role in

---

4. Charvat, "Introduction" to *The Scarlet Letter*, xv. This introduction is printed in the very first volume completed and published of what—as the Center for Editions of American Authors—became an ambitious attempt to produce critical texts of the American classics by applying the same methodologies developed for editing the works of the English renaissance, especially those of Shakespeare.

† From *Novel* 30.2 (Winter 1997): 193–217. Copyright © 1997 NOVEL Corp. Reprinted with permission. Page numbers in square brackets refer to this Norton Critical Edition.

dealing with crime.[1] The conflation of religious, political, legislative, and judicial power in Hawthorne's early New England is total: the monolith rules and sentences. The people may mutter, but they must also unhesitatingly obey.

As Hawthorne well knew, however, the legal and judicial authority of the magistrates, particularly during the tumultuous decade in which he situates his tale, was anything but unassailable.[2] The colony's criminal justice system had been intentionally structured to counterpoint magistratical power with the peer-group power of grand and petit juries and elected legislators who were not magistrates. And, wherever magistrates nevertheless attempted to exert hegemonic power, their authority was under persistent siege. Juries brought in verdicts which frustrated and undermined magistrates' judicial authority. Agitators for legislative reform worked to set prescribed penalties for crimes with the explicit goal of circumscribing the magistrates' discretionary sentencing authority. In short, the historical magistrates were neither as powerful nor as awe-inspiring as their fictional counterparts.

The wealth of excellent recent scholarship focusing on Hawthorne's Puritan sources has explicated a host of issues underlying the Puritan world of Hawthorne's fiction: the religion, sexuality, and politics of prominent Puritans Anne Hutchinson, Richard Bellingham, and John Winthrop have all been persuasively detailed (Colacurcio, *Essays*; Arac; Bercovitch; Berlant). But what has not been adequately explored in this most legal of novels is Hawthorne's ahistorical imaging of the machinery of Puritan criminal law. At the same time that the novel seems obsessed with crime and punishment, it avoids—indeed erases—the institutions and procedures that constitute public criminal process. This essay applies a process of double historicization to the novel's exploration of the relation of crime and law to the private individual. The first level of inquiry compares case histories, statutes, and legal disputes of the 1640s to Hawthorne's fictional Boston, to locate points of significant variance. Hawthorne's occasional inaccuracies have been the subject of critical discussion for more than thirty years; as recently as 1988 Michael Colacurcio declared that the novel's "major historical fabrication" was casting Bellingham rather than Winthrop as governor in June of 1642 (110). I argue that a great deal more was changed or eliminated, and that the text consequently bears the traces of a series of historical figures it struggles to suppress. These include, most significantly, the shadows of three: the townsman juror, the whipped woman, and the political malcontent.

Focusing historical analysis on what Hawthorne's text omits will re-

1. Virtually all of the townspeople who comment on Hester's punishment note, in one form or another, "the worshipful magistrates" who have "awarded" Hester's sentence. One says the magistrates are "God-fearing" but "merciful overmuch," while another wishes that they, not the magistrates, had been in charge of determining the penalty (51) [38–39]. Every comment testifies to the magistrates' power: none mentions a trial.

2. Hawthorne's scholarly familiarity is attested to not only by the historical details used throughout his Puritan fiction, but by existing library records of the Salem Athenaeum, listing the source books he borrowed. See Ryskamp 257–58, Kesselring passim, and Colacurcio, "Footsteps" 462 n6. On the persistent efforts of the colonists to circumscribe magistratical power throughout this period, see Haskins 29–42.

quire a reevaluation of the novel's traditional villains, the "grim-visag'd" magistrates whose sentence binds Hester to the red letter of the law. Hawthorne's narrator characterizes them as rigid, severe, and frostbitten, incapable of judging a woman's heart; surprisingly, critics who specialize in exposing this narrator's ironic doublespeak in other areas have accepted such epithets.[3] Measured against their historical counterparts, however, Hawthorne's magistrates emerge as distinctly progressive; if they are more autocratic, they exercise their power with compassion and restraint.

If Puritan history makes Hawthorne's historical manipulations visible, the politics of 1850 make them comprehensible. My focus here is on two law-related issues *The Scarlet Letter* profoundly meditates: First, what obligations do individuals have to obey laws regulating private behavior, laws that directly conflict with individuals' deeply held principles, and which they have had no hand in making? And second, must submission to such a law be viewed as integrity-destroying cowardice, or can it be understood as courageous and even beneficial to the individual? These questions sounded with particular resonance in 1850, when the legitimacy of public law and criminal process was a matter of intense national debate. In the same month that *The Scarlet Letter* appeared, Senator Daniel Webster irrevocably destroyed his almost mythic reputation by arguing that the Compromise Act of 1850 was a reasonable means to preserve the nation and should be adopted. Abolitionists thundered against him from newspapers, pulpits, and platforms. Citizens were urged to defy the Compromise's Fugitive Slave Law provisions, with violence if necessary.

As Jonathan Arac and Sacvan Bercovitch have shown, *The Scarlet Letter* was written in a time of intense concern about the Fugitive Slave Laws. Like Arac and Bercovitch, I read *The Scarlet Letter* as a response to the political anxieties of 1850. My focus, however, is not (or not exclusively) on Hawthorne's attitude toward slavery or the necessity for broad political compromise, but on the specific crisis faced by Northerners who had to decide whether or not to cooperate with the provisions of the Fugitive Slave Law. That law, passed by federal legislators in Washington, placed all citizens under affirmative legal obligations not only to permit but to assist in the capture and return of fugitive slaves. Significantly, the federal Compromise Act of 1850 conflicted with, and overturned, state-level protections for runaway slaves that had been provided for by such laws as the Massachusetts Personal Liberty Acts of 1843 (Schwartz 191). Throughout most of the 1840s these laws made it virtually impossible to recover a runaway slave in many Northeastern states; after 1850, federal law would force New Englanders to become passive witnesses to the capture, imprisonment, and rendition of the runaways in their midst. Abolitionist fervor intensified in response. The battle cry of violent resistance in the

---

3. See, e.g. Shulman, who argues that Hawthorne placed Hester in a "joyless, punitive society" run by men who are "capable but insensitive, heartless" (86–88), or Berlant, who characterizes Bellingham in the child custody scene as showing "symptomatic Puritan inability to adjudicate properly, due to his oversaturation with juridical consciousness" (78).

name of a Higher Law was preached to enthusiastic crowds by the Boston Vigilance Committee, which also undertook to rescue imprisoned fugitives. From the pulpit, abolitionist minister Theodore Parker "adjured" his parishioners to "reverence a government that is right, statutes that are right . . . but to disobey every thing that is wrong" in the name of the "higher law," the "law of God" (40).

Recent articles by Jean Fagan Yellin and Jennifer Fleischner have productively explored Hawthorne's refusal to represent slavery in his works and documented his belief that the enslavement of African-Americans was in general neither outrageous nor inhumane. As Yellin has shown, the sufferings and dilemmas that interested Hawthorne were those of whites, not blacks. In this context, I will argue that in designing Hester's punishment, Hawthorne eliminated whatever would have suggested a resemblance between her situation and that of the slave. As a figure for white northerners, Hester's behavior becomes all the more controversial. To a member of the Vigilance Commitee, Hester's outward submission to the strictures of Puritan law might well appear a shameful knuckling under, the kind of failure of the will that buys safety at the price of personal integrity. Yet Hawthorne convinces us that Hester's behavioral acquiescence is both truly heroic and intellectually liberating. With Hester as a model, the novel suggests, readers may find the courage not to rebel but to forego rebellion. In the 1838 speech that set the pro-law terms of the debate over obedience to law, Lincoln had warned that if "the laws be continually despised and disregarded" by "mobs" who take it on themselves to judge the acceptability of each law, order, reason and the Government itself must eventually fall ("Address" 22). Yet it was precisely the choice to submit to law rather than to follow the dictates of private conscience that Parker, Thoreau and others found absolutely unacceptable.

After exploring this historical context, the final section of this essay will argue that the debate over obedience to law is crucial to reading *The Scarlet Letter*. By entering such debates through the medium of fiction, a novel can significantly influence readers' responses to the challenges presented by contemporary events without requiring them to read the novel in explicitly political terms. Where contemporary speeches and editorials impelled readers to respond by adopting or refuting the specific position argued in the text, Hester Prynne's hard-won freedom and serenity could elicit admiration and a desire for emulation even from readers who would ordinarily have resisted the novel's underlying attitude toward law and obedience. This is not to reduce the novel to the status of an essay or a narrow political allegory; instead, it is precisely the literary qualities of evocativeness, complexity, and imaginative richness that make its impact on these law-related issues possible, just as those same qualities have produced an extraordinary range of "purely literary" interpretations. But if fiction's fundamental openness to interpretation distinguishes it from most forms of discursive advocacy, I will also argue that it makes it *like* rather than unlike most forms of law, which also depend on a process

of continuing interpretation for their power. Though law is often imaged as fixed and rigid in contrast to literature's interpretive fluidity, I
will argue that *The Scarlet Letter*'s contribution to the American cultural dialogue about law and obedience owes as much to its narrative
specificity, boundedness, and closure as to its interpretive ambiguities.

II.

Explaining Hester's appearance on the scaffold to a just-arrived Roger
Chillingworth, a townsman says that

> our Massachusetts magistracy, bethinking themselves that this
> woman is youthful and fair, and doubtless was strongly tempted
> to her fall;—and that, moreover, as is most likely, her husband
> may be at the bottom of the sea;—they have not been bold to put
> in force the extremity of our righteous law against her. The
> penalty thereof is death. But, in their great mercy and tenderness
> of heart, they have doomed Mistress Prynne to stand only a space
> of three hours on the platform of the pillory, and then and there-
> after, for the remainder of her natural life, to wear a mark of
> shame upon her bosom. (62–63) [46]

While Hawthorne's fictional magistrates *are* the criminal justice system, their historical counterparts' authority was significantly limited
by the colonial jury's verdict-making powers, on one hand, and the
colony's prescribed criminal procedures, on the other. A person accused of crime was not a passive or disempowered object to whom law
was "done." Rather, under the 1641 Body of Liberties, a hard-won definition of the civil rights of colonists, the defendant enjoyed a series of
important rights, including the right to choose a jury or bench trial, to
challenge jurors for cause, to have another person speak on her behalf, to a speedy trial at which written records were made, and to appeal the verdict to a higher court (see paragraphs 29, 30, 36, 41, 64 of
the Body of Liberties in Powers's appendix [533–48]). The range of
available punishments, and the circumstances in which they could be
imposed were also regulated by the Body of Liberties, which guaran-
teed in its first paragraph that "no mans life shall be taken away, no
mans honour or good name shall be stayned, no mans person shall be
arrested, restrayned, banished, dismembred, nor any wayes punished
. . . unlesse it be by vertue or equitie of some expresse law of the
Country waranting the same," and in its forty-sixth outlawed punishments "that are inhumane, Barbarous or cruell." A person accused of
adultery would have been tried by a jury of twelve freemen in a trial
court where magistrates sat as judges. The jury would have decided, in
private, not only the general question whether to convict or acquit but
also, because the conviction must be for a specific crime, what crime
had been provably committed. Only the return of the verdict triggered
the judge's sentencing powers (Konig 33, Haskins 32–36).

Death was the mandatory penalty for adultery in the Massachusetts
Bay Colony in 1642, though it was not then a capital crime either in
England or in the colony at Plymouth (Powers 78, 261–62, 300).

Once the jury returned a verdict for adultery, the magistrate-judges had no discretionary authority to demonstrate "tenderness and mercy" by imposing a lesser penalty. Conversely, if the jury chose to return a verdict for a lesser sexual offense such as "lewd and lascivious behavior," the death penalty could not be imposed.

The power of juries to control sentencing by determining verdicts was frequently commented on at the time. In John Winthrop's Journal, recently argued to be not only Hawthorne's "prime and obvious source" for *The Scarlet Letter*, but to have furnished "the novel's most essential themes" as well (Colacurcio, "Woman's" 103), Winthrop describes a "sad business" that "fell out" in the spring of 1645, in which a churchgoing young man went to England, leaving his wife in the care of another "pious" and "sincere" member,

> who in time grew over familiar with his master's wife, (a young woman no member of the church) so as she would be with him oft in his chamber, etc. and one night two of the servants, being up, perceived him to go up into their dame's chamber, which coming to the magistrate's knowledge, they were both sent for and examined . . . and confessed not only that he was in her chamber with her in such a suspicious manner, but also that he was in bed with her, but both denied any carnal knowledge, and being tried by a jury upon their lives by our law, which makes adultery death, the jury acquitted them of adultery, but found them guilty of adulterous behavior. This was much against the minds of many, both of the magistrates and elders, who judged them worthy of death. . . . [A]ll that the evidence could evince was but suspicion of adultery, but neither God's law nor ours doth make suspicion of adultery (though never so strong) to be death; whereupon the case seeming doubtful to the jury, they judged it safest in case of life to find as they did. So the court adjudged them to stand upon the ladder at the place of execution with halters about their necks one hour, and then to be whipped or each of them to pay 20 pounds. (2:305–306)

Clearly, the locus of power in this case is the jury, not the magistrates; unless the jury convicts, the magistrates cannot execute, however much they may deem an offender "worthy of death." Where the jury in this 1645 case used the "expresse law" requirement to avoid the death penalty many magistrates would have preferred, a jury three years earlier had used its verdict to require an execution the magistrates would gladly have avoided. In 1642, the same year Hester received her red A, Mary Latham and James Britton became the only persons executed for adultery in the history of the Massachusetts Bay Colony. Describing the case in his journal, Winthrop noted that "some of the magistrates thought the evidence not sufficient against her, because there were not two direct witnesses, but the jury cast her, and then she confessed the fact, and accused twelve others, whereof two were married men" (2: 190–91). Britton petitioned the general court for his life, "but they would not grant it, though some of the magistrates spake much for it, and questioned the letter, whether adultery was death by God's law now" (2:191) No discretion was available once a jury verdict for adultery had been returned. Latham and Britton were hanged.

Did Hester have a trial? If she chose a jury rather than a bench trial, of what specific crime did the jurors convict her? Did the grim crowd that watched her mount the scaffold include jurors whose votes helped put her there? And, perhaps most significantly, why did Hawthorne invent a criminal case in which the determination of guilt or innocence would have been made by a jury and then carefully construct the impression that the magistrates acted as a law unto themselves?

For one thing, we should note that the execution of Britton and Latham was by no means characteristic of Puritan justice. Although indictments on capital offenses were fairly common, convictions were rare.[4] The Body of Liberties specified twelve capital crimes; yet, as Edwin Powers puts it, "time after time, juries refused to bring in verdicts that might have led to the scaffold" (279). Instead, they used their verdict-controlling power as modern juries do, to bring in verdicts for lesser-included offenses when death seemed too extreme a punishment. The Records of the Court of Assistants, the court of general jurisdiction of the Bay Colony, reflect numerous cases in which juries effectively circumscribed judges' sentencing powers, eliminating possible infliction of the death penalty. In cases charging adultery, verdicts were returned reading "not legally guilty but guilty of very filthy carriage, etc.," "not guilty according to Indictment but found him Guilty of vile, filthy and abominably libidinous Actions," and "not legally Guilty according to Indictment but doe find hir Guilty of Prostituting hir body to him to Committ Adultery" (Powers 103, 279).

The real power to determine sentencing in adultery cases thus often lay with the jury, who rarely used it to its harshest capacity. Yet Hawthorne's townspeople suggest that whipping, branding, or death would have been more appropriate punishment for Hester's crime. Clearly, she is better off in the magistrates' hands than left to the townspeople's mercy. While Hawthorne's narrator suggests that "out of the whole human family" it would be difficult to find persons "less capable of sitting in judgment on an erring woman's heart" than the magistrates (64) [47], he situates Hester, with characteristic irony, above a throng of neighbors whose judgment would have been far harsher and more vengeful. Erasing the Puritan jury not only makes the magistrates the sole source of judgment, it also increases the ambit of their sentencing discretion. This helps explain why the "expresse

---

4. This clemency did not, unfortunately, extend to cases for witchcraft, as the fate of Mistress Hibbins, the sister of Governor Bellingham who invites Hester to witches' meeting in the forest, demonstrates. Her case is described in Caleb Snow's *History of Boston*, which Ryskamp has shown was Hawthorne's primary source for historical details. As Snow tells it, "the jury brought her in guilty [of witchcraft], but the magistrates refused to accept the verdict; so the cause came to the general court, where the popular clamour prevailed against her, and the miserable old lady was condemned and executed in June 1656" (qtd. in Ryskamp 267). As this account shows, where conflicts occurred between juries and magistrates the "popular clamour" of those at the juror level could win out, even if it meant executing the governor's sister. Such power in the populace contrasts sharply with the impotence of those who "clamour" against Hester in the novel's opening scene.

law" for which Hester is convicted is never mentioned, and why the word "adultery" never appears in the text. Hester is apparently convicted of adultery, a capital crime, but she receives a sentence which could only have been imposed for a much less serious infraction. By implying that the magistrates' range of options included these much harsher punishments, Hawthorne both inflates the magistrates' powers and highlights their compassionate consideration for Hester's circumstances.

This reallocation of power has three important effects. As already discussed, it enlarges and concentrates the magistrates' power over the townspeople while putting in their hands enormous discretionary authority. This erases any semblance of participatory or democratic government and replaces it with an image of authoritarian oligarchy. Second, it exacerbates the distance, in terms of class and power, between the lone woman on the scaffold and those who decide her fate. Finally, it disconnects the townspeople from any involvement in or responsibility for judging and sentencing Hester. Because I will explore the implications of the first two later in this essay, I want to look now at the third point, the non-participatory status of the witnessing bystanders in the opening scene.

To have Hester's guilt determined by a jury of her peers would suggest that the power to judge crime and assign penalties is not limited to those on high but shared or mediated among the community as a whole. And, of course, sharing the power to judge is precisely what juries are all about. As Alexis de Tocqueville noted in his brief paean to the American jury, the jury system

> places the real direction of society in the hands of the governed, or of a portion of the governed, and not in that of the government. . . . The true sanction of political laws is to be found in penal legislation; and if that sanction is wanting, the law will sooner or later lose its cogency. He who punishes the criminal is therefore the real master of society. Now the institution of the jury raises the people itself, or at least a class of citizens, to the bench of judges. The institution of the jury consequently invests the people, or that class of citizens, with the direction of society. (1: 293)

Hawthorne's deliberate elimination of the jury is, in de Tocqueville's terms, an inversion designed to make the magistrates rather than the townspeople "the real master of society." Hawthorne's irony in dubbing one opinionated townswoman a "self-constituted judge" is thus double: her presumption in taking on the magistratical job of judging a neighbor's guilt is an example of comic overreaching as much because she is an ordinary citizen as because she is a woman.

Hawthorne's townspeople judge—but their judgments trigger no consequences. No matter how extreme a punishment they call for, they are not responsible for any sufferings that result. Because their "verdicts" float free from liability for the burdens they impose, they can judge and, more importantly, rejudge Hester, until the harshness of those early judgments melts into later admiration for her modesty and usefulness. By the novel's end, the once reviled adulteress has become a woman respected for her wisdom as well as her sufferings, as those who once reviled her (or their daughters) now seek out her advice.

What I am suggesting is that the townspeople's freedom to interpret Hester is enabled by their position outside the concentration of power up on that balcony. Indeed, the novel insists in a variety of ways that mental development is always fullest and freest when liberated from the crushing weight of behavior's consequences. Readers raised on *The Plague* and *Man's Fate*—or for that matter, on *Middlemarch*—may find paradoxical at best the suggestion that personal development is fully possible only when the thinker is not required to act in consistency with his beliefs. But for Hester, as well as for the townspeople, it is precisely the unlinking of mental freedom from any obligation toward consonant action that makes her intellectual growth possible. In "Another View of Hester" we learn that in the isolation of her lonely cottage Hester's extraordinary "freedom of speculation" has led her to believe that "the whole system of society is to be torn down, and built up anew" (164–65) [107, 108]. Yet Hester's conclusion that "the world's law was no law for her mind" is antinomian only in the theoretical sense. An Anne Hutchinson of the mind alone, Hester does not behave as if she believes that the world's law is no law for her body. She submits. She counsels young women to submit. Whatever she may be feeling, she walks through the streets of Boston with her head modestly down, and her outward obedience buys her the unassaulted privacy in which to continue thinking. She hopes that some bright future time will resolve the world's inequities, but in the here and now her freedom exists in the realm of thought, not action.[5]

There is an important connection between Hester's restricted behavior and her unrestricted thoughts. Her position outside the web of normal social obligation and activity permits her to see and judge society whole. Also, and perhaps more significantly, Hawthorne implies that it is precisely because she need not think about practical action that her mental explorations can be so far-reaching. The energies dammed up by her life of enforced outward conformity can flow freely only in this interior realm, where their penetration of unexplored terrain will not be cut off by the confrontations and compromises that would inevitably ensue were they to be translated into radical action. While Hawthorne suggests that in different circumstances Hester might have been a

---

5. In this context, it is important to note that Hester's one moment of rebellion—the plan to leave the colony with Arthur Dimmesdale—is presented within the novel as not simply doomed but wrongful. Just as Dimmesdale's presence has been a primary reason for Hester's remaining in Boston, so his failing health and spirits under Chillingworth's predatory attentions convince her to leave. Motivated by his personal weakness, characterized by secrecy, fear, and deception, the proposed flight is not a courageous challenge to authority but an attempt to run away from its adverse effects. While we admire Hester's strength and compassion, and yearn, on her behalf, for some means of escape from the pressures of community, law, and responsibility, everything in the novel suggests that such flight is neither viable nor admirable. Because even private sexual misconduct is a violation of community norms and laws, expiation and reintegration can only be achieved through a public process that involves both wrongdoer and the community in which the wrong was committed.

prophetess or a revolutionary, it is quite clear that in Hester's world, the satisfactions of philosophical exploration are made available through her life of privation and are one of its few compensations. Like the widely various juridical opinions of the milling crowd beneath the scaffold, Hester's philosophical and historical conclusions can be radical, even revolutionary, precisely because they are not muddied by the messy and corrupting process of attempting change in the real world.[6] It is significant too that outward obedience is all that the Puritan rule of law requires; its justice system punishes only acts, not thoughts. Because community stability depends on each member's self-restraint, Hester's conformity to behavioral expectations helps hold the community together even when her thoughts may be at their bitterest. If protecting society from disruptive assaults is a paramount goal, then such a system helps preserve order, while leaving each individual the sanctum of his or her own mind. Whether that very limited freedom is enough is of course quite another question.

III.

If Hawthorne's elimination of the Puritan jury suggests that he wanted his magistrates to be more powerful than their historical counterparts, his handling of Hester's sentence suggests that he also wanted them to be more responsive. Let us return briefly to Puritan legal history. In 1641, the general court of the Colony of New Plymouth sentenced Thomas Bray and Anne, the wife of Francis Linceford, for the "crime of adultery and uncleanesse," to which both had confessed publicly. Much of the court's sentence will be familiar:

> [T]he Court doth censure them as followeth: that they be severely whipt immediately at the publik post, & that they shall weare (whilst they remayne in the government) two letters, viz. an AD, for Adulterers, daily, upon the outeside of their uppermost garment, in a most emenent place thereof; and if they shalbe found at any tyme in any towne or place within the government without them so worne upon their uppermost garment as aforesaid, that the constable of the towne or place shall take them, or either of them omitting so to weare the said two letters, and shall forthwith whip them for their negligence and shall cause them to be immediately put on againe, and so worne by them and either of them; and also that they shalbe both whipt at Yarmouth, publikely, where the offence was committed, in such fitt season as shalbe thought meete by Mr. Edmond Freeman & such others as are authorized for the keepeing of the Courts in these partes. (*Records of Plymouth* 2:28)

---

6. Like Bercovitch, I place major emphasis on the moment of Hester's return, though my focus does not read it as the defining moment in the creation of a liberal ideology of compromise. While I agree with Arac's argument that the novel "is propaganda—*not* to change your life," I argue that it offers the rule of law rather than simple "character" as the central enabling and positive value. Like Fleischner, I argue that Hawthorne sees dissociation from public political action as privately beneficial; I want to suggest, however, that Hester represents the situation of the ordinary reader rather than, as Fleischner suggests, the artist.

The similarities between Anne Linceford's sentence and Hester Prynne's are obvious. Yet the discovery that Hester's lifetime letter-wearing sentence has a precise historical analogue should not obscure the fundamental difference between the two: like virtually all Puritan sexual offenders, Anne Linceford was publicly stripped and severely whipped, most probably receiving the Biblically allowable maximum of forty lashes. Hester receives no physical punishment. If *The Scarlet Letter* is the painstakingly accurate representation of Puritan life it is often assumed to be, the example of Anne Linceford is troubling. Why did Hawthorne, whose historical research was nit-picking enough to permit him to provide correct street addresses for his historically prominent characters, eliminate what was for the Puritans a fundamental component of all serious punishment? In short, why isn't Hester whipped?

In 1844, Hawthorne noted as a story idea in his journal "the life of a woman, who, by the old colony law, was condemned always to wear the letter A, sewed on her garment, in token of having comitted adultery" (*American* 254) [215]. Two colonial statutes have generally been accepted as Hawthorne's possible source; significantly, each mandates a severe public whipping before the offender begins a life of sartorial humiliation. The penalty not only shames the sinful spirit, but harshly mortifies its fleshly container. The first, a 1658 act of the colony of New Plymouth, provided: "whosoever shall committ Adultery shalbee severely punished by whipping two several times; . . . and likewise to weare two Capital letters viz. AD cut out in cloth and sewed on theire uppermost garments on their arme or backe; and iff att any time they shalbee taken without the said letter whiles they are in the Government soe worn to bee forthwith taken and publickly whipt" (*Compact* 42–43). The second, a 1694 act described in Joseph Felt's 1827 *Annals of Salem*, provides that adulterers be made "to sit an hour on the gallows, with ropes about their necks, be severely whip't not above 40 stripes and forever after to wear a capital A 2 inches long, cut out of cloth colored differently from their clothes and sewed on the arms or back parts of their garments so as always to be seen when they were about" (317). Whichever statute Hawthorne may have seen, his fascination with the psychological possibilities of the sentence did not extend to its corporal component. Hester is humiliated, first by being made to stand three hours on the scaffold, and then by her lifetime of letter wearing; she is also apparently imprisoned, since Pearl is born in prison, and Hester returns to the prison after her morning exposure. But she is not whipped. Hester's red A, frequently characterized as a happily vanished instance of Puritan severity, is most noteworthy for its extraordinary *leniency*, its complete avoidance of the physical chastisement so essential to Puritan programs for spiritual correction.

Whipping was the standard colonial punishment for bastardy and other sex crimes. As Powers notes: "a review of the Colonial court records gives one the impression that one who held the sex mores of the times in light esteem would sooner or later have an engagement with the constable at the whipping post" (172). Unless the defendant was rich enough to substitute payment of a fine, a whipping of up to forty lashes might be expected. The *Records of the Court of Assistants* in Boston in 1642, the year Hester mounted her scaffold, contain numerous examples of such punishment. Robert Wyar and John Garland, for instance, for "ravishing" two young girls, "the fact confessed by the girles, & the girles both upon search found to have bin defloured, & filthy dalliance confessed by the boyes," were sentenced to be severely and publicly whipped, the girls to be whipped also, but privately (121). The denouement to the 1645 case from Winthrop's Journal, described earlier, provides a further example. The court sentenced the pair to an hour on the gallows with halters around their necks, and then either to pay 20 pounds, or be whipped. "The husband (although he condemned his wife's immodest behavior, yet) was so confident of her innocency in point of adultery, as he would have paid 20 pounds rather than she should have been whipped; but their estate being but mean, she chose rather to submit to the rest of her punishment than that her husband should suffer so much for her folly. So he received her again, and they lived lovingly together" (2:258). Even where letter-wearing penalties were inflicted for long periods of time, they began with a whipping.[7] Hawthorne's avoidance of physical punishment is thus stunningly ahistorical, whether considered in light of the typical punishment for lesser sex crimes or as an example of an "old colony law" on adultery.

Whipping was not only the most historically common punishment for adultery and other sex crimes in Boston in 1642, it was also one of the hottest social and literary subjects of Hawthorne's day. As Richard Brodhead has demonstrated in his examination of antebellum America's obsession with the subject, Hawthorne's audience was embroiled in controversy over corporal versus psychological punishment. Psychological punishment, touted as "discipline through love," was associated with progress and reform (70). Originating in family-based disciplinary instruction, such methods substituted the infliction of guilt for the infliction of physical pain, thereby internalizing parental authority. Controversies over methods of punishment were played out in every medium, both fictional and journalistic. Throughout the 1840s and 1850s, Brodhead declares, "the picturing of scenes of physical correction emerges as a major form of imaginative activity in America, and arguing the merits of such discipline becomes a major item on the American public agenda" (67). Furors over inflammatory scenes of whipping in novels like *Two Years Before the Mast* (1840) and *Uncle Tom's Cabin* (1852) stimulated book sales enormously.

7. In 1657, for example, the Plymouth Court again imposed its "old colony law," this time on Katherine Alnes, who, "for unclean and lascivious behavior," was sentenced to be twice publicly whipped and then forever after to wear "a Roman B" on her clothes (*Records of Plymouth* 3:111, Powers 198). In 1639, in Boston, John Davies was sentenced "for groase offences in attempting lewdness with divers women" to be severely whipped, both in Boston and at Ipswich, and then "to weare the letter V upon his breast upon his uppermost garment untill the Court do discharge him," which it did, in recognition of his good behavior, some six months later (*Records of Court* 2:81, 87).

Why then isn't Hester whipped? Paradoxically, the very topicality of corporal punishment may have prevented Hawthorne from consigning Hester to the whipping post. Brodhead begins his general analysis by establishing that in the ante-bellum period, "whipping *means* slavery . . . and considerable evidence suggests that the more general imaging of such punishment at this time has slavery as its ultimate referent" (68). If we connect this perception about the 1840s to the anomalous absence of a whipping from Hester's 1642 sentence—a juxtaposition Brodhead does not make—we see that to have Hester receive a historically accurate forty lashes would have irrevocably positioned her as a slave surrogate, an object of pity and a spur to activism. To put it simply, had Hester's punishment begun with a whipping, *The Scarlet Letter* would have been a book about slavery. As a white victim of the type of cruelties associated with slavery, Hester would have made those horrors immediate and accessible. "Hester Prynne" would have been a sign pointing toward an absent and unrepresented character—the American slave—and the novel might have joined the decade's greatest bestseller, *Uncle Tom's Cabin*, as a passionate abolitionist manifesto.

But that was precisely what the novel is structured to prevent. Hawthorne's discomfort with abolitionism is well known; although not a defender of slavery, he rejected the notion of kinship with slaves or identification with their plight. In an 1851 letter to Longfellow, he declared that he never "did, nor ever shall, feel any pre-eminent ardor for the cause" of abolitionism. Two months later, he assured Zachariah Burchmore that he had "not . . . the slightest sympathy for the slaves; or, at least, not half so much as for the laboring whites, who, I believe, as a general thing, are ten times worse off than the Southern negroes" (Mellow 409–10). Where Hawthorne feared to tread, he discouraged his readers from rushing in: his heroine is neither stripped nor whipped. The phantom figure of the oppressed slave is kept out of his text, and his heroine does not become, as Stowe's light-skinned Eliza would two years later, a slave surrogate with whom readers could identify.

If Hawthorne must reinvent history in order to make Hester a stand-in for the reader herself rather than a figure for enslaved African-Americans, he cannot entirely eradicate what Toni Morrison has called the "Africanist presence" in the shadowy margins of canonical American texts (44–46). Two recent critics, Mara Dukats and Caroline Woidat, have identified Hester as a slave figure, and have suggested that contemporary novels such as Maryse Condé's *I, Tituba* and Morrison's *Beloved* rewrite her story with all the violence and racial confrontation the earlier novel suppresses (and, as Sethe's chokecherry-tree back testifies, with all the horrors of whipping made manifest as well). Viewed through the lens of slavery, Hester is indeed the "allegorical figure of patient submission to tyranny" Woidat constructs, "a white, female" Uncle Tom whose refusal to rebel ensures her continuing victimization (537). But if it is important to recognize that the racialized context of *The Scarlet Letter* is unavoidable, it is equally important to explore the consequences for the novel of Hawthorne's insistence that Hester's choices and burdens are those of whites, not blacks.

Morrison's evocative essay articulates the racialized ground in which American literary narratives construct affirmative "American" values such as independence and freedom by contrasting the position of white Americans with those of enslaved blacks. In *The Scarlet Letter*, Hawthorne's efforts to maintain Hester's racial separation are twofold. Not only does he attempt to eliminate those characteristics of Hester's situation—like whipping—that would link her to enslaved African-Americans, he also tries to overcome the assumption, created by the omnipresence of slavery in antebellum American thought, that a person whose behavior is severely restricted by the force of law must be mentally enslaved as well. Castigating fellow Massachusetts citizens as virtual slaves because they would not resist the Fugitive Slave Law, Henry David Thoreau fumed that "there are some, who, if they were tied to a whipping-post, and could but get one hand free, would use it to ring the bells and fire the cannons to celebrate *their* liberty" (30). That Hester, though harshly constrained, both avoids the whipping post and enjoys a substantial measure of intellectual liberty suggests that Hawthorne's point is the inverse of Thoreau's: for Hawthorne, no amount of legal repression can eradicate the essential capacity for inner freedom he believes to be inherent in whites. Nor can it merge their situation with that of slaves.

Through Hester then, white readers may well have encountered their own legal/political situation, de-familiarized, perhaps, but recognizable nevertheless. Like New England citizens, but not like the whipped slave, Hester must decide whether or not to obey a harsh law imposed on her by distant, all-powerful lawmakers who are more concerned with the fate of the entire community than with any erring individual. Like them, but not like the slave, she has the freedom ultimately to *consent*, rather than merely submit, to the weight of Law she neither approves of nor has had any hand in making. She is thus a monitory model for the reader, and her progress toward inner freedom lights the way for our own. That the repugnant laws Hawthorne believed in the necessity of obeying were primarily fugitive slave laws argues even more strongly the importance of excluding the shadow slave from a position of possible reader-identification. In his 1852 campaign biography of Franklin Pierce, Hawthorne would declare that "merely human wisdom and human efforts" could not overcome the evils of slavery "except by tearing to pieces the Constitution, breaking the pledges which it sanctions, and severing into distracted fragments" the whole country (415). From his anxious viewpoint, excessive sympathy for slave-victims might lead to attempted rescues, confrontations, and violence, which in turn would undermine the cohesion and security of the national union. As his rhetoric clearly reveals, abolitionism is firmly equated in Hawthorne's mind with destructiveness; it is a force which "tears," "breaks," and "severs" the already vulnerable legal structures binding the states together.[8]

If readers are to be persuaded that the crushing weight of law should be borne uncomplainingly, those who administer that law must not be monsters. Harsh whippings inflicted on lovely heroines prevent readers from respecting those who call for the lash. Hester is spared her turn at the whipping post because, beneath their "grim-visaged" exteriors, Hawthorne's quasi-federal magistrates must be humane. They eschew violence and retribution in favor of inducements toward self-reformation. Because such psychological punishments were widely perceived as progressive, the magistrates are subtly aligned with forces of reform familiar to readers through debates over educational and military discipline.[9]

While Hawthorne's narrator primly recoils from these "sages of rigid aspect," Hawthorne is thus hard at work rewriting history to improve their authority and compassion. They may appear cold, distant, cruel, and unfair, and in the short run, they may be so, but the novel as a whole exhibits a powerful underlying faith in the notions of order, authority, and non-participatory law-making which the magistrates represent. Somehow the whole point is that their immediate unfairness is *not* the point: we must suffer and obey what appears today to be harsh and oppressive law because in the long run maintaining the community is more important than protesting injustice. As several commentators have noted, Hawthorne's defense of the Fugitive Slave Law in *The Life of Pierce* parallels Hester's counsel to the unhappy women who seek her out in the novel's final chapter: systemic injustice cannot be "remedied by human contrivance" but must be left to "Heaven's own time" when it will "vanish like a dream." To rebel against present unfairness is not only arrogant and unnecessary, but dangerous.

IV.

Just as the "real world" of Hawthorne's fiction is constructed at least partially by excluding figures like the townsman juror and the whipped woman whose presence would undermine the magistrates' justness and authority, it also suppresses all evidence of popular challenges to the magistrates' powers. 1642, the year Hester mounted her scaffold,

8. Arac also discusses aspects of Hawthorne's treatment of slavery in the *Life of Pierce* (253–54), as does Bercovitch (86–88). While the biography was, unlike the novel, an explicitly political act written for a particular campaign, and, on Hawthorne's part, written too with hopes of reaping a political appointment as a reward, its attitude toward the possible consequences of violent abolitionism is consistent with that expressed elsewhere in his writings.

9. Because Brodhead's analysis of nineteenth-century discipline uses antebellum but not Puritan materials, his discussion of the various forms of punishment in *The Scarlet Letter* misses this crucial aspect of Hester's punishment. Because his methodology prevents his recognizing the significance of Hester's unwhipped back—the affirmative marker of meaning here constituted by an unmarked surface—Brodhead mis-characterizes Hester's letter as a harsh instance of "corporal correction," "correction performed through the external, visible marking of the body" (77–78), rather than as a splendid example of the very shift from corporal to psychological punishment which his article so persuasively documents as having occurred in the 1840s and 1850s. Berlant too refers to Hester's "marked body," as if the letter were a brand or tattoo (65).

saw intense attacks on the magistrates' undemocratic authority, attacks fully characteristic of the decade in which they occurred. At least two such disputes—the infamous squabble over Goody Sherman's sow and the debate over the magistrates' unlimited sentencing discretion—hover influentially just below the surface of Hawthorne's narrative. Nowhere is his historical sleight of hand more visible than in these efforts to strip volatile conflicts of their politically problematic content while recasting them so as to enhance and entrench the power of his magistrates.

When Hester visits the governor's mansion to protest Pearl's rumored removal from her custody, Hawthorne's narrator explains the "ludicrous" involvement of such eminent figures in a small-scale dispute of this kind:

> At that epoch of pristine simplicity, however, matters of even slighter public interest, and of far less intrinsic weight than the welfare of Hester and her child, were strangely mixed up with the deliberations of legislators and acts of state. The period was hardly, if at all, earlier than that of our story, when a dispute concerning the right of property in a pig, not only caused a fierce and bitter contest in the legislative body of the colony, but resulted in an important modification of the framework itself of the legislature. (101) [68]

Hawthorne's narrator smiles a bit condescendingly at this trivial dispute in a charmingly simpler era, memorable as much for the magistrates' magnanimous concern for petty squabbles as for the unspecified legislative reform it occasioned. In fact, it was not only one of the most complex and contorted lawsuits in Massachusetts history, but also, as Winthrop's lengthy account (dated June, 1642, the month Hawthorne's narrative begins) makes clear, "gave occasion to many to speak unreverently of the court, especially of the magistrates."[1] Goody Sherman, a poor widow, apparently egged on by her unscrupulous lodger, one Story, sued Captain Keayne, a sharp and much disliked merchant, for the value of a sow she claimed he had mistakenly slaughtered. Suits (for damages) and countersuits (for libel) wound through an astonishing variety of trial and appeals courts for more than two years. More than seven days of testimony were eventually heard by the full Court of Assistants, comprising 9 Magistrates and 30 Deputies. Sympathy ran high for the widow against the rich merchant, although everyone seems to have known that much of the evidence and testimony had been manufactured after the fact. Although a majority of the deputies sided with Mrs. Sherman, the case was determined in Captain Keayne's favor when the magistrates exercised their "Negative Voice," a device permitting them to nullify the votes of non-magistrate assistants by returning a verdict in favor of the party receiving a majority of the magistrates' votes. This exercise of magistratical

---

1. In Robert C. Winthrop's *Life*, "The Stray Sow and the Negative Voice" warrants an entire chapter, which traces in detail the course of the dispute, the extended litigation it triggered, and its consequences within the community (2:280–95).

supremacy only made matters worse with the public, for, as Winthrop tells it, "the report went, that their negative voice had hindered the course of justice, and that these magistrates must be put out, that the power of the negative voice might be taken away" (qtd. in R. Winthrop 282). Because "there was much laboring under a false supposition," Winthrop published a "declaration of the true state of the cause" and a defense of the Negative Voice (qtd. in R. Winthrop 283). The following year he managed to defeat efforts to abolish it, but the bad taste lingered in many mouths; the consequent separation of the deputies and magistrates into two legislative bodies speaks as much of persistent resentment and conflict as it does of triumphant resolution.

Like widow Sherman, Hester Prynne receives personal attention from powerful magistrates. Unlike the widow whose litigation exploited the availability of public process and judicial review almost beyond human capacity, Hester's custody case is resolved immediately, through an ad-hoc informal conversation in the ex-governor's garden. Hawthorne's magistrates hold neither criminal trials for adultery nor legal hearings on child custody. Applying their discretionary authority to the circumstances of the case at the moment it is presented, they appear rigid but behave with compassion, leaving Hester her child as they left her unmarked skin. Hawthorne's ambivalent handling of the sow case—gratuitously intruding it into his narrative while suppressing its subversive resonance—suggests the ultimate goal of his re-inventions of Puritan history. On the one hand, he wants the aura of historical accuracy and authorial erudition that such references to long-forgotten cases can produce. On the other hand, he wants to present the Puritan magistracy as unassailably secure in their powers, a type of idealized federal bureaucracy. The result is the same as in his handling of the absent jury trial: all challenges to magistratical authority disappear. Instead of providing evidence that the magistrates were under attack, the case is refigured as a comic example of the magistrates' willingness to stoop responsively to aid a poor widow, just as they deign to listen to Hester's plea for continued custody of Pearl.

The challenge to the magistrates' Negative Voice was not the only, or even the most serious, attack on the powers of the magistrates during the period of Hawthorne's fiction. As Mark D. Cahn has shown, the unlimited discretionary powers of the magistrates—precisely the aspect of their authority Hawthorne is at greatest pains to present as entrenched—were the focus of the intense debates over the codification of non-capital criminal sentences. Colonists outside the inner circle of power fought to circumscribe the magistrate-judges sentencing authority by establishing pre-set penalties for specific crimes. While there were several reasons for the movement to codify, "none . . . was more significant than the freemen's desire to curb the discretionary powers of the magistrates. The freemen feared that unless penalties were established by statute and rules regarding punishment made public, the magistrates could not be trusted to impose penalties fairly and with regularity" (108). Without pre-set penalties, challengers argued, judges imposed widely varying sentences for the same crime, making the outcome of cases dependent on judicial bias or whim, and undermining the system's consistency and predictability. The magistrates (led by the indomitable Winthrop) fought vigorously to retain their discretionary authority, insisting that as God's representatives on earth they were specially empowered, and that through their discretion God's law was harmonized with the diversity of human experience. As Cahn notes, "the leitmotif of Winthrop's political writings was that God intended certain men to be magistrates—and for these individuals, once elected, to govern unimpeded by dictates and restrictions imposed by those less fit to rule" (121). In 1644, Winthrop lost the battle when the General Court voted to accept the validity of prescribed punishments and restrict the penalties magistrates could impose, though the magistrates managed to delay the adoption of an extensive code until 1648.

The period between 1641 and 1648—roughly the period covered by the events of *The Scarlet Letter*—was thus permeated by this bitter challenge to the arbitrariness of magistratical power. Though there is no explicit reference in Hawthorne's text to the battle over codification, I believe that the extraordinary emphasis in the opening scene —and indeed, throughout the novel—on the sole and unlimited discretion of the magistrates in dealing with Hester is more than coincidental. Hawthorne's narrative both illustrates and argues Winthrop's case for the legitimacy of discretionary authority. In Hawthorne's Boston you can trust the powers that be, however far-away, grim-visaged, and sealed off from popular input, because they are ultimately compassionate, reasonable, and devoted to the community's welfare.

The influence of the codification dispute on Hawthorne's text can best be understood by seeing judicial discretion in sentencing as a form of interpretation. Codification supporters were suspicious of authority, which they saw as arbitrary and subjective. So long as magistrates could decide for themselves what penalty should be imposed in a non-capital case, they could "interpret" the circumstances of the case to mete out punishments based on political or personal bias. Inflexible statutory penalties were proposed as means to curb judicial inconsistency by eliminating the judge's power to interpret. Interpretation was thus imaged negatively; consistent justice could be grounded only in the predictability afforded by black-letter pre-set penalties. The same infraction should produce the same penalty, regardless of who was the judge, who the defendant. In direct opposition, the magistrates championed case-by-case interpretation of the law. They presented their authority as objective, skillful, and sensitive. Arguing that it was the defendants, not the magistrates, who were likely to be variable, the magistrates wanted the power to mold sentences to the circumstances of each case. Though the sentence once imposed would not change, it would be the product of an interpretive response to particular circumstances.

In this context, Hester's scarlet A is Winthrop's best case. The letter, a seemingly rigid and unalterable sign of objective authority, in practice represents flexibility and openness to interpretation, both past and future. While the letter A stands for the crime she has committed, it is also "the letter of the law," the penalty for that crime. Created before the novel's action begins through a process of compassionate interpretation, the letter has been carefully shaped to fit the circumstances of Hester's case, a case which calls, not for whipping or execution, but for this sentence only. The letter also opens to a future of reinterpretation, as the seemingly unchangeable A comes over time to signify Hester's admirable qualities rather than her past behavior. The letter itself cannot change, of course, but its meaning can. As Hester's personal sign, the way the letter is read tracks her changing relations with the Puritan community. Ultimately, she claims the letter as the marker of her identity, beyond the power of the magistrates to remove. In a typical Hawthorne paradox, what is most rigid signifies what is most fluid; what is most fungible, abstract, impersonal—a letter of the alphabet—becomes what is most personal, unique, and identity-bound. The A represents the potential for compassionate interpretation which lies within seeming inflexibility, and which can best be achieved by granting broad discretionary authority to magistratical decision-makers.

V.

If the changing course of Hester's relationship with the Puritan legal establishment demonstrates that accepting the law's strictures can strengthen both the individual and the community, the terrifying counter-example set by Roger Chillingworth completes the lesson. Upon discovering his wife being publicly punished for adultery, Roger Prynne could have taken action against Hester by divorcing her, an option he is never described as considering.[2] With respect to her lover, however, he was legally obligated to leave the prosecution and punishment of the crime to the colony's courts. Instead of doing so, he devotes his life to the secret discovery and punishment of her partner. In what seems to be an act of kindness, he assures Hester that though he will make it his business to find out the identity of her lover, he will never "betray him to the gripe of human law" (75) [54]. In actuality, his preservation of secrecy is anything but kind. Unlike Hester, who protects Dimmesdale's identity in order to spare him pain, Chillingworth's aim is to monopolize the power to investigate, condemn, and punish the wrongdoer. Policeman, magistrate, judge, jury, and executioner in one, Chillingworth usurps every governmental role in the criminal justice system. Though his methods do not include the actual use of whips or stocks, Hawthorne describes his interaction with Dimmesdale as the ongoing infliction of torture: "Would he arouse [his victim] with a throb of agony? The victim was for ever on the rack; it needed only to know the spring that controlled the engine;—and the physician knew it well!" (140) [93]. If we assess Chillingworth's be-

---

2. While divorce was virtually unavailable, and socially unacceptable, in England in the seventeenth century, colonial American courts occasionally issued divorce decrees from their earliest years, and partners were free to remarry. See Haskins 63, 81, 194–95.

havior in terms of its attitude toward law, it is clear that his rejection of public magistratical process in favor of fanatical service to the private law of vengeance marks him as the novel's vigilante figure. If Hester models the ultimate benefits to be derived from accepting the workings of legal process, her husband presents the necessary disaster—both to the community and to the vigilante himself—that results when individuals reject public process in favor of private action.

To one who believes in the unifying powers of the rule of law, the vigilante is a destabilizing threat: an anarchic evader of legal structures who is willing to employ violence. Lincoln had warned in the "Address to Young Men" in 1838 that when individuals arrogate to themselves the right to punish even genuine wrongdoers, mob violence is often the result, and, in turn, the destruction of government through a gradual weakening of the people's respect for it. The "lawless in spirit" become "lawless in practice," he charged, until those who have "ever regarded the Government as their deadliest bane . . . make a jubilee of the suspension of its operations; and pray for nothing so much as its total annihilation," while even good men lose their attachment to law and thus "the strongest bulwark of any government" is destroyed (30–31). In Lincoln's apocalyptic vision, dis-interested judgment, due process, indeed, all the forces of cohesion in society disappear when such figures are ascendant. To prevent such harm, Lincoln called for "every American, every lover of liberty" to swear "never to violate in the least particular, the laws of the country," and to teach reverence for the laws in every home, school, and college until it should become "the political religion of the nation" (32).

Significantly, Hawthorne's imaging of the vigilante figure's destructiveness focuses as much on the vigilante himself as on his victim. As a one-man criminal justice system, Chillingworth's rage to punish is unrestricted. None of the colony's institutional safeguards, such as statutorily limited penalties, judges uninvolved in the case, public records and public scrutiny, operate to keep his drive for vengeance within civilized bounds. When he makes what he thinks is a principled decision to retain control of Dimmesdale's prosecution rather than turn it over to the magistrates, he loses all the community-directed restraints that are designed to make the rule of law both rational and humane. The fact that Chillingworth feels so deeply the insult of Hester's adultery, far from conferring an obligation to judge or punish, should disqualify him from both roles. Yet he takes on the roles of judge and executioner, roles which, because his relationship to them is so inappropriate, cause the corruption of his own soul, "striking evidence of man's faculty of transforming himself into a devil, if he will only, for a reasonable space of time, undertake a devil's office" (170) [110]. Instead of a heightened integrity and a strengthened individualism, his actions lead to a loss of perspective, self-control, and qualitative humanness.

It is highly significant that the "devil's office" the good doctor assumes is precisely that role which the rule of law most triumphantly eliminates: that of torturer. The rack and other such "engines" were the kind of "inhumane, barbarous and cruel" punishments outlawed by the 1641 Body of Liberties. Hester, dealt with by the public authorities, receives a humane sentence most striking in its failure to include physical punishment.

In Hawthorne's grim utopia, the justice system is administered by men who rise above any personal drive for revenge, eschew violence, and illustrate the superiority of disinterested lawmaking over the "barbarity" of private justice. The magistrates' cold distance protects Hester from both her husband's and the townspeople's outrage. If the magistrates' sentence inflicts years of lonely suffering on Hester, her submission to the discipline of law also enables her intellectual growth and, the final chapter suggests, something like serenity. Those who evade "the gripe of law" are destroyed, either by falling victim to vengeance and private self-punishment, like Dimmesdale, or by suffering the self-destructiveness of unregulated and inappropriately assumed punitive power, like Chillingworth.[3]

That Chillingworth is positioned as a vigilante suggests that the spectre of violent disdain for law was one of Hawthorne's motivating fears in writing the novel. The public discourse of New England abolitionism in the late 1840s and 1850s preached just such vigilanteism, and it is useful to read Hawthorne's fiction within this larger cultural conversation about decisions to obey or resist the strictures of law. In an 1852 speech, for instance, Frederick Douglass thundered to a largely white political audience that "the only way to make the Fugitive Slave Law a dead letter is to make half a dozen or more dead kidnappers" (*Life* 207). His words were received with laughter and applause. Two years later, when a white federal guard was killed in a botched attempt to rescue Anthony Burns, a fugitive, Douglass defended the act in an article titled "Is it Right and Wise to Kill a Kidnapper?" by arguing that the guard's "slaughter" "was as innocent in the sight of God, as would be the slaughter of a ravenous wolf in the act of throttling an infant. We hold that he had forfeited his right to live, and that his death was necessary, as a warning to others liable to pursue a like course" (*Life* 287). In a sermon preached two days after the incident, Theodore Parker justified the killing, while laying the blame for violence not on those who sought to free Burns but on the state and federal officials who had imprisoned him.[4] While the use of violence was certainly not universally accepted within Abolitionist circles, it was condoned, justified, and encouraged by many as the only

3. Chillingworth's attempt to achieve a wholly private revenge on Dimmesdale is ultimately unsuccessful, for the minister not only resists the doctor's continual efforts to elicit for himself alone what in Puritan terms must be a public confession, but "escapes" into the realm of the public to confess and die in the midst of his congregation. In this rule of law analysis, it is fitting that Dimmesdale's ultimate sanctuary is not a private but a public place, where relief from the burden of past deeds is found through permitting the community, however ambiguously, to know and assess his sin. Dimmesdale can defeat—though not survive—Chillingworth's lawless surveillance by mounting the scaffold in the presence of magistrates and townspeople. Similarly, his attempts to take on the governmental role of judge and punisher through self-flagellation must fail, because they do not proceed from a public assessment by uninvolved decision-makers.

4. It was Parker himself who, on the night of the attempt to free Burns, had roused the crowd at Boston's Faneuil Hall and made the motion to "adjourn to Court Square" where Burns

way to conscientiously resist the rendition of fugitives. Douglass and others preached that each individual has the obligation to judge man-made law against the Higher Law of right and wrong set by God. Where that law is judged and condemned as profoundly wrong, the individual must not only refuse to obey it, he should be willing to take on himself the infliction of punishment for that wrongdoing, even if such punishment leads to fatal violence. So Douglass calls on fellow abolitionists to execute slaveowning "kidnappers" whose capture of fugitives is lawful under the Compromise Act of 1850, and Parker refuses to condemn those who caused the death of a guard while attempting to free a fugitive awaiting rendition.

Read in the context of such calls for independent judgment of laws and violent resistance to their enforcement, *The Scarlet Letter* becomes a creative brief in support of Lincoln's doctrine of obedience to law. This is not to say that the story of Hester Prynne's willed submission to the harsh but compassionate law of the Puritan magistrates is no more than a response to contemporary political anxieties. If colonial and antebellum politics make this reading visible, they do not restrict its relevance for readers from Hawthorne's day to our own. Along with the many other issues the novel raises, *The Scarlet Letter* is a powerful and imaginative meditation on the larger issues implicated in every individual's continuing relation to governmental law, authority, and enforcement. The power to judge and punish wrongdoing, the novel suggests, must remain with the public authorities because, whereas vigilanteism undermines the peaceful order of society, the rule of law is the best hope of preserving it. Only the magistrates can translate judgment into action without becoming contaminated by passion. The novel suggests that we, the reader-peers figuratively participating in the crowd around Hester's scaffold, should accept the ultimate usefulness to society even of some deeply repugnant laws instead of challenging their immediate harshness.

Positioned within the novel as a sympathetic heroine, Hester certainly does not reap the traditional heroine's rewards of amatory and economic success. She is loved but not permitted to live with or marry her lover, and the wealth that Chillingworth possesses is left to Pearl, not to her. While Hester's heroism in resisting the temptation to rebel does bring such benefits as privacy, intellectual independence, and an apparently useful wisdom, each is achieved as a direct consequence of her suffering, isolation, and shame. If the violent resister proves his commitment by his willingness to suffer imprisonment and public condemnation, perhaps the person who chooses to obey in a time of general resistance must also be prepared to pay a severe price. The novel resists providing any simplistic vision of happiness for those who might follow in Hester's footsteps, insisting instead that this form of heroic compromise is anything but an easy way out.

---

was being held. His sermon, along with journalistic reports of the events and coverage of the legal proceedings, was published in pamphlet form as *Boston Slave Riot and Trial of Anthony Burns*. The sermon is on 30–33.

The novel makes no explicit connections to the Compromise Act of 1850, and there is no evidence that contemporary readers made such connections, or even, for that matter, that Hawthorne himself did.[5] Yet the national controversy that swirled around the Fugitive Slave provisions of the Act, the intense anxieties about possible disruptive violence, sectional fragmentation, and the obligations of individuals to obey unpalatable laws were very much part of the atmosphere in which the text was both written and read, and I believe it is reasonable to suggest that the novel both expressed and shaped the direction of those concerns. To make such a claim raises two important and connected questions with which I want to end this essay. First, how can a novel—especially one that does not make its politics a matter of explicit concern—play an important role in such an ongoing cultural dialogue? And second, if it can, does it do so only by ignoring or sidestepping the novel's essential literariness, reducing it to a species of political discourse? While a full answer to these questions would require another essay, a few points can be noted.

In my view, it is precisely *The Scarlet Letter*'s "literariness" that empowered it to play a critical role in shaping its readers' views, even if the dimensions of that role may be impossible to verify or recover. Obviously, a novel is neither a political essay nor a proposed statute. Perhaps less obviously, its unlikeness from each of these is different. A political essay that argues strongly for a specific position requires its audience to take an equally specific position in response—not just to agree or disagree with its assertions, but to restrict the ambit of that agreement to the particular issue and questions framed for debate. The story of Hester Prynne remains open in precisely the ways that such an essay is circumscribed. Like the letter she wears, the novel itself opens out to a range of interpretive responses among readers and invites a change in such responses over time. We can read the novel as being about passion, repression, and hypocrisy, without being required to accept or reject its implicit claims about civic obligation. Further, because the novel does not force readers to defend previously articulated political stands—does not, in fact, appear to be about contemporary politics at all—it can make new ways of thinking about those issues more easily acceptable. Through Hester readers can come to see freely chosen acceptance of the law's strictures as heroic. The transformation of such submission from cowardice into courage can elicit admiration and evoke a desire for emulation without forcing readers into a debate about the provisions of any statute. Among the many things it accomplishes, *The Scarlet Letter* permits its readers to explore the courage that can sometimes be required to obey the law

---

5. The contemporary reviews of *The Scarlet Letter* collected by Scharnhorst suggest that readers of Hawthorne's day singled out the novel's poetry and passion, its study of the human heart and its handling of the consequences of adultery. Hester's heroic obedience and the magistrates' compassion were noted, as when the Portland Transcript applauded Hester's "almost proud submission to the indignities inflicted upon her" (24), and Orestes Brownson critiqued Hawthorne's failure to condemn the adultery, declaring that the magistrates' "treatment of the adulteress was far more Christian than [Hawthorne's] ridicule of it" (34–39) [253]. I have, however, found no reviews connecting the novel to agitation about the Compromise Act.

without conducting that exploration in the already-tainted context of discussions about controversial fugitive slave laws. Once affected by these underlying issues in the novel's powerful story, it seems to me quite reasonable to suggest that, without necessarily attributing it to the novel, a reader might find herself responding differently to subsequent calls for violent resistance to divisive and unpalatable laws.

If evocative power and openness to interpretation distinguish the novel from position papers of any kind, boundedness, narrative closure, and moral inflection mark fiction's difference from most discursive forms of law. In juxtaposing law and literature, writers have sometimes imaged law as the kind of fixed text that determines and closes down the process of interpretation, while literature offers an openness to interpretation derived from its imaginative complexity.[6] Such dichotomies, though useful, erase important continuities connecting the two discourses.[7] What is significant is that legal texts, whether statute, constitutional provision or judicial decision, are necessarily part of an ongoing process of interpretation as the language of impersonal rules and previous interpretations is applied in specific, often unforeseeable cases. When the fugitive slave provisions of the Compromise Act of 1850 were drafted, legislators could sketch out a statutory scheme for recovering runaway slaves, but until the law was applied in a variety of states and contexts, its ambiguities, enforceability and consequences could not be known. It required, and received, judicial interpretation in a variety of adversarial contexts, interpretation that varied over time and with the identity of the judicial interpreter. Just as recent Supreme Court decisions have significantly changed "the law" in many areas by reinterpreting such textually fixed Constitutional provisions as the Fourth Amendment's protection against unreasonable search and seizure, so state and federal courts are continually called on to interpret and reinterpret in new contexts the meaning of statutes, codes, and earlier decisions. This openness to a necessary and evolving process of interpretation suggests a profound continuity that links law to literature through a shared dependence on language and rhetoric, with all the richness, complexity and ambiguity inherent in any discursive enterprise. Hester's red "letter of the law" is an apt symbol of that continuity: like the text of the novel in which it appears, it is both the product of and the textual stimulus for continuing interpretation.

But if law and literature both require interpretive readings, literary narratives can provide a degree of specificity and closure unavailable

6. See, for instance, Tanner, who positions marriage law as non-narrative and rigid, in contrast to the emotional responsiveness of fiction: "In the bourgeois novel we can find a strictness that works to maintain the law, and a sympathy and understanding with the adulterous violator that works to undermine it," he claims, adding later that "you can't have a society without laws, and you can't have a novel without sympathy (or empathy, or understanding, etc.)" (14, 24). Another good example is Dimock, who distinguishes the criminal law's "impulse toward precision" and narrowness, "whose operative terms were to become specific and explicit, without nuance or ambiguity," from the novel's "signifying latitude," which produces a symbolic amplitude and a "continuing (or perhaps even expanding) capacity for symbolization" (215–17).

7. The equal openness of both legal and literary texts to interpretation has been forcefully argued by Fish and explored in Brooks and Gewirtz's collection of essays.

to law. Faced with Hester's adultery, Hawthorne's Puritan magistrates, like Winthrop's contemporaries who fought hard to retain the privilege, had the power to fashion a discretionary sentence responsive to her unique circumstances; they could not, however, predict with certainty its effect on Hester's future life. Similarly, the Compromise Act of 1850 could provide the occasion for debate and dire prediction, but it could not determine the outcome of a particular fugitive's quest for freedom or trace the particular series of events that would implicate that Act in the eventual outbreak of the Civil War. The connection of legal cause to ultimate practical effect, the vivid, particular way that a harsh law will change the lived experience of those it affects, can only be imagined as among the possibilities that may ensue if this or that legal text becomes law. Literary narratives, in contrast, provide not just beginnings but endings, sequences of events in which the consequences of actions can be traced through time. If we are used to recognizing that a novel like *The Scarlet Letter* presents a complex and richly imagined world characterized by ambiguity and multiple possibilities for interpretation, it is also true that the story of Hester Prynne, Arthur Dimmesdale, and Roger Chillingworth describes not an infinity of paths but a course of connected events, producing *these* results and conflicts, and, finally, *this* particular form of closure. In 1850 it was the novel, not the statute, that could present a definite story of how the law affects the individual.

WORKS CITED

Arac, Jonathan. "The Politics of *The Scarlet Letter*." *Ideology and Classic American Literature.* Ed. Sacvan Bercovitch and Myra Jehlen. Cambridge: Cambridge UP, 1986. 247–66.
Bercovitch, Sacvan. *The Office of the Scarlet Letter.* Baltimore: Johns Hopkins UP, 1991.
Berlant, Lauren. *The Anatomy of National Fantasy: Hawthorne, Utopia, and Everyday Life.* Chicago: U of Chicago P, 1991.
Boston Slave Riot and Trial of Anthony Burns. Boston: Fetridge, 1854.
Brodhead, Richard H. "Sparing the Rod: Discipline and Fiction in Antebellum America." *Representations* 21 (1988): 67–93.
Brooks, Peter, and Paul Gewirtz, eds. *Law's Stories: Narrative and Rhetoric in the Law.* New Haven: Yale UP, 1996.
Cahn, Mark D. "Punishment, Discretion, and the Codification of Prescribed Penalties in Colonial Massachusetts." *The American Journal of Legal History* 33.2 (1989): 107–36.
Colacurcio, Michael. "Footsteps of Ann Hutchinson: The Context of *The Scarlet Letter*." *ELH* 39 (1972): 459–94.
———. " 'The Woman's Own Choice': Sex, Metaphor, and the Puritan 'Sources' of *The Scarlet Letter*." Colacurcio, *Essays* 101–35.
Colacurcio, Michael, ed. *New Essays on* The Scarlet Letter. Cambridge: Cambridge UP, 1985.
The Compact with the Charter and Laws of the Colony of New Plymouth. Boston: Dutton, 1836.
Dimock, Wai Chee. "Criminal Law, Female Virtue, and the Rise of Liberalism." *The Yale Journal of Law & the Humanities* 4 (1992): 209–47.
Dukats, Mara L. "The Hybrid Terrain of Literary Imagination: Maryse Condé's Black Witch of Salem, Nathaniel Hawthorne's Hester Prynne, and Aime Cesaire's Heroic Poetic Voice." *College Literature* 22 (1995): 51–61.
Douglass, Frederick. *Life and Writings of Frederick Douglass.* Ed. Philip S. Foner. New York: International, 1950.
Felt, Joseph. *Annals of Salem.* Salem, 1827.
Fish, Stanley. "Working on the Chain Gang: Interpretation in Law and Literature." *Doing What Comes Naturally: Change, Rhetoric, and the Practice of Theory in Literary and Legal Studies.* Durham: Duke UP, 1989. 87–102.
Fleischner, Jennifer. "Hawthorne and the Politics of Slavery." *Studies in the Novel* 23.1 (1991): 96–106.
Haskins, George Lee. *Law and Authority in Early Massachusetts.* New York: Macmillan, 1960.
Hawthorne, Nathaniel. *The American Notebooks.* Ed. Claude M. Simpson. Columbus: Ohio State UP, 1962.

————. *Life of Franklin Pierce. Works.* Vol. 12. Ed. G.P. Lathrop. Boston: Houghton, 1883.
————. *The Scarlet Letter.* Columbus: Ohio State UP, 1962.
Kesselring, Marion. *Hawthorne's Reading 1828–1850.* New York: NY Public Library, 1949.
Konig, David T. *Law and Society in Puritan Massachusetts: Essex County 1629–1692.* Chapel Hill: U of North Carolina P, 1979.
Lincoln, Abraham. "Address to the Young Men's Lyceum of Springfield, Illinois." *Abraham Lincoln, Speeches and Writings 1832–1858.* New York: Library of America, 1989.
Mellow, James R. *Nathaniel Hawthorne in his Times.* Boston: Houghton, 1980.
Morrison, Toni. *Playing in the Dark: Whiteness and the Literary Imagination.* Cambridge: Harvard UP, 1990.
Parker, Theodore. "The Three Chief Safeguards of Society, Considered in a Sermon." Boston: Crosby, 1851.
Powers, Edwin. *Crime and Punishment in Early Massachusetts.* Boston: Beacon, 1966.
Ryskamp, Charles. "The New England Sources of *The Scarlet Letter.*" *American Literature* 31.3 (1959): 257–72.
Records of the Court of Assistants of the Colony of the Massachusetts Bay 1630–1692. Vol. 12. Boston: County of Suffolk, 1904.
Records of the Plymouth Colony: Court Orders. Ed. Nathaniel Shurtleff. Boston: White, 1855.
Scharnhorst, Gary, ed. *The Critical Response to Nathaniel Hawthorne's* The Scarlet Letter. New York: Greenwood, 1992.
Schwartz, Harold. "Fugitive Slave Days in Boston." *New England Quarterly* 27 (1954): 191–212.
Shulman, Robert. "The Artist in the Slammer: Hawthorne, Melville, Poe and the Prison of their Times." *Modern Literary Studies* 14.1 (1984): 79–88.
Tanner, Tony. *Adultery in the Novel: Contract and Transgression.* Baltimore: Johns Hopkins UP, 1979.
Thoreau, Henry David. "Slavery in Massachusetts." *Anti-Slavery and Reform Papers.* Montreal: Harvest, 1963. 26–41.
Tocqueville, Alexis de. *Democracy in America.* 1835. Ed. Phillips Bradley. Trans. Henry Reeve, Francis Bowen. 2 vols. New York: Random, 1945.
Winthrop, John. *The History of New England from 1630 to 1649.* 4 vols. Ed. James Savage. Boston: Little, 1853.
Winthrop, Robert C. *Life and Letters of John Winthrop.* New York: Da Capo, 1971.
Woidat, Caroline M. "Talking Back to Schoolteacher: Morrison's Confrontation with Hawthorne's *Beloved.*" *Modern Fiction Studies* 39.3–4 (1993): 527–46.
Yellin, Jean Fagan. "Hawthorne and the American National Sin." *The Green American Tradition: Essays and Poems for Sherman Paul.* Ed. Daniel Peck. Baton Rouge: Louisiana State UP, 1989. 75–97.

MILLICENT BELL

The Obliquity of Signs: *The Scarlet Letter*†

It is not wrong to identify in this famous short novel the subjects that lie so clearly upon its surface—the effect of concealed and admitted sin, or the opposed conditions of isolation and community, or the antithetic viewpoints of romantic individualism and puritan moral pessimism or the dictates of nature and law. But—and perhaps it is the current self-consciousness of literature that makes this so—it may now be possible to find in this work a primary preoccupation with the rendering of reality into a system of signs. Hawthorne may have had similar reasons to our own for questioning—while performing—the interpretation of experience as a species of message. It is a general human impulse to seek coherence—a syntax—in life, but it is the artist above all who does so most heroically, who is the champion of our general endeavor. When that endeavor becomes dubious, art itself becomes questionable. Like ourselves, Hawthorne may have come to feel

† From *The Massachusetts Review* 23.1 (1982): 9–26. Reprinted by permission. Page numbers in square brackets refer to this Norton Critical Edition.

that the universe at large speaks an incomprehensible babble in which it merely amuses us to suppose we hear communicating voices, explanation—even consolation.

The very title of the book is a sign, the smallest of literary units, the character "standing for" no more than a speech sound. The letter "A" is the first letter, moreover, of the alphabet, which Pearl recognizes as having seen in her horn book, and represents the beginning, therefore, of literacy. Reading will be given the broadest meaning in this novel. It will become a trope for the decipherment of the world as a text. *The Scarlet Letter*, then, is, as much as any work of fiction can be, an essay in semiology. Its theme is the obliquity or indeterminacy of signs. From this source comes an energy present in every part of the book; from it derives the peculiar life of those other themes which might otherwise seem lacking in modern interest.

That the status of signs is especially important to Hawthorne is evident in a peculiar stylistic feature of *The Scarlet Letter*. Though the reader has the impression of a constant encouragement to symbolic interpretation, it turns out, upon examination, that Hawthorne's prose contains only occasional metaphor or simile and no true allegorical cohesion. What in fact happens is something else: we are frequently *asked to consider* things as symbolic; objects, persons and events are *called* signs rather than being silently presented as such. Hawthorne undertakes a narrative putatively historical, to begin with, introducing it in the Custom House Preface as a redaction from a documentary record, to reinforce the sense of a reconstructed literal past. But again and again he deliberately declares that the actualities of his tale are or may be taken as signs, and he uses repeatedly such words as "type," "emblem," "token," or "hieroglyph." All these words are used in a sense roughly synonymous.

"Type" is almost invariably employed to mean "that by which something is symbolized or figured; anything having a symbolic signification; a symbol, emblem" (*OED*), a sense which had been current already in English during the Renaissance and can be found in one of Hawthorne's favorite older writers, Spenser. The word was still used in this way in the mid-nineteenth century when the meaning more common with us, of a general form or of a kind or class, arose, and Hawthorne, who is conservative in language, almost always seems to be employing the older rather than the newer of these two senses. He even occasionally hints the special theological usage which identifies in the Old Testament events in the New of which they are "types"—or rather he employs a reversed adaptation of this which labels something in his story a "type" of a Bible element—as when Hester Prynne is called "a scarlet woman and a worthy type of her of Babylon" [74]. But it should be observed that this particular description comes not from the narrator but from one of the tale's seventeenth century Puritans who might be expected to typologize in this way, just as it is the Puritan authority that has affixed upon Hester the signifying letter which is invariably described as being not red but scarlet. She is called a "type" in a non-scriptural sense by the Hawthorne-narrator. At such

times she can be associated with traditional figures of moral personification when he comments, "It may seem marvellous that this woman
should call that place her home, where, and where only, she must
needs be the type of shame" [55]—which still implicitly refers to the
viewpoint of the Boston community or, again, when Chillingworth is
said to have come home to behold "the woman, in whom he hoped to
find embodied the warmth and cheerfulness of home, set up as a type
of sin before the people" [79]. Other occurrences of the term, however,
are closer to the simpler meaning of a symbol. Such is the early designation of the infant Pearl as "a forcible type, in its little frame, of the
moral agony which Hester Prynne had borne throughout the day" [50].

"Token," i.e., "something that serves to indicate a fact, event, object,
feeling, etc.; a sign, a symbol" (*OED*) also serves to indicate a sign,
with the added implication that the sign is an evidence, even a consequence of the signified. Dimmesdale's distaste for Chillingworth's appearance is "a token, implicitly to be relied on, of a deeper antipathy
in the breast of the latter" [93]. "Emblem" is another name for a symbolic signifier, more exclusively visual, deriving from the seventeenth
century taste for expressing abstractions by means of objects or pictured objects, but since used as another synonym for symbol as well as
for an armorial device or even for a badge that might be worn on
clothing. Hester's "A" is all these—a badge she wears, a device for the
escutcheon on her tombstone—"On a field sable, the letter A, gules"
[166] and the "emblem of her guilt" [69].

Finally, there is "hieroglyph," which more than any of the terms just
glanced at suggests the art of writing at the same time that it suggests
the pictorial figure, in the reference to the picture-writing of the Egyp-
tians. By extension, too, a hieroglyph is "a figure, device, or sign, having some hidden meaning; a secret or enigmatical symbol" (*OED*), and
so more than any of the others expresses Hawthorne's feelings about
the signifiers he has marked out in his tale. Such a mystery is the child
Pearl, as we shall shortly consider. As Hester and Dimmesdale watch
her in the forest, it is observed, "She had been offered to the world,
these seven years past, as the living hieroglyphic, in which was revealed the secret they so darkly sought to hide,—all written in this
symbol,—all plainly manifest,—had there been a prophet or magician
skilled to read the character of flame" [132]. Pearl, the animate letter
or character, is truly the hieroglyphic figure which hides an elusive
meaning.

Like a rhetorician, Hawthorne has, in the examples I have given, labelled his subjects as though they were figures of speech in a spoken
or written text. But, of course, these types, emblems, tokens, and hi-
eroglyphs are not really supposed to be products of the human imagination. They belong to the category of privileged signs deriving from a
transcendent presence. They are "written" by a spiritual force which
expresses itself in the secret language of appearances. To read such
texts one must be gifted with a prophet's or a magician's power to see
beyond actuality. As Chillingworth says of the "riddle" ("a question or
statement intentionally worded in a dark or puzzling manner" [*OED*])

of the identity of Hester's lover, "the Daniel who shall expound it is yet a-wanting" [45]. The surface of life which he beholds is thus compared to the most famous of dark texts, the writing on the wall at Belshazzar's feast.

For us, there may no longer be a center, as Jacques Derrida would call it, to assure to such—or any—appearances the status of signs. With our loss of confidence in the sacred grounding of signs we have lost confidence in their objectivity, and see them only as games of the mind. Hawthorne may have been at the threshold of our condition, though he was still formally committed to older views. The Puritan ontology as well as the Puritan morality haunted the American mind in Hawthorne's day, and haunted his in particular. We think more usually of the moral imperatives of Puritanism as a lingering presence in Hawthorne's writing—and where more than in this tale of transgression and penance? But it is the Puritan understanding of the relation of natural to divine reality that was more important to him. The Puritans regarded reality textually; a long tradition of Christian thought which spoke through them analogized the world as a book which might be compared to scripture as an act of divine writing. What God had written in the creation was a cryptic language, yet one could be confident nonetheless that no phenomenon but had its sacred sense. Such a viewpoint was older than Christianity, having its roots in platonism. It was, too, enjoying a new life in the secularized religion of romantic transcendentalism of which Hawthorne was aware at close hand.

Hawthorne knew perfectly well his difference and distance from the Puritans, though "strong traits of their nature," he said, had "intertwined themselves" with his [12]. He was skeptical as well about the convictions of his Concord neighbors, Emerson and Thoreau. His temperamental nominalism, which is so visible in the determined abstention from all interpretation practiced in his Notebooks with their tireless recording of trivial realities, made him a man for whom the world is exactly what it is and no more. Yet, as for so many mid-nineteenth century minds the loss of the visionary sense, the draining of significance from the mundane, was felt with a certain anguish, at best a wry humor, and the viewpoint of science seemed to him pitiably meager and even morally dangerous. In *The Scarlet Letter* he gives play to all of his mingled feelings—his tenderness for the poetry of a lost faith in essences, his ironic detachment and disbelief, and his fear of such disbelief in himself or others.

The agency of these complex feelings is, in the novel, a persona about whom too little has been said. His divided attitudes are made clear in the Custom House Preface—making the Preface a necessary part of the fictional whole, giving a character to the narrating voice. This narrator appears to us in the Preface as a man undecided in his view of reality between the Puritan-transcendental conviction that the invisible speaks ceaselessly behind the visible and the materialism that finds the explanation of things merely in accident and physical laws. He admits his deviation from the beliefs of his "grave, bearded, sable-

cloaked and steeple-crowned" [11] progenitors, yet declares a legitimate descent from them. He values his experiences at the Custom
House as an antidote to transcendental associations and inclinations.
Even the old inspector, a personality of unillumined materiality, was,
he tells us, "desirable as a change of diet, to a man who had known Alcott" [22]. Yet his final and most moving words are a tribute to the art
that discerns the spirit essence in the quotidian.

In this well-known section of the Preface he discusses his aesthetic
problems while striving, in the Custom House, to overcome his creative torpor. But it should be noted that his problem is as much ontological as aesthetic: it involves his unsuccessful struggle to attain the
transcendental sense. In the nighttime vigil in the parlor of his Salem
house, the moonlight "making every object so minutely visible, yet so
unlike a morning or noontide visibility," the homely details of the
room were completely seen, he recalls, "yet spiritualized by the unusual light." The room became a neutral territory where "the Actual
and the Imaginary may meet" [29]. It was the sort of meeting he
would have liked to bring about in his writing yet could not, though
the "wiser effort would have been, to diffuse thought and imagination
through the opaque substance of today . . . to seek, resolutely, the true
and indestructible value that lay hidden in the petty and wearisome incidents, and ordinary characters" [30]. His failure was no matter
merely of skill or of artistic imagination, as it has seemed to most
readers. The requisite imagination that he lacked was the prophet or
magician's—or if the poet's, then the romantic poet's seer-like power
to discern higher truth. Unable to find essence in his surroundings he
could only retreat to the unsubstantiality of the past or the fanciful, in
which one might play with the idea of significance in the mode of romance.

Nevertheless, nothing is more serious than *The Scarlet Letter*, despite the charge of Henry James that its faults are "a want of reality
and an abuse of the fanciful element—of a certain superficial symbolism" which "grazes triviality." James did not see that Hawthorne's
method in the book was to express his own profoundest problem. In a
way that is seldom understood and seems sometimes merely coy, he
offers and withdraws, denies and provides the sense of the spirituality
of life—and so suggests the opacity or unreliability of its signs. Many
a reader has been irritated by the narrator's reluctance to decide what,
if anything, Chillingworth saw on Dimmesdale's bosom, or what, if
anything, was seen in the sky during the night-scaffold scene in Chapter 12 or what, if anything, was seen on Dimmesdale's bosom, again,
by the assembled multitude in the final scaffold scene. These are only
the most memorable instances of Hawthorne's reluctance to settle a
simple question of appearances. More important, however, is his refusal to help us to assign final significance to these phenomena, even
if granted. Repeatedly, he seems only willing to say, as at the conclusion of the final scene after summarizing the conflicting reports of witnesses, "The reader may choose among these theories."

Nowhere is this insistent ambiguity more conspicuous than in the central scaffold scene—which James, it may be noted, particularly disliked. Here are duplicated the conditions of the moonlit chamber of the Preface; the scene is bathed in a supernal light which makes each detail both completely visible and radiant with meaning. In the light cast from the sky during the minister's night-vigil, he sees for the first time that Roger Chillingworth is no friend, he pierces the veil. Yet this is also the occasion for the narrator's most skeptical discussion of the delusiveness of signs. He comments upon the "messages" read into nature by man and the egotism of the assumption that they are addressed to our particular selves. "We impute it, therefore, solely to the disease in his own eye and heart that the minister, looking upward toward the zenith, beheld there the appearance of an immense letter,— the letter A" [102], he seems to conclude. But, immediately after, we hear that the sexton reported the next day that "a great red letter in the sky,—the letter A" [104], was seen by others also, and by them taken to stand for Angel, to signify the governor's passing. So, what are we to make of the reading of signs? The sexton, who has found Dimmesdale's glove on the scaffold, says that Satan must have dropped it there, intending—falsely—to impute that Dimmesdale belongs where evil-doers are set up to public shame. Signs may be only the mischief-making of Satan, then, and no true tokens? Except, of course, that this token *is* well placed!

Hester's letter is the central example of the almost infinite potentialities of semantic variety. A material object, a piece of embroidered cloth held in the finder's hand, it is the one irreducible reality which connects the intangible historic past with the narrator's present sensation; it authenticates, is an evidence of its vanished substantiality. As an abstract sign on Hester's bosom, it purports to speak both for the nature of her past and for the present condition of the wearer. It is a letter of the alphabet, but also, presumably, an initial, a sign of a sign, since it represents a word, the next larger linguistic unit after the letter. But "adultery" is never "spelled out." The word, like the act it designates, is invisible in the text—the act held inaccessibly out of the reader's sight while the word only hovers in his mind. The merely implied word becomes somehow less explicit, and when we are told that the letter is a "talisman" (a magic object generally engraved with figures or characters) of the Fiend, we suspect a more generalized significance. It is said to throb in sympathy with all sin of whatever kind beheld by Hester. It seems to represent an absolute and undenotable evil.

The letter may indicate the presence in Hester of Original Sin, and refer to a common corruption which requires no outward demonstration, which does not manifest itself in true signs, which even the most virtuous in deed must share. The old Calvinist mystery is really the mystery of signs—there is an inner reality that cannot be signified by deed, while deeds, good works or the reverse, are without inner meaning. Trapped in this disjunction the Puritans themselves forget the original significance of Hester's letter and take it to stand for "able"— which is, unlike "adultery," enunciated in the text—because of her good works. But Hester, when the magistrates consider removing the stigma, says, "were I worthy to be quit of it, it would fall away of its own nature, or be transformed into something that should speak a different purport" [110]. She seems, still, to insist upon its relation to her inner self. Yet she will try to comfort Dimmesdale by pointing out *his* good works—"Is there no reality in the penitence thus sealed and witnessed by good works?" [123]—until he tells her that *his* scarlet letter still "burns in secret."

On Dimmesdale, where the letter may be guessed to have appeared for a similar signifying function as on Hester, it is, however, as invisible as the act or condition it refers to. Society has placed no token upon him and when Chillingworth opens the sleeping minister's vestment he sees "something" which is not pictured or named for the reader. Even in the final scene when he tears his own garment from his chest we are told only, "It was revealed! But it were irreverent to describe that revelation" [161], and the reader is cheated again of the confirming spectacle. Although some spectators testified to having seen that the minister did bear a letter like Hester's, others saw nothing. And the sign, if it had really been there, might, anyhow, our narrator remarks, have been only the medical symptom of Dimmesdale's psychic distress, "the effect of the ever active tooth of remorse gnawing from the inmost heart outwardly" [163], an instance of psychosomatic symptomology (another sign theory which greatly interested Hawthorne, as we shall see in a moment).

Pearl, the asker of so many preternaturally pertinent questions, asks her mother to explain the meaning of the sign she wears and is not answered—plausibly because the answer would be beyond her grasp but also so that the reader may still not hear the signified, the unutterable. When she asks, "What does the letter mean, mother," Hester says evasively, "I wear it for the sake of its gold thread" [117]. Pearl says that she has been told that the scarlet letter is the Black Man's mark, an expression she repeats when she asks if the minister holds his hand upon his bosom because the Black Man has "set his mark" there. "Mark," for which the root sense is, once again, token or sign, implies here, as a special meaning, a signature, the personal sign of a signer set in stead of his name. As such it signifies not the wearer but the writer, the author of all sin. Pearl connects this guessed-at sign with Hester's A when she asks, "Is this his mark?" and extracts from her mother the acknowledgment, "Once in my life I met the Black Man! This scarlet letter is his mark!" [120]. And Pearl then guesses, when she sees the minister's hand over his heart, "Is it because, when the minister wrote his name in the book, the Black Man set his mark in that place?" [121].

Both symbol and consequence of Hester's and Dimmesdale's sin, Pearl is herself an instance of the ambiguity of signs. She is the animate letter, the child dressed in gold-embroidered scarlet, "the scarlet letter in another form, the scarlet letter endowed with life" [69]. Yet when she dances about in the final scene in the city square, "her dress, so proper was it to little Pearl, seemed an effluence or inevitable development and outward manifestation of her character, no more to be separated from her than the many-hued brilliancy from a butterfly's wing, or the painted glory from the leaf of a bright flower" [145]. Her appearance, once the sign, the "effluence" of her parents' sin, is now an exterior organically developed from her own airy nature, as the rest of nature's signs emanate from transcendent being. Earlier, she reverses or nullifies Hester's sign when she places it, made of eel grass, upon herself. It is the color of nature, green, the eidetic image of her mother's token, and Pearl waggishly reflects as though to mock the meaning-searcher, "I wonder if mother will ask me what it means!" But Hester refuses to see it as a sign, and says, "The green letter on thy childish bosom has no purport" [115].

The mystery of meaning is expressed in the obliquity of Pearl's own answers to the question of what she is. Hester wonders, "Child, what are thou?" and is answered, "O, I am your little Pearl" [66], which is no answer for her name is her sign not her significance. Hester asks, "Tell me, then what thou art and who sent thee hither?" and then answers this question herself, but Pearl demurs, "I have no Heavenly Father" [67], the animate sign denying its source in the divine. A little later, the Reverend Wilson asks again, "Who made thee?" [75] and Pearl's answer is that she has not been made but plucked from the prison rose-bush, an answer at once improbably arch and informed with a pantheistic view of nature, dispensing with the myth of express creation. Hawthorne's ironic dubiety can be felt in his presentation of the Governor's shocked, "a child of three years old, and she cannot tell who made her!" [76]—for how many among his readers would have had perfect confidence in the catechism reply? Of course, all the while that we have had this play of alternative semiologies, of Puritan and transcendental explanations of origin, it is obvious that Pearl's pert remarks are naturalistically explicable; she has just seen the roses in the governor's garden, has already been called "red rose" by Wilson himself, who also calls her "little bird of scarlet plumage" [74], the natural creature she will be likened to in the last scene.

Our first view of Hester and her child occurs, nevertheless, when they emerge from the prison door passing the rose-bush and the weeds "which evidently found something congenial in the soil that had so early borne the black flower of civilized society, a prison" [36]. Weeds and prison are linked by a resemblance that is not merely metaphor but attributable to the generative force of which they are both products. Nearby, the rose-bush holds up "delicate gems" which "might be imagined to offer" sweetness to the condemned "in token that the deep heart of Nature could pity and be kind to him" [36]. Nature, the symbolizer, proffers a token from the realm of spirit in the same way as the Christian godhead has sent Pearl as "emblem and product of sin" [64]. But Hawthorne does not assert either source of signification uncontrovertibly: his weak copula, "might be imagined," is a reminder that such symbolizing may be only the result of the human imagination.

It is quite "significant," therefore, that the artistic imagination appears centrally in Hester herself who is an artist of needlework, the only medium available to a woman in her day. Her works are distinguished by their power of symbolic exhibition, her first oeuvre of note having been her letter. She is afterwards called upon to show the meaning of other human situations, the pomp of public ceremonies, the sorrow of funerals which she would "typify by manifold emblematic devices" [57]. Her art is also *self*-expressive, "a mode of expressing and therefore soothing the passion of her life" [58]. Pearl has something of her mother's instinct: her creativity operates upon "a stick, a bunch of rags, a flower" [65], adapting them to her inner drama. Her art is harmless play. But Hester collaborates with Puritan society in converting Pearl herself into a symbol by clothing her in her symbolizing, signifying costume. She thus does violence to the irreducible being of the child who is shown repeatedly to be a natural phenomenon, a whimsical child and nothing else. All art, all symbolizing, is reductive.

In the mirror of art the truth is distorted from its natural proportions, as Hester's own image is when she sees herself in the polished armor in the Governor's house. The monstrously enlarged "A" upon her breast, her face reduced to insignificance by the convex surface of the breastplate, represent her reduction as the woman behind the scarlet letter. And in time, "all the light and graceful foliage of her character had been withered by this red hot brand, and had long fallen away, leaving a bare and harsh outline" [106–07], the person *becoming* the symbol. Yet the narrative shows at the same time that Hester resists this simplification, remaining a complex, developing personality. An opposite process takes place in the case of Chillingworth who, as his history advances, becomes more and more an abstract symbol of infernal malice until at the end he simply shrivels to nothing, all his humanity gone.

But Hawthorne does not dismiss or disparage the reading of signs altogether. He continues throughout the narrative to find ways of exploring the relation of phenomenon and meaning, of outerness and inwardness; his narrative discovers and tests other pairs of terms that represent signifier and signified. One example is the theory of disease by which he anticipates psychosomatic medicine. Chillingworth, it will be recalled, ascribes his patient's malady to a spiritual cause. "He to whom only the outward and physical evil is laid open knoweth, oftentimes, but half the evil which he is called upon to cure. A bodily disease, which we look upon as whole and entire within itself, may, after all, be but a symptom of some ailment in the spiritual part . . . a sickness, a sore place, if we may so call it, in your spirit, hath immediately its appropriate manifestation in your bodily frame" [91]. Bodily disease, then, is a "manifestation" of spirit, another instance of the sign language of all phenomena. Hawthorne's interest in the general science of signs, extends, logically, to the branch of medicine having to do with symptoms, which is also called semiology. Older medical concepts and even modern ones, of course, imply a dualism in the patient whose disease is defined as a manifestation of some hidden meaning— and a meaning that was truly inaccessible, for the most part, before the germ theory and modern knowledge of physiology. And so the source of disease, though presumed to be spiritual in Dimmesdale's case, will not, after all, be accessible to the probing of his physician-enemy.

Dimmesdale himself subscribes to his physicians' theories when he attributes his own distrust of Chillingworth to his inner spiritual disorder—"the poison of one morbid spot was infecting his heart's entire substance" [93]. In fact, his perceptions are accurate. But his inner condition does produce hallucinations, delusive signs. These seem to demonstrate, again, Hawthorne's view of the effects of the Puritan-transcendental view of a superior spiritual reality, his preference for the matter-of-fact: "It is the unspeakable misery of a life so false as his, that it steals the pith and substance out of whatever realities there are around us . . . To the untrue man, the whole universe is false,—and it is impalpable,—it shrinks to nothing within his grasp" [96–97].

All things hidden and all things exposed become antonyms in the novel to reflect the opposition of outer and inner. The forest, where the lovers meet alone save for little Pearl who does not understand what she sees except by occult instinct, is the place of a seclusive truth, difficult to read; the forest path, like a hard text, is "obscure." The public scenes in which Hester and Dimmesdale are together are the locus of communal truth, that which is perceived by all. "We must not talk in the market-place of what happens to us in the forest" [152], Hester warns Pearl, distinguishing between the unutterable inner world and the world of speech. Hester's "A", Mistress Hibbins says, is a "token" that Hester has been to the forest many times, but the minister's visit is ultimately incommunicable. His election sermon is best understood when, in fact, its *words* are indistinguishable and only the mournful tone of his voice conveys his state to Hester as she stands outside. Language, by implication, misleads us, tells us nothing of the heart, which has no language. Dimmesdale's unintelligible murmur is like Pearl's babble or the gibberish she speaks in his ear in the night scaffold scene—perhaps a sacred speaking in tongues, perhaps the non-sense of a message-less world.

Nature, too, only babbles. The forest keeps its secrets though the babbling brook would seem to want to "speak" them: "All these giant trees and boulders of granite seemed intent on making a mystery of the course of this small brook: fearing, perhaps, that, within its never-ceasing loquacity, it should whisper tales out of the heart of the old forest whence it flowed, or mirror its revelations on the smooth surface of a pool" [120]. Pearl asks what the brook says, but Hester replies that if she had a sorrow of her own the brook would tell her of it, "even as it is telling me of mine!" [121], implying that she has understood the brook as the brook has understood her, but also that one hears in Nature's babble what one's own experience suggests. And as Pearl continues to play by the side of the brook her own cheerful babble mingles with its melancholy one, we are told, and "the little stream would not be comforted and still kept telling its unintelligible secret of some mournful mystery" [121].

Hawthorne's antithesis between the solitary soul and society is a variation upon the theme of an inexpressible inner reality. Hester is one of the great American isolatoes, who cannot speak the language of community. At his extremest, this loner is Melville's Bartleby, who withdraws from language altogether. By embracing silence he acknowledges the lapse of a common truth which unites not only men with one another but which, by a language of signs, unites the universe to mankind. Hester's sin is not only unutterable but involves a name, that of her partner, which she refuses to utter. Her sexual history is so private that it cannot be imagined when we gaze at her in the chaste aftermath of Hawthorne's novel. And yet that privacy has its public manifestation, the child Pearl. And Hester's sin is outrageously publicized by her exposure in the most public of places, the town pillory. The opening scene of the novel draws thrilling intensity from this paradox. From the hidden interior of her prison cell, from the secrecy of her own heart, Hester emerges with the child upon her arm, isolated and silent, to stand upon the most public site in Boston. A special piece of cruel machinery, a vise to hold the head upright, is available on the scaffold so that the condemned may be forced to face those who look upon him, and Hawthorne comments, "There is no outrage more flagrant than to forbid the culprit to hide his face for shame" [42]. But Hester voluntarily faces her viewers. Nevertheless, her exposure reveals nothing. Indeed, the spectator is prompted to find her an "image of Divine Maternity" [42], to read the scarlet woman as her opposite.

"Secret" is a key word in *The Scarlet Letter*. All the principal personages have secrets—Hester, the identity of her lover, Dimmesdale his sin, Chillingworth his own identity and motive. Chillingworth's name is like Hester's sin in never being enunciated in the text—though we may guess that it is Prynne. Perhaps the most important of these secrets, in terms of the progressive tension of the plot is Dimmesdale's. Chillingworth's struggle to bring to the surface what lies hidden in the minister's heart is the primary conflict of the story (James was right in saying that the essential drama is there, between the two men, and not in Hester). This is also because more is involved in their struggle than the story tells: theirs is the contest between two views of the communicability of meaning. Chillingworth had asked Hester to name her lover and she had refused, eliciting from him the comment, "there are few things,—whether in the outward world, or the invisible sphere of thought—few things hidden from the man, who devotes himself earnestly and unreservedly to the solution of a mystery" [53]. By profession a scientist, an investigator of nature and mankind, he is confident that he can compel all mysteries to yield to him. From the "prying multitude," from even the magistrates and ministers, Hester's secret may be hidden, but, Chillingworth declares, "I come to the inquest with other senses than they possess. I shall seek this man as I have sought truth in books, as I have sought gold in alchemy" [53].

Chillingworth is defined as a materialist, one of a species of men who have lost the sense of spiritual meanings. "In their researches into the human frame, it may be that the higher and more subtle faculties of such men were materialized, and that they lost the spiritual view of existence amid the intricacies of that wondrous mechanism which seemed to involve art enough to comprise all of life within itself" [80]. The newcomer becomes the community physician, replacing the aged deacon and apothecary, "whose piety and deportment were stronger testimonials in his favor" than a medical diploma, for he is learned in both "antique physic" [80] and the Indians' homeopathic medicine.

He believes, consequently, that the inner condition of his patient, the meaning of his disease can be understood. The narrator seems to agree: "Few secrets can escape an investigator who has opportunity and license to undertake such a quest" [83]. Like a researcher into a difficult scientific problem he is described "prying into his patient's bosom, delving among his principles, prying into his recollections, proving everything with a cautious touch, like a treasure-seeker in a dark cavern" [83]. Hawthorne even goes on to say, "A man burdened with a secret should especially avoid the intimacy of his physician" for "at some inevitable moment, will the soul of the sufferer be dissolved, and flow forth in a dark and transparent stream, bringing all its mysteries into the daylight" [83]. The doctor—more investigator than therapist—is said to be "desirous only of truth, even as if the question involved no more than the air-drawn lines and figures of a geometrical problem, instead of human passions, and wrongs inflicted on himself" [86].

His contest with Dimmesdale, who steadfastly protects his secret, is dramatically illustrated in their conversation in the graveyard in chapter 10. Upon a grave without identifying tombstone the physician finds weeds that "grew out of the [buried man's] heart" and "typify, it may be, some hideous secret that was buried with him." They have sprung up there, Chillingworth declares, "to make manifest an unspoken crime" [87]. Dimmesdale, however, insists upon the inaccessibility and sacredness of the dead man's secrets. "There can be . . . no power, short of the Divine mercy, to disclose, whether by uttered words, or by type or emblem, the secrets that may be buried with a human heart. The heart . . . must perforce hold them, until the day when all hidden things shall be revealed. . . . These revelations . . . are meant merely to promote the intellectual satisfaction of all intelligent beings, who will stand waiting, on that day, to see the dark problem of this life made plain" [88]. Not merely, then, does he not choose to tell his secret; it cannot ever be revealed to men until Judgment Day. It is a mystery too profound for us before that. And, Hawthorne's language seems to suggest, it is a mystery which is only part of the general mystery of "hidden things" for which "type or emblem" [88]—the language of appearances—provide no clue. As the methodical indeterminacy of *The Scarlet Letter* suggests, there is no present disclosure of "the dark problem of this life" [88].

To presume otherwise by trying to penetrate the mystery of another soul is Chillingworth's sin, as Dimmesdale tells Hester. He "violated in cold blood the sanctity of a human heart" [125–26]. This statement is not usually understood, though invariably quoted in discussions of the novel. We tend to think that Chillingworth has sinned because he has criminally used the knowledge he has gained in order to manipulate and destroy the minister. But this is not what the words say. The insistence upon illicit discovery, the assault by Chillingworth upon sacred knowledge, is itself illegitimate.

Here perhaps is the pious man's reply to the problem of the obliquity of signs. Hawthorne may have felt that it was his only stay against skepticism to believe in an ultimate revelation, an ultimate deciphering of what is beyond our comprehension in this life. But he may also have entertained the suspicion that no ultimate meanings exist. Perhaps he sometimes felt bold enough to share the thought expressed by Melville in a letter he got from him only a year after *The Scarlet Letter* was published: "If any of those other Powers choose to withhold certain secrets, let them; that does not impair my sovereignty in myself; that does not make me tributary. And perhaps after all, there is *no* secret."

DAVID LEVERENZ

Mrs. Hawthorne's Headache: Reading *The Scarlet Letter*†

When Hawthorne read the end of *The Scarlet Letter* to his wife, it "broke her heart and sent her to bed with a grievous headache—which I look upon as a triumphant success!" His Chillingworth-like tone belies his own feelings. Ostensibly his "triumphant" sense of professional satisfaction depends on breaking a woman's heart and mind, much as his narrative pacifies the heart and mind of its heroine. But Hawthorne's "success" also depends on evoking great sympathy for female suffering. Several years later he vividly recalled "my emotions when I read the last scene of the Scarlet Letter to my wife, just after writing it—tried to read it, rather, for my voice swelled and heaved, as if I were tossed up and down on an ocean, as it subsides after a storm." As Randall Stewart notes, "Hawthorne was not in the habit of breaking down." This scene, and the shaking sobs that overcame him at his dying mother's bedside, "are the only recorded instances of uncontrolled emotion" in Hawthorne's career.[1]

Mrs. Hawthorne's headache is a rare moment in the history of American reader responses. It reveals not only a spouse's ambiguously painful reaction but also the author's incompatible accounts of his own first reading. Both responses seem deeply divided: one with a splitting headache, the other with a split self-presentation. If we accept at face

---

† From *Nineteenth-Century Literature* 37.4 (1983): 552–75. Copyright © 1999 by the Regents of the University of California. Reprinted by permission. Page numbers in square brackets refer to this Norton Critical Edition.
1. Randall Stewart, *Nathaniel Hawthorne: A Biography* (New Haven: Yale UP, 1948), 95, cites both the first quotation, which is from a letter to Horatio Bridge, 4 Feb. 1850, rpt. in *Hawthorne: The Critical Heritage*, ed. J. Donald Crowley (New York: Barnes and Noble Books, 1970), 151, and the second quotation, which is from Hawthorne's *English Notebooks*, 14 Sept. 1855.

value the goal announced by Hawthorne's narrator in the first paragraph of "The Custom-House," to seek a self-completing communion with his readers, his quest to discover "the divided segment of the writer's own nature" ends in frustration. Both Hawthorne and his most intimate sympathizer experience inward turmoil and self-controlled withdrawal. As several first readers commented in print, Hawthorne's romance left them with similarly intense and unresolved feelings—of sadness, pain, annoyance, and almost hypnotic fascination.

The Scarlet Letter's strange power over its contemporary readers derives from its unresolved tensions. What starts as a feminist revolt against punitive patriarchal authority ends in a muddle of sympathetic pity for ambiguous victims. Throughout, a gentlemanly moralist frames the story so curiously as to ally his empathies with his inquisitions. Ostensibly he voices Hawthorne's controlling moral surface, where oscillations of concern both induce and evade interpretive judgments. Yet his characterizations of Hester and Chillingworth bring out Hawthorne's profoundly contradictory affinities with a rebellious, autonomous female psyche and an intrusive male accuser. The narrative's increasing preoccupation with Dimmesdale's guilt both blankets and discovers that fearful inward intercourse. D. H. Lawrence's directive to trust the tale, not the teller, rightly challenges the narrator's inauthentic moral stance.[2] But that becomes a complicating insight, not a simplifying dismissal. In learning to see beyond Hawthorne's narrator, readers can see what lies beneath the author's distrust of any coercive authority, especially his own. Though the narrator sometimes seems quite self-consciously fictionalized, he functions less as a character than as a screen for the play of textual energies.

The plot establishes incompatible centers of psychological power: Hester's fierce private passion, at once radically independent and voluptuously loving, and Chillingworth's equally private rage to expose, control, and accuse. These centers have surfaced in modern criticism as feminist or psychoanalytic responses to the text. The narrator's voice acts as a safety valve, releasing and containing feelings in socially acceptable ways. His very self-conscious relation to his readers, whom he frequently appeals to and fictionalizes, both abets, displaces, and conceals his story's unresolved tensions.

The narrator also mirrors the limits of his contemporary American reader's toleration for strong subjectivity, especially anger. As Trollope noted, "there is never a page written by Hawthorne not tinged by satire." The narrator of The Scarlet Letter skillfully intermingles earnest appeals for sympathy with mocking exposure of rage, distanced as cruelty.[3] His tolerance for human frailty, his addiction to

---

2. Studies in Classic American Literature (Garden City, N.Y.: Doubleday, 1951), 13; see also his discussion of The Scarlet Letter as a "colossal satire" full of "inner diabolism" (92–110).

3. "The Genius of The Scarlet Letter," in The Scarlet Letter: An Annotated Text, Backgrounds and Sources, Essays in Criticism, ed. Sculley Bradley, Richmond Croom Beatty, and E. Hudson Long, 1st ed. (New York: W. W. Norton & Company, 1962), 242; see also "He is always laughing at something with his weird, mocking spirit" (244). The article in the Norton edition is a partial reprint of Trollope's "The Genius of Nathaniel Hawthorne," North American Review, Sept. 1879, 203–22.

multiple interpretations, and his veiled hints at self-disgust deflect his fear that anger destroys a lovable self. In claiming that art should veil self-exposure, he invites both sympathy and self-accusation. He is a Dimmesdale who doesn't quite know he is a Chillingworth.

Several nineteenth-century readers sensed Chillingworth's ascendance in the narrator as well as his narrative. Trollope and Henry James both noted with some surprise that the romance was oddly a hate story, and James speaks of Hawthorne's constant struggle between "his evasive and his inquisitive tendencies."[4] Anne Abbott felt "cheated into a false regard and interest" by Hester's seeming suffering and Dimmesdale's seeming faith, because Hester's pride destroys her Christian character, while Dimmesdale's suffering becomes "aimless and without effect for purification or blessing to the soul." "A most obstinate and unhuman passion, or a most unwearying conscience it must be," she continues, ". . . but such a prolonged application of the scourge." Finally, the man whom Hawthorne considered his most astute critic, E. P. Whipple, concluded that the narrator's tendency to "put his victims on the rack" establishes an uncomfortably compelling despotism. Though the morbid suffering appalls sensible readers, he said, they yield despite themselves to "the guidance of an author who is personally good-natured, but intellectually and morally relentless."[5]

The narrator is protected by his duplicitous stance from full exposure, as he half admits. The rhetorical strategies that can give his reader a headache preserve his good name. Yet under his interpretive equivocations, unresolved conflicts about anger, authority, and female autonomy continuously impel the contradictions in his voice as well as his story. A close reading of *The Scarlet Letter* along these lines, as I try to offer here, raises the possibility of using formalist methods to explore the text's intimate, ambivalent relationship to the author's own life and the contemporary interpretive community.[6]

4. Trollope, "The Genius of *The Scarlet Letter*," 243. James, *Hawthorne*, introd. Tony Tanner (London: Macmillan, 1967), 109–10. Taylor Stoehr, *Hawthorne's Mad Scientists: Pseudoscience and Social Science in Nineteenth-Century Life and Letters* (Hamden, Conn.: Archon Books, 1978), 116, stresses Chillingworth's function as "an evil chorus figure whose perspective has much in common with that of the reader and the author." An angry Salem Whig found nothing but Chillingworth in Hawthorne; see Benjamin Lease, "Salem vs. Hawthorne: An Early Review of *The Scarlet Letter*," *New England Quarterly*, 44(1971): 110–17.
5. Anne W. Abbott, review of *The Scarlet Letter*, in *North American Review*, July 1850, rpt. in *Hawthorne: The Critical Heritage*, 164–67; see 166 [245–46]. E. P. Whipple. "Nathaniel Hawthorne," *Atlantic Monthly*, May 1860, rpt. in *Hawthorne: The Critical Heritage*, 340–50; see 344, 346. Whipple's 1850 review of *The Scarlet Letter* is also reprinted in *The Critical Heritage*, 160–62.
6. In arguing that close reading opens out to questions of social history, I am opposing the antiformalist stance taken by Jane Tompkins in her December 1981 MLA talk on how critics have preserved Hawthorne's reputation at the expense of say, Susan Warner's. I agree with Tompkins's larger contention that textual meanings are established by readers at any historical moment. But if I am right to say that *The Scarlet Letter* both induces, replicates, and undermines the interpretive expectations of its contemporary readers, that posits a more ambivalent relation between text and community than the theory of interpretive community so far allows. Various writings by Tompkins, Stanley Fish, and Walter Benn Michaels have been developing the theory; Steven Mailloux usefully summarizes the theory and others in *Interpretive Conventions: The Reader in the Study of American Fiction* (Ithaca and London: Cornell UP, 1982). Mailloux uses Hawthorne to orient the theory toward how texts constitute complex ethical judgments.

I

A surprisingly aggressive feminist interpretation seems self-consciously mandated as the storytelling begins. The narrator's first sentence deflates church and state to "steeple-crowned hats," while the first paragraph associates those hats with the iron spikes on the prison door. As the next paragraph explains, the colony's patriarchs have appropriated "the virgin soil" for graves and a prison, while stifling their utopian hopes with a grave distrust of human nature. Hats and "sad-colored garments" blend with the "beetle-browed and gloomy front" of the prison in a shared exterior gloom.[7] Inwardness has been shut up and spiked, along with youthful hopes and the virgin land.

The narrator's implicit symbolic advocacy becomes overt with his presentation of the "wild rose-bush," growing beside "the black flower of civilized society." If the prison is massive, forbidding, even "ugly," the rose bush brings out feminine delicacy and "fragile beauty." It also promises to awaken the body to imaginative life. It "might be imagined" to offer fragrance to a prisoner, "in token that the deep heart of Nature could pity and be kind to him." Perhaps, the narrator muses, this rose bush "survived out of the stern old wilderness, so long after the fall of the gigantic pines and oaks that originally overshadowed it" (39–40) [37]. Without pinning himself down, he allegorically intimates that patriarchs will die while tender flowers endure.

Or perhaps, he continues, the rose bush sprang up under the footsteps of "the sainted Ann Hutchinson"—the adjective lets loose his anti-Puritan, even Papist bias—as she walked through the prison door. In either case, his interpretive alternatives evoke a woman's triumphant survival beyond her towering, glowering elders, or at least her stubborn public opposition. As new elders die the natural death of Isaac Johnson, the first dead Puritan patriarch, they will retreat to "the congregated sepulchres" that define their eternity as interchangeably as their gravity defines their lives, while the rose and true womanhood may persevere toward a more naturally blossoming future.

Taking a final swerve from patriarchal authority by abdicating his own, the narrator refuses to "determine" which alternative should hold. Instead he presents the rose to his reader, since it grows "so directly on the threshold of our narrative, which is now about to issue from that inauspicious portal" (40) [37]. With a lushly symbolic self-consciousness the narrator has established a broad array of sympathies joining feminism, nature, youth, the body, and imaginative life. This associational array opposes patriarchal oppression, which doubly oppresses itself. The narrator's rhetorical strategies awaken reader expectations as well as sympathies. When Hester walks through the prison door, she will "issue" as the narrative itself, with all the hopes embodied in what is now the reader's wild red rose.

---

7. *The Scarlet Letter: An Authoritative Text, Backgrounds and Sources, Criticism,* ed. Sculley Bradley, Richmond Croom Beatty, E. Hudson Long, Seymour Gross, 2nd ed. (New York: W. W. Norton & Company, 1978), 39 [36]; further page references in the text are to this edition.

Yet Hester also walks forth into narrative hopelessness. With a hand even heavier than his heart the narrator suddenly imposes his gloomy end on her brave beginning. He tells us that the rose may "relieve the darkening close of a tale of human frailty and sorrow" [37]. That portentous phrase shuts the door on her wild possibilities as massively as the prison door dwarfs the rose. His plot will undercut the hopes his voice has just raised. His other alternative, that the rose bush might symbolize "some sweet moral blossom," seems deliberately anemic beside the contending passions his introduction promises. The narrator's sudden deflection from the rose's prospects suggests his fatalistic alliance with the prison's "darkening close." His narrative will be both, inextricably. He opens and shuts the door.

What seems here to be only a slight discomfort with the rose's radical implications eventually becomes an ambivalent inquisition into the dangers of Hester's lawless passion. The narrative issues forth as Chillingworth as well as Hester. Chillingworth's probing brings out the reader's powers of psychological detection while Hester's character encourages feminist responses. At once rebel and inquisitor, the narrator falsely joins these poles in a mystifying voice-over. He implies that the law can be transcended through Dimmesdale's growth toward spiritual purity or softened through Hester's growth toward maternal sympathy. To the degree that we can also perceive his own voice as an "issue" we can locate the unresolved tensions under his still more mystified "sweet moral blossom" of being true to oneself.

Hester Prynne's first gesture, to repel the beadle's authority, refocuses narrative sympathies. Her radical feminism goes further than Hyatt Waggoner's sense of her as a champion of the oppressed, and beyond Nina Baym's various arguments that she champions the private imagination.[8] In chapter 13 she goes so far as to imagine the "hopeless task" of building the whole social system anew, changing sex roles so completely that both womanhood and manhood will become unrecognizable to themselves (120) [108]. It seems an extraordinary instance of negative capability that Hawthorne, who forbade his daughter to write because it was unfeminine, could imagine the most radical woman in nineteenth-century New England, even retrospectively.[9] Though his narrator several times interjects that Hester's mind has gone so astray only because her heart "had lost its regular and healthy throb" (120) [108], his abstracted, fitful cavils seem to heighten our sense of her sustained independence.

Hester's private question about the "race" of women can still leap

---

8. Hyatt H. Waggoner, *Hawthorne: A Critical Study*, rev. ed. (Cambridge, Mass.: Harvard UP, 1963), 145; Nina Baym, *The Shape of Hawthorne's Career* (Ithaca and London: Cornell UP, 1976), 124–35. Judith Fryer makes a more dubious argument for Hester's potential "androgyny" in *The Faces of Eve: Women in the Nineteenth Century American Novel* (New York: Oxford UP, 1976), 74–84. See also Baym's "The Significance of Plot in Hawthorne's Romances," in *Ruined Eden of the Present: Hawthorne, Melville, and Poe: Critical Essays in Honor of Darrel Abel*, ed. G. R. Thompson and Virgil L. Lokke (West Lafayette, Ind.: Purdue UP, 1981), 49–70.

9. See Edward Wagenknecht, *Nathaniel Hawthorne: Man and Writer* (New York: Oxford UP, 1961), 17–18 and 150–53, for various remarks about Hawthorne's ambivalence concerning strong women.

off the page for modern readers: "Was existence worth accepting, even to the happiest among them?" (120) [108]. She has long since "decided in the negative" this question for herself. Later, from her radical freedom of fresh perception, she sees all social institutions "with hardly more reverence than the Indian would feel for the clerical band, the judicial robe, the pillory, the gallows, the fireside, or the church" (143) [128]. Not even Melville, with his more impulsive extremes of negation, offers such a laconic, liberating list. For Hester the comforts of fireside and church grow from the punitive powers of the clergy and judiciary, as interlocked and equivalent institutions.

Yet Hester's rebellious autonomy shields two very different kinds of loving. Why is it, the narrator asks in chapter 5, that Hester does not leave Salem? She could go to Europe, where she could "hide her character and identity under a new exterior," or she could enter the forest, "where the wildness of her nature might assimilate itself with a people whose customs and life were alien from the law that had condemned her" [55]. In rejecting both these ways of abandoning herself, whether to a civilized mask or to diffused natural passion, Hester consciously chooses to define her "roots" as her "chain" [56]. Her identity is the sin so "galling to her inmost soul." But the clear separation of outer sin from inner soul shows how unrepentant her desire remains. She becomes the jailer of a fearful secret: her dream of "a union, that, unrecognized on earth, would bring them together before the bar of final judgment, and make that their marriage-altar, for a joint futurity of endless retribution." I do not think any commentator has noticed the sacrilegious force of the hope that really impels her heart: to be united with Dimmesdale forever, in hell. A Dante-esque fantasy of condemned love lurks in her depths "like a serpent" (61) [56].[1] It terrifies her more consciously self-reliant conceptions of herself.

Hester's dream of a love forever framed by patriarchal punishment allows the narrator to present her as more victim than rebel. She is a woman more sinned against than sinning. Moreover, she is a mother as well as a woman in love. Her daughter's existence providentially prevents her from becoming a radical prophetess like Ann Hutchinson. The narrator observes that mothering, like knitting, fortunately "soothes" Hester's tendency toward conflict. In the task of educating Pearl, "the mother's enthusiasm of thought had something to wreak itself upon" (120) [108].[2] To reduce her ideas to an "enthusiasm" ready to be "wreaked" shows the narrator's bias. As a solitary, victimized woman Hester can rethink all social relations. But as a mother she has to nurture conventional womanhood, in herself as well as her daughter. As Dimmesdale says to John Wilson in chapter 8, the child "was

1. Every Hawthorne commentator I have read has missed Hester's secret dream of reunion in hell. They assume she hopes for heavenly reconciliation. See, for example, Richard H. Brodhead, *Hawthorne, Melville, and the Novel* (Chicago and London: U of Chicago P, 1976), 66; and Michael Davitt Bell, *The Development of American Romance: The Sacrifice of Relation* (Chicago and London: U of Chicago P, 1980), 178.
2. I am indebted here and throughout this essay to Richard Brodhead's incisive commentary on an earlier draft, as well as to helpful responses from Walter Herbert and *Nineteenth-Century Fiction*'s two readers.

meant, above all things else, to keep the mother's soul alive" (85) [77]. The narrator recurrently echoes the minister's sense of this "softening" charge: "Providence, in the person of this little girl, had assigned to Hester's charge the germ and blossom of womanhood, to be cherished and developed amid a host of difficulties" (120) [108]. The narrator veils his ambivalence about Hester's intellectual independence and her passionate desire by reinforcing what Nancy Chodorow has called "the institution of mothering" as the cure for all her ills.[3]

A less ambivalent narrator would see himself as part of his heroine's problem. Hester is far from liberated, even inwardly, despite her extraordinary perceptiveness about social repression. She avoids any struggle for public power except to preserve her conventional role as mother. She realizes that her winning advice to Dimmesdale— "Preach! Write! Act! Do anything, save to lie down and die!" (142) [127]—can apply only to men, not to herself. Yet she does not realize how grossly inadequate a man Dimmesdale turns out to be, as lover, parent, and friend. While the narrator seeks to shift Hester's ground from radical thought and sexual intimacy to more acceptable maternal love, Hester's tenacious affirmation of her continuously punished union holds fast despite increasingly glaring flaws in her man as well as the man who tells her story.

One scene in particular becomes a graphic paradigm of the forces converging to bring her strength within the sphere of Dimmesdale's weakness. In "The Child at the Brook-Side" Pearl stands across the brook from the two lovers, deliberately disregarding Hester's anxious pleas to come to them. When Hester tries to coax her across by saying that Pearl will have twice as much love as before with Dimmesdale beside her, the child fixes her eyes on her mother and the minister "as if to detect and explain to herself the relation which they bore to one another." Then, "assuming a singular air of authority, Pearl stretche[s] out her hand, with the small forefinger extended." She stamps her foot and "burst[s] into a fit of passion," with "piercing shrieks," her finger seeming to point at Hester's bosom, which now lacks the scarlet letter. Dimmesdale, never one to relish strong feelings, erupts with the immemorial plea of a father bent on adult matters: "Pacify her, if thou lovest me!" (149, 150) [133, 134].

As with any key scene, the incident focuses larger issues. To demand that Hester pacify Pearl if she loves him implies, most immediately, that Dimmesdale will continue to avoid the role of parent himself. Hester has to accept his abdication as part of loving him. More subtly, Dimmesdale's "if" is both a bargain and a threat. He can measure Hester's love for him by her success or failure in disciplining Pearl. Dimmesdale's habit of mind here reflects town values of authority and accounting, what the narrator satirizes in "The Custom-House," rather than wilderness intimacy. It is one of the narrator's more sympathetic cues, here and elsewhere, that we know Hester by

---

3. *The Reproduction of Mothering: Psychoanalysis and the Sociology of Gender* (Berkeley and Los Angeles: U of California P, 1978).

her first name and Dimmesdale by his last. Using her first name encourages intimacy with her freedom from her husband, and from
other imposed self-definitions, while the near-impossibility of calling
him "Arthur" indicates his anxious conformity to inherited social
codes.[4]

Yet the scene prefigures Hester's own accommodation to those
codes. The narrator already has taken some care to assert that Pearl is
Hester's hidden nature. She is a classic female double, in terms that
Sandra Gilbert and Susan Gubar have made familiar. She embodies
the lawless passion and impetuous rages constrained in her mother.
But as Hester senses from the first, her disturbingly alien "imp" also
embodies society's punishing judgment, as well as the letter's own imperiousness.[5] To pacify these contending elements in Pearl, Hester re-
assumes the scarlet letter. That acceptance of Pearl's pointing finger
means accepting love defined in Dimmesdale's terms, as a self-
pacification.[6]

As the story continues, Dimmesdale becomes the primary agent for
Hester's change from perceptive radical to sad-eyed sympathizer. In
their forest colloquy, for instance, Hester seems not to notice that the
minister prefaces her heretical claim to their wilderness "consecration" by comparing their "sin" to Chillingworth's "blacker" sin (140)
[125]. His mind still hovers anxiously in a patriarchal hierarchy of sin,
guilt, and violation. Equally symptomatic, his first response to her urgent assertion of mutual sanctity is "Hush, Hester!" For him to rise
and say he has not forgotten, as he then does, avoids confronting the
impasse between his sense of violation and her sense of holiness. His
association of intimacy with violation also connects him to the narrator. The very first paragraph of "The Custom-House" both solicits and
denies the possibility of "perfect sympathy" between writer and reader
by associating knowledge of "the inmost Me" with veils and violation.

A comprehensive fear of public anger, suffusing the entire narrative,
generates Dimmesdale's self-accusations. His obsessive guilt for a moment of consummated desire masks a deeper reluctance to expose aspects of himself that might displease authority. His pain becomes a
mystified accommodation that internalizes authority as self-
punishment. Overtly the narrator disengages himself from Dimmesdale's morbid self-scrutiny. He accuses the minister of selfishness,

4. This view of first name as implying intimacy and last name as social code should be qualified
by the fact that in early American culture one way of patronizing a woman was to call her by
her first name, whereas use of the last name implied respect.

5. Brodhead, Hawthorne, Melville, and the Novel, 56–57, emphasizes Pearl's oscillation between incompatible modes, especially in this scene. Most critics simply see Pearl as Hester's
double. On doubles in general see Sandra M. Gilbert and Susan Gubar, The Madwoman in
the Attic: The Woman Writer and the Nineteenth-Century Literary Imagination (New Haven
and London: Yale UP, 1979), esp. 69–92.

6. My analysis of this scene opposes the more narcissistic readings offered by John Irwin,
American Hieroglyphics: The Symbol of the Egyptian Hieroglyphics in the American Renaissance (New Haven and London: Yale UP, 1980), 250–51, which stresses the interplay of
mirrors with absence; and by Sharon Cameron, The Corporeal Self: Allegories of the Body in
Melville and Hawthorne (Baltimore and London: Johns Hopkins UP, 1981), 84, which
stresses Pearl's connection to the letter as part of Hester's body. Both readings illuminate
narrative doublings and problems of identity but avoid the interpersonal issues that generate
narcissistic fears. Cameron in particular reduces feelings of anger to acts of violence.

egotism, and cowardice, while presenting Dimmesdale's closet self-flagellations as bizarre. Yet the narrator frequently locates the sources of both art and truth within Dimmesdale's "anguish." When the minister speaks publicly, as he does several times "in tongues of flame," his eloquence becomes analogous to the writer's capacity for "addressing the whole human brotherhood in the heart's native language." Such eloquence must "gush" with "its own throb of pain" (104) [94]. For the narrator all art seeks ways of sharing that pain, without full self-exposure. "The only truth, that continued to give Mr. Dimmesdale a real existence on this earth," the narrator concludes in chapter 11, "was the anguish in his inmost soul" (107) [97]. This anguish, he explains a few pages later, is not guilt but "all the dread of public exposure" (112) [101].[7]

Twice in the narrative Dimmesdale allows flashes of anger to break through, and twice the feelings subside to a guilty sadness. In chapter 10 the minister suddenly demands of Chillingworth. "But who art thou, that meddlest in this matter?—that dares thrust himself between the sufferer and his God?" He rushes from the room with a "frantic gesture." But after secluding himself for several hours, he makes "the amplest apologies" to "the kind old man" for the "violence" of his "unseemly outbreak of temper." As Chillingworth calculates, manipulating his anger is a "step" toward exposing "the hot passion of his heart." The physician's cool malice toys with the minister's heated wrath to show the dangers of self-exposure. "As with one passion, so with another!" Chillingworth says to himself (101) [91].

When Hester tells Dimmesdale that Chillingworth is her husband, her lover explodes with rage. Now the frightening extremes of his anger disturb the narrator as well as Hester. Suddenly imposing a hierarchical interpretive frame, the narrator associates violence, blackness, and intermixture with the Devil's "portion."

> "The minister looked at her, for an instant, with all that violence of passion, which—intermixed, in more shapes than one, with his higher, purer, softer qualities—was, in fact, the portion of him which the Devil claimed, and through which he sought to win the rest. Never was there a blacker or a fiercer frown, than Hester now encountered. For the brief space that it lasted, it was a dark transfiguration." (139) [125]

Dimmesdale's "lower energies" yield, but only because he "had been so much enfeebled by suffering." "Woman, woman, thou art accountable for this!" he cries, again invoking the town's habit of punitive accounting. "I cannot forgive thee!" But when Hester throws her arms around him with "sudden and desperate tenderness," he allows his forgiveness to emerge, "out of an abyss of sadness, but no anger." God, they agree,

---

7. This reading differs from Christian readings that see Dimmesdale's "tongues of flame" eloquence as the romance's central truth; e.g., see Roy Male's essay on "Hawthorne's Literal Figures," in *Ruined Eden of the Present*, 90. My reading also differs from those who see Dimmesdale's guilt in primarily sexual terms; see Joel Porte, *The Romance in America: Studies in Cooper, Poe, Hawthorne, Melville, and James* (Middletown, Conn.: Wesleyan UP, 1969), 98–114.

should be the punisher (139, 140) [125]. The narrator's recoil from his character's rage diminishes Dimmesdale's passion to guilt and constricts Hester's passion to tenderness.

Outwardly Hester seems to have long since accepted her "stain," a taint that at last precludes any role for her as prophetess. In some respects, as Nina Baym and others have emphasized, her compromise compels the townspeople to soften their harsh views of her. Her "power to do," when she restricts it to the "power to sympathize," makes "the world's heavy hand" ordain her a Sister of Mercy, her last Papist transfiguration (117) [105]. At the end Hester returns to Boston to live out her life as a quiet force for sympathy if not immediate change, invigorating other despondent women with the hope of some future prophetess.[8]

But her real passions remain buried except for one last try. On the scaffold with her lover, she desperately resurrects her secret dream of union in hell: "Shall we not meet again? . . . Shall we not spend our immortal life together? Surely, surely, we have ransomed one another, with all this woe!" (181) [162]. Once again she claims that their relation can be "ransoming" in its own terms, though now through the more equivocal authority of martyrdom.

Characteristically, Dimmesdale's first response again is "Hush, Hester, hush!" He has set his "bright, dying eyes" on higher spiritual possibilities for himself. As he cites God, soul, reverence, and the impossibility of "an everlasting and pure reunion," his language shows an ascendant selfishness. Hester, willing to sacrifice purity for love, finds her love sacrificed for his purity. Once again she is abandoned, as Roger Prynne had abandoned his wife for almost two years, as her lover abandoned both her and her daughter for much longer.[9] The men in her life have maintained their intellectual or spiritual self-control by rejecting intimacy. The last she hears from her lover's lips is not her name but "Praised be his name! His will be done! Farewell!" (181) [162].

Hester's experience here finally does to Hester what Dimmesdale demands for Pearl in that scene by the brookside. It pacifies her. Her capacity to love diminishes to a tender mothering, the defeated residue of a passionate equality. Pearl's own change toward tenderness, when she kisses the minister on the scaffold, has been foreshadowed by several narrative admonitions about her dangerous lack of "heart," as Hester was found wanting. Now Pearl gains her narrator's praise for returning to femininity. Her tears, beyond anger at last, indicate her "pledge" that she will no longer "do battle with the world,

8. Baym, "The Significance of Plot," in *Ruined Eden of the Present*, makes a strong argument for Hester's consistent social power. Baym also stresses Dimmesdale's moral inadequacy, though the sexism she attributes to Darrel Abel should be lodged with the narrator. I think Baym overstates Hester's consistency and underplays the narrator's ambivalence. The narrator's Catholic associations for Hester—the "sainted" Ann Hutchinson, the "madonna" that a "Papist" would have seen, and here a "Sister of Mercy" whose letter "had the effect of the cross on a nun's bosom" (118) [106]—may be meant to evoke suspiciousness as well as approval, given the anti-Catholic feelings running so high in the 1850s.
9. The narrator implies twice that Chillingworth had been detained against his will by Indians for much of that time. Chillingworth is called "Master Prynne" by a townsman in chapter 3. His "Peace, Hester, peace!" concluding chapter 14 parallels Dimmesdale's later formula.

but be a woman in it" (181) [162]. Similarly, Hester realizes that her future prophetess must never be stained with sin, shame, or even a lifelong burden of sorrow. Mutely accepting the conflation of town with narrative values, she must be content with conflating all the traditional female roles: nurse, seamstress, mother, helpmeet, confidante, and tender heart.

Several critics, notably Nina Baym and Michael Colacurcio, have argued that the ending shows Hester achieving at least partial self-fulfillment.[1] That may be true in terms that the town can recognize. But it seems to me that the narrative ponderously thwarts the twin sources of her rebellious strength: her tenacious desire and her fierce mind. More specifically, the narrator breaks his explicit promise of reunion with Dimmesdale.

As the minister assures Pearl on the midnight scaffold, all three will stand together "At the great judgment day!" The narrator, too, sees them illuminated in "the light that is to reveal all secrets, and the daybreak that shall unite all who belong to one another" (112) [101]. But Dimmesdale's revelation leads to eternal separation, not reunion. In the procession he had seemed "unattainable in his worldly position, and still more so in that far vista of his unsympathizing thoughts, through which she now beheld him" (170) [152]. Now the narrator's final words bury Hester's hopes in a permanent gloom, nervously commented on by the most sensitive early reviewers and symbolized by her tombstone's legend of red based on black. That tombstone is all that unites the two graves, whose dust, as the narrator at last concludes, "had no right to mingle" (186) [166]. After the child who danced on Isaac Johnson's grave in chapter 10 is reduced to tears, the narrator escorts Hester to her "darkening close" among the congregated sepulchres. Hester's life has been a motherly survival among imprisoned possibilities.

II

A narrative that begins by challenging patriarchal punishment ends by accepting punishment as a prelude to kindness. From Anthony Trollope to Frederic Carpenter and beyond, the ending has disturbed many readers who like Hester's spirited subjectivity. As one critic noted in 1954, "unlike his judicial ancestor, who consigned a witch to the gallows with an undismayed countenance, Hawthorne would have sprung the trap with a sigh. If one were the witch, one might well wonder wherein lay the vital difference."[2]

Though my reading continues that tradition, I question whether the

1. See Baym. "The Significance of Plot." in *Ruined Eden of the Present*; and Michael J. Colacurcio, "Footsteps of Ann Hutchinson: The Context of *The Scarlet Letter*," *ELH*, 39 (1972): 459–94, an essay which rightly connects Hester to Ann Hutchinson and Dimmesdale to John Cotton but wrongly reduces Hester's radical perceptions to her sexuality. He concludes that both the teller and the tale force Hester to abandon conclusions to which we are sympathetic.
2. Morton Cronin, "Hawthorne on Romantic Love and the Status of Women," *PMLA*, 69 (1954): 98. See also Frederic I. Carpenter's fine essay, "Scarlet A Minus," *College English*, 5 (1944): 173–80.

narrator represents all of Hawthorne. While he provides a safely over-arching frame of moral values to which both Hawthorne and his audi-ence could consciously assent, the narrator's evasive mixture of sympathy and judgment also provides a safe way of going beyond so-cially responsible norms to investigate dangerously attractive interior states of mind. From the first paragraph of "The Custom-House" Hawthorne presents his "intrusive author" as a solicitous, sensible, yet receptive interpreter whose movement from torpid business surround-ings to a romantic sensibility opens the door for Hester's story. His first reaction to the scarlet letter, after all, is hilariously inappropriate: he measures it, and finds that "each limb proved to be precisely three inches and a quarter in length" (27) [26]. This habit of precise ac-counting would seem perfectly natural to the "man of business," the "main-spring" of the Custom-House, who could "make the incompre-hensible as clear as daylight," and for whom a "stain on his con-science" would be no more troublesome than an error in his accounts or an ink-blot in his record books (22) [21–22]. But the scarlet letter takes the narrator beyond his own more satirical accounts. Its mean-ings "streamed forth from the mystic symbol, subtly communicating it-self to my sensibilities, but evading the analysis of my mind" (28) [26].

This tension between sensibility and analysis persists through the narrative. The power of authority to take the shameful measure of vul-nerable subjectivity terrifies the narrator. Yet he seems equally terrified of the heart-freezing isolation inherent in aggressive autonomy. Flee-ing coercive authority, including his own, he defines himself simply as an imaginative re-creator of Surveyor Pue's manuscript and imagines Hester's rebellious self-reliance with sustained flights of empathy. Fleeing self-reliance, he chastises Hester's pride and relentlessly ac-cuses Chillingworth's self-possessed malice. For him subjectivity seems always vulnerable to alien invasion. Chillingworth's own inva-sion of Dimmesdale's soul manifests the devil's entry into the scholar-physician. Perpetually oscillating between subjectivity and authority, the narrator dodges being pinned down to one mode or the other. To commit himself either way might expose his fearful cruelty of heart or his equally fearful vulnerability to violation.[3]

His solution, for both himself and his heroine, is the fluidity of sym-pathetic relationship. He strives to "stand in some true relation with his audience," fictionalizing his reader as "a kind and apprehensive, though not the closest friend." Without such a relation, he says, "thoughts are frozen and utterance benumbed" (7) [7]. The metaphor comes close to self-exposure. Seeking a nonthreatening communica-tion that protects him from real intimacy, he indicates his fear of a solidifying self-possession. The audience has to warm the intrinsic coldness of his heart and tongue.

3. Recent criticism has begun to explore these oscillations. See esp. Brodhead, *Hawthorne, Melville, and the Novel*; Kenneth Dauber, *Rediscovering Hawthorne* (Princeton: Princeton UP, 1977), though Dauber is taken in by the narrator's claims for intimacy; and Edgar A. Dryden, *Nathaniel Hawthorne: The Poetics of Enchantment* (Ithaca and London: Cornell UP, 1977), which argues for Hawthorne's alternation between postures as his way of managing "a menacing otherness at his own center" (21).

Similarly, the coldness of Hester's radical speculations must be warmed by her mothering heart. "A woman," he concludes, "never overcomes these problems by any exercise of thought"; they can be solved only be letting the heart "come uppermost" (120) [108]. Having established Hester's radical potential, the narrator now undercuts her force by dramatizing her transformation back to lovability, not toward public combat. The "magic touch" to bring about her "transfiguration," as he says earlier (119) [107], sets the second half of the narrative in motion. She vows to redeem Dimmesdale from his own weakness and his malevolent tormentor. She will accomplish "the rescue of the victim" from her husband's "power" (121) [109].

Why the sudden swerve toward selfless liberation of a man whom, even near the end, she can hardly forgive for deserting her? As the narrator says so empathetically in one of his last oscillations, "thus much of woman was there in Hester, that she could scarcely forgive him . . . for being able so completely to withdraw himself from their mutual world; while she groped darkly, and stretched forth her cold hands, and found him not" (170) [152]. Yet here, nine chapters earlier, she resolves to rescue her self-absorbed lover. In part the narrator advocates a maternal sympathy that can subdue Hester for her own good. More deeply, by both investigating and identifying with the victim, the narrator encourages a Chillingworth-like interpretive mode that intensifies punitive perceptions of guilt, on all sides. In its latest form this mode has become psychoanalytic detection of the Chillingworth-Dimmesdale relation.

It seems obvious to post-Freudian readers that Chillingworth's revengeful penetration into Dimmesdale's bosom constitutes the climatic moment of physical intimacy in the story. His intrusive, sadistic rape first awakens protracted "throb[s] of pain," then culminates in the "moment of his ecstasy," when his discovery of what lies on the sleeping minister's chest sends Dimmesdale into a "shudder" and Chillingworth into a "ghastly rapture" of riotous gestures (102) [92]. The sexualization of revenge accompanies the desexing of love. More broadly, the narrator's overt language of sympathy frequently masks his fascination with the violation of inward spheres. Various readers have noted that Chillingworth bears the same relation to Dimmesdale that Pearl often has to Hester: the unrestrained underside of socially conforming energies.[4] Dimmesdale's self-preoccupied guilt, to take this view further, licenses Chillingworth's rage for penetration, possession, and violation even as it recalls the minister's own moment of violation in the past. In the psychological allegory to which the narrator seems increasingly disposed, malicious intrusion is guilt's double.

The narrative itself becomes a further stage for contrary energies, as Richard Brodhead's fine discussion of its mixed modes indicates. After establishing initially intense sympathies with Hester's resolute in-

---

4. See Leslie A. Fiedler, *Love and Death in the American Novel*, rev. ed. (New York: Stein and Day, 1966), 437; and Baym, *The Shape of Hawthorne's Career*, who differs from my view in saying that at the end "the two shattered personalities become whole again and the symbolic characters disappear" (130).

tegrity and defiant creativity, it moves toward framing her, in several senses. It also induces a covert fascination with violating her inwardness and humbling her strength. This drama is displaced from Hester to Dimmesdale. The sexuality of victimization and the intellectualized control of rage move Hester's subjectivity toward the margins of Hawthorne's romance.

Psychoanalytic readings tend to suppress Hester's struggle for autonomy to reflect the Chillingworth-Dimmesdale connection. Both Frederick Crews and John Irwin, the two most prominent psychoanalytic investigators, assume the role of detective on the trail of a narcissist. Crews presents the story entirely as if it were the narrator's ambiguously ironic relation to Dimmesdale's libidinal repression, while Irwin's Lacanian reading finds narcissistic mirroring doubled and redoubled throughout the text. But Dimmesdale's growth from narcissism to sublimated independence, like the narrator's ironic pursuit, is a flight from feeling. Whether seeing Freudian desire or Lacanian absence at the heart of the text, both Crews and Irwin mistake the narrator's defenses for narrative truths.[5]

Anxiety about anger, more fearful to him than sexual desire, generates the narrator's incompatible fascinations with Hester's independence and Chillingworth's malice. Both these frozen stances intimate anger, in opposite ways. But because Chillingworth's rage has its base in intimacy, unlike Hester's more generalized social rebellion, he is punished far more severely by the narrator, who makes the cuckolded husband his prime villain. To the narrator anger and desire are the same thing: low, base, the devil's plaything. They lead to violence and violation, not love. Yet his idea of love is finally a mystified self-projection. In affirming sympathy as the key, he defines it as the capacity to complete one's divided self without undue self-exposure, from the first paragraph of "The Custom-House" to the last pages of the story. That narcissistic definition avoids acknowledging conflict as part of intimacy. In fact it avoids otherness altogether, because for the narrator otherness brings a terror of unloving regard. For him, anger is the terror of unloving strangeness within oneself. In rigidifying Chillingworth's anger as possessive malice the narrator controls that terror as allegory, while in transforming Hester's more complicated subjectivity to maternal sympathy he diffuses that terror as romance.[6]

---

5. Irwin, *American Hieroglyphics*, 239–84; Frederick C. Crews, *The Sins of the Fathers: Hawthorne's Psychological Themes* (New York: Oxford UP, 1966), 136–53. Irwin sees Dimmesdale's guilt as the "true" self opposing his false public role and presents Hester as the double for a Dimmesdale-like narrator. Crews mocks Hester for "prating" of freedom and finds that the minister's anxious egotism finally achieves "heroic independence" of Hester by sublimating desire into oratory (143, 149). Baym, *The Shape of Hawthorne's Career*, 138–39, briefly suggests a Freudian perspective, that Pearl might be Hester's id and Chillingworth Dimmesdale's superego.

6. In *Rediscovering Hawthorne* Dauber astutely discusses the shift toward Dimmesdale as allegory's socialization of the forest's romance world. Brodhead, *Hawthorne, Melville, and the Novel*, associates interpretive openness with Hester's symbolic mode, while Chillingworth embodies tendencies toward allegorical rigidity and the punitive realism of a hierarchic male society. Bell, *The Development of American Romance*, 176–77, similarly argues that Hester's rebellion is "the central 'story' " but that she, as well as society, represses herself to become a "victim of allegory." Both Poe and Henry James vehemently opposed Hawthorne's allegorizing as artistically destructive, a perspective sometimes adopted by Hawthorne himself.

By the end of the story both Dimmesdale and the narrator release emotions only through an ascension of words that nobody quite understands. Dimmesdale's new power of unclear statement, in his sermon and his confession, mirrors a broader narrative mystification of pain as the source of eloquence and transfiguration. From an initial appreciation of Hester's strength and fascination with Chillingworth's power, the narrator has moved toward exalting Dimmesdale's weakness. The minister's diffuse anguish displaces Hester's clearheaded suffering. Through insistent narrative framing, his masochism becomes the scaffold for self-magnifying transcendence, culminating in the narrator's advocacy of spiritualized male narcissism as the way to complete one's divided self.

Dimmesdale's feminized pain first brings some traditional male rewards. Though he forsakes his own fatherhood from the moment of conception, he ascends to meet his heavenly father after receiving a weepy kiss from his daughter, whom he barely has time to acknowledge before his death. Pearl's childhood is an extreme instance of the absent father and the over-present mother so basic to American middle-class society, and experienced by Hawthorne in his own life.[7] Consider her father as an American success story, made possible by his flight from woman and child. He has no distractions from his work, and he can exercise to the full his intellectual powers. He makes an extraordinary social impact, gains respect as a public and private adviser, and after a satisfactory dark night of the soul he gains his final reward of celestial approval. Meanwhile Hester, like a good mistress, remains bonded to her child, her duties, her isolation, her marginal status, and her hopeless dreams of union.

The narrator's astonishing corollary to Hester's decline into sympathy unites Chillingworth, Dimmesdale, and himself in a loving ascension. After Dimmesdale spurns Hester to gain an uncontaminated integration for his purified maleness, we are asked to imagine him united in heaven not just with God but with Chillingworth as well. In the middle of the story the narrator oddly interpolates that "hatred, by a gradual and quiet process, will even be transformed to love," if new irritations of hostility do not impede the process (116) [105]. At several other points he implies that rage and desire fuse as violent passion. Now the narrator inverts the devil's work. He takes the ability to transform hate into love as his final test of the reader's tender capacities.

Asking his readers to be merciful to Chillingworth, he wonders "whether hatred and love be not the same thing at bottom." Each supposes "intimacy and heart-knowledge." Each needs dependence. Each dies if the object withdraws.

> Philosophically considered, therefore, the two passions seem essentially the same, except that one happens to be seen in a celes-

---

7. See Chodorow, *The Reproduction of Mothering*; also see the last chapter of David Leverenz, *The Language of Puritan Feeling: An Exploration in Literature, Psychology, and Social History* (New Brunswick, N.J.: Rutgers UP, 1980), 258–71.

tial radiance, and the other in a dusky and lurid glow. In the spiritual world, the old physician and the minister—mutual victims
as they have been—may, unawares, have found their earthly stock
of hatred and antipathy transmuted into golden love. (183–84)
[164]

The passage still seems to me the strangest in all of Hawthorne.
Transforming devilish rage into divine love, it takes Dimmesdale's hierarchy of high and low to its highest extreme. If the narrator hesitates
to assert their fanciful union as spiritual fact, he has no qualms about
describing them as "mutual victims." Anne Abbott cited this passage as
a prime example of Hawthorne's "mistborn ideas" and asked "if there
be any firm ground at all" here. Yet she also mused, in some perplexity,
that Hawthorne seems to share that "doubt."[8] Her reaction is quite
right, because the passage substitutes loving victims for strong selves
in conflict. Its several levels of meaning bring the reader's contrary responses to their final suspended inversion.

The possibility of spiritual union in heaven joins the two whose intercourse on earth comes to center the story: revengeful father and vi-
olated/violating son. The cuckold and the lover rise together to an
all-male paradise, while Hester mutely returns to Salem. The narrator's fantasized embrace of father and son gives a more openly Oedipal
dimension to the classic American fantasy, first described by Leslie
Fiedler, of two men in flight from strong women. Moreover, the trans-
mutation suggests an integration of the male self as well, if only in
coupling two sides of a self-falsification. Intrusive sadism and guilty
vulnerability come together at last, released from any pressure to
come to terms with anger, love, or fear.

Most significantly, the union occurs not in the plot but in the narrator's relation to his audience. He sets his readers a last challenge: can
you take your sympathy that far? In asking readers to sympathize with
Dimmesdale and Chillingworth as "mutual victims" and to imagine
hate transmuted into golden love, the narrator brings himself into that
embrace, with his reader as witness. All three male voices, ironically at
odds on earth, escape together, free from the body's sexuality and the
mind's conflicts, and free from genuine intimacy.[9]

Yet this narrative flight, like all his extremes, is momentary. Returning to earth, he sympathetically concludes with Hester's solitude, not
Dimmesdale's transcendence. Part of the narrator's strategy for recon-
ciling conflicts is to condemn fixity of any kind, physical or spiritual. If
rigidity seems fearfully demonic, associated with anger and the lower
parts of the soul or body, flexible sympathy becomes the narrator's
vague placebo. This tactic allows him momentary participations in his

8. Abbott, review of *The Scarlet Letter*, in *Hawthorne: The Critical Heritage*, 165 [245]. Bell,
   The Development of American Romance, 178, suggests that even God "becomes a kind of allegorical double" for Dimmesdale's "guilty self-justification." Leslie Fiedler, *Love and Death
   in the American Novel*, 235, describes this passage as "an equivocation which undercuts, at
   the last moment, the whole suggested meaning of his book."
9. See Hélène Cixous, "sorties," in *New French Feminisms: An Anthology*, ed. Elaine Marks and
   Isabelle de Courtivron (Amherst: U of Massachusetts P, 1980), 91–92, on the reduction of
   the woman to the maternal implied in the ascension of man to the father.

contradictory extremes. But it also establishes multiple authorial interpretations as a shifting medium for the plot. His self-dramatizing
ceaselessly pacifies and resurrects his plot's tensions, while deflecting
attention from his punitive plotting to the sympathetic puppeteer.

Pearl represents what most needs pacification: her rebellious impulses toward creative autonomy and her aggressive impulses to detect
and accuse. Dimmesdale, far from being the "true self" of the romance, unites two weak contemporary defenses against Pearl's strong
impulses. He embodies a male accommodation to public role and a female sense of self as vulnerable victim. If Pearl joins contradictory
strengths, Dimmesdale joins fragile defenses. As the narrative awakens
contrary energies of rebellion and intrusion, the narrator's voice quells
these polarized versions of anger and authority through his rhetoric of
sympathy and his intimacy with what he often calls Dimmesdale's
"tremulous" voice. His feminized hero, a dimmed valley even in his
name, becomes both the narrator and the object of his inquisition.

In the narrator's increasingly Oedipal allegory, a regressive, inquisitorial family triangle of cruel impersonal father, kind despairing
mother, and tortured triumphant son all but drives out early expectations for Hester's adult subjectivity against public patriarchy. A sado-
masochistic symbiosis of father and son becomes a vision of
transcendent, victimized love. Yet the narrative insistently returns to
its latent subversion of male inauthenticity. Hester's integrity mutely
survives. If Pearl ceases to do battle with the world, she finds a wider
world unimaginable to Boston, or for that matter to the narrator himself, whose Puritan roots "have intertwined themselves" with his own
nature (12) [12]. This is as close as he comes to directly acknowledging his Chillingworth side. At the same time, however, his presentation
of himself gives access to strong subjectivities beyond his conscious
accommodations.

A psychoanalytic focus on anger and dependence might illuminate
Hawthorne's biography here, especially if complemented by a feminist
analysis of the polarized sex role expectations so basic to his time.
Hawthorne's remarkable empathy with a solitary woman, and his fear of
an unloving other insinuated into his own psyche, probably have their
contradictory sources in his ties to his mother, whose death helped to
impel Hester's creation. The intensities of that bond go deeper than the
more obvious Oedipal guilt for having possessed a woman whose husband strangely disappeared.[1] Yet the complexities of narrative dissociation in *The Scarlet Letter* have as much to do with Hawthorne's canny
relation to his audience as with his uncanny relation to himself.

1. As John Franzosa has established for "The Custom-House," anger and dependence are issues more basic than guilt and sexuality. See " 'The Custom-House,' *The Scarlet Letter*, and
   Hawthorne's Separation from Salem," *ESQ*, 24 (1978): 57–71 [pp. 387–404 in this Norton
   Critical Edition]. Franzosa argues that a guilty identity balances impulses toward hostile intrusion and isolated self-possession, and allows inauthentic identity with the narrator's community. Baym defends Hawthorne's mother from Hawthorne in "Nathaniel Hawthorne and
   His Mother: A Biographical Speculation," *American Literature*, 54 (1982): 1–27. While suggesting that Hawthorne's various presentations of her mask her "oppressive" presence in his
   psyche, Baym sees *The Scarlet Letter* as a creative reversal that temporarily frees Hawthorne
   from dependency on maternal power.

In conforming to his audience's expectations for a morally comfortable narrator, Hawthorne fictionalizes himself so as to partially undermine his own characterization. His fragmenting empathies outstrip the narrator's growing alliances with Dimmesdale's self-centering scrutiny and Chillingworth's intrusive detection. He seems fully aware that his readers will accept Hester only while she suffers for her sin; as no less than three reviewers remarked, the narrator avoids the dangers of "the French school" by making his heroine satisfactorily miserable.[2] Yet while silencing Hester with values he and his audience hold dear, he makes his readers uncomfortable with those values.

When he at last offers his "sweet moral blossom," it turns out to be a version of Dimmesdale's anguish over self-display: "Be true! Be true! Be true! Show freely to the world, if not your worst, yet some trait whereby the worst may be inferred!" (183) [163]. This is the hesitant exhibitionism of a disembodied Boston Flasher, who encourages his readers to imagine his worst while showing their own. He assumes that his readers share with him not only a self worth hating but also the ambivalent desire to detect, to be detected, and to stay respectably hidden. A mutual revelation of guilty subjectivity constitutes his idea of true sympathy, true community, and true interpretation. As he quietly observes, just after Dimmesdale has seen his A flash across the sky, "another's guilt might have seen another symbol in it" (113) [102]. At such moments, while interpretive authority disintegrates, writing and reading converge. They become equivalent, equivocal acts of shared self-exposure and accusation. Uneasy lies the tale that wears that crown.

Finally, however, The Scarlet Letter takes readers beyond its narrator and his imagined audience. Dimmesdale's guilt, like the narrator's, conceals a fear of losing approval. But Hawthorne's romance evokes strong subjectivity in opposition to dependence of any kind. Throughout, like an anxious referee, the interpreter's voice strives to rise above the fray. Trying to sympathize, judge, and reconcile, he imposes the masks he wants to lift. Yet while the storyteller oscillates between guilt and decorum, his story brings out a much more risky inwardness, whose unresolved tensions sent Mrs. Hawthorne to bed and Hester to a deeper solitude. Hester's epitaph suitably blazons forth her red strength against her black background. By contrast, the narrator's epitaph could be the remark he addresses to "the minister in a maze": "No man, for any considerable period, can wear one face to himself, and another to the multitude, without finally getting bewildered as to which may be the true" (154) [137]. In accommodating his voice to

2. The phrase is Whipple's (Hawthorne: The Critical Heritage, 161–62). Henry F. Chorley, in a review in the Athenaeum, 15 June 1850, praised The Scarlet Letter for being "so clear of fever and of prurient excitement" because "the misery of the woman" is always present (rpt. in Hawthorne: The Critical Heritage, see 163), while E. A. Duyckinck, in a review in Literary World, 30 Mar. 1850, was happy to see a "writer who has lived so much among the new school" handle "this delicate subject without an infusion of George Sand" (rpt. in Hawthorne: The Critical Heritage, see 156–57) [239]. On the other hand, both Abbott's review and the review by Orestes Brownson in Brownson's Quarterly Review. Oct. 1850, condemn the romance because Hester is not sufficiently repentant, as does the infamous review by Arthur Cleveland Coxe in the Church Review, Jan. 1851 (rpt. in Hawthorne: The Critical Heritage; see 165–66; 177–78; and 183) [254–63].

the contradictions of public authority, the narrator joins Salem's congregated sepulchres, while Hester's life continues to speak with embattled vitality.

STEPHEN RAILTON

The Address of *The Scarlet Letter*†

Reader-response critics often use "reader" and "audience" as synonymous terms, but it is worthwhile preserving a distinction between them. We could use the term "reader" for anyone who at any time opens a book and begins processing a text. "Audience," on the other hand, could be reserved to designate the specific group, the contemporary reading public, to whom an author originally addresses the text. All readers, of course, can be identified with larger groups, which Stanley Fish has taught us to call "interpretive communities."[1] But as an author writes a text, there is one particular group for whom he or she is writing; let us call that group the author's "audience." Thus, the readers of *The Scarlet Letter* have all come into existence after the novel was written. The novel's audience, though, was there before Hawthorne sat down to write it. As reader-response criticism shows, any reader's ideological allegiances as a member of a particular community play a crucial role in determining the way that reader produces meaning from a work of literature. But only the "audience," as I am suggesting we define it, can play a role in the creation of the work itself. The reader responds to the text, but first, in the very act of literary conception, there is the response of the text to its audience: the way the text is shaped by the author's ambitions and anxieties about performing for a particular group.

Because the role that this audience plays in the text is a subjective one, we have to make further distinctions. The contemporary audience for *The Scarlet Letter* was there, both sociologically and psychologically, before Hawthorne sat down to write his novel: it was "there" in America in 1850 as the actual reading public available to him as a professional writer and "there" in Hawthorne's mind as his internalized construct of the people he hoped would buy, read, and understand his novel. As Walter J. Ong has pointed out, any writer's sense of audience is an imaginative abstraction, a "fiction."[2] But Ong's emphasis needs to be qualified and historicized. For Hawthorne, or for any writer who hopes to perform successfully for his or her audience, this

---

† From *Readers in History: Nineteenth-Century American Literature and the Contexts of Response*, ed. James L. Machor (Baltimore: Johns Hopkins UP, 1993), 138–63. Reprinted by permission of the publisher. Parts of this essay are derived from the author's chapter on Hawthorne and *The Scarlet Letter* in *Authorship and Audience: Literary Performance and the American Renaissance* (Princeton: Princeton UP, 1991). Page numbers in square brackets refer to this Norton Critical Edition.

1. See Stanley Fish, "Interpreting the *Variorum*," *Critical Inquiry* 2 (1976): 465–85; also Fish, *Is There a Text in This Class? The Authority of Interpretive Communities* (Cambridge: Harvard UP, 1980).

2. Walter J. Ong, "The Writer's Audience Is Always a Fiction," *PMLA* 90 (1975): 9–21.

"fiction" is dialectically constructed by inescapable cultural facts. How Hawthorne conceptualized his audience had to start with his sense of the readers, real rather than ideal, who constituted the reading public in mid-nineteenth-century America.[3] Thus, it was this historically given audience, as I shall try to show in the first half of my essay, that inhabited his imagination and that presided over the fiction that he wrote as *The Scarlet Letter*.

In the second part of this essay, I will focus on the difference between the way a text originally responds to its audience and the way readers subsequently respond to a text. Because a text's audience and its readers are constructed in historically different ways, there is necessarily a distance between their potentialities as responders.[4] Secure in our chronological place as the latest arrivals on the literary historical scene, we are likely to think that we are better equipped to understand or appreciate a text than its original audience, that we know better. This seems especially true of our attitude toward the Victorian Americans for whom Hawthorne wrote. As readers, after all, we have rescued *Moby-Dick*, *Walden*, and *Leaves of Grass* from their benighted failure as an audience. It is certainly true that we know differently. *The Scarlet Letter* was the first novel to use a woman's sexuality to explore and challenge the structures of society; in the hundred and forty years since, many other writers have followed Hawthorne's lead. We could say that we have the benefit of this additional experience, but we should also acknowledge what we have lost. Just as it is apparently impossible for anyone these days to read Hawthorne's book without already knowing that Dimmesdale had been Hester's lover—a fact that even the most perceptive contemporary reader could not have suspected until the book's third chapter,[5] and would not know for sure until the middle—so it is almost impossible for us to imagine how

---

3. More than one kind of reading public was available to Hawthorne. Henry Nash Smith has suggested distinguishing the readers of the early 1850s by "brow levels"—i.e., high-, middle-, and lowbrow audiences (*Democracy and the Novel* [New York: Oxford UP, 1978], 6–10). And David S. Reynolds's *Beneath the American Renaissance* (New York: Knopf, 1988) shows us how the literary expectations and appetites of the type of audience that Smith would call "lowbrow" differed from the values we associate with the genteel culture. I am assuming that Hawthorne wrote *The Scarlet Letter* for the same kind of audience that had read his tales and sketches for twenty-five years in such "middlebrow" publications as *Godey's*; in "The Custom-House," for instance, when he describes the place where his imagination works, the environment is that of an unmistakably genteel parlor.

4. See Hans Robert Jauss, "Literary History as a Challenge to Literary Theory," in *Toward an Aesthetic of Reception*, trans. Timothy Bahti (Minneapolis: U Minnesota P, 1982). Jauss's great contribution is to remind us that at any given literary-historical moment, readers approach a new text from within a certain "horizon of expectations," which will determine their response to a work of art; once read, a text can in turn begin to reshape or expand that horizon, so that at subsequent literary-historical moments it can be read in previously unthought of ways (see 21–25).

5. Chapter 3 is called "The Recognition." Since it begins by describing Chillingworth's deformed appearance as he emerges from the forest to see Hester on the scaffold, while chapter 2 ended by describing the man Hester had married as "slightly deformed" (*The Scarlet Letter*, ed. William Charvat et al. [Columbus: Ohio State UP, 1962], 58) [43], the novel tempts its reader to jump to the conclusion that *this* is the recognition. For Hester and Chillingworth to see each other after two years in such a setting is a dramatic recognition, but *the* recognition occurs much later in the chapter: when Dimmesdale speaks to Hester, and Pearl somehow recognizes her father's voice: "The poor baby . . . directed its hitherto vacant gaze towards Mr. Dimmesdale, and held up its little arms, with a half pleased, half plaintive murmur" (67) [49]. Since the immediate question of the chapter—for Chillingworth, for the Puritans, and for the uninitiated reader—is who is Pearl's father, Hawthorne is thus very subtly

those contemporary readers would have initially reacted to Hester Prynne. We know otherwise than the readers of 1850. We cannot help but bring to the novel a very different set of preconceptions—about someone like Hester, about adultery, about Christianity.

And we should admit that we often know less. At Petroglyph Point in Mesa Verde National Park is a rock covered with signs scratched by the Anasazi who lived there 700 years ago. No one now can interpret them. They communicated without ambiguity to the people for whom they were "written" but are perfectly opaque to us. As itself a hieroglyphic emblem, *The Scarlet Letter* looks like a much more accessible sign. That it works for and speaks so powerfully to modern readers is a measure of its achievement. But Hawthorne was not writing for us or for the theoretical reader of much reader-response criticism. Every reader's responses are relevant to any attempt to determine the ultimate significance of the text. We can, however, gain a lot by trying to reconstruct the way Hawthorne wrote it for his contemporary audience, by trying to understand how it was meant to speak to and work on the readers of his day.

There is no question about the force of his concern with the response of his contemporary audience. In the letters he wrote as he was finishing the novel, the emphasis is not on whether his novel had succeeded on its own terms—he seemed to know he'd written a great book, though a "dark and dismal" one. For him the question was whether it would succeed with its audience.[6] He was urgently worried about material success: he had lost his job at the Custom House; he was broke with a family to support. He was, however, equally anxious about rhetorical success. He and his publisher arranged with Melville's friend Duyckinck to publish an excerpt from the book in *The Literary World* as a kind of promotional device. Hawthorne's one stipulation was that the excerpt come from "The Custom-House," not from *The Scarlet Letter*: "I don't think it advisable to give any thing from the story itself; because I know of no passage that would not throw too much light on the plan of the book."[7] He says "plan," not "plot," which suggests that he had organized the novel strategically to work on its contemporary audience in a specific way. Given his concern here with a kind of secrecy, we could even say that the novel's deepest "plot" was somehow against its audience. That leads to the question I want to try to answer first: how did *The Scarlet Letter* address its audience? That question in turn leads to a more theoretical one. *The Scarlet Letter* reaches us a century and a half after it was addressed. Can readers in the 1990s respond according to plan, when the plan was worked out in 1850?

---

rewarding readers who do not jump to interpretive conclusions, who keep open a question like "What does the recognition mean?" Of course, readers who cannot delay interpretive closure will not recognize the recognition. Throughout my essay, references to *The Scarlet Letter* will be to the Ohio State edition and will be cited in parentheses in my text.

6. See his letters to J. T. Fields, January 20, 1850, and to Horatio Bridge, February 4, 1850, in *Nathaniel Hawthorne: The Letters, 1843–1853*, ed. Thomas Woodson et al. (Columbus: Ohio State UP, 1985), 307–308, 311–12 [pp. 226–29 in this Norton Critical Edition].

7. *Letters, 1843–1853*, 322.

I

There is in fact an aboriginal audience inscribed into the text. Before Hester appears in the marketplace, the narrative puts in place the throng of Puritan men and women for whom the scarlet letter is first "published." Putting a "crowd of spectators" (54) [41] in place before the story itself begins is Hawthorne's acknowledgment of the point that the audience precedes the text. His preoccupation with audience response is signaled by the way he puts those Puritans at the center of his stage: both chapter 1 *and* chapter 2 begin by drawing our attention to them. How historical *The Scarlet Letter* is, how much it is "about" the Puritan culture that provides its occasion, is a question that has long been debated by the commentators.[8] But the main role the "Puritans" play in the text is that of audience to its drama: they exist chiefly as an interpretive community.[9] Hawthorne regularly pauses the narrative to elaborate on how the people of Boston react to a new development in the story, how they "see" Hester and the other central characters, how they interpret the scarlet letter. And as an audience, the "Puritans" are not very historical. Although they dress like seventeenth-century colonists, their reactions, and the assumptions behind those reactions, are those of the genteel readers who formed Hawthorne's mid-nineteenth-century audience. The first step in appreciating Hawthorne's "plan" is to recognize the way he writes into the novel a version of his reading public, disguised in period costumes.

The "Puritans' " understanding of human nature is hardly Calvinist. Rather, it reflects the polarizations of the moral melodramas that were the most popular works of Hawthorne's time. *Uncle Tom's Cabin*, usually considered the best-selling book of this period, began appearing a year after *The Scarlet Letter*.[1] One characteristic Stowe's novel shares

---

8. The most ingenious recent advocate for reading the novel as an examination of colonial Puritanism is Michael J. Colacurcio; see his "Footsteps of Ann Hutchinson: The Context of *The Scarlet Letter*," *ELH* 39 (1972): 459–94 [pp. 304–31 in this Norton Critical Edition], and "The Woman's Own Choice: Sex, Metaphor, and the Puritan 'Sources' of *The Scarlet Letter*," in *New Essays on "The Scarlet Letter*," ed. Michael J. Colacurcio (Cambridge: Cambridge UP, 1985), 101–36.

9. I am not so much borrowing Fish's idea of "interpretive communities" here as trying to co-opt it. Hawthorne would have liked Fish's phrase but not his relativism. For him there is a right and a wrong interpretive community. The Puritans' reading of the scarlet letter defines the wrong one. Yet his faith in the possibility of a definitive interpretation—one that finds, not makes meaning—is announced at the very start of "The Custom-House," where he says he writes for "the few who will understand him, better than most of his school-mates and life-mates" (35). The community adumbrated here eventually emerges, as we will see, within the text itself.

1. To develop my analysis of how Hawthorne's novel addresses his audience's preoccupations, I will be comparing *The Scarlet Letter* to *Uncle Tom's Cabin*. Because my emphasis is on the way Hawthorne's vision of human nature set him outside and at odds with those preconceptions, the comparison may seem an invidious one, a mere reformulation of what Jane Tompkins refers to as a "long tradition of academic parochialism" that "assigns Hawthorne and Melville the role of heroes, the sentimental novelists the role of villains" (*Sensational Designs: The Cultural Work of American Fiction* [New York: Oxford UP, 1985], 125, 149). That is not my intention. The contempt Hawthorne could at moments feel for the contemporary audience that made "sentimental novels" the best-selling fiction of his time and place is notorious these days and certainly has to be included in our understanding of his hypostatization of his audience. But comparing Hawthorne's and Stowe's novel does not require one to assent to his frustrated vilification of "that damned mob of scribbling women." I am in complete agreement with what Tompkins says elsewhere, that "the work of the sentimental writ-

with the more conventional genteel best-sellers is its distribution of characters into the fixed patterns of melodramatic allegory: little Eva St. Clare is wholly angelic, Simon Legree is the incarnation of evil. These are also the patterns into which the Puritans of Hawthorne's novel keep trying to fit the central characters. To them, in that first scene, the A Hester wears "seemed to derive its scarlet hue from the flames of the infernal pit" (69) [50]. To them Dimmesdale appears as if robed in the spotless white Eva invariably wears: "They deemed the young clergyman a miracle of holiness. . . . In their eyes, the very ground on which he trod was sanctified" (142) [94]. When in the penultimate chapter they realize Dimmesdale is about to die, "it [would not] have seemed a miracle too high to be wrought for one so holy, had he ascended before their eyes, waxing dimmer and brighter, and fading at last into the light of heaven!" (252) [159]. Such an image would have been inconceivable to a Calvinist. It was, however, a very familiar one to Hawthorne's contemporaries: the first staged version of *Uncle Tom's Cabin*, which opened to eager throngs of spectators in 1852, actually ended with little Eva rising up from the stage into heaven.[2] The Puritans cannot settle on an interpretation of Chillingworth—to some he has been sent miraculously by "Heaven" to cure their saintly minister's body (121) [81]; to others, he is either "Satan himself, or Satan's emissary," come to plot against the saintly minister's soul (128) [86]—but in either case their reading of his character relies on the type of moral dichotomies found in genteel fiction.

Why Hawthorne felt he had to plan carefully for his own audience becomes clear when we realize that the Puritans are a terrible audience. Their responses, and the assumptions behind them, are wholly inadequate to either the moral or the interpretive demands of his story. In that opening scene the novel explicitly condemns them for their failure of sympathy: they see Hester as an Other and cast her out of their society, even though the novel shows us that she is still essentially governed by their values: "She knew that her deed had been evil" (89) [61]. In the second half, they take "Another View of Hester." Since she quietly goes about her charitable duties as "a Sister of Mercy" to the

---

ers is complex and significant in ways *other than* those that characterize the established masterpieces" such as *The Scarlet Letter* (126). (I have registered my own appreciation for the greatness of Stowe's novel in "Mothers, Husbands and *Uncle Tom*," *Georgia Review* 38 [1984]: 129–44.) "Conventionality" is also a term with many possible referents: if we were to focus on the politics of Hawthorne's and Stowe's novels rather than on what Hawthorne defined as his central thematic concern, the truth of the human heart, I could be comparing the radicalism of *Uncle Tom's Cabin* to the conventionality of *The Scarlet Letter* (see, for example, Sacvan Bercovitch, "The A-Politics of Ambiguity in *The Scarlet Letter*," *New Literary History* 19 [1988]: 629–54). What my comparison does depend on, however, is the cultural-historical legitimacy of Hawthorne's belief that his conception of the human self was in conflict with the genteel self-image that Stowe's readers found reflected and confirmed in her novel. While Stowe brilliantly challenges her audience's assumptions about a social evil, Hawthorne is trying to complicate and change that audience's assumptions about themselves.

2. The dramatization was written by George L. Aikens. The ascent into heaven was an impressive piece of stagecraft—and an impressive instance of Victorian faith, which did not require wires and a winch to make the trick believable. Even in Stowe's novel, Tom twice has a vision of Eva being directly translated, in a radiant cloud of glory, into heaven (*Uncle Tom's Cabin* [New York: Library of America, 1982], 368 and 406–407).

poor and sick (161) [105], they see her as "our Hester,—the town's own Hester" (162) [106]. But when the chapter titled "Another View of Hester" goes on to show us still *another* view of Hester,[3] we see how profoundly estranged from the town she has become: "She cast away the fragments of a broken chain. The world's law was no law for her mind" (164) [107]. The Puritans' utter failure as "readers" of the story is brought home to them dramatically at the climax, which depicts another publication of the scarlet letter while again they stand around the scaffold as a literal audience. Hawthorne, as he does throughout the novel, divides his focus in this scene between the action and their reaction. As we noted, they expect to see Dimmesdale ascend in glory to heaven. Instead, he goes up the steps of the scaffold to take his shame upon him. This not only explodes their predictions about the plot of Dimmesdale's life; it also razes the structure of assumptions by which they have understood reality. When Hester "published" her letter at the start, they stood in self-righteous certainty of their judgment on her. When Dimmesdale reveals his letter at the end, however, they are thrown into the "tumult" of interpretive chaos, "so taken by surprise, and so perplexed as to the purport of what they saw,—unable to receive the explanation which most readily presented itself, or to imagine any other,—that they remained silent and inactive spectators of the judgment which Providence seemed about to work" (253) [160].

Hawthorne put this surrogate audience into the text to guide his own audience's responses. His readers could watch them watching the story, and learn from them how not to read *The Scarlet Letter*. That explains why those Puritans are disguised Victorian Americans, for the assumptions that Hawthorne plots against are those that he identifies with his contemporary readers. He valued fiction for the truth that it could tell, but also said he wrote "to open up an intercourse with the world."[4] He summed up his thematic project as a writer by referring to himself as "a person, who has been burrowing, to his utmost ability, into the depths of our common nature, for the purposes of psychological romance."[5] But inseparable from this was his rhetorical project, the "apostolic errand" he refers to obliquely in "The Custom-House" (7) [10]. His "plan" for *The Scarlet Letter* was to communicate as well as to explore the depths of our common nature, the truths of the human heart. What he felt standing between him and the achievement of that plan were just the kind of moral and psychological simplifications that the book's Puritans accept as true. Their superficial judgments cut them off from the depths of our common nature.

When Dimmesdale gets back to his study after the breathtaking re-

3. This chapter's title is another instance of the kind of punning in which Hawthorne engages in "The Recognition"; once again, the reader who suspends closure is rewarded.
4. Hawthorne, Preface to the 1851 edition of *Twice-Told Tales*, ed. Roy Harvey Pearce et al. (Columbus: Ohio State UP, 1974), 6. That Hawthorne felt fiction had to tell the truth is an idea that appears in many places throughout his work. In the preface to *The House of the Seven Gables*, for instance, he writes that even fiction that claims the "latitude" of Romance "sins unpardonably" if it "swerve[s] aside from the truth of the human heart" (*The House of the Seven Gables*, ed. William Charvat et al. [Columbus: Ohio State UP, 1965], 1).
5. Hawthorne, Preface, *The Snow-Image* (1852), in *The Snow-Image and Uncollected Tales*, ed. Roy Harvey Pearce et al. (Columbus: Ohio State UP, 1974), 4.

union with Hester in the woods, the narrative provides a final gloss on what has happened to him: "Another man had returned out of the forest; a wiser one; with a knowledge of hidden mysteries which the simplicity of the former never could have reached" (223) [142]. This characterization links Dimmesdale with such earlier figures in Hawthorne's fiction as Young Goodman Brown and Ethan Brand, both of whom also learn the dark secrets of the heart (Brown in the forest). By their knowledge Brown and Brand are estranged from the world. In the first paragraph of "The Custom-House," however, Hawthorne announces his desire as a "speaker" to "stand in some true relation with his audience" (4) [7]. It is this desire to publish the truth—about himself, about the hidden mysteries his own experience has taught him— that carries Dimmesdale at the end up the scaffold's steps. There he becomes, at last, a true preacher, trying to stand in a true relation with *his* audience, and his text (like Hawthorne's) is "The Revelation of the Scarlet Letter." But Dimmesdale's revelation falls on blind eyes as his audience proves unwilling to abandon the "simplicities" of their former interpretation. To sum up the Puritans' failure even in this scene, we can invoke the novel's tersest paragraph: "The scarlet letter had not done its office" (166) [108]. As a sign of the truth of the human heart, the letter remains opaque to its aboriginal audience. By letting his audience see this other audience's blindness, however, Hawthorne is looking for a way to enable the scarlet letter to perform its office as a letter: to communicate.

For we are meant to consider the reason for the Puritans' failure. It is not simply their lack of sympathy for Hester as a sinner; that is but the symptom of a deeper cause: their failure to be honest with themselves and each other about the truths of their own nature. By means of the "sympathetic knowledge of the hidden sin in other hearts" that Hester's letter gives her, we see the people of Boston in much the same light that reveals Salem to Goodman Brown in the wilderness, as a brotherhood of shame and guilt: "If truth were everywhere to be shown, a scarlet letter would blaze forth on many a bosom besides Hester Prynne's" (86) [60]. Like Brown, however, the Puritans self-righteously reject this community: he exiles himself from society; they project their hidden sinfulness onto Hester and then, as a kind of repression, banish her and her A from their knowledge of themselves. In this unwillingness to "Be true" (260) [163] to the truth of their common nature lies the source of their inadequacies as "spectators." They see the world in the simplistic terms on which the repression of self-knowledge depends. Their reading of Dimmesdale's character is the obverse side of their repression of Hester. Onto the minister they project their image of the pure, angelic self, the self-gratulatory image that is fostered by their denial of the sinful self. Their misreading of Dimmesdale is as egregious as their inability to sympathize or identify with Hester, and it is treated even more explicitly as their failure as an audience. The minister achieves "a brilliant popularity in his sacred office," but "the people knew not the power that moved them thus." On the other hand, we're told exactly what that power consists of—the burden of guilty self-knowledge: "This very burden it was, that gave him sympathies so intimate with the sinful brotherhood of mankind: so that his heart vibrated in unison with theirs, and received their pain into itself, and sent its own throb of pain through a thousand other hearts, in gushes of sad, persuasive eloquence" (142) [94].

What Hawthorne is describing here is the basis of the "true relation" in which, as the "speaker" of *The Scarlet Letter*, he hopes to "stand with his audience": a fellowship of seekers for the truth of the heart, united by a knowledge of their mutual human frailties.[6] It is this way of "reading" the scarlet letter that he models for every reader in "The Custom-House," when he depicts himself taking up the *A* and placing it on his own breast (31–32) [26]. This is exactly the opposite of what the Puritans do, when they condemn an Other to wear the letter as their scapegoat. This, though, is what Dimmesdale himself will finally do, when he reveals his letter to them. And this is the lesson Hester ultimately learns from Dimmesdale, when at the very end she voluntarily puts the *A* back on. It is, we learn in "The Custom-House," and learn authoritatively, the true way to interpret the novel: we must not merely pick up *The Scarlet Letter*—we must wear it, must admit the truth it tells us about ourselves. In terms of Hawthorne's "plan," this means he must lead his audience beyond the psychological "simplicities" reflected in their conventional, melodramatic moral categories. In this sense, the whole rhetorical problem of the novel is summed up, anxiously, in the last three sentences of chapter 22, the chapter that precedes "The Revelation of the Scarlet Letter": "The sainted minister in the church! The woman of the scarlet letter in the market-place! What imagination would have been irreverent enough to surmise that the same scorching stigma was on them both?" (247) [156]. The answer, of course, is Hawthorne's imagination. But that answer only locates the point from which, as a Victorian American author, he felt he had to begin. The end toward which he worked depended upon his audience's willingness to accept the terms of his imagination. Given the pieties of his genteel audience, "irreverent" is a good term for those terms. He wants to unite those aspects of human nature which his culture kept asunder—the most saintly and the most debased, the best and worst.

6. Hawthorne repeats this passage at the end, when he describes the source of Dimmesdale's oratorical power in the Election Day sermon: "If the auditor listened intently, and for the purpose, he could detect the same cry of pain. What was it? The complaint of a human heart, sorrow-laden, perchance guilty, telling its secret, whether of guilt or sorrow, to the great heart of mankind; beseeching its sympathy or forgiveness,—at every moment,—in each accent,—and never in vain! It was this profound and continual undertone that gave the clergyman his most appropriate power" (243–44) [154–55]. Hawthorne's repetition of this idea, not to mention the evident earnestness of the passage itself, indicates how crucial to him was the ideal of sympathy for mutual human frailty as the basis of the bond between author and audience. I do not have space in this essay to contrast this with the basis on which Emerson put the relation between himself as speaker and his American audience; suffice it to say that it was diametrically opposed. To Emerson, every heart vibrates, not to human frailty, but to godlike self-reliance; the power of the Emersonian orator flows from the way he addresses himself to "the better part" of every auditor, not the worst. I point this out just to indicate that if one draws a wider circle around Hawthorne's available audience than I limit myself to—if one were to include the people who listened so enthusiastically to Emerson in 1850 as well as those who read genteel fiction—one would still be staring at the problem Hawthorne knew he was up against: that his truths of the human heart were at odds with the popular assumptions of his culture.

Among the culture's most devout pieties was the idea of true womanhood, which insisted on the segregation of heroines from sin, especially from sinful sexuality.[7] Thus, Hawthorne knew, his audience was likely to put almost as much distance as the Puritans do between themselves and Hester as a convicted adulteress. The literary type to which contemporary readers would have referred her was not the one that probably comes first to the modern reader's mind—the feminist protagonist, whom they had never met—but rather the Dark Heroine, a figure familiar from other books. Victorian American preconceptions about such a figure define the second step in Hawthorne's rhetorical plan: to create sympathy for Hester. The first eight chapters of the novel are largely devoted to this task. When Hester enters the story through the prison door, before describing her, before describing the *A* to which all the Puritans' eyes are drawn, Hawthorne describes the baby in her arms. His audience meets her first as "the mother of this child" (52) [40]. Stowe, who had her own rhetorical design on the same reading public, and knew as much as Hawthorne about how to achieve it, relies on exactly the same strategy. To that audience, a male black slave was as much an Other as a convicted adulteress. To close the gap between her hero and her readers, Stowe lets them meet for the first time in Tom's cabin, where he is meekly learning how to write from the master's child while his wife cooks in the foreground and his children play in the background. As if these domestic emanations weren't enough, Stowe allows only a few pages to pass before Tom too has a baby in his arms.[8] Both Hester's and Tom's babies are intended as passports to admit their bearers into the region where genteel readers and their sympathies were already at home.

By continually referring to Hester as a "mother"—as sacred a category to contemporary readers as minister was to the Puritans—and by developing in detail her struggles both to make her way as a woman in the wider world and to raise a daughter (the focus of chapters 5 and 6), Hawthorne seeks to complicate his readers' response to "this poor victim of her own frailty, and man's hard law" (87) [60]. This strategy culminates in chapters 7 and 8, the most dramatic episode of the novel's first half. Hester, "a lonely woman, backed by the sympathies of nature" (101) [68], goes to the Governor's Hall to argue "a mother's rights" (113) [76] before the men who intend to take Pearl from her. This scene goes after the sympathies of contemporary readers as directly and as shrewdly as Stowe does in her novel, where the forced separation of mothers and children is restaged again and again as the surest way to get white women readers to identify with the sufferings of slaves. The brilliantly plotted intention of this episode in which Hester fights "the public" (101) [68] to keep her child is once and for all to split Hawthorne's audience's responses from the Puritans' admonitory attitude: Victorian readers can only take Hester's side *against* the Puritans, and thus have been compelled to identify with her. The-

7. See Barbara Welter, "The Cult of True Womanhood: 1820–1860," *American Quarterly* 18 (1966): 151–74.
8. See *Uncle Tom's Cabin*, chap. 4, "An Evening in Uncle Tom's Cabin," 32–44.

matically, this means that they have been forced to include the Dark Heroine inside their sense of what it is to be human, even to be a mother.

Hawthorne works toward the same end in other ways. A major component of his plan could be called his strategy of narrative delay. Perhaps the most remarkable trait of the book's opening is the way it stalls and stutters before allowing the story proper to begin. We have already seen how chapter 2 restates the opening of chapter 1, by redescribing the audience before the prison door. Then chapter 2 goes on for about 300 words to wonder what this waiting throng "might be" assembled to see (49–50) [37]. Who is about to emerge from the prison? The narrative actually offers eight different answers to this question, none of which is accurate. It then keeps its audience waiting eight paragraphs more before Hester herself appears. This pattern of asking questions but delaying the answers recurs in many different contexts. Hawthorne leaves open such trivial questions as whether Hester cut her hair off, or just confined it under her cap (163) [107], and such crucial questions as "where was [Dimmesdale's] mind" as he marches forward to give the Election Sermon after having agreed to run away with Hester (239) [152]. In a sense this pattern organizes the whole novel. In the opening scene, both Chillingworth privately and the Puritans publicly ask who is the father of Hester's infant (62, 65) [45, 48]; the answer to this question is withheld—from Chillingworth (and the reader) until the middle, from the Puritans until the end.

Much more is at stake here than narrative suspense. One part of the reputation Puritanism had in the nineteenth century was its intolerance. Hawthorne's concern, as I have said, was with his contemporaries' assumptions, but as a means of addressing his concern he exploits the association of Puritanism with intolerance for all it is worth to him as a writer trying to complicate and enlarge those assumptions. At the heart of the Puritans' failure as interpreters of the scarlet letter is their inability to tolerate any kind of ambiguity. They cannot profit from the delay the narrative provides at the start: they "know" who is coming out of jail and how they should respond to her. When they see her—pointedly, they see only the letter she wears— Hester's appearance simply reconfirms their preconceptions. On the other hand, what Hawthorne's own audience is meant to learn from the narrative's habit of postponing answers to the questions it raises is how to suspend judgment—how, for example, to take another view of Hester. Hawthorne models this too in "The Custom-House," when he recounts how, after finding the A, he tried many different ways to solve the "riddle" of what it might mean (see 31–32) [26].

Closely allied to this pattern of narrative delay are the novel's stylistic or syntactic habits. In the book's second paragraph we are told that "it may safely be assumed that" the Puritans picked a site for their prison early in Boston's history (47) [36]. Such a point, we might think, could easily have been determined; his use of this construction

(I mean the syntactic one, not the jail) indicates again how much more interested he is in his contemporary audience than in New England history. Indeed, the syntactic construction stands in opposition to the jail: it opens up rather than locks in possibility. By emphasizing the uncertainty of even so factual a matter as a date, Hawthorne is calling attention to the problematic relationship between "assumption" and truth. Just as his narrative delays answers, his style withholds certainties. "We shall not take it upon us to determine," he writes in the last paragraph of chapter 1, "whether" the rose beside the prison door is merely natural, "or whether, as there is fair authority for believing," it supernaturally symbolizes Ann Hutchinson's antinomianism (48) [37]. In the first paragraph of chapter 2, he has no sooner suggested that "some noted culprit" might be about to emerge from the prison than he qualifies himself: "An inference of this kind could not so indubitably be drawn" (49) [37]. Instances of this stylistic indefiniteness could be multiplied almost indefinitely. Very little in *The Scarlet Letter* is stated as unequivocal fact. "It may be," "it might be," "perchance," "perhaps," "it seemed," "according to some," "it was reported"—these or similar locutions appear in almost every paragraph. While the Puritans cannot tolerate ambiguity, Hawthorne requires his audience to live with it. What "may safely be assumed" or what "kind of inference" should be drawn remains much of the time an explicitly open question, which is how this stylistic trait echoes the narrative one we looked at. The audience, forced in this way to abandon any privileged position as mere spectators, must become an active part of Hawthorne's interpretive community. Hawthorne separates his audience from the "simplicity" of the Puritans' responses and from the black-and-white terms of contemporary moral melodrama, and initiates them instead into the problematic realm of the "hidden mysteries" that is his subject.

"Simplicity" versus "hidden mysteries"—these are the antitheses he uses to measure the difference between the assumptions Dimmesdale takes into the woods and the knowledge which, after meeting Hester, he brings back. In terms of his "plan," the great scene between the lovers is the one for which Hawthorne has been carefully preparing his audience all along. Structurally, it occupies the same position in the novel's second half that Hester's confrontation in the Governor's Hall occupies in the first; thematically, it completes the project that he began by enabling the audience to sympathize, and thus identify, with Hester. Now he is ready dramatically to expose them to what meeting Hester in the wilderness can reveal about the truths of their own hearts.

Like the scene in which Hester fights to keep her child, her meeting with Dimmesdale in the forest evokes a paradigm readers would have met frequently in the period's best-selling melodramas. According to the biblical archetypes on which those stories relied, it is a temptation in the wilderness. *Uncle Tom's Cabin* offers a parallel scene at Simon Legree's, when Cassy, Stowe's version of the Dark Heroine and Hester's sister in passion and despair, exhorts Tom to choose a better life. With "a wild and peculiar glare" in her "large, black eyes," with "a flash of sudden energy," Cassy urges him to murder Legree and be free.[9] When Hester uses "her own energy" to exhort Dimmesdale to break with "these iron men" who "have kept thy better part in bondage too long already," she too "fix[es] her deep eyes on the minister's, and instinctively exercis[es] a magnetic power" over his spirit (197–98) [127]. "Any life is better than this," cries Cassy; Hester exclaims, "Do any thing, save to lie down and die!" (198) [127].

There is, of course, an apparently crucial difference between these two exhortations. Cassy, full of hate, tempts Tom to murder, but Hester's voice, which sounds so full of love, seems to summon Dimmesdale toward a "new life" of "human affection and sympathy" (200) [129]. It might seem beside any point Hawthorne had in mind to note that the Decalogue equally forbids killing and committing adultery. Yet Hawthorne's novel goes on to show decisively, in its own terms, which are psychological rather than Mosaic, that the passions Hester arouses in the woods are just as destructive as Cassy's murderous rage at Legree's. Hawthorne takes his audience into the woods with Hester, but he brings them back out with Dimmesdale. Chapter 20, "The Minister in a Maze," follows him homeward, which allows Hawthorne carefully to explore the "revolution in the sphere of [his] thought and feeling" that breaks loose after he yields his "will" to "Hester's will" (217) [138]. Chapter 20 also forces a sudden change in the text's representation of the Puritans. Hawthorne abruptly individualizes them. Instead of an aggregate, admonitory audience or an iron-visaged, repressive society, they are converted into men and women, as Dimmesdale meets an aged, venerable deacon, a "poor, widowed, lonely" old mother, and a maiden "fair and pure" (217–20) [139–40]. In the woods Hester rejects society as scornfully as it originally exiled her, but when Dimmesdale comes out of the woods society is portrayed as individuals with sympathetically human faces. And in each encounter with these members of his congregation, Dimmesdale feels "incited to do some strange, wild, wicked thing or other" (217) [138]—not premeditated murder, certainly, but something equally destructive of "human affection and sympathy." Dimmesdale, horrified to discover the anarchic violence of his own desires, wonders if he has somehow sold his soul to Satan in the woods. In the passage that follows, Hawthorne offers his own interpretive gloss on the meeting with Hester and states conclusively that indeed it was a temptation in the wilderness:

> The wretched minister! He had made a bargain very like it! Tempted by a dream of happiness, he had yielded himself with deliberate choice, as he had never done before, to what he knew was deadly sin. And the infectious poison of that sin had been thus rapidly diffused throughout his moral system. It had stupefied all blessed impulses, and awakened into vivid life the whole brotherhood of bad ones. Scorn, bitterness, unprovoked malignity, gratu-

9. *Uncle Tom's Cabin*, 461–63.

itous desire of ill, ridicule of whatever was good and holy, all awoke, to tempt, even while they frightened him. (222) [141–42]

We have yet to note the real distinction between Stowe's and Hawthorne's versions of this temptation scene. If there is not finally much difference in the kind of lawless, selfish, violent energies that fuel Cassy's and Hester's exhortations, there is nonetheless a vast difference in the larger role that meeting the Dark Heroine plays in the novels' thematic economies. Despite Cassy's attractiveness, Tom is never really tempted, nor is Stowe's audience. When she comes with her murderous scheme and Tom hastily replies, "Don't sell your precious soul to the devil, that way!" Stowe's audience is reminded of what evil is; when a few seconds later Tom asks God to "help us follow in His steps, and love our enemies," Stowe's audience is reminded what good is. At no point during Tom's temptation in Legree's wilderness does the narrative challenge that audience's preconceptions. Hawthorne, though, in keeping with his pattern of openness and delay, withholds his definitive interpretation of what transpired in the woods until three chapters after Hester seduces Dimmesdale with that "dream of happiness." Because Dimmesdale at first succumbs to the temptation, he is forced to realize firsthand the "hidden mysteries" of his own heart: that is the maze he gets lost in, and at the center of it is "a profounder self" (217) [139] than he had previously suspected.

Within this pattern—and we had better be explicit about this—Hawthorne allows Hester to seduce the audience as well. Probably every reader's hopes for her and Dimmesdale's happiness, and something fiercer and profounder too, are aroused when she lets down her magnificent hair in the woods. By letting desire loose inside the narrative, Hawthorne attempts a radical challenge to the Victorian audience's self-image. At the very start of the scene he quietly insinuates what meeting Hester in the woods should mean: "The soul beheld its features in the mirror of the passing moment" (190) [122]. By withholding his authoritative reading of the scene for twenty pages, he gives his audience an opportunity to follow Dimmesdale through the maze; for when he realizes what has been let loose *in himself*, "the Reverend Mr. Dimmesdale thus communed with himself" (221) [141], and it is by thus communing with his self, with his own previously hidden impulses, that Dimmesdale discovers his "profounder self" and becomes "another man," and "a wiser one." The conventional temptation-in-the-wilderness scene of popular fiction, by signaling itself as such, allowed readers to shield themselves against any disturbing response. In Stowe's novel, the true way depends on rejecting the Dark Heroine—and so remaining safe from any self-knowledge her character might reveal. Evil remains an abstraction to be resisted; Cassy is allowed to learn from Tom, but not to teach him anything. In Hawthorne's novel, though, the truth depends on communing first with Hester and then with oneself. The encounter in the woods is ultimately a *self*-recognition scene. The way it works on its audience makes lawless desire a fact of human nature that, as a fact of human nature, cannot be denied. In place of the straight lines and neat polarities of moral melodrama, Hawthorne has led his audience deep into the maze of their own hearts.[1]

II

We know who the first "reader" of *The Scarlet Letter* was, and as it happens, we also know a bit about her response. The day Hawthorne finished writing the manuscript, he finished reading it aloud to his wife. "It broke her heart," he wrote a friend, "and sent her to bed with a grievous headache—which I look upon as triumphant success!"[2] Signs of her distress are still evident in a letter she wrote to a friend a week later: "I do not know what you will think of the Romance. It is most powerful, & contains a moral as terrific & stunning as a thunderbolt. It shows that the Law cannot be broken."[3] As modern readers we may be tempted to smile here and congratulate ourselves on our increased sophistication. Despite Sophia Hawthorne's credentials—both as an intimate of the author, and as a reader herself (Melville, for example, was very impressed with her response to *Moby-Dick*)[4]—we are likely to dismiss her reading as naive. Her insistence on "the Law" sounds too much like the narrow-minded reading the "Puritans" try to impose on the story. And we have outgrown her quaint Victorian reductiveness, which values a work of art for the "moral" it supplies—as if literature, Ezra Pound wrote contemptuously in 1918, were merely "the ox-cart and post-chaise for transmitting thoughts poetic or otherwise."[5]

I want to end this essay by considering the gap between the way *The Scarlet Letter* addressed its contemporary audience and the way it seems to speak to us at the end of the twentieth century. Let me start with a reconsideration of Sophia Hawthorne's response. Behind her assertion of "the Law" is nothing like the Puritans' self-righteous smugness. They take the law for granted, but it is clear from her reactions—the grief, the headache, the mixed emotions she betrays even a week later with words like "terrific" and "stunning"—that as a reader she has been fully open to the experience of the text. As far as the Law goes, she is clearly right about the values Hawthorne's novel ultimately privileges. It was post-Victorian writers like Henry James and Pound who taught us to look for the meaning of form in works of lit-

1. Chillingworth is vouchsafed such a chance as well. Just before she seeks out Dimmesdale in the woods, Hester goes to talk with Chillingworth at the seashore. Here, too, meeting Hester represents an opportunity to see one's self: "The unfortunate physician . . . lifted his hands with a look of horror, as if he had beheld some frightful shape, which he could not recognize, usurping the place of his own image in a glass. It was one of those moments—which sometimes occur only at the interval of years—when a man's moral aspect is faithfully revealed to his mind's eye. Not improbably, he had never before viewed himself as he did now" (172) [112]. Hawthorne's emphases here underscore the centrality of this kind of self-recognition scene to his project in the novel.
2. Hawthorne to Horatio Bridge, February 4, 1850, *Letters, 1843–1853*, 311 [pp. 228–29 in this Norton Critical Edition].
3. Sophia Hawthorne to Mary Mann, February 12, 1850, quoted ibid., 313.
4. See Melville's letter to Sophia Hawthorne, January 8, 1852, *The Letters of Herman Melville*, ed. M. R. Davis and W. H. Gilman (New Haven: Yale UP, 1960), 145–47.
5. Ezra Pound, "A Retrospect," rpt. in *Literary Essays of Ezra Pound*, ed. T. S. Eliot (New York: New Directions, 1968), 11.

erature; when we approach *The Scarlet Letter* from that perspective, it seems even more inexorably, less ambiguously to affirm the Law. At the start, in the absolute middle, and again at the end the novel returns to the scaffold that represents the Law. From a strictly formal point of view, we should never have been tempted in the wilderness; the structural placement of that scene, given the logic of returning to the scaffold that the narrative has already established, is enough to indicate that in the "wild, heathen Nature of the forest" (203) [130], we have gone astray. Of course, it is by vicariously going astray with Hester in "the mystery of the primeval forest" (183) [118] that readers can discover the truth of their hearts—but it is from Dimmesdale, whose attempt to come home from the woods leads him too to return to the scaffold, that Hawthorne expects his audience to learn how to live with that knowledge. Even Hester eventually agrees, as we can tell from her decision to resume the letter that Dimmesdale has taught her must be revealed.

One reason to value Sophia's response is that it registers Hawthorne's radical achievement even as an apostle of the moral law. The law must be obeyed—this, in one form or another, is the moral of every genteel fiction of his time. But Hawthorne's exploration of this truth in *The Scarlet Letter* more closely resembles (and anticipates) the severe wisdom of Freud's *Civilization and Its Discontents*: the law must be obeyed, and therein lies the tragedy of our instinctual lives. Sophia's broken heart indicates that she too was seduced by Hester's "dream of happiness" in the woods. The novel's deepest power flows from the way it enacts, not simply moralizes on, its theme. When the anarchic desires that the forest represents get let loose in the novel, we want to live there. To the palpable promise of erotic fulfillment that Hester's lawless energy summons up in us we are prepared to sacrifice everything—even, to take the human fact with which the narrative immediately daunts the lovers in the woods, to sacrifice Pearl. Amidst the imperious claims of their re-aroused passion, Hester and Dimmesdale, and probably even the Victorian audience, forgot about this child. But if in the first half Hawthorne uses Pearl's presence to encourage his audience to sympathize with Hester, here he uses her absence to keep a kind of moral distance from Hester's exhortation. When Pearl comes back into view, which happens even before the lovers leave the woods, she points the way that Dimmesdale later realizes he must take. When he climbs up to the scaffold, he sacrifices his own desires to the claims of his relationships as an adult to other people: to Pearl as her father, to his parishioners as their minister, even to Hester as her partner in shame. But embracing the Law instead of Hester is hard, even tragic, as *The Scarlet Letter* almost alone among the period's fictions acknowledges. Like most best-selling novels, including *Uncle Tom's Cabin*, it ends with a recovered family: on the scaffold at the end are Dimmesdale, Hester, Pearl, and Chillingworth, finally united in public. But unlike all those other endings, Hawthorne's fully reckons the cost, in terms of an individual's instinctual desires, by which a family is achieved and maintained.

The law must be obeyed, but this is a terrific truth, not a conventional truism: Mrs. Hawthorne's reading seems both critically and emotionally sound. Yet because the terms it relies on—a moral, the Law—seem so distant from those that modern readers bring to a text, such terms also establish the cultural gap across which the novel speaks to us. For example, published modern readings of it often regret or more often simply ignore the moral that Hawthorne himself provides. We know he was pleased with his wife's reaction as an audience. We cannot say exactly how he felt about her conclusions as a critic. Presumably he knew literature could not do police work, could not lay down or enforce laws. But we also know that he wanted his work to explore and express truths. The moral he offers his audience exhorts them to the same project: "Be true! Be true! Be true! Show freely to the world, if not your worst, yet some trait whereby the worst may be inferred" (260) [163]. It is true that he offers this as only one among the "many morals" that may be drawn from the tale he has told, but this is one of those points in the text where he abandons his technique of narrative and stylistic ambiguity. Instead of offering us a number of morals to choose from, he insists, with all the unequivocality of the imperative mood, on this one. This moral does bring toward a conclusion the rhetorical project that governs Hawthorne's intentions throughout the book: to initiate contemporary readers into the truths about themselves that their culture has repressed. But in our time there remains our distrust, not to say positive distaste, for a moral. Do readers have the right of re-vision? Can we ignore or reject the author's own reading, offered inside the text itself?

Well, we could say that this enjoinment is not addressed to "us." Given the way our century began, for instance, with Freud's revelations about the truths of the human psyche, we do not approach Hawthorne's "drama of guilt and sorrow" (253) [160] with anything like the self-image of his Victorian American readers. Since we do not share their pieties, we cannot easily appreciate the "irreverence" of the burden he puts on his imagination by tasking it to show that the scarlet woman and the saintly minister both wear the "same scorching stigma." It is analogous to the way that every modern reader already knows that Dimmesdale is Hester's lover: the "hidden mysteries" into which Hawthorne felt obliged to guide his audience so carefully are not hidden for us. The "profounder self" that Dimmesdale is amazed to discover, and that Hawthorne's contemporaries did not consciously recognize either, is a fact of human nature that our culture largely takes for granted. Or think how differently a Victorian and a modern reader are apt to react to Hester in that first scene. In both cases the reflexes are conditioned by cultural experience. But whereas Hawthorne's culture had conditioned his audience, as they valued the image of themselves that the genteel culture sanctioned, to reject any identification with so dark a heroine, our own cultural experience, including the high ideological status accorded the dissatisfied wife, leads today's readers to prejudge Hester, so passionate a victim of a bad marriage and a repressive society, almost antithetically.

We need not judge such differences as either for better or for worse. But we should take account of them. Americans going to Latin America have to be warned not to use their thumb and forefinger to signal "OK"—because in Mexico or Brazil that friendly sign stands for something very different. Similarly, the gestures Hawthorne uses to communicate his vision to his contemporaries speak to postmodern readers in ways he could not have anticipated. The context in which he wrote was defined by his audience's mid-nineteenth-century faiths; for our part, we cannot help but read from within the context of late-twentieth-century doubts. Thus to post-deconstructionist critics, the various maneuvers by which Hawthorne sought to recondition the responses of Victorian readers—delay, withholding, equivocation, ambiguity—may look definitive. What for Hawthorne was a means—a strategy to change his audience's preconceptions—now seems, given our preconceptions, to be an end. Within the past ten years, as could have been expected, have appeared critical readings that argue the "indeterminacy," the "illegibility," the "pervasive ambiguity" of the novel.[6] That ambiguity was a means for Hawthorne seems clear from the care he takes eventually to provide interpretive closure, as in that sequence we examined where, twenty pages after Hester's urging instinctual fulfillment in the wilderness has had a chance to work on Dimmesdale (and on us), the narrator tells us unambiguously that Dimmesdale (and we) have been seduced by our own profoundest self. But such authoritative passages, though written in the language that spoke most authoritatively to his contemporaries, fall deafly on our modern ears. Satanic bargain, deadly sin, whatever was good and holy—post-deconstructionist readers can ignore such locutions or dismiss them as inauthentic. It is an irony of literary history that Hawthorne begins by acknowledging the problem of trying to speak the truth to a culture of euphemism, which means there are many words he cannot use without "startl[ing]" his "present day" readers (51) [38]. He manages to solve that problem brilliantly, writing one of the nineteenth century's most mature explorations of adult sexuality so tactfully that only a few extremists were upset. But he could not have anticipated the problem of trying to define the truth for a culture of doubt, and so the novel cannot defend itself from the postmodern emptiness of the words it ultimately relies on to make its truths persuasive to its audience.

Feminist readings of the novel are also likely to confuse Hawthorne's means with ends. The strategic care he takes in the first third to nurture his Victorian audience's sympathy for Hester can similarly seem definitive, so that the passions she arouses in the forest can seem exemplary, the novel's ultimate act of visionary witness. Modern readers, unlike Victorian ones, are prepared to go as deep into the

6. These epithets are from, respectively, Millicent Bell's "The Obliquity of Signs: *The Scarlet Letter*," *Massachusetts Review* 23 (1982): 9–26 [pp. 451–63 in this Norton Critical Edition]; Norman Bryson's "Hawthorne's Illegible Letter," in *Teaching the Text*, ed. Susanne Kappeler and Norman Bryson (London: Routledge, 1983), 92–108, rpt. in *Nathaniel Hawthorne's "The Scarlet Letter*," ed. Harold Bloom (New York: Chelsea, 1986), 81–95; and Evan Carton's *The Rhetoric of American Romance* (Baltimore: Johns Hopkins UP, 1985), 191–227.

wilderness as Hester can take them, but are often simply unwilling to follow Dimmesdale back from the woods to the scaffold, although that is the ground, the ground of moral duty, that Victorian readers were most familiar with.[7] Never mind that the narrative decisively defines the "dream of happiness" in the woods as a "temptation"; to such recent readers, Dimmesdale's decision to stand with Hester in "shame" rather than live with her in "joy," his decision to "reveal" the scarlet letter, does not look like moral heroism, but rather psychological cowardice or emotional betrayal. When Hawthorne makes Dimmesdale Christ-like in this scene of "triumphant ignominy before the people" (257) [162]—he submits to "the will which God hath granted [him]"; he forgives his enemy; he stands (in fact, we are told explicitly that though he tottered on the way to the scaffold, he "did not fall!") "as one who, in the crisis of acutest pain, had won a victory" (251–55) [159–61]—the novel again relies on the most definitive terms available at the time to convince a contemporary audience. Uncle Tom dies a similarly Christ-like death when he wins his "victory" at the end of Stowe's novel. But the Christian scaffolding with which Hawthorne props up Dimmesdale's actions no longer resonates with us. For many modern readers, Dimmesdale dies—and publishes the truth—in vain.

Certainly for most readers, in Hawthorne's time and ours, the tragic waste of Hester's powers and passions is what resonates most deeply as we close the tale. Doubtless it was this that broke Mrs. Hawthorne's heart. The novel redeems this loss, however, in two ways. Neither is the redemption that contemporary readers may have been looking for. When Sambo and Quimbo witness Tom's martyrdom at Legree's, we are told explicitly that by this means their souls are saved.[8] Yet we are not told about the eternal fate of Hester's soul. (Indeed, Hawthorne leaves out this detail so conspicuously that we seem warranted in thinking that his use of Christian iconography at Dimmesdale's death is largely a means too: his means of giving Dimmesdale's act of "being true" the highest possible stature in his audience's eyes.) Rather, the most immediate event that redeems Hester's, Dimmesdale's, and our anguish at being on the scaffold instead of in the woods is the earthly fate of Pearl's self. By living up to his responsibilities as her father, Dimmesdale frees her from her "errand as a messenger of anguish" to "grow up amid human joy and sorrow" (256) [162]. This is probably the one place where the novel backs down from its commitment to tell the truth, however tragic—for the notion that parents, by doing the right thing, can somehow spare their children from the tragedies of their own lives is hopelessly naive, however attractive. The happy ending permitted Pearl is another place where the novel would have spoken more convincingly to Victorian than to modern readers.

7. Recent critics who find the book's imaginative center with Hester in the woods or who reject Dimmesdale's revelation on the scaffold include Nina Baym, *The Shape of Hawthorne's Career* (Ithaca: Cornell UP, 1976), 123–51; and David Leverenz, "Mrs. Hawthorne's Headache: Reading *The Scarlet Letter*," *Nineteenth-Century Fiction* 37 (1983): 552–75 [pp. 463–81 in this Norton Critical Edition].
8. Stowe, *Uncle Tom's Cabin*, 481–82.

The novel, though, does not quite end with the prospect of Pearl as "married, and happy, and mindful of her mother" (262) [165]. It goes on to describe Hester's earthly fate as well. Having learned from Dimmesdale how to "be true," Hester settles permanently in Boston and puts on the letter "of her own free will" (263) [165]. To modern readers who see the letter as "illegible" or as only the badge of Hester's "victimization by patriarchy,"[9] this ending must seem absurd or grotesque. But in terms of the novel's rhetorical project, the most redemptive thing that happens when Hester resumes the A is the growth of a new interpretive community around it. As we noted, Dimmesdale's revelation of the scarlet letter confounds rather than communicates to the Puritans who make up the novel's internal audience. At the very end, however, another group of viewers emerges to see the A in a wholly new way: "The scarlet letter ceased to be a stigma which attracted the world's scorn and bitterness, and became a type of something to be sorrowed over, and looked upon with awe, yet with reverence too" (263) [165].

Like the first time we see someone seeing the letter—when Hawthorne puts it on his own breast in "The Custom-House"—this last time is exemplary. This is how to read the scarlet letter: with sorrow for human frailty, awe at the hidden mysteries of the heart, reverence for another soul as equally human. By interpreting the letter in this spirit, the community that gathers around Hester at the end forms a third term to mediate between the repressive injustices of society and the lawless desires of the wilderness. The bases for this community's interpretation are sympathy and self-knowledge, and in their sensitivity as interpreters we see the basis for the belief that Hester prophetically embodies at the end: that "a new truth would be revealed, in order to establish the whole relation between man and woman on a surer ground of mutual happiness" (263) [166]. Is not this "new truth" the truth that Hawthorne has tried to express in *The Scarlet Letter*? If the profounder self he reveals in the wilderness had been recognized and rightly understood, the Puritans never would have banished Hester. In fact, if we think about it, is it not likely that if the needs and desires of that profounder self had been acknowledged, Hester and Chillingworth never would have married? Hester, we have to remember, had to repress the truth about herself and her own desires to marry Chillingworth in the first place, and in a sense it is from that first act of repression that the tragedy of her life follows.

But if the novel reaches interpretive closure at the end, in this sympathetic community's reading of the A, it does not reach stasis. Restoring the status quo is not the end of Hawthorne's rhetorical project. For just as the ultimate interpretive community in the novel has been brought into existence by the experience of the tale itself, so Hawthorne hopes to change his audience by the "new truth" he has revealed and carefully enabled them to experience by reading the tale.

9. This is the feminist reading offered by Cynthia S. Jordan, *Second Stories: The Politics of Language, Form, and Gender in Early American Fictions* (Chapel Hill: U of North Carolina P, 1989), 152–72.

The novel's very last line leaves his readers staring at the A. It leaves them, that is, with a project of their own: to join the community that sees the letter as the sign that speaks to all of us about our own profounder self. What Mrs. Hawthorne read in the novel—that life is tragic, but redeemed by moral significance—would qualify her, I think, for membership in that community. Self-knowledge and sympathy are not outdated virtues, but it is legitimate to ask whether many modern readers are interested in belonging to the particular interpretive community into which Hawthorne sought to turn his contemporary audience. He addresses himself to their nineteenth-century assumptions and leads them to the new truths revealed at the end, in the woods and on the scaffold. We start with different assumptions. His novel is bound to lead us to other, different ends.

LOUISE DeSALVO

Nathaniel Hawthorne and the Feminists: *The Scarlet Letter*†

On Saturday, 27 July 1844, Nathaniel Hawthorne made an entry in his notebook that was the germ for his most famous and most critically acclaimed novel, *The Scarlet Letter*: 'The life of a woman, who by old colony law, was condemned always to wear the letter A, sewed on her garment, in token of her having committed adultery.'[1]

Between the publication of *Fanshawe* in 1828, until the time he began working on *The Scarlet Letter*, in 1849, when he was in his midforties, Hawthorne had confined his writing to short works,[2] many of which were published in periodicals such as *The Token* and the *Salem Gazette*, and later collected in *Twice-Told Tales* and *Mosses from an Old Manse*.[3] Although Hawthorne was prolific, he found it impossible to

---

† From *Nathaniel Hawthorne* (Atlantic Highlands: Humanities Press International, 1987), 57–76. Copyright © 1987 by Louise DeSalvo. Reprinted by permission of the author. Page numbers in square brackets refer to this Norton Critical Edition.

1. N. Hawthorne, *The American Notebooks*, 254 [215].
2. N. Arvin, Introduction to *Hawthorne's Short Stories*, 254.
3. For a history of the publication of these volumes, see F. Bowers's 'Textual commentary' in N. Hawthorne, *Twice-Told Tales*, *The Centenary Edition of the Works of Nathaniel Hawthorne*, vol. IX, and J. D. Crowley's 'Historical commentary' in *Mosses from an Old Manse*, *The Centenary Edition of the Works of Nathaniel Hawthorne*, vol. X. The final collection to appear in Hawthorne's lifetime was *The Snow-Image* (1851). *See* J. D. Crowley, 'Historical commentary' in *The Snow-Image and Uncollected Tales*, *The Centenary Edition of the Works of Nathaniel Hawthorne*, vol. XI.

   Virtually all of Hawthorne's short fiction is of interest to the feminist reader, and a complete study of his short works from a feminist perspective is sorely needed. * * * A considerable number of the stories deal with the issue of love and marriage, such as 'The Wedding Knell', 'The Minister's Black Veil', 'The Birth-mark', 'The New Adam and Eve', to name but a few, and they offer superb insights, not only into Hawthorne's attitudes, but also to the prevailing attitudes of the time. Others, such as 'Rappaccini's Daughter' and 'The Snow-Image,' deal with the issue of the condition of daughterhood within the patriarchal family as Hawthorne conceived it, which illuminates his treatment of Una. Still others, like 'The Gentle Boy' and 'My Kinsman, Major Molineux,' express Hawthorne's often ambivalent attitudes to his patriarchal forebears. Certain tales, such as 'Alice Doane's Appeal,' treat the issue of incest. A sketch which castigates a woman for modesty, and which illustrates Hawthorne's vacillating attitude to women's sexuality, in addition to demonstrating his voyeurism, is 'The

support his family on the paltry amounts he earned from his writing—
he was paid only 'an average of $1.00 per page'[4] for his contributions
to *The Token*—so that by the time he began *The Scarlet Letter*, he and
Sophia had experienced periods of financial destitution, which had
forced them to move in with Hawthorne's mother, then living on Mall
Street in Salem, and had led Hawthorne to accept, on 3 April 1846,
the position of Surveyor of the Custom-House in Salem.[5]

Hawthorne worked at the Custom-House until his dismissal, on
8 June 1849, as a result of the Whigs electoral victory. His wife,
Sophia, 'greeted the first news of his dismissal with the remark, "Oh,
then, you can write your book!"'

It was an extremely difficult time for him, for, on 30 July, his mother
died. On the day before her death, in a journal entry, Hawthorne described the time that he spent at her bedside as 'the darkest hour I
ever lived'. After her death he became seriously ill, but in September,
after he recovered, he began writing *The Scarlet Letter* in 'response to
his mother's death',[6] and as a kind of elegy to her. Like his heroine
Hester Prynne, Elizabeth Hawthorne had become pregnant with her
first child outside of marriage and had been socially ostracized; like
Hester, his mother was husbandless, a single parent, raising her offspring alone, on the fringes of society. But it is also likely that his
mother's death provided a kind of creative release, for he worked 'with
an intensity that almost frightened his wife, and with a speed that
brought the book to completion before the year ended'.[7] His wife
Sophia certainly made the writing of the novel possible because without the money she had saved, 'a hundred and fifty dollars in bills, in
silver, even in coppers',[8] her earnings from her decorative work,
Hawthorne would have had to find another form of employment. The
novel was composed quickly, and was completed on 3 February 1850.[9]

'The Custom-House' which serves as an introduction to and pro-

---

Canal-Boat' which, according to J. R. Mellow, presents a 'devastating sketch' (54) of the
American woman but which also presents as devastating a sketch of Hawthorne's persecu-
tory attitude towards women. In addition, a number of the tales discuss the relationship of
women to learning and education: among them, 'The Birth-mark' and 'Rappaccini's Daughter'. Several tales deal with the witchcraft era in American history: 'Young Goodman Brown',
'Alice Doane's Appeal', 'The Hollow of the Three Hills', 'The Prophetic Pictures', 'Edward
Randolph's Portrait', 'Drowne's Wooden Image', for example. According to the feminist
critic, N. Baym, a number of the tales uncover the psychopathology of the rejection of
women, or of the feminine—'Rappaccini's Daughter', 'The Birth-mark', 'Wakefield', 'The
Man of Adamant', 'The Prophetic Pictures', 'Roger Malvin's Burial', 'Young Goodman
Brown', 'The Minister's Black Veil', 'The Shaker Bridal'.

For illuminating discussion of the tales, see N. Baym, 'Hawthorne's women'; M. D. Bell,
Hawthorne and the Historical Romance of New England; C. M. Bensick, *La Nouvelle Béa-
trice*; F. Crews, *The Sins of the Fathers*; J. Fetterley, *The Resisting Reader* (on 'The Birthmark'); J. R. Mellow, *Nathaniel Hawthorne*; N. F. Doubleday, *Hawthorne's Early Tales*.

4. J. D. Crowley, 'Historical commentary' to *Twice-told Tales*, *The Centenary Edition of the
Works of Nathaniel Hawthorne*, 497.

5. R. Stewart, *Nathaniel Hawthorne*, 79. See G. C. Erlich, *Family Themes and Hawthorne's Fiction*.

6. H. H. Hoeltje, 'The writing of *The Scarlet Letter*', 342; N. Baym, 'Nathaniel Hawthorne and
his mother', 20, 21. For a discussion of the effect of his mother's death on the creation of
the novel, see, especially, N. Baym and G. C. Erlich. * * *

7. N. Baym, 1. See G. C. Erlich for a discussion of how his mother's death freed him to write
his masterpiece.

8. L. H. Tharp, *The Peabody Sisters of Salem*, 190.

9. H. H. Hoeltje, 344.

vides a frame for *The Scarlet Letter* was intended by Hawthorne to be a deliberate act of aggression and revenge against the Whigs who were responsible for his dismissal from his post. As author of the piece, he saw himself as a 'hunter', and he described the act of writing as the loading of a 'gun with a bullet and several buckshot'; reading his work, moreover, would 'kill the public . . . with my biggest and heaviest lump of lead'.[1] 'The Custom-House' is a savage, even vicious, satire against government service, and the kind of men who enter it. The Custom-House officers talk 'with that lack of energy that distinguishes the oc-cupants of alms-houses, and all other human beings who depend for subsistence on charity . . . or any thing else but their own independent exertions' (7) [9]; the veterans under Hawthorne's orders, largely Whigs, whom he has not dismissed, although he should have, 'go lazily about what they termed duty, and, at their own leisure and conve-nience, betake themselves to bed again' (13) [14]. Hawthorne clearly feels that if he has tolerated them, and allowed them to continue in government service, because he 'could never quite find in my heart to act upon the knowledge' (14) [15] that they should be dismissed, the Whigs should have allowed him to retain his position.

Hawthorne reserves his most acid attack for the Permanent Inspec-tor, animal-like, with 'no soul, no heart, no mind; nothing, as I have al-ready said, but instincts' (18) [17] whose main attribute was his ability to recollect 'the ghosts of bygone meals', 'while all the subsequent ex-perience of our race . . . had gone over him with as little permanent ef-fect as the passing breeze' (19) [18].

Although Hawthorne makes it quite clear that he believes that he has been betrayed by *male* politicians, and that he intends to take his revenge upon them, none the less, the image which introduces 'The Custom-House' and dominates it, is the image of the American eagle, which Hawthorne depicts as a negative *female* image. It is worth quot-ing in its entirety, because the tale that Hawthorne tells of betrayal by the political system is enacted against the backdrop of this image of female betrayal. Over the entrance to the Custom-House,

> hovers an enormous specimen of the American eagle, with out-spread wings, a shield before her breast, and, . . . a bunch of in-termingled thunderbolts and barbed arrows in each claw. With the customary infirmity of temper that characterizes this unhappy fowl, she appears, by the fierceness of her beak and eye and the general truculency of her attitude, to threaten mischief to the in-offensive community; and especially to warn all citizens, careful of their safety, against intruding on the premises which she over-looks with her wings. Nevertheless, vixenly as she looks, many people are seeking, at this very moment, to shelter themselves un-der the wing of the federal eagle; imagining, I presume, that her bosom has all the softness and snugness of an eider-down pillow. But she has no great tenderness, even in her best of moods, and,

---

1. W. Charvat, 'Introduction to *The Scarlet Letter*', *The Scarlet Letter. The Centenary Edition of the Works of Nathaniel Hawthorne*, xxii. Citations from this edition will be placed within parentheses throughout this essay.

> sooner or later, . . . is apt to fling off her nestlings with a scratch of her claw, a dab of her beak, or a rankling wound from her barbed arrows. (5) [8–9]

This image is extraordinary not only because it transforms the American eagle (the symbol of American might and strength) into a *female* image, but also because the effect of this transformation is subtly yet bitterly misogynist. It states that this female eagle is potentially and unpredictably vicious 'to the inoffensive community' precisely because she is female, and it is in the nature of females to be unpredictable; moreover, this female eagle is doubly vicious and unpredictable because she is an *unhappy* female who might lash out, with her 'thunderbolts' and her 'barbed arrows' at any one, at any time, whether or not they deserve it.

What Hawthorne accomplishes by rendering the national American symbol as female, is, in effect, a shifting of the responsibility and blame for his dismissal from the Custom-House away from the men who were responsible (and, by extension, away from the male-dominated patriarchal political system). Instead, despite his acerbic and rancorous remarks about men in government service, it is clear from this image of the female federal eagle, that, at some deep level, Hawthorne experienced his dismissal as *maternal* rejection, rather than as the result of a male political wrangle. Thus, the female federal eagle becomes the bad mother. She does not offer 'great tenderness, even in her best of moods', but rather flings her nestlings (one of whom was Hawthorne himself) from the nest 'with a scratch of her claw', or, even worse, 'a rankling wound from her barbed arrows' (5) [9]. This image subtly, but effectively, indicates that, at some deep level, Hawthorne irrationally blamed his mother for having abandoned him through her death, and that he also blamed her for losing his position at the Custom-House. What the feminist reader of 'The Custom-House' must note is how this image misrepresents political power as female, and how it blames a maternal figure for what is, in reality, the action of a male-dominated political machine.

Near the beginning of 'The Custom-House', Hawthorne announces that one of his reasons for writing the sketch is to 'put myself in my true position as editor' (4) [8] of Hester Prynne's tale, and to explain 'how a large portion of the following pages came into my possession, and as offering proofs of authenticity of a narrative contained therein' (4) [8]. Hawthorne describes finding barrels in the second story of the Custom House, containing bundles of documents of Jonathan Pue, a surveyor and local antiquarian, which could be used for 'a regular history of Salem' (31) [26]. In the bundle, Hawthorne discovers 'a certain affair of fine red cloth, much worn and faded . . . [which] on careful examination assumed the shape of a letter. It was the capital letter A' (31) [26] together with 'a small roll of dingy paper' containing 'a reasonably complete explanation of the whole affair' (32) [26–27].

This fictive posture of Hawthorne as editor of an historical document is an attempt to persuade the reader that the story that he tells, though embellished, is in effect an authentic, if not true account of Hester Prynne's fate in Puritan New England, and that the novel is the 'representation of a mode of life not heretofore described' (4) [8]. 'What I contend for is the authenticity of the outline' (33) [27]. Thus Hester's story comes to represent a model for describing the ways in which women who deviated from Puritan law were treated in Puritan New England and a model for understanding the character of the male élite Puritan oligarchy.

Although, ostensibly, *The Scarlet Letter* is a novel about a woman, what is insisted upon in the purported autobiography at the beginning of the novel, is that writing the history of a culture, that writing the history of a woman's fate within a culture, is, and ought to be, a strictly male enterprise. Attributing Hester's tale to the researches of Jonathan Pue effectively serves to write out his wife Sophia's, his mother Elizabeth's, and his daughter Una's relationship to the creation of the novel. If Hawthorne's prologue is, in fact, what it purports to be—an autobiographical account of how *The Scarlet Letter* came into being—it seems curious that Hawthorne would create Surveyor Pue and then credit him for the novel, rather than the women to whom he was indebted. Why bother to invent the fiction of the autobiographical frame at all if the autobiographical frame is, in fact, a fiction? In fact, what Hawthorne is doing, although he may not be aware of it, is creating his own autobiography by disavowing the facts of his life: he is creating what he would like the reader to know about himself: he is creating himself even as he creates Hester Prynne.

So convincing is Hawthorne's ploy that the reader rarely notices that the introduction provides a fascinating account of how the writing of romance or history *must* be articulated as if it proceeds from male to male even when (or perhaps especially when) women are the subject of that history, even when women have, in fact, made the writing of that work possible. In one very important scene, Hawthorne has a fantasy about Pue handing him Hester's story, and he describes Pue here as a ghostly father:

> With his own ghostly hand, the obscurely seen, but majestic figure had imparted to me the scarlet symbol, and the little roll of explanatory manuscript. With his own ghostly voice, he had exhorted me, on the sacred consideration of my filial duty and reverence towards him,—who might reasonably regard himself as my official ancestor to bring his mouldy and moth-eaten lucubrations before the public. (33) [27–28]

Thus, Hawthorne does not perceive the function of telling his tale as serving the causes of women's history; rather, Hawthorne is using one woman's story to serve the purposes of *male* history, both his own and men in general—a fact that has been overlooked by feminist literary critics. As Pue's ghost instructs Hawthorne: '. . . I charge you, in this matter of old Mistress Prynne, give to your predecessor's memory the credit which will be rightfully its due!' (33–34) [28].

The fundamental assumption about the nature of history that is embedded here is that woman's history is, and ought to be, the *property* of the male historian. Indeed, in the first moments of the novel, as Hester is about to emerge from the prison, Hawthorne uses the word 'narrative' to describe her: just as she is about to emerge from the jail, so is 'our narrative, . . . about to issue from that inauspicious portal' (48) [37]. She is not a character, she is a narrative, and in the language that Hawthorne insists upon, Hester and the narrative are, in fact, the same.

Moreover it is absolutely necessary that this history be presented as if it were authentic *especially if* that account grossly misrepresents woman's history, as the life story of Hester Prynne in *The Scarlet Letter* grossly distorts the fate of women who committed adultery in Puritan New England. In one very important sense, depicting Hester's strength and her resilience in the face of her punishment serves to nullify the effects of such persecution. If Hester could endure, and triumph (as women who were persecuted for adultery surely did not), then the negative consequences of the persecution itself are blunted, and the persecuting fathers rendered less virulent than they in fact were.

Critics, such as Charles Ryskamp and William Charvat have documented the fact that Hawthorne read widely in the history of Puritan New England of the 1640s, and that his notebooks indicate his concern with getting the details of that time precisely correct. Sources such as Caleb H. Snow's *History of Boston* and Joseph Felt's *Annals of Salem* were read and used 'to create an authentic picture of the seventeenth century'.[2] But despite Hawthorne's concern for accurate details, what has been glossed is the fundamental inaccuracy of the substance of Hawthorne's tale. Although Hawthorne would have known that Plymouth law decreed two whippings and the wearing of the letters 'AD' on the arm or back of the adulteress,[3] he has omitted the whippings from his romance and has Hester embellish the 'A' into an object of great beauty; although 'Governor John Winthrop's journal of 1644 records the execution, in the Bay Colony, of Mary Latham, eighteen, who having married an "ancient man . . . whom she had no affection unto," committed adultery with "divers young men"'[4] as the fate of the adulteress, Hawthorne writes, instead, how Hester's pun-

---

2. C. Ryskamp, 'The New England sources of *The Scarlet Letter*,' 269 [292].
3. W. Charvat, xxvi.
4. W. Charvat, xxvii. An entry in Hawthorne's *The American Notebooks* for 28 August 1837 details a visit to Eben Hathorne, who might have been the model for Surveyor Pue:

> The pride of ancestry seems to be his great hobby; he had a good many old papers in his desk at the custom-house, which he produced and dissertated upon, and afterwards went with me to his sister's in Howard place; and showed me an old book, with a record of the first emigrants (who came over 200 years ago) children in his own handwriting. . . . As we walked, he kept telling stories of the family. . . . (74)

An entry for 15 June 1838 describes going to the burial-ground in Charter Street, and seeing a gravestone 'to the memory of "Colonel John Hathorne, Esq.," who died in 1717. This was the witch-judge. . . . Other Hathornes lie buried in a range with him on either side' (172). Hawthorne concludes: 'It gives strange ideas, to think how convenient to Dr. Peabody's family this burial-ground is,—the monuments standing almost within arm's reach of the side windows of the parlor' (172). In my judgement, Nathaniel's marriage to Sophia Peabody was, in part, an attempt to forge a connection with his own past, and I use, as evidence, this quotation from his diaries.

ishment is to endure the stares of the townspeople as she stands on
the scaffold; although a real Hester Craford, in '1668 was found guilty
of fornication', a 'lesser sin than adultery', and was 'whipped, and had
her child taken from her', Hester is neither whipped, nor deprived of
her child (xxvii); although Felt's *Annals* records that in 1694, 'adultery
was punishable by an hour on the gallows, forty stripes' (xxvii), and the
wearing of a capital 'A', Hawthorne has omitted the forty stripes from
his tale. At the end of the novel, Hawthorne has Hester returning to
the place of her punishment and *voluntarily* resuming her persecution, for 'not the sternest magistrate of that iron period would have
imposed it,—[she] resumed the symbol of which we have related so
dark a tale' (262) [165]. This is certainly a bizarre touch—to state that
even the most iron-handed Puritan magistrate would not persecute
her is falsifying history; to state that she willingly puts on the letter 'A'
makes her *self*-persecuting, rather than persecuted. If Hawthorne, as
he himself stated, was striving for *authenticity* in writing Hester's tale,
The Scarlet Letter must be adjudged a woefully inaccurate failure.

In fact, even rendering the character of Dimmesdale as so pathetic, so
ineffectual, so self-destructive effectively serves to dim the ferocity of
his historical counterparts: it is impossible to read Hawthorne's
Dimmesdale and conceptualize the Puritan oligarchy as avenging
avatars. Instead of a persecuting angel, inspired by the wrath of the
righteous, we are given the portrait of a bumbling lover, a portrait of a
man who beats himself with 'a bloody scourge' (144) [96], who punishes
himself for hiding his sin, rather than a man who persecutes others.

Hawthorne substitutes Dimmesdale's refusal to acknowledge the
fact of his paternity (which is surely interesting in light of Hawthorne's biography) and Chillingworth's probing into the secrets of
Dimmesdale's heart as greater evils than the evils suffered by those
persecuted by Puritan justice! And so, in the context of *The Scarlet
Letter*, in a fascinating reversal of the facts of history, Dimmesdale, the
representative of the Puritan state and Puritan power in the novel, becomes more sinned against than sinning—he is described as the 'victim . . . for ever on the rack' (140) [93]—and his victimization at the
hands of Chillingworth becomes of greater consequence and has more
dire results than Hester's punishment! Hawthorne, in his revisionist
history, thus substitutes a portrait of a male victim for an accurate portrait of a female victim of the Puritan oligarchy.

One of his primary arguments that blunts the effect of the persecution of women is that grief and suffering, rather than being destructive
to a woman, is, in fact, ennobling, so long as she does not become a
social reformer as a result of it: Hester wears 'a halo of misfortune'
(53) [40]; when Hester sees Pearl's gaiety, what she wants for her, is 'a
grief that should deeply touch her, and thus humanize and make her
capable of sympathy' (184) [119].

As the novel progresses, Hawthorne subtly shifts the blame for what
happens to Chillingworth and to Dimmesdale onto the shoulders of
Hester. The effect of this is to render Hester completely responsible
for the physical, emotional and spiritual well-being of the men in her

life. Chillingworth tells her 'Woman, woman, thou art accountable for this' (194) [125] and Dimmesdale repeatedly insists that his salvation is her responsibility: 'Think for me Hester! Thou art strong' (196) [126]. In one very important scene, Chillingworth blames Hester, and not the rigid system of Puritan justice, or his own actions, for Dimmesdale's slow demise: he tells her 'you [Hester] cause him to die daily a living death' (171) [111]; and she accepts the blame for Chillingworth's obsession with revenge—when he asks her who is responsible, she says 'It was myself' (173) [112] just as she accounts herself responsible for Dimmesdale: she becomes 'sensible of the deep injury for which she was responsible to this unhappy man, in permitting him to lie for so many years' (192) [124]. Thus, Hester, the person with the least amount of real power in the novel is made, symbolically, the person with the most power, and the most responsibility for the outcome of the tale. This move deflects attention away from the reality of Hester's utter powerlessness in the Puritan scheme. Just as Hawthorne fixes our attention on Dimmesdale's dying, and on Hester's heroism and her responsibility for the well-being of the men in her life, to blunt the facts of Puritan history, so he employs a similar strategy when, in 'The Custom-House', his symbolic language presents *his* persecution at the hands of the Whigs as having a greater consequence than Hester's suffering: he aligns himself with the benighted Dimmesdale when he describes writing Hester's story 'from beyond the grave' (44) [34], and he states, in bold, attention-getting letters, that her tale 'may be considered as the POSTHUMOUS PAPERS OF A DECAPITATED SURVEYOR' (43) [34]; the 'A' that he finds in the pack of old papers sears *his* breast, not hers.

In 'The Custom-House', Hawthorne describes his very real connection with the historical figures in the novel by relating his family history, 'the deep and aged roots which my family has struck into the soil' (8) [11]. It is important to note that he conceptualizes his family history in completely male terms; in the family tree that he outlines here for himself, not one woman is mentioned. He describes the 'figure of that first ancestor, invested by family tradition with a dim and dusky grandeur, was present to my boyish imagination, as far back as I can remember' (9) [11] and how the figure of this 'grave, bearded, sable-cloaked, and steeple-crowned progenitor,—who came so early with his Bible and his sword' haunted his imagination. Hawthorne describes this forebear as a 'bitter persecutor', and he relates how his son 'inherited the persecuting spirit' by making 'himself so conspicuous in the martyrdom of the witches' (9) [11].

Although Hawthorne admits that his male ancestors were 'bitter persecutors', and although he admits that they indulged in 'cruelties', he blunts the effect of this admission by various narrative strategies. One strategy is to describe actual historical events as hypothetical events. For example, he does not describe the persecution of heterodox believers and so-called witches as *having* taken place: he describes those persecutions as if they *might* have taken place: 'It might be, that an Antinomian, a Quaker, or other heterodox religionist, was to be scourged out of town . . . It might be, too, that a witch like old Mistress Hibbins . . . was to die upon the gallows' (48) [37]. Or he blunts the effect of persecution, when he describes it, by employing neutral language: offenders are not beaten, they are 'corrected at the whipping-post' (49) [37]; the pillory is 'an agent in the promotion of good citizenship' (55) [41]; Hester's 'A' is not a punishment, but a 'fitting decoration to the apparel which she wore' (53) [40].

Thus, the effect of Hawthorne's description of the Puritan oligarchs is to render them as having been simply intolerant men, rather than as sadists and misogynists, the only conclusion that can be reached after reading a history of the Hawthorne family, such as that by Vernon Loggins. In Loggins, the bearded, sable-cloaked Hathorne's typical punishments are described: he 'ordered a constable to cut off a convicted burglar's ear and brand the letter B on his forehead'; he sentenced a woman accused of fornication to a whipping, but simply fined a man who routinely beat his wife; he ordered into slavery the children of Quakers; he ordered 'hangings, the cutting off of men's ears, the boring of holes through women's tongues with red hot irons' and the starving to death of imprisoned Quakers (63). Nor can Hathorne's punishments be explained away by stating that they were typical of the time: indeed, so excessive was his zeal, that in 1661, because of his behaviour, Charles II commanded that any case involving a Quaker should be transferred to English courts. Hathorne's son was equally guilty of excesses; by 1692, as the magistrate responsible for the preliminary hearings in the Salem witchcraft trials, he had crowded the prisons with 'supposed witches and wizards'; on 19 July 1692 five women were hanged.[5]

Hawthorne's purpose in writing *The Scarlet Letter* is overtly announced in 'The Custom-House'. He states:

> I know not whether these ancestors of mine bethought themselves to repent, and ask pardon of Heaven for their cruelties; or whether they are not groaning under the heavy consequences of them, in another state of being. At all events, I, the present writer, as their representative, hereby take shame upon myself for their sakes, and pray that any curse incurred by them . . . may now and henceforth be removed. (9–10) [11–12]

The act of writing the novel, will, therefore, exculpate Hawthorne's Puritan forebears 'now and henceforth'. It is no wonder, therefore, given his self-admitted reason for writing the novel, why he revises what Hester's fate would have been into the tale that he tells. In order to remove the burden of guilt and responsibility from his male forebears, he must rewrite woman's history. Instead of presenting a vicious tale of brandings and beatings, what Hawthorne presents instead is the pargeted[6] tale of Hester Prynne: 'her beauty shone out, and made a halo of the misfortune and ignominy in which she was enveloped' (53) [40].

---

5. V. Loggins, *The Hawthornes*, 130–303.
6. J. Marcus has used the term in reference to Virginia Woolf's process of composition in *The Years*. See J. Marcus, '*The Years* as Greek drama, domestic novel, and Götterdämmerung'.

Hawthorne's principal strategy, at the beginning of the novel itself, is to deflect attention away from the Puritan patriarchs who have voted Hester's punishment, the patriarchs who have made the laws and who enforce them. They scarcely exist as far as the novel is concerned. Rather, as Hester Prynne emerges from the jail, Hawthorne focuses all of his narrative attention, and for several pages, upon the vengeful response of the Puritan *women*. They take 'a peculiar interest in whatever penal infliction might be expected to ensue' (50) [38]. In the novel, it is not the oligarchs, Hawthorne's forebears, who punish, it is the goodwives who demand justice:

> 'Goodwives', said a hard-featured dame of fifty, 'I'll tell ye a piece of my mind. It would be greatly for the public behoof, if we women, being of mature age and church-members in good repute, should have the handling of such malefactresses as this Hester Prynne. What think ye, gossips? If the hussy stood up for judgment before us five, that are now here in a knot together, would she come off with such a sentence as the worshipful magistrates have awarded? Marry, I trow not!' (51) [38]

Although Hawthorne appears to be arguing for gender-determined punishment, he is also stating that the male judges who did exist were fairer than any woman would have been. A man in the crowd who overhears the women says 'is there no virtue in woman, save what springs from a wholesome fear of the gallows?' (52) [39]. And Hawthorne states that the uglier a woman is, the more vengeance she would exact from criminals: 'the ugliest as well as the most pitiless of these self-constituted judges' says 'This woman has brought shame upon us all and ought to die. Is there not law for it?' (51) [39]. All the vengeance at the beginning of the novel has been female; when a beadle finally appears, he seems far less severe than the women; in contrast to their graphic desire to 'put the brand of a hot iron on Hester Prynne's forehead' (51) [39], he simply 'prefigured and represented in his aspect the whole dismal severity of the Puritanic code of law' (52) [39].

This is a fascinating strategy. Hawthorne denies history by misrepresenting Hester's punishment as if it would have been essentially fair and judicious. Then he argues that if women had had political power, they would have been harsher to adulteresses than his fictional Puritan leaders had been to Hester. Hawthorne therefore creates a romance about judicious Puritan rule which denies the reality of the abuse of power by Puritan rulers, and then he uses the fiction he has created to argue that men are essentially more fair-minded than women would be! This literary strategy, though highly persuasive, is extraordinarily illogical and misleading for Hawthorne draws ethical conclusions about justice being fair-minded if it is male, and vengeful if it is female from a universe which he himself has created, and which is a misrepresentation of historical reality.

In the context of the Puritan cosmology developed in *The Scarlet Letter*, Hester Prynne is enormously concerned about what will happen to her child Pearl, as well she should be because the children of miscreants were not treated well in Puritan New England. Throughout the novel, Pearl is repeatedly associated with the devil, with evil, with sin, and with witchcraft: her looks are 'perverse' and 'malicious' (92) [63]; she is an 'imp of evil' (93) [64], 'fiend-like', an 'evil spirit' (97) [66], 'a shadowy reflection of evil' (94) [64], a 'demon offspring' (99) [67], a 'demon-child' (100) [68]; there is a 'fire in her' (101) [68]; her cries are 'a witch's anathemas in some unknown tongue' (94) [64], she is a 'little baggage [who] hath witchcraft in her' (116) [78], there is 'witchcraft in little Pearl's eyes' (154) [101]; she is 'a shadowy reflection of evil' (94) [64], the 'effluence of her mother's lawless passion' (165) [108]; her imaginary playmates are 'the puppets of Pearl's witchcraft' (95) [65]. And Hawthorne makes it clear that she has inherited these tendencies from her mother: although, *in utero*, Pearl's character was at first unblemished, her 'mother's impassioned state had been the medium through which were transmitted to the unborn infant the rays of its mortal life; and, however white and clear originally, they had taken the deep stains of crimson and gold, the fiery lustre, the black shadow' (91) [62].

The character who is repeatedly associated with Pearl is Mistress Hibbins, who is based upon an actual woman, who, the narrative records, will be accused of witchcraft and who will 'die upon the gallows' (49) [37]. In the forest, Dimmesdale likens Pearl's cries to 'the cankered wrath of an old witch, like Mistress Hibbins' (210) [134]. Nor can Hester civilize Pearl. Hawthorne suggests that, without a man in the house, Hester is incapable of controlling Pearl's bad behaviour—raising Pearl is described as a process which is identical to an exorcism which Hester is not capable of performing, an attitude towards childrearing that Hawthorne certainly manifested in his journal descriptions in reference to his daughter Una who is described in terms very like those used to describe Pearl: 'The child could not be made amenable to rules', her 'elements were perhaps beautiful and brilliant, but all in disorder' (91) [62].[7]

The process of caring for Pearl, however, leads to Hester's salvation, because through caring for Pearl she avoids becoming a latter-day Anne Hutchinson, and accepts her womanly role, which, according to Hawthorne, is essential if a woman is to be saved. But it is the absent father Dimmesdale who is responsible for Pearl's salvation: as Pearl kisses him at the end of the novel, she feels grief for the first time, and it is this grief, and not her mother's care, which humanizes her:

7. T. Walter Herbert, 'Nathaniel Hawthorne, Una Hawthorne, and *The Scarlet Letter*: Interactive Selfhoods and the Cultural Construction of Gender,' *PMLA* 103 (1988): 285–97 [pp. 522–41 in this Norton Critical Edition]. Hawthorne's entries in *The American Notebooks* from 19 March 1848 to 30 July 1849 are illuminating, as Herbert argues brilliantly in his article. *See, especially*: 'The children have been playing ball together; and Una, heated by the violence with which she plays, sits down on the floor, and complains grievously of warmth—opens her breast. This is the physical manifestation of the evil spirit that struggles for the mastery of her; he is not a spirit at all, but an earthy monster, who lays his grasp on her spinal marrow, her brain, and other parts of her body that lie in closest contiguity to her soul; so that the soul has the discredit of evil deeds' (420–1) [218]. It seems bizarre to see the spectacle of the devil inhabiting one's daughter as she undoes her clothes because she has been playing with gusto.

Pearl kissed his lips. A spell was broken. The great scene of grief, in which the wild infant bore a part, had developed all her sympathies; and as her tears fell upon her father's cheek, they were the pledge that she would grow up amid human joy and sorrow, nor for ever do battle with the world, but be a woman in it. (256) [162]

This scene effectively obliterates all the years of Hester's mothering. Just as Hawthorne has written his own mother and his wife out of "The Custom-House', so he writes Hester out of the cause for Pearl's salvation in *The Scarlet Letter*. It is not all the years of Hester's toil which saves Pearl from a life of evil in Puritan New England, or from being persecuted as a witch, like Mistress Hibbins. Rather, Pearl becomes a happy woman because of this single moment that she shares with her father Dimmesdale which unlocks her ability to feel grief. Salvation comes, not as a result of Pearl and Hester working together through the years to make a reasonably good life for themselves despite persecution. No, salvation comes, in Hawthorne's world, from being humanized as a result of feeling sorry for the suffering your *father* has experienced! And even the reprehensible Chillingworth, in leaving Pearl 'a very considerable amount of property, both here and in England' (261) [164] is made even more responsible for Pearl's good fortune, than all the years of Hester's toil as a single parent, raising her child alone. Hawthorne, therefore, privileges the effect of the absent father upon the good fortune of the child over the labour of the present mother.

It is no wonder, then, that heaven is described in the novel as an all-male paradise, with no room for Hester, a paradise where no women are permitted. Although Hester is buried near Dimmesdale, in paradise, however, in 'the spiritual world, the old physician and the minister—mutual victims as they have been—may . . . have found their earthly stock of hatred and antipathy transmuted into golden love' (261) [164].

* * *

* * * In 'The Custom-House', when Hawthorne picks up Hester's scarlet A and places it on his breast, he 'experienced a sensation not altogether physical, yet almost so, as of burning heat; and as if the letter were not of red cloth, but red-hot iron', he 'shuddered, and involuntarily let it fall upon the floor' (32) [26]. Although branding was, in fact, a rather typical Puritan punishment for transgressors, it is important to note that Hawthorne records the branding as having occurred (symbolically) to himself, and not to Hester, which serves to focus attention upon himself, and to deflect attention away from her. As she is an adulteress, he becomes an adulterator, as he misleads his audience into thinking that his Puritan forebears were simply intolerant men, rather than sadistic persecutors who repeatedly sentenced adulteresses either to banishment (which meant certain death) or to 'thirty stripes from a knotted whip',[8] which usually led to festering wounds,

8. V. Loggins, p. 69.

serious infection, and a long, lingering, painful illness, often resulting in death. Hawthorne has therefore used the novel to control his own past, to rewrite his past into a version that would provide him with less virulent male ancestors and that would present them to the world as less sadistic than they in fact were. And Hawthorne's desire in writing *The Scarlet Letter*, to remove the curse from his Puritan forebears 'now and henceforth' (10) [12] was so immensely successful that his rewritten, highly inaccurate version of Puritan history, which blunts the reality of the persecutions of the time, is the version that most Americans believe, because most Americans learn their Puritan history, not through a history which graphically describes the savagery of the Hathornes, but instead, through reading *The Scarlet Letter*. *The Scarlet Letter* has, indeed, absolved Hawthorne's forebears from guilt, 'now and henceforth'.

ROBERT K. MARTIN

Hester Prynne, *C'est Moi*: Nathaniel Hawthorne and the Anxieties of Gender†

Serving time as U.S. consul in Liverpool, Nathaniel Hawthorne wrote a now infamous note to his publisher complaining about the competition from "a damned mob of scribbing women"[1]—a much quoted remark that has led some critics to speculate about the conflict between Hawthorne and writers such as Susan Warner or Maria Cummins and others to speculate about Hawthorne's misogyny. But an account of misogyny in Hawthorne that takes no account of his own and his culture's gender anxieties is necessarily inadequate: to assess his conflicting views of women, one must first place them in the context of his anxieties about his own masculinity. For, much like the very women from whom he sought to distance himself, Hawthorne described himself as a "scribbler,"[2] at once trivial (a scribbler, not a writer) and threatening (part of a "mob"). Even as Hawthorne's success as a canonical author increased, he felt that he was not the "man" he ought to be. In part this was a lingering view that art itself was an unmanly, hence trivial, occupation, while in part this anxiety grew out of his own success as a professional author—success that increasingly aligned him with the professional women he scorned and feared. If

---

† From *Engendering Men: The Question of Male Feminist Criticism*, ed. Joseph A. Boone and Michael Cadden (New York: Routledge, 1990), 122–31. Copyright © 1990. Reproduced by permission of Routledge/Taylor & Francis Books, Inc. Page numbers in square brackets refer to this Norton Critical Edition.

1. Letter to Ticknor, 19 January 1855, in *Letters of Hawthorne to William D. Ticknor* (Newark: Carteret Book Club, 1910), 1:75
2. See Hawthorne's description of himself as a young man as "a scribbler by profession" in a letter dated 12 April 1838, as well as his youthful description of British writers as "the scribbling sons of John Bull" in a letter of 13 March 1821. Both letters are in *The Centenary Edition of the Works of Nathaniel Hawthorne*, ed. William Charvat et al. (Columbus: Ohio State UP, 1962), 15:270 and 15:139, respectively. All further quotations from Hawthorne's works are from this edition and are indicated in the text by volume number and page number.

critics have rarely examined Hawthorne's relationships to women in the light of his own constructions of masculinity,[3] they have also rarely investigated the class implications suggested by that word *mob*, in which a Carlylean fear of the French Revolution conflates the uncontrolled political expression of the lower classes with the threat of an unbridled sexuality—a conflation already evident in "My Kinsman, Major Molineux."

Rather than dwelling with the biographical Hawthorne's attitudes toward women, I want to examine the "scribbling women" *in* Hawthorne's fiction, to look at some of his representations of female artists and their relation to changing patterns of gender and class in nineteenth-century America. By focusing on *The Scarlet Letter* * * * with [its] reworkings of the figure of the strong erotic woman artist and [its] triangulations of desire, I hope to make clear that Hawthorne's anxieties were as much about his intrusion, as a man, into a female world as about women's intrusions into his male world. This exploration of Hawthorne's response to questions of art and gender seeks to locate that response at the precise moment in the history of the construction of gender in which he wrote, a moment well-captured in his apparently indirect-free-discourse rendering of Hester's thoughts on the relationship of gender to historical change: "the very nature of the opposite sex, or of its long hereditary habit, which has become like nature, is to be essentially modified" (1:165) [108]. Following Hester's cue, I want to reexamine masculinity in its social and historical contexts—the essential task facing men as feminists, and one made possible by the feminist critique of gender and culture. As Hélène Cixous has put the challenge, "woman must write woman. And man, man . . . it's up to him to say where his masculinity and femininity are at."[4]

Hawthorne's career coincided with major changes in the social structures of American life. His early dispossession, through his father's death and his mother's subsequent dependence on her relatives for financial support, and the consequent loss of certainty about his social standing reflect a pattern repeated frequently throughout the 1820s and 1830s as the traditional elite gave way to a new commercial class. These social shifts were closely linked to issues of gender, for the decline of a rural domestic economy, largely self-sufficient and based on home labor, allowed for economic expansion through *men's* work and required the increased seclusion of women and their transformation into objects of display. Thus during this period sexual politics meant the creation of a domestic ideal of women at the moment

3. For instance, Nina Baym's very important work on Hawthorne has by-and-large dealt with the question of Hawthorne's representation of women without raising larger issues across gender. Recently, there have been a few exceptions, notably Leland S. Person, Jr.'s *Aesthetic Headaches: Women and a Masculine Poetics in Poe, Melville, and Hawthorne* (Athens: U of Georgia P; 1988). His explorations of Hawthorne's "feminized masculine poetics" (174) are intriguing, and he more than anyone has shown Hawthorne's attempt to subvert a traditional masculine poetics. His study seems to me nonetheless too optimistic in its evaluation of this subversion, largely because of his relative neglect of the anxieties it produces, particularly with regard to gender identity and heterosexual certainty.
4. Hélène Cixous, "The Laugh of the Medusa," trans. Keith Cohen and Paula Cohen, first published in *Signs* (Summer 1976) and reprinted in *New French Feminisms*, ed. Elaine Marks and Isabelle de Courtivron (New York: Schocken, 1981), 247.

when the demarcation between "the domestic" and "the economic" was most rigid. Hawthorne might best be seen, in this light, as a child of pre-Jacksonian America who found it difficult to accept the radical reordering of society that made his own later career as a novelist possible. The violent tales of his early years ("Roger Malvin's Burial," "My Kinsman, Major Molineux," "The Gentle Boy") all give some indication of the sense of rupture with the past that dominated the young Hawthorne. All is always lost, they seem to repeat.

As the author of such tales for gift book annuals, Hawthorne's early career was at once genteel and feminine. His future sister-in-law Elizabeth Peabody thought his sister Elizabeth had written the early stories, and Margaret Fuller assumed the author of "The Gentle Boy," whom she had not yet met, "to be a woman."[5] As late as 1843, he published "Drowne's Wooden Image" in *Godey's Lady's Book* for a female audience. Hence, by birth and early professional profile, Hawthorne was still part of the genteel generation of Irving, even if he would continue writing long enough to be the friend and sometime muse for that decidedly "masculine" post-Jacksonian author, Herman Melville. By becoming a writer of novels (even if he called them romances), however, Hawthorne entered another world, a more competitive, public world that by its very professional nature may have seemed more "manly." Yet even though Hawthorne triumphed in this new arena, his triumph came at considerable psychic cost, since it meant betraying the fathers by abandoning the gentility of anonymity and domestic seclusion and by becoming—as publishing author and emblazoned artist—the scarlet woman.

I

Many of these historical tensions are evident in "The Custom-House" preface to *The Scarlet Letter*. Once read largely as a mix of anecdotal background and political revenge, the essay has been increasingly seen as an integral part of the novel, establishing its narrative voice and historical theme. But the essay does much more than that, and in ways that have gone largely unexplored. "The Custom-House" is above all an essay in sexual politics, as implied by Hawthorne's description of the most prominent feature of the building itself—an enormous *female* American eagle over the entrance. This eagle is treacherous precisely because, like Hester's A, its meaning is not fixed: although the eagle is "vixenly," she attracts those who imagine "that her bosom has all the softness and snugness of an eider-down pillow." They may soon encounter her ire, however, in the form of "a scratch of her claw, a dab of her beak, or a rankling wound from her barbed arrows" (1:5) [9]. Now it may well be that Hawthorne's main purpose here is political revenge, but the language in which he seeks to accomplish it could hardly be more gendered. Underneath the "feminine" exterior there lurks a fantasy of violence rooted in a primitive fear of the empowered

5. *The Letters of Margaret Fuller*, ed. Robert N. Hudspeth (Ithaca: Cornell UP, 1983–1987), 1:198.

woman. So it was, apparently, with the women of Hawthorne's time—that "damned mob" of which he complained to his publisher: you just couldn't count on them always to be ladies. Hawthorne's fiction repeatedly represents the sexual (and cultural) appeal of these "vixens" while regularly deploying plots that require their suppression.

Hawthorne was not, of course, unacquainted with the revolutionary women of his time. He knew Margaret Fuller well enough to express repeated fear and anger; his own wife Sophia was the sister of one of the most important feminists of the period, Elizabeth Peabody; in his Roman years he was associated not only with the Browning circle but also with the noted American sculptress Harriet Hosmer, the center of a lesbian circle of artists termed the "harem (scarem)" by William Wetmore Story. Such strong women found their way into Hawthorne's fictions, where, from Hester Prynne and Zenobia to Miriam, they occupy prominent positions. Hawthorne's works betray an extraordinary ambivalence about these heroines, even as his fictions reflect the cultural plot that will enforce the effacement of such women by the figure of the domestic angel. It is as if Hawthorne wrote over and over again his own choice of the invalid Sophia over her sister, expressing the fears of emasculation that strong women produced in him (and in his culture) while regularly failing to convince us that the sickly maiden was an adequate alternative either in life or art.

The dilemma of the custom-house is one that concerns not only men's relationship to women, but men's relationship to other men, for the custom-house is a male preserve, "a sanctuary into which womankind, with her tools of magic, the broom and mop, has very infrequent access" (1:7) [10]. But this separate sphere, like Irving's dream of life in a Dutch genre painting, is already a spoiled Eden, threatened, on the one hand, by the claims of women and, on the other, by Hawthorne's own sense of unworthiness to succeed his male "progenitors." Thinking back over the power of the past and reflecting on the absence of transplantation that might have improved the "stock," Hawthorne laments that the venerable "old trunk" of his family tree should only "have born, as its topmost bough, an idler like myself" (1:10) [12].

These anxieties about sterility mark Hawthorne's career in the custom-house as a return to his ancestors, an attempt to rejoin the "patriarchal body," as he calls it, in "Uncle Sam's brick edifice." His scorn for his colleagues and superiors and his recognition of their uselessness barely conceal his recurring anxiety about filial relationships and authority. The Inspector, for example, is "the father," "the patriarch," but also "a legitimate son" of the revenue system itself as well as of "a Revolutionary colonel" (1:16) [16]. As we know from "My Kinsman, Major Molineux," to be the son of a revolutionary officer is to be at once patriarch and parricide. There can be no easy relationship with the past, for all Americans are in some sense "illegitimate" children of "nature" as a result of the revolution, the event that haunts this preface (and the event, not insignificantly, that is indirectly responsible for Hawthorne's discovery of the packet containing Hester's scarlet letter, apparently forgotten in the flight to Halifax by the royal officials). American history, then, is founded upon a violation of authority, a refusal of the king-father's rule; and yet descent from those original parricides, ironically, becomes a mark of legitimating authority, by means of which one becomes a son or daughter of the revolution. In the mid-nineteenth century, the "old families" increasingly drew upon such a claim of descent as a way of marking themselves off from foreign intrusions. If Hawthorne's Inspector is a figure of fun, a comic version of the patriarch, the older man's exaggerated virility nonetheless attests to the anxieties of the fatherless Hawthorne, author now of a fatherless book, of which he claims to be "editor, or very little more" (1:4) [8]. Hence the lustiness of the Inspector's voice and laugh, which come "strutting out of his lungs, like the crow of a cock, or the blast of a clarion"; nor are these his only active organs, for he is also "the husband of three wives, all long since dead; [and] the father of twenty children" (1:17) [17].

If such biblical fertility is out of date, the Inspector and the Collector are both remnants of another era, one that Hawthorne prizes in part as a period *before politics* and before the decline from the past. The Collector, for instance, although hopelessly conservative and ruled by habit, has a "fondness for the sight and fragrance of flowers," "a trait . . . seldom seen in the masculine character after childhood or early youth" (1:22) [20]. If such figures are "patriarchal," they are not driven by the anxieties of mid nineteenth-century sexual ideology, with its increasingly rigid division of gender roles. Hawthorne yearns for an older world of gentlemen who can retain their sensibilities, even as he sees their greater marginalization (violently enacted, for instance, in the conflict of the Pyncheons in *The House of the Seven Gables*). He, like Hester, is a victim in part of a changed system and a new *American* cultural identity that allows little place for the aesthetic.

For the custom-house is now the realm of the "man of business," a place where Hawthorne feels he *ought* to be. His sense of manliness requires that he leave behind "the dreamy brethren of Brook Farm," the "fastidious[ness]" and "refinement" of New England literary culture, and return to "[un]lettered intercourse" (1:25) [22]. His own fate there, his dismissal from his post, marks a renewed expulsion from patrilineal succession and casts an ironic shadow over the attempt to return to the fathers. Ill at ease among the Transcendentalists and above all unwilling to pursue the implications of their plans for social and sexual reorganization, Hawthorne has retreated to the world of "men," only to find himself judged wanting. " 'What is he?' " Hawthorne imagines the "gray shadow" of one of his "forefathers" murmuring to the other. " 'A writer of storybooks! What kind of business in life . . . may that be? Why, the degenerate fellow might as well have been a fiddler!' " (1:10) [12]. As John Irwin has astutely noted, the text's "implied patriarchal censure of the author seems to raise the question of whether masculinity is compatible with the role of the artist."[6] In this

6. John Irwin, *American Hieroglyphics* (New Haven: Yale UP, 1980), 276.

preface to a story of a woman scorned by her community for a sexual transgression, Hawthorne dramatizes his own inability to find a place to locate safely both his vocation and his gender.

It is striking that the descent from the past depicted in "The Custom-House" is strictly male. Aside from the eagle that guards the entrance (and the jocular reference to cleaning women), no woman ever enters these precincts—except of course the author of the A. In a similar way Hawthorne defines his own descent as a male genealogy, identifying his ancestors only as William and John Hathorne. In calling on "the earliest emigrant of [his] name" (1:8) [11], however, he simultaneously reminds the reader of his willed *difference* from the fathers, his "embroidering" of the family name's spelling. Choosing to be a writer, he now rewrites the name as "Hawthorne," thereby placing his heritage at a distance that he can control. If the fathers have made him a Salemite, Ha(w)thorne alone can claim responsibility for making himself an author.

This exclusively male genealogy serves as the framework for a story that is just the opposite, a story of a mother and a daughter with no visible father. Likewise the narrator of "The Custom-House"—clearly identified in many ways as Hawthorne himself—denies paternity, claiming to be only the editor and not the author of the tale, which is "authorized and authenticated by the [entirely fictive, of course] document of Mr. Surveyor Pue" (1:32) [27]. Not unlike the silent Dimmesdale, he disclaims responsibility; he didn't write it, he didn't conceive it. He can't have written it, because patriarchs don't write, they merely record, and because Hester's story is inscribed in a "rag of scarlet cloth" that requires knowledge not available to men. Consistent with her role in a female-authored world, Hester will conclude the novel not only the figurative daughter of Ann Hutchinson but a literal mother (of Pearl) and grandmother as well. We learn that she hears from the grown-up Pearl in a language that is private and unreadable by the community: "Letters came, with armorial seals upon them, though of bearings unknown to English heraldy" (1:262) [165]. These signs, known to Pearl and Hester, stand in counterpoint to those that conclude the novel a few pages later, which are written, like the letter, to assign meaning for the community. Hester's woman's tale is framed by men and their meanings, but gains a space within, a space emblematized by her own writing/embroidering and by the letters of her daughter.

The custom-house is of course the site of Hawthorne's discovery of the mysterious package that contains the scarlet letter. The package, we are told, pertains to the *"private* capacity" of Surveyor Pue, and contains "a certain affair of fine red cloth" (1:30–31; emphasis added) [25–26]. This object is thus associated with the private domain increasingly defined in the nineteenth century with domestic femininity, and it is itself an object of feminine art. Wrought "with wonderful skill of needlework" (a skill associated in Hawthorne's fiction not only with Hester but with Priscilla and Miriam as well), it exemplifies an art form "now forgotten," as "ladies conversant with such mysteries" have

informed the narrator. The letter, hence, is not merely of female man-
ufacture but indeed part of a private, mysterious female realm to
which one can only have access through the mysterious knowledge of
certain "ladies" (1:31) [26]. In taking up the task of reading the letter,
of reconstituting its secret stitches, Hawthorne thus inscribes himself
on the feminine side of the boundary separating male and female
"realms," allying himself with those who understand the mysteries of
women. And yet this task of telling the tale is given to him not by the
"female" letter but by the ghost of the old Surveyor, who appears like
Hamlet's father to insist upon "filial duty." But if in his time "a man's
office was a life-lease" (1:33) [28], that authority has now been
usurped. So, in yet another engendered transgression, in order to be a
true son of the Surveyor, Hawthorne, it turns out, must be loyal not to
the custom-house but to his vocation as artist; he must repudiate "Uncle Sam's gold" and "the Devil's wages" (1:39) [31]. Only by making
art out of gold—not by creating art for gold—can he revive a lost and
miraculous skill.

Although the act of authorship is transgressive, telling this tale
nonetheless constitutes a curious act of fidelity to the fathers; for it
transforms the assignment of the letter by the ancestral fathers into a
punishment with ample recompense, an A that can be made over into
a proclamation of worth rather than a badge of shame. But telling the
tale is also the metaphorical equivalent of putting on the letter—an
act equivalent, as Hawthorne explains, to branding himself with a
"red-hot iron" (1:32) [26]. Hawthorne's assumption of the letter aligns
him not only with Dimmesdale and his apparent self-administration of
the "silent" letter on his chest, but more significantly with Hester, for
it is she above all who both wears and "writes" the letter.[7] However
much Hawthorne may fear the power of Hester, he is deeply identified
with her as an outcast from his own community—publicly humiliated,
accused of improper conduct, and expelled from the place of the fathers.

For Hawthorne this outcast state is epitomized when he loses his
job (the opposing party has won the presidential election), a state that
he likens to decapitation by the guillotine. Deliberately leaving the
image hanging between "literal fact" and "metaphor" (1:41) [32],
Hawthorne represents himself as at once castrated and assassinated,
for the image invites itself to be read both personally and politically.
Once more, then, the image of the revolution comes to mean for Hawthorne the death of the fathers, and hence his own, at least threatened, death. For as a "DECAPITATED SURVEYOR," Hawthorne
presents himself, humorously to be sure, as one who has assumed the
role of his predecessors, figuratively died for it, and now simply
"long[s] to buried, as a politically dead man ought" (1:43) [34]. Has he

7. There may be another complex relationship between Hawthorne and Hester here. Both
names begin with H, of course, and the transformation of an H into an "A requires only a
"steeple-crown." Perhaps more significantly, both names involve a missing, or supplementary, letter. Hester recovers her biblical origins if her H is shifted to Esther, while Hawthorne
marks off his distance from his origins by adding a W. The W, we might say, is his scarlet letter, one that seeks to unwrite the legend of past evil, even while reminding us of it.

not worked in the house of the patriarch? How then is he not guilty? As Hawthorne sketches the inevitable death of the fathers and his own ambivalent relationship to them, he seeks to escape the punishment meted out to them by becoming the daughter-bride, that is, by becoming Hester Prynne. For it is precisely the story of "one Hester Prynne" that begins to fire his imagination upon his dismissal from the custom-house, transforming that "unpleasant" "predicament" into a cause for "congratulations" (1:41) [33] and, indeed, the precondition of the fictional recreation of the wearer of the scarlet letter that now follows.

It is in Hester's voice, therefore, that Hawthorne speaks as a revolutionary, as the parricide he faces execution for being because he is a man. Figuratively resurrected in Hester, he must assume his crime and add to it that of transvestism, both as the author of her tale, which he has "dress[ed] up" (1:33) [27], and as the wearer of the letter. For in a passionate moment of identification, affected by a "deep meaning" that touches his "sensibilities, but evad[es] the analysis of [his] mind," he places the letter "on [his] breast" (1:31–32) [26], thereby re-eroticizing the male body. Wearing her clothes and speaking in her voice, he becomes a hieroglyph of the crime of art by representing that crime precisely as a refusal of the gender boundaries instilled in everyday life, the habits and customs that have overridden the ambiguities of nature.

II

These issues run throughout the narrative of *The Scarlet Letter*, where art is repeatedly presented as a sexual crime, the production of an illegitimate child. Pearl and the letter are, we are often reminded, identical, given that the production of the text and the production of the child both take place outside the law of patriarchy. Who is the father? the ministers ask Hester to confess. But she will not speak; for to speak would be to give the child a father (1:68) [49]. The Hawthornean text also refuses acknowledgment of paternity; it almost obsessively insists upon the relativity of reading. The scene before the prison—as the crowd awaits Hester's appearance—"could have betokened" one thing in England, but in New England "an inference of this kind could not so indubitably be drawn"; "it might be" the scene of punishment of a religious heretic or a drunken Indian, then again "it might be, too," the anticipated execution of a witch (1:49) [37]. Tokens do not have fixed meanings in Hawthorne, where everything works by metonymy. Perhaps the punishment of Quakers, Indians, and witches can be seen as analogous things, as refusals of otherness. As such Hawthorne's text frustrates the desire for paternity, for certitude, by allowing space only for what "might be"; meaning, like paternity, is rendered putative. Hence, although often discussed as allegory, Hawthorne's art represents a world in which no meanings are fixed, in which everything is always a polysemous surface awaiting interpretation. This is of course precisely the import of his reference to hieroglyphics, and it is stressed one last time in the famous tombstone inscription that closes the work. Although John McWilliams, following a long tradition of Hawthorne criticism in his certainty if not his conclusions, claims that this final inscription is "the conclusive sign that the prevalence of the symbolic letter overwhelms any hope of progress,"[8] in fact it is a signifier without any fixed signified, a set of words requiring "translation." * * * The reader is left at the end not with a meaning, but with a pointer toward meaning in a language most readers cannot read. It remains another mystery upon which to speculate, like Melville's doubloon, another failure of the belief in the power to interpret Hester's life (or any other) for her.

The artist's function resembles Hester's fantastic embroidery of the letter. Her art may be presented as transgressively criminal, but it is also a response to a crime. Indeed, Hester's artistry is to write her "crime" in a way that disguises it, that makes it no crime at all. Hester does this by embroidering her letter, and hence disguising or displacing the univocal sense assigned to it by the letter of the law. Her embroidered letter is the permanent display of her condemned sexuality that unsettles the terms of her condemnation. At the same time, Hester acts in part out of a need to survive, for her art is also a very material means of producing income: she is, we should not forget, a single mother with a child and few opportunities for self-supporting work. So Hester survives by embroidering, that is, by copying her own story in a disguised form.[9] Her art, Hawthorne notes, "[was] then, as now, almost the only one within a woman's grasp" (1:81) [57]. The remark may be taken in a number of ways, but even its most misogynistic implications may be alleviated if we think of them in the context of Judy Chicago's *The Dinner Party* (1979), with its attempt to reclaim the "minor" female arts. Hawthorne clearly sees Hester as an artist, if in a different medium, and he takes her task as central to all art. Hester's art, though, is flawed, for it cannot celebrate passion: "like all other joys, she rejected it as sin" (1:84) [58]. But if *her* art cannot celebrate passion, *Hawthorne's* at least occasionally can, especially when he undertakes to speak through her.

And yet Hawthorne's is an art that gives with one hand as it takes with the other. His equivocations about possible meanings are echoed in his alternative plots. Although this double-plotting is especially evident in his treatment of strong women throughout his canon, it is most striking in *The Scarlet Letter*, where he locates all female attributes within a single character. Hester's scene in the woods, when she asserts the power and even sanctity of her love for Dimmesdale, is thus not to be seen either as an ideal or an object of scorn; Hawthorne speaks his Romantic desire through Hester as he also speaks his sense of guilt and shame. She becomes his voice because she speaks so clearly for the kind of freedom that Hawthorne would not allow her *or*

8. John P. McWilliams, Jr., *Hawthorne, Melville, and the American Character: A Looking-Glass Business* (Cambridge: Cambridge UP, 1984), 68.
9. On needlework and narrative, see Elaine Showalter, "Piecing and Writing," in *The Poetics of Gender*, ed. Nancy K. Miller (New York: Columbia UP, 1986), 222–47. She terms the quilt a "hieroglyphic or diary" (241).

himself. As a sexual outlaw, Hester gains a freedom of the imagination, and it is this power that Hawthorne simultaneously seeks to employ and control:

> Her intellect and heart had their home, as it were, in desert
> places, where she roamed as freely as the wild Indian in his
> woods. For years past she had looked from this estranged point of
> view at human institutions, and whatever priests or legislators
> had established; criticizing all with hardly more reverence than
> the Indian would feel for the clerical band, the judicial robe, the
> pillory, the gallows, the fireside, or the church. The tendency of
> her fate and fortunes had been to set her free. The scarlet letter
> was her passport into regions where other women dared not
> tread. (1:199) [128]

As an "Indian," Hester escapes the social control and surveillance of the community. She has, at least temporarily, access to the forest—not the demonized forest of the Puritans, but the "mother-forest" (1:204) [131] of nature rather than custom.[1] Made into a stranger, she gains the stranger's ability to see the arbitrariness of signs. It is precisely this estrangement that was foreclosed to most American women of Hawthorne's time, who were increasingly bound to the familiar limitations of the domestic. The fallen woman, like the prostitute to whom she is linked, sees into the mystery of the social order and understands at first hand its hypocrisies. Hester has, after all, slept with the minister and suffered the effects of his silence, as well as those of her husband's revenge. Hawthorne knows this and makes Hester know it, but then he takes that knowledge away: the brave paragraph that I have just cited ends, almost piously, "Shame, Despair, Solitude! These had been her teachers,—stern and wild ones,—and they had made her strong, but taught her much amiss" (1:199–200) [128]. What a dying fall!

Hawthorne's scheme seems to require masochism; he simply will not let the "crime" go unpunished, and so he must ascribe the willingness to suffer to the victim. Hence, to the degree that Hester's embroidered A can be seen as the pained writing of her own body, in her own blood, we must also see this "female" masochism as the function of a desperate male need to "authorize" female desire—a need that, figuratively speaking, supplies the needlework that closes and then opens the female body to male possession. The analogy between Hester's bleeding body and her red letter is heightened, of course, by the original description of the letter as a "rag of scarlet cloth," with its associations of menstruation and defloration.[2] But while Hester writes

---

1. Nina Baym is right, I think, to link the Indian woman in Hawthorne to a suppressed matriarchy, although she does not pursue the point, especially in *The Marble Faun*, where the idea of matriarchy is crucial as the Etruscan counterpoint to papal Rome. See Baym, *The Shape of Hawthorne's Career* (Ithaca: Cornell UP, 1976), 120.
2. See, for example, Joanne Feit Diehl, "Re-Reading *The Letter*: Hawthorne, the Fetish, and the (Family) Romance," *New Literary History* 19 (Spring 1988): 655–73. Diehl's emphasis on Hawthorne's desire for the mother seems to me somewhat overstated, especially since it entails neglect of the male relationships in his fiction. It was, after all, Hawthorne's *father* who died when he was young. (The figure of the sea-captain father is almost certainly pres-

out of her suffering, she does not escape it. Hester's public performance of her sexuality, enacted in the initial scene of the novel and repeated throughout her life by her wearing of the letter, confirms her
role, woman's role, as the embodiment of a sexuality that is at once
silent and always spoken. As such she becomes a marvelous instance
of Foucault's understanding of the transformation of sexuality into discourse. Her every appearance is to speak her story, to repeat almost
obsessively the story of her pain and loss, and yet never to complete
that story.[3]

For Hester's story has no origins (no visible husband, since Chillingworth chooses not to reveal himself to anyone but her, and no visible
lover to acknowledge the paternity of her child) and is thus always
self-made and remakeable. Her work is an art of "fertility" (1:53) [40],
her own and that of an endlessly reproducing, self-generating art.
Forced to perform a role in the male drama of guilt and sin, Hester simultaneously plays her own part, refusing to speak the lines others
have written for her. Her proud assertion of her A is an acknowledgment of the fact that even the actor or actress on the stage is always
performing his or her own text. In a society that insists that silence
surround sexuality, Hester's body becomes the stage on which she constantly refuses silence. What she cannot say is the one thing she is expected to say, to name the father. Hester writes her own text and
remains a sign without a transcendent author.

T. WALTER HERBERT, JR.

Nathaniel Hawthorne, Una Hawthorne, and *The Scarlet Letter*: Interactive Selfhoods and the Cultural Construction of Gender†

In the months before Hawthorne began writing *The Scarlet Letter*, he
was troubled by something in the character of his daughter Una that
he had difficulty defining. He made a series of entries in his notebook
during this period that record her daily activities, adding up to an extended meditation on the enigma that her personality presented to
him. Here is one of several uneasy summaries:

> [T]here is something that almost frightens me about the child—I
> know not whether elfish or angelic, but, at all events, supernatu-

---

ent in the sea captain of *The Scarlet Letter*, who would take Hester and Dimmesdale away,
but who will inevitably bring Chillingworth along as well. What ship could take Dimmesdale
and Chillingworth away? Only, one might answer, one captained by Melville.)

3. In Peggy Kamuf's very acute commentary, Hester's embroidery is "a speculation . . . on the
position of the symbol of the guilty subject, the subject of nonidentity, the 'woman' presented in *Appliquée*" ("Sexual Politics and Critical Judgment," in *After Strange Texts: The
Role of Theory in the Study of Literature*, ed. Gregory S. Jay and David L. Miller [U of Alabama P, 1985], 83).

† From *PMLA* 103 (1988): 285–97. Page numbers in square brackets refer to this Norton
Critical Edition.

ral. She steps so boldly into the midst of everything, shrinks from nothing, has such a comprehension of everything, seems at times to have but little delicacy, and anon shows that she possesses the finest essence of it; now so hard, now so tender; now so perfectly unreasonable, soon again so wise. In short, I now and then catch an aspect of her, in which I cannot believe her to be my own human child, but a spirit strangely mingled with good and evil, haunting the house where I dwell. (*American*, 430–31) [218–19]

Hawthorne's perplexity illustrates a leading feature of the cultural construction of gender, the way in which perceptions of human reality are concerted—and disconcerted—by the systems of meaning through which gender is construed. Hawthorne's mind was the arena, in this respect, of an unresolvable contest of significations. The conceptions of gender informing his consciousness proposed womanhood and manhood as complementary opposites, in keeping with the domestic ideal emerging in the early nineteenth century, which assigned to women the destiny of fulfilling themselves through tender self-sacrifice in the private roles of wife and mother. This womanly selfhood is now recognized as a derivative counterpart of the self-sufficing combative style of manhood then acquiring supremacy, as called forth by the competitive requirements of a capitalist democratic culture.[1]

Prominent in Hawthorne's description of Una is the confounding of these gender categories: the child's masculine boldness and hardness and unshrinking "comprehension of everything" is amalgamated with tenderness, wisdom, and the finest essence of delicacy. The child appears to him an anomaly, neither male nor female and yet both. She strikes him as not human, in uncanny moments, because she does not conform to the definitions that organize his perceptions of the human. Yet Hawthorne seems incipiently aware of this: he places emphasis on the uneasy play of his perceptions, pointing to the connection between his shifting vision of Una and a disturbance internal to his mind. He attempts again and again to put on paper a description of the way she appears to him because her presence "seems to embarrass the springs of spiritual life and the movement of the soul" (*American*, 414).

Hawthorne's anxieties were easily aroused on these issues because he felt his own character to be anomalous in relation to the prevailing standard of masterful public manhood. Hawthorne's painful shyness—to take the most obvious external marker—was a "feminine" trait; Henry Wadsworth Longfellow spoke for the commonplace response

---

1. Douglas's *Purity and Danger* describes the shaping of perception by culturally constituted systems of ordering reality. Literary studies like those of Greenblatt, Herbert, and Mullaney, making use of interpretive anthropology as pioneered in works by Douglas, Geertz, and Turner, are now converging as "cultural poetics" and "the new historicism." Gender as a cultural construction is treated in Chodorow's *Reproduction of Mothering: Psychoanalysis and the Sociology of Gender* and in the anthologies *Sexual Meanings: The Cultural Construction of Gender and Sexuality*, edited by Ortner and Whitehead, and *Woman, Culture, and Society*, edited by Rosaldo and Lamphere. The definitions of womanhood and manhood emerging in early nineteenth-century America are discussed in the studies by Cott, Degler, Ryan, and Smith-Rosenberg.

when he observed that "to converse with Hawthorne was like talking with a woman" (Lathrop, 559). Hawthorne was aware, moreover, that the self-hood expressed in his writing is a tremulous connoisseur of emotion, subtly responsive to inward experience, who is preoccupied with keeping the "inmost Me behind its veil" (*Scarlet*, 4) [7] while establishing an intimate communion with the reader.[2] In defense of this artistic character, Hawthorne covertly yet persistently resisted conventional definitions of manhood, and this rebellion gave him strong sympathies with the feminist protest against the restricted role assigned to women. Yet by the same token Hawthorne was profoundly disconcerted by women who displayed the forthright public assertiveness that he himself lacked, as he shows in his famous venomous assaults on women writers and in the postmortem denigration of his erstwhile friend Margaret Fuller. Hawthorne's unstable fusion of feminism and misogyny is one feature of the interference pattern set up by ceaselessly colliding self-appraisals, the convulsive uncertainties regarding his sexual identity that permanently characterized his emotional life.

Hawthorne's behavior on the day his daughter was born reflects his characteristic inward tension. He is hesitant to confront the child, even fearful: "I have not yet seen the baby, and am almost afraid to look at it," he writes to his sister. Hawthorne transcribes impressions of the newborn he has collected from the attending physician, Dr. Bartlett; his mother-in-law, Mrs. Peabody; the housekeeper, Mary O'Brien; and a neighbor, Mrs. Prescott. Yet even as he points out that he has formed no judgment of his own, his mind fixes on a detail sharply at odds with his concept of feminine delicacy. "Of my own personal knowledge I can say nothing, except that it already roars very lustily" (*Letters 1843–1853*, 15).

Such moments of troubled response had a fateful import for Una Hawthorne. She was not a chance acquaintance or a literary rival or a sometime friend, like Margaret Fuller, to be given a temporary role in the ambivalent drama of Hawthorne's mind. She was his own human child, and her character—so uncanny and so alien—was shaped by the way she was reared in his household. It would be an oversimplification to say that Una became merely a creature of her father's imagination, no more than the embodiment of his gender conflicts, as projected onto her. Yet her character, like his, was a cultural construction, and it was one in which Hawthorne had a hand.

This is not the occasion for a detailed treatment of the pattern of solicitude and discipline that the Hawthornes organized about their baby daughter,[3] but crucial issues of the selfhood they sought to impart are disclosed in their naming her Una, after Spenser's maiden of holiness. This decision provoked a controversy among family and

2. In this respect Hawthorne's relation to himself and his public is strongly analogous to that of the women writers Kelley discusses in *Private Woman, Public Stage*. Baym and Carton provide excellent discussions of Hawthorne's ambivalence about gender.
3. A discussion of Sophia Hawthorne's role in the formation of Una's mental life lies beyond the scope of this essay. Sophia's exceptional response to the emerging norms of gender, the marriage she made to Nathaniel, and her place in the constellation of family relations are complex subjects that bear on this question, which I treat in *Dearest Beloved*.

friends that illuminates the larger cultural processes of gender definition that were then taking place.

In studying the contradictions in womanly experience during the nineteenth century, Sandra Gilbert and Susan Gubar fix on Spenser's Una as an image of the feminine peculiarly attuned to masculine dread. Intelligence, aggression, sexuality, and creative enterprise are all stripped away from this passive and angelic doll, and are attributed to her hideous counterpart, the shape-shifting monster Duessa, whose loathsome duplicity, secret erotic filth, and quest for domination suitably embody male horror. A projection of male derangement, Duessa has also a potentially constructive meaning for women. She emerges as a precursor of "the madwoman in the attic," symbolizing womanly autonomy in its earliest struggles toward self-expression, when it knows itself only in the form dictated by the symbolic apparatus that brands autonomy in women as monstrous (Gilbert and Gubar, 27–30).

In focusing on Una and Duessa, Gilbert and Gubar extend discussions that took place in Hawthorne's America. While autonomous individuality gained preeminence as an ideal of masculine character in the Victorian age, Spenser's mythological diagram was invoked to illustrate the splitting of woman's reality into two centers of psychic force: the polar tension between the derivative position of the domestic angel and the tormented assertion by women of the autonomy that men increasingly claimed for themselves. John Bell's statue of Una and the lion, for example, which was displayed at the Crystal Palace in 1851, celebrates the magical power of blameless feminine gentleness to subdue the brute ferocity of males (Gay, 414–15), a theme that Nina Auerbach elaborates in *Woman and the Demon*.

Closer to home was the uneasy debate Margaret Fuller conducted with the ideal she found in Spenser's unearthly maiden. No American woman of the period struggled more vigorously than she to realize herself as an individual in her own right. She was also an intimate of the Hawthorne household before and after Una's birth, when the Hawthornes were reading Spenser together. The summer Una was born Fuller published "The Great Lawsuit," her preliminary draft of *Woman in the Nineteenth Century*, which discusses Una as occupying a notably limited place in the "range of female character in Spenser." So long as "Britomart and Belphoebe have as much room on the canvass as Florimel," Fuller observes, ". . . the haughtiest Amazon will not murmur that Una should be felt to be the highest type" (25). The restlessness audible in Fuller's carefully conditional "should be felt to be" is accentuated in the final version of this passage, published the following year, which demotes Una from the pinnacle of womanhood: no longer the "highest" type, she becomes merely the "fairest" (66).

Hawthorne's friend George Hillard, who had also published a discussion of Spenser's *Faerie Queene* (Hull, 112), objected that the spiritual forces associated with Una should be kept within the boundaries of myth, not applied directly to human experience. The name was "too imaginative"; it should "rather be kept and hallowed in the holy crypts of the mind, than brought into the garish light of common day"

(J. Hawthorne, 1:276). Replying to Hillard, Hawthorne insists that in his own eyes the child perfectly incarnates what her name means and that its appropriateness will become generally apparent as she leads her life:

> . . . the name has never before been warmed with human life, and therefore may not seem appropriate to real flesh and blood. But for us, our child has already given it a natural warmth; and when she has worn it through her lifetime, and perhaps transmitted it to descendants of her own, this beautiful name will have become naturalized on earth;—whereby we shall have done a good deed in first bringing it out of the realm of Faery.   (*Letters 1843–1853*, 22)

Hawthorne depends here on a "naturalization" that will come about automatically simply because the child is female. The gender system that ascribed nurturant tenderness to women and combative individuality to males was conventionally regarded in Hawthorne's time as a law of nature and of nature's God, a matter of universal essences that were at once biological and ethereal—inherent and transcendent gender identities that would assert themselves no matter what deviations individual men or women might indulge in. Because he recognized that his own character was in some respects deeply at odds with these definitions of normality, Hawthorne persistently queried the natural foundation of manhood and womanhood.[4] Yet he sought to quell his uneasiness about his lustily roaring newborn daughter by insisting that the natural properties of womanhood had already been secured and would emerge inevitably as the child grew up. There is "something so especially piquant," he observes, "about having helped to create a future woman" (*Letters 1843–1853*, 25).

In the five years that elapsed between his letter to Hillard and his writing *The Scarlet Letter*, Hawthorne lost his confidence that the child would naturalize the identity he had ascribed to her. Instead of displaying tender holiness suited to allaying masculine dread, her character now intensified his initial fears. Bringing Una out of "the realm of Faery" had also brought Duessa, and by a simultaneous reverse movement his own flesh and blood had slipped into fairyland and was now surrounded by an uncanny aura of the supernatural. The work of naturalization remained to be accomplished, both for himself and for her.

Una's role as a source for Pearl has played a useful part in critical studies of *The Scarlet Letter*. One tradition—summarized by Barbara Garlitz—treats the text as a work of art whose self-contained whole-

---

4. *The Scarlet Letter* has been the subject of vigorous discussions that adopt various understandings of familial relations as universals. Male asserts that Hawthorne deals in the "timeless abstractions" that inform the biblical narrative of Eve's transgression, so that Hester departs from her divinely ordained sexual role in seeking masculine knowledge (99–100). Whelan pursues this line so far as to claim that, after repenting her effort to usurp man's place, Hester will rejoin Arthur in Heaven, in "what is to be her Eternal Home and Fireside" (504). Ragussis, in quite a different vein, grounds his trenchant and compelling discussion on linguistic universals, the constitutive properties of "writing" and "fiction," as these define a "family discourse" in Hawthorne notably distinct from any particular time and locality.

ness fuses quotidian raw materials into a dynamic system of resolved stresses, so that the meaning of Una-Pearl takes form with reference to the other elements of the aesthetic totality. Or the imaginative life of the artist himself may be the focus of attention, as in Evan Carton's acute and powerful * * * essay, where Una and *The Scarlet Letter* both bear witness to the conflicted sexuality inherent in Hawthorne's unfolding conception of Romance. It would also be possible, and instructive, to place the center of gravity in Una's story. She is the only one of Hawthorne's three children who has not inspired a book-length biography; her short, unhappy life has not seemed to have the requisite importance. As one who lives out the torment of Gilbert and Gubar's *Madwoman in the Attic*, however, she merits intensive study, and her doom could well occasion a comprehensive summary judgment on her father's life and work.

Instead of finding an autonomous sovereign significance in one of these three centers of interest, I treat them as interactive, as contingent and interdependent participants in a collective process. In the cultural construction of gender both the builders and the building materials are human beings who are at work on one another and whose intercourse is mysteriously conveyed and contained in works of art. Stephen Greenblatt has given the name *cultural poetics* to the study of this interdefining activity as a cultural process at large, and it is a study that—however broad its implications—requires the careful examination of local particulars, here the particulars of gender conflict interlinking Nathaniel Hawthorne, Una Hawthorne, and *The Scarlet Letter*.

Instead of reifying Hawthorne's entangled brooding on Una's character into transcendent aesthetic terms, *The Scarlet Letter* extends that brooding and complicates the entanglement. Little Pearl is made to enact the qualities that most troubled Hawthorne in his daughter, and she is eventually delivered from them. Hawthorne surrounds little Pearl, that is to say, with a therapeutic program, which includes a diagnosis of her difficulty and a prescription for cure, grounded on the gender categories that he considered natural and that defined a femininity he hoped his daughter would grow into.

Yet his ambivalence about gender issues leads Hawthorne to subvert these categories even as he invokes them, so that to trace the process by which he restores Pearl to "normality" is to single out but one movement in a continuous scrimmage of meanings. As David Leverenz's subtly nuanced discussion shows, unresolved emotional conflicts are at the heart of *The Scarlet Letter*'s magical power over its readers; a close reading of the text leads both inward, toward its reverberating interior resonances, and outward to social history. The thematic conflicts in Hawthorne's text receive comment from the conflicts in his own experience, and they also receive comment from the discordant form Una's life finally assumes. Far from attaining the natural womanhood Hawthorne wished for her, Una becomes a ravaged battleground where the opposing forces inherent in that ideal carry on their ceaseless warfare.

To investigate the contests of gender signification that take place within Nathaniel Hawthorne, Una Hawthorne, and *The Scarlet Letter* is to find that these three theaters of conflict are not sharply bounded entities. The differences among them are vivid—the difference among a man, a woman, and a book. Yet the cunningly interlinked differences within them give us access to their joint engagement in the cultural construction of gender and subvert any effort to view them as autonomous individualities. They play against each other in a cultural politics, such that the assertion of a total comprehensive vision always turns out to be rhetorical, and is delusory if taken to be final. They are not self-contained selfhoods shedding light, as solitary lighthouses might shed light, one on the other. Nor do they finally stand apart from ourselves, illuminating our own gender conflicts. They are moments in an interactive texture of semantic relations, the cultural metabolism of meanings by which gender is constructed in America, outside which there is no place to stand.

Pearl's inhuman nature results from the sin of her parents, so the narrative manifestly asserts, and that sin is rooted in distortions of gender. In the story of Hester and Arthur a manly woman and a womanly man repair their aberrant characters; they reciprocally enable one another to attain "true" manhood and "true" womanhood, and this fulfillment redeems their child.

Hester is a vigorous and independent-minded woman who bitterly resents the oppression she has suffered and sees it as bearing on "the whole race of womanhood. Was existence worth accepting, even to the happiest among them?" Fundamental social changes, she recognizes, are necessary to remove the injustice women suffer:

> As a first step, the whole system of society is to be torn down, and built up anew. Then, the very nature of the opposite sex, or its long hereditary habit, which has become like nature, is to be essentially modified, before woman can be allowed to assume what seems a fair and suitable position. Finally, all other difficulties being obviated, woman cannot take advantage of these preliminary reforms until she herself shall have undergone an even mightier change; in which, perhaps, the ethereal essence, wherein she has her truest life, will be found to have evaporated.   (165–66) [108]

This passage illustrates Hawthorne's restlessness with the definition of gender as a natural ethereal essence. Is it the "nature" of the male sex that must be changed or merely its "long hereditary habit"? Is it necessary for the "truest life" of woman to be sacrificed, or is that only a danger? Is the psychosocial revolution Hester contemplates a perversion, distorting the "ethereal essence" of woman, or is it simply very difficult?

Hester's pursuit of such speculations is itself presented as an "exercise of thought" at odds with her feminine nature. In taking up this frustrating intellectual quest, she departs from the woman's natural engagement with concerns of the heart and as a result creates a personal impression of "marble coldness":

> There seemed to be no longer any thing in Hester's face for Love to dwell upon; nothing in Hester's form, though majestic and statue-like, that Passion would ever dream of clasping in its embrace; nothing in Hester's bosom, to make it ever again the pillow of Affection. Some attribute had departed from her, the permanence of which had been essential to keep her a woman. (163) [107]

Yet Hester's femininity has not been altogether destroyed. Looking forward to her meeting with Arthur in the forest, Hawthorne observes: "She who has once been woman, and ceased to be so, might at any moment become a woman, again, if there were only the magic touch to effect the transfiguration" (164) [107].

Well before that climactic meeting, however, Hester gives evidence of an "innate womanliness" prevailing still among the circumstances tending to replace it with an "unnatural" masculinity. She is preserved from the wilder excesses of rebellion by the devotion that she can pour into the rearing of Pearl; and in her relation to the community at large she displays the quality of compassionate self-sacrifice belonging to woman's "ethereal essence." Hawthorne speaks of her uncomplaining submission to the abuse she receives from the public, of the "blameless purity" of her life. He points out that she lives with extreme frugality, giving all her surplus to the poor. The scenes in which this distinctive "feminine" virtue most exercises itself are those of the sickbed and the deathbed, where "Hester's nature showed itself warm and rich; a well-spring of human tenderness, unfailing to every real demand, and inexhaustible by the largest" (161) [105].

The compelling reality of this "womanly" trait, Hawthorne affirms, is felt by the community at large, so that the townsfolk begin to say that the scarlet A "meant Able, so strong was Hester Prynne, with a woman's strength" (161) [106].

Enacted in the forest, accordingly, is the reciprocal "magic touch," in which Hester recovers her "womanhood" and, in the consummate exercise of her woman's strength, makes a "man" out of Arthur Dimmesdale. As Hester sees Arthur approaching on the forest path, she observes his "nerveless despondency"; and his behavior throughout the scene reveals his loss of the ascribed masculine qualities of public initiative and self-possession, of rational judgment and resolute will. As Arthur begins to grasp the scale of his dilemma, he turns to Hester for guidance: "Think for me, Hester! Thou art strong. Resolve for me!" (196) [126].

Hester, of course, has already contrived the plan that she now persuades Arthur to adopt, that of leaving the colony for a better life elsewhere, and in the course of advocating this plan, she asserts her psychological dominion over him. " 'Is the world then so narrow?' ex-

claimed Hester Prynne, fixing her deep eyes on the minister's, and instinctively exercising a magnetic power over a spirit so shattered and
subdued, that it could hardly hold itself erect" (197) [127].

The ultimate result of this encounter is not to bring Arthur into
compliance with her plan but to empower him to conceive and execute a plan of his own, which is gauged to extend and indeed to culminate his public responsibilities. Hester is startled and dismayed
when, after his Election Day sermon, Arthur approaches the scaffold
to proclaim his guilt. Yet something within her compels her to acquiesce: "slowly, as if impelled by inevitable fate, and against her
strongest will" (252) [159], Hester joins him. The role of submission
for which nature had framed her undermines the long-practiced assertion of her will, now that Arthur assumes command. She has rendered
him capable of fulfilling his manhood, which includes taking charge of
her.

He continues to depend at this final moment on her "woman's
strength," now in its proper place, subordinated to the purpose he has
chosen. As they mount the scaffold together, they form a tableau in
which the complementarity of natural genders is triumphant; essential
manhood and essential womanhood have been mutually re-created
and are reciprocally confirmed. "Come hither now, and twine thy
strength about me! Thy strength, Hester; but let it be guided by the
will which God hath granted me!" (253) [160].

Pearl's redemption occurs at this moment of confession and expiation and fulfillment; and the conception of gender as a natural essence
supports Pearl's transformation here, even as it structures Hawthorne's diagnosis of the aberration he saw in Una, which he elaborates in detail as Pearl goes through the therapeutic process
Hawthorne envisions for her.

Pearl has inherited the defiance that climaxes in Hester's bitterness
at the lot of women, and the child seems to anticipate that she too will
eventually be at odds with the world. Instead of playing with the children of the town, Pearl invents imaginary playmates, whom she regards with vehement hostility:

> She never created a friend, but seemed always to be sowing
> broadcast the dragon's teeth, whence sprung a harvest of armed
> enemies, against whom she rushed to battle. It was inexpressibly
> sad—then what depth of sorrow to a mother, who felt in her own
> heart the cause!—to observe, in one so young, this constant
> recognition of an adverse world, and so fierce a training of the en-
> ergies that were to make good her cause, in the contest that must
> ensue. (95–96) [65]

Just as Hester's rebellion brings on a conflict with her own "womanly" nature, so Pearl suffers from internal contradictions. On the one
hand, she is an agent of Hester's punishment, upholding the validity of
the order that Hester violates. Pearl's preoccupation with the scarlet
letter, her persistent allusions to it, and her eerily apt questions to

Hester about Arthur fill out her character as an enforcer of the lawful order of society. Yet she herself "could not be made amenable to rules" (91) [62].

This contradictory situation comes to a head in the forest, after Hester has removed the scarlet letter from her breast, and has also removed the severe cap from her head, so that her rich dark hair gushes voluptuously down over her shoulder, stirring Arthur to a resumption of his manhood. Having agreed to flee the colony, they call the child to join them, but instead of responding with sympathy, Pearl throws a tantrum that is at once commanding and uncontrolled. "Assuming a singular air of authority, Pearl stretched out her hand, with the small forefinger extended, and pointing evidently toward her mother's breast." When her mother seemed not to comprehend her meaning, "the child stamped her foot with a yet more imperious look and gesture." And when Hester sternly repeated her demand that the child come to her, Pearl "suddenly burst into a fit of passion, gesticulating violently, and throwing her small figure into the most extravagant contortions. She accompanied this wild outbreak with piercing shrieks" (209–10) [134], with the result that Hester was compelled to obey the child's command.

Pearl's domineering manner in this scene, as elsewhere, recapitulates Hawthorne's uneasy observations of Una:

> To-day Una is exceedingly ungracious in her mode of asking, or rather demanding favors. For instance, wishing to have a story read to her, she has just said, "Now I'm going to have some reading"; and she always seems to adopt the imperative mood, in this manner. She uses it to me, I think, more than to her mother, and, from what I observe of some of her collateral predecessors, I believe it to be an hereditary trait to assume the government of her father. (*American*, 414)

Hawthorne's "feminine" self-consciousness made him especially touchy about being dominated by "a future woman."

The compounded paradox in which Pearl gains control of others by losing control of herself, enforcing a lawful decorum that she herself cannot observe, is markedly evident in Hawthorne's descriptions of Una. He returns again and again to what he terms the "tempestuous" character of Una's personality, which erupts when her will is crossed (*American*, 411). Here is Hawthorne's terse summary of a battle between them: "—she resists—father insists—there is a terrible struggle—and she gets into almost a frenzy; which is now gradually subsiding and sobbing itself away in her mother's arms" (*American*, 406). Sophia was often called on to mediate deadlocks between Una and her father, who found the child's rages peculiarly disconcerting. While traveling in the summer of 1848, he writes home about how much he misses the children, wryly observing that he would even like to see "little Tornada in one of her tantrums" (*Letters 1843–1853*, 231). If Hawthorne was psychologically vulnerable to Una's fury, perhaps even overawed by it on occasion, we hear an echo of his response in Arthur's words to Hester: "I know nothing that I would not sooner encounter than this passion in a child. In Pearl's young beauty, as in the wrinkled witch, it has a preternatural effect. Pacify her, if thou lovest me" (210) [134].

Una's preternatural rage, Hawthorne's language suggests, collapses the dichotomy that her name was meant to safeguard: her fury invokes the essential unity of the womanly qualities polarized in Spenser's figures—the lovely innocence of the holy maiden and the ferocity of the wrinkled witch, Duessa. As Una shrieked and raged, she aroused in Hawthorne the terrors inherent in the manhood by which these versions of womanhood were produced, the dread manifestly projected onto the monster-woman but hidden within reverence for the woman as angel.

Yet Una herself had internalized this gender system, so that her response to her aggressive impulses—like Hawthorne's—was shaped by the doctrine that pronounced them unnatural in a girl. As Hawthorne reflected on the manifold indelicacies in her conduct, it seemed to him that she was possessed by an "earthy monster, who lays his grasp on her spinal marrow, her brain, and other parts of her body that lie in closest contiguity to her soul" (*American*, 420–21) [218]. Una too gives evidence of having experienced herself—or the "indelicate" part of herself—as monstrous.

Pearl, as noted, insists on the lawful order of things with hysterical passion, which takes on an eerie self-propelling quality—the scream of the bewitched at being bewitched. Una also asserts with lurid intensity a standard she herself violates, in a way that voices the terror within her own mind.

Once when her mother was reading her a children's story called "The Bear and the Skrattel," Sophia's attempt to imitate the unearthly shrillness of the Skrattel's voice filled Una with horror, conjuring up the "earthy monster" within her. "Little Una cries 'No; no!' with a kind of dread," Hawthorne observes; and he specifies with unnerving serenity the chronic inner torment of which this outcry was an instance.

> It is rather singular that she should so strongly oppose herself to whatever is unbeautiful or even unusual, while she is continually doing unbeautiful things in her own person. I think, if she were to see a little girl who behaved in all respects like herself, it would be a continual horror and misery to her, and would ultimately drive her mad.   (*American* 419)

In Pearl these unearthly contradictions are resolved as Hester helps Arthur mount the scaffold:

> The great scene of grief, in which the wild infant bore a part, had developed all her sympathies; and as her tears fell upon her father's cheek, they were the pledge that she would grow up amid human joy and sorrow, nor for ever do battle with the world, but be a woman in it.   (256) [162]

The "manlike" imperiousness gives way to tears of sympathy, and the "elflike" inhuman remoteness gives way to warm human relations.

Like Pinnochio, Pearl is transformed from an unnatural creature, endowed with life but not truly human, into a "real little girl." "Her wild,
rich nature had been softened and subdued," Hawthorne tells us, "and
made capable of a woman's gentle happiness" (262) [165].

Yet this moment of naturalization neither transcends the contest of
gender definitions in *The Scarlet Letter* nor provides a stable vantage
from which to view it. No reader attuned to Hawthorne's ambivalence
toward Arthur's "feminine" traits and Hester's "masculine" traits would
long believe that the conclusion of their amorous entanglement unambiguously celebrates self-reliant manhood and angelic womanly
submission, even by implication. Instead of presenting a confident vision of domestic felicity organized around natural models of maleness
and femaleness, the work emerges from a troubled conflict over those
issues—a conflict in which apparent virtues are subverted and apparent vices furtively endorsed. Hawthorne's guilty admiration for
Hester's "manfulness" and his uneasy identification with Arthur's lan-
guishing, introspective, and timorous nature are most evident in his
intimate and detailed depiction of these ostensibly perverse traits.

As many critics have observed, moreover, Pearl's domestic felicity is
not located in the United States or in any other clearly definable
place. It is supported by the fabulous wealth that she inherits from
Chillingworth, which makes her "the richest heiress of her day," and
Hawthorne is careful to point out that the armorial seals on the letters
Hester receives have "bearings unknown to English heraldry"
(261–62) [165]. Hawthorne's conclusion effectively exempts Pearl
from the dilemmas that the book portrays, but it does not resolve
them. Rescued momentarily from unreality, Pearl slips back into a
fairy-tale world.

The work at large embodies, that is, a strong covert resistance to the
gender system Hawthorne uses in analyzing Pearl's "unnatural" character and in dramatizing her redemption. This scheme of thematic
conflicts, once recognized, uncovers a tangled nest of kindred para-
doxes involving Hawthorne, his daughter, and *The Scarlet Letter*. Pre-
scribing a cure for the aberrations of Pearl-Una, Hawthorne invokes
the complex of gender symbols that actually produced those aberrations: he proposes the source of the disease as a remedy for it. Yet he
subverts that recommendation—and presumably aggravates the disease—by undermining the gender doctrines in question; he had reason to feel that in writing *The Scarlet Letter* he had indulged the very
qualities in himself—his own unnatural feminine qualities—that gave
rise to his daughter's miseries. It is well known that he looked upon
his masterwork with guilt, as a "a h-ll-fired story" that was not "natural" for him to write (*Letters 1843–1853*, 312, 461). Far from offering
The Scarlet Letter as a pattern for addressing Una's troubles,
Hawthorne forbade his daughter to read the book and kept up the pro-
hibition as late as her sixteenth year.[5]

* * *

5. Letter from Una Hawthorne to her aunt Elizabeth P. Peabody, 10 Apr. 1860.

Una's difficulties became acute when she was fourteen years old, when the physical developments of puberty were far enough advanced to force the issues about the sort of woman she would become. The Hawthornes were living in Rome at the time, where Una, like her father, became fascinated by the young American women who lived on their own studying art, enjoying a degree of personal freedom not available in the United States. Madame de Staël's *Corinne: Or, Italy* had made Rome famous as an environment fostering possibilities of womanhood sharply at odds with the conventions prevailing in England and America, a culture in which women of artistic talent could take roles of public consequence instead of being confined to the domestic sphere. Margaret Fuller, nicknamed the "American Corinna," was part of a steady migration of gifted and spirited women who saw in Italian society a more generous atmosphere than they could enjoy at home and larger horizons in which to find themselves. Hawthorne responded to Rome with his characteristic ambivalence, haunted by a sense of pervading moral disease, yet strongly intrigued. In Una the experience precipitated a psychic crisis, as Hawthorne notes in his journal:

> Una has taken what seems to be a Roman fever by sitting down to sketch in the Coliseum. It is not a severe attack, yet attended with fits of exceeding discomfort, occasional comatoseness, and even delirium to the extent of making the poor child talk in rhythmical measure, like a tragic heroine.   (*French*, 495)

The physicians concluded that Una's illness was in part psychological, so that she was said to have a "nervous fever" as well as the "Roman fever."

On 13 November 1858, eleven days after Una took to her bed, she wrote to her cousin Richard Manning in Salem:

> My ideal of existence would be to live in Italy in a house built and furnished after my own taste, often paying long visits to England, and sometimes to America, & pursue my studies and other occupations unmolested by mankind in general. But people seldom, if ever, realize their ideal of life, and I fancy I shall never see the fulfillment of mine.

Una knew that her father was determined to have the family return to the United States, and in touching on this issue she discloses something of the guilt she felt in opposing his plan. "I don't mind telling you," she admits to Richard in the same letter, "what a high treasonable countryman you have, but you know I may be brought back to the ways of righteousness when I return, tho' it is my private opinion that my feelings will be still more confirmed."

Una's psychological difficulties arose not because her father had imposed the external necessity of returning to America but because the potential conflict between them spoke to the cultural contradictions inherent in her experience of herself. She was conscientiously devoted to "the ways of righteousness," which included living in conformity with the ideal of "true womanhood" in America. Yet she also abhorred the prospect. It is as though she had been covertly encouraged to repudiate, by some communication of Hawthorne's own ambivalence, the very model of womanly fulfillment she had been enjoined to follow. Hawthorne's remark that she sounded like a "tragic heroine" suggests his intuition that she was trapped in a predicament having eerily literary dimensions, including his authorship of what was unreadable, and was becoming unendurable, in her story.

Sophia watched incessantly by her daughter's bedside, and in a letter to her sister Elizabeth P. Peabody, written 3 July 1859, she remarked on Una's seeming withdrawal from life:

> She looked at me once with particularly wide open eyes . . . & said in a natural voice—"I am going to die now. There is no use in living."—"Goodbye,—dear—" As I did not reply to this she more earnestly repeated, "Goodbye, dear" & deliberately turned with her face to the wall & lay perfectly still. . . . Sometimes she would lie on her back & stretch out her feet & lay her arms by her side, & with unwinking glassy eyes look straight at the bed's foot with no speculation & as if already cold & lifeless.

As soon as Una could travel, the Hawthornes left Rome and, after a year in England, set sail for America. On 20 July 1860, shortly after their arrival at Concord, Una wrote to her cousin Richard about the difficulties produced by "my rebellious feelings," informing him that she would soon come to stay in Salem. A physician had confirmed her expectation that she would suffer another attack of "brain fever" unless she could get away from her family. "He is going to talk to papa and tell him his mind, and then I shall be free as air! Think how happy I must be!" Looking forward to her trip to Salem, she exclaimed, "Oh, I long to be there, out of this killing place."

The anticipated visit in Salem did not occur; and five days later Una again wrote to Richard: "I was very unwell from many causes, and I knew my only safety was in keeping my mind off myself. From having followed that wise course until now & keeping away from home (!) I have greatly improved." Her further comment focuses attention on the "masculine" assertiveness at the heart of her conflict. "Though I appear, & am, perfectly well while I do as I please, (did you ever know such a wilful & headstrong young woman as I am?) there is a certain little group of events & sights & minds that in a minute by a most wonderful magic make me faint & sick & all over shooting pains."

Una's imprisonment within the family's conception of proper young womanhood was dramatized in early September, when her younger brother, Julian, was enrolled in a school at Concord to prepare him for college. The school itself welcomed young women as students; yet, against the advice of friends, the Hawthornes steadfastly refused to permit Una to attend (Bassan, 26). Within the month she became violent and had to be restrained by force.

The Hawthornes then turned for help to a practitioner of medical electricity, a therapy that viewed a wide variety of diseases—especially "nervous" diseases—as suitable for treatment with electric shocks (Beard and Rockwell; Shecut; Leithead; Luke). This method was developed in the nineteenth century to a high level of sophistication, with a formidable array of batteries, generators, and electrodes manufactured for complex uses in the two principal forms of therapy: "faradization," which involved shocking tissue directly, and "galvanization," which produced spasmodic muscular responses by running electricity down motor nerves. Advocates of electrotherapeutics held that the "nervous principle" in the body was linked to an electrical fluid pervading the universe, whose activities produced earthquakes as well as thunderstorms; they envisioned electricity as the physical substance of the individual soul in relation to the world soul. Patients were given multiple applications of the electrodes over a period of days, which cured them by restoring a natural equilibrium, attuned to the universal electrical harmony. Because women were viewed as naturally delicate, their "susceptibility" to electrical influence was thought to be "higher" than men's; medical electricians boasted that "many of the most delightful results of general faradization and central galvanization, have been obtained in neurasthenic, anemic, hysterical women" (Beard and Rockwell, 292). The treatment was, in short, a lurid parody of the naturalization to natural womanhood that Hawthorne had counted on when Una was a baby, had envisioned in *The Scarlet Letter*, and had sought to bring about by getting her out of Rome.

At first Hawthorne took a skeptical tone toward the procedure, alluding to the "incantations of a certain electrical witch"—the "Doctoress" being a Mrs. Rollins of Cambridge (*Letters 1857–1864*, 323). But as the days passed he began to believe the treatments had worked. "All the violent symptoms were allayed," Hawthorne wrote two weeks later, "by the first application of electricity, and within two days she was in such a condition as to require no further restraint. Since then, there has been no relapse, and now, for many days, she has seemed entirely well, in mind." "Her derangement," Rollins had informed them, "was the result of a liver-complaint and a slight affection of the heart, probably produced or strengthened by the Roman fever." These maladies being "perfectly within the control of medical electricity," Rollins had assured the Hawthornes "that we need have no apprehension of future mental disturbance" (*Letters 1857–1864*, 327).

Hawthorne responded to Una's difficulties with severe anxiety. During the worst period of her illness in Rome he became so distraught, Sophia recalled, that he "expected every morning to find his hair turned to snow upon his head" (letter to Peabody, 3 July 1859). Unable to endure the alternations of hope and dread concerning Una's prognosis, Hawthorne had settled his mind on the prospect that his daughter would not survive. During Una's breakdown in Concord, he sought to relieve his torment by taking a turn on Mrs. Rollins's battery (*Letters 1857–1864*, 325).

It is fair to say, and Sophia more than once did say, that Hawthorne himself never recovered from Una's illness, suffering as he did the de-

clining health that ended with his death in 1864. In 1862 she wrote to
Annie Fields:

> I was quite alarmed when I returned that evening to find Mr.
> Hawthorne very ill. It was a Roman cold, with fever and utter
> restlessness, and it has hardly left him yet. . . . Alas the Roman
> days were melancholy days for him, and he thinks he shall never
> recover from them. Even when he looks at his Rose of Sharon so
> firm and strong now, I think he feels uncertain that she still lives
> and blooms, so deeply scored into his soul was the expectation of
> her death. It was his first acquaintance with suffering, and it
> seemed to rend him asunder.

Hawthorne's anticipation of continuing trouble for Una was quite
accurate, in contrast to the medical electrician's confident words
about future mental disturbances. After his death Una suffered further bouts of mental illness, in circumstances bespeaking her
dilemma: she could neither live out nor repudiate the womanly role
she had made her own, and her torment over this inward contradiction sometimes became overwhelming. When her younger sister, Rose,
married George Lathrop in the fall of 1871, Una responded as though
the event signaled her own failure to achieve this presumptive sine
qua non of womanly fulfillment. Her psychological disturbance on this
occasion was so acute that those close to her, setting aside references
to "nervous fever," described her condition as "insanity" and placed
her for a time in an asylum (Hull, 105).

Una was twice engaged to be married, both times to notably unlikely prospects, as she both obeyed and disobeyed the imperative to
take up the roles of wife and mother. The first engagement was to a
young man named Storrow Higginson, who professed himself not to
believe in marriage (and in the event displayed the courage of this
conviction); and the second was to Albert Webster, a tubercular poet
of modest means, who set off for the Sandwich Islands to regain his
health and died on the voyage (Hull, 101, 107–108).[6] Una's brother,
Julian, describes her response to the news of Webster's death: " 'Ah—
yes!' she said, slowly, with a slight sigh. She made no complaint, nor
gave way to any passion of grief; but she seemed to become spiritualized,—to relinquish the world, along with her hopes of happiness in it"
(2:373). Within six months Una was dead, at the age of thirty-three.

The principals at the center of attention here—Una Hawthorne,
Nathaniel Hawthorne, and *The Scarlet Letter*—take part in an ecology
of signs: each has its distinctive identity amid the environment provided by the others. I do not mean that they form a natural ecosystem,
as though a biological necessity ordained the gender arrangement of
which Una was a victim and her father a tormented beneficiary, with
The Scarlet Letter innocently mirroring the arrangement's rich, ironic

---

6. On Storrow Higginson's view of marriage see the letter written by Nathaniel's sister Elizabeth to "My dear Maria [Manning?]" on 20 Feb. 1868 (30–31).

complexities. The very act of circumscribing the semantic interplay I have described emphasizes the historical contingency of the cultural construction of gender. It is a process whose boundaries cannot be brought clearly into focus.

It is apparent, first, that Una's rage, grief, and madness were not a private affair. They formed her own version of a collective response to the domestic ideal shared by middle-class northeastern women right through the nineteenth century, particularly women of enterprise and cultural attainments, whose lives prominently featured dramas of thwarted strength. Charlotte Gilman's story "The Yellow Wall-paper" provides a consummate articulation of the inward meaning of such misery, including the "rest cure," a therapy often complemented with applications of medical electricity. A more involuted enactment of the bitter dilemmas at stake here is provided in Jean Strouse's and Ruth Bernard Yeazell's accounts of Alice James, a brilliant and forceful woman who fashioned an identity from the experience of being incurable and spoke of the effort "to get myself dead" as the climax of her career (Yeazell, 2). Catharine Beecher, it appears, took her own periodic collapses at face value—simply as illness of the sort women contract—and sought recourse to the "water cures" that proliferated during the early part of the century. But, as Kathryn Kish Sklar observes, the spas that Beecher frequented offered an environment in which women could share their sorrow and anger with one another and experience a collective validation of the anguished consciousness that seemed altogether aberrant in institutional settings dominated by male concerns. Hidden within this womanly suffering were the ingredients of liberation for women and the harbingers of its advent.

In the concluding passages of *The Scarlet Letter*, Hester's cottage provides a locale in which a sisterhood of unresolved misery has an opportunity to take form:

> People brought all their sorrows and perplexities, and besought her counsel, as one who had herself gone through a mighty trouble. Women, more especially,—in the continually recurring trials of wounded, wasted, wronged, misplaced, or erring and sinful passion,—or with the dreary burden of a heart unyielded, because unvalued and unsought,—came to Hester's cottage, demanding why they were so wretched, and what the remedy! (263) [165]

To these women Hester provides the hope of a future consummation, a new order of gender relations within which such troubles would be resolved:

> She assured them . . . of her firm belief, that, at some brighter period, when the world should have grown ripe for it, in Heaven's own time, a new truth would be revealed, in order to establish the whole relation of man and woman on a surer ground of mutual happiness. (263) [165–66]

Casting his romance in Puritan times, Hawthorne creates a rhetorical schema in which this scene of unresolved conflict—and the whole tormented story of Hester, Pearl, and Arthur—is seen as typical of an era safely in the past, to which nineteenth-century Americans might look back from the vantage point supplied by the "new truth" about women and men that they claimed for their own.

The agent of the coming revelation, Hester foresees, will be a woman who is also an angel, since this "mission of divine and mysterious truth" could never be confided to a sinful creature like herself (263) [166]. The divine woman to whom Hester looks forward from the dark confusions that beset her in the seventeenth century is in fact the domestic angel of the nineteenth century, the epiphany of ethereal womanhood ordained by nature and nature's God, living happily in accordance with the inner truth of her being.

> The angel and apostle of the coming revelation must be a woman, indeed, but lofty, pure, and beautiful; and wise, moreover, not through dusky grief, but the ethereal medium of joy; and showing how sacred love should make us happy, by the truest test of a life successful to such an end!   (263) [166]

Hawthorne looked upon his wife as just such an angel and apostle of domestic felicity as Hester's vision describes, and in keeping with the interior dilemmas of this selfhood, she suffered throughout her adult life from nervous ailments, including episodes of complete prostration. When Hawthorne read her the conclusion of *The Scarlet Letter*, he observed, "it broke her heart and sent her to bed with a grievous headache" (*Letters 1843–1853*, 311) [228]. Yet Sophia construed this headache, like her other sufferings, as evidence of the ethereal delicacy she considered inherent in her womanly nature.

The Scarlet Letter struck her like a jolt of medical electricity, confirming the absoluteness of this inward moral law. "I do not know what you will think of the Romance," she wrote to her sister a few days later. "It is most powerful & contains a moral as terrific & stunning as a thunder bolt. It shows that the Law cannot be broken" (*Letters 1843–1853*, 313). Sophia does not mean that the law cannot be broken with impunity but that—like a natural law—it cannot be broken at all. The overpowering shock transmitted by *The Scarlet Letter* restores her mind, so she affirms, to its own intrinsic order: disabling sickness and natural therapy here perfectly united.

I do not mean to parade Sophia's response as a deplorable misreading—as though I had at hand a final correct reading against which to measure it—but as bespeaking her version of the thematic conflicts at work in her husband's mind, her daughter's mind, and in *The Scarlet Letter* itself. The sacred force locked up in the natural order of genders brought a measure of coherence to the troubles of her consciousness, even as it acted in Una's disintegration.

To relate *The Scarlet Letter* to the cultural construction of gender is thus to examine the specific terms on which selfhoods were made and unmade in Hawthorne's time within the patterns of meaning by which sexual identity was then coming to be defined. To acknowledge the power of such cultural processes, and of literary art within those processes, is to recognize that the problems we have explored cannot be sequestered in the early nineteenth century, as though we ourselves had at last attained the "surer ground of mutual happiness" that Hester foretold.

The Scarlet Letter is a powerful book not because it resolves our gender conflicts but because it draws us into them and forces us to deploy our own ways of seeking to manage them. The work becomes implicated in our predicaments, inviting us to recognize that we cannot read it unless we also read ourselves, without any guarantee of what outcomes will result, without any sure way to demarcate what we have seen from what we are, or are becoming, or are seeking no longer to be.[7]

WORKS CITED

Auerbach, Nina. *Woman and the Demon: The Life of a Victorian Myth.* Cambridge: Harvard UP, 1982.

Bassan, Maurice. *Hawthorne's Son: The Life and Literary Career of Julian Hawthorne.* Columbus: Ohio State UP, 1970.

Baym, Nina. "Thwarted Nature: Nathaniel Hawthorne as Feminist." *American Novelists Revisited.* Ed. Fritz Fleishmann. Boston: Hall, 1982. 58–77.

Beard, George M., and A. D. Rockwell. *A Practical Treatise on the Medical and Surgical Uses of Electricity.* New York: Wood, 1875.

Carton, Evan. " 'A Daughter of the Puritans' and Her Old Master: Hawthorne, Una, and the Sexuality of Romance." *Daughters and Fathers.* Ed. Linda Boose and Betty Sue Flowers. Baltimore: Johns Hopkins UP, 1989. 208–32.

Chodorow, Nancy. *The Reproduction of Mothering: Psychoanalysis and the Sociology of Gender.* Berkeley: U of California P, 1978.

Cott, Nancy. *The Bonds of Womanhood: "Woman's Sphere" in New England, 1790–1835.* New Haven: Yale UP, 1980.

Degler, Carl. *At Odds: Women and the Family in America from the Revolution to the Present.* New York: Oxford UP, 1980.

Douglas, Mary. *Purity and Danger: An Analysis of Concepts of Pollution and Taboo.* New York: Praeger, 1966.

Fuller, Margaret. "The Great Lawsuit." *Dial* 4 (1843): 1–47.

———. *Woman in the Nineteenth Century.* Introd. Bernard Rosenthal. New York: W. W. Norton & Company, 1971.

Garlitz, Barbara. "Pearl: 1850–1955." *PMLA* 72 (1957): 689–99.

Gay, Peter. *The Tender Passion.* Vol. 2 of *The Bourgeois Experience: Victoria to Freud.* 2 vols. New York: Oxford UP, 1986.

Geertz, Clifford. *The Interpretation of Cultures.* New York: Basic, 1973.

———. *Local Knowledge: Further Essays in Interpretive Anthropology.* New York: Basic, 1983.

Gilbert, Sandra M., and Susan Gubar. *The Madwoman in the Attic: The Woman Writer and the Nineteenth-Century Literary Imagination.* New Haven: Yale UP, 1979.

Gilman, Charlotte Perkins. "The Yellow Wall-paper." *The Norton Anthology of Literature by Women.* Ed. Sandra M. Gilbert and Susan Gubar. New York: W. W. Norton & Company, 1985. 1148–61.

Greenblatt, Stephen. *Renaissance Self-Fashioning, from More to Shakespeare.* Chicago: U of Chicago P, 1980.

———. *Shakespearean Negotiations: The Circulation of Social Energy in Renaissance England.* Berkeley: U of California P, 1988.

Hawthorne, Elizabeth. Letters, ts. Hawthorne-Manning Collection, Essex Inst., Salem.

Hawthorne, Julian. *Nathaniel Hawthorne and His Wife.* 2 vols. Boston: Houghton, 1885.

Hawthorne, Nathaniel. *The American Notebooks.* Ed. Claude M. Simpson. Vol. 8 of Hawthorne, *Centenary Edition.* 1972.

———. *The Centenary Edition of the Works of Nathaniel Hawthorne.* Ed. William Charvat, Roy Harvey Pearce, and Claude M. Simpson. Columbus: Ohio State UP, 1962–23 vols.

———. *The French and Italian Notebooks.* Ed. Thomas Woodson. Vol. 14 of Hawthorne, *Centenary Edition.* 1980.

———. *The Letters 1843–1853.* Ed. Thomas Woodson, L. Neal Smith, and Norman Holmes Pearson. Vol. 16 of Hawthorne, *Centenary Edition.* 1985.

7. For helpful suggestions on this essay I am indebted to Warwick Wadlington, Joan Lidoff, David Leverenz, and Stephen Greenblatt, as well as to my colleagues in the Writer's Group at Southwestern University.

———. *The Letters 1857–1864*. Ed. Thomas Woodson, James A. Rubino, L. Neal Smith, and Norman Holmes Pearson. Vol. 18 of Hawthorne, *Centenary Edition*. 1987.

———. *The Scarlet Letter*. Ed. Fredson Bowers and Matthew J. Bruccoli. Vol. 1 of Hawthorne, *Centenary Edition*. 1962.

Herbert, T. Walter, Jr. *Marquesan Encounters: Melville and the Meaning of Civilization*. Cambridge: Harvard UP, 1980.

Hull, Raymona. "Una Hawthorne: A Biographical Sketch." *Nathaniel Hawthorne Journal* 6 (1976): 87–119.

Kelley, Mary. *Private Woman, Public Stage: Literary Domesticity in Nineteenth-Century America*. New York: Oxford UP, 1984.

Lathrop, George Parsons. "Biographical Sketch." *Tales, Sketches, and Other Papers by Nathaniel Hawthorne with a Biographical Sketch by George Parsons Lathrop*. 1883. Freeport: Books for Libraries, 1972. 441–569.

Leithead, William. *Electricity: Its Nature, Operation, and Importance in the Phenomena of the Universe*. London: Longman, 1837.

Leverenz, David. "Mrs. Hawthorne's Headache: Reading *The Scarlet Letter*." *Nineteenth-Century Fiction* 37 (1983): 552–75.

Luke, Thomas Davey. *Manual of Physio-Therapeutics*. New York: Wood, 1926.

Male, Roy R. *Hawthorne's Tragic Vision*. 1957. New York: W. W. Norton & Company, 1964.

Mullaney, Stephen. "Lying like Truth: Riddle, Representation and Treason in Renaissance England." *ELH* 47 (1980): 32–47.

———. "Strange Things, Gross Terms, Curious Customs: The Rehearsal of Cultures in the Late Renaissance." *Representations* 3 (1983): 40–67.

Ortner, Sherry B., and Harriet Whitehead, eds. *Sexual Meanings: The Cultural Construction of Gender and Sexuality*. Cambridge: Cambridge UP, 1981.

Ragussis, Michael. "Family Discourse and Fiction in *The Scarlet Letter*." *ELH* 49 (1982): 863–88.

Rosaldo, Michelle Zimbalist, and Louise Lamphere, eds. *Woman, Culture, and Society*. Stanford: Stanford UP, 1974.

Ryan, Mary P. *Cradle of the Middle Class: The Family in Oneida County, New York, 1790–1865*. Cambridge: Cambridge UP, 1981.

———. *The Empire of the Mother: American Writing about Domesticity, 1830–1860*. New York: Haworth, 1982.

Shecut, J. L. E. W. "An Essay on the Principles and Properties of the Electric Fluid." *Shecut's Medical and Philosophical Essays*. Charleston, 1819. 184–259.

Sklar, Kathryn Kish. *Catharine Beecher: A Study in American Domesticity*. New Haven: Yale UP, 1973.

Smith-Rosenberg, Carroll. *Disorderly Conduct: Visions of Gender in Victorian America*. New York: Knopf, 1985.

Spenser, Edmund. *The Faerie Queene*. 2 vols. London: Dent, 1910.

Strouse, Jean. *Alice James: A Biography*. New York: Bantam, 1980.

Turner, Victor. *Dramas, Fields, and Metaphors: Symbolic Action in Human Society*. Ithaca: Cornell UP, 1974.

———. *The Ritual Process: Structure and Anti-Structure*. Chicago: Aldine, 1969.

Whelan, Robert Emmet, Jr. "Hester Prynne's Little Pearl: Sacred and Profane Love." *American Literature* 39 (1967): 488–505.

Yeazell, Ruth Bernard. *The Death and Letters of Alice James*. Berkeley: U of California P, 1981.

NINA BAYM

Revisiting Hawthorne's Feminism†

In this essay I swim against the tide to argue—again—for Hawthorne as a feminist writer from *The Scarlet Letter* onward. I argued this in essays published throughout the 1970s and 1980s, as well as in *The Shape of Hawthorne's Career* (1976). My readings have been contested, debated, revised, extended; the idea of Hawthorne as a feminist has been overwhelmingly rejected. In what follows I'll describe my original positions, summarize the important critical challenges to

† From the *Nathaniel Hawthorne Review* 30 (Spring & Fall 2004), 32–55. Reprinted by permission of the author. Page numbers in square brackets refer to this Norton Critical Edition.

them, and finally—in view of these challenges—propose the idea of a feminist Hawthorne anew.

* * *

The Shape of Hawthorne's Career pointed to a significant change in Hawthorne's thematic emphasis around the time of *Mosses from an Old Manse* (1846). He began publishing as a Neoclassicist strongly critical of non-conforming individualism, became increasingly Romantic during the 1840s, and emerged with *The Scarlet Letter* into full daylight as a partisan of his outcast heroine, Hester Prynne. The character type faulted by the Neoclassicist, however, did not now earn the approval of the Romanticist. That Hester was a woman made all the difference. With one exception (Catharine in "The Gentle Boy"), the denigrated Romantic characters had been men. The later, admired Romantic characters were women.

Guided by my perception of this important distinction, I made several claims about Hawthorne and women characters, about Hawthorne and the feminine (defining the feminine as an assemblage of traits associated with persons socially identified as women), and about Hawthorne and feminism. I proposed that as the fiction increasingly centered on sympathetic women characters struggling against a murderous male authority, Hawthorne frequently contrasted such characters to an alternative female type. This structure deployed the traditional literary contrast between "dark" and "fair" ladies. I called the dark lady a "real" woman and the fair lady a "social myth" invented by patriarchal culture to discipline "real" women; I proposed that real women embodied creative force while fair women, if favored by men, destroyed not only the women they had bested but also the men who chose them. I also suggested that Hawthorne linked artistic creativity, including his own, with traits that might be fairly called "feminine" because they were represented by these sympathetic, embattled "real" women as natural expressions of their womanhood. I further proposed in two essays—"Hawthorne's Women" (1971) and "Thwarted Nature" (1982)—that, because Hawthorne represented women simultaneously as embodiments of misogynistic male fantasies about women and as "real" women struggling against these fantasies, it was appropriate to call him a feminist.

I excepted Hawthorne from feminist arguments that the canonized authors were patriarchal sexists, even though it was he who infamously referred to literary women as a "d——d mob of scribbling women." No true patriarch, I thought, could have invented Hester. In proposing Hester as the novel's protagonist—initially in "Passion and Authority" (1970)—I was not offering a new reading but reviving an approach that had languished under Perry Miller's powerful influence. The "Miller" line understood Hawthorne to be writing about Puritan theology from a perspective close to the Puritans themselves, and criticizing his own culture for foolish optimism about human nature. This approach assumed that Arthur Dimmesdale was *The Scarlet Letter*'s protagonist. If *The Scarlet Letter* retold Genesis, Hester was the temptress Eve; if it retold Puritan history, she was Anne Hutchinson.

Yes, Hawthorne began *The Scarlet Letter* with reference to "the sainted Ann Hutchinson"; but that was irony, as recourse to his early, uncollected "Mrs. Hutchinson" (1830) made clear. No matter that twenty years had elapsed between the works; Hester was no more than a sexual and doctrinal temptress whose scheming led poor Arthur Dimmesdale, the novel's beset hero, astray.

Having interpreted the novel as a story about Hester (an interpretation which, no matter how my feminist angle has been rejected, is now standard in discussions of the novel), I then reread "The Custom-House" as an autobiographical allegory about a blocked artist breaking out by identifying himself with an imaginary, stigmatized woman ("The Romantic Malgré Lui," 1973). When "Hawthorne" wanders into the upper floor of the Custom-House, finds the letter, puts it on his chest, and feels it burn, he is saying in several senses, "this is my character." He associates the creative flood that sweeps him out of the Custom-House backwater with the life force inhering in this admirable woman. For, as the novel unfolds, the letter, intended by the Authorities to signify harsh but just condemnation, is made by Hester to signify something entirely different—able, admirable. From this perspective, I thought at the time, the novel's feminism was self-evident.

I interpreted Dimmesdale as Hester's foil—weak, orthodox, conventional—and as her temptation rather than she his. As an actor in his own story, Dimmesdale, like so many other Hawthorne male characters, rejects the woman at his own cost as well as hers. In *The Scarlet Letter*, oppression or rejection of women, rather than surrender to them, led to male downfall. This motif, incipient in earlier stories like "Young Goodman Brown" (1835) and "The Minister's Black Veil" (1836), became dominant in the 1840s; this change gave Hawthorne's career its "shape."

How to explain this development? Between 1841 and 1846 he encountered the Transcendentalists via his eight-month sojourn at Brook Farm and several years in Concord. He came into close contact with Romantic ideas as they were vividly articulated by living people. The iconoclastic idealists who became his friends—Thoreau, Fuller, Emerson—had an intellectual vigor and courage he could not help but admire. These provocations coincided with his marriage. They also coincided with his recognition that New England literary culture was itself moving in a more liberal direction.

Then, in 1849, having returned to Salem three years earlier to work in a dull job secured through political patronage, he suffered two bereavements. He lost this boring yet remunerative occupation when his party lost the elections, and his mother died. According to Sophia, Hawthorne's wife, and also according to Hawthorne's courtship letters, his mother was reclusive and remote. Julian Hawthorne's biography of his parents affirmed the characterization; but Hawthorne's journals, along with his letters to his mother and sisters, testify to her strong and much-loved presence. Her loss was shattering. In "Hawthorne and His Mother" (1982) I proposed that this death, in complex ways, might have motivated *The Scarlet Letter*. I imagined

Hester as a version of the mother, and the novel as allying with her—she who had always supported his literary ambitions—rather than with the stultifying, untrustworthy authority of Uncle Sam's Custom-House.

* * *

Challenges to these readings have countered that Hawthorne's use of the feminine was always in the service of masculinity issues, that he viewed assertive or aggressive or rebellious women as threats to masculinity; that his inevitable punishing or containing of truant women demonstrated deep hostility to them and a profoundly conservative view of their proper place; that this penalizing reflected discomfort over the ongoing feminization of the literary profession; that women characters are tools of the state, upholding or instilling conservative, bourgeois values, "naturalizing" the capitalist agenda by a politics of domesticity. These points recur and overlap throughout six critical approaches, of which I now offer representative examples: Puritan/traditionalist, masculinity, gay/queer, feminist, political, and biographical studies.

Puritan/traditionalist criticism, masculinity studies, and gay/queer studies converge in Hawthorne studies by agreeing that men are central and women ancillary in his writings. Traditionalist studies of Hawthorne took the male center for granted; Baym (as I will now call myself) questioned this. Traditional critics now started insisting that, yes, Hawthorne's main characters were, indeed, male. Michael Colacurcio's "Woman's Own Choice" (1985) reads *The Scarlet Letter* as Dimmesdale's overcoming Hester's literalist temptation. Saying that "the fiercely logical structure of *The Scarlet Letter* points to Dimmesdale as the indubitable center of literary organization" (119), that "structural analysis . . . must always privilege Dimmesdale" (133), Colacurcio thinks Hester's choice of "a human lover" rather than "the figure of salvation in covenant" (Dimmesdale's choice) demonstrates her female incapacity for abstract thought. When her moment to choose comes, "she passionately chooses the literal. To which she almost converts even Dimmesdale" (124). Dimmesdale, however, demonstrates his manhood and admirable orthodoxy by rejecting her temptation.

Masculinity studies and gay/queer studies also focus on men. Masculinity critics identify "feminine" tendencies in the self or the culture, and consider how masculinity is defined as their opposite. Some critics in this mode—e.g., Leland S. Person, who writes that Coverdale, Kenyon, and Dimmesdale briefly "enjoy creative relationships with women before repressing the self-creative impulse within themselves which the woman evokes" (115)—take the Baym-like position that men need the feminine; others, like T. Walter Herbert (*Dearest Beloved*) and David Leverenz, argue that rejecting women is (unfortunately) necessary for men dedicated to Jacksonian masculinity. Leverenz writes: "story after story presents conventional manliness as aggressive, insensitive, and murderously dominant" (231); "as male

rivalry takes center stage, the narrators disengage from their heroines.
. . . They put up a fog of ambiguities, ironies, self-consciousness, and
multiple points of view to screen their covert participation in the
men's struggle for narcissistic self-empowering" (246–47). Some critics propose that the biographical Hawthorne is uncomfortable about
operating in an increasingly feminine profession (the opposite of
Baym's point that a good male artist has to accept the inner feminine).
Millicent Bell observes that "his authorial mode was that of the feminized male author who knows he has entered a female world in becoming a writer rather than a businessman or politician" (15).
Kenneth Egan proposes that Hawthorne made Hester an adulteress
specifically to express the author's sense that to be a male writer in his
culture "was necessarily to be an adulteress or feminized adulterer of
the truth" (41). James D. Wallace says that Hawthorne's hostile reaction to women writers originates in his uneasy identification with
them. Herbert brings the lessons of *The Scarlet Letter* home to men:
"Men whose manhood compels them to hate what they conceive as
the womanhood in them lead psychic lives that are characterized by a
continuous internal assault that is gendered male-on-female. . . .
[Men] may find inspiration in Hester, as we seek to rework the manhood that dooms us to pornographic enchantments and cripples our
capacity for intimacy with real women" ("Pornographic," 116, 119).

Gay/queer criticism is male-centered by definition. Homosocial and
homoerotic moments are excavated and attributed either to Hawthorne's own suppressed sexual inclinations or to the sublimated,
affect-laden idealizations of male-male relationships in antebellum
culture. Robert K. Martin points to "the dynamics of male relationship" in *The Scarlet Letter* and *The Blithedale Romance*—noting for
example the "extraordinarily erotic moment" when Chillingworth half-
undresses the sleeping Dimmesdale, and claiming that Coverdale's
disquisitions on polymorphous sexuality at Blithedale register his attraction to Hollingsworth (132). Lauren Berlant also finds Coverdale's
attraction to Hollingsworth central in *The Blithedale Romance* ("Fantasies"). Scott S. Derrick identifies the erotic connection between
Dimmesdale and Chillingworth as the affective center of *The Scarlet
Letter*; Leverenz writes, "the cuckold and the lover rise together to an
all-male paradise, while Hester mutely returns to Boston" (275).
Karen L. Kilcup argues that the relationship of author to reader in
Hawthorne's work is erotically charged and—supposing that Hawthorne imagines his reader as male—specifically homoerotic.

Although academic feminism is rife with internal dissention, most
self-identified Hawthorne feminists agree in rejecting Baym's readings.
Stressing the way Hawthorne inevitably punishes and/or silences unconventional women, they find his plots antifeminist, reinforcing a
culturally conservative agenda, and testimony to authorial misogyny. A
preponderance of feminist criticism thinks Hawthorne felt threatened
by emergent feminism, female activism, female sexuality, and women
writers—in fact, by any sign of women's desire to improve their lot or

determine their own lives. For this group, Hawthorne's narratorial hand-wringing over the intractability of social institutions and the misery of women is a sentimental sham.

The first scholar to make this argument was probably Judith Fetterley, who sees "The Birth-mark" as illustration of "the great American dream of eliminating women" (24) [717]. Louise DeSalvo concedes that Hawthorne "portrayed, with superb accuracy, the condition of women in the nineteenth century and the psychological processes of men who could not tolerate the notion of female equality" but decides that because "he shared the misogynistic view of his age, he could not condemn what he saw and drew back from defining the implications, for society, of what he so astutely observed about the reality of women's lives" (121–22). Barbara Bardes and Suzanne Gossett use *The Blithedale Romance* and *The Scarlet Letter* to observe that while Hawthorne's novels reveal "distrust of almost anyone with the power of speech," he was especially wary of "women with 'tongues' because he connected women's public speech with sexual exposure and expression" (59). Joyce W. Warren finds him especially severe on strong women, who "are never allowed to pursue what might seem to be the implications of their characters; they do not become heroic leaders or independent public figures. . . . This hesitation is owing in part to Hawthorne's belief in a conventional image of feminine behavior" (189). Jean Yellin thinks *The Scarlet Letter* "seriously considers the new feminist definitions of womanhood and, rejecting them, replicates traditional imagery and endorses patriarchal notions" (126). Amy Schrager Lang complains about Hester's unfeminist subsidence into a "vague politics of patience and inaction" (191).

More recently, Jamie Barlowe's "Rereading Women" (1997) and follow-up *Scarlet Mob* (2002) coins the term "Hester Prynnism" to denote antifeminist silencing and ignoring of women's voices, of which the first and most egregious practitioner was Hawthorne himself. Barlowe idealizes the Hester of Roland Joffé's 1995 film; she sees Joffé's plot—in which Hester spends a lot of time naked, Dimmesdale professes undying love, and the couple (with Pearl recently born rather than seven years old) successfully run off together—as a feminist way to tell Hester's story. Although the idea of an entirely different Hester in an entirely different narrative (along with an entirely different Dimmesdale) may seem bizarre, and although not every feminist will share Barlowe's idea of feminism, most feminist criticism does fantasize a different ending to Hester's story. Sandra Tomc, invoking Hawthorne's "notoriously conservative ideas about women [and] feminism," agrees that Hawthorne "repudiates both his heroine and the genre [of seduction novel] that inspired her" (469, 472). Todd Onderdonk imputes an obsession with sexual purity to Hawthorne deriving from the author's conviction that women have only one "necessary function—motherhood" (97).

Political, new-historical, and ideological critics perceive Hawthorne's women as servants of bourgeois capitalism. Gendered spheres, here, are key to the consolidation of middle-class, capitalist culture in Hawthorne's era; women were pressed into bourgeois service by persuading them that their natural abilities suit them for the domestic sphere, where they are cherished and protected. And Hawthorne went along with this project, which relies heavily on what such critics consider sentimental hocus-pocus. Michael Davitt Bell calls sentimentalism "a medium of psychological repression and social control" that, in his view, the conservative Hawthorne deployed against women's rights and other movements for social change (191). Gillian Brown argues that a female domestic subculture "based on self-denial and collectivity—the ethos of sympathy customarily and disparagingly called sentimentalism" (6)—has not produced "an antithetical model of selfhood" but only further domesticated "an already domesticated selfhood. . . . Far from an account of the female subject, domesticity signifies a feminization of selfhood in service to an individualism most available to (white) men" (7). The novel most suited to this approach is *The House of the Seven Gables*; but other novels also figure. Lori Merish, for example, reads *The Blithedale Romance* as an exposure of "the extent to which the bourgeois ideology of romantic love and consensual familial ties produces new species of patriarchal power, reconfiguring, rather than undermining, women's construction as property" (172). Ellen Weinauer says that "Despite his effort to situate himself in an alternative and indeed antipatriarchal history, *The Scarlet Letter* taken as a whole suggests that . . . Hawthorne needs the possessed female body" (107) [386].

Psychologizing this political class-and-gender analysis, Joel Pfister thinks Hawthorne's plots about "the feminization of women" (8) reflect and contribute to a middle-class discourse of sexuality. Still, Pfister says that Hawthorne recognizes the artificiality of this discourse: he is "product, agent, and critic of an emerging middle-class interiority, and is aware that his participation in reproducing the forms of subjectivity of his class is political" (183). Herbert (*Dearest Beloved*) interweaves Hawthorne's fiction with family letters to show how internalized social ideas of true woman and manly man are experienced as authentic. He develops a poignant portrait of a Sophia who has violently disciplined herself to become the woman Nathaniel required as the condition of his adoration. And he shows a Nathaniel imprisoned in turn by the surveillance of the monstrous woman he created. According to Herbert, this paradigm implicates the entire culture; the Hawthornes "vividly exemplified the domestic ideal of family relations that became dominant in the early nineteenth century" (xvi). For Herbert, Hawthorne is both participant and critic of the represented scene, seeking to "contain his material within the rhetoric of the domestic ideal, even as he lays open the dilemmas intrinsic to that ideal" (199).

Three important ideological readings make Hester into a problem or opportunity for the state. Sacvan Bercovitch reads Hester's return to Boston and resumption of the letter as the novel's most important event. In a "woman's own choice" quite unlike Colacurcio's, Hester elects "to become the agent of her own domestication" (11); "in the most carefully prepared-for reversal in classic American literature, Hester herself imposes the symbol" (92). Her choice, he says, illustrates the workings of liberal capitalism, a political form "designed to make subjectivity the primary agency of change while keeping the subject under control," a double function accomplished "by representing interpretation as multiplicity flowing naturally into consensus" (23–24). Where Bercovitch finds Hester a type of the citizen in her free acceptance of social control, Berlant describes her citizen type less forgivingly as a "mutual articulation of woman, privacy, and political submission" (*Anatomy*, 106) and proposes that "woman" is a "manifest public problem of law and order" that is solved by containment (108). Brook Thomas likens Hester's final community of women to Habermas's public sphere, a zone of independent activity that guarantees the state's democratic functioning. Curiously, of these three readings only Berlant makes a point of Hester's gender, and even she perceives "the male body" (Dimmesdale's male body) as "the major stress point in the social order" (115).

All lines of criticism fret over Hawthorne's self-awareness. Even Bercovitch, in a troubled and troubling footnote, remarks that Hawthorne, not liberal culture, ultimately "compels Hester to resume the A"; this "sense of compulsion . . . adds a discordant note to Hawthorne's orchestration of pluralist points of view" (157). For if Hawthorne knew about the woman-centered reform initiatives in antebellum culture, if he knew well some of the women actively involved in such efforts, if he knew that the literary market he sought to enter and dominate was filled with women authors, then it becomes likely that his strategies of plot containment represent his own intentions rather unthinkingly reproducing social platitudes. Hawthorne was well acquainted with, even close to, many women who lived undomestic lives but neither killed themselves nor kept silent. He knew women scholars, writers, artists, and activists: among others, Elizabeth Peabody, Mary Peabody Mann, Sarah Josepha Hale, Grace Greenwood, and, perhaps above all, Margaret Fuller. Thomas R. Mitchell has written compellingly about traces of Fuller in Hawthorne's writing; he sees her in Hester, Zenobia, and Miriam. He finds sentences in *The Scarlet Letter* appropriating "The Great Lawsuit" almost verbatim. It would seem to follow that if he created powerful women only to silence them, he did so as a way of rejecting the signs of the times that he saw all around him.

* * *

To suggest a feminist Hawthorne in the face of all this criticism is foolhardy. Nevertheless, I will give it a try. I grant at the outset—a point that criticism usually ignores, perhaps because it's so obvious— that he stopped with white American women resident in New England, presumably heterosexual, of English descent. Hawthorne knew his own limits in this regard; when he wrote "women this" and "men that," he asked to be understood as an interpreter of New England life and character, not the universe. I grant too that if a feminist position must be manifested by plots wherein women live happily ever after on their own terms, Hawthorne fails. Happy endings on such terms are impossible in his novels—men are not what women imagine. One might argue that, given the kind of man Dimmesdale is, *The Scarlet Letter* is far more feminist for refusing the bogus finale of a happy escape than had it allowed the two (three, actually) to make their getaway. The mismatch between women's illusions and the realities of male character is a leading motif in the later romances.

Hawthorne's observation that smart women often make foolish choices is not erroneous; the problem is still with us. There are, of course, other imaginable endings than a happy marriage; much feminist writing today exists to show how women might get along without men (or, more strategically, to show what social reforms are necessary so that women can actually get along without men). In which case, since Hawthorne's work exactly fits this description, his feminism should be obvious. Smart, independent women like Hester, Zenobia, and Miriam are his heroines in *The Scarlet Letter, The Blithedale Romance*, and *The Marble Faun*. But even the more conventional women—Phoebe, Priscilla, and Hilda, not to mention the amazing Hepzibah, who deserves much more careful appraisal than I have space for here—are women used to living alone and fending for themselves.

They can and do get along without men, but they would prefer not to. No question: this author is preoccupied with the heterosexual couple and the obstacles that make of a supposedly fulfilling social form something so fraught with misery. Why this is so, and what to do about it, are questions his plots repeatedly ask. But if his plots do not—cannot—lead to happy outcomes in a conventional romantic sense, neither do they end in utter social futility. They offer limited, incremental change, although often at a great cost to the agent of such change.

By the time he wrote *The Scarlet Letter* Hawthorne had become aware of and deeply involved in ideas about women's grievances as they were expressed by articulate women he knew, especially Margaret Fuller. He understood that, since he had chosen to write fiction, many if not most of his readers would be women; he anticipated their thoughtful familiarity with these ideas. Virtually alone among male authors of his generation, he made space for feminist analysis in his fiction. Hester is made to introduce feminist ideas at least twice in *The Scarlet Letter*: once in chapter 13, where, brooding over the situation of woman, she wonders whether existence was "worth accepting, even to the happiest among them" (165) [108], and again in chapter 24, where she tells sorrowful women about her hope for a new truth that would "establish the whole relation between man and woman on a surer ground of mutual happiness" (263) [166].

The subject runs constantly through *The Blithedale Romance*, especially in chapter 14, where Zenobia insists that "when my sex shall achieve its rights, there will be ten eloquent women, where there is now one eloquent man" and goes on to say that "thus far, no woman in the world has ever once spoken out her whole heart and her whole mind! The mistrust and disapproval of the vast bulk of society throttles us, as with two gigantic hands at our throats!" (120). True, Coverdale attributes "the animosity with which she now took up the general quarrel of women against men" to "Zenobia's inward trouble"—but this is at least to concede that such a quarrel exists. When Coverdale adds that he personally would be happy to give woman "all she asks, and add a great deal more, which she will not be the party to demand, but men, if they were generous and wise, would grant of their own free motion" (121), he is saying men are neither generous nor wise. Hollingsworth's behavior (and his own) bear this out.

Feminist ideas typical of Hawthorne's era also circulate through *The Marble Faun*, as in chapter 13, when Miriam tells Kenyon that men wrongly believe "Nature has made women especially prone to throw their whole being into what is technically called Love. We have, to say the least, no more necessity for it than yourselves—only, we have nothing else to do with our hearts. . . . I can think of many women, distinguished in art, literature, and science—and multitudes whose hearts and minds find good employment in less ostentatious ways— who lead high, lonely lives, and are conscious of no sacrifice, so far as your sex is concerned" (121). Miriam's reference to distinguished professional women, which Kenyon does not contest, alludes to a situation that few male authors of Hawthorne's day recognized in print.

Certainly, Hawthorne's novels point to errors that reform-minded women typically make—mainly through lack of self-understanding and unwitting complicity in the conditions they deplore. But unless a feminist perspective requires asserting that women are perfect, his observations might be seen as attempts to intervene on the feminist side. That feminist ideas are uttered by flawed women, that activist women generalize from their own situations, does not invalidate the ideas. The imperfect women who utter feminist sentiments are treated sympathetically and admiringly. They have enormous courage and considerable intellect. Even when defeated, they make things happen. Bercovitch presumes that the liberal polity absorbs Hester's dissent; but I think her resumption of the letter permanently changes her public world. Hawthorne writes: "The scarlet letter ceased to be a stigma which attracted the world's scorn and bitterness, and became a type of something to be sorrowed over, and looked upon with awe, yet with reverence too" (263) [165].

Had Hester never returned, she would have been forgotten. Had she returned and not worn the letter, she would have escaped the letter's meaning without changing it. Returning and wearing the letter when "not the sternest magistrate of that iron period would have imposed it" alters the way the letter is perceived, changes its definition. People look on the letter "with reverence." Hester preaches a model of change involving sudden revelation from a sinless apostle of joy, but she practices a model of slow change brought about by persons visibly scarred by battles fought and ignominy endured. This is not entirely a sentimental outcome, resulting from pity ("sorrowed over"); it is also the outcome of reverence, of awe. Re-entering civil life adorned with the letter by her own choice, Hester moves Puritan Boston from the Dark Ages towards enlightened modernity. Now, a century and a half after *The Scarlet Letter*, popular references to a scarlet letter invariably imply unjust stigmatization. In the wider world, this novel has performed that cultural work.

One concedes that Hester and Hawthorne understand women's plight in reference to intimacy with men. This was the overwhelming focus of feminist reformers of his day, the overwhelming subject of the novel (his chosen genre), and (after all) the overwhelming concern of feminist reformers now. The underlying sources of the difficulty in thinking of a feminist Hawthorne, as I see it now, are his beliefs in such a thing as human nature and, worse still, in essential differences between human nature in the two sexes. The key point is that, for Hawthorne, the age-old, relentless history of male exploitation of women could only be explained as the outgrowth of essential characteristics of human selves.

If the two sexes are essentially different, as I now think Hawthorne thinks they are, then the social change sought by feminism would seem impossible to achieve. But, oddly, Hawthorne's work does not offer these essentialist beliefs as conservative excuses to keep women down. On the contrary, it struggles to plot a way in which, given these "facts" about the human, women may be raised up. His novels are replete with objections against social arrangements that tell so heavily and unjustly against women. I used to think that Hawthorne presented romantic love as a social myth invented to ensnare women, because woman after woman in his texts suffers from what might be called "a broken heart." Passages in the novels seem to support this idea of love as a social myth; for example, Coverdale, at the end of *Blithedale*, laments that "It is nonsense, and a miserable wrong—the result, like so many others, of masculine egotism—that the success or failure of woman's existence should be made to depend wholly on the affections, and on one species of affection; while man has such a multitude of other chances, that this seems but an incident. For its own sake, if it will do no more, the world should throw open all its avenues to the passport of a woman's bleeding heart" (241). But now I notice that this social asymmetry stems from "masculine egotism," not a constructed condition but a fact about men, and see that these sentences argue explicitly for social change.

Hawthorne's point, one might say, is not that essentialism makes social change impossible but that it makes social change impossible unless differences between women and men are taken into account. The slow, uneven pace of social change occupies Hawthorne much in these later works wherein—unlike so much antifeminist rhetoric of his day, of which Hollingsworth's tirade in chapter 14 of *The Blithedale Romance* is a splendid example—inequality of physical strength is unimportant. What matters is the internal difference to which Hollingsworth refers when, after threatening violence against female reformers ("petticoated monstrosities," as he calls them), he says that force is unnecessary because "the heart of true womanhood knows where its own sphere is, and never seeks to stray beyond it" (123). That the heart of womanhood knows its sphere, as Hollingsworth would define it, is repeatedly given the lie in Hawthorne's writings; but that women have more heart than men is something he counts on. In women's excess of heart, compared to men—or in men's deficiency of heart, compared to women—lies the explanation for an asymmetrical culture.

Male egotism and its associated cold-heartedness had been a Hawthorne obsession from far back in his career: "Wakefield" (1835), implicitly in "Young Goodman Brown" (1835) and "The Minister's Black Veil" (1837), "The Man of Adamant" (1837), and "The Shaker Bridal" (1838); on through the 1840s: "Egotism; or, the Bosom Serpent" (1843), "The Birth-mark" (1843), and "Rappaccini's Daughter" (1844). Still prominent in three of the four later romances (the contrast between Hepzibah and Clifford introduces it into *Seven Gables* as well)—these traits are now considered entirely in terms of their meaning for women's lives. In *The Blithedale Romance*, Coverdale's speculations about Hollingsworth in chapter 7—"Sad, indeed, but by no means unusual" that he has mistaken his "terrible egotism" for "an angel of God" (55)—and in chapter 9: "Men who have surrendered themselves to an over-ruling purpose" are almost never able to "recognize the process, by which godlike benevolence has been debased into all-devouring egotism" (70–71)—acquire their significance because of the way this man behaves towards women. In chapter 28, as noted above, he deplores the masculine egotism that makes women's success wholly dependent on love (241). Most memorably, in chapter 14, he interprets Hollingsworth's antifeminist tirade as an

> outrageous affirmation of what struck me as the intensity of masculine egotism. It centred everything in itself, and deprived woman of her very soul, her inexpressible and unfathomable all, to make it a mere incident in the great sum of man. Hollingsworth had boldly uttered what he, and millions of despots like him, really felt. Without intending it, he had disclosed the wellspring of all these troubled waters. (123)

Masculine self-absorption is the source, but it prevails because women lack a corresponding self-absorption. When, rather than rising to Hollingsworth's challenge, Zenobia mildly counters that, if man were "but manly and godlike," woman would be "only too ready to become to him what you say" (124), she demonstrates the other side of the intractable equation. Coverdale, appalled, wonders whether her words express women's "nature" or "the result of ages of compelled degradation" and whether, in either case, it could "be possible ever to redeem them." He does not, however, notice that this meditation has been sparked by his peevish awareness that the women are more attracted to Hollingsworth than to him: "how little did these two women care for me, who had freely conceded all their claims, and a great deal more, out of the fullness of my heart" (124). Hawthorne lets readers see that Coverdale's self-labeled feminism is also exploitative of women; he is not exempt from the situation that he analyzes so cannily.

Nor is Zenobia exempt; her capitulation here puts a feminist conundrum squarely before us. If millions of men behave like Hollingsworth and millions of women behave like Zenobia (and their gendered behavior is reproduced more palely in Coverdale and Priscilla), what can be hoped for? The intransigency of the problem, rather than their weakness of intellect, baffles his women characters. The more acute their minds, the more they recognize the conundrum. When the narrator comments on Hester's meditations, he says: "A woman never overcomes these problems by any exercise of thought. They are not to be solved, or only in one way. If her heart chance to come uppermost, they vanish" (166). This passage has been read as a misogynistic dismissal of female intellectuality. But it can be read to mean, not that women lack intellect, but that nobody can solve these problems by sheer intellectual force, and that a woman happily in love will likely stop worrying about them. Yes, but how many women are happily in love in Hawthorne's world? Too, if unhappiness makes women into reformers, it does the same with men. As Holgrave says, "The world owes all its onward impulse to men ill at ease. The happy man inevitably confines himself within ancient limits" (306–07).

Thus, to say that Hawthorne's women have more heart than his men does not imply that they have less brain. Mind does not unsex a woman; Zenobia is smarter than Hollingsworth, Miriam than Kenyon. Hester leaves Dimmesdale in the dust. True, all that thinking in Hester's case is associated with an apparent loss of beauty, insofar as female beauty means sexual attractiveness to heterosexual men. That Hawthorne might have reconsidered this facile association is inferable from the fact that neither Zenobia nor Miriam is less sexually appealing because of her intellect. With these two later heroines Hawthorne seems to propose that beauty and braininess are different expressions of the same force, a force lacking in the counter-heroines Priscilla and Hilda whose appeal lies in both their physical plainness and intellectual timidity.

But if Hester's thinking makes her less conventionally sexy, it does not make her less loving, and if motherhood is Hawthorne's test for true womanhood, then Hester is a paragon. I read *The Scarlet Letter* as an "antiseduction" novel. The protagonist does not die; she succeeds as a single mother supporting herself and her child and, when her child is grown, becomes a valued and valuable member of the community.

In the plot's unfolding, the significant result of Hester's independent thinking is a profoundly womanly decision (in Hawthorne's terms) to "rescue" Dimmesdale by telling him who Chillingworth is. Thus the forest meeting where Dimmesdale's cold heart triumphs over her warm one, his appeal to the great heart of womanhood effectively seducing Hester for a second time.

Herbert, like other critics, says "Hester has already contrived the plan that she now persuades Arthur to adopt. She wants them to leave the colony" (*Dearest Beloved*, 201). No; she wants *him* to leave the colony. Horrified by Dimmesdale's condition as she sees it in the second scaffold scene, inferring that Chillingworth is somehow to blame, Hester determines first to "meet her former husband"—not her former lover—and "do what might be in her power for the rescue of the victim on whom he had so evidently set his gripe" (167) [109]. "I must reveal the secret," she tells Chillingworth; "what may be the result, I know not" (173) [112]. Chillingworth releases her from her oath of secrecy, freeing her to follow her conscience: "Go thy ways, and deal as thou wilt with yonder man" (174) [113].

As chapter 16 tells us, Hester's one intention is "to make known to Mr. Dimmesdale, at whatever risk of present pain or ulterior consequences, the true character of the man who had crept into his intimacy" (182) [118]. Beyond this she has no plan. Their forest meeting makes her, at last, "fully sensible of the deep injury for which she was responsible to this unhappy man" (192) [124]. No plan already decided on, even if she had one, could possibly be useful in view of what she sees Dimmesdale to be: "She now read his heart more accurately" (193) [124].

Dimmesdale then commandeers the conversation in typical passive-aggressive fashion by pleading for her help: "Be thou strong for me! . . . Advise me what to do" (196) [127]. She answers by counseling him to leave Boston—whether heading west into the forest or east over the ocean—in ringing rhetoric that implies no intention to go with him: "Leave this wreck and ruin here where it hath happened! Meddle no more with it! Begin all anew. . . . The future is yet full of trial and success. There is happiness to be enjoyed! There is good to be done! . . . Up, and away!" (198) [128]. But then Dimmesdale replies, "There is not the strength or courage left me to venture into the wide, strange, difficult world, alone!" and, as the narrator stresses, repeats the word *alone*. Hester hears his unvoiced plea and responds to it: "Thou shalt not go alone!" (198) [128]. In this exchange Dimmesdale manipulates Hester—no doubt sincerely—through a sentimental appeal to (as he put it earlier) the "wondrous strength and generosity of a woman's heart" (68) [50]. Only a woman's heart can be so worked upon.

Dimmesdale's thoughts in this scene are all for himself, Hester's all for him. He is, after all, a true man as she is a true woman. One might suppose that it was always thus for these two—the woman in love with the man, the man in love with himself. Few seduced women get the chance to express the point with more intensity than Zenobia in her great attack on Hollingsworth: "It is all self! . . . Nothing else but self, self, self! . . . I see it now! I am awake, disenchanted, disenthralled! Self, self, self!" (218). Certainly, Hester never approaches this level of feminist rage, even though Dimmesdale's death amounts to yet another disavowal of human love. What Hester achieves through Dimmesdale's death, however, is unique in that it is a loving—that is, womanly—life without a man. It prefigures and registers the eruption of women into the public sphere through various forms of culturally acceptable womanly activity, what historians have come to call "domestic feminism."

Herbert writes that *The Scarlet Letter* "does not work out a solution to the male-on-female sexual abuse that it so pervasively depicts, but in Hester Prynne [Hawthorne] dramatizes the struggle of women to disentangle themselves from this enslavement, and to find lives of independent self-respect, and to define an autonomous sexual selfhood" ("Pornographic," 119). What Herbert calls male-on-female sexual abuse, Hawthorne would call the inequality of egotism versus love; I see no male character in the whole Hawthorne repertory who "loves" a woman the way a woman loves him. However, that Hester is struggling to find a life of independent self-respect is not so clear, still less that she is trying to define an "autonomous sexual selfhood"; on the contrary, Hawthorne proposes, exactly her disregard for self (including, yes, her celibacy) changes the public mind. Because Hester "had no selfish ends, nor lived in any measure for her own profit and enjoyment," people look up to her (263) [165].

This change is not a reversal, but a continuation of what had been happening over the seven years of her earlier sojourn in Boston:

> She was self-ordained a Sister of Mercy; or, we may rather say, the world's heavy hand had so ordained her, when neither the world nor she looked forward to this result. The letter was the symbol of her calling. Such helpfulness was found in her—so much power to do, and power to sympathize—that many people refused to interpret the scarlet A by its original signification. They said that it meant Able; so strong was Hester Prynne, with a woman's strength. (161) [105–06]

Pearl, too, is crucial to understanding Hester as a loving woman in the less heterosexualized sense that Hawthorne represents in *The Scarlet Letter*. Much has been written about Pearl as her mother's disciplinarian, the externalization of her mother's sin, and so on (e.g., Emily Budick, Franny Nudelman). But Pearl is also a human person, somebody for Hester to love, her child. The quiet and outwardly compliant Hester explodes furiously when the Governor threatens to take Pearl from her. "Hester caught hold of Pearl, and drew her forcibly into her arms, confronting the old Puritan magistrate with almost a fierce expression. Alone in the world, cast off by it, and with this sole treasure to keep her heart alive, she felt that she possessed indefeasible rights against the world, and was ready to defend them to the death. . . . 'Ye shall not take her! I will die first!' " To Dimmesdale she cries out, "thou knowest what is in my heart, and what are a mother's rights, and how much the stronger they are, when that mother has but her child and the scarlet letter! Look thou to it! I will not lose the child! Look to it!" (113) [76].

Leaving the governor's hall, her mother's rights confirmed, Hester declines Mistress Hibbens's invitation to a witches' gathering. "I must tarry at home, and keep watch over my little Pearl. Had they taken her from me, I would willingly have gone with thee into the forest, and signed my name in the Black Man's book too, and that with mine own blood!" (117) [79]. Had Pearl been taken from her, Hester would have embraced her social identity as a bad woman; Pearl keeps Hester's loving heart—her identity as a good woman—alive. She thinks, the narrator reports: "How strange, indeed! Man had marked this woman's sin by a scarlet letter. . . . God, as a direct consequence of the sin which man thus punished, had given her a lovely child, whose place was on that same dishonored bosom, to connect her parent for ever with the race and descent of mortals, and to be finally a blessed soul in heaven!" (89) [61]. Not incidentally, that same dishonored bosom is where people in extreme situations come over time to rest: "Hester's nature showed itself warm and rich; a well-spring of human tenderness, unfailing to every real demand, and inexhaustible by the largest. Her breast, with its badge of shame, was but the softer pillow for the head that needed one" (162) [105].

Hester's character cannot be explained through allusions to ideology or social expectations. If anything, the course of her life shows that ideology and social expectations should have made her a very different person from the one she is. As a seduced ingénue, she should have died; as an evil temptress, she should have recanted, gone mad, or been murdered by the mob. Instead, she survives as love's incarnation. Yet, or because of this, she does not find happiness with one man. A new model of love between woman and man is needed, a new kind of couple—"sacred love" Hawthorne calls it at the novel's end (263) [166]. If only a love of this sort can guarantee mutual happiness between men and women, only a love like this could underpin a society of equals that might supersede present-day exploitation. As long as there are two sexes in the world, a just and humane polity must perceive each as equal to the other. But the very difference between the sexes that demands better forms of human intimacy also impedes their realization.

Awareness of the recalcitrant reality of human nature occupies Hester's meditations on reconstructing the social system, which include the tasks—in order—of tearing down society and rebuilding it, altering what in men is either their "very nature or its long hereditary habit, which has become like nature"; and finally producing, somehow, a "still mightier change" in woman herself—a change "in which, perhaps, the ethereal essence, wherein she has her truest life, will be found to have evaporated" (165–66) [108]. This "ethereal essence" is her capacity of loving. Should that be destroyed, then the social formation of which Hester dreams is an impossibility, because it is grounded in exactly that love, the only counter to male self-love. The "whole new truth," the "coming revelation" of which Hester later speaks (263) [166], would then be beyond human reach.

What, then, is to be done? The only possible changes Hawthorne can imagine—and he does imagine them—are palliative and far from romantic. Society can begin to compensate for the trials and consequences of woman's greater heart. Women's lot can be eased; they can be helped rather than punished; their humanity can be affirmed by

recognizing their equality with men, their intellects respected, possibilities opened for them other than the domesticity that has failed
them. Above all, perhaps, the institution of marriage needs to be freely
elected; neither men nor women should be required to marry. *The
Scarlet Letter, The Blithedale Romance,* and *The Marble Faun* all make
space for emancipated female rhetoric, place transgressing women at
the center, insist on women's equality with men, and deny the universal applicability of domestic ideals. But none imagines different men
and different women from the ones Hawthorne believes people foun-
dationally are, or opportunistically describes social outcomes that the
author thinks cannot possibly come to pass.

WORKS CITED

Bardes, Barbara, and Suzanne Gossett. *Declarations of Independence: Women and Political Power in Nineteenth-Century American Fiction.* New Brunswick: Rutgers UP, 1990.

Barlowe, Jamie. "Rereading Women: Hester Prynne-ism and the Scarlet Mob of Scribblers." *American Literary History* 9 (1997): 197–225.

———. *The Scarlet Mob of Scribblers: Rereading Hester Prynne.* Carbondale: Southern Illinois UP, 2000.

Baym, Nina. *The Shape of Hawthorne's Career.* Ithaca and London: Cornell UP, 1976.

———. "Passion and Authority in The Scarlet Letter." *The New England Quarterly* 43 (1970): 209–30.

———. "Hawthorne's Women: The Tyranny of Social Myths." *Centennial Review* 15 (1971): 250–72.

———. "The Romantic Malgré Lui: Hawthorne in the Custom-House." *ESQ* 19 (1973): 14–25.

———. "Thwarted Nature: Nathaniel Hawthorne as Feminist." In *American Novelists Revisited: Essays in Feminist Criticism* Ed. Fritz Fleischmann. Boston: G. K. Hall, 1982, 58–77.

———. "Nathaniel Hawthorne and His Mother: A Biographical Speculation." *American Literature* 54 (1982): 1–27.

Bell, Michael Davitt. *The Development of American Romance: The Sacrifice of Relation.* Chicago: U of Chicago P, 1980.

Bell, Millicent, "Introduction." *New Essays on Hawthorne's Major Tales.* New York: Cambridge UP, 1993.

Bercovitch, Sacvan. *The Office of the Scarlet Letter.* Baltimore: The Johns Hopkins UP, 1991.

Berlant, Lauren. "Fantasies of Utopia in The Blithedale Romance." *American Literary History* 1 (1989): 30–62.

———. *The Anatomy of National Fantasy.* Chicago: U of Chicago P, 1991.

Brown, Gillian. *Domestic Individualism: Imagining Self in Nineteenth-Century America.* Berkeley: U of California P, 1990.

Budick, Emily Miller. *Engendering Romance: Women Writers and the Hawthorne Tradition, 1850–1990.* New Haven: Yale UP, 1994.

Colacurcio, Michael J. " 'The Woman's Own Choice': Sex, Metaphor, and the Puritan 'Sources' of *The Scarlet Letter.*" In *New Essays on* The Scarlet Letter. Ed. Colacurcio. New York: Cambridge UP, 1985, 101–36.

Derrick, Scott S. " 'A Curious Subject of Observation and Inquiry': Homoeroticism, the Body, and Authorship in Hawthorne's *The Scarlet Letter.*" *Novel* 28 (1995): 308–26.

DeSalvo, Louise. *Nathaniel Hawthorne.* Atlantic Highlands, NJ: Humanities Press International, 1987.

Egan, Ken. "The Adulteress in the Market-Place: Hawthorne and *The Scarlet Letter.*" *Studies in the Novel* 27 (1995): 26–41.

Fetterley, Judith. *The Resisting Reader: A Feminist Approach to American Fiction.* Bloomington: Indiana UP, 1978.

Hawthorne, Nathaniel. *The Scarlet Letter.* Vol. 1 of the *Centenary Edition of the Works of Nathaniel Hawthorne.* Ohio State UP, 1962.

———. *The House of the Seven Gables.* Vol. 2 of the *Centenary Edition of the Works of Nathaniel Hawthorne.* Ohio State UP, 1965.

———. *The Blithedale Romance.* Vol. 3 of the *Centenary Edition of the Works of Nathaniel Hawthorne.* Ohio State UP, 1964.

———. *The Marble Faun.* Vol. 4 of the *Centenary Edition of the Works of Nathaniel Hawthorne.* Ohio State UP, 1968.

Herbert, T. Walter. *Dearest Beloved: The Hawthornes and the Making of the Middle-Class Family.* Berkeley: U of California P, 1993.

———. "Pornographic Manhood and *The Scarlet Letter.*" *Studies in American Fiction* 29 (2001): 113–20.

Kilcup, Karen L. " 'Ourself behind Ourself, Concealed': The Homoerotics of Reading in *The Scarlet Letter*." *ESQ* 42 (1996): 1–28.

Lang, Amy Schrager. *Prophetic Woman: Anne Hutchinson and the Problem of Dissent in the Literature of New England*. Berkeley: U of California P, 1987.

Leverenz, David. *Manhood and the American Renaissance*. Ithaca: Cornell UP, 1989.

Martin, Robert K. "Hester Prynne, *C'est Moi*: Nathaniel Hawthorne and the Anxieties of Gender." In *Engendering Men: The Question of Male Feminist Criticism*. Ed. Joseph A. Boone and Michael Cadden. New York: Routledge, 1990, 122–39, 304–306.

Merish, Lori. *Sentimental Materialism: Gender, Commodity Culture, and Nineteenth-Century American Literature*. Durham: Duke UP, 2000.

Mitchell, Thomas R. *Hawthorne's Fuller Mystery*. Amherst: U of Massachusetts P, 1998.

Nudelman, Franny. " 'Emblem and Product of Sin': The Poisoned Child in *The Scarlet Letter* and Domestic Advice Literature." *Yale Journal of Criticism* 10 (1997): 193–213.

Onderdonk, Todd. "The Marble Mothers: Hawthorne's Iconographies of the Feminine." *Studies in American Fiction* 31 (2003): 73–100.

Person, Leland S. *Aesthetic Headaches: Women and a Masculine Poetics in Poe, Melville, and Hawthorne*. Athens: U of Georgia P, 1988.

Pfister, Joel. *The Production of Personal Life: Class, Gender, and the Psychological in Hawthorne's Fiction*. Stanford: Stanford UP, 1991.

Thomas, Brook. "Citizen Hester: *The Scarlet Letter* as Civic Myth." *American Literary History* 13 (2001): 181–211.

Tomc, Sandra. "A Change of Art: Hester, Hawthorne, and the Service of Love." *Nineteenth-Century Literature* 56 (2002): 466–94.

Wallace, James D. "Hawthorne and the Scribbling Women Reconsidered." *American Literature* 62 (1990): 201–22.

Warren, Joyce W. *The American Narcissus: Individualism and Women in Nineteenth-Century American Fiction*. New Brunswick: Rutgers UP, 1984.

Weinauer, Ellen. "Considering Possession in *The Scarlet Letter*." *Studies in American Fiction* 29 (2001): 93–112.

Yellin, Jean Fagan. *Women and Sisters: The Antislavery Feminists in American Culture*. New Haven: Yale UP, 1989.

BETHANY REID

Narrative of the Captivity and Redemption of Roger Prynne: Rereading *The Scarlet Letter*†

Pearl's lack of a father lies at the heart of *The Scarlet Letter*. It is not surprising, then, that many scholars find *The Scarlet Letter* resolved when Pearl's biological father, the minister Arthur Dimmesdale, publicly acknowledges her. My reading differs. One effect of Pearl's illegitimacy, her fatherlessness, is that it leaves her available to claims from numerous potential fathers. Her existence is threatened by her unknown biological father as well as by an invisible heavenly father (an alternative she finds especially appalling). The Puritan elder John Wilson suggests a host of fathers for little Pearl, remarking to Chillingworth, "every good Christian man hath a title to show a father's kindness towards the poor, deserted babe."[1] "I am Mother's child" (76) [74], Pearl argues, but because fatherlessness and its inherent result, a vaguely menacing multiplicity of fathers, was a problem in Hawthorne's life as well, I propose that considering *The Scarlet Letter* in light of Hawthorne's biography creates an opportunity to explore

---

† From *Studies in the Novel* 33 (Fall 2001): 247–67. Copyright © 2001 by the University of North Texas. Reprinted by permission of the publisher. Page numbers in square brackets refer to this Norton Critical Edition.

1. Nathaniel Hawthorne, *The Scarlet Letter*, Norton Critical Edition (New York: W. W. Norton and Company, 1988), 80 [78].

Pearl's relationship to her mother's husband, Roger Chillingworth, and changes the way we understand the novel's apparent resolution.

A scene near the novel's conclusion clarifies for me the significance of the collapse of Hawthorne's biography (his lack of a father combined with multiple father figures) into story (Pearl's lack of a father combined with multiple potential father figures). It is Election Day and, as Hester, Pearl, Dimmesdale, and Chillingworth all pass through or linger in the marketplace, a "shipmaster" appears (158) [149]. Because we know that Hawthorne's father, Nathaniel Hathorne, was a ship captain who died away at sea when the future author was not yet four years old, we can understand the shipmaster of *The Scarlet Letter* to be a revenant, a ghost speaking out of Hawthorne's personal past. Additionally, notice that Hawthorne's substitution of "shipmaster" for the more commonly used "ship captain" (his father's title) plays on Chillingworth's lost name of "Master Prynne"—something I will bring out more fully. Like a long absent father, the shipmaster is captivated by Pearl and grabs for her, trying to "snatch a kiss" (165) [155]. He fails: "Finding it as impossible to touch her as to catch a humming-bird in the air, he took from his hat the gold chain that was twisted about it, and threw it to the child. Pearl immediately twined it around her neck and waist, with such happy skill, that, once seen there, it became a part of her, and it was difficult to imagine her without it" (165–66) [155]. This shipmaster can no more touch her than can a dead father touch a living child. What he can do, as this passage underscores, is invest Pearl with his possession—an improvisation that Chillingworth will repeat.

Captain Nathaniel Hathorne left an insubstantial material inheritance to his family. A gun and a ship's log were saved for Nathaniel, but the legacy was, largely, impoverishment, with the result that his widow, the former Elizabeth Manning, was forced to live off her family. His Grandfather Manning, however, did eventually leave Nathaniel Hawthorne an inheritance, with which Hawthorne began the highly mythologized internship writing in his mother's attic. The psychological drama suggested by these details adds symbolic weight to my reading of the shipmaster scene. Pearl's gold chain is ostensibly precious while highly ambivalent. Symbolizing wealth, the gold chain also symbolizes bondage—a perverse though apt metaphor for inheritance. "[T]wined . . . around her neck" (166) [155], the gold chain is like a hangman's noose that may have threatened Hester, and it is like an iron chain that oppresses a slave or drags a body to the ocean floor. The connection between the shipmaster and his gold chain and Chillingworth, AKA Master Prynne, tightens when the shipmaster makes Pearl the bearer of a message for her mother from "the black-a-visaged, hump-shouldered old doctor." For most readers of the novel, this gesture is ominous. When we invest the shipmaster with the presence of Hawthorne's dead ship-captain father, we see that Hawthorne has subverted a more obvious equation between biological fathers (his and Pearl's). He draws out the menace of being fathered by a spectre.

Literal or legal illegitimacy is Pearl's special challenge, but figurative illegitimacy—which I claim as Hawthorne's special burden—pervades each characterization in the novel; thus, innumerable scholars have been able to demonstrate how Dimmesdale's recognition resolves difficulties for Pearl, for Dimmesdale, and to some extent for Hester. However, I wish to demonstrate that Nathaniel Hawthorne's paternal deprivation and ambivalence toward other father figures is mirrored and distorted not only in the biological family group of *The Scarlet Letter*, but also in the figure of Roger Chillingworth. The ways in which Chillingworth's portrayal shadows the story of the lost Captain Hathorne are also important here. Overall, I'm concerned to show how Hawthorne's ambivalence creates images that disturb readers, fend off interpretation, and cause us to fail to acknowledge Chillingworth's full potential in the novel, particularly in the novel's closing images.

The Family Romance

Born in Salem, Massachusetts, 4 July 1804, Nathaniel Hawthorne was the legitimate second child and only son of his parents. For many years he was also the only male heir of his generation in both the Manning and Hathorne families.[2] Despite his hyper-legitimacy, a theme of figurative illegitimacy was present in his family romance. At the time of his birth, his mother lived in the Hathorne family home with Nathaniel Sr.'s widowed mother and unmarried sisters. A seagoing brother made his home there as well, but, in the phrase of Arlin Turner, the Hathorne home was "only rarely and temporarily invaded by the father."[3] According to Nina Baym, First Mate and later Captain Hathorne spent only seven months at home during his seven-year marriage.[4] On 28 December 1807, when Nathaniel was three years and five months old, Captain Hathorne sailed on yet another trading expedition, this time bound for South America. A third child and second daughter was born two weeks later, but Captain Hathorne was never to see her. In January he contracted yellow fever and, brought ashore, he died in a boarding house in Surinam. When his ship returned to Salem harbor in early April, it bore news of his death, but no body. Biographers pinpoint his father's death as the originating event for Hawthorne's lack of a conclusive identity; Edwin Haviland Miller, for instance, calls the death of Captain Hathorne "traumatic," and the "worst" of events for the young child,[5] but, only three years and nine

2. As is well known in Hawthorne studies. Hawthorne added the W sometime in the 1820s. The W either restored the name to its British and thus more aristocratic spelling (perhaps enhancing the correct pronunciation), or it repudiated his father's identity along with that of Hawthorne's severely Puritan paternal ancestors depicted—though not named—in "The Custom-House." In small, then, the drama of Hawthorne's name reflects his life-long struggle with being the male scion of his family while feeling a pervasive sense of alienation from both houses.

3. Arlin Turner, *Nathaniel Hawthorne: A Biography* (New York: Oxford UP, 1980), 11.

4. Nina Baym, "Nathaniel Hawthorne and His Mother: A Biographical Speculation," *Feminism and American Literary History* (New Brunswick, NJ: Rutgers UP, 1992), 42.

5. Edwin Haviland Miller, *Salem is My Dwelling Place: A Life of Nathaniel Hawthorne* (Iowa City: Iowa UP, 1991), 25. In addition to Miller, I have relied on a number of biographies, particularly on James Mellow, *Nathaniel Hawthorne in His Times* (Boston: Houghton Mifflin, 1980), who makes the earliest thorough examination of Hawthorne's ambivalence toward father figures; Gloria Erlich's *Family Themes and Hawthorne's Fiction: The Tenacious Web* (New Brunswick, NJ: Rutgers UP, 1984), with her presentation of Hawthorne's psychological themes, has been another valuable resource.

months old when he learned of his father's demise, Nathaniel may
have had no conscious memory of him. If he remembered Captain
Hathorne's occasional disruptions of the household, had he enjoyed or
resented them? Did he feel anguished when he learned of his father's
death, or omnipotent—or both?

In later life, Hawthorne claimed to remember nothing of his father's
death. His older sister, Ebe, fortunately, remembered the day well
enough to give us a glimpse into Hathorne and Manning family dynamics: "[M]y mother called my brother into her room, next to the
one where we slept, and told him that his father was dead. He left very
little property and my Grandfather Manning took us home."[6] Ebe's
memory sets the two families on opposing sides of a skirmish: Captain
Nathaniel Hathorne, deceased, was "his" (Nathaniel's) father; their
mother's father was "my [Ebe's] Grandfather Manning." At their
father's house the children slept in a "room" (not "our bedroom" or
"nursery") as if they were boarders; conversely, "Grandfather Manning
took us *home*" (emphasis added). One wonders why Ebe, at age six
probably better able to process such information, wasn't given the
news directly, along with or instead of Nathaniel. According to other
sources, Ebe's recollection is unreliable: Elizabeth did not immediately move her young family from one house to the other, but only after several months. I imagine young Nathaniel, who turned four in
July, experiencing the awakening of his conscious life and memory as
the singular male of the Hathorne household. The move to the Manning home considerably altered his position.

Little is known of Hawthorne's relations with the Hathornes. They
lived only a few houses away from the Mannings, but Ebe avoided
them and Nathaniel, too, seldom visited. In "Nathaniel Hawthorne
and His Mother: a Biographical Speculation," Baym argues that a
germ of illegitimacy infects even this circumstance. In his preface to
The Scarlet Letter, "The Custom-House," Hawthorne describes his
Hathorne ancestors as rigorously Puritanical, leading Baym to speculate that because Ebe was born after her parents had been married
only seven months, her paternal grandmother and aunts may have
looked askance on her birth, and on her mother (43). Elizabeth Manning and Nathaniel Hathorne enjoyed a long and apparently affectionate engagement (at least, Nathaniel's logbook includes affectionate
remarks), but Baym asserts that "the old-fashioned and pious
Hathornes" must certainly have believed Elizabeth Manning had re-
sorted to a feminine trick to speed her wedding date (42–43). To push
Baym's speculation further, did the Hathornes consider Elizabeth a
loose woman because of her bridal pregnancy and thus question the
paternity of all her children? Whatever the case, Elizabeth, a widow at
age twenty-eight, was not to benefit from any Hathorne largesse.

Whether her move a few months after hearing of her husband's
death was a symbolic repudiation of the father who left them impoverished, or a rejection of—or by—the Hathornes, the Hathorne children

6. Quoted in Mellow, *Nathaniel Hawthorne in His Times*, 14.

now became wards of the more generous and more overwhelming
Mannings. In 1808, Elizabeth's parents and seven of her eight brothers and sisters still occupied the family home. His mother and sisters
slept in a room together, but Nathaniel went upstairs to sleep with his
uncles. Complicating matters, Elizabeth, reportedly, became a recluse.
She wore black for the rest of her life, seldom if ever ventured out of
doors, and conferred at least a portion of her parental responsibilities
onto her family. (Baym persuasively argues that Elizabeth took a more
active role in her children's lives than other biographers have believed.)

Robert Manning, one of Elizabeth's bachelor brothers, bore the
most responsibility toward her children as well as to the family business. According to their letters, the Mannings regarded Robert as the
children's social father. Gloria Erlich employs tonal evidence from
Robert's letters to Elizabeth ("warm" and "solicitous" versus the
"brief" and "functional" tone of letters to his wife) to suggest that
Robert's "most intimate feelings [were] preempted by his sister and
her family" (47). Although Robert and Elizabeth's relationship is not
my topic here, I agree that Hawthorne's ambivalence toward father
figures in his fiction was fostered in part by his confusion about his
uncle's affection and fatherly discipline. Determined to educate his
nephew to follow in his footsteps, Uncle Robert became the father figure against whom young Nathaniel rebelled.

In *The Bastard Hero in the Novel*, Margaret Bözenna Goscilo argues
that illegitimacy empowers characters.[7] And Hawthorne's pervasive
sense of figurative illegitimacy can be understood as an empowering
factor in his success at writing his way out of the family script: though
later political appointments seem to resonate with his first American
ancestors, he did not go to sea in the manner of the Hathorne men of
the two generations prior to his own; and he did not go into the Manning family business despite Uncle Robert's having educated him for
exactly that purpose. Hawthorne wrote his way out of the family script
in other ways as well. In "The Custom-House" he avoids the question
of his Manning ancestors altogether and assumes his Hathorne ancestors would not recognize him as their descendant: "No aim, that I
have ever cherished, would they recognize as laudable; no success of
mine—if my life, beyond its domestic scope, had ever been brightened
by success—would they deem otherwise than worthless, if not positively disgraceful."[8] He takes on their mantle of guilt, but eschews any
other inheritance.

Written upon the death of Hawthorne's mother, *The Scarlet Letter*
mirrors both aspects of Hawthorne's sense of illegitimacy—his physical lack of a father and his emotional ambivalence toward father
figures. Thus the romance's resolution in a chain of interlocking re-
legitimations would seem to be the point of its denouement: Dimmesdale recognizes his child and reconciles with his God; Pearl kisses her

7. Margaret Bözenna Goscilo, *The Bastard Hero in the Novel* (New York: Garland, 1990).
8. Nathaniel Hawthorne, "The Custom-House," *The Scarlet Letter*, Norton Critical Edition
(New York: W. W. Norton and Company, 1988), 9–10 [12].

father and thereby claims a right to "grow up amid human joy and sorrow, nor for ever do battle with the world, but be a woman in it" (173) [162]; Hester atones for her sin first by publicly recognizing her daughter's father, then by returning to America and mentoring unhappy young women. And Hawthorne seems to further resolve the plot in its closing image of the single tombstone engraved with Hester's infamous A. On the surface of these legitimations, Hawthorne has been thought to recuperate the union of his biological mother and father— even going so far as to bury them side by side in the cemetery at King's Chapel. The father's body has been redeemed at last. Or so it would seem.

Hawthorne's biographical tensions suggest that one's illegitimacy is not so easily resolved. Illegitimacy, figurative or literal, raises anxiety about all precursors. Can "old Roger Chillingworth," the former "Master Prynne" remain, then, outside the reforged bonds of the other primary characters, and outside the resolution? Although many critics notice that Chillingworth invests Pearl with his estate, enabling her to travel to Europe and, perhaps, to marry well, they persist in imagining him at the romance's end as a devilish entity stripped of all power, separated from humanity, unmourned in a forgotten grave. Gillian Brown, in "Hawthorne, Inheritance, and Women's Property," acknowledges Chillingworth's agency, but then writes of "Hester's legacy to Pearl [which] deeds her daughter entry into future narratives of property."[9] Emily Budick argues that Chillingworth symbolically legitimates Dimmesdale via his descendants.[1] I find, however, that Hawthorne's extreme ambivalence toward father figures creates a potential for Chillingworth's recuperation as a type of Captain Hathorne. Indeed, I argue that we can understand *The Scarlet Letter* as the tale of Chillingworth's fall and redemption—enacted through a series of opportunities to claim Pearl as his child.

"My home is where thou art . . ."

To begin with, even though she is not his biological daughter, Pearl resembles Chillingworth. Excrescences of the biological parents' relationship (as someone has said of Pearl), both characters function to test Hester Prynne and Arthur Dimmesdale. Chillingworth, like Pearl, has dubious parentage. While both Hester and Arthur reflect on legitimate family histories and, albeit briefly, invoke for the reader their birthrights of genteel upbringings, Roger Chillingworth does not. He seems never to have been a child, but to have sprung up from "the nether earth" (83) [81].[2] Like Pearl and like the scarlet letter she embodies, Chillingworth is a palimpsest or, better, a Rorschach blot, par-

9. Gillian Brown, "Hawthorne, Inheritance, and Women's Property," *Studies in the Novel* 23 (1991): 116.
1. Emily Budick, *Engendering Romance: Women Writers and the Hawthorne Tradition, 1850–1990* (New Haven: Yale UP, 1994), 38.
2. Christopher Bigsby, in his 1994 novel *Hester* (New York: Penguin, 1994), accents Chillingworth's figurative illegitimacy by making him illegitimate and Jewish, though he misses an opportunity (and misreads *The Scarlet Letter*) in making Chillingworth his legal name and Prynne, Hester's chosen pseudonym.

adoxically unreadable and multiply read.[3] Furthermore, when he exchanges his patronymic, Prynne, for a pseudonym, he undergoes a metamorphosis (apart from the freezing of his assets that "Chillingworth" implies). His "old studies in alchemy" define his character (51) [51]. Not stability but transformation is his hallmark, as it will become Pearl's.

This is not to deny his primary role in the novel. Despite his mutability (or as another sign of it), Chillingworth holds a perverse authority over the other characters and represents the most legitimate class in their Puritan society. The patriarchal leaders and historical figures Governor Bellingham and the Reverend John Wilson keep company with him, and though they do not necessarily believe Chillingworth to be of the Elect (one of God's chosen for salvation), the "elder ministers of Boston and deacons of [Dimmesdale's] church" deem it "providential" that Chillingworth should be Dimmesdale's private physician (84) [81]. "Providential": so if Chillingworth is not exactly of God, he is at least commissioned by God. Additionally, Chillingworth in seeking revenge appoints himself to a God-like, law-bearing role. His mission is to uncover the name of the father who has transgressed against Puritan law. In short, his function is to name Pearl. Naming is central not merely to *The Scarlet Letter* but to illegitimacy generally. Furthermore, it suggests Puritan Election—having one's name written on God's invisible roll—a concept relevant to the story's setting and suggestive of another way in which this theme resonates throughout the novel.

Our first view of Chillingworth, like later views, is filtered through Hester's considerable bias against him. Even so, what we first observe about him underscores his mutable nature. When he steps out of the wilderness and into the Boston marketplace, he is positioned so as to appear figuratively illegitimate, standing beside his "Indian attendant" at the forest verge, physically marginalized at the "outskirts" of a crowd, hoping to be "redeemed out of [his] captivity" (43) [44]. He arrives at a place where he expects to discover his wife and property and reclaim his identity as a member of a family. Separated from Hester for two years, he shouldn't be surprised to discover that they have produced a child of two or three years of age. As he comes to understand that the object of the crowd's attention is a young mother—his wife—standing on a scaffold and holding not a toddler but a squalling infant, he is stripped of any hope of re-identification.

Beneath the surface of this non-reunion lies the Hathorne family romance. We can imagine Elizabeth and her children—Ebe and the

3. Lauren Berlant, in *The Anatomy of National Fantasy: Hawthorne, Utopia, and Everyday Life* (Chicago: U of Chicago P, 1991), argues that all of Hawthorne's heroines are "uncanny, paradoxical, politically unintelligible" (9), and David S. Reynolds, in *Beneath the American Renaissance: The Subversive Imagination in the Age of Emerson and Melville* (Cambridge: Harvard UP, 1988), asserts that Hester has "no absolute meaning or distinct authorial attitude" but is instead a "multifaceted heroine in whom [numerous] types [are] artistically fused" (375). I find these interpretations useful, but in comparison to Pearl, Hester seems to tend toward stasis, becoming rigid in her beliefs and statue-like in her appearance as a result of wearing the scarlet letter. Her eventual return to Puritan America confirms this interpretation.

five-month old Nathaniel—greeting Captain Hathorne in the fall of 1804. Unlike the captain, Chillingworth reacts to the sight of his wife with a child with a repulsion physically manifested as a "writhing horror" that twists "itself across his features, like a snake gliding swiftly over them" (44) [44].[4] T. Walter Herbert describes Chillingworth's response as masturbatory; the "snake-like writhing" is an intimation of the "erotic energy invested both in the hidden feelings and in the compulsion to keep them concealed."[5] According to Herbert, Chillingworth's reaction imitates the sexual transgression and consummation that have resulted in Hester's infamy. But Herbert's analysis is especially astute if we imagine Chillingworth unconsciously replicating Pearl's procreation: claiming her on a visceral level.

Recovering his rational faculties, Chillingworth begins his interrogation of the scene by asking a townsman, "tell me of Hester Prynne— have I her name rightly?—of this woman's offences" (44) [45]. He, by rights, does "have" her name. The Bostonian's reply is worth noting in full:

> Yonder woman, Sir, you must know, was the wife of a certain learned man, English by birth, but who had long dwelt in Amsterdam, whence, some good time agone, he was minded to cross over and cast in his lot with us of the Massachusetts. To this purpose, he sent his wife before him, remaining himself to look after some necessary affairs. Marry good Sir, in some two years, or less, that the woman has been a dweller here in Boston, no tidings have come of this learned gentleman, Master Prynne; and his young wife, look you, being left to her own misguidance—(45) [45].

Hawthorne's verbal playfulness here, "you must know," "necessary affairs," and "Marry good Sir," feeds into Chillingworth's surprised response, a climactic "Ah—aha!—I conceive you," and sets up additional symbolic engenderings. The Bostonian continues, speculating as to whether Master Prynne is alive or dead: "If he be still in life," or "at the bottom of the sea." Which is it? Chillingworth could immediately decide the question by asserting his legitimate identity. Instead, he joins Hester's silence, opening the door for his abandonment of the former name and mastery of "Master Prynne." In other words, he seizes on the coincidence of his anonymous arrival with Hester's humiliation as an opportunity to de-legitimate himself. By vacating his name, Chillingworth drains it of significance, un-naming both Hester and Pearl, announcing, in effect, "this woman is not my wife" and "this child is not my child."

4. One assumes, at least, that Captain Hathorne did not react with repulsion to his infant son, but this is only an assumption. One possible conclusion of Baym's bridal pregnancy hypothesis is to infer that Elizabeth's husband came to share his family's coolness toward her. To view the situation from another direction, as Hawthorne's employment was inadequate to support a family, he may have been distressed to discover that they had produced a second child. Such conjectures, though tentative, suggest further possibilities for the deep ambivalence inherent in Hawthorne's fictional father figures.
5. T. Walter Herbert, *Dearest Beloved: The Hawthornes and the Making of the Middle-Class Family* (Berkeley: U of California P, 1993), 192.

Hawthorne's ambivalence manifests itself here as hesitation. Chill-ingworth's attire—a strange disarray of civilized and savage costume—and Indian escort open a small window of opportunity through which we may imagine him as an emerging American hero—earthborn like Cooper's Natty Bumppo, adopting a pseudonym like Melville's Ish-mael, possibly about to turn around and light out for the territories like Twain's Huck Finn.[6] He could also return to the Old World where, as the inheritance with which he endows Pearl later informs us, he has amassed property. He takes none of these actions; instead, he is a study in ambivalence. He first gestures to Hester to keep silent, but then calls out, "Speak; and give your child a father!" (49) [49], risking that she will identify him. Does he invite her to do so? Hester, "turn-ing pale as death" at the sound of his voice, "which she too surely recognized," invokes instead a "Heavenly Father" for her child and promises that "she will never know an earthly one."

Though he would seem to have made his choice, Chillingworth con-tinues to hesitate on the threshold of possibility. The apparent unrav-eling of identity and legitimacy begun in the marketplace where he first encounters his wife continues when they share a residence in the Boston prison. This lodging represents to Chillingworth merely a real-istic aspect of Puritan hospitality, "the most convenient and suitable mode of disposing of him" until his "ransom" has been agreed upon (50) [51]. For Hester, the prison is mercilessly oppressive. Within her cell she considers both suicide and infanticide. Oddly, it is Chilling-worth's mission to restore mother and child. And he does. In fact, here we witness a "male birth" typical in the literature of bastardy, nearly so dramatic a male birth as when Mr. Earnshaw in *Wuthering Heights* opens his coat to reveal the child Heathcliff. The scene in *The Scarlet Letter* again underscores the resemblance between Chillingworth and Pearl. Earlier, Chillingworth was crippled by "a writhing horror," a "convulsion" (44) [45]; now the infant "writhe[s] in convulsions" (50) [50], as much a "forcible type" of Chillingworth's earlier "moral agony," as she is of her mother's. Called on for his medical skills, Chillingworth balks: "Here, woman! The child is yours,—she is none of mine, neither will she recognize my voice or aspect as a father's" (51) [51]. Hawthorne could have omitted "as a father's"; he could have written, "as a physician's" or "as a friend's." The authorial choice nudges us to notice Chillingworth's loss. When Hester refuses to give her husband's potion to Pearl, he must concede to give it himself and he expresses what I construe as longing: "were it my child,—yea, mine own, as well as thine!—I could do no better for it."

Hawthorne presents Chillingworth ambivalently. He has Chilling-worth speak to Hester "half coldly, *half soothingly*" (51; emphasis added) [51]. "Thy acts are like mercy," Hester notices, though she continues, "But thy words interpret thee as a terror!" (54) [54]. Most readers agree with her second finding: they declare Chillingworth nas-

6. Not so far-fetched a thought—in his 1972 film adaptation of the novel, *Der Scharlachrote Buchstabe*, Wim Wenders does cast Chillingworth as a frontiersman.

tily asexual and react with horror to any suggestion of his parenting Pearl. David Reynolds lumps him with other "frigid villains" such as Rappaccini who poisons his beautiful, motherless daughter in the earlier Hawthorne tale.[7] The notion that Chillingworth is inherently evil leads some readers to believe that Hester escaped from her husband to come to Boston; Chillingworth's aforementioned surprise at the Bostonian's story perhaps allows us to think so.[8] However, she has kept his name, and her neighbors know her story. Hawthorne's narrator tells us that she had come ahead of her husband to prepare a home. Furthermore, on our first glimpse of him back in the marketplace, Chillingworth is neither crippled nor old, nor is he monstrously deformed as he appears to Hester seven years later. George Eliot's characters Adam Bede and Silas Marner overcome similar deficiencies, but in this novel, physical incapacity is damning. Notice, though, that despite Chillingworth's appearance in Hester's memory—"well-stricken in years"—Hawthorne's narrator remonstrates that he "could hardly be termed aged" (43) [44]. As to whether Chillingworth is asexual or impotent (arguments that various readers have made), he has chosen a given name, Roger, which was a colonial epithet for adulterous intercourse or rape.[9] Regardless of how we view him, he views himself as a potent force, a male rival of Hester's unnamed lover.

In the prison Chillingworth says that if Pearl were his own, he could "do no better" for her (51) [51]. Nonetheless, I am building a case in which he could do better for his wife's child. Hester has offended her husband by having an adulterous affair, yet her lover has done nothing to support her emotionally or financially. Despite her later assertion of the "consecration" of her sexual union with Dimmesdale (133) [126], she has formed neither a new marriage nor any lasting bond. What would happen if Chillingworth, invoking the colonial laws of coverture,[1] declared his true identity, and reunited with Hester? Such a resolution would be, one assumes, not in Hester's best interests. Even so, Hawthorne has embedded his characters in an era when the governing bodies nearly insisted that a husband take responsibility for his wife's actions. As the character most allied to the office of law-giver, this seems Chillingworth's obvious duty. Could Hester acquiesce to be rescued? Would Master Prynne then spend his autumnal years at the hearth he feels robbed of, entertained by the antics of a lively and legitimate(d) child (like Silas Marner), doted on by a grateful wife?

I meet with considerable resistance when presenting Chillingworth as an alternative for Pearl's social father. But, while *The Scarlet Letter* does not encourage the likelihood of Chillingworth's reintegration into the human family, other novels do admit such possibilities and

---

7. Reynolds, 178.
8. See for instance Bigsby's *Hester*, in which Hester indeed comes to America to escape from Chillingworth.
9. See John D'Emilio and Estelle B. Freedman, *Intimate Matters: A History of Sexuality in America* (New York: Harper and Row, 1988), for a history of the term "roger'd." Demi Moore's movie adaptation of *The Scarlet Letter* also makes use of rogered as a vulgarity for rape or rough intercourse, as, I am told, do British detective novels.
1. Coverture, a concept borrowed in America from English common law, means simply that a husband's identity incorporated that of the wife, making them one legal body.

thus they demonstrate choices Hawthorne doesn't make. In *Hobomok* (1824), L. Maria Child allows one lover, the heroine's Narragansett Indian husband and the father of her child, to step aside when her former lover, an Englishman, returns. Because he has been thought lost at sea and given up for dead (as has Chillingworth), the Englishman views his fiancée's infidelity in the most generous light. In *Silas Marner* (1853), George Eliot seems deliberately to recuperate and redeem Chillingworth, writing of a crippled protagonist who has been duped and jilted, a miser who one day finds his gold happily replaced by a golden-haired toddler. In *Adam Bede* (1859), Eliot makes the interloper her protagonist, describing Adam at the novel's beginning as older and with a shoulder deformed similarly to Chillingworth's as he first appears in the marketplace. The allusion seems deliberate (Eliot's adulterous characters are named Arthur and Hester), yet Adam overcomes this description to emerge as a heroic protagonist. A much darker British vision is Thomas Hardy's *The Mayor of Casterbridge* (1886) in which the protagonist in a drunken rage sells his wife and daughter to a stranger, only to make a home for them years later when his ailing wife returns with a teenaged girl—a girl whom he vainly wishes were his lost biological child. In Henry James's *Portrait of a Lady* (1881), Isabel Archer sacrifices her romantic potential in order to parent her adolescent step-daughter, her husband's bastard child. Similarly, Edith Wharton's *Summer* (1917) can be read as a recuperation of Hawthorne's theme, a story resolved—albeit unsatisfactorily—when a young woman's foster father marries her after she is impregnated and abandoned by another, younger lover. Wharton's Charity and lawyer Royall carry on Hawthorne's vexing ambiguity and ambivalence. Although some readers are incensed by Royall's apparent entrapment of his stupefied ward, others applaud Charity's good sense in appropriating Royall's legitimacy for her unborn child.[2]

Is there any likelihood that the Chillingworth Hawthorne presents to us could be reintegrated into the human family—even in so vexed a manner? If we are led by Hester's repugnance at reunion with her husband (though her repugnance can be no greater than Isabel's at rejoining Osmond, or Charity's at marrying lawyer Royall), Chillingworth seems nonetheless perched on the verge of just such an action. The narration lingers over the image of Pearl fallen into a "dewy slumber" in his arms (51) [52]. Having ministered to Pearl and Hester's physical needs (the sort of act, after all, that builds attachment), Chillingworth suggests an even more radical alternate family than one in which an emotional or societal parent takes the place of a biological one: "Here on the wild outskirt of the earth, I shall pitch my tent; for, elsewhere a wanderer, and isolated from human interests, I find here a woman, a man, a child, amongst whom and myself there exist the closest ligaments . . . Thou and thine, Hester Prynne, belong to me. My

2. For a discussion of conflicting reactions to Charity's marriage to Royall, see Rhonda Skillern, "Becoming a Good Girl: Law Language, and Ritual in Edith Wharton's 'Summer,'" *The Cambridge Companion to Edith Wharton*, ed. Millicent Bell (Cambridge: Cambridge UP, 1995), 117–36.

home is where thou art, and where he is" (54) [54]. Despite all else that transpires in this scene, here Chillingworth has said, explicitly, that Hester, her child, and her lover comprise his *home*. They are his family. Read unsympathetically, his pledge to her seems wholly perverse—he uses the language of ownership and slavery. Read sympathetically, Chillingworth's oath creates an important moment for my argument. For good or ill, ownership underlies patriarchal conceptions of the family, and in using the intimate pronouns "thou" and "thine," Chillingworth seems to be reimagining a family for himself. Similarly, Chillingworth's "closest ligaments" resonate with the "lig" of religion, both of which derive from *ligare*, to bind. His diction may remind us of the biblical story of Ruth who, despite her husband's death without progeny, remains loyal to her mother-in-law: "Intreat me not to leave thee, or to return from following after thee: for whither thou goest, I will go; and where thou lodgest, I will lodge: thy people shall be my people, and thy God, my God: where thou diest, will I die, and there will I be buried: the Lord do so to me, and more also, if ought but death part thee and me" (Ruth 1:16–17). Chillingworth, too, is loyal: he will remain by Hester's side until death parts them.

A reconstituted family along the lines of *Silas Marner* does not seem possible here. In the same speech, Prynne-Chillingworth overturns his chance for a new domestic religion, refusing to "encounter the dishonor that besmirches the husband of a faithless woman" (54) [54]. Possessing "the lock and key of her silence" (81) [79], Master Prynne then "vanish[es] out of life as completely as if he indeed lay at the bottom of the ocean whither rumor had long ago consigned him" (82) [79]. That his identity should be lost in the vastness of the ocean is, of course, significant to Hawthorne's early loss of his father. And, like the lost father, Chillingworth—in abandoning this family group potentially encompassing himself, his wife, her lover, and her child—takes on a tremendous power to haunt.

Chillingworth's symbolic power exacts a steep price. Consider, in contrast, Pearl's effect on Hester. Although Sacvan Bercovitch (along with Hawthorne's narrator) argues that it is the office of the scarlet letter to domesticate Hester,[3] I find (as does Baym) that what stitches Hester back into the fabric of the human family is not the letter, but Pearl. Helping her to command her more radical instincts, the child softens Hester's heart and enables her to endure and partake in her oppressive community. Hester is a model for reintegration in more ways than one, for, as Michael Ragussis asserts in *Acts of Naming: The Family Plot in Fiction*, "to recognize publicly one's kindred is the moral concomitant to engendering, defining the family not merely biologically but morally."[4] In these terms, refusing to publicly recognize Pearl and Hester is disastrous for Dimmesdale, but refusing Pearl is equally disastrous for Chillingworth. His tragedy is Dimmesdale's, and more,

---

3. Sacvan Bercovitch, *Rites of Assent: Transformations in the Symbolic Construction of America* (New York: Routledge, 1993).
4. Michael Ragussis, *Acts of Naming: The Family Plot in Fiction* (New York: Oxford UP, 1986), 65.

for while Dimmesdale knows unambiguously that he must confess his sin and paternity (though he takes seven years to do it), Chillingworth fails to understand the nature of his own tragedy. In attempting to reveal the genetic father of his wife's child, he works toward the wrong end, and he obscures his own potential. Although she is solely burdened with Pearl's care and financial support, Hester, the illegitimated mother, has a more legitimate life than either Dimmesdale or Chillingworth.

His adoption of a pseudonym does not end Chillingworth's opportunities to name himself Hester's husband and Pearl's father. Moreover, in later scenes we continue to glimpse a potential for Hester to reassess Chillingworth. The first opportunity occurs when Pearl is three years old and refuses to be catechized by the Puritan elders. Chillingworth is, arguably, her only sympathetic onlooker, showing a grandfather's amusement at Pearl's antics. Despite his smiles—I'm stubbornly interpreting his smile as genuine rather than devilish—Hester perceives only how ugly Chillingworth is, "how his dark complexion seemed to have grown duskier, and his figure more misshapen" (77) [76]. Hawthorne demurs to depict her consciously assessing Chillingworth's potential to assist her, but the images convey exactly this potential: about to lose her child, desperate for some action, Hester turns to Dimmesdale only after first appraising and rejecting Chillingworth.

Another opportunity for appraisal occurs in the second scaffold scene when Pearl is seven years old and Chillingworth stands once more at the margin of the biologically bound group. Again, the images conjure the possibility for his acceptance, this time by little Pearl. While Pearl and Hester stand at midnight with Dimmesdale, Pearl twice draws her hand out of Dimmesdale's to point at "old Roger Chillingworth" (106, 107) [102]. Her gesture both accuses and includes him. For his part, Chillingworth stands watching as if "to claim his own" (107) [103]. As in the Governor's hall, the ambiguity and ambivalence of his interest render his appearance ghastly. We cannot understand his motives, though we may guess at them, particularly because in this scene Dimmesdale perceives him for the first time as an "arch-fiend." The uncanny vividness of his expression, or the intensity of "the minister's perception of it," remains "painted on the darkness," a Cheshire cat grin. This would seem to complicate any hope of reinterpretation. Through whose perspective, however, do we view Chillingworth?

Soon after the second scaffold scene, when Hester confronts him on the ocean shore, Chillingworth undergoes a moment of tragic self-recognition. Legitimacy is identity, and mirrors are literal and figurative reflections of identity; thus, in The Scarlet Letter (as in "The Custom-House"), mirrors are unreliable. While speechifying about human hearts and fiends, Chillingworth is suddenly stopped—he sees another face "usurping the place of his own image in a glass" (117) [112]. The moment resembles an earlier one in which Hester seems to glimpse a fiend "peeping out" from Pearl's eyes (68) [66]. The earlier scene matters. Both Chillingworth and Dimmesdale look at Pearl, hoping and dreading to see a reflection of her genetic father; Hester, on the other hand, gazes into the lens of her daughter's eyes and sees what she does not expect. I have always thought that she sees a "fiend" where she would expect to see her own image reflected, but Budick suggests another possibility: that Hester expects to see Dimmesdale reflected in Pearl's features and instead sees Chillingworth (26).[5] In the scene on the seashore as well, the gazer looks as if into a mirror and sees something other than what ought to be reflected there. For Chillingworth, "It was one of those moments . . . when a man's moral aspect is faithfully revealed to his mind's eye" (117) [112]. A humanist would call him fortunate: "Not improbably, he had never before viewed himself as he did now." It is a potential turning point, another chance for redemption.

This brief moment at which the novel reveals Chillingworth's perspective has consequences for the scene that unfolds from it. Hester's response to Chillingworth's discomfort suggests an extent to Mr. and Mrs. Prynne's previous intimacy not previously revealed. Despite their estrangement of nine years, she discerns his vulnerability and takes advantage, asking mercy: "Has he [Dimmesdale] not paid thee all?" (117) [112]. "No!" Chillingworth responds, "He has but increased the debt!" (118) [112]. But then, Chillingworth, grappling with his identity, abandons the economic metaphor and reminds Hester, "Dost thou remember me? Was I not, though you might deem me cold, nevertheless a man thoughtful of others, craving little for himself,—kind, true, just, and of constant, if not warm affections. Was I not all this?" Hester's response should surprise us: "All this, and more." If she doesn't consider re-legitimating her marriage, Hester at the very least in this scene invokes an honest emotional response from Chillingworth. She anguishes that there is "no good" for anyone involved, but Chillingworth admits pity for Hester and feels "a thrill of admiration" for her. Her speech becomes conciliatory. She seems about to bargain with Chillingworth. Would she offer her companionship and that of her daughter for Chillingworth's pardon of her lover? "[B]e once more human" she entreats him, and, overturning her previous exclamation, promises, "There might be good for thee, and for thee alone" (119) [113]. Reconciliation seems an unlikely extremity, yet she attempts to enlist Chillingworth's support and uses the vocabulary of her daughter's naming (the Pearl of great price) when she asks, "Wilt thou reject that priceless benefit?" If Chillingworth hears duplicity in her offer, he ignores it. Responding to the sympathy he chooses instead to discern, he offers absolution: "Ye . . . are not sinful . . . neither am I fiend-like."

His priestly words of compassion leave Hester unconvinced. Illegitimate, unredeemed, cuckolded, stripped of his proper name, Chillingworth has, indeed, become a fiend. His eyes glare red. His appearance

---

5. Elaborating on yet another non-biological family—Joseph, Mary, and Jesus—Budick further corroborates my view of Chillingworth: "By seeing Chillingworth in Pearl, Hester [repairs] her broken marriage to Chillingworth. Hester would reestablish the child's legitimacy by fantasizing a new law of reproduction" (27).

is monstrous: "a deformed old figure, with a face that haunted men's memories longer than they liked" (119) [113]. When he parts from Hester, he goes "stooping away along the earth" more like a devil than a man. We may wish to notice that Hawthorne, like Hester, has consistently marshaled conventional prejudices against Chillingworth—he is ugly, "dusky," deformed, and he spends too much time thinking. For some readers, these are reasons enough to dislike him. I want to make obvious, however, our reaction. Particularly because our sympathy is here entwined with Hester's, it is suspect. Without pausing to analyze the exchange between them, she resists the domestic peace she previously admitted of her marriage. "Be it sin or no," she now says bitterly, "I hate the man!" (120) [114].

Perhaps it is Chillingworth's fiend-like appearance that prompts Hawthorne to have him described next by the shipmaster, who, as I have suggested, also stands in for him. The interaction between the shipmaster and Pearl encapsulates the relationship that soon unfolds between Pearl and Chillingworth. Signifying Chillingworth's wealth, the gold chain given to her by the shipmaster is perfectly suited to Pearl's form. That she should possess it, we are told, is natural, like a genetic inheritance (166) [155]. Booking passage with Dimmesdale, Hester, and Pearl back to the Old World, Chillingworth suggests— once more—that the four principal characters form a family unit.

A Family "at last"

One important result of *The Scarlet Letter*'s infamous ambiguity resides in how critics persist in choosing and rechoosing Pearl's "real" father. They persist despite Hawthorne's explicit revelation to the reader of the relationships between Hester, Dimmesdale, and Chillingworth and despite Hawthorne's explicit refusal to favor one father over the other. Most favor Dimmesdale: Myra Jehlen says of "the minister, the adulteress and their child" that they are "at last a family";[6] Bercovitch proclaims Dimmesdale to be "now openly [Pearl's] father at last" (202). Budick seems to claim just the opposite when she asserts that "fathers may be official ancestors rather than genetic ones" (19). She adds, "The confrontation with illegitimacy and doubt does not mean that the son ought now to divest himself of his parents. On the contrary, he has to acknowledge and affirm both of them."

I find Hawthorne invoking neither an official nor a genetic father. Not choosing reiterates Hawthorne's childhood drama, in a sense affirms it, by leaving Pearl unfathered. With this humanizing kiss, Dimmesdale does claim Pearl and acknowledge her as a daughter—"at last" in the words of Jehlen and Bercovitch. I find it interesting that the language and imagery of the final scaffold scene manipulate our impression of Pearl's fate even when subsequent events contradict it. It's an iconic scene, heavily freighted as if with religious imagery. Like a painted tile bearing a saint's image, the moment makes a powerful

6. Myra Jehlen, "Introduction: Beyond Transcendence," *Ideology and Classic American Literature* (Cambridge: Cambridge UP, 1986), 9.

impression on observers: "Pearl kissed his lips. A spell was broken. The great scene of grief, in which the wild infant bore a part, had developed all her sympathies; and as her tears fell upon her father's cheek, they were the pledge that she would grow up amid human joy and sorrow, nor for ever do battle with the world, but be a woman in it" (173) [162].

Like an icon, however, what transpires here is frangible. Despite his ownership of "her father's cheek," and the passive extraction of Pearl's "pledge," Dimmesdale's confession is penultimate to Chillingworth's final word, the willing of a "very considerable amount of property, both here and in England" to Pearl (176) [164]. Dimmesdale may claim Pearl, but the aftermath, his death, orphans her. He leaves Pearl no estate, physical or spiritual. He leaves her even less than Hawthorne's father left him (a ship's log and a gun, remember, but also a family beyond his mother). Regardless of its attempt to resonate, Chillingworth's legacy shatters the image communicated through Dimmesdale's reception of Pearl's kiss. The kiss may have enabled Pearl to grow up to "be a woman" (173) [162], but she is not fully human until she receives Chillingworth's legacy: "So Pearl—the elf-child,—the demon offspring, as some people, up to that epoch [i.e., beyond the scaffold scene], persisted in considering her—became the richest heiress of her day, in the New World" (176) [164]. More important, Chillingworth's estate effects "a material change" so that, "little Pearl, at a marriageable period of life, might have mingled her wild blood with the lineage of the devoutest Puritan among them all." Dimmesdale's kiss fails to confer such legitimacy as this.

Only Chillingworth can turn wild Pearl into "Pearl Prynne." In death, he becomes her social father, the father who endows her, the father society recognizes. What change does he effect on his own behalf? A final, usually ignored difficulty with the inheritance he leaves Pearl is the paper trail that must accompany it. (And one function of "The Custom-House" is to emphasize that paper trails existed in the seventeenth century.) Has Chillingworth been steadily amassing his fortune in land while also pursuing his revenge? Or has he managed to alter his name from "Prynne" to "Chillingworth" on previously held deeds? His legal executors, Governor Bellingham and Reverend Wilson (176) [164], are booked for surprising discoveries. Legitimacy for Chillingworth has far-reaching consequences, for a reassessment of his status must undo the motive and inspiration of how we have understood Hester's self-imposed, nun-like devotion to the Puritan community. Noticing Chillingworth's late-won legitimacy also shatters our faith in the apparent legitimating effect of Dimmesdale's confession.

Although its effects on Hester and Dimmesdale often slip by without comment, Chillingworth's final action, when we pay attention to it, begets an alteration of identity deeply upsetting to our understanding of Pearl's character. Harry Levin transports her to a new aesthetic altogether, suggesting that when we learn "that [Pearl] grew up an heiress and traveled abroad, we realize that we can pursue her further adventures through the novels of Henry James," and Edwin Haviland

Miller calls this a "happy suggestion"; however, those familiar with James's Daisy Miller, Isabel Archer, or Catherine Sloper know only too well the reasons why a Jamesian father sends a daughter to Europe, and what happens to her there.[7] Europe is anticipated as a civilizing adventure, a way to cultivate class in a young woman ostensibly from a class-less society. It is also a way to break her spirit. James's Daisy, for instance, becomes too well contained, bounded by "the little Protestant cemetery, in an angle of the wall of imperial Rome."[8] Catherine Sloper's fate seems no better. James's only literally illegitimate female figure, Pansy Osmond in *Portrait of a Lady* (even called "Pearl" at some point), is similarly contained—locked up in a convent because she will not agree to make the sort of brilliant, financially advantageous marriage her father prefers for her. Budick writes of Isabel Archer, whom she calls James's "latter-day Pearl," that she "comes back to the land of her fathers" (Europe?) and makes a marriage that "characterizes Hester's own marriage to Chillingworth [and] anticipates elements of Freud's family romance" (22).

Speculation about Pearl's life can, unfortunately, go no further than do any of James's unfortunate young women. The bequest may return her to a "fatherland," but Pearl returns neither to England, nor to Chillingworth's specific property which is unambiguously located "here and in England" (176) [164]. Nor does she return to Hester's "paternal home" in "Old England" (42) [43]. Whether she is "gone untimely to a maiden grave," or "still in life" (with Hawthorne as with James, to be "still" is not an attractive alternative to the maiden grave), we can say for certain only that Pearl has lost her attractive mutability (the flip side of Chillingworth's unattractive mutability) and is no longer part of the American democratic project. Looked at in this way, the previous, nearly tacit assumption that Roger Chillingworth's legacy enables Pearl to escape Puritan America becomes problematic. Hawthorne's conception of Pearl's inheritance is ambiguous. Like the shipmaster's chain, it destroys her autonomy. In the context of Hawthorne's personal history as well (the denial of his father's body and a Salem gravesite), it matters that Pearl's body does not return home to New England.[9]

Hawthorne's imaginative construct of America is so pervasive throughout the novel that Pearl's exemption, merely of itself, is troubling. How can we imagine in *The Scarlet Letter* any resolution outside America, or indeed—in Richard Poirier's phrase—any "world elsewhere"? Scholars quibble about why Hester returns to New En-

7. Harry Levin, *The Power of Blackness: Hawthorne, Poe, Melville* (New York: Knopf, 1958), 78. Edwin Haviland Miller, *Salem Is My Dwelling Place: A Life of Nathaniel Hawthorne* (Iowa City: Iowa UP, 1991), 16.
8. Henry James. "Daisy Miller: A Study," *The Turn of the Screw and Other Short Fiction by Henry James* (New York: Bantam, 1981), 320.
9. I should credit *Adam Bede* for provoking my thoughts on this subject. When Eliot's Hester, Hetty Sorrel, unwittingly causes the death of her premature, illegitimate child, Eliot first condemns her to death then banishes her for life to Australia. When her sentence is commuted seven years later (a number of years significant to the plot of *The Scarlet Letter*), Hetty attempts to return but dies in a shipwreck. As a conflation of Hester and Pearl, Hetty underscores the significance of Hester's return to America and Pearl's failure to return.

gland, but to my mind, she can no more escape Puritan American than can Milton's Satan escape Hell. Yet Pearl, we are asked to believe, escapes—even transcends—the lessons her peculiar culture has inculcated in her. The impact of Pearl's absence is attenuated via Hester's return, but as surely as the name of the father was withheld at the outset, the body of the new mother—for whose infant, the narrator suggests, Hester "embroider[s] a baby-garment, with . . . a lavish richness of golden fancy" (177) [165]—is also withheld. Banished, Pearl continues to dramatize the crisis that the presence of two fathers implies: she belongs nowhere. As Herbert notes, "Hawthorne's conclusion exempts Pearl from the dilemmas that the book portrays but fails to resolve them" (204). Under scrutiny, her exemption only heightens those dilemmas.

As I have said, few readers are willing to long entertain the thought that Chillingworth could claim Pearl. Nonetheless, Hawthorne (unlike Hester) seems to me careful never to completely disallow his potential. And the limits of Hawthorne's refusal to turn completely against his fiendish villain reach to the novel's closing words. Here he further "resolves" the plot of *The Scarlet Letter* by laying his heroine to rest beside a grave, "an old and sunken one," but set apart—"with a space between as though [the graves] had no right to touch" (178) [166], and beneath a single tombstone engraved with the letter A. More than one scholar has noted that with this conclusion Hawthorne imaginatively reconstructs his mother's death and reunites his parents. But whose grave is this?

Our refusal to credit Chillingworth with human potential causes us to look away as Hawthorne's ambivalence unfolds into the final image of the grave. Although generations of readers have assumed that she shares the A with Dimmesdale, should we assume that Puritan Boston would lay to rest even their able, angelic adulteress beside their late, beloved pastor? That we persist in choosing this option for Hester is a credit to Hawthorne's ambivalence—and craft. Warning us that "the curious investigator may still discern, and perplex himself with the purport," Hawthorne describes the "engraved escutcheon" bearing the legend, "ON A FIELD, SABLE, THE LETTER A, GULES" (178) [166]. Readers are not willing to be perplexed. For instance, in an otherwise excellent psychoanalytic reading of *The Scarlet Letter*, Joanne Feit Diehl assumes that in the graves "the two lovers [rest] . . . side by side."[1] Via this closing image, Diehl writes, "Hawthorne reiterates the resilience of what the A symbolizes: the desire for contract and reunion with the forbidden" (250). But wouldn't Puritan Boston more likely bury Hester beside the man who—in endowing her daughter—has named himself "husband," and named himself "Roger Prynne"? The A would then symbolize the importance of the letter of the law. I find insufficient evidence to make this claim any stronger. However,

---

1. Joanne Feit Diehl, "Re-Reading The Letter: Hawthorne, the Fetish, and the (Family) Romance," *The Scarlet Letter: Complete, Authoritative Text With Biographical Background and Critical History*, ed. Ross C. Murfin (New York: Bedford Books of St. Martin's Press, 1991), 250.

rather than affirming the A's resilience, as Diehl argues, the now apparent ambivalence of the graves may challenge us to rethink our assumptions. Perhaps Surveyor Pue's exhumed body in "The Custom-House" is meant to suggest the necessity and utility of another exhumation?

Like the sexualized motif of the grave marker, Hawthorne's ambivalence toward Chillingworth's character fosters not resolution but increased ambiguity. The idea of Chillingworth reunited with his lawful wife is, after all, thoroughly ambiguous and thoroughly pessimistic: "Prynne" does not appear on the tombstone any more than it graces the names of Pearl's legitimate descendents (who will bear her husband's name).[2] Neither can we settle (or unsettle) the question in favor of Chillingworth's body over Dimmesdale's. Hawthorne doesn't say which man's body lies beside Hester's. Perhaps it doesn't matter.[3]

Finally, I find resting in the mystery of this moment a more satisfying alternative than the false critical resolution usually ascribed. I find it so because it bears more psychological truth in regard to Hawthorne's identity theme than does a clearly unambiguous reunion of the lovers' bodies. Was Hawthorne's "father" the never present sea-captain whose genetic material he shared, or was it a father figure such as Robert Manning, his paternalistic, intrusive uncle? Once realized, the seemingly perverse sleight of hand in the King's Chapel burying ground, and in The Scarlet Letter's closing idea, compels us to reexamine the biography while insisting that we will find no answers there. Via this refusal to name, Hawthorne inscribes not a father so much, or fathers, as his own inconquerable ambvialence toward them.

SACVAN BERCOVITCH

The A-Politics of Ambiguity in *The Scarlet Letter*†

The drama of Hester Prynne's return has gone unappreciated, no doubt because it is absent from the novel. At a certain missing point in the narrative, through an unrecorded process of introspection, Hester abandons the high, sustained self-reliance by which we have come to identify her, from her opening gesture of defiance, when she repels the beadle and walks proudly "into the open air" (162) [40], to the forest scene seven years later, when she casts off her A and urges Dimmesdale to a new life—choosing for no clear reason to abandon her heroic independence and acquiescing to the A after all. Voluntarily she returns to the colony that had tried to make her (she once believed) a "life-long bond-slave," although Hawthorne pointedly records the ru-

2. In which case, Chillingworth's gravestone with "Prynne" prominently displayed is one detail Demi Moore's 1997 movie almost got right.
3. Having once looked at the grave site in this way, I have difficulty seeing it in any other. I have in mind a *Wuthering Heights*, Heathcliff-like contention of the dead Chillingworth for proximity to his wife's body.
† From *The Office of* The Scarlet Letter (Baltimore: Johns Hopkins UP, 1991), 1–31. Page numbers in square brackets refer to this Norton Critical Edition.

mors that Pearl "would most joyfully have entertained [her] . . .
mother at her fireside" (313–14, 344) [144, 165]. And voluntarily
Hester resumes the letter as a "woman stained with sin, bowed down
with shame," although, he adds, "not the sternest magistrate of that
iron period would have imposed it" (344) [165]. As in a camera ob-
scura, isolation and schism are inverted into vehicles of moral, political, and historical continuity:

> Women, more especially . . . came to Hester's cottage, demanding
> why they were so wretched, and what the remedy! Hester com-
> forted and counseled them, as best she might. She assured them,
> too, of her firm belief, that, at some brighter period, when the
> world should have grown ripe for it, in Heaven's own time, a new
> truth would be revealed, in order to establish the whole relation
> between man and woman on a surer ground of mutual happiness.
> Earlier in life, Hester had vainly imagined that she herself might
> be the destined prophetess, but had long since recognized the im-
> possibility that any mission of divine and mysterious truth should
> be confided to a woman stained with sin, bowed down with
> shame, or even burdened with a life-long sorrow. The angel and
> apostle of the coming revelation must be a woman, indeed, but
> lofty, pure, and beautiful; and wise, moreover, not through dusky
> grief, but the ethereal medium of joy; and showing how sacred
> love should make us happy, by the truest test of a life successful
> to such an end! (344–45) [165–66]

The entire novel tends toward this moment of reconciliation, but
the basis for reconciliation, the source of Hester's revision, remains
entirely unexplained. The issue is not that Hester returns, which
Hawthorne does account for, in his way: "There was a more real life
for Hester Prynne, here, in New England" (344) [165]. Nor is it that
she resumes the A: we might anticipate that return to beginnings, by
the principles of narrative closure. What remains problematic, what
Hawthorne compels us to explain for ourselves (as well as on Hester's
behalf), is her dramatic change of purpose and belief. Throughout her
"seven years of outlaw and ignominy," Hester had considered her A
a "scorching stigma" and herself "the people's victim" (291, 331,
313–14) [129, 156, 144]. Only some "galling" combination of fatalism
and love, Hawthorne tells us early in the novel, had kept her from
leaving the colony at once, after her condemnation (188) [55]. She
had been "free to return" to England; she had also had

> the passes of the dark, inscrutable forest open to her, where the
> wildness of her nature might assimilate itself with a people whose
> customs and life were alien from the law that had condemned
> her. . . . But [Hester was possessed by] . . . a fatality, a feeling so
> irresistible and inevitable that it ha[d] the force of doom. . . . Her
> sin, her ignominy, were the roots which she had struck into the
> soil. It was as if a new birth, with stronger assimilations than the
> first, had converted the forest-land . . . into Hester Prynne's wild
> and dreary, but life-long home. . . . The chain that bound her here
> was of iron links, and galling to her inmost soul. . . . What she

> compelled herself to believe,—what, finally, she reasoned upon,
> as her motive for continuing a resident of New England,—was
> half a truth, and half a self-delusion. Here, she said to herself,
> had been the scene of her guilt, and here should be the scene of
> her daily punishment; and so, perchance, the torture of her daily
> shame would at length purge her soul, and work out another pu-
> rity than that which she had lost; more saint-like, because the re-
> sult of martyrdom. (186–87) [55–56]

Something of that force of necessity attends Hester's return, together with that earlier self-denying, self-aggrandizing quest for martyrdom. But it now conveys a far less "wild and dreary" prospect.
Hester chooses to make herself not only an object of the law, "saint-
like" by her resignation to "daily punishment," but more largely an
agent of the law, the sainted guide toward "another purity," "some
brighter period" of "sacred love" foreshadowed by her agon (344–45)
[166]. What had been half-truth, half-delusion is rendered whole as a
vision of progress through due process. And the bond she thus forges
anew with the community lends another moral interpretation to her
"new birth" as American. It recasts her adopted "forest-land" into the
site of prophecy, home-to-be of the "angel and apostle of the coming
revelation"; it reconstitutes Hester herself, *as a marginal dissenter,* into
an exemplum of historical continuity (344–45) [166].

We accept all this as inevitable, as readers did from the start, because Hawthorne has prepared us for it. His strategies of ambiguity
and irony *require* Hester's conversion to the letter. And since the magistrates themselves do not impose the A; since the community has long
since come to regard Hester as an "angel or apostle" in her own right;
since, moreover, we never learn the process of her conversion to the A
(while her development through the novel tends in exactly the opposite direction); since, in short, neither author nor characters help
us—we must meet the requirement ourselves.

"The scarlet letter had not done its office," and, when it has, its office depends on our interpretation—or, more precisely, on our capacities to respond to Hawthorne's directives for interpretation. The
burden this imposes can be specified by contrast with Dimmesdale's
metamorphosis, earlier in the story, from secret rebel into prophet of
New Israel. Hawthorne details the state of despair in which the minister agrees to leave, elaborates the disordered fantasies that follow, and
yet leaves it to us to explain Dimmesdale's recantation. In this case,
however, the explanation emerges directly from character and plot.
"The minister," Hawthorne writes, "had never gone through an experience calculated to lead him beyond the scope of generally received
laws; although, in a single instance, he had so fearfully transgressed
one of the most sacred of them. But this had been a sin of passion, not
of principle, nor even purpose" (290) [128]. When, accordingly,
Dimmesdale decides to leave with Hester, he does so only because he
believes he is "irrevocably doomed" (291) [129], and we infer upon his
return that he has regained his faith after all—that he has made peace
at last with the Puritan ambiguities of mercy and justice, good and

evil, head and heart, which he had abandoned momentarily in the forest.

The reasons for Hester's reversal are far more complex. It takes the whole story to work them through. To begin with, there is the problem of form, since in her case (unlike Dimmesdale's) the reversal so conspicuously defies tradition. I refer to the genre of tragic love to which *The Scarlet Letter* belongs. Had Hester returned for love alone (the A for Arthur) or under the cloud of disaster abroad (the A for adversity), we could follow her reasoning readily enough. But Hawthorne asks us to consider the disparity between these familiar tragic endings and Hester's choice. The familiar endings, from *Antigone* and *Medea* through *Antony and Cleopatra* and *Tristan and Isolde*, are variations on the theme of love against the world. Hester's return merges love *and* the world. In this aspect (as in others) it offers a dramatic contrast with European novels of adultery, which narrative theorists have classified in terms either of subversion or of containment, as implying "a fatal break in the rigid system of bourgeois realism," or as "work[ing] to subvert what [the novel] aims to celebrate," or else (because of the "nearly universal *failure* of the adulterous affair") as serving "closurally to reinstate social norms."[1] *Madame Bovary* and *Anna Karenina* can be said to fit any of these descriptions. *The Scarlet Letter* fits none. Hester neither reaffirms her adulterous affair nor disavows it; her actions neither undermine the social order nor celebrate it; and at the end she neither reinstates the old norms nor breaks with them. Instead, she projects her dream of love onto some "surer ground" in the future, when "the whole relation between man and woman" can be reestablished. In other words, her return deliberately breaks with tradition by its emphasis on the political implications of process as closure.

The political emphasis is appropriate for the same reason that it is problematic: Hawthorne's portrait of Hester is a study of the lover as social rebel. Not as antinomian or witch, as he explicitly tells us, and certainly not as adulteress—if anything Hester errs at the opposite extreme, by her utter repression of eros. This emphasis on the non- or even antierotic is also to highlight sexual transgression, of course, but wholly by contrast; and it is to reinforce the contrast that Hawthorne insinuates by his often-remarked parallels between Hester and "unnatural" Anne Hutchinson, mother of "monstrous misconceptions"[2] as well as imperious, "bitter-tempered" Mistress Hibbins (217) [78]. Hawthorne remarks, with a note of disgust, that Hester had lost her "womanly" qualities, had become almost manlike in her harshness of manner and feature:

> Even the attractiveness of her person had undergone a . . . sad
> transformation . . . [so that] there seemed to be no longer any

---

1. Joseph Allen Boone, *Tradition Counter Tradition: Love and the Form of Fiction* (Chicago: U of Chicago P, 1987), 48; Tony Tanner, *Adultery in the Novel: Contract and Transgression* (Baltimore: Johns Hopkins UP, 1979), 13.
2. Amy S. Lang, *Prophetic Woman: Anne Hutchinson and the Problem of Dissent in the Literature of New England* (Berkeley: U of California P, 1987), 58, 67.

thing in Hester's face for Love to dwell upon; nothing in Hester's form, though majestic and statue-like, that Passion could ever dream of clasping it its embrace; nothing in Hester's bosom, to make it ever again the pillow of Affection. Some attribute had departed from her, the permanence of which had been essential to keep her a woman. (258–59) [107]

Hester errs, then, not in her sexual transgression but in her "stern development" as an individualist of increasingly revolutionary commitment (259) [107]. At the novel's center is a subtle and devastating critique of radicalism that might be titled "The 'Martyrdom' of Hester Prynne." It leads from her bitter sense of herself as victim to her self-conscious manipulation of the townspeople, and it reveals an ego nourished by antagonism; self-protected from guilt by a refusal to look inward; using penance as a refuge from penitence; feeding on shame, self-pity, and hatred; and motivated by the conviction that society is the enemy of the self.

Let me recall the scene I began with, in the chapter midway through the novel. Seven years have passed and the townspeople have come to regard Hester with affection, admiration, even reverence. On her part, Hester has masked her pride as humility, has repeatedly reminded them, by gesture and look, of her "saint-*like*" suffering, and in general has played upon their guilt and generosity until "society was inclined to show its *former* victim a more benign countenance than she cared to be favored with, or, perchance, than she deserved" (187, 257; my emphasis) [56, 106]. And like other hypocrites in Hawthorne's work, Hester pays a heavy price for success. "All the light and graceful foliage of her character had been withered up," he tells us, "leaving a bare and harsh outline, which might have been repulsive, had she possessed friends or companions to be repelled by it" (258) [106–07]. She has none because she wants none. The "links that united her to the rest of human kind had all been broken," save for "the iron link of mutual crime" (255) [104]. She considers Pearl, whom she loves, an instrument of "retribution" (273) [117]. Concerning those to whom she ministers— not only "her enemies" but also those for whom "the scarlet letter had the effect of a cross on a nun's bosom"—Hawthorne points out that Hester "forebore to pray for [them], lest, in spite of her forgiving aspirations, the words of the blessing should stubbornly twist themselves into a curse" (258, 191) [106, 59].

It is worth stressing the severity of Hawthorne's critique. After seven years Hester has become an avenging angel, a figure of penance unrepentant, a so-called Sister of Mercy who not only scorns those who call her so but who has developed contempt for all "human institutions," "whatever priests or legislators had established" (257, 290) [105, 128]. Despairing, therefore, of any improvement short of tearing down "the whole system of society" and doubtful even of that "remedy," she turns her energies first against "the world's law" and then against her daughter and herself (260, 259) [108, 107]. Her heart, Hawthorne tells us,

> had lost its regular and healthy throb, [and she] wandered with-
> out a clew in the dark labyrinth of mind; now turned aside by an
> insurmountable precipice; now starting back from a deep chasm.
> There was wild and ghastly scenery all around her, and a home
> and comfort nowhere. At times, a fearful doubt strove to possess
> her soul, whether it were not better to send Pearl at once to
> heaven, and go herself to such futurity as Eternal Justice should
> provide. (261) [108]

Here is the allegorical landscape of misguided rebellion: a wild, self-
vaunting independence leading by a ghastly logic of its own to the
brink of murder and suicide. No wonder Hawthorne remarks at this
point that "the scarlet letter had not done its office."

I do not mean by this to deny the obvious. Hester is a romantic
heroine. She is endowed with all the attributes this term implies of
natural dignity, generosity of instinct, and what Hawthorne calls "a
woman's strength" (257) [106]. Although she persistently abuses or represses these qualities, nonetheless they remain potential in her—dormant but felt in her every thought and action—and Hawthorne clearly
means them to move us all the more forcefully for the contrast. As he
remarks after detailing her "sad transformation," "She who has once
been a woman, and ceased to be so, might at any moment become a
woman again, if there were only the magic touch to effect the transfiguration. We shall see whether Hester Prynne were ever afterwards
so touched, and so transfigured" (259) [107]. While we wait to see,
Hester persistently invites our pity and praise, and by and large she
succeeds, as she did with the Puritans. But to take her point of view is
to prevent the scarlet letter from doing its office. It leads us, as it did
Hester, into conflict—compels us to choose between the reasons of
the heart and the claims of institutions—and conflict is precisely what
the letter is designed to eliminate.

Again, a distinction is called for. Conflict is also a form of process,
of course, but one that assumes inherent antagonism; it derives from a
partiality that inspires partisanship. Conflict forces us to take positions and thus issues in active oppositions: one certainty against another, one generation against the next, one class or gender against
another. Process (for Hawthorne) is a form of partiality that accepts
limitation, acknowledges its own incompleteness, and so tends toward
tolerance, accommodation, pluralism, acquiescence, inaction.

The contrary tendency toward conflict is the dark side of Hawthorne's chiaroscuro portrait of Hester. Her black eyes and hair—always a danger signal in Hawthorne's (culture's) symbolic system—are
complemented, so to speak, by his relentless critical commentary on
her every misstep into independence. We feel it the moment she
crosses the prison threshold to his gently mocking "*as if* by her own
free-will" (162; my emphasis) [40]. We see it detailed in her radical
speculations, when her mind wanders

> without rule or guidance, in a moral wilderness as vast, as intri-
> cate and shadowy, as the untamed forest. . . . Her intellect and

heart had their home, as it were, in desert places, where she
roamed as *freely* as the wild Indian in his woods. . . . Shame, Despair, Solitude! These had been her teachers,—stern and wild
ones,—and they had made her strong, but taught her much
amiss. (290; my emphasis) [128]

This running gloss on the ways that the letter has not done its office
reaches its nadir in her forest meeting with Dimmesdale. Amidst the
fallen autumn leaves, Hester discards the A in a gesture of defiance for
which (Hawthorne reminds us) her entire seven years had been the
preparation. "The past is gone!" she exclaims. "With this symbol, I
undo it all, and make it as it had never been!" (292) [130]. And the
narrator adds, with characteristic irony (characteristic, among other
things, in that the irony borders on moralism):

O exquisite relief! She had not known the weight, until she felt
the *freedom!* . . . All at once, *as with* a sudden smile of heaven,
burst forth the sunshine.
Such was the sympathy of Nature—that wild, heathen Nature
of the forest never subjugated by human law, nor illumined by
higher truth—with the bliss of these two spirits! (292–93; my emphasis) [130]

The narrator's ironies are not Hawthorne's precisely, and the difference, as we shall see, allows for a significant leeway in interpretation.
But even within this larger perspective the contrast in forms of
process is unmistakable. The radicalization of Hester Prynne builds on
the politics of either/or. Hawthorne's symbolic method requires the
politics of both/and. To that end, in the forest scene, Pearl keeps Hester from disavowing the office of the A, as earlier she had kept her
from becoming another antinomian Anne or Witch Hibbins. Indeed, it
is worth digressing for a moment to point out how closely for these
purposes Pearl is bound to the A—with what painstaking care this *almost* anarchic figure is molded into a force for integration. Hawthorne
presents in Pearl a profound challenge to the boundaries of socialization,[3] but he also details her restraining role with a consistency that
verges on the didactic. He sustains this technique through virtually all

---

3. * * * It may be noted here, as intrinsic to Hawthorne's mode of ambiguity, that Pearl, who
forces Hester to restore the A, is among other things an incarnation of Emersonian whim
(not to say Poesque perversity)—a figure of "infinite variety," "mutability," and "caprice,"
with "wild, desperate, defiant" proclivities; the very spirit of negation, toward her inwardly
rebellious mother no less than toward the apparent consensus of Puritan Boston (269–74)
[113–18]—and that all these traits, including the most "freakish" ("fiend-like," "demon offspring"), give symbolic substance to the "imperious gesture" with which Pearl asserts her
"authority" in the forest scene (298–99) [133–34]:

Pearl still pointed with her forefinger; and a frown gathered on her brow; the more impressive from the childish . . . aspect of the features that conveyed it. . . .
"Hasten Pearl; or I shall be angry with thee!" cried Hester Prynne. . . .
But Pearl, not a whit startled at her mother's threats, any more than mollified by her
entreaties, now suddenly burst into a fit of passion, gesticulating violently, and throwing
her small figure into the most extravagant contortions. . . . Seen in the brook, once
more, was the shadowy wrath of Pearl's image, crowned and girdled with flowers, but
stamping its foot, wildly gesticulating, and, in the midst of it all, still pointing its small
forefinger at Hester's bosom! . . .
"Come thou and take it up!" (298–300) [134–35]

her dialogues, with their conspicuously emblematic messages. And he reinforces it with his every definition of Pearl: as "imp" of the "perverse" *and* "pearl of great price," as "demon offspring," "Red Rose," "elf-child," and "mother's child" (Hester's "blessing" and "retribution" all in one); as the image simultaneously of "untamed nature" and the "angel of judgment," and, at the climactic election-day ritual, as (successively) "sin-born child," "witch-baby," the quintessential outsider who engages with and so weaves together all sections of the diverse holiday crowd—"even as a bird of bright plumage illuminates a whole tree of dusky foliage"—and, finally, as the fully "human" daughter who breaks once and for all the "spell" of mutual isolation (208, 211, 210, 215, 202–203, 205, 329, 330, 336, 339) [72, 74, 73, 77, 67, 69, 155, 156, 160, 162]. Throughout this *development*—in effect, our developing sense of Pearl as "the scarlet letter endowed with life"—Pearl serves increasingly to underscore what is wrong with Hester's radicalism, what remains "womanly" about Hester despite her manlike "freedom of speculation," and what sort of politics Hester must adopt if she is to help effect the changes that history calls for (204, 210, 259) [69, 73, 107].

No other character in the novel, not even the shadowy Roger Chillingworth, is more carefully orchestrated into the narrative design or more single-mindedly rendered a means of orchestration. Midway through the story, at the midnight scaffold, Hawthorne pointedly presents us with a *figura* of things to come: "There stood the minister, with his hand over his heart; and Hester Prynne, with the embroidered letter glimmering on her bosom; and little Pearl, herself a symbol, and the connecting link between those two" (251) [101]. At the last scaffold scene Pearl kisses the minister, now openly her father at last, and Hawthorne remarks: "Towards her mother, too, Pearl's errand as a messenger of anguish was all fulfilled" (339) [162]. And with that office accomplished—by the one character, it will bear repeating, who might be imagined to offer an alternative vision in the novel—Hester can choose in due time to become the agent of her own domestication.

There is a certain irony here, to be sure, but it functions to support Hester's choice by reminding us of the burden of free will, when freedom is properly willed, for, although the burden is a tragic one, it alone carries the prospect of progressive (because incremental, nonconflictual) change. * * * Let me say * * * that [this irony] pertains above all to historical process and that it is perhaps especially prominent in Hawthorne's tales of the Puritans. The obvious contrast to Hester's return in this respect is the fate of Young Goodman Brown. Unlike Hester, Brown insists on alternatives when he rejoins the settlement—innocence or guilt, the truths of the town or those of the

---

Pearl's reflection in the brook is a memorable representation of the reciprocities of process and telos. It stands for nature (and the natural) as an office of repression. Equally and *simultaneously*, it stands for the demands of social conformity, indifferent to threat and entreaty, and conveyed through an impassioned willfulness. It is the letter of the law conceived in the spirit of resistant individuality, and vice versa.

forest—and so finds himself in a hermeneutical impasse, a paralysis of thought and action whose issue is unambiguous "gloom." The no less obvious parallel (in view of Hester's propensities for the unillumined "sympathy of Nature") is the lovers' choice that ends "The May-Pole of Merry Mount." Strictly speaking, it is John Endicott, "the Puritan of Puritans," who forces the former "Lord and Lady of the May" into history. But in fact, Hawthorne emphasizes, they had started on that harsh, necessary road to progress long before, of their own free will: "From the moment they truly loved, they had subjected themselves to earth's doom of care, and sorrow, and troubled joy, and had no more a home at Merry Mount."[4]

Much the same might be said of Hester and Dimmesdale, although they must learn the lesson for themselves, separately, and offstage as it were—Dimmesdale, in the privacy of his study (following a "maze" of Goodman Brown–like temptations); Hester across the ocean, in the "merry old England" that the Puritans had rejected together with the Maypole (303, 211) [137, 74]. Like Dimmesdale, she comes back home as a mixed figure of "pathos" and promise (333) [157]—"angel of judgment" and mercy, "messenger of anguish" and hope. Hawthorne writes of the fully humanized Pearl, the former "wild child" who has at last "developed all her sympathies," that she would no longer need to "do battle with the world, but [could] be a woman in it" (339) [157]. It might be said of Hester upon her return that she can leave Pearl behind because she has taught herself to play Pearl to her own former Hester. She no longer needs restrictions because, after her long battle with the world, she has learned how to restrict herself—how to obviate the conflict between self and society, between the certainty of love and certain prospects of social change, between prophetic hope and politics as usual. As a woman in the world, she has learned to deflect, defuse, or at least defer that inherently explosive conflict and at best to transmute it, freely, into a faith that identifies continuity with progress.

This political level of meaning is closely connected to the moral. What I just called Hawthorne's politics of both/and is directly based upon his concept of truth. Critics often remark on the moral he draws from Dimmesdale's experience: "Be true! Be true! Be true!" (341) [163]. But, as usual with Hawthorne, it is hinged to the narrative by ambiguities. He tells us that he has culled the moral ("among many" others) from "a manuscript of old date," which he has "*chiefly* followed" (341; my italics) [163]. And he prefaces the moral with a dazzling variety of reports about the scarlet letter (or the absence of it) on the minister's breast. For Hawthorne, partiality is to process what multiplicity is to truth—a series of limited perspectives whose effectiveness depends on their being partial without becoming exclusive and partisan in such a way as gradually, by complementarity rather than conflict, to represent

---

4. Hawthorne, "The May-Pole of Merry Mount," in *Tales and Sketches*, ed. Roy Harvey Pearce (New York: Library of America, 1982), 370, 367, 363.

the whole. His political meaning here points us toward the premises of liberal society. His moral meaning is grounded in the premises of Puritan thought. The connection between the two is that between the Hobbist and the Calvinist meanings of the Fall. *The Scarlet Letter* is a story of concealment and revelation, where the point of revelation is not to know the truth but to embrace many truths and where concealment is not a crime, but a sin.

Not crime, but sin: Hawthorne adopts this fine theological distinction for his own liberal purposes. A crime pertains to externals, and, as a rule, it involves others, as in the case of murder or adultery. A sin pertains to the spiritual and internal, to an act of will. It may or may not involve crime, just as a crime (murder, for example, or adultery) *may* not involve sin. It depends on the inner cause, the motive. The issue, that is, is guilt, not shame: not the deceiving of others, but the skewing of one's own point of view. The political office of the A is to make partisanship an agent of reciprocity. Its moral office is to lead from the willful self-binding of a truth—paradigmatically, a truth of one's own—to the redemptive vision of many possible truths.

In the next-to-last chapter, that office is rendered (as the chapter title tells us) through "The Revelation of the Scarlet Letter" (332) [157]. The action centers on the scaffold, as it does twice previously. The first time is at Hester's midday "public exposure" (172) [46], where the A denotes various kinds of division (within the community, within Dimmesdale, and, most dramatically, between Hester and the community). The second scaffold scene comes midway through the novel, in the midnight meeting that draws the main characters together, and by implication, the townspeople as well, for the A that flashes across the night sky lights up the entire town "with the distinctness of mid-day . . . [lending] another moral interpretation to the things of this world than they had ever borne before . . . as if [this] . . . were the light that is to reveal all secrets, and the day-break that shall unite all who belong to one another" (251) [101].

In short, the novel tends increasingly toward reconciliation through a series of ambiguous unveilings, each of which might be titled "The Revelation of the Scarlet Letter." In that penultimate chapter Dimmesdale reconciles himself with his guilt, with Pearl, with Hester, with Chillingworth, and, in "words of flame," with the destiny of New Israel (332) [157]. Now it only remains for Hester to join the telos in process. When she does so, in the conclusion, her moral interpretation of things past and future may be seen to reverse her first misstep across the prison threshold. Indeed, the scene deliberately echoes that initiation into concealment so as emphatically to invert it. When Hester returns, she pauses "on the threshold" of her old home—as many years before she had paused "on the threshold of the prison door"— long enough to display to the onlookers a scarlet letter on her breast (162, 343) [39, 164]. It is a nice instance of liminality serving its proper conservative function at last. Then, at the start of her trials, Hester had repelled the beadle, representative of "the Puritanic code of law" (162) [39], in order to assert "her own free-will." Now she returns as representative of the need for law and the limits of free will. Having abandoned the hope of erasing the past, Hester internalizes the past in all its shame and sorrow. Franz Kafka's penal colony requires a fatal mechanism of authority in order to make the prisoner accept his guilt; Hester preempts the mechanism by authorizing her own punishment and inscribing her guilt upon herself. In a gesture that both declares her independence *and* honors her superiors, she reforms herself, voluntarily, as the vehicle of social order.

This moral design parallels the political process I outlined, but with an important difference. Hester's radicalism sets her apart and sustains her marginality to the end. The sin she commits (her double act of concealment, first of her lover, then of her husband) links her to everyone else. She is unique as a rebel but typical as a liar. Indeed, telling lies is the donnée of the novel as for the Puritans the prison is the donnée of their venture in utopia. It establishes the terms of human possibility in an adulterated world. Directly or indirectly—as deception, concealment, or hypocrisy, through silence (in Hester's case), cunning (in Chillingworth's), eloquence (in Dimmesdale's), or perversity (in Pearl's)—lies constitute the very texture of community in *The Scarlet Letter*. But the texture itself is not *simply* evil. All of Hawthorne's main characters are good people trapped by circumstance, all are helping others in spite of themselves, and all are doing harm for what might justifiably be considered the best of reasons: Hester for love, Dimmesdale for duty, and the Puritan magistrates for moral order. Even Chillingworth, that least ambiguous of villains, is essentially a good man who has been wronged, who lies in order to find the truth, who prods his victim to confess (partly, perhaps, through love), and who, in leaving his wealth to Pearl (gratuitously), provides the basis for whatever there is of a happy ending to the story.

Hawthorne owes this *complex* view of evil—good and evil entwined, the visible "power of blackness" symbiotically augmented by the pervasive if sometimes oblique power of light—to Puritan theology. As the New England primer put it, Adam's fall did much more than fell us all. It also brought the promise of grace through Christ, the Second Adam. Justice *and* mercy, law *and* love: from these twin perspectives, the Puritans built the scaffold and imposed the A. Restrictions were necessary because the Fall had sundered the affections from the intellect; it had set the truths of the heart at odds with the truths of the mind. Now only faith could reconcile the two kinds of truth. They who bound themselves to a single view, *either* justice *or* mercy, were entering into a Devil's pact. They were committing themselves to a lie by concealing a part of reality from themselves, including the reality of the self in all its ambiguity, both human and divine—hence, the degeneration of Chillingworth, "demon of the intellect" (321) [149], and Dimmesdale, until he manages to harmonize the minister's gospel of love with the lover's self-punishment. Hence, too, Pearl's fragmented identity: she is a shifting collage of retribution and love, seeking integration; and, hence, the reciprocal movement of Hester and the community, from opposition to mutuality. As she acts the Sister of Mercy toward those who merely judged her, and so judged too harshly, Hester increasingly touches the people's "great and warm heart" (226) [85]. At the end, after she has passed judgment on herself, Hester gains a fuller, more generous vision of reality than she dreamed possible in the forest. Then it was love with a consecration of its own. Now her love has the consecration of justice, morality, and community.

I rehearse this familiar pattern in order to point out that nothing in it is random or arbitrary. Not a single aspect of this apparent multiplicity (reversals, revisions, and diverse points of view) permits free choice. Hawthorne's celebrated evasiveness comes with a stern imperative. Penitence, he would urge us, has more substance than the absolutism of either/or. Drab though it seems, the morality of both/and heightens personal vision by grounding it in the facts of experience. It takes more courage to compromise. It is a greater act of self-assertion to recognize our limits—to "be true" to what we most deeply are while admitting the fragmentary quality of our truth—to keep faith in our boldest convictions while acknowledging the incompleteness of those convictions, and so to discipline ourselves, of our "own free-will," to the pluralist forms of progress.

It amounts to a code of liberal heroics. Hawthorne's focus is first and last upon the individual; his emphasis on perspective assumes faith in ambiguity; and his ambiguities compel resolution through the higher laws of both/and. Through those higher laws we learn how to sustain certain ideals *and* deny the immediate claims of their certainty upon us; how to possess the self by being self-possessed (which is to say, to hold the self intact by holding it in check); and, from both of these perspectives, how voluntarily to embrace gradualism and consensus in the expectation that, gradually, "when the world should have grown ripe for it," consensus will yield proximate justice for the community and, for the individual, the prospect of unadulterated love.

The prospect leads from the moral to the aesthetic level of the novel. Again, Hawthorne himself provides the link—in this case through the parallel he assumes between moral bivalence and symbolic ambiguity. Consider the title he gives to that chapter midway through the novel. "Another View of Hester" means an inside view of her secret radicalism; it also means a public view of Hester through her acts of charity, which in turn involves a distinction between the view of the many, who consider her "angelic," and the view of the few, "the wise and learned men" who were reluctant to give up earlier "prejudices" (257) [106]. "Another view" means a true sight of Hester, as she really is (rather than as she appears), *and* it means a glimpse of Hester in medias res, in the process of development. Above all, it means another view in the sense of differences of interpretation: interpretation in the form of rumor and legend (the A that magically protects Hester "amid all peril"); interpretation as a mode of sacralization (the A as a nun's cross); interpretation as agent of social change; and interpretation as vehicle of manipulation (Hester "never raised her head to receive their greeting. If they were resolute to accost her, she laid her finger on the scarlet letter, and passed on. This might be pride, but was so like humility that it produced all the softening effects of the latter quality on the public mind"); and, of course, interpretation as the avenue to multiple meanings—the A as sign of infamy, pillow for the sick, shield against Indian arrows, "glittering" and "fantastic" work of art (257–58, 255) [106, 105].

All this and more. No critical term is more firmly associated with *The Scarlet Letter* than ambiguity. What has not been adequately remarked, and questioned, is the persistent, almost pedantic pointedness of Hawthorne's technique. F. O. Matthiessen defined Hawthorne's ambiguity as "the device of multiple-choice"[5]—and so it is, if we recognize it as a device for enclosure and control. That strategy can be traced on every page of the novel, from start to finish, in Hawthorne's innumerable directives for interpretation: from the wild rose he presents to his readers in chapter I—in a virtuoso performance of multiple choice that is meant to preclude choice (for it instructs us *not* to choose between the local flower, the figural passion flower, and the legacy of the ambiguously "sainted Anne Hutchinson")—to the heraldic device with which the novel ends: the "engraved escutcheon" whose endlessly interpretable design (one "ever-glowing point of light gloomier than the shadow" but a source of relief nonetheless) *"might* serve for a motto *or* brief description of our now concluded tale" (345; my emphasis) [166]. Concluded *then,* but, by authorial direction, it is *now* in process, a prod to our continuing speculations. The "curious investigator may still discern [it]," Hawthorne remarks, "and perplex himself with the purport" (345) [166], and the interplay between our perplexity and its purport, like that between process and telos in the description of the rose ("It *may* serve, let us hope, to symbolize *some* sweet moral blossom, that *may* be found along the track, *or* relieve the darkening close tale of human frailty and suffering"), tells us that meaning, while indefinite, is neither random nor arbitrary; rather, it is gradual, cumulative, and increasingly comprehensive (159; my emphasis) [37].

The Scarlet Letter is an interpreter's guide into perplexity. As critics have long pointed out, virtually every scene in the novel is symbolic, virtually every symbol demands interpretation, and virtually every interpretation takes the form of a question that opens out into a variety of possible answers, none of them entirely wrong, and none in itself satisfactory. But the result (to repeat) is neither random nor arbitrary. It is a strategy of pluralism—issuing, on the reader's part, in a mystifying sense of multiplicity—through which each set of questions and answers is turned toward the same solution: all meanings are partly true, hence, interpreters must choose as many parts as possible of the truth and/or as many truths as they can possibly find in the symbol.

Let me illustrate my point through the single most straightforward instance of choice in the novel. Describing Hester's "sad transformation" (midway through the story), Hawthorne remarks that her "rich

5. F. O. Matthiessen, *American Renaissance: Art and Expression in the Age of Emerson and Whitman* (New York: Oxford UP, 1941), 276.

and luxuriant hair had either been cut off, or was . . . completely hidden by the cap" (259) [107]. For once, it seems, we have a plain truth to discover. Something has been hidden, a question about it has been raised, and we await the moment of disclosure; that moment reveals, of course, in "a flood of sunshine" (292) [130], that Hester had *not* cut off her hair. But of course, too, Hawthorne means for us to recognize that in some sense she *had*—had cut off her "essential womanhood," had cut herself off from community, and had cut away her natural luxuriance of character by willfully hiding it beneath an Odysseus' cloak of conformity. These are metaphors, not facts. But in Hawthorne's ambiguous world a main function of choice is to blur the commonsense lines between metaphor and fact, and nowhere is that blurring process better demonstrated than at the moment of revelation, during her forest meeting with Dimmesdale, when Hester discards the A:

> By another impulse, she took off the formal cap that confined her hair; and down it fell upon her shoulders, dark and rich, with at once a shadow and a light in its abundance, and imparting the charm of softness to her features. There played around her mouth, and beamed out of her eyes, a radiant and tender smile, that *seemed* gushing from the very heart of womanhood. . . . Her sex, her youth, and the whole richness of her beauty, came back from *what men call* the irrevocable past. (292–93; my emphasis) [130]

Shadow and light, seemed and was, irrevocable and renewed, womanhood cut off/hidden/lost/restored: *The Scarlet Letter* is a novel of endless points of view that together conspire to deprive us of choice. We are enticed by questions so that we can be allowed to see the polarity between seeking *the* answer, any answer, and undertaking an interpretation. The option is never one thing or another; it is all or nothing. We are offered an alternative, not between different meanings, but between meaning or meaninglessness, and it is meaning in that processual, pluralistic, and therefore (we are asked to believe) progressivist sense that Hester opts for when she returns to New England.

In that option lies the moral-aesthetic significance of Hawthorne's representation of crime as sin. Crime involves social transgression, as in the tradition of the detective story, which centers on the discovery of the criminal. Or, more equivocally, it might involve a conflict of rights that must be decided one way or another, as in the tradition of the novel of adultery, which opposes the claims of the heart to those of civic order. Hawthorne makes use of both kinds of plot, only to absorb them—climactically, through Hester's return—into a story about the trials and triumphs of ambiguity. Through the office of the scarlet letter, all particulars of the criminal act, together with the conflicts they entail, dissolve into a widening series of reciprocities. We come to see that the issue is not a breach of commandment, but (as Hawthorne signals by the conspicuous absence from the novel of the word "adultery") an incremental process of interpretation by which we discern the purport of the broken law for ourselves, and we do so by turning speculation against the tendency either to take sides or to view conflicting sides as irreconcilable.

To represent crime as sin is first of all to universalize the legal problem. It forces us to read a particular transgression in terms of innate human defects and the recurrent conflict of good and evil. But more comprehensively it makes the universal itself a curious object of interpretation—not in order to demystify it, not even to analyze it (in any cognitive sense), but, on the contrary, to invest it with richer significance and a more compelling universality. The ambiguities of *The Scarlet Letter* lead us systematically forward, from the political to the moral or religious to the aesthetic levels, toward what we are meant to understand is a series of broader and ampler meanings. *Always* ampler, and therefore at any given point indefinite: a spiral of ambiguities whose tendency to expand in scope and depth is all the more decisive for the fact that the process occurs in unexpected ways. The result is a liberal hierarchy of meaning, a series of unfoldings from simple to complex, "superficial" to "profound," which is as schematic, comprehensive, and coercive as the medieval fourfold system. Hawthorne's representation of crime as sin requires us to remain vague about all issues of good versus evil (except the evils of partiality and partisanship) in order to teach us that the Puritans' final, relatively nonconflictual view of Hester is deeper than the single-minded judgment reflected in the governor's iron breastplate, just as her final, relatively nonconflictual position toward their bigotry opens the way for both personal and historical development.

I have been using the term "option" in connection with Hester's return in order to stress the overriding distinction in Hawthorne's "device of multiple-choice" between making choices and having choice. His point is not that Hester finally makes a choice against adultery. It is that she has no choice but to resume the A. To make choices involves alternatives; it requires us to reject or exclude on the ground that certain meanings are wrong or incompatible or mutually contradictory. To have choice (in Hawthorne's fiction) is to keep open the prospects for interpretation on the grounds that reality never means either one thing or another but, rather, is Meaning fragmented by plural points of view, for, although the fragmentation is a source of many a "tale of frailty and sorrow," such as *The Scarlet Letter*, it is also, as *The Scarlet Letter* demonstrates, the source of an enriched sense of unity, provided we attend to the principles of liberal exegesis. And by these principles, to opt for meaning in all its multifariousness—to have your adulterous love and do the work of society too—is to obviate not only the conflicts embodied in opposing views but also the contradictions implicit in the very act of personal interpretation between the fact of multiple meaning and the imperative of self-assertion.

In other words, to interpret is willfully, in the interests of some larger truth, *not to choose*. Ambiguity is a function of prescriptiveness. To entertain plural possibilities is to eliminate possible divisions. We are forced to find meaning in the letter, but we cannot choose one meaning out of many: Chillingworth's fate cautions us against that self-destructive act of exclusion. Nor can we choose to interpret any of the novel's uncertainties as contradictions: the antagonism between Hester and the townspeople (or between Chillingworth and Dimmesdale, or between the minister and his conscience) cautions us repeatedly against that abuse of free will. What remains, then, is the alternative that symbols are lies, multiple choice is a mask for absence of meaning, and the letter is an arbitrary sign of transient social structures. And Hester's incipient nihilism cautions us at every turn against that flight from responsibility: in the first scene, by her instinctive attempt to conceal the letter; then, three years later, by concealing its meaning from Pearl (to Hawthorne's suggestion that "some new evil had crept into [her heart], or some old one had never been expelled"); later, in the forest scene, by flinging the letter "into infinite space" and drawing an (infinitely illusory) "hour's free breath"; and, finally, at the election day ritual, by gloating secretly at the prospect of its annihilation, a prospect that Hawthorne opens to her imagination so that, by absorbing it into what the entire novel makes us think *must* be some larger, truer interpretation, we can effectually exclude it as an alternative from our own (162, 274, 300) [40, 117, 135].

If we refuse to exclude it—if we are tempted like Hester in the forest to reject meaning, if we make Chillingworth's choice at the scaffold against mercy or Dimmesdale's in his "secret closet" for contradiction (242) [96]—then interpretation has not done its office. And lest, like these characters, we find ourselves wandering in a maze, Hawthorne points us toward the true path, midway in our journey through the novel. In "Another View of Hester" he impresses upon us: the need for personal interpretation; the inevitably partial nature of such interpretation; the richly varied experiential bases of interpretation; the tendency of these partial and shifting interpretations to polarize into symbolic oppositions, such as rumor and event, metaphor and fact, natural and supernatural, good and evil, head and heart, concealment and revelation, fusion and fragmentation; the need to recognize that these polarities, because symbolic, are never an inherent source of conflict, but instead they are always entwined in symbiotic antagonism and therefore mutually sustaining; and, as the key to it all, the *clavis symbolistica*, the need for faith both in the value of experience (shifting, private, and partial though it is) and in some ultimate hermeneutical complementarity, as in an ideal prospect that impels us toward an ever-larger truth.

That faith involves a *certain* activity on the reader's part. We need to make sense of the entire process for ourselves so that the process can in turn make sense of our partial contributions. The text elicits personal response in order to allow each of us to contribute to the expanding continuum of liberal reciprocity. It is a hermeneutics designed to make subjectivity the primary agency of change while keeping the subject under control, and it accomplishes this double function by representing interpretation as multiplicity flowing naturally into consensus. For, as oppositions interchange and fuse in the text, they yield a synthesis that is itself a symbol in process, an office not yet done. It is a richer symbol now than it was before, a higher office, but still veiled in the winding *perhapses, ors*, and *mights* that simultaneously open new vistas of meaning and dictate the terms of closure.

It may be helpful to distinguish this strategy from others to which it has been compared. Hawthorne does not deconstruct the A; he does not anticipate the principle of indeterminacy; and he offers neither an aesthetics of relativism nor a dialectics of conflict. We might say that in some sense he is doing all of these things, but only in the sense that to do so is to dissipate the integral force of each. His purpose is to rechannel indeterminacy into pluralism, conflict into correspondence, and relativism into consensus. Insofar as terms such as "instability" and "self-reflexiveness" apply to *The Scarlet Letter*, they are agencies of a certain kind of interpretation, much as private enterprise and self-interest were said to be agencies of the general good in antebellum America. Frank Kermode's claim for Hawthorne's modernity—"his texts . . . are meant as invitations to co-production on the part of the reader"—is accurate in a sense quite different from that which he intended. Kermode speaks of "a virtually infinite set of questions." *The Scarlet Letter* holds out that mystifying prospect, much as Jacksonian liberals held out the prospect of infinite possibility, in order to implicate us as coproducers of meaning in a single, coherent moral-political-aesthetic design.[6]

This contrast pertains even more pointedly to Mikhail Bakhtin's concept of the dialogic imagination, which it has recently become fashionable to apply to American novels, and *The Scarlet Letter* in particular. Dialogics is the process by which a singular authorial vision unfolds as a "polyphony" of distinct voices. It entails a sustained open-ended tension between fundamentally conflicting outlooks. They are said to be conflicting insofar as they are *not* partial reflections (such as good or evil) of a more complex truth but each of them, rather, the expression of a separate and distinct way of understanding, a substantially different conception or configuration of good and evil. And they are said to be open-ended because the tension this involves is sustained *not* through the incremental layers of meaning but through the dynamics of diversity itself, which is, by definition, subversive of any culturally prescribed set of designs, including those of group pluralism. Bakhtin's dialogics denies telos through a "modernist" recognition of difference. Hawthorne's ambiguities imply telos through the evasion of conflict. They are modernist in the sense of modern middle-class culture—which is to say, in their *use* of difference (including marginality, complexity, and displacement) for purposes of social cohesion. Recent theorists such as Paul Ricoeur and Hans Blumenberg tell us that the novel (the genre par excellence of the dialogic) "legitimates

---

6. Frank Kermode, *The Classic: Literary Images of Permanence and Change* (New York: Knopf, 1975), 43.

the aesthetic qualities of *novitas*, . . . removes the dubiousness from what is new, and so *terra incognita*, or the *munda novus*, becomes possible."[7] Hawthorne seeks precisely to rein in what becomes possible. Aesthetically, it is the letter's office, as *novitas*, to enclose "the new world," whether as alternative order or as Bakhtinian carnival, within culture, *as* culture.

We might term this strategy the "monologics of liberal ambiguity." It serves to mystify hierarchy as multiplicity and diversity as harmony in process. Dialogics unsettles the link between process and closure. Hawthorne details the manifold discrepancies between process and closure in order to make discrepancy itself—incompleteness, concealment, the distance between penance and penitence—a vehicle of acculturation. To that end he guides his readers (as he does his errant heroine) to a *certain* belief in the unity of the symbol. He shows us that, precisely by insisting on difference, we can fuse an apparently (but not really) fragmented reality. Augustine's answer to Manichaean dualism was to redefine evil as the absence of good. Hawthorne's answer to the threat of multiplicity is to redefine conflict as the absence of ambiguity, and ambiguity, therefore, as the absence of conflict.

Ambiguity is the absence of conflict: Hawthorne's logic is as simple in theory as it is complicated in application. Historical facts tend toward fragmentation, but ambiguity brings this tendency under control, gives it purpose and direction, by ordering the facts into general polarities. Fragmentation itself thus becomes a function of consensus. For once the fragments have been ordered into polarities, the polarities can be multiplied ad infinitum, since each polarity entails or engenders other parallel, contrasting, or subsidiary sets of polarities. The process is one of endless variation upon a theme. And vice versa: it is a process of variation endlessly restricted to a single theme, because (in Hawthorne's fiction) all polarity is by definition ambiguous, all ambiguity is symbolic, and all symbols tend toward reconciliation— hence, the distinctly narrowing effect of Hawthorne's technique, in spite of his persistent allusions and deliberate elusiveness. He himself wrote of *The Scarlet Letter* to his publisher, James T. Fields, on November 3, 1850, that since the novel was "all in one tone" it could have gone on "interminably."[8] We might reverse this to say that what makes the novel hermeneutically interminable also makes it formally and thematically hermetic. In that sustained counterpoint between endlessness and monotone lies the dynamic behind Hawthorne's model of pluralist containment. Process for him is a means of converting the *threat* of multiplicity (fragmentation, irreconcilability, discontinuity) into the pleasures of multiple choice, where the implied answer, "all of the above," guarantees consensus.

The process of conversion follows the symbolic logic of the scarlet

7. Mikhail Bakhtin, *Problems in Dostoevsky's Poetics*, ed. and trans. Caryl Emerson (Minneapolis: U of Minnesota P, 1984), passim; Hans Blumenberg, "The Concept of Reality and the Possibility of the Novel," in *New Perspectives in German Literary Criticism*, ed. Richard Amacher and Victor Lange (Princeton: Princeton UP, 1979), 32.
8. Hawthorne, *Letters, 1843–1853*, ed. Thomas Woodson, L. Neal Smith, and Norman Holmes Pearson, in *Works*, Centenary Edition, 23 vols. (Columbus: Ohio State UP, 1985), 16:371.

letter. It is the office of the A to demonstrate that naturally, organically, pluralism tends to absorb differences into polar opposites, and that bipolarity, properly interpreted, tends of its own accord toward integration. So conceived, the monologics of ambiguity in *The Scarlet Letter* extend to structures of gender, religion, history, psychology, aesthetics, morality, and epistemology. One instance, a minor one but suggestive of Hawthorne's range, is the imaginary "Papist" at the first scaffold scene (166) [42], who sees Hester as the Virgin Mother and who seems to offer an option—an oppositional view, in Raymond Williams's sense, or, more accurately (in light of Hawthorne's emphasis on the relative newness in 1642 of the Reformation), a residual view—that goes deeper than personal and partial differences of perspective.[9] But here, as elsewhere, Hawthorne's point is to intrigue us with notions of conflict in order to disperse them. He can be said to have invented the Papist (that Puritan symbol of irreconcilable antagonism) on our behalf as an early step in our education in ambiguity, and the education proceeds through our recognition, in due time, that the putative contrast is really just one pole in the reciprocity between justice and love. Thus, Catholic and Protestant outlooks merge, midway through the novel, in the townspeople who interpret the A sympathetically as "a cross on a nun's bosom" and, more powerfully, at the final scaffold scene, in the apparent pietà, where Hester (in an image that prepares us for her final role as prophet) plays Sacred Mother to Dimmesdale's Christ (258, 339) [106, 161].

It makes for a rich fusion of polarities, with multiple implications for Hawthorne's symbolic method. For example, the papist perspective (if I may call it so) clearly parallels the compassionate view of Hester expressed by the young mother at the prison door, and clearly, Hawthorne presents *her* view mainly for purposes of contrast, as he does the Papist's, to highlight the harshness of Puritan judgment, whether from magistrates or from "matrons" (161) [38]. In each case the contrast turns out to be a form of symbolic doubling. The "young wife, holding a child by the hand," in some sense mirrors Hester; the embittered matrons in some sense preview Hester's later "injustice"— her impenitent, sometimes brutal judgments (variously motivated by "scorn," "hatred," and "asperity") of her perceived "enemies," her husband, and even her daughter (162, 269, 274) [38, 114, 118]. The result is a spiral of symbolic reciprocities, reinforced by principles of psychology (head-heart) and morality (good-evil), which grow increasingly comprehensive in their image of womanhood—increasingly comprehensive and, proportionately, increasingly positive. They find their high point in Hester the prophet: the rehumanized (because refeminized) heroine whose fall, though it warrants "strict" and "severe" censure (274) [117], augments the promise she represents of future good things. The revelation is still to come, but Hester at last has reached the proper *womanly* vantage point for perceiving something of its import; she has earned the privilege of paying homage, if not directly to

---

9. Raymond Williams, *Marxism and Literature* (Oxford: Oxford UP, 1977), 121–27.

Hawthorne's "little Dove, Sophia," as several critics have argued, then to the dream of "sacred love," which Sophia shared with Nathaniel and which largely derived from the mid-nineteenth-century cult of domesticity (344) [166].[1]

A similar strategy of incorporation applies to the parallel between the Papists and the other non-Puritan culture represented at the first scaffold scene. I refer to the local Indians, who judge from Hester's "brilliantly embroidered badge" that she "must needs be a personage of high dignity among her people" (330) [156]. Hawthorne invests the story's Indians with much the same processual-symbolic effect as he does the Catholic. He juxtaposes the outsider's perspective, in both cases, to that of the Puritans in order to absorb historical difference into what we are meant to think of as broader, universal categories. To that end he deploys the keywords of savagism: "stone-headed" implements, "snake-like" features, "savage finery," "painted barbarians," and, most frequently, "wild"—"wild Indian," "wild men . . . of the land," the "wildness" of their "native garb" (318, 329, 315, 330, 169) [147, 155, 145, 155, 44].

It makes for an all-too-familiar Romantic-Jacksonian configuration: the primitive as an early stage of social growth, which the civilized state not only supersedes but (in the process) ingests, so that its best society combines the "natural" state with the "higher" advantages of culture. Hence, the Indian aspect of Pearl, the "wild child" (329) [155], and, above all, the Indian wildness of Hester's radicalization:

> Her intellect and heart had their home, as it were, in desert places, where she roamed as freely as the wild Indian in his woods . . . criticizing all with hardly more reverence than the Indian would feel for the clerical band, the judicial robe, the pillory, the gallows, the fireside, or the church. (290) [128]

An entire culture is represented in these cunningly compressed polarities. Hawthorne appreciates the natural freedom of the "red men" (287) [127], just as he deplores the civilized excesses of the Puritan pillory—and vice versa; he recognizes the dangers of "desert places" just as he acknowledges the need for fireside and church. It is an ambiguity that effectually deprives the Indians of both nature and civilization, a high literary variation on an imperial rhetoric that ranges from Francis Parkman's elegies for a "noble," "primitive," "dying" race to what Herman Melville satirized as "the metaphysics of Indian-hating."[2] Here it serves to empty the "savages" of their own history so as to universalize them as metaphors for Hester's development.

As all of these examples suggest, the basic symbolic opposition in *The Scarlet Letter* is that between self and society. I said earlier that

---

1. T. Walter Herbert, Jr., "Nathaniel Hawthorne, Una Hawthorne, and *The Scarlet Letter:* Interactive Selfhoods and the Cultural Construction of Gender," *PMLA* 103 (1988): 285–97 [pp. 522–41 in this Norton Critical Edition].

2. Francis Parkman, *The Jesuits in North America in the Seventeenth Century* (1867), in *France and England in North America*, ed. David Levin (New York: Library of America, 1983), 1:343, 461, 466; Herman Melville, *The Confidence-Man: His Masquerade*, in *Pierre, Israel Potter, The Confidence-Man, Tales, and Billy Budd*, ed. Harrison Hayford (New York: Library of America, 1984). 994.

Hawthorne portrays Hester as an individualist of increasingly radical commitment. I might as well have said a radical of increasingly individualist commitment, for Hawthorne's aim is to counter the dangerously diverse social possibilities to which she has access, in fantasy or fact—Indian society, witch covens, Elizabethan hierarchy, Leveler and Ranter utopia (289, 313–30) [127, 143–56]—to bring all such unruly alternatives under control, rhetorically and hence morally and politically, by implicating them all under the symbol of the unrestrained self.

No symbol was better calculated to rechannel dissent into the gradualism of process. And no symbol was more deeply rooted in the culture. As *The Scarlet Letter* reminds us, it served as a major Puritan strategy of socialization, through a process of inversion that typifies all such strategies. Society in this polar opposition became the symbol of unity, and the unsocialized self was designated the symbol of chaos unleashed—"sin, in all its branches," as the Reverend John Wilson details them in the first scaffold scene for "the poor culprit's" sake (176) [50]. Or, mutatis mutandis, the unsocialized self was a morass of "monstrous misconceptions," as John Winthrop labeled Anne Hutchinson, and society stood not just for legal order (as against antinomianism), but for Order at large—"the laws of nature and the laws of grace" (to quote Winthrop again) through which "we are bound together as one man."[3]

In either case, the polarity of self and society remained central through the successive discourses of libertarianism, federalism, republicanism, and Jacksonian individualism. Its negative pressures, implicit in Hawthorne's reference to "the sainted Anne Hutchinson" (and explicit in his essay on "Mrs. Hutchinson")—as well as in recurrent charges of antinomianism against those who were said to have "sprung up under her footsteps" [37], from Edwards through Emerson—are memorably conveyed in Alexis de Tocqueville's contrast between "traditional" and "modern" modes of control: "The ruler no longer says: 'You must think as I do or die.' He says: 'You are free to think differently, and to retain your life, your property, and all that you possess; but from this day on you are a stranger among us.'" Its positive form can be inferred from Edwin Chapin's Massachusetts election day sermon of 1844, *The Relation of the Individual to the Republic*. The self, Chapin argues, denotes "matters of *principle*" and society entails "matters of *compromise*," but in the American way of "self-government" (as nowhere else) it is "compromise not *of* principle but *for* principle."[4]

The Scarlet Letter is the story of a stranger who rejoins the community by compromising for principle, and her resolution has far-reaching implications about the symbolic structures of the American ideology. First, the only plausible modes of American dissent are those

3. John Winthrop, *The History of New England*, ed. James Savage (Boston: Phelps and Farnham, 1825), 1:166; and "A Model of Christian Charity" (1630), in *Winthrop Papers*, ed. Stewart Mitchell (Boston: Massachusetts Historical Society, 1931), 2:124.
4. Alexis de Tocqueville, *Democracy in America*, ed. J. T. Mayer, trans. George Lawrence (Garden City, N.Y.: Doubleday, 1969), 72; Edwin Chapin, *The Relation of the Individual to the Republic* (Boston: Dutton and Wentworth, 1844), 27, 31.

that center on self: as stranger or prophet, rebel or revolutionary, law-breaker or Truth seeker, or any other adversarial or oppositional form of individualism. Second, whatever good we imagine must emerge—and, properly understood, *has* emerged and is continuing to emerge—from things as they are, insofar as these are conducive to independence, progress, and other norms of group pluralism. And third, radicalism has a place in society, after all, as the example of Hester demonstrates—radicalism, that is, in the American grain, defined through the ambiguities of both/and, consecrated by the tropes of theology ("heaven's time," "justice and mercy," "divine providence"), and interpreted through the polar unities at the heart of American liberalism: fusion and fragmentation, diversity as consensus, process through closure.

MICHAEL T. GILMORE

Hawthorne and the Making of the Middle Class†

The currently fashionable triad of American literary studies, race, gender, and class, a triad born of the egalitarian dethroning of the white, male, largely Anglo-Saxon canon, contains its own tacit hierarchy and rests on its own unenunciated principles of exclusion and privileging. Disagreements abound over whether race or gender should occupy the top tier in the new cultural ranking, but about the subordination, even the effacement, of class, there can be no doubt. Few working-class authors have been recuperated—George Lippard, author of *The Quaker City* (1845), is a notable exception from the antebellum period—and no programs in class and its multifarious manifestations have entered college curricula to compete for students with women's studies and African-American studies. Class as a thematic or formal consideration, once the obligatory nod has been made, usually recedes to the background, if it does not vanish altogether, while the critic goes about the business of interpreting *Uncle Tom's Cabin* (1852), *Clotel* (1853), or *Pierre* (1852) in the light of racial and feminist concerns.

One might speculate about the reasons for this omission. It could be argued that the assimilation of the children of working-class parents into the white-collar professoriate has dulled academic sensitivity to the reality of socioeconomic difference. Or it might be claimed that the historic dominance of the middle class in the United States has produced a relatively homogeneous society in which class conflicts have been muted to the point of unimportance. Or if one balks at the notion of an ideological monolith, a related hypothesis offers itself. One might still hold that the United States, in contrast to the stratified nations of Europe where social and economic alterity erupted into armed combat in 1848, subsumes its class divisions under the sign of

† From *Discovering Difference: Contemporary Essays in American Culture*, ed. Christoph K. Lohmann (Bloomington: Indiana UP, 1993), 88–104. Reprinted by permission of Indiana University Press and the author. Page numbers in square brackets refer to this Norton Critical Edition.

gender and/or race. What we find in nineteenth-century American writing, goes a version of this argument, is not economic struggle but a clash of gender styles, not a confrontation between social groups but the displacement of a patrician ideal of masculinity by an entrepreneurial or marketplace model.[1]

This paper takes issue with the critical consensus that relegates class to the margins of antebellum American literature. It does so not by examining the novels of a certified labor activist like Lippard, but rather by turning to a familiar and much-analyzed classic of the American Renaissance, *The Scarlet Letter* (1850). Nathaniel Hawthorne, perhaps our most "canonical" nineteenth-century novelist, the writer, indeed, in whom the canon is given birth, maps the emergence of middle-class identity and simultaneously reveals the self-contradictory and unsettled nature of the new configuration. Behind this claim lies the work of historians and students of gender and the family who have shown, convincingly to my mind, that the period when Hawthorne was writing saw the appearance of the middle class in its recognizably modern form. These scholars dispute the idea of an unbroken ideological or class hegemony in the United States. They recount the development of a social formation that declared itself, in part, through gender arrangements, the separation of public and private spheres, and the substitution of naturalism for historical contingency. Their work suggests not so much that class was submerged in gender, but rather that gender and the family were imbued with the determinants of class.[2]

Yet Hawthorne's text complicates the findings of these scholars. *The Scarlet Letter* points not simply to the development of an American middle class but also to the highly ambiguous character of that construction. It makes clear that the category of class, at least as the category arises in the Age of Jackson, does not march under the banner of essentialism. Hawthorne's masterpiece amounts to a warning that, in rescuing class from erasure, we must dispel any notion of its being a self-consistent entity.

The social indeterminacies of *The Scarlet Letter* problematize the current view of Hawthorne as an important figure in the formulation

1. I refer here specifically to the formulation of David Leverenz. See his book, *Manhood and the American Renaissance* (Ithaca: Cornell UP, 1989). The elision of class, usually in favor of gender or race, is so pervasive in criticism on antebellum literature that to illustrate the practice, one could simply call the roll of leading Americanists: Jane Tompkins, Philip Fisher, Richard Brodhead, etc. Some "second generation" New Historicists have argued for greater attention to class, although their own writing tends to marginalize it. See, for instance, Gillian Brown, *Domestic Individualism: Imagining Self in Nineteenth-Century America* (Berkeley: U of California P, 1990). A recent article that attempts to recuperate class more centrally in relation to several Hawthorne short stories is Nicholas K. Bromell, " 'The Bloody Hand' of Labor: Work, Class, and Gender in Three Stories by Hawthorne," *American Quarterly* 42 (1990): 542–64.

2. Of the many writers who could be mentioned here, I would single out Stuart Blumin, *The Emergence of the Middle Class: Social Experience in the American City, 1760–1900* (New York: Cambridge UP, 1989); Bruce Laurie, *Artisans into Workers: Labor in Nineteenth-Century America* (New York: Noonday, 1989); Mary P. Ryan, *The Cradle of the Middle Class: The Family in Oneida County, New York, 1790–1865* (New York: Cambridge UP, 1981); and Eli Zaretsky, *Capitalism, The Family, and Personal Life*, rev. ed. (New York: Harper, 1986). On the English side, see Leonore Davidoff and Catherine Hall, *Family Fortunes: Men and Women of the English Middle Class 1750–1850* (Chicago: U of Chicago P, 1987).

of a conservative brand of liberal individualism. According to the interpretation put forward most forcefully by Sacvan Bercovitch, Hawthorne contributed to the building of an ideological consensus that complemented the middle class's coalescence.[3] But the class loyalties knitted into *The Scarlet Letter* seem altogether too unstable to authorize so unambiguous a cultural function for the narrative. And recognizing the textual vacillations fosters a certain skepticism about the critical method of reasoning by analogy or homology. The case for Hawthorne's "liberalism" often seems to rest on structural resemblances between literary and social states of affairs, a mode of demonstration that commonly suppresses evidence of dissimilarity.[4] The resemblances are undeniably there in *The Scarlet Letter*, but the differences are no less real, and Hawthorne's text can be usefully studied to bring out the historical and gender oppositions concealed within literary-social congruity.

It remains true that *The Scarlet Letter* participates in the project of shaping middle-class identity. The novel registers the exfoliation of a socially specific way of life. It encodes the deep structures of the middle class within its discursive patternings and to some degree labors to win consent to that class's dominance by validating its claims to universal legitimacy. But at the same time *The Scarlet Letter* obscures the boundary lines it seems to posit as impermeable. The book undoes its own synchronizations of gender roles, private and public spaces, and socioeconomic categories. Hawthorne's notion of what constitutes middle-class personhood turns out to be internally beleaguered. Patterns of male and female behavior, as pictured in the novel, slide into inversions of themselves, and the tale's image of the present is disrupted by pressure from the past and foreshadowings of the future. To borrow the terminology of Raymond Williams, we might say that Hawthorne's middle class incorporates both residual and proleptically oppositional elements,[5] but because gender is so integral to middle-class character as it crystallizes in the text, sexual ambiguation necessarily accompanies ideological and vocational exchange. The middle-class mother assumes a relation to the social like that of a free-market individualist, while the middle-class father embraces feminized sentiment. Hawthorne's new class threatens to come apart even as it comes into being.

Doubtless these inconsistencies can be traced in part to Hawthorne's own anomalous class position, a matter to which I will return

3. Bercovitch has developed his position in essays published over a number of years and drawn together in *The Office of "The Scarlet Letter"* (Baltimore: Johns Hopkins UP, 1991). A somewhat similar interpretation of Hawthorne's novel as a document of ideological compromise has been advanced by Jonathan Arac in "The Politics of *The Scarlet Letter*," in *Ideology and Classic American Literature*, ed. Sacvan Bercovitch and Myra Jehlen (New York: Cambridge UP, 1986), 247–66.

4. This form of argumentation has become identified with the New Historicism and is illustrated, in criticism on Hawthorne, by Walter Benn Michael's essay, "Romance and Real Estate," reprinted in his *The Gold Standard and the Logic of Naturalism: American Literature at the Turn of the Century* (Berkeley: U of California P, 1987), 85–112. On the totalizing character of Michael's book, see Brook Thomas, *The New Historicism and Other Old-Fashioned Topics* (Princeton: Princeton UP, 1991), 117–50.

5. See Williams, *Marxism and Literature* (Oxford: Oxford UP, 1977), esp. 108–27.

at the end of the paper. But insofar as Hawthorne can be taken as an influential maker and articulator of nineteenth-century American culture, it is possible to generalize from the inconstant allegiances of his greatest work. The reversals and impasses of *The Scarlet Letter* betoken not merely his own unsettled status as an impoverished patrician trying to earn a livelihood by literature. They attest to the instability, the persistent vulnerability, of the ideological closure of the antebellum middle class.

I.

Like the word adultery, the name of the middle class is never mentioned in *The Scarlet Letter*. The only socioeconomic groupings Hawthorne refers to are the rich and the poor, or, in the antiquated vocabulary the novel sometimes adopts, the high and the low. Hester Prynne is said to receive abuse equally from the poor on whom she bestows her charity and from the "[d]ames of elevated rank" for whom she plies her needle.[6] The mass of Puritans are distinguished from their rulers only by being designated "the people," with little detail provided about their material condition.

Yet like the act of adultery, the middle class occupies a crucial position in Hawthorne's narrative. Following Roland Barthes—who defined the bourgeoisie as the class *"which does not want to be named"*—one might see the avoidance of nomination as the proof of textual centrality.[7] Hawthorne's labeling of those who are presumably neither rich nor poor as "the people" would be in keeping with this universalizing or self-excising impulse. Fortunately, there is more to go on than deletion. Hawthorne writes that the Puritan order supplanted the "system of ancient prejudice" associated with "nobles and kings" (164) [107]. He invites us to view the inhabitants of seventeenth-century Boston as the precursors of post-feudal—that is, bourgeois—civilization. But historical commonplace dissolves into anachronism, and anticipation gets conflated with actuality as the Puritan past merges into the American present. For Hawthorne presents colonial Boston as a preindustrial settlement sheltering a contemporaneous middle class, and he inscribes his major characters, above all Hester, with attitudes and modes of behavior that did not become normative until the entrenchment of commercial and industrial capitalism in the nineteenth century.

It might be useful to summarize some of the salient features of that emergent social and economic organization. Perhaps most important for *The Scarlet Letter* is the increasingly rigid segregation of work from the household, a divorce accelerated by the decline of domestic production and by the rise of factories and offices. Along with this change came a revaluation of female personality. Excluded from the public

6. Nathaniel Hawthorne, *The Scarlet Letter* (Columbus: Ohio State UP, 1962), vol. I of *The Centenary Edition of the Works of Nathaniel Hawthorne*, 84 [59]. Subsequent page numbers given in the text refer to this edition.
7. See Barthes, *Mythologies*, trans. Annette Lavers (New York: Hill and Wang, 1972), 138.

and male preserve of "productive" labor, women began to be identified with, and supposedly to derive their nature from, the private space of the home. They shed their traditional image as lustful and socially disruptive and were now believed to find fulfillment in moral purity, self-sacrifice, and caring for others. This revision, it should be emphasized, centered on middle-class women, who have been pictured—by, among others, Mary Ryan in history, and Nancy Armstrong in literature[8]—as the principal makers of middle-class lifestyle. The dominant values obviously penetrated working-class culture as well, but many laboring people retained residual or eighteenth-century perspectives on work and the family. Working-class women, for instance, were slower to assimilate domestic ideology because they typically sought employment in manufactories or carried paid work into the home.

The Puritan commonwealth depicted in Hawthorne's early chapters, and at various subsequent moments throughout the text, looks decidedly premodern in its emphasis on hierarchy and patriarchy and in its blurring of the boundaries between public and private. It is a community of rulers and ruled, of ministers, magistrates, and soldiers exercising authority over a deferential and largely undifferentiated people. Hawthorne says that seventeenth-century Boston takes its character from "the stern and tempered energies of manhood, and the sombre sagacity of age" (64) [47]. He distances its customs from his own time by observing that the Puritan elders regularly intervene in the most intimate details of moral and family existence. This patriarchal world antedates the Victorian model of domesticity and assumes the primacy of fathers in governing the family. Governor Bellingham, the Reverend Mr. Wilson, and other civil authorities contemplate removing Pearl from Hester's care because they assume the public's right to oversee the socialization of children. And just as the public intrudes into what came to be seen as a private and female enclave, so Puritan women in the novel think nothing of "stepping forth into the public ways" and loudly proclaiming their opinions of Hester's misdeed. For these New England matrons, writes Hawthorne, "the man-like Elizabeth"—not, one might add, the modest and sentimental Victoria—"had been the not altogether unsuitable representative of the sex" (50) [38].

Although Hester emerges out of the seventeenth-century past, her Elizabethan qualities belong mainly to the narrative's prehistory. Hester, the sexually sinful female, exemplar of traditional womanhood, seems outdated when the action commences. Her refusal to identify her lover in the marketplace reveals the heroine as someone who is already in transition toward a post-Puritan order which guards the private from public exposure. Dimmesdale is also revealed in this opening scene as a Janus-like figure with one eye on a future respectful of the separate spheres. He tells the Reverend Mr. Wilson, much to the older man's bewilderment, "that it were wronging the very na-

---

8. I refer to Ryan's *Cradle of the Middle Class* and to Nancy Armstrong, *Desire and Domestic Fiction: A Political History of the Novel* (New York: Oxford UP, 1987).

ture of woman to force her to lay open her heart's secret in such broad daylight, and in the presence of so great a multitude" (65) [48].

The later pages on Hester's psychological metamorphosis are read too narrowly if we make out in them only the account of one unhappy woman's accommodation to repression. The celebrated descriptions of Hester's change "from passion and feeling, to thought," of her once sensual but now forbidding aspect "that Passion would never dream of clasping in its embrace" (163–64) [107], condense into the span of a few years and a single chapter the reconstruction of feminine nature that required roughly a century to complete. Hawthorne dissolves the transgressive, appetitive Eve into her sexless opposite, replacing concupiscence with the condition that Nancy Cott has accurately labeled "passionlessness" and that underwrites the age's ascendent ideal of self-negating motherhood.[9] He historicizes, as it were, the dark lady/ fair lady split in classic American literature by portraying Hester as a dangerous adulteress recasting herself into a model Victorian saint. In the course of the story, she assumes all those mother-related callings available to nineteenth-century middle-class women, winning the people's reverence for her selflessness as a volunteer nurse and self-ordained "Sister of Mercy." The townspeople forget the "original signification" (161) [105–06] of Hester's letter because that original meaning—of woman as fallen Eve—has been eclipsed historically by middle-class woman's role as self-sacrificing dispenser of nurturance.

Just as Hester is a woman in transition, so *The Scarlet Letter* itself can be understood as a text mutating from one generic category to a second, historically posterior, literary form. The tale, like the heroine, appears anachronistic at first, an eighteenth-century seduction story that has somehow strayed into the age of *Uncle Tom's Cabin* and *The Wide, Wide World* (1850). But Hawthorne's narrative quickly shows its hybrid character as a contemporaneous sentimental novel superimposed upon that obsolete seduction plot. It is remarkable how much of the book approximates the fiction of the "scribbling women" Hawthorne famously disparaged in his correspondence. The structure of the antebellum middle-class family is replicated, or rather disfigured, in the novel's central human reality, the mother and daughter who spend all their time together while the father absents himself at work. The many scenes involving Hester and Pearl parallel the sometimes affectionate, sometimes troubled, mother-daughter relationships familiar to readers of domestic literature. Hawthorne admits that the wearer of the letter behaves more like a mother from the permissive present than from the rigid Puritan past. Loving her daughter "with the intensity of a sole affection," she lacks the resolve to discipline Pearl severely and expects little return for her tenderness other "than the waywardness of an April breeze" (179) [116]. This domestic Hester almost lives up to Hawthorne's description of her as "the image of Divine Maternity" (56) [42].

But Hester, even in her maternal avatar, is not, or not merely, the

9. See Cott's essay, "Passionlessness: An Interpretation of Victorian Sexual Ideology, 1790–1850," in *A Heritage of Her Own*, ed. Nancy Cott and Elizabeth H. Pleck (New York: Simon, 1979), 162–81.

Victorian angel in the house, the woman Dimmesdale hails as his "better angel" (201) [129]. The proto-feminism into which her alienation modulates is, in Hawthorne's treatment, the corollary to her solitary mothering and doing of good. Thrust into a modernized family arrangement by her infraction, Hester experiences as compressed personal history the gradual sundering of realms—public disjoined from private, male separated from female—that by the mid-nineteenth century constituted middle-class existence. One need only contrast the gawking, vociferous matrons who surround the scaffold in the early chapters with the mother and daughter who retire into the background while Dimmesdale delivers his election sermon. The now fully modern heroine, clinging to the margins of the marketplace, feels overwhelmed by a sense of her lover's remoteness "from her own sphere." Despite their private interview in the forest, Dimmesdale seems to have no connection to her; in his public, professional capacity, he is "utterly beyond her reach" (239) [152]. Such stark compartmentalizing underlines the rigid genderization against which antebellum feminism rebels but which simultaneously empowers feminist protest by making women cognizant of themselves as a separate human category and interest group. Hester is a female reformer two hundred years before her time because alone among the Puritans she is able to conceptualize "the whole race of womanhood" (165) [108] as a branch of the human race apart from men.[1]

Dimmesdale is Hester's male counterpart as middle-class father and "new man" emancipated from the paradigms of an earlier cultural system. Unlike the Puritan patriarchs, he expresses admiration for Hester's unwillingness to speak in public: what for them is a failure of religious and civil duty is for him the mark of true womanhood. The split between public and private defines masculine identity for Dimmesdale too. He internalizes the fundamental rupture of modern social life as a division between his inner and outer selves. The self he displays in public to his parishioners is sharply differentiated from—it is the contradiction of—the private self that the reader knows to be Pearl's unacknowledged father and Hester's soulmate. The minister is tortured by "the contrast between what I seem and what I am" (191) [123] and struggles to take his place beside his "wife" and child before the public gaze. But every attempt to confess, to overcome the breach between family and workplace, founders on his fear of the consequences of exposure. As we shall see, Dimmesdale does succeed in mediating between the private and the public, but he does so in ways that controvert his characterization as middle-class male.

Dimmesdale is further set apart from Boston's ruling elders by his having risen in the community through ambition and ability. "It was an age," Hawthorne writes, "when what we call talent had far less consideration than now, but the massive materials which produce stability

---

1. I should perhaps qualify this statement by noting the conspicuous seventeenth-century exception (that proves the nineteenth-century rule?) of Anne Hutchinson. On the continuities between Hutchinson and Hester, see Amy Lang, *Prophetic Woman: Anne Hutchinson and the Problem of Dissent in the Literature of New England* (Berkeley: U of California P, 1987).

and dignity of character a great deal more" (237) [150]. Dimmesdale has acted the part of a Jacksonian man on the make and pushed ahead of his seniors through assiduous cultivation of crowd-pleasing verbal skills. The homology to Hawthorne's own situation as a professional author trying to win fame and affluence through his linguistic gifts is evident enough.

Indeed, Dimmesdale's curious dwelling arrangements both highlight his post-Puritan professionalism and epitomize the text's enforcement of gender sequestration. The minister lives not with his "family" but with Hester's former husband, Roger Chillingworth, a man who, like himself, has a university education and practices an intellectual calling. Their lodgings resemble a workspace or office building more than a home. In one half is Dimmesdale's library, crammed with "parchment-bound folios" and writing materials, in the other the physician has installed his "study and laboratory," and the "two learned persons" daily settle down to their specialized vocations, at the same time "bestowing a mutual and not incurious inspection into one another's business" (126) [84–85]. Hawthorne has written into the narrative a graphic image of male professionals "married" to their work in the era after family production, when mental and manual forms of labor were segregated almost as sharply as men and women. Or better yet, he has given us a picture of the intensifying rivalry between the two great healing professions of the nineteenth century, the clerical attendants of the soul and the medical doctors of the body. Only Hester, in her gendered and unpaid role as charity worker, is entitled to treat spiritual as well as physical ailments.

Hawthorne is able to render the world of middle-class professionalism so vividly because he endeavors to enter it. His ambition to write for a livelihood, to become that invention of modernity, an independent author, gives him sympathetic understanding of his two male characters even as it figuratively places him in competition with them for status and income. As a young man about to matriculate at Bowdoin College, Hawthorne already pictured himself as a professional; in a well-known letter to his mother, he weighed the pros and cons of a career in law, medicine, and the ministry, ending with the question, "What would you think of my becoming an Author, and relying for support upon my pen?" As a writer who specialized in character analysis, Hawthorne did not flinch from rivalry with the other professions but positively cultivated it, as he ventured into territory traditionally reserved for clergymen and doctors. Reviewers, repelled or amazed by his psychological penetration, regularly compared him to a preacher, a Puritan, or an anatomist. "[H]e shows the skillful touches of a physician in probing the depths of human sorrow," exclaimed an admirer of the tales, and a reader of *The Scarlet Letter* was uttering a commonplace when he remarked that "of all laymen he [Hawthorne] will preach to you the closest sermons."[2]

2. Letter to Elizabeth C. Hawthorne, 13 March 1821, *Letters, 1813–1843* (Columbus: Ohio State UP, 1984), vol. 15 of *The Centenary Edition*, 139; see the reviews collected in *Hawthorne: The Critical Heritage*, ed. J. Donald Crowley (New York: Barnes, 1970), esp. 78, 193.

Just as Hawthorne the novelist would lay claim to professional standing, so his novel apes the mores of the white-collar paradigm. *The Scarlet Letter* is formed by the same structural divisions that beset Hawthorne's principal characters. The book reproduces the separation of spheres most palpably in the line isolating "The Custom House— Introductory" from the ensuing narrative. The preface encloses the reader in the public and male domain of the Salem customhouse, "Uncle Sam's brick edifice" (12) [13] symbolizing government and commerce. Here Hawthorne introduces us to his fellow workers, all of them men, describes his duties as Surveyor of the Revenue, and sets forth a kind of professional primer for writers, a detailed account of the genesis and composition of his romance. This sketch abuts but does not encroach upon the family romance of Hester, Pearl, and Arthur. Affective life quarantines itself in the tale of frustrated love, with its copious notation of female domesticity and private suffering. Holding in tension the oppositions endemic to nineteenth-century capitalism, the text as an entirety organizes itself as an instantiation of middle-class experience.

A similar splitting operates on a smaller scale within the romance proper, once the opening scene of Hester's punishment on the scaffold has run its course. Thereafter imperceptible lines of gender division radiate throughout the plot and give the tale its exemplary character as a kind of microcosm of the divergent forms of antebellum American storytelling. Chapters track Hester and/or Pearl on the one side, and Dimmesdale and/or Chillingworth on the other; mother and daughter inhabit one fictional space, the two males work and reside in another. When gender intersections occur, they do so outside society or in highly privatized settings that do not disturb the developing barrier between the familial and the public—places such as a jail cell, the scaffold at midnight, the seashore, or the forest. *The Scarlet Letter's* spatial demarcations point to its double character as feminized domestic tale and canonical "drama of beset manhood."[3] The novel's divisions miniaturize respectable—that is, middle-class—literary culture's bifurcation into the two subgenres of sentimental fiction and the fiction of male bonding and competition.

2.

Thus far we have been concerned with the parallels or homologies between Hawthorne's fictional universe and the historical details of middle-class formation. *The Scarlet Letter*, according to the argument, reinscribes the spatial and gender divisions constitutive of middle-class identity in the era of its rise. A change of focus is now in order, for it will bring to light some of the dark spots that concentration on similarity has ignored. The "dark spots" are complications and contra-

3. I am paraphrasing the title of Nina Baym's article, "Melodramas of Beset Manhood: How Theories of American Fiction Exclude Women Authors," *American Quarterly* 33 (1981): 123–39. *The Scarlet Letter* is fairly unusual among the classics of the American Renaissance in encompassing both male and female domains.

dictions whose effect is to destabilize the particular alignments posited between textual and historical patterns. A first step toward correcting these occlusions would be to note that the gendered locus of class membership wavers in the novel and that Hester and Dimmesdale change places by donning the other sex's social characteristics.

The Scarlet Letter, for example, contains an American Adam figure who bears comparison to other Adamic heroes of nineteenth-century male sagas, heroes like Natty Bumppo, Ishmael, and Henry David Thoreau. This character, writes Hawthorne, "roamed as freely as the wild Indian in the woods" and criticizes the institutions of Puritan Boston "with hardly more reverence than the Indian would feel for the clerical band, the judicial robe, the pillory, the gallows, the fireside, or the church" (199) [128]. The character conceptualizes freedom and autonomy as qualities existing apart from the social order. For Hawthorne's Adam figure, the individual is defined not as a member of some larger unit but primarily in opposition to community; he is self-made and owes allegiance only to his own values and interests.

The character, of course, is Hester, but Hawthorne's account of her fierce independence suggests less Victorian womanhood than the Jacksonian individualist. It is appropriate to use the pronoun "he" in describing such a person because to Hawthorne's contemporaries, the solitary subject was necessarily a man. Ralph Waldo Emerson's representations stand as typical. In that most famous of treatises on the mid-century summons to autonomy, "Self-Reliance" (1841), the seeker after independence is always gendered as male. The iterated nouns and pronouns do not mask but instead proclaim the cultural exclusions: "The nonchalance of boys who are sure of a dinner, and would disdain as much as a lord to do or say aught to conciliate one, is the healthy attitude of human nature." Emerson's masculine insistences implicitly invert the clauses in his declaration, "Whoso would be a man, must be a non-conformist."[4]

In actuality, this virile nonconformist conformed to the social practices of his time. He was more entrepreneur than Transcendentalist or sourceless Adam. Karl Marx's comments in *Grundrisse* on Robinson Crusoe, a literary avatar for the Adam myth, are illuminating not just about Hawthorne's tale but about the disjunction between the individual and civil society generally, a separation which provides so recurrent a feature of American masculine writing. Marx explains that the presence in eighteenth- and nineteenth-century literature of the isolated, apparently pre-social individual—a figure he himself likens to Adam or Prometheus—entails a massive forgetting or ignorance. Entering the novel "[n]ot as a historic result but as history's point of departure," the Robinson Crusoe character reverses the actual circumstances of his appearance. He belongs to, and can only arise in, a "society of free competition" where "the individual appears detached from the natural bonds etc. which in earlier historical periods make

---

4. The quotations are from *Essays: First Series* (Cambridge: Belknap Press of Harvard UP, 1979), vol. 2 of *The Collected Works of Ralph Waldo Emerson*, 29.

him the accessory of a definite and limited human conglomerate."[5] Some of the bonds Marx has in mind, like clans or feudal hierarchies, never existed in America, but Hawthorne's rendering of the Puritan commonwealth reminds us that on this continent too the human community involved a dense network of responsibilities and connections. The autonomous individual who dominates antebellum narratives of male rivalry and maturation is a corollary to the acceleration of market capitalism in the Age of Jackson, not a reflection of humanity unencumbered by history but a product of the breakdown of republican commitment to the common welfare and its displacement over the century by laissez-faire ideology. The bearer of this historical change was Jackson's man-on-the-make, vocal opponent of customary restrictions on economic development and building block of the new middle class. But in *The Scarlet Letter*, paradoxically enough, this quintessential individualist and free-thinking pioneer in regions forbidden to women is herself a woman and otherwise the antithesis of Jacksonian man.

Hester's dissident side, as noted earlier, associates her with antebellum feminism. Recent critics have construed Hawthorne's strictures on his heroine as a repudiation of the movement for women's rights that was gathering force while he composed his romance, less than two years after the Seneca Falls Convention of 1848.[6] While this may be an accurate appraisal of Hawthorne's conscious purpose, it slights the historical volatility of his characterization of Hester. The heroine's assumption of masculine traits—which Hawthorne obviously intends as a disparagement—encodes a shadowy hint of future developments in female reformism. For a brief moment at the end of the story, Hester appears to overshoot, as it were, the domestic feminism of Hawthorne's own day and to verge on the androgynous "New Woman" of the post-Civil War period.

As Carol Smith-Rosenberg has pointed out,[7] the feminism of the late nineteenth and early twentieth centuries thrived outside conventional social arrangements. It broke with the ideology of domesticity. The "New Woman" differentiated herself from her mother's generation by rejecting marriage and opting for a career. She braved the charge of "mannishness" by choosing a life not in the traditional family but in female institutions like women's colleges and social settlements, the best-known example of which was Hull House in Chicago, and she strove to cultivate autonomy as in a nondomestic environment.

Hester's denial of her (hetero)sexuality can thus be viewed not simply as a de-eroticizing but as a prefiguration of the Gilded Age woman reformer. Such a reading would be patently anachronistic, but

5. References are to the selection from *Foundations (Grundrisse) of the Critique of Political Economy, The Marx-Engels Reader*, ed. Robert C. Tucker, 2nd ed. (New York: W. W. Norton & Company, 1978), 222.

6. See Bercovitch, *The Office of "The Scarlet Letter,"* 106.

7. See particularly Smith-Rosenberg, "The New Woman as Androgyne: Social Disorder and the Gender Crisis, 1870–1936," *Disorderly Conduct: Visions of Gender in Victorian America* (New York: Oxford UP, 1985), 245–96.

my point is that Hawthorne's portrait of Hester as self-reliant individualist converts her, in the novel's "Conclusion," into a prophecy of supercession. She never remarries after Arthur's death and, upon returning to New England from Europe, assembles around her a community of women who console and advise each other in the face of masculine oppression. In this liminal, nonfamilial setting, Hester creates an alternative institution to patriarchal structures. Her stated message, in which she assures her followers of a "brighter period" when "the whole relation between man and woman" will be established "on a surer ground of mutual happiness" (263) [165–66], is far less radical and less meaningful than her example. Hester endures as an independent being who separates herself from the prevailing social order—her cottage lies on the distant periphery of the Puritan settlement—and who finds fulfillment in the company of other females. The image of her in the book's final pages seems as much an historical postscript as a textual coda to the action.[8]

Just as Hester undergoes a series of social and sexual mutations, so Dimmesdale, exemplar of mid-century manhood, alchemizes into a communal being who looks remarkably like a sentimental novelist. The minister, according to Hawthorne, could never join Hester—or the Deerslayer, or the hermit of Walden Pond—in "the hardships of a forest life." His "culture, and his entire development" as a man of the cloth forbid it (215) [137]. Standing at "the head of the social system," Dimmesdale derives his very identity from its framework; he internalizes the community's "regulations, its principles, and even its prejudices" (200) [128]. Whereas Hester discovers her authentic self in isolation from the Puritan colony, Dimmesdale—to revert to Marx's formulation—knows himself to be "the accessory to a definite and limited human conglomerate." He is a residual presence in the commercial and industrial middle class, a product as much of the eighteenth or seventeenth century as of the Age of Jackson and Hawthorne. The minister can be seen as demonstrating the accuracy of Hawthorne's historical imagination—he is supposed to be a Puritan, after all—but more interestingly, his portrayal underscores the persistence in the text of loyalties and assumptions about individuality that clash with the ideology of liberalism. As a man, Dimmesdale is an anachronism from the past, as Hester as a woman is a potential anachronism from the future.

But Dimmesdale is not just a man; he also completes Hawthorne's fictionalization of middle-class womanhood. From the outset, he is delineated in terms that typify nineteenth-century femininity more than conventional maleness. First beheld on the balcony during Hester's punishment, he has "large, brown, melancholy eyes," a "tremulous" mouth, and a "nervous sensibility." His diffidence ill suits public office and causes him to feel most at ease in "shadowy by-paths." Dimmes-

8. This is not to suggest that the argument for a nondomestic feminism wasn't made in Hawthorne's day. Margaret Fuller's *Woman in the Nineteenth Century* (1845) is a case in point. But as a widespread cultural movement, the phenomenon belongs to the latter third of the century.

dale is said to keep himself "simple and childlike" and to retain "a freshness, and fragrance, and dewy purity of thought" that affects many people as the manner of "an angel" (66) [48]. It would appear from his description that the angel is domestic, the pure and retiring homemaker of Victorian ideology.

Besides physically resembling a woman—much as Hawthorne does in surviving daguerreotypes—Dimmesdale is identified with the female realm of the emotions. His feminine qualities tally with his (residual) immersion in the social; he and Hester swap positions dramatically in this respect. Hawthorne, speaking in his most naturalizing mode, observes that her years of isolation have stripped Hester of the capacity for affection and passion, the preservation "of which had been essential to keep her a woman" (163) [107]. But what Hester has temporarily forsaken, Dimmesdale, nominally a man, has possessed all along. The feeling evident in his voice when he addresses the Puritan populace works so powerfully on the hearts of his auditors, that the minister's words weld them "into one accord of sympathy" (67) [49].

Dimmesdale's skill at deploying and manipulating sentiment enables him, like the popular women novelists of the 1850s, to bridge the gap between private affect and public occupation. The young preacher is conscious of the rift between the two realms, an awareness that certifies his modernity and places him apart from the Puritan patriarchs, who act as though the closet and the marketplace are synonymous. Dimmesdale's attempt to surmount the division rhetorically, through the mediation of language appealing to the emotions, inflects his nineteenth-century contemporaneousness toward the feminine and allies him, as an artist figure, with Stowe or Warner rather than Cooper or Melville. For the minister's sermons, delivered "in a tongue native to the human heart" (243) [154], constitute a sentimental literature; they validate and make public—they publish—the inner feelings that the text denominates as female or domestic. Hawthorne tropes the heart as a chamber or residence, a space that only a woman can humanize and make inhabitable. He has Chillingworth observe to Hester, "My heart was a habitation large enough for many guests, but lonely and chill, and without a household fire" (74) [53]. Dimmesdale's "Tongue of Flame" suffuses the public world with affectivity; he feminizes culture by lighting a hearth fire in the popular heart.

Dimmesdale's volte-face, from rising male professional to domestic novelist reaching out from the private sphere to engage "the whole human brotherhood" in the language of sentiment (142) [94], alerts us to the fact that the neat structural divisions of Hawthorne's own novel tend to lose their resolution upon closer scrutiny. Hawthorne himself is a male fiction writer redoing the seduction formula as a domestic love story of mother, daughter, and missing father. Moreover, the partition between public and private, male and female, encapsulated in the break between "The Custom-House" and the romance proper, inverts itself with a slight alteration of perspective. Hawthorne terms the preface an indiscreet surrender to the "autobiographical impulse" (3) [7]. Not only does he lay out his theory of romance, he divulges intimate details about his struggles with a writer's block. He gives an account of his personal affairs, including his resentment at being dismissed from office—the kind of washing one's laundry in public that Hawthorne well knew would create a stir. He even conducts the reader into a chamber of his home, with its "little domestic scenery" of doll, child's shoe, and hobbyhorse (35) [29]. The tale that follows, on the other hand, is an impersonal commodity contrived for sale on the literary marketplace. Hawthorne, who addressed his readers as "I" in the introduction, now extinguishes the private self and assumes the mask of omniscience as a third-person narrator. The pigeonholing on which the text seemed to rest its articulation of social life under expanding capitalism proves impossible to maintain. *The Scarlet Letter's* formal separation into preface and narrative operates to exhibit *and* to dissolve the structures of middle-class existence.

These migrations demonstrate the lability of structural parallels between text and history. They testify to the overflow or supplement that class brings to gender. Hester is a female denizen of the private sphere, but she is also an isolated individualist whose stance toward the social mimics laissez-faire doctrine rather than the cult of domesticity. Dimmesdale is an absent father and male co-worker, but he is also a domestic author. Both characters, in both their avatars, inhabit positions in the middle class—positions that did not emerge as ubiquitous until that class jelled in the Jacksonian Era. Yet the two characters hold those places as occupational and ideological transvestites.

Class refuses to be permanently absorbed into gender in Hawthorne's text. For while gender style is always tethered to class, class exceeds the capacity of gender to contain it. The refusal of fixed gender roles returns upon class, as it were, to advertise a problem in Hawthorne's attitude toward middle-class identity. The mid-century middle class proscribed the very gender ambiguity he sponsors in his novel. To be a "masculine" woman was to veer toward the attributes of the working class; to be a feminized male was to ape the manner of the social aristocracy. Hawthorne's sense of occupational and gender mutability connotes a refusal to abide by the dominant class's sexual and spatial requirements. The novel's constant shifting of boundaries betrays authorial doubts about the middle-class ethos. The shifts intimate, not Hawthorne's collusion in the liberal consensus, but rather his indecision about an historical emergence that his art commemorates but simultaneously chafes at as stultifying.

3.

The ending of Hawthorne's novel precipitates a last effort to confront the compartmentalizations of market culture. The ending can be read in either of two ways, as an undoing of middle-class conventions or as their apotheosis. The final tableau on the scaffold, with Dimmesdale joining Hester and Pearl as he had failed to do at the beginning, reconstitutes the intimate nuclear family. T. Walter Herbert, in an influential article on gender in Hawthorne, calls this scene a recreation of "essential manhood and essential womanhood."[9] And there's no doubt that the last chapters contain some of the narrative's most ideologically sanitized pronouncements. A consolidating of gender stereotypes and cultural boundaries appears to signal Hawthorne's complete capitulation to middle-class ideals. He projects the fissures of his time into the afterlife. Not Hester and Dimmesdale, he suggests, but Dimmesdale and his male rival, "the old physician," will find themselves reunited in the "spiritual world," their "antipathy transmuted into golden love" (260–61) [164]. Pearl's shedding of tears at her father's dying kiss is construed, in the best sentimental fashion, as "the pledge" that she will cease to "do battle with the world, but be a woman in it" (256) [162]. The reader learns that Hester's hope of reforming gender relations will have to wait upon an "angel" of unblemished character, "a woman indeed, but lofty, pure, and beautiful"; and capable of "showing how sacred love should make us happy, by the truest test of a life successful to such an end!" (263) [166]. Though Hester delivers this prophecy to a community of women, Hawthorne's words imply that his heroine's feminist longings are to find fulfillment in the dream of a perfect marriage.

If at moments the ending strives to naturalize the doctrine of pure womanhood, however, it never does so without equivocation. Pearl's defection to Europe, where she reenters the gentry from which her mother's family descended, hints at a persistent and unmastered distaste for the confinements of middle-class life. The same impatience hovers behind Hawthorne's disclosure, in the tale's final paragraph, that on the tombstone of his ill-starred lovers "there appeared the semblance of an engraved escutcheon" bearing a heraldic device (264) [166]—feudal and aristocratic residues that affront middle-class closure. Moreover, Hester's insistence on reassuming the scarlet letter, on advertising her youthful sinfulness, acts as a reminder of the premodern understanding of woman's character. The letter reminds us that nineteenth-century female essentialism is a temporally bounded, post-Puritan construct, not an eternally existing ideal. Contemporaneous gender roles can be thought of as universally desirable only by repressing the historical differences that the tale itself has documented.

To put this more positively, Hawthorne seems as intent on rending the barriers of Jacksonian culture as he is on legitimating its norms. The scaffold scene, with its reuniting of the middle-class family unit, illustrates the point. The apparent essentialism of this episode is qualified, not to say undermined by the physical setting of its occurrence. Hawthorne brings together the Victorian trinity of mother, father, and child in the very site where domestic ideology proscribes it: before the stares of the multitude in the marketplace or public stage. Understood in this way, the building of the entire narrative toward the climactic reconstruction of the family indicates a wish on Hawthorne's part, not to uphold, but to challenge nineteenth-century binary logic. The scaf-

---

9. Herbert, "Nathaniel Hawthorne, Una Hawthorne, and *The Scarlet Letter*: Interactive Selfhoods and the Cultural Construction of Gender," *PMLA* 103 (1988): 285–97, esp. 289 [pp. 522–41 in this Norton Critical Edition].

fold scene marks a trespassing of the industrial order's boundaries, a reversion to older patterns of behavior and an anticipation of future struggles to insert familial or domestic issues into the political sphere.

A glance at Hawthorne's own circumstances, and another look at Hester's standing in the community, may help to elucidate his oscillations. The author of *The Scarlet Letter* occupied a highly irregular class position. As he impresses upon us in "The Custom-House," he was descended from one of New England's most distinguished families. The Hathornes (spelled without the "w") were long-standing members of the Massachusetts elite and perhaps the closest thing the non-slave-holding states boasted to an aristocracy. The novelist's ancestors journeyed to the New World with the first wave of Puritan immigrants. They were prominent jurists and magistrates whose deeds—or rather, misdeeds—were recorded in histories of the country's earliest settlement. But like Poe's mythical Ushers, the line's fortunes have declined precipitously. When the future novelist was a child of three, his own father, a merchant, died at sea, and he was raised on the charity of relatives. As an author, he has not escaped dependency. He has continued to receive handouts to support his family; indeed, as we know from the preface, he has failed so miserably as a writer that he has had to accept employment as a government functionary. Little wonder that he imagines his forefathers dismissing him as a mere "writer of story-books! . . . Why, the degenerate fellow might as well have been a fiddler!" (10) [12].

Like his fictional minister, Hawthorne the dependent patrician seemed to have an equivocal sexual identity that inclined toward the female. Many contemporaries commented on his extraordinary good looks, Elizabeth Peabody (the sister of his wife) pronouncing him "handsomer than Lord Byron"—another aristocratic figure renowned for almost feminine beauty. Reviewers detected "a large proportion of feminine elements" in the work—to quote Henry Wadsworth Longfellow—and heaped up adjectives like quiet, passive, pure, arch, delicate, lovely, and sensitive. They called the novelist "Gentle Hawthorne" in recognition both of his genteel roots and demeanor and of his womanly tenderness. Hawthorne's celebrated reclusiveness reinforced these impressions. The description of Dimmesdale as lingering in "shadowy by-paths" can be applied to the notoriously shy and aloof creator who withdrew into his mother's home for a decade after graduating from college. And of course Hawthorne's lack of financial independence cast him in a feminized position. Like women throughout history, he had to rely on others to provide the money for his family's maintenance.[1]

Compounding the feminizing of aristocracy, Hawthorne's pauperism highlights the mutability of his location in the social order. He repre-

1. Peabody is quoted in James R. Mellow, *Nathaniel Hawthorne in His Times* (Boston: Houghton, 1980), 6; the Longfellow review appears in *Hawthorne: The Critical Heritage*, 80–83, esp. 81. Although I invert his emphases, I wish to acknowledge here the work of David Leverenz on types of antebellum masculinity. See *Manhood and the American Renaissance*.

sents a notable instance of antebellum declassing: he is an impoverished scion of the American patriciate, an aristocrat driven to subsist
on public charity. But he is also, precisely as the author of the text we
are reading, on the verge of redefining his social position as a member
of the rising professional class. He aspires to, and with this fiction finally attains, the economic independence that comes from appeal to
the marketplace and not to a patron. He belongs to the first generation of self-supporting writers in the nation's history, the men and
women of the 1850s who proved it possible to live by the pen.
Hawthorne is at once a professional male, an erstwhile aristocrat, and
a failed laborer at literature reeling from the loss of his government
sinecure. Ideological uncertainty and ambivalence toward the new
middle class seem hardly surprising in his case. He stands within the
emergent social formation, but he stands above it and below it as well.

And Hester shares his categorical instability as *declassé* aristocrat.
When first forced to mount the scaffold, she thinks back to her paternal English home, "a poverty-stricken" dwelling over the portal of
which hangs "a half-obliterated shield of arms . . . , in token of ancient
gentility" (58) [43]. Convicted of adultery, required to wear the badge
of shame, Hester's regal bearing nevertheless invests her with an aristocratic air. The servant who admits the heroine to Governor Bellingham's mansion is so struck by her manner, and by "the glittering
symbol on her bosom," that he imagines she must be "a great lady in
the land" (104) [70]. But in fact Hester's sexual transgression only
completes her family's social collapse, arguably into the laboring class.
She ekes out a subsistence for herself and Pearl with her needlework,
a Puritan forerunner of the nineteenth century's favorite emblem of
downtrodden womanhood, the seamstress.

Seen from a different angle, Hester evokes the middle class in the
making, but, like her creator, she stands outside as well as within the
nascent configuration. Her ties to the working class are particularly
significant in this regard. For the Jacksonian working class was both
residual and sexually problematic in its behavior; its female members
were mannish and unfeminine, as well as old-fashioned, by bourgeois
standards. They departed the family for workshops or toiled in the
home for wages at the very moment when the middle-class dwelling
was becoming equated with leisure and with exemption from the rapacity of the marketplace. Female laborers approximated women of
the past or men of the present more than the wives of antebellum
lawyers, retailers, and manufacturers. Hester's erasure of her femininity and adoption of free-market attitudes may thus stem as much from
the ambiguities of her class status as from the sliding of her gender
position and historical specificity.

But these ambiguities do not negate the evidence linking Hester
and Arthur to middle-class formation. As much as the overt allegiances, the instabilities in their respective characterizations announce the entrance into American literature of a new historical
phenomenon. For the slippages are not unique but were in actuality
common to the antebellum middle class. It is hardly a coincidence

that the novel's version of that class materializes as a consequence of
sin. To Hawthorne, middle-class emergence is a fraught difficulty, not
a matter for congratulation. His two principal actors reflect his own,
and presumably many other people's, incomplete incorporation into,
and continuing uneasiness with, the social revolution of his time.
Hawthorne's lovers proclaim the circumstance that at a time of profound sociological dislocation, Americans who were acquiring middle-
class values and lifestyle were by no means unanimous about the
process. Some retained older loyalties and patterns of behavior that
could generate internal disaffection; others developed commitments
that could lead to open resistance. Hester and Arthur's permutations
bespeak the still fluid nature of an ideological ascendancy that hardened into dominance only after the Civil War—and did so, moreover,
in relation to an increasingly restive and militant working class.

Gender and race have been rightly reinstated at the center of American literary history. We have learned, thanks to the insights of feminists and African Americanists, to revise our thinking about the
supposedly essential qualities that determine those two rubrics. It is
now accepted that gender and race are social contructions with indeterminate boundaries that fluctuate over time and are shaped by historical circumstances rather than by anything innate. In the case of
class, the situation in the United States has traditionally been the reverse. Americans have long taken for granted the proposition that
there was no such thing as class in the country's past; unlike gender
and race, it simply didn't exist. If this reading of *The Scarlet Letter* accomplishes nothing else, it is meant to suggest that here too change is
necessary. Class, no less a social construction than gender and race,
has been just as fluid and difficult to ascertain exactly. But its existence has been just as real, and it is time that we admitted its importance in the making of our cultural inheritance.

LARRY J. REYNOLDS

The Scarlet Letter and Revolutions Abroad†

When Hawthorne wrote *The Scarlet Letter* in the fall of 1849, the fact
and idea of revolution were much on his mind. In "The Custom-
House" sketch, while forewarning the reader of the darkness in the
story to follow, he explains that "this uncaptivating effect is perhaps
due to the period of hardly accomplished revolution and still seething
turmoil, in which the story shaped itself."[1] His explicit reference is to
his recent ouster from the Salem Custom House, his "beheading" as

---

† From *American Literature* 57.1 (March 1985): 44–67. Copyright © 1985 by Duke University Press. All rights reserved. Used by permission of the publisher. Page numbers in square
brackets refer to this Norton Critical Edition.
1. *The Scarlet Letter*, ed. William Charvat, Roy Harvey Pearce, and Claude Simpson (Columbus: Ohio State UP, 1962), 43 [34]. Hereafter cited parenthetically in the text.

he calls it, but we know that the death of his mother and anxiety about where and how he would support his family added to his sense of upheaval. Lying behind all these referents, however, are additional ones that have gone unnoticed: actual revolutions, past and present, which Hawthorne had been reading about and pondering for almost twenty consecutive months. These provided the political context for *The Scarlet Letter* and shaped the structure, characterizations, and themes of the work.

I

ROME YET UNCONQUERED! FRANCE TRANQUIL. LEDRU-ROLLIN NOT TAKEN. THE HUNGARIANS TRIUMPH! GREAT BATTLE NEAR RAAB! THE AUSTRIANS AND RUSSIANS BEATEN. CONFLICTS AT PETERWARDEIN AND JORDANOW. SOUTHERN GERMANY REPUBLICAN. BATTLE WITH THE PRUSSIANS AT MANHEIM. RESULT UNDECIDED. These are the headlines of the *New York Tribune* for 5 July 1849; and because they are typical, they suggest the excitement and interest generated in America by the wave upon wave of revolution that swept across Europe during the years 1848 and 1849. In Naples, Sicily, Paris, Berlin, Vienna, Milan, Venice, Munich, Rome, and nearly all the other cities and states of continental Europe, rulers and their unpopular ministers were overthrown, most notably Louis Philippe and Guizot in France, Ferdinand I and Metternich in Austria, and Pope Pius IX and Rossi in the Papal States.[2] Meanwhile revolutionary leaders such as Lamartine, Kossuth, and Mazzini became heroes in American eyes as they tried to institute representative governments and alleviate the poverty and oppression that precipitated the revolutions.

By the fall of 1849, all of the fledgling republics had been crushed by conservative and reactionary forces, and this fact explains in part why the influence of the revolutions upon *The Scarlet Letter* in particular and the American literary renaissance in general has been overlooked. Unlike the American Revolution (whose influence has received thorough study), the revolutions of 1848–49 came to naught, making them appear inconsequential in retrospect. In addition, the excitement generated in America, while intense, was short lived and soon forgotten; national attention soon turned to the turmoil generated by the slavery issue, which obscured Europe's role as the previous focus of this attention. A third explanation for the neglect is that studies of the literature of this period have tended to focus on native themes and materials. Concomitantly, reference works such as James D. Hart's *Oxford Companion to American Literature* and John C. Gerber's *Twentieth Century Interpretations of "The Scarlet Letter"* have provided chronological indexes that correlate only American history with the lives and works of American authors, despite the fact that the

2. Useful overviews of the revolutions of 1848–49 are provided by *The Opening of An Era: 1848 An Historical Symposium*, ed. François Fejto (1948; rpt. New York: Howard Fertig, 1966), and *The Revolutions of 1848–49*, ed. Frank Eyck (New York: Barnes & Noble, 1972).

major newspapers of the day devoted three-fourths of their front-page coverage to European events.

Although the European revolutions all failed, from the spring of 1848 to the fall of 1849, the American public displayed its interest and sympathy by mass gatherings, parades, fireworks, proclamations, speeches, and constant newspaper coverage, which swelled with the arrival of each steamer.[3] Members of the American *literati*, Hawthorne's friends among them, also responded with ardor. To celebrate the French Revolution, Lowell wrote two poems, "Ode to France, 1848," in which he linked American Freedom with the fires burning in the streets of Paris, and "To Lamartine, 1848," in which he sang the praises of the poet-statesman who headed the new provisional government. Evert Duyckinck, Hawthorne's editor at Wiley & Putnam's, declared himself *"en rapport"* with the French Revolution;[4] and S. G. Goodrich, Hawthorne's former publisher, who witnessed events in Paris, wrote an enthusiastic account for the *Boston Courier*. Emerson, who visited Paris in May 1848, expressed reservations about the posturings of the mobs in the streets but was impressed by Lamartine and sympathized with the social activists. "The deep sincerity of the speakers," he wrote, "who are agitating social not political questions, and who are studying how to secure a fair share of bread to every man, and to get the God's justice done through the land, is very good to hear."[5]

Margaret Fuller, who served as one model for Hester, became, as is well known, more intently engaged in the European revolutions than any of her countrymen. As a witness to the rise and fall of the Roman Republic, she wrote impassioned letters to the *New York Tribune* praising the efforts of her friend Mazzini, describing the defense of Rome, and pleading for American support. "The struggle is now fairly, thoroughly commenced between the principle of democracy and the old powers, no longer legitimate," she wrote in the spring of 1849. "Every struggle made by the old tyrannies, all their Jesuitical deceptions, their rapacity, their imprisonments and executions of the most generous men, only sow more dragon's teeth; the crop shoots up daily more and more plenteous." When the battle of Rome was fought, Fuller served tirelessly as a nurse and watched the warfare surrounding her. "Men are daily slain," she wrote on June 21, "and this state of suspense is agonizing. In the evening 't is pretty, though terrible, to see the bombs, fiery meteors, springing from the horizon line upon their bright path, to do their wicked message." After the French had invaded the city, she wrote, "I see you have meetings, where you speak of the Italians,

---

3. A comprehensive study of the American response to the revolutions has yet to be published; however, the specialized studies of Elizabeth B. White, *American Opinion of France, from Lafayette to Poincaré* (New York: Knopf, 1927), Arthur James May, *Contemporary American Opinion of the Mid-Century Revolutions in Central Europe* (Philadelphia: U of Pennsylvania P, 1927), and Howard R. Marraro, *American Opinion of the Unification of Italy, 1846–1861* (New York: Columbia UP, 1932), when placed side by side, cover most of the salient features of this response, as it revealed itself publicly.
4. Letter to George Duyckinck, 18 March 1848. All of the letters from the brothers Duyckinck are quoted with the kind permission of the Duyckinck Family Papers, Rare Books and Manuscript Division, The New York Public Library, Astor, Lenox and Tilden Foundations.
5. *The Letters of Ralph Waldo Emerson*, ed. Ralph L. Rusk, IV (New York: Columbia UP, 1939), 73–74.

the Hungarians. I pray you *do something.* . . . Send money, send cheer,—acknowledge as the legitimate leaders and rulers those men who represent the people. . . .[6]

As Hawthorne was defending himself from the attacks of the Salem Whigs and battling to be reinstated as surveyor, the developments in Italy received a predominant amount of American attention. On June 20, the *Boston Daily Advertiser* reported that the French, in order to restore the power of the Pope, were marching on Rome with 80,000 men, and it quoted Mazzini's declaration that "We shall fight to the last against all projects of a restoration." The following day, alongside of Hawthorne's public letter to Hillard, this same newspaper reported Garibaldi's arrival upon Neapolitan territory and printed Louis Napoleon's lengthy speech explaining his government's support of the Pope. During the next two months, as Hawthorne ceased careering through the public prints in his decapitated state, accounts of the defeat of the Roman revolutionaries made their way to the United States, where they were greeted by most with sadness or outrage.

Although Margaret Fuller's former devotee Sophia Hawthorne (in her dutifully childlike manner) expressed approval of the republican successes in Europe as they were occurring in 1848,[7] her husband most likely shared neither her optimism nor the enthusiasm of their literary friends, particularly Fuller. In fact, the book that he wrote in the wake of the revolutions in 1849 indicates that they reaffirmed his scepticism about revolution and reform and inspired a strong reactionary spirit which underlies the work.

Revolution had been a fearful thing in Hawthorne's mind for some time, even though he found the ends it wrought at times admirable.[8] Violent reform and the behavior of mobs particularly disturbed him,[9] as the final scene of "My Kinsman, Major Molineux" makes clear. This story may celebrate the beginnings of a new democratic era, as some have suggested, but it cannot be denied that Molineux is presented as a noble victim of a hellish mob. "On they went," Hawthorne wrote, "like fiends that throng in mockery round some dead potentate,

6. *At Home and Abroad, or Things and Thoughts in America and Europe*, ed. Arthur B. Fuller (1856; rpt. Port Washington, N.Y.: Kennikat, 1971), 380, 381, 409, 421.
7. In a December 1848 letter to her mother, Sophia declared, "What good news from France! . . . There seems to be a fine fresh air in France just now. . . . it is very pretty when the people do not hurt the kings, but merely make them run. Since Prince Metternich has resigned, I conceive that monarchy is in its decline," quoted in Julian Hawthorne, *Nathaniel Hawthorne and His Wife*, I (1884; rpt. n.p.: Archon Books, 1968), 331.
8. See Celeste Loughman, "Hawthorne's Patriarchs and the American Revolution," *American Transcendental Quarterly*, 40 (1979): 340–41, and John P. McWilliams, Jr., " 'Thorough-Going Democrat' and 'Modern Tory': Hawthorne and the Puritan Revolution of 1776," *Studies in Romanticism*, 15 (1976): 551.
9. Hawthorne's reservations about the behavior of revolutionary mobs can also be seen in his sketches "The Old Tory" (1835) and "Liberty Tree" (1840). His manuscript "Septimius Felton" contains some of his final thoughts on the subject. "In times of Revolution and public disturbance," he writes, "all absurdities are more unrestrained; the measure of calm sense, the habits, the orderly decency, are in a measure lost. More people become insane, I should suppose; offenses against public morality, female license, are more numerous; suicides, murders, all ungovernable outbreaks of men's thoughts, embodying themselves in wild acts, take place more frequently, and with less horror to the lookers-on." See *The Elixir of Life Manuscripts*, ed. Edward H. Davidson, Claude M. Simpson, and L. Neal Smith (Columbus: Ohio State UP, 1977), 67.

mighty no more, but majestic still in his agony."[1] Similarly, in "The Custom-House" sketch, Hawthorne presents himself as the victim of another "bloodthirsty" mob, the Whigs, who, acting out of a "fierce and bitter spirit of malice and revenge," have struck off his head with the political guillotine and ignominiously kicked it about. This presentation, humorous in tone but serious in intent, gives *The Scarlet Letter* its alternate title of "THE POSTHUMOUS PAPERS OF A DECAPITATED SURVEYOR" and foreshadows the use and treatment of revolutionary imagery in the novel proper.

This imagery, of course, is drawn from the French Revolution of 1789, which was at the forefront of Hawthorne's mind for several reasons. First of all, the spectacular excesses of that revolution provided the language and metaphors used by conservatives to describe events in 1848–49. In a letter to the *New York Courier and Enquirer*, Bishop Hughes, a supporter of Pope Pius IX, denounced the revolutionaries of Rome and claimed, "They have established, according to what I regard as the truest accounts, a reign of terror over the Roman people, which they call a government." Alluding to Margaret Fuller, Hughes added that "no ambassador from foreign countries has recognized such a republic, except it be the female plenipotentiary who furnishes the *Tribune* with diplomatic correspondence."[2] Evert Duyckinck, keeping his brother George (who was in Paris) abreast of American attitudes in the spring of 1848, reported that "People look at this Revolution with recollections of the Era of Robespierre and suspect every revival of the old political phraseology of that period. An article attributed to Alison is going the rounds from Blackwoods in which he sets Satan grinning over the shoulders of Lamartine."[3] The *Blackwood's* article referred to had echoed the theme of "Earth's Holocaust" as it declared, "Experience will prove whether, by discarding all former institutions, we have cast off at the same time the slough of corruption which has descended to all from our first parents. We shall see whether the effects of the fall can be shaken off by changing the institutions of society; whether the devil cannot find as many agents among the Socialists as the Jacobins; whether he cannot mount on the shoulders of Lamartine and Arago as well as he did on those of Robespierre and Marat."[4]

The bloody June Days of 1848 seemed to confirm such scepticism, and even George Duyckinck, an ardent supporter of the French people, was reminded of the Reign of Terror and the role women played in it as he reflected upon recent events. "Human nature," he wrote his brother, "seems to be the same it was sixty years ago. Heads were stuck on pikes or swords and women danced about them as they did then and who can doubt but that if the insurgents had succeeded the guillotine would have been as busily at work today as it was then."[5]

1. "My Kinsman, Major Molineux," in *The Snow-Image and Uncollected Tales*, ed. J. Donald Crowley (Columbus: Ohio State UP, 1974), 230.
2. Rpt. *Boston Post*, 29 June 1849, p. 1, col. 6.
3. Letter to George Duyckinck, 18 April 1848; Duyckinck Family Papers, New York Public Library.
4. "Fall of the Throne of the Barricades," *Blackwood's*, 63 (1848): 399.
5. Letter to Evert Duyckinck, 30 June 1848; Duyckinck Family Papers, New York Public Library.

Although use of the guillotine had been discontinued (General Cavaignac used the firing squad during the June Days, when an estimated 10,000 died), the shadow of that instrument loomed over all, and after Louis Napoleon came to power, it became unwise even to mention this symbol of revolution. Under Napoleon's administration in 1849, the owner of a Paris newspaper called *Le Peuple*, for an article entitled "The Restoration of the Guillotine," was fined and sentenced to five years imprisonment, while the proprietor of *La Revolution Democratique et Sociale*, for an article entitled "The Political Scaffold," was fined and sentenced to three years imprisonment.[6] In America, the guillotine and the scaffold carried not quite so much import, except, of course, in the mind of one decapitated surveyor.

Predictably, the American press drew careless comparisons between the European revolutions and the American political scene. When Zachary Taylor began his series of political appointments in the spring and summer of 1849, they were reported in the Democratic papers as revolutionary acts, as symbolic beheadings of Democratic party members. Some seven times in May and June, for example, the *Boston Post* printed, in conjunction with the announcement of a political appointment and removal, a small drawing presumably of General Taylor standing beside a guillotine, puffing a cigar, surrounded by heads (presumably of Democrats) at his feet. One of these drawings appeared on 11 June and on the following day, a letter to the editor appeared objecting to Hawthorne's removal from the Salem Custom House. "This is one of the most heartless acts of this heartless administration," the anonymous writer declared. "The head of the poet and the scholar is stricken off to gratify and reward some greedy partizan! . . . There stands, at the guillotine, beside the headless trunk of a pure minded, faithful and well deserving officer, sacrificed to the worth of party proscription, Gen. Zachary Taylor, now President." As Arlin Turner has pointed out, this letter was probably a source of Hawthorne's "beheading" metaphor;[7] however, behind the reference were two years of revolutionary events in Europe, two years of revolutionary rhetoric and imagery.

II

Such rhetoric and imagery appeared not only in the newspapers, of course, but also in contemporary books, some of which dealt with revolution in a serious historical manner. Although *The Scarlet Letter* has often been praised for its fidelity to New England history, the central setting of the novel, the scaffold, is, I believe, an historical inaccuracy intentionally used by Hawthorne to develop the theme of revolution. The Puritans occasionally sentenced a malefactor to stand upon a shoulder-high block or upon the ladder of the gallows (at times with a halter about the neck),[8] but in none of the New England histories

6. See the review "Lamartine's Histoire des Girondins," *Southern Quarterly Review*, 16 (1849): 58.
7. *Nathaniel Hawthorne: A Biography* (New York: Oxford UP, 1980), 181.
8. See Joseph B. Felt, *The Annals of Salem, from Its First Settlement* (Salem: W. & S. B. Ives, 1827), 176, 317.

Hawthorne used as sources (viz., Felt, Snow, Mather, Hutchinson, and Winthrop) are these structures called scaffolds. In fact, I have been unable to find the word "scaffold" in them. The common instruments of punishment in the Massachusetts Bay Colony were, as Hawthorne shows in "Endicott and the Red Cross," the whipping post, the stocks, and the pillory. (The gallows, located in Boston at the end of town,[9] was used for hangings and serious public humiliations.) Although Hawthorne in his romance identifies the scaffold as part of the pillory, his narrator and his characters refer to it by the former term alone some twenty-six times, calling it the scaffold of the pillory only four times and the pillory only once.[1]

As early as 1557 and then later with increasing frequency during the first French Revolution, the word "scaffold" served as a synecdoche for a public beheading—by the executioner's axe or the guillotine. And, because of its role in the regicides of overthrown kings, the word acquired powerful political associations, which it still retains.[2] When King Charles I was beheaded with an axe following the successful rebellion led by Cromwell, Andrew Marvell in his "An Horation Ode" used the word in the following tribute to his king:

> . . . . thence the royal actor born
> The tragic scaffold might adorn:
>   While round the armed bands
>   Did clap their bloody hands.
>   *He* nothing common did or mean
> Upon that memorable scene:
>   But bowed his comely head
>   Down, as upon a bed.[3]

One hundred and forty-four years later, when Louis XVI became a liability to the new French republic, he too, of course, mounted what was termed the "scaffold" and there became one of the victims of the new device being advocated by Dr. Guillotin. The association of a scaffold with revolution and beheading, particularly the beheading of Charles I and Louis XVI, explains, I think, why Hawthorne uses it as his central and dominant setting. It links the narrator of "The Custom-House" sketch with the two main characters in the romance proper, and it raises their common predicaments above the plane of the personal into the helix of history.

9. See Caleb H. Snow, *A History of Boston, the Metropolis of Massachusetts* (Boston: A. Bowen, 1825), 169.
1. See John R. Byers, Jr., and James J. Owen, *A Concordance to the Five Novels of Nathaniel Hawthorne*, II (New York: Garland, 1979), 667, 579.
2. *Oxford English Dictionary*, IX (Oxford: Clarendon Press, 1933), 159. Beheading was not a common form of punishment in the Massachusetts Bay Colony. The only mention I have found of it involved the punishment of an Indian found guilty of theft and of striking a settler's wife in the head with a hammer, causing her to lose her senses. Neither a block nor a scaffold was used in his execution, however. "The executioner would strike off his head with a falchion," John Winthrop reported, "but he had eight blows at it before he could effect it, and the Indian sat upright and stirred not all the time," *The History of New England from 1630 to 1649*, ed. James Savage, 2 vols. (1825–1826; rpt. New York: Arno Press, 1972), II, 189.
3. *The Complete English Poems*, ed. Elizabeth Story Donno (New York: St. Martin's Press, 1972), 56.

Hawthorne's desire to connect his narrative with historic revolutions abroad is further shown by the time frame he uses. The opening scenes of the novel take place in May 1642 and the closing ones in May 1649.[4] These dates coincide almost exactly with those of the English Civil War fought between King Charles I and his Puritan Parliament. Hawthorne was familiar with histories of this subject and had recently (June 1848) checked out of the Salem Atheneum François Guizot's *History of the English Revolution of 1640, Commonly Called the Great Rebellion.*[5] Guizot, Professor of Modern History of the Sorbonne when he wrote this work, became, of course, Louis Philippe's Prime Minister whose policies provoked the French Revolution of 1848. During the spring of 1848 Guizot's name became familiar to Americans, and probably the man's recent notoriety led Hawthorne to a reading of his work in the summer of 1848.

Examination of the simultaneity between fictional events in *The Scarlet Letter* and historical events in America and England verifies that the 1642–1649 time frame for events in the romance was carefully chosen to enhance the treatment of revolutionary themes. When Hester Prynne is led from the prison by the beadle who cries, "Make way, good people, make way, in the King's name," less than a month has passed since Charles's Puritan Parliament had sent him what amounted to a declaration of war. Five months later, in October, 1642, the first battle between Roundheads and Cavaliers was fought at Edgehill, and word of the open hostilities reached America in December.[6] Then and in the years that followed, the Bay Colony fasted and prayed for victory by Parliament, but these became times of political anxiety and stress in America as well as England. According to one of Hawthorne's sources, Felt's *Annals of Salem*, in November 1646 the General Court (presided over by Messrs. Bartholomew and Hathorne) ordered "a fast on Dec. 24th, for the hazardous state of England . . . and difficulties of Church and State among themselves, both of which, say they, some strive to undermine."[7] By the final scenes of the novel, when Arthur is deciding to die as a martyr, Charles I has just been beheaded (on 30 January 1649); thus, when Chillingworth sarcastically thanks Arthur for his prayers, calling them "golden recompense" and "the current gold coin of the New Jerusalem, with the King's own mint-mark on them" (224) [143], Hawthorne adds to Chillingworth's irony with his own. Furthermore, given the novel's time frame, the tableau of Arthur bowing "his head forward on the cushions of the pulpit, at the close of his Election Sermon" (250) [158], while Hester stands waiting beside the scaffold, radiates with ominous import, particularly when one recalls that Arthur is not a graduate of Cambridge, as most of the Puritan ministers of New En-

4. See Edward Dawson, *Hawthorne's Knowledge and Use of New England History: A Study of Sources* (Nashville: Joint Univ. Libraries, 1939), 17.
5. Marion L. Kesselring, *Hawthorne's Reading, 1828–1850* (1949; rpt. New York: Norwood, 1976), 52.
6. See Winthrop, II, 85.
7. Felt, 175.

gland were,[8] but rather of Oxford, the center of Laudian and Royalist sympathies and the place of refuge for King Charles during the Revolution.

By thus setting events in an age when "men of the sword had overthrown nobles and kings" (164) [107], Hawthorne provides a potent historical backdrop for the revolutionary and counter-revolutionary battles fought, with shifting allegiances, among the four main characters and the Puritan leadership. Furthermore, his battle imagery, such as Governor Bellingham's armor and Pearl's simulated slaying of the Puritan children, draws upon and reflects the actual warfare abroad and thus illuminates the struggles being fought on social, moral, and metaphysical grounds in Boston.

Bearing upon the novel perhaps even more than its connections with the English "Rebellion" and its attendant regicide are its connections with the first French Revolution and the execution of Louis XVI. In the romance itself, Hawthorne first alludes to one tie when he describes the scaffold in the opening scenes; "it constituted," he writes, "a portion of a penal machine, which . . . was held, in the old time, to be as effectual an agent in the promotion of good citizenship, as ever was the guillotine among the terrorists of France" (55) [41–42]. This allusion may be derived from the imagery appearing, as discussed above, in the contemporary press; but it is also shaped, in a more profound way, by an overlooked source of *The Scarlet Letter*, Alphonse de Lamartine's *History of the Girondists*, a history of the first French Revolution published in France in 1847, translated into English by H. T. Ryde and published in the United States in three volumes in 1847–48.[9]

Lamartine, the poet-statesman who had risen to the head of the Provisional Government in Paris following the February 1848 Revolution, became a well-known figure in America during 1848–49 and was widely admired for his idealism, courage, and eloquence. Numerous Americans expressed high regard for him;[1] the *New York Herald*, deviating from its usual format, ran an engraving of him on its front page;[2] and one New York City speculator, trying to dignify a venture, even

8. See Frederick Newberry, "Tradition and Disinheritance in *The Scarlet Letter*," *ESQ*, 23 (1977): 13.
9. The relationship between the French and English revolutions is one point emphasized in Lamartine's work; he points out that "Louis XVI had read much history, especially the history of England. . . . The portrait of Charles I., by Van Dyck, was constantly before his eyes in the closet in the Tuileries; his history continually open on his table. He had been struck by two circumstances; that James II. had lost his throne because he had left his kingdom, and that Charles I. had been beheaded for having made war against his parliament and his people," (New York: Harper, 1847–48) I, 52. (This edition of Lamartine will hereafter be cited parenthetically in the text.)
1. Evert Duyckinck in a letter to his brother George, reported that from the point of view of Americans "Lamartine stands out nobly" and speculated that if the new republic progressed well then Lamartine "will be the Washington of France" (3 April 1848, Duyckinck Family Papers, New York Public Library). Emerson, while in Paris, attended a session of the National Assembly and heard Lamartine's speech on Poland. "He did not speak . . . with much energy," Emerson wrote his wife, "but is a manly handsome greyhaired gentleman with nothing of the rust of the man of letters, and delivers himself with great ease & superiority (*Letters*, IV, 77).
2. On 29 March 1848.

named a street of sixpenny shanties "Lamartine's Row."[3] After he had fallen from power due to his unwillingness to align himself with the radical republicans or the right-wing Bonapartists, Lamartine was treated as a noble martyr in the American press. The *New York Evening Post* on 23 June 1849, the day after Bryant's editorial on Hawthorne's behalf appeared there, devoted two and a half front-page columns to a glowing summary of Lamartine's literary and political career. "[His] brief administration," the article concluded, "born of the barricades of February, expired amidst the roar of the cannon of June," proved "that Lamartine is too righteous a man to be a politician." "He was no demagogue; he appreciated the crisis, approved the revolution, but dreaded its excess. To save his country from terrorism and communism, he cheerfully laid down his popularity, as he would have laid down his life."

Before this political martyrdom, which would have engaged Hawthorne's sympathy, Lamartine's career had been advanced by his writings; his *Histoire des Girondins* established his credentials as a republican leader, helped inspire the Revolution of 1848 that he struggled to lead and moderate, and acquired much international renown. "We doubt whether this is not already the most popular *book*, as its author is the most popular *man* of the day," a reviewer for the *New York Courier and Enquirer* proclaimed,[4] when the English translation appeared. Unlike Guizot, Lamartine was not a scholarly historian, and his account of the first French Revolution is an imaginative and dramatic construct that gains much of its power from its sympathetic treatment of Louis XVI and its suspenseful narrative structure, which includes a tableau at the scaffold as its climactic scene. Throughout the first volume and a half of his history, Lamartine, while detailing the political infighting of the National Assembly and their struggle with the king for power, generates sympathy for Louis. He and his family are seldom free from danger, and the two high points of Volume I are their unsuccessful attempt to flee the country and their confrontation with a mob of thousands at the Chateau of the Tuileries. In Volume II, Lamartine shows the situation of the royal family becoming more desperate and the king acquiring strength and character as his fate unfolds. In terms a decapitated surveyor could appreciate, Lamartine observes that "all the faults of preceding administrations, all the vices of kings, all the shame of courts, all the griefs of the people, were accumulated on his head and marked his innocent brow for the expiation of many ages" (I, 27). "He was the scape-goat of olden time, that bore the sins of all" (II, 323).

Lamartine shifts from third-person omniscient narration to third-person limited after the National Assembly renders its verdict of guilty and its judgment of death. Thus, unlike Carlyle's clipped, brusque, and almost sarcastic account of the regicide, Lamartine's treatment

3. See *The Diary of George Templeton Strong*, ed. Allan Nevins and Milton Halsey Thomas, I (New York: Macmillan, 1952), 344.
4. 17 May 1848, p. 2, c. 3.

generates sympathy; the reader is beside the king for some thirty intensely moving pages—as he parts with his family, as he rides in the carriage with his priest, who hears his confession, and as he sees and enters the Place de la Révolution to be beheaded. "There," Lamartine writes, "a ray of the winter's sun . . . showed the place filled by 100,000 heads, the regiments of the garrison of Paris drawn up round all sides of the scaffold, the executioners, awaiting the victim, and the instrument of death prominent above the mob, with its beams and posts painted blood-color. It was the guillotine!" (II, 370). Stationed around the scaffold are "unscrupulous and pitiless ruffians," who desire "the punishment should be consummated and applauded" (II, 371). In contrast, the king steps forward composed and aloof. Humiliated by being bound, he regains his composure, mounts the scaffold, faces the multitude, casts a farewell glance on his priest, and meets his death. "The plank sunk, the blade glided, the head fell" (II, 373), Lamartine writes, as this chilling and memorable scene comes to an end. Appearing in almost the exact center of the narrative, on the 867th page of 1578, the scene dominates the history; all that goes before anticipates it; all that follows refers back to it. The rest of Volume II and all of III detail the excesses of the Revolution: the assassination of Marat, the Reign of Terror, the wave upon wave of bloodletting, and so on, all of which become horrifyingly repetitive.

Lamartine's stirring treatment of revolutionary events and political martyrdom and especially his unprecedented use of the scaffold as both a dramatic setting and a unifying structural device lead one to speculate that Hawthorne may have read this work before he wrote *The Scarlet Letter*; however, speculation is unnecessary. He did. The records of the Salem Atheneum reveal that on 13 September 1849, he checked out the first two volumes of Lamartine's *History*.[5] Moreover, Sophia Hawthorne's letters to her sister and mother, combined with Hawthorne's notebook entries, reveal, as no biographer has yet pointed out, that it was about ten days later, most likely between 21 September and 25 September, that Hawthorne began work in earnest on *The Scarlet Letter*.[6] On 27 September he checked out the third volume of Lamartine's *History*, and on that date Sophia, in an often-quoted letter, informed her mother, "Mr. Hawthorne is writing morning & afternoon. . . . He writes immensely—I am almost frightened about it—But he is well now & looks very shining."[7] (He re-

5. Kesselring, 42.
6. Hawthorne and his wife spent much of the last half of August and the first part of September househunting, first on the Atlantic shore near Kittery Point, and then in the Berkshires near Lenox. Hawthorne may have worked on *The Scarlet Letter* during the second week in September after Sophia returned from Lenox, but if he did, it was not with the commitment he later displayed, for on 17 September he set out with his friend Ephraim Miller on a leisurely three-day journey to Temple, New Hampshire. Assuming he rested on the 20th, the day after his return, and knowing it was the 27th when Sophia first said he was writing "immensely" mornings and afternoons, it seems likely that between 21 September and 25 September he became absorbed in the writing of his romance. All of the letters from Sophia Hawthorne to her mother Elizabeth P. Peabody and her sister Mary Mann are quoted with the kind permission of the Henry W. and Albert A. Berg Collection, The New York Public Library, Astor, Lenox and Tilden Foundation.
7. Letter to Elizabeth P. Peabody (mother); Berg Collection, New York Public Library.

turned the first two volumes of the *History* 6 November and the third volume 12 November.) This correlation in dates plus Hawthorne's allusions to the terrorists of France suggests that what has become one of the most celebrated settings in American literature, the scaffold of *The Scarlet Letter*, was taken from the Place de la Révolution of eighteenth-century Paris, as described by Lamartine, and transported to the Marketplace of seventeenth-century Boston, where it became the focal point of Hawthorne's narrative. Along with it came, most likely, a reinforced scepticism about violent reform.

III

Recognition that revolutionary struggle stirred at the front of Hawthorne's consciousness as he wrote *The Scarlet Letter* not only accounts for many structural and thematic details in the novel but also explains some of the apparent inconsistencies in his treatment of his characters, especially Hester and Arthur. The issue of the degree and nature of Hawthorne's sympathies in the novel has been debated for years, at times heatedly, and I have no hope of resolving the debate here; however, I think the revolutionary context of events provides a key for sorting out Hawthorne's sympathies, or more accurately those of his narrator (whose biases closely resemble Hawthorne's). The narrator, as a member of a toppled established order, an *ancien régime* so to speak, possesses instincts that are conservative and antirevolutionary, consistently so, but the individuals he regards undergo considerable change, thus evoking inconsistent attitudes on his part. Specifically, when Hester or Arthur battle to maintain or regain their rightful place in the social or spiritual order, the narrator sympathizes with them; when they become revolutionary instead and attempt to overthrow an established order, he becomes unsympathetic.[8] The scaffold serves to clarify the political and spiritual issues raised by events in the novel, and the decapitated surveyor of the Custom House, not surprisingly, identifies with whoever becomes a martyr upon it.

Hawthorne's use of the scaffold as a structural device has long been recognized; in 1944 Leland Schubert pointed out that the novel "is built around the scaffold. At the beginning, in the middle and at the end of the story the scaffold is the dominating point."[9] The way in which the scaffold serves as a touchstone for the narrator's sympathies, however, has not been fully explored, particularly with reference to the matter of revolution.

As every reader notices, at the beginning of the story, Hester is accorded much sympathy. Her beauty, her courage, her pride, all receive emphasis; and the scaffold, meant to degrade her, elevates her, figura-

8. Nina Baym in her discussion of "The Custom-House" sketch posits that "like Hester, [Hawthorne] becomes a rebel because he is thrown out of society, by society. . . . The direct attack of 'The Custom-House' on some of the citizens of Salem adds a fillip of personal revenge to the theoretical rebellion that it dramatizes," *The Shape of Hawthorne's Career* (Ithaca: Cornell UP, 1976), 148–49. Hawthorne's attack, I think, can be more accurately termed a counterattack and seen as dramatizing not a rebellion but his reaction to a rebellion.
9. *Hawthorne the Artist* (Chapel Hill: U of North Carolina P, 1944), 137–38.

tively as well as literally. The narrator presents her as an image of Divine Maternity, and more importantly, as a member of the old order of nobility suffering at the hands of a vulgar mob. Her recollection of her paternal home, "poverty-stricken," but "retaining a half-obliterated shield of arms over the portal" (58) [43] establishes her link to aristocracy. Furthermore, although she has been sentenced by the Puritan magistrates, her worst enemies are the coarse, beefy, pitiless "gossips" who surround the scaffold and argue that she should be hanged or at least branded on the forehead. The magistrates, whom Hawthorne characterizes as "good men, just, and sage" have shown clemency in their sentence, and that clemency is unpopular with the chorus of matrons who apparently speak for the people.

Through the first twelve chapters, half of the book, the narrator's sympathies remain with Hester, for she continues to represent, like Charles I, Louis XVI, and Surveyor Hawthorne, a fallen aristocratic order struggling in defense of her rights against an antagonistic populace. The poor, the well-to-do, adults, children, laymen, clergy, all torment her in various ways; but she, the narrator tells us, "was patient,—a martyr, indeed" (85) [59]. It is Pearl, of course, who anticipates what Hester will become—a revolutionary—and reveals the combative streak her mother possesses. "The warfare of Hester's spirit," Hawthorne writes, "was perpetuated in Pearl" (91) [62], and this is shown by Pearl's throwing stones at the Puritan children ("the most intolerant brood that ever lived" [94] [64]), her smiting and uprooting the weeds that represent these children, and her splashing the Governor himself with water. "She never created a friend, but seemed always to be sowing broadcast the dragon's teeth, whence sprung a harvest of armed enemies, against whom she rushed to battle" (95) [65]. (The echo here of Margaret Fuller's dispatch from Rome is probably not coincidental.)

Hester's own martial spirit comes to the fore in the confrontation with Bellingham, but here she fights only to maintain the *status quo* and thus keeps the narrator's sympathies. She visits the Governor not to attack him in any way but to defend her right to raise Pearl. Undaunted by Bellingham's shining armor, which "was not meant for mere idle show," Hester triumphs, because she has the natural order upon her side and because Arthur comes to her aid. Drawing Pearl forcibly into her arms, she confronts "the old Puritan magistrate with almost a fierce expression"; and Arthur, prompted into action by Hester's veiled threats, responds like a valiant Cavalier. His voice, as he speaks on her behalf, is "sweet, tremulous, but powerful, insomuch that the hall reechoed, and the hollow armour rang with it" (114) [77].

In the central chapters of the novel, when the narrator turns his attention toward Arthur and evidences antipathy toward him, it is not only because of the minister's obvious hypocrisy but also because of the intellectual change that he has undergone at Chillingworth's hands. Subtly, Arthur becomes radicalized and anticipates Hester's ventures into the realm of speculative and revolutionary thought.

"There was a fascination for the minister," Hawthorne writes, "in the company of the man of science, in whom he recognized an intellectual cultivation of no moderate depth or scope; together with a range and freedom of ideas, that he would have vainly looked for among the members of his own profession" (123) [82]. And if Arthur is the victim of the leech's herbs and poisons, he is also a victim of more deadly intellectual brews as well. The central scene of the novel, Arthur's "vigil" on the scaffold, is inspired, apparently, by the "liberal views" he has begun to entertain. "On one of those ugly nights," we are told, "the minister started from his chair. A new thought had struck him" (146) [97]. This thought is to stand on the scaffold in the middle of the night, but by so doing he joins the ranks of Satan's rebellious legions. As he indulges in "the mockery of penitence" upon the scaffold, his guilt becomes "heaven-defying" and reprehensible, in the narrator's eyes. Rather than seeking to reestablish his moral force, which has been "abased into more than childish weakness," Arthur, in his imagination, mocks the Reverend Wilson, the people of Boston, and God himself. Furthermore, as Henry Nash Smith has pointed out, the "lurid playfulness" Arthur indulges in upon the scaffold, calls into question "the very idea of a solid, orderly universe existing independently of consciousness."[1] The questioning remains Arthur's, however, not the narrator's, and the scene itself, with the scaffold as its setting, serves to reveal the cowardice and licentiousness Arthur has been reduced to. The blazing A in the sky, which Arthur sees "addressed to himself alone," marks Governor Winthrop's death, according to the townspeople, and thus further emphasizes (by its reference to Winthrop's famous leadership and integrity) the nadir Arthur has reached by his indulgence in defiant thought and behavior.

The transformation Hester undergoes in the middle of the novel (which only appears to be from sinner to saint) is a stronger version of that which Arthur has undergone at her husband's hands; she too becomes, like the French revolutionaries of 1789 and the Italian revolutionaries of 1849, a radical thinker engaged in a revolutionary struggle against an established political-religious order. And as such, she loses the narrator's sympathies (while gaining those of most readers). The transformation begins with her regaining, over the course of seven years, the goodwill of the public, which "was inclined to show its former victim a more benign countenance than she cared to be favored with, or, perchance, than she deserved" (162) [106]. The rulers of the community, who "were longer in acknowledging the influence of Hester's good qualities than the people," become, as time passes, not her antagonists but rather the objects of her antagonism. We first see her impulse to challenge their authority when Chillingworth tells her that the magistrates have discussed allowing her to remove the scarlet letter from her bosom. "It lies not in the pleasure of the magistrates to take off this badge" (169) [110], she tells him. Similarly, when she

1. *Democracy and the Novel: Popular Resistance to Classic American Writers* (New York: Oxford UP, 1978), 25.

meets Arthur in the forest several days later, she subversively asks, "What hast thou to do with all these iron men and their opinions? They have kept thy better part in bondage too long already!" (197) [127].

The new direction Hester's combativeness has taken is political in nature and flows from her isolation and indulgence in speculation. In a passage often quoted, but seldom viewed as consistent with the rest of the novel, because of its unsympathetic tone, the narrator explains that Hester Prynne "had wandered, without rule or guidance, in a moral wilderness. . . . Shame, Despair, Solitude! These had been her teachers,—stern and wild ones,—and they had made her strong, but taught her much amiss" (199–200) [128]. Hester's ventures into new areas of thought link her, significantly, with the overthrow of governments and the overthrow of "ancient prejudice, wherewith was linked much of ancient principle." "She assumed," the narrator points out, "a freedom of speculation, then common enough on the other side of the Atlantic, but which our forefathers, had they known of it, would have held to be a deadlier crime than that stigmatized by the scarlet letter" (164) [107]. Referring for the second time to the antinomian Anne Hutchinson, whom Hawthorne in another work had treated with little sympathy, the narrator speculates that if Pearl had not become the object of her mother's devotion, Hester "might, and not improbably would, have suffered death from the stern tribunals of the period, for attempting to undermine the foundations of the Puritan establishment" (165) [108].[2]

Although Hester does not lead a political-religious revolt against the Puritan leadership, these speculations are quite relevant to the action which follows, for Hawthorne shows her radicalism finding an outlet in her renewed relationship with Arthur, which assumes revolutionary form. When they hold their colloquy in the forest, during which she reenacts her role as Eve the subversive temptress, we learn that "the whole seven years of outlaw and ignominy had been little other than a preparation for this very hour" (200) [129]. What Hester accomplishes during this hour (other than raising the reader's hopes) is once again to overthrow Arthur's system and undermine his loyalty to the Puritan community and the Puritan God. She establishes a temporary provisional government within him, so to speak, which fails to sustain itself. Although Hester obviously loves Arthur and seeks only their happiness together, her plan, which most readers heartily endorse, challenges, in the narrator's eyes, the social order of the community and the spiritual order of the universe, and thus earns his explicit disapproval.

When Hester tells Arthur that the magistrates have kept his better part in bondage, the narrator makes it clear that it is Arthur's better

---

2. For excellent discussions of Hawthorne's attitudes toward women activists, see Neal F. Doubleday, "Hawthorne's Hester and Feminism," *PMLA*, 54 (1939): 825–28; Morton Cronin, "Hawthorne on Romantic Love and the Status of Women," *PMLA*, 69 (1954): 89–98; and Darrel Abel, "Hawthorne on the Strong Dividing Lines of Nature," *American Transcendental Quarterly* 14 (1972): 23–31.

part that has actually kept his worse and lawless self imprisoned. For some time the prison has proved sound, but "the breach which guilt has once made into the human soul is never, in this mortal state, repaired," the narrator declares. "It may be watched and guarded; so that the enemy shall not force his way again into the citadel. . . . But there is still the ruined wall" (200–201) [129]. Thus, as Hawthorne draws upon the popular revolutionary imagery of 1848–49 to present Hester as a goddess of Liberty leading a military assault, she prevails; however, her victory, like that of the first Bastille day, sets loose forces of anarchy and wickedness. Arthur experiences "a glow of strange enjoyment" after he agrees to flee with her, but to clarify the moral dimensions of this freedom, Hawthorne adds, "It was the exhilarating effect—upon a prisoner just escaped from the dungeon of his own heart—of breathing the wild, free atmosphere of an unredeemed, unchristianized, lawless region" (201) [129].

Unlike the earlier struggle that Hester and Arthur had fought together to maintain the *status quo*—the traditional relationship between mother and child—this struggle accomplishes something far more pernicious: "a revolution in the sphere of thought and feeling." And because it does, it receives unsympathetic treatment. "In truth," Hawthorne writes, "nothing short of a total change of dynasty and moral code, in that interior kingdom, was adequate to account for the impulses now communicated to the unfortunate and startled minister. At every step he was incited to do some strange, wild, wicked thing or other, with a sense that it would be at once involuntary and intentional" (217) [138–39].

Donald A. Ringe among others has suggested that this abrupt change in Arthur's system is beneficent, a fortunate fall, in other words, that gives him insight and powers of expression;[3] however, the narrative emphasizes that it is unfortunate and unholy. Arthur's impulses to blaspheme, curse, and lead innocence astray are a stronger version of those seen during his vigil, and they confirm the narrator's assertion that the minister has acquired "sympathy and fellowship with wicked mortals and the world of perverted spirits" (222) [142]. It is important to notice also that the success of Arthur's sermon, which is so eloquent, so filled with compassion and wisdom, depends ultimately not upon his new revolutionary impulses but upon older counter-revolutionary sources that are spiritually conservative. He draws upon the "energy—or say, rather, the inspiration which had held him up, until he should have delivered the sacred message that brought its own strength along with it from heaven" (251) [158].

The final change of heart and spirit that Arthur undergoes and that leads him to his death on the scaffold is foreshadowed by events in the marketplace prior to his sermon. There the exhibition of broadswords upon the scaffold plus Pearl's sense of "impending revolution" suggests that while the minister's better self has been overthrown, it will reassert itself shortly. The procession in which Arthur appears drama-

---

3. "Hawthorne's Psychology of the Head and Heart," *PMLA* 65 (1950): 129.

tizes the alternative to the lawless freedom Hester has offered. Here, as Michael Davitt Bell has observed, we have "the greatest tribute in all of Hawthorne's writing to the nobility of the founders."[4] The people, we are told, had bestowed their reverence "on the white hair and venerable brow of age; on long-tried integrity; on solid wisdom and sad-colored experience; on endowments of that grave and weighty order, which gives the idea of permanence, and comes under the general definition of respectability" (237–38) [151]. These are the qualities that distinguish Bradstreet, Endicott, Dudley, Bellingham, and their compeers. And, although we are not told who the new governor is (it was Endicott), we know that his election represents orderly change, in contrast to the rebellion and regicide that has recently occurred in England. "Today," Hester tells Pearl, "a new man is beginning to rule over them," and, in harmony with this event, Arthur acts to reestablish his place within the order of the community and within the order of the kingdom of God.

During the sermon Arthur seems to regain some of his spiritual stature and is described as an angel, who, "in his passage to the skies, had shaken his bright wings over the people for an instant,—at once a shadow and a splendor." Because Arthur is still a hypocrite, considerable irony exists within this description; however, when the minister walks to and mounts the scaffold, the narrator's irony turns to sincerity. Arthur attempts, before he dies, to regain God's favor, and as he nears the scaffold, where Hester and Chillingworth will both oppose his effort to confess, we are told that "it was hardly a man with life in him, that tottered on his path so nervelessly, yet tottered, and did not fall!" The exclamation mark indicates the double sense of "fall" Hawthorne wishes to suggest, and at the end Arthur seems to escape from the provisional control over him that both Chillingworth and Hester have had.

"Is not this better than what we dreamed of in the forest?" he asks Hester, and although she replies "I know not! I know not!" the revolutionary context of the novel, the bias toward restoration and order, indicate we are supposed to agree that it is.[5] Arthur's final scene upon the scaffold mirrors Hester's first scene there, even though he proceeds from the church whereas she had proceeded from the prison. But, unlike Hester, Arthur through humility and faith seems to achieve peace, whereas she, through "the combative energy of her character," had achieved only "a kind of lurid triumph" (78) [55]. In the final scaffold scene, Pearl acts as an ethical agent once again and emphasizes Hawthorne's themes about peace and battle, order and revolt. At the moment of his death, Arthur kisses Pearl, and the tears she then sheds are "the pledge that she would grow up amid human joy and sorrow, nor for ever do battle with the world, but be a woman in

4. *Hawthorne and the Historical Romance of New England* (Princeton: Princeton UP, 1971), 140.
5. A number of critics have read this scene as ironic and seen Dimmesdale as deluded or damned; however, the *Pietà* tableau, Arthur's Christlike foregiveness of Chillingworth, and Hawthorne's own emotional response to the scene (when he read it to Sophia) make it difficult to agree with such a reading.

it." In what seems to be a reward for her docility, she marries into European nobility (thereby accomplishing a restoration of the ties with aristocracy her maternal relatives once enjoyed); similarly, Hester at last, we are told in a summary, forsakes her radicalism and recognizes that the woman who would lead the reform movements of the future and establish women's rights must be less "stained with sin," less "bowed down with shame" than she. This woman must be "lofty, pure, and beautiful, and wise, moreover, not through dusky grief, but the ethereal medium of joy" (263) [166].

More than one reader has correctly surmised that this ending to the novel constitutes a veiled compliment to Hawthorne's little Dove, Sophia, and a veiled criticism of Margaret Fuller, America's foremost advocate of women's rights and, at the time, one suffering from a sullied reputation due to gossip about her child and questionable marriage. Hawthorne's long and ambivalent relationship with Fuller and his response to her activities as a radical and revolutionary in 1849 had a decided effect upon the novel. There are several parallels which indicate Fuller served as a model for Hester: both had the problem of facing a Puritan society encumbered by a child of questionable legitimacy; both were concerned with social reform and the role of woman in society; both functioned as counsellor and comforter to women; and both had children entitled to use the armorial seals of a non-English noble family. All of these Francis E. Kearns has pointed out;[6] however, a more important parallel Kearns fails to mention is that for Hawthorne both women were associated with the ideas of temptation and revolution, with the figures of Eve and Liberty. Fuller was not only the most intelligent, articulate, and passionate woman Hawthorne had ever spent so many hours alone with,[7] she was also, as he began *The Scarlet Letter*, an ardent revolutionary supporting the overthrow of the most prominent political-religious leader in the world.

Certainly Hawthorne's knowledge of and interest in the New England past were considerable; however, as Thomas Woodson has pointed out, his interest in his contemporary world was far greater than the critical emphases of recent decades would indicate.[8] In his writing of *The Scarlet Letter* he drew upon the issues and rhetoric he was encountering in the present, especially those relating to himself as a public figure. Moreover, he responded strongly and creatively to accounts of foreign revolutions and revolutionaries that he found in the newspapers, the periodicals, and books new to the libraries. Although to most of his countrymen the overthrow of kings and the triumph of republicanism were exhilarating events, to a man of Hawthorne's temperament, the violence, the bloodshed, the extended chaos that accompanied the revolutions of 1848–49 were deeply disturbing. As-

---

6. "Margaret Fuller as a Model for Hester Prynne," *Jahrbuch für Amerikastudien*, 10 (1965): 191–97.
7. The most revealing information about the Hawthorne-Fuller relationship is contained in Margaret Fuller's 1844 Commonplace Book, which deserves to be edited and published. The manuscript is on deposit by Mrs. Lewis F. Perry at the Massachusetts Historical Society.
8. "Hawthorne's Interest in the Contemporary," *Nathaniel Hawthorne Society Newsletter*, 7 (1981): 1.

sociated in his own mind with his personal plight, they, along with his reading in Guizot and Lamartine, shaped *The Scarlet Letter* in Burkean ways the reader of today finds difficult to accept. We value too highly Thomas Paine and the rights of woman.

JEAN FAGAN YELLIN

The Scarlet Letter and the Antislavery Feminists†

Picture . . . Hawthorne's grand woman, in all her native dignity, standing calm and self-poised.
—*Elizabeth Cady Stanton*[1]

Perhaps the most complex and influential literary work that uses the antislavery women's iconography to reject their ideology is *The Scarlet Letter*.[2] Tracing the abolitionists' discursive codes in literary works is, obviously, different from tracing them in sculptural icons. In Hawthorne's romance, the emblem of the antislavery women functions as a subtext to Hester Prynne's emblem.

The narrator of *The Scarlet Letter* addresses, and invites his audience to address, the issue of signification by overtly playing with the meanings of Hester's "A." Intended to brand her as an adultress, after

† From *Women and Sisters: The Antislavery Feminists in American Culture* (New Haven: Yale UP, 1989), 125–150. Page numbers in square brackets refer to this Norton Critical Edition.
1. Elizabeth Cady Stanton, "Hester Vaughn," *The Revolution* (10 December 1868): 360–61.
2. Hawthorne scholarship has been transformed by the appearance of *The Centenary Edition of the Works of Nathaniel Hawthorne*, ed. William Charvat, Roy Harvey Pearce, and Claude M. Simpson, 23 vols. (Columbus: Ohio State UP, 1962–). References to *The Scarlet Letter* and other works by Hawthorne are to this edition. References to the *American Notebooks* are to volume 8 of this edition. See also *Hawthorne's Lost Notebook, 1835–1841*, transcribed by Barbara S. Mouffe (University Park: Pennsylvania State UP, 1978).

Hawthorne's letters are designated by dates and addresses in the text or in the notes; quoted passages follow the texts established for *The Centenary Edition*. I am grateful to L. Neal Smith, associate textual editor of *The Centenary Edition*, who made typescripts and notes relating to this correspondence available to me before these texts appeared in print.

Building on Robert Cantwell's *Nathaniel Hawthorne, the American Years* (New York: Rinehart, 1948), relevant biographical studies include Arlin Turner's "Hawthorne and Reform," *New England Quarterly* 15 (1942): 700–14; his "Needs in Hawthorne Biography," *Nathaniel Hawthorne Journal* 2 (1972): 43–45; and his *Nathaniel Hawthorne: A Biography* (New York: Oxford UP, 1980); as well as James R. Mellow, *Nathaniel Hawthorne in His Times* (Boston: Houghton Mifflin, 1980). In addition to works mentioned in the notes that follow, I have found the following critical studies particularly useful: Nina Baym's "Hawthorne's Women: The Tyranny of Social Myths," *Centennial Review* 15 (1971): 250–72; her "The Significance of Plot in Hawthorne's Romances," in G. R. Thompson et al., eds., *The Ruined Eden of the Present: Hawthorne, Melville, Poe* (Lafayette, Ind.: Purdue UP, 1981), 44–70; her "Passion and Authority in *The Scarlet Letter*," *New England Quarterly* 43 (1970): 209–30; and her full-length study, *The Shape of Hawthorne's Career* (Ithaca, N.Y.: Cornell UP, 1976); Michael D. Bell's *Hawthorne and the Historical Romance of New England* (Princeton: Princeton UP, 1971); Millicent Bell, "The Obliquity of Signs: *The Scarlet Letter*," *Massachusetts Review* 23 (1982): 9–26; Sacvan Bercovitch's *The American Jeremiad* (Wisconsin: U of Wisconsin P, 1978); Richard Brodhead's *Hawthorne, Melville and the Novel* (Chicago: U of Chicago P, 1976); Michael Colacurcio's "Footsteps of Anne Hutchinson: The Context of *The Scarlet Letter*," *ELH* 39 (1972): 459–94; and his *The Province of Piety* (Cambridge, Mass.: Harvard UP, 1984); Ronald J. Gervais, "A Papist Among the Puritans: Icon and Logos in *The Scarlet Letter*," *Journal of the American Renaissance* 25 (1979): 11–16; Lawrence S. Hall, *Hawthorne, Critic of Society* (New Haven: Yale UP, 1944); Harry B. Henderson III, *Versions of the Past: The Historical Imagination in American Fiction* (New York: Oxford UP, 1974); and Tony Tanner, *Adultery in the Novel: Contract and Transgression* (Baltimore: Johns Hopkins UP, 1979).

seven years it means *able* to a portion of Boston's population. Hester herself, the narrator tells us, has been encoded to signify "woman's frailty and sinful passion," and at times this is how she understands herself (79) [55]. But behind these shifting interpretations of Hester and her emblem lie the shifting interpretations of the emblem of the female slave. Dramatizing the notion that womanhood is not a natural but a conventional construct—as Sojourner Truth, Harriet Jacobs, and the other female slaves excluded from this category testified— Hawthorne's book begins by presenting a woman publicly exposed, a figure made familiar by the abolitionists. Hester Prynne's ordeal on the scaffold, and the events that follow, signal her exclusion from the category of true womanhood. Although its focus later shifts, *The Scarlet Letter* recurrently presents the structures of the antislavery women's discourse. Repeatedly addressing the concerns of the anti- slavery women, the book explores Hester's ideas, and those of the narrator, in relation to her identity (her womanhood) and her mem- bership in the community (her sisterhood).

In *The Scarlet Letter*, as in the speeches, writings, and images of the antislavery feminists, enchaining and exposure signify woman's op- pression. Hawthorne, however, does not use them as a signal that woman should mount a public effort for self-liberation. Although his book ends with a kind of restoration of Hester as a Woman and a Sis- ter, she does not achieve this identity by asserting the antislavery fem- inists' ideology or by struggling for her rights in the public sphere. Instead, learning that she should accept her lot, confident that some- day, somehow, things will change for the better, Hester conforms at last to patriarchal definitions of womanhood. *The Scarlet Letter* is, on one level, a critique of patriarchal ideologies and structures, but it is a critique that seriously considers the new feminist definitions of wom- anhood and, rejecting them, replicates traditional imagery and en- dorses patriarchal notions. Hawthorne's narrator openly discusses the reencoding of both the embroidered emblem and of Hester herself. But the presence of the emblem of the enchained female slave, which functions as a subtext of Hawthorne's emblem, is never mentioned; its reencoding is covert.

Recently, studies of Hawthorne's life and of the selfhood that he ex- pressed in his writings have explored beyond the walls of his legendary "dismal and squalid chamber" at Salem. They have, for example, es- tablished that, like other white Americans of his place and time, he had everyday contact with African-Americans and that, in addition to sharing the common awareness of the slavery question, he was more than routinely familiar with Cuban slavery and something of an expert concerning African colonization and the slave trade.[3]

As a writer of fiction, Hawthorne chose to center his work on moral issues; repeatedly, on one level, his subject was psychological slavery. Although the antislavery activists were denouncing slavery as a tyr-

---

3. See my "Hawthorne and the American National Sin," in *The Green Tradition in American Culture*, ed. H. Daniel Peck (Baton Rouge: Louisiana State UP, 1989).

anny of both flesh and spirit—and his brother-in-law Horace Mann was condemning slavery on the floor of Congress as a system in which "man claims authority over the body, mind, and soul of his fellow-men"—Hawthorne never did connect slavery with the bondage that was his chosen subject. He never did identify the "unpardonable sin" that obsessed him with "the American national sin" that the Garrisonians were denouncing.[4] Where Hiram Powers had distanced an enchained white woman in space and called her a *Greek Slave*, Nathaniel Hawthorne distanced an enchained white woman in time and called her Hester Prynne.

Hawthorne was, of course, familiar with the abolitionists. Even conservative Salem, although not a Garrisonian center like Boston, had its share of antislavery controversy. His black townswomen had been first in the nation to organize a female antislavery society, and they later joined an interracial organization that sent delegates to all three Conventions of American Women Against Slavery. At the 1839 convention, Clarissa C. Lawrence, a black Salem delegate, took the floor to point out that she, and other blacks, "meet the monster prejudice *every where*." She urged the white delegates, "Place yourselves, dear friends, in our stead." Four years earlier, racist, antiabolitionist white Salem-ites had mobbed an antislavery meeting planned for Howard Street Church. When the Grimkés had come to town in 1837, however, local antislavery women successfully scheduled four full days of activities. Angelina Grimké wrote that she and her sister spoke at the Friends' Meeting House, met with "colored members of the Seaman's and Moral Reform Society," addressed an audience of more than a thousand at the Howard Street Meeting House, and talked with children and adults at the "colored Sabbath School."[5]

Although Sophia Peabody, the townswoman Hawthorne would later marry, represented just the sort of person that the abolitionist activists were trying to influence, she did not involve herself in the female antislavery movement in Salem or elsewhere. Long before her marriage, the invalided Sophia had lived for a year and a half on a Cuban sugar plantation. In the "Cuba Journals" (letters she and her sister Mary, her companion, had written home to Salem), the Peabody sisters recorded their experiences and impressions of slavery. They commented on the overwhelming black presence and on the picturesqueness of the Africans at play, on the oppressiveness of slave labor, on the brutality of the system, on the sexual exploitation of slave women, and even on the practice of infanticide. This Cuban experience motivated Mary Peabody to become an active abolitionist, but it prompted Sophia to decide not even to think about slavery. Dwelling on this subject, she

4. Horace Mann, speech of 23 February 1849, *Slavery: Writings and Speeches* (New York: Burt Franklin, 1969), 153–54.
5. Although well documented in the holdings of the Essex Institute, the history of the Salem, Massachusetts, Female Anti-Slavery Society has not been written. See *The Liberator*, 7 January 1832 and 17 November 1832; *Proceedings, Third Anti-Slavery Convention of American Women 1839* (Philadelphia: Merrihew and Thompson, 1839), 8–9; and Angelina Grimké to Jane Smith, 16 July 1837, Grimké-Weld papers, Clements Memorial Library, University of Michigan.

wrote, "would certainly counteract the beneficent influences" of her Cuban visit; and her faith in God reassured her "that he makes up to every being the measure of happiness which he loses thro' the instrumentality of others. I try to realize how much shorter time is, than eternity and then endeavour to lose myself in other subjects of thought."[6]

Back in Boston, before her marriage, Sophia Peabody was part of a grouping that included Maria White, who converted her fiancé James Russell Lowell to abolitionism, and the Sturgis sisters, members, as was White, of the Female Anti-Slavery Society. At the bookstore of her sister Elizabeth, she met with other "advanced" women to attend Margaret Fuller's Conversations and discuss topics such as art, ethics, great men—and Woman. After marrying Hawthorne and moving to Concord, her circle included the Alcotts and Lydian Emerson, members of the local society. But Sophia Peabody Hawthorne distanced herself from abolitionism. She expressed her hostility to women's antislavery activities when, during her pregnancy, she wrote to her mother that she planned to engage "the ladies of the antislavery society" to sew a layette because "I have no manner of scruple about making them take as little as possible; while I could not think of not giving full and ample price to a poor person, or a seamstress by profession."[7]

She rejected not only the work of the female abolitionists, but also the feminist ideas Margaret Fuller voiced in "The Great Lawsuit," the most important statement on the "woman question" to follow Sarah Grimké's Letters on the Equality of the Sexes. Commenting to her mother about Fuller's polemic, Sophia Peabody Hawthorne writes that Fuller fails to understand that "Had there never been false and profane marriages, there would not only be no commotion about woman's rights, but it would be Heaven here at once. Even before I was married, however, I could never feel the slightest interest in this movement [women's rights]."[8] Sophia Peabody Hawthorne then voiced her disapproval of women who, following in the Grimkés' footsteps, brave the public sphere and speak from the platform: "it was always a shock to me to have women mount the rostrum. Home, I think, is the greatest arena for women."[9]

Years later, she indignantly responded when her sister Elizabeth Peabody, who had written an antislavery pamphlet, mailed it to the Hawthornes' young daughter, Una. Attacking radicals like the abolitionists and the feminists who advocated breaking oppressive laws in

6. "Cuba Journal," 1; Sophia Peabody letters, 20 December [1833]–2 July [1834], Mary Peabody letters, 8 January–31 May [1834], Sophia Peabody to Mrs. Elizabeth Palmer Peabody, 21 March [1834], Henry W. and Albert A. Berg Collection, The New York Public Library, Astor, Lenox and Tilden Foundations. Used by permission.
7. Sophia Peabody Hawthorne to her mother, Mrs. Elizabeth Peabody, 15 November 1843. Unless otherwise stated, quoted passages from Sophia Peabody Hawthorne's correspondence are from The Henry W. and Albert A. Berg Collection, The New York Public Library, Astor, Lenox and Tilden Foundations, and are used by permission.
8. "The Great Lawsuit: Man versus Men; Woman versus Women," The Dial (July 1843); revised and republished as Woman in the Nineteenth Century, ed. Arthur B. Fuller (New York: Tribune P, 1845). Sophia Peabody Hawthorne to her mother, Elizabeth P. Peabody, quoted in Julian Hawthorne, Nathaniel Hawthorne and His Wife: A Biography (Boston: Houghton Mifflin, 1884), 1:257.
9. Sophia Peabody Hawthorne to her mother, in Julian Hawthorne, Nathaniel Hawthorne and His Wife, 1:257.

the name of a higher law, Sophia Peabody Hawthorne wrote, "I consider it a very dangerous and demoralizing doctrine and have always called it 'transcendental slang.' " Announcing that she had not shown the pamphlet to Una and that she would not, she stated that she was familiar with reports of slave sales and did not believe her sister's accusations that slave women were routinely subjected to sexual abuse: "And you would display before . . . [my daughter's] great, innocent eyes a naked slave girl on a block at auction (which I am sure is an exaggeration for I have read of those auctions often and even the worst facts are never so bad as absolute nudity)."[1] This correspondence reveals that Sophia Peabody Hawthorne followed neither Angelina Grimké's advice to act against slavery nor Catharine Beecher's advice to influence men to take action against it.

Some of the Hawthornes' neighbors, however, were deeply involved in antislavery feminist activities. In Salem in the spring of 1848—shortly after Hawthorne's persistence had won him an appointment as surveyor of the Custom House and the family had moved from Concord back to their home town—the first women's rights petitions in Massachusetts were circulated. For six years, with the help of Phebe King of Danvers, Mary Upton Ferrin drafted, circulated, and submitted petitions. Literally standing in Angelina Grimké's footsteps, in 1850 she addressed a committee of the Massachusetts legislature. Using what was by now a staple of feminist rhetoric, Ferrin likened the condition of woman to that of the slave. Although widely ridiculed, Ferrin was encouraged by a local minister turned politician, Rev. Charles W. Upham—the same man who led the local Whig attack against Hawthorne's federal appointment in 1849. Aiding him was Phebe King's son Daniel, a U.S. congressman. Salem politics dictated that feminism's strongest supporters were Hawthorne's bitterest political enemies.[2]

The reformers made consistent gains in their efforts to bring the slavery question home to New England throughout the years of Hawthorne's literary apprenticeship. They succeeded in alerting everyone to the 1835 attack on the antislavery women, and many agreed with Angelina Grimké that the mobbed women were martyrs. This was the term that the British writer Harriet Martineau, who had met the members of the Boston Female Anti-Slavery Society, used to describe them in the *London and Westminster Review*. Attacked in the newspapers for endorsing the women's antislavery principles, Martineau cut short her American excursion shortly after the riot. Four years later, when the women were again mobbed in Philadelphia, reform Boston gossiped

---

1. Sophia Peabody Hawthorne to her sister Elizabeth P. Peabody [Spring 1860], quoted in Louise Hall Tharp, *The Peabody Sisters of Salem* (Boston: Little, Brown, 1950), 288; and in Rose Hawthorne Lathrop, *Memories of Hawthorne* (Boston: Houghton Mifflin, 1923), 358.
2. Independently of Ferrin's efforts, the Know-Nothings, who dominated the legislature, passed a Married Woman's Property Act in 1853; a liberalized divorce law followed in 1855. See *History of Woman Suffrage*, ed. Elizabeth Cady Stanton et al., 6 vols. (New York, 1881–1922), 1:208–15. For Hawthorne and Upham, see Hawthorne to Horace Mann, Salem, 26 June 1849 and 8 August 1849; and to Burchmore, 17 September 1850, and 7 April 1851, in *Letters*, 16:284–86, 291–95; 364–66; 415–16. Also see Stephen Nissenbaum, "The Firing of Nathaniel Hawthorne," Essex Institute *Historical Collections* 114 (April 1978): 57–86.

about Maria Weston Chapman's collapse after her failed attempt to speak at Pennsylvania Hall—her voice drowned out by the mob surrounding the building and her red shawl flaming against the Quaker gray worn by the besieged abolitionists trapped within.[3]

Other well-publicized incidents involved abolitionist efforts to rescue fugitive slaves. In 1845, Jonathan Walker, a white Massachusetts sea captain, was arrested and jailed in Florida for aiding fugitives. Convicted, Walker was punished by being enchained, displayed on the pillory, and branded on the hand with the letters SS (slave stealer). Back home, he went on the antislavery lecture circuit, recounting his harrowing experience and displaying his "branded hand," which was daguerrotyped by Southworth and Hawes. Walker's ordeal inspired John Greenleaf Whittier to write a poem that elevates the brand by likening it to armorial hatchments and reversing its signification from negative to positive, from "slave stealer" to "salvation to the slave." In 1848, the slave emblem was transformed into a living tableau by the capture of the schooner *Pearl*. Mary and Emily Edmondson, two young black sisters, had been seized when the schooner was caught transporting a group of fugitive slaves to freedom. To raise money for their manumission, Henry Ward Beecher invited his congregation to attend a mock slave auction where the audience could simultaneously experience the delights of beneficence by helping emancipate slaves while experiencing the delights of sin by bidding for females standing on the block. The widely publicized Plymouth Church "auction" of the Edmondsons—and later, of other fugitive slave women and girls—caused a sensation. The Edmondsons' would-be rescuers, however, were not so fortunate as Beecher's "slaves." After a celebrated trial, Captain Edward Sayer and Mate Daniel Dreyton were convicted. Sentenced to heavy fines they could not pay, the men spent four years in jail before being pardoned.[4]

3. For commentary that blamed the abolitionists for inciting the mob, see "Reported Riot in Boston" in the *American Monthly Magazine*, which Hawthorne would edit the following year, vol. 2 (1835): 164. Harriet Martineau, "The Martyr Age of the United States," *London and Westminster Review* (December 1838; republ. Newcastle upon Tyne: Finlay and Charlton, 1840): 43; *Autobiography of Harriet Martineau*, ed. Maria W. Chapman, 3 vols. (Boston: J. R. Osgood, 1877), 1:347–57. For Garrison's description of Chapman at Pennsylvania Hall, and of her subsequent illness, see his letter to his mother dated 19 May 1838; and to George Benson, 25 May 1838, in the *Letters of William Lloyd Garrison*, ed. Walter M. Merrill and Louis Ruchames, 6 vols. (Cambridge, Mass.: Harvard UP, 1971–1981), 2:363, 366. Also see Lydia Maria Child to Caroline Weston, 28 July 1838, in *Selected Letters, 1817–1880*, ed. Milton Meltzer and Patricia G. Holland (Amherst: U of Massachusetts P, 1982), 79–82; Child to Louisa Loring, 3 June 1838; and to Lydia B. Child, 7 August 1838, in *The Collected Correspondence of Lydia Maria Child, 1817–1880*, ed. Patricia G. Holland and Milton Meltzer (Millwood, N.Y.: Kraus Microform, 1980).

4. For Whittier's poem, "The Branded Hand," see *The Complete Poetical Works of John Greenleaf Whittier*, Cambridge Edition (Boston and New York: Houghton Mifflin, Riverside P, 1894), 296. Walker later lectured with Harriet Jacobs's brother, John S. Jacobs. Daniel Drayton, too, later spoke for the abolitionists; he published an account of his ordeal in *Personal Memoirs* (Boston: Bella Marsh, 1855). For Mann's defense of Drayton, see Louisa Hall Tharp, *Until Victory: Horace Mann and Mary Peabody Mann* (Boston: Little, Brown, 1953), 224–34. For the *Pearl* refugees, see Harriet Beecher Stowe, *Key to Uncle Tom's Cabin* (1853; reprint, New York: Arno, 1968), 306–30. For Beecher's "slave sales," see William C. Beecher and Rev. Samuel Scoville, *A Biography of Henry Ward Beecher* (New York: C. L. Webster, 1888), 292–300; and William G. McLaughlen, *The Meaning of Henry Ward Beecher* (New York: Knopf, 1970), 200–201. Eastman Johnson, who had painted Hawthorne's portrait in 1846, made the Plymouth Church "slave sale" the subject of his oil painting *The Freedom Ring* after the magazinist Rose Terry Cooke, who was in the church, heard Beecher's plea and dropped her ring into the collection plate.

Two of these sensational events personally involved members of Sophia Peabody Hawthorne's family. In 1835, Hawthorne's future sister-in-law Elizabeth Peabody had been a guest in the house where Martineau was staying and had burned the Boston newspapers to spare the Englishwoman the embarrassment of reading their attacks. Martineau later wrote that Peabody had begged her to modify her antislavery sentiments in order to retrieve at least a degree of respectability. When Martineau refused, her American tour collapsed. In the case of the *Pearl*, Hawthorne's brother-in-law Horace Mann defended Sayers and Drayton in court. As a literate New Englander, Hawthorne would doubtless have been aware of these highly publicized incidents; as Sophia Peabody's husband, he had direct knowledge of two of them.[5]

Hawthorne knew the reformers well. He did not like them much. An 1835 journal entry testifies to his lack of sympathy for them and for their causes:

> A sketch to be given of a modern reformer—a type of the extreme doctrines on the subject of slaves, cold-water, and all that. He goes about the street haranguing most eloquently, and is on the point of making many converts, when his labors are suddenly interrupted by the appearance of a keeper of a madhouse, where he has escaped. Much may be made of this idea.[6]

After his brief stay at Brook Farm, Hawthorne sketched the reformers in more than a half-dozen short pieces. "Earth's Holocaust," which condemns them most fully, presents a vision of ultimate destruction not uncommon in his time, and commonplace in our own. Here the world is destroyed not by accident or by oppressors desperate to maintain their power, but by reformers whose attacks on social corruption ultimately consume mankind's most valuable achievements.[7]

Women's rights reformers appeared repeatedly in Hawthorne's writings years before he created in Zenobia of *The Blithedale Romance* a fictional feminist who betrays both her sister and herself. As early as 1830, he published a biographical piece so unsympathetic to Anne Hutchinson that it mandates a careful examination of his apparent approval of her in *The Scarlet Letter*. In this early work, Hawthorne's narrator states that he is repelled by women who make themselves intellectually visible—even by writing for publication: "There is a delicacy . . . that perceives, or fancies, a sort of impropriety in the display of a woman's natal mind to the gaze of the

---

5. *The Autobiography of Harriet Martineau*, vol. 2, 33–35. For the Manns, see Louise Tharp, *Until Victory*, especially 224–34; and Jonathan Messerli, *Horace Mann* (New York: Knopf, 1972).

6. 1835 entry, *American Notebooks*, 10.

7. Hawthorne lived at Brook Farm from April to November 1841. For his critical private views of reformers, see, for example, *American Notebooks*, 10, 136. For his critical public views, see, for example, "The Hall of Fantasy," *Pioneer* (February 1843), and a series of pieces in *The Democratic Review*, including "The New Adam and Eve" (February 1843); "The Procession of Life" (April 1843); "The Celestial Rail-road" (May 1843); "The Christmas Banquet" (January 1844); "The Intelligence Office" (March 1844); and "A Select Party" (July 1844). "Earth's Holocaust" appeared in *Graham's Magazine* in May 1844. All of these were collected in the 1846 edition of *Mosses from an Old Manse*.

world, with indications by which its inmost secrets may be searched out."[8]

In "The Gentle Boy" (1832), Hawthorne cast as a woman the most prominent Quaker exemplar of "unbridled fanaticism." Ilbrahim's mother, Catharine, "neglectful of the holiest trust which can be committed to a woman," abandons her son in response to her driving need to testify against persecution (and to experience it).[9] In "A New Adam and Eve" (1843), Hawthorne follows a pair of newly created innocents through nineteenth-century Boston. Entering the legislature, Adam seats Eve in the speaker's chair, and the narrator comments that "he thus exemplifies Man's intellect, moderated by Woman's tenderness and moral sense! Were such the legislation of the world, there would be no need of State Houses, Capitols, Halls of Parliament." These words, although appearing to endorse political feminism, also enunciate a gendered ideology that assigns intellect to males and morality and emotion to females.[1]

The opposition to feminism is more direct in "The Hall of Fantasy," also published in 1843. Despite a disclaimer, by identifying only Abigail Folsom among the reformers, Hawthorne's narrator suggests that women who defy tradition are insane. (Famous for speechifying at antislavery meetings, Folsom was generally considered quite mad; Emerson called her "the flea of the conventions.") Female reformers concerned with women's rights are openly criticized in Hawthorne's "A Christmas Banquet" (1844). Here the narrator includes among his misfits an ideological feminist who has "driven herself to the verge of madness by dark broodings on the wrongs of her sex, and its exclusion from a proper field of action."[2]

In light of this hostility to feminist reformers, it is surprising that in *The Scarlet Letter* the first view of Hester standing on the pillory recalls the antislavery feminists and their emblem of the Woman and Sister. Of course, Hawthorne's terms are different from theirs: he identifies a different cast of characters and locates them within a different temporal framework.

8. *The Blithedale Romance* (1852); "Mrs. Hutchinson," Salem *Gazette*, 7 December 1830, republished in *Biographical Sketches*, Riverside Edition, vol. 17, 217–26. Evidently Hawthorne did not think that female artists exposed themselves as female writers did. Yet while courting Sophia Peabody, long before *The Scarlet Letter*, he alternately fantasized about a life in which both of them would create art and expressed concern that efforts to do serious work as an artist would jeopardize her health. See Hawthorne to Sophia Peabody, 21 and 23 August 1839; 3 January 1840; 15 April 1840; 12 August 1841, in *The Letters*, vol. 15. 339, 397, 440, 557. For Sophia Peabody Hawthorne as an artist, see Josephine Withers, "Artistic Women and Women Artists," *Art Journal*, 35 (1976): 330–36.
9. "The Gentle Boy" first appeared in *The Token* for 1832; it was collected in *Twice-Told Tales*. For an informed discussion, see Michael J. Colacurcio, *The Province of Piety*; 63, 66–68 suggest connections among this text, "Mrs. Hutchinson," and *The Scarlet Letter*.
1. "The New Adam and Eve" first appeared in the *United States Magazine and Democratic Review* (12 February 1843); it was collected into *Mosses* in 1846 and 1854; see *The Centenary Edition*, vol. 10.
2. "The Hall of Fantasy," which first appeared in *The Pioneer* (1843), and "A Christmas Banquet," which first appeared in *Democratic Review* in 1844, were collected into *Mosses* in 1846 and 1854; for all, see *The Centenary Edition*, vol. 10. For Abby Folsom, see *The National Cyclopaedia of American Biography* (New York: James T. White, 1921), 2:394. Hawthorne's reference to Folsom—like his other references to contemporaries—was dropped when this piece was anthologized.

Yet the women we have been examining had repeatedly related their struggle for self-definition to similar struggles in the seventeenth century, the period Hawthorne chose for his romance. Responding to the clerical attack against women's participation in public life, in *Letters on the Equality of the Sexes* Sarah Grimké had likened the Puritan persecution of "witches" to the abuse heaped on her and the other antislavery feminists. Grimké predicted that in a freer future, "the sentiments contained in the Pastoral Letter will be referred to with as much astonishment as . . . that judges should have sat on the trials of witches, and solemnly condemned nineteen persons and one dog to death for witchcraft."[3] Similarly, Abby Kelley Foster, appearing before hostile audiences, had routinely discussed the martyrdom that Mary Dyer and others had suffered at the hands of the New England Puritans in relation to the hostility directed against her for deviating from established norms: "A century ago my Quaker ancestors were acquainted with the Deacons of New England. Their backs were stripped and whipped until the skin was torn off, and their ears were cut off, and they were sometimes even put to death. . . . I have no doubt you would commit similar barbarities upon my person if you thought public sentiment would allow it."[4]

The Scarlet Letter encodes not only connections between repression in seventeenth-century Boston and in nineteenth-century Salem—between the public punishment of Hester Prynne and the exposure and "beheading" of the "Custom House" narrator—it also encodes the public attacks on the antislavery women, Hawthorne's contemporaries.[5] One of their central icons is displayed in the opening scene: the figure of a woman forcibly exposed in public. Although Hester is not marked by an iron chain but by a piece of needlework, recurrent references to the scarlet letter as a brand force the connections between the embroidered symbol and the instruments of slavery. Later, presenting abolitionist iconography in its fullness, the narrator irrevocably links Hester, his seventeenth-century adultress, to the antislavery feminists, his contemporaries, by using their image of an enchained woman to describe Hester's condition in Boston: "The chain that bound her . . . was of iron links and galling to her inmost soul" (80) [56].

Perhaps the opening view of Hester on the scaffold of the pillory seemed familiar to the antislavery feminists among Hawthorne's earliest readers. Some might have reacted to the color of Hester's embroidery by recalling the red shawl of Maria Weston Chapman at Pennsylvania Hall; others perhaps associated Hester's symbolic branding to Jonathan Walker's barbarous punishment. Certainly Elizabeth Cady Stanton was responding to the feminist subtext of *The Scarlet*

---

3. Sarah M. Grimké, *Letters on the Equality of the Sexes* (Boston: Isaac Knapp, 1838), letter 3, 14.
4. Margaret Hope Bacon, *I Speak for my Slave Sister: The Life of Abby Kelley Foster* (New York: Thomas Crowell, 1974), 131.
5. For echoes in *The Scarlet Letter* of the French Revolution, and of the European revolutions of 1848, see Larry J. Reynolds, "*The Scarlet Letter* and Revolutions Abroad," *American Literature* 57 (March 1985): 44–67 [pp. 614–31 in this Norton Critical Edition]. For the "decapitated surveyor" Hawthorne and Hester, see Stephen Nissenbaum, "The Firing of Nathaniel Hawthorne," *Essex Institute Historical Collections* 114 (April 1978): 57–86.

Letter when she evoked Hester as "Hawthorne's . . . grand woman, in all her native dignity, standing calm and self-poised through long years of dreary isolation from all her kind."[6] This regal conquered female figure is best depicted, in nineteenth-century American sculpture, by Harriet Hosmer's *Zenobia*. Shown exhibited as a trophy by the Roman emperor Aurelian and wearing the chains of her conquerers, Hosmer's Queen of Palmyra submits to public display.[7] In Hawthorne's writings, however (despite her name), it is not the disappointed suicide—the Zenobia of *Blithedale*—but the defiant adultress, Hester of *The Scarlet Letter*, who embodies the energy of the captive queen.

When the sculptor Howard Roberts created his full-length figure of Hester, he, too, incorporated the abolitionists' iconography of link chains. Like Hawthorne's creation, Roberts's Hester stands at once fully disclosed and completely unrevealed. Although she is forcibly displayed before us, her gaze does not meet ours. She is not nude but fully clothed. Her left arm cradles her sleeping baby, whose head rests against a large badge ornamented with a capital *A* on Hester's breast. Roberts's Hester does not try to hide either the letter or the babe. Like Hawthorne's creation, she is apparently concentrating on some painful reality, and her posture and expression suggest strain. Standing on rough wooden boards, she rests her right hand on a wooden post, and below that hand, Roberts carved the two hanging links of chain. These links connect his pilloried Puritan with Powers's *Greek Slave* and Hosmer's *Zenobia*—and all of them with antislavery iconography.[8]

From the moment Hawthorne's Hester emerges from prison, her regal impression underscored both by her person, "tall, with a figure of perfect elegance, on a large scale," and by her manner, "characterized by a certain state and dignity," she is presented in terms of the conquered queen (53) [40]. The description of the letter branding her emphasizes this identification. "Glittering like a . . . jewel" (202) [130], it is characterized as an ornament appropriate for "dames of a court" (81) [57], as "fitting decoration" (53) [40] for royalty. In response to the magnificence of her badge and her regal presence, those unfamiliar with Puritan customs judge Hester "a great lady in the land" (104) [70], "a personage of high dignity among her people" (246) [156]. Like Hosmer's *Zenobia*, who wears her manacles as if they were bracelets, and named for Esther, the captive biblical queen whose defiant courage the antislavery women admired, Hawthorne's Hester wears her embroidered brand like conquered royalty.

6. "Hester Vaughn," *The Revolution* (10 December 1868): 360–61.
7. For Harriet Hosmer's *Zenobia* (1858), see *Harriet Hosmer: Letters and Memories*, ed. Cornelia Carr (London: J. Lane, The Bodley Head, 1913), 191–93, 199–204, 363–68; Lorado Taft, *History of American Sculpture* (New York: Macmillan, 1930); and Margaret F. Thorp, *The Literary Sculptors* (Durham: Duke UP, 1965), 87–88. A version of this work is at the Wadsworth Atheneum, Hartford. The subject of Zenobia, Queen of Palmyra, was of interest to the American feminists; Child discusses her in *History of the Condition of Woman*, 2 vols. (Boston: J. Allen, 1835). William Ware's 1837 novel is best known by its second title, *Zenobia: or, the Queen of Palmyra*. *The Blithedale Romance*, Hawthorne's comment on Brook Farm, was published in 1852.
8. Roberts's 1869 sculpture is in the collection of the Library Company of Philadelphia. See *Philadelphia: Three Centuries of American Art. Bicentennial Exhibition*, catalog (Philadelphia: Philadelphia Museum of Art, 1976), 34.

The Scarlet Letter is linked to the discourse of the antislavery women not only by these iconographic motifs, but also by its central concerns. In *Letters on the Equality of the Sexes*, Sarah Grimké had argued that after the fall in Eden woman was the first victim. Although the action of Hawthorne's book takes place in America, almost with his first words the narrator characterizes this new world as fallen. Describing Hester's appearance on the pillory, he notes that while "a Papist" "might have seen in this beautiful . . . woman with the infant at her bosom, an object to remind him of the image of Divine Maternity," she actually resembles Mary only "by contrast" [42]. Hester, we are told, is not like that second sinless Eve, but the first, and it is as a type of fallen woman, he tells us, that she is condemned to be identified by the people. Hawthorne's opening pages present a repressive new society practicing institutionalized violence against a woman.

The first scaffold scene showing Hester, her infant in her arms, displayed in public as punishment for the crime of adultery, of course focuses a number of issues. The problem Hawthorne's Puritan theocracy addresses (a problem central in nineteenth-century American fiction) is that the family on the scaffold is incomplete. This woman lacks a husband; this child lacks a father. The solution to this problem, the emergence of the absent male figure, like the solution to the problem of Arthur Dimmesdale, the polluted priest, is figured in the three scaffold scenes as the story unfolds.

But this initial view of Hester on the scaffold also dramatizes the issues that the antislavery women were addressing. *The Scarlet Letter*, no less than *Uncle Tom's Cabin*, published three years later, portrays an American society where publicly, officially, and institutionally, one of God's reasoning creatures is transformed into a thing; and where, privately, one individual tyrannizes over another in this world and threatens his salvation in the next. Here a human being is branded, displayed before the community, and dehumanized. It is perhaps not surprising that, written as the abolitionists labored to convince Americans that slavery was the national sin and as the feminists intensified their characterization of woman's condition as slavery, *The Scarlet Letter* dramatizes the problem of the institutional violation of an individual, the problem central to the notion of slavery, in the person of a woman. Hawthorne's intermittent use of the discourse of the antislavery women to present the twin issues of Hester's dehumanization and her isolation—which relate to the issues of womanhood and sisterhood the antislavery women were raising—results in a series of images that periodically push against the static symmetry of the scaffold scenes.

At the beginning of the book, the drama in Hawthorne's Market Place is heightened because the community condemning Hester is shown as monolithic. While Native Americans are present, here their society is not seen as an alternative to Boston (although Hester will later suggest this to Arthur). Further, as Hawthorne knew, in addition to the Native Americans and transplanted Europeans his narrator shows in the Market Place, the population of seventeenth-century

New England had included another group: the Africans. By obliterating this historic black presence, Hawthorne's narrator helps guarantee Hester's absolute isolation.[9]

He does, of course, suggest a black community of a kind. *The Scarlet Letter* presents a classic displacement: color is the sign not of race, but of grace—and of its absence. Black skin is seen as blackened soul. Instead of presenting an African-American alternative to white Boston, it hints at a diabolical reversal. This satanic conspiracy, like establishment Boston, is male-dominated; it is ruled by the Black Man whose purpose seems to be to enslave others—particularly women. (That he wants their bodies as well as their souls is suggested by Hester's statement to Pearl that the Black Man is the child's father. It is tempting to play with connections between dark unpredictable Pearl and the untamed exotic dark females of American nineteenth-century letters. Subtexts concerning women and the sinfulness of female sexuality on the one hand, and blacks and the sinfulness of black sexuality on the other, lend added significance to the nineteenth-century phrase coupling "women and Negroes.")

Members of this subversive group live in the town, but their activities in the forest suggest the international slave trade with the colors of the participants reversed: the names of whites are signed in a book belonging to the Black Man, and whites are branded with the Black Man's mark. They suggest, too, white reports of black Africans—of wild dancing in the woods.[1] Although this diabolical society is never taken seriously, when "black" is read as describing skin color and not moral status, the text of *The Scarlet Letter* reveals the obsessive concern with blacks and blackness, with the presence of a dangerous dark group within society's midst, that is characteristic of American political discourse in the last decades before Emancipation.

By choosing to obliterate the historic black presence and by choosing not to show Native American culture as an alternative to the society of white Boston, Hawthorne's narrator helps guarantee Hester's absolute isolation. With the negation of these potential alternative communities, her ostracism will be complete if the women—the one group within Boston society who might possibly sympathize with her—endorse Hester's official condemnation.

9. For blacks in seventeenth-century Massachusetts, see, for example, Robert C. Twombly and Robert H. Moore, "Black Puritan: The Negro in Seventeenth-Century Massachusetts," *William and Mary Quarterly*, 3d series (April 1967): 224–42; and George H. Moore, *Notes on the History of Slavery in Massachusetts* (1866; reprint, New York: Negro Universities P, 1968). For Hawthorne's early awareness of this historic black presence, see, for example, *American Notebooks* 21, 150; his continued interest in the history of African-Americans is expressed (550). Also see "Old News," *The New-England Magazine* 1–3 (February–May 1835) in *The Snow Image* (1852); and *Grandfather's Chair* 2 (1841) in *True Stories: Writings for Children*, Centenary Edition, vol. 6; for more, see my essay "Hawthorne and the American National Sin," *The Green American Tradition*, ed. H. Daniel Peck.

1. The convergence of western structures signifying diabolism and spiritual enslavement, and western structures signifying Africans and the African slave trade, is discussed in *The Image of the Black in Western Art*, vol. 2, *From the Early Church to the "Age of Discovery,"* pt. 1, Jean Devisse, *From the Demonic Threat to the Incarnation of Sainthood* (New York: William Morrow, 1979); and in *The Image of the Black in Western Art*, vol. 2, *From the Early Christian Era to the "Age of Discovery,"* pt. 2, Jean Devisse and Michel Mollat, *Africans in the Christian Ordinance of the World*, Fourteenth to the Sixteenth Century (New York: William Morrow, 1979).

The opening pages of *The Scarlet Letter* dramatize these women rejecting their common sisterhood with Hester. Demonstrating that they
have thoroughly internalized the patriarchal values of the community,
the women in the Market Place judge Hester's punishment not as too
harsh but as too lenient. Even while condemning the criminal more
severely than do the male officials of the colony, however, they implicitly acknowledge that although they do not recognize Hester as one of
themselves, they are nevertheless her sisters in the eyes of the patriarchy: "This woman has brought shame upon us all, and ought to die"
(51) [39]. Further, they acknowledge that as a representative female,
Hester must be punished if society is to continue to control the
women. If she is reprieved, "Then let the magistrates, who have made
. . . [the law] of no effect, thank themselves if their own wives and
daughters go astray!" (52) [39]. Their fury is an index of their oppression. One of the clearest measures of the lack of true community in
the Boston of *The Scarlet Letter* is the women's determination to deny
Hester's sisterhood.[2]

As the narrative progresses, the issue of sisterhood takes several
forms. After Hester's release from jail, isolated and reviled, the narrator writes that she intermittently "felt or fancied . . . [that] a mystic
sisterhood would contumaciously assert itself." This sisterhood would
apparently link her to other sinners, particularly to women who, although never accused, seemed to her to have engaged in forbidden
sexual activity (86–87) [60]. But while noting that she felt herself a
member of a sisterhood of sinners, the narrator comments that she
fought against this sense of community, "struggling to believe that no
fellow-mortal was guilty like herself" (87) [60].

He later discusses another kind of sisterhood. The people of Boston,
he writes,

> perceived . . . that . . . Hester . . . was quick to acknowledge her
> sisterhood with the race of man, whenever benefits were to be
> conferred. . . . She came, not as a guest, but as a rightful inmate,
> into the household that was darkened by trouble . . . as if its
> gloomy twilight were a medium in which she was entitled to hold
> intercourse with her fellow-creatures. . . . She was a self-ordained
> Sister of Mercy. (160–61) [105]

Hester willingly shares a sense not of mutual sin, but of sickness; she
shares the sorrow common to fallen humans in a fallen world.

Although Hester denies any knowledge of the community led by the
Black Man, at least one Boston woman welcomes her membership in
this grouping. This diabolical secret society is an assembly to which
many thought Hester belonged. The reputed witch Mistress Hibbins,
believing Hester's brand a sign of her membership and affirming their

2. These women are so punitive that an anonymous man chides them. One, however—a young
mother—sympathizes with Hester. Her comment about the badge—"Not a stitch in that embroidered letter, but she has felt it in her heart" (54) [41]—recalls a motto of the sewing circles organized by the female antislavery societies: "May the points of our needles prick the
slaveholders' consciences."

common sisterhood, interprets Hester's rejection as a clumsy effort to preserve organizational secrecy.

Despite these actual or imagined communities, however, near the end of *The Scarlet Letter*, when Hester stands at the foot of the scaffold as Arthur preaches his Election Sermon, she is again the center of a "magic circle of ignominy," and the women who had earlier condemned her are again among those surrounding her (246) [156]. Their "cool, well-acquainted gaze at her familiar shame," along with that of the other townspeople, "tormented Hester Prynne, perhaps more than all the rest" (246) [156]. Seven years—and twenty chapters—after her branding on the pillory, Hester remains rejected as a sister by the women of Boston.[3]

In addition to dramatizing the women's informal denial of Hester's sisterhood, the first scaffold scene also dramatizes the institutional denial of her identity. Hester's official transformation from woman to thing enacts the negation central to the institution of slavery—the denial of the humanity of one of God's reasoning creatures, the denial the abolitionists saw as sin. "Giving up her individuality," the narrator says, "she would become the general symbol at which the preacher and the moralist might point, and in which they might vivify and embody their images of woman's frailty and sinful passion" (79) [55].

The discourse of the antislavery feminists also functions as a subtext of *The Scarlet Letter* in connection with the question of Hester's womanhood. This is most apparent in the chapter called "Another View of Hester." At this point in the narrative, Hester, shocked by Arthur's distraught appearance in the second scaffold scene, has decided to try to rescue him from Roger's torture. Here the narrator pauses to explore Hester's identity seven years after her sentence and punishment. He places his examination within the context of a general discussion of the nature and condition of woman—a topic which by 1849 the antislavery feminists had been considering for more than a dozen years and which some of them had recently addressed in new, revolutionary ways at Seneca Falls.

Using a series of buried images and convoluted formulations, Hawthorne's narrator characterizes womanhood as conditional and woman as passive, fragile, and endangered. Imaging Hester first in terms of a group of static free-standing vertical objects—a blasted tree, a neoclassical sculpture—and generalizing on her nature, he comments that as a result of undergoing "an experience of peculiar severity" (figured as being crushed), a woman frequently loses "some attribute . . . the permanence of which has been essential to keep her a woman" (163) [107]. He assures us that this lost womanhood can, however, be restored by another physical contact, "the magic touch to effect the transfiguration" (164) [107].

---

3. If anything, Hester's isolation is now more complete. Although some have come to believe her *A* signifies "Able," we are not told that the women have stopped behaving like witches and distilling their poison for her ears; the tender-hearted young mother who initially sympathized with her has died in the seven-year interval.

This description of Hester, which notes her "marble coldness" (seen as a result of her life having "turned . . . from passion and feeling, to thought") and observes that she is "standing alone," suggests a sculpture (164) [107]. Activating this freestanding marble-like figure, the narrator evokes Hiram Powers's enchained *Greek Slave* as he describes Hester engaging in action: "She cast away the fragments of a broken chain. The world's law was not law for her mind."[4] This apparently revolutionary act, however, does not free her. Hester's chains, the narrator explains, were already broken.

> It was an age in which the human intellect, newly emancipated, had taken a more active and a wider range than for many centuries before. Men of the sword had overthrown nobles and kings. Men bolder than these had overthrown and rearranged—not actually, but within the sphere of theory, which was their most real abode—the whole system of ancient prejudice, wherewith was linked much of ancient principle. (164) [107]

Hester is presented as the beneficiary of these male revolutionaries, not as a revolutionist herself. Likened to an intellectual whose radicalism stops short of "the flesh and blood of action," she might have been a revolutionist, it is suggested, but for the birth of her child (164) [108]. The characterization of this event as "providential" implies that it may be a blessing that woman's reproductive role prevents her from becoming an activist. Had Pearl not been born, the narrator suggests, Hester might have become a religious leader or prophet, might have "come down to us in history, hand in hand with Ann Hutchinson, as the foundress of a religious sect. She might, in one of her phases, have become a prophetess. She might, and not improbably would, have suffered death from the stern tribunals of the period, for attempting to undermine the foundations of the Puritan establishment" (165) [108]. But Hester does not become a link in this extraordinary chain of female revolutionists, the foremothers Abby Kelley Foster had eulogized, whom Hawthorne had condemned as fanatics in "The Gentle Boy." Instead, learning the lesson Ilbrahim's mother had failed to learn, Hester focuses her energies on motherhood.

Ironically, however, her efforts to fulfill this traditional female role inevitably raise precisely the line of revolutionary inquiry that the narrator suggests characterized the thought of women who assumed untraditional public roles. Concerning Pearl, "in bitterness of heart" Hester asks "whether it were for ill or good that the poor little creature had been born at all" (165) [108]. It might seem peculiar that she had not become desperate much earlier. Hester had given birth to an illegitimate child before *The Scarlet Letter* begins. However, unlike the drowned Martha Hunt (whom Hawthorne and the others had pulled out of the dark pond in 1845), and unlike the countless deceived maidens of American nineteenth-century fiction, she evidently had not

---

4. Miner Kellogg's promotional pamphlet *Powers' Statue of The Greek Slave* (New York: R. Craigshead, 1847) underscores Hester's connections with Powers's work; see especially p. 125.

attempted abortion, infanticide, or suicide. Only after seven years of dehumanization and ostracism does Hawthorne's female sexual rebel apparently consider adopting the destructive and self-destructive patterns assigned to "fallen women" in nineteenth-century American life and letters.

The questions she poses make clear that, despite her continued ostracism, she does not see her condition as fundamentally different from that of other women. "Indeed, the same dark question often rose into her mind, with reference to the whole race of womanhood. Was existence worth accepting, even to the happiest among them? As concerned her own individual existence, she had long ago decided in the negative, and dismissed the point as settled" (165) [108].

In the discussion that follows, the narrator initially intimates that the origins of the "woman question" may be social; this implies that public activity, like that of the antislavery feminists, could change woman's situation. But while suggesting that intense activity might result in reforms, this passage does not present woman as an active agent. Note the use of the passive voice:

> As a first step, the whole system of society is to be torn down, and built up anew. Then, the very nature of the opposite sex, or its long hereditary habit, which has become like nature, is to be essentially modified, before woman can be allowed to assume what seems a fair and suitable position. Finally, all other difficulties being obviated, woman cannot take advantage of these preliminary reforms, until she herself shall have undergone a still mightier change, in which, perhaps, the ethereal essence, wherein she has her truest life, will be found to have evaporated. (166) [108][5]

This analysis of woman's condition—that she is not permitted "a fair and suitable position"—appears similar to the analysis of the antislavery feminists. But here the cause of woman's oppression is identified differently, and the solution proposed is different from theirs.

Feminists such as Sarah Grimké, arguing that male domination is the source of woman's problems, had proposed that women actively oppose patriarchal restrictions and reassert their God-given role as corulers of the earth. Hawthorne's narrator suggests, however, that woman's condition is somehow a consequence of her female essence, of her essential nature. Accordingly, she can rectify her oppressed social status neither by acting (like those "men of the sword" who had toppled aristocratic political structures), nor by thinking (like the "bold" men who had transformed ancient ideological structures). Instead, using an absolute negation and an equally absolute assertion, the narrator suggests that women remain passive and trust their phys-

5. The danger of women's evaporation was again voiced following the October 1851 Woman's Rights Convention at Worcester. When an article in the *Christian Inquirer* queried, "Place woman unbonneted and unshawled before the public gaze and what becomes of her modesty and her virtue?" feminist Ernestine Rose responded: "In [the writer's] benighted mind, the modesty and virtue of woman is of so fragile a nature, that when it is in contact with the atmosphere, it evaporates like chloroform. Such a sentiment," she continued, "carries its own deep condemnation" (*History of Woman Suffrage*, 1:245–46).

iology and their luck. Although women are ephemeral and in danger of "evaporation," he writes, their problems are equally ephemeral: "A woman never overcomes these problems by any exercise of thought. They are not to be solved, or only in one way. If her heart chance to come uppermost, they vanish" (166) [108].

Hester—"whose heart," we are told, "has lost its regular and healthy throb," now is seen not as a defeated queen or an enchained sculpture, but as a lost and fallen Eve (166) [108]. The consequence of her single act toward self-liberation—throwing away her broken ideological chains—is not freedom, as it had been for Angelina Grimké. Although no longer bound by a repressive ideology, she is enslaved by her own nature. Tyrannized by her own ideas, tortured by thoughts of infanticide and suicide, she now wanders alone, a fallen Eve in a fallen world: "There was wild and ghastly scenery all around her, and a home and comfort nowhere" (166) [108]. This entire passage, which recalls Angelina Grimké's early sense of bewilderment at finding herself on an "untrodden path," demonstrates the complex use, in *The Scarlet Letter*, of the antislavery feminists' structures of ideology and discourse. Unlike Grimké, who pursued her innovative course and redefined herself, Hester cannot successfully achieve womanhood and sisterhood unless Hawthorne's narrator changes his definition of woman or presents a narrative that contradicts these constructions.[6] Despite this, however, in the balance of the text we are intermittently presented with fragmentary views of Hester that figure her efforts to achieve these dual goals.

Hester's attempts to act out traditional female roles involve her with a number of issues Hawthorne's feminist contemporaries were raising. Her situation as Roger's wife, for example, dramatizes their demand for more adequate divorce laws, and her plight as a mother accused of unfitness addresses the feminist issue of a woman's right to her child.[7]

Hester's relationship to Arthur, it would appear, is by definition unconventional. Instead, however, it follows a standard pattern. Her functional role as Arthur's true wife becomes clear in the forest scene when she tells him that Roger is her legal husband. Here the question of a wife's duty, a question of deep interest to the feminists, is raised. Earlier, the narrator has revealed that Hester felt connected to Arthur in ways that the patriarchy mandated that true women be connected to their husbands—as primarily defined by this relationship, as primarily wives, and not (as the antislavery women urged) as primarily God's creatures or as citizens. In this scene, the narrator articulates Hester's lack of a sense of autonomy, her crucial dependence on her perception of Arthur's estimate of her: "All the world had frowned on her. . . . Heaven, likewise, had frowned upon her. . . . But the frown of this pale, weak, sinful, and sorrow-stricken man was what Hester could not bear, and live!" (194–95) [125]. When Hester deliberately

---

6. Angelina Grimké to Jane Smith, 9 May–5 June–7 June 1837. For Nathaniel Hawthorne's ambivalence concerning the construction of gender, see Walter Herbert, Jr., "Nathaniel Hawthorne, Una Hawthorne, and *The Scarlet Letter*," *PMLA* 103 (May 1988): 285–97.
7. "Declaration of Sentiments," *History of Woman Suffrage*, 1:70–73.

risks Arthur's anger in an attempt to rescue him, she risks what—as every traditional wife knows—amounts to annihilation. This explains the wildness of her plea, following his fury: "Let God punish! Thou shalt forgive!" (194) [125]. Arthur's response, "I freely forgive you now. May God forgive us both!" articulates his acceptance of the traditional husband's role as mediator between his erring wife and the Creator (195) [125].[8]

Their reconciliation, however, results in a reversal of the traditional marital relationship. Fearing Arthur is endangered both physically and spiritually as a result of his prolonged torture, Hester initially acts as a traditional wife by urging him to save himself. But when Arthur claims he is unable to choose, to act independently, when he urges her to assume a dominant role—"Think for me . . . thou art strong. Resolve for me!" (196) [126]; she does so—"Thou shalt not go alone!" (198) [128].

Following this exchange, the narrator pauses to present another detailed view of Hester. She is no longer seen as a fallen, wandering Eve, but as the quintessential enemy of Puritan civilization, an Indian at home in the vast wild. "Her intellect and heart had their home, as it were, in desert places, where she roamed as freely as the wild Indian in his woods" (199) [128]. Hester's new perspective recalls her shift in vision on the scaffold seven years earlier. Then, she had reviewed her life in an effort to comprehend her current situation and to validate her immediate perceptions. Now, however, Hester looks outward. Her new vision of society is perhaps analogous to the prospect viewed by Hawthorne's narrator after he was forced from the Custom House, or to the prospect from Henry David Thoreau's jail cell. "It was," Thoreau had written, "like travelling into a far country. . . . It was to see my native village in light of the middle ages. . . . It was a closer view of my native town. . . . I had not seen its institutions before."[9]

From this new perspective, Hester identifies the institutional struc-

8. For a contemporary feminist discussion of the duties of a wife and of the traditional role of a Christian husband as mediator between his wife and her Creator, see Sarah Grimké's *Letters on the Equality of the Sexes.* For a very different reading of Hester's relationship with Arthur and of the book's conclusion, see Nina Baym, "Thwarted Nature: Nathaniel Hawthorne as Feminist," *American Novelists Revisited: Essays in Feminist Criticism,* ed. Fritz Fleischmann (Boston: G. K. Hall, 1982), 58–77.

Hester's self-identification as Arthur's true wife is demonstrated by her refusal to name him in the first scaffold scene and in her prison interview with Roger; by the narrator's insinuation that her decision to remain in Boston after being released from prison is at least partially based on her feeling "connected in a union, that, unrecognized on earth, would bring them together before the bar of final judgment, and make that their marriage-altar" (80) [56]; by her tenacious appeal to Arthur to intervene on her behalf with the Governor when her custody of Pearl is jeopardized; and by her sense of a responsibility and commitment to Arthur, her only "significant link" to anyone in the community. This commitment leads her to tell Roger that she has decided to break her promise and reveal his identity to Arthur.

Hester's revelation of Roger's identity comments not only on her earlier promise to keep that identity secret and her refusal to name her lover to him, it also underscores her sense of herself as Arthur's wife by reversing the stock literary situation in which an adulterous wife finally identifies a secret lover to her husband.

9. In 1848, Thoreau had included these ideas in his talk on "Civil Disobedience" at the Concord Lyceum; Elizabeth Peabody had published his essay—along with Hawthorne's sketch "Main Street"—in *Aesthetic Papers* (May 1849); reprint, Gainesville, Fla.: Scholar's Facsimiles and Reprints, 1957.

tures of Boston, domestic as well as religious and political, with enemy eyes. She now examines, we are told, "whatever priests or legislators had established; criticizing all with hardly more reverence than the Indian would feel for the clerical band, the judicial robe, the pillory, the gallows, the fireside, or the church" (199) [128]. Hester is no longer like other women. The narrator explains: "The tendency of her fate and fortunes had been to set her free. The scarlet letter was her passport into regions where other women dared not tread" (199) [128].[1]

If, at this stage, Hester's development were to replicate the pattern described by the antislavery feminists, her new-found ability to identify the patriarchal society as her enemy would spark a new assertion of her identity, her womanhood. But Hester does not remain a wild Indian for long. Although after her agreement with Arthur she casts aside the dehumanizing scarlet letter and in the forest with him again becomes a woman, this renewal is presented as a consequence of her restored relationship with a man, as a result of his "magic touch." It is not shown as the result of her reawakened sense of her own identity— a consciousness that, in the case of the deeply religious antislavery feminists, grew from a sense of a renewed relationship with the Creator. Nevertheless, in the forest Hester appears an unfallen Eve in tune with Nature. When she again takes up the scarlet letter to suffer the "dreary change" into a thing, it is, she thinks, merely to "bear its torture . . . only a few days longer," until she can drown the dehumanizing brand in the deep sea (211) [135].

Her return is quickly followed by the third scaffold scene, which presents the carefully prefigured resolution of many of the problems the first scaffold scene had figured. Arthur confesses his crime in public; the spell binding Pearl is broken; the family is made complete; and Hester's relationship with Arthur is reordered to conform to a conventional marital pattern. When he calls, "Hester . . . come hither!" (252) [159], the woman who seven years earlier had defied the demands of husband, church, and state to name her partner in adultery—the woman who, we have just been told, sees all of Boston through the eyes of a "wild Indian"—obeys wordlessly "as if impelled by inevitable fate, and against her strongest will" (252) [159].

When Hester momentarily hesitates before reaching his side, Arthur reformulates and repeats his command: "Hester Prynne . . . in the name of Him, so terrible and so merciful, who gives me grace . . . come hither now, and twine thy strength about me!" (253) [160]. Arthur's language gains added significance in the context of this display of female obedience and of Hester's unanswered question, "Shall we not spend our immortal life together?" (256) [162]. His choice of words underscores the impression that this display of the completed nuclear family figures the standard wedding scene that climaxes much of our nineteenth-century fiction.

As Hawthorne wrote, use of the trope of the marriage of vine and

---

1. The narrator does not entirely approve. He comments, "Shame, Despair, Solitude! These had been her teachers,—and they had made her strong, but taught her much amiss" (199–200) [128].

elm became common in discussions of the woman question. The authors of the 1837 Pastoral Letter had used it to attack the Grimké sisters:

> If the vine, whose strength and beauty is to lean upon the trellis-work, and half conceal its clusters, thinks to assume the independence and the overshadowing nature of the elm, it will not only cease to bear fruit, but fall in shame and dishonor into the dust. We can not, therefore, but regret the mistaken conduct of those who encourage females to bear an obtrusive and ostentatious part in measures of reform, and countenance any of that sex who so far forget themselves as to itinerate in the character of public lecturers and teachers.[2]

In response, Sarah Grimké had presented a startling feminist variant. In her version, phallic objects that suggest both pastoral and military life apparently guard woman against some unnamed threat; but actually, they are woman's oppressors, not her defenders. Grimké's prose suggests that women who look to men for protection discover that males are at best weak and impotent, at worst dangerously rapacious. "Ah! How many of my sex feel in the dominion, thus unrighteously exercised over them, under the gentle appelation of *protection*, that what they have leaned upon has proved a broken reed at best, and oft a spear."[3]

The version of the trope presented in *The Scarlet Letter* is peculiar because in the third scaffold scene traditional gender roles are apparently reversed. The female vine is physically strong and the male elm, weak. Nonetheless, the physically stronger female submits against her will to the weaker male, who acts out the traditional husband's role of intermediary between his wife and the Creator. Thus Arthur: "Thy strength, Hester; but let it be guided by the will which God hath granted me. . . . Come, Hester, come! Support me up yonder scaffold!" (253) [160].[4]

Critics have pointed out that the final scaffold scene resolves many of the issues implicit in the first. But this scene fails to figure the resolution of the problems encoded in the earlier image of Hester ex-

---

2. The 1837 Pastoral Letter of "The General Association of Massachusetts (Orthodox) to the Churches under Their Care" is extracted in Stanton, *History of Woman Suffrage*, 1:81–82. The figure of the marriage of weak female vine and strong male elm appeared in classical writings by Virgil, in medieval emblem books, and in English masterworks by Spenser, Shakespeare, and Milton. I am indebted to A. Bartlett Giamatti for bringing to my attention Peter Demetz's "Elm and Vine: Notes Toward the History of a Marriage Topos," *PMLA* 73 (1958): 521–32.

3. Sarah Grimké, *Letters on the Equality of the Sexes* (Boston: Isaac Knapp, 1838), 21.

4. The comments of Hawthorne's narrator about the events following Arthur's spectacular death reinforce the impression that Hester, like a true wife, has grounded her sense of self in her relationship with her man. Reporting that after the minister's death Roger "positively withered up" because revenge was "the very principle of his life" and with Arthur's death there was "no further material to support it" (260) [163–64], he comments on the similarities between love and hate and defines both as parasitic: "Each renders one individual dependent for the food of his affections and spiritual life upon another; each leaves the passionate lover, or the no less passionate hater, forlorn and desolate by the withdrawal of his object" (260) [164]. References to connections between marriage and mosses and references to wives as "gentle parasites" recur throughout Hawthorne's work. Here his account of Hester's disappearance after Arthur's death underscores the notion that she is a true wife, a gentle parasite deprived of her host.

posed and enchained. Nor does it resolve the issues we have been examining: the official denial of Hester's womanhood and the informal denial of her sisterhood. As if acknowledging this, in the last chapter the narrator again turns to the twin issues of Hester's womanhood and sisterhood. Long after Pearl's humanization and Arthur's death on the scaffold, and long after Hester had taken Pearl away from Boston, he says, "Hester Prynne had returned, and taken up her long-forgotten shame. . . . [T]here was more real life for Hester Prynne, here, in New England, than in that unknown region where Pearl had found a home. Here had been her sin; here, her sorrow; and here was yet to be her penitence" (262–63) [165]. Hawthorne's feminist readers might find this promising. Despite the narrator's earlier statements about women, perhaps here, in contrast to most nineteenth-century fiction, a woman's life will not be seen as defined by a single event; perhaps here a female character will finally be treated as autonomous. While Hester's womanhood has been seen as contingent on her relationship with a man, and while her sisterhood is still denied, despite stirrings in the community, surely now that the narrator has returned to these issues, he will resolve them—although the comment that she must still become penitent perhaps presents a problem.

But the book ends on the next page. Her "real life" (262) [165]—inevitably involving her womanhood and sisterhood, inevitably involving her "sin . . . sorrow and . . . penitence" (263) [165], inevitably involving the sequence of views of Hester that we have been charting—is disposed of in eleven sentences in the next to last paragraph of *The Scarlet Letter*.

This passage begins with an announcement that the signification of her brand has been transformed. The "scarlet letter ceased to be a stigma which attracted the world's scorn and bitterness, and became a type of something to be sorrowed over, and looked upon with awe, yet with reverence too" (263) [165]. Its changed signification, however, alters neither the form nor the force of Hester's dehumanizing brand. Although she is no longer identified as a threat but as a source of support, as "one who had herself gone through a mighty trouble," Hester evidently has not again regained the womanhood stripped from her on the scaffold and so briefly restored during her forest meeting with Arthur (263) [165]. Apparently in the world of *The Scarlet Letter*, only a man's potent touch can restore lost womanhood; here a woman is defined neither as God's moral creature nor as a female member of society, but as the object of a man's love.

This passage reveals a triple vision. At its center, in a scene that finally does function as a pendant to the opening scene of Hester exhibited in the Market Place, the narrator shows her inside her hut, surrounded by the women of Boston. This glimpse of Hester among the women appears to resolve many of the tensions figured by the denial of her sisterhood in that first scaffold scene, and it perhaps even suggests the kind of women's discussion group that Margaret Fuller had created, which Sophia Peabody Hawthorne had attended. Actually, however, it is very different. What troubles the "wretched" "demanding" females surrounding Hester are not the complexities of the woman question that we are told had once tortured her, complexities that, by 1849, feminist intellectuals and activists had been addressing for years: the nature of woman as God's creature and the character of woman's oppression by the patriarchy. Instead, the women around Hester focus on private problems resulting from their sexual experiences with men: on the consequences of breaking the patriarchal rules restraining female "passion," or on the sense of worthlessness they feel because they are "unvalued and unsought" by men (263) [165]. Like the women surrounding her, Hester now focuses on these private and domestic aspects of women's lives. And like them, she does so in private.

Leaving implicit an assertion with which the feminists certainly agreed—that "the whole relation between man and woman" requires basic change—Hester makes explicit a series of ideas about how this change is to come about, ideas with which they certainly disagreed (263) [166]. What she says counters feminist assertions that women are competent to analyze their situation and to conceptualize the changes needed, that the time for these changes is now, and that women acting together can successfully achieve the necessary reforms. Instead, Hawthorne's narrator writes that Hester assures the women around her that the inevitable change must be based on a new revelation, that it will not occur now, and that it will not result from any actions of hers or of their own: "at some brighter period, when the world should have grown ripe for it, in Heaven's own time, a new truth will be revealed" (263) [166]. Hawthorne would repeat both the meter and the matter of these phrases. Four years later, rejecting antislavery activism in his campaign biography of Franklin Pierce, he would echo his rejection of feminist activism in *The Scarlet Letter*. A wise man, he would assert, "looks upon slavery as one of those evils which divine Providence does not leave to be remedied by human contrivances, but which, in its own good time, by some means impossible to be anticipated, but of the simplest and easiest operation, when all its uses shall have been fulfilled, it causes to vanish like a dream."[5]

At the end of *The Scarlet Letter*, we are told that Hester sketches, for the women around her, alternative versions of the female figure who, she asserts, will herald the "new truth." She dismisses the first: It is a vision of Hester herself as a "destined prophetess" (263) [166] publicly proclaiming a revolution in "the whole relation between man and woman." She rejects this figure although it would appear to climax and to culminate the fragmentary series of views of Hester that we have been tracing—as queen, as woman, and as sculpture, all in chains; as fallen, lost Eve; as wild Indian; and as prelapsarian Eve. And she rejects it although the narrator's comment that she herself had once "vainly imagined" (263) [166] she might fulfill this role underscores the intellectual and aesthetic inevitability of Hester's transformation into the "destined prophetess."

5. *Life of Franklin Pierce*, Centenary Edition, 5:416–17 [232–34].

In refusing this vision of herself, Hester evidently repudiates the feminist subtext—the language and iconography of the antislavery women, the images of women in chains, of female figures erect in space—that has fueled *The Scarlet Letter*. Clearly, she now repudiates tactics like those of the antislavery feminists who were defying social taboos in an effort to move other women to action, polemicizing, lecturing, and preaching in public, and prophesying a change in "this whole relation between man and woman."

Just as clearly, she repudiates their ideology. Although finally surrounded by women and acknowledging her connections with these everyday sinners (and thus by extension with women like those who, in Hawthorne's time, were held in slavery and with those who, although legally free, identified so deeply with their sisters in chains that they figured themselves as slaves), she now denies the central assertion of the antislavery feminists: "that any mission of divine and mysterious truth should be confided to a woman stained with sin, bowed down with shame, or even burdened with a life-long sorrow" (263) [166]. With these words, Hester denies that any of them (she herself, the women around her, or by extension nineteenth-century women literally and figuratively in chains) can act to end patriarchal oppression, can break her own chains and the chains of her sisters.

Instead, we are told that Hester has endorsed a different ideology. She now asserts that a woman unlike herself and her audience will function as "the angel and apostle of the coming revelation" (263) [166]. In accordance with this new idea, she projects a new iconography. The figure she envisions, the antithesis of the woman in chains, is a divine female rescuer "lofty, pure, and beautiful; and wise . . . through . . . the ethereal medium of joy" (263) [166]. Instead of proselytizing in public like the "destined prophetess"—and like the antislavery feminists who figured themselves as self-liberated liberators—this rescuer will deliver her message in private. Instead of engaging in debate and agitation like the antislavery feminists, the rescuer will present her message by example, simply showing "how sacred love can make us happy, by the truest test of a life successful to such an end!" (263) [166]. Five years after publication of *The Scarlet Letter*, Coventry Patmore's poem would provide this female culture figure with a name. The image Hester here envisions and endorses, a superhuman, privatized, and domesticated version of the Liberator of the double antislavery emblem, is the patriarchy's paradigm of true womanhood, the Angel in the House.[6]

Ironically, Hester's new vision does not resolve the division between

6. Coventry Patmore, *The Angel in the House*, 2 vols. (London: Macmillan, 1863); Patmore's poem had been published in sections in 1854, 1856, 1860, and 1863. Hawthorne, who was familiar with Patmore's poetry, wrote that "The Angel in the House" was "a favorite" of his and of Sophia; he judged it "a poem for married people to read together." See Mellow, *Nathaniel Hawthorne in His Times*, 40, 439; and *English Notebooks*, 620. I am deeply grateful to Milton R. Stern, whose comments, made so long ago, moved me to attempt an adequate reading of this passage, and who explores some of the complexities of Hawthorne's thought and production in "Nathaniel Hawthorne: Conservative After Heaven's Own Fashion," in Joseph Waldmeier, ed., *Essays in Honor of Russel B. Nye* (East Lansing, Mich.: Michigan State UP, 1978), 195–225.

women that the first scaffold scene had dramatized; it simply reverses it. Now on one side is a happy lone figure; on the other, among women "stained . . . bowed down . . . and burdened," crouches Hester. She counsels those around her to comfort each other in private, to be patient, and to have faith. Formulated in the terms of the antislavery emblem, she advises them to function as sisters, as members of their human community, but not as women, God's autonomous moral creatures.

The final lines of *The Scarlet Letter* powerfully reinforce its opening scene. The free-standing vertical "slab of slate"—placed not over Hester's grave but between it and Arthur's, marked not with her name or his or even the word naming their relationship, but with the brand that signaled, for her, the denial of both womanhood and sisterhood—this gravestone recalls our first view of Hester Prynne (264) [166]. Then, on the scaffold of the pillory, a young woman dressed in gray and branded with red was forced to expose herself as a punishment for breaking patriarchal laws restricting sexuality and as a device for controlling the behavior of other women in the colony. As then in the Market Place, so now in the cemetery, both her womanhood and her sisterhood are denied. Marked with a symbol whose meanings "perplex" (264) [166] their nineteenth-century viewers (and become available to us only through the intervention of Surveyor Pue and his decapitated successor, male officials of governments succeeding the Puritan theocracy), this "slab of slate" represents the ultimate denial of Hester's humanity and her membership in the community.[7] What we remember is the reassertion of the iconography of the antislavery feminists, now used to counter their definitions of true womanhood; we remember Hester's final exclusion from sisterhood with the dead, her final reduction from woman to nameless thing.

With the *Greek Slave* and *The Scarlet Letter*, the emblem of a woman exposed and enchained, of a woman pleading, again signifies a female victim, as it had before Angelina Grimké's excited realization that to appeal is to assert power. The antislavery feminists had recorded the supplicant image to express woman's struggle against oppression and to announce their own self-liberation. But the emblem of the female in chains was reappropriated and again recorded. Over time, as patriarchal discourse became utterly dominant, the speeches and writings of the antislavery feminists were marginalized. Then they disappeared from the page.

7. For an awareness of the role of the government officials, I am indebted to Nina Baym's "George Sand in American Periodicals" (Paper delivered at the meetings of the Nathaniel Hawthorne Society, New York, 1983).

LELAND S. PERSON

The Dark Labyrinth of Mind: Hawthorne, Hester, and the Ironies of Racial Mothering†

> If a pastor has offspring by a woman not his wife, the church dismiss him, if she is a white woman; but if she is colored, it does not hinder his continuing to be their good shepherd.
> —Harriet Jacobs, *Incidents in the Life of a Slave Girl*

"Explicit or implicit, the Africanist presence informs in compelling and inescapable ways the texture of American literature," argues Toni Morrison. "It is a dark and abiding presence, there for the literary imagination as both a visible and an invisible mediating force. Even, and especially, when American texts are not 'about' Africanist presences or characters or narrative or idiom, the shadow hovers in implication, in sign, in line of demarcation."[1] In this essay I want to accept the challenge Morrison issues to American literary scholars and to explore the "dark labyrinth of mind," as Hawthorne calls it, that constitutes Hester Prynne's subjectivity and subject position in *The Scarlet Letter*.[2] With some uncanny inspiration from the epigraph I have taken from Harriet Jacobs's *Incidents in the Life of a Slave Girl*,[3] I want to examine Hester within a historical context formed by the intersection of motherhood and race and to ask some questions about how discourses of motherhood, slavery, miscegenation, abolition, women's rights, child custody, and so on contend with one another at the site of Hester's character. Hawthorne referred to the importation of slaves as a "monstrous birth," and in this essay I wish to see how and what Hester's maternal behavior signifies within a racial context of "other," if not monstrous, mothering.[4]

Hester Prynne's adulterous behavior and the scarlet letter that initially represents it also deform her motherhood. Examined within a nineteenth-century context, moreover, Hester's deviant mothering can be understood more particularly within a framework of slave motherhood. Sociologist Patricia Hill Collins, for example, describes a "distinctly Afrocentric ideology of motherhood" that slave women adapted to the oppressive conditions of slavery: community-based childcare, informal adoption, reliance on *"othermothers"*—traditions, she emphasizes, rooted in very different life experiences from the prevalent cult

---

† From *Studies in American Fiction* 29 (Spring 2001): 33–48. Copyright © Northeastern University. Reprinted by permission of the publisher and the author. Page numbers in square brackets refer to this Norton Critical Edition.

1. Toni Morrison, *Playing in the Dark: Whiteness and the Literary Imagination* (Cambridge: Harvard UP, 1992), 46–47.
2. Nathaniel Hawthorne, *The Scarlet Letter*, ed. William Charvat et al., *The Centenary Edition of the Works of Nathaniel Hawthorne*, vol. 1 (Columbus: Ohio State UP, 1962), 166 [108]. Hereafter cited parenthetically by volume and page number.
3. Harriet Jacobs, *Incidents in the Life of a Slave Girl* (1861), ed. Jean Fagan Yellin (Cambridge: Harvard UP, 1987), 74.
4. Nathaniel Hawthorne, "Chiefly about War-Matters," *Miscellaneous Prose and Verse*, ed. Thomas Woodson, Claude M. Simpson, and L. Neal Smith, *The Centenary Edition of the Works of Nathaniel Hawthorne*, vol. 23 (Columbus: Ohio State UP, 1994), 420.

of true womanhood, with its dependency on a world of separate male and female spheres.[5] Hazel Carby points out, in this respect, that Harriet Jacobs's *Incidents in the Life of a Slave Girl* contradicts and transforms an ideology of true womanhood and motherhood "that could not take account of her experience."[6] Linda Brent abandons her children in order to save them—convinced that they have better chances of survival and success with "others." In Carby's view, "Jacobs developed an alternative set of definitions of womanhood and motherhood in the text which remained in tension with the cult of true womanhood."[7] Deborah Gray White, furthermore, documents cases from the 1830s and 1840s of slave mothers who actually killed their children. Some "claimed to have done so because of their intense concern for their offspring." One mother claimed that "her master was the father of the child, and that her mistress knew it and treated it so cruelly that she had to kill it to save it from further suffering."[8] Whether or not a mother actually commits infanticide, as Cassy does in *Uncle Tom's Cabin* or as the slave mother does in Frances Harper's poem of that title, slavery radically altered motherhood—inverting or ironizing it.[9] "I made up my mind," Stowe's Cassy explains. "I would never again let a child live to grow up! I took the little fellow in my arms, when he was two weeks old, and kissed him, and cried over him; and then I gave him laudanum, and held him close to my bosom, while he slept to death."[1] Converting the maternal breast into a source of poison rather than nourishment—being a good mother in the deforming context of slavery can actually mean killing, not nurturing, one's child. Killing the child to save it, giving it up to ensure it a better life: both forms of

5. Patricia Hill Collins, "The Meaning of Motherhood in Black Culture and Black Mother/Daughter Relationships," *SAGE* 4, no. 2 (Fall 1987): 3, 5.
6. Hazel V. Carby, *Reconstructing Womanhood: The Emergence of the Afro-American Woman Novelist* (New York: Oxford UP, 1987), 49.
7. Carby, 56. In Stephanie Smith's felicitous terms, Jacobs's "desertion will translate into devotion." *Conceived by Liberty: Maternal Figures and Nineteenth-Century American Literature* (Ithaca: Cornell UP, 1994), 146.
8. Deborah Gray White, *Ar'n't I a Woman? Female Slaves in the Plantation South* (New York: W. W. Norton & Company, 1985), 88.
9. Frances Harper, "The Slave Mother." *A Brighter Coming Day: A Frances Ellen Watkins Harper Reader*, ed. Frances Smith Foster (New York: Feminist P, 1990), 85:

> Then, said the mournful mother,
>   If Ohio cannot save,
> I will do a deed for freedom,
>   She shall find each child a grave.
>
> I will save my precious children
>   From their darkly threatened doom,
> I will hew their path to freedom
>   Through the portals of the tomb.
>
> A moment in the sunlight,
>   She held a glimmering knife,
> The next moment she had bathed it
>   In the crimson fount of life.
>
> They snatched away the fatal knife,
>   Her boys shrieked wild with Dread;
> The baby girl was pale and cold,
>   They raised it up, the child was dead. (lines 41–56)

1. Harriet Beecher Stowe, *Uncle Tom's Cabin*, ed. Elizabeth Ammons (New York: W. W. Norton & Company, 1994), 318.

ironic mothering suggest a perverse inversion—what Jean Wyatt, referring to Sethe's murder of Beloved in Toni Morrison's novel, calls the
"ultimate contradiction of mothering under slavery."[2]

If not quite in such terrible terms, the question of bad and even infanticidal mothering arises in *The Scarlet Letter*. After the opening
scene in the market place, when Pearl is newborn, Hester returns
from the scaffold "in a state of nervous excitement that demanded
constant watchfulness, lest she should perpetrate violence on herself,
or do some half-frenzied mischief to the poor babe" (*CE* 1:70) [50].
Later, at the Governor's Hall, when Pearl is three, Hester vows to kill
herself before allowing the magistrates to remove Pearl from her care
(*CE* 1:113) [76]. Later still, when Pearl is seven, a "fearful doubt
strove to possess [Hester's] soul, whether it were not better to send
Pearl at once to heaven, and go herself to such futurity as Eternal Justice should provide" (*CE* 1:166) [108]. This last thought proceeds
directly out of the "dark labyrinth of mind" in which Hester has wandered during her seven years of ostracism from the Puritan community, and this infanticidal impulse leads directly into Hawthorne's
observation that the "scarlet letter had not done its office" (*CE* 1:166)
[108]. Among other features of her character, in other words,
Hawthorne makes Hester's motherhood and its deviant tendencies—
over the entire seven-year period of the novel—issues for careful observation.

Hawthorne could have found numerous examples of infanticidal
mothers in the Puritan sources from which he composed *The Scarlet
Letter*, including several that occurred during the period that com-
prises the novel's historical setting. Peter Hoffer and N. E. H. Hull
cite the case of Dorothy Talbie of Salem, who was hanged in 1638 for
murdering her three-year-old daughter. Recording this incident in his
journal, John Winthrop noted that Talbie was "so possessed with Satan that he persuaded her (by his delusions, which she listened to as
revelations from God) to break the neck of her own child, that she
might free it from future misery."[3] Winthrop's explanation and the motive he attributes to Talbie anticipate Hester's thoughts of saving Pearl
and herself from earthly pain. In another case Allice Bishop was executed in Plymouth in 1648 for murdering her four-year-old daughter,
whom she had apparently conceived in an act of adultery.[4] In the same
year another Massachusetts court condemned Mary Martin to death
for killing her newborn daughter. The circumstances of the case bear
some similarities to those in *The Scarlet Letter*. As recorded by
Winthrop, Mary Martin's father had returned to England without ar-
ranging for proper supervision for his two daughters. Mary, the elder,
promptly committed adultery with the married Mr. Mitton of Casco
and, "her time being come, she was delivered of a woman child in a

2. Jean Wyatt, "Giving Body to the Word: The Maternal Symbolic in Toni Morrison's *Beloved*."
PMLA 108 (May 1993): 476.
3. Quoted in Peter C. Hoffer and N. E. H. Hull, *Murdering Mothers: Infanticide in England
and New England 1558–1803* (New York: New York UP, 1981), 40.
4. Hoffer and Hull, 42.

back room by herself." Martin attempted to kill the child by kneeling upon its head and then ultimately "put it into the fire."[5] Abandonment by a father (Martin) or father-like husband (Chillingworth), followed by adultery, the birth of an "illegitimate" child, and thoughts of infanticide—the resemblances seem compelling. Cotton Mather, moreover, preached two sermons inspired by the execution of Margaret Gaulacher, an Irish servant who had murdered her illegitimate newborn child. Mather cared less about the details of Gaulacher's case, which he scarcely mentioned, than about the frequency of bastard neonaticide. "I cannot but think," he concluded, "That there is a *Voice of God* unto the Country in this Thing; That there should be so many Instances of Women Executed for the Murder of their *Bastard-Children*. There are now Six or Seven such unhappy Instances."[6]

One of the most striking was the case of Esther Rodgers of Kittery, Maine, who confessed to being "defiled by a *Negro* Lad" at the age of seventeen, to murdering the resulting child, and to giving it a "Private Burial in the Garden."[7] Some time after committing this infanticide, which she did "in Secret" and without being caught, Rodgers moved to Newbury, where she repeated the crime. In her own words:

> And there I fell into the like Horrible Pit (as before) *viz.* of Carnal Pollution with the *Negro* man belonging to that House. And being with Child again, I was in as great concern to know how to hide this as the former. Yet did not so soon resolve the Murdering of it, but was continually hurried in my thoughts, and undetermined till the last hour. I went forth to be delivered in the Field, and dropping my Child by the side of a little Pond, (whether alive, or still Born I cannot tell) I covered it over with Dirt and Snow, and speedily returned home again. (124)

Rodgers was caught immediately and ultimately executed (on July 31, 1701) for both crimes, and the remainder of her brief confession, like the three sermons John Rogers preached upon the subject of her sinfulness, recounts her repentance and conversion. I cannot tell if Hawthorne knew this text, but Esther Rodgers' situation certainly bears some similarities to Hester's. Rogers emphasizes Rodgers' public presence in and for the Puritan community—the visitors she receives in prison, the round of visits she makes to "private Meetings of Christians in the Town" (131), the freedom and openness with which she discusses her situation (132), the "invincible Courage" she maintains on the verge of her execution (144), the public spectacle of the execution itself, which draws a crowd of 4,000–5,000 (153), and even her insistence to the High Sheriff that she be allowed "the liberty to walk on Foot" to the gallows rather than being carried in a cart (143). In his

5. Hoffer and Hull, 43.
6. Cotton Mather, A Sorrowful Spectacle, in Two Sermons Occasioned by the Just Sentence of Death, on a Miserable Woman, for the Murder of a Spurious Offspring (Boston: T. Fleet & T. Crump, 1715), 90.
7. Esther Rodgers, "The Declaration and Confession of Esther Rodgers." In John Rogers, Death the Certain Wages of Sin to the Impenitent: Three Lecture Sermons; Occasioned by the Execution of a Young Woman, Guilty of Murdering Her Infant Begotten in Whoredom (Boston: Green and Allen, 1701), 122. Hereafter cited parenthetically.

preface to Rodgers' "confession" Samuel Belcher calls her a "poor wretch, entering into Prison a Bloody Malefactor, her Conscience *laden with Sins of a Scarlet Die*" (italics added, 118). Whether or not this scarlet Esther inspired Hawthorne's Hester, Esther Rodgers' case does evidence an Africanist presence in the seventeenth-century background of *The Scarlet Letter*. Whereas Rodgers resorts to infanticide, of course, Hester Prynne rejects that final solution and chooses instead to raise Pearl by herself.

Nineteenth-century as well as seventeenth-century materials comprise Hester's character, of course. While these seventeenth-century examples of fornication, adultery, and infanticide offer important evidence that Hawthorne had ample material to underwrite the Puritan features of Hester's maternal situation, the most striking examples of maternal infanticide in nineteenth-century literature involve slave mothers killing (or some times simply abandoning) their children in order to save them from enslavement. *The Scarlet Letter* has increasingly been examined in its nineteenth-century context, and its participation in a conversation about slavery and abolition has become almost axiomatic. For the most part, however, critics such as Jonathan Arac, Sacvan Bercovitch, Jennifer Fleischner, and Deborah Madsen have revealed Hawthorne's historicism in order to confirm his conservatism—his failure to oppose slavery and embrace abolition. Arguing that Hester's scarlet A resembles the United States Constitution as a contested text, Arac, for example, considers the "indeterminacy" of the letter's meaning a strategy on Hawthorne's part for avoiding political action and change. *The Scarlet Letter*, he believes, is "propaganda—*not* to change your life."[8] Bercovitch makes a more abstract case, but he too considers *The Scarlet Letter* to be "thick propaganda," and he cites Hawthorne's "ironies of reconciliation" and laissez-faire "strategy of inaction" as key ingredients in the liberal ideology that sponsored numerous compromises with slavery, especially in 1850, the year of *The Scarlet Letter*'s publication.[9]

Jean Fagan Yellin has gone furthest in exploring the novel's inscription by slavery and abolitionist discourses and convincingly established Hawthorne's knowledge of anti-slavery feminism.[1] She has linked Hester iconographically to female slaves as sisters in bondage even as she stresses Hawthorne's refusal to let Hester function as a full-fledged anti-slavery feminist. "*The Scarlet Letter* presents a classic displace-

8. Jonathan Arac, "The Politics of *The Scarlet Letter*." *Ideology and Classic American Literature*, ed. Sacvan Bercovitch and Myra Jehlen (New York: Cambridge UP, 1986), 251.
9. Sacvan Bercovitch, *The Office of The Scarlet Letter* (Baltimore: Johns Hopkins UP, 1991), 89, 109, 110. Fleischner also argues that *The Scarlet Letter* reflects an "ideology that is related to the belief in compromise toward slavery adopted by Hawthorne and other Northerners at mid-century who, although anti-slavery, were above all pro-union." See "Hawthorne and the Politics of Slavery," *Studies in the Novel* 23 (1991): 97. Deborah L. Madsen, " 'A for Abolition': Hawthorne's Bond-servant and the Shadow of Slavery," *Journal of American Studies* 25 (1991): 225–59, focuses on Governor Bellingham's bond-servant to claim that Hawthorne "complicates the vision of American liberty by representing, in 'typical' form, the entire generation of Founding Fathers who were slave owners" (257).
1. Jean Fagan Yellin, "Hawthorne and the American National Sin." *The Green American Tradition: Essays and Poems for Sherman Paul*, ed. H. Daniel Peck (Baton Rouge: Louisiana State UP, 1989), 75–97, and *Women and Sisters: The Antislavery Feminists in American Culture* (New Haven: Yale UP, 1989) [pp. 632–55 in this Norton Critical Edition].

ment," Yellin points out: "color is the sign not of race, but of grace—and of its absence. Black skin is seen as blackened soul." When "black' is read as describing skin color and not moral status, the text of *The Scarlet Letter* reveals the obsessive concern with blacks and blackness, with the presence of a dangerous dark group within society's midst, that is characteristic of American political discourse in the last decades before Emancipation."[2] Even though she explicitly links Hester to slave womanhood, Yellin ignores one of the key parallels. She focuses briefly on Hester's single motherhood but only in order to link her to other "fallen women" in nineteenth-century life and letters.[3] Complaining of Hester's erstwhile feminism obscures her position on the "other" side of the slavery/abolition equation—as a single mother whose racial identity helps illustrate the politics of racial mothering.

Jay Grossman offers an even more particularized reading of race in *The Scarlet Letter* by arguing that, in its fixation on the figure of the black man, the novel becomes "profoundly implicated" in "antebellum discourses of miscegenation." The "novel's depiction of miscegenation does not merely reproduce the terms of the Southern confrontation between a white master and a female slave," he argues. "Rather, the novel shifts the genders of that equation, with the effect ultimately of revealing the white fears that linked North and South: a shared belief in the unbridled sexuality of African men and the vulnerability of white women, a shared panic when confronted with the possibility of racial mixing."[4] In the allegorical terms that Grossman uses, Hester is a "victimized woman and Pearl the illegitimate child of a father-master"—Dimmesdale, whom the text obsessively figures as black.[5] Although he does not say so explicitly, Grossman seems to recognize the ambiguities, or doubleness, of Hawthorne's symbolic representation of race in *The Scarlet Letter*. Hester and Dimmesdale can be both black and white.

Similarly, I am not interested in identifying Hester Prynne as a slave mother or a black woman who has "passed" as white all these years. To be sure, our current critical interest in the representation of race and gender in literary texts provides a lens through which previously invisible textual features, such as Morrison's "Africanist presence," come to light. But the issue is not Hester's blackness or the Africanist "shadow" (to use another of Morrison's suggestive terms) that may "hover" over her character. The question is Hester's connection as a woman and a mother to other nineteenth-century female "characters"—in particular, to slave mothers and anti-slavery feminists. That connection is tricky. Hazel Carby, for example, has cautioned that "any feminist history that seeks to establish the sisterhood of white and

2. Yellin, *Women and Sisters*, 138 [643]. Yellin goes on, however, to argue that Hester's refusal to become a prophetess at the end of the novel reflects Hawthorne's repudiation of the "antislavery feminists who were defying social taboos in an effort to move other women to action" (149).
3. Yellin, *Women and Sisters*, 142 [646].
4. Jay Grossman, " 'A' is for Abolition?: Race, Authorship, *The Scarlet Letter*," *Textual Practice* 7 (Spring 1993): 14, 15.
5. Grossman, 14, 17.

black women as allies in the struggle against the oppression of all
women must also reveal the complexity of the social and economic differences between women," so I want to be careful in examining how
Hawthorne's representation of Hester as a mother engages and addresses contemporary issues of slave motherhood.[6] While Hester's
motherhood, constructed discursively and intertextually, does link her
with slave mothers, she also enjoys some privileges by virtue of her
white racial identity. Insofar as she embodies racial identities, Hester
represents an amalgam, or amalgamation. Hawthorne does link her
situation closely enough with that of slave mothers that he tacitly invites us to discover an Africanist "presence" in her character. Describing the Puritans' expectations outside the prison door in the opening
scene of *The Scarlet Letter*, Hawthorne observes that it

> might be that a sluggish bond-servant, or an undutiful child,
> whom his parents had given over to civil authority, was to be cor-
> rected at the whipping post. It might be, that an Antinomian, a
> Quaker, or other heterodox religionist, was to be scourged out of
> town, or an idle and vagrant Indian, whom the white man's fire-
> water had made riotous about the streets, was to be driven with
> stripes into the shadow of the forest. It might be, too, that a
> witch, like old Mistress Hibbins, the bitter-tempered widow of the
> magistrate, was to die upon the gallows. (CE 1:49) [37]

Hawthorne's catalog makes clear the Puritans' conflation of various
outlaw groups into a single figure of alterity—Hester herself. As an object of the Puritan's collective gaze, Hester embodies multiple forms of
otherness, certainly including race. As a subject, therefore, Hester
finds it difficult to escape her objectified being. Contemplating the
"entire track along which she had been treading, since her happy infancy," she finds herself focusing on the scarlet letter and all that it
signifies: "these were realties,—all else had vanished!" (CE 1:59) [44].

This is not to say that Hester's objective status entirely eclipses her
subjectivity—or, in the terms that concern me here, that her objectified status as an "other" woman colors her character completely in
racial terms. Hester carries ambiguous racial markings, and I think
Hawthorne exploits that ambiguity—the whiteness of her blackness—
to shine an interesting and ironic light on the presumptions of white
female abolitionists like Margaret Fuller and his sister-in-law, Elizabeth Peabody. In arguing the case for women's emancipation, for example, Fuller links women and slaves, effectively commandeering the
subject position of black women for her own rhetorical and political
purpose.[7] Elizabeth Peabody had long irritated Hawthorne with her

6. Carby, 53. See also Margaret M. R. Kellow, "The Divided Mind of Antislavery Feminism: Ly-
    dia Maria Child and the Construction of African American Womanhood." *Discovering the
    Women in Slavery: Emancipating Perspectives on the American Past*, ed. Patricia Morton
    (Athens: U of Georgia P, 1996), 107–26. Kellow concludes that the "discourse of indepen-
    dence and self-reliance as constructed by Child, crucial though it was to undermining the
    defense of slavery, had very little to do with black women" (113).
7. Fuller asserts, for example, that "there exists in the minds of men a tone of feeling towards
    women as toward slaves," and makes her case for women's emancipation by placing women
    in the same position as "Negroes": "As the friend of the negro assumes that one man cannot,

abolitionist views. When she sent the Hawthornes an abolitionist pamphlet she had written, Hawthorne returned it to her without even showing it to Sophia. "No doubt it seems the truest of truth to you," he told his sister-in-law, "but I do assure you that, like every other Abolitionist, you look at matters with an awful squint, which distorts everything within your line of vision."[8] Three months later, after Peabody apparently sent him the same pamphlet, Hawthorne returned it again with a curt note:

> I read your manuscript abolition pamphlet, supposing it to be a new production, and only discovered afterwards that it was the one I had sent back. Upon my word, it is not very good; not worthy of being sent three times across the ocean; not so good as I supposed you would always write on a subject in which your mind and heart were interested.[9]

This correspondence occurred in 1857 while the Hawthornes were living in Liverpool and, thus, years after publication of *The Scarlet Letter*, but the Hawthornes' arguments with Peabody over slavery and abolition were longstanding.[1] To whatever extent he was aware of it, then, Hawthorne had personal reasons to criticize the feminist antislavery position and to situate Hester Prynne within the ideological context that discourse created. Considered as both subject and object, Hester occupies a symbolic position, it seems to me, on the dividing line between black and white feminism—the line that some white nineteenth-century feminists either ignored or erased. Objectified in a way that associates her with slave mothers, Hester retains some privileges of her status as a white feminist who, like Fuller and Peabody, presumed to occupy the subject position of slave women.

When he referred to slavery as a "monstrous birth" in "Chiefly about War-Matters," Hawthorne was playing upon the odd fact that, some time after carrying the Pilgrims to Plymouth, the *Mayflower* had become a slave ship. "There is an historical circumstance, known to few," he observed, "that connects the children of the Puritans with these Africans of Virginia in a singular way. They are our brethren, as being lineal descendents from the May Flower, the fated womb of which, in her first voyage, sent forth a brood of Pilgrims upon Plymouth Rock, and, in a subsequent one, spawned slaves upon the southern soil;—a monstrous birth, but with which we have an instinctive sense of kindred, and so are stirred by an irresistible impulse to attempt their rescue, even at the cost of blood and ruin."[2] We "must let her white progeny offset her dark one," Hawthorne concludes, and I

---

by right, hold another in bondage, so should the friend of woman assume that man cannot, by right, lay even well-meant restrictions on woman," *Woman in the Nineteenth Century*, ed. Larry J. Reynolds (New York: W. W. Norton & Company, 1998), 18, 20.

8. Nathaniel Hawthorne, *The Letters, 1857–1864*, ed. William Charvat et al., *The Centenary Edition of the Works of Nathaniel Hawthorne*, vol. 18 (Columbus: Ohio State UP, 1987), 89.

9. *The Letters, 1857–1864*, 115.

1. In his biography of Peabody, Bruce Ronda discusses the conflict between Hawthorne and Peabody, as well as Hawthorne's "hostility to antislavery advocates." See *Elizabeth Palmer Peabody: A Reformer on Her Own Terms* (Cambridge: Harvard UP, 1999), 265.

2. Hawthorne, "Chiefly about War-Matters," 420.

would like to speculate further on the black and white doubleness to which he refers by suggesting that he had already explored the "singular" connection between Puritans and Africans—that in Hester he had discovered a vehicle for letting the "white progeny" of the *Mayflower* "offset her dark one." Hester Prynne embodies the racial doubleness that Hawthorne cites. Objectively and subjectively considered, she may be considered both black and white, and the challenge Hawthorne poses for the reader is how to deal with the Africanist presence (in Morrison's term) that shadows the white feminist subject.

Yellin has demonstrated conclusively that Hawthorne "became intimately acquainted with the essential facts of chattel slavery, as well as with the debate raging around it."[3] The Peabody sisters' Cuba Journals describe the sexual exploitation of slave women, for example, and even the frequency of infanticide—twenty or thirty deaths on the plantation where they stayed.[4] Hawthorne's 1835 sketch "Old News" not only mentions the slave population of Salem, but also includes the observation that "when the slaves of a family were inconveniently prolific, it being not quite orthodox to drown the superfluous offspring, like a litter of kittens, notice was promulgated of a 'negro child to be given away.' "[5] Although Yellin concludes that Hawthorne "deliberately avoided thinking about black slavery in antebellum America," I want to argue that, in identifying Hester with slave motherhood, Hawthorne interrogates and critiques the familiar identification of women and slaves—the conflation in nineteenth-century victimology of white mothers and slave mothers.[6] Illustrating the ironies of racialized maternal signification, Hawthorne undermines an anti-slavery feminist discourse that pretends to occupy the subject position of the slave woman and mother.

Dimmesdale's impregnation of Hester—after the "middle passage" that separates her from her husband—resembles a white master's miscegenetic coupling with a slave woman, at least in its analogous imbalance of power. Hester and Dimmesdale's action, even as it recalls the seventeenth-century predicaments catalogued by Mather and Winthrop, places Hester in a position that was beginning to register with nineteenth-century readers of abolitionist tracts and fugitive slave narratives. "Thou wast my pastor, and hadst charge of my soul," Hester reminds Dimmesdale at the Governor's Hall (*CE* 1:113) [76], as she implores him to intercede with the Puritan magistrates and convince them to let her retain custody of Pearl. In *Incidents in the Life of a Slave Girl* (1861) Harriet Jacobs comments that "there is a great difference between Christianity and religion at the south. . . . If a pastor has offspring by a woman not his wife, the church dismiss him, if she is a white woman; but if she is colored, it does not hinder his continuing to be their good shepherd."[7] Much like a slave mother,

3. Yellin, "Hawthorne and the American National Sin," 76.
4. Yellin, "Hawthorne and the American National Sin," 84.
5. Nathaniel Hawthorne, "Old News," *The Snow-Image and Uncollected Tales*, ed. William Charvat et al., *The Centenary Edition of the Works of Nathaniel Hawthorne*, vol. 11 (Columbus: Ohio State UP, 1974), 139.
6. Yellin, "Hawthorne and the American National Sin," 89.
7. Jacobs, 74.

whose only hope for keeping her child resided in her ties to white male authority, Hester must plead her case at secondhand. Harriet Jacobs maintains some leverage over Dr. Flint by threatening to expose his licentiousness to his wife and to the community. Similarly, Hester has gained leverage over Dimmesdale by refusing to name him as Pearl's father. According to a similar, absolute authority that separated slave mothers from their children and converted children into property subject to sale by the very fathers who denied their blood ties, Hester and Pearl remain subject to patriarchal law. Ultimately, however, Hester's feminist victory at the Governor's Hall offers a model that slave mothers like Jacobs were hard-pressed to emulate. Jacobs's many appeals to Mr. Sands, the biological father of her two children, repeatedly fall on deaf ears. Indeed, when she finally gets safely to New York, she is astonished to learn that, instead of freeing the daughter whose freedom she pressured him into buying, he has given Ellen to the daughter of a friend.

Like the mulatto children of slaveholders, Pearl follows the condition of her mother, and the parental triangle Hawthorne describes around Pearl resembles the common triangle on southern plantations if "Good Master Dimmesdale" occupies the position of the slave master, who fathers an illegitimate child upon one of his slaves, cuckolding her husband and then denying the child whom he fathers—even as, in his role as magistrate, he retains the power to remove her from her mother. In the terms that Hortense Spillers uses about fatherhood under slavery, "a dual fatherhood is set in motion, comprised of the African father's *banished* name and body and the captor father's mocking presence."[8] Not unlike a paranoid slave owner, determined to erase all traces of his miscegenetic paternity, furthermore, Dimmesdale worries about Pearl's maturing appearance. His refusal to acknowledge Pearl in any way, his dread that his "own features were partly repeated" in her face (*CE* 1:206) [132], parallels the paradoxical relation between fatherhood and master-hood that writers such as Frederick Douglass and Harriet Jacobs describe. Douglass explains that slave women's children "in all cases follow the condition of their mothers," in order to make the slave-owning father's "wicked desires profitable as well as pleasurable; for by this cunning arrangement, the slaveholder, in cases not a few, sustains to his slaves the double relation of master and father."[9] And Jacobs tells the story of a Congressman who insists that his six mulatto children be sent away from the "great house" before he visits with his friends. "The existence of the colored children did not trouble this gentleman," she observes; "it was only the fear that friends might recognize in their features a resemblance to him."[1]

In the scaffold scene that opens *The Scarlet Letter* Hester seems uncannily linked to her sisters in bondage through a similar relationship to patriarchal power. Yellin notes the iconographic link to anti-

8. Spillers, "Mama's Baby, Papa's Maybe: An American Grammar Book," *diacritics* 17, no. 2 (Summer 1987): 80.
9. Douglass, *Narrative of the Life of Frederick Douglass* (New York: Penguin, 1982), 49.
1. Jacobs, *Incidents in the Life of Slave Girl*, 142.

slavery emblems of women on the auction block: "Hawthorne's book begins by presenting a woman publicly exposed, a figure made familiar by the abolitionists."[2] The narrator himself wonders before Hester's entrance if a "sluggish bond-servant" is about to appear (CE 1:49) [37]. Hester's stubborn refusal to name her child's father, furthermore, links her uncannily, if ironically, with slave mothers. Monika Elbert celebrates this refusal as a feminist gesture of defiance, a defiant "sin against patriarchy" along the lines Julia Kristeva marks out in "Stabat Mater."[3] The "Virgin assumes her feminine denial of the other sex (of man) but overcomes him by setting up a third person," Kristeva says: "I do not conceive with *you* but with *Him*."[4] For Hester, compared if "only by contrast" to the "image of Divine Maternity" (CE 1:56) [42], denial of Dimmesdale promises transcendence—for Pearl—of the mother's condition. "My child must seek a heavenly Father," Hester insists; "she shall never know an earthly one!" (CE 1:68) [49]. Hester's refusal to name Pearl's father highlights the ironies of racial mothering, however, for in the inverted world of slavery, as Harriet Jacobs notes, "it was a crime for a slave to tell who was the father of her child."[5] While Hester's repeated refusals to name the father link her with the black sisterhood Jacobs identifies, such refusals signify very differently within different discursive and legal communities. The sort of heroic feminist action that Elbert celebrates signifies a *slave* mother's compliance *with* rather than rebellion *against* slave law. Parthenogenesis—Kristeva's feminist ideal, a male slaveholder's economic strategy. The condition and race of the mother make the difference.

While "Good Master Dimmesdale" may not be a *slave* master, his repudiation of Pearl resembles a slave master's behavior and subjects his daughter, as the Governor's Hall scene makes clear, to a similar patriarchal authority. Fatherhood, in Douglass's terms, gives way to "masterhood." Slave owners "controlled virtually all dimensions of their children's lives," Patricia Hill Collins observes; "they could be sold at will, whipped, even killed, all with no recourse by their mothers. In such a situation, simply keeping and rearing one's children becomes empowerment."[6] The Puritan magistrates, "Good Master Dimmesdale" included, claim a similar authority to dispose of Pearl. Hester claims a mother's power not to let them, and as her desperation increases in the face of her powerlessness, her subjectivity and her subject position resemble those of nineteenth-century slave mothers like Harriet Jacobs. The "fact that slave society did not condemn

2. Yellin, *Women and Sisters*, 126.
3. Monika M. Elbert, "Hester's Maternity: Stigma or Weapon?" *ESQ* 36 (1990): 179.
4. Julia Kristeva, "Stabat Mater." *The Kristeva Reader*, ed. Toril Moi (New York: Columbia UP, 1986), 180.
5. Jacobs, 13. "The secrets of slavery are concealed like those of the Inquisition," Jacobs observes. "My master was, to my knowledge, the father of eleven slaves. But did the mothers dare to tell who was the father of their children? Did the other slaves dare to allude to it, except in whispers among themselves? No, indeed! They knew too well the terrible consequences" (35).
6. Collins, "Shifting the Center: Race, Class, and Feminist Theorizing about Motherhood." *Representations of Motherhood*, ed. Donna Bassin, Margaret Honey, and Meryle Mahrer Kaplan (New Haven: Yale UP, 1994), 66.

'illegitimacy' indicates the centrality of the mother role," observes Deborah Gray White, "a role which was presumed legitimate independent of the father's or husband's role."[7] Hester's situation in *The Scarlet Letter*, of course, tests the legitimacy of her maternal role. She does not commit infanticide, choosing heroically to live apart from her husband and to be the single mother of an "illegitimate" child, but she still confronts many of the same issues faced by slave mothers.

"What are a mother's rights," Hester asks Dimmesdale at the Governor's Hall, and "how much stronger they are, when that mother has but her child and the scarlet letter!"—that is, no husband/father and no political or legal standing (*CE* 1:113) [76]. Although Hester has successfully marked out a marginal space of her own in which to *be* a mother, the Puritan magistrates remind her that she mothers, so to speak, at the pleasure of the patriarchs; for they retain the power, *in loco Parentis*, to take Pearl away from her in much the same way that slave owners—fathers or not—possessed that absolute power. Michael Grossberg has shown that custody rulings in the nineteenth century, however, "increasingly devalued paternally oriented, property-based welfare considerations and emphasized maternally biased child nurture ones."[8] Interpolating such changes anachronistically into his Puritan setting, Hawthorne conducts a "custody trial" (in Elbert's terms) at the Governor's Hall.[9] The Massachusetts legislature, in fact, enacted a law in the 1840s instructing the courts that "the rights of the parents to their children, in the absence of misconduct, are equal and the happiness and welfare of the child are to determine its care and custody."[1] As if quoting the statute—albeit for selfish as much as altruistic reasons—Dimmesdale argues that, "for Hester Prynne's sake, and no less for the poor child's sake, let us leave them as Providence hath seen fit to place them!" (*CE* 1:115) [77]. But even as the Governor's Hall scene dramatizes changes in nineteenth-century custody law, it addresses itself—if only in ironic contrast—to scenes of slave mothers begging for their maternal rights before intransigent slave owners, who had no legal obligation to care about the welfare of mothers or children. Harriet Jacobs, therefore, in contrast to Hester, must prevent her children from following their mother's condition—ironically, by giving them up or sending them away. "Poor little ones! fatherless and motherless!" she exclaims, as she bends over her sleeping children at the moment she leaves them for her solitary hiding place; "I knelt and prayed for the innocent little sleepers. I kissed them lightly, and turned away."[2]

Hester's admission to Mistress Hibbins that, had the magistrates taken Pearl from her, she would "willingly" have gone into the forest and signed her name—in her "own blood"—in the "Black Man's book" acquires an uncanny new meaning in this context, as if Hester ac-

7. White, 159.
8. Michael Grossberg, "Who Gets the Child? Custody, Guardianship, and the Rise of a Judicial Patriarchy in Nineteenth-Century America," *Feminist Studies* 9 (1983): 240–41.
9. Elbert, 194.
1. Grossberg, 241.
2. Jacobs, 96.

knowledges her racial difference, her narrow escape from the horrors of black slave motherhood—the privilege she has been granted, as it were, to *pass* as a white mother. Surely this scene and its threat to single motherhood might have struck a responsive emotional chord in a readership of anti-slavery feminists who might have appreciated the ironies of racial mothering Hawthorne highlights—the ironic signification of similar maternal acts. Following the condition of even the single mother means different things. In nineteenth-century America, Hawthorne instructs us, maternal differences are rooted in race.

Sacvan Bercovitch links the ending of The Scarlet Letter to the Liberian solution (the repatriation of slaves) promoted at the end of Uncle Tom's Cabin—largely, however, for its enactment of political gradualism or denial.[3] He might have found a more particularized similarity by following, if you will, the condition of the mothers. For like Linda Brent or Stowe's Eliza and George Harris, Hester flees America with her daughter. In the wake of the Fugitive Slave Law of 1850, Linda Brent feared that she and her children could be kidnapped on the streets of New York and returned to the South. Indeed, "many a poor washerwoman who, by hard labor, had made herself a comfortable home," she comments, "was obliged to sacrifice her furniture, bid a hurried farewell to friends, and seek her fortune among strangers in Canada."[4] Hester, too, considers a kind of Underground Railroad journey to freedom from white men's power. Deeper and deeper goes the path into the wilderness, she tells Dimmesdale, "less plainly to be seen at every step; until, some few miles hence, the yellow leaves will show no vestige of the white man's tread. There thou art free" (CE 1:197) [127]. After Dimmesdale's death, however, Hester seeks asylum in England, much as Jacobs—ironically—leaves New York for New England to avoid the likelihood of capture and then travels to England with her mistress's daughter Mary. "For the first time in my life," Jacobs observes, "I was in a place where I was treated according to my deportment, without reference to my complexion. I felt as if a great millstone had been lifted from my breast" and experienced for the first time "the delightful consciousness of pure, unadulterated freedom."[5] Even Pearl's inheritance from Chillingworth rather than from Dimmesdale makes a kind of sense—if Dimmesdale, with his exaggerated paleness, plays the role of slave-owning father. While Dimmesdale seems to acknowledge his paternity, his death enables Pearl's repatriation away from her father's world. She follows the condition of her mother. Linda Brent's children receive nothing from their white father, Mr. Sands. In bypassing her biological father in favor of her mother's legal husband, Pearl (despite her generous behavior to Dimmesdale on the scaffold) can be liberated from a "slave" economy and can return to her "step" father's estate—to a patrimony associated with the Black Man in the forest.

The case I have been making for reading Hawthorne's representa-

3. Bercovitch, The Office of The Scarlet Letter, 89.
4. Jacobs, 191.
5. Jacobs, 183.

tion of Hester Prynne within a context of slave mothering does not mitigate recent criticism of his politics—his gradualist, providential views on slavery and its abolition. His interest in the experience and psychology of motherhood has its own political dimensions. If only through instructive analogy, Hawthorne situates Hester's maternal behavior within a context in which mothering signifies in racial terms. Refusing to name her child's father, resisting the efforts of the good masters to take her child away, planning an escape to freedom—Hester resembles slave mothers like Harriet Jacobs even as her actions signify and thereby underline the politics of racial difference. Situating Hester in a complex subject and object position in which slave motherhood and anti-slavery feminism come together, he represents the dangers of a presumption—the identification of black and white women's experiences and politics—that cuts as sharply today as it would have in the nineteenth century. Hester's abject dependence upon patriarchal sufferance for her mothering rights links her to her slave sisters, but her ability to mother at all marks her feminist difference from slave mothers like Harriet Jacobs. Hester Prynne is not a slave mother, but in representing her maternally, Hawthorne shows more sympathy and ironic understanding of the politics of her motherhood than his nineteenth- and twentieth-century detractors have allowed.

Other Writings

AMY SCHRAGER LANG

Anne Hutchinson†

In 1830 the Salem *Gazette* printed a biographical sketch of Anne Hutchinson written by Nathaniel Hawthorne, native son and aspiring young author. The sketch, entitled "Mrs. Hutchinson," is a curious one. Not only does Hawthorne assume that his readers will recognize his Mrs. Hutchinson and remember her history but he assumes as well the immediacy of her story. Nowhere in the sketch does he detail the story of Hutchinson's excommunication from the First Church of Boston or her banishment from Massachusetts Bay in 1638. Instead, "Mrs. Hutchinson," ostensibly a portrait of the seventeenth-century heretic, begins with an attack on the "public women" of the nineteenth century, in whose ranks one might, Hawthorne suggests, find Hutchinson's "living resemblance." Hawthorne acknowledges the peculiarity of this opening—excusing "any want of present applicability" by the "general soundness of the moral"—but insists nonetheless on the aptness of his comparison. Hutchinson, that public woman of the past "whereof one was a burthen too grievous for our fathers,"[1] has been succeeded by a new breed of woman no less burdensome and far more numerous. Paradoxically, the religious heretic of the 1630s is reincarnated in the female sentimental novelist of the 1830s.

Twenty-five years before writing his famous letter to William Ticknor bemoaning the domination of the literary marketplace by the "d—d mob of scribbling women," Hawthorne introduces his reader to Anne Hutchinson by deploring the "irregularity" of the "ink-stained Amazons" who present themselves at the bar of literary criticism. In Hawthorne's estimation the "false liberality and . . . courtesy" accorded these women by their reviewers combine to "add a girlish feebleness to the tottering infancy of [American] literature" (*TS*, 18) [167]. All too clearly, the Amazons will "expel their rivals . . . and petticoats [will] wave triumphantly over all the field" (*TS*, 18) [167].

Hawthorne himself realized that the juxtaposition of seventeenth-

---

† From *Prophetic Woman: Anne Hutchinson and the Problem of Dissent in the Literature of New England* (Berkeley: U of California P, 1987), 1–14. Page numbers in square brackets refer to this Norton Critical Edition.
1. Nathaniel Hawthorne, *Tales and Sketches* (New York: Library of America, 1982), 18. Additional references to this edition will be cited in the text and identified by the abbreviation *TS* followed by the page number.

century antinomian and nineteenth-century author demanded explanation, particularly since the latter, rather than promulgating "strange
and dangerous opinions," consistently urged the virtues of home and
hearth. What links these disparate figures is "feminine ambition."
Both Hutchinson and her literary counterpart of the nineteenth century have abandoned their embroidery for careers as public speakers.
As prophetess in one case and novelist in the other, each has stepped
out of her appointed place and indelicately displayed her "naked mind
to the gaze of the world, with indications by which its inmost secrets
may be searched out" (TS, 19) [168]. This unseemly exposure of a private self to the public gaze—indecorous at best and at worst positively
lewd—is urged on antinomian and sentimental author alike by an apparently irresistible "inward voice." Like the errant Anne Hutchinson,
who, according to Hawthorne, confused "carnal pride" with the gift of
prophecy, so the misguided author yields to the "impulse of genius like
a command of Heaven within her" (TS, 19) [168].

The similarity between antinomian and sentimentalist, both of
whom appeal to an inner voice to rationalize their intrusion into the
public arena, casts the literary critic in the role of the Puritan magistrate. The court of literary opinion must, Hawthorne insists, "examine
with a stricter . . . eye the merits of females at its bar, because they are
to justify themselves for an irregularity which men do not commit in
appearing there" (TS, 19) [168]. Likewise, Hawthorne refuses to dismiss the Puritans' judgment against Anne Hutchinson as the action of
an "illiberal age." On the contrary, "worldly policy and enlightened
wisdom" would also dictate her banishment (TS, 21) [170]. In the interest of the rising culture, the literary critics of the nineteenth century would do well to banish from the American literary scene those
whose "slender fingers" enfeeble it.

The energy of Hawthorne's sketch comes from his intuitive recognition of a resemblance between Anne Hutchinson and the scribbling
women. The story of "the Woman," as Hawthorne invariably calls
Hutchinson, is offered as the quintessential story of female empowerment—of its origin in an erroneous "inward voice," its unseemly public expression, and its disastrous social effect. Inevitably, that story is
fraught with tension. In fact, insofar as one term points toward the
broad masculine realm of autonomous action in the world while the
other calls us home again, the phrase "public women" captures a crucial contradiction. This contradiction is similarly reflected in the competing images of unnatural strength and equally unnatural weakness
in Hawthorne's sketch. The female author, with an Amazon-like disregard for feminine decorum, expels her male rivals from the literary
field, but the flag her "slender fingers" hoist over that field is only, after all, a "petticoat": the woman warrior writes domestic fiction.

On the one hand, the act of female authorship constitutes an assertion of autonomy and, thus, a challenge to authority as dramatic as
Hutchinson's antinomianism. By choosing "the path of feverish hope,
of tremulous success, of bitter and ignominious disappointment" (TS,
19) [168], the woman writer defies her place. On the other hand, it is

not strength but rather the "girlish feebleness" of the sentimental domestic novel penned by the Amazon that threatens to undermine the
national literature. In other words, the trouble with the Amazon, ink-
stained or otherwise, is that she remains a woman and, as Woman, implies an order that, as Amazon, she violates. Insofar as Woman
contains in herself the possibility of Amazonian defiance, she suggests
the further—and more frightening—possibility that men too might
step out of their places.

In this sense the gender-specific problem of the public woman figures the larger dilemma of maintaining the law in a culture that simultaneously celebrates and fears the authority of the individual. That
dilemma has long been identified with antinomianism, but Hawthorne's sketch calls our attention to the fact that the problem of
individual autonomy is especially problematic when the individual
is female. The fact that Anne Hutchinson, the classic American
representative of a radical and socially destructive self-trust, is a
woman compounds and complicates her heresy. In "Mrs. Hutchinson"
the problem of antinomianism is propounded as the problem of Anne
Hutchinson, which is, in turn, the problem of the public woman.

It is precisely this sequence in which I am interested. What little information exists about the historical Anne Hutchinson has long since
been unearthed; likewise, the term *antinomian* has been appropriated
by scholars in a wide variety of disciplines to mark the outer limits of
American individualism. But in all the work that has been done on antinomianism, both as Puritan and as American heresy, the fact that the
antinomian is embodied as a woman has received scant attention. Another history of antinomianism needs to be written, one focusing on
the special relevance of "the Woman" to the nature of antinomian
heresy and depending less on the historical record than on the "literary" one. In the context of this history, Hawthorne's sketch seems less
odd than inevitable.

The contours of Hutchinson's story are familiar. In 1634 Anne
Hutchinson, a woman in middle age, left England with her large family
to follow the much-admired Reverend John Cotton to New England. Admitted to the church, her husband elected to the high office
of deputy to the Massachusetts General Court, Hutchinson set about
establishing herself in her new home. Her first prominence was as a
nurse-midwife and spiritual adviser to women, but sometime during
her first two years in Boston she began to hold weekly gatherings for
the purpose of reviewing and commenting on the sermon of the previous Sunday. These meetings, first attended exclusively by women,
quickly grew to include men and soon drew a regular attendance of
sixty or more of the town's inhabitants, including the young governor,
Henry Vane, and a number of other men of power and prominence. As
her following changed in both size and prestige, so too, apparently, did
Hutchinson's message. Rather than simply recapitulating the weekly
sermon, she undertook to reproach the Massachusetts clergy. The leaders of the church, she claimed, had fallen into a covenant of works.

"Legalists" all, they mistakenly took sanctification—the successful struggle of the saint against sin—as evidence of election, failing to understand that works and redemption bear no necessary connection. In essence Hutchinson spoke for a doctrine of free grace, characterized by the inefficacy of works and the absolute assurance of the saint. Until the arrival in 1636 of her brother-in-law and supporter, the Reverend John Wheelwright, John Cotton alone was exempt from her criticism.

Hutchinson's followers, convinced that the Massachusetts Bay ministers were guilty of preaching a covenant of works, were moved to action. Efforts were made to replace the Reverend John Wilson, then pastor of the Boston church, with John Wheelwright. The animosity between Hutchinson's supporters and her opponents grew until, in January 1637, a Fast Day was set aside in an effort to restore the peace. In a conciliatory move John Wheelwright was asked to deliver the Fast Day sermon. His sermon provoked a charge of sedition, and this charge, in turn, brought petitions on his behalf to the General Court. Accusations of antinomianism from one side were met with thinly veiled charges of papism from the other. Between the two the errand of the New Israel seemed doomed. As disruption and contention spread, affecting participation in colonial elections and the conduct of the Pequot War, not even the prominence of Hutchinson's followers could protect her. The authorities of the Bay moved into action, first meeting privately with Hutchinson, Cotton, and Wheelwright to inquire into their difference with the orthodox ministers. Discontented with the answers they received, the ministers convened a synod—the first in the colonies—for the purpose of formulating and responding to the errors of the antinomians. The General Court followed suit with sterner measures: the leaders among the antinomians were variously disenfranchised and banished, their male supporters disarmed. Considered by most the ringleader, Hutchinson was herself brought to trial by the Court in the fall of 1637 and by the church the following spring. Exiled and excommunicated, she fled to Rhode Island in 1638, moving five years later to New York, where, apparently in providential vindication of her judges, she and all but one member of her family were killed in an Indian raid.

The rapidity with which the Massachusetts Bay community fell into dissension has captured the interest of a wide range of modern scholars. In a period in which scarcity and inflation were intensified by a steady increase in population, the disproportionate affiliation of merchants with the "Hutchinsonians" has been explained as a response to the "insupportable pressures" suffered by those who would be both pious and successful in commerce. The merchants, it is claimed, used antinomianism as their way to rebel against an authoritarian Puritan regime, which tended to constrain their economic behavior.[2] The spe-

2. The most thorough exploration of the role of merchants in the antinomian controversy can be found in Emory Battis, *Saints and Sectaries: Anne Hutchinson and the Antinomian Controversy in the Massachusetts Bay Colony* (Chapel Hill: University of North Carolina Press, 1962). Other versions of this argument appear in Bernard Bailyn, *The New England Merchant in the Seventeenth Century* (New York: Harper and Row, 1955), and Larzer Ziff, *Puritanism in America: New Culture in a New World* (New York: Viking, 1973).

cial appeal of Hutchinson's "primitive feminism" to women has also
been explored. In her "new theology," one scholar argues, "*both* men
and women were relegated, vis-à-vis God, to the status that women occupied in Puritan society vis-à-vis men."[3] Social and intellectual historians have mined the antinomian controversy for information about
the limits of Puritan orthodoxy, social "boundary-marking" in the
colonies, Puritan attitudes toward dissent, and the status of women in
early New England. Literary critics have adopted the term *antinomian*
to describe the oppositional quality they find in the classic literature of
the American Renaissance and have taken the antinomian impulse to
enable literary production in a Puritan culture. Important as it is,
however, this wealth of historical data and literary conjecture does relatively little to advance our understanding of the symbolic value of the
story of Anne Hutchinson beyond reinforcing what the early narratives
tell us more forcefully—that is, that antinomianism represented a rejected alternative to the New England Way.

While the orthodox struggled to bring together citizen and saint, to
establish a connection between private and public realms of experience, the antinomian, building on the ambiguous status of the individual in Reformed theology, proposed a new relationship between the
two central facts of Christianity—the unmerited redemption of
mankind by Christ and the continued existence of sin and misery in
the world. Justification, the antinomian claimed, is a gift freely given
to fallen man without which all his pious endeavor is to no purpose. At
the moment of conversion, the saint, like an empty vessel, is cleansed
and filled with Christ's love, and by this motion of the divine, the chosen are at once freed from accountability under the Law and assured
of election. Individual identity is subsumed in divinity; the works of
the saint are one with Christ's. As one English antinomian explained
it, "in all your acts Christ acts, and in all Christ acts within you, you
act . . . and in your lowest acts Christ acts as well as in your highest."[4]
Man's sinful nature remains unaltered by the influx of grace, but the
antinomian's perception of his sinfulness is radically changed. Secure
in his election, the antinomian ascribes neither real nor symbolic
value to deeds: sin exists only "that there may be a place for faith." Instead of the orthodox notion of "visible sainthood," which proposed
that grace would emanate in good works and which thus nicely ac-
commodated the exigencies of community, antinomianism offered a
perfectionist theology wherein election is witnessed and sealed by the
spirit and cannot be tested by outward means.

Even in this brief description of the heresy, it is possible to discern
both the paradoxical nature of the antinomian as he presents himself
to the world and the larger problem of authority that antinomianism
engages. The antinomian regards the saint as indissolubly joined with
Christ. Individuality is merely the medium through which God exerts

3. Lyle Koehler, *A Search for Power: The "Weaker Sex" in Seventeenth-Century New England*
(Chicago: University of Illinois Press, 1980), 221.
4. Quoted in Gertrude Huehns, *Antinomianism in English History* (London: Cresset Press,
1951), 44.

himself. Because this is equally true of all the saints and because the nature of divinity is necessarily constant, the experiences of the saints answer one another "as face answers face in a glass."[5] Thus, those who "belong to God" are able to distinguish between God's people and the reprobate. On these grounds the American antinomians rejected the colonists' view of themselves as a chosen people, bound by covenant to fulfill God's work in the New World, and offered in its place the notion of a mystical community of the elect. The system of rewards and punishments adduced from the Law and embodied in temporal authority is, for the antinomian, irrelevant. Sin and sanctity alike are transient, inconsequential events, their significance lost in the very moment of the Spirit's invisible witness to election.

From this moment forward, the antinomian lives in a world free of the sometimes productive, sometimes disabling anxiety characteristic of the Puritan saint. Election is, for him, a condition of self-abnegation, his individuality no longer individual, his labors at an end, his destiny secure. In this sense, as the Puritans were wont to point out, antinomianism "quenches all endeavor." Yet rather than appearing passive, the antinomian seemed, even to the Puritans, to indulge the furthest extremes of self-assertion. For those who did not share their belief in the immediate union of the elect with Christ, the antinomian's claim to invisible witness, absolute assurance, and exemption from the Law could only seem like sheer arrogance. Abandoning the social for the teleological, then, the antinomian elevates the self to a new status precisely by insisting on the dissolution of the self in Christ.

The theological idea that the covenant of grace releases the elect from accountability under the Law is not indigenous to the United States. The idea is generally traced back to Paul's epistles, while the term *antinomian* is said to have been coined by Luther, who used it in reference to the German Johannes Agricola.[6] The charge of antinomianism was leveled against John of Leyden and the Anabaptist leaders of the Münster Rebellion in 1533, and concern with the heresy burgeoned during the English Civil War as writers like John Eaton, the "father of English antinomianism," produced tract after tract with titles like *The Honey-combe of free Justification by Christ Alone*. The persistence of the term into the nineteenth century likewise is not peculiar to America, nor is its appearance in literary guise. James Hogg's 1824 *Confessions of a Justified Sinner* relates the fall into antinomianism of the unrepentant Robert Colwan; Mike Hartley, the "Antinomian weaver," makes his appearance twenty-five years later in Charlotte Brontë's *Shirley*. Yet there is reason to speak of American antinomianism as a separate phenomenon, for here the heresy is encoded in the story of Anne Hutchinson's conflict with the authorities of the Massachusetts

5. Quoted in Huehns, *Antinomianism*, 93.
6. The biblical text most generally cited is Romans 6. For a discussion of the history of antinomianism as a term, see Ronald A. Knox, *Enthusiasm* (New York: Oxford University Press, 1950), and Huehns, *Antinomianism*.

Bay as this was repeated and elaborated from one generation to the next. Tied to the figure-legend of Anne Hutchinson, the local history of antinomianism is distinct from its universal one. Moreover, it is gendered female from the outset.

New World antinomianism was suppressed in 1638 and the authority of the ministers and magistrates restored. Yet the recurrent and pejorative use of both the figure of Anne Hutchinson and the term *antinomian* into the nineteenth century suggests that the tensions ostensibly resolved at the time lingered on, transformed. Celebratory or even apologetic accounts of the antinomian controversy are rare even though precedents exist for the celebration of if not heresy then at least certain heretics. The Romantic historian George Bancroft reconstructed Roger Williams, for example, as a "lark" giving voice to the "clear carols" of intellectual liberty, thus suggesting that some forms of Puritan heresy could be absorbed into a future consensus. Hutchinson resists just such renovation. Arrogant, rebellious, enthusiastic, the American Jezebel remains "tinged with fanaticism" throughout her history.[7] She is striking largely for her ability to rouse anxiety. If only because it remained so disturbing to Americans for so long, Hutchinson's story tells us a great deal about the unspoken concerns of her countrymen. But to account for its longevity and its force, we will need terms other than those commonly used. Most crucially, we must distinguish between the antinomian controversy itself—a historical event important largely because it sheds light on the social reality of the early colonies—and the narrative accounts of that controversy— the stories told about it (or more loosely, drawn from it), sometimes in self-defense, sometimes in indignation, but always to caution against present or future danger. While representing themselves for the most part as "histories," these narratives contribute less to our knowledge of the "real" controversy than they do to our understanding of how Americans have formulated and lent meaning to a series of events, local in nature and removed in time.

John Winthrop, for instance, goes to some lengths to insist that the Hutchinsonians were summoned before the Court not as heretics but because they "disturb[ed] the Churches . . . interrupt[ed] the civill Peace . . . and began to raise sedition amongst us, to the indangering of the Commonwealth." "Hereupon for these grounds named, (and not for their opinion . . .)," he goes on, "for these reasons (I say) being civill disturbances, the Magistrate convents . . . and censures them."[8] Winthrop's vehemence on this point has quite reasonably been taken as a response to English accusations that the colonists prosecuted cases of conscience as civil crimes, accusations he feared would be politically damaging to the Bay colony. Like his ministerial colleagues, the official historian of the controversy knew that in antinomianism he was faced with an interpretation of doctrine that proposed not only an

---

7. George Bancroft, *History of the United States of America* (Boston: Little, Brown, 1879), 6 vols., 1:298, 296.
8. David D. Hall, ed., *The Antinomian Controversy, 1636–1638: A Documentary History* (Middletown, Conn.: Wesleyan University Press, 1968), 213–14.

alternative conception of the self but also, by implication at least, a radically different order of society.

It would seem that gender is of no concern here, but the immediate political motive and the larger ideological one do not entirely explain Winthrop's narrative. They fail to account for the zeal with which Winthrop details such matters as the physical deformities of Hutchinson's friend Mary Dyer's stillborn child or Hutchinson's own "misconceptions." In order to talk about these elements of Winthrop's narrative, we must think not of history but of story, not of the heretic but of the woman who promises a stable, familial community yet remains capable of producing monsters.

Even in Winthrop's narrative, the historical Anne Hutchinson is swallowed up in the monitory figure of the American Jezebel as narrative history is overwhelmed by cautionary tale. Much as the accounts of the antinomian controversy respond to changes in political climate, shift in their emphasis, and vary in their form, they nonetheless document an urgent and continuing need to choose against antinomianism that can best be understood if we consider the evolution and the place of Hutchinson's story in an American pattern of meaning. Like that story, this study begins with history and ends with literature. It does not treat every account of the antinomian controversy, nor does it trace all representations of the antinomian impulse in the literature of the United States. It focuses instead on the cautionary tale of Anne Hutchinson, a tale that does not simply recast the past for the purposes of the present but continually reenlivens the female heretic only to banish her once again. As an exploration of the strategies Americans used to contain antinomianism, this study is designed not to move away from the larger issues of American individualism engaged by the antinomian controversy but to ground these in a specific story. Insofar as antinomianism presumes, as one scholar has put it, "that social benefit [can] arise from an a-social orientation of the component parts of . . . society,"[9] the story of Anne Hutchinson sets in relief a continuing tension in American culture over the relationship between private and public realms of experience expressed concurrently in the figure of the antinomian and that of "the Woman."

The concurrence of these figures is particularly apparent in Hawthorne's "Mrs. Hutchinson." Hawthorne organizes his sketch into two vignettes, one centering on Hutchinson's crime, the other on her punishment. The first vignette is set at dusk in the Hutchinsons' crude house, newly built at the "extremity of the village," on a street "yet roughened by the roots of the trees, as if the forest . . . had left its reluctant footprints behind" (TS, 20) [168]. As we enter the "thronged doorway," we sense that everything about this scene is wrong. Positioned at the furthest margin of the settlement where the wilderness still encroaches, "the Woman" faces her distinguished and predominantly male audience: Governor Henry Vane, in whose eyes Hutchinson's "dark enthusiasm" is mirrored; John Cotton, "no young and hot

9. Huehns, *Antinomianism*, 169.

enthusiast" but nonetheless "deceived by the strange fire now laid upon the altar"; the Reverend Hugh Peters, "full of holy wrath"; the "shuddering and weeping" women, and the young men, "fiery and impatient, fit instruments for whatever rash deed may be suggested" (*TS*, 20–21 [169]). No one, Hawthorne emphasizes, is indifferent to Hutchinson's words, yet the meeting proceeds in utter silence as far as the reader is concerned. This silencing of Hutchinson measures the tension in Hawthorne's sketch.

The threat of an Anne Hutchinson is captured not in overt statement but in the small disjunctive elements that fill the scene. Hutchinson's proper attire, for example, is belied by the inappropriateness of her preaching. Likewise, her eloquence stands in sharp contrast to the "quiet voice of prayer" we overhear elsewhere in the settlement. Her house is thronged with disciples but devoid of domestic comforts. The household hearth has been supplanted by a "strange fire" that inflames rather than warms; the family board is replaced by an altar. Instead of offering maternal reassurance to the "infant colony," Hutchinson reduces her audience to frightened "children who . . . enticed far from home . . . see the features of their guides . . . assuming a fiendish shape" (*TS*, 21) [170]. The woman of this house is no Daughter of Zion but instead a "disturber of Israel" unfolding "seditious doctrines" designed to persuade her neighbors that "they have put their trust in unregenerate and uncommissioned men, and have followed them into the wilderness for naught" (*TS*, 21) [170].

Like the first vignette, the second one begins not with Hutchinson but with another audience, this one sitting in judgment, not in awe. Once again the mood is ominous: a "sleety shower beats fitfully against the windows, driven by the November blast, which comes howling onward from the northern desert" (*TS*, 22) [170]. And once again the events of the controversy are associated with that threatening wilderness against which the Puritan community did constant battle. Before us are ranged those "blessed fathers of the land" whom we Americans, Hawthorne reminds us with characteristic irony, rank next only to the "Evangelists of Holy Writ" (*TS*, 22) [170]. Hutchinson faces this venerable company with "a flash of carnal pride half hidden in her eye, as she surveys the many learned and famous men whom her doctrines have put in fear" (*TS*, 23) [171]. Hutchinson's eloquence is, in some sense, the subject of the first vignette; her arrogance is the theme of the second. We watch first as Hutchinson exults in her contest with the "deepest controversialists" of the day and then as exultation leads inevitably to self-incrimination. With victory in sight, she arrogates to herself the role of judge, claiming "the peculiar power of distinguishing between the chosen of man and the Sealed of Heaven. . . . She declares herself commissioned to separate the true shepherds from the false, and denounces present and future judgments on the land, if she be disturbed in her celestial errand. Thus," says Hawthorne, "the accusations are proved from her own mouth" (*TS*, 23) [171]. He means, of course, that Hutchinson's words reveal her antinomian tendencies, but the impact of the vignette depends heavily on the Woman's usurpation of man's place as judge and on her arrogant assertion of a superior knowledge of God's will.

Like the words that inspire her audience to turn against minister and magistrate, the theological demonstration that stands behind Hutchinson's condemnation of the Bay leaders—that is, antinomianism as the Puritans understood it—is absent from Hawthorne's sketch. Both omissions work to define Hutchinson's crime as social rather than theological and, in this way, to broaden its relevance. She is guilty of resistance to lawful authority, on the one hand, and of refusing to play the part of woman, on the other. The failure of domesticity that Hawthorne associates with the eloquence of "the Woman," because he regards it as a violation of the law that governs her nature, points inevitably to heresy and sedition. In Hawthorne's sketch, then, antinomianism names a pattern of opposition shared by the "public woman" of the nineteenth century and the heretic of the seventeenth.

The antinomian lays claim to an unassailable inner knowledge, and the moment when Hutchinson alleges her peculiar powers is both the moment of her condemnation and the dramatic climax of Hawthorne's sketch. As Hawthorne understood, knowledge of the kind Hutchinson claimed respects no authority outside itself and is susceptible to no proof. Witnessed by an invisible spirit taken to be divine, it supersedes all other forms of knowledge. The antinomian regards this knowledge as a product of the influx of divinity and herself merely as the organ of its expression. Potentially, at least, the inner certainty this knowledge lends empowers the individual to act without reference to external authority or even against it. But the antinomian's knowledge transcends her condition. She must continue to live in the world and act the part of the sinner. Having relinquished the old natural self to God, however, she no longer attributes the usual significance to her words and deeds, for these cannot adequately represent the new self that belongs to God. Her deeds are hers only in the most provisional sense.

The uncomfortable resemblance between the language of antinomianism and a dominant American rhetoric committed to the values of individualism and the unfettered expression of the self in the political and economic arenas as well as the private one has encouraged scholars to generalize the problem of antinomianism into one simply of authority, of how the claims of the individual are to be balanced against those of the community. And, in fact, translated into the secular language of self and community, the problem of antinomianism might be said to stand at the heart of liberal ideology. But this shift in terms suppresses the role of gender in our formulation of the heresy and, in this way, replicates earlier versions of Hutchinson's story in which gender is likewise the suppressed issue. In other words, by generalizing the problem of antinomianism, we set aside the very story that has defined antinomianism for Americans. By placing "the Woman" in the "centre of all eyes" (TS, 23) [171]. Hawthorne's sketch recalls us to that story. It reminds us that the problem of antinomianism and the problem of female empowerment are entwined from the very beginning.

JOHN NICKEL

Hawthorne's Demystification of History in "Endicott and the Red Cross"†

Since the "return to history," one of Hawthorne's tales of Puritan history, "Endicott and the Red Cross" (1837), has received increased critical attention. Michael Colacurcio, in his study of Hawthorne's role as a moral historian in the early tales, argues that " 'Endicott and the Red Cross' dramatizes, from the seventeenth-century point of view . . . that two very different sorts of specifically religious separations have been unleashed on the colony of the Massachusetts in the 1630's": the figure of John Endicott, according to Colacurcio, represents the "Puritanic" idea of separation from popery, while the character of Roger Williams primarily stands for the more radical separation of spiritual concerns from social and political powers.[1] John Franzosa, employing an Eriksonian model of psychohistory, suggests that Hawthorne sought fame by writing historical tales such as "Endicott and the Red Cross" and that the figure of Williams serves as a "vehicle for Hawthorne's self-presentation."[2] Joining these recent interpreters of the tale, Harold Bush states that, through the negative portrayal of Endicott, Hawthorne "presented historical challenges and corrections to the prominent and pervasive romantic constructions of Puritanism."[3] In their studies all three critics focus on Hawthorne's depiction of the Puritans, on his participation in the historical debate over the import of New England's forebears.

"Endicott and the Red Cross," however, instructs its readers not solely about Puritan history but also about the writing of history itself. Composing the tale during the first boom period of U.S. historiography, Hawthorne is wary of contemporary histories' tendency to produce myths, to represent what Hawthorne considers to be subjective interpretations of the past as revelations of natural, eternal laws.[4] This

---

† From *Texas Studies in Literature and Language* 42.4 (2000): 347–62. Page numbers in square brackets refer to this Norton Critical Edition.
1. Michael Colacurcio, *The Province of Piety: Moral History in Hawthorne's Early Tales* (Cambridge: Harvard UP, 1984), 230.
2. John Franzosa, "Young Man Hawthorne: Scrutinizing the Discourse of History," in *Self, Sign, and Symbol*, ed. Mark Neuman and Michael Payne (Lewisburg, Penn.: Bucknell UP, 1987), 86.
3. Harold Bush, "Re-Inventing the Puritan Fathers: George Bancroft, Nathaniel Hawthorne, and the Birth of Endicott's Ghost," *ATQ* 9 (June 1995): 132.
4. Hawthorne's view of romantic historiography resembles Roland Barthes's description of myth as a system of communications that hides its ideological message. In contrast to a straightforward political statement, a myth relies on images or formulas whose associations communicate the myth's critique of romantic meaning. As we will see, moreover, Hawthorne's critique of romantic histories bears similarities to what Barthes describes in *Mythologies* as a way to attack myths: "the best weapon against myth is perhaps to mythify it in its turn, and to produce an *artificial myth*: and this reconstituted myth will in fact be a mythology." The "artificial myth," according to Barthes, differs from other myths in that it reveals itself to be a myth, a mode of communication. For this effect to occur, another point of view is offered that enables the readers to see the myth as not innocent but motivated; thus, Barthes writes, the artificial-myth maker "has strewn his reconstitution with supplementary ornaments which demystify it" (Roland Barthes, *Mythologies*, trans. Annette Lavers [New York: Hill and Wang, 1972], 136).

tendency characterizes romantic historiography, the dominant, coeval mode of narrating the past, exemplified in the writings of George Bancroft and William Prescott. As we will see, by employing and subverting the conventions of romantic historiography in the tale, Hawthorne exposes their biased character and process of producing myth. Hawthorne's own narration of the past, I believe, both converges with and diverges from romantic historiography.

My reading of Hawthorne departs, in turn, from the few studies that examine his fiction in relation to the historiography of the time in that I see Hawthorne directly engaging with and challenging contemporary modes of constructing history.[5] A pointed satire of romantic historiography, "Endicott and the Red Cross" presents us with an opportunity to explore how Hawthorne intervenes in the social arena through his romance art, which was once thought to be hardly concerned with "*history as history*."[6] Only by situating "Endicott and the Red Cross" in the context of contemporary historiography can we understand the curious formal features of the tale: deliberate self-contradiction in the conclusion; narration of a historical event that appears more like an imaginative reverie than a historical account; and abundance of symbols including the red cross, which is defaced because of its symbolism.

Imagination, Objectivity, and the Writing of History

The most influential romantic history in the U.S., of course, is Bancroft's *History of the United States*, the first volume of which was published in 1834 and quickly became a success. A biographer of Bancroft, Russel Nye, notes that "within a year [of the first volume's publication] Bancroft's book had found its way into nearly a third of the homes of New England, and the author's name was well on the way to becoming a household word."[7] One of the first U.S. historians to study in Germany, where he was taught by Heeren, Hegel, Savigny, and Böckh, Bancroft narrates in his *History* the struggle for freedom in the colonization and revolution. For the patriotic and melioristic Bancroft, the role of the historian is to reveal his country's divinely inspired liberation, as he insists in the famous introduction to the 1834 volume of *History of the United States*:

5. See Harry B. Henderson, *Versions of the Past: The Historical Imagination in American Fiction* (New York: Oxford UP, 1974), 91–126; and Susan Mizruchi, *The Power of Historical Knowledge: Narrating the Past in Hawthorne, James, and Dreiser* (Princeton: Princeton UP, 1988), 83–134.

6. Seymour Gross's often-quoted formulation—"*history as history* had but very little meaning for Hawthorne artistically"—has been challenged by many Hawthorne critics (Seymour Gross, "Hawthorne's 'My Kinsman, Major Molineux': History as Moral Adventure," *Nineteenth-Century Fiction* 12 [September 1957]: 99). Some discussions of the treatment of history in Hawthorne's fiction include Emily Miller Budick, *Fiction and Historical Consciousness: The American Romance Tradition* (New Haven: Yale UP, 1989), 36–54, 79–142; Alide Cagidemetrio, *Fictions of the Past: Hawthorne & Melville* (Amherst: Institute for Advanced Study in the Humanities, 1992), 25–48; and Robert Daly, " 'We Have Really No Country at All': Hawthorne's Reoccupations of History," *Arachne* 3 (1996): 67; George Dekker, *The American Historical Romance* (Cambridge: Cambridge UP, 1987), 129–85; John P. McWilliams, *Hawthorne, Melville, and the American Character: A Looking-Glass Business* (Cambridge: Cambridge UP, 1984), 25–48; and Alan O. Weltzien, "The Picture of History in 'The May-Pole of Merry Mount,' " *Arizona Quarterly* 45 (Spring 1989): 29–48.

7. Russel B. Nye, *George Bancroft: Brahmin Rebel* (New York: Knopf, 1945), 102.

It is the object of the present work to explain how the change in
the condition of our land has been accomplished; and, as the fortunes of a nation are not under the control of blind destiny, to follow the steps by which a favouring Providence, calling our
institutions into being, has conducted the country to its present
happiness and glory.[8]

Bancroft's *History*, with its treatment of national progress, serves to
defend the present state of affairs of Jacksonian America and presents
an idealized vision of the future.

Like other romantic historians, especially Prescott, Bancroft views
past events through a transcendental, systematic framework, locating
what he believes to be moral laws operating in the past and then
tracing their evolution. Discussing U.S. histories at this time, de
Tocqueville notes their tendency to present a "single great historical
system"; he writes that "historians who live in democratic ages are not
only prone to assign a great cause to every incident, but they are also
given to connect incidents together to deduce a system from them."[9]
Similarly, David Levin, in his study of U.S. romantic historians, states
that they tried to abstract a principle behind every major action, and
this principle or moral is what gave unity to the past and what the historian kept constantly before the reader.[1]

To recreate the past, romantic historians use their imagination as
well as literary conventions found in novels such as symbolism, character types and sketches, and picturesque scenery. As part of their effort to appeal to audiences, romantic historians also employ dramatic
techniques, including dialogue and stirring incidents: Bancroft even
received critical praise for his dramatic ability.[2] While often emulating
the writing techniques of historical fiction, romantic historians make
sure to distinguish their history from historical romance, noting, for
example, their avoidance of "imaginary" conversations and their fidelity to documents.[3] The rigorous, systematic examination of historical documents, for romantic historians, gives their endeavors scientific
authenticity. As Richard Vitzthum writes, Bancroft, for instance, posits
that "the historian approaches a historical subject the way an as-
tronomer views an unknown constellation or a biologist studies a new
species of plant": the historian observes the subject as accurately as
possible, exhaustively analyzes and compares all available documents,
and then extracts the cause of historical events and, most importantly,
the moral law present in the past.[4] A romantic historian like Bancroft

---

8. George Bancroft, *History of the United States from the Discovery of the American Continent*,
   vol. 1 (1834; rpt., Boston: Little, Brown, and Co., 1855), 4.
9. Alexis de Tocqueville, *Democracy in America*, ed. Richard Heffner (New York: Mentor,
   1956), 186.
1. David Levin, *History as Romantic Art: Bancroft, Prescott, Motley, and Parkman* (New York:
   AMS, 1967), 27.
2. On romantic historians' use of literary conventions, see Levin, *History*, 7–22.
3. Levin, *History*, 11.
4. Richard C. Vitzthum, *The American Compromise: Theme and Method in the Histories of Bancroft, Parkman, and Adams* (Norman: U of Oklahoma P, 1974), 34. Vitzthum discusses Bancroft's claim that history in general and his *History* in particular are scientific, drawing on
   many of the ten volumes of Bancroft's *History* (32–36).

believes that the historical narrative is a natural extension of the scientific analysis of documents, an objective, truthful representation of the discovered natural laws of the past. Conceived as such, romantic histories—especially in the narrative proper—hide rather than call attention to their invented or constructed character.

The romantic histories of New England and the U.S. were read extensively by Hawthorne, as Marion Kesselring's well-known account of Hawthorne's reading reveals. In fact, according to Kesselring, a few months before he wrote "Endicott and the Red Cross," Hawthorne borrowed the first volume of Bancroft's *History* from the Salem Athenaeum (from April 13 to May 6, 1837).[5] Based on the assumption, shared by romantic historians, that a historical re-creation will most engage and involve the reader in the past, Hawthorne's own mode of historical writing also uses imagination to recreate history. In the opening of an early sketch, "Sir William Phips" (1830), Hawthorne defends his fictional writing of history. Historical figures, he states, "seldom stand up in our imaginations like men." "So," he asserts,

> a license must be assumed in brightening the materials which time has rusted and in tracing out the half-obliterated inscriptions on the columns of antiquity: fancy must throw her reviving light on the faded incidents that indicate character, whence a ray will be reflected, more or less vividly, on the person to be described.[6]

In this work, Hawthorne distinguishes his historical writing from the chronicle or record of past events, as he does in "My Kinsman, Major Molineux" (1831), where he states that his tale differs from the "long and dry detail of colonial affairs" (11:209).

Whereas romantic historians like Bancroft view their histories as objective representations of the past, Hawthorne acknowledges and embraces his historical writing as a subjective creation. Since original events in the past as they actually occurred are inaccessible and history is received only through textual traces, Hawthorne believes the imagination to be crucial, not just in the process of writing but in the very act of constructing meaning for the past. Hawthorne, writes Johannes Kjørven, "regards any experience of a historical fact in terms of a reading imposed upon the fact."[7] Imaginative historical interpreta-

5. Kesselring's study shows the dates that Hawthorne checked out Bancroft's *History* (Marion L. Kesselring, *Hawthorne's Reading, 1828–1850: A Transcription and Identification of Titles Recorded in the Charge-Books of the Salem Athenaeum* [1949; rpt., Folcraft, Penn.: Folcraft, 1969], 39). Following Neal Frank Doubleday, Lea Bertani Vozar Newman notes that the tale was probably composed in the early fall of 1837. See Neal Frank Doubleday, *Hawthorne's Early Tales: A Critical Study* (Durham: Duke UP, 1972), 101; and Lea Bertani Vozar Newman, *A Reader's Guide to the Short Stories of Nathaniel Hawthorne* (Boston: G. K. Hall, 1979), 89.

6. Nathaniel Hawthorne, "Sir William Phips," in *Miscellaneous Prose and Verse*, ed. Thomas Woodson, vol. 23 of *The Centenary Edition of the Works of Nathaniel Hawthorne* (Columbus, Ohio: Ohio State UP, 1994), 59. All the following quotations from Hawthorne's works are from this edition and will be cited parenthetically (Nathaniel Hawthorne, *The Centenary Edition of the Works of Nathaniel Hawthorne*, ed. William Charvat, 23 vols. [Columbus: Ohio State UP, 1963–1994]).

7. Johannes Kjørven, "Hawthorne and the Significance of *History*," in *Americana Norvegica: Norwegian Contributions to American Studies*, vol. 1, ed. Sigmund Skard and Henry Wasser (Philadelphia: U of Pennsylvania P, 1966), 112.

tions, though, for Hawthorne, should not completely divorce themselves from past reality. Attempting to connect the past and imaginative associations of it, Hawthorne's historical romance is written, as he states in the "Custom-House" (1850), in "a neutral territory, somewhere between the real world and fairy-land, where the Actual and the Imaginary may meet, and each imbue itself with the nature of the other" (1:36) [29]. Although Hawthorne's stories are not literally true and do not objectively represent the "Actual," Hawthorne would claim that his mode of telling history still contains truth about the past—an imaginative truth.

A Critique of Romantic Historiography

Hawthorne would agree with Hayden White that historical narratives are "verbal fictions, the contents of which are as much invented as found and the forms of which have more in common with their counterparts in literature than they have with those in science."[8] Romantic histories in particular, Hawthorne perceives, are constructs that often present distorted views of the past, masked as natural and divine laws, and socialize their readers to these views. In "Endicott and the Red Cross," first published in *The Salem Gazette* on November 4, 1837,[9] Hawthorne employs conventions of romantic historiography and reveals them for what they are—literary conventions manipulated to suit the author's subjective perspective. Hawthorne, in telling the tale, provides his readers with interpretive tools to recognize the literary and rhetorical techniques of romantic historiography and immunize themselves against the power of these techniques to spread ideology. In this way, Hawthorne uses his historical romance to teach his audience how to read romantic history.[1]

One literary device that romantic histories often rely on—and one that Hawthorne employs subversively in his tale—is the representative hero, a figure who embodies the pervading principle of the time. Levin describes the representative hero in romantic historiography:

> The ideally representative man . . . was the incarnation of the People. He represented national ideals. He acted in the name of the People, and they acted through him. The relationship was emotional, often mystical. However lofty the leader was, he loved the People. When he had to, he reprimanded them, and he often rejuvenated them in a moment of peril. Every one of the histori-

8. Hayden White, "The Historical Text as Literary Artifact," in *The Writing of History: Literary Form and Historical Understanding*, ed. Robert Canary and Henry Kozicki (Madison: U of Wisconsin P, 1978), 42. One of the foremost critics on historical writing, White discusses the literary nature of historical narratives in this essay. For an extensive analysis of the rhetorical tropes employed by the leading European historians of the nineteenth century, see his *Metahistory: The Historical Imagination in Nineteenth-Century Europe* (Baltimore: John Hopkins UP, 1973).
9. "Endicott and the Red Cross" was also printed in the 1838 edition of *The Token*, which appeared in 1837, and in the second series of *Twice Told Tales*, which came out in 1842.
1. By Hawthorne's "readers" and "audience," I am referring to his ideal audience. The satirical critique, we will see, of romantic histories in "Endicott and the Red Cross" is subtle, and, as a reviewer of this essay noted, it is uncertain whether Hawthorne's intention would have been generally recognizable to an actual contemporary audience.

ans iterated a cliché that dramatizes this relationship: in battle after battle the leader "infused his spirit" into his men, or "animated them with his own spirit," or "inspired them with his own
energy," or "breathed his own spirit into them."[2]

Bancroft, following the lead of the many biographies of George Washington published in the early part of the century, treats Washington as
such a hero, particularly in the ninth volume when Bancroft describes
Washington rallying his troops after their loss in the Battle of Long Island. To the same effect, Prescott in *History of the Reign of Ferdinand
and Isabella, the Catholic*, which appeared in three volumes from
1837 to 1841, describes the ability of the Spanish commander, Gon-
salvo de Cordova, to "infuse heart into his followers" and display "that
inflexible constancy which enables the strong mind in the hour of
darkness and peril to buoy up the sinking spirits around it."[3]

Hawthorne parodies this convention in his treatment of Endicott as
a representative hero, with Endicott resembling more an ill-tempered
tyrant bent on securing his own authority than a true leader of the
people. As Endicott, who is in charge of the Salem community and its
militia, reads Governor Winthrop's letter that reports the plans of
Charles I to send a governor-general to the colonies, a "wrathful
change came over his manly countenance," and his "blood glowed
through it, till it seemed to be kindling with an internal heat; nor was
it unnatural to suppose that his breastplate would likewise become red
hot, with the angry fire of the bosom which it covered" (9:437) [175].
As opposed to the heroes depicted in romantic histories who keep
their composure, remaining calm in drastic situations, Endicott allows
anger to overwhelm him—anger that, along with his desire to assert
power, prompts his supposedly courageous deed.

After summoning the villagers and militia, he delivers an emotion-
filled speech, in which he tells them about the letter and calls on them
to resist the king's tyranny. Endicott's speech is interrupted by a male
villager being punished for offering his own interpretation of the New
Testament, different from that of the church leaders, and forced to
wear the label, "a wanton gospeller." Endicott "in the excitement of
the moment, shook his sword wrathfully at the culprit,—an ominous
gesture from a man like him" and threatens, "Break not in upon my
speech; or I will lay thee neck and heels this time till tomorrow" (439)
[176]. At the continuation of Endicott's agitative speech, according to
the narrator, a "deep groan from the auditors,—responded to the intelligence" (440) [177]. Declaring the colony's independence just prior
to his triumphant act—the rending of the red cross from the militia's
royal banner—Endicott "gazed round at the excited countenances of
the people, now full of his own spirit" (440). [177]. The crowd has become imbued with his "spirit," though not because of his heroism but
because of his fanatical and menacing character. Through this depic-

2. Levin, *History*, 50–51.
3. William H. Prescott, *History of the Reign of Ferdinand and Isabella, the Catholic*, vol. 3
(1841; rpt., Philadelphia: Lippincott, 1872), 131.

tion of Endicott, Hawthorne, in effect, warns his readers against un-critically accepting romantic histories' portrayals of heroic figures.

Symbolizing the principle of liberty, the representative hero's actions in romantic histories usually foreshadow future events in which liberty triumphs over tyranny. The romantic historians' treatment of the hero's deeds functions as part of the historians' application of typol-ogy—the Christian theological doctrine that events of the Old Testa-ment predict events in the New Testament—to historical writings. Romantic historians view New England colonial history in light of the revolution, searching for types of the victory of liberty. In Michael Davitt Bell's words, "Each instance of the struggle between liberty and tyranny, each emergence of embryonic democracy, could be regarded as a type of the great culminating example of the victory of liberty over tyranny—the American Revolution."[4] While reviewing a volume of Bancroft's *History*, Prescott, for instance, claims that the "principle" of American colonial history was the "tendency to independence." "It is this struggle with the mother-country," Prescott states, "this constant assertion of the right of self-government, this tendency—feeble in the beginning, increasing with increasing age—towards republican institu-tions, which connects the Colonial history with that of the Union and forms the true point of view from which it is to be regarded."[5] To Prescott's comments Bancroft would add that Jacksonian democracy, in particular, is a further extension of revolutionary teleology.

Rendering Endicott as a precursor of the American revolution, Hawthorne unveils how romantic historians impose their revolutionary interpretations on the past. At times, in fact, the tale's narrator, anti-quarian and usually uncritical, resembles a romantic historian. After dramatically describing the increasing tyranny of Charles I at the outset of the tale, the narrator maintains: "There is evidence on record, that our forefathers perceived their danger, but were resolved that their in-fant country should not fall without a struggle, even beneath the giant strength of the King's right arm" (9:433) [173]. The narrator reveals himself to be a patriotic member of the New England community, one who might not be objective in narrating a historical event of the Salem colony. The bias of the narrator's history, however, becomes clear in En-dicott's incendiary speech. The rhetoric of the speech is anachronistic to New England in the 1630s. Endicott's invocations of "liberty" and "civil rights" and his rhetorical questions—"Who shall enslave us here?" and "What have we to do with England?"—belong rather to the 1760s and 1770s,[6] the implication being that the narrator has embellished Endi-cott's speech by inserting this revolutionary language (9: 439–40) [177].

The prejudiced, constructed nature of the tale's typological history is also apparent in its conclusion, where, after Endicott has excised the flag's red cross because it represents royal tyranny and popery, the narrator proclaims:

---

4. Michael Davitt Bell, *Hawthorne and the Historical Romance of New England* (Princeton: Princeton UP, 1971), 8.
5. Quoted in Michael Davitt Bell, *Hawthorne*, 8.
6. Colacurcio, *Province of Piety*, notes the historically incorrect rhetoric of the speech (232).

> We look back through the mist of ages, and recognise, in the rending of the Red Cross from New England's banner, the first omen of that deliverance which our fathers consummated, after the bones of the stern Puritan had lain more than a century in the dust. (9:441) [178].

The tale's earlier depiction of the leader's own tyranny points to the unreliability of the narrator's final claim, that Endicott's action prefigures the revolution. Moreover, the reference to Endicott's "bones" in the "dust" undercuts the loftiness of the theme, revealing a discrepancy between the Salem leader's actual legacy, a decayed corpse, and its idealized glorification by the narrator.

Hawthorne further subverts romantic historians' use of typology in his treatment of Endicott's breastplate, which Sacvan Bercovitch identifies as the "dominant symbol" of the tale. The breastplate, Bercovitch notes, appears in the Old Testament as an emblem of Israelite theocracy: Moses gave his brother, Aaron, a breastplate in fulfillment of God's commandment to establish a sanctuary for God among God's people.[7] On one hand, then, the breastplate in Hawthorne's tale signals that Endicott is a descendent, a typological fulfillment, of the Israelites who is carrying out God's mission in the New Canaan of America. But in the tale, the breastplate does not just function symbolically; it reflects the scene in the village—"This piece of armour was so highly polished, that the whole scene had its image in the glittering steel" (9:434) [173]. When looking at Endicott, one sees the breastplate's reflection of the fierce punishments in the village: on the steps of the church are the "wanton gospeller" and a woman wearing a "cleft stick on her tongue" because she criticized the church elders; a suspected Catholic and a royalist are confined to a pillory and the stocks, respectively; and in the crowd in the square are villagers with cropped ears, branded cheeks, and slit and seared nostrils, and a woman who, resembling Hester Prynne, is forced to wear the letter "A" on her dress (9:435) [173–74]. Showing Endicott to be a cruel fanatic who is not divinely inspired or fulfilling a providential mission, the breastplate, as a self-contradictory symbol, casts suspicion on the mythic symbols and typology employed in historical accounts.

In the portrayal of Endicott, Hawthorne deliberately constructs a false myth (with enough traces of Endicott's cruelty to enable his readers to deconstruct it). Hawthorne's historical sources for the tale clearly show that Endicott's reason for rending the red cross was not political but religious. For New England Puritans, it was idolatrous to use any sacred symbol, and the cross, furthermore, was associated with the Roman Catholic Church.[8] Hawthorne's knowledge of Endi-

7. Sacvan Bercovitch, "Endicott's Breastplate: Symbolism and Typology in 'Endicott and the Red Cross,' " *Studies in Short Fiction* 4 (Summer 1967): 289–91.
8. Doubleday, *Hawthorne's Early Tales*, analyzes Hawthorne's relation to his historical sources in the early tales and provides an informative discussion of the subject in "Endicott and the Red Cross" (101–108). For an examination of the religious contexts of Endicott's action, though one that only addresses Hawthorne's tale by way of introduction, see Francis J. Bremer, "Endicott and the Red Cross: Puritan Iconoclasm in the New World," *Journal of American Studies* 24 (April 1990): 5–22.

cott's true motivation appears in the account of Endicott's action in *Grandfather's Chair*, Hawthorne's book of stories of New England history for children, which was published in 1840. In this work, when the child asks her grandfather whether Endicott's action was "meant to imply that Massachusetts was independent of England," the elderly storyteller replies: "I doubt whether he had given the matter much consideration except in its religious bearing" (6:24).

In Hawthorne's tale the subjectively constructed nature of mythic histories is illustrated not only in the narrator's account of Endicott's action but also in Endicott's telling of the colony's history in his speech. Like the narrator and romantic historians, Endicott narrates a highly rhetorical and evocative history, first asking the colonists,

> Wherefore, I say, have we left the green and fertile fields, the cottages, or, perchance, the old gray halls, where we were born and bred, the church-yards where our forefathers lie buried? Wherefore have we come hither to set up our tombstones in a wilderness?

"A howling wilderness it is!" he continues, invoking threatening images of the colony's surroundings. "The wolf and the bear meet us within halloo of our dwellings. The savage lieth in wait for us in the dismal shadow of the woods" (9:438) [176]. Though Endicott treats his account as objective, the reader of "Endicott and the Red Cross" cannot help but notice its misrepresentation of the colony's situation. The head of a "slain" wolf, for instance, has just been nailed to the steps of the church—"The blood was still plashing on the door-step" (434) [173]—evincing that the colony endangers wild animals and not the converse. In addition, American Indians are not hiding in the forest but openly watching Endicott lead the militia in its drills. Earlier in the tale, the narrator stated that the Indians' "flint-headed arrows were but childish weapons, compared with the matchlocks of the Puritans," and Endicott even boasted of the militia's clear military superiority to the Indians (436) [174].

Endicott's interpretation of the colony's history is soon contested openly. Endicott, similar to romantic historians, ascribes ideal motives to the founding of the colony: "Wherefore, I say again, have we sought this country of a rugged soil and wintry sky? Was it not for the enjoyment of our civil rights?" He then adds, "Was it not for the liberty to worship God according to our conscience?" To which, the "wanton gospeller" responds, "Call you this liberty of conscience?" (439) [176]. Roger Williams's reaction to this interruption is a "sad and quiet smile," an indication that he also believes that Endicott's actions belie his historical interpretation. After threatening the young man, as we have seen, Endicott, resuming his history, symbolically calls the continent a "new world" where they can "seek a path from hence to Heaven" (439) [176].

By incorporating a figure of a mythmaker in Endicott, Hawthorne takes his early-nineteenth-century readers back to the 1630s to show them that the grand, ideal mission of the New England colony's founding was not inherent in the spirit of the colony but was invented. This skillful maneuver demystifies history by historicizing the myth of American colonization, revealing—albeit fictionally—when and how it originated.[9] The specific, historically determined context of Endicott's mythic history of the colonization is his fear of losing his authority in the Salem community, and the import of his history is that he should remain in power in order to lead the colony's resistance. Hawthorne, then, implicitly criticizes not only Endicott's role as a leader but also his manner of history telling: the hegemonic Endicott constructs a deceitful analogy between the history's images and message, between the revolutionary associations of the colony and his self-serving agenda. By invoking the colonists' collective experience of their journey to the "new world" and promoting values and images that seemingly transcend the differences between himself and the other colonists, Endicott conceals his own social and political dominance. "Endicott and the Red Cross" evinces that mythic histories—such as those of Endicott and romantic historians—have social implications and an underlying ideological meaning despite appearing to express common sense or universal values. Consenting to Endicott's reading of history for his Salem audience is, in effect, to accept his position of power, just as agreeing with romantic historians' interpretations of the past is also to assent to their praising view of present affairs.

Endicott's mythic history resembles romantic histories in another way, the relation between himself as a historian and the audience. Both the romantic historian and Endicott narrate monological histories, imposing their interpretation of the past on the reader by suppressing differing viewpoints and providing the reader only with their perspective. Vitzthum describes the relation between the speaker and the reader in Bancroft's *History of the United States*: "As in all the volumes of the *History*, the speaker in Volume I stands between the reader and the past, telling him in no uncertain terms what it means, how it should be judged, how much it is worth."[1] Endicott, after reading Winthrop's letter, tells Williams that "if John Endicott's voice be loud enough, man, woman, and child shall hear" the contents of the letter (9:438) [176]. We soon realize that Endicott's voice has to be loud enough to drown out competing voices, such as the "voice" of the "wanton gospeller" (439) [176]. Already punished for giving his own interpretation of the Bible, the young man will be punished further if he offers his own history of the colony's past. When Williams rebukes Endicott for crudely referring to the beheading of Queen Mary Stuart, Endicott "imperiously" responds: "Hold thy peace, Roger Williams!" (439) [177]. A symbolic tyrant, Endicott suppresses dialogue in order to protect his mythic interpretation of

9. I echo Richard Slotkin's statement on the relation of history and myth, influenced by Barthes's *Mythologies*: "We can only demystify our history by historicizing our myths—that is, by treating them as human creations, produced in a specific historical time and place, in response to the contingencies of social and historical life" (Slotkin, "Myth and the Production of History," in *Ideology and Classic American Literature*, ed. Sacvan Bercovitch and Myra Jehlen [Cambridge: Cambridge UP, 1986], 80).

1. Vitzthum, *American Compromise*, 44.

the colony's history and to construct for the colonists their connection with the past.

Historical Romance

What Hawthorne earnestly seeks to avoid in "Endicott and the Red Cross" is forcing his subjective view of the past on the reader. In order to prevent the mythicizing of his history and the reader's uncritical acceptance of the narrative as an accurate reflection of the past, Hawthorne highlights the fictional quality of his historical writing. In "Endicott and the Red Cross," the narrator first describes the village as it appears through the "mirrored picture" of Endicott's breastplate, and it remains unclear whether the whole tale is told from this perspective (9:434) [173]. Endicott's breastplate, like the breastplate hanging in the governor's mansion in *The Scarlet Letter*, is convex, presenting a distorted reflection of the surrounding scene, signaling that the tale is not a transparent medium for the expression of the Salem colony's past. Furthermore, while romantic histories do not refer to the historian in the narrative, providing no signs that the author is organizing the history's materials, Hawthorne's tale calls attention to the antiquarian narrator as a producer of meanings: "There happened to be visible, at the same noontide hour, so many other characteristics of the times and manners of the Puritans, that we must endeavor to represent them in a sketch" (434) [173]. This tale, in contrast to romantic histories, does not give its readers the sense of a direct relation between themselves and the past. The constituted nature of the tale is heightened in the conclusion when the narrator states that "[w]e look back through the mist of ages" at Endicott's action, suggesting that the tale may have been a dream or an imaginative meditation of the past, which has been perceived through a cloudy "mist" (441) [178].

Another strategy Hawthorne utilizes to keep his readers from passively accepting his representations of history is to refuse to provide them with a reliable moral or interpretation of past events. In the preface to *The House of Seven Gables* (1851), Hawthorne distinguishes himself from writers who "relentlessly . . . impale the story with its moral" (2:2). "When romances do really teach anything," he insists, "or produce any effective operation, it is usually through a far more subtle process than the ostensible one" (2:2). The "subtile process" in "Endicott and the Red Cross" is to encourage readers to create their own morals from history, to participate in the production of meaning. By leaving the readers with a conclusion that contradicts the rest of the tale—a conclusion that ironically celebrates a fanatic tyrant—Hawthorne invites the readers to scrutinize the judgments of the antiquarian narrator and become historians, in effect, who sort through the evidence in the narrative. Complicating the reader's task, Hawthorne presents a dialogic or polyphonic history, one that offers several different ideological voices or perspective—those of Endicott, the narrator, the "wanton gospeller," and Williams, among others—for the reader to compare and evaluate.[2] In doing so, Hawthorne rejects romantic historians' tendency to reduce American colonial history to a set of essences, and, unlike these historians, he involves his readers in a hermeneutic problem, in which they must create history rather than simply reading about it.[3]

Hawthorne's history-making reader also becomes a symbol producer. The symbol, for Hawthorne, expresses the imaginary relation to the past—it is a literary construct used to endow a past event with meaning.[4] Hawthorne's use of symbolism is evident in his favorable depiction of William's entrance into the Salem village: with "apostolic dignity" Williams appears as a pious shepherd and Christ-like figure and drinks from a natural spring fountain, a traditional emblem of wisdom and divinity (9:436) [175]. In contrast to romantic historians' employment of mythic symbolism, the always self-reflexive Hawthorne calls attention to his symbols—as well as other literary conventions—as creations. In "Endicott and the Red Cross," the reader is asked to analyze the tale's symbols and select those appropriate to represent the past. In this way the reader partakes in the process of historical symbol invention, as Roy Harvey Pearce argues. Symbolism in Hawthorne's fiction, Pearce suggests, is "expressed as process rather than as source or product."[5]

Through the many symbols in the tale,[6] Hawthorne conveys that human experience relies on sign and symbol production to make sense of the world. The punishments in the colony, for instance, all involve

2. Hawthorne's tale is similar to what Mikhail Bakhtin describes as the chief characteristic of Dostoevsky's novels: the "plurality of independent and unmerged voices and consciousnesses, a genuine polyphony of fully valid voices" (M. M. Bakhtin, *Problems of Dostoevsky's Poetics*, ed. and trans. Caryl Emerson [Minneapolis: U of Minnesota P, 1984], 6). For Bakhtin, multivocal or polyphonic works, like Dostoevsky's novels, allow the voices of the main characters as much authority as the narrator's voice, which engages in dialogue with the characters' voices. For an extended discussion of his theory of polyphony and dialogue, see M. M. Bakhtin, "Discourse in the Novel," in *The Dialogic Imagination: Four Essays by M. M. Bakhtin*, trans. Caryl Emerson and Michael Holquist (Austin: U of Texas P, 1981), 259–422.

3. My thinking on the relation between reading and the performance of history has been influenced by J. Hillis Miller's interpretation of "The Minister's Black Veil." Miller argues that the act of reading the tale involves the process of producing history (*Hawthorne and History: Defacing It* [Cambridge, Mass.: Basil Blackwell, 1991)], 45–132).

4. I do not intend to enter the much discussed debate over whether Hawthorne was more of a symbolist than an allegorist, or vice versa. Millicent Bell has recently summarized the different critical views on this subject and states: "[i]t would appear that for Melville and Hawthorne, as for Emerson, allegory was not distinguished from symbolism with any precision" (introduction to *New Essays on Hawthorne's Major Tales*, ed. Millicent Bell [Cambridge: Cambridge UP, 1993], 23). For a discussion of Hawthorne's role as a symbolist or allegorist, see, for example, F. O. Matthiessen, *American Renaissance: Art and Expression in the Age of Emerson and Whitman* (London: Oxford UP, 1941), 242–315; Charles Feidelson, *Symbolism and American Literature* (Chicago: U of Chicago P, 1953), 6–16; and Ursula Brumm, *American Thought and Religious Typology* (New Brunswick: Rutgers UP, 1970), 11–128.

5. Roy Harvey Pearce, "Romance and the Study of History," in *Hawthorne Centenary Essays*, ed. Pearce (Columbus: Ohio State UP, 1964), 238.

6. Stephen Orton, in "De-centered Symbols in 'Endicott and the Red Cross,'" *Studies in Short Fiction* 30 (Fall 1993): 565–73, provides a Derridean deconstructive reading of some of the symbols in "Endicott and the Red Cross." While this interpretation helps explain on a linguistic level how Hawthorne subverts some of the tale's negative symbols, such as the breastplate and royal flag, it cannot explain more positive symbols, such as those in the description of Williams.

physical manifestations of the purported crime; in the case of the young man accused of providing his own interpretation of the New Testament, the punishment is literally a sign, which reads "a wanton gospeller." The church at first appears to lack a signifier: it has "neither steeple nor bell to proclaim it,—what nevertheless it was,—the house of prayer" (9:434) [173]. The narrator then points out the wolf's head nailed to its porch, which, recalling the animals sacrificed to consecrate altars in the Old Testament, reveals that the church has a symbol after all. When Endicott defaces the royal banner because of the symbolism of its red cross, he deliberately performs an act that stands for the colony's resistance to royal tyranny: the act of destroying a symbol thus becomes a symbol. The readers of the tale, Hawthorne hopes, will recognize that symbols are inevitable and constructed and will then consciously create their own symbols.

To reinforce the importance of an active, creative mode of interpretation, Hawthorne, we can say finally, presents two characters as his ideal readers. The "wanton gospeller," as we have seen, is a resistant reader, who views Endicott's history as a misrepresentation, not a seamless whole, and gives his own interpretation of the Bible, "unsanctioned by the infallible judgment of the civil and religious leaders" (9:435) [173]. The second ideal reader is the woman with the symbolic letter A imposed on her. Though "even her own children knew what the initial signified," she refuses to accept passively the meaning attached to it (435) [174]. As the narrator states,

> Sporting with her infamy, the lost and desperate creature had embroidered the fatal token in scarlet cloth, with golden thread and the nicest art of needle-work; so that the capital A might have been thought to mean Admirable, or any thing rather than Adulteress. (435) [174]

The reference to the "art" of the needleworker identifies her as an artist, an interpreter who recreates symbols. Depicted in situations of reading, these characters come closest to expressing Hawthorne's pedagogic message about the proper way to interpret romantic histories.[7]

An astute critic of contemporary writings and reading assumptions and expectations, Hawthorne sought to disrupt the interpretive conventions of antebellum audiences and give them new reading strategies. While modern critics have often contrasted Hawthorne with contemporary writers who are more overtly socially and politically oriented such as Harriet Beecher Stowe, Hawthorne shares with these

---

7. We can begin to reexamine the ubiquitous figures of reading in Hawthorne's fiction as responses to specific coeval discourses. Given the similarities between the needleworker and Hester Prynne, *The Scarlet Letter* seems a likely place to start, and an interpretation would assume that Hester is a resistant reader. In an influential interpretation of the romance, Bercovitch argues to the contrary and suggests that Hester, as she reveals in her return to the Puritan village, abandons her earlier self-reliance and defiance, internalizes society's constricting values, and "has no choice but to resume the A" (*The Office of The Scarlet Letter* [Baltimore: Johns Hopkins UP, 1991], 21). Bercovitch's reading, which is more complex than I have presented it, does not consider, though, that Pearl's departure to an "unknown region" (1: 262) [165] represents an alternative to the consensus-dominated, Puritan village. Recognizing this alternative before her return, Hester, I would argue, continues to perceive the limits of hegemonic views of her and attach her own meanings to the scarlet letter.

writers a strong didactic motivation, an intention to effect cultural change.[8] Though Hawthorne does not provide "Endicott and the Red Cross" with a reliable, central message, we, as the tale's interpreters, can: instead of reading romantic histories in complicity with their authors, we should follow the examples of the "wanton gospeller" and needleworker, challenge these histories' symbolic representations and masked ideologies, and construct our own interpretation of the past.

DAVID LEVIN

Shadows of Doubt: Specter Evidence in Hawthorne's "Young Goodman Brown"†

I choose for my text two statements written in the autumn of 1692, after twenty Massachusetts men and women accused of witchcraft had been executed. The first is by Increase Mather, the second by Thomas Brattle.

> . . . the Father of Lies [Mather declared] is never to be believed: He will utter twenty great truths to make way for one lie: He will accuse twenty Witches, if he can thereby bring one honest Person into trouble: He mixeth Truths with Lies, that so those truths giving credit unto lies, Men may believe both, and so be deceived.[1]

Brattle was astonished by the ease with which witnesses avoided a crucial distinction:

> And here I think it observable [he wrote], that often, when the afflicted [witnesses] do mean and intend only the appearance and shape of such an one, (say G[oodman]. Proctor) yet they positively swear that G. Proctor did afflict them; and they have been allowed so to do; as tho' there was no real difference between G. Proctor and the shape of G. Proctor.[2]

Nathaniel Hawthorne's protagonist Goodman Brown commits the very mistakes that Brattle and Mather belatedly deplored in 1692. He lets the Devil's true statements about the mistreatment of Indians and Quakers prepare him to accept counterfeit evidence, and he fails to insist on the difference between a person and the person's "shape," or

---

8. In her well-known study, Jane Tompkins discusses the rise of Hawthorne's literary reputation and argues that to Hawthorne's contemporaries "his fiction did not distinguish itself at all clearly from that of the sentimental novelists—whose work we now see as occupying an entirely separate category" (*Sensational Designs: The Cultural Work of American Fiction, 1790–1860* [New York: Oxford UP, 1985], 17). For reasons that Tompkins explains, modern critics have tended to oppose his writing to the popular fiction of his time, praising Hawthorne for his psychological depth and density of composition. See Tompkins, 3–39.

† From *American Literature* 34 (1962): 344–52. Copyright © Duke University Press. All rights reserved. Used by permission of the publisher. Page numbers in square brackets refer to this Norton Critical Edition.

1. Increase Mather, *Cases of Conscience Concerning Evil Spirits Personating Men* (Boston, 1693), reprinted in *What Happened in Salem?*, David Levin, ed. (New York, 1960), 122.

2. Letter of Thomas Brattle, dated October 8, 1692, and reprinted in *ibid.*, 130. The letter was probably circulated in manuscript; the name of the addressee is unknown.

specter. Most modern critics who have discussed the story have repeated both these errors, even though Hawthorne clearly identifies the
chief witness as the Devil and the setting as the Salem Village of
witchcraft days. In the last decade, several articles have rightly contended that Hawthorne meant to reveal the faultiness of Goodman
Brown's judgment;[3] but the first and most cogent of these did not prevent so distinguished a critic as Harry Levin from alluding to "the
pharisaical elders" whom Goodman Brown sees "doing the devil's work
while professing righteousness."[4] And the cogent article itself insists
that "it is not necessary to choose between interpreting the story literally and taking it as a dream"; that Brown neither goes into a forest
nor dreams that he goes into a forest. What Brown does, says D. M.
McKeithan, is "to indulge in sin (represented by the journey . . .)."[5]

I believe that one must first of all interpret the story literally. The
forest cannot effectively represent sin, or the unconscious mind of
Goodman Brown, or the heart of the dark moral wilderness, until one
has understood the literal statements about the forest in regard to the
literal actions that occur therein. Instead of agreeing with one critic
that "the only solution to the problem" of what happens in the forest
"lies in the tale's complex symbolic pattern,"[6] let us try to accept
Hawthorne's explicit statements of fact. Instead of inventing a new
definition of the word "witch," as another critic has done,[7] let us try to
read the story in the terms that were available to Hawthorne. A proper
reading of the literal action removes some of the ambiguity that it is
now so fashionable to admire, but it should leave open a sufficient variety of interpretations to satisfy those who insist on multiple meanings, and it will clarify the fine skill with which Hawthorne made the
historical materials dramatize his psychological insights and his allegory.

Hawthorne knew the facts and lore of the Salem witchcraft "delusion," and he used them liberally in this story as well as others. He set
the story specifically, as the opening line reveals, not in his native
Salem, but in Salem Village, the cantankerous hamlet (now Danvers)
in which the afflictions, the accusations, and the diabolical sabbaths
centered in 1692. Among the supposedly guilty are the minister of
Salem Village and two women who were actually hanged in that terrible summer. Hawthorne not only cites testimony that Martha Carrier
"had received the Devil's promise to be queen of hell" [186]; he also
quotes Cotton Mather's description of her as a "rampant hag" [186],
and he even violates Goodman Brown's point of view in order to introduce another actual rumor of 1692: "Some affirm that the lady of the
governor was there [at the witches' sabbath]" [185]. He takes great

3. D. M. McKeithan, "Hawthorne's 'Young Goodman Brown': An Interpretation," *Modern Language Notes*, LXVII, 93–96 (Feb. 1952); Thomas F. Walsh, Jr., "The Bedeviling of Young
   Goodman Brown," *Modern Language Quarterly*, XIX, 331–36 (Dec. 1958); Paul W. Miller,
   'Hawthorne's 'Young Goodman Brown': Cynicism or Meliorism?," *Nineteenth-Century Fiction*, XIV, 255–64 (Dec. 1959).
4. Harry T. Levin, *The Power of Blackness: Hawthorne, Poe, Melville* (New York, 1958), 54.
5. McKeithan, 96.
6. Walsh, 336.
7. Miller, 259 n. 10.

care to emphasize the seeming presence at the witches' sabbath of the best and the worst of the community—noting with superbly appropriate vagueness, just before the climax, that the "figure"[8] who prepares to baptize Goodman Brown "bore no slight similitude, both in garb and manner, to some grave divine of the New England churches" [186].

There can be no doubt that Hawthorne understood clearly the importance of what was called "specter evidence" in the actual trials. This was evidence that a specter, or shape, or apparition, representing Goodman Proctor, for instance, had tormented the witness or had been present at a witches' meeting. Hawthorne knew that there had been a debate about whether the Devil could, as the saying went, "take the shape of an angel of light," and in both "Alice Doane's Appeal" and "Main Street" he explicitly mentioned the Devil's ability to impersonate innocent people.[9] He was well aware that Cotton Mather had warned against putting too much confidence in this sort of evidence; he also knew that after the Mathers and Thomas Brattle had opposed even the admission of specter evidence (the Mathers on the ground that it was the Devil's testimony), the court had convicted almost no one and not a single convict had been executed. It seems certain, moreover, that Hawthorne had read Cotton Mather's biography of Sir William Phips, in which Mather the historian not only echoes his father's language about truths and lies, but clearly suggests that one of the Devil's purposes had been the traducing of Faith.

> On the other Part [Mather wrote in 1697], there were many persons of great Judgment, Piety and Experience, who from the beginning were very much dissatisfied at these Proceedings; they feared lest the *Devil* would get so far into the *Faith* of the People, that for the sake of many *Truths*, which they might find him telling of them, they would come at length to believe all his *Lies*, whereupon what a Desolation of *Names*, yea, and of *Lives* also, would ensue, a Man might without much *Witchcraft* be able to Prognosticate; and they feared, lest in such an extraordinary Descent of *Wicked Spirits* from their *High Places* upon us, there might such *Principles* be taken up, as, when put into *Practice*, would unavoidably cause the *Righteous to perish with the Wicked*, and procure the Blood-shed of Persons like the *Gibeonites*, whom

---

8. The first published versions of the story used the word "apparition" here. See *The New-England Magazine* VIII, 257 (April 1835); and *Mosses from an Old Manse* (New York, 1846), 80. The word was changed to "figure" in Hawthorne's last revision of *Mosses from an Old Manse* (Boston, 1857).

    The text of this story has often been erroneously printed. One important change seems to have been made by George P. Lathrop in the edition he published nineteen years after Hawthorne's death. Every earlier version that I have seen, including Hawthorne's last revision, says that "the chorus of the desert" at the spectral meeting in the forest seemed to include "the roaring wind, the rushing streams, the howling beasts, and every other voice of the unconverted wilderness. . . ." Lathrop and almost every editor after him changed the word "unconverted" to "unconcerted." I have been following Hawthorne's last revision.

9. Hawthorne even joked casually about this kind of imposture. Of his participation in the experiment at Brook Farm he wrote: "The real me was never an associate of the community; there has been a spectral Appearance there, sounding the horn at day-break, and milking the cows . . . and doing me the honor to assume my name." Quoted in Randall Stewart, *Nathaniel Hawthorne, A Biography* (New Haven, 1949), 60.

some learned Men suppose to be under a false Pretence of *Witch-craft*, by *Saul* exterminated.[1]

If we set aside the alternative possibilities for a while and examine the story from the seventeenth-century point of view—the perception of Goodman Brown through which Hawthorne asks us to see almost all the action—we will find a perfectly clear, consistent portrayal of a spectral adventure into evil. Goodman Brown goes into the forest on an "evil" errand, promising himself that after this night he will "cling" to the skirts of his wife, Faith, "and follow her to heaven." Once in the wilderness, he himself conjures the Devil by exclaiming, "What if the Devil himself should be at my very elbow!" [179]. Immediately, he beholds "the figure of a man" [179], and this figure quite unambiguously tells him that it has made the trip from Boston to the woods near Salem Village—at least fifteen or twenty miles—in fifteen minutes. Brown refuses the Devil's staff and announces that he is going back to Faith, but the Devil, "smiling apart," suggests that they "walk on, nevertheless, reasoning as we go" [180].

The reasoning proceeds from this point, as the Devil tries to convince Brown that the best men are wholly evil. Most of the argument that follows corresponds to the traditional sophistry of the Devil—the kind of accusation with which Satan nearly discourages Edward Taylor's saint from joining the church in *God's Determinations Touching His Elect*. It is here that the Devil mentions true sins (the mistreatment of Indians and Quakers) in order to induce despair: men are so wicked that nothing can save them.[2] Against this first argument Goodman Brown resists longer than some modern critics have resisted, for he sees that the alleged hypocrisy of elders and statesmen is "no rule for a simple husbandman like me" [180]. Foolishly, however, he believes the Devil's testimony (as his neighbors did in 1692), and he frankly tells him that "my wife, Faith" [181], is the foundation of his reluctance to become a witch.

This admission invites the Devil to proceed, and it determines the organization of the rest of his argument. With typical subtlety he pretends to give up at once, because

> ". . . I would not for *twenty* old women like the one hobbling before us that Faith should come to any harm."
> As he spoke he *pointed his staff at a female figure* on the path, *in whom Goodman Brown recognized* a very pious and exemplary old dame. . . .[3] [181]

---

1. Cotton Mather, *Magnalia Christi Americana: or, The Ecclesiastical History of New-England* (London, 1702), Book II, 62.
2. Here again we should notice that Cotton Mather had used language very close to Hawthorne's. In a sermon called "The Door of Hope," Mather cautioned against "A sinful and woful Despair." Some men, he said, "rashly conclude" that "because they see no *help* to their Souls in themselves, . . . there is no *hope* for their Souls any where else." And among several "*Reasons* of Despair" to which he offered answers at the end of the sermon, the fifth reads: "I doubt I have committed the *unpardonable Sin*; and then, all my hope is lost forevermore." *Batteries Upon the Kingdom of the Devil* (London, 1695), 100 ff.
3. The italics are mine.

The Devil has of course conjured this "figure," which moves "with singular speed for so aged a woman," and he appears to it in "the very image"—soon afterward, "the shape"—"of old Goodman Brown, the
grandfather of the silly fellow that now is" [181]. When the woman's
figure has served his purpose, the Devil throws his staff "down at her
feet" [182], and she immediately disappears. Brown accepts this evidence without question, for by this time the Devil is "discoursing so
aptly that his arguments [seem] rather to spring up in the bosom of his
auditor than to be suggested by himself" [182].

But Goodman Brown holds back once again, and the Devil, assuring
him that "You will think better of this by and by" [182], vanishes. Just
as Brown is "applauding himself greatly" [182], he is assaulted by another kind of airy evidence: disembodied voices. The "mingled sounds"
appear to pass "within a few yards," and although the "figures" of the
minister and deacon "brushed the small boughs by the wayside, it
could not be seen that they intercepted, even for a moment, the faint
gleam from the strip of bright sky athwart which they must have
passed" [183]. Brown cannot see "so much as a shadow," but "he
could have sworn"—as witnesses in 1692 did indeed swear—that he
recognized the deacon and the minister in "the voices, talking so
strangely in the empty air" [183].

Now, as Brown doubts that "there really [is] a heaven above him"
[183], the Devil has only to produce evidence that Faith, too, is guilty.
Hearing the voice of Faith from a "black mass" of cloud that "hurried"
across the sky although no wind is stirring, Brown calls out to her in
agony, and the "echoes of the forest" [184]—always under the Devil's
control—mock him. Then the Devil sends his final argument, Faith's
pink ribbon, as her voice fades into the far-off laughter of fiends. At
the end of the story we learn that this evidence, too, was spectral, for
Faith wears her ribbons when her husband returns home in the morning; but now, in the forest, Brown is convinced that his "Faith is gone"
[184], that the world belongs to the Devil. He takes up the Devil's
staff and "seems to fly along the forest path rather than to walk or run,
. . . rushing onward with the instinct that guides mortal man to evil"
[184].

With beautiful care Hawthorne makes his descriptive language reinforce these meanings through the rest of the horrible experience. "Flying" among the black pines, Brown finally sees the "lurid blaze" of the
witch-meeting and pauses "in a lull of the tempest that had driven him
onward" [185]. The verse that he hears is sung "by a chorus, not of
human voices, but of all the sounds of the benighted wilderness, pealing in awful harmony together" [185], and his own cry sounds in "unison with the cry of the desert" [185]. At the sabbath itself he sees,
"quivering between gloom and splendor" [185], *faces* belonging to the
best people of the colony. A congregation shines forth, then disappears
in shadow, and again grows, "as it were, *out of the darkness, peopling
the heart of the solitary woods at once*" [185].[4] Brown believes that he

4. The italics are mine.

recognizes "a score" of Salem Village church members before he is "well nigh ready to swear" that he sees "the figure" of the minister, "the shape of his own dead father," "the dim features" of his mother, and "the slender form" [186] of his wife. When he stands with the form of Faith, they are "the only [human] pair, *as it seemed*," who hesitate "on the verge of wickedness in this dark world" [187]. It is "the shape of evil" [187] that prepares to baptize them, and the figure that stands beside Brown is that of his "pale" wife.[5] When he implores her to "look up to heaven and resist the wicked one" [187] the whole communion disappears, and he cannot learn "whether Faith obeyed" [187].

The clarification that this reading achieves for the story should remove some of the objections that have been raised against it even by its admirers. When we recognize that the Devil is consistently presenting evidence to a prospective convert who is only too willing to be convinced, we do not need to complain with F. O. Matthiessen against Hawthorne's "literal insistence on that damaging pink ribbon"; nor need we try, with R. H. Fogle, to explain the ribbon away.[6] One might insist that even here Hawthorne restricts his language admirably to Brown's perception, for he says that *something* fluttered lightly down through the air and that Brown, after seizing it, *beheld* a pink ribbon. Brown's sensory perception of the ribbon is no more literal or material than his perception of the Devil, his clutching of the staff, or his hearing of the Devil's statement about the fifteen-minute trip from Boston to the woods near Salem Village. But such an argument is really unnecessary. The seventeenth-century Devil could produce specters, with or without the consent of the people they resembled, and he could make cats, birds, and other familiars seem to materialize before terrified witnesses.[7] For such a being, and with a witness overcome by "grief, rage, and terror," a ribbon posed no great difficulty.

Hawthorne's technique thus gives a clear view of his meaning. When we stop looking for what we may wish to believe about Puritans who whipped Quakers and burned Indian villages, we can recognize just what it is that Goodman Brown sees. Hawthorne does not tell us that none of the people whom Brown comes to suspect is indeed a diabolical agent, but he makes it clear that Brown has no justification

5. Here it might be argued that Hawthorne says Faith was actually present, for he writes that "the wretched man beheld his Faith, and the wife her husband," and just before Brown cries out Hawthorne writes, "The husband cast one look at his pale wife, and Faith at him. What polluted wretches would the next glance show them to each other . . ." It is more consistent with Hawthorne's practice throughout the story to read these references to Faith's observation as Goodman Brown's view of her reaction. All the action has been seen from Brown's point of view, and Hawthorne has never entered Faith's mind. Surely the exclamation is in Brown's mind only, for it prompts him to act, and his plea that she look up to heaven leaves him standing alone. Her specter vanishes with the others.

6. F. O. Matthiessen, *American Renaissance: Art and Expression in the Age of Emerson and Whitman* (New York, 1941), 284; and R. H. Fogle, "Ambiguity and Clarity in Hawthorne's 'Young Goodman Brown,' " *New England Quarterly* XVIII, 451 (Dec. 1945).

7. Cf. Cotton Mather, *Magnalia Christi Americana*, Book II, 60; and Cotton Mather, in *Memorable Providences, Relating to Witchcraft and Possessions* (Boston, 1689), reprinted in Levin, *What Happened in Salem?*, 96–97: "Other *strange* things are done by them in a way of *Crafty Illusion*. They do craftily make of the *Air*, the *Figures* and *Colors* of things that never can be truly created by them. All men might *see*, but, I believe, no man could *feel* some of the Things which the *Magicians of Egypt*, exhibited of old."

for condemning any of them—and no justification for suspecting them, except for the shadowy vista that this experience has opened into his own capacity for evil. Asking whether these people were "really" evil is impertinent, for it leads us beyond the limits of fiction. The story is not about the evil of other people but about Brown's doubt, his discovery of the *possibility* of universal evil. Before reading the Devil's statements here in the light of ideas that Hawthorne suggested elsewhere, we must read them in their immediate context. At the witch-meeting, the "shape of evil" invites Goodman Brown to "the communion" of the human "race," the communion of evil, but we have no more right than Brown himself to believe the Father of Lies. Indeed, Hawthorne's brilliant success depends on this distinction. He gives us an irresistible picture of a "crisis of faith and an agony of doubt";[8] we must notice that Brown finally does exorcise the spectral meeting, but that he can never forget his view of the specters or the abandon in which he himself became "the chief horror" in the dark wilderness. He lives the rest of his life in doubt, and the literal doubt depends on his uncertainty about whether his wife and others are really evil. If he were certain that they had been present in the forest, he would not treat them even so civilly as he does during the rest of his life. It is the spectral quality of the experience—both its uncertainty and its unforgettable impression—that makes the doubt permanent.

The question, then, is not whether Faith and the others were really there, in their own persons, at the witch meeting. When Hawthorne asks whether Goodman Brown had "fallen asleep in the forest and only dreamed a wild dream of a witch meeting," and replies, "Be it so if you will," he offers an alternative possibility to the nineteenth-century reader who refuses to take devils seriously even in historical fiction. The choice lies between dream and a reality that is unquestionably spectral. Neither Hawthorne nor (at the end) even Goodman Brown suggests that the church members were present in their own persons. Brown's question is whether the Devil, when he took on their shapes, had their permission to represent them. That is why Hawthorne can say, "Be it so if you will." For the meaning remains the same even if Brown, having for some odd reason fallen asleep in the woods before the story begins, has dreamed the entire experience.

By recognizing that Hawthorne built "Young Goodman Brown" firmly on his historical knowledge, we perceive that the tale has a social as well as an allegorical and a psychological dimension. Hawthorne condemns that graceless perversion of true Calvinism which, in universal suspicion, actually led a community to the unjust destruction of twenty men and women. But we ought also to be reminded of some general truths about proper ways to read this wonderfully shrewd writer. We must not underestimate his use of historical materials, even when he is writing allegory; nor should we let an interest in patterns of image and symbol or an awareness that he repeatedly uses the same types of character obscure the clear literal significance of in-

---

8. The phrase is Harry Levin's. See *The Power of Blackness*, 54.

dividual stories. Working over an amazingly—some critics have said, an obsessively—narrow range of types and subjects, he nevertheless achieves a remarkable variety of insights into human experience.

FREDERICK CREWS

Escapism in "Young Goodman Brown" and "The Minister's Black Veil"†

* * *

These conflicts are perhaps most fully observable in "Young Goodman Brown," a patently symbolic story whose atmosphere and import resemble those of "My Kinsman, Major Molineux." Like Robin's, Brown's ordeal is useful for us because it is uncomplicated by assertions of high conscious purpose; the hero simply and "inexplicably" undergoes a dreamlike or dreamed experience that permanently alters him. Yet he becomes what other and seemingly nobler Hawthornian escapists become: "a stern, a sad, a darkly meditative, a distrustful, if not a desperate man" (II, 106) [188]. This fact suggests, but of course does not prove, that Brown's case offers a psychological paradigm for the others; and this is just what we shall argue.

It is worth stressing that "Young Goodman Brown," which has teased its numerous critics with ambiguous hints of religious allegory, has a reasonably literal starting-point for its dream experience. If Brown loses his "faith" in mankind or salvation, he does so by fleeing from a normal, loving wife named Faith. These newlyweds are not yet fully acquainted with each other's minds—and, we can infer, not yet sure of each other's commitment to marriage. This is established with some subtlety:

> "Dearest heart," whispered [Faith], softly and rather sadly, when her lips were close to his ear, "prithee put off your journey until sunrise and sleep in your own bed to-night. A lone woman is troubled with such dreams and such thoughts that she's afeard of herself sometimes. Pray tarry with me this night, dear husband, of all nights in the year."
>
> "My love and my Faith," replied young Goodman Brown, "of all nights in the year, this one night must I tarry away from thee. My journey, as thou callest it, forth and back again, must needs be done 'twixt now and sunrise. What, my sweet, pretty wife, dost thou doubt me already, and we but three months married?" (II, 89) [178]

Here, as so often in Hawthorne, the two-dimensionality of the scene, with its stylized reply and its want of overt motivation, has the effect of guiding and heightening our psychological expectations.

† From *The Sins of the Fathers: Hawthorne's Psychological Themes* (Berkeley: U of California P, 1989), 98–111. Copyright © 1966 by Frederick C. Crews. Used by permission of Oxford University Press, Inc. Page numbers in square brackets refer to this Norton Critical Edition.

Faith's whispered plea to Brown, "sleep in your own bed," has a distinctly sensual overtone that Brown himself picks up in his mocking question about "doubt"; a causal connection appears to subsist between Brown's mysterious rendezvous with the Devil and his flight from his wife's embraces. The very absoluteness and seeming arbitrariness of his decision to leave makes us look for such a hidden connection. Again, Faith's confessing that "a lone woman is troubled with such dreams and such thoughts that she's afeard of herself sometimes" places the ensuing plot in a suggestive light. Brown, too, will be troubled with a "dream" that will make him afraid of himself and indeed afraid of Faith. Hawthorne is evidently implying that when a newly married pair are separated, each may become subject to unpleasant ideas that under ordinary circumstances are kept in check only by the reassuring presence of the other.

Hawthorne reminds us in various ways that Brown is facing embodiments of his own thoughts in the characters he meets in the forest. The Devil's inducements are spoken "so aptly that his arguments seemed rather to spring up in the bosom of his auditor than to be suggested by himself" (II, 95) [182]. The haunted forest is horrible to Brown, "but he was himself the chief horror of the scene . . ." (II, 99) [184], and he races toward the witches' sabbath screaming blasphemies and giving vent to demonic laughter. Hawthorne comments: "The fiend in his own shape is less hideous than when he rages in the breast of man" (II, 100) [184]. This makes it clear that the presumptive appearance of devils in the story is meant to refer to Brown's subjective thoughts. No wonder that when he arrives at the sabbath and sees the damned congregation, "he felt a loathful brotherhood [with them] by the sympathy of all that was wicked in his heart" (II, 102) [186]. Under these conditions the appearance of Faith in this company can have no bearing on her actual virtue or lack of it; she is there because Brown's inner *Walpurgisnacht* has reserved a special role for her.[1]

What does the Devil offer Goodman Brown? There is no ambiguity here. Having assembled likenesses of all the figures of authority and holiness in Salem village and treated them as proselytes of hell, the Devil points them out to Brown and his fellow initiates:

> "There," resumed the sable form, "are all whom ye have reverenced from youth. Ye deemed them holier than yourselves, and shrank from your own sin, contrasting it with their lives of righteousness and prayerful aspirations heavenward. Yet here are they all in my worshipping assembly. This night it shall be granted you to know their secret deeds: how hoary-bearded elders of the

---

1. Some critics have argued otherwise on the basis of Faith's pink ribbons, whose tangible reality in the forest is taken as evidence that she is "really" there. As David Levin correctly maintains, however, if the Devil is anything more than a fantasy of Brown's he can conjure pink ribbons as easily as the more visionary part of his spectacle. See "Shadows of Doubt: Specter Evidence in Hawthorne's 'Young Goodman Brown,'" *American Literature* XXXIV (November 1962): 344–52 [pp. 693–99 in this Norton Critical Edition]. Brown shares Othello's fatuous concern for "ocular proof," and the proof that is seized upon is no more substantial in one case than in the other.

church have whispered wanton words to the young maids of their households; how many a woman, eager for widows' weeds, has given her husband a drink at bedtime and let him sleep his last sleep in her bosom; how beardless youths have made haste to inherit their fathers' wealth; and how fair damsels—blush not, sweet ones—have dug little graves in the garden, and bidden me, the sole guest, to an infant's funeral. By the sympathy of your human hearts for sin ye shall scent out all the places—whether in church, bed-chamber, street, field, or forest—where crime has been committed, and shall exult to behold the whole earth one stain of guilt, one mighty blood spot. Far more than this. It shall be yours to penetrate, in every bosom, the deep mystery of sin, the fountain of all wicked arts, and which inexhaustibly supplies more evil impulses than human power—than my power at its utmost—can make manifest in deeds." (II, 103f.) [186–87]

Knowledge of sin, then, and most often of sexual sin, is the prize for which Goodman Brown seems tempted to barter his soul. In this version of the Faustian pact, the offered power is unrelated to any practical influence in the world; what Brown aspires to, if we can take this bargain as emanating from his own wishes, is an acme of voyeurism, a prurience so effective in its ferreting for scandal that it can uncover wicked thoughts before they have been enacted.

Thus Goodman Brown, a curiously preoccupied bridegroom, escapes from his wife's embraces to a vision of general nastiness. The accusation that Brown's Devil makes against all mankind, and then more pointedly against Faith, clearly issues from Brown's own horror of adulthood, his inability to accept the place of sexuality in married love. Brown remains the little boy who has heard rumors about the polluted pleasures of adults, and who wants to learn more about them despite or because of the fact that he finds them disgusting. His forest journey, in fact, amounts to a vicarious and lurid sexual adventure. Without insisting on the extraordinary redundancy of phallic objects in the tale, I shall merely cite the judgment of critics who do not share the bias of this study. Roy R. Male finds that "almost everything in the forest scene suggests that the communion of sinners is essentially sexual . . . ," and Daniel G. Hoffman, after reminding us that a witches' coven is, *prima facie*, an orgy with the Devil, finds that "phallic and psychosexual associations are made intrinsic to the thematic development of [Hawthorne's] story. . . . Brown's whole experience is described as a penetration of a dark and lonely way through a branched forest. . . . At journey's end is the orgiastic communion amid leaping flames."[2]

If Brown's sexual attitude is that of a young boy rather than a normal bridegroom, we may be permitted to wonder if parental, not wifely, sexuality is not the true object of his prurience. This supposition is strengthened by the virtual identity between the Devil's convocation of damned Salem dignitaries here and the comparable scene in

2. *Hawthorne's Tragic Vision*, 78; *Form and Fable in American Fiction*, 165f.

"Alice Doane's Appeal." In both cases the exposé is of "all whom ye have reverenced from youth," and in the earlier story an Oedipal theme is made all but explicit. "Young Goodman Brown" is subtler but not essentially different. The Devil, the carnal initiator, happens to look exactly like Brown's grandfather, and he and Brown "might have been taken for father and son" (II, 91) [179]. This Devil, furthermore, persuades Brown to join the coven by feeding his cynicism about all his male ancestors—who turn out to have a connection with Hawthorne's own ancestors. After declaring himself to be as well acquainted with the Browns as any other Puritan family, the Devil adds, "I helped your grandfather, the constable, when he lashed the Quaker woman so smartly through the streets of Salem" (II, 92) [180]. If forefathers are fathers at a slight remove, both Brown and Hawthorne are leveling circuitously filial charges of sexual irregularity here. And the charges become more pointed when the witch Goody Cloyse recognizes that the Devil is "in the very image of my old gossip, Goodman Brown . . ." (II, 94) [181]. It is not difficult to see the sense in which Brown's grandfather is alleged to have been the "gossip" or confidant of a witch who is met on the way to an orgy. If Brown must now believe this of his grandfather, he must also have some doubts about his father; for his earlier statement, "My father never went into the woods on such an errand, nor his father before him" (II, 92) [180], has already been half-refuted.

It would seem, then, that "Young Goodman Brown" offers yet another instance of Hawthorne's practice of denigrating fathers *in absentia*. As usual, too, the missing literal father is replaced by numerous authority figures who can be regarded as his surrogates. Few pages in the tale lack some accusatory reference to a king, a governor, a minister, a deacon, or an elder of the church. When Brown, in a frenzy of self-induced despair, cries "Come witch, come wizard, come Indian powwow, come devil himself, and here comes Goodman Brown" (II, 99) [184], he has not simply given himself over to hell, but has done so by aligning himself with unscrupulous male authorities—the evil counterparts of "all whom ye have reverenced from youth." Having recognized in his elders the very impulses that filial respect has inhibited in himself, he declares himself free to indulge those impulses without punishment. "You may as well fear him [i.e., himself]," he tells the anti-authorities, "as he fear you" (II, 99) [184].

Brown's fantasy-experience, like that of Robin Molineux, follows the classic Oedipal pattern: resentment of paternal authority is conjoined with ambiguous sexual temptation. In both instances, furthermore, the hero's attitude toward womankind is violently ambivalent. A general slur on women is implied when Brown sees that the forest sinners include virtually all the respectable women he has known, from the Governor's wife and her friends through "wives of honored husbands, and widows, a great multitude, and ancient maidens, all of excellent repute, and fair young girls, who trembled lest their mothers should espy them" (II, 101) [185]. The near-universality of this company reminds us of the two critical figures who are missing: Brown's mother and his wife. Yet Faith does arrive, only to disappear at the hideous moment of initiation—as if Brown were not able to stand a final confrontation of his suspicions about her. And he has been led to this moment by reflecting that the woman who taught him his catechism as a boy, Goody Cloyse, is a witch; this is to say that maternal authority is as questionable as paternal authority.[3] Like Ilbrahim, however, Brown finally absolves his mother, but not his father. Just as he is about to join the congregation of sinners, "He could have well-nigh sworn that the shape of his own dead father beckoned him to advance, looking downward from a smoke wreath, while a woman, with dim features of despair, threw out her hand to warn him back. Was it his mother?" (II, 102) [186].

The general pattern of "Young Goodman Brown" is that fathers are degraded to devils and mothers to witches (both attributions, of course, are confirmed in psychoanalysis). Yet the outcome of that pattern, as is always true of Hawthorne's plots, is not simple degradation but a perpetuated ambivalence. Brown lives out a long life with Faith and has children by her, but entertains continual suspicions about her virtue. In retrospect we can say that the source of his uncertainty has been discernible from the beginning—namely, his insistence upon seeing Faith more as an idealized mother than as a wife. She has been his "blessed angel on earth," and he has nurtured a transparently filial desire to "cling to her skirts and follow her to heaven" (II, 90) [178]. A bridegroom with such notions is well prepared for an appointment with the Devil.

Nothing can be gained from disputing whether Brown's forest experience was real or dreamed, for in either case it serves his private need to make lurid sexual complaints against mankind. Yet the richness of Hawthorne's irony is such that, when Brown turns to a Gulliver-like misanthropy and spends the rest of his days shrinking from wife and neighbors, we cannot quite dismiss his attitude as unfounded. Like Gulliver's, his distinctly pathological abhorrence has come from a deeper initiation into human depravity than his normal townsmen will ever know. Who is to say that they are exempt from the fantasies that have warped him? The only sure point is that by indulging those fantasies Brown *has* become different; at least one case of human foulheartedness has been amply documented, and for all we know, Salem may be teeming with latent Goodman Browns. In examining his own mind, I imagine, Hawthorne found good reasons for thinking that this might be so.

---

3. Brown resembles Robin in allowing his general faith in women to be shaken by his acquaintance with one degenerate woman. In reply to his objection that Faith's heart would be broken by his joining the sabbath, the Devil says, "I would not for twenty old women like the one hobbling before us that Faith should come to any harm" (II, 93) [181]. This insinuation that the loved woman is somehow linked to the despised one is picked up by Brown. "What if a wretched old woman do choose to go to the devil when I thought she was going to heaven," he tells himself; "is that any reason why I should quit my dear Faith and go after her?" (II, 96) [182]. Like Reuben Bourne's anguished question as to whether he should desert Roger Malvin *because* Roger has been a father to him, this sentence hints at unconscious motivation. Brown is beginning to see Faith under the aspect of the evil-maternal Goody Cloyse; and he puts "a world of meaning" (II, 95) [182] into his astonished reflection that it was she who taught him his catechism.

* * *

Exactly parallel to Young Goodman Brown's case is that of the Reverend Hooper in "The Minister's Black Veil"—a story that has provided much doctrinal ammunition for critics who are predisposed to see Hawthorne's ideal as a mild-mannered bachelor in clerical garb. If Hooper is not, as some maintain, "a preacher who preaches on behalf of the author," neither is he a perfect Antichrist in his pride and despair.[4] Both interpretations ignore Hawthorne's evasiveness about ultimate truth and his meticulous concern with ironies of motivation. As in Brown's case, what we learn about secret sin from Hooper is only what Hooper *becomes*, not what he believes. He is a pathetically self-deluded idealist who, goaded into monomania by a certain incompleteness in his nature, ends by becoming the one obvious exemplar of the vice he rightly or wrongly attributes to everyone else.[5]

Perhaps the best way to see the parallelism between Hooper's case and Goodman Brown's is to remind ourselves of the religious consequences of the two revulsions against mankind. We are not likely to call Brown a religious sage, yet his attitudes are no less "holy" than Hooper's. Why should we lend a transcendent aura to Hooper's gloom while regarding Brown's, quite rightly, as pathological? The fact is that Brown's mania takes the form of a super-piety scarcely distinguishable from Hooper's:

> On the Sabbath day, when the congregation were singing a holy psalm, he could not listen because an anthem of sin rushed loudly upon his ear and drowned all the blessed strain. When the minister spoke from the pulpit with power and fervid eloquence, and, with his hand on the open Bible, of the sacred truths of our religion, and of saint-like lives and triumphant deaths, and of future bliss or misery unutterable, then did Goodman Brown turn pale, dreading lest the roof should thunder down upon the gray blasphemer and his hearers. (II, 106) [188]

It is fairly clear that the "anthem of sin" assaulting Brown's ears is a projection of his own half-repressed fantasies. Yet in taking a radical view of man's sinfulness Brown is being an orthodox Calvinist; as several critics have noted, one of the beauties of "Young Goodman Brown" is that the Devil's role is to persuade the hero to take his religion seriously. We might therefore say that the tale is psychologically if not theologically anti-Puritan. But if this is so, it follows that we are under no obligation to admire the same radical pessimism in Hooper simply because Hooper is a Puritan minister.

In one sense Hooper's "eccentricity" (I, 52n.) [189] appears to be without direct motive. Like other Hawthornian monomaniacs, he points to a mysterious external necessity when asked to explain his be-

---

4. See Levin, *The Power of Blackness*, 42, and William Bysshe Stein, "The Parable of the Antichrist in 'The Minister's Black Veil,'" *American Literature* XXVII (November 1955): 386–92.

5. Of all readings of the tale, that of E. Earle Stibitz does best justice to this quintessentially Hawthornian situation. See "Ironic Unity in Hawthorne's 'The Minister's Black Veil,'" *American Literature* XXXIV (May 1962): 182–90.

havior, and we are permitted no glimpse of his mind before he dons the veil. Yet Hawthorne's visual presentation of him is a distinct sketch of a familiar character-type. The minister is "a gentlemanly person, of about thirty, though still a bachelor . . . dressed with due clerical neatness, as if a careful wife had starched his band, and brushed the weekly dust from his Sunday garb" (I, 53) [189]. From these few words we would expect Hooper to display a fastidiousness in his personal relations as well as in his dress. And indeed, the note of tidy womanliness here runs through the tale in a faint, suggestive undercurrent, particularly in the continual mention of the veil. As one parishioner remarks with unconscious acuteness, "How strange . . . that a simple black veil, *such as any woman might wear on her bonnet,* should become such a terrible thing on Mr. Hooper's face!" (I, 56f.; my italics) [191].

Such innuendoes become significant when we learn that Hooper is engaged to be married. His consummately normal fiancée, Elizabeth, cannot persuade him to remove the veil, with the predictable result that the marriage is called off. Hooper's reaction to Elizabeth's farewell is to smile, despite his grief, at the thought that "only a material emblem had separated him from happiness, though the horrors, which it shadowed forth, must be drawn darkly between the fondest of lovers" (I, 63f.) [195]. This smile, which recurs so often that it acquires a quality of daffy abstractedness, is Hooper's substitute for considering Elizabeth's reasonable plea. It could be plausibly argued, I think, that Hooper has donned the veil in order to prevent his marriage. On the one hand we see that he is already quite prim enough without a woman in the house, and on the other we find that he broods over dark, unspecified horrors that must separate the fondest of lovers. Where have these horrors come from, if not from his own imagination? It is possible that Hooper, who like Goodman Brown is obliged to confront the sexual aspects of womanhood, shares Brown's fears and has hit upon a means of forestalling their realization in marriage. His literal wearing of a veil, like Brown's figurative removal of it to leer at the horrid sexuality underneath, acts as a defense against normal adult love. No wonder that the topic of his first "veiled" sermon is "secret sin, and those sad mysteries which we hide from our nearest and dearest, *and would fain conceal from our own consciousness* . . ." (I, 55; my italics) [190].

Now, I do not care to lay very much stress on the indications of sexual squeamishness in Hooper. They are there, but they command much less attention than the comparable elements in "Young Goodman Brown." But the very ambiguity in Hooper's motivation enables Hawthorne to offer us glimpses into the minds of the people who must form their own theories about their minister. This is true, for example, at the funeral of the young lady with whom Hooper seems to have had some connection, if only in his thoughts. Poe and others have made much of Hooper's uneasiness in the presence of the corpse, and have intimated that Hooper, like his later counterpart

Dimmesdale, must have been tempted into sexual indulgence at least once in his career. Yet the hints of an explicit liaison are supplied by the highly suggestive bystanders to the scene. It is "a superstitious old woman" (I, 58) [192] who thinks that the corpse has shuddered at Hooper's aspect, and it is "a fancy" (I, 58) [192] of two parishioners that Hooper and the girl's spirit are marching hand in hand in the procession. That the fancy is shared is no sign of its truth. Simply, Hawthorne is exposing a preoccupation in the collective mind of the town.

This preoccupation might be said to be the chief object of Hawthorne's scrutiny in "The Minister's Black Veil." From the beginning he is concerned with the telltale responses that Hooper's "ambiguity of sin or sorrow" (I, 65) [196] elicits from his fellow men. In the sermon on buried sin "each member of the congregation, the most innocent girl, and the man of hardened breast, felt as if the preacher had crept upon them, behind his awful veil, and discovered their hoarded iniquity of deed or thought" (I, 55) [190–91]. By joining young virgins with old sinners Hawthorne is placing his customary emphasis on the universality of human nature; no one is completely free from the urges that are gratified by only a few. Hooper's parishioners would prefer not to acknowledge these urges of which he has become a visible reminder. They begin slighting him,[6] making fun of him, fleeing his presence, calling him insane, and inventing sexual rumors about him that will cancel the relevance of the veil to their own latent thoughts. Of all the busybodies in the town, including a special delegation whose task is to uncover the mystery, no one is able to face Hooper directly—and even Elizabeth herself susceptible to the "whispers" (I, 62) [194] of an obviously sexual scandal. When she too is suddenly terrified by a hidden meaning in the veil, Hawthorne has capped his demonstration of general *malaise*, for Elizabeth possesses a steady, cleansing love that seems unique in the town. Hooper is doubtless the supreme example of isolation "in that saddest of all prisons, his own heart" (I, 67) [197], but his difference from the others is only a matter of degree.

Thus the world of "The Minister's Black Veil" is one in which a man can reasonably be "afraid to be alone with himself" (I, 57) [191]. The real struggle in the tale is not between Hooper and the others but between conscious and unconscious thoughts within each individual. Total repression is restored in everyone but Hooper, and in his case, as in Goodman Brown's, the truth is permitted utterance only in the form of symbolism and accusation. Hooper has a sympathy with "all dark affections" (I, 65) [196], but he lacks the courage to confess their hold upon his own imagination. He too is one of those who are frightened by the veil, and understandably so, for he has had clear intima-

---

6. A particularly interesting early example is Old Squire Saunders's forgetting to invite Hooper to dinner after the Sunday service—a slip that is said to occur "doubtless by an accidental lapse of memory" (I, 56) [191]. It is clear that Hawthorne's interest in such "accidents" was parallel to Freud's in *The Psychopathology of Everyday Life*.

tions of what the force of civilization must contend with in its effort to
remain the master. Hawthorne leaves us with the Swiftian idea that a
little self-knowledge is worse than none, and that the best approximation to happiness rests in an ignorant, busy involvement with a society
of unconscious hypocrites.

In proceeding from sexual fear to obsession and misanthropy,
Brown and Hooper may stand for Hawthorne's escapists generally.
Sometimes, as with Ethan Brand, the hint of twisted sexuality is offered almost as an irrelevant afterthought; we learn in passing that in
his search for the Unpardonable Sin, which is of course finally located
in his own breast, Brand has taken an innocent girl and made her "the
subject of a psychological experiment, and wasted, absorbed, and perhaps annihilated her soul, in the process" (III, 489). More often, as in
"Egotism; or, The Bosom Serpent," "The Birthmark," "The Artist of
the Beautiful," and "The Man of Adamant," the hero is facing a matrimonial challenge like Brown's or Hooper's. Either he is evading marriage, or he has been discarded for a better lover, or he is a strangely
uneasy newlywed, or his wife is simply temporarily absent. However
sketchy the connection between the hero's lovelessness and his zealous project or phobia, that connection is always indicated.[7]

J. HILLIS MILLER

The Problem of History in
"The Minister's Black Veil"†

* * *

Just why does the simple act of wearing the black veil cause all this
devastation in the little community of Milford? The catastrophic effect
seems outrageously incommensurate with its trivial cause. The wearing of the veil, I answer, suspends two of the basic assumptions that
make society possible: the assumption that a person's face is the sign
of his selfhood and the accompanying presumption that this sign can
in one way or another be read. A whole series of presuppositions accompany those assumptions: the presupposition that there are natural
as opposed to arbitrary signs, in this case the face; the presupposition
that the face as exterior and visible natural sign refers to an interior,
nonlinguistic entity, the consciousness, subjectivity, soul, or selfhood
of the person who presents that face to the world; the presupposition
that the procedure whereby we read a person's selfhood by his or her
face is paradigmatic for sign-reading in general. The reading of person

---

7. As Harry Levin remarks, Hawthorne's tales are "rife with matrimonial fears" (*The Power of
Blackness*, 58). Levin alludes to "Mrs. Bullfrog," "The Wedding Knell," "The Shaker Bridal,"
"Edward Fane's Rosebud," "The Wives of the Dead," and "The White Old Maid"—a modest
beginning for an inventory of the relevant works.
† From *Hawthorne and History: Defacing It* (Oxford: Basil Blackwell, 1991), 92–106. Copyright © J. Hillis Miller. Reprinted by permission of the author. Page numbers in square
brackets refer to this Norton Critical Edition.

by face can then be universally extended to the reading of all natural and supernatural entities, all entities not persons—the absent, the inanimate, the dead. This reading would be expressed by those most basic of tropes, prosopopoeia and apostrophe, as in Wordsworth's opening address in "The Boy of Winander": "There was a boy: ye knew him well, ye cliffs / And islands of Winander!" It is all very well to say that of course we know that reading a personality by a face is a precarious dependence on an unreliable trope, but we go on knowing, choosing, and deciding in daily life as if this were not the case. Hawthorne's story shows that if the originary figure of reading self by face is put in question, then the whole set of assumptions making individual and social life possible are suspended.

When he puts on the black veil the Reverend Hooper is as if he were already dead. Or, rather, he seems already to have withdrawn to that realm where signs cannot reach, for which "death" is one name. Or, rather, it is as if the simple act of putting on the black veil had revealed the unverifiable possibility that each of us already dwells in that realm, both as we are for other people and even as we are for ourselves. The black veil reveals in these effects the possibility that unveiling, apocalyptic or otherwise, is impossible.

The most literal and direct effect of the veil is to suspend for Hooper's parishioners access to his subjectivity. His "figure" becomes ambiguous, disquietingly attractive, fascinating, just because his face has become invisible. This is expressed by a regular distinction between "face" and "figure" that Hawthorne borrows from common parlance: "Strangers came long distances to attend services at his church, with the mere idle purpose of gazing at his figure, because it was forbidden them to behold his face" (381) [196].

Hooper's last words, "I look around me, and, lo! on every visage a Black Veil" (384) [198], assert that the face itself is a veil. Hooper's corpse mouldering in the earth, still veiled, is a veiled veil, a veil on top of a veil. There is no reason to assume that even the most extravagant series of unveilings would ever reach anything but another veil. Death, as Paul de Man says, is "a displaced name for a linguistic predicament."[1] This is the predicament of never being able to name the realities we most want to name—the self, nature, God, the realm beyond the borders of life—except in that unverifiable trope called a catachresis. Catachresis often takes the form of a prosopopoeia, as in "face of a mountain" or "eye of a storm." Such a trope defaces or disfigures in the very act whereby it ascribes a face to what has none.

Hawthorne gives striking typological expression to this predicament in his image of the veiled face as a veil behind a veil. The black veil is literally a de-facement or dis-figurement. It deprives Hooper of the face whereby his neighbours assume they know him. However one wishes to describe it generically, as allegorical personification, or as parabolic realism, or as apocalyptic prophecy, the veil as type or sym-

1. Paul de Man, "Autobiography as De-Facement," *The Rhetoric of Romanticism* (New York: Columbia University Press, 1984), p. 81.

bol de-faces that for which it stands. At the same time the veil disfigures its referent in another way. The veil between us and that for
which it is a type and a symbol is an enigmatic sign that appears to
give access to what it stands for while forbidding the one who confronts it to move behind it by any effort of hermeneutic interpretation.
If Hooper's face behind the veil, like that of all his neighbours, is yet
another veil, then it can be said that the real face too is not a valid
sign but another de-facement. The face de-faces . . . it.

Systematic narrative and figurative notations in the story of the things
that are covered by a black veil extend the meaning of veiling to cover
the whole repertoire of those entities that are the outside grounding of
social life: nature, God, death, or the realm we shall enter after death.
It is as if the inaccessibility of what the black veil covers makes it
spread out to include not just Hooper's face as the sign of his selfhood
but the whole array of things that are the threatening exterior of social
life, while at the same time presumed to be its secure foundation.
    When Hooper's subjectivity becomes inaccessible by way of his
face, his veil covers a kind of floating location of the unlocatable. The
spectator's speculations about what may be behind the veil drifts from
consciousness to the place of death, to God, to nature. Hawthorne's
story implicitly recognizes that prosopopoeia is the primary means by
which mankind names and tames all that is outside the human. We
give nature, God, or death a human face in order to give ourselves the
illusion that we can have access to them, understand them, appropriate them as the grounds of our social intercourse. But Hooper's wearing the black veil, by suspending that primary "literal" prosopopoeia
whereby we interpret a person's facial features as the signs of his or
her selfhood, suspends also those extensions of prosopopoeia that are
ordinarily so taken for granted as not even to be recognizable as
tropes, for example when we call nature "she."
    When Hooper is affrighted by his own face in the mirror during the
wedding service, he rushes forth into the darkness: "For the Earth,
too, had on her Black Veil." "Dying sinners" shudder when Hooper
puts his veiled face near their own, "such were the terrors of the black
veil, even when Death had bared his visage" (381) [196]. In his
deathbed speech Hooper speaks of the way man now does "vainly
shrink from the eye of his Creator" (384) [198]. All these prosopopoeias—Earth as a woman, Death as man, God as possessing an
all-seeing eye—discreetly signalled by capitals, by pronouns, or by the
projection on what is not human of parts of the human body, are so inextricably woven into everyday speech as to be almost invisible. They
are almost effaced or "dead" metaphors. Of course we speak of the
earth as "she." Of course we speak of being face to face with death, or
of being under the eye of God. How could we speak at all of these
things otherwise? Such universal tropes become visible only when
they are suspended. Prosopopoeia is essential to allegory, as in the
capitalizations of Earth, Death, and Creator here. How could there be
allegory without abstractions personified and capitalized, "Orgoglio" in

Spenser, or "Caritas" and the rest in Giotto's Allegory of the Virtues and Vices at Padua? Prosopopoeia is the catachrestic trope that covers our ignorance of nature, death, and God. Prosopopoeia makes everything we say of these, like what we say of the human heart, an allegory. They are allegorical in the sense of being simultaneously an unveiling (speaking of Mother Earth opens up the possibility of incorporating nature into our discourse), and a veiling (speaking of Mother Earth covers over the otherness of nature by ascribing to it a spurious similarity to ourselves).

Much is at stake in being able to go on seeing these effaced prosopopoeias as valid. At stake is our ability to go on living with a modest sense of security as mortals in an alien and threatening universe. At stake also is even our sense of ourselves *as* selves, since to question those ubiquitous personifications of nature, God, and death is, by a reciprocal putting in question, to suspend that "literal" prosopopoeia whereby a human face, our own or that of another, is an index to a self behind the face. It is no wonder the good citizens of Milford are appalled.

Hooper performs all this putting-in-question not by a disarticulating process using language against language. Such an effort always fails by smuggling back into the effort of disarticulation the very thing that is being disarticulated, as in my almost effaced prosopopoeia in "smuggling." Hooper's act works because it is done in perhaps the only way such an act can be effectively performed: in a silent "gesture" that is not really a gesture, since it is not part of a usual system of bodily movements, and by the proffering of a sign that is not really a sign, since its referent and its signification remain forever unverifiable. He appears wearing a black veil.

The performative effect of this silent act can be compared to the equally devastating effect of Bartleby's "I would prefer not to," in Melville's "Bartleby the Scrivener."[2] In both cases, once by an act of language, once by an act outside of language, language is brought to a stop, rendered powerless. This inhibition includes all kinds of language: narrative language, language conceptual, dialectical, critical, historical, biographical, and so on. In the "The Minister's Black Veil" it can be said that the efforts of Hooper's parishioners, of Hooper himself, of the narrator of his story, of Hawthorne, and of all readings of the story, including this one, are unavailing attempts to find language adequate to reincorporate into our everyday world the mute sign Hooper displays as an affront to his community.

It is now possible to answer the question, "Of what, then, is The 'Minister's Black Veil' a parable?" The story is not simply a parable of the working of parable, as opposed to being the parabolic expression of a "spiritual" meaning, a meaning capable of being expressed in no other way. Biblical scholars and critics of secular parables, such as those of Kafka, have observed that all parables tend to be about their

---

2. I have discussed Melville's story in *Versions of Pygmalion* (Cambridge: Harvard University Press, 1990), pp. 141–78.

own working. Jesus's parable of the sower is the paradigmatic example. This would not be enough to say about "The Minister's Black Veil." Of this story it would be better to say that it is the indirect, veiled expression of the impossibility of expressing anything verifiable at all in parable except the impossibility of expressing anything verifiable.

The veil is the type and symbol of the fact that all signs are potentially unreadable, or that the reading of them is potentially unverifiable. If the reader has no access to what lies behind a sign but another sign, then all reading of signs cannot be sure whether or not it is in error. Reading would then be a perpetual wandering or displacement that can never be checked against anything except another sign. If the artwork should be, in Kant's formulation, the indispensable bridge between epistemology and ethics, from knowledge to justified action, Hawthorne's story, it can be said, puts all its readers together on that bridge, stuck there without entrance or egress, able to go neither forward nor backward, neither back to certain knowledge of what the story means nor forward to conscientious ethical or political action in the real world.

This situation is intolerable. To live is to act, to need to act, and to need to act with a sense that we are justified in what we do. We would do anything to escape from this situation or to persuade ourselves that we are not in it. "The Minister's Black Veil" presents the reader with a full repertoire of the ways this attempt can be made. All critical essays on the story are so many more attempts to put something verifiable behind the veil, to make the veil the type and symbol of something definite one can confront directly, face to face, *through* the veil, by means of the veil. Each of these attempts proffers an hypothesis about the meaning of the veil. Each proposes or posits some entity there. This is followed, in each case, by unsuccessful attempts to verify this hypothesis, or by an implicit recognition in the act of positing the hypothesis that it is intrinsically unverifiable.

I have already cited passages in which Hooper's parishioners imagine that some stranger may have changed places with their pastor. I have also cited the discussion with Elizabeth in which Hooper answers the direct request to "take away the veil" if not from his face then from the enigmatic or "mysterious" words he uses to explain the veil. He answers only in terms of riddling "ifs": "Know, then, this veil is a type and a symbol . . . *If* it be a sign of mourning . . . *If* I hide my face for sorrow . . . and *if* I cover it for secret sin" (378–79, my italics) [194–95]. But Elizabeth, Hooper's parishioners, the narrator, Hooper himself, and the reader do not want "ifs" and "perhapses". We want certainty. In response to that hermeneutic need the good citizens of Milford suppose there must be some specific cause or explanation for Hooper's taking the veil. They conclude, for example, from the fact that he avoids looking at his own veiled face that, like the Reverend Moody of York, though by intent rather than by accident, he must have performed some deeply guilty act: "This was what gave plausibility to the whispers, that Mr Hooper's conscience tortured him for some great crime, too horrible to be entirely concealed, or otherwise than so obscurely intimated" (380) [196]. On the other hand, according to another hypothesis, they suppose that Hooper must be possessed and may be consorting with the devil behind the veil: "It was said, that ghost or fiend consorted with him there" (380) [196]. Another possibility, proposed to herself earlier by Elizabeth, is that the wearing of the veil "was perhaps a symptom of mental disease" (379) [195]. The operative words here are *perhaps, obscurely,* and *or.* It may be this or it may be that. There is no way to tell. Whatever hypothesis anyone makes about what is behind the veil, whatever proposal, proposition, or positing anyone makes, remains just that, an unverifiable hypothesis. There is no way, in this life, once you have accepted the complex ideology of the veil, to get behind the veil to find out what is really going on back there, though this is what that ideology leads us to want to do.

If, after death, good Mr Hooper's face "mouldered beneath the Black Veil," this suggests the inextricable involvement of the inaccessibility of death in the ideological system of veiling. It confirms that death is indeed a displaced name for a linguistic predicament, the predicament of being able to posit or project names freely, in primal personifying apostrophes, but unable to validate those names by any direct experience of what is named. The positing itself erects a barrier or veil. Such naming is premimetic or pre-representational, that is, it does not point toward anything that can be directly experienced. At the same time such naming forbids ever entering a representational or mimetic domain where words can be matched with things known directly, prior to language. The face is a defacing, as the *pro* ("in front of, before") in *prosopon* or *prosopopoeia* suggests. *Prosopon* means face *or* mask, the face as mask put in front of an unfathomable enigma. The figure of the face as that which is "in front" of something behind is present still in all our English words in "front": "confront," "affront," "frontal," and "front" itself. These come from Latin *frons*: "forehead," "brow." The title of Hardy's "In Front of the Landscape," for example, is already a covert prosopopoeia, as is a colloquial phrase like "the front of the house." The most disquieting effect of Hooper's veil, as the story makes clear in Hooper's last speech, is to show that the face itself is already an impenetrable veil. A veiled face is a veil over a veil, a veiling of what is already veiled.

Even for Hooper, who lives behind the veil and should therefore know what it typifies, the sight of his veiled face is terrifying. This is the case not because the veil signifies a secret guilt of which he is aware, nor because he knows that he consorts with the devil behind it—no textual support is given to these hypotheses—but because for him too its meaning cannot be specified and then verified. Though he is behind the veil, when he catches a glimpse of his veiled face in the mirror he is as much outside the veil as anyone else. For Hooper too the meaning of the veil is a matter of "if," of "perhaps," and of the "or" of ambiguity.

Nor is Hooper himself exempt from the irresistible temptation to

make the veil typify something definite in order to escape from the unbearable suspension of not knowing for sure. His proposal involves
speculations not about what is within his own hidden subjectivity, except insofar as it is hidden even from himself, but rather speculations
about what is beyond the grave, beyond even that apocalyptic unveiling when all shall be revealed: "What, but the mystery which it obscurely typifies, has made this piece of crape so awful? When the
friend shows his inmost heart to his friend; the lover to his best-
beloved; when man does not vainly shrink from the eye of his Creator,
loathsomely treasuring up the secret of his sin; then deem me a monster, for the symbol beneath which I have lived, and die!" (384) [198].

The black veil is the presentation not so much of a secular symbol
as of a spiritual symbol that has only an individual authority, just as,
within Protestantism generally, or New England Puritanism in particular, every man may be his own priest, his own validation for a testimony that goes beyond biblical precedent and institutional authority.
The minister's veil extrapolates beyond the biblical texts about veils,
just as Hawthorne's story is a parable added in supplement to the
canonical parables of Jesus in the New Testament. * * * Hooper
nowhere claims that his authority for wearing the veil is some special
mission, election, or calling that has commanded him to do so as witness to some peculiar insight mediated to his congregation by means
of the veil. He is conspicuously silent where he might speak out, by
saying "God commanded me to do it," or "A still small voice told me to
do it," or even, "The devil made me do it." He just does it. Though
Hooper becomes an awesome power in the New England church, a famous preacher who strikes religious terror into the hearts of all who
hear him, that church dispatches a representative to his deathbed to
try (unsuccessfully) to persuade Hooper to remove the veil before he
dies. His stubborn refusal is seen as a scandal by his church.

Moreover, the traditional theological terminology of Hooper's refusal (in the words "mystery" and "obscurely typifies") is displaced to
name the linguistic predicament I have identified. The emphasis is on
that particular form of this predicament so fascinating to Hawthorne:
the incommensurability of solitary consciousness and any language
whatsoever that "may be understood and felt by anybody, who will give
himself the trouble to read it" (Preface to *Twice-told Tales*, 1152). The
logic of Hooper's formulation turns on "when" and "then." *When* each
of us does not hide his inmost heart from God, from those closest to
him, even from himself, or as Hooper has put it in his initial sermon
after he dons the Black Veil, when we no longer cover "those sad mysteries which we hide from our nearest and dearest, and would fain
conceal from our own consciousness, even forgetting that the Omniscient can detect them" (373) [190], *then* "deem me a monster, for the
symbol beneath which I have lived, and die!" The now of that "then",
however, has not yet come. In this life it remains the imminence of a
perpetual "not quite yet" within which "every visage" is a Black Veil, as
impenetrable as Hooper's literal veil of crape. Within the time of waiting for that perpetually deferred uncovering, Hooper is not a monster,

or not yet a monster, unless all others are monsters too, though it *would* be monstrous to wear the black veil still, after the universal unveiling at the apocalypse.

Monster: the word means "showing forth," the demonstration of something hideously unlawful or unique, for example, a monstrous birth. Now Hooper is not a monster because all men and women are monsters. All manifest, in spite of themselves, the sign of the nameless and unattainable secrets all hide in their hearts, secrets monstrously different in each case. The singularity of selfhood, its uniqueness, the impossibility of fitting selfhood into any categories of genre or species, and the impossibility of saying anything definite about it are, as I have said, perhaps that "Unpardonable Sin" Ethan Brand seeks everywhere in the world and then finds in his own heart. The unpardonable sin is that sin beyond the reach of language, beyond even that particular form of performative language called a pardon, beyond even God's speech of pardon, if not beyond God's all-seeing eye. How awful to be visible to God but beyond the reach of God's pardoning word!

Hooper dies not only still veiled, but still with "a faint smile lingering on the lips" (384) [198]. This dimly glimmering smile is the sign of his characteristic irony, meaning by irony a perpetual suspension of definite meaning. Hooper's smile accompanies the unresolvable ambiguity of the veil itself and of everything that is said about it, by the narrator, by the people of Milford, and by Hooper himself, however desperate all of these are to put an end to that ambiguity by saying something definite and verifiable about the meaning of the veil. Hooper's neighbours, the narrator, and the readers of the story are driven to extravagant unverifiable hypotheses by the juxtaposition of that faint smile and the surmounting blank black veil, marked only by its fold. I suggested earlier that the fold in the veil may perhaps be related to the twice-telling of this tale and to the way a secondary parabolic meaning is superimposed on the primary literal meaning. It would be just as plausible to relate the folding to the double meaning of irony. The two signs, the dim smile without a face and the folded veil above it, would then mean the same thing or would double one another. They would be the type and symbol of the radical undecidability of all ironic expression, even of that form of ironic expression that is not verbal but facial. Irony keeps its own counsel. It responds to our interrogations only with a further ironic smile or with an ominously permissive, "Of course, if you say so."

Insofar as Hooper's sin is the sin of irony, it is appropriate that the story should end with his death, since death and irony have a secret and unsettling alliance. Though Hooper, unlike Socrates, is not put to death for being an ironist, in both cases irony is shown to be lethal. It is deadly both for the ironist and for those on whom the irony is inflicted. Irony puts both the ironist and his victims in proximity to death, but it ironically survives the death of the ironist to go on through perhaps centuries of human history effecting its deadly work of the suspension of that definite meaning for which we all long and which we all think we ought to have. The putting to death of Socrates did not put an end to the effect of Socrates's irony, as the citizens of Athens may have hoped. Quite the contrary, as any good reader of the Platonic dialogues knows. And the citizens of Milford, like the narrator, who in his last sentence places the events he has been telling at a firm historical distance ("The grass of many years has sprung up and withered on that grave" [394] [198–99]), are still haunted by the memory of Hooper's smile and by the image of his face mouldering beneath the veil.

The attempt by the characters and by the narrator to put an end to painful hermeneutic suspension is continued by all the commentaries on Hawthorne's story that propose some definite explanation of it. One example would be an explanation in terms of history: "The Minister's Black Veil" is a representation by Hawthorne of the historical situation of New England Puritanism surviving into a Franklinian society. Another explanation would appeal to the psychology of the author: "The Minister's Black Veil" expresses Hawthorne's obsession with the theme of secret sin or guilt. Another explanation would be based on intertextual analogies: "The Minister's Black Veil" is to be read in terms of its echoes of similar themes and figures in other works by Hawthorne, for example the motif of the veil in *The Blithedale Romance* and *The Marble Faun*, or the motif of secret sexual transgression in *The Scarlet Letter*, or the theme of unpardonable sin in "Ethan Brand." D. A. Miller's Foucauldian interpretation of the story * * * argues that the story is made definite in meaning when it is placed in the context of nineteenth-century ideas about sexual secrets. My reading differs in principle from all these in being an unveiling and putting in question of the ideology of unveiling that inveigles Hooper, his community, and most readers of the story into believing that there must be something definite behind the veil—both Hooper's veil and the veil of the text as the words on the page—and that our business as readers is to identify it.

"The Minister's Black Veil," both the veil itself, *in* the story, and the text of the story in the sense of the materiality of the letter, the words there on the page, patiently endures all these positings and projections of meaning, but it does not unequivocally endorse any of them. It offers itself to be read. If there is a veil in the text that all those inside the story want desperately to pierce or to lift so they can name once and for all what is behind it, for readers of "The Minister's Black Veil," here and now in 1990, the text itself is a veil we would pierce or lift. This desire to establish a definitive meaning for the black veil by relating it to something behind it for which it stands is an example of the hermeneutic desire as such. This desire would put a stop to the endless drifting of interpretation by saying, once and for all, "The veil means so and so." The reader shares this desire with Hooper's congregation, with his fiancée, with Hooper himself. This might be expressed by saying that the story is an allegory of the reader's own situation in reading it. If this hermeneutic desire could be appeased, then example could be a confirmation of theory, or a means of adjusting it so it could be confirmed. Allegory and realism would then be reconciled, since the realistic story would be the unambiguous carrier of a definite allegorical meaning. Language and history would be brought to touch one another, merge, overlap.

This happy reconciliation, this crossing over by means of parable into the land of parable, behind the veil, does not in this case occur. One remembers Lewis Carroll's poem of "The Walrus and the Carpenter." To the final interrogation of the oysters, "answer came there none, / Which was not surprising since / They'd eaten every one." Of all our interrogations of the veil of "The Minister's Black Veil," as of the interrogations of the veil itself within the story, it can be said "answer came there none." This is not because the text is a self-consuming artifact that eats itself up through some internal contradiction or undecidability. Rather, the attempt to turn the opacity of parabolic symbol into transparent concept is the eating up of the text. The text says what it says, if it says anything, in the way parable does, that is, by way of opaque symbols that resist translation into perspicuous concepts. To say of the veil it is a symbol of sin, it is sorrow, it is madness, it is New England Puritanism in a Franklinian culture, or it is the cover for sexual secrets is to receive no response from the text.

The text remains silent. It gives no answer to our questions, though it endures being translated into the unverifiable concepts which eat it up. Such translations make the story disappear from the page and become those blank pages in the sunlight Hawthorne feared all his works were. To alter the metaphor again: "The Minister's Black Veil," like Bartleby in Melville's story, answers to all our demands: "I should prefer not to." Like Bartleby's phrase, with its conditional "should," its gently indecisive "prefer," both inhibiting the "not" from being the negative of some positive and thereby something we can make part of some dialectical reasoning, "The Minister's Black Veil" is neither positive nor negative. It is patiently neutral. It says neither yes nor no to whatever hypotheses about it the reader proposes. The text offers neither confirmation nor disconfirmation of any speculative formulation about its meaning.

In this the text is like the black veil itself. The performative efficacy of "The Minister's Black Veil" lies in this similarity. It works. Like the veil, the story is a strange kind of efficacious speech act. It is a way of doing things with proffered signs. But it does to undo, to take away foundation or authority from anything any reader can say of it.

JUDITH FETTERLEY

Women Beware Science: "The Birthmark"†

The scientist Aylmer in Nathaniel Hawthorne's "The Birthmark" provides another stage in the psychological history of the American protagonist. Aylmer is [Washington] Irving's Rip and [Sherwood] Anderson's boy [in "I Want to Know Why"] discovered in that middle age which Rip evades and the boy rejects. Aylmer is squarely confronted with the realities of marriage, sex, and women. There are compensations, however, for as an adult he has access to a complex set of mechanisms for accomplishing the great American dream of eliminating women. It is testimony at once to Hawthorne's ambivalence, his seeking to cover with one hand what he uncovers with the other, and to the pervasive sexism of our culture that most readers would describe "The Birthmark" as a story of failure rather than as the success story it really is—the demonstration of how to murder your wife and get away with it. It is, of course, possible to read "The Birthmark" as a story of misguided idealism, a tale of the unhappy consequences of man's nevertheless worthy passion for perfecting and transcending nature; and this is the reading usually given it.[1] This reading, however,

---

† From *The Resisting Reader: A Feminist Approach to American Fiction* (Bloomington: Indiana UP, 1978), 22–33. Page numbers in square brackets refer to this Norton Critical Edition.

1. See, for example, Brooks and Warren, *Understanding Fiction* (New York: Appleton-Century-Croft, 1943), pp. 103–106: "We are not, of course, to conceive of Aylmer as a monster, a man who would experiment on his own wife for his own greater glory. Hawthorne does not mean to suggest that Aylmer is depraved and heartless. . . . Aylmer has not realized that perfection is something never achieved on earth and in terms of mortality"; Richard Harter Fogle, *Hawthorne's Fiction: The Light and The Dark*, rev. ed. (Norman, Okla. University of Oklahoma Press, 1964), pp. 117–31; Robert Heilman, "Hawthorne's 'The Birthmark': Science as Religion," *South Atlantic Quarterly* 48 (1949), 574–83: "Aylmer, the overweening scientist, resembles less the villain than the tragic hero: in his catastrophic attempt to improve on human actuality there is not only pride and a deficient sense of reality but also disinterested aspiration"; F. O. Matthiessen, *American Renaissance* (New York: Oxford University Press, 1941), pp. 253–55; Arlin Turner, *Nathaniel Hawthorne* (New York: Holt, Rinehart, and Winston, 1961), pp. 88, 98, 132: "In 'The Birthmark' he applauded Aylmer's noble pursuit of perfection, in contrast to Aminadab's ready acceptance of earthiness, but Aylmer's achievement was tragic failure because he had not realized that perfection is not of this world." The major variation in these readings occurs as a result of the degree to which individual critics see Hawthorne as critical of Aylmer. Still, those who see Hawthorne as critical of Aylmer locate the source of his criticism in Aylmer's idealistic pursuit of perfection—e.g., Millicent Bell, *Hawthorne's View of the Artist* (New York: State University of New York, 1962), pp. 182–85: "Hawthorne, with his powerful Christian sense of the inextricable mixture of evil in the human compound, regards Aylmer as a dangerous perfectibilitarian"; William Bysshe Stein, *Hawthorne's Faust* (Gainesville: University of Florida Press, 1953), pp. 91–92: "Thus the first of Hawthorne's Fausts, in a purely symbolic line of action sacrifices his soul to conquer nature, the universal force of which man is but a tool." Even Simon Lesser, *Fiction and the Unconscious* (1957; rpt. New York: Vintage-Random, 1962), pp. 87–90 and pp. 94–98, who is clearly aware of the sexual implications of the story, subsumes his analysis under the reading of misguided idealism and in so doing provides a fine instance of phallic criticism in action: "The ultimate purpose of Hawthorne's attempt to present Aylmer in balanced perspective is to quiet our fears so that the wishes which motivate his experiment, which are also urgent, can be given their opportunity. Aylmer's sincerity and idealism give us a sense of kinship with him. We see that the plan takes shape gradually in his mind, almost against his conscious intention. We are reassured by the fact that he loves Georgiana and feels confident that his attempt to remove the birthmark will succeed. Thus at the same time that we recoil we can identify with Aylmer and through him act out some of our secret desires. . . . The story not only gives expression to impulses which are ordinarily repressed; it gives them a sympathetic hearing—an opportunity to show whether they can

ignores the significance of the form idealism takes in the story. It is not irrelevant that "The Birthmark" is about a man's desire to perfect his wife, nor is it accidental that the consequence of this idealism is the wife's death. In fact, "The Birthmark" provides a brilliant analysis of the sexual politics of idealization and a brilliant exposure of the mechanisms whereby hatred can be disguised as love, neurosis can be disguised as science, murder can be disguised as idealization, and success can be disguised as failure. Thus, Hawthorne's insistence in his story on the metaphor of disguise serves as both warning and clue to a feminist reading.

Even a brief outline is suggestive. A man, dedicated to the pursuit of science, puts aside his passion in order to marry a beautiful woman. Shortly after the marriage he discovers that he is deeply troubled by a tiny birthmark on her left cheek. Of negligible importance to him before marriage, the birthmark now assumes the proportions of an obsession. He reads it as a sign of the inevitable imperfection of all things in nature and sees in it a challenge to man's ability to transcend nature. So nearly perfect as she is, he would have her be completely perfect. In pursuit of this lofty aim, he secludes her in chambers that he has converted for the purpose, subjects her to a series of influences, and finally presents her with a potion which, as she drinks it, removes at last the hated birthmark but kills her in the process. At the end of the story Georgiana is both perfect and dead.

One cannot imagine this story in reverse—that is, a woman's discovering an obsessive need to perfect her husband and deciding to perform experiments on him—nor can one imagine the story being about a man's conceiving such an obsession for another man. It is woman, and specifically woman as wife, who elicits the obsession with imperfection and the compulsion to achieve perfection, just as it is man, and specifically man as husband, who is thus obsessed and compelled. In addition, it is clear from the summary that the imagined perfection is purely physical. Aylmer is not concerned with the quality of Georgiana's character or with the state of her soul, for he considers her "fit for heaven without tasting death" [209]. Rather, he is absorbed in her physical appearance, and perfection for him is equivalent to physical beauty. Georgiana is an exemplum of woman as beautiful object, reduced to and defined by her body. And finally, the conjunction of perfection and nonexistence, while reminding us of Anderson's story in which the good girl is the one you never see, develops what is only implicit in that story: namely, that the only good woman is a dead one and that the motive underlying the desire to perfect is the need to eliminate. "The Birthmark" demonstrates the fact that the idealization of women has its source in a profound hostility toward women and that it

be gratified without causing trouble or pain. There are obvious gains in being able to conduct tests of this kind with no more danger and no greater expenditure of effort than is involved in reading a story." The one significant dissenting view is offered by Frederick Crews, *The Sins of the Fathers* (New York: Oxford University Press, 1966), whose scattered comments on the story focus on the specific form of Aylmer's idealism and its implications for his secret motives.

is at once a disguise for this hostility and the fullest expression of it.

The emotion that generates the drama of "The Birthmark" is revulsion. Aylmer is moved not by the vision of Georgiana's potential perfection but by his horror at her present condition. His revulsion for the birthmark is insistent: he can't bear to see it or touch it; he has nightmares about it; he has to get it out. Until she is "fixed," he can hardly bear the sight of her and must hide her away in secluded chambers which he visits only intermittently, so great is his fear of contamination. Aylmer's compulsion to perfect Georgiana is a result of his horrified perception of what she actually is, and all his lofty talk about wanting her to be perfect so that just this once the potential of Nature will be fulfilled is but a cover for his central emotion of revulsion. But Aylmer is a creature of disguise and illusion. In order to persuade this beautiful woman to become his wife, he "left his laboratory to the care of an assistant, cleared his fine countenance from the furnace smoke, washed the stains of acid from his fingers" [199]. Best not to let her know who he really is or what he really feels, lest she might say before the marriage instead of after, "You cannot love what shocks you!" [199]. In the chambers where Aylmer secludes Georgiana, "airy figures, absolutely bodiless ideas, and forms of unsubstantial beauty" [204] come disguised as substance in an illusion so nearly perfect as to "warrant the belief that her husband possessed sway over the spiritual world" [204]. While Aylmer does not really possess sway over the spiritual world, he certainly controls Georgiana and he does so in great part because of his mastery of the art of illusion.

If the motive force for Aylmer's action in the story is repulsion, it is the birthmark that is the symbolic location of all that repels him. And it is important that the birthmark is just that: a birth *mark*, that is, something physical; and a *birth* mark, that is, something not acquired but inherent, one of Georgiana's givens, in fact equivalent to her.[2] The close connection between Georgiana and her birthmark is continually emphasized. As her emotions change, so does the birthmark, fading or deepening in response to her feelings and providing a precise clue to her state of mind. Similarly, when her senses are aroused, stroked by the influences that pervade her chamber, the birthmark throbs sympathetically. In his efforts to get rid of the birthmark Aylmer has "administered agents powerful enough to do aught except change your entire physical system" [209], and these have failed. The object of Aylmer's obsessive revulsion, then, is Georgiana's "physical system," and what defines this particular system is the fact that it is female. It is Georgiana's female physiology, which is to say her sexuality, that is the object of Aylmer's relentless attack. The link between Georgiana's birthmark and her sexuality is implicit in the birthmark's role as her emotional barometer, but one specific characteristic of the birthmark makes the connection explicit: the hand which shaped Georgiana's

---

2. In the conventional reading of the story Georgiana's birthmark is seen as the symbol of original sin—see, for example, Heilman, p. 579; Bell, p. 185. But what this reading ignores are, of course, the implications of the fact that the symbol of original sin is female and that the story only "works" because men have the power to project that definition onto women.

birth has left its mark on her in *blood*. The birthmark is redolent with references to the particular nature of female sexuality; we hardly need Aylmer's insistence on seclusion, with its reminiscences of the treatment of women when they are "unclean," to point us in this direction. What repels Aylmer is Georgiana's sexuality; what is imperfect in her is the fact that she is female; and what perfection means is elimination.

In Hawthorne's analysis the idealization of women stems from a vision of them as hideous and unnatural; it is a form of compensation, an attempt to bring them up to the level of nature. To symbolize female physiology as a blemish, a deformity, a birthmark suggests that women are in need of some such redemption. Indeed, "The Birthmark" is a parable of woman's relation to the cult of female beauty, a cult whose political function is to remind women that they are, in their natural state, unacceptable, imperfect, monstrous. Una Stannard in "The Mask of Beauty" has done a brilliant job of analyzing the implications of this cult:

> Every day, in every way, the billion-dollar beauty business tells women they are monsters in disguise. Every ad for bras tells a woman that her breasts need lifting, every ad for padded bras that what she's got isn't big enough, every ad for girdles that her belly sags and her hips are too wide, every ad for high heels that her legs need propping, every ad for cosmetics that her skin is too dry, too oily, too pale, or too ruddy, or her lips are not bright enough, or her lashes not long enough, every ad for deodorants and perfumes that her natural odors all need disguising, every ad for hair dye, curlers, and permanents that the hair she was born with is the wrong color or too straight or too curly, and lately ads for wigs tell her that she would be better off covering up nature's mistake completely. In this culture women are told they are the fair sex, but at the same time that their "beauty" needs lifting, shaping, dyeing, painting, curling, padding. Women are really being told that "the beauty" is a beast.[3]

The dynamics of idealization are beautifully contained in an analogy which Hawthorne, in typical fashion, remarks on casually: "But it would be as reasonable to say that one of those small blue stains which sometimes occur in the purest statuary marble would convert the Eve of Powers to a monster" [200]. This comparison, despite its apparent protest against just such a conclusion, implies that where women are concerned it doesn't take much to convert purity into monstrosity; Eve herself is a classic example of the ease with which such a transition can occur. And the transition is easy because the presentation of woman's image in marble is essentially an attempt to disguise and cover a monstrous reality. Thus, the slightest flaw will have an immense effect, for it serves as a reminder of the reality that produces the continual need to cast Eve in the form of purest marble and women in the molds of idealization.

3. Vivian Gornick and Barbara K. Moran, eds., *Woman in Sexist Society: Studies in Power and Powerlessness* (New York: Basic Books, 1971), p. 192.

In exploring the sources of men's compulsion to idealize women Hawthorne is writing a story about the sickness of men, not a story about the flawed and imperfect nature of women. There is a hint of the nature of Aylmer's ailment in the description of his relation to "mother" Nature, a suggestion that his revulsion for Georgiana has its root in part in a jealousy of the power which her sexuality represents and a frustration in the face of its inpenetrable mystery. Aylmer's scientific aspirations have as their ultimate goal the desire to create human life, but "the latter pursuit, however, Aylmer had long laid aside in unwilling recognition of the truth—against which all seekers sooner or later stumble—that our great creative Mother, while she amuses us with apparently working in the broadest sunshine, is yet severely careful to keep her own secrets, and, in spite of her pretended openness, shows us nothing but results. She permits us, indeed, to mar, but seldom to mend, and, like a jealous patentee, on no account to make" [203]. This passage is striking for its undercurrent of jealousy, hostility, and frustration toward a specifically female force. In the vision of Nature as playing with man, deluding him into thinking he can acquire her power, and then at the last minute closing him off and allowing him only the role of one who mars, Hawthorne provides another version of woman as enemy, the force that interposes between man and the accomplishment of his deepest desires. Yet Hawthorne locates the source of this attitude in man's jealousy of woman's having something he does not and his rage at being excluded from participating in it.

Out of Aylmer's jealousy at feeling less than Nature and thus less than woman—for if Nature is woman, woman is also Nature and has, by virtue of her biology, a power he does not—comes his obsessional program for perfecting Georgiana. Believing he is less, he has to convince himself he is more: "and then, most beloved, what will be my triumph when I shall have corrected what Nature left imperfect in her fairest work! Even Pygmalion, when his sculptured woman assumed life, felt not greater ecstasy than mine will be" [202]. What a triumph indeed to upstage and outdo Nature and make himself superior to her. The function of the fantasy that underlies the myth of Pygmalion, as it underlies the myth of Genesis (making Adam, in the words of Mary Daly, "the first among history's unmarried pregnant males"[4]), is obvious from the reality which it seeks to invert. Such myths are powerful image builders, salving man's injured ego by convincing him that he is not only equal to but better than woman, for he creates in spite of, against, and finally better than nature. Yet Aylmer's failure here is as certain as the failure of his other "experiments," for the sickness which he carries within him makes him able only to destroy, not to create.

4. Mary Daly, *Beyond God the Father* (Boston: Beacon P, 1973), p. 195. It is useful to compare Daly's analysis of "Male Mothers" with Ellmann's discussion of the "imagined motherhood of the male" in *Thinking About Women*, pp. 15ff. It is obvious that this myth is prevalent in patriarchal culture, and it would seem reasonable to suggest that the patterns of cooptation noticed in "Rip Van Winkle" and "I Want to Know Why" are minor manifestations of it. *An American Dream* provides a major manifestation, in fact a tour de force, of the myth of male motherhood.

If Georgiana is envied and hated because she represents what is different from Aylmer and reminds him of what he is not and cannot be, she is feared for her similarity to him and for the fact that she represents aspects of himself that he finds intolerable. Georgiana is as much a reminder to Aylmer of what he is as of what he is not. This apparently contradictory pattern of double-duty is understandable in the light of feminist analyses of female characters in literature, who frequently function this way. Mirrors for men, they serve to indicate the involutions of the male psyche with which literature is primarily concerned, and their characters and identities shift accordingly. They are projections, not people; and thus coherence of characterization is a concept that often makes sense only when applied to the male characters of a particular work. Hawthorne's tale is a classic example of the woman as mirror, for, despite Aylmer's belief that his response to Georgiana is an objective concern for the intellectual and spiritual problem she presents, it is obvious that his reaction to her is intensely subjective. "Shocks you, my husband?" queries Georgiana [199], thus neatly exposing his mask, for one is not shocked by objective perceptions. Indeed, Aylmer views Georgiana's existence as a personal insult and threat to him, which, of course, it is, because what he sees in her is that part of himself he cannot tolerate. By the desire she elicits in him to marry her and possess her birthmark, she forces him to confront his own earthiness and "imperfection."

But it is precisely to avoid such a confrontation that Aylmer has fled to the kingdom of science, where he can project himself as a "type of the spiritual element." Unlike Georgiana, in whom the physical and the spiritual are complexly intertwined, Aylmer is hopelessly alienated from himself. Through the figure of Aminadab, the shaggy creature of clay, Hawthorne presents sharply the image of Aylmer's alienation. Aminadab symbolizes that earthly, physical, erotic self that has been split off from Aylmer, that he refuses to recognize as part of himself, and that has become monstrous and grotesque as a result: "With his vast strength, his shaggy hair, his smoky aspect, and the indescribable earthiness that incrusted him, he seemed to represent man's physical nature; while Aylmer's slender figure, and pale, intellectual face, were no less apt a type of the spiritual element" [203]. Aminadab's allegorical function is obvious and so is his connection to Aylmer, for while Aylmer may project himself as objective, intellectual, and scientific and while he may pretend to be totally unrelated to the creature whom he keeps locked up in his dark room to do his dirty work, he cannot function without him. It is Aminadab, after all, who fires the furnace for Aylmer's experiments; physicality provides the energy for Aylmer's "science" just as revulsion generates his investment in idealization. Aylmer is, despite his pretenses to the contrary, a highly emotional man: his scientific interests tend suspiciously toward fires and volcanoes; he is given to intense emotional outbursts; and his obsession with his wife's birthmark is a feeling so profound as to disrupt his entire life. Unable to accept himself for what he is, Aylmer constructs a mythology of science and adopts the character of a scientist to disguise his true nature and to hide his real motives, from himself as well as others. As a consequence, he acquires a way of acting out these motives without in fact having to be aware of them. One might describe "The Birthmark" as an exposé of science because it demonstrates the ease with which science can be invoked to conceal highly subjective motives. "The Birthmark" is an exposure of the realities that underlie the scientist's posture of objectivity and rationality and the claims of science to operate in an amoral and value-free world. Pale Aylmer, the intellectual scientist, is a mask for the brutish, earthy, soot-smeared Aminadab, just as the mythology of scientific research and objectivity finally masks murder, disguising Georgiana's death as just one more experiment that failed.

Hawthorne's attitude toward men and their fantasies is more critical than either Irving's or Anderson's. One responds to Aylmer not with pity but with horror. For, unlike Irving and Anderson, Hawthorne has not omitted from his treatment of men an image of the consequences of their ailments for the women who are involved with them. The result of Aylmer's massive self-deception is to live in an unreal world, a world filled with illusions, semblances, and appearances, one which admits of no sunlight and makes no contact with anything outside itself and at whose center is a laboratory, the physical correlative of his utter solipsism. Nevertheless, Hawthorne makes it clear that Aylmer has got someone locked up in that laboratory with him. While "The Birthmark" is by no means explicitly feminist, since Hawthorne seems as eager to be misread and to conceal as he is to be read and to reveal, still it is impossible to read his story without being aware that Georgiana is completely in Aylmer's power. For the subject is finally power. Aylmer is able to project himself onto Georgiana and to work out his obsession through her because as woman and as wife she is his possession and in his power; and because as man he has access to the language and structures of that science which provides the mechanisms for such a process and legitimizes it. In addition, since the power of definition and the authority to make those definitions stick is vested in men, Aylmer can endow his illusions with the weight of spiritual aspiration and universal truth.

The implicit feminism in "The Birthmark" is considerable. On one level the story is a study of sexual politics, of the powerlessness of women and of the psychology which results from that powerlessness. Hawthorne dramatizes the fact that woman's identity is a product of men's responses to her: "It must not be concealed, however, that the impression wrought by this fairy sign manual varied exceedingly, according to the difference of temperament in the beholders" [200]. To those who love Georgiana, her birthmark is evidence of her beauty; to those who envy or hate her, it is an object of disgust. It is Aylmer's repugnance for the birthmark that makes Georgiana blanch, thus causing the mark to emerge as a sharply defined blemish against the whiteness of her cheek. Clearly, the birthmark takes on its character from the eye of the beholder. And just as clearly Georgiana's attitude toward her birthmark varies in response to different observers and definers. Her self-image derives from internalizing the attitudes toward her of the man or men around her. Since what surrounds Georgiana is an obsessional attraction expressed as a total revulsion, the result is not surprising: continual self-consciousness that leads to a pervasive sense of shame and a self-hatred that terminates in an utter readiness to be killed. "The Birthmark" demonstrates the consequences to women of being trapped in the laboratory of man's mind, the object of unrelenting scrutiny, examination, and experimentation.

In addition, "The Birthmark" reveals an implicit understanding of the consequences for women of a linguistic system in which the word "man" refers to both male people and all people. Because of the conventions of this system, Aylmer is able to equate his peculiarly male needs with the needs of all human beings, men and women. And since Aylmer can present his compulsion to idealize and perfect Georgiana as a human aspiration, Georgiana is forced to identify with it. Yet to identify with his aspiration is in fact to identify with his hatred of her and his need to eliminate her. Georgiana's situation is a fictional version of the experience that women undergo when they read a story like "Rip Van Winkle." Under the influence of Aylmer's mind, in the laboratory where she is subjected to his subliminal messages, Georgiana is co-opted into a view of herself as flawed and comes to hate herself as an impediment to Aylmer's aspiration; eventually she wishes to be dead rather than to remain alive as an irritant to him and as a reminder of his failure. And as she identifies with him in her attitude toward herself, so she comes to worship him for his hatred of her and for his refusal to tolerate her existence. The process of projection is neatly reversed: he locates in her everything he cannot accept in himself, and she attributes to him all that is good and then worships in him the image of her own humanity.

Through the system of sexual politics that is Aylmer's compensation for growing up, Hawthorne shows how men gain power over women, the power to create and kill, to "mar," "mend," and "make," without ever having to relinquish their image as "nice guys." Under such a system there need be very few power struggles, because women are programmed to deny the validity of their own perceptions and responses and to accept male illusions as truth. Georgiana does faint when she first enters Aylmer's laboratory and sees it for one second with her own eyes; she is also aware that Aylmer is filling her chamber with appearances, not realities; and she is finally aware that his scientific record is in his own terms one of continual failure. Yet so perfect is the program that she comes to respect him even more for these failures and to aspire to be yet another of them.

Hawthorne's unrelenting emphasis on "seems" and his complex use of the metaphors and structures of disguise imply that women are being deceived and destroyed by man's system. And perhaps the most vicious part of this system is its definition of what constitutes nobility in women: "Drink, then, thou lofty creature," exclaims Aylmer with "fervid admiration" as he hands Georgiana the cup that will kill her [210].

Loftiness in women is directly equivalent to the willingness with which they die at the hands of their husbands, and since such loftiness is the only thing about Georgiana which does elicit admiration from Aylmer, it is no wonder she is willing. Georgiana plays well the one role allowed her, yet one might be justified in suggesting that Hawthorne grants her at the end a slight touch of the satisfaction of revenge: " 'My poor Aylmer,' she repeated, with a more than human tenderness, 'you have aimed loftily; you have done nobly. Do not repent that with so high and pure a feeling, you have rejected the best the earth could offer' " [211]. Since dying is the only option, best to make the most of it.

CINDY WEINSTEIN

The Invisible Hand Made Visible: "The Birth-mark"†

"The Custom-House" places us firmly in the world of antebellum America, even as "The Market-Place," chapter 2 of *The Scarlet Letter*, situates us "not less than two centuries ago" (77) [37]. The culture of the nineteenth century unmistakably takes precedence over that of the seventeenth. "The Birth-mark," to the contrary, directs us quite clearly back to "the latter part of the last century" (764) [199]. It is thus not beside the point to consider the ways in which economic analyses of the eighteenth century, particularly those relating to the issue of circulation, might pertain to the economic circulations in "The Birth-mark." Another reading of the birthmark that adds to the debate about the "Crimson Hand" (766) [200], the "spectral Hand" (766) [201], the "odious Hand" (767) [201], and the "Bloody Hand" (765) [200] yet one more hand could be construed as this critic's obsessive reproduction of Aylmer's fetishism. To this end, a glance at the invisible hand of Adam Smith, which makes its appearance in perhaps this most famous passage from *The Wealth of Nations*, permits us to view Aylmer's actions from a different and enlightening perspective: "By preferring the support of domestic to that of foreign industry, he intends only his own security; and by directing that industry in such a manner as its produce may be of the greatest value, he intends only his own gain, and he is in this, as in many other cases, led by an invisible hand to promote an end which was no part of his intention."[1] According to Smith, consequences often have little to do with one's intentions, because one's self-interested intention "frequently promotes [the interest] of the society more effectually than when [one] really intends to promote it" (28). This is clearly not the case in "The Birth-mark," where Aylmer's self-interested intentions bring about self-interested results that do every-

† From *The Literature of Labor and the Labors of Literature: Allegory in Nineteenth-Century American Fiction* (New York: Cambridge UP, 1995), 82–86. Page numbers in square brackets refer to this Norton Critical Edition.
1. Adam Smith, *An Inquiry into the Nature and Causes of the Wealth of Nations*, ed. James Rogers (Oxford: Clarendon Press, 1880), vol. 2, 28.

thing to preserve "his own security" and nothing to promote "the public good" (28). Have the goals of 1776, the year which saw the publication of *The Wealth of Nations* and the birth pangs of an American nation, been both forsaken by and made unavailable to America in the 1840s? If so, are we to read "The Birth-mark" as a nineteenth-century corrective to the misguided optimism of political economists like Adam Smith and John Locke, who believed that self-interest and the public good were not mutually exclusive in a society that functioned according to a laissez-faire market economy?[2] Tempting as this reading might be, Hawthorne's story seems less an indictment of a laissez-faire economy than of an economy that isn't laissez-faire enough. The tension at the heart of "The Birth-mark" is this: Aylmer's desired end is the invisible hand of Smith's market economy, but the means he deploys in achieving it fly in the face of Smith's economic directives.

What Hawthorne thought of Smith or whether he even read *The Wealth of Nations* has unfortunately not been documented. Sacvan Bercovitch, however, has recently claimed that the brand of irony at work in Hawthorne's representations of the Puritan past is an "historiographical equivalent of laissez-faire," a "counterpart to Adam Smith's concept of the invisible hand."[3] In following Bercovitch's lead, I want to argue that the free-market ideology at work in Smith's ideal of the invisible hand is, in part, what motivates Aylmer to erase the visible hand that is Georgiana's birthmark. But in living up to Smith's principles, Aylmer uses all the wrong strategies: not only is his task deeply intentional, which is antithetical to the unintentionality that governs the marketplace in *The Wealth of Nations*, but Aylmer's active intervention into Georgiana's body is, to say the least, the furthest thing from a policy of laissez-faire. Aylmer's antimarket means, in other words, will make it impossible for him to attain what he desires, the invisible hand and the subsequent power of the market, or something will go awry in the attempt to fulfill his wishes.

My discussion of the circulations in "The Birth-mark" and Georgiana's body, in particular, has thus far focused on the problematics of gender and signification raised by this state of instability. In moving to a discussion of the economic issues suggested by this thematic of circulation, it will be useful to consider another somewhat lengthier passage from *The Wealth of Nations* in which Smith figures the economic circulations of late-eighteenth-century Great Britain in blatantly physiological terms:

2. Although I emphasize Smith for the obvious reason that the figure of the hand so powerfully conjoins *The Wealth of Nations* and "The Birth-mark," the presence of Locke should also be noted. In *The Second Treatise of Government* (New York: Bobbs-Merrill, 1952), Locke notes that "a state of liberty . . . is not a state of license; though man in that state have an uncontrollable liberty to dispose of his person or possessions, yet he has not liberty to destroy himself, or so much as any creature in his possession" (5). The best discussion of Locke and antebellum configurations of the self can be found in Howard Horwitz's *By the Law of Nature: Form and Value in Nineteenth-Century America* (Oxford: Oxford Univ. Press, 1991).

3. Bercovitch, *The Office of The Scarlet Letter*, 41. For a brilliant discussion of Smith's thought, see Jean-Christophe Agnew, *Worlds Apart: The Market and the Theater in Anglo-American Thought, 1550–1750* (Cambridge: Cambridge Univ. Press, 1986), esp. 149–94. For a brief discussion of Smith's impact on American economic theory and the late-nineteenth-century novel, see Horwitz, *By the Law of Nature*, 126–8.

In her present condition, Great Britain resembles one of those unwholesome bodies in which some of the vital parts are overgrown, and which, upon that account, are liable to many dangerous disorders scarce incident to those in which all the parts are more properly proportioned. A small stop in that great bloodvessel, which has been artificially swelled beyond its natural dimensions, and through which an unnatural proportion of the industry and commerce of the country has been forced to circulate, is very likely to bring on the most dangerous disorders upon the whole body politic. . . . The blood, of which the circulation is stopped in some of the smaller vessels, easily disgorges itself into the greater, without occasioning any dangerous disorder; but, when it is stopped in any of the greater vessels, convulsions, apoplexy, or death are the immediate and unavoidable consequences. (186–87)

According to this description, Georgiana's birthmark could be registering a deeply disordered market. And this is indeed the case; not, however, because Georgiana's fluctuating blood supply manifests any disorder (her paling and blushing would be evidence of a healthy and mobile physiological state) but rather because Aylmer's inability to focus on anything but Georgiana's birthmark brings about a state not unlike the one described by Smith, in which "convulsions, apoplexy," *and* death are the "unavoidable consequences." We are frequently reminded of Aylmer's Ahab-like monomania: "Without intending it—nay, in spite of a purpose to the contrary—[he] reverted to this one disastrous topic" (766) [201] and a page later, "He had not been aware of the tyrannizing influence acquired by one idea over his mind" (767) [202].[4] The problem with the birthmark is not its instability or its uncontrollability or its mobility but the fact that Georgiana has it and Aylmer seems to want it. The birthmark registers Georgiana's ineluctable and successful participation in the market economy. As something Georgiana possesses, the birthmark is also Georgiana, and as such it represents Georgiana's capacity to possess more, and thus it becomes what Aylmer must have. Whereas Georgiana both possesses the "charm" (764) [199] of the birthmark and is possessed by it, Aylmer is clearly possessed by it but receives none of the benefits of possession. He possesses it at the end of the story, when, after receiving assurances from Georgiana that she will drink a potentially fatal elixir, Aylmer has appropriated the power of the market that had been located in the birthmark: "His spirit was ever on the march—ever ascending—and each instant required something that was beyond the scope of the instant before" (777) [209]. Capturing the spirit of [Henry Ward] Beecher and [William Ellery] Channing, Aylmer has recaptured his ever mobile spirit and transcendent identity by immobilizing and appropriating Georgiana's.

He succeeds in doing this by strategically manipulating the competitive principles of the market economy that inform the relations

4. Whereas Aylmer depends upon the fluctuating meanings of the birthmark to exert his power, Ahab attempts to empower himself by hypostatizing the meanings of Moby Dick.

among Georgiana, himself, and her/the birthmark. Aylmer's anxieties about the hermeneutic fluctuations of the birthmark are, as has already been suggested, further exacerbated by the fact of its proprietary indeterminacy; in other words, to whom does the birthmark belong? Is it Georgiana? Is Georgiana the birthmark's? These questions underscore the inextricable relation between matters of economy and the self at the same time as they bring us back to the task of defining Hawthorne's economics of allegory. Aylmer's commitment to erasure is also a commitment to ownership, requiring precisely those hermeneutic and proprietary indeterminacies that had seemed most worrisome. Anxiety producing as they may be, these indeterminacies nevertheless enable him to sustain the belief that Georgiana and her property, that is the birthmark, can be disengaged from one another through a process of disembodiment and thus permit Aylmer's territorial raids upon and into Georgiana's body. Aylmer's relation to Georgiana illustrates what Macpherson has called a "possessive market society," where "a man's energy and skill are his own, yet are regarded not as integral parts of his personality, but as possessions."[5] According to this logic, Aylmer assumes that Georgiana cannot both be the birthmark and possess it; therefore, he has an opportunity to own it. Similarly, in order for Georgiana to own the birthmark, she cannot be the birthmark. It is only by not owning the birthmark that she has a chance of owning it. Because her body has been constituted in the name of private property, the issue arises as to whose property she is now and whose she might become; Georgiana's body therefore functions as the site upon which the competitive spirit of the market economy plays itself out. The birthmark is Georgiana's property, and as property its ownership is transferrable or vulnerable, in this case to scientific experimentation. Yet as the ending of the story makes painfully clear, Georgiana *is* her property, or the birthmark. She both is it and owns it. Property that is not alienable is ultimately self-destructive. Because possession and identity are inextricable in the case of the birthmark, Georgiana commits a grave mistake in hoping that they might be separate. Interestingly enough, Aminadab puts his own finger on this logic when he first sees Georgiana lying unconscious in the laboratory: "If she were my wife, I'd never part with that birth-mark" (770) [203]. Aminadab might simply be communicating his aesthetic preference for Georgiana with a birthmark as opposed to Georgiana without one, but one can also hear in this sentence the inextricable connection between Georgiana's identity and the birthmark. She thinks, however, that in giving up the birthmark she can still be a person: "Either remove this dreadful Hand, or take my wretched life!" (768) [202]. Only when she realizes that her "or" will have to be an "and" will she understand what is at stake in the removal of the birthmark. The problem is not with alienable property but with property that won't be alienable.

Whereas in "The Celestial Rail-road" the disjunction between name

5. Macpherson, *The Political Theory of Possessive Individualism: Hobbes to Locke* (Oxford: Oxford UP, 1962), 48.

and character constituted allegorical subjects who either were controlled by the market or transcended it (and thereby most fully exemplified it), "The Birth-mark" produces allegorical subjects as a
consequence of applying the principles of the market economy to the
relation between persons and (their) bodies. Georgiana's birthmark
marks the surplus of meaning generated by the circulations of her
body, which are then transformed by Aylmer into a problem both of allegorical interpretation and economic possessiveness. What does her
birthmark signify, and who owns it? That these two questions follow
from one another, at least for Aylmer, suggests that allegory and the
market economy share the mechanism of generating and containing
surplus meaning (or value) in order to make that surplus available for
possession. Once Georgiana's proprietary relation to her body unravels
as a consequence of Aylmer's successful manipulation of the rules of
property, an economics of allegory reveals a configuration in which the
omnipotence and transcendence of one character, in this case Aylmer,
depend upon the geographical and characterological immobility of
others, namely Georgiana and to a lesser extent Aminadab. Like Mr.
Smooth-it-away [in Hawthorne's "The Celestial Rail-Road"], who in
seeming to have escaped the exigencies of the market most clearly represented it, Aylmer controls the instabilities of the market, which were
most clearly embodied by Georgiana, but the market cannot exist
without precisely those instabilities that continually present the occasions for his acts of transcendence.

    In making visible the circulations of the physiological and economic
systems that define the late-eighteenth-century world of Aylmer and
Georgiana, the birthmark locates upon Georgiana's body a version of
the market's circulatory system, whose movements are nicely depicted
as Georgiana experiences "a stirring up of her system,—a strange
indefinite sensation creeping through her veins, and tingling, half
painfully, half pleasurably, at her heart" (773–4) [206]. Having destroyed the birthmark as well as his wife, Aylmer has returned the market to its rightful owner—himself. His antipathy to the birthmark was
never really the fact of its uncontrollability but rather the fact that
Georgiana was both the possessor of and the one possessed by the
market's powerful uncontrollability. In the true spirit of Adam Smith,
Aylmer has restored the invisibility to the hand that Georgiana had
made visible.

Nathaniel Hawthorne:
A Chronology

1804	Born July 4 in Salem, Massachusetts.
1808	Hawthorne's father, a ship captain, dies of yellow fever in Surinam (Dutch Guiana). Hawthorne's mother moves her three children in with her parents, the Mannings.
1813	Receives a mysterious leg injury that lays him up for months.
1816	Hawthornes visit the family property in Raymond, Maine, where Hawthorne enjoyed hunting and fishing.
1820	With his sister Louisa publishes a neighborhood paper, the *Spectator*.
1821	Enters Bowdoin College in Brunswick, Maine, where his classmates include lifelong friends Franklin Pierce, Horatio Bridge, and Henry Wadsworth Longfellow, among others.
1825	An undistinguished student, Hawthorne graduates from Bowdoin in September just barely in the top half of his class; returns to Salem after graduation and lives with his mother and sisters in the Manning household.
1828	Pays $100 to have his first novel, *Fanshawe*, published, but he would subsequently repudiate the novel, which is loosely based on his experiences at Bowdoin.
1830	Publishes sketches (including "Mrs. Hutchinson") and tales ("The Hollow of Three Hills" and "An Old Woman's Tale") in the *Salem Gazette*.
1831–36	Publishes many tales and sketches, most of them in *The Token*, an annual gift book by Samuel Goodrich, but is unsuccessful in finding a publisher for three different collections of tales during this period (*Seven Tales of My Native Land*, *Provincial Tales*, and *The Story Teller*).
1836	Edits the short-lived *American Magazine of Useful and Entertaining Knowledge*. Publishes Peter Parley's *Universal History on the Basis of Geography* for Samuel Goodrich.
1837	The American Stationers Company of Boston publishes *Twice-Told Tales*, a collection of eighteen tales and sketches that includes "The Gentle Boy," "Wakefield," "The May-Pole of Merry Mount," and "The Minister's Black Veil." Franklin Pierce tries to have Hawthorne appointed historiographer on the South Seas Expedition commanded by Charles Wilkes. Meets Sophia Peabody.

1838   Begins publishing tales in the *United States Magazine and Democratic Review*, founded and edited by John Louis O'Sullivan. Hawthorne becomes romantically involved with Mary Silsbee and considers challenging O'Sullivan to a duel on her account. During the summer, Hawthorne spends two months in western Massachusetts. He also begins his courtship of Sophia Peabody.

1839   Appointed inspector in the Boston Custom House at an annual salary of $1100. Publishes *The Gentle Boy: A Thrice-Told Tale*, featuring an engraving by Sophia.

1840   Publishes *Grandfather's Chair*, a collection of historical sketches for children.

1841   Publishes *Famous Old People* and *Liberty Tree*, two more children's books. Leaving his job at the Boston Custom House, Hawthorne buys two $500 shares in Brook Farm, a utopian community founded by George Ripley, with the idea that he and Sophia can live there when they marry. Hawthorne lives at Brook Farm from April to November.

1842   A second, expanded edition of *Twice-Told Tales* appears. Marries Sophia Peabody (July 9) and moves into the Old Manse in Concord, Massachusetts, adjacent to the field where the first battle of the Revolutionary War was fought. Henry David Thoreau had planted a vegetable garden for the newlyweds. During his three years in Concord, Hawthorne gets to know Ralph Waldo Emerson, Margaret Fuller, William Ellery Channing, and Thoreau, among others.

1844   The Hawthornes' daughter Una is born (March 3).

1845   Publishes the *Journal of an African Cruiser*, an edited account of his Bowdoin friend Horatio Bridge's journey to Africa. Leaves Concord in November, largely for financial reasons, and moves his family back to Salem.

1846   Appointed surveyor of the Salem Custom House (April) at an annual salary of $1,200. The Hawthornes' son Julian is born on June 22. Publishes *Mosses from an Old Manse*, which includes such tales as "Young Goodman Brown," "The Birth-mark," "The Artist of the Beautiful," "Rappaccini's Daughter," and "Roger Malvin's Burial."

1847   Moves his family into a larger house on Mall Street in Salem.

1849   Removed from his job in the Custom House by the newly elected Whig administration. Mother dies on July 31. Begins writing *The Scarlet Letter*.

1850   *The Scarlet Letter* is published on March 16 and goes through three editions in nine months. The Hawthornes move to Lenox in western Massachusetts, where Hawthorne meets Herman Melville on August 5. Melville's essay, "Hawthorne and His Mosses," appears in the August 17 and 24 issues of Evert Duyckinck's *Literary World*.

1851   Publishes *The House of the Seven Gables, The Snow Image and Other Twice-Told Tales,* and *The Wonder Book.* The Hawthornes' daughter Rose is born on May 20. Hawthornes leave Lenox in November for West Newton, Massachusetts, outside of Boston.

1852   Publishes *The Blithedale Romance* and a campaign biography for his old friend, presidential candidate Franklin Pierce. Buys the only house he will ever own in Concord, Massachusetts, and names it the Wayside.

1853   Publishes *Tanglewood Tales.* Appointed U.S. consul in Liverpool by President Pierce. Hawthornes leave for England in July.

1857–59   After resigning the consulship, Hawthorne briefly tours the British Isles and France before settling in Italy (Rome and Florence), prolonging his stay when Una contracts "Roman fever."

1859   Returns to England.

1860   Publishes *The Marble Faun.* Returns to the United States and to the Wayside in Concord after seven years abroad.

1862   Journeys to Washington, D.C., with publisher William Ticknor. Meets President Abraham Lincoln. Publishes "Chiefly About War-Matters" in the *Atlantic Monthly.*

1863   Publishes *Our Old Home,* a book of reminiscences about England, and dedicates it to Franklin Pierce.

1864   Dies on May 19 in Plymouth, New Hampshire, where he had traveled with Franklin Pierce. Buried in Concord's Sleepy Hollow cemetery on May 23.

Selected Bibliography

• indicates works included, excerpted, or adapted in this volume.

WEB SITES

Hawthorne in Salem.
Nathaniel Hawthorne Society. <asweb.artsci.uc.edu/english/HawthorneSociety/nh.html >

BIBLIOGRAPHIES AND OTHER SCHOLARLY RESOURCES

Boswell, Jeanetta. *Nathaniel Hawthorne and the Critics: A Checklist of Criticism, 1900–1978.* Metuchen: Scarecrow, 1982.

Clark, C. E. Frazer, Jr. *Nathaniel Hawthorne: A Descriptive Bibliography.* Pittsburgh: U of Pittsburgh P, 1978.

Cohen, B. Bernard, ed. *The Recognition of Nathaniel Hawthorne.* Ann Arbor: U of Michigan P, 1969.

Crowley, J. Donald, ed. *Hawthorne: The Critical Heritage.* New York: Barnes and Noble, 1970.

Gale, Robert L. *A Nathaniel Hawthorne Encyclopedia.* Westport: Greenwood, 1991.

Idol, John L., Jr., and Buford Jones, eds. *Nathaniel Hawthorne: The Contemporary Reviews.* New York: Cambridge UP, 1994.

Ricks, Beatrice, Joseph D. Adams, and Jack O. Hazlerig, eds. *Nathaniel Hawthorne: A Reference Bibliography, 1900–1971.* Boston: G. K. Hall, 1972.

Scharnhorst, Gary, ed. *The Critical Response to Nathaniel Hawthorne's* The Scarlet Letter. Westport: Greenwood, 1992.

———, ed. *Nathaniel Hawthorne: An Annotated Bibliography of Commentary and Criticism before 1900.* Metuchen: Scarecrow, 1988.

BIOGRAPHY

Bridge, Horatio. *Personal Recollections of Nathaniel Hawthorne.* New York: Harper, 1893.

Cantwell, Robert. *Nathaniel Hawthorne: The American Years.* New York: 1948.

Conway, Moncure D. *Life of Nathaniel Hawthorne.* New York: Lovell, 1890.

Fields, James T. *Yesterdays with Authors.* Boston: Houghton Mifflin, 1871.

Hawthorne, Julian. *Nathaniel Hawthorne and His Circle.* New York: Harper & Brothers, 1903.

———. *Nathaniel Hawthorne and His Wife: A Biography.* 2nd ed. 2 vols. Boston: James Osgood, 1885.

Herbert, T. Walter. *Dearest Beloved: The Hawthornes and the Making of the Middle-Class Family.* Berkeley: U of California P, 1993.

Lathrop, Rose Hawthorne. *Memories of Hawthorne* (1897). Boston: Houghton Mifflin, 1923.

Loggins, Vernon. *The Hawthornes: The Story of Seven Generations of an American Family.* New York: Columbia UP, 1951.

Mellow, James R. *Nathaniel Hawthorne in His Times.* Boston: Houghton Mifflin, 1980.

Miller, Edwin Haviland. *Salem Is My Dwelling Place: The Life of Nathaniel Hawthorne.* Iowa City: U of Iowa P, 1991.

Moore, Margaret. *The Salem World of Nathaniel Hawthorne.* Columbia: U of Missouri P, 1997.

Stewart, Randall. *Nathaniel Hawthorne: A Biography.* New Haven: Yale UP, 1948.

Ticknor, Caroline. *Hawthorne and His Publisher.* Boston: Houghton Mifflin, 1913.

Turner, Arlin. *Nathaniel Hawthorne: A Biography.* New York: Oxford UP, 1980.

Van Doren, Mark. *Nathaniel Hawthorne: A Critical Biography.* New York: William Sloane, 1949.

Wineapple, Brenda. *Hawthorne: A Life.* New York: Knopf, 2003.

Woodberry, George E. *Nathaniel Hawthorne* (1902). New York: Chelsea House, 1980.

SELECTED CRITICISM OF *THE SCARLET LETTER*

Abel, Darrel. "Hawthorne's Pearl: Symbol and Character." *ELH* 18 (1951): 50–66.

———. *The Moral Picturesque: Studies in Hawthorne's Fiction.* West Lafayette: Purdue UP, 1988.

• Anderson, Douglas. "Jefferson, Hawthorne, and 'The Custom-House.' " *Nineteenth-Century Literature* 46 (1991): 309–26.

Arac, Jonathan. "The Politics of *The Scarlet Letter*." In *Ideology and Classic American Literature*. Ed. Sacvan Bercovitch and Myra Jehlen. New York: Cambridge UP, 1986. 247–66.

Arvin, Newton. *Hawthorne*. Boston: Little, Brown, 1929.

Barlowe, Jamie. *The Scarlet Mob of Scribblers: Rereading Hester Prynne*. Carbondale: Southern Illinois UP, 2000.

Barnett, Louise K. "Speech and Society in *The Scarlet Letter*." *ESQ* 29 (1983): 16–24.

Bayer, John. "Narrative Technique and the Oral Tradition in *The Scarlet Letter*." *American Literature* 52 (1980): 250–63.

Baym, Nina. "Passion and Authority in *The Scarlet Letter*." *New England Quarterly* 43 (1970): 209–30.

———. "Revisiting Hawthorne's Feminism." *Nathaniel Hawthorne Review* 30 (Fall & Spring 2004): 32–55.

———. "The Romantic *Malgré Lui*: Hawthorne in 'The Custom-House.' " *ESQ* 19 (1973): 14–25.

———. *The Scarlet Letter: A Reading*. Boston: Twayne, 1986.

———. *The Shape of Hawthorne's Career*. Ithaca: Cornell UP, 1976.

Becker, John E. *Hawthorne's Historical Allegory: An Examination of the American Conscience*. Port Washington, NY: Kennikat, 1971.

Bell, Michael Davitt. "Arts of Deception: Hawthorne, 'Romance,' and *The Scarlet Letter*." *New Essays on* The Scarlet Letter. Ed. Michael J. Colacurcio. New York: Cambridge UP, 1985. 29–56.

———. *Hawthorne and the Historical Romance of New England*. Princeton: Princeton UP, 1971.

Bell, Millicent. *Hawthorne's View of the Artist*. New York: State U of New York P, 1962.

———, ed. *New Essays on Hawthorne's Major Tales*. New York: Cambridge UP, 1993.

———. "The Obliquity of Signs: *The Scarlet Letter*." *Massachusetts Review* 23 (1982): 9–26.

Bensick, Carol M. "Dimmesdale and His Bachelorhood: 'Priestly Celibacy' in *The Scarlet Letter*." *Studies in American Fiction* 21 (1993): 103–10.

———. "His Folly, Her Weakness: Demystified Adultery in *The Scarlet Letter*." *New Essays on* The Scarlet Letter. Ed. Michael J. Colacurcio. New York: Cambridge UP, 1985. 137–59.

Bentley, Nancy. *The Ethnography of Manners: Hawthorne, James, Wharton*. Cambridge: Cambridge UP, 1995.

• Bercovitch, Sacvan. *The Office of* The Scarlet Letter. Baltimore: Johns Hopkins UP, 1991.

———. "*The Scarlet Letter*: A Twice-Told Tale." *Nathaniel Hawthorne Review* 22.2 (1996): 1–20.

Berlant, Lauren. *The Anatomy of National Fantasy: Hawthorne, Utopia, and Everyday Life*. Chicago: U of Chicago P, 1991.

Bernstein, Cynthia. "Reading *The Scarlet Letter*: Against Hawthorne's Fictional Interpretive Communities." *Language and Literature* 18 (1993): 1–20.

Boewe, Charles, and Murray G. Murphy. "Hester Prynne in History." *American Literature* 32 (1960): 202–04.

Boudreau, Kristin. "*The Scarlet Letter* and the 1833 Murder Trial of the Reverend Ephraim Avery." *ESQ* 47 (2001): 89–112.

•———. *Sympathy in American Literature: American Sentiments from Jefferson to the Jameses*. Gainesville: UP of Florida, 2002. 49–82.

Branch, Watson. "From Allegory to Romance: Hawthorne's Transformation of *The Scarlet Letter*." *Modern Philology* 80.2 (Nov. 1982): 145–60.

Brodhead, Richard H. *Cultures of Letters: Scenes of Reading and Writing in Nineteenth-Century America*. Chicago: U of Chicago P, 1993.

———. *Hawthorne, Melville, and the Novel*. Chicago: U of Chicago P, 1976.

———. *The School of Hawthorne*. New York: Oxford UP, 1986.

Bronstein, Zelda. "The Parabolic Ploys of *The Scarlet Letter*." *American Quarterly* 39 (1987): 193–210.

Brooke-Rose, Christine. "A for But: 'The Custom-House' in Hawthorne's *The Scarlet Letter*." *Word and Image* 3 (1987): 143–55.

Brown, Gillian. *Domestic Individualism: Imagining Self in Nineteenth-Century America*. Berkeley: U of California P, 1990.

———. "Hawthorne, Inheritance, and Women's Property." *Studies in the Novel* 23 (Spring 1991): 107–18.

Browner, Stephanie P. "Authorizing the Body: Scientific Medicine and *The Scarlet Letter*." *Literature and Medicine* 12 (1993): 139–60.

Budick, Emily Miller. *Engendering Romance: Women Writers and the Hawthorne Tradition, 1850–1990*. New Haven: Yale UP, 1994.

———. "Hester's Skepticism, Hawthorne's Faith: Or, What Does a Woman Doubt? Instituting the American Romance Tradition." *New Literary History* 22 (1991): 199–211.

———. "Pearl's Feet and the Real of Hawthorean R/romance." *Nathaniel Hawthorne Review* 30 (Fall & Spring 2004): 187–216.

Cameron, Sharon. *The Corporeal Self: Allegories of the Body in Melville and Hawthorne*. Baltimore: Johns Hopkins UP, 1981.

Carpenter, Frederic I. "Scarlet A Minus." *College English* 5 (1944): 173–80.

Carton, Evan. " 'A Daughter of the Puritans' and Her Old Master: Hawthorne, Una, and the Sexuality of Romance." In *Daughters and Fathers*. Ed. Lynda E. Boose and Betty S. Flowers. Baltimore: Johns Hopkins UP, 1989. 208–32.

———. *The Rhetoric of American Romance*. Baltimore: Johns Hopkins UP, 1985.

Cheyfitz, Eric. "The Irresistibleness of Great Literature: Reconstructing Hawthorne's Politics." *American Literary History* 6 (Fall 1994): 539–58.

Clark, C. E. Fraser. " 'Posthumous Papers of a Decapitated Surveyor.' " *Studies in the Novel* 2 (1970): 395–419.

Coale, Samuel Chase. *Mesmerism and Hawthorne: Mediums of American Romance*. Tuscaloosa: U of Alabama P, 1998.

———. "*The Scarlet Letter* as Icon." *ATQ* 6 (1992): 251–62.

• Colacurcio, Michael J. "Footsteps of Ann Hutchinson: The Context of *The Scarlet Letter*." *ELH* 39 (1972): 459–94.

———. *The Province of Piety: Moral History in Hawthorne's Early Tales*. Cambridge: Harvard UP, 1984.

———. "The Woman's Own Choice: Sex, Metaphor, and the Puritan 'Sources' of *The Scarlet Letter*." In *New Essays on* The Scarlet Letter. Ed. Michael J. Colacurcio. Cambridge: Cambridge UP, 1985. 101–35.

Cottom, Daniel. "Hawthorne versus Hester: The Ghostly Dialectic of Romance in *The Scarlet Letter*." *Texas Studies in Literature and Language* 24 (1981): 47–67.

Cox, James M. "*The Scarlet Letter*: Through the Old Manse and the Custom House." *Virginia Quarterly Review* 51 (1975): 432–47.

Crain, Patricia. *The Story of A: The Alphabetization of America from the New England Primer to* The Scarlet Letter. Stanford: Stanford UP, 2000.

Crews, Frederick. *The Sins of the Fathers: Hawthorne's Psychological Themes*. New York: Oxford UP, 1966.

Cronin, Morton. "Hawthorne on Romantic Love and the Status of Women." *PMLA* 69 (1954): 89–98.

Cuddy, Lois A. "Mother-Daughter Identification in *The Scarlet Letter*." *Mosaic* 19 (1986): 101–15.

Dauber, Kenneth. *Rediscovering Hawthorne*. Princeton: Princeton UP, 1977.

Davidson, Edward H. *Hawthorne's Last Phase*. New Haven: Yale UP, 1949.

Davis, Sarah I. "Another View of Hester and the Antinomians." *Studies in American Fiction* 12 (1984): 189–98.

Dekker, George. *The American Historical Romance*. Cambridge: Cambridge UP, 1987.

Derrick, Scott S. " 'A Curious Subject of Observation and Inquiry': Homoeroticism, the Body, and Authorship in Hawthorne's *The Scarlet Letter*." *Novel* 28 (1995): 308–26.

• DeSalvo, Louise. *Nathaniel Hawthorne*. Atlantic Highlands: Humanities P, 1987. 57–76.

Diehl, Joanne Feit. "Re-Reading *The Letter*: Hawthorne, the Fetish, and the (Family) Romance." *New Literary History* 19 (1988): 655–73.

Diffee, Christopher. "Postponing Politics in Hawthorne's *Scarlet Letter*." *Modern Language Notes* 111 (1996): 835–71.

Dolis, John. *The Style of Hawthorne's Gaze: Regarding Subjectivity*. Tuscaloosa: U of Alabama P, 1993.

Donahue, Agnes McNeil. *Hawthorne: Calvin's Ironic Stepchild*. Kent, OH: Kent State UP, 1985.

Doubleday, Neil Frank. *Hawthorne's Early Tales: A Critical Study*. Durham: Duke UP, 1972.

Dryden, Edgar A. *Nathaniel Hawthorne: The Poetics of Enchantment*. Ithaca: Cornell UP, 1977.

Dunne, Michael. *Hawthorne's Narrative Strategies*. Jackson: UP of Mississippi, 1995.

Egan, Ken. "The Adultress in the Market-Place: Hawthorne and *The Scarlet Letter*." *Studies in the Novel* 27 (1995): 26–41.

Eakin, Paul John. "Hawthorne's Imagination and the Structure of 'The Custom-House.' " *American Literature* 43 (1971): 346–58.

Easton, Alison. *The Making of the Hawthorne Subject*. Columbia: U of Missouri P, 1996.

Elbert, Monica M. *Encoding the Letter "A": Gender and Authority in Hawthorne's Early Fiction*. Frankfurt: Haag & Herchen, 1990.

———. "Hester on the Scaffold, Dimmesdale in the Closet: Hawthorne's Seven-Year Itch." *Essays in Literature* 16 (1989): 234–55.

———. "Hester's Maternity: Stigma or Weapon?" *ESQ* 36 (1990): 175–208.

Elder, Marjorie J. *Nathaniel Hawthorne: Transcendental Symbolist*. Athens: Ohio UP, 1969.

Erlich, Gloria C. *Family Themes and Hawthorne's Fiction: The Tenacious Web*. New Brunswick: Rutgers UP, 1984.

Faust, Bertha. *Hawthorne's Contemporaneous Reputation: A Study of Literary Opinion in America and England, 1828–1864*. New York: Octagon Books, 1968.

Feidelson, Charles, Jr. "*The Scarlet Letter*." In *Hawthorne Centenary Essays*. Ed. Roy Harvey Pearce. Columbus: Ohio State UP, 1964. 31–77.

Fick, Rev. Leonard J. *The Light Beyond: A Study of Hawthorne's Theology*. Westminster: Newman, 1955.

Fleischner, Jennifer. "Hawthorne and the Politics of Slavery." *Studies in the Novel* 23 (1991): 96–106.

Fogle, Richard H. *Hawthorne's Fiction: The Light and the Dark*. Norman: U of Oklahoma P, 1964.

————. *Hawthorne's Imagery: The "Proper Light and Shadow" in the Major Romances*. Norman: U of Oklahoma P, 1969.

Foster, Dennis. "The Embroidered Sin: Confessional Evasion in *The Scarlet Letter*." *Criticism* 25 (1983): 141–63.

• Franzosa, John. " 'The Custom-House,' *The Scarlet Letter*, and Hawthorne's Separation from Salem." *ESQ* 24 (1978): 57–71.

Freed, Richard C. "Hawthorne's Reflexive Imagination: *The Scarlet Letter* as Compositional Allegory." *ATQ* 56 (1985): 31–54.

Fryer, Judith. *The Faces of Eve: Women in the Nineteenth-Century American Novel*. New York: Oxford UP, 1976.

Gable, Harvey L., Jr. *Liquid Fire: Transcendental Mysticism in the Romances of Nathaniel Hawthorne*. New York: Peter Lang, 1998.

Garlitz, Barbara. "Pearl: 1850–1955." *PMLA* 72 (1957): 689–99.

Gartner, Matthew. "*The Scarlet Letter* and the Book of Esther: Scriptural Letter and Narrative Life." *Studies in American Fiction* 23.2 (1995): 131–51.

Gilmore, Michael T. *American Romanticism and the Marketplace*. Chicago: U of Chicago P, 1985.

• ————. "Hawthorne and the Making of the Middle Class." In *Discovering Difference: Contemporary Essays in American Culture*. Ed. Christoph Lohmann. Bloomington: Indiana UP, 1993. 88–104.

————. "Hidden in Plain Sight: *The Scarlet Letter* and American Legibility." *Studies in American Fiction* 29 (Spring 2001): 121–28.

Ginsberg, Lesley. "The ABCs of *The Scarlet Letter*." *Studies in American Fiction* 29 (Spring 2001): 13–31.

Goddu, Teresa A. "Letters Turned to Gold: Hawthorne, Authorship, and Slavery." *Studies in American Fiction* 29 (Spring 2001): 49–76.

Gollin, Rita K. *Nathaniel Hawthorne and the Truth of Dreams*. Baton Rouge: Louisiana State UP, 1979.

————, and John L. Idol, Jr., eds. *Prophetic Pictures: Nathaniel Hawthorne's Knowledge and Uses of the Visual Arts*. Westport: Greenwood P, 1991.

Green, Carlanda. " 'The Custom-House': Hawthorne's Dark Wood of Error." *New England Quarterly* 53 (1980): 184–95.

Grossman, Jay. " 'A' is for Abolition?: Race, Authorship, *The Scarlet Letter*." *Textual Practice* 7 (1993): 13–30.

Hall, Lawrence Sargent. *Hawthorne: Critic of Society*. New Haven: Yale UP, 1944.

Harris, Kenneth Marc. *Hypocrisy and Self-Deception in Hawthorne's Fiction*. Charlottesville: UP of Virginia, 1988.

Harshbarger, Scott. "A 'H-ll-Fired Story': Hawthorne's Rhetoric of Rumor." *College English* 56 (1994): 30–45.

Hennelly, Mark M., Jr. "*The Scarlet Letter*: 'A Play-Day for the Whole World?' " *New England Quarterly* 61 (1988): 530–54.

Herbert, T. Walter. *Dearest Beloved: The Hawthornes and the Making of the Middle-Class Family*. Berkeley: U of California P, 1993.

• ————. "Nathaniel Hawthorne, Una Hawthorne, and *The Scarlet Letter*: Interactive Selfhoods and the Cultural Construction of Gender." *PMLA* 103 (1988): 285–97.

————. "Pornographic Manhood and *The Scarlet Letter*." *Studies in American Fiction* 29 (Spring 2001): 113–20.

Hewitt, Elizabeth. "Scarlet Letters, Dead Letters: Correspondence and the Poetics of Democracy in Melville and Hawthorne." *Yale Journal of Criticism* 12.2 (1999): 295–319.

Hilgers, Thomas L. "The Psychological Conflict Resolution in *The Scarlet Letter*." *ATQ* 43 (Summer 1979): 211–24.

Hodges, Elizabeth Perry. "The Letter of the Law: Reading Hawthorne and the Law of Adultery." In *Law and Literature Perspectives*. Ed. Bruce L. Rockwood and Roberta Kevelson. New York: Peter Lang, 1996. 133–68.

Hoeltje, H. H. *Inward Sky: The Mind and Heart of Nathaniel Hawthorne*. Durham: Duke UP, 1962.

Hoffman, Daniel G. *Form and Fable in American Fiction*. New York: Oxford UP, 1961.

Hull, Richard. "Sent Meaning vs. Attached Meaning: Two Interpretations of Interpretation in *The Scarlet Letter*." *ATQ* 14.2 (2000): 143–58.

Hutner, Gordon. *Secrets and Sympathy: Forms of Disclosure in Hawthorne's Novels*. Athens: U of Georgia P, 1988.

Idol, John L., Jr., and Melinda Ponder, eds. *Hawthorne and Women: Engendering and Expanding the Hawthorne Tradition*. Amherst: U of Massachusetts P, 1999.

Irwin, John T. *American Hieroglyphics: The Symbol of the Egyptian Hieroglyphics in the American Renaissance*. New Haven: Yale UP, 1980.

Isani, Mukhtar Ali. "Hawthorne and the Branding of William Prynne." *New England Quarterly* 45 (1972): 182–95.

Jacobson, Richard J. *Hawthorne's Conception of the Creative Process*. Cambridge: Harvard UP, 1965.

James, Henry. *Hawthorne*. London: Macmillan, 1879.

Johnson, Claudia Durst. "Impotence and Omnipotence in *The Scarlet Letter*." *New England Quarterly* 66 (1993): 594–612.

———. *The Productive Tension of Hawthorne's Art*. University: U of Alabama P, 1981.

———, ed. *Understanding* The Scarlet Letter: *A Student Casebook to Issues, Sources, and Historical Documents*. Westport, CT: Greenwood, 1995.

Kamuf, Peggy. "Hawthorne's Genres: The Letter of the Law *Appliquée*." In *After Strange Texts: The Role of Theory in the Study of Literature*. Ed. Gregory S. Jay and David L. Miller. Tuscaloosa: U of Alabama P, 1985. 69–84.

Kesselring, Marion L. *Hawthorne's Reading, 1828–1850*. New York: New York Public Library, 1949.

Kesterson, David B., ed. *Critical Essays on Hawthorne's* The Scarlet Letter. Boston: G. K. Hall, 1988.

Kilcup, Karen L. " 'Ourself behind Ourself, Concealed—': The Homoerotics of Reading in *The Scarlet Letter*." *ESQ* 42 (1996): 1–28.

Kimball, Samuel. "Countersigning Aristotle: The Amimetic Challenge of *The Scarlet Letter*." *ATQ* 7 (1993): 141–58.

Kopley, Richard. "Hawthorne's Transplanting and Transforming 'The Tell-Tale Heart.' " *Studies in American Fiction* 23 (1995): 231–41.

———. *The Threads of* The Scarlet Letter: *A Study of Hawthorne's Transformative Art*. Newark: U of Delaware P, 2003.

Korobkin, Laura Hanft. "The Scarlet Letter of the Law: Hawthorne and Criminal Justice." *Novel* 30 (1997): 193–217.

Kramer, Michael P. "Beyond Symbolism: Philosophy of Language in *The Scarlet Letter*." In *Imagining Language in America: From the Revolution to the Civil War*. Princeton: Princeton UP, 1992. 162–97.

Kreger, Erika M. " 'Depravity Dressed Up in a Fascinating Garb': Sentimental Motifs and the Seduced Hero(ine) in *The Scarlet Letter*." *Nineteenth-Century Literature* 54.3 (1999): 308–35.

Lang, Amy Schrager. *Prophetic Woman: Anne Hutchinson and the Problem of Dissent in the Literature of New England*. Berkeley: U of California P, 1987. 161–92.

Last, Suzan. "Hawthorne's Feminine Voices: Reading *The Scarlet Letter* as a Woman." *Journal of Narrative Technique* 27.3 (1997): 349–76.

Lathrop, George P. *A Study of Hawthorne*. Boston: Osgood, 1876.

Lawrence, D. H. *Studies in Classic American Literature*. 1923. Garden City, NY: Doubleday, 1953.

Lee, A. Robert. *Nathaniel Hawthorne: New Critical Essays*. New York: Barnes and Noble, 1982.

Lefcowitz, Allan. "*Apologia* Pro Roger Prynne: A Psychological Study." *Literature and Psychology* 24 (1974): 34–44.

Leverenz, David. *Manhood and the American Renaissance*. Ithaca: Cornell UP, 1989.

• ———. "Mrs. Hawthorne's Headache: Reading *The Scarlet Letter*." *Nineteenth-Century Fiction* 37 (1983): 552–73.

• Levine, Robert S. "Antebellum Feminists on Hawthorne: Reconsidering the Reception of *The Scarlet Letter*." An essay written for this Norton Critical Edition and published here for the first time.

Loving, Jerome. "Hawthorne's Awakening in the Customhouse." In *Lost in the Customhouse: Authorship in the American Renaissance*. Iowa City: U of Iowa P, 1993. 19–34.

Luedtke, Luther S. *Nathaniel Hawthorne and the Romance of the Orient*. Bloomington: Indiana UP, 1989.

Lundblad, Jane. *Nathaniel Hawthorne and European Literary Tradition*. New York: Russell and Russell, 1965.

Maddox, Lucy. *Removals: Nineteenth-Century American Literature and the Politics of Indian Affairs*. New York: Oxford UP, 1991.

Madsen, Deborah L. " 'A for Abolition': Hawthorne's Bond-servant and the Shadow of Slavery." *Journal of American Studies* 25 (1991): 255–59.

Male, Roy R. *Hawthorne's Tragic Vision*. New York: W. W. Norton & Company, 1957.

• Martin, Robert K. "Hester Prynne, *C'est Moi*: Nathaniel Hawthorne and the Anxieties of Gender." In *Engendering Men: The Question of Male Feminist Criticism*. Ed. Joseph A. Boone and Michael Cadden. New York: Routledge, 1990. 122–31.

Martin, Terence. "Dimmesdale's Ultimate Sermon." *Arizona Quarterly* 27 (1971): 230–40.

———. *Nathaniel Hawthorne*. Revised Edition. Boston: Twayne, 1983.

Matthiessen, F. O. *American Renaissance: Art and Expression in the Age of Emerson and Whitman*. New York: Oxford UP, 1941.

McGill, Meredith. "The Problem of Hawthorne's Popularity." In *Reciprocal Influences: Literary Production, Distribution, and Consumption in America*. Ed. Steven Fink and Susan S. Williams. Columbus: Ohio State UP, 1999. 24–54.

McNamara, Anne Marie. "The Character of Flame: The Function of Pearl in *The Scarlet Letter*." *American Literature* 27 (1956): 537–53.

McPherson, Hugo. *Hawthorne as Myth-Maker: A Study in Imagination*. Toronto: U of Toronto P, 1969.

McWilliams, John P., Jr. *Hawthorne, Melville, and the American Character: A Looking-Glass Business*. Cambridge: Cambridge UP, 1984.

Mellard, James M. "Inscriptions of the Subject: *The Scarlet Letter*." In *Using Lacan, Reading Fiction*. Urbana: U of Illinois P, 1991. 69–106.

Milder, Robert. "*The Scarlet Letter* and Its Discontents." *Nathaniel Hawthorne Review* 22.1 (1996): 9–25.

Miller, J. Hillis. *Hawthorne and History: Defacing It*. Cambridge: Basil Blackwell, 1991.

Millington, Richard H. *Practicing Romance: Narrative Form and Cultural Engagement in Hawthorne's Fiction*. Princeton: Princeton UP, 1992.

Mitchell, Thomas R. *Hawthorne's Fuller Mystery*. Amherst: U of Massachusetts P, 1998.

Mizruchi, Susan L. *The Power of Historical Knowledge: Narrating the Past in Hawthorne, James, and Dreiser*. Princeton: Princeton UP, 1988.

Moers, Ellen. "*The Scarlet Letter*: A Political Reading." *Prospects* 9 (1985): 49–70.

Nevins, Winfield S. "Nathaniel Hawthorne's Removal from the Salem Custom House." *Essex Institute Historical Collections* 53 (1917): 97–132.

Newberry, Frederick. *Hawthorne's Divided Loyalties: England and America in His Works*. Rutherford, NJ: Fairleigh Dickinson UP, 1987.

• ———. "A Red-Hot 'A' and a Lusting Divine: Sources for *The Scarlet Letter*." *New England Quarterly* 60.2 (June 1987): 256–64.

———. "Tradition and Disinheritance in *The Scarlet Letter*." *ESQ* 23 (1977): 1–26.

Newman, Lea B. V. *A Reader's Guide to the Short Stories of Nathaniel Hawthorne*. Boston: G. K. Hall, 1979.

Nissenbaum, Stephen. "The Firing of Nathaniel Hawthorne." *Essex Institute Historical Collections* 114 (1978): 57–86.

Norman, Jean. *Nathaniel Hawthorne: An Approach to an Analysis of Artistic Creation*. Trans. Derek Coltman. Cleveland: P of Case Western U, 1970.

Nudelman, Franny. " 'Emblem and Product of Sin': The Poisoned Child in *The Scarlet Letter* and Domestic Advice Literature." *Yale Journal of Criticism* 10.1 (1997): 193–213.

Pearce, Roy Harvey, ed. *Hawthorne Centenary Essays*. Columbus: Ohio State UP, 1964.

Person, Leland S. *Aesthetic Headaches: Women and a Masculine Poetics in Poe, Melville, and Hawthorne*. Athens: U of Georgia P, 1988. 122–38.

• ———. "The Dark Labyrinth of Mind: Hawthorne, Hester, and the Ironies of Racial Mothering." *Studies in American Fiction* 29 (Spring 2001): 33–48.

———. "Hester's Revenge: The Power of Silence in *The Scarlet Letter*." *Nineteenth-Century Literature* 43 (1989): 465–83.

———. "*The Scarlet Letter* and the Myth of the Divine Child." *ATQ* 44 (1979): 295–309.

Pfister, Joel. *The Production of Personal Life: Class, Gender, and the Psychological in Hawthorne's Fiction*. Stanford: Stanford UP, 1991.

Pimple, Kenneth D. " 'Subtle, but Remorseful Hypocrite': Dimmesdale's Moral Character." *Studies in the Novel* 25 (1993): 257–71.

Pryse, Marjorie. *The Mark and the Knowledge: Social Stigma in Classic American Fiction*. Columbus: Ohio State UP, 1979. 15–48.

Quirk, Tom. "Hawthorne's Last Tales and 'The Custom-House.' " *ESQ* 30 (1984): 220–31.

Ragussis, Michael. *Acts of Naming: The Family Plot in Fiction*. New York: Oxford UP, 1986. 65–68.

• Railton, Stephen. "The Address of *The Scarlet Letter*." In *Readers in History: Nineteenth-Century American Literature and the Contexts of Response*. Ed. James L. Machor. Baltimore: Johns Hopkins UP, 1993. 138–63.

• Reid, Bethany. "Narrative of the Captivity and Redemption of Roger Prynne: Rereading *The Scarlet Letter*." *Studies in the Novel* 33 (Fall 2001): 247–67.

Reid, Alfred S. *The Yellow Ruff and The Scarlet Letter: A Source of Hawthorne's Novel*. Gainesville: U of Florida P, 1955.

Reynolds, David S. "Hawthorne's Cultural Demons: History, Popular Culture, and *The Scarlet Letter*." In *Novel History: Historians and Novelists Confront America's Past (and Each Other)*. Ed. Mark C. Carnes. New York: Simon & Schuster, 2001. 229–34.

Reynolds, Larry J. *European Revolutions and the American Literary Renaissance*. New Haven: Yale UP, 1988.

———, ed. *A Historical Guide to Nathaniel Hawthorne*. New York: Oxford UP, 2001.

• ———. "*The Scarlet Letter* and Revolutions Abroad." *American Literature* 57.1 (March 1985): 44–67.

Rozakis, Laurie N. "Another Possible Source of Hawthorne's Hester Prynne." *ATQ* 59 (1986): 63–71. [Elizabeth Pain is the source.]

Sandeen, Ernest. "*The Scarlet Letter* as a Love Story." *PMLA* 77 (1962): 425–35.

Sanderlin, Reed. "Hawthorne's *Scarlet Letter*: A Study of the Meaning of Meaning." *Southern Humanities Review* 9 (1975): 145–57.

Savoy, Eric. " 'Filial Duty': Reading the Patriarchal Body in 'The Custom-House.' " *Studies in the Novel* 25 (1993): 397–417.

Scheiber, Andrew J. "Public Force, Private Sentiment: Hawthorne and the Gender of Politics." *ATQ* 2.4 (1988): 285–99.

Schiff, James. *Updike's Version: Rewriting The Scarlet Letter*. Columbia: U of Missouri P, 1992.

Schubert, Leland. *Hawthorne the Artist: Fine-Art Devices in Fiction*. Chapel Hill: U of North Carolina P, 1944.

Schwab, Gabriele. "Seduced by Witches: Nathaniel Hawthorne's *The Scarlet Letter* in the Context of New England Witchcraft Fictions." In *Seduction and Theory: Readings of Gender, Representation, and Rhetoric*. Ed. Diane Hunter. Urbana: U of Illinois P, 1989. 170–91.

Small, Michel. "Hawthorne's *The Scarlet Letter*: Arthur Dimmesdale's Manipulation of Language." *American Imago* 37 (1980): 113–23.

Smith, Allan Gardner Lloyd. *Eve Tempted: Writing and Sexuality in Hawthorne's Fiction*. Totowa, NJ: Barnes and Noble, 1984.

Stein, William Bysshe. *Hawthorne's Faust: A Study of the Devil Archetype*. Gainesville: U of Florida P, 1953.

Sterling, Laurie A. "Paternal Gold: Translating Inheritance in *The Scarlet Letter*." *ATQ* 6 (1992): 17–30.

Stoehr, Taylor. *Hawthorne's Mad Scientists: Pseudoscience and Social Science in Nineteenth-Century Life and Letters*. Hamden: Archon, 1978.

Stubbs, John Caldwell. *The Pursuit of Form: A Study of Hawthorne and the Romance*. Urbana: U of Illinois P, 1970.

Swann, Charles. *Nathaniel Hawthorne: Tradition and Revolution*. New York: Cambridge UP, 1991.

Sweeney, Susan Elizabeth. "The Madonna, the Women's Room, and *The Scarlet Letter*." *College English* 57 (1995): 410–25.

Thomas, Brook. "Citizen Hester: *The Scarlet Letter* as Civic Myth." *ALH* 13 (Summer 2001): 181–211.

Thompson, G. R. *The Art of Authorial Presence: Hawthorne's Provincial Tales*. Durham: Duke UP, 1993.

Tomc, Sandra. "A Change of Art: Hester, Hawthorne, and the Service of Love." *Nineteenth-Century Literature* 56 (2002): 466–94.

———. " 'The Sanctity of the Priesthood': Hawthorne's 'Custom-House.' " *ESQ* 39 (1993): 161–84.

Tompkins, Jane. *Sensational Designs: The Cultural Work of American Fiction, 1790–1860*. New York: Oxford UP, 1985.

Traister, Bryce. "The Bureaucratic Origins of *The Scarlet Letter*." *Studies in American Fiction* 29 (Spring 2001): 77–92.

Van Leer, David. "Hester's Labyrinth: Transcendental Rhetoric in Puritan Boston." In *New Essays on* The Scarlet Letter. Ed. Michael J. Colacurcio. New York: Cambridge UP, 1985. 57–100.

von Abele, Rudolph. *The Death of the Artist: A Study of Hawthorne's Disintegration*. The Hague: Martinus Nijhoff, 1955.

von Frank, Albert J., ed. *Critical Essays on Hawthorne's Short Stories*. Boston: G. K. Hall, 1991.

Waggoner, Hyatt H. *Hawthorne: A Critical Study*. Revised Edition. Cambridge: Harvard UP, 1963.

———. *The Presence of Hawthorne*. Baton Rouge: Louisiana State UP, 1979.

Wamser, Garry. "The Scarlet Contract: Puritan Resurgence, The Unwed Mother, and Her Child." In *Law and Literature Perspectives*. Ed. Bruce L. Rockwood and Roberta Kevelson. New York: Peter Lang, 1996. 381–406.

• Weinauer, Ellen. "Considering Possession in *The Scarlet Letter*." *Studies in American Fiction* 29 (Spring 2001): 93–112.

Weldon, Roberta F. "From 'The Old Manse' to 'The Custom-House': The Growth of the Artist's Mind." *Texas Studies in Literature and Language* 20 (1978): 36–47.

Whelan, Robert Emmet, Jr. "Hester Prynne's Little Pearl: Sacred and Profane Love." *American Literature* 39 (1967): 488–505.

• Winship, Michael. "Hawthorne and the 'Scribbling Women': Publishing *The Scarlet Letter* in the Nineteenth-Century United States." *Studies in American Fiction* 29 (Spring 2001): 3–11.

Yellin, Jean Fagan. "Hawthorne and the American National Sin." In *The Green Tradition: Essays and Poems for Sherman Paul*. Ed. H. Daniel Peck. Baton Rouge: Louisiana State UP, 1989. 75–97.

• ———. *Women and Sisters: The Antislavery Feminists in American Culture*. New Haven: Yale UP, 1989. 125–50.

SELECTED CRITICISM FOR "MRS. HUTCHINSON"

Colacurcio, Michael J. *The Province of Piety: Moral History in Hawthorne's Early Tales*. Cambridge: Harvard UP, 1984. 63–68.

Davis, Sarah I. "Another View of Hester and the Antinomians." *Studies in American Fiction* 12 (1984): 189–98.

• Lang, Amy Schrager. *Prophetic Woman: Anne Hutchinson and the Problem of Dissent in the Literature of New England*. Berkeley: U of California P, 1987.

Maddox, Lucy. *Removals: Nineteenth-Century American Literature and the Politics of Indian Affairs*. New York: Oxford UP, 1991. 110–25.

SELECTED CRITICISM FOR "ENDICOTT AND THE RED CROSS"

Bercovitch, Sacvan. "Endicott's Breastplate: Symbolism and Typology in 'Endicott and the Red Cross.' " *Studies in Short Fiction* 4 (1967): 289–99.

Bremer, Francis J. "Endecott and the Red Cross: Puritan Iconoclasm in the New World." *Journal of American Studies* 24.1 (1990): 5–22.

Bush, Harold K. "Re-Inventing the Puritan Fathers: George Bancroft, Nathaniel Hawthorne, and the Birth of Endicott's Ghost." *ATQ* 9.2 (1995): 131–52.

Colacurcio, Michael J. *The Province of Piety: Moral History in Hawthorne's Early Tales*. Cambridge: Harvard UP, 1984. 221–38.

Franzosa, John. "Young Man Hawthorne: Scrutinizing the Discourse of History." *Bucknell Review* 30.2 (1987): 72–94.

• Nickel, John. "Hawthorne's Demystification of History in 'Endicott and the Red Cross.' " *Texas Studies in Literature and Language* 42.4 (2000): 347–62.

Orton, Stephen. "De-Centered Symbols in 'Endicott and the Red Cross.' " *Studies in Short Fiction* 30.4 (1993): 565–74.

Royer, Diana. "Puritan Constructs and Nineteenth-Century Politics: Allegory, Rhetoric, and Law in Three Hawthorne Tales." In *Worldmaking*. Ed. William Pencak. New York: Peter Lang, 1996. 211–40.

SELECTED CRITICISM FOR "YOUNG GOODMAN BROWN"

Berkove, Lawrence I. " 'Reasoning as We Go': The Flawed Logic of 'Young Goodman Brown.' " *Nathaniel Hawthorne Review* 24.1 (1998): 46–52.

Clark, James W. "Hawthorne's Use of Evidence in 'Young Goodman Brown.' " *Essex Institute Historical Collections* 111 (1975): 12–34.

Colacurcio, Michael J. "Visible Sanctity and Specter Evidence: The Moral World of Hawthorne's 'Young Goodman Brown.' " *Essex Institute Historical Collections* 110 (1974): 259–99. Revised version in Colacurcio, *The Province of Piety: Moral History in Hawthorne's Early Tales*. Cambridge: Harvard UP, 1984. 283–313.

Cook, Reginald L. "The Forest of Goodman Brown's Night: A Reading of Hawthorne's 'Young Goodman Brown.' " *New England Quarterly* 43 (1970): 473–81.

• Crews, Frederick. *The Sins of the Fathers: Hawthorne's Psychological Themes*. New York: Oxford UP, 1966. 98–106.

Eberwein, Jane Donahue. " 'My Faith Is Gone!': 'Young Goodman Brown' and Puritan Conversion." *Christianity and Literature* 32 (1982): 23–32.

Franklin, Benjamin V. "Goodman Brown and the Puritan Catechism." *ESQ* 40 (1994): 67–88.

Hostetler, Norman H. "Narrative Structure and Theme in 'Young Goodman Brown.' " *Journal of Narrative Technique* 12 (1982): 221–28.

Jayne, Edward. "Pray Tarry with Me Young Goodman Brown." *Literature and Psychology* 29 (1979): 100–113.

Keil, James C. "Hawthorne's 'Young Goodman Brown': Early Nineteenth-Century and Puritan Constructions of Gender." *New England Quarterly* 69.1 (1996): 33–55.

• Levin, David. "Shadows of Doubt: Specter Evidence in Hawthorne's 'Young Goodman Brown.' " *American Literature* 34 (1962): 344–52.

Levy, Leo B. "The Problem of Faith in 'Young Goodman Brown.' " *JEGP* 74 (1975): 375–87.

Loving, Jerome. "Pretty in Pink: 'Young Goodman Brown' and New-World Dreams." In *Critical Essays on Hawthorne's Short Stories*. Ed. J. Albert von Frank. Boston: G. K. Hall, 1991. 219–31.

Morris, Christopher. "Deconstructing 'Young Goodman Brown.' " *ATQ* 2 (1988): 23–33.

Mosher, Harold F. "The Sources of Ambiguity in Hawthorne's 'Young Goodman Brown': A Structuralist Approach." *ESQ* 26 (1980): 16–25.

Paulits, Walter J. "Ambivalence in 'Young Goodman Brown.' " *American Literature* 41 (1970): 577–84.

Reynolds, Larry J. "Melville's Use of 'Young Goodman Brown.' " *ATQ* 31 (1976): 12–14.

Shuffleton, Frank. "Nathaniel Hawthorne and the Revival Movement." *ATQ* 44 (1979): 311–23.

Stoehr, Taylor. " 'Young Goodman Brown' and Hawthorne's Theory of Mimesis." *Nineteenth-Century Fiction* 23 (1969): 393–412.

Wright, Elizabeth. "The New Psychoanalysis and Literary Criticism: A Reading of Hawthorne and Melville." *Poetics Today* 3 (1982): 89–105.

SELECTED CRITICISM FOR "THE MINISTER'S BLACK VEIL"

Barry, Elaine. "Beyond the Veil: A Reading of Hawthorne's 'The Minister's Black Veil.' " *Studies in Short Fiction* 17 (1980): 15–20.

Benoit, Raymond. "Hawthorne's Psychology of Death: 'The Minister's Black Veil.' " *Studies in Short Fiction* 8 (1971): 553–60.

Birk, John F. "Hawthorne's Mister Hooper: The Veil of Ham." *Prospects* 21 (1996): 1–11.

Carnochan, W. B. " 'The Minister's Black Veil': Symbol, Meaning, and the Context of Hawthorne's Art." *Nineteenth-Century Fiction* 24 (1969): 182–92.

Coale, Samuel. "Hawthorne's Black Veil: From Image to Icon." *CEA Critic* 55 (1993): 79–87.

Colacurcio, Michael J. "Parson Hooper's Power of Blackness: Sin and Self in 'The Minister's Black Veil.' " *Prospects* 5 (1980): 331–411. Also in *The Province of Piety: Moral History in Hawthorne's Early Tales*. Cambridge: Harvard UP, 1984. 314–85.

- Crews, Frederick. *The Sins of the Fathers: Hawthorne's Psychological Themes*. New York: Oxford UP, 1966. 106–11.
Crie, Robert P. " 'The Minister's Black Veil': Mr. Hooper's Symbolic Fig Leaf." *Literature and Psychology* 17 (1969): 211–18.
Danow, David K. "The Semiotic Significance of 'The Minister's Black Veil.' " *Semiotica* 113.3–4 (1997): 337–346.
Davis, Clark. "Facing the Veil: Hawthorne, Hooper, and Ethics." *Arizona Quarterly* 55 (Winter 1999): 1–19.
Franklin, Rosemary F. " 'The Minister's Black Veil': A Parable." *Studies in Short Fiction* 56 (1985): 55–63.
Freedman, William. "The Artist's Symbol and Hawthorne's Veil: 'The Minister's Black Veil' Resartus." *Studies in Short Fiction* 29 (1992): 353–62.
German, Norman. "The Veil of Words in 'The Minister's Black Veil.' " *Studies in Short Fiction* 25 (1988): 41–47.
McCarthy, Judy. " 'The Minister's Black Veil': Concealing Moses and the Holy of Holies." *Studies in Short Fiction* 24 (1987): 131–38.
- Miller, J. Hillis. *Hawthorne and History*. Cambridge: Basil Blackwell, 1991. 73–102.
Morsberger, Robert E. " 'The Minister's Black Veil': 'Shrouded in a Blackness, Ten Times Black.' " *New England Quarterly* 46 (1973): 454–63.
Newberry, Frederick. "The Biblical Veil: Sources and Typology in Hawthorne's 'The Minister's Black Veil.' " *Texas Studies in Literature and Language* 31 (1989): 169–95.
Newman, Lea Bertani Vozar. "One Hundred and Fifty Years of Looking at, through, behind, beyond, and around 'The Minister's Black Veil.' " *Nathaniel Hawthorne Review* 13:2 (1987): 5–12.
Ostrowski, Carl. "The Minister's 'Grievous Affliction': Diagnosing Hawthorne's Parson Hooper." *Literature and Medicine* 17.2 (1998): 197–211.
Quinn, James, and Ross Baldessarini. "Literary Technique and Psychological Effect in Hawthorne's 'The Minister's Black Veil.' " *Literature and Psychology* 24 (1974): 115–23.
Randall, Dale B. "Image-Making and Image-Breaking: Seeing 'The Minister's Black Veil' through a Miltonic Glass, Darkly." *Resources for American Literary Study* 23.1 (1997): 19–27.
Reece, James B. "Mr. Hooper's Vow." *ESQ* 21 (1975): 93–102.
Seigel, Catherine F. "Jumping Through Hawthorne's Hoop(er)s." *Short Story* 2.1 (1994): 79–88.
Wallace, James D. "Stowe and Hawthorne." In *Hawthorne and Women: Engendering and Expanding the Hawthorne Tradition*. Ed. John L. Idol, Jr., and Melinda M. Ponder. Amherst: U Massachusetts P, 1999. 92–103.

SELECTED CRITICISM FOR "THE BIRTH-MARK"

Arner, Robert D. "The Legend of Pygmalion in 'The Birthmark.' " *ATQ* 12 (1972): 168–71.
Bromell, Nicholas K. " 'The Bloody Hand' of Labor: Work, Class, and Gender in Three Stories by Hawthorne." *American Quarterly* 42 (1990): 542–64. Also in Bromell, *By the Sweat of the Brow: Literature and Labor in Antebellum America*. Chicago: U of Chicago P, 1993.
Eckstein, Barbara. "Hawthorne's 'The Birthmark': Science and Romance as Belief." *Studies in Short Fiction* 26 (1989): 511–19.
- Fetterley, Judith. *The Resisting Reader: A Feminist Approach to American Fiction*. Bloomington: Indiana UP, 1978. 22–33.
Gatta, John. "Aylmer's Alchemy in 'The Birthmark.' " *Philological Quarterly* 57 (1978): 399–413.
Johnson, Barbara. "Is Female to Male as Ground Is to Figure?" In *Feminism and Psychoanalysis*. Ed. Richard Feldstein and Judith Roof. Ithaca: Cornell UP, 1989. 255–68.
Micklaus, Robert. "Hawthorne's Jekyll and Hyde: The Aminadab in Aylmer." *Literature and Psychology* 29 (1979): 148–59.
Person, Leland S. *Aesthetic Headaches: Women and a Masculine Poetics in Poe, Melville, and Hawthorne*. Athens: U of Georgia P, 1988. 108–12.
Pfister, Joel. *The Production of Personal Life: Class, Gender, and the Psychological in Hawthorne's Fiction*. Stanford: Stanford UP, 1991. 29–48.
Pribek, Thomas. "Hawthorne's Aminadab: Sources and Influence." *Studies in the American Renaissance* (1987): 177–86.
Proudfit, Charles L. "Eroticization of Intellectual Functions as an Oedipal Defence: A Psychoanalytic View of Nathaniel Hawthorne's 'The Birthmark.' " *International Review of Psychoanalysis* 7 (1980): 375–83.
Quinn, James, and Ross Baldessarini. " 'The Birth-mark': A Deathmark." *University of Hartford Studies in Literature* 13 (1981): 91–98.
Reid, Alfred S. "Hawthorne's Humanism: 'The Birthmark' and Sir Kenelm Digby." *American Literature* 38 (1966): 337–51.
Rosenberg, Liz. " 'The Best That Earth Could Offer': 'The Birthmark,' a Newlywed's Story." *Studies in Short Fiction* 30 (1993): 145–51.
Rucker, Mary F. "Science and Art in Hawthorne's 'The Birthmark.' " *Nineteenth-Century Literature* 41 (1987): 445–61.

Shakinovsky, Lynn. "The Return of the Repressed: Illiteracy and the Death of the Narrative in Hawthorne's 'The Birthmark.' " *ATQ* 9 (1995): 269–81.

Smith, Allan Gardner Lloyd. *Eve Tempted: Writing and Sexuality in Hawthorne's Fiction*. Totowa, NJ: Barnes & Noble, 1983. 95–100.

Van Leer, David. "Aylmer's Library: Transcendental Alchemy in Hawthorne's 'The Birthmark.' " *ATQ* 25 (1975): 211–20.